Not For Loan

A Dictionary of
Scottish Phrase and Fable

A Dictionary of
Scottish Phrase and Fable

Ian Crofton

BIRLINN

First published in 2012 by
Birlinn Limited
West Newington House
10 Newington Road
Edinburgh
EH9 1QS

www.birlinn.co.uk

ISBN: 978 1 184158 977 0

British Library Cataloguing-in-Publication Data
A catalogue record for this book is available from the British Library

Designed by James Hutcheson
Typeset by Iolaire Typesetting, Newtonmore
Printed and bound by Gutenberg Press, Malta

In fondest memory of my parents

JOHN CROFTON (1912–2009)

and

EILEEN CROFTON (1919–2010)

who had the good sense to settle in Scotland before I was
born, and who shared with me their deep love and
fascination for their adopted country

INTRODUCTION

Confessions of a Justified Scotsman

I feel a certain presumption in offering the present volume to the public.

Firstly, it takes a fair amount of hard-necked *heichtynes* (that fine old Scots word for 'temerity') to wrap oneself in the mantle of the Revd Dr Ebenezer Cobham Brewer, who back in the Victorian era initiated the whole phrase-and-fable industry. For many years Dr Brewer beavered for obscure allusions in the arcana of ancient texts, checked out the unread footnotes of dusty tomes, wandered, notebook in hand, through the baffling mazes of the world's mythologies, gradually filling his study with card upon card, piling scholarly serendipity upon scholarly serendipity, until in 1870 he eventually gave birth to his eponymous *Dictionary of Phrase and Fable*. Dr Brewer modestly stated that this work – almost certainly the most browsable (and possibly the most idiosyncratic) reference book ever published – contained nothing but 'trifles too insignificant to find a place in books of higher pretension'. Posterity has begged to differ, and his work is now in its 18th edition.

In defence of my authorship of the present volume, I should say that I have served a long apprenticeship in this line of work. My first proper job, beginning back in 1977, was as an editor with Wm Collins and Sons, the Glasgow-based publishers, for whom I worked on all kinds of general reference books, including encyclopedias and dictionaries of quotations, and also on books of Scottish interest. Another decade with various London publishers followed, before this particular gamekeeper turned poacher, and set up as a freelance writer. In this capacity I contributed extensively to the first and second editions of *Brewer's Dictionary of Modern Phrase and Fable*, compiled *Brewer's Dictionary of Curious Titles*

and *Brewer's Cabinet of Curiosities*, and wrote the Scottish (and the Irish, Welsh and Northern English) entries for *Brewer's Britain and Ireland*, a phrase-and-fable gazetteer of these islands. It was while co-authoring the latter volume that I came to realize what a wealth of material there was for a dedicatedly Scottish dictionary of phrase and fable. I started to make notes ... and to wave my antennae about ... and the notes piled up, and stretched out, and found other notes to talk to ...

Secondly, on the presumption front, there is the question of my identity. I have sometimes wondered whether I am sufficiently Scottish to undertake such a task as this. Although I was born and raised in Edinburgh, my father was Anglo-Irish (born in Dublin, educated in England) and my mother reared in London, the daughter of a Liverpudlian father and a Scottish mother (a Mackay whose ancestors came from Rogart in eastern Sutherland). Two years before I was born, my father took up a post at Edinburgh University (see the entry herein on the EDINBURGH METHOD); so of my parents' five children, the three eldest were born in London and the two youngest in Scotland. I was sent to an independent day school in Edinburgh, which, by the time I got there, had an English rector with ambitions to turn the place into an English public school. He was echoing the aspirations of the founders, among them Sir Walter Scott (whose ghost, more than any other, haunts the pages of this volume), to turn 'Scots lads into English gentlemen'. Well, I wasn't sure whether I was, with my parentage, a genuine Scots lad, but I was damn well sure I didn't want to be an English gentleman ...

One thing I never did acquire – as every new acquaintance south of the Border immediately remarks when I inform them where I come from – was a Scottish accent. So, although I wrote my MA dissertation on that masterpiece of synthetic Scots, Hugh MacDiarmid's *A Drunk Man Looks at the Thistle*, and have immersed myself over the years in the cities, landscapes and cultures of Scotland, I must remain a mongrel outsider, no more than an adopted Scot – in short, something of a fraud. But I hope that readers of the present volume will find that the proof of the pudding is in the eating.

This *Dictionary of Scottish Phrase and Fable* is not an encyclopedia. For those who are after a comprehensive and authoritative (and sober) reference work on Scottish people and places, nothing serves better than the admirable *Collins Encyclopedia of Scotland* (HarperCollins, 1994, 2000), edited by John and Julia Keay; or, for a phrase-and-fable gazetteer of Scotland, together with an elucidation of the meanings of Scottish place names, then I would suggest consulting the relevant entries in the aforementioned *Brewer's Britain and Ireland* (Weidenfeld, 2005).

A Dictionary of Scottish Phrase and Fable does not have entries on notable Scots *per se*, unless they have some sobriquet or nickname as a nail to hang them on. Thus there is an entry for ROBERT THE BRUCE, in so far that it explains the sobriquet 'the Bruce', but does not offer a full account of his career; there is also an entry for his hostile English nickname KING HOBBE, and for the story of BRUCE AND THE SPIDER and for BRUCE'S CAVE – not to mention the phenomenon of WALLACETHEBRUCEISM. Likewise, there is an entry for the YOUNG PRETENDER, but not for 'Stuart, Charles Edward'; and an entry for BROON, THE and the MISERY FROM THE MANSE, but not for 'Brown, Gordon'; for BIG ECK but not for 'McLeish, Alex' (nor for that matter for 'Salmond, Alex' – though WEE ECK does get a look in). There is the occasional entry for historical (or legendary) characters whose stories have become so iconic (or, indeed, fabular) as to demand inclusion: thus we have the very real Flora MACDONALD (as well as her supposed maidservant, Betty BURKE); the possibly real Jenny GEDDES; and the almost certainly mythical Sawney BEAN. Some characters, such as R.L. Stevenson's Bonny Fighter Alan BRECK, and Scott's Meg MERRILIES (based on two actual gypsies, Jean Gordon and Flora Marshal), bridge the gap between fact and fiction.

Similarly with places: only nicknames, sobriquets and curiosities with a tale to tell are included. Thus there are entries for AULD REEKIE and ATHENS OF THE NORTH, and even for DUNEDIN, but not for 'Edinburgh'; for ARTHUR'S SEAT but not 'Ben Nevis' (and for that matter for the GREY MAN OF BEN MACDUI but not for 'Ben Macdui'); for ARCHIE'S ROCK, the COCK OF ARRAN and the GUTTIT HADDIE, but not for 'Bass Rock', 'Campsie Fells' or 'North Berwick Law'; and for BLYTHE ABERDEANE, the BRAIF TOUN, the CITY OF BON ACCORD, the CITY OF ST NICHOLAS, FURRY BOOTS CITY, the GRANITE CITY and the SILVER CITY – but not for 'Aberdeen' itself. Following similar principles, battles only appear if their name is not simply geographical (or if the battle is not strictly a battle): so there is the BATTLE OF THE SHIRTS and the BATTLE OF GEORGE SQUARE and the BATTLE OF THE CLANS – but no Bannockburn, Flodden, Pinkie or Culloden.

Nor is the present volume a lexicon of the Scots language. For a more conventional Scots dictionary, readers will find the *Concise Scots Dictionary* (Aberdeen University Press, 1985; Polygon 1999) invaluable. The CSD was prepared under the chief editorship of Mairi Robinson, and draws on two vast and magisterial publications, the *Scottish National Dictionary* (SND), begun in 1931 under the editorship of William Grant, who was succeeded in 1946 by David Murison, who saw the project through to completion in 1976; and the *Dictionary of the Older Scottish Tongue* (DOST), compiled under a series of editors, beginning with William A. Craigie, between 1931 and 2002. Both works, plus more recent supplements, have (under the editorship of Susan Rennie) been combined into a freely accessible online database, under the title of the *Dictionary of the Scottish Language* (DSL); it can be found at www.dsl.ac.uk. Needless to say, both the CSD and the DSL have proved invaluable resources to the present compiler. Earlier lexicographical works have also proved of great interest, especially John Jamieson's *Etymological Dictionary of the Scottish Language* (1808; Supplement 1825). A more recent offering, Michael Munro's *The Complete Patter* (1996), should also be mentioned, giving as it does an entertaining and illuminating survey of the colourful and endlessly creative contemporary patois of Glasgow. For the most part, the above volumes concentrate on single words, but they also include phrases, and it is with the latter that the present volume concerns itself (when it is not dealing with fables). And to all the above – as well as to numerous individuals who have shared with me some of their favourite turns of phrase and figures of speech – I owe a great debt of gratitude.

So if the present volume is neither a conventional encyclopedia of people and places nor a comprehensive lexicon, what (to borrow an old Scots euphemism) the HECKIEBIRNIE is it? The word *Dictionary* in the title serves to indicate that the entries are arranged alphabetically, and that the book is interested, one way or another, with words and phrases; in truth, this book is above all a gallimaufry, a miscellany of colourful and interesting phrases and names and stories that accumulate one upon the other, linked by a web of cross-references (indicated by SMALL CAPITALS), to build a kaleidoscopic view of Scottish traditions, legends, folklore, customs, cultures and contemporary consciousness, with no pretence at thorough inclusivity, completion or final authority. Matters of language and national identity are constantly in flux, the stories we tell ourselves about our past (historical or fictional) endlessly evolve – and thus this is 'A' not 'The' *Dictionary of Scottish Phrase and Fable*. It is a work in progress, an ongoing project that I hope will extend far into the future, a rolling stone that will continue to gather all kinds of interesting and hitherto unidentified mosses as it rolls ponderously along forgotten stalkers' tracks and old drove roads grown over with heather – not to mention the unexpected gems to be found in the unlit, graffiti-spattered wynds and closes of our modern cities.

So, what will the reader find inside this great baggy monster (to violently switch metaphors), as it drags itself along? Above all else, I hope the reader will find endless diversion. You may not locate the particular thing you thought you might look up, but I'd be very disappointed if you didn't come across half a dozen other unsuspected items that caught your attention, and detained you from more important business for a while. That is pretty much how I went about putting this book together, over a period of a decade or so: if something intrigued me, I would see if I could find a way of fitting it in. If it was a dull word, or phrase, or person, without some kind of a story to tell, then I wouldn't want to bother you with it. The important

thing was that whatever it was, it should be interesting enough to divert me for a while from getting on with more important business (although what that business might have been I have now forgotten).

What kind of entries have I included, then? Time for some categories and some lists:

- Colourful turns of phrase, insults, put-downs, ejaculations and so on, both contemporary and historical, are scattered throughout the book, from an ABERDEEN SWEETIE to a GLASGOW KISS, from BAGGY AGGIE to TEENIE FAE TROON, from DANCE THE REEL O' BOGIE to DING DOON TANTALLON, from MIXTER-MAXTER to MIM AS A MAY PUDDOCK, from AW FUR COAT AN NAE KNICKERS to AWA AN BILE YER HEID ... There is even a smattering of Gaelic (though this is *not* a Gaelic work, and I am no Gaelic scholar), from OCHONE to CEUD MÌLE FÀILTE ...
- A selection of proverbs, from MONY A MICKLE MAKS A MUCKLE to IF IT'S NO' THE SKITTER, IT'S THE SPEW (for an exhaustive collection, the reader is referred to Colin Walker's *Scottish Proverbs*, Birlinn, 2000) ...
- RHYMING SLANG, from Tony Blairs (flares) to Duke of Argylls (piles), from Friar Tucked (in deep trouble) to Hampden roar (score), from Mars Bar (scar) to Radio Rental (mental) ...
- A certain amount of FAUX JOCKERY, such as IT'S A BRAW BRICHT MUNELICHT NICHT ... JINGS, CRIVENS, HELP MA BOAB ... OCH AYE THE NOO ... etc., etc. ...
- Toasts, prayers, mottoes, etc., from HERE'S TO US and the SELKIRK GRACE ('Some hae meat ...'), to WHA DAUR MEDDLE WI ME? and MAY PRICK NOR PURSE NE'ER FAIL YOU ...
- Quotations and sayings that have entered the national consciousness, from 'The END OF AN OLD SONG' to 'IT CAME WITH A LASS AND IT WILL PASS WITH A LASS', from 'FREEDOM AND WHISKY GANG THEGITHER' to 'A MAN'S A MAN FOR A' THAT', plus some lesser-known quotations that are worth including for reasons of colour, such as the characterization of St Andrews by a Victorian missionary as a 'MASS OF MORAL PUTRESCENCE', and the description of James V by the poet Sir David Lindsay as 'AY FUCKAND LYKE ANE

FURIOUS FORNICATOR' (a fuller collection will be found in David Ross's *Scottish Quotations*, Birlinn, 2001) ...

- Well-known songs, poems, novels, TV shows, etc. that have become cultural icons, from 'YE BANKS AND BRAES O' BONNIE DOON' to 'YE CANNA SHOVE YER GRANNY AFF A BUS', from 'LAMENT FOR THE MAKARIS' and *THE MERRY MUSES OF CALEDONIA* to *The WHITE HEATHER CLUB*, OOR WULLIE and *RAB C. NESBITT*, from the real story that inspired the kidnap in *KIDNAPPED* and the original HEART OF MIDLOTHIAN to a tentative exploration of the meaning of the title of *TRAINSPOTTING* ...

Moving to the fabular side of things, the reader will find in these pages:

- All kinds of creatures, both real and imaginary, from BERNIE THE BULL and DOLLY THE SHEEP to GREYFRIARS BOBBIE, the TURRA COO and the BEAST OF BALMORAL, from the WALRUS OF THE HEBRIDES to the LAST WOLF IN SCOTLAND ... together with a collection of Scots names for various animals, listed under FAUNA CALEDONIA ...
- Plants and trees, from the DEIL'S SNUFFBOX and the FLOWER WHICH GREW AT THE FOOT OF THE CROSS to WALLACE'S OAK and the FORTINGALL YEW ... plus numerous Scots names for flowers, listed under FLORA CALEDONIA ...
- Buildings and other structures, from the BUS SHELTER OF UNST, the BLACK DWARF'S COTTAGE and the BRIDGE TO NOWHERE, to EDINBURGH'S FOLLY and that infamous Aberdonian triumvirate, EDUCATION, SALVATION and DAMNATION ...
- Roads, from the STRING and the LANG WHANG to the DEVIL'S ELBOW and the REST AND BE THANKFUL, from ROSE STREET and SAUCHIEHALL STREET to DANUBE STREET and BLYTHSWOOD SQUARE (the last two included for reasons that will become apparent) ...
- Symbols, from the SALTIRE and the THISTLE to the WHITE ROSE OF SCOTLAND, the LION RAMPANT and the TREE THAT NEVER GREW ...
- Ceremonies and customs, fairs, festivals and feasts, from the BELLS and BLOOD-DRINKING (not usually conducted simultaneously) to BANNOCKBURN

DAY and the BRAW LADS' GATHERING, from the BURRYMAN and the FIREBALLS to the FALKIRK TRYST and FISHERMEN'S TABOOS, from DOOKING FOR APPLES to RIDING THE STANG ...
- Charms and amulets, from BARBRECK'S BONE to TOAD STONES, from the LEE PENNY to the FAIRY FLAG OF DUNVEGAN ...
- Supernatural beings, from the BLUE MEN OF THE MINCH to the GOLDEN HORSE OF LOCH LUNDIE, from BROWNIES and FATLIPS and REDCAPS to the GORBALS VAMPIRE, the SILKIE FOLK, the *SLUAGH* and the troublesome WORRICOW ...
- Items of clothing from BLUE BONNETS and INVERNESS CAPES to NICKY TAMS and PEERIE HEELS ...
- Clubs and societies, from the HORSEMAN'S WORD to the CROCHALLAN FENCIBLES, from the BEGGAR'S BENISON to the SIX-FOOT HIGH CLUB ...
- Crimes and outrages, from BURNT CANDLEMAS and the HERSCHIP OF BUCHAN to the ROUGH WOOING and SLAIN MEN'S LEA, from the APPIN MURDER to the MASSACRE OF TRANENT ...
- Disasters and other tragedies, from BLACK FRIDAY and the LOSS OF GAICK to the MUCKLE SPATE and the LOCKERBIE BOMBING ...
- Eponymous places, from AGASSIZ ROCK and BALFOUR BAY to RANDOLPH'S LEAP and DAFT ANN'S STEPS ...

Take a breath, and maybe a bite to eat, and something to drink?

- Try some ARBROATH SMOKIES, or maybe some CRAPPIT HEIDS, FREE KIRK PUDDING or RUMBLEDETHUMP, and perhaps, as a *DEOCH-AN-DORUS*, you might wash all this down with a glass of CHEEKY WATTER or a shot of STAIRHEID SHANDY?
- Then have a go at some games and dances, from BABBITY BOWSTER and the GAY GORDONS to SCOTCH HORSES and that old favourite, TWISTING THE FOUR LEGS FROM A COW ...
- Sample some matters pertaining to the Kirk, from AULD LICHTS AND NEW LICHTS and the SERMON ON THE MOUND to the DOOKIT FOLK, the HILL FOLK and the LAND O' THE LEAL ... but don't mention the AULD ENEMY, His Nibs the EARL O' HELL, aka the BLACK THIEF, aka the

MUCKLE CHIELD, aka *AM FEAR TH'AIR AN T-SLABHRUIDH* ...

- Scotland, of course, is never short of weather, from BANFF BAILLIES and GOWK STORMS to a TOUCH OF LIDDESDALE DROW and a splash of the LAUCHIN RAIN ... and, then of course, Scotland has had its very own, gloriously named, HURRICANE BAWBAG ...

As mentioned before, nicknames are a core component of the book, and are not just restricted to places and individuals ...

- So here are the nicknames of various groups of citizens, including the RED LICHTIES of Arbroath, Dumbarton's (and Stirling's) SONS OF THE ROCK, the BLACK BITCHES of Linlithgow, the DOONHAMERS of Dumfries, and many more ...
- Some of these names have spilled into the nicknames of local football teams, but other club names require further elucidation, such as the Bears, the Blue Brazil and the Bully Wee, the Cabbage, the Warriors and the Maryhill Magyars – all explained, along with many others, under FOOTBALL CLUB NICKNAMES.
- Scottish regiments have also attracted a great host of nicknames – the Ladies from Hell, Hell's Latest Invention, the Poison Dwarves, the First and Worst, Pontius Pilate's Bodyguard, etc., etc. – a lengthy list will be found under REGIMENTAL NICKNAMES.
- Then there are a host of miscellaneous nicknames, such as BLACK BREEKS (a minister), the BUBBLY BABIES (the Boys' Brigade), the FOUR-FOOTED CLANSMEN (the sheep that replaced people during the Clearances), the KISHORN COMMANDOS (who built many of Scotland's North Sea oil rigs), the MEMAWS (the boys in blue once dubbed SILLITOE'S COSSACKS), the SEVEN MEN OF MOIDART, the SEVEN MEN OF KNOYDART and the SEVEN MEN OF GLEN MORISTON, the STROMA PIRATES, the TUNNEL TIGERS and, of course, the TARTAN ARMY ...

All these items accumulate, I hope, into some kind of picture of Scotland as we know it (and as we once might have known it, but have possibly forgotten). The snapshot is momentary, the framing provisional, the work continuing. I hope and expect that the book's (hopefully innumerable) readers will play their part in furthering the work, and the author hereby invites you to enter into a dialogue with him via email (scottishpandf@gmail.com) to suggest amendments and additions, to provide fascinating elaborations – and to deliver no-doubt justified castigations. Although, in this last respect I hope I might avoid, to borrow a phrase, *gettin' ma heid in ma hands an' ma teeth tae play wi'*.

Many people have encouraged me to persist with this monstrous endeavour. Two former colleagues at Collins, Edwin Moore and Michael Munro – who, like me, have long turned poacher – responded to my early efforts with considerable enthusiasm, and pointed me towards Neville Moir, publishing director at Birlinn, who championed the idea and has proved a much valued flying buttress to the whole creaking edifice. Andrew Simmons, managing editor at Birlinn, has seen the project through to press calmly and efficiently, and has not only listened to my views on such matters as format and typography, but has (with great tact) actually elicited them. Finally, Michael Munro returned to the fray to undertake the heroic task of editing the entire manuscript. This he did assiduously, suggesting numerous additions, and steering me diplomatically away from a number of potentially foul solecisms. It goes without saying that any errors that remain rest entirely at my own door.

Ian Crofton
July 2012

A

Aald Rock, da 'The Old Rock', the affectionate name given by Shetlanders (especially Shetlanders in exile) to their native islands.

> A thing for oppenin tins wi an da wirds a me
>   favourite hyme,
> Five mottos oota crackers at wis poo'd at
>   Christmastime,
> Twa boanie coloured postcairds at I'd bowt o wir
>   Aald Rock,
> An therty-two letters at I wis gotten fae different
>   fok.
>   – Rhoda Bulter, 'Clearin Oot Da Handbag',
>   www.shetlanddialect.org.uk

Abbey lairds A jocular name for debtors who sought refuge in the Abbey SANCTUARY at Holyrood in Edinburgh. The sanctuary, which extended over a large area including ARTHUR'S SEAT, was first established by David I in the 12th century, but the first record of a debtor taking advantage of it dates from 1531. Within the bounds of the sanctuary, debtors were beyond the reach of the magistrates of the city, and law and order were maintained by a functionary known as the Bailie of Holyrood. The 'lairds' could leave the sanctuary once a week on the Sabbath, when no legal proceedings could be brought against them. Among the hundreds or even thousands who benefited from the Abbey Sanctuary was Thomas de Quincey, author of *Confessions of an English Opium-Eater*, who had reason to spend time here on a number of occasions in the 1830s. (It turned out that his visits were not strictly necessary; he had plenty of pound notes hidden about his lodgings – tucked into mattresses, marking the page in books, and so on – but he had entirely forgotten their existence.) The sanctuary ceased to exist when imprisonment for debt was abolished in 1880, but its boundary can still be seen in the Canongate, marked by a circle of cobbles in the middle of the road where the old Girth ('sanctuary') Cross, consisting of a pillar on top of a three-stepped base, stood until some time after 1767.

Abbot and Prior of Bonaccord *See* CITY OF BON ACCORD.

Abbot of Unreason The master of ceremonies or lord of misrule who organized the revels – often parodying religious rituals – during festivals such as Christmas. Such carryings-on tended to be suppressed following the Reformation. Various other titles were borne by these MCs, such as *Abbot of Na Rent* (i.e. having no benefice), or in the case of Aberdeen, *Abbot of Bonaccord* or *Abbot Out of Reason* (*see* CITY OF BON ACCORD). As part of the plan for Mary Queen of Scots to escape from Lochleven Castle in 1568, ORPHAN WILLIE Douglas took on the role of Abbot of Unreason in order to distract the queen's jailers.

Aberdeen *See* ABERDONIAN JOKES; BLYTH ABERDEANE; BRAIF TOUN, THE; CITY OF BON ACCORD, THE; CITY OF ST NICHOLAS, THE; FURRY BOOTS CITY; GRANITE CITY, THE; 'NORTHERN LIGHTS OF OLD ABERDEEN, THE'; SILVER CITY, THE.

Aberdeen awa The city of Aberdeen and its environs, *awa* being an abbreviation of *thereawa*, 'thereabouts'. The term, dating from the 19th century, is also applied to the local dialect.

> When he alighted from the Edinburgh coach at the canny twa and twae toun of Aberdeen awa, he had some doubt if the inhabitants spoke any Christian language.
>   – John Galt, *The Entail* (1823)

Aberdeen bow A hull design developed by Alexander Hall & Sons, shipbuilders of Aberdeen. The

1

aim was to reduce the depth of the hull, so saving on tax (which was related to the depth of the hull). In the Aberdeen bow, the bow was extended forward above the waterline, which incidentally provided the ship with greater speed and seaworthiness. The design was adopted by many shipbuilders around the world, and used in the Aberdeen-built clipper *Thermopylae* (launched 1868), which sailed from Gravesend to Melbourne, Australia, in a record 60 days (still unbroken by a sailing vessel). It was only rivalled for speed by the *CUTTY SARK*.

Aberdeen chocolates A name given by school-children during the Second World War to mint imperials, presumably with some reference to the reputed meanness of Aberdonians. Not to be confused with ABERDEEN SWEETIES.

Aberdeen haddie *See* HADDIE.

Aberdeen Shore Porters Society, the A removals company established in Aberdeen in 1498, and thus one of the oldest companies in the UK. It started as a cooperative of porters at Aberdeen harbour, who combined together for mutual protection. For centuries the Society was controlled by the city council, but it is now a private partnership.

Aberdeen sweetie A painful thumb-flick against someone's head. *Compare* GLASGOW KISS.

Aberdonian jokes The Aberdonians have long been suspected by their fellow countrymen of particular MEANNESS – a prejudice also picked up by some curmudgeonly foreigners:

> It was only in Aberdeen that I saw kilts and eightsome reels and the sort of tartan tightfistedness that made me think of the average Aberdonian as a person who would gladly pick a halfpenny out of a dunghill with his teeth.
> – Paul Theroux, *The Kingdom by the Sea* (1983)

Jokes about Aberdonian stinginess have been around since at least the 1920s, as the following examples from that decade attest:

> A drouthy Aberdonian desirous of quenching his thirst found that he only had sixpence all told, whereas

ninepence was necessary. He solved the problem by pawning the sixpence for fivepence and selling the pawn ticket for fourpence. He thus obtained ninepence and got his pint of beer.

> It was at another bar that another son of the Granite City lingered a long time while examining his change. 'Is it no' right?' asked the barmaid. 'Aye,' the man replied. 'Just.'

All very regrettable.

Aberdonians of Germany, the *See* SWABIANS.

Aberdonians of Ireland, the The citizens of Portadown, so-called because of their alleged meanness.

Abyssinian, the A nickname of the explorer James Bruce of Kinnaird (1730–94), who travelled across Ethiopia (then known as Abyssinia), initially disguised as a Syrian physician called El Hakim Yagoube, with the aim of discovering the source of the Nile. He claimed that he found this in a swamp at Gish on 4 November 1770, whereupon, replete with the 'sublime of discovery', he raised a glass to George III, Catherine the Great and an unknown woman called Maria. His account of his journey, published in 1790 as *Travels to Discover the Source of the Nile in the Years 1768–73*, met with considerable scepticism, as so much of what he related seemed outlandish – so much so that Rudolph Raspe made him the dedicatee of his sequel to *The Surprising Adventures of Baron Münchhausen*. Bruce claimed that the Abyssinians ate raw beef cut straight from the cow, that he cured the empress of smallpox, that the emperor made him a provincial governor, that he broke in a wild horse and that he won the hearts of innumerable native women. All this was in fact probably true. Unfortunately, though, the stream emanating from the swamp at Gish turned out to be only one of several tributaries of the Blue Nile, and it was not until the following century that the source of the major branch, the White Nile, was found to be Lake Victoria. Bruce himself, having survived wars, desert crossings and countless other tribulations, died following a fall down the stairs in his home at Kinnaird.

> We just read thro' Bruce's Travels, with infinite delight where all is alive & novel & about kings & Queens &

fabulous Heads of Rivers, Abyssinian wars & the line of Solomon & he's a fine dashing fellow & intrigues with Empresses & gets into Harems of Black Women & was himself descended from Kings of Scotland ...
– Charles Lamb, letter, 1806

Accidental Club, the A convivial Glasgow gentlemen's club that flourished in the later 18th century, meeting in its club room in the Gallowgate. To become a member, it was sufficient that an existing member affirmed that one was his friend, 'and no foe to jocularity'. When a teacher called John Taylor produced a poem entitled 'Nonsense', which was 'declared by Professor Hamilton to be destitute of a single idea', the members of the Accidental Club awarded the poet a leaden crown. Regarding the name, the authority on the Glasgow clubs of the period has this to say:

Whether this appellation arose from its members being only by some accident present, or never by any accident absent; whether from their accidentally becoming gay upon ale, or accidentally keeping sober on toddy; or whether from their accidentally stealing softly home to bed, or accidentally being carried *riotous* to the Laigh Kirk Session-house – at that period, as we have hinted, the only *civil* watchhouse in the City – it is now of little moment to inquire. All we need say is, that no one who, at any time and by any accident, joined the fraternity, ever gave it up till he, and at length the whole Club, became one day connected, we would hope, with another, more happy, and more enduring brotherhood!
– John Strang, *Glasgow and its Clubs* (1856)

See also HODGE PODGE CLUB; PIG CLUB.

Accies, the *See* FOOTBALL CLUB NICKNAMES.

Act of Proscription (1746) *See* PROSCRIPTION, ACT OF.

Act of Union Beeches, the A group of straggly beech trees on the windswept slopes of North Berwick Law, East Lothian. They were planted by Sir Hew Dalrymple, a local laird and signatory of the 1707 Act of Union.

Adam and Eve A pair of Sitka spruces planted in the grounds of Culzean Castle around 1836, some four years after the species was first introduced to Scotland by David Douglas.

Addison of the North, the A sobriquet given to the novelist Henry Mackenzie (1745–1831), author of *The Man of Feeling*. In this influential novel of sentiment, Harley, the eponymous hero, is presented in a series of disjointed episodes, in a similar fashion as the English writer Joseph Addison (1672–1719) portrayed Sir Roger de Coverley in his famous *Spectator* essays. Mackenzie also edited two weekly periodicals modelled on Addison's *Spectator*, namely *The Mirror* (1779–80) and *The Lounger* (1785–7), to which he contributed most of the essays, upholding the values of natural sentiment and harmony. The name 'Addison of the North' may originate in the dedication that ends Sir Walter Scott's *Waverley* (1814): 'These volumes being respectfully inscribed to our Scottish Addison, Henry Mackenzie, by an unknown admirer of his genius.'

Admirable Crichton, the The sobriquet given to the polymath James Crichton of Clunie (1560–82) by the poet John Johnston in his *Heroes Scoti* (1603). Crichton was the son of the Lord Advocate of Scotland, and by the age of 14 or 15 had completed his master's degree at the University at St Andrews. At some point he studied under the great humanist scholar George Buchanan. Crichton left Scotland around 1577, and according to his own account served for two years in the French army before arriving in Genoa in 1579, where he was invited to deliver an oration on the occasion of the election of the magistrates. The following year he proceeded to Venice, where he was taken up by the renowned printer Aldo Manuzio (Aldus Manutius), who had been impressed by a Latin ode penned by the young man. Manuzio promoted his protégé in a handbill, in which Crichton's talents are enumerated at length: fluent in ten languages; masterly in philosophy, theology, astrology and mathematics; quick to improvise Latin verses in all metres and all subjects; prodigious in his ability to recall the entirety of the works of Aristotle and his commentators; eloquent and witty, handsome and athletic; as skilled in the arts of war as the arts of peace. As his reputation grew, Crichton was invited to participate in public debates with leading scholars in Venice and Padua, and by early 1582 he had entered the service of the Duke of Mantua. Here he attracted the jealousy of the duke's son, Vincenzo Gonzaga, and in the early hours of 3 July 1582 it seems that Crichton became involved in a brawl with Vincenzo and one of his cronies, in which he received a mortal wound. The circumstances of his death remain murky.

In Britain, Crichton's reputation was picked up and embellished by Sir Thomas Urquhart in *The Discovery of a Most Exquisite Jewel* (1652), which includes a considerably romanticized account of the life and achievements of 'the admirable Crichtoun'. In the 19th century the legend was revisited by Harrison Ainsworth in his novel *Crichton* (1837), while the sobriquet but not the man was borrowed by J.M. Barrie for his social comedy *The Admirable Crichton* (1902), about an aristocratic family shipwrecked on a desert island, in which circumstances a resourceful manservant proves to be their saviour.

Adventurers of Fife, the *See* GENTLEMEN ADVENTURERS OF FIFE, THE.

Adversity Hume The sobriquet given by William Cobbett to the Scottish radical MP, Joseph Hume (1777–1855), on account of his advocacy of economic retrenchment in the 1820s. Cobbett contrasted Hume with the politician he dubbed 'Prosperity Robinson': Frederick John Robinson, Viscount Goderich, who in 1825, as Chancellor of the Exchequer, told the House that the country had never been more prosperous. This announcement was followed by bank failures and a collapse in the value of stocks and shares. Hume was also known as 'the Apothecary', having apprenticed as a surgeon in 1790, and worked in that capacity for the East India Company.

Advocates' Library *See* FACULTY OF ADVOCATES.

'Ae Fond Kiss' A poem by Burns, probably written in December 1791, and published the following year. The opening and closing stanzas are the same:

Ae fond kiss, and then we sever, –
Ae fareweel, and then – for ever

Deep in heart-wrung tears I'll pledge thee!
Warring sighs and groans I'll wage thee!

The poem was addressed to 'my Nancy' – Agnes McLehose (1758–1841), whom he had met during his visit to Edinburgh in 1786, and with whom he carried on a passionate correspondence, in which he called her 'Clarinda' and himself 'Sylvander'. Although she was separated from her husband, she refused to consummate the affair, and Burns comforted himself in the arms of Nancy's servant Jenny Clow, who bore him a son. Burns was still strongly attached to Nancy, however, and when, in November 1791, after a lengthy hiatus in their correspondence, she wrote to him to tell him that she intended to accept the invitation of her estranged husband to join him in Jamaica, Burns rushed over to Edinburgh and had one last meeting with her, on 6 December. He then returned to Dumfries, and on 27 December sent her 'Ae Fond Kiss' and two other poems, accompanied by a brief note:

> I have yours, my ever-dearest madam, this moment. I have just ten minutes before the post goes, and these I shall employ in sending you some songs I have just been composing to different tunes for the *Collection of Songs*, of which you have three volumes, and of which you shall have the fourth.

Nancy sailed from Leith in February 1792 in the *Roselle*, the same ship in which Burns himself had intended to sail for Jamaica with his HIGHLAND MARY in 1786, a plan forestalled by Mary's death of a fever. Once in Jamaica, Nancy found her husband no kinder than he had been, and returned home, arriving in Edinburgh in August 1792. She and Burns never met again, although they exchanged a few letters. Nancy survived the poet by 45 years, and after her death the following note was found among her papers:

> 6th Dec., 1831. This day I never can forget. Parted with Burns in the year 1791, never more to meet in this world. Oh, may we meet in Heaven!

Byron selected the fourth stanza of 'Ae Fond Kiss' as the epigraph of *The Bride of Abydos*, while Scott considered 'that one verse is worth a thousand romances':

Had we never lov'd sae kindly –
Had we never lov'd sae blindly –
Never met – or never parted,
We had ne'er been broken-hearted!

The title *Ae Fond Kiss* ... was adopted by Ken Loach for his 2004 film set in Glasgow about an affair between an Asian DJ and an Irish teacher.

Aff an on aboot Approximately. *Aff an on* on its own means 'off and on', i.e. intermittently.

Aff one's eggs (1) In error. (2) In a state of anxiety. John Jamieson, in his *Etymological Dictionary of the Scottish Language* (1825 Supplement), explains the expression thus:

> The allusion is evidently to a fowl leaving her eggs, or sitting on something else, supposing they are under her.

Afore ye go! The slogan of Bell's Whisky, first registered in 1925. The phrase actually originated during the First World War, when the Bell family sent cases of their wares down to the docks to be consumed by soldiers about to embark for France. The slogan was perhaps inspired by Ian Sinclair's song 'Tak a Dram', the chorus of which goes:

> So button up and aye be cheery
> Tak a dram afore ye go.

The spirit is that of the *DEOCH-AN-DORUS*, as immortalized by Harry Lauder.

Afton *See* SWEET AFTON.

Agassiz Rock A small crag on the south side of Blackford Hill, Edinburgh. In 1840 the Swiss geologist Louis Agassiz (1807–73) examined the striations on the andesite lava of the rock and declared, 'This is the work of the ice' – the first recognition that Scotland had once been covered in glaciers.

A gaun fit's aye gettin' *See* GAUN FIT'S AYE GETTIN', A.

Agile and Suffering Highlanders, the A nickname for the Argyll and Sutherland Highlanders.

A' guts and gyangals *See* DEVIL'S BIRD, THE.

Ah could sleep on the edge ae a razor A colourful Glaswegian expression indicating that the speaker is extremely fatigued.

Ah could sook the face right aff ye Another colourful Glaswegian expression, this time indicating the speaker's amorousness and osculatory intentions. From the female point-of-view, the opposite attitude was formerly indicated in the expression *Ah widnae snog him if he fartit ten-bob notes*. Equally to the point is the female put-down, *Ah widnae pull it fur a pension*.

Ah kent his faither A standard put-down, implying that anyone who has achieved anything of note, or who has any pretensions, is really no better than anyone else, and has almost certainly got above themselves. It shares the democratic sentiment of Burns's 'A MAN'S A MAN FOR A' THAT', and yet still manages to convey a certain meanness of spirit.

> He supposed it was a variant on the old put-down. *Him? A writer? He couldnae be. I kent his faither!*
> – Alan Spence, *The Magic Flute* (1990)

> It is part of that old Scottish 'Ah kent his faither' syndrome, for he knows I am no better than he is.
> – Dave Brown and Ian R. Mitchell, *A View from the Ridge* (1991)

> In Lowland families, children as a rule have not been encouraged to speak their minds in the presence of their elders ... Even in later life, when they have established themselves in their own villages and towns, they feel the glances of appraisal following them and hear the whispers of 'Mphm, that'll be Sandy Thomson's Jimmie.'
> – Ian Finlay, *Scotland* (1945)

See also JOCK TAMSON'S BAIRNS; THINKS HE'S BIG, BUT A WEE COAT FITS HIM.

Ah'm that hungry ah could eat ... A number of items that the ravenous of Glasgow might eat are recorded in Michael Munro's *The Complete Patter* (1996), including a *farmer's arse through a hedge*, a *scabby dug* and a *scabby-heidit wean* (child).

Ah've no got ma sorras tae seek I have quite enough troubles already, thank you.

Ah wouldnae piss doon his throat if his chest was on fire Rodney Bickerstaffe (b.1945), leader of NUPE (now UNISON), the public employees' union, claimed this 'Scottish insult' as the inspiration for a line in his speech at the Labour Party Conference on 30 September 1992:

> John Major, Norman Lamont – I wouldn't spit in their mouths if their teeth were on fire.

Aikenhead, Thomas *See* RHAPSODY OF ILL-INVENTED NONSENSE, A.

Ailsa cock The puffin, which breeds on the rocky Ailsa Craig in the Firth of Clyde.

> ... the very poorest people eat ... sea fowles, which are brought from Ailra [a former name for Ailsa Craig] of the bigness of ducks and of the tast of solan geese [gannets], and are called Abbanacks or Ailra cocks and Tarnachans of which there is so great a multitude about that Isle, that when by a shot of a piece, they are put upon the wing, they will darken the heavens above the spectators.
> – *A Description of Carrict by Mr Abercrummie, Minister of Minibole* (1696)

Ailsa Craig *See* DEAF AS AILSA CRAIG; PADDY'S MILESTONE.

Airts and pairts *See* IN AIRTS AND PAIRTS.

Alba The Gaelic name for Scotland, possibly deriving from the Old Celtic word *alp*, meaning 'rock' or 'crag', and applied to the whole country since the 9th century, when Kenneth MacAlpin united the Scots of DALRIADA with the PICTS of the east. By the end of the 11th century the kings of the united kingdom were referring to themselves not as kings of Alba but as *Rex Scotiae*, although the old name lives on in place-names such as Breadalbane. The name ALBANY is related.

> Beloved land of the east,
> Alba of marvels ...
> – Anon., 'The Song of Deirdre', from the Gaelic of the Glanmason MS (1238).

To the Irish Deirdre, Alba was of course 'the land of the east', whither she fled with her lover Naoise (*see* DEIRDRE OF THE SORROWS).

Albania A Latinized variant of ALBANY, a former name for Scotland. It was used by, among others, Geoffrey of Monmouth, who, in his *Historia Regum Brittaniae*, Book VII, chapter iii, quotes the prophecy of Merlin:

> Albania shall be enraged, and assembling her neighbours, shall be employed in shedding blood ...

Geoffrey of Monmouth asserted that the founder of Albania – long before the arrival of either Picts or Scots – was Albanactus, the youngest son of Brutus, who in turn was descended from the Trojan prince Aeneas. According to Geoffrey of Monmouth, Albanactus was killed by the King of the Huns shortly after he began his reign. The name Albanactus was, of course, a back formation from Albany and ALBA.

The name 'Albania' was later also used in anglophone contexts, such as the poem 'River of Forth Feasting' by William Drummond of Hawthornden (1585–1649):

> Whate'er beneath Albania's hills do run,
> Which sees the rising or the setting sun,
> Which drink stern Graupius' mists or Ochil's snows,
> Stone-rolling Tay, Tyne tortoise-like that flows ...

Albany An anglicized form of *Albyn* or *Albainn*, variants of ALBA, the Gaelic name for Scotland, and possibly related to Albion, a pseudo-classical name for Britain as a whole. (The latter name survives in Scotland in the names of two football teams: Stirling Albion, and Albion Rovers, of Coatbridge.) Since 1398 the second eldest son of the Scottish monarch has borne the title 'Duke of Albany', while the Albany Herald is an officer of the LYON COURT. *See also* BONNIE LASS OF ALBANY, THE.

Alcoholism vs Communism The legend on a banner seen at a Scotland vs Soviet Union football match in 1982. *See also* FREEDOM AND WHISKY GANG THEGITHER.

Alexander the Corrector The sobriquet of Alexander Cruden (1699–1770), the highly eccentric compiler of an early Biblical concordance. Cruden was born and educated in Aberdeen, where at Marischal College he shone as an outstanding scholar of Latin, Greek and the Bible. He had intended a career in the Kirk, but experienced a setback when his suit was rejected by a minister's daughter, who subsequently became pregnant by her brother. Cruden's mental health appears to have suffered as a result of these unusual circumstances, and he was confined for a fortnight in the Aberdeen tolbooth. Following this shock, he left for London and only returned to Aberdeen once, shortly before his death. After a spell as a tutor, he worked as a proofreader and bookseller, and published his *Complete Concordance to the Holy Scriptures* in 1737. Shortly after this his importunate wooing of a widow led to his incarceration in a private madhouse for nine weeks, until he made good his escape. Another spell in an asylum followed in 1753, after Cruden had intervened in a street brawl and been so incensed when a young man swore in front of him that he 'corrected him with some severity', with the aid of a shovel. He related all this in *The Adventures of Alexander the Corrector* (1754), and – blending his role as proofreader and moral crusader – embarked on a one-man campaign to restore the nation's moral health by correcting its spelling and grammar. To this end he carried with him a sponge, with which he wiped out any signs or graffiti that he regarded as incorrect or immoral. At the same time he laid siege to Elizabeth Abney, the daughter of the Lord Mayor of London, a young lady to whom he had not been introduced but whom he recognized as destined to be his helpmeet. Miss Abney took a contrary view of the matter, and fled the capital. Undaunted, Cruden continued to work with extraordinary energy, publishing *The Corrector's Earnest Address to the Inhabitants of Great Britain*, together with corrected editions of his concordance. He was buried in the non-conformist burial ground at Dead Man's Place, Southwark, and left money to fund a bursary at the University of Aberdeen.

All ... *See also* AW ... or A' ...

All Stuarts are not sib to the king An old saying indicating that one is not necessarily of any consequence just because one shares the name of a famous person – in this case the Stuart kings. *Sib* means 'related'. According to tradition, it was James VI who first issued this rebuke.

All the comforts of the Saltmarket An ironic expression denoting a singular absence of luxury, or anything like it. The Saltmarket, the street running south from Glasgow Cross, was once renowned for its poverty.

All to the one side like Gourock Said of anything asymmetrical or lopsided, alluding to the fact that the town on the Firth of Clyde is largely built on one side of a hill.

Alluterlie barbares James VI's description of the inhabitants of the Hebrides, in his *Basilikon Doron* (1597):

> As for the Hie-lands, I shortly comprehend them all into two sorts of people: the one, that dwelleth in our maine land, that are barbarous for the most parte yet mixed with some shewe of civilitie: the other that dwelleth in the Iles and are alluterlie barbares ... reforme and civilize the best inclined among them, rooting out or transporting the barbarous and stubborne sort and planting civilitie in their roomes.

For James's attempt to carry out this last policy, *see* GENTLEMEN ADVENTURERS OF FIFE, THE.

Ally's Tartan Army *See* TARTAN ARMY.

Almanie whistle A kind of high-pitched flageolet or recorder, apparently imported from *Almanie*, i.e. Germany (*cf.* French *Allemagne*). In 1574 the town council of Aberdeen decreed that one John Coupar should be paid by the burgesses and craftsmen of the city to play his 'Almany quhissil', accompanied by a servant 'playand upon the tambourine', at four in the morning and eight in the evening to mark the beginning and end of the working day. By 1630, however, the din had become something of an embarrassment, and in ending the practice the council condemned it as 'ane uncivill form to be usit within sic ane famous burgh, and often fund falt with, alsweill be sindrie nichtbouris of the toun as be strangeris'.

Aloreburn The motto of the burgh of Dumfries, used 'during centuries of struggle', according to *The Ordnance Gazetteer of Scotland* (ed. Francis H. Groome, 1882–5), 'as a war-cry to muster the townsmen':

The side toward the English border being that whence invasion usually came, a place of rendezvous was appointed there on the banks of a rill called the Lower Burn, nearly in the line of the present Loreburn Street; and when the townsmen were summoned to the gathering, the cry was raised, 'All at the Lower Burn', – a phrase that passed by elision into the word 'A'loreburn'.

The last occasion on which the rallying cry was used to summon all males between the ages of 16 and 60 was during the 1715 Rebellion. In response, the Jacobites left the town alone.

Alt Clut See KINGDOM OF THE ROCK, THE.

Am Ah richt or am Ah wrang? A rhetorical question asserting the infallibility of the speaker regarding the point in question. The expected answer is 'You're richt.' A variant is 'Am Ah richt or am Ah richt?' to which the answer is the same, but more so.

Amber Mile, the See ROSE STREET.

Americans, gullible See HAGGIS.

Am fear th'air an t-slabhruidh (Gaelic, 'the man on the chain) A name for the Devil in the Outer Hebrides, according to George Henderson in his *Survivals in Belief Among the Celts* (1911). The chain in question was that over the fire, which was said to be cursed, and thus touching it was taboo. *Cf* WAG-AT-THE-WA'

Amsterdam was built on the back of Bressay A saying relating to the Shetland island of Bressay, off the east coast of Mainland. In the 17th and 18th centuries large fleets of Dutch vessels fished in Bressay Sound and thereabouts, reputedly making fortunes for their owners. Fort Charlotte in Lerwick was built in 1665 to protect the Sound of Bressay from the Dutch navy at the outbreak of the Second Anglo–Dutch War, but was burnt by them in 1673, during the Third Anglo–Dutch War. The present structure, named after the queen consort of George III, dates from 1781.

Anacreon, the Scotch See SCOTCH ANACREON, THE.

Andrew Ferrary or **Andro Ferrara** A Scottish broadsword. Some authorities say that the term refers to Andrea dei Ferrari ('Andrew of the Armourers'), a 16th-century swordsmith from Belluno, a town in the Dolomites north of Venice, while others suggest one Andrew Ferrars or Ferrier, possibly an Italian swordsmith resident in Arbroath.

Angelical Thomas See MAJOR WEIR.

Angel's Peak See DEVIL'S POINT, THE.

Angel's share, the That portion of all whiskies that is lost through evaporation through the oak of the barrels during the maturation process, amounting to some 2 per cent of the volume each year. *The Angel's Share* is also the title of a 2012 comic heist movie directed by Ken Loach with a screenplay by Paul Laverty, about a young offender from Glasgow who is found to have a connoisseur's nose for fine whisky.

Angus Og The anglicized version of the Gaelic Aonghas Òg, 'young Angus', the name of a number of notable characters. Aengus Òg (variously spelt) was the Celtic god of love, and looms large in Irish mythology. In Scottish history, Aonghas Òg (d. 1328) was Lord of Islay and head of Clan Donald, and fought alongside Robert the Bruce at Bannockburn. Another Aonghas Òg (d.1490) was the bastard son of the last independent LORD OF THE ISLES, and fought his father at BLOODY BAY. He met a violent end when his Irish harpist cut his throat while he was sleeping. Finally, Angus Og was the hero of a cartoon strip that appeared for many years in the *Daily Record* and *Sunday Mail*. Drawn by Ewen Bain, a Glasgow art teacher who originally came from Skye and who died in 1990, Angus Og was an archetypal TEUCHTER, who lived on the non-existent island of Drambeg, 'fairest island in the Utter Hebrides'.

Annacker's midden A complete mess; a *midden* is a dunghill or refuse heap. The allusion is to a firm of Glasgow butchers and sausage manufacturers, in business in various parts of the city from 1853 to 1942, whose refuse bins for sub-standard bits and pieces were regularly gone through by the destitute for scraps of sustenance, leaving behind messes that were to become proverbial. *See also* MIDGIE-RAKER.

Annan, Tweed and Clyde Three of Scotland's principal rivers rise relatively close together in the Southern Uplands, giving rise to the old rhyme:

Annan, Tweed and Clyde
Rise oot o' ane hillside.
Tweed ran, Annan wan,
Clyde fell, and brak its neck owre Corra Linn.

(Corra Linn is one of the Falls of Clyde.) There is some poetic licence in the rhyme, however. Although the Tweed and Annan both rise in the Moffat Hills close to the DEVIL'S BEEF TUB, the Clyde has its headwaters in the Lowther Hills a few miles to the west. Nevertheless, the triadic image seems to have fixed itself in many an imagination. For example, the explorer James Bruce (the ABYS-SINIAN) found the supposed source of the Blue Nile (which he discovered in 1770) something of a disappointment in comparison:

The marsh and fountains, upon comparison with the rise of many of our rivers, became now a trifling object in my sight. I remembered that majestic scene in my own country, where Tweed, Clyde and Annan rise on one hill ...
  – James Bruce, *Travels to Discover the Source of the Nile* (1790)

Annie Laurie *See* 'BONNIE ANNIE LAURIE'.

Annie McShuggle frae Ochintoogle An archety-pical clippy on the old Glasgow tramcars (or *caurs*), as in the rhyme:

Fares please, fares please,
You can hear me say,
As Ah collect ma money
Aw the day.

Ah work in the corporation,
You can tell it by ma dress,
Ah'm Annie McShuggle frae Ochintoogle,
The caur conductoress.

Annie Rooney, to have an To exhibit a fit of temper; the expression is current in Glasgow.

The identity of Ms Rooney is unknown, and she may just be a stereotypically hot-tempered Irish person.

Another clean shirt an' that'll be me A phrase prognosticating imminent extinction. It is to be heard on the lips of the more gloomy hypochon-driacs of Glasgow, when someone makes the mis-take of asking them how they are.

Another for Hector! *See* HEDGES OF DEATH, THE.

An' that And so on. The phrase is often added as a suffix to a proposition or discourse that the speaker cannot be bothered to complete.

An' then yer arse fell aff An appropriate response to someone who is indulging in insufferable brag-gadocio.

Anthrax Island The nickname of Gruinard Island, a small, somewhat featureless island in the beautiful Gruinard Bay, between Poolewe and Ullapool. In 1942 government scientists used the island for an experiment in biological warfare, exploding a bomb that spread the spores of anthrax. The disease killed off the resident sheep in a matter of days. The government was persuaded of the effectiveness of anthrax as a weapon of mass destruction, and con-tingency plans, authorized by Churchill, were drawn up in 1944 to bomb German cities with anthrax bombs should the Germans themselves employ bacteriological weapons. After the war, various at-tempts were made to decontaminate the island, all unsuccessful until 1986, when the island was soused in sea water and formaldehyde. In 1990 the Ministry of Defence lifted the long-standing quarantine, and people were once more allowed to land on Gruinard Island.

Antiburghers *See* BURGHERS VERSUS ANTIBUR-GHERS.

Anti-Panties *See* KNICKERBOCKER POLITICIAN, THE.

Antonine Wall *See* GRYME'S DYKE.

Ant-tossing A form of divination formerly practised in Gaeldom:

> This animal is shaken between the palms of the hand and laid upon the table. It is believed by boys to indicate the weather of the following day, by lighting on its back or belly and the alacrity with which it moves away.
>
> – John G. Campbell, *Superstitions of the Highlands and Islands of Scotland* (1900)

Aperitif A set of dentures.

Apostle of the Highlanders St Columba (521–97), who, arriving in Iona from Ireland, proceeded to convert the inhabitants of DALRIADA.

Apothecary, the *See* ADVERSITY HUME.

Appin Murder, the A notorious assassination that took place in the wake of the failed '45 Jacobite Rising, in the region of northwest Argyll known as Appin. On 14 May 1752 Colin Roy Campbell of Glenure, known as the Red Fox because of his hair colour and flushed face, was shot on the road between Ballachulish and Duror in the wood of Lettermore by an unknown gunman on the hillside above. In Robert Louis Stevenson's *Kidnapped* (1886), chapter xvii, the murder is witnessed by the hero, David Balfour:

> But just as he turned there came the shot of a firelock from higher up the hill; and with the very sound of it Glenure fell upon the road.
>
> 'O, I am dead!' he cried, several times over.
>
> The lawyer had caught him up and held him in his arms, the servant standing over and clasping his hands. And now the wounded man looked from one to another with scared eyes, and there was a change in his voice, that went to the heart.
>
> 'Take care of yourselves,' says he. 'I am dead.'
>
> He tried to open his clothes as if to look for the wound, but his fingers slipped on the buttons. With that he gave a great sigh, his head rolled on his shoulder, and he passed away.

Young David sets off up the hill in pursuit of the assassin:

> So little a time had elapsed, that when I got to the top of the first steepness, and could see some part of the open mountain, the murderer was still moving away at no great distance. He was a big man, in a black coat, with metal buttons, and carried a long fowling-piece.
>
> 'Here!' I cried. 'I see him!'
>
> At that the murderer gave a little, quick look over his shoulder, and began to run. The next moment he was lost in a fringe of birches; then he came out again on the upper side, where I could see him climbing like a jackanapes, for that part was again very steep; and then he dipped behind a shoulder, and I saw him no more.

David, rather than being credited with helping to catch the killer, is suspected of being an accomplice, and is obliged to flee.

Apart from the involvement of Balfour, which is pure fiction, Stevenson based his version of events on the historical record. Campbell of Glenure had been appointed factor of the estate of the Jacobite supporter Stewart of Ardshiel, which had been forfeited by the government. The Stewarts were immediately suspected of having a hand in the murder. The main suspect was the man who had returned undercover from exile to collect Ardshiel's rents – Allan Breck Stewart (the basis for the character of Alan BRECK in *Kidnapped*). But he evaded capture, and the authorities seized in his place his former guardian, James Stewart, known as *Seumas a' Ghlinne* or James of the Glen, and put him on trial at Inverary before a Campbell-dominated jury, with the Duke of Argyll, chief of the Campbells, as judge. James was found guilty IN AIRTS AND PAIRTS (i.e. as an accessory to the crime) and on 8 November 1752 was hanged on Gallows Hill at Ballachulish.

It is said that the identity of the actual killer is known to the Stewarts of Appin, but that the secret has been kept secure within the family for the past 250 years. The antipathy of the Stewarts of Appin towards the Campbells is reflected in this anecdote related by the novelist Henry Mackenzie (1745–1831):

> A jocular anecdote of old blind Mr Stewart [of Appin]. The boy who was reading to him from the Book of Job mispronounced the word *camels*. 'If he had so many Cawmells in his household,' said Mr Stewart, 'I do not wonder at his misthriving.'

Apprentice's Pillar, the *See* PRENTICE PILLAR, THE.

April gowk The victim of an April fool; *see* HUNTEGOWK.

Arabs Self-appointed nickname for supporters of Dundee United FC.

Arbroath smokie Haddock that is smoked over hardwood unsplit (unlike, for example, FINNAN HADDIE) until it is a beautiful golden or coppery colour. There is a tale that the smokie was born when a haddock was found in the smouldering remains of a cottage that had burnt down – and was found to be delicious. Arbroath smokies actually originated in the nearby fishing village of Auchmithie, and were originally known as *Auchmithie lucken* or *pinwiddies*. In the early 19th century several families from Auchmithie settled in Arbroath, and eventually production in the latter outstripped that in the former. In 2004 the European Commission gave the Arbroath smokie Protective Geographical Indication, meaning that only haddock smoked in the traditional fashion within 8 km (5 miles) of the centre of Arbroath could bear the name. A special Arbroath smokie tartan was created to celebrate this prestigious status, shared with the likes of Parma ham and Champagne.

Arch of heaven An old term for a RAINBOW.

Archibald the Grim Archibald, Earl of Douglas, Earl of Wigtown and Lord of Galloway (*c*.1328–1400), also known as Black Archibald, the bastard son of the BLACK DOUGLAS. In accordance with the AULD ALLIANCE he fought for the French at the Battle of Poitiers, where he was captured by the English but escaped. Back in Scotland he was made Lord Warden of the Marches, and succeeded in ridding Annandale of the English. He does not appear to have been outstandingly fierce or bloodthirsty by the standards of his day, so his nickname may reflect the description of him by the 15th-century chronicler Walter Bower as 'dark and ugly more like a coco [cook-boy] than a Noble'.

Another 'Archie the Grim' was Archibald Campbell, 7th Earl of Argyll (1575–1638), known in Gaelic as *Gillespie Gruamach*, so-called because of the ferocity with which he dealt with his enemies, notably the Macdonalds and the MacGregors.

Archibald the Tineman *See* TINEMAN, THE.

Archie's Rock A crag near Inchlaggan in Glen Garry. It is named after Archibald MacDonald, who, with his two brothers, owned Glen Garry in the 13th century. Their land was coveted by their neighbours, Cameron of Lochiel, Fraser of Lovat and Duncan MacDonell of Morar, who conspired together to kill off the brothers. One was murdered by Lovat while dining, another ambushed and dispatched by Lochiel's followers. The third brother, Archibald, was out hunting with MacDonell when they came to the eponymous rock. MacDonell asked Archibald if he could tell the time by the sun, and when the latter looked up, MacDonell drew his sword and sliced off his head – which, as it bounced down the rock, gasped out 'Two o'clock.'

Argyll's Bowling Green A humorous (in a Victorian sort of way) name applied to the far-from-flat, indeed notably nubbly, peninsula between Loch Long and Loch Goil. It was coined in the early 19th century. Sometimes the area referred to extends northward to take in the ARROCHAR ALPS:

> Up betimes next morning, you are on the beautiful road which runs between Tarbet and Arrochar, and begin, through broken, white up-streaming mists, to make acquaintance with the 'Cobbler' and some other peaks of that rolling country to which Celtic facetiousness has given the name of 'The Duke of Argyle's Bowling-green'.
> – Alexander Smith, *A Summer in Skye* (1865)

Argyll's Eyeglass *See* COBBLER, THE.

Ariosto of the North, the Byron's characterization of Sir Walter Scott:

> Great as thou art, yet paralleled by those
> Thy countrymen, before thee born to shine,
> The bards of Hell and Chivalry: first rose
> The Tuscan father's comedy divine;
> Then, not unequal to the Florentine,

The Southern Scott, the minstrel who called forth
A new creation with his magic line,
And, like the Ariosto of the North,
Sang ladye-love and war, romance and knightly
    worth.
    – *Childe Harold's Pilgrimage* (1818), canto IV, xl

The Italian poet Ludovico Ariosto (1474–1533) was the author of the romance epic *Orlando Furioso* (1516). The 'Tuscan father' is, of course, Dante, author of *The Divine Comedy*. *See also* SCOTCH ANACREON, THE.

Arkaig, Treasure of Loch *See* TREASURE OF LOCH ARKAIG.

Army of the Congregation of Christ *See* LORDS OF THE CONGREGATION.

Arran water A humorous euphemism for whisky (usually illicit) distilled on the isle of Arran. *See also* MOUNTAIN DEW.

Arrochar Alps, the The name given to the group of craggy mountains rising above the village of Arrochar, at the north end of Loch Long in Argyll, including the COBBLER, Beinn Ime, Beinn Narnain and the Brack. The name was first used by the working-class climbers of Clydeside who from the 1930s found Arrochar an accessible sort of Mecca; it is thus a less sarcastic coinage than the WEST LOTHIAN ALPS. The name was first used in print in 1946, by Ben Humble, an Arrochar aficionado. The coinage was not entirely original:

Our Scottish Alps …
Fu' aft disdain to doff their dun
Snaw-tooried bannets to the sun.
    – J. Young, *Lochlomondside* (1872)

Arrow of Glen Lyon, the A sobriquet of Alasdair MacGregor of Glen Strae (1567–1604), chief of his clan and son of Gregor MacGregor, who made the famous MACGREGOR'S LEAP over the River Lyon. 'The Arrow of Glen Lyon' is the title of an anonymous Gaelic poem addressed to Alasdair MacGregor, who was a keen hunter, skilled in the making of arrows:

Terror of all our foes, pride of Glen Lyon!
Thou wert a skilled fletcher, thy quiver ever full.
See how the sharp arrow is winged with the eagle's
    plume,
Bound with silken thread, red and green, from
    Ireland,
Waxed to shield the polished shaft from the heat of
    the sun.

In 1602 MacGregor led his men against the Colquhouns of Luss in Glen Fruin – resulting in the so-called Slaughter of Lennox (*see* MACGREGOR, PROSCRIPTION OF CLAN). Following his capture, MacGregor was taken to Edinburgh where in 1604 he was hanged his own height above his fellows in honour of his rank.

Arse, as hard as Hinnerson's *See* HARD AS HINNERSON'S ERSE, AS.

Arse, they shall also see my *See* WISEST FOOL IN CHRISTENDOM, THE.

Arthur o' Bower A personification of the wind, as in this verse collected in Robert Chambers's *Popular Rhymes of Scotland* (1842 edition):

Arthur o' Bower has broken his band,
And he's come roaring owre the lands;
The king o' Scots, and a' his power
Canna turn Arthur o' Bower.

Arthur's Oon or **Arthuris Hufe** 'Arthur's oven' or 'Arthur's hall', a beehive-shaped Roman building that stood on the north bank of the River Carron, near to the Carron Ironworks, until demolished in 1743 by Sir Michael Bruce, Laird of Stenhouse, in order that the stones could be used to make a new weir. When detailed drawings were made in 1726, it was described as 'the Roman Sacellum of Mars Signifier, vulgarly called Arthur's Oon'. Quite how it became associated with King Arthur is unknown; it was also known as *Julius' Hoff* (after Julius Caesar). The name *Arthuris Hufe* was also applied to the constellation Arcturus, for example by Gavin Douglas in his Scots version of *The Aeneid* (1513).

Arthur's Seat Edinburgh's mini-mountain, resembling from various perspectives the form of a lion couchant. It is a remnant, like Castle Rock and Calton Hill, of the vast 'Edinburgh Volcano' that blew its top some 325 million years ago. The hill has been identified with Arthur, the legendary British king, since at least the 12th century, when the Anglo-Norman chronicler Gerald of Wales called it *Cathedra Arturii* ('Arthur's throne'). The association may be even older: the ancient Brythonic tribe, the Votadini, had their capital on Castle Rock, and are the subject of the poem *Y GODODDIN*, which was written *c*. AD 600 and which mentions Arthur – although this mention may be a later addition. There certainly is a broadly contemporary Iron Age hill fort on the summit. By the 16th century the name had become anglicized, as attested in Walter Kennedy's 1508 FLYTING with Dunbar:

> Do thou not thus, brigane, thou sall be brynt,
> With pik, tar, fire, gunpoldre, and lynt
> On Arthuris-Sete, or on a hyar hyll.

In his *Itinerary* of 1617, the English traveller Fynes Morison calls it 'the Chair of Arthur'. William Maitland in his *History of Edinburgh* (1753) suggests the origin of the name is in fact *Ard-na-Saighead* (Gaelic, 'height of the arrows'). Less plausible is the suggestion that the name is a corruption of 'Archers' Seat'.

Arthur's Seat and environs feature in Scott's HEART OF MIDLOTHIAN (1818), Hogg's *Private Memoirs and Confessions of a Justified Sinner* (1824), Stevenson's unfinished *Weir of Hermiston* (*see* HUNTER'S BOG) and Ian Rankin's *The Falls* (2001), to name but a few literary appearances, while the poet Thomas Campbell composed much of *The Pleasures of Hope* (1799) while taking energetic walks about the hill. In *The Heart of Midlothian*, Scott quotes a fine old song, said to describe the fate of Barbara Erskine, daughter of the Earl of Mar, who was abandoned by her husband, the Marquess of Douglas (for more details of the case, *see under* WALY):

> Now Arthur's Seat shall be my bed,
> The sheets shall ne'er be pressed by me;
> St Anton's Well shall be my drink,
> Since my true love has forsaken me.
>
> Martinmas wind, when wilt thou blaw,
> And shake the green leaves aff the tree?
> O gentle death, when wilt thou come?
> For of my life I am wearie.

In 1784 the famous quack and sex therapist Dr James Graham returned to his native Edinburgh, having run into debt in London despite the success of his Temple of Hymen and his Celestial Bed (in which couples, for a fee of £50, had the opportunity to be 'agitated in the delights of love' with the aid of electricity; other treatments favoured by Dr Graham included ice-cold champagne douches). In Edinburgh, in support of his belief that disease was caused by excess heat, he proposed to build a huge and presumably draughty Temple of Health on the summit of Arthur's Seat, 'in order to try how far the utmost degree of cold in the locality of Edinburgh could be borne' (James Grant, *Cassell's Old and New Edinburgh*, 1880s). Fortunately, his proposal was rejected by the authorities.

There is an old pagan custom, still observed, that every Mayday young women climb Arthur's Seat to wash their faces in the dew at sunrise, hoping to ensure their beauty endures. The custom is not just confined to young women: on 1 May 1826, at the age of 81, Dr Andrew Duncan, founder of the Morningside Asylum, made the ascent, and survived another two years.

> Who indeed, that has once seen Edinburgh, with its couchant lion crag, but must see it again in dreams, waking or sleeping.
> – Charlotte Brontë, letter

See also GUTTIT HADDIE (for the Waterspout of Arthur's Seat); HANGMAN'S CRAIG; RADICAL ROAD; SALISBURY CRAGS; WELLS OF WEARIE.

There is also an Arthur's Seat in Dumfriesshire; it is a subsidiary top (731 m) of Hart Fell, north of Moffat.

As deep and dirty as the Clyde (Of a person) completely untrustworthy.

As gross an imposition as ever the world was troubled with *See* OSSIAN FORGERIES, THE.

Assured Scots Those Scots who, for a financial consideration, collaborated with the English during the ROUGH WOOING of the 1540s. After the war some of them were put on trial; 192 citizens of Dundee were acquitted, and the entire town of Dumfries received a pardon.

As weel soon as syne The sooner the better; both *soon* and *syne* suggest PDQ.

Asylum of railway lunatics, an Lord Cockburn's description of Scotland as the railway boom got under way in the 1840s: 'The country is an asylum of railway lunatics.' He was in particular referring to the financial speculation surrounding the new industry, as schemes were launched to create direct links between innumerable small towns with innumerable other small towns, more with an eye to gathering up investment than yielding a profit. The inevitable crash occurred in October 1847, with railway shares losing 85 per cent of their peak value.

Athens of the North, the A somewhat self-regarding sobriquet first adopted by Edinburgh in the later 18th century, when it was the centre of the SCOTTISH ENLIGHTENMENT, and indeed a new Athens in the intellectual sphere. An early version of the name appears in a letter dated 29 July 1761 from Alexander Carlyle to Sir Gilbert Elliot, in which the former refers to Edinburgh as 'the Athens of Great Britain'. The name also reflects the classical architecture of the NEW TOWN, in particular the old Royal High School, which is modelled on the Temple of Theseus in Athens, and EDINBURGH'S FOLLY, based on the Parthenon. Topographically, the SEVEN HILLS OF EDINBURGH make it in this respect 'the Rome of the North'. Not all have been convinced by Edinburgh's claim – or indeed the claim of Scotland more generally – to have inherited the mantle of ancient Athens:

REVD DR FOLLIOTT. Sir, I say every nation has some eximious virtue; and your country is pre-eminent in the glory of fish for breakfast. We have much to learn from you in that line at any rate.

MR MAC QUEDY. And in many others, sir, I believe. Morals and metaphysics, politics and political economy, the way to make the most of all the modifications of smoke; steam, gas, and paper currency; you have all these to learn from us; in short, all the arts and sciences. We are the modern Athenians.

REVD DR FOLLIOTT. I, for one, sir, am content to learn nothing from you but the art and science of fish for breakfast. Be content, sir, to rival the Boeotians, whose redeeming virtue was in fish … and leave the name of

Athenians to those who have a sense of the beautiful, and a perception of metrical quantity.
– Thomas Love Peacock, *Crotchet Castle* (1831)

The Irish journalist William Maginn (1794–1842) was equally dismissive:

This Edinburgh some call Metropolis,
And Capital, and Athens of the North –
I know not what they mean.

See also AULD REEKIE; LITTLE SPARTA; REYKJAVIK OF THE SOUTH, THE.

Atholl, Sow of *See* BOAR OF BADENOCH.

Atholl brose A dish comprising oatmeal, honey and whisky, sometimes with cream, traditionally stirred with a silver spoon. It was formerly used as a cure for colds and is now served as a dessert in restaurants specializing in Scottish cuisine. (*Cranachan* is a similar dessert, although it always includes cream, and often raspberries.) The name is said to derive from a story from the reign of James III (1460–88). This relates how in 1475 the Earl of Atholl captured the rebel John MacDonald, Earl of Ross and LORD OF THE ISLES, by filling a small well in Skye (from which the latter was wont to drink) with honey and whisky. The rebel earl, duly duped, dallied too long by this Hippocrene spring and was taken in his cups. Others less convincingly date the story to the '45 Rebellion, when the Duke of Atholl is said to have used this ploy against his Jacobite enemies. The dish furnished the English poet Thomas Hood (1799–1845) – whose father's family hailed from Errol in the Carse of Gowrie – with the title of a poem and a satisfying pun:

Charm'd with a drink which Highlanders compose,
A German traveller exclaim'd with glee, –
Potzausend! sare, if dis is Athol Brose,
How goot dere Athol Boetry must be!

BROSE on its own is basically either oatmeal or peasemeal porridge. *See also* KAIL BROSE; PEASE BROSE.

Atholl Crescent Formerly an informal name for the Edinburgh College of Domestic Science, which was located in this elegant New Town street between 1891 and 1970.

Atholl Highlanders, the The only legal private army in the UK. The first Atholl Highlanders was the 77th Regiment of Foot, a regular unit raised by the 4th Duke of Atholl in 1777. It was disbanded in 1783 following a mutiny. In 1839 the 6th Duke, then Lord Glenlyon, raised a ceremonial body called the Atholl Highlanders, which escorted Queen Victoria on her tour of Perthshire in 1842 and provided her with a guard during her stay at Blair Castle (the seat of the dukes of Atholl) in 1844. In gratitude (and in the fevered spirit of tartanry then prevalent), Victoria gave the Atholl Highlanders official status by presenting them with colours. The Atholl Highlanders make regular ceremonial appearances at Blair Castle, but have never seen active service as such.

At the knag and the widdie At loggerheads; in strong disagreement; failing to sing from the same hymn sheet. A *knag* is a lump of knotty wood or a hook (hence *knaggit* can mean ill-tempered or sour), while a *widdie* is literally a willow (sometimes a willow wand used as a latch or door fastening), and is used figuratively of someone who is very stubborn or contrary.

At the length an lang At last. In Orkney and Shetland they say *at de lang an de lent*. The phrase *at lang length* means the same.

At the lug o' the law Having the ear (*lug*) of the court; having one's finger on the pulse of events; being at the centre of affairs. The expression has fallen out of use.

Attila the Hen *See* STALIN'S GRANNY.

Atween the wind an the wa Literally, 'between the wind and the wave', i.e. between the Devil and deep blue sea.

Auchengeich Disaster The worst pit disaster in Scotland in the 20th century. It took place at the Auchengeich Colliery, Lanarkshire, on 18 September 1959. An electrical fault caused an underground

fire, in which 47 men lost their lives owing to carbon monoxide poisoning. It was not the first major accident at Auchengeich: on 22 January 1931 six miners were killed in an explosion.

Auchenshoogle The home town of the BROONS, who live in a tenement flat at number 10 Glebe Street. The name (sometimes Auchentogle) only came into use in the comic strip in the 1990s, prior to which the locality was nameless. It is also the home of OOR WULLIE. The fictional Auchenshoogle contains elements of both Dundee and Glasgow, and its name is now used to denote the archetypal small Scottish town, both jocularly and seriously. For an example of the former, visit the website of Auchenshoogle Library (auchenshoogle.bravehost. com), and for an example of the latter, see the essay on territorial designations on scotshistory.online. co.uk by Stuart Morris of Balgonie and Eddergoll:

> Once a territorial designation has been recognized by the Lord Lyon (who, in all matters to do with titles and heraldry in Scotland, uses the Royal prerogative), it must be used and not played with. James MacTavish of Auchenshoogle cannot be James MacTavish through the week and MacTavish of Auchenshoogle at the weekend or at Highland Balls.

The name was no doubt inspired by the Glasgow district of Auchenshuggle (from Gaelic *Achadh an t-Seagail*, 'the field of rye'); in the fictional place name, the element *shoogle* is the Scots word for 'to shake'.

Auchterarder Creed, the A doctrine adopted by the presbytery of Auchterarder in Perthshire in 1717. It held that 'It is not sound and orthodox to teach that we must forsake sin in order to our coming to Christ.' This was interpreted by some to imply that God's chosen elect can do what they damn well please. This was one of the key points of dispute in the MARROW CONTROVERSY, and the creed was condemned by the General Assembly as 'unsound and detestable doctrine'.

Auld Alliance, the The longstanding alliance between Scotland and France against the common enemy, England. Although legend suggests that it originated in 809, when a Scots king called Achaius or Eochaid supposedly agreed to help Charlemagne fight the Saxons, historically speaking the alliance originated in the treaty signed between John de Balliol and Philip IV of France in 1295. It was regularly renewed (usually on the accession of a new monarch to the throne of either kingdom) until finally abandoned in 1560. Ironically, the first known written reference to 'the auld allyance' dates from 1566.

The Auld Alliance bound each party to invade English territory should England attack either of them, and Scots armies fought in France during the Hundred Years' War against England (and it was a company of Scots soldiers who formed the French monarch's bodyguard, the GARDE ECOSSAISE). However, the Auld Alliance could lead the Scots into rash invasions of England: in 1346 David II was captured at the Battle of Neville's Cross; and in 1513 James IV was killed alongside 10,000 of his fellow countrymen at Flodden Field, having invaded the north of England at the request of the French. Nevertheless, the diplomatic pieties continued, and in 1525 we find the French regent, Louise de Savoie, Duchesse d'Angoulême, in a letter to the Estates of Scotland, expressing 'the ancient and inviolable love, alliance, federation and affinity which has been from the earliest times, and is now, between the House of France and that of Scotland'.

The Alliance was at its strongest following James V's marriage to the French noblewoman Mary of Guise, and the English invasion known as the ROUGH WOOING, after which French troops were stationed in Scotland and the infant Mary Queen of Scots was married off to the French dauphin. However, the Reformation in Scotland persuaded the Protestant Scots that they shared greater common cause with the Protestant English than with the Catholic French – and also closer trading ties – resulting in a diplomatic revolution and the Anglo–Scottish accord embodied in the Treaty of Edinburgh of 1560.

Although the Auld Alliance may not always have worked out in favour of the Scots' own best interests in political or military terms, it did lead to a great enrichment of Scottish culture, as attested by the French vocabulary and international outlook found in the works of Dunbar and other poets of the Scottish Renaissance, and in the impact on law, architecture (as can be seen, for example, in the older parts of Holyroodhouse) and cuisine – for example, to this day in Scotland a *gigot* (the Old French word for a leg of lamb or mutton) will be served on an *ashet* (from French *assiette*, 'plate'). (For other instances of French influence on vocabulary, *see for example* BEJAN; DINNAE FASH YERSEL; GARDYLOO; HOGMANAY; JAW-PISH.) Such influences were strengthened by the large numbers of Scots – such as John Mair or Major (*HADDINGTONUS SCOTUS*) and John Ireland (*see MEROURE OF WYSSDOME, THE*) – who attended the University of Paris, or served as mercenaries for the French crown. And the taste of Scotland's elite for claret survived the formal ending of the Auld Alliance, and even in the late 17th century, Scottish wine merchants visiting Bordeaux were given first choice of the region's wines.

> Good claret best keeps out the cauld,
> And drives away the winter sorn;
> It makes a man baith gash and bauld,
> And heaves his saul beyond the morn.
> – Allan Ramsay, 'To the Ph——'

(Lord Cockburn recalled that in 1798, as Britain fought Revolutionary France, the Edinburgh city fathers 'passed a self-denying ordinance, by which they resolved to ruin France by abstaining from claret at this and all other municipal festivals. The vow, however, was not kept; and so the French were not ruined.')

The Auld Alliance has long provided a reference point in diplomatic exchanges. In 1427, Alain Chartier, Chancellor of Bayeux, gave the following speech (in French) while on a mission to Scotland to propose a marriage between the dauphin and the daughter of James I:

> We have tested the faith of the Scots in adverse times – a faithful nation, a people most worthy of friendship and renown, tried in manhood, whom we cannot honour enough or praise worthily. Nor is the league between us written in parchment of sheepskin, but rather in the flesh and skin of men, traced not in ink but in blood shed in many places.

Half a millennium later, in a speech given in Edinburgh in 1942, Charles de Gaulle, leader of the Free French, referred to 'the oldest alliance in the world':

> In every combat where for five centuries the destiny of France was at stake, there were always men of Scotland to fight side by side with men of France, and what Frenchmen feel is that no people has ever been more generous than yours with its friendship.

The relationship has continued to have its ambivalences. At the height of the banking crisis in 2009, President Nicolas Sarkozy of France reportedly told Prime Minister Gordon Brown:

> You know, Gordon, I should not like you. You are Scottish, we have nothing in common and you are an economist. But somehow, Gordon, I love you ... But not in a sexual way.

Auld Bleary A nickname of Robert II (reigned 1371–90), who in 1384, when he was 68, was effectively deposed in a palace coup by his eldest son, John, Earl of Carrick. John became Guardian of Scotland, while his father retired to Dundonald Castle in Ayrshire. Although by the time he lost power Robert was by the standards of the day a very old man (hence, presumably, the nickname), he had shown his vigour by siring 14 children by his two wives, plus perhaps 20 illegitimate children by a variety of mistresses. His son John ascended the throne as Robert III; he was to prove, in his own words, the WORST OF KINGS AND MOST MISERABLE OF MEN.

Auld claiths and cauld porritch The epitome of enforced austerity. For example, in those impoverished January days after Christmas excess, it is back to *auld claiths and cauld porritch*.

Auld Clootie The Devil. A *cloot* is a hoof, two of which are supposedly to be found at the base of Auld Clootie's shaggy legs. A variant on the name is *Daddy Cloots*. For Clootie's croft, *see* GOODMAN'S CROFT.

> O thou! whatever title suit thee,
> Auld Hornie, Satan, Nick, or Clootie.
> – Robert Burns, 'Address to the Deil' (1786)

A report spread in town and country that a man, dressed in a bullock's skin, with the horns fastened on his forehead, had robbed the house of a maiden lady, under the character of 'Auld Clootie', compelling her to give up her goods, or be carried off by him. A rumour was circulated of his apprehension and trial, and that he had been sentenced to stand in the pillory in the High Street of Edinburgh on a day specified.

> – John Strathesk (ed.), Hawkie, *The Autobiography of a Gangrel* (1888)

There are a plethora of similar semi-jocular familiar names for the Devil, including the Auld Yin, the Auld Boy, the Auld Black Lad, the Auld Chiel, the AULD ENEMY, Auld Bobbie, Auld Harry, Auld Hornie, the Auld Man, Auld Mishanter (*mishanter*, 'disaster'), Auld Nick, Auld Nicky Blue-Thooms, Auld Roughy, Auld Sandy, Auld Simmy, Auld Sootie, the Auld Thief and Auld Whaap-neb. *See also* DEVIL, THE.

Auld Enemy, the England. The phrase is now mostly used jocularly, especially in sporting contexts.

> Our Scottish identity ... is, at the heart, constructed out of our hatred of England, our profound sense of injustice, our massive chip on the shoulder; take away the Auld Enemy, and there is nothing left.
> – *The Scotsman*, 16 April 1992

The Auld Enemy, or just *the Enemy*, formerly denoted the Devil:

> The peasantry in Scotland ... having a strong impression of the necessity of decency of language ... have employed a variety of denominations, to avoid that familiar use that might either indicate or produce trivial views of the eternal world. Thus he [the Devil] is sometimes called, *the Ill man, the Fiend ... the Enemy*.
> – John Jamieson, *An Etymological Dictionary of the Scottish Language* (1825 supplement)

Auld Grey Toon, the A sobriquet awarded to at least three Scottish burghs: Dunfermline, St Andrews and Hawick (aka the Grey Auld Toon, and known to the tourist industry as *the Queen o' the Borders*).

> They're but cauld kail an' soor dook [sour milk] beside the burgers o' the Auld Grey Toon!
> – S.R. Crockett, *The Stickit Minister* (1893)

Auld hech how, the The same old routine, circumstances, state of health, etc., with a suggestion that returning to or continuing with same is a prospect not to be welcomed – *hech how* being an interjection expressing despondency and sorrow. John Jamieson, in his *Etymological Dictionary of the Scottish Language* (1825 supplement), cites the following lines from 'A. Scott's Poems, 1811' (it has not so far proved possible to identify this poet):

> O Richie Gall! cauld 'mang the dead, –
> Thou's left us a' without remead
>   To sigh hech howe,
> That on that heart the worms should feed,
>   Or gowan grow.

Auld Hornie Another name for the Devil; *see* AULD CLOOTIE.

Auld in the horn Experienced and wise; the phrase derives from the practice of telling a cow or a sheep's age by the markings on its horns, and their length.

Auld Kirk, the The established Church of Scotland, as distinct from the Free Church of Scotland that broke away in the DISRUPTION OF 1843.

> The gude auld Kirk o' Scotland,
> The wild winds round her blaw,
> And when her foemen hear her sough,
> They prophecy her fa';
> But what although her fate has been
> Amang the floods to sit –
> The gude auld Kirk o' Scotland,
> She's nae in ruins yet!
>   – George Murray (1819–68), 'The Auld Kirk o' Scotland'

Auld Kirk also became a euphemism for whisky, perhaps because the established Church was less condemnatory of strong liquor than the Free Church, or alternatively because in many places the income of Church of Scotland ministers depended on the price of barley, from which whisky is made.

> Now what will you tak? A glass of wine or a wee drappie of the 'Auld Kirk'?
>   – John Plenderleith, *The Kittlegairy Vacancy; or, a New Way of Getting Rid of Old Ministers* (1884)

See also WEE FREES.

'Auld Lang Syne' An old Scottish song, collected by Robert Burns, but not original to him, as he himself acknowledged (although the verses beginning 'We twa hae run about the braes' and 'We twa hae paidl'd in the burn' appear to be Burns's own creations). The title literally means 'old long since', i.e. 'times past', sentimentally viewed. The song, to the tune of 'Can ye labour lea', is universally sung just after the BELLS on New Year's Day – a custom that goes back to at least the late 19th century.

> Should auld acquaintance be forgot,
>   And never brought to mind?
> Should auld acquaintance be forgot,
>   And auld lang syne!
>
> *For auld lang syne, my dear,*
>   *For auld lang syne.*
> *We'll tak a cup o' kindness yet,*
>   *For auld lang syne.*
>
> And surely ye'll be your pint-stoup!
>   And surely I'll be mine!
> And we'll tak a cup o' kindness yet,
>   For auld lang syne.
> *For auld, &c.*
>
> We twa hae run about the braes,
>   And pou'd the gowans fine;
> But we've wander'd mony a weary fit,
>   Sin' auld lang syne.
> *For auld, &c.*
>
> We twa hae paidl'd in the burn,
>   Frae morning sun till dine;
> But seas between us braid hae roar'd
>   Sin' auld lang syne.
> *For auld, &c.*
>
> And there's a hand, my trusty fiere!
>   And gie's a hand o' thine!
> And we'll tak a right gude-willie waught,
>   For auld lang syne.
> *For auld, &c.*

[*be your pint-stoup*, buy your pint cup; *braes*, hillsides; *gowans*, daisies; *fit*, foot; *paidl'd*, paddled; *braid*, broad; *fiere*, friend; *good-willie waught*, goodwill draught]

The first known reference to the song is in James Watson's *Choice Collection of Comic and Serious Scots Poems* (1711), where it appears as 'Old Longsyne', although its origins may well go much further back. Burns himself, who found the phrase *auld lang syne* 'exceedingly expressive', acknowledged the antiquity of the song in a letter dated September 1793:

Light be the turf on the breast of the heaven-inspired poet who composed this glorious fragment! There is more of the fire of native genius in it than half-a-dozen of modern English Bacchanalians.

Burns was however in error when he claimed that this 'song of the olden times'

... has never been in print, nor even in manuscript, until I took it down from an old man singing ...

– as, in addition to Watson's version, the phrase had appeared in similar poems by Robert Ayton (1570–1638) and Allan Ramsay (1686–1757).

Regarding the third verse, there are a number of mentions of 'plucking the gowans fine' in the comic novels of P.G. Wodehouse, while in Dickens's *David Copperfield* Mr Micawber quotes the line about gowans, adding, 'I am not exactly aware ... what gowans may be, but I have no doubt that Copperfield and myself would frequently have taken a pull at them, had it been feasible.'

Auld Lichts and New Lichts The nicknames given to opposing factions within the Kirk and its various secessionist groupings in the 18th and 19th centuries (*see for example* BURGHERS VERSUS ANTIBURGHERS). The more Calvinist and conservative Auld Lichts adhered to the obligations of the Solemn League and Covenant (*see* COVENANTERS), while the New Lichts were more liberal in theological terms. The various breakaway churches founded at various times by both Auld Lichts and New Lichts have long been reabsorbed into the Church of Scotland. Burns alludes to the schism in 'The Twa Herds' (posthumously published in 1801):

He fine a mangy sheep could scrub
Or nobly fling the gospel club,
And New-Light herds could nicely drub,
    Or pay their skin,
Could shake them o'er the burning dub,
    Or heave them in.

'The Twa Herds' is a satire on two mutually antipathetic contemporary ministers, both zealous Auld

Lichts, namely the Revd Alexander Moodie (whose face, Burns tells us in 'The Holy Fair', would have frightened the Devil) and the Revd John Russell, whose voice 'roared every note of the damned'. Outsiders often found the niceties of what distinguished the Auld Lichts and the New Lichts difficult to fathom:

Who or what the 'New Lichts' were is somewhat difficult to define, as they might belong to any denomination; but, generally speaking, it was the 'Revivalists' and their followers who came under the category of 'New Lichts'. 'Salvation made easy' was the head and front of their offendings.
    – C.M. Thomson, *Drummeldale* (1899)

Auld maid's bairn or **wean** The perfectly behaved child of an elderly spinster's imagining, invoked when she is expressing disapproval of the carryings-on of real children.

'Twas true, as aft his granny said,
That auld maids' weans were aye weel-bred.
    – J.G. Horne, *Lan'wart Loon* (1928)

Auld Reekie An affectionate nickname for Edinburgh, meaning 'old smoky', referring to the wreaths of smoke that once hung permanently over the city.

When chitterin' cauld the day sall daw,
Loud may your bonny bugles blaw
    And loud your drums may beat.
Hie owre the land at evenfa'
Your lamps may glitter raw by raw,
    Along the gowsty street.

I gang nae mair where ance I gaed,
By Brunston, Fairmileheid, or Braid;
    But far frae Kirk and Tron.
O still ayont the muckle sea,
Still are ye dear, and dear to me,
    Auld Reekie, still and on!
    – Robert Louis Stevenson, 'Auld Reekie'

Tradition has it that it was James VI who coined the name, while viewing Edinburgh across the Forth from the coast of Fife. However, Robert Chambers, in his *Traditions of Edinburgh* (1824), states that:

This highly appropriate popular sobriquet cannot be traced beyond the reign of Charles the Second. A curious and recondite tradition assigns the following as the origin of the phrase. An old patriarchal gentleman in Fife, designated Durham of Largo, was in the habit, at the period mentioned, of regulating the time of evening-worship by the appearance of the smoke of Edinburgh, which he could easily see, through the clear summer twilight, from his own door. When he observed the smoke increase in density, in consequence of the good folks of the city preparing their supper, he would call all the family into the house, saying – 'It's time noo, bairns, to tak the beuks, and gang to our beds, for yonder's Auld Reekie, I see, putting on her nicht-cap!'

The poet Coleridge's first impression of the city was of 'the smoke ... rising from ten thousand homes' (letter to Robert Southey, 13 September 1803). Burns referred to the city fondly as 'Auld chuckie Reekie' ('To William Creech', 1787), while Robert Fergusson's poem 'Auld Reikie' (1773) is a satirical celebration of the city's stinks (*reek* also meaning 'to give off a stench'), in particular those associated with the emptying of bedpans in the morning (*see* GARDYLOO), which were also known as the FLOW-ERS OF EDINBURGH:

> On stair wi' tub, or pat [pot] in hand,
> The barefoot housemaids looe to stand,
> That antrin [wandering] fock may ken how snell [sharp]
> Auld Reikie will at morning smell:
> Then, with an inundation big as
> The burn that 'neath the Nore Loch Brig is,
> They kindly shower Edina's roses,
> To quicken and regale our noses.

A century later things had not improved much:

> We devoutly believe that no smell in Europe or Asia – not in Aleppo or Damascus in the present day – can equal in depth and intensity, in concentration and power, the diabolical combination of sulphurated hydrogen we came upon one evening about ten o'clock in a place called Toddrick's Wynd.
> – *The Builder*, 1856

Although the provision of more effective sanitation and the Clean Air Act of 1956 have done much to clear Edinburgh's air, the city may still, on a windless winter's day, when viewed from any of its hills, be part obliterated by a pall of pollution.

> Edina – Reekie – mon amour.
> Dae't, or I'll skelp your airse, ye hoor.
> – Hamish Henderson, 'Floret Silva Undique', from *Auld Reekie's Roses*

Auld Ringan Oliver A militant and mighty COVEN-ANTER about whom many tales were once told in his native Border country. A man celebrated as much for the strength of his physique as the strength of his convictions, he farmed at Smailcleuchfoot on the River Jed, and it was said he could take 'a ten half-fou boll of barley in the wield of his arm and fling it across a horse's back with the utmost ease'. He fought at Bothwell Brig in 1679, and after that bloody rout was forced to hide out in the wilds. A decade later he fought against the Jacobites at Killiecrankie, and again was on the losing side, but the day after, in Dunkeld, he accepted a challenge to fight the High-land champion, Rory Dhu Mhor. Rory almost got the better of him, but Oliver, bleeding from many wounds, took advantage of a momentary lapse of concentration on the part of his opponent and ran him clean through.

Thereafter, Oliver lived a quieter life as a tenant farmer at Smailcleuchfoot. Such was his reputation for integrity that his neighbour and landlord, the Marquess of Lothian, who had business in London, entrusted Oliver with the key of the room in which he kept private papers and other valuable docu-ments, with the instruction that he should let no one else enter the room on any account. The Marquess's son, believing this prohibition could not possibly apply to himself, demanded the key from Oliver, who stoutly (and no doubt undiplomatically) re-fused. Not long after, the son inherited the mar-quessate, and determined to even the score with that 'dour old Cameronian devil'. To this end, one day the young Marquess and some friends came riding through Oliver's farm, ostensibly hunting hares, but it soon became obvious that they were out to trample down the old Covenanter's crops. His protests being haughtily ignored, on the grounds that this was the Marquess's own land, Oliver took up an old musket and shot one of the Marquess's dogs dead. The young lord, incensed, complained to the sheriff at Jedburgh, who duly issued a summons. This Oliver stubbornly refused to obey. Eventually the sheriff and a posse came to

Smailcleuchfoot to arrest Oliver, who barricaded himself in, determined to resist. Shots were exchanged, but it seemed a stalemate might result until a young woman who was living in the house, perhaps as Oliver's housekeeper, was drawn out of curiosity from the hiding place whither Oliver had sent her for safety, and peered over the old man's shoulder. She instantly received a bullet in the throat, and Oliver realized he could do nothing to save her. Roused to battle-fury, the old man pulled down the barricades and rushed his tormentors, bent on revenge. A terrible hand-to-hand struggle ensued, until Oliver was struck in the face by a hammer, which smashed his jaw. Subdued and bound, he was taken to the Tolbooth in Edinburgh, where he festered for eight years, in constant pain from his broken jaw and his old battle wounds, which opened up again and would not heal. At length he was released, but never returned to Smailcleuchfoot. He died in 1736 and was buried in Greyfriars Kirkyard.

> The crystal Jed by Smailcleuchfoot
> Flows on with murmuring din;
> It seems to sing a dowie dirge
> For him that dwelt therein.
> – James Telfer, *Border Ballads* (1824)

Auld Ringan Oliver, alongside Billy Marshall, the CAIRD O' BARULLION, is held up as a heroic antecedent by Hugh MacDiarmid in *First Hymn to Lenin* (1931).

Auld Robin Gray The eponymous hero of a ballad composed by Lady Anne Lindsay in 1772. The young female narrator relates how her lover, Jamie, has gone to sea, and then her father breaks his arm, her mother falls sick, and the cow's 'stown awa' (a detail suggested by Lady Anne's little sister). Seeing her distress, Auld Robin Gray offers to marry her and support the family, and the narrator agrees, believing that Jamie is drowned. However, a month later Jamie turns up, causing tears all round, but the narrator stays faithful to her husband, 'For auld Robin Gray he is kind to me.' The original Robin Gray was the herdsman of Lady Anne's father, the Earl of Balcarres.

Auld Wat Walter Scott of Harden, one of the most notorious of the BORDER REIVERS, who died at a ripe old age in 1629. He was married to Mary Scott, the FLOWER OF YARROW, and one of his sons-in-law was Scott of Tushielaw, the so-called KING OF THE BORDER. Auld Wat himself was an ancestor of Sir Walter Scott, and his castle at Harden, just west of Hawick, is well preserved; its setting is vividly described in John Leyden's *Scenes of Infancy* (Leyden helped Sir Walter in the compilation of *MINSTRELSY OF THE SCOTTISH BORDER*):

> Where Bortha hoarse, that loads the meads with
>   sand,
> Rolls her red tide to Teviot's western strand,
> Through slaty hills, whose sides are shagg'd with
>   thorn,
> Where springs in scattered tufts the dark green
>   corn,
> Towers wood-girt Harden, far above the vale,
> And clouds of ravens o'er the turrets sail;
> A hardy race, who never shrunk from war,
> The *Scott*, to rival realms a mighty bar,
> Here fixed his mountain home – a wide domain,
> And rich the soil, had purple heath been grain.

(Borth is the Borthwick, a tributary of the Teviot.) Auld Wat is celebrated in a number of ballads, for example 'Jamie Telfer', in which he falls into a rage of grief after his kinsman, Willie Scott of Gorrinberry, is killed:

> But he's taen aff his gude steel cap,
> And thrice he's waved it in the air;
> The Dinlay snaw was ne'er mair white,
> Nor the lyart locks of Harden's hair.
>
> 'Revenge! revenge!' Auld Watt 'gan cry;
> 'Fye, lads, lay on them cruellie!
> We'll ne'er see Teviotside again,
> Or Willie's death revenged sall be.'

Auld Wat also appears in Sir Walter's own *Lay of the Last Minstrel*:

> An aged knight, to danger steel'd,
> With many a moss-trooper came on;
> And azure in a golden field,
> The stars and crescent graced his shield,
> Without the bend of Murdieston.
> Wide lay his lands round Oakwood tower,
> And wide round haunted Castle-Ower;

High over Borthwick's mountain flood,
His wood-embosom'd mansion stood;
In the dark glen, so deep below,
The herds of plundered England low;
His bold retainers' daily food,
And bought with danger, blows, and blood.
Marauding chief! his sole delight
The moonlight raid, the morning fight;
Not even the Flower of Yarrow's charms
In youth, might tame his rage for arms.
And still, in age, he spurn'd at rest,
And still his brows the helmet press'd,
Albeit the blanched locks below
Were white as Dinlay's spotless snow.
Five stately warriors drew the sword
Before their father's band;
A braver knight than Harden's lord,
Ne'er belted on a brand.

The Scotts of Harden are also celebrated in 'The Blades of Harden' by William H. Ogilvie (1869–1963):

Ho! For the blades of Harden!
Ho! For the driven kye!
The broken gate and the lances' hate
And the banner red on the sky!
The rough road runs by the Carter;
The white foam creams on the rein;
Ho! For the blades of Harden!
'There will be moonlight again!'

(In fact, THERE WILL BE MOONLIGHT AGAIN was the motto of the Armstrongs, not the Scotts.)

Auld wifie's or **grannie's soukers** Mint imperials or pan drops (from *souk*, 'suck').

Auld Year's Nicht Another name for HOGMANAY.

Auld Yule Christmas Day, Old Style, variously dated 5, 6 or 7 January.

Auntie Beenie An older woman who is somewhat old-fashioned both in dress and manner.

Author of *Waverley*, the The anonymous tag under which Sir Walter Scott published many of his novels after *Waverley* (1814), his first effort in prose fiction.

Waverley is set at the time of the 1745 Jacobite Rebellion, and its hero, Edward Waverley ('a sneaking piece of imbecility', according to Scott), derives his name from Waverley Abbey, near Farnham in Surrey. Scott's intention in opting for anonymity was to protect his reputation as a poet, although before long the identity of the author of what became known as the 'Waverley novels' became an open secret, and something of a joke, which Scott maintained until coming clean in 1827. Prior to his unveiling he was often referred to as 'the Wizard of the North' or 'the Great Unknown' (the latter coined by his publisher, James Ballantyne).

The name Waverley subsequently became a popular brand name, attaching itself to Edinburgh's main railway station, a train service between London and Edinburgh, a species of biscuit (sticky white goo nestling between two wafers and rimmed with chocolate), and a pen manufactured by the firm of MacNiven and H. Cameron Ltd in the 1870s, famously promoted by the following rhyme:

They come as a boon and a blessing to men,
The Pickwick, the Owl and the Waverley pen.

Awa an bile yer heid Be off with you (literally, 'go away and boil your head'). Alternatively, you may say to the person who is proving an irritation *Awa an pap peas at yer granny* or *Awa an play in the traffic* or *Awa an peddle yer arse*, etc., etc.

Awa an raffle yer doughnut Go and offer your bodily delights to paying customers; i.e. get lost.

Aw ae oo *See* WE'RE A' AE OO.

Awa in a dwam Lost in a reverie; daydreaming. *Dwam* can also denote a swoon or a nap.

Awa i' the heid Mentally unstable.

Awa the Crow Road *See* CROW ROAD.

Awa wi' it Drunk, or otherwise out of one's head.

Awa ye go (1) Get away with you; said to someone considered to be havering (talking foolishly), or saying something unbelievable or pretentious.

Part of him always stood back, dismissive of any pretension, a wee crabbit Scottish gremlin that narked in his head. *Ach away ye go! Don't kid yourself. I know fine what you really are.*
– Alan Spence, *The Magic Flute* (1990)

A variant is 'Awa wi ye'.
(2) There you are then; that's that.

When I die ther'll be no whirlmagees aboot me, but just a pennyworth o' blackball on my coffin, and away ye go.
– G. Fraser, *Sketches* (1877)

Awbody's body Everybody's friend; a sycophant. *Body* in this context denotes a person.

Awful Hand, the The fanciful name sometimes given to a range of Galloway hills, the highest of which, Merrick, is, at 843 m (2766 ft), the highest hill in the Southern Uplands. The name Merrick itself comes from Gaelic *meurach*, meaning 'fingered', and the range (as seen from the air, at least) is said to resemble the fingers of an outstretched hand: Merrick is the index finger, Benyellary the thumb, Kirriereoch Hill and Tarfessock the middle fingers, and Shalloch on Minnoch the little finger. 'Awful' presumably refers to the remoteness and bleakness of the terrain.

Aw fur coat an nae knickers All surface sophistication and respectability, but 'common' and/or raunchy underneath – with the implied comparison to a high-class prostitute (*cf.* DANUBE STREET). In Glasgow they say that Edinburgh people are 'Aw fur coat an nae knickers'; this certainly chimes in with the city's reputation as the embodiment of CALEDONIAN ANTISYZYGY.

People used to say this ['Aw fur coat an nae knickers'] about genteel ladies from Morningside who kept up

the appearance of being well-off when they were in fact poor. It's now more widely used to describe someone pretentious – and is sometimes used to describe Edinburgh itself.
– Jennifer Veitch, in *The Scotsman*, 1 May 2006

Aw the nice! A Glaswegian expression uttered when something regarded as cute or sweet comes into view or is mentioned. It has a similarly cloying effect on the hard-nosed as the geographically more widespread 'Bless!' *See also* VOMIT.

Avalanche overwhelms the Black Officer *See* LOSS OF GAICK, THE.

Averse to pleasure What the Scots are, according to William Hazlitt; *see* PARTICULARLY DISAGREEABLE.

Aye ma Aunt Fannie Pull the other one. Often abbreviated to *Aye ma auntie.*

Ay fuckand lyke ane furious fornicator How Sir David Lindsay (*c.*1486–1555) describes James V in his 'Answer to the King's Flyting':

… lyke ane boisterous bull, ye run and ryde
Ryatouslie lyke ane rude rubiatoure [scoundrel]
Ay fuckand lyke ane furious fornicator.

See also FLYTING; GOODMAN OF BALLENGEICH, THE.

Ayrshire Bull, the *See* BROON FRAE TROON.

Ayrshire shortbread A type of shortbread that includes cream amongst its ingredients. The name may reflect the fact that Ayrshire is famed for its dairy industry.

B

Babbity bowster A country dance that traditionally provided the finale for a ball, wedding reception or other celebration. It was also known as *bab at the bowster* or *bab in the bowster* or *bumpkin brawly*. *Babbity* means 'bob', while a *bowster* means 'bolster'. The relevance of the latter becomes clear in the following description of the dance published in *Notes and Queries*, 18 January 1851:

> ... the company having formed itself into a circle, one, either male or female, goes into the centre, carrying a pillow, and dances round the circle with a sort of shuffling quick step, while the others sing, – 'Wha learn'd you to dance, you to dance, you to dance, Wha learn'd you to dance, Bab in the Bowster brawly?' To which the dancer replies: 'Mother learn'd me to dance, me to dance, me to dance, Mother learn'd me to dance, Bab in the Bowster brawly.' He or she then lays down the pillow before one of the opposite sex, when they both kneel on it and kiss; the person to whom the pillow has been presented going over the above again, etc., till the company tires.

Another version of the words is as follows:

> Wha learned you to dance,
> Babbity Bowster, Babbity Bowster?
> Wha learned you to dance,
> Babbity Bowster, brawly?
>
> My minny learned me to dance,
> Babbity Bowster, Babbity Bowster,
> My minny learned me to dance,
> Babbity Bowster, brawly.

Various forms of the name are also applied to a variety of children's games, the rules of which differ from region to region. In particular, there is a kissing game called *bee-baw-babbity*, during which the following is sung:

> Bee baw babbity,
> Babbity, babbity,

> Bee baw babbity,
> Kiss the bonnie wee lassie.
>
> Bee baw babbity, babbity, babbity,
> Bee baw babbity, babbity, busty barley.
> Kneel down, kiss the ground,
> Kiss the ground, kiss the ground,
> Kneel down, kiss the ground,
> Kiss a bonnie lassie ... [etc.]

Backdoor trot An attack of diarrhoea. The euphemism, still in use, is first recorded in the 18th century.

Back feast or **back treat** In Orkney and Shetland, a party laid on by the best man and his friends a few weeks after the wedding to thank the bride and her family for the wedding feast. The young women who were still unmarried were sat along either side of the hall or barn where the party was being held, while two older men, known as 'ministers' or 'priests', would march each bachelor in turn up and down reciting various rhymes before pushing him onto the lap of one of the waiting maidens. Each couple thus 'married' would partner each other in all the dances that night, and the young woman would share the food she had brought along with her beau, who would escort her home at the end of the festivities. *See also* HAME-FARE.

Back green or **back court** An area of lawn, bin shelters and washing lines found at the back of tenement flats, usually so positioned as to avoid the scorching sun of a Scottish summer. *See also* HAMELLDAEME; SUMMER HAS LEAPED SUDDENLY UPON EDINBURGH LIKE A TIGER.

Back o' the mune, at the A long way away.

Back tae auld claiths and cauld porritch *See* AULD CLAITHS AND CAULD PORRITCH.

Bad Boys, the *See* BUBBLY BABIES, THE.

Bad Man, the A children's euphemism for the Devil, whose home is the *Bad Place* or the *Ill Place* or the *Bad Fire*.

> I was sure the devil was lurking there, ready to pounce and take me away with him to the bad fire.
> – Molly Weir, *Best Foot Forward* (1974)

The white campion, *Lychnis verspertina*, is known, for some reason, as the *Bad Man's bonnie flooer*.

Badger A nickname of the Labour politician Alistair Darling (b.1953), MP for Edinburgh South West, Chancellor of the Exchequer 2007–10, and paid-up member of the Westminster SCOTIA NOSTRA. The nickname refers to his badger-like appearance: white hair and black eyebrows.

Ba games *See* HANDBA.

Baggy Aggie A derisive term for any woman wearing over-large, ill-fitting clothes. Similarly, any girl or woman regarded as possessing poor personal hygiene is dubbed *Scabby Aggie*.

Ba Green A strip of meadow (grid reference NT 845 385) about a mile south of Coldstream. What is remarkable about it is that, even though it is positioned on the south bank of the Tweed, it is marked by the Ordnance Survey as belonging to Scotland – an exception to the line of the Border in these parts, which otherwise runs along the middle of the river. The story is that formerly the men of Coldstream on the Scottish side and the men of Wark on the English side played a version of the game of HANDBA on the meadow once a year, and for the following year the Ba Green belonged to whichever country won. However, when Coldstream became much bigger than the hamlet of Wark, it became clear that the Scottish side would never be beaten, owing to sheer weight of numbers – so the Ba Green became part of Scotland in perpetuity.

Ba-heid Literally 'ball-head', i.e. someone with an inflated ego. Such a person may also be referred to as a *big balloon*. *See also* HEID-THE-BA.

Bahookie freezer A somewhat contrived term for a 'bum freezer', i.e. a short jacket. The more down-to-earth Scots word *bahookie* or *behouchie*, meaning the bottom, is thought to be a conflation of English 'behind' and Scots *houch* or *hoch*, the back of the thigh.

Baillie Vass *Private Eye*'s nickname for Sir Alec Douglas-Home, Conservative prime minister in 1963–4, previously 14th Earl of Home and subsequently Baron Home of the Hirsel. The name arose from a mix-up in the *Aberdeen Evening Express*, which inadvertently used a photograph of the prime minister above a caption relating to a baillie (municipal magistrate) called Vass.

Bairns, the (1) A nickname for the Scots Guards. (2) A nickname for Falkirk FC (*see* BAIRNS O' FALKIRK).

Bairns o' Falkirk The inhabitants of Falkirk have become known as *bairns*, from the town's motto: 'Better meddle wi' the Deil than the bairns o' Falkirk.' Hence Falkirk FC are nicknamed 'the Bairns'.

> The town coat of arms which had the well-known motto 'Better meddle wi' the deil than the bairns o' Falkirk,' indicates a phase of temperament which will be better left unexplained.
> – R. Gillespie, *Roundabout Falkirk* (1879)

The term *bairn* for a baby or child is used widely in Scotland, apart from Glasgow and other western parts of the Central Belt, where the word *wean* (pronounced 'wain', and derived from *wee ane*, 'small one') is preferred.

Bald Iain *See* LOM, IAIN.

Baldy Bain or **Bane** or **Bayne** A contemporary nickname for any man with a shiny pate, as in the children's rhyme:

> 'What's yer name?'
> 'Baldy Bane'
> 'What's yer other?'
> 'Breid an butter.'

The Baldy Bane Theatre Company, which puts on productions and workshops in schools and community venues around Glasgow and elsewhere, was formed in 1991.

Balefire A funeral pyre or beacon fire. In the Borders balefires were lit to warn of raids or invasions: a single fire denoted a warning of an enemy approaching; two fires meant they were certainly on their way; four fires together denoted that they were of great power and menace. The *bale-* element is from Old English *bæl*, 'pyre', and ultimately from Sanskrit *bhala*, 'brightness', and is cognate with the first element of BELTANE, the Mayday festival celebrated with bonfires.

Balfour Bay The unofficial name of a beautiful sandy bay, in Gaelic called Tràigh Gheal, on the otherwise rocky south coast of the tidal isle of Erraid, off the west coast of the Ross of Mull. The English name refers to David Balfour, the hero of Robert Louis Stevenson's *Kidnapped* (1886), who, having been shipwrecked on the Torran Rocks, is carried by a tidal race towards the island:

> The shores of Earraid were close in; I could see in the moonlight the dots of heather and the sparkling of the mica in the rocks ... in about an hour of kicking and splashing, I had got well in between the points of a sandy bay surrounded by low hills.
> The sea was here quite quiet; there was no sound of any surf; the moon shone clear; and I thought in my heart I had never seen a place so desert and desolate. But it was dry land ...
> – chapter xiii

Balfour's hopes fade, however, when he finds he is apparently stranded on the island, and it is only after surviving on limpets and buckies (periwinkles) for some days that he realizes that the narrows between the island and the mainland of the Ross can be crossed, dry-shod, at low tide.

Balmoral, Beast of *See* BEAST OF BALMORAL.

Balmoral, chicken *See* HAGGIS.

Balmoral bonnet A floppy, lopsided beret with a tassel or pompom on the crown and a band with a chequered red-and-white pattern or other design. Such bonnets – in black or khaki – have been

adopted by various Scottish regiments. It takes its name from Queen Victoria's Deeside residence, Balmoral Castle – 'this dear paradise', as she called it – where she and Albert could indulge their passion for unrestrained tartanry. *See also* BLUE BONNET; GLENGARRY; SCOTCH BONNET.

Balmorality A term coined in 1932 by George Scott-Moncrieff in an article in *Scotland in Quest of Her Youth* (ed. D.C. Thomson):

> Sir Walter Scott re-discovered Scotland, and ... unwittingly paved the way for Victoria and the cult of Balmorality ... a glutinous compound of hypocrisy, false sentiment, industrialism, ugliness, and clammy pseudo-Calvinism.

The term has come to denote an obsession with the outer trappings of Scottishness while neglecting the deeper concerns and problems that face the people and nation of Scotland. The word refers to Victoria's residence at Balmoral Castle.

Baltic A Glaswegian expression denoting 'very cold'.

Banff bailies Fluffy white clouds on the horizon.

> It was a common saying in parts of Banffshire that the snow of the coming winter made its appearance – 'cast up' – during harvest in the large, white, snowy-looking clouds that rise along the horizon. They were called 'Banff bailies', and at all seasons of the year were looked upon as the forerunners of foul weather.
> – Walter Gregor, *The Folk-Lore of the North-East of Scotland* (1881)

Banging it out bravely What James VI accused the Scottish magnates of doing to each other (a tradition that extended back many centuries before James's time):

> ... for any displeasure that they apprehend to be done against them by their neighbour, to take up a plain feud against him and without respect to God, King or Commonweal bang it out bravely, he and all his kin against him and all his.
> – James VI, *Basilikon Doron* (1597)

Bankie An inhabitant of Clydebank.

Bankies, the *See* FOOTBALL CLUB NICKNAMES.

Bannatyne Club A club founded in 1823 by Sir Walter Scott, the publisher Archibald Constable and others with the purpose of printing rare works of Scottish literary or historical interest. It was named after George Bannatyne (1545–1608), an Edinburgh merchant who in 1568, while plague raged in the city, retreated to his native Angus, where he occupied his time by copying out Scottish poems from the 15th and early 16th century. It is to his manuscript that we owe the preservation of many of the poems of Robert Henryson, William Dunbar, David Lyndsay and Alexander Scott (the SCOTCH ANACREON). The Bannatyne Club issued 116 volumes, and was dissolved in 1861. A club with similar aims, the Maitland Club, was founded in Glasgow in 1828. It was named after Sir Richard Maitland of Lethington (1496–1586), a poet and judge who compiled an important early collection of Scottish poetry. His son William was Secretary of State to Mary Queen of Scots, while another son, John, was Lord Chancellor.

Bannock A round, flattened scone-like bread, made from barley flour, oatmeal or peasemeal, and cooked on a griddle or girdle (*see* CULROSS GIRDLE). Bannocks are baked in Scotland, Ireland and the north of England, and the word comes from the Gaelic *bannach*, which is possibly related to Latin *panicium*, from *panis*, 'bread'. In the past bannocks were unleavened, but today they are usually leavened using baking powder or baking soda. Various types of bannock were associated with particular festivals, whether Celtic or Christian, for example, *harvest bannock* was made from grain from the last sheaf cut (and *bannock hive* was a rash caused by oatmeal newly ground after harvest). In Aberdeenshire in the past, *Bannock Nicht* was Shrove Tuesday (*see also* FASTERN EVE). Different recipes are associated with different places. Although bannock-shaped, *Pitcaithly bannock* (first recorded in 1831, and named after a locality near Bridge of Earn) is more like shortbread, and filled with citron peel and chopped almonds. *Selkirk bannock*, made with wheat flour, is spongy and buttery and full of raisins; it was created by Robbie Douglas, who opened a bakery shop in Selkirk in 1859. Selkirk bannock secured immortality when it was served to Queen Victoria on her visit to Sir Walter Scott's granddaughter at Abbotsford.

Bannockburn Day An annual celebration by the Scottish National Party to commemorate Robert the Bruce's victory over the English on 24 June 1314, usually held on the nearest Saturday to the anniversary. The celebration consists of a procession to the giant statue of Bruce at the battlefield, accompanied by speeches, music, etc.

Banshee or **benshie** A female spirit, often associated with a particular family, whose wailing prophesies an imminent death or other catastrophe. In Gaelic she is a *ban-sith*, 'fairy woman', and banshees are also encountered in Ireland. It has been suggested that the wailing attributed to banshees may actually have been the sounds emitted by female WILDCATS seeking to attract the attention of a mate, although the fact that wildcats have never been indigenous to Ireland throws a *soupçon* of cold water on this theory.

Barbreck's Bone A charm, in the form of a plate of elephant ivory, which was in the possession of the Campbells of Barbreck (by Loch Awe in Argyll) until 1829. It was reputed to have fallen from the sky, landing in the cemetery of Inverliver, by Loch Etive in Argyll. It acquired a reputation as a cure for madness, and such was its value that anyone borrowing it had to leave a deposit of £100. The object dates from the 11th or 12th century, and may have originally been a book cover. It is now in the care of the National Museums of Scotland.

Bard of Keppoch, the *See* LOM, IAIN.

Bard of the Silvery Tay, the William McGonagall (1825–1902), Dundee handloom weaver and writer of appalling verse. The sobriquet refers to a phrase deployed in his most famous poem, that on the TAY BRIDGE DISASTER. McGonagall himself recalled that 'The most startling incident in my life was the time I discovered myself to be a poet, which was in the year 1877.' The occasion for this discovery was an effusion he penned that year, in the form of 'An Address to the Rev. George Gilfillan'; in response, Gilfillan inadvertently encouraged further outpourings by remarking that 'Shakespeare never wrote anything like this.' McGonagall's performances of his verses proved very popular, although audiences primarily regarded him as a comic turn, rather than the serious poet he took himself for. After the death of the poet laureate, Alfred, Lord Tennyson, in 1892, McGonagall walked 60 miles through heavy rain to Balmoral to ask Queen Victoria to appoint him to the post. Had he not penned 'An Ode to the Queen on her Jubilee Year', a poem that includes the following verse?

> And as this is her first Jubilee year,
> And will be her last, I rather fear:
> Therefore, sound drums and trumpets cheerfully,
> Until the echoes are heard o'er land and sea.

He was told that Her Majesty was not in residence. McGonagall consoled himself with the fact that two years later the King of Burma, Thibaw Min, made him a Knight of the White Elephant. Ironically, McGonagall's works have never been out of print, perhaps because, according to Stephen Pile in his *Book of Heroic Failures* (1979), the man was 'so giftedly bad he backed unwittingly into genius'.

Barisdall Either a form of torture, or a verb meaning 'to imprison'. In the LYON IN MOURNING there is a reference to someone being 'barisdall'd in a dark dungeon', and another to 'that racking machine which [MacDonald of] Barisdale invented and made use of to extort confession from thieves'. Barisdale is a remote settlement on Loch Hourn, Knoydart.

Barking and fleeing Heading for ruin, owing to fecklessness and prodigality. John Jamieson, in *An Etymological Dictionary of the Scottish Language* (1808), suggests the allusion is 'to the *barking* of dogs, and the *flight* of birds, in consequence of the alarm given'. In his 1825 Supplement, Jamieson cites the following:

> 'O, the lands of Milnwood! – the bonny lands of Milnwood, that have been in the name of Morton for twa hundred years!' exclaimed his uncle; 'they are barking and fleeing, outfield and infield, haugh and holme!'
> – Sir Walter Scott, *Old Mortality* (1816), chapter vii

It has been suggested there may be a link to Swedish *barka*, 'to fly, run quickly', as in the phrase *det barkar åt skogen*, literally meaning 'it runs to the wood', but implying that things are going from bad to worse.

Bar-L, the A nickname for Barlinnie, the infamous high-security prison in the Riddrie area of Glasgow, built in 1880. It is also known as the *Riddrie Hilton*. The pioneering Special Unit at Barlinnie, set up in the 1970s, successfully rehabilitated a number of hardened, violent criminals, notably Jimmy Boyle, who entered the unit a gangster and convicted murderer, and left it a respected sculptor and author of the admired autobiography, *A Sense of Freedom* (1977).

> He's obviously been residing in one ay the Windsor group hotels, Saughton, Bar L, Perth, Peterhead, etc.
> – Irvine Welsh, *Trainspotting* (1993)

A *Barlinnie drumstick* is a vicious weapon comprising a length of lead piping studded with nails.

Barlass, Kate The nickname given to Catherine Douglas in honour of her role in trying to save the life of James I. She was a lady-in-waiting to Joan, James's queen consort, and in 1437, while James and his retinue were staying at the Blackfriars Monastery in Perth, assassins led by Sir Robert Graham (at the behest of Walter, Earl of Atholl) came to murder the king. According to legend, someone in on the plot had removed the bolt from the door of the royal chamber. So, to prevent the entry of the assassins, Catherine 'schott hir arm into the place quhair the bar sould haif passit', i.e. used her own arm to bar the door (this detail appears to have been added by Hector Boece in his *Historia Gentis Scotorum*, written 90 years after the event; the quote above is from John Bellenden's 1527 translation). It was to no avail: the killers burst in, breaking her arm, forcing the king to try to make his escape in an undignified fashion. According to the account of John Shirley, transcribed in the 1440s, James

> ... entered low down among the ordure of the privy, that was all of hard stone and none window nor issue thereupon save a little square hole even at the side of the bottom of the privy, that at the making thereof of old time was left open to cleanse and ferme the said

privy, by which the said King might well have escaped, but he made to let stop it well three days afore ... because that when he played at the paume [tennis] the balls that he played with often ran in that foul hole.

James was thus trapped, and dispatched with a number of dagger thrusts. In Dante Gabriel Rossetti's ballad 'The King's Tragedy' (1881) it is Catherine who relates the events, although the privy is decorously converted into a 'crypt' or 'vault'. The poem begins thus:

I Catherine am a Douglas born,
A name to all Scots dear;
And Kate Barlass they've called me now
Through many a waning year.

This old arm's withered now. 'Twas once
Most deft 'mong maidens all
To rein the steed, to wing the shaft,
To smite the palm-play ball.

In hall adown the close-linked dance
It has shone most white and fair;
It has been the rest for a true lord's head,
And many a sweet babe's nursing-bed,
And the bar to a King's chambère ...

It has been suggested that the common US phrase 'Katie bar the door', meaning that action should be taken to avert imminent trouble, originates in the story of Kate Barlass, particularly Rossetti's line 'Catherine, keep the door' (spoken by the queen), but this is by no means certain.

Barr's cat A proverbially formidable feline, whose reputation still persists in the southwest.

It was a very large monster of a *bawdrons*, that was known about the farm of Barr, in the parish of Pennigame, about sixty years ago ... the size of it became proverbial all over the country, and everything larger than it should be, was said to be a *rouser*, like *Barr's Cat*.
– John MacTaggart, *The Scottish Gallovidian Encyclopaedia* (1824)

Bars o' Ayr, like the Fast and furiously. The simile was once applied to any action or phenomenon involving speed and roaring, such as a river in spate. The reference is to the sand bar that formerly stood

at the mouth of the River Ayr, now cleared by dredging.

What's set the man a snoring like the bars o' Ayr, at this time o' day, I won'er?
– John Galt, *The Entail* (1823)

Bar-the-door or **barley-door** A children's game in which one chases after the others, and any caught are confined in a 'den' by the catcher shouting 'Bar the door'. Prisoners can be freed if another on their own side reaches them and shouts 'Break the door'. In another variant, one player seeks to dodge the catcher to reach a touchline, whereupon he or she shouts 'Bar the door' (or, in Forfar, 'Schoolie'). The others then rush across en masse, hoping to avoid capture. The game is also known as *leave-o*, from *relieve*, a release from captivity.

Barlinnie drumstick See BAR-L, THE.

Barra A barrow. To *set doon the barra* is to go bankrupt, to be unable to pay one's debts. If you *fancy yer barra*, then you have a high regard for yourself, and if something is *right into yer barra* then it's right up your street, just what you want. *The Barras* (the Glasgow Barrowland Market) is Glasgow's flea market, situated just east of the city centre in Calton, an area informally known as Barrowland. When the market opened after the First World War, traders sold their wares from barrows, but now the market is housed in the same building as the Barrowland Ballroom, although there are still plenty of outside stalls. The Barrowland Ballroom was opened in 1934, burnt down in 1958 and was replaced in 1960 by a new building, which now plays host to rock and pop concerts. In the popular imagination, the Barrowland Ballroom is inextricably connected to the murderer BIBLE JOHN.

Barras, the See BARRA.

Barrowland Ballroom See BARRA.

Barry Backpass The nickname of the footballer Barry Ferguson (b.1978), captain of Rangers and the national side. He is also known as 'Squarebaw'.

Bartle Fair The St Bartholomew's Day Fair held from the 15th century at Kincardine O'Neil, Aberdeenshire. The village was the site of an important ford across the River Dee, used by drovers taking cattle south via the Cairn O' Mounth to the markets at Crieff and Falkirk (*see* FALKIRK TRYST, THE). Although St Bartholomew's Day falls on 24 August, Kincardine's Bartle Fair took place over three days in early September, and thousands of cattle were bought and sold on Bartle Muir, a little to the north of the village, accompanied by much drunken revelry. An attempt by the authorities in 1777 to suppress the 'cursing, lying, tricking, stealing, brawling, fighting and every indecency at every corner' that was taking place in the kirkyard was resisted by those local residents who were doing well out of selling food and liquor to the crowds. The Fair declined after it moved to Potarch Common in 1815, a couple of miles downstream, and was finally extinguished with the arrival of the railway in Deeside in the 1860s.

Bass cock A puffin. The name derives from the Bass Rock in the Firth of Forth, where many breed – although the Bass Rock is more famous for its 100,000-strong gannet colony, to such an extent that the scientific name for a gannet is *Sula* or *Morus bassana*, while in French it is a *fou de bassan* and in German a *Basstölpel*. Compare AILSA COCK.

Bathing the bride in whisky *See* PENNY BRIDAL.

Battle of Bonnymuir, the *See* RADICAL WAR, THE.

Battle of Garelochhead, the A confrontation that took place on Sunday 22 August 1853 at the resort of Garelochhead, at the head of the Gare Loch, beyond Helensburgh. In order to enforce the Sabbath, Sir James Colquhoun and his keepers attempted to prevent the disembarkation from the paddle steamer *Emperor* of Glasgow day-trippers on a foray DOON THE WATTER. They failed in this attempt, but Sir James subsequently won the battle in the courts, and Sunday cruises were banned for some years.

Battle of George Square On Friday 31 January 1919 – also known as Bloody or Black Friday – the trade unionists of RED CLYDESIDE summoned some tens of thousands of striking workers to gather in George Square, Glasgow, to call for improved working conditions and a 40-hour week. The Red Flag was raised, and fighting broke out with the police, leading to a reading of the Riot Act. The government, apparently expecting revolution to break out at any moment (the Secretary of State for Scotland called it a 'Bolshevist uprising'), confined the Highland Light Infantry to their barracks in Maryhill, mistrusting their allegiances, and sent in perhaps as many as 10,000 English troops and tanks to patrol Glasgow's streets, with the aim of deterring further unrest. Some of the left-wing leaders, including Manny Shinwell and Willie Gallacher, were jailed; agreement was eventually reached on a 47-hour week.

Battle of Glen Tilt A confrontation that took place on 21 August 1847 between Professor Balfour and a party of Edinburgh University botany students on the one hand and, on the other, the gamekeepers and gillies of the Duke of Atholl, who was determined to prevent people using the old drove road through the glen, which he regarded as his private fiefdom. The case was taken up by the Society for the Protection of Public Rights of Roadways in Scotland, and the right of access was eventually established. The victory was commemorated in a ballad:

> There's ne'er a kilted chiel
> Shall drive us back this day, man.
> It's justice and it's public richt
> We'll pass Glen Tilt afore the nicht,
> For dukes shall we care ae bawbee?
> The road's as free to you and me
> As to his Grace himself, man.

Battle of Little Sparta *See* LITTLE SPARTA.

Battle of the Braes The name awarded by the press at the time to a violent encounter in 1882 between around 100 crofters from the township of Braes, south of Portree in Skye, and a large force of policemen. The original issue was the grazing rights on Ben Lee. After the expiry of their old lease, the crofters had volunteered to pay a generous rent, but

Lord MacDonald wanted the land for his own sheep. The crofters decided to ignore this and continued to graze their stock on Ben Lee, and in retaliation Lord MacDonald determined to evict the ringleaders. When the sheriff's officer, Angus Martin, was dispatched to deliver eviction orders on 7 April 1882, he was waylaid by a group of crofters, who forced him to burn the papers. The authorities then drafted in 50 extra policemen from Glasgow, and early on a cold, wet morning on 19 April the forces of law and order, with Sheriff Ivory of Inverness bringing up the rear, marched on Braes. Initially the crofters were taken by surprise, but soon men, women and children met the baton-wielding policemen with missiles and sticks. The confrontation was followed by a number of arrests, convictions and modest fines – and considerable publicity for the crofters' cause. The whole affair was celebrated in a song, which includes the following verses:

All day the cruel battle raged,
We showed them we could fight.
But five brave men were taken off
To Inverness that night.

The judge he found them guilty men
And fined them two pounds ten,
In half a minute it was paid
And off they went again.

Once more Macdonald's anger broke.
'Invade the Isle of Skye!
Two thousand soldiers, boats and guns
The people must comply!'

'Oh, if we send one million men'
In London they declared,
'We'll never clear the Isle of Skye.
The people are not scared.'

It is said by some that it was the Battle of the Braes, and not Culloden, that was the last battle fought on British soil. In any case, the incident marked the near end of the CLEARANCES. The following year a Royal Commission was set up to look into 'the conditions of the crofters and cottars in the Highlands ... and everything concerning them', which in turn gave rise to the Crofters Act (1886), which protected crofters' rights, notably security of tenure.

The site of the Battle of the Braes is today marked by a memorial, with the following inscription: 'Near this cairn on 19 April 1882 ended the battle fought by the people of Braes on behalf of the crofters of Gaeldom.' *See also* SEVEN MEN OF KNOYDART, THE.

Battle of the Clans An encounter that took place on the North Inch of Perth in 1396 to settle a territorial dispute between Clan Chattan (a confederation that included Mackintoshes and Macphersons) and Clan Key (or Quhele), identified by some with the Camerons. King Robert III (the self-styled WORST OF KINGS AND MOST MISERABLE OF MEN) had endeavoured, via the Earl of Crawford and the Earl of Dunbar, to get the clans to settle the matter amicably, but to no avail. The respective chiefs instead suggested a staged battle before the king and his court, with each side fielding 30 men bearing LOCHABER AXES, CLAYMORES, crossbows and dirks; they were prohibited from wearing armour. When the appointed day came, the Chattans found themselves a man short, and refused to fight until the numbers should be made up. At this point a local Perth armourer and harness-maker called Henry Smith (aka Hal o' the Wynd or Gow-Chrom, meaning 'crooked smith') volunteered his services in exchange for half a gold crown and the promise of a pension for life. He survived, along with nine others on the Chattan side, while only two from Clan Key left the field alive (one of them diving into the Tay to make good his escape). The episode features in Scott's *The Fair Maid of Perth* (1828), and the author somewhat gleefully describes the carnage at half-time:

About twenty of both sides lay on the field, dead or dying; arms and legs lopped off, heads cleft to the chin, slashes deep through the shoulder to the breast, showed at once the fury of the combat, the ghastly character of the weapons used, and the fatal strength of the arms which wielded them.

Hal o' the Wynd apparently played a key role in the Chattan victory, although afterwards he could not name the clan he'd fought for; rather, he had 'fought for his own hand'. It is said that he went north to live in Chattan territory, where he became the ancestor of numerous Smiths and Gows (presumably including Neil Gow, the celebrated 18th-century Dunkeld fiddler).

Battle of the Seven Sleepers Another name for the Battle of Dunsinane, fought in 1054 on 27 July, the Day of the Seven Sleepers. The Seven Sleepers were a legendary group of Christian youths of Ephesus who around AD 250 sought to escape persecution by hiding in a cave, where they fell asleep, awakening a couple of centuries later. At the Battle of the Seven Sleepers, Macbeth was defeated by MALCOLM CAN-MORE and his Northumbrian allies under Siward, although, *contra* Shakespeare, he was not killed at Dunsinane but at Lumphanan three years later (*see* BIRNAM WOOD).

Battle of the Shirts A bloody contest fought between Clan Ranald, under its chief John of Moidart, and its Macdonald and Cameron allies on the one hand, and, on the other, an army of Frasers under Hugh, Lord Lovat, and Ranald Gallda. It took place on 15 July 1544, in the Great Glen between Loch Lochy and Loch Oich. According to legend, the day was so hot that the men discarded their plaids and fought in their shirts, eventually taking refuge from the heat in the cold waters of the loch, where they kept up the bloody work. It was said that out of some 800 participants, only a dozen survived. The Gaelic name of the battle, *Blar na Léine* ('field of the shirts'), is, however, a corruption of *Blar na Leana*, 'field of the marshy meadow', so the story may be a retrospective explanation of a philological misinterpretation.

Battle of the Spoiled Dyke *See* MASSACRE CAVE, THE.

Battle of the Standard A battle fought on Cowton Moor, near Northallerton, Yorkshire, on 22 August 1138, in which the Scots under David I were defeated by an English army commanded by Walter Espec and William of Aumale. The name refers to the mast erected by the English on a wagon from which flew the banners of St Peter of York, St Cuthbert of Durham, St Wilfrid of Ripon and St John of Beverley. The aftermath was possibly bloodier than the battle, as the local peasantry took its revenge on the invaders, one chronicler recording that 'wherever [Scotsmen] were discovered they were put to death like sheep'.

Bauchle, to mak a *See* MAK A BAUCHLE O (SOMETHING).

Bauchling and reproaching *See* TRUCE DAYS.

Baudrons *See* PUSSY-BAUDRONS.

Bawbee Originally, in the reign of James V, a silver sixpence, but subsequently debased to a halfpenny. Hence the word also came to be applied to the John Dory, a fish which on its side bears a round mark, associated with the coin taken from a fish by St Peter (Matthew 17:27; *see also* PETER'S THUMB). The *Bawbee Bible* is the Shorter Catechism, while a *bawbee jo* is a prostitute who solicits on the streets. Various bridges (such as one at Bonill in Dunbartonshire and another linking Leven and Methil in Fife) are called the *Bawbee Bridge*, from the toll that used to be levied.

The word *bawbee* is familiar to generations of children from the lullaby by the Galashiels weaver, part-time poet and confectionery salesman Robert Coltart, who died in 1880, aged 43, of a brain tumour, and was buried in an unmarked grave:

> Ally, bally, ally bally bee,
> Sittin' on yer mammy's knee
> Waitin' for a wee bawbee
> Tae buy mair Coltart's candy.

The word *bawbee* is thought to derive from the territorial designation of Alexander Orrok of Sillebawbe, who was appointed master of the mint in 1538. Another suggestion is that it is a corruption of French *bas-billon*, a base copper coin. *See also* BONNET PIECE.

Bawd bree Hare soup (*bawd*, 'hare'; *bree*, 'broth'). The noted songwriter Lady Grisell Baillie (1665–1746) described *bawd bree* as 'hare soup with hares in it'.

Bawling Campbells, the The daughters of the 2nd Duke of Argyll (RED JOHN OF THE BATTLES) and his second wife, Jane Warburton, whom he married in 1717. According to the duke's great-niece, Lady Louisa Stuart (*Some Account of John, Duke of Argyll, and his Family*, 1863), the Campbell daughters who survived into adulthood acquired a reputation for their 'loud shrill voice common to the four, which gained them a variety of nicknames, such as the Screaming Sisterhood, the Bawling Campbells, and so forth'.

Bean, Sawney A legendary cannibal who is said to have lived at some time between the 13th and 16th centuries. The earliest popular account of the story is in the 18th-century *Newgate Calendar*, which states that Alexander Beane was born in East Lothian during the reign of James VI, but was too lazy to take up his father's occupation of ditch digger and hedge trimmer, so, accompanied by a feckless woman from the locality, set off for the west to pursue an alternative career. He set up home in a sea cave on a remote part of the southwest coast (both Bennane Head in Ayrshire and the Mull of Galloway are mentioned) and here he and his wife bred a large, incestuous family. They would ambush unwary travellers, kill them and eat them, pickling any body parts they were too full to consume on the spot. In all, they were said to have eaten over 1000 people. When one traveller escaped from their clutches and informed the authorities, the king led a force of 400 men and a pack of bloodhounds to extirpate the clan, who were seized and taken to Edinburgh, Glasgow or Leith. Here, without trial, the men had their extremities – including their genitalia – cut off, and bled to death, while the women and children were forced to watch, before themselves being burnt alive. The story was probably intended as a combination of anti-Scots propaganda at the time of the Jacobite rebellions, and a warning to the young of the perils of avoiding hard work. In the 21st century the legend resurfaced in the 2010 comedy-horror film, *Hotel Caledonia*, written, produced and directed by Nicholas David Lean. *See also* SAWNEY.

Bears, the *See* FOOTBALL CLUB NICKNAMES.

Beast of Balmoral, the Reports of a creature resembling a black panther in the vicinity of Balmoral Castle in Deeside began to appear in the 1990s. In December 1997 a local gamekeeper, believing he had the beast in his sights, shot the tortoiseshell cat of the Revd Robert Sloan, minister of Craithie Kirk, where the queen worships while staying at Balmoral. His employers ordered the unfortunate gamekeeper to apologise to the Revd Sloan and his family, and to study the difference between domestic and feral cats.

Beasts and beast lore The reader is referred to the following entries:

- BARR'S CAT
- BEAST OF BALMORAL, the
- BERNIE THE BULL
- BLUE WHALE OF BRAGAR, the
- BOOBRIE
- CAMEL OF THE CANONGATE, the
- COWS, NOTABLE
- CRAWS' COURT
- DINMONT, DANDIE
- DOLLY THE SHEEP
- DRAGONS
- EELS
- ELEPHANT OF BROUGHTY FERRY, the
- ERTH HUNS
- FAUNA CALEDONIA (which includes numerous Scots names for various animals)
- FLOUNDERS
- GHOST-BIRD, the
- GIGELORUM
- GOATS, SUPERNATURAL
- GOLDEN HORSE OF LOCH LUNDIE, the
- GORDON SETTER
- GOWK
- GREYFRIARS BOBBY
- HAIRY COOS
- HALKERTON'S COW
- HARES
- HORSE OF THE WOODS
- HUMLE or HUMMEL COW
- JENKIN'S HEN
- KELPIE
- LAMMERMUIR LION
- LAST WOLF IN SCOTLAND, THE
- LAVELLAN
- LOCH NESS MONSTER
- LOWRIE
- LUATH
- MESTER STOOR WORM
- MORAG
- NUCKELAVEE
- PUSSY-BAUDRONS

- SANDY CAMPBELL
- SEA SERPENTS
- SEAWEED-EATING SHEEP
- SWAN OF CLOSEBURN, the
- TOURIST EAGLE
- TURRA COO, the
- UNICORN
- WALRUS OF THE HEBRIDES, the
- WATER COW
- WEST HIGHLAND TERRIER
- *WESTLOTHIANA LIZZIAE*
- WHITE PET
- WILDCAT
- WIZARD SHACKLE

See also SUPERNATURAL BEINGS.

Beasts of Holm, the *See IOLAIRE* DISASTER.

Bedesman, King's *See* GABERLUNZIE.

Bedlam after importunate wooing of widow, incarcerated in. *See* ALEXANDER THE CORRECTOR.

Bedlam rather than the gallows, deserving *See* SWEET SINGERS, THE.

Bee-baw-babbity *See* BABBITY BOWSTER.

Beer As elsewhere, both the authorities and the public have long been anxious that the product offered by brewers is of the highest quality. A law first issued in the 13th century stated that any brew-wife who failed to 'maik guid ale' should be fined eight shillings, or 'be put on the kukestule' (ducking stool), and the ale given away to the poor and the sick. An anonymous 16th-century song suggests the following punishment:

Quha hes guid malt and makis ill drink,
Wo mot be hir weird [fate]!
I pray to God scho rot and stink
Sevin year abune the erd.

– subsequent to which, the guilty party is to sink 'quik to Hell'.

Any attempt to tax beer or ale was deeply resented, and the eightpence-per-pint levy instituted in Edinburgh in 1659 even provoked divine dis-

pleasure, at least according to the diary of John Nicoll, a Covenanter:

Yet this imposition upon the ale and beer seemed not to thrive, for at the same instant, viz., upon the 1st, 2nd, 3rd and 4th days of September, God from the heavens declared His anger by sending thunder, fire and unheard tempest and storms and inundations of waters, which destroyed their common mills, dams and works, to the Town's great charges and expense.

The malt tax of 1725, which pushed up the price of beer, led not to divine displeasure, but to the SHAWFIELD RIOTS.

By the 18th century two main types of beer were being brewed in Scotland: strong, dark, slightly sweet 'Scotch ale' drunk by the wealthy, and the weaker and thinner 'tuppeny' (the price per pint in 1707) consumed by everybody else. ('Scotch ale' is today a designation of strong Scottish beers exported to the USA; in Scotland, such beers are often sold as 'wee heavy'.) The later 19th century saw the introduction of a third main type, the 'pale ale'. The names of beers and ales brewed in Scotland use both descriptive terms and the 'shilling' categories, which originally reflected the price per barrel in the 19th century. Generally speaking, although 'shilling' names were never precisely tied to alcoholic strength, brewers broadly followed the categorization below:

Light	60 shilling	under 3.5% abv
Heavy	70 shilling	3.5–4.5% abv
Export	80 shilling	4.0–5.5% abv
Wee heavy	90 shilling	over 6.0% abv

The 'shilling' categories were revived in the 1970s to denote cask rather than keg beers, and generally reflect alcoholic strength. *See also* GROANING MALT; HEATHER ALE.

Beeswing A small village between Dumfries and Dalbeattie, formerly known as Lochend, but renamed after the renowned racehorse and broodmare Beeswing, who between 1835 and 1842 won 51 of the 63 races she ran in.

Beezer A word, probably originating in the early 20th century but of obscure origin, applied to anything excellent, either as noun or adjective. It can also be an exclamation, and provided the title of the Dundee-published D.C. Thomson comic *The Beezer*, which ran from 1956 until it was merged into *The Beano* in 1993.

Before the Lord left Partick A long time ago. In *The Complete Patter* (1996), Michael Munro suggests the expression may allude to 'the area's high density of Glasgow University students'. A variant is *since God left Govan*, that being an impoverished area of Glasgow.

> It's crazy! It's the best idea since God left Govan. I love it.
> – Andrew Greig, *The Return of John Macnab* (1996)

Beggar's Benison, the A club for libertines founded in Anstruther in Fife in 1732 by John McNachtane, a minor Highland chieftain and adherent of Enlightenment values, who also doubled up as a customs officer. The club, which came to have branches in Edinburgh and Glasgow, initially drew its members from the ranks of customs officers, merchants and well-off artisans, but by the end of the century churchmen and aristocrats such as the Earl of Elgin, the Earl of Lauderdale and the Duke of Gordon were also represented. The members enjoyed dining and drinking together, singing ribald songs and toasting ribald toasts. Sex seems to have been an obsession, and the club hosted instructional lectures in that field, sometimes illustrated by naked 'posture girls'. It also maintained an extensive library of pornography. The initiation ceremony appears to have involved bouts of collective masturbation, apparently as an expression of free thinking. The club's symbol was a phallus with a small bag dangling beneath it, reflecting the club's motto: 'May prick nor purse ne'er fail you.' George IV became an honorary member, and donated a snuffbox containing the pubic hair of one of his mistresses. It is said that the club's many relics were once offered to a museum curator, who, shocked by their explicit nature, fell into a faint.

Beggar's mantle fringed wi' gowd, a James VI's description of the KINGDOM OF FIFE. At that time, Fife's ports flourished on fishing and extensive trade with the Low Countries, while its interior remained poor – a situation that later changed with the development of the county's rich agricultural land, and its extensive resources of coal.

Beginning of all sorrow, the How the *Liber Pluscardensis* – a history of Scotland written at Pluscarden Abbey, Moray, in 1461 – characterized the death of Alexander III, who was killed on 19 March 1286 when his horse stumbled over a cliff at Kinghorn in Fife:

> Oh how dolorous, bitter and dark that unlooked-for day, how mournful and disastrous, how pregnant with tears, calamity and grief, forecasting such a time of unrest and dule. Truly it might be said, 'Woe to the folk of Scotland, for here is the beginning of all sorrow.'

As Alexander left no male heir, the disaster encouraged Edward I of England (the HAMMER OF THE SCOTS) to try to impose his own choice of king on Scotland (*see* MAID OF NORWAY; GREAT CAUSE, THE), leading to the long years of conflict known as the Scottish Wars of Independence, ending at Bannockburn in 1314. The *Liber Pluscardensis* recounts how THOMAS THE RHYMER had predicted the disaster:

> Now, concerning this grief and unforeseen misfortune, a certain country prophet, called Thomas the Rhymer (we do not know by what spirit he was moved), the day before the sorrowful death of the King, said to the Earl of March, certain English being present, 'Alas the morrow, for it will be a day of grief and disaster, a great and most bitter day for the kingdom of Scotland. Before the twelfth hour there shall blow such a storm through the kingdom as men have never heard for a long time past: it shall appal the hearers, bring low high hearts, and overthrow the tall and fast-rooted mountains.'
>
> The Earl of March, who was at Dunbar, knew not what this could mean, and wondered greatly. And on the morrow, when the time had come, there was no sign of wind showing in the air, and he thought that Thomas was wrong and had told him falsely. But then, while he dined, came suddenly a messenger from the North, who beat violently on the door, seeking to enter and straightway brought the formal news of the King's death, whereat they were all stricken with amazement, and stood there stupefied like men in a trance.

Bejan, bejaune, bejaunt, etc A first-year under-graduate. The term was formerly used at Edinburgh and Aberdeen, but is now only in use at St Andrews University, where the female version is a *bejantine* (in Aberdeen it was *bejanella*). The term derives from the French *béjaune*, 'greenhorn, callow youth', a term in use at the Sorbonne in Paris from the Middle Ages; this in turn derives from *bec jaune*, 'yellow beak', i.e. a young bird. *See also* BUTTERY WULLIE COLLIE; RAISIN WEEKEND.

Belle of Mauchline, the Jean Armour (1765–1834), so called by Burns, whose wife she eventually became. Jean was the daughter of James Armour, a master mason in the Ayrshire village of Mauchline, and in the period 1777–89 Burns lived at the nearby farm of Lochlea, then at Mossgiel, which he and his brother Gilbert took over on the death of their father in February 1784. Shortly afterwards 'Rob Mossgiel' issued a warning to the 'Mauchline belles':

> Beware a tongue that's smoothly hung,
>   A heart that warmly seems to feel;
> That feeling heart but acts a part, –
>   'Tis rakish art in Rob Mossgiel.

The young women of the neighbourhood failed to listen: Elizabeth Paton bore Burns's first illegitimate child in May 1785, and by the end of the year Jean Armour herself was pregnant by him. She had first met Burns when she'd been obliged to chase away his dog LUATH while she was hanging up her washing on a drying green. This was probably in 1784. Sometime later Burns launched his poetical courtship:

> In Mauchline there dwells six proper young belles,
>   The pride of the place and its neighbourhood a';
> Their carriage and dress, a stranger would guess,
>   In Lon'on or Paris they'd gotten it a':
> *Miss Miller* is fine, *Miss Markland*'s divine,
>   *Miss Smith* she has wit, and *Miss Betty* is braw;
> There's beauty and fortune to get wi' *Miss Morton*;
>   But *Armour*'s the jewel for me o' them a'.
>   – 'The Belles of Mauchline'

In March 1786 Jean told her father that she was pregnant. He fainted, then packed her off to Paisley before her condition became too obvious. It seems that she and Burns fully intended to get married (and were perhaps so already, in an irregular fash-

ion; *see* MARRIAGE *SUBSEQUENTE COPULA*), but James Armour opposed the match. Word of the pregnancy leaked out, and in June first Jean and then Burns were summoned before the Mauchline Kirk to confess their sins. Faced with the opposition of James Armour, Burns had his tragically foreshortened fling with HIGHLAND MARY. After Mary's death he resumed relations with Jean, who proceeded to give birth to two sets of twins (although three out of the four children died in infancy). After the success of the Kilmarnock Edition of his poems, Burns became a better marital prospect. James Armour withdrew his opposition, and the marriage was registered in August 1788. Jean and Burns went on to have another five children together, the last of whom was born on the day of Burns's funeral in July 1796. Jean outlived the poet by 38 years, and she and the children, who were left more or less destitute, were eventually supported by a charitable fund. She was buried beside her husband in his mausoleum in Dumfries.

> When first I came to Stewart Kyle,
>   My mind it was na steady;
> Where'er I gaed, where'er I rade,
>   A mistress still I had aye:
> But when I came roun' by Mauchline town,
>   Not dreadin' onie body,
> My heart was caught before I thought –
>   And by a Mauchline lady.
>   – Robert Burns, 'The Mauchline Lady' (sung to the tune
>   of 'I had a horse, and I had nae mair')

Belle Stuart, La Frances Teresa Stuart (1647–1702), a maid of honour to Catherine of Braganza, queen to Charles II, whose sister had described Frances to him as 'the prettiest girl in the world and the most fitted to adorn a court'. Samuel Pepys admired 'her sweet eye, little Roman nose, and excellent taille', while another observer described her as 'the only blazing star'. As far as her personality was concerned, one contemporary described her as 'cunning', while another complained that she was 'infantile'. Certainly, she eschewed court politics for her preferred pastimes of blind man's buff, hunt the slipper and building houses out of cards. She also refused to become Charles's mistress, and in 1667 married Charles Stewart, 3rd Duke of Richmond and 6th Duke of Lennox. She was said to be the model for Britannia that graced a medal commissioned by King Charles to commemorate the Peace of Breda:

> The king's new medal, where, in little, is Mrs Stewart's face ... and a pretty thing it is, that he should choose her face to represent Britannia by.
> – Samuel Pepys, Diary, 25 February 1667

This figure of Britannia, first engraved by John Roettier, continued to appear on copper pennies until decimalization in 1971, when she was transferred to the 50 pence piece. The childless Duchess of Lennox, who died in 1702, stipulated that money she left in her will to her 'near and dear kinsman', Lord Blantyre, should be used for the purchase of an estate to be called 'Lennox's Love to Blantyre'. The property in question was Lethington, near Haddington, and the house there, previously the seat of the Maitlands and dating back to the 14th century, has ever since been known as Lennoxlove.

Bell Geordie The nickname of George Gibson, the Glasgow city bellman during the later years of the 18th century and the early years of the 19th. In 1790 a vacancy for assistant bellman came up, and the candidates for the job were invited to speak the following lines to see whose voice carried best:

> Notice. – There has just arrived at the Broomielaw a boat-load of fine fresh herrings, selling at three a penny.

Geordie duly spoke the announcement in a fine, clear voice, then recited some lines of his own composition:

> Now, my gude folks, this cry is all hum,
> For herrings in the boat are not yet come
> Therefore you needna fash to gang awa
> To seek sic dainties at the Broomielaw;
> But if they come, and I'm town-crier then,
> I'll tinkle thrice my bell and let ye ken.

He was duly awarded the job, and for many years entertained the citizens with the witty and original way in which he delivered his public announcements and advertisements. His downfall came when he uttered the following lines within earshot of some of the city's magistrates, whose origins had been humble:

> If in our Courts a stranger keeks,
> His eye meets neither squires nor bankers;
> But judges wha shape leather breeks,
> And justices wha sowther tankers.
> [*sowther tankers*, 'solder tankards']

This affront to magisterial dignity resulted in Geordie's immediate dismissal, his red coat of office being stripped from his back and his bell seized from his hand. He subsequently took to the bottle, lost his sight, and was to be seen being led around the streets by a little girl, his granddaughter, and begging for bread on the sites of his former glories.

Bell hoose, the See FISHERMEN'S TABOOS.

Bell Rock An infamous reef in the North Sea, a dozen miles or so off the Angus coast, and long a hazard for shipping as only a small part of it protrudes above the water. Both the name Bell Rock and the alternative name Inchcape Rock (Gaelic *innis*, 'island', possibly with either Old Norse *skeppa*, 'basket', or Gaelic *sgeip*, 'beehive') may refer to its shape, although according to tradition a medieval abbot of Arbroath (formerly Aberbrothock) placed a bell on the rock to warn sailors of the danger. The story is that the bell was later removed by a pirate, who, according to John Monipennie (writing in 1633), one year later 'perished upon the same rock, with ship and goods, in the righteous judgement of God'. This tale inspired Robert Southey's famous ballad, 'The Inchcape Rock', in which Ralph the Rover meets just such a well-deserved fate:

> They hear no sound, the swell is strong;
> Though the wind hath fallen they drift along,
> Till the vessel strikes with a shivering shock –
> 'Oh, Christ! It is the Inchcape Rock!'

> Sir Ralph the Rover tore his hair,
> He curst himself in his despair;
> The waves rush in on every side,
> The ship is sinking beneath the tide.

> But even in his dying fear,
> One dreadful sound could the Rover hear;
> A sound as if with the Inchcape Bell,
> The Devil below was ringing his knell.

Work began on the construction of a lighthouse on the rock in 1807 and finished in 1811 – a considerable engineering achievement, undertaken by John Rennie and Robert Stevenson, grandfather of RLS. The new light was celebrated in a poem called 'Pharos Loquitur' by Sir Walter Scott, written when he visited the Bell Rock in 1814:

> Far in the bosom of the deep,
> O'er these wild shelves my watch I keep;
> A ruddy gem of changeful light
> Bound on the dusky brow of night.

Bell-the-Cat The nickname of Archibald Douglas, Earl of Angus (1453–1513), deriving from an incident in 1482. Douglas and his fellow nobles had long complained about James III's favouring of masons and musicians, and while they sat in Lauder Kirk, ostensibly en route to fight the English, Douglas declared, 'I'll bell the cat.' He was referring to the fable of Aesop, in which the mice are pondering how to deal with the danger of the cat, when one suggests that they tie a bell round its neck to warn them of its approach. This is thought to be an excellent idea by the other mice, until one of them asks who precisely will undertake this perilous task. Douglas was of course volunteering himself, and went straight to James's tent where he demanded the king dismiss his favourites. When this was refused, Douglas and the other nobles seized six of the favourites and hanged them from the bridge over the Leader Water. Robert Cochrane, the architect whom the king had made Earl of Mar, demanded to be suspended from a silken cord, not by a hempen rope 'like ane thief'. His request was refused. Archibald Bell-the-Cat's son, Gavin Douglas, was of a gentler disposition: he was Bishop of Dunkeld and a great poet, noted for his translation into Scots of Virgil's *Aeneid*. *See also* BLUE BLANKET.

Bells, the The church bells that mark midnight at HOGMANAY. Ships docked in harbour or anchored in the Forth or Clyde sound their foghorns at the same moment. Complete strangers, the worse for wear, embrace and kiss each other in the street. Without prompting, those at New Year parties cross their arms, link hands, form a circle, sway in and out, singing AULD LANG SYNE with a smile on their lips and a tear in their eye. John Knox turns in his grave.

Bell that never rang, the *See* TREE THAT NEVER GREW, THE.

Bellum Episcopale *See* BISHOPS' WARS, THE.

Belly-blind The game of blind man's buff, or the blindfolded person in the game, or any blindfolded person. The reason for the *belly* element is obscure, but may be a corruption of the name *Billie*. Another name for the game is *bellie-mantie*, where the second element may be from French *manteau*, a cloak, which would have been used as a blindfold.

Belt, the *See* TAWSE.

Beltane The ancient Celtic Mayday festival, celebrated in Scotland, Ireland and the Isle of Man with bonfires lit on the tops of mountains and hills, and possibly originally accompanied by human sacrifice. The word is an anglicization of Gaelic *bealltainn*, of which the first element is cognate with the *bale*-element in BALEFIRE, ultimately derived from Sanskrit *bhala*, 'brightness'. Sir James Frazer, in *The Golden Bough*, quotes an account by the Perthshire laird, John Ramsay of Ochtertyre (1736–1814), the patron of Burns and friend of Sir Walter Scott, indicating that celebrations of Beltane continued in the Highlands and Islands well into the early modern period:

> Like the other public worship of the Druids, the Beltane feast seems to have been performed on hills or eminences. They thought it degrading to him whose temple is the universe, to suppose that he would dwell in any house made with hands. Their sacrifices were therefore offered in the open air, frequently upon the tops of hills, where they were presented with the grandest views of nature, and were nearest the seat of warmth and order. And, according to tradition, such was the manner of celebrating this festival in the Highlands within the last hundred years. But since the decline of superstition, it has been celebrated by the people of each hamlet on some hill or rising ground around which their cattle were pasturing. Thither the young folks repaired in the morning, and cut a trench, on the summit of which a seat of turf was formed for the company. And in the middle a pile of wood or other fuel was placed ...

The fire was started from nothing by spinning a stick in a hole bored into a plank of oak, or similar methods, thus having 'the appearance of being immediately derived from heaven'. If the fire did not take, it implied someone in the company was guilty of some secret crime. Once the fire was alight, much feasting, singing and dancing followed. Towards the end of the proceedings, according to Ramsay, the master of ceremonies produced the *Beltane cake*, and the ritual associated with this may recall earlier human sacrifices:

> ... the Beltane cake ... was divided into a number of pieces, and distributed in great form to the company. There was one particular piece which whoever got was called cailleach beal-tine – i.e., the Beltane carline, a term of great reproach. Upon his being known, part of the company laid hold of him and made a show of putting him into the fire; but the majority interposing, he was rescued. And in some places they laid him flat on the ground, making as if they would quarter him. Afterwards, he was pelted with egg-shells, and retained the odious appellation during the whole year. And while the feast was fresh in people's memory, they affected to speak of the cailleach beal-tine as dead.

In the Hebrides, the Beltane cake was baked with a hole in the middle, through which the cows were milked. Frazer goes on to cite Beltane celebrations still in use in the parish of Callander up to the end of the 18th century. Inevitably, there have been various modern revivals – every year since 1988, for example, thousands of people have attended a fire festival on the top of Calton Hill in Edinburgh, on the night of 30 April. *See also* SAMHAIN.

Ben Alder Cottage A remote and supposedly haunted bothy on the western shore of Loch Ericht, to the south of Ben Alder, and at the foot of the slope containing Prince Charlie's Cave. The full story – an object lesson in how fictions can take on a life of their own – was unravelled by Paddy Buckley in 'Strange Happenings at Ben Alder Cottage' (*Scottish Mountaineering Club Journal*, 2011), of which the following is a brief outline.

Ben Alder Cottage was last inhabited on a permanent basis by a gamekeeper called Joseph McCook, who lived there for nearly 40 years with his family, until just after the First World War.

Thereafter, the cottage was used occasionally by estate gillies and stalkers, and by tramps and hill-walkers. One of the estate gillies, Ian McPherson, admitted that he had made up a story about a ghost in Ben Alder Cottage:

> The house was haunted by a woman who once took refuge there from a storm. She was storm-stayed until hunger crazed her and she killed and ate her child. She was seen passing through Rannoch so wild-eyed with despair that no one dared to cross her path. Some said that she returned to the wastes of Rannoch, driven by remorse, and was lost in the morasses of that place.
>
> – Elizabeth and Ian McPherson, *Happy Hawkers* (1937)

Apparently, McPherson's intention with this story had been to scare away unwelcome visitors – and, entering into the spirit of it, the head stalker of the time, Finlay McIntosh, would give sinisterly ambivalent answers to those who asked him about the ghost. Possibly as a consequence, from the late 1930s various overnight visitors at the cottage reported hearing strange sounds – footsteps, tappings, scratching and groans – and even experienced phenomena of a *poltergeistische* persuasion. A rumour circulated that the cottage was haunted by the old stalker, McCook, who had allegedly hanged himself on the back of the front door. This rumour appeared in print in W.H. Murray's *Undiscovered Scotland* (1951), to the distress of McCook's descendants, obliging Murray to publish an apology. Despite this, the story continued to appear in print – for example in an article in the *Scotsman* published in July 1973. In fact, McCook had died peacefully in 1933 at the ripe of old age of 85, in the Cottage Hospital, Newtonmore, and was described by his minister, the Revd A.E. Robertson (the first person to complete all the MUNROS) as 'a very fine type of Highland stalker, level-headed and sensible'.

For another strange (but true) tale from Ben Alder, *see* MAN WITH NO NAME, THE.

Benches & Hedges The nickname, playing on a well-known brand of cigarette, given since the 2006 indoor smoking ban in Scotland, to an outside area at Glasgow Airport where smoking is allowed. The area is provisioned with benches, and surrounded by a plastic privet hedge.

Bendy juice Glaswegian slang for any kind of alcoholic drink liable to render one's legs bendy.

Bendy Wendy A nickname of Wendy Alexander (b.1963), leader of the Labour opposition in the Scottish Parliament from September 2007 until she resigned in June 2008. The nickname refers to her contortions in May 2008 around the issue of whether there should be a referendum on Scottish independence. Her challenge to the SNP to 'bring it on' was at odds with the policy of her boss, Gordon Brown.

Ben Loyal *See* QUEEN OF THE SCOTTISH PEAKS, THE.

Ben Macdui, Grey Man of *See* GREY MAN OF BEN MACDUI, THE.

Ben Nevis *See* REAL BIG BEN, THE.

Ben Wyvis, snows of *See* SNOWS OF BEN WYVIS.

Bereans A Presbyterian sect that was founded in Fettercairn, Kincardineshire in 1773 by the Revd John Barclay. They took their name from the inhabitants of Berea (modern Veria) in northern Greece, who in Acts 17:11 'received the word with all readiness of mind, and searched the scriptures daily, whether those things were so'.

> The last of the sect in Laurencekirk were two old women, and when one of them died the other feelingly remarked – 'Wae's me! when I gang too the Bereans'll be clean licket aff!'
> – A.C. Cameron, *Fettercairn* (1899)

Bernera Riot *See* HIS POLYONYMOUS OMNIPOTENCE.

Bernie the Bull Perhaps the only animal in Scotland that has provided the impetus for a major piece of civil engineering. The small island of Vatersay – since 1911 the most southerly inhabited island in the Outer Hebrides – is separated from Barra by a narrow sea channel. Traditionally, the crofters of Vatersay would swim their cattle across, but agitation for a safer crossing erupted in 1986 following

the drowning of Bernie, a prize bull, who, after performing his many and varied duties on the island, succumbed to exhaustion on the return swim. Government was obliged to act, and a new causeway was opened in 1991. It is hoped this will prevent the depopulation of Vatersay, a fate that has befallen all the islands to the south – Sandray, Pabbay, Mingulay and Bearnaraigh.

Berwick cockles Peppermint-flavoured sweeties, coloured white with pink stripes and formed in the shape of the cockles harvested around Tweedmouth harbour.

Berwick-upon-Tweed The Border town long suffered something of an identity crisis, having changed hands 13 times between Scotland and England, until ending up on the wrong side of the Border in 1482. In 1551 an Anglo–Scottish treaty made it a free burgh, a status it maintained until 1885, when an act of Parliament incorporated it into the English county of Northumberland. Before the act, some official documents included 'Berwick-upon-Tweed' alongside 'Great Britain and Ireland'. There is a persistent rumour that this was the case in the declaration of hostilities against Russia at the beginning of the Crimean War, but that the peace treaty omitted to mention Berwick-upon-Tweed, which is thus still technically at war with Russia. For the record, Berwick Rangers FC play in the Scottish rather than the English League. In 2008 a local paper polled residents and found 79 per cent in favour of being governed from Edinburgh, rather than London. *See also* LITTLE DOOR TO THE WIDE HOUSE OF ENGLAND, THE; SECOND ALEXANDRIA, THE.

Beside the Bonnie Brier Bush *See* KAILYARD SCHOOL; 'THERE GROWS A BONNIE BRIER BUSH'.

'Bessie Bell and Mary Gray' A ballad that recalls the fate of Bessie Bell, the daughter of the Laird of Kinvaid, who was visiting Mary Gray at her house at Lednock (Lynedoch), in the valley of the River Almond west of Perth, when the plague of 1645 (or 1666) broke out. To avoid infection, the two friends secluded themselves in a remote bower on the Burn Braes, but they caught the plague when visited by a young man from Perth, who was in love with one or other of them. All three died, and their bodies were left to rot until only the bones were left, and these were then buried by the River Almond. Towards the end of the 18th century, Thomas Graham, the new owner of the estate, repaired their burial place, surrounding it with iron railings and installing a slab inscribed with the words, 'They lived, they loved, they died.' According to one account, the Duke of Abercorn was so moved by the ballad that he gave the names Bessie Bell and Mary Gray to two hills in County Tyrone, Ulster; other accounts suggest that these were the names of two nannies in the Abercorn household.

Best laid schemes ... Burns's lines from 'To a Mouse' (subtitled: 'on turning her up in her nest, with the plough, November, 1785') have become proverbial:

> The best laid schemes o' mice an' men
> Gang aft agley,
> An' lea'e us nought but grief an' pain,
> For promis'd joy.

The phrase *Of Mice and Men* became the title of a 1937 novella by John Steinbeck. *See also* WEE, SLEEKIT, COW'RIN', TIM'ROUS BEASTIE.

Best MP Scotland never had, the *See* RAT RACE IS FOR RATS, THE.

Better meddle wi' the deil than the bairns o' Falkirk *See* BAIRNS O' FALKIRK.

Better to marry than hang *See* MUCKLE MOU'D MEG.

Better that bairns should weep than bearded men The callous observation made by the Master of Glamis on the tears shed by the 16-year-old James VI after he had been seized in the RUTHVEN RAID of August 1582, and so separated forever from his first love, the handsome Esmé Stuart, Duke of Lennox. One contemporary observed that Glamis's words 'entered so deeply into the king's heart, as he did never forget them'.

Between the lichts Between the lights of day and night, i.e. twilight, the time of day that creatures

such as BROWNIES might be glimpsed. The French have an evocative expression that also suggests the inbetween-ness of this time: *Entre chien et loup* ('between dog and wolf').

Bhoys, the *See* FOOTBALL CLUB NICKNAMES.

Bible, only football team to be mentioned in the *See* QUEEN OF THE SOUTH.

Bible John The nickname of an unknown serial killer who was blamed for the murders of three young women in Glasgow in 1968 and 1969. All three victims had been dancing at the Barrowland Ballroom (*see under* BARRA) just before their deaths, and witnesses said that the man with whom the last victim left the Barrowland made a number of references to the Bible, and described the dance hall as a 'den of iniquity'. All the women were menstruating at the time of their deaths, and they were all strangled with their stockings; two of them were raped. The handbags of all three were missing. A similar killer, called Johnny Bible, is investigated by Inspector REBUS in Ian Rankin's novel *Black and Blue* (1997).

Biddy *See* RED BIDDY.

Bide a wee Wait a moment; stay a while; be patient. The phrase, found for example in the works of S.R. Crockett, James Bridie and Neil Munro, has a whiff of the KAILYARD SCHOOL about it, and hovers on the fringes of FAUX JOCKERY.

Bidie-in or **bidey-in** One who *bides in* (lives in), i.e. an unmarried cohabitee, a common-law husband or wife.

Bierricht *See* ORDEAL BY BLOOD.

Big Eck The nickname of the footballer and manager Alex McLeish (b.1959), 'Eck' being an affectionate version of Alec or Alex (as in WEE ECK, aka Alex Salmond, who is also, confusingly, sometimes known as Big Eck). In the 1980s McLeish was one of Aberdeen's leading stars, and also won 77 Scottish caps. He has since managed a number of clubs, including Motherwell, Hibs, Rangers and Birmingham City, and for ten months in 2007 managed the national side.

> Wee Eck watched Big Eck address his players in the Hampden dressing room on Saturday and knew he was the right man to lead the country – in a footballing sense at least.
>
> First Minister Alex Salmond looked on in awe as Alex McLeish commanded the respect of every one of Scotland's stars in the final moments before they stepped on to the hallowed turf to face Italy ...
>
> – Neil Cameron, 'Wee Eck is Backing Big Eck', in the *Daily Record*, 21 November 2007

Big hoose (1) The laird's mansion; (2) a town hall or city chambers; (3) a euphemism for prison.

Biggar's bigger The citizens of the Lanarkshire market town are fond of the old saw: 'London and Edinburgh are big, but Biggar's bigger.' Biggar is famous for the huge bonfire that is lit in the main street every Hogmanay, a custom going back hundreds of years and only interrupted during the blackout in the Second World War, when the locals had to content themselves with burning a candle in a tin.

Big Jessie *See* JESSIE.

Big man A respectful form of address for a man.

> Frankie White's calling him 'big man' hadn't helped. Big man. The implied stature beyond the physical the words sought to bestow on him was an embarrassment.
>
> – William McIlvanney, *The Big Man* (1985)

Conversely, *wee man* is a friendly form of address to someone smaller than oneself or to a little boy. *See also* IN THE NAME OF THE WEE MAN.

Big Man, the The nickname of Jock Stein (1922–85), regarded by many as the most successful Scottish football manager ever, having won the European Cup, 11 Scottish League Championships, 11 Scottish Cups and 6 Scottish League Cups. In 1965, after stints at Dunfermline and Hibs, he became the first non-Catholic manager of Celtic, and between 1966 and 1974 led the team to nine Scottish League championships in a row. Under his management Celtic also won the European Cup in

1967: 'We did it by playing football,' Stein said afterwards, 'Pure, beautiful, inventive football.' He became full-time Scotland manager in 1978. Stein had long suffered from ill health, and his last words, after he collapsed in the dugout at Ninian Park in Cardiff on 10 September 1985 were 'It's all right, doc. I'm feeling better now.'

Big Red Shed, the The descriptive nickname of Glasgow's Scottish National Exhibition and Conference Centre, built in the 1980s. The nickname is now obsolete, as the building has been painted grey for some years.

Big Sam The nickname of Samuel McDonald (d.1802), Scottish footman to the Prince of Wales (the future George IV). He was 6 ft 10 in (2.05 m) tall.

Big Yin, the 'The Big One', the nickname of the comedian Billy Connolly, born in Anderston, Glasgow, in 1942. The nickname originated when Connolly was a teenager, to differentiate him from his father, also called Billy. 'My father was a very strong man,' he recalls:

> He was 'Big Billy' and I was 'Wee Billy'. And then I got bigger than him, and the whole fucking thing got out of control. And then I became 'the Big Yin' in Scotland. So, we'd go into the pub and someone would say, 'Billy Connolly was in.' 'Oh, Big Billy or Wee Billy?' 'The Big Yin.' 'Oh, Wee Billy.'
>
> – *Billy Connolly's World Tour of Australia* (1996)

Bill, the *See* FORT, THE.

Billy A Glaswegian name for any Protestant, especially of the more bigoted sort – as in the street rhyme:

> Are ye a Billy or a Dan
> Or an auld tin can?

See also DAN.

Billy Boys A notorious Protestant gang of the 1920s and 1930s, whose base was Bridgeton ('Brigton') in Glasgow. These and other similar gangs did little to enhance the city's reputation:

The gangsters have come to Britain. Glasgow, second city of the Empire, frankly acknowledges their reign of terror. A thousand young men ... rule the poorer districts. Their insignia of office are the broken bottle, the razor blade, the cosh, the knife and – newest and most effective of all – the bayonet.
– *Sunday Express*, 1935

The name 'the Billy Boys' both reflects that of the great Protestant hero, 'King Billy' (William of Orange), and that of the gang's leader, Billy Fullerton. Fullerton founded the gang in 1924, reputedly after he was hit on the head with a hammer having made the mistake of scoring a goal in a friendly football match against a Catholic team. The gang – just one of many in the area – took on rival Catholic gangs in Bridgeton such as the Norman Conks – who took their name from Norman Street, a Catholic neighbourhood. On Catholic holy days and saints' days, the Billy Boys would parade down Norman Street. What happened next is described by Sir Percy Sillitoe, the police chief whose men – SILLITOE'S COSSACKS – took on the gangs in the 1930s:

As soon as the distant strains of this offensive music were heard by the Conks, they manned all upper windows, and even the roofs in their street, and when the Billy Boys' band tried to march past, it was met with a downpour of bricks, missiles, buckets of filth, and broken glass. If the Norman Conks could have made boiling lead, I am sure they would not have hesitated to use that too. It was certainly all that would have been needed to complete the picture of a medieval siege.

Fullerton and some of his followers were strike breakers during the 1926 General Strike, and he later joined the British Union of Fascists and attacked Communist gatherings. When he died in 1962 his cortège was accompanied by 1000 people. Edwin Morgan wrote a poem to commemorate the death of 'King Billy of Brigton', dying alone in a box bed:

... it isn't the violence they remember
but the legend of a violent man ...

The Billy Boys had their own theme song, 'The Billy Boys', sung to the tune of 'Marching Through Georgia':

Hullo! Hullo!
We are the Billy Boys!
Hullo! Hullo!
You'll know us by our noise!
We're up to our knees in Fenian blood,
Surrender or you'll die!
For we are the Brigton Billy Boys.

This anti-Catholic song was subsequently taken up by Loyalists in both Glasgow and Belfast, and is a particular favourite among supporters of Rangers FC – although in 2006 UEFA, in an effort to stamp out sectarianism, ordered the club to ban the singing of the song during matches. *See also* FAMINE SONG, THE; NINETY-MINUTE BIGOTS.

Binos, the *See* FOOTBALL CLUB NICKNAMES.

Bird-Catchers, the A nickname for the Royal Scots Greys; *see* REGIMENTAL NICKNAMES.

Birdman of Stirling Castle, the Father John Damian, a noted alchemist, charlatan and quack at the court of James IV. He was known to his enemies as the 'French leach', although according to Bishop John Leslie (*De Origine, Moribus, et Rebus Gestis Scotorum*, 1578) he was an Italian. In 1504, in return for a promise to turn lead into gold, James IV made Damian abbot of Tongland Abbey. In 1507, witnessed by the king, Damian attempted to fly from the walls of Stirling Castle to France, but shortly after take-off ended up in a dunghill with a broken thigh bone. He blamed this ignominious outcome on the feathers he had used in his wings (apparently based on a design by Leonardo da Vinci); he had chosen hens' feathers, and realized too late that hens are creatures who 'covet the middens and not the skies'.

The poet William Dunbar, perhaps jealous of the king's bounty towards the abbot, was delighted, and mocked Damian in a couple of satires. In the first satire, Dame Fortune shows the poet a vision of an abbot resembling a horrific griffin, who takes to the air and mates with a female dragon, so begetting the Antichrist:

He sall ascend as ane horrebble grephoun,
Him meit sall in the air ane scho dragoun;
Thir terrible monsteris sall togidder thrist
And in the cludis get the Antechrist,
Quhill all the air infeck of thair pusoun.

In the other satire, Damian, having killed many of his patients with his quack medicines, is attacked in the air by all sorts of species of bird:

> Thay set aupone him with a yowle
> And gaif him dynt for dynt.

Thus battered until all his feathers 'war drownd and drawkit' he plunges to the earth,

> And in a myre up to the ene
> Amang the glar did glyd.

More recently, another poet, Edwin Morgan, wrote of the events 'At Stirling Castle, 1507':

> Damian, D'Amiens, Damiano –
> we never found out his true name, but there
> he crouched, swarthy, and slowly sawed the air
> with large strapped-on bat-membrane wings.
> – *Sonnets from Scotland* (1984)

According to the architectural historian Professor Charles McKean, Damian's flight may not have been quite so laughable, and in fact he may have flown up to half a mile. McKean points out that if the wings had not worked, Damian would almost certainly have been killed, given the drop from the castle's walls and the crags beneath. Certainly the king was pleased enough to award Damian a pension after he retired from Tongland Abbey in 1509.

Bird that never flew, the *See* TREE THAT NEVER GREW, THE.

Birks and briars If *birks* (birches) and briars grew on the graves of two lovers, it was believed that death had not divided them.

Birks of Aberfeldy, the The scenic glen of the Urlar Burn at Aberfeldy, so-called because lined with birch trees (Scots *birk*). Robert Burns visited on 30 August 1787 and celebrated the scenery in his poem 'The Birks of Aberfeldy':

> The braes ascend like lofty wa's,
> The foaming stream deep-roaring fa's,
> O'erhung wi' fragrant spreading shaws –
> The birks of Aberfeldy.

> Bonie lassie, will ye go,
> Will ye go, will ye go,
> Bonie lassie, will ye go
> To the birks of Aberfeldy!

Birlinn of Clanranald, The The English-language title of *Birlinn Chlann-Raghnail*, the masterpiece of the Gaelic poet Alasdair MacMaighstir Alasdair (Captain Alasdair MacDonald, *c.* 1698–1770). Written at some point after 1751, it recounts the voyage of the *birlinn* (a type of boat similar to a Viking longship) of the Chief of Clanranald from South Uist to Carrickfergus in Ulster.

> The waves grew dark, thick, dun-bellied,
> angry and sallow
> the sky had every single hue
> you find in tartan …

> The ocean then donned completely
> its black grey cloak,
> its rough, shaggy sable mantle
> of horrid surging.
> – trans. Derick Thomson (Ruaraidh MacThòmais) (1996)

There is also a translation by Hugh MacDiarmid (1935).

Birnam Wood A wooded area a little to the south of the Perthshire village of Birnam, itself just across the Tay from Dunkeld. It was at Birnam that the historical MACBETH, once he had assumed the throne, defeated a rebel army in 1045, so this may have inspired Shakespeare to introduce the place into his tragedy. In *Macbeth* he thus has the Third Apparition conjured by the Weird Sisters to prophesy:

> Macbeth shall never vanquish'd be until
> Great Birnam Wood to high Dunsinane Hill
> Shall come against him.
> – IV.i

This of course comes to pass when Malcolm has his troops cut branches from Birnam Wood to camouflage their approach to Macbeth's redoubt on Dunsinane Hill, where Macbeth is killed. Dunsinane, about a dozen miles to the southeast, is the location of an ancient hill fort, and the real Macbeth *did* suffer a defeat here, on 27 July 1054 (*see* BATTLE OF

THE SEVEN SLEEPERS), but he was not killed until the Battle of Lumphanan (near Banchory in Aberdeenshire) on 15 August 1057, the supposed spot being marked by Macbeth's Cairn. *See also* SCOTTISH PLAY, THE.

Bishops' Wars, the Two wars (1639 and 1640) resulting from Charles I's attempt to impose episcopacy on predominantly Presbyterian Scotland. The wars were also collectively known by the Latin name *Bellum Episcopale*. Charles's requirement for funds to fight the Scots obliged him to summon the English Parliament (which had not sat for 11 years), so paving the way for the outbreak of the Civil War in England. *See also* DUNSE DINGS A'.

The unpopularity of bishops in Scotland is attested in the name *bishop's weed* for ground elder (an invasive weed), and in the saying *The bishop's foot has been in the broth*, meaning the food has been burnt. A *bishop* was a heavy wooden implement for compacting and levelling stones and earth; it could also denote a second-hand horseshoe, or a person who is full of sound and fury signifying nothing.

Bit and the buffet, the Literally the food and the blows, i.e. the good with the bad.

Bucklaw, who had never been at all scrupulous in choosing his companions, was accustomed to, and entertained by, a fellow whom he could either laugh with or laugh at as he had a mind, who would take, according to Scottish phrase, 'the bit and the buffet,' understood all sports, whether within or without doors, and, when the laird had a mind for a bottle of wine (no infrequent circumstance), was always ready to save him from the scandal of getting drunk by himself.
– Sir Walter Scott, *The Bride of Lammermoor* (1819), chapter xxi

Bite the glove or **thumb, to** In the Borders, such a gesture was once akin to throwing down the gauntlet as a challenge to fight a duel.

To bite the thumb or the glove seems not to have been considered, upon the Border, as a gesture of contempt, though so used by Shakespeare [in *Romeo and Juliet*, I.i], but as a pledge of mortal revenge. It is yet remembered that a young gentleman of Teviotdale, on the morning after a hard drinking bout, observed

that he had bitten his glove. He instantly demanded of his companions with whom he had quarrelled? and learning that he had had words with one of the party, insisted on instant satisfaction, asserting that, though he remembered nothing of the dispute, yet he never would have bitten his glove without he had received some unpardonable insult. He fell in the duel ...
– Sir Walter Scott, *The Lay of the Last Minstrel* (1805), note

The incident in question took place near Selkirk in 1721.

Blaand A Shetland concoction comprising buttermilk whey fermented until it is slightly *pétillant*.

Black affrontit (1) Seriously offended. (2) Highly embarrassed. The use of the word *black* as an intensifier goes back to at least the early 17th century:

O fie, sirs, for black burning shame,
Ye'll bring a blunder on your name!
– Anon., 'Bonny Heck' (1706)

However, the earliest recorded usages in the *DSL* of the now-common collocation *black affrontit* date only from the end of the 19th century:

What needs I care whuther fowk kens a' aboot it, or no'? I've been black affrontit that often, I dinna care a doaken noo what happens.
– J.B. Salmond, *My Man Sandy* (1899)

Black Agnes Agnes Dunbar, née Randolph (*c.* 1312–69), wife of Patrick, Earl of Dunbar and March, and so-called 'be ressone sho was blak skynnit', according to the 16th-century chronicler Robert Lindsay of Pitscottie. She is remembered for her refusal, during the absence of her husband, to surrender Dunbar Castle in 1338 to an English force led by the Earl of Salisbury, defiantly declaring (in the words of the old ballad):

Of Scotland's king I haud my house,
He pays me meat and fee,
And I will keep my gude auld house,
While my house will keep me.

When the English catapulted rocks into the castle, she had her maids dress up in their Sunday best and dust the battlements; when they brought up a kind of siege engine known as a sow, she had one of the catapulted rocks dropped on it, smashing it to pieces, and as the English troops manning it scattered, she shouted 'Behold the litter of English pigs'; when they paraded her brother, the Earl of Moray, before the castle with a rope round his neck, she urged them to go on and hang him, so she would inherit his earldom (he survived). Eventually, on 10 June, Salisbury withdrew, complaining (according to the ballad):

> She kept a stir in tower and trench,
> That brawling, boisterous Scottish wench;
> Cam I early, cam I late,
> There was Agnes at the gate.

Pitscottie concluded that Agnes was 'of greater spirit than it became a woman to be'. When her brother died without issue in 1347, she duly became Countess of Moray, and she and her younger sister inherited his considerable lands.

Mary Queen of Scots had a palfrey called Black Agnes, named after the countess and given to her by her half-brother, the Earl of Moray. Mary's favourite palfrey, however, was called Rosabelle.

See also SENGA.

Black as the Earl o' Hell's waistcoat *See* EARL O' HELL, THE.

Black bitch (1) According to John Jamieson, in *An Etymological Dictionary of the Scottish Language* (1825 supplement), this was a miller's trick for cheating his customers, to wit:

> A bag which, in former times at least, was clandestinely attached to the lower part of the mill-spout, that through a hole in the spout, part of the meal might be abstracted as it came down into the trough.

(2) A pejorative nickname for an inhabitant of Linlithgow, from the dog on the burgh's coat-of-arms.

Black Bob The nickname of General Robert Craufurd (1764–1812), a brilliant but flawed army officer. Born in Newark Castle, Ayrshire, Craufurd served in India against Tipu Sultan; in Ireland at the time of the 1798 rebellion; and under Wellington in the Peninsular War, during which he commanded the Light Division. His nickname alludes to his violent mood swings and his harsh discipline. Regarding the former, his friend General Sir George Napier wrote of him in his memoirs:

> Brilliant as some of the traits of his character were, and notwithstanding the good and generous feelings which often burst forth like a bright gleam of sunshine from behind a dark and heavy cloud, still there was a sullenness which seemed to brood in his innermost soul and generate passions which knew no bounds.

His reputation as a fearsome martinet is attested, for example, in one address he made to the entire Light Division, insisting that every man maintain a straight line of march:

> If I ever have any occasion to observe any man of the Brigade pick his road and go round a pool of water instead of marching through it I am fully determined to bring the officer commanding the company to which that man belongs to court martial. Should the court acquit the officer it shall not deter me from repeating the same ceremony on any other officer again and again ... I will insist on every soldier marching through water and I will flog any man attempting to avoid it.

Craufurd was mortally wounded on 19 January 1812 while storming the breach during the Siege of Ciudad Rodrigo, and died in agony five days later.

Black books, in the To be in debt.

Black Boo Man The bogeyman, who supposedly goes 'boo!' to frighten children; *cf.* the American equivalent, the *bugaboo* – a word thought to be of Celtic origin, as in the Cornish *buccaboo*, the Devil.

> Then dinna fright your laddie wi' the 'black boo' man,
> But let him douk his lugs in his wee parritch pan;
> Lay ye his rosy cheek upon his mou' a wee,
> How the rogue will laugh when his minny's in his ee.
> – James Ballantine, *The Gaberlunzie's Wallet* (1843)

Black breeks Literally 'black trousers', but figuratively either a minister of the kirk, or a coffin. In some places ministers were referred to as *black coats*, for example at sea, where the word 'minister' was taboo (*see also* FISHERMEN'S TABOOS). However, the term *black coat* was in wider use, as the following attests:

O Gowdie, terror o' the whigs,
Dread o' blackcoats and rev'rend wigs!
— Robert Burns, 'Epistle to John Goldie, in Kilmarnock' (1785)

The association of ministers with dark and sober garments goes back at least to a 1575 act of the General Assembly, which specified that 'thair haill habitis sall be of grave colour, as black, russet, sad gray, sad broun …'

Black bun A traditional Scottish baked good, also known as *Scotch bun*, consisting of a fruit cake enclosed in pastry. Originally it was served on Twelfth Night (hence an alternative name, *twelfth-cake*), but now it traditionally makes its appearance at Hogmanay, accompanying first-footers (see FIRST FOOT). Robert Louis Stevenson described it as 'a dense black substance, inimical to life'.

Black Child, the See SON OF THE BONES.

Black coat See BLACK BREEKS.

Black Colonel, the Colonel John Farquharson of Inverey (d. c. 1698), a fiery Jacobite; see COLONEL'S BED, THE.

Black Comyn, the See RED COMYN, THE.

Black cork Porter, the dark ale brewed from black malt.

Black cow, to be trodden on by the To suffer a severe misfortune.

The black cow on your foot ne'er trod,
Which gars you sing alang the road.
— David Herd, ed., *Ancient Scottish Songs, Heroic Ballads, etc.* (1776)

The *black ox* performs a similarly malevolent function:

'I'm fain to see ye looking sae weel, cummer; the mair, that the black ox has tramped on ye since I was aneath your roof-tree.'
'Ay,' said Elspeth; but rather from a general idea of

misfortune, than any exact recollection of what had happened, – 'there has been distress amang us of late …'
— Sir Walter Scott, *The Antiquary* (1816), xl

Black Dinner, the An infamous episode that took place in Edinburgh Castle during the minority of James II. After the death in 1439 of Archibald Douglas, 5th Earl of Douglas, the effective regent, power was shared uneasily between three men: Lord Chancellor Crichton; James 'the Gross' Douglas, 1st Earl of Avondale; and Sir Alexander Livingston of Callendar, the warden of Stirling Castle. On 24 November 1440 Crichton invited the young William Douglas, 6th Earl of Douglas, then aged only about 16, and his younger brother David to dine at Edinburgh Castle. But when a black bull's head was brought to the table the young Douglases were apprehended, accused of treason and beheaded in the presence of the king, then only ten years old. Crichton, Livingston and Avondale are all thought to have been behind this attempt to neutralize the power of the Black Douglases (see BLACK DOUGLAS, THE); Avondale particularly benefited from the deaths of his great-nephews, as he inherited the earldom as 7th Earl of Douglas. Some historians have suggested that the details of the dinner and the bull's head may be later embellishments (see BULL'S HEAD).

Edinburgh Castle, toun and tower,
God grant thou sink for sin;
And that even for the black dinner
Earl Douglas gat therein.
— Traditional rhyme

Black doctor A horse leech, formerly used for medicinal purposes.

Black dog The unwelcome companion of those who are in a deep depression. Churchill famously had his own black dog, and Samuel Johnson before him. What is perhaps less well known is that Sir Walter Scott was also visited by the beast, as recorded in his journal in March 1828 (quoted in Lockhart's *Life*):

I was sadly worried by the black dog this morning, that vile palpitation of the heart – that *tremor cordis* – that hysterical passion which forces unbidden sighs and

BLACK DONALD

tears, and falls upon a contented life like a drop of ink on white paper, which is not the less a stain because it carries no meaning.

The term *black dog* has also been applied (in Queen Anne's reign) to a bad shilling, and also to a large type of fly used by anglers. The phrase *butter in the black dog's house* denotes something irretrievably lost.

Black Donald (Gaelic *Domnhuill Dubh, Domhnall Dubh* or *Domnuill-dhu*). The Devil, who assumes many disguises, including that of an old man in black clothing. The 11th chief of Clan Cameron, who fought for the Lord of Isles at the REID HAR-LAW in 1411, was also known as *Domnhuill Dubh*.

Black Douglas, the The byname of Sir James Douglas (*c.*1286–1330), Robert the Bruce's right-hand man during the Wars of Independence. John Barbour, in *The Brus* (*c.* 1375), calls him 'the guid Schir James':

All men luffit him for his bounté,
For he was of full fair affeir,
Wys, curteis and deboneir,
Large and luffand als was he.

Barbour suggests that the name 'Black Douglas' derives from the fact that Douglas's hair was black, although it is also said the name was awarded him by the English, who described him as 'mair fell than wes ony devill in hell' on account of such gruesome exploits as the DOUGLAS LARDER. Another notable *coup de guerre* was his capture in February 1314 of Roxburgh Castle, using the subterfuge of having his men wrap their cloaks round them in the dark, in which guise they crawled towards the walls and were mistaken for harmless cattle. When Douglas himself silently ap-peared within the castle walls, he heard (according to legend) an English mother singing to her child:

Hush ye, hush ye, little pet, ye,
The Black Douglas shall not get ye.

Indeed he didn't, as both mother and child were spared. Douglas also played his part at Bannock-burn, pursuing the fleeing English with such re-morselessness that his quarry, according to Barbour, had not even leisure to make a comfort stop ('He leyt thaim nocht haff sic layser / As anys water for to

ma [i.e. make]'). For some years after, 'the Blak Dowglas' led cross-Border raids deep into England, as far south as the Humber. On one of these incursions he took part in the so-called CHAPTER OF MYTON (1319).

After Bruce's death in 1329, Douglas set out to fulfil his promise to his king to take his heart on crusade to the Holy Land, in order to atone for the murder of the RED COMYN in church. Douglas's route took him to Spain, where he fought alongside Alfonso XI of Castile against the Moors of Granada. Finding himself surrounded and impossibly out-numbered, Douglas – at least according to legend – took the silver casket containing Bruce's heart from around his neck and flung it into the enemy host, shouting, 'Now pass thou onward before us, as thou wert wont, and I will follow thee or die!' With that he hurled himself forward to death and glory – and thereafter the Douglas motto became 'Doe or Die.' After the battle, the Moorish commander recovered his body and the casket, and returned them to Alfonso. Douglas's corpse was then boiled, the flesh buried in Spain and the bones taken back to Scotland, where they were buried in St Bride's Church, Douglas. Bruce's heart was interred in Melrose Abbey. Subsequently, the Douglas family arms incorporated a bloody heart.

He thought rather to be with the foremost than with the hindermost ... [He] was reputed for the most hardy knight and greatest adventurer in all the two kingdoms.
   – Jean Froissart, *Chroniques* (later 14th century), on Sir James Douglas

Sir James's descendants, including his bastard son ARCHIBALD THE GRIM, became known as the Black Douglases, to distinguish them from the Earls of Angus, their junior cousins, who were known as the Red Douglases. Sir James's younger brother was HUGH THE DULL. The Douglases went on to become one of the most powerful and turbulent families in medieval Scotland.

In all nations it is observed that there are some families fatal to the ruin of the commonwealth and some persons fatal to the ruin of the house and race of which they are descended.
   – William Drummond of Hawthornden (1585–1649), on the Douglases

48

See also BLACK DINNER, THE; and for the meaning of the name *see* DOUGLAS.

Black Dwarf, the David Ritchie (1740–1811), also known as Bow'd or Crooked David, a person of restricted growth born at Stobo, where his father laboured in the slate quarries. Ritchie, after some wanderings, eventually settled in the Manor Valley, near Peebles, building a sturdy shelter for himself on a piece of moorland on Woodhouse Farm. In 1802 Sir James Nasmyth, the local laird, built Ritchie a cottage (known as the Black Dwarf's Cottage), which includes a door only 3 ft 10 in (115 cm) high. Walter Scott (himself lame) had visited Ritchie in 1797, and was later inspired to write his novel *The Black Dwarf* (1816), set in Liddesdale around the time of the abortive Jacobite rising in 1708. In the novel the eponymous hero becomes Elshender the Recluse or Elshie of the Mucklestanes – referring to the hovel he builds himself out of huge stones. Elshie is a misanthrope whom the locals believe to be in league with the Devil; however, unbeknownst to others, he intervenes for the good in various situations, and turns out to be the wealthy Sir Edward Mauley. In his introduction, Scott discusses the character of Ritchie, quoting Robert Chambers's description of him in the *Scots Magazine* for 1817:

> His skull, which was of an oblong and rather unusual shape, was said to be of such strength, that he could strike it with ease through the panel of a door, or the end of a barrel. His laugh is said to have been quite horrible; and his screech-owl voice, shrill, uncouth, and dissonant, corresponded well with his other peculiarities ... A jealous, misanthropical, and irritable temper, was his prominent characteristic. The sense of his deformity haunted him like a phantom. And the insults and scorn to which this exposed him, had poisoned his heart with fierce and bitter feelings, which, from other points in his character, do not appear to have been more largely infused into his original temperament than that of his fellow-men.

The novel also draws on the legend of the Brown Man of the Moors, who apparently only appears when troubled times are imminent, and for whom Elshender is mistaken when he is first seen on Mucklestane Moor:

> 'Auld Peght!' exclaimed the grand-dame; 'na, na – bless thee frae scathe, my bairn, it's been nae Peght that – it's been the Brown Man of the Moors! ... My father aften tauld me he was seen in the year o' the bloody fight at Marston-Moor, and then again in Montrose's troubles, and again before the rout o' Dunbar, and, in my ain time, he was seen about the time o' Bothwell-Brigg ... O, bairns, he's never permitted but in an ill time, sae mind ilka ane o' ye to draw to Him that can help in the day of trouble.'
> – chapter iii

Neither critics nor public thought much of the novel; Scott himself confessed that in writing it he had 'tired of the ground I had trod so often before ... I quarrelled with my story, & bungled up a conclusion'.

Blackening A prenuptial ritual still practised in various parts of Scotland, such as Orkney and Aberdeenshire. The future bridegroom or bride is seized by friends and covered in treacle, flour, soot, feathers, etc. The victim is then paraded around the town or village on the back of a pickup truck to the accompaniment of blowing whistles, banging drums, yells and general cacophony. The victim is generally rendered insensible by drink, and often ends up in the sea or tied to a lamppost in a prominent place. *See also* PENNY BRIDAL.

Black Friday (1) A name given by Jacobites to 6 December 1745 when Lord George Murray and others in his army persuaded the YOUNG PRETENDER that, in the absence of English support and a French intervention, they should turn back north from Derby rather than advancing on London. 'No one,' commented Horace Walpole, 'is afraid of a rebellion that runs away.'

(2) Friday 14 October 1881, the day a severe storm hit the Berwickshire coast. The morning had dawned fine, but with the weatherglass showing a very low reading, suggesting trouble ahead. With families to feed, the fishermen of Eyemouth decided to risk it, but as 45 boats set out from the harbour in tight formation, one old fisherman standing on the pier was heard to mutter, 'They'll nae be sae close thegither when they cam hame.' The storm hit in the late morning. On land, 30,000 trees were flattened, while at sea 19 boats were lost – foundering in the huge waves or smashed against rocks. In

49

all, 189 fishermen perished, 129 of them from Eyemouth. A national collection raised £54,000 to support the widows and children. The memorial to the disaster in the village features a broken mast carved from granite, while that in nearby St Abbs consists of a number of bronze figures of women and children looking out to sea.

(3) For a third Black Friday, *see* BATTLE OF GEORGE SQUARE.

Black Gate, the The slippery slope, the road to perdition (*gate* here is 'way, road', from Old Norse *gata*, 'path').

Black Hope A narrow, steep-sided and craggy valley on the southeast side of Hart Fell, in the Moffat Hills. 'Hope' in this instance derives from Old English *hop*, meaning a small enclosed valley. A few miles to the southeast, now enclosed within the dark recesses of Eskdalemuir Forest, may be found Muckle White Hope.

Black house (Gaelic *taigh dubh*). A style of cottage formerly found widely in the Highlands and Islands. It had a thatched roof and double unmortared walls with turf squeezed between; the fire burnt in the middle of the earthen floor, the smoke hopefully reaching a hole in the ceiling. 'Black' may have denoted inferior to the newer houses with slates and mortared stone walls; alternatively *dubh*, 'black', may have been confused with the similar-sounding *tughadh*, 'thatch'. Black houses had generally been abandoned by the later 20th century, although some are preserved as heritage attractions.

Black Isle, the A peninsula between the Moray and Cromarty firths. It is neither black nor an isle. Although some say 'black' refers to its appearance (the dark soil, the trees seen in winter), others suggest that Duthuc, a local saint, was misread as Gaelic *dubh*, 'black'. More fancifully, some have asserted that 'black' refers to the area's past association with witchcraft and the dark arts.

Black Jock Johnnie Armstrong of Gilnockie, south of Langholm, one of the more notorious of the BORDER REIVERS, hanged in 1530. One contemporary account tells how,

... from the Scottis bordour to Newcastell of England, thair was not ane of quhatsoevir estate bot payed [BLACKMAIL] to this John Armestrange ane tribut to be frae of his cumber ... and albeit that he was ane lous leivand man ... he was als guid ane chieftane as evir was upon the borderis.

During James V's campaign to bring law and order to the Borders, the young king personally led a force of 8,000 men into Teviotdale, where, at Carlenrig, some ten miles southwest of Hawick, he met up with Armstrong and some two score of his men. Armstrong appears to have gone willingly to the meeting, presumably under a guarantee of safe conduct – one account suggests that the king had asked Armstrong to join him for a day's hunting. But the hot-tempered young king and the seasoned, flashy hardman soon fell to bad-mouthing each other – at least, so it is suggested in the ballad of 'Johnnie Armstrong', in which the king is outraged by Armstrong's ostentation and presumption of equality:

Johnnie wore a girdle about his middle,
Imbroidered ower wi' burning gold,
Bespangled wi' the same metal;
Maist beautiful it was to behold.

There hang nine tassles at Johnnie's hat,
And ilk ane worth three hundred pound.
'What wants that Knave that a King should have,
But the sword of honour and the Crown?'

'O, where got thou these tassles, Johnnie,
That blink sae brawlie abune thy brow?'
'I gat them in the field fechting,
Where, cruel king, thou durst not be!'

The king takes extreme umbrage, and Armstrong has to plead for his life:

To seek het water beneath cauld ice,
Surely it is a great folie –
I have asked grace at a graceless face,
But there is nane for my men and me.

To no avail – he and his men, rather than being taken for trial and public execution on the scaffold, are hanged there and then from 'growand trees'. Subsequently, Armstrong became the subject of popular mythologizing: he was a Robin Hood figure; he left his fellow Scots in peace, only ever raiding over the Border into England; he was a romantic lover. None of this appears to have been the case, but Black Jock Armstrong has cast a long shadow, appearing, for example, in John Arden's 1964 play, *Armstrong's Last Goodnight*.

Blackmail A word that owes its origin to the time of the BORDER REIVERS, and in this specific context the term is defined by John Jamieson, in his *Etymological Dictionary of the Scottish Language* (1808), as follows:

> A tax or contribution paid by heritors or tenants, for the security of their property, to those freebooters who were wont to make inroads on estates, destroying the corns, or driving away cattle.

The practice was also popular in parts of the Highlands – it was a speciality of Clan Macgregor, for example (*see* ROB ROY). In Scots, and in some northern English dialects, the word *mail* or *meal* (from Old Norse *mal*, 'agreement') formerly denoted a monetary payment, usually of rent or taxes. *Black* almost certainly connotes the criminal nature of the transaction, although it has been suggested that the 'tax' paid was in black cattle rather than white (i.e. silver) money.

Black man (1) The bogeyman. (2) Liquorice. (3) Dark toffee. (4) A block of ice cream held between a thin wafer and a wafer biscuit with a chocolate rim and marshmallow interior. Regarding sense (3), in *The Scots Kitchen* (1929) Marian McNeill quotes 'a native of Kilmarnock':

> In the pan, in the little shop where we bought it, it looked like gingerbread, but when it was broken up, it was a crispy crunch, like a petrified sponge, but once it was in the mouth, it melted into the most soul-satisfying, delectable sweet. (It was about an inch thick.) Even after sixty years, I can still taste it in my memory.

Black Mausoleum, the *See* BLUIDY MACKENZIE.

Black nebbie or **nebboch** A Northeastern term for a kettle, the second element being a diminutive of *neb*, a beak or snout.

Blackness and darkness, brimstone and burning *See* MAJOR WEIR.

Black Officer, the *See* LOSS OF GAICK, THE.

Black o' the e'e The apple of someone's eye.

Black ox *See* BLACK COW.

Black Ravens of Lochcarron A translation of the Gaelic *Fithich dhubha Loch Carrann*, a term once applied to the inhabitants of the village of Lochcarron in Wester Ross, apparently on account of their dark skin.

Black Saturday The name that the Scots gave to their defeat at the Battle of Pinkie, fought on Saturday 10 September 1547 during the course of the ROUGH WOOING. The name was also applied to 4 August 1621, the day the Scottish Parliament ratified the FIVE ARTICLES OF PERTH.

Black saxpence A coin of sinister significance, as explained by John Jamieson in his *Etymological Dictionary of the Scottish Language* (1825 Supplement):

> Black Saxpence, a sixpence, supposed by the credulous to be received from the devil, as a pledge of an engagement to be his, soul and body. It is always of a black colour, as not being legal currency; but it is said to possess this singular virtue, that the person who keeps it constantly in his pocket, how much soever he spend, will always find another sixpence beside it.

Black stool The STOOL OF REPENTANCE.

Black-strippit ba A bull's eye, a black-and-white-striped hard toffee flavoured with peppermint. They were apparently popularly consumed during church services, with the length of the sermon being measured in the number of ba's required to see one to the end (three for forty minutes).

Black Thief, the The Devil, aka *the Auld Thief, the Ill Thief* or the FOUL THIEF.

Black Vault of Dunure Castle, the *See* KING OF CARRICK.

Black Watch, the Now the 3rd Battalion, Royal Regiment of Scotland, but prior to 2006 an independent regiment, the Black Watch (Royal High-

land Regiment), nicknamed the LADIES FROM
HELL; before 1881 they were the 42nd Highland
Regiment of Foot, nicknamed the *Forty-twa* (as
celebrated in the popular 19th-century ballad,
'The Gallant Forty-twa'). The Black Watch was
formed in Aberfeldy in October 1739 from a number of 'Independent Companies' of Highland
troops, some of which dated back to 1662. The
name refers to the dark green and blue regimental
tartan and from the fact that the regiment was
originally tasked to keep peace between the clans
in the Highlands. The 1739 gathering was
commemorated in 1887 by a memorial in Aberfeldy
and by a poem by William McGonagall:

> The monument I hope will stand secure for many a
> long day,
> And may the people of Aberfeldy always feel gay;
> As they gaze upon the beautiful Black Watch
> monument,
> I hope they will think of the brave soldiers and feel
> content.

Apparently in the 1990s English officers began to
refer to the regiment as 'That Fine English Regiment Spoiled by the Presence of a Few Jocks'.

Gregory Burke's 2006 play *Black Watch*, performed by the National Theatre of Scotland, was
based on interviews with members of the regiment,
and was a popular and critical success both in
Scotland and London.

Blackwood's Magazine *See* MAGA.

Black yarn In the Northeast, a fishing trip resulting
in a meagre or non-existent catch: when the net was
lifted from the water, only the 'black yarn' of the net
could be seen, rather than the silver of fish.

Blar na Léine *See* BATTLE OF THE SHIRTS.

Blantyre Pit Disaster The worst mining disaster in
Scottish history. It took place on 22 October 1877,
when an underground explosion led to the deaths of
207 miners, the youngest of whom was aged only 11.
Local MP Alexander Macdonald, also president of
the Miners' National Association, stepped in to stop
survivors from mounting a rescue, as conditions were
too dangerous. Earlier concerns about safety at the

mine had been ignored by the owner, William Dixon,
but calls to prosecute him came to nothing. Two
years later there was another explosion in the 'Fiery
Mine', costing the lives of 28 men.

Blasphemous buffoon Pastor Jack Glass's description of Billy Connolly. *See* HEROD OF HILLHEAD,
THE.

Blasphemy, last person to be hanged for *See*
RHAPSODY OF ILL-INVENTED NONSENSE, A.

Blaw a cauld coal, to Literally, to blow on a cold
coal, i.e. to fail, or embark on a course of action with
no hope of success. The expression fell out of use in
the 19th century.

> 'Aweel,' said Cuddie, after a little consideration, 'I see
> but ae gate for't, and that's a cauld coal to blaw at,
> mither.'
> – Sir Walter Scott, *Old Mortality* (1816), chapter vii

Blaw in someone's lug, to Literally, to blow in
someone's ear, i.e. to flatter them. The expression
survived into the 20th century.

Blind Harper, the (Gaelic *An Clàrsair Dall*). The
Gaelic poet and harper Roderick Morrison (*c.* 1656–
1713/14), of Bragar, Lewis. He was said to have lost
his sight after contracting smallpox when at school
in Inverness. Morrison enjoyed the patronage of
Iain Breac, 18th Chief of the MacLeods of Dunvegan, after meeting him in Edinburgh in 1681, and
on the chief's death in 1693 Morrison wrote a fine
elegy:

> Wrapped in the linen shroud did I leave the strength of
> the weak, the journey's end of men of song, as also the
> wealth of men of ancient lore, and the treasury of
> learned poets – your death has set them in disarray;
> and since you went into the coffin I am no object of
> envy.
> – 'Creach na Ciadaoin' ('Wednesday's Bereavement',
> translated by William Matheson)

Only a few of Morrison's poems – and none of his
harp compositions – survive.

Blind Harry or **Hary** A Scottish poet (?1440–?92),
also known as Harry the Minstrel, celebrated as the

author of the 12,000-line poem in couplets recounting, without great regard for historical accuracy, the
deeds of William Wallace, hero of the Wars of
Independence. *The Actes and Deidis of the Illustre
and Vallyeant Campioun Schir William Wallace*, or
The Wallace for short, was most likely composed in
the 1470s. Little is known of Harry, although he
earns a mention in Dunbar's 'LAMENT FOR THE
MAKARIS'. The historian John Major, writing in the
early 16th century, states that Harry was blind from
birth, but the vivid visual imagery in the poem, and
the apparent first-hand experience of warfare it
conveys, indicates otherwise. His alternative name,
Henry the Minstrel, appears only to have come into
common usage after the publication of John Jamieson's edition of *The Wallace* in 1820. The name
Blind Harry is also applied to the game of blind
man's buff or BELLY-BLIND.

Blind Saturday The Saturday of the week in which
those paid their wages fortnightly received nothing.
The other Saturday was *pay Saturday*.

Blithemeat The food provided to celebrate the
birth of a child, or given to the mother, or given
by the mother to the first person she meets when
taking her child to church for the first time. *Blithe*
here means 'joyful'.

Blobberlips, Queen of the Gypsies *See under*
SHELLYCOAT.

Block, hammer and nail A boys' game, formerly
played in the Northeast, and involving seven
players. The boy representing the block went down
on all fours, while the boy representing the nail did
the same, with his head close to the former's
backside. The boy representing the hammer lay
on his back behind the nail, while the remaining
four boys each took a limb of the hammer, lifted him
up and swung him into the backside of the nail, to
see whether the nail would be driven into the block.

Blood-drinking Martin Martin, in his *Description of
the Western Isles of Scotland* (1695), describes how
the islanders made blood-covenants:

> Their ancient leagues of friendship were ratified by
> drinking a drop of each other's blood, which was

commonly drawn out of the little finger. This bond
was religiously observed as a sacred bond; and if any
person after such an alliance happened to violate the
same, he was from that time reputed unworthy of all
honest men's conversation.

After a violent death, the bereaved in their dis-
tractions of grief sometimes appear to have drunk
the blood of the slaughtered loved one, as in this
lament by a foster-mother for a Macdonald killed at
the Battle of Cairinish in 1601, quoted by George
Henderson in *Survivals in Belief Among the Celts*
(1911):

> Thy body's blood flagrantly
> a-soaking thy linen
> And I myself sucking it
> till hoarse were my breath.

Bloodthirsty Dee The Aberdeenshire river had
a reputation for taking human lives, hence the
following rhyme about the Dee and its gentler
neighbour:

> Bloodthirsty Dee
> Each year needs three,
> But bonny Don
> She needs none.

In the past, according to George Henderson in his
Survivals in Belief Among the Celts (1911), 'A plaid
has several times been made an offering to the
water-spirit of the Dee.' The Till, a Northumbrian
tributary of the Tweed, had a similar reputation:

> Says Tweed to Till –
> 'Wha gars ye run sae still?'
> Says Till to Tweed –
> 'Though ye rin wi' speed,
> And I rin slaw,
> For ae man that ye droon
> I droon twa.'
> – Anon., 'Twa Rivers' (17th century)

See also DEE VS DON.

Bloody ... *See also* BLUIDY ...

Bloody Bay A bay on the northeast coast of Mull,
north of Tobermory, so-called because of the naval
battle fought here in either 1480 or 1483 between

John MacDonald, Earl of Ross and LORD OF THE ISLES, and his rebel son ANGUS OG. Angus won the day, and took power from his father, maintaining it until his murder in 1490. All this disorderly conduct led James IV to forfeit the Lordship of the Isles from John MacDonald in 1493.

Bloody Butcher An alternative nickname for BUTCHER CUMBERLAND.

Bloody Clavers *See* BONNIE DUNDEE.

Bloody Friday *See* BATTLE OF GEORGE SQUARE.

Bloody Harlaw *See* REID HARLAW, THE.

Bloody Orkney The archipelago was so characterized by Hamish Blair in lines written during the Second World War and quoted in Arnold Silcock's *Verse and Worse* (1952):

> The bloody roads are bloody bad,
> The bloody folks are bloody mad,
> They'd make the brightest bloody sad,
> In bloody Orkney …
>
> No bloody sport, no bloody games,
> No bloody fun: the bloody dames
> Won't even give their bloody names
> In bloody Orkney.

The rhyme soon caught on, and was applied to many other places, including the remote village of Halkirk in Caithness – 'a dreary little interruption to the general emptiness around it', according to Bill Bryson's *Notes from a Small Island* (1995). Halkirk was the site of a vast POW camp in the Second World War, and guard duty here was an unpopular posting with British troops – hence:

> This fucking town's a fucking cuss,
> No fucking trams, no fucking bus,
> Nobody cares for fucking us
> In fucking Halkirk.

Bloody puddings A nickname for the inhabitants of Stromness, Orkney, a *bloody pudding* being a black pudding. The name supposedly refers to the food-stuffs that workers from the parish took with them while building St Magnus' Cathedral in Kirkwall. *See* TEU-NEEMS.

Bloody Vespers, the A melée in Moray on New Year's Day 1555, in which 172 members of the Dunbar and Innes families set upon each other in Elgin Cathedral. The Innes posse had it in for David Dunbar, Dean of Moray, and Alexander Dunbar, Prior of Pluscarden, while the Dunbars were after the head of the Innes family. Contemporary opinion held that the sacrilege involved was worse than the bloodshed.

Blowing one's nose in one's neighbour's soup *See under* SNITE SOMEONE'S NEB, TO.

Blowing Saturday, the The day of a great storm that took place on 20 February 1799.

Blowup Nose Pleasingly, the name of a coastal headland just north of the village of Findon, Aberdeenshire.

Blubber-totum In the Northeast, any drink, such as tea, soup, etc., that is regarded as too weak, thin or wishy-washy. *Blubber* in this context is a bubble of air, while *totum* comes from *teetotum*, a game involving a polygonal top inscribed with a number of different letters. Small wagers are made as to which of the letters the top will come to rest on.

Bluebell of Scotland, the The harebell (*Campanula rotundifolia*), considered one of Scotland's national flowers, alongside HEATHER, the THISTLE and the WHITE ROSE OF SCOTLAND.

> Oh where, tell me where, did your Highland laddie dwell?
> Oh where, tell me where, did your Highland laddie dwell?
> He dwelt in bonnie Scotland where bloom the sweet bluebells,
> And it's oh! in my heart I rue my laddie well.
> – Traditional, 'The Bluebells of Scotland'
>
> I love a lassie, a bonnie, bonnie lassie,
> She's as pure as the lily in the dell.
> She's as sweet as the heather, the bonnie bloomin' heather –
> Mary, ma Scotch Bluebell.
> – Harry Lauder, 'I Love a Lassie' (1905)

For some alternative names, *see under* FLORA CALEDONIA.

Blue Blanket, the The traditional nickname of the banner of the craftsmen of Edinburgh. According to legend the original banner, bearing the motto 'In thy good pleasure build thou the walls of Jerusalem' (Psalm 51), was taken on the First Crusade (1096–9) by some Scottish craftsmen, who hoped to raise it on the walls of Jerusalem. It is more likely, however, that the banner had its origins in 1482, when King James III was faced with an invading English army and the rebellion of a number of his nobles. The king was seized by two of his uncles and imprisoned in Edinburgh Castle, but was somehow liberated by his wife, Margaret of Denmark, together with a number of others, including the craftsmen of Edinburgh. The latter raised the money to repay the dowry of Lady Cecil, the daughter of Edward IV, the English king, and so ended the English invasion. The Edinburgh craftsmen were perhaps also angered by the treatment meted out to their fellow craftsmen by Archibald Douglas, Earl of Angus, and the other rebel nobles (*see* BELL-THE-CAT). As a reward for their loyalty, the king gave the city of Edinburgh its 'Golden Charter' and presented the Edinburgh craftsmen with a banner, swallowtailed in shape and measuring 10 ft 2 in by 6 ft 6 ins (305 × 195 cm), with a blue saltire, a thistle, a crown and a hammer, and the the following words:

> Fear God and honour the King with a long lyffe and prosperous reigne and we that is Trades shall ever pray to be faithfull for the defence of his sacred Maiesties royal person till Death.

This banner became known as the 'Blue Blanket', and was entrusted to the care of the Incorporation of Hammermen of Edinburgh, a guild of blacksmiths, goldsmiths, cutlers, armourers and other workers in metal. In 1496 the Hammermen were granted the use of the Chapel of St Eloi in St Giles' Cathedral, and the banner was hung there. When it was unfurled by the Deacon Convenor of Trades, the burgesses of the city were bound to come out in arms in support of their king; the banner was taken to Flodden in 1513, and the citizens rallied to it again during the ROUGH WOOING. The Scottish monarchs were not always as grateful as they might be; in *Basilikon Doron* (1599) James VI wrote:

> The craftsmen think we should be content with their work how bad and dear so ever it be; and if in anything they be controlled, up goeth the Blue Blanket!

Today, at least two of versions of the banner exist: one in the Trades Maiden Hospital, and one in the National Museum of Scotland. There is a Blue Blanket public house in the Canongate, Edinburgh.

Blue bonnet The traditional Scottish headgear, also known as a tam o' shanter. They used to be predominantly blue, as attested by this description in his *Itinerary* (1617) by the English traveller Fynes Morison, who had visited Scotland in 1598:

> The husbandmen in Scotland, the servants, and almost all in the country did wear coarse cloth made at home, of grey or sky-colour, and flat blue caps, very broad.

A blue bonnet is also a metonym for the wearer, and the term became associated both with wild Highland clansmen (*see* HIGHLAND LADDIE, THE) and with the equally wild BORDER REIVERS:

> March, march, Ettrick and Teviotdale,
> Why the deil dinna ye march forward in order?
> March, march, Eskdale and Liddesdale,
> All the Blue Bonnets are bound for the Border.
> – Sir Walter Scott, *The Monastery* (1820).

The ballad 'Blue Bonnets Over the Border' predates the version just quoted, however, as Scott himself refers to it in *Marmion* (1808), with the suggestion that it was already being sung to an established tune (later to become the official march of a number of Scottish and Canadian regiments):

> And minstrels, at the royal order,
> Rung out – 'Blue Bonnets o'er the Border'.
> – Sir Walter Scott, *Marmion* (1808), canto V, xvii

The tune has been played on the pipes on a number of significant occasions in military history, for example as the rearguard of the Argyll and Sutherland Highlanders retreated from the Japanese across the causeway to Singapore, on 31 January 1942. On D-Day, 6 June 1944, Bill Millin aka the MAD PIPER, personal piper to Lord Lovat, commander of 1st Special Service Brigade, played 'Blue Bonnets Over the Border' as the commandos crossed Pegasus Bridge, the strategic bridge over the River Orne, having landed at Sword Beach and linked up with the paratroops who had taken the bridge just after midnight. *See also* BALMORAL BONNET; GLENGARRY; SCOTCH BONNET.

Blue Brazil, the Cowdenbeath FC; *see* FOOTBALL
CLUB NICKNAMES.

Blue Gown *See* GABERLUNZIE.

Blue hen Formerly, a euphemism for a decanter of
whisky; *compare* TAPPIT HEN.

Blue Men of the Minch Supernatural sea creatures,
known as *Na Fir Ghorm* in Gaelic, who haunt the
Minch (the stretch of water between mainland
Scotland and the Outer Hebrides), occasionally
preying on sailors.

> When the chief of the Blue Men had all his men
> gathered about him, ready to attack a ship, he rose high
> in the water and shouted to the skipper two lines of
> poetry, and if the skipper did not reply at once by
> adding two lines to complete the verse, the Blue Men
> seized the ship and upset it. Many a ship was lost in
> days of old because the skipper had no skill at verse.
> – Donald Alexander Mackenzie, *Wonder Tales from
> Scottish Myth and Legend* (1917)

It is possible that the Blue Men originated as
personifications of the notoriously dangerous waters
of the Minch, particularly those around the Shiant
Isles.

> ... the strait which lies between the Island of Lewis and
> the Shant [sic] Isles (the charmed islands) ... is called
> the 'Sea-stream of the Blue Men'. They are ... of
> human size, and they have great strength. By day and
> by night they swim round and between the Shant Isles,
> and the sea there is never at rest. The Blue Men wear
> blue caps and have grey faces which appear above the
> waves that they raise with their long restless arms. In
> summer weather they skim lightly below the surface,
> but when the wind is high they revel in the storm and
> swim with heads erect, splashing the waters with mad
> delight. Sometimes they are seen floating from the
> waist out of the sea, and sometimes turning round like
> porpoises as they dive.
> – Donald Alexander Mackenzie, *Wonder Tales from
> Scottish Myth and Legend* (1917)

John Campbell, minister of Tiree between 1861 and
1891, reported that on one voyage his boat had
been followed by 'a blue-covered man', but the
reverend gentleman came to no harm.

Blue Mogganers *See* BLUE TOON, THE.

Bluenose A pejorative word for a Protestant used
by some Roman Catholics, especially in the west of
Scotland. Blue (with white) is the colour of Rangers
FC, hence associated with Protestantism. *See also*
BLUE RIBBON; TRUE BLUE.

Blue ribbon The badge of the Covenanters, inspired by a passage in the Old Testament:

> Speak unto the children of Israel, and bid them that
> they make them fringes in the borders of their gar-
> ments throughout their generations, and that they
> put upon the fringe of the borders a ribband of
> blue.
> – Numbers 15:38

In his *History of the Troubles and Memorable Transactions in Scotland, 1624–45*, John Spalding describes how when the Covenanters occupied
Aberdeen in 1639 they slaughtered all the dogs
they could find:

> The reason was, when first the army came here, ilk
> captain, commander, servant and soldier had ane blue
> ribbon about his craig [neck]: in despite and derision
> whereof, when they removed from Aberdeen, some
> women of Aberdeen, as was alleged, knit blue ribbons
> about their messans' [lap dogs'] craigs: whereat the
> soldiers took offence, and killed all their dogs for this
> very cause.

See also TRUE BLUE.

Blues, the *See* FOOTBALL CLUB NICKNAMES.

Blue Saltire, the *See* SALTIRE, THE.

Blue Toon, the A nickname for Peterhead, perhaps
in reference to its maritime setting, or its position
on the COLD SHOULDER OF SCOTLAND. The natives of Peterhead – especially its fishermen – are
called Blue Mogganers, presumably related to *mog-
gan*, a woollen stocking or stocking foot, worn over
a stocking in the house, or over one's shoe in cold
weather outside.

Blue Whale of Bragar, the In September 1920 a
group of lads out fishing off the northwest coast of

Lewis spotted what they thought was the upturned hull of a wrecked boat. The next day, locals spotted the 'boat' stuck in rocks on the shore, and realized that it was a long-dead blue whale, 80 feet (24 m) long and with a harpoon sticking out of its back. The carcase was towed in to Bragar Bay, where it was left on the shore while the authorities were notified – all whales beached on the foreshore being 'royal fish', i.e. the property of the crown. As the authorities dithered and delayed, the stench from the foreshore increasingly troubled the nostrils of the villagers of Bragar, and eventually they were given permission to dispose of the remains. The guts were towed out to sea, while the blubber was used for all kinds of purposes, from fuel oil to medicine. In 1921 Murdo Morrison, the local postmaster and spokesperson for the village in dealing with the authorities, erected an arch at his property in Bragar consisting of the lower jawbone of the whale. The harpoon, while being cleaned and polished in a garage, suddenly detonated, blowing a large hole in the wall. It seems likely that the whale had been caught but not killed by the harpoon, and that the whalers, fearing for their safety, had cut the lines. Quite how long the unfortunate animal had lumbered through the oceans before finally expiring is unknown, but it presumably originated somewhere in the waters off the Antarctic, thousands of miles south of Lewis. Markings on the harpoon, which now adorns the whalebone arch, are said to indicate 'oriental origins'. See also CAMEL OF THE CANONGATE, THE; ELEPHANT OF BROUGHTY FERRY, THE; WALRUS OF HARRIS, THE.

Bluidy Clavers See BONNIE DUNDEE.

Bluidy Harlaw See REID HARLAW, THE.

Bluidy Mackenzie The sobriquet bestowed on the politician, judge and jurist Sir George Mackenzie of Rosehaugh (c. 1638–91), partly because of his involvement as Justice-Depute in the mass witch trials of 1661–2, and more particularly for his role as Lord Advocate under Charles II in the prosecution of the COVENANTERS during the KILLING TIME. He was also known as 'the Bluidy Advocate'. In 1680 the extreme Covenanter, Richard Cargill, condemned Mackenzie for his 'constant pleading against, and

persecuting to death, the people of God' and for his 'ungodly, erroneous, phantastic, and blasphemous tenets, printed to the world in his pamphlets and pasquils'. In court, Mackenzie was notoriously fiery as well as eloquent, and in the face of civil unrest was prepared to defend Stuart absolutism and dispense with legal niceties, stating that 'the Necessity of State is that supereminent Law, to which upon occasions all particular Acts must bow', and damning those 'Jesuitical and Fanatical Principles, that every man is born free, and at Liberty to choose what form of government he pleaseth'. At the Glorious Revolution Mackenzie retired to England, fearing assassination attempts by Covenanters out for revenge.

Outside the courtroom Mackenzie showed himself to be a cultured man, helping to found the library of the FACULTY OF ADVOCATES and writing a number of notable works, including *Aretina, or, The Serious Romance* (1660; said to be 'the first Scottish novel'), *A Moral Essay preferring Solitude to Public Employment* (1665) and *Institutions of the Law of Scotland* (1684), the standard text for over a century. He is buried in the supposedly heavily haunted 'Black Mausoleum' in Greyfriars Kirkyard in Edinburgh, before which the local boys used to chant:

> Bluidy Mackingie, cam oot if ye daur,
> Lift the sneck an' draw the bar.

It was Mackenzie who may have given rise to the now obsolete expression *to gie fair mackaingie*, 'to give a free hand'. (For the explanation of the pronuniation of 'enz' as 'ing', *see under* MING THE MERCILESS.)

Bluidy puddings See BLOODY PUDDINGS.

Bluidy Tam How his enemies referred to General Thomas or Tam Dalyell (or Dalzell or Dalziel, c. 1599–1685). A lifelong supporter of the Stuart cause, Dalyell fought for Charles II at Worcester (1651), was taken prisoner, escaped from the Tower of London to the Continent and in 1655 entered the service of the Russian tsar, earning the nickname 'the Muscovy Beast' or 'Muscovy Deil' (with a pun on his surname). Returning to Scotland at the Restoration, he earned the particular enmity of the COVENANTERS for his role in suppressing the

1666 PENTLAND RISING at Rullion Green, and in the bloody aftermath. Even Bishop Gilbert Burnet, in his *History of My Own Time*, was shocked at Dalyell's ruthlessness, saying he

> ... acted the Muscovite too grossly. He threatened to spit men, and to roast them: and he killed some in cold blood, or rather in hot blood; for he was then drunk, when he ordered one to be hanged, because he would not tell where his father was.

Dalyell's reputation for severity – which he may have deliberately cultivated in order to intimidate would-be dissidents – was reinforced in the wake of the defeat of another Covenanting army at the Battle of Bothwell Brig in 1679, and the KILLING TIME that followed. It is on the eve of Bothwell Brig that Scott introduces Dalyell into *Old Mortality* (1816), providing the following pen portrait partly based on the *Memoirs* of Dalyell's subordinate, Captain John Creighton (which were edited by Jonathan Swift):

> His dress was of the antique fashion of Charles the First's time, and composed of chamois leather, curiously slashed, and covered with antique lace and garniture. His boots and spurs might be referred to the same distant period. He wore a breastplate, over which descended a grey beard of venerable length, which he cherished as a mark of mourning for Charles the First, having never shaved since that monarch was brought to the scaffold. His head was uncovered, and almost perfectly bald. His high and wrinkled forehead, piercing grey eyes, and marked features, evinced age unbroken by infirmity, and stern resolution unsoftened by humanity. Such is the outline, however feebly expressed, of the celebrated General Thomas Dalzell, a man more feared and hated by the whigs than even Claverhouse [James Graham of Claverhouse, aka BONNIE DUNDEE] himself, and who executed the same violences against them out of a detestation of their persons, or perhaps an innate severity of temper, which Graham only resorted to on political accounts, as the best means of intimidating the followers of presbytery, and of destroying that sect entirely.
> – chapter xxx

In 1681 Dalyell raised the Royal Scots Greys at his ancestral home, the House of Binns in West Lothian. His enemies asserted that he built the towers of the house to stop the Devil from blowing it away. They also told a tale of how Dalyell and the Devil were playing cards one night, and the latter was so infuriated when his opponent won that he hurled a marble table at him. This missed its target, and sailed through the window to land in Sergeant's Pond, from where it was retrieved in 1878 and restored to the house. Dalyell continued in royal service until his death of apoplexy at his town house in Edinburgh, on 23 August 1685.

Blyth Aberdeane William Dunbar thus apostrophized the city in his 1511 poem 'The Queenis Progress at Aberdeen', which describes the visit of James IV's consort, Margaret Tudor.

> Blyth Aberdeane, thow beriall of all tounis,
> The lamp of bewtie, bountie, and blythnes;
> Unto the heaven [ascendit] thy renoun is
> Off vertew, wisdome, and of worthiness;
> He nottit is thy name of nobilnes.
> [*beriall* = beryl; *He* = high]

Blythswood Square An elegant square in central Glasgow, built in 1823, which during the day is a home for respectable businesses, but whose pavements at night at one time transmuted into promenades where prostitutes plied their trade, before they were 'moved down the hill' by the police. The following exchange occurred on 1 June 2004 during a debate about prostitution tolerance zones at the Local Government and Transport Committee of the Scottish Parliament:

> *Margo MacDonald:* You are not nearly old enough to remember when it [the area for prostitution in Glasgow] was Blythswood Square, but I am looking at the two Glasgow members who are present to see whether either of them is old enough to remember that, but they obviously are not.
> *Michael McMahon:* Ma mammy told me tae stay away from it.

More apocryphal, perhaps, is the story of the elderly gentleman who was accosted by a lady in Blythswood Square and asked if he would like 'super sex'. To which he replied, 'Ooh, I don't know. What kind of soup is it?' Almost certainly without foundation is the allegation that this same gentleman later booked into a hotel, where he was asked whether he would like the Tartan Room. 'Ooh no,' he said. 'Just the room'll do fine.' *See also* DANUBE STREET.

Boak *See* VOMIT.

Boar of Badenoch, the An Torc (Gaelic, 'the boar'), a GRAHAM of 2424 ft (739 m) on the west side of the Drumochter Pass, on the southern border of the region of Badenoch. Its name refers to its shape, somewhat like a hog's back, and to a legend that the mountain was once haunted by a phantom boar. Its slightly higher (2634 ft /803 m) companion to the south, Meall an Dòbhraichean (Gaelic, 'hill of the watercress'), has become known as the Sow of Atholl, Atholl being the territory to the south of Badenoch. *See also* WOLF OF BADENOCH.

Boar's head A Northeastern term for a fragment of a RAINBOW.

Boars of Duncansby A dangerous reef in the Pentland Firth, to the north of Duncansby Head in Caithness, the most northerly point on the mainland of Britain.

Bob-at-the-bowster *See* BABBITY BOWSTER.

Bobbing John The nickname of John Erskine, 6th (or 11th) Earl of Mar (1675–1732), military leader of the '15 Rising. The nickname refers to his wandering allegiances (and may also have some ribald connotations). He had been one of the commissioners sent to London to negotiate the Union, and in 1714 was Secretary of State for Scotland. Although pledging his allegiance to Queen Anne's Hanoverian successor, he was dismissed, and in a short space of time found himself a Jacobite. Calling the Highlanders to arms, he told his own tenants in Deeside that he would turn them out and raze their homes should they fail to respond. As a military commander, Mar was inept, failing to achieve victory at SHERIFFMUIR despite his numerical superiority. As the Rising fizzled out, he fled with the OLD PRETENDER to France, and in 1721 accepted a pension of £3500 per annum from George I. It was said that Mar went on to betray

the suspected Jacobite, Francis Atterbury, Bishop of Rochester, who in 1723 was forced into exile.

Bodach Glas The family spectre of the Grants of Rothiemurchus. In Gaelic *Bodach Glas* literally means 'grey (or pale and wan) old man'; an alternative name appears to be *Bodach An Duin*. Several other Highland families had their own ghostly familiar or *bodach*. For example, the Macleans of Lochbuie were attended by a mounted spectre, the ghost of one of their ancestors killed in battle, who, on the occasion of the death of a Maclean, would ride three times round the house, ringing his fairy bridle. This figure was known as *Eoghan a chinn bhig*, 'Hugh of the Little Head'. In *Waverley* (1814), Sir Walter Scott gives Fergus MacIvor (Vich Ian Vohr), the young Highland chieftain, his own Bodach Glas, 'a tall figure in a grey plaid'. This Bodach Glas is supposedly the revenant of Halbert Hall, a Lowlander whom MacIvor's ancestor, Ian nan Chaistel, had killed over disputed booty some three centuries before, and who had subsequently appeared to successive MacIvor chiefs to announce death or catastrophe.

> 'O,' answered Fergus, with a melancholy air, 'my fate is settled. Dead or captive I must be before tomorrow.'
> 'What do you mean by that, my friend?' said Edward. 'The enemy is still a day's march in our rear, and if he comes up, we are still strong enough to keep him in check. Remember Gladsmuir.'
> 'What I tell you is true notwithstanding, so far as I am individually concerned.'
> 'Upon what authority can you found so melancholy a prediction?' asked Waverley.
> 'On one which never failed a person of my house. I have seen,' he said, lowering his voice, 'I have seen the Bodach Glas.'
> – Chapter xxx

See also MEG MULLACH; SWAN OF CLOSEBURN, THE.

Bodach-rocais *See* TATTIE-BOGLE.

Bodhisattva of the Cairngorms, the In Buddhism, a Bodhisattva is a being who is worthy of nirvana but who remains on the mortal plane to help humans to find salvation. The eccentric baronet

Sir Hugh Rankin (1899–1988), who variously worked as a riveter's mate and a sheepshearer, and who became a Muslim and then a Buddhist, made the following pronouncement in 1959:

> It is part of our known belief that five Bodhisattvas (Perfected Men) control the destiny of the world. They meet once a year in a cave in the Himalayas to make their decisions. One of them lives in the Scottish Cairngorms.

It is possible, of course, that Rankin may have misidentified the GREY MAN OF BEN MACDUI.

Body-snatching See BURKE AND HARE.

Bogan of Bogan, Mrs See FLOWER OF STRATHEARN, THE.

Boghead coal See PARAFFIN YOUNG.

Boglies See MONARCH OF THE GLEN.

Bog that walked, the In 1629 the Privy Council recorded a disaster that occurred in the flat Angus farmland just south of where the River South Esk enters the Montrose Basin:

> ... the like was never heard of in any kingdom or age, in so far as ane great and large moss of the thickness of ane spear has been driven by the force and violence of wind and water fra the firm ground and bounds where from all beginning it immoveably stood to the lands of Powis and Powmilne and other lands [Corsbruik and Woodside] ... and has overflowed and covered the saids whole lands and has tane ane solid firm and settled stand thereon, and has overturned the whole houses for the most part of the saids lands, so that twenty families were constrained for life and deid, and with the extreme hazard of their lives, to flee and leave their houses and all within the same to the violence of the moss.

As Powis and Woodside are some 3 miles (5 km) apart, the area affected must have been substantial.

In his *Book of Days* (1864), Robert Chambers records Thomas Pennant's description of a similar event that occurred in 1771, near the shore of the Solway Firth:

When he passed the spot during his First Journey to Scotland in 1768, he saw it a smiling valley; on his Second Journey, four years afterwards, it was a dismal waste. The Solway Moss was an expanse of semi-liquid bog covering 1600 acres, and lying somewhat higher than a valley of fertile land near Netherby. So long as the moderately hard crust near the edge was preserved, the moss did not flow over: but on one occasion some peat-diggers imprudently tampered with this crust; and the moss, moistened with very heavy rain, overcame further control.

It was on the night of the 17th of November 1771, that a farmer who lived near the Moss was suddenly alarmed by an unusual noise. The crust had given way, and the black deluge was rolling towards his house while he was searching with a lantern for the cause of the noise. When he caught sight of a small dark stream, he thought it came from his own farmyard dung hill, which by some strange cause had been set in motion. The truth soon flashed upon him, however. He gave notice to his neighbours with all expedition. 'Others,' said Pennant, 'received no other advice than what this Stygian tide gave them: some by its noise, many by its entrance into their houses; and I have been assured that some were surprised with it even in their beds. These passed a horrible night, remaining totally ignorant of their fate, and the cause of their calamity, till the morning, when their neighbors with difficulty got them out through the roof.' About 300 acres of bog flowed over 400 acres of land, utterly ruining and even burying the farms, overturning the buildings, filling some of the cottages up to the roof, and suffocating many cattle. The stuff flowed along like thick black paint, studded with lumps of more solid peat; and it filled every nook and crevice in its passage. 'The disaster of a cow was so singular as to deserve mention. She was the only one, out of eight in the same cow-house, that was saved, after having stood sixty hours up to the neck in mud and water. When she was relieved she did not refuse to eat, but would not touch water, nor would even look at it without manifest signs of horror.'

Bogle A ghost, bugbear or any other terrifying and hideous supernatural creature.

> Caald blaws the nippin' north wi' angry sough,
> And showers his hailstanes frae the Castle Cleugh

Owre the Greyfriars, whare, at mirkest hour.
Bogles and spectres wont to tak their tour ...
– Robert Fergusson, 'The Ghaists: A Kirk-Yard Eclogue'
(1773)

A *bogle* or *craw bogle* can also be a scarecrow (*see* TATTIE-BOGLE), while the game of *bogle about the stacks* was a form of hide-and-seek. Bogle is also a surname, originally applied as a nickname to anyone with a scary appearance. The Revd Albert Bogle of St Andrew's Parish Church in Bo'ness came to national prominence in 2010 when he began to broadcast his services to mobile phones; he had already been streaming his services on the internet for some years.

Boil yer heid *See* AWA AN BILE YER HEID.

Boke *See* VOMIT.

Bold Buccleuch Walter Scott of Buccleuch (1565–1611), Keeper of Liddesdale, and an ancestor of his namesake, Sir Walter Scott the writer. He earned his sobriquet from his role in breaking KINMONT WILLIE out of Carlisle Castle in 1596. The incident temporarily dented Anglo-Scottish relations, and to smooth things over, James VI asked Buccleuch to surrender himself to the English, which he duly did. In London he was presented to Elizabeth I, who quizzed him as to why he had dared to undertake such a desperate and presumptuous enterprise. He reportedly replied, 'What is it that a man dare not do?' For her part, Elizabeth observed, 'With ten thousand such men, our brother in Scotland might shake the firmest throne in Europe.'

Bold, hardy race, much inured to war, a A description of the Scots by the 14th-century French chronicler Jean Froissart.

Bolshevik consul in Scotland, the first *See* FIGHTING DOMINIE, THE.

Bolt the cadger A Northeastern expression meaning to vomit; a *cadger* is an itinerant hawker or fish seller, and is also applied to a bad-tempered person. A variant is *cowp the cadger*. *See also* KING'S ERRAND MAY COME IN THE CADGER'S GATE.

Bon accord *See* CITY OF BON ACCORD.

Bonaily *See* DEOCH-AN-DORUS.

Bond, James The fictional Secret Service agent who features in a series of thrillers by the English writer Ian Fleming, starting with *Casino Royale* (1953). Bond is supposedly the son of a Scottish father, a certain Andrew Bond of Glencoe, and after being expelled from Eton following a dalliance with a maid, is schooled at Fettes College, the so-called SCOTS ETON. The character of Bond is based on a range of men Fleming met during the Second World War while working in naval intelligence; a particular inspiration was the Scottish diplomat, soldier, politician and author Fitzroy Maclean (1911–96), who operated with Tito's partisans behind enemy lines in Yugoslavia. In the first few film adapatations of the novels, Bond was played by the Scottish actor Sean Connery.

Bond of manrent A quasi-feudal institution by which minor barons or knights received the protection of a more powerful, senior magnate in return for helping to further the great man's interests, this service often involving violent action. The institution, which effectively created a bond of kinship between unrelated nobles, and which helped to prolong aristocratic factionalism and feuding in Scotland for so long, was still in evidence in the 16th century. In one such bond, that made in 1502 between Alexander, Earl of Huntly and Alexander Seton of Tullibody, the latter avowed: 'And I shall keep service and manrent to my said Lord in all his actions, matters, and quarrels ... and I shall keep his counsel secret, &c.'

B1, to do a To head off somewhere else. The Glaswegian expression derives from the official form B1, presented to those recently made unemployed who cannot wait a week for their first dole money, and who need to apply for urgent income support from another office.

Boneless Wonder, the Winston Churchill's description of the Lossiemouth-born Labour prime minister, Ramsay MacDonald, during his second term in government (1929–31):

I remember when I was a child, being taken to the celebrated Barnum's Circus, which contained an exhibition of freaks and monstrosities, but the exhibit on the program which I most desired to see was the one described as 'The Boneless Wonder'. My parents judged that the spectacle would be too demoralizing and revolting for my youthful eye and I have waited fifty years, to see The Boneless Wonder sitting on the Treasury Bench.

To his friends, MacDonald was *Ramsay Mac*.

Bones blamed for virgin birth *See* SON OF THE BONES.

Bonglies A derogatory name given to tourists (or any outsiders, including WHITE SETTLERS) in the Highlands. The expression is of relatively recent origin.

Bonnet *See* BALMORAL BONNET; BLUE BONNET; GLENGARRY; STEEL BONNET. In Glasgow, a *bunnit* is a cloth cap, and *to do one's bunnit* is to throw a major wobbly, while a *bunnit-hustler* is any comfortably-off person who boasts about their impoverished working-class roots.

Bonnet laird A small-scale farmer who owned his own land (or sometimes rented it for a nominal fee). The bonnet was the favoured headgear of the yeoman class. Such lairds were also known as *cock lairds*.

Bonnet piece A nickname given to a gold ducat, worth 40 shillings Scots, issued in 1540 during the reign of James V, showing the king wearing a bonnet. It was the first gold coin minted in Scotland to bear a portrait of the monarch. It was also at this time that the BAWBEE was first issued.

Bonnet Toun, the A sobriquet of the Ayrshire town of Stewarton, alluding to its former fame for bonnet-making. Today, the Bonnet Guild organizes the town's annual gala.

'Bonnie Annie Laurie' A song, dating from the later 17th or early 18th century, traditionally attributed to William Douglas of Fingland. It is addressed to Anne or Anna Laurie (born sometime in the 1680s), daughter of Sir Robert Laurie of Maxwelton House, near Thornhill in Dumfriesshire (the song is also known as 'Maxwelton Braes'):

> Maxwelton's braes are bonnie
> Where early fa's the dew
> And 'twas there that Annie Laurie
> Gave me her promise true,
> Gave me her promise true
> Which ne'er forgot will be,
> And for bonnie Annie Laurie
> I'd lay me doon and dee.

Anne's father opposed the match, perhaps because she was very young at the time, and in 1710 she married a neighbour and relative of Douglas, namely Alexander Ferguson of Craigdarroch. In 1706 Douglas himself, who had served abroad with the Royal Scots and was an ardent Jacobite (another reason Sir Robert may have turned him down), had married an heiress, Elizabeth Clerk of Glendroth. Later, hearing news of Douglas, Anne wrote, 'I trust that he has forsaken his treasonable opinions, and that he is content.'

The version of the song we have today owes much to the rewriting of Lady John Scott (1810–1900), who also supplied the tune; she said her version was based on one by Allan Cunningham she found in an 1825 collection entitled *Songs of Scotland*. It is possible that at least some of the first stanza may owe something to Douglas, who is known to have been acquainted with Miss Laurie, and to have written other verse.

For the species of Scottish sentiment known as Laymedoonandeeism, *see* WALLACETHEBRUCEISM.

'Annie Laurie' was the pen name adopted by the pioneering US investigative journalist (or 'stunt girl') Winifred S. Black (1863–1936), who pulled off a number of scoops, such as obtaining an interview with President Harrison by sneaking onto his private train and hiding under a table, or, on another occasion, disguising herself as a boy to mingle with the troops dealing with the floods in Galveston, Texas.

Bonnie Brier Bush *See* THERE GROWS A BONNIE BRIER BUSH; KAILYARD SCHOOL.

Bonnie Dundee A nickname of John Graham of Claverhouse, 1st Viscount Dundee (?1649–89), who led a Jacobite Highland army to victory over the forces of William III at the Battle of Killiecrankie, but was himself killed in the fighting. Macaulay, in his *History of England from the Accession of James the Second* (1848), describes how Dundee was fatally hit by a musket ball, and as he slid from the saddle was caught by a man called Johnstone:

'How goes the day?' said Dundee. 'Well for King James,' answered Johnstone: 'but I am sorry for your Lordship.' 'If it is well for him,' answered the dying man, 'it matters the less for me.'

His earlier role in suppressing the COVENANTERS in southwest Scotland during the KILLING TIME of the 1670s and 1680s earned him his viscountcy in 1688, and the less admiring nickname of *Bluidy Clavers* – although he was apparently responsible for few deaths himself, and recommended leniency towards the persecuted. His enemies held that he could only be killed with a silver bullet – as Scott relates in his description of the Battle of Drumclog (1679):

Many a whig that day loaded his musket with a dollar cut into slugs, in order that a silver bullet (such was their belief) might bring down the persecutor of the holy kirk, on whom lead had no power.
– *Old Mortality* (1816), chapter xvi

This belief arose from the conviction that Dundee was in league with the Devil, as recorded in this anonymous verse:

I fought at land, I fought at sea,
At hame I fought my aunty, O;
But I met the Devil and Dundee,
On the braes o' Killiecrankie, O.

After his death, 'Bonnie Dundee' became a Jacobite hero, and was famously celebrated by Scott in a poem that was later set to music:

To the Lords of Convention 'twas Claver'se who spoke
'Ere the King's crown shall fall there are crowns to be broke
So let each cavalier who loves honour and me,
Come follow the bonnet of Bonny Dundee.

Come fill up my cup, come fill up my can,
Come saddle your horses, and call up your men;
Come open the West Port, and let me gang free,
And it's room for the bonnets of Bonny Dundee!

Dr Brewer included Dundee in his list of 'Noted men of short stature' in the 1896 edition of his *Dictionary of Phrase and Fable*, although he does not divulge his precise height.

The phrase 'bonnie Dundee' has also been applied to the city itself, as recorded by Daniel Defoe in his *Tour Through the Whole Island of Great Britain* (1724–6): 'Dundee, a pleasant, large, populous city ... well deserves the title of Bonny Dundee, so often given it in discourse, as well as in song.' William McGonagall, the BARD OF THE SILVERY TAY, picked up the theme in his poem, 'Bonnie Dundee in 1878':

There's no other town I know of with you can compare
For spinning mills and lasses fair,
And for stately buildings there's none can excel
The beautiful Albert Institute or the Queen's Hotel ...

'Bonnie Banks o' Loch Lomond, The' *See* TAKE THE HIGH ROAD.

Bonnie Doon *See* 'YE BANKS AND BRAES O' BONNIE DOON'.

'Bonnie Earl o' Moray, The' A celebrated ballad on the murder of the ambitious and handsome James Stewart, 2nd Earl of Moray, at Donibristle, Fife, on 7 February 1592, by followers of George Gordon, 1st Marquess of Huntly, whose power in the Northeast he had threatened. Moray was renowned for his good looks, and according to tradition, when Huntly slashed his face with his dagger, the Bonnie Earl retorted, 'Ye hae spoilt a better face than your ain, my lord!' Although popular feeling called for justice, Huntly was held under house arrest for just a week, and never brought to trial. In the ballad, the motive for the slaughter of 'the Bonnie Earl' was his favour with Anne of Denmark, queen to James VI, but the latter was probably more concerned that Moray might be plotting against him alongside the turbulent Francis Stewart, Earl of Bothwell (*see* WIZARD EARL, THE).

The ballad, which may go back to the 17th century, famously opens:

Ye Highlands and ye Lawlands,
Oh where hae ye been?
They hae slain the Earl o' Moray
And laid him on the green.

In 1954 the American writer Sylvia Wright described in *Harper's Magazine* how as a girl she had misheard this last line as 'And Lady Mondegreen', and the coinage *mondegreen* has subsequently been adopted to denote any such mishearing (such as, in 'Onward Christian Soldiers', the words 'Christ the royal master' being construed as 'Castor-oil master').

Bonnie fechter *See* BRECK, ALAN.

Bonnie Lass of Albany, the In 1787 the exiled and nearly dead-from-drink Charles Edward Stuart legitimized his bastard daughter by awarding her the title Duchess of ALBANY. This brought out the anti-Hanoverian in Robert Burns and induced him to write 'The Bonnie Lass of Albany':

My heart is wae, and unco wae,
To think upon the raging sea,
That roars between her gardens green
An' the bonnie Lass of Albany.

Bonnie Prince Charlie *See* YOUNG PRETENDER, THE.

Bonnybridge, UFOs over *See* FALKIRK TRIANGLE.

Bonny fighter, a *See* BRECK, ALAN.

Bonny Sunday In Shetland, the Sunday before Christmas; the first term is alternatively spelt *Benna* or *Benni* or *Beainer* (from Old Norse *bæn*, 'prayer').

Bonspiel A curling tournament between different clubs, districts or parishes. The origin of the term, which was once also applied to other sports, is uncertain; it may come from Dutch *bondspel* (*verbond*, 'covenant, alliance', and *spel*, 'play'). Outdoor bonspiels held on frozen lochs are increasingly uncommon in Scotland, owing to global warming.

The most famous bonspiel ('the Bonspiel' or 'Grand Match'), in which thousands of players take part, is that called by the Royal Caledonian Curling Club on the LAKE OF MENTEITH on those rare occasions when the ice reaches a thickness of 7 inches (17.5 cm). This last occurred in 1979, only the third time since 1945. In January 2010 a sufficient thickness of ice was again achieved, but the Royal Caledonian Curling Club, having been advised not to proceed by the local authority and the emergency services, could not obtain insurance, and thus declined to proceed. Plans to hold an unofficial match had to be abandoned when a thaw set in on 11/12 January.

In the 18th century a certain John Cairney penned the following lines on the harmonious nature of the Bonspiel:

No party politics around our Tee,
For Whig and Tory on the ice agree;
Glory we play for, may it be our lot,
To gain the Bonspiel by a single shot.

See also ROARING GAME, THE.

Boobrie, the A creature of Gaelic folklore, which emerges from deep lochs, and which may take the form of a bird, a horse or a bull. A detailed account was left in manuscript form by the folklorist John Francis Campbell of Islay (1822–85), to whom eyewitnesses reported their encounters with the beast:

This species of animal which within the last century was by no means rare in the districts of Upper Lochaber and Argyll, has for many years been totally extinct, the assigned cause being the extent to which heather burning has been practised in those districts for so many years past. Very long heather was the natural resting place and shelter of the Boobrie ... In form and colour the Boobrie strongly resembles the Great Northern Diver, with the exception of the white on the neck and breast; the wings of both, bearing about the same proportion to the size of their bodies, appear to have been given them by nature more for the purpose of assisting them in swimming under water, than flying. In size of body he is larger than seventeen of the biggest eagles put together. His neck is two feet eleven inches long, and twenty-three inches in circumference, his bill is about seventeen inches long, black in colour, measuring round the root about eleven inches; for the first twelve inches the bill is straight, but after that assumes the shape of an eagle's, and of proportionate strength. His legs are remarkably short for his size, black in colour, but tremendously powerful, the feet are webbed till within five inches of the toes, which then terminate in immense claws of most destructive nature. The print of his foot on the mud at the east end of the lake (as accurately measured by an authority) covers the space generally contained within the span of a large wide-spreading pair of red deer's horns. The sound he utters resembles that of a large bull in his most angry humours, but much superior in strength. The favourite food of the Boobrie is the flesh of calves; failing them he feeds upon sheep or lambs, as suits him, or seizing his prey he carries it off to the largest neighbouring muir loch, swims out to the deepest part, where he dives, carrying his victim along with him, and there feeds, returning on shore at pleasure. He is also particularly fond of otters, which he swallows in great numbers, and with considerable avidity.

Campbell says that the Boobrie prefers to assume this bird-form, but may also appear in the form 'of a water-horse or *each-uisg*, and of a water-bull or *tarbh-uisg*'. The water-horse is akin to the KELPIE, and Campbell tells the story of a farmer ploughing some hard ground by Loch Frisa on Mull, who harnesses an unknown horse he finds feeding by the loch to replace one of his three horses, which has cast a shoe.

> On an attempt to turn the horses this borrowed one became rather restive, which brought the whip into use, though lightly; no sooner had the thong touched him than he instantly assumed the form of a most enormous Boobrie, and uttering a shout which appeared to shake the earth, plunged into the loch, carrying with him the three horses and plough.

The *tarbh-uisg* appears to be a more benevolent manifestation of the Boobrie, and Campbell tells the story of this water-bull saving a maiden from the unwanted attentions of a rejected suitor. Just as the latter has thrown his plaid over the young woman's head, the *tarbh-uisg* suddenly appears, crushes the man to the ground, and invites the startled young woman to climb onto his back. He then deposits her safely at her mother's door. The suggestion is that the *tarbh-uisg* is in fact a spirit imprisoned in bull-form for some previous misdemeanour, and that this good deed liberates the trapped soul – for the *tarbh-uisg* is never seen again.

The word *boobrie* may be from the Gaelic *bubaire*, the great bittern, which has a loud booming call – similar to the bull-like bellow of the boobrie. Indeed, the Latin name for the great bittern is *Botaurus stellaris*, 'the starred or speckled bird which bellows like an ox-bull'; in French it is the *bœuf du marais*, 'ox of the swamp', or *taureau d'étang*, 'bull of the pond', and one of the older English names for the bird was *bog-bull*. By the time that Campbell of Islay was writing, the bittern was a very rare bird in the Highlands, as elsewhere. *See also* GOLDEN HORSE OF LOCH LUNDIE, THE.

Bookmarks Sir Walter Scott is said to have had a special bookmark printed and inserted into volumes in his library that he lent to others. On it was the following instruction: 'Please return this book: I find that though many of my friends are poor arithmeticians, they are nearly all good book-keepers.' *See also* ERRATA.

Book of Common Order, The *See* KNOX'S LITURGY.

Book of Discipline Either of two books – *The First Book of Discipline* (1560) and *The Second Book of Discipline* (1578) – compiled by John Knox and others that regulated the doctrine, governance and patrimony of the Church of Scotland.

> For let your honours be assuredly persuaded, that where idolatry is maintained or permitted (where it may be suppressed), that there shall God's wrath reign, not only upon the blind and obstinate idolater, but also upon the negligent sufferers [of the same]; especially if God has armed their hands with power to suppress such abomination.
> – *The First Book of Discipline* (1560), 'The Third Head: Touching the Abolition of Idolatry'. The book was addressed to the Great Council of Scotland.

Book of the Dean of Lismore, The An important collection of Gaelic poetry from both Scotland and Ireland compiled between 1512 and 1526 by James MacGregor (Seumas MacGriogair), vicar of Fortingall in Perthshire and absentee Dean of Lismore Cathedral. Others, including his brother Duncan

(Donnchadh), may also have had a hand in the compilation. The collection also includes texts in Scots and Latin.

Bool in one's moo, to have a To speak in an affected fashion, as if one were TEENIE FAE TROON, or a denizen of MORNINGSIDE. A *bool* is a marble, or a bowl, as in the game of bowls.

Boots Corner The corner of Union Street and Argyle Street in Glasgow was formerly given this nickname, from the presence there of a Boots pharmacy (now replaced by a branch of KFC). It was once famous as a rendezvous point for dating couples, hence its alternative name, *Dizzy Corner*: to *give someone a dizzy* means to stand them up.

Borderers, the *See* FOOTBALL CLUB NICKNAMES.

Border Game, the A variation on Mornington Crescent, that game of cunning and strategy played on the Radio 4 panel show, *I'm Sorry, I Haven't a Clue*. Scotland to serve, starting at the northeastern end:

Scotland	England
Meg's Dub	Marshall Meadows Bay
Witches Knowe	Folly Farm
Clappers	Brow of the Hill
Foulden Deans	High Cocklaw
Cawderstanes	Low Cocklaw
Nabdean	Honey Farm
Fishwick Mains	Horncliffe
New Ladykirk	Hangman's Land
Uppsettlington	Norham
Milne Graden	Dreeper Island
Tweedmill	Twizel
Oxenrig	Peter's Plantation
Coldstream	Cornhill on Tweed
Lees	Lamb Knowe
Fireburn Mill	Wark
Homebank	Gallows Hill
Birgham	Carham
Nottylees	Howburn
Hoselaw Mains	Horse Rigg
Wideopen Moor	Bowmont Hill
Venchen Hill	Shotton Hill
Halfway House	Elsdonburn Shank
Witchcleugh Burn	Madam Law
Wildgoose Hill	Blackhaggs Rigg
The Curr	The Schil
Birnie Brae	Mounthooly
Dod Hill	Hen Hole
Crooksike Head	Hanging Stone
Windy Rig	Davidson's Linn
Philip Hope	Beef Stand
Peelinick	Yearning Law
Watch Knowe	Deel's Hill
Corse Slack	Ogre Hill
Crooked Hope	The Hearts Toe
Peat Shank	Tate's Well
Lamblair Edge	Ramshope Lodge
Wooplaw Rig	Redesdale
Butter Bog	Black Cleugh
Dand's Pike	Limestone Knowe
Carlin Tooth	The Trouting
Hartshorn Pike	Upper Stony Holes
Blackhope	Deadwater
Foulmire Heights	Bellsburnfoot
Buckside	Cat Cairn
Bloodybush Burn	Clinty Sike
Flight Moss	Hobbis Flow
Scotch Knowe	Lazy Knowe
Kaim Brae	Kershopehead
Scotch Kershope	English Kershope
Blinkbonny Height	Burnt Shields
Greena Hill	Stonegarthside Hall
Longrow	Nook
Harelawslack	Peter's Crook
Archerbeck	Beyond-the-Wood
Canonbie	Liddel Strength
Glenzierfoot	Campers' Corner
Scotland Gate	Englishtown
Campingholm	Moss Side
Black Sark	Solway Moss
Gretna Green	Plumpe Farm
Gretna	Mill Hill
Lochmaben Stone	Sarkfoot Point

A draw, so far.

Border reivers The mounted irregulars who from the later Middle Ages to the end of the 16th century made cross-Border raids (or raids against their fellow countrymen) in search of plunder (usually of cattle), loot and rapine. *Reive* is a Scottish and northern English variant of *reave*, 'to carry off by force', from Old English *reafian*. Those reivers on the Scottish side were also known as BLUE BONNETS or steel bonnets (from their headgear). Their *modus operandi* was described by John Leslie, Bishop of Ross, in his *History of Scotland* (1572–6):

They sally out of their own borders, in the night, through unfrequented by-ways, and many intricate windings. All the day time, they refresh themselves and their horses, in lurking holes they had pitched upon before, till they arrive at the dark in those places they have a design upon. As soon as they have seized upon the booty, they, in like manner, return home in the night, through blind ways, and fetching many a compass [taking many circuitous routes]. The more skilful any captain is to pass through these wild deserts, crooked turnings and deep precipices, in the thickest mists and darkness, his reputation is the greater, and he is looked upon as a man of an excellent head.

The more notorious Scottish families involved in raiding included the Elliots (memorably Little Jock Elliot; *see* WHA DAUR MEDDLE WI ME?), the Kerrs, the Maxwells, the Armstrongs (notably KINMONT WILLIE), the Johnstones and the Scotts (famously AULD WAT of Harden and BOLD BUCCLEUCH, both ancestors of Sir Walter), together with their sundry GRAINS (branches). These 'surnames', like their counterparts further north, the Highland clans, owed greater loyalty to their own 'heidsmen' (chiefs) and kin than to the usually rather feeble authority of the Scottish Crown.

The Border reivers were a tough breed: the contemporary historian William Camden said it was the harsh Scottish weather that had 'hardened their carcasses'. Their horsemanship and their soldierly qualities were much admired, Queen Elizabeth herself observing that 'with ten thousand such men, James [VI] could shake any throne in Europe'. However, when incorporated into a regular army they were unreliable, both because their top priority tended to be plunder, and because they were likely to change allegiance to the winning side (as happened at Ancrum Moor in 1545). Many had relatives on the other side of the Border; at the Battle of Pinkie in 1547 Borderers from both Scotland and England were observed chatting to each other, but when they realized that someone was watching they put on a show of fighting.

When the two countries were not at war, March Wardens (*see* MARCHES) were appointed by both kingdoms to keep the peace, and every 40 days would hold TRUCE DAYS to resolve disputes – sometimes unsuccessfully. In 1575, for example, the meeting degenerated into a fight known as the REDESWIRE FRAY. James V had made a concerted effort to bring law and order to the Borders in 1528–30, capturing and executing such notorious figures as William Cockburn of Henderland, Adam Scott of Tushielaw (the so-called KING OF THE BORDER) and Johnnie Armstrong of Gilnockie (known as BLACK JOCK). With his accession to the throne of England in 1603, and the outrages of ILL WEEK, James VI set about suppressing the turbulent Border families once and for all, and had a proclamation read in all the Marches announcing his intentions:

The foul and insolent outrages lately committed upon the Border of our realms of England and Scotland by persons accustomed in former times to live by rapine and spoil, preying daily upon our good and loving subjects, without fear of God or man, hath given us just cause to use all means convenient, both for the relief of our subjects damnified, and for prevention of the like mischief hereafter.

The reivers were successfully suppressed, and many went on to participate in the plantation of Ulster; the Borders themselves were to be renamed the MIDDLE SHIRES.

An insight into the life of a reiver comes to us in the account that Sir Robert Carey, the Warden of the English East March, made of the confessions of Geordie Burn, whom he had captured returning from a raid in 1596, and condemned to hang:

He voluntarily of himself said that he had lived long enough to do so many villainies as he had done; and told us that he had lain with about forty men's wives, some in England, some in Scotland, and that he had killed seven Englishmen with his own hands, cruelly murdering them; that he had spent his whole time in whoring, drinking, stealing, and taking deep revenge for slight offences. He seemed to be very penitent, and much desired a minister for the comfort of his soul.

Two centuries later, Sir Walter Scott collected many of the ballads that tell of the doings of the reivers, which he published in his *MINSTRELSY OF*

THE SCOTTISH BORDER. 'The Lament of the Border Widow', for example, is supposed to refer to the execution of Cockburn of Henderland, who by tradition was hanged over the gate of his own tower:

> My love he built me a bonny bower,
> And clad it a' wi' lilye flour;
> A brawer bower ye ne'er did see,
> Than my true love he built for me.
>
> There came a man, by middle day,
> He spied his sport, and went away;
> And brought the king that very night,
> Who brake my bower, and slew my knight.

The reivers have cast their spell further down the centuries, for example in 'The Raiders' by Will H. Ogilvie (1869–1963), which opens:

> Last night a wind from Lammermuir came roaring
>   up the glen
> With the tramp of trooping horses and the laugh of
>   reckless men
> And struck a mailed hand on the gate and cried in
>   rebel glee
> 'Come forth, come forth, my Borderer, and ride the
>   March with me!'

Not all have been seduced by the romantic image of these lawless Borderers. In his 1971 study of the reivers, *The Steel Bonnets*, George Macdonald Fraser sought to correct the perception:

> There is a tendency to regard the high midnight of the Border Reiver as a stirring, gallant episode in British history. It was not like that; it was as cruel and horrible in its way as Biafra or Vietnam.

The experience of those on the receiving end is reflected in the anonymous ballad, 'The Death of Parcy Reed':

> God send the land deliverance
> Frae every reiving, riding Scot;
> We'll sune hae neither cow nor ewe,
> We'll sune hae neither staig nor stot.

See also CURSE ON THE REIVERS, THE; DISH OF SPURS; HELL SHALL HAVE HER AIN AGAIN THIS NICHT; KING OF THE BORDER, THE; MOSS TROOPERS; RED COCK CROW ON THE ROOFTREE, TO MAKE THE; THERE WILL BE MOONLIGHT AGAIN; WHA DAUR MEDDLE WI ME?

Bore Stane, the (1) A weathered piece of red sandstone that stands on a pedestal in the boundary wall of Morningside Parish Church in Edinburgh. It was in this stone that the Royal Standard (*see* LION RAMPANT) was supposedly pitched as the Scottish army mustered on the Borough Muir prior to marching to destruction at Flodden in 1513 – a *bore stane* being one in which a hole has been drilled for such a purpose.

> Highest, and midmost, was descried
> The royal banner floating wide;
> The staff, a pine-tree, strong and straight,
> Pitch'd deeply in a massive stone ...
>   – Sir Walter Scott, *Marmion* (1808), canto IV

The stone lay in an adjacent field until moved to its present position on the orders of Sir John Stuart Forbes of Pitsligo in 1852. However, there appears to be no firm evidence of such a muster on the Borough Muir, and it is possible that the stone was once an ancient grave slab or cist cover.

(2) There is another Bore Stane, a natural rock outcrop on the col between East Cairn Hill and Cock Rig in the Pentland Hills. It may have once functioned as a boundary marker.

Born a virgin and died a harlot The verdict on a long-dead daughter of the GRANITE CITY, whose (almost certainly apocryphal) epitaph is quoted in Donald and Catherine Carswell's *The Scots Week-End* (1936):

> Here lie the bones of Elizabeth Charlotte,
> That was born a virgin and died a harlot.
> She was aye a virgin till seventeen –
> An extraordinary thing for Aberdeen.

See also EPITAPHS.

Borrowed days, the The last three days of March, supposedly characterized by unpleasant wintry weather. According to Robert Chambers in his *Book of Days* (1862–4): 'The popular notion is, that they were borrowed by March from April, with a view to the destruction of a parcel of unoffending young sheep – a purpose, however, in which March was not successful.' Chambers goes on to quote a rhyme 'given at the firesides of the Scottish peasantry':

March said to Aperill,
I see three hoggs upon a hill,
And if you'll lend me dayes three,
I'll find a way to make them dee.
The first o' them was wind and weet,
The second o' them was snaw and sleet,
The third o' them was sic a freeze,
It froze the birds' nebs to the trees:
When the three days were past and gane,
The three silly hoggs came hirpling hame.

Chambers cites an earlier mention, in *The Complaynt of Scotland* (1548):

There eftir I entrit in ane grene forest, to contempill the tender yong frutes of grene treis, becaus the borial blastis of the thre borouing dais of March hed chaissit fragrant flureise of evyrie frut-tree far athourt the fieldis.

Chambers continues:

No one has yet pretended fully to explain the origin or meaning of this fable. Most probably, in our opinion, it has taken its rise in the observation of a certain character of weather prevailing about the close of March, somewhat different from what the season justifies; one of those many wintry relapses which belong to the nature of a British spring.

In the Highlands, the borrowed days or *Faoilteach* occur in February:

The Faoilteach, or those first days of February, serve many poetical purposes in the Highlands. They are said to have been borrowed for some purpose by February from January, who was bribed by February with three young sheep. These three days, by Highland reckoning, occur between the 11th and 15th of February; and it is accounted a most favourable prognostic for the ensuing year that they should be as stormy as possible. If these days should be fair, then there is no more good weather to be expected through the spring. Hence the Faoilteach is used to signify the very ultimatum of bad weather.

– Anne MacVicar Grant, *Essays on the Superstitions of the Highlanders of Scotland* (1811)

Bosjesman A bushman (from the Dutch word *boschjesman*), i.e. a member of the San people, nomadic hunters in southwestern Africa. In Glasgow in 1844 a total of 96,000 people paid a penny each to see a show featuring 'Bosjesmans' – although, as Alasdair Cameron tells us in his *Popular Entertainments in 19th Century Glasgow* (1990):

... they were rumoured to be Irish labourers dressed in feathers and rabbit-skins whose primitive language was Gaelic. It was also said that one of the Bosjesmans ate live rats as part of their performance. This certainly outdid another showman who merely bit off their heads and skinned them with his teeth.

Bo tae yer blanket, to say *See* SAY BO TAE YER BLANKET, TO.

Botherers, the A nickname for the King's Own Scottish Borderers; *see* REGIMENTAL NICKNAMES.

Bothy ballads Traditional songs once sung by farm labourers in the Northeast, especially in Buchan. A *bothy* was an outhouse on a farm providing Spartan accommodation for the unmarried male workers, who were hired for six months at a time. (Today, the term is more often applied to a rough mountain shelter used by climbers, fishermen, etc.) In *Eleven Years of Farm Work* (1879), James Taylor describes typical conditions:

The bothy is an old dirty-looking thatched house, joined on to the end of a cow byre and scarcely one yard from the door there is a large dung-hill ... an empty dark, filthy, sooty place ...

During the long nights the men would entertain themselves by singing ballads, many of them bawdy, especially where the sexual prowess of the ploughman was concerned (*cf.* PLOUGHMAN POET, THE). A number of ballads are critical of the harsh working conditions or of individual employers, for example one 'Swaggers' (identified as James Hay, who farmed at Newmill near Auchterless):

Come all ye jolly ploughboys, that whistle through the glen,
Beware on going to Swaggers, for he'll be at Porter Fair.
He'll be aye lauch lauchin', he'll aye be lauchin' here,
An' he'll hae on the blithest face, in a' Porter Fair.

Others list the achievements of individual workers, such as victories in ploughing matches, or otherwise recount the life of an agricultural labourer:

'Twas in the merry month of May
When flowers had clad the landscape gay
To Ellon Fair I bent my way
With hopes to find amusement.

A scrankie chiel to me cam near
And quickly he began to spier
If I wid for the neist half year
Engage to be his servant.

I'll need you as my orra loon
Four poun' ten I will lay doon
To you, when Martinmas comes roon
To close out your engagement.
            – 'Ellon Fair'

So rich was the tradition in the Northeast that Francis Child stated that of the 305 ballads in his *English and Scottish Popular Ballads* (1882–98), 91 were collected in Aberdeenshire. The successor to the traditional bothy ballad was the CORN-KISTER.

Bottomless breeks A jocular term for a kilt, once disparagingly used by Lowlanders.

I'd rather keep Cadwaller's goats,
And feast upon toasted cheese and leeks
Than go back again to the beggarly North
Tae herd 'mang loons with bottomless breeks.
        – William Maginn, 'Sir Malcolm O'Doherty's Farewell to
          Scotland' (1830s)

… the country's weel eneugh, an it werena that dour deevil, Claver'se (they ca' him Dundee now), that's stirring about yet in the Highlands, they say, wi' a' the Donalds and Duncans and Dugalds, that ever wore bottomless breeks, driving about wi' him, to set things asteer again, now we hae gotten them a' reasonably weel settled.
        – Sir Walter Scott, *Old Mortality* (1816), chapter xxxvii

Bouley Bashers A name given in Aberdeen to those boy racers who caused noise and nuisance in their high-powered cars on the city's Beach Boulevard, until they were subjected to an antisocial dispersal order in 2005.

Bounty A man goes to his doctor with a piece of chocolate stuck in one ear and a bit of coconut stuck in the other. 'Aw, doctor, it fair hurts,' moans the man. 'Bounty,' replies the doctor.

Bow'd David *See* BLACK DWARF, THE.

Bow-head Saint, the *See* MAJOR WEIR.

Boy David, the An early nickname for the Liberal (later Liberal Democrat) politician David (now Lord) Steel, born in Kirkcaldy in 1938. He was only 26 when he was first elected to the Westminster Parliament for Roxburgh, Selkirk and Peebles in a 1965 by-election, and only 38 when he took over the leadership of the Liberal Party in 1976. He was the first presiding officer of the Scottish Parliament (1999–2003).

Boys-a-day! A once common but now obsolete exclamation.

Bradog *See* GOWK.

Brae, gang doon the *See* GANG DOON THE BRAE.

Braeman An old term for an inhabitant of a hilly region, especially the southern fringes of the Grampians, a *brae* being a hillside. The term was used into the 19th century.

Braemar Gathering *See* HIGHLAND GAMES.

Braes, Battle of the *See* BATTLE OF THE BRAES.

Brahan Seer, the A shadowy figure who first emerged in print under this name in Alexander Mackenzie's *Prophecies of the Brahan Seer* (1877). Quite who the original Brahan Seer was (if he existed at all) is far from clear. Alexander Mackenzie names him as 'Kenneth Mackenzie, better known as Coinneach Odhar, the Brahan Seer'. Brahan is an estate near Dingwall that once belonged to the Mackenzie Earls of Seaforth, while *Coinneach Odhar* is Gaelic for 'dun-coloured Kenneth'. Some have suggested that such a Coinneach Odhar was born in Uig on the isle of Lewis on Seaforth lands in the middle of the 17th century, and that he later worked as a labourer on the Brahan estate, although there is no clear evidence either that he came from Lewis or that he was a Mackenzie. Others have pointed to a commission of justice from 1577 ordering the arrest of six men and twenty-six women on charges of witchcraft, their leader being one 'Kennoch Owir'; subsequently two or more of the women were burnt at Chanonry in Easter Ross. In legend, Chanonry is also associated with the death of Coinneach Odhar, who had apparently irritated the Countess of Seaforth in the reign of Charles II by informing her that her husband, then in France, was finding comfort in the arms of another. She took the news badly, and had him burnt to death in a barrel of tar on Chanonry Point. Before he died, he prophesied that the Seaforth line would end with an Earl who was both deaf and dumb. According to Sir Walter Scott, the last Lord Seaforth died in 1815 'in paralytic imbecility'.

The prophecies of the Brahan Seer – which in some accounts he made with the aid of a crystal – appear to have come down through oral tradition, and it is likely that various other traditional predictions accumulated round his name. Those that deal with places near Brahan are more likely to be his. For example, he foresaw that Strathpeffer would become a magnet for crowds seeking health and pleasure, and this was deemed to have come to pass when in the later 18th century the village became a popular spa. Another prediction concerning Strathpeffer stated that if five churches were built in the town, then ships would anchor themselves to their spires. In the mid-19th century, against the wishes of the inhabitants, a fifth church *was* built; the prophecy was considered fulfilled shortly after the First World War when an airship flew over the town, and its grappling iron became caught on one of the spires. Another local prediction was that 'One day ships will sail round the back of Tomnahurich Hill'; this is taken to predict the building of the Caledonian Canal, which takes this route between Loch Ness and Inverness. One of his most famous predictions concerns Culloden, the battlefield being located on Drummossie Muir:

> Oh! Drummossie, thy bleak moor shall, ere many generations have passed, be stained with the best blood of the Highlands.

For a Brahanic prophecy concerning a cow giving birth at the top of Fairburn Tower, *see under* COWS, NOTABLE. For other seers, *see* LADY OF LAWERS, THE; THOMAS THE RHYMER.

Braif Toun, the A sobriquet of Aberdeen, alluding to the occasion when Provost Davidson led the tradesmen of Aberdeen against the Highlanders of Donald, Lord of the Isles, at the REID HARLAW in 1411. Davidson was among the many killed in the battle.

Brandane An inhabitant of Bute. An early mention comes in John of Fordun's *Gesta Annalia* (14th century), in which the people of Bute are referred to as *Brandani*. The name most probably alludes to St Brendan of Clonfert, who built a cell here in the 6th century.

Branks The Scottish term for the scold's bridle. The branks consisted of an iron muzzle fitted over the head, with a plate inserted into the mouth, on top of the tongue. Sometimes the plate had a spike underneath, so that any attempt to speak brought about a jab of pain. The punishment was imposed upon those found guilty of blasphemy, witchcraft, slander, nagging, gossiping, or other behaviour regarded as antisocial. Although often thought of as a punishment meted out exclusively to women, one of the earliest recorded references, dating from 1559, refers to a Dundee man being sentenced to 'be put in the branks'. A typical case, from Lanark in 1653, records that:

> Iff evir the said Elizabeth sal be fund scolding or railling ... scho sal be sett upone the trone in the brankis and be banishit the toun thaireftir.

The word *branks* originally denoted a form of horse's bridle, and later also came to denote mumps. *See also* FORFAR BRIDIE.

Braveheart A 1995 Oscar-winning film about the Scottish national hero William Wallace (*c.* 1270–1305), directed by the Australian Mel Gibson, who also plays Wallace. While to many the film and its hero became a symbol of Scottish resistance to nearly two decades of Conservative rule from Westminster, to others it merely served to encourage the most aggressive and irrational aspects of Scottish Anglophobia. To anyone with even a slight knowledge of Scottish history, it appeared as a typically opportunistic Hollywood trifling with the truth, with a kilt-clad Wallace (the historical figure was in fact a Lowlander) becoming romantically involved with Isabella of France, wife of the future Edward II of England – to mention just two examples. In 2009 *The Times* ranked it second in a list of the 'most historically inaccurate movies' of all time, while Billy Connolly more pithily opined that the film was 'pure Australian shite'. For a while, journalists applied the phrase 'Braveheart spirit' to any Scottish national side in football or rugby that was taking its customary thrashing.

Braw bricht munelicht nicht, It's a *See* IT'S A BRAW BRICHT MUNELICHT NICHT.

Braw Lads' Gathering, the An annual event in Galashiels, held since 1930, in which riders parade on horseback around the town to celebrate the granting of the burgh charter in 1599. The riders – each presented with a sprig from a plum tree to commemorate the 1337 victory over English raiders (*see* SOOR PLOOM) – are led by the year's Braw Lad, who carries the burgh flag, and leads his followers to the Auld Town Cross for the ceremony of the Mixing of the Roses, carried out by the year's Braw Lass. The ceremony, in which red and white roses are commingled on a bed of thistles, commemorates the marriage in 1503 between James IV and Margaret Tudor, who received the Ettrick Forest as a wedding present. At midday, the Braw Lad dips the burgh flag at the war memorial, where in the evening the Braw Lass lays the mixed roses in tribute to the fallen of the two World Wars. The association of 'braw lads' with the burgh is embodied in a well-known traditional song, sung to a tune that was Haydn's favourite Scottish melody:

> Braw lads o' Galla Water!
> Bonnie lads o' Galla Water!
> Lothian lads will ne'er compare
> Wi' the braw lads o' Galla Water.

Robert Burns reworked the idea in 'Galla Water' (1793):

> Braw, braw lads on Yarrow braes,
> Ye wander thro' the blooming heather;
> But Yarrow braes, nor Ettrick shaws,
> Can match the lads o' Galla Water.

See also RIDING THE MARCHES.

Braxfield, Lord *See* WEIR OF HERMISTON.

Breakfast Although Dr Johnson is better known for his snide comments about oats and Scotsmen, he was struck, in his *Journey to the Western Isles of Scotland* (1775), by the quality of the hospitality he was offered – particularly the breakfasts:

> In the breakfast the Scots, whether of the Lowlands or mountains, must be confessed to excel us. The tea and coffee are accompanied not only with butter, but with honey, conserves, and marmalades. If an epicure could remove by a wish, in quest of sensual gratifications, wherever he had supped he would breakfast in Scotland.

Of course, Johnson was writing in the era before HIGH TEA had come to embody Scottish culinary abundance.

Breath like a burst lavvy A Glaswegian expression that needs no explanation.

Breck, Alan The 'bonny fighter', flamboyant Jacobite and friend to the Hanoverian hero, David Balfour, in Robert Louis Stevenson's novel *Kidnapped* (1886). He is closely modelled on the historical figure, Allan Breck Stewart, who was widely suspected of responsibility for the 1752 APPIN MURDER, a notorious incident that is vividly recreated in the novel. 'Breck' is an Anglicization of Gaelic *breac*, 'speckled', referring to his pockmarked face.

> He came up to me with open arms. 'Come to my arms!' he cried, and embraced and kissed me hard upon both cheeks. 'David,' said he, 'I love you like a brother. And O, man,' he cried in a kind of ecstasy, 'am I no a bonny fighter?'
> Thereupon he turned to the four enemies, passed his sword clean through each of them, and tumbled them out of doors one after the other. As he did so, he kept humming and singing and whistling to himself,

like a man trying to recall an air; only what he was trying was to make one. All the while, the flush was in his face, and his eyes were as bright as a five-year-old child's with a new toy.

– *Kidnapped* (1886), chapter x

In a note to *Rob Roy*, Sir Walter Scott describes how a friend of his had supposedly encountered Allan Breck Stewart around 1789 in Paris, where he had become a Benedictine priest. He is described in the note as 'a tall, thin, raw-boned, grim-looking, old man', who says, 'with a sigh, in a sharp Highland accent, "Deil ane o' them a' is worth the Hie Street of Edinburgh!"'

The expression *bonnie fechter* is used more generally for an enthusiastic advocate of a particular cause, as well as someone who is handy with their fists.

Breek-brothers Rivals in love; *breeks* are trousers. The term was still in use in the early 20th century.

Bridie *See* FORFAR BRIDIE.

Bridge For those with an interest in bridges, the following entries may prove enlightening:

- BRIDGE OVER THE ATLANTIC, THE
- BRIDGE TO NOWHERE, THE
- *BRIGADOON* and TAM O' SHANTER (for Brig o' Doon).
- BRIGGERS, THE
- DEVIL'S BRIDGE
- Devorgilla's Bridge (*see under* SWEETHEART ABBEY)
- FAIRY FLAG, THE (for Fairy Bridge)
- HIELANMAN'S UMBRELLA, THE
- PAINTING THE FORTH BRIDGE
- SQUINTY BRIDGE
- TAY BRIDGE DISASTER

Bridge over the Atlantic, the The jocular nickname of Clachan Bridge, a stone-built, single-arch bridge over the Clachan Sound, linking the mainland Argyll with the island of Seil, south of Oban. The bridge, designed by Thomas Telford, was completed in 1793, and has a span of some 22 m (72 ft).

Bridge to Nowhere, the The nickname of a pedestrian bridge over the M8 in the Anderston district of Glasgow, which stops in mid-air. Built in the 1960s, it was originally intended to link to an elevated shopping centre, which was never built. There are plans to complete the bridge, for use by pedestrians and cyclists. *See also* GORBALS MICK.

There is another 'Bridge to Nowhere' at Belhaven Bay in Dunbar, East Lothian. At high tide, steps at either end lead mysteriously down into the sea; but at low tide it is clear that the bridge crosses the outflow of the Biel Water, which cuts a channel through the sand flats.

Brigadoon The Lerner and Lowe musical, first staged on Broadway in 1947 and filmed in 1954, has come to epitomize the Hollywood vision of all things Caledonian. The story concerns two New Yorkers holidaying in Scotland who stumble upon a mysterious Highland village called Brigadoon. To keep it safe from the outside world, the village only appears for one day every hundred years, so when it does manifest itself it is heavily accoutred with kilts, heather, bagpipes, sporrans, Highland flings and other items of haute tartanry, including a character called, appropriately enough, Angus McGuffie. The most likely inspiration for the name is the medieval Brig o' Doon in (non-Highland) Ayrshire, where in Burns's poem TAM O'SHANTER the eponymous hero manages to escape the clutches of his pursuers, for, as the poet explains, 'It is a well-known fact that witches, or any evil spirits, have no power to follow a poor wight any farther than the middle of the next running stream.' Such a bridge, marking the frontier between the otherworld and the everyday, would seem to be a suitable source for the Brigadoon name. As it happens, Lerner in fact based his book on a story by the German novelist Friedrich Gerstäcker (1816–72) about a fictional village called Germelshausen, but a German setting for a Broadway confection so soon after the Second World War was about as promising as Zero Mostel and Gene Wilder in *The Producers* putting on a musical called *Springtime for Hitler*, so the action was switched to Bonnie Scotchland. Arthur Freed, the producer of the film, is on record as saying:

I went to Scotland but I could find nothing that looked like Scotland.

Briggers, the The men who built the Forth Bridge (*brig* in Scots), one of the marvels of Victorian engineering, constructed between 1883 and 1890.

> A monument o' strength and grace
> Til the dour age o' coal and steam.
> – Sydney Goodsir Smith, 'The Two Brigs'

At its peak, the workforce totalled 4600 men; 98 lost their lives, while hundreds more were seriously injured. *See also* PAINTING THE FORTH BRIDGE.

Brighton of the North, the A title awarded to the seaside resort of Nairn in its Victorian heyday. The first bathing-machine offering salt baths was established on Nairn beach in 1793, and visitor numbers boomed following the arrival of the railway in 1855. Things have gone downhill in recent years, and in 2011 Nairn was nominated for the Plook on the Plinth trophy for 'most dismal town in Scotland' (*see* CARBUNCLE AWARDS). The reason for the nomination was given as follows:

> Described in Victorian times as 'the Brighton of the North', the cumulative effects of decades of poor planning, official indecision, developer greed and bad design have turned Nairn from an attractive seaside resort with interesting architecture and great facilities, into a depressing transit route for visitors with a town centre that is dying.

See also NAIRRRRRN.

British Solomon, the A flattering sobriquet of James VI and I, who prided himself on his learning; *see* WISEST FOOL IN CHRISTENDOM, THE.

Broch A round drystone tower, with hollow walls. Brochs are found in the Northern Isles, the Hebrides and the coast of the northwestern mainland. They date from the Iron Age, mostly the 1st century BC to the 2nd century AD. The word is a variant of *burgh*, and is related to Old Norse *borg*, 'castle, stronghold'.

Broch, the The local name for Fraserburgh, and also Burghead. The word is a variant of *burgh*, and was formerly applied to any local town. More generally, fishing crews from up and down the east coast are known as *Brochers*.

Brodie, William *See* DEACON BRODIE.

Broken men Those men without lands, clans or lords who led a violent existence as mercenaries or outlaws in the wilder parts of Scotland. In the ballad 'KINMONT WILLIE', recalling events in the later 16th century, the term is applied to the BORDER REIVERS who set out to rescue the eponymous hero:

> 'Where be ye gaun, ye broken men?'
> Quo' fause Sakelde; 'Come tell to me!'

The *Domestic Annals of Scotland* for 26 February 1602 records a raid on Moy by 'thieves, broken men and sorners [extorters of free board and lodging] of clans, bodin and furnist with bows, habershons, twa-handit swords, and other weapons invasive, and with hagbuts and pistolets'. In 1603 James VI declared the entire Clan MacGregor to be broken men, and banned their very name (*see* MACGREGOR, PROSCRIPTION OF CLAN). The religious troubles and violent dislocations during the reign of Charles I gave the broken men – also at this period known in the Borders as MOSS TROOPERS – further opportunities for mayhem and plunder, and many rallied round such freebooting, nominally royalist leaders as Lord Kenmure in Kirkcudbrightshire, who had as his standard a barrel of brandy atop a pole. Broken men were still apparently a source of fear in the wake of the '45, a century later:

> At the door of the first house we came to, Alan knocked, which was no very safe enterprise in such a part of the Highlands as the Braes of Balquhidder. No great clan held rule there; it was filled and disputed by small septs, and broken remnants, and what they call 'chiefless folk', driven into the wild country about the springs of Forth and Teith by the advance of the Campbells.
> – Robert Louis Stevenson, *Kidnapped* (1886),
>   chapter xxv

See also PUT TO THE HORN.

Broken Reid *See* RAT RACE IS FOR RATS, THE.

Broo or **Buroo, the** Originally short for 'Unemployment Bureau', i.e. the Labour Exchange, and now applied to its successor, the social security office. If one is in receipt of state unemployment benefits, etc., one is *on the broo. See also* ON THE BOX.

Brooch of Lorn, the (Gaelic *Braiste Lathurna*) An heirloom of the MacDougalls of Lorn in Argyll, consisting of an oval-shaped rock crystal set in a silver disc of Celtic design and surrounded by pearls. According to legend, it was originally owned by Robert the Bruce, but when Bruce and 300 men retreated into Argyll after the Battle of Methven in 1306, they were ambushed at Dalrigh by Lord Lorn and 1000 of his MacDougall clansmen, in revenge for the murder of Lorn's nephew, the RED COMYN. Outnumbered, Bruce only escaped by leaving his cloak and brooch in the hands of his attackers. Thereafter the MacDougalls kept the brooch at Dunollie Castle until the religious wars of the 1640s, when it was moved to Gylen Castle on Kerrera. Here it remained until the castle was captured by General David Leslie in 1647, and the brooch was assumed to have been lost. In 1819 the brooch was found in a chest after the death of Major Campbell of Bragleen, and in 1825 General Sir Duncan Campbell, a descendant of Campbell of Inverawe, one of Leslie's officers, returned the brooch to MacDougall of Dunollie.

Broomie Law The acerbic five-year-old heroine of Cinders McLeod's cartoon strip which ran for some years in the *Herald*. She is named after the Broomie-law, the once busy waterfront of the north bank of the Clyde in Glasgow. Other characters, also named after Glasgow places, include Broomie's handbag Hags Castle, her dolly Annie Land (after Anniesland), and grumpy old Mary Hill.

Broon, Mrs A nickname for Buckfast Tonic Wine; *see* BUCKFAST TRIANGLE.

Broon, the A journalistic nickname for Gordon Brown (aka the MISERY FROM THE MANSE), styled as if he were a Highland chieftain, and with a nod to Scotland's First Family, the *BROONS*. After he became Prime Minister in 2007, Brown featured in *Private Eye* as a dour and gaffe-prone Paw Broon in a pastiche of *The Broons* cartoon strip, while on 25 January 2009, Burns Night, he made a guest appearance in the original strip in the *Sunday Post*, alongside the Scottish First Minister, Alex Salmond (the twins, expecting salmon for tea, are disappointed when Salmond turns up instead). It was Salmond who suggested that he appear in the strip to mark the launch of the Scottish government's HOMECOMING SCOTLAND CAMPAIGN, and the *Post* agreed, but for the sake of political balance also invited Brown to that other Number 10 – the Broons' tenement flat at 10 Glebe Street, AUCHENSHOOGLE.

Broon frae Troon The nickname of the rugby union player Gordon Brown (1947–2001), a native of Troon in Ayrshire. He won 30 caps as a lock for Scotland between 1969 and 1976, but no points. In the epigraph to his poem to Gordon Brown, the late Mick Imlah dubs him 'the Ayrshire Bull':

> You knew two bits of Burns. Still you pretended
> Poems would outlast what the British Lions did,
> You, who had beaten Springbok and All Black ...
> – Mick Imlah, 'Gordon Brown', from *The Lost Leader* (2008)

Broonie *See* BROWNIE.

Broons, The A comic strip in D.C. Thomson's *Sunday Post* featuring 'Scotland's First Family', the Broons. It has appeared every week since 8 March 1936. The Broons also star in their own annual every other year, alternating with OOR WULLIE. They were the creation of Dudley D. Watkins, the first newspaper illustrator in the UK who was permitted to sign his own work. The family, who speak in broad Scots, consists of Granpaw Broon, Paw Broon (still sporting an Edwardian walrus moustache), his sensible, matriarchal wife Maw Broon, and their children: Hen (Henry), Daphne, Joe, Maggie, Horace, the Twins (one of whom is called Eck) and the Bairn. The Broons all live in a tenement at 10 Glebe Street in the fictional town of AUCHENSHOOGLE (or Auchentogle), and also have a humble Highland seat – the BUT AND BEN. Watkins died in 1969, and for five years the *Post* reprinted old strips (with some updating), before employing new artists and writers. In 2007 *Private Eye* started to run a parody strip featuring

Prime Minister Gordon Brown as Paw Broon (*see* BROON, THE).

Brose A staple rural dish into the 19th century, comprising oatmeal and pease-meal boiled in vegetable stock. *See also* ATHOLL BROSE; KAIL BROSE; PEASE BROSE.

Brothels, busy times for Edinburgh *See* DANUBE STREET; GENERAL ASSEMBLY.

Brother of man *See* EVOLUTION.

Broughty Ferry *See* RICHEST SQUARE MILE IN EUROPE, THE.

Brownie A domestic sprite, generally regarded as benevolent, although occasionally prone to mischief. They supposedly help with household chores (hence the name of the junior wing of the Girl Guides), which they perform during the night. Brownies are recorded in the Lowlands and the Borders from the 16th century, and have various southern cousins, such as pixies, hobs and pucks. They do not like to be rewarded too directly for their work, as the following rhyme attests:

> Gie Brownie coat, gie Brownie sark [shirt],
> Ye'se get nae mair o' Brownie's wark!

Brownies were quick to take offence, and when they did they would depart the household forever, taking their luck with them. One such offended Brownie was that of Cranshaws, on the Whiteadder Water in Berwickshire, who used to help with the harvest until one year someone remarked that the corn was 'not well mowed' (heaped up). To which the Brownie indignantly retorted:

> It's no weel mowed! It's no weel mowed!
> Then it's ne'er be mowed by me again;
> I'll scatter it oure the Raven stane,
> And they'll hae some wark e'er it's mowed again.
> – from George Henderson, *Popular Rhymes of Berwickshire* (1856)

That Brownies belonged to an older dispensation is attested by the tale of a Brownie in Nithsdale around the time of the Reformation. The sprite was surprised by the local minister, who, attempting to baptize him,

flung some holy water in his face. The Brownie yelled in dismay, and was seen no more.

The demon-obsessed James VI thought Brownies were devils in disguise:

> The spirit called Brownie appeared like a rough man, and haunted divers houses without doing any evil, but doing, as it were, necessarie turns up and down the house; yet some are so blinded as to believe that their house was all the sonsier, as they called it, that such spirits resorted there.
> – James VI, *Daemonologie* (1597)

Victorian folklorists have left a number of descriptions:

> Brownie is a personage of small stature, wrinkled visage, covered with short curly brown hair, and wearing a brown mantle and hood. His residence is the hollow of the old tree, a ruined castle, or the abode of man. He is attached to particular families, with whom he has been known to reside, even for centuries, threshing the corn, cleaning the house, and doing everything done by his northern and English brethren. He is, to a certain degree, disinterested; like many great personages, he is shocked at anything approaching to the name of a bribe or *douceur*, yet, like them, allows his scruples to be overcome if the thing be done in a genteel, delicate, and secret way. Thus, offer Brownie a piece of bread, a cup of drink, or a new coat and hood, and he flouted at it, and perhaps, in his huff, quitted the place for ever; but leave a nice bowl of cream, and some fresh honeycomb, in a snug private corner, and they soon disappeared, though Brownie, it was to be supposed, never knew anything of them.
> – Thomas Keightley, *The Fairy Mythology: Illustrative of the Romance and Superstition of Various Countries* (1870)

The characteristic rough humour of the Scottish peasant, as it affects the creations of the fancy, embodies itself almost exclusively in the Brownie. This was a half-human creature, of uncouth appearance.

> His matted head on his breast did rest;
> A lang blue beard wan'er'd down like a vest;–
> But the glare o' his e'e hath nae bard exprest.

During the day he would lurk in out-of-the-way corners of some old house which he had chosen to inhabit; and in the night-time would make himself useful to the family to which he had attached himself. But the conditions of his service were the most disinterested ever drawn up, and on the slightest attempt being made to reward him for his labours he would disappear for ever.

> – Sir George Douglas, *Scottish Folk and Fairy Tales* (1901), introduction

For the Brownie of Tullochgorum, *see* MEG MULLACH. *See also* URISK.

Brown Man of the Moors, the *See* BLACK DWARF, THE.

Bruce and the spider A fable long told about ROBERT THE BRUCE. In the winter of 1305–6 Bruce was forced to take refuge from the English in a cave or cabin on the island of Rathlin, off the north coast of Ulster, leading some unknown contemporary English songwriter to crow (in Latin):

> Run away, Scots, and hide in a cave
> Lest you catch the eye of Edward the Brave.
> England, rejoice!

While secluded in the cave, according to the story, Bruce watched as a spider attempted to complete its web, and failed six times to secure a thread to the roof. But on the seventh attempt it succeeded, which inspired Bruce with the idea that if he persevered he would succeed. Soon afterwards he returned to Scotland, rallied support, and began the campaign that would eventually lead to decisive victory at Bannockburn.

Whether the fable predates the version told in Sir Walter Scott's *Tales of a Grandfather* (1828–30), a child's history of Scotland, is unclear. In Scott's version, Bruce is trying to decide whether he should fight for his country's freedom or abandon it forever for the Crusades. He too has suffered six defeats, but the example of the spider gives him hope that his luck is about to turn. Scott adds:

> I have often met with people of the name of Bruce, so completely persuaded of the truth of this story, that they would not on any account kill a spider; because it was that insect which had shown the example of perseverance, and given a signal of good luck to their great namesake.

The fable is so well-known that it was used in a 1991 TV advertisement regarding the privatization of Scottish Power. In this, the spider addresses the king thus: 'Hello there, big man, how's it gaun?'

Buarach bhaoi *See* WIZARD SHACKLE.

Bubbly Babies or **Bubbly Bairns, the** Disparaging nicknames for the Boys' Brigade, the church-based uniformed youth group who are often referred to simply as the B.B. Another mischievous misinterpretation of the initials yields *Bad Boys*. Compare HALLELUJAHS, THE.

Bubbly-jock A turkey-cock. John Jamieson, in his *Etymological Dictionary of the Scottish Language* (1808) says 'The name seems to have originated from the shape of his comb, which has considerable resemblance to the snot collected at a dirty child's nose', and cites the northern English dialect term *snotergob* for 'the red part of a turkey's head'. The *Dictionary of the Scots Language* opines that the word is 'More prob. imitative of the sound made by the turkey.' Hugh MacDiarmid, in his 1926 poem 'The Bubblyjock', describes the turkey as 'hauf like a bird and hauf like a bogle', and says it sounds as if it had swallowed the bagpipes, and 'the blether stuck in its throat'.

> So that's the way o' it! Yuletide's comin'!
> Haverin' hypocrites, hear them talk:
> Peace and goodwill to men and women,
> But thraw the neck o' the bubbly-jock.
> – W.D. Cocker (1882–1970), 'The Bubbly-Jock'

The word is also used figuratively of something to be feared, which may explain the habit formerly observed in Fife of greeting a turkey-cock with the execration: 'Bubbly-jock, your wife's a witch, and a' your bairns are warlocks.' To be *sair hauden doon by the bubbly-jock* denoted that one had far too much on one's plate. The Royal Scots Greys were nicknamed the 'Bubbly Jocks'; *see* REGIMENTAL NICKNAMES.

Buchan *See* COLD SHOULDER OF SCOTLAND, THE; HERSCHIP OF BUCHAN.

Buchan Chield, the The byname of George Smith Morris (1876–1958), an Aberdeen-born blacksmith who became one of the most famous writers and singers of CORNKISTERS (comic songs in the DORIC). In 1912 he married Agnes Kemp, sister of Willie Kemp, so-called KING OF THE CORNKISTERS, with whom he collaborated. For an example of Morris's work, *see under* NICKY TAMS. *Chield* can mean 'boy', 'young man' or 'fellow'.

Buchanites A millenarian sect, named after Elspeth Buchan, née Simpson (1738–1791), the daughter of an inn-keeper in Banffshire, who had left her husband and subsequently been inspired by the preaching of the Revd Hugh White of the Irvine Relief Church to believe that she was the woman described in Revelation 12:1:

> And there appeared a great wonder in heaven, a woman clothed with the sun, and the moon under her feet, and upon her head a crown of twelve stars.

White was censured by the presbytery, and in 1784 he and Buchan and fewer than four dozen followers moved to a farm at New Cample in Dumfriesshire. According to one story, when Mrs Buchan adjured one old man to 'Come and toil in the garden of the Lord', he replied, 'Thank ye, but He wasna ower kind to the first gairdner that he had.' Mrs Buchan, who claimed that she gave her followers the Holy Ghost by breathing on them, liked to be known as 'Friend Mother in the Lord', but outsiders called her 'Luckie Buchan, the witch-wife'. Once settled on their modest farm, the Buchanites were rumoured to practise sexual promiscuity, leading the poet Robert Burns to describe them as 'idle and immoral', and their beliefs 'a strange jumble of enthusiastic jargon'; however, neither marriage nor any sort of 'love-dealings' were permitted by Mrs Buchan. Rather, she encouraged her disciples to believe that after 40 days' fasting they would be taken up to heaven, while still alive. In *The Scottish Gallovidian Encyclopaedia* (1824), John MacTaggart describes what happened when 'at last the glorious day arrived':

> Platforms were erected for them to wait on, and Mrs Buchan's platform was exalted above all the others. The hair of each head was cut short, all but a tuft on the top, for the angels to catch by when drawing them up. The momentous hour came. Every station for ascension was instantly occupied. Thus they stood, expecting to be wafted every moment into the land of bliss, when a gust of wind came; but instead of wafting them upwards, it capsized Mrs Buchan, platform and all.

After this disappointment, many of Mrs Buchan's followers fell away, but some stayed loyal until her death seven years later. The Revd White insisted she was not dead, but merely in a trance – although even he realized his error when her body began to putrefy. As the Buchanites were committed to celibacy, their number was steadily diminished. The last of them, Andrew Innes, died in 1846, having left instructions that Mrs Buchan's coffin should be buried beneath his own, so that he would be awakened when she arose.

Buckfast Triangle, the A disparaging term applied to the area east of Glasgow incorporating Cumbernauld, Coatbridge and Airdrie. The allusion is to the supposed popularity there of the cheap alcoholic beverage Buckfast Tonic Wine, made by the Benedictine monks of Buckfast Abbey, Devon. Based on red wine, the strong, sweet and sticky drink goes under various nicknames in Scotland, including Mrs Broon, Buckie, Bo, Electric Soup, Commotion Lotion and Wreck-the-Hoose Juice. Originally produced in the 1880s as a medicinal drink, it has in recent decades been blamed for encouraging binge drinking and aggressive behaviour – hence the expression *Buckfast commando* for a fearless drunk spoiling for a fight. *See also* LANNY; RED BIDDY.

Buckhaven pie *See* FAUNA CALEDONIA.

Buckie, gang tae *See* GANG TAE BUCKIE!

Buckieman's tooth, a A fragment of a RAINBOW (presumably alluding to the Moray fishing village).

Buddies, the *See* FOOTBALL CLUB NICKNAMES.

Buddy A native of Paisley, *buddy* being the local pronunciation of 'body', i.e. a person, as in 'Gin a body meet a body / COMIN' THRO' THE RYE'. By transference, St Mirren FC, the town's football club, is nicknamed the Buddies. *See also* FOOTBALL CLUB NICKNAMES.

Buff the Beggars The nickname of an 18th-century Glasgow worthy, Dr William Porteous, who became minister of the Wynd Church in 1776.

He was a tall, dark-complexioned man, with a commanding appearance and an enormous wig, and he made himself somewhat unpopular among the poorer classes, by looking strictly after parties claiming relief at the Town's Hospital. At length the worthy doctor got the cognomen of 'Buff the Beggars', and the common cry in the streets was

Porteous and the deil,
Buff the beggars weel!

During the excitement of the French Revolution, Dr Porteous preached a sermon before the Glasgow Volunteers, in which he compared the orgies of the revolutionists to scenes in the bottomless pit, 'when Satan gave the signal and all hell rose in a mass!'

– The 'Rambling Reporter', notes to the 1887 reprint of *Jones's Directory for the Year 1787* – the first Glasgow directory, by Nathaniel Jones

Buildings and other structures In addition to those entries listed under BRIDGE and ROADS ..., the reader is referred to the following:

- ARTHUR'S OON
- BIG RED SHED, the
- BLACK DWARF'S COTTAGE, the
- BROCH
- BUS SHELTER OF UNST, the
- CANNONBALL HOUSE
- CLUNY'S CAGE
- DWARFIE STANE, the
- EDINBURGH'S FOLLY
- EDUCATION, SALVATION AND DAMNATION
- FAITH, HOPE AND CHARITY
- FIR CHREIG
- FLODDEN WALL, the
- FORT WEETABIX
- GOBLIN HA'
- GRYME'S DYKE
- HEART OF MIDLOTHIAN, the
- HEAVE AWA' HOUSE
- HOLYROOD
- HOUSE OF TERROR, the
- ITALIAN CHAPEL, the
- JEAN'S HUT
- KING SCHAW'S GRAVE
- LALLY'S PALAIS
- LAMP OF LOTHIAN, the

- LANTERN OF THE NORTH, the
- LITTLE BELSEN
- LIVE AND LET LIVE MONUMENT, the
- METHODOME, the
- MINISTERS' ALTAR, the
- NEPTUNE'S STAIRCASE
- NOLLIE, the
- O OF ARBROATH, the
- PELE TOWER
- PEOPLE'S PALACE, the
- PICTS' HOUSES
- PINEAPPLE, the
- PRENTICE PILLAR, the
- REPENTANCE TOWER
- ROTTENROW
- ST ANDREW'S HOUSE
- SARRY HEID, the
- SCOTT MONUMENT, the
- STALAG LUFT BUTLINS
- SUFFERIN GENERAL, the
- TENNANT'S STALK
- TIBBIE SHIEL'S INN
- TOMB OF THE EAGLES, the
- WALLACE MONUMENT, the
- WATER HOLE, the
- WELL OF THE HEADS
- WINDHOUSE

Bukhara Burnes The nickname of the Montrose-born explorer and linguist Sir Alexander Burnes (1805–41), first cousin once removed of Robert Burns and an early player in the Great Game. Burnes made his reputation when in 1832, as an officer of the East India Company, he travelled in disguise across Afghanistan to Bukhara in Central Asia. He advised against British military intervention in Afghanistan, but nevertheless accompanied the expeditionary force in 1841 as deputy British envoy. Along with his younger brother and another officer, he was murdered on 2 November 1841 when an angry mob broke into the British residency in Kabul – although he killed six of his attackers before being cut down himself. In the subsequent retreat, only one British officer made it back to India.

Bull, Peg The sister of John Bull in *The Famous History of John Bull* (1712) by the Kincardineshire-born satirist John Arbuthnot. As John Bull is the personification of England, so his sister is the personification of Scotland:

John had a sister, a poor girl that had been starved at nurse. Anybody would have guessed Miss to have been bred up under the influence of a cruel stepdame, and John to be the fondling of a tender mother. John looked ruddy and plump, with a pair of cheeks like a trumpeter; Miss looked pale and wan, as if she had the green sickness; and no wonder, for John was the darling: he had all the good bits, was crammed with good pullet, chicken, pig, goose, and capon; while Miss had only a little oatmeal and water, or a dry crust without butter. John had his golden pippins, peaches, and nectarines; poor Miss, a crab-apple, sloe, or a blackberry. Master lay in the best apartment, with his bedchamber towards the south sun. Miss lodged in a garret exposed to the north wind, which shrivelled her countenance. However, this usage, though it stunted the girl in her growth, gave her a hardy constitution; she had life and spirit in abundance, and knew when she was ill-used. Now and then she would seize upon John's commons, snatch a leg of a pullet, or a bit of good beef, for which they were sure to go to fisticuffs. Master was indeed too strong for her, but Miss would not yield in the least point; but even when Master had got her down, she would scratch and bite like a tiger; when he gave her a cuff on the ear, she would prick him with her knitting-needle. John brought a great chain one day to tie her to the bedpost, for which affront Miss aimed a penknife at his heart. In short, these quarrels grew up to rooted aversions; they gave one another nicknames, though the girl was a tight clever wench as any was, and through her pale looks you might discern spirit and vivacity, which made her not, indeed, a perfect beauty, but something that was agreeable.

Bullers of Buchan, the A spectacular feature on the coast between Peterhead and Aberdeen, near Cruden Bay. It takes the form of a former sea cave whose roof has collapsed, leaving a circular pot surrounded by cliffs some 150 ft (45 m) high, into which the sea rushes through a natural arch, and furiously swirls about. *Buller* in Scots (perhaps related to French *bouillir*, 'to boil') can denote a bubble, thence a boiling up of water, or a loud gurgling noise, and thence a whirlpool. James Boswell, who visited the Bullers in 1773, described the place as a 'monstrous cauldron', while his companion, Samuel Johnson, considered that 'No man can see it with indifference who has either sense of

danger or delight in rarity.' He had to stretch his vast vocabulary to describe the topography: 'It is a rock perpendicularly tubulated, united on one side with a high shore, and on the other rising steep to a great height, above the main sea.'

Bullion's Day The old name in Scotland for 4 July, the feast of the transference of the remains of St Martin (d. AD 397) to the cathedral at Tours. St Martin became known in Scotland as 'St Martin of Bullion' from the French *Saint Martin le bouillant*, referring to his emblem, a globe of fire that was seen over his head while he said Mass. In the entry for 4 July in his *Book of Days* (1862–4), Robert Chambers notes:

> In Scotland, this used to be called St Martin of Bullion's Day, and the weather which prevailed upon it was supposed to have a prophetic character. It was a proverb, that if the deer rise dry and lie down dry on Bullion's Day, it was a sign there would be a good gose-harvest – gose being a term for the latter end of summer; hence gose-harvest was an early harvest. It was believed generally over Europe that rain on this day betokened wet weather for the twenty ensuing days.

Bullion's Day is thus the equivalent of the English St Swithin's Day (15 July).

Bull's head 'A signal of condemnation, and prelude of immediate execution, said to have been anciently used in Scotland', according to John Jamieson in the 1825 Supplement to his *Etymological Dictionary of the Scottish Language*. Jamieson cites Lindsay of Pitscottie's account of the presentation of the bull's head at the infamous BLACK DINNER in Edinburgh Castle prior to the slaughter of the Earl of Douglas and his younger brother, but he also cites other authorities who suggest that this was a one-off, and that the bull's head was produced to betoken the stupidity of the young Douglases in falling into the trap laid for them. Jamieson points out that no other instances of the 'custom' are recorded, and suggests that the early historians – Lindsay of Pitscottie, Hector Boece, Drummond of Hawthornden and others – were merely following each other in asserting that the bull's head was, in Drummond's words, 'a sign of present death in these times'.

Bully Wee, the *See* FOOTBALL CLUB NICKNAMES.

Bumpkin brawly *See* BABBITY BOWSTER.

Bum's oot the windae, yer Literally, 'Your posterior is hanging out of the window', i.e. you are making an exhibition of yourself by talking utter nonsense.

Bunchy knobs of papist flesh A contemporary Scots pamphleteer's characterization of Charles I's bishops.

Bunnit *See* BONNET.

Burghers versus Antiburghers A controversy in the 18th century regarding the *burgher* or *burgess oath*, which anyone wishing to become a *burgher* or *burgess* (citizen or freeman) of a royal burgh was required to swear. The *Burghers* held that it was incumbent upon those who swore the burgher oath to uphold the Established Church of Scotland, while the *Antiburghers*, who belonged to various seceding denominations, disagreed. By the early 19th century, both Burghers and Antiburghers had split into factions known as AULD LICHTS AND NEW LICHTS. This seems to have overcome previous enmities to the extent that in 1820 the New Licht Burghers and the New Licht Antiburghers came together to form the United Secession Church. Further schisms and reconciliations recurred among the various factions through the decades and centuries that followed.

Burial, beliefs regarding *See* GRAVEYARD WATCH.

Burke, Betty The name adopted by Bonnie Prince Charlie, the YOUNG PRETENDER, when in June 1746 he dressed up as Flora MACDONALD's maid, to sail 'OVER THE SEA TO SKYE' in an effort to escape the Redcoats after Culloden. Dressed in a calico gown, quilted petticoat, waterproof cape, a cap and women's shoes and stockings, he determined to hide a pistol in his petticoat, but Miss Macdonald vetoed the idea, saying that if they were searched they would surely be found out. The prince retorted that if he were searched that close, they would 'certainly discover me at any rate'. In his *Journal of a Tour to the Hebrides* (for 13 September 1773), James Boswell describes Miss Burke tramping across the bogs of northern Skye on his/her way to Kingsburgh, the house of Alexander Macdonald, the factor of Macdonald of Sleat:

The wanderer, forgetting his assumed sex, that his clothes might not be wet, held them up a great deal too high. [Macdonald of] Kingsburgh mentioned this to him, observing, it might make a discovery. He said he would be more careful for the future. He was as good as his word; for the next brook they crossed, he did not hold up his clothes at all, but let them float upon the water. He was very awkward in his female dress. His size was so large, and his strides so great, that some women whom they met reported that they had seen a very big woman, who looked like a man in woman's clothes, and that perhaps it was (as they expressed themselves) the PRINCE, after whom so much search was making.

Once at Kingsburgh, Miss Burke was described by Macdonald's daughter as 'a very odd, muckle ill-shapen up wife as ever I saw', while his wife recalled: 'I saw such an odd muckle trallup of a carlin [hag, witch, old woman] making lang, wide steps through the hall that I could not like her appearance at all.' She was particularly taken aback when Miss Burke, who had not shaved for some days, kissed her cheek. When Macdonald informed her of Miss Burke's true identity, she became hysterical: 'O Lord,' she cried, 'we are a' ruin'd and undone for ever! We will a' be hang'd now!' Her husband merely observed that death comes to us all, 'and if we are hanged for this, I am sure we will die in a good cause'.

Burke and Hare Two notorious murderers, William Burke and William Hare, who in 1827–8 supplied the Edinburgh Medical School, notably Dr Robert Knox, with 17 of their murder victims, to be used for dissection. Burke and Hare were both Irish immigrants, the former a tenant in the latter's lodging house in the West Port area of Edinburgh. In embarking on the body-snatching business, they eschewed the hard work undertaken by more conventional 'Resurrectionists', who would at night surreptitiously disinter recently buried corpses to sell to the anatomists – prompting the building of castellated watch towers in more than one Edinburgh cemetery, the construction of bars or mortsafes over graves, and the following lines by a local poet, James Thomson:

Of a' articles for sale,
Whilk bodies think is lawfu',
To sell the dead, it bangs the hale –
There's something in't that's awfu'!

The first body sold by the Burke and Hare was that of a tenant who had expired owing rent, but after that they did not bother to wait for nature to take its course, and instead plied their victims with whisky before smothering them – a process later known as 'burking'. When they were eventually arrested, Hare turned King's evidence on Burke, who was hanged and his body publicly dissected. A wallet made from his skin is on display at the Royal College of Surgeons, Edinburgh. Hare was released, and his ultimate fate is unknown, although some identified him with a blind beggar who once haunted Oxford Street in London. Despite a public outcry, Knox avoided prosecution. At the time of the trial, the following rhyme was in popular circulation:

> Up the close and doun the stair,
> But an' ben wi' Burke an' Hare.
> Burke's the butcher, Hare's the thief,
> Knox the boy that buys the beef.

In *Murder for Profit* (1926), William Bolitho described Knox as 'One of those intelligent eccentrics of whom Scotland has the manufacturing secret.' He became the subject of James Bridie's play *The Anatomist* (1930).

Burleigh, Burley or **Burly, Captain** See CAPTAIN BURLY.

Burning the clavie A midwinter fire ceremony celebrated in Burghead on the south shore of the Moray Firth. It takes place on 11 January, the first day of the year in the old Julian Calendar, and the intention is to ensure good luck for the year that follows. The *clavie* in question is a tar barrel, which is set alight and carried aloft on a *spoke* (a pole used by salmon fishermen) around the village and then taken up to Doorie Hill, where it becomes part of a large bonfire. The word *clavie* may come from Gaelic *cliabh*, a basket for holding firewood etc., or from Latin *clavis*, a nail – the same large nail is used to attach the barrel to the pole every year, and local tradition holds that the Romans had a fort and altar on Doorie Hill (though they probably did not come this far north). In the past the Kirk condemned the ceremony as 'superstitious, idolatrous and sinful, an abominable heathenish practice', but it survived all efforts to extinguish it. Similar cere-

monies were formerly practised in other fishing villages in Moray, in which the clavie was carried from boat to boat so that the fishing season would be a good one. *See also* FIREBALLS, THE; UP-HELLY-AA.

Burn of Sorrow and Burn of Care See CASTLE GLOOM.

Burns, Robert See PLOUGHMAN POET, THE; THREE ROBBIES, SCOTLAND'S; and *passim*.

Burns of Gaeldom, the See ROBERT BURNS OF GAELDOM, THE.

Burns Night An annual celebration on the evening of 25 January, the birthday of Robert Burns, usually regarded as Scotland's national poet. On the menu is HAGGIS, accompanied by CHAMPIT TATTIES and bashit neeps (mashed potatoes and turnips), all washed down with whisky. Formal Burns Nights have acquired a prescribed order of ceremonies: a grace is said, often the SELKIRK GRACE; the haggis is piped in, and then subjected to a recitation of Burns's 'Address to a Haggis' (*see* GREAT CHIEFTAIN O' THE PUDDIN'-RACE), during which the haggis is cut open at the appropriate point; the 'Loyal Toast' is then given, if the company are not in sympathy with the poet's republican sentiments; there follows a speech on some Burns-related topic, and a toast to the 'Immortal Memory' of the poet; a male speaker then gives a speech proposing the 'Toast to the Lassies'; then a female speaker gives a reply to this. Various further recitations and songs may follow, and the evening ends with the company standing, joining hands and singing AULD LANG SYNE.

Not all are in sympathy with these rituals. In a forward to a short anthology of Burns's poems in 2010, the poet Don Paterson wrote:

> Many of us dread Burns Night. Address to a bloody Haggis; recitations of Tam O'Shanter that should, by rights, have their speakers automatically sectioned or arrested; much talk of 'our Rabbie' – but as Hugh MacDiarmid said: 'No wan in fifty kens a wurd Burns wrote / But misapplied is aabody's property.'

Burnt Candlemas A punitive English raid at Candlemas (2 February) 1356, when Edward III of

England cut a swathe through the Lothians, putting Haddington and Edinburgh to the torch. Then, running short of supplies and having failed to force the Scots to come to terms, he withdrew southward.

Burnt-nebbit tawse *See* TAWSE.

Buroo, the *See* BROO, THE.

Burryman, the Formerly the central figure in traditional ceremonies in a number of Scottish fishing ports along the East coast, such as Buckie and Fraserburgh, but now only found in South Queensferry on the Firth of Forth. The Burryman was a local man who was dressed up in a costume covered with thousands of sticky burrs and then chased out of town, apparently taking any bad luck with him. The intention was to improve the fishing, and if such an improvement followed, the Burryman got the credit. The last recorded Burryman ceremony in Fraserburgh was in 1864. In South Queensferry, the Burryman – dressed head to foot in burrs, with only three small holes for eyes and mouth – is still paraded round the town on the second Friday of August, accompanied by two attendants. They follow a seven-mile route, calling in at pubs, factories and the provost's house, and the Burryman now and again manages to sip a proffered glass of whisky through a straw. The burrs in the Burryman's costume may originally have symbolized the evil spirits that cling to the skins of the living.

Bus Shelter of Unst, the Britain's most northerly inhabited island is also home to the world's most unusual bus shelter. It contains a sofa, a vase of flowers, a carpet, a computer and a hot snacks counter. All this is thanks to local schoolboy Bobby Macaulay, who, several years ago, wrote to the local newspaper to ask for a new bus shelter, as the old one was derelict and leaking. Once the new bus shelter arrived, Bobby decided to make it a little more homely, and involved his family and friends in turning it into a must-see tourist attraction for all visitors to the island. It has since been named 'Best Bus Shelter in Britain' by *Buses Magazine*.

But An intensifier attached in Glasgow to the end of sentences to denote 'though' or 'however'.

> Naw I'm no. Wish to christ I was but. That's the trouble with nowadays, you can't even get fucking drunk.
> – James Kelman, *The Busconductor Hines* (1984)

But and ben A small two-roomed cottage, a sized-down version of the 'two-up, two-down'. A *but* is the outer room (from the preposition and adverb *but*, meaning 'in or into the outer part of a house'), while a *ben* is the inner room (from the preposition and adverb *ben*, 'within' or 'into the inner part of a house'). The original collocation of 'but and ben', in the sense of 'inside and out', is found, for example, in Allan Ramsay's 'To the Phiz: An Ode':

> Then fling on coals, and ripe the ribs,
> And beik the house both but and ben:
> That mutchkin stoup it hauds but drips,
> Then let's get in the tappit-hen.

The aura of cosiness and good fellowship associated with the phrase made the but and ben, in its full-blown cottage sense, a staple of the KAILYARD SCHOOL and FAUX JOCKERY, in which it becomes the repository of modest ambition, virtuous restraint and domestic content, as celebrated in Sir Harry Lauder's 'Just a Wee DEOCH AN DORUS':

> There's a wee wifie awaiting
> In a wee but and ben ...

The *BROONS*, of *Sunday Post* fame, have a but and ben as their country retreat or 'hame fae hame', and Maw Broon has even gone so far as to produce her very own *But An' Ben Cookbook*. Of a different bent is *But n Ben A-Go-Go*, Matthew Fitt's dystopian sci-fi novel in Scots, published in 2000.

Butcher Cumberland The sobriquet awarded by Jacobites to William Augustus, Duke of Cumberland (1721–65), younger son of George II and commander of Hanoverian forces during the '45 Rising. The epithet refers in particular to his ruthless hunting down of the defeated Highlanders after Culloden. In consequence of his atrocities, the Highlanders gave the name Stinking Billy to common ragwort, a plant famously poisonous to horses and cows. (For their part, the English named a pleasant garden flower Sweet William in his honour.)

Cumberland inspired John Roy Stuart to pen the following curse (here translated from the Gaelic):

May William, the son of George, be as a leafless splintered tree, rootless, branchless, sproutless. May there be no joy on his hearth, no wife, no brother, no son, no sounding harp of blazing wax.

The curse seems to have had some effect: although Cumberland had many mistresses, he never married, and thus had no legitimate issue; and his elder brother, Frederick, Prince of Wales, died in 1751.

Cumberland was the object of many more Jacobite animadversions. The following was collected by Bishop Forbes in The LYON IN MOURNING:

Here continueth to stink
The memory of the Duke of Cumberland
Who with unparalleled barbarity,
And inflexible hardness of heart,
In spite of all motives to lenity
That policy or humanity could suggest,
Endeavoured to ruin Scotland
By all the ways a Tyrant could invent.

Forbes also found this, which damns not only Cumberland but also Sir John Murray of Broughton, the secretary to Bonnie Prince Charlie who subsequently turned king's evidence, leading to the execution of SIMON THE FOX:

Auld Satan cleekit him by the spaul
And stappit him in the dub o' Hell.
The foulest fiend there doughtna bide him,
The damned they wadna fry beside him,
Till the bluidy Duke cam trysting thither,
And the ae fat butcher fried the ither.

For a gastronomic association of Cumberland with blood pudding, see YOUNG CHEVALIER, THE.

Butter in the black dog's house See BLACK DOG.

Buttery or **buttery rowie** An Aberdeen speciality, consisting of a rich, flaky bread roll made with lots of butter. Some assert that the rowie, with its rounded bottom, should be distinguished from the flat-bottomed buttery.

Buttery-lippit 'Butter-lipped', i.e. sycophantic, flattering.

Buttery Wullie Collie How the townspeople and urchins of Aberdeen used to refer to the students of the city's university. Collie may be derived from 'college' (in Glasgow students were Collie dougs), and Buttery possibly refers to a tavern called Buttery College near Slains, Aberdeenshire, owned by a man called Butter, where it was said that students assiduously studied tippling. First-year students at Aberdeen were known as Buttery Benjies, the latter element being a corruption of BEJAN, the term formerly used for first-years at Aberdeen (and still used at St Andrews).

I shall not enlarge on the feeling of pride, and the sense of incipient manliness with which, like most of my youthful fellows, I donned the red gown worn at the college, glorying in the epithet of 'Butterie,' bestowed by the street urchins on freshmen at Aberdeen.
– J. Riddell, Aberdeen and Its Folk (1868)

Buttock-mail The term applied from the 16th century to the fines formerly levied on fornicators (see FORNICATION ... BUT A PASTIME). Presumably this was a jockular allusion to BLACKMAIL. A first offence attracted a fine of £4 (Scotch), while for a second offence the fine was doubled. Adulterers could expect a fine of £20 (Scotch), and double that for a second offence. In the 20th century, the term was in use in the Northeast for a spanking.

Byochy-byochy See VOMIT.

By the lug and the horn By brute strength; the reference is to manhandling a recalcitrant sheep (lug, 'ear'). In contrast, if one has the wrang soo by the lug, one has blamed the wrong person, or got the wrong end of the stick.

By the way or **byraway** A phrase added at the end of statements by Glaswegians as an intensifying addendum, or simply as a full stop. The effect can be somewhat aggressive, e.g.: 'Hey, pal, that's ma pint, by the way.' So distinctive is the phrase that Glaswegians are sometimes referred to by other Scots as 'By-the-ways'.

C

Cabbage, the A nickname for Hibernian FC: Cabbage and Ribs is rhyming slang for Hibs. *See also* FOOTBALL CLUB NICKNAMES; RHYMING SLANG; KAIL.

Cabbages, detailed depictions of *See* GLASGOW BOYS, THE.

Cabbieclaw A traditional dish of cod in a sauce of egg and horseradish. The word derives either, via the AULD ALLIANCE connections (especially James V's marriage to Mary of Guise), from French *cabillaud*, 'cod'; or, via the trade with the Low Countries, Dutch *kabeljauw*, meaning the same (in Orkney dialect *kabbilow* is 'codling').

Cabby-labby or **kebbie-lebbie** A kerfuffle, a brouhaha, a noisy disputation.

> A while in silence scowl'd the crowd,
> And syne a kebby-lebby loud
> Gat up, an' twenty at a time
> Gae their opinions of the crime.
> – William Anderson, *The Piper of Peebles* (1794)

Caber *See* TOSSING THE CABER.

Cabrach, the *See* SIBERIA OF SCOTLAND, THE.

Ca' canny An adjuration to proceed cautiously.

> I made it a rule, after giving the blessing at the end of the ceremony, to admonish the bride and bridegroom to ca' canny, and join trembling with their mirth.
> – John Galt, *Annals of the Parish* (1821), chapter xlviii, year 1807

In the context of industrial relations, the expression means to work to rule.

Cadger's news Stale news, a *cadger* being an itinerant hawker. *Fiddler's news* or *piper's news* is equally old hat; the reference is to itinerant musicians. *See also* BOLT THE CADGER; KING'S ERRAND MAY COME IN THE CADGER'S GATE.

Caesar *See* CESAR.

Caird o' Barullion, the The sobriquet of Billy Marshall (?1671–1792), self-proclaimed king of the Galloway gypsies; among his many wives was Flora Marshall, an inspiration for the character of Meg MERRILIES in Scott's *Guy Mannering*. A *caird* is a gypsy or tinker, and *Barullion* refers to the location of one of his retreats, the Fell of Barhullion between Port William and Whithorn in the Machars of Wigtownshire. Marshall and his gang preyed upon travellers on remote mountain passes in Galloway (notably the Corse o' Slakes between Cairnsmore and Cairnhattie), and were also much involved in the local smuggling trade, using the Fell of Barhullion and a cave high on Cairnsmore to conceal the booty. Marshall may have been associated with the infamous Captain Yawkins – who appears under his own name in S.R. Crockett's *The Raiders* (1894), and as Dirk Hatteraick in *Guy Mannering* (*see* DIRK HATTERAICK'S CAVE). In an 'additional note' to the latter novel, Scott gives some more details on Billy Marshall (whom he calls Willie Marshal):

> He was born in the parish of Kirkmichael about the year 1671; and, as he died at Kirkcudbright 23rd November 1792, he must then have been in the one hundred and twentieth year of his age. It cannot be said that this unusually long lease of existence was noted by any peculiar excellence of conduct or habits of life. Willie had been pressed or enlisted in the army seven times, and had deserted as often; besides three times running away from the naval service. He had been seventeen times lawfully married; and, besides, such a reasonably large share of matrimonial comforts,

was, after his hundredth year, the avowed father of four children by less legitimate affections.

Marshall himself claimed to have fought for King William at the Battle of the Boyne in 1690, and became king of the Galloway gypsies when he stabbed the previous king, Isaac Miller, to death. In 1712 he made a bid to extend his fiefdom deeper into Ayrshire, but was defeated in a battle at Newton of Ayr by a force of gypsies from Argyll and Dunbartonshire. Twelve years later he was said to be the ringleader of the LEVELLERS' RISING in Galloway. When this was suppressed by troops, Marshall was taken prisoner, but escaped with the aid of Andrew Gemmil (on whom Scott modelled the character of Edie Ochiltree). His later life was less eventful, as Scott notes:

> He subsisted in his extreme old age by a pension from the present Earl of Selkirk's grandfather. Will Marshal is buried in Kirkcudbright church, where his monument is still shown, decorated with a scutcheon suitably blazoned with two tups' horns and two cutty spoons.

Marking his passing, the *Annual Register* noted that of 'all the thievish wandering geniuses, who ... led forth their various gangs to plunder, and alarm the country, he was by far the most honourable of his profession'.

In *The Tinkler-Gypsies of Galloway* (1908), Andrew McCormick portrays Marshall as a man out of his time:

> In the light of aristocratic ideals, if Billy sinned it was only because he arrived a little late upon the scene ... A curious mixture Billy undoubtedly must have been – a law unto himself when the country was almost devoid of policemen or executive officers to enforce properly the laws such as they were. He gave many occasion to hate him ... Others treated him kindly ... and in return he appears to have proved grateful to them. In that state of matters we must not fail to note what he accomplished. In point of fact, 'frae the braes o' Glenapp to the Brig-en' o' Dumfries' he played the part of an overlord – though his was a kind of catholic superiority for which he could produce no title ... His life was in a manner a final protest against usurpation and aggrandisement on the part of the white race over the dark. Might had despoiled and was despoiling the dark of their rights, and Billy raised a last unavailing

protest on behalf of his race against the law that 'Might (or its modern equivalent, money and brain power) is right.' The kindlier nature in us applauds his protest, but civilization shrieking 'Might is right', and with hands oft-times dripping with blood, marches forward, fulfilling the destiny of the world.

As McCormick's tribute anticipates, Billy Marshall has become something of a hero of the Left. His entry in the *Dictionary of National Biography* was written by Hamish Henderson (*see* 'FREEDOM COME-ALL-YE, THE'), and in his poem 'Pedigree', from *First Hymn to Lenin* (1931), Hugh MacDiarmid proclaims that if he could choose his ancestors, 'I'd ha'e Auld Ringan Oliver and the Caird o' Barullion.' *See also* AULD RINGAN OLIVER; KING OF THE GYPSIES.

Cairngorm Tragedy, the Britain's worst mountaineering disaster took place on 21–22 November 1971, when a school party was caught out on the plateau en route from the summit of Cairn Gorm to Corrour Bothy as a blizzard set in. Five schoolchildren and a trainee instructor died of exposure. Only one instructor and one pupil from the party survived.

Cairry-oot *See* CARRY-OOT.

Cairter Mary *See* KERTIN MARY.

Caisean-uchd According to Macleod and Dewar's *Gaelic–English Dictionary* of 1831, this was 'the breast-strip of a sheep killed at Christmas or New Year's Eve, and singed and smelled by each member of the family as a charm against fairies and spirits'. Macleod and Dewar state that *caisean* denotes 'anything curled, wrinkled or hairy, the dewlap or skin that hangs down from the breasts of cows ...', while *uchd* is 'breast, bosom'. Alexander Carmichael provides more detail in his *Carmina Gadelica* (1900):

> The strip is oval, and no knife must be used in removing it from the flesh. It is carried by the carollers when they visit the houses of the townland, and when lit by the head of the house it is given to each person in turn to smell, going sunwise [*DEISEIL*]. Should it go out, it is a bad omen for the person in whose hand it

becomes extinguished. The inhaling of the fumes of the burning skin and wool is a talisman to safeguard the family from fairies, witches, demons and other uncanny creatures during the year.

Cait Sith *See* WILDCAT.

Cake Day *See* HOGMANAY.

Calcutta Cup A trophy awarded to the winner of the annual rugby union match between Scotland and England. The cup owes its origins to the rugby match played on Christmas Day 1872 in Calcutta (now Kolkata), India, between a team of 20 Englishmen and a team of 20 Scottish, Irish and Welsh players. The following January saw the formation of the Calcutta Football Club, but the game of rugby turned out to be unsuited to the local climate, especially after the abolition of the free bar, and after four years the club disbanded and withdrew its funds from the bank. The funds were in the form of silver rupees, and these were melted down and made into a cup, which the former members presented to the Rugby Football Union back in Britain. They specified that it should be competed for annually in a club knock-out competition (like soccer's FA Cup), but the RFU frowned on competitiveness of this sort, and decided to hold an annual England vs Scotland match instead. The first match for which the cup was awarded was played at Raeburn Place, Edinburgh, on 10 March 1879, and ended in a draw. It has been played for every year since, apart from the war years 1915–19 and 1940–6. The original cup, of ornate workmanship, features three cobras as the handles, and a lid surmounted by an elephant. Both nations hold replicas, as the original is somewhat fragile, particularly after certain drunken players used it in an impromptu post-match game of football along Princes Street, Edinburgh, in 1988.

Caledonia The Roman name, first used by Tacitus, for the land to the north of the Antonine Wall (aka GRYME'S DYKE). The name came from the Caledones, a small tribe in Perthshire, although the name *Caledones* – possibly derived from a pre-Celtic word meaning 'hard people' or 'noisy people' – was

soon applied by the Romans to all the inhabitants of Caledonia. (The term *Picti* for these people first came into use by Roman writers at the end of the 3rd century AD; *see* PICTS.) After the Roman period, the name Caledonia was superseded by ALBA, ALBANY, SCOTIA and Scotland, although it surreptitiously survived in a number of place names: for example, Schiehallion, the Perthshire mountain, is from Gaelic *Sith Chailleann*, 'fairy hill of the Caledonians'; while Dunkeld is from Gaelic *Dùn Chailleann*, 'fort of the Caledonians'.

The name Caledonia was patriotically revived as a personification in the 18th century, starting with the anti-Unionist Lord Belhaven (1656–1708), who in the last days of the Scottish Parliament addressed his fellow members thus:

> I think I see our ancient mother Caledonia, like Caesar, sitting in the midst of our senate ... attending the final blow.

Tobias Smollett, in the wake of Culloden, wrote:

> Mourn, hapless Caledonia, mourn
> Thy banished peace, thy laurels torn.

Burns talks of 'brave Caledonia, the chief of her line', while Scott famously apostrophizes her in 'The LAND OF THE MOUNTAIN AND THE FLOOD':

> O Caledonia! stern and wild,
> Meet nurse for a poetic child!

By the 19th century 'Caledonia' had become a marketing brand: for example, the steamship company Caledonian MacBrayne (CAL-MAC), founded in 1878; the Caledonian express passenger service running between London and Glasgow in the 1950s and 1960s; and the five-star Caledonian Hotel in Edinburgh, opened in 1903. Caledonian FC, one of the precursors of Inverness Caledonian Thistle (*see* SUPER CALEY GO BALLISTIC, CELTIC ARE ATROCIOUS), was formed in 1885 or 1886. *See also* NEW CALEDONIA; OLD CALEDONIAN FOREST.

Caledonian antisyzygy, the A term coined by Gregory Smith in 1919 in *Scottish Literature: Character and Influence*. In this book Smith describes the 'antisyzygy' – the yoking together of opposites, the 'zigzag of contradictions' – that he sees as central to the Scottish character. This characteristic, according to Smith, is strongly represented in the national literature:

> Perhaps in the very combination of opposites – what either of the two Thomases, of Norwich and Cromarty, might have been willing to call 'the Caledonian antisyzygy' – we have a reflection of the contrasts which the Scot shows at every turn, in his political and ecclesiastical history, in his polemical restlessness, in his adaptability, which is another way of saying that he has made allowance for new conditions, in his practical judgement, which is the admission that two sides of the matter have been considered. If therefore, Scottish history and life are, as an old northern writer said of something else, 'varied with a clean contrair spirit', we need not be surprised to find that in his literature the Scot presents two aspects which appear contradictory. Oxymoron was ever the bravest figure, and we must not forget that disorderly order is order after all.

The yoking together of opposites – the respectable and the reprehensible, the romantic and the realist, the sentimental and the grotesque, the down-to-earth and the fantastical – is found in many Scottish writers, Scott and Hogg among them (notably in the latter's *Private Memoirs and Confessions of a Justified Sinner*). Byron found it in full measure in Burns, as he recorded in his journal in 1813:

> What an antithetical mind! – tenderness, roughness – delicacy, coarseness – sentiment, sensuality – soaring and grovelling, dirt and deity – all mixed up in that one compound of inspired clay.

The antisyzygy finds its most sharp-focused expression in Stevenson's 1886 novella, *The Strange Case of Dr Jekyll and Mr Hyde*, in which two violently contrasted characters are embodied in the same man. Subsequently, Hugh MacDiarmid became fascinated with the idea of the Caledonian antisyzygy, and consciously worked it into the mutating imagery, antitheses variable moods and contrasting planes of *A Drunk Man Looks at the Thistle* (1926). More recently, writers such as Irvine Welsh and Ian Rankin have sought to explore under the skirts of Scotland's tight-buttoned, matronly capital, to see whether Edinburgh really is AW FUR COAT AN NAE KNICKERS.

> ... drunken decency and sober violence,
> Our paradox of ways.
>   – Douglas Dunn, 'The Apple Tree', from *St Kilda's Parliament* (1981)

Caledonian Forest, the See OLD CALEDONIAN FOREST, THE.

Caledonian Orogeny, the A vast geological process responsible for building a belt of mountains extending from Ireland and Wales through northern England and Scotland (south and east of the Great Glen) to Norway. It took place from the late Silurian to the middle Devonian periods, as the landmasses gathered to form the supercontinent of Pangaea, some 420 to 390 million years ago.

More recent Caledonian orogenies have been proposed, but have come to nought. After Ordnance Survey measurements in 1846–7 demonstrated for the first time that Ben Nevis was higher than Ben Macdui, which previously held the crown as Britain's highest mountain, Macdui's owner, the Earl of Fife, decreed that he was to be buried on the mountain's summit under a vast cairn that would take its height from 4295 ft to something in excess of Nevis's 4406 ft. The plan never came to pass. Half a century later, in 1891, a correspondent, disappointed with Ben Nevis's generally lumpish demeanour, wrote to the *Glasgow Herald* suggesting Britain's loftiest peak might be enhanced

> ... by blasting with dynamite some of the neighbouring hills, where the excavation would not be noticed, and obtaining a supply of ... stones to be piled up to form a more lofty and graceful summit to the hill, bringing it to the full height of 5,000 feet, and giving the British tourist a finer mountain to look at and to ascend; the view would be superb.

See also WEST LOTHIAN ALPS.

Caley See FOOTBALL CLUB NICKNAMES.

Callanish Stone Circle See FIR CHREIG.

Callant's Festival, the The festivities associated with RIDING THE MARCHES in Jedburgh, in which the principal is known as the Jethart Callant (*callant*, 'youth, fellow'). The present form of the pageant dates from 1946. *See also* CAPON TREE, THE.

Caller herrin Freshly caught herring. 'Caller herrin' was a common cry by street vendors in former times, as celebrated in the famous song by Lady Nairne, the FLOWER OF STRATHEARN, to a tune by the fiddler Nathaniel Gow (son of the more famous Neil), a tune that blended Newhaven fishermen's cries with the chimes of the bells of St Andrews:

Wha'll buy caller herrin'?
They're bonny fish and halesome fairin';
Wha'll buy caller herrin'?
New-drawn frae the Forth?

Caller was also applied to other fresh foods. Robert Fergusson has a poem entitled 'Caller Oysters':

Auld Reekie's sons blyth faces wear;
September's merry month is near,
That brings in Neptune's caller chere,
New oysters fresh;
The halesomest and nicest gear
Of fish and flesh.

In one of his tales James Hogg rhetorically asked whether a man of taste could not distinguish 'sweet, callar, fresh lamb frae auld crock mutton' (*Tales and Sketches by the Ettrick Shepherd*, 1837), while the novelist Henry Mackenzie (1745–1831) recalled that 'The cry of *Caller Laverocks* [larks] was always heard in severe winters.' The word can also mean 'cool', and also 'healthy' or 'lively', as in:

O luely, luely cam she in
And luely she lay doun:
I kent her be her caller lips
And her breists sae sma' and roun'.
    – William Soutar (1898–1943), 'The Tryst'
    [*luely*, softly]

Call Ghàdhaig See LOSS OF GAICK, THE.

Cally Contemporary slang for Carlsberg Special Brew, a particularly potent brand of lager, often purchased in the morning by those who feel the need to top up on the night before.

Cal-Mac The familiar name for Caledonian Mac-Brayne, the shipping company that provides the vast majority of the ferry services around the Firth of Clyde and to and from the Hebrides.

The earth belongs unto the Lord,
And all that it contains;
Except the Kyles and the Western Isles,
And they are all MacBrayne's.
    – Anon. (20th century)

The company was founded in 1851 as David Hutcheson & Co, and in the 1870s was taken over by David MacBrayne. In 1973 most of the ships and routes operated by MacBrayne's were acquired by the Caledonian Steam Packet Co., to form Caledonian MacBrayne, with headquarters in Gourock. The company is now publicly owned by the Scottish Executive.

The end of the world is near when the MacBrayne's ship will be on time.
    – Iain Crichton Smith, 'Thoughts of Murdo'

Calton Hill, supernatural goings-on under See FAIRY BOY OF LEITH, THE.

Calton Weavers, the The handloom weavers of the village of Calton (now part of Glasgow), who in the summer of 1787 agitated for higher pay, destroying the work of those who worked for the old rates. The city magistrates tried to restore order, but were driven back by a crowd of some 7000 weavers and their families. Soldiers were sent in, and the Riot Act was read. Three weavers were killed in a volley of musket fire, and three died later of their wounds, becoming Scotland's first proletarian martyrs.

O, I'm a weaver, a Calton weaver;
I'm a rash and roving blade.
    – Anon., 'The Calton Weaver'

Camel of the Canongate, the A beast whose presence in Edinburgh was noted by John Nicoll, Writer to the Signet, in a diary entry for January 1659:

At this time there was brought to the nation ane high great beast called an Dromedary, whilk being keeped close in the Canongate, none had a sight of it without three pennies the person, whilk produced much gain to the keeper, in respect of the great numbers of people that resorted to it for the sight thereof. It was very big, and of great height, and cloven footed like unto a cow, and on the back ane seat, as it were a saddle to sit on.

There was brought in with it ane little baboon, faced like unto an ape.

Cameronians A strict sect of COVENANTERS, named after their founder, the Presbyterian 'field preacher' Richard Cameron (1648–80), known as 'the Lion of the Covenant'. Cameron's opposition to Charles II's attempt to impose episcopacy in Scotland led him to spend some years in exile in the Netherlands. He returned to Scotland in 1680, and on 22 June, in the town square of Sanquhar in Dumfriesshire, accompanied by a small band of armed men, issued the so-called Sanquhar Declaration. In this, he declared that the king 'and the men of his practices' were 'enemies to our Lord and His Crown, and the true Protestant and Presbyterian interest in this land'. He continued:

> As also we, being under the standard of our Lord Jesus Christ, Captain of Salvation, do declare a war with such a tyrant and usurper, and all the men of his practices, as enemies to our Lord Jesus Christ, and His cause and covenants; and against all such as have strengthened him, sided with, or anywise acknowledged him in his tyranny, civil or ecclesiastic; yea, against all such as shall strengthen, side with, or anywise acknowledge any other in like usurpation and tyranny – far more against such as would betray or deliver up our free reformed mother Kirk unto the bondage of Antichrist the Pope of Rome.

This declaration of war against the king brought about a swift and savage response – the beginning of the so-called KILLING TIME. Together with a number of other prominent Covenanters, Cameron himself was killed on 22 July, exactly a month later, in a skirmish at Airds Moss in east Ayrshire. Just before the fight, Cameron had uttered the following brief prayer: 'Lord, spare the green and take the ripe.' After his death his head was displayed on a pike, between his two hands, as if in prayer. A stone at Aird's Moss is inscribed with the following lines:

> Halt, curious passenger, come here and read,
> Our souls triumph with Christ our glorious Heid.
> In self-defence we murdered here do lie
> To witness 'gainst the nation's perjury.

After the Glorious Revolution, Cameron's armed followers were recruited into the army of William of Orange to fight against the forces of the Catholic James VII, whose exclusion from the succession Cameron had called for. On 16 April 1689 they were formed into a new regiment, called the 'Cameronian Regiment' by their enemies, 'whose oppression against all such as were not of their own sentiment made them generally hated and feared in the northern counties', according to one contemporary. The Cameronians played a key role in defeating the Jacobites at Dunkeld on 21 August 1689, and were later named the 26th (The Cameronian) Regiment of Foot. In 1881 this unit was merged with the 90th Perthshire Light Infantry to form the Cameronians (Scottish Rifles). In 1968, rather than amalgamate with another regiment, the Cameronians disbanded.

The Cameronian sect, meanwhile, had been unhappy with the religious settlement of 1690 and refused to take oaths of allegiance to a monarch who had not accepted the Covenant. They opposed the Union of 1707, and were subsequently suspected of intriguing with the Jacobites, although there is no evidence that they did. In 1743 a group called the Macmillanites – so-named after their leader, John Macmillan (1670–1753) – seceded from the mainstream Cameronians, believing the latter had strayed from the true path of the Reformation. Most Cameronian congregations united with the Free Church of Scotland in 1876.

Cam I early, cam I late ... *See* BLACK AGNES.

Campbellites Followers of the Revd John McLeod Campbell (1800–76), who was expelled from the ministry in 1831 for preaching the universality of atonement, which contradicted the received doctrine in the Kirk that God loved only the elect. However, in 1868 his abilities as a theologian were recognized when he was awarded an honorary doctorate by Glasgow University.

'Campbells Are Coming, The' A rousing marching song said to date from the 1715 Jacobite Rebellion, in which the Hanoverian forces under John Campbell, Duke of Argyll, were victorious over the insurgents:

> The Great Argyll he goes before,
> He makes the cannons and guns to roar,
> With sound o' trumpet, pipe and drum,
> The Campbells are coming, ho-ro, ho-ro!

The tune became the regimental march of the Sutherland Highlanders, and of its successor, the Argyll and Sutherland Highlanders. In 1857 during the Siege of Lucknow those trapped in the residency knew relief was at hand when they heard the distant pipes of Sir Colin Campbell's Sutherland Highlanders playing 'The Campbells Are Coming'.

In the late 18th century the tune became popular among the Anglo-Irish hell-raisers of Limerick, where it was known as 'Garryowen' (the name of an area of the city), and in 1807 Thomas Moore supplied some lyrics describing the riotous behaviour of the young gentlemen. The tune was subsequently adopted as its regimental march by the Royal Irish Lancers, and by many other regiments in Britain, Canada and the USA. It was played as General Custer led the US 7th Cavalry to annihilation at Little Big Horn.

Campbeltown See HAME; NEAREST PLACE TO NOWHERE, THE.

Camp Meg An eccentric character who in the early 19th century left her husband and a life of gentle-womanly comfort in the west of Scotland to live in a Napoleonic-era beacon house in Camp Wood, near Gorebridge, Midlothian. She made her living as a horse-doctor, and rode her horse Skewball in local races dressed as a man. A somewhat different account is found in *Cassell's Old and New Edinburgh* (1880s), although the author, James Grant, may possibly be confusing the village of Currie to the west of Edinburgh with the various 'Currie' place names to the southeast of Gorebridge:

> About the year 1820 there was found dead in one of the old camps near Currie a peculiar kind of recluse, who had a craze for haunting such places, and was known by the name of 'Camp Meg'. She was a strange, half-witted creature, weird, wild-looking, and bronzed by exposure; but as she spoke with a good English accent, was supposed to have been a soldier's widow. With no companion but a cat, she was first found occupying a little hut she had constructed for herself in an angle of the trenches of the Roman camp above Dalkeith [a few miles north of Gorebridge]. Of this place she constituted herself cicerone, and was wont to speak of Julius Agricola [the Roman general who had

campaigned in Scotland in the 1st century AD] and his officers as if she had known them all intimately. Dewar of Vogrie [a couple of miles northeast of Gorebridge], taking pity upon her, had a little hut properly built for her occupation; but a storm demolished it, on which she returned to her old den in the trenches. Then, after a time, she wandered away westward to another camp near Currie, also said to be one of Agricola's, and there 'Camp Meg' was found in her old age, dead of exposure and destitution.

Candy King of Glasgow, the See CHEUGH JEAN.

Cannibalistic Idiot, the See UNION DUKE, THE.

Cannibals Although Sawney BEAN remains Scotland's most famous cannibal (even if his actual existence remains problematic), various other cases of Caledonian anthropophagy have been recorded. In his *Book of Days* (1862–4), Robert Chambers mentions a number of such reports (which should equally be taken with a pinch of salt). First of all, Chambers cites a passage from St Jerome, who, on a visit to Gaul around 380, 'learned that the Attacotti, the people of the country now called Scotland, when hunting in the woods, preferred the shepherd to his flocks, and chose only the most fleshy and delicate parts for eating'.

Chambers goes on to quote from the *Orygynale Chronykil of Scotland* of Andrew of Wyntoun, who mentions a case from around the year 1339, not long before his own time, when the English armies of Edward III had laid waste some of the most fertile areas of Scotland:

> About Perth thare was the countrie
> Sae waste, that wonder wes to see;
> For intill well-great space thereby,
> Wes nother house left nor herb'ry.
> Of deer thare wes then sic foison [abundance],
> That they wold near come to the town.
> Sae great default was near that stead,
> That mony were in hunger dead.
>
> A Carle they said was near thereby,
> That wold set settis [traps] commonly,
> Children and women for to slay,
> And swains that he might over-ta;
> And ate them all that he get might:
> Chrysten Cleek till name be bight.

> That sa'ry life continued he,
> While waste but folk was the countrie.

In later folklore (not mentioned by Chambers) Chrysten Cleek became Christie-Cleek, supposedly the nickname of Andrew Christie, a butcher from Perth, who with his *cleek* (i.e. crook, or hooked staff) would pull his victims from their horses in the southern foothills of the Grampians, before butchering and devouring them. Christie-Cleek eventually became a sort of bogeyman to scare children into behaving themselves.

Finally, Chambers quotes from Lindsay of Pitscottie's *Historie and Chronicles of Scotland, 1436–1565*, regarding an instance from around 1460:

> About this time there was ane brigand ta'en, with his haill family, who haunted a place in Angus. This mischievous man had ane execrable fashion, to tak all young men and children he could steal away quietly, or tak away without knowledge, and eat them, and the younger they were, esteemed them the mair tender and delicious. For the whilk cause and damnable abuse, he with his wife and bairns were all burnt, except ane young wench of a year old, wha was saved and brought to Dundee, where she was brought up and fostered; and when she cam to a woman's years, she was condemned and burnt quick for that crime. It is said that when she was coming to the place of execution, there gathered ane huge multitude of people, and specially of women, cursing her that she was so unhappy to commit so damnable deeds. To whom she turned about with an ireful countenance, saying, 'Wherefore chide ye with me, as if I had committed ane unworthy act. Give me credence, and trow me, if ye had experience of eating men and women's flesh, ye wold think it so delicious, that ye wold never forbear it again.' So, but [without] any sign of repentance, this unhappy traitor died in the sight of the people.

For the so-called 'Cannibalistic Idiot', *see under* UNION DUKE, THE. *See also* MAC AN T-SRÒNAICH.

Cannonball House A 15th-century tenement building near the top of Edinburgh's Royal Mile, so named because high in its western gable wall is lodged a cannonball. Romantic fancy has it that it was fired from Edinburgh Castle by a pro-Hanoverian gunner aiming at Holyroodhouse, where Bonnie Prince Charlie was in residence in 1745. However, the more prosaic truth appears to be that it was inserted by engineers around 1620 to mark the precise height of the springs at Comiston, several miles to the south, from where fresh water was piped to fill the old Castlehill Reservoir, which supplied much of the Old Town.

Canntaireachd (Gaelic, 'chanting') A traditional and now rarely used method of notating classical bagpipe music using syllables. Vowels usually represented the notes of the melody, while consonants stood for grace notes, although there was no single standard system. *Canntaireachd* was transmitted entirely orally until first transcribed in the late 18th century. It has now largely been replaced by conventional staff notation.

Canongate breeks A euphemism, in use in the 17th and 18th centuries, for any sexually transmitted disease. *Breeks* are breeches, while the Canongate is the lower part of the Royal Mile in Edinburgh, once known as a resort of prostitutes and their clients. The phrase was used by, among others, the eccentric pamphleteer known as the TINCLARIAN DOCTOR:

> It is commonly called the Clap, or Glengore, and now under the Name of the *Canongate* Breeks.
> – William Mitchel, *A wonderful sermon, preached by the Tinclarian doctor, upon the nineteenth day of January 1734, and the sixty fourth year of his age, before hundreds of students of divinity, in … the College of Edinburgh* (1734)

Cant It is possible that the word *cant*, in the sense of insincere or hypocritical preaching on religious issues, accompanied by many a pious platitude, derives from the name of the Scottish Presbyterian minister, Andrew Cant (1590–1663). Although a staunch advocate of the National Covenant, Cant was also an enthusiastic Royalist who called for the Restoration of Charles II. His last ministry was in Aberdeen, where in 1660 a complaint was lodged with the magistrates, charging Cant with 'denouncing *anathemas* and *imprecations* against many of his congregation in the course of performing his religious duties' (Robert Chambers and Thos. Thomson, eds, *Biographical Dictionary of Eminent*

Scotsmen, 1856). Although proceedings commenced, Cant resigned before a judgement could be given.

The association of cant with Cant goes back at least to the early 18th century:

> Cant is, by some People, derived from one *Andrew Cant*, who, they say, was a Presbyterian Minister in some illiterate Part of *Scotland*, who by Exercise and Use had obtained the Faculty, *alias* Gift, of Talking in the Pulpit in such a Dialect, that it's said he was understood by none but his own Congregation, and not by all of them. Since *Mas. Cant's* time, it has been understood in a larger Sense, and signifies all sudden Exclamations, Whinings, unusual Tones, and in fine all Praying and Preaching, like the unlearned of the Presbyterians.
> – *The Spectator* No. 147, 18 August 1711

An alternative – and, sadly, more plausible – etymology for the word suggests a derivation from Norman French *canter*, Latin *cantare*, 'to sing', which since the 12th century had been used pejoratively of the chanting in church services. Certainly *cant* in the sense of the jargon or argot of an underworld or professional group can be dated prior to the Revd Cant:

> As far as I can learn or understand by the examination of a number of them, their language – which they term peddler's French or canting – began within these thirty years.
> – Thomas Harman, *Caveat, or Warning for Common Cursetors, Vulgarly Called Vagabonds* (1567)

See also UNCO GUID.

Caoir na mara Gaelic, 'flame of the sea'; *see* KERTIN MARY.

Caomhan Gaelic for 'dear one, darling', and formerly used as a propitiatory euphemism for the Devil. *Cf.* the Eumenides, 'the kindly ones', the name the ancient Greeks gave to the Furies.

Capercaillie See HORSE OF THE WOODS.

Capon Tree, the An 800-year-old oak near Jedburgh. The name possibly derives from the Capuchin monks who used to shelter under it en route to Jedburgh Abbey. The Jedburgh callants rallied here in times of trouble, and still do during the annual Callant's Festival. Nearby is another notable tree, the KING OF THE WOOD.

Cap's aye oot fin it's rainin' kail, (one's) Literally, '(one's) cup is always out when it's raining cabbage', i.e. one has one's eye on the main chance. The expression is from the Northeast.

Captain Burly A sobriquet of John Balfour of Kinloch, an extreme COVENANTER, and one of the murderers of Archbishop Sharp in 1679. Following the assassination, Balfour appears to have fought at Drumclog the same year, and participated in Argyll's Rising in 1685, after which he disappears from the annals of history. His nickname referred to his build, but sometimes led to him being confused with one of the Balfours of Burleigh. Scott made this mistake in *Old Mortality*, in which one of Sharp's assassins, and one of the central characters of the novel, is Balfour of Burley.

Carbonari claim Scottish origin *See* NEXT YEAR IN SCOTLAND.

Carbuncle Awards A series of trophies awarded since 2001 to bleak localities in Scotland by a panel appointed by *Urban Realm*, a Scottish on-line architectural magazine. The trophies include the Plook on the Plinth Award (*plook* being the contemporary Scots word for 'pimple'), given to Scotland's most dismal town (winners have included Cumbernauld, Coatbridge, Glenrothes and JOHN O'GROATS), the Pock Mark Award for worst planning disaster, and the Zit Building Award for worst new building.

Carbuncle of Ward Hill, the A legend pertaining to Ward Hill on the island of Hoy, Orkney. It was said that on the slope of the hill above the DWARFIE STANE there was a carbuncle (gemstone) that could be seen from below, but which disappeared when one climbed towards it. The *Orkneyinga Saga* weaves the story of the carbuncle into that of Snorro the Dwarf. In *The Cruise of the Betsey* (1857), the geologist Hugh Miller sadly records that he could see no sign of it on his visit:

The sun broke out in great beauty after the shower, glistening on a thousand minute runnels that came streaming down the precipices, and revealing, through the thin vapoury haze, the horizontal lines of strata that bar the hill-sides, like courses of ashlar in a building. I failed, however, to detect, amid the general many-pointed glitter by which the blue gauze-like mist was bespangled, the light of the great carbuncle for which the Ward Hill has long been famous, – that wondrous gem, according to Sir Walter [Scott, in *The Pirate* (1821)], 'that, though it gleams ruddy as a furnace to them that view it from beneath, ever becomes invisible to him whose daring foot scales the precipices whence it darts its splendour.'

The Northern Sutor of Cromarty was once supposed to hold a similar jewel; *see under* SOUTAR.

Carcake *See* FASTERN EVE; CULROSS GIRDLE.

Care's ma case Woe is me. The expression comes from the Northeast.

Carlin An old hag or witch. The word forms part of the name of a number of topographic features. *Carlin's Leap* (or Witch's Step), a translation of Gaelic Ceum na Caillich, is a gash in Arran's main mountain ridge; *Carlin Maggie* is a pinnacle on Bishop Hill, Fife; while *Carlin's Cairn* is a subsidiary top of Corserine, a high hill in Galloway. *Carlin's Loup* ('witch's leap') is the prominent rock in the Pentland village of Carlops (which is named after it), from where women suspected of being witches were formerly thrown. If they flew they were guilty, and if they plunged to their deaths they were clearly innocent. *See also* FAIRIES O' CARLOPS.

The word *carlin* also denoted the last sheaf cut at harvest, or the corn dolly made from this. *Carlin heather* was bell heather, and *carlin spurs* gorse.

Carnwath-like A term current in the 19th century for 'awkward', 'wild-looking', 'distorted', after the Lanarkshire village, home of the RED HOSE RACE, and whose inhabitants are locally known as WHITE CRAWS. In the past various theories were put forward as to the reason for the phrase: from the wild appearance of the surrounding country; from 'the tortuous nature of the village, which twists like a

snake and has five exits in different directions'; because, according to Robert Chambers, 'The old church of Carnwath had its bell at the wrong end, namely the east.'

Carried into France or Holland in a night *See* FAIRY BOY OF LEITH, THE.

Carritch The catechism, sanctioned by the General Assembly in 1648. The Shorter Catechism was known as the *Single Carritch* or *Mither's Carritch*.

> My mother gar'd me learn the Single Carritch, whilk was a great vex ...
> – Sir Walter Scott, *Old Mortality* (1816), chapter xxxvii

Carronade A species of light, short-range naval cannon, taking its name from its place of manufacture, the Carron Ironworks, established in 1760 on the River Carron near Falkirk. The carronade was adopted by the Royal Navy in 1779, and remained in service until the mid-19th century.

There are two connections between Robert Burns on the one hand and the carronade and the Carron Ironworks on the other. In 1787, en route to the Highlands, the poet called at the Ironworks, but was declined admission. That evening, with a diamond pen, he scratched a riposte on a window in the inn where he was staying:

> We cam na here to view your warks,
> In hopes to be mair wise,
> But only, lest we gang to hell,
> It may be nae surprise:
> But when we tirl'd at your door
> Your porter dought na hear us;
> Sae may, shou'd we to Hell's yetts come,
> Your billy Satan sair us!
> [*yetts*, gates; *sair*, serve]

The second connection came five years later, in 1792, when Burns sent a gift of four carronades to the French Convention, which landed him in some trouble (*see* 'DEIL'S AWA' WI' TH'EXCISEMAN, THE').

Carrot Sunday (Gaelic *Domhnach Curran*) The Sunday before Michaelmas (29 September), when in the Highlands and Islands the women traditionally dug up the carrots, which were regarded as symbols of fertility. The harvesting was accompanied by appropriate songs, such as the following, recorded in the later 19th century by Alexander Carmichael in his *Carmina Gadelica*:

Torcan torrach, torrach, torrach,
Sonas curran corr orm,
Michael mil a bhi dha m'chonuil,
Bride gheal dha m'chonradh.
Piseach linn gach piseach,
Piseach dha mo bhroinn,
Piseach linn gach piseach,
Piseach dha mo chloinn.
(Cleft fruitful, fruitful, fruitful,
Joy of carrots surpassing upon me,
Michael the brave endowing me,
Bride the fair be aiding me.
Progeny pre-eminent over every progeny,
Progeny on my womb,
Progeny pre-eminent over every progeny,
Progeny on my progeny.)

The disinterment of a forked carrot provoked particular delight.

Carrying up the baby An old custom, described in this account from the west of Scotland, dated 1879:

When a child was taken from its mother and carried outside the bedroom for the first time after its birth, it was lucky to take it up stairs, and unlucky to take it down stairs.

If there were no stairs, then carrying the baby up three steps of a ladder, or up onto a box or chair, would suffice.

Carry-oot (1) Alcoholic drink purchased from an off-licence, pub, etc., for consumption elsewhere. (2) Takeaway food.

It started t dawn on them that th drink wis runnin oot. Bit o a stooshie, that. 'We'll hae to go fur a cairry-oot' says Erchie. 'Oan new years morning! Whaur'll we get that?' 'The co-op. It's aye got drink!' So, aff they aw went – in drag – roond tae the co-op. Wisnae open, of coorse ...
– Helen Ross, 'The Stookie', www.tachras.co.uk/journal/ articles3/kirklands/kirk1.htm

Foodwise, the opposite to a carry-oot is a *sittie-doon* or a *sittie-in*.

Casket Letters, the A collection of letters supposedly sent by Mary Queen of Scots to the man who became her third husband – James Hepburn, Earl of Bothwell. Many among the Scottish aristocracy were infuriated at Mary's choice of husband, which they feared eclipsed their own power and influence. Bothwell was widely held responsible for the murder of the queen's second husband, Lord Darnley. By June 1567 the nobles, led by the Earl of Morton and Maitland of Lethington, had come out in rebellion; Bothwell fled, and Mary was taken prisoner, and the following month was forced to abdicate. The casket in question was said to have been found in the possession of one of Bothwell's servants, and the contents were produced as evidence in December 1568 at the inquiry in Westminster into Mary's alleged complicity in Darnley's murder. The originals had disappeared by the end of the 16th century, but copies made by the Westminster clerks remain. The consensus among historians is that some of the letters *were* from Mary to Bothwell, others were from Mary to someone else, some were written to Bothwell by a third party, and that several contain a degree of forgery by a person unknown.

Castle, a smile and a song, a The Glaswegians have a saying: 'Edinburgh! A castle, a smile and a song ... One out of three isn't bad.' *See also* WISE MEN.

Castlecary Rail Disaster A serious accident in which 35 people were killed and 179 injured. It occurred in dark and snowy conditions on the evening of 10 December 1937, when the Edinburgh–Glasgow express crashed into the rear of the stationary Dundee–Glasgow local. The former was travelling at some 70 mph, too fast for the conditions, although the official inquiry concluded the signalman was to blame.

Castle Gloom The original name of Castle Campbell, a partly restored and loftily positioned ruin perched in the Ochil Hills at the head of Dollar Glen, above the Clackmannanshire town of Dollar. The place is first recorded in a papal bull of 1466, which mentions 'a tower of the place of Glowm'; it acquired its present name in 1489 after it came, via marriage, into the hands of the Campbells of Argyll, and was burnt down by the Marquess of Montrose in 1645, and again in 1654 by General Monck. Nearby, overlooking the castle, is Gloom Hill, reputedly once a favourite venue for witches' covens, while below the castle is the confluence of the Burn of Sorrow and the Burn of Care, names presumably inspired by the 'Gloom' connection; similarly, romantics have interpreted the name Dollar as deriving from 'dolour', although, more prosaically, it is in fact an old Brythonic name meaning 'arable field'.

> Oh, Castell Gloom! Thy strength is gone,
> The green grass o'er thee growin';
> On Hill of Care thou art alone,
> The Sorrow round thee flowin'.
>
> O Castell Gloom! on thy fair wa's
> Nae banners now are streamin.
> The houlet flings amang thy ha's,
> And wild birds there are screamin'.
>   – Lady Carolina Nairne, 'Castell Gloom' [*houlet*, 'owl']
>
> Thy green old Castle Campbell stands,
>   Majesticly on high;
> Though part hath crumbled into sand,
>   In waste and ruin lie,
> Its lofty walls hath sheltered friends,
>   And foes they did beguile,
> Yea, shelter they did oftimes lend
>   Unto the great Argyle.
>   – Sylvester H. Neil, 'Rural Walks Near Dollar' (1873)

Castration William Daniell, in his *Voyage Round Great Britain* (1815–25), tells the story of a Macnaughten clansman on Lewis who attracted the jealous suspicions of his chieftain, who 'doomed him to the fate of Abelard'. The unfortunate man thereafter suffered 'the pitying derision of his fellows', but he seemed patiently reconciled to his fate until one day he seized the son of the chieftain and carried him away to the top of a precipice at Dunoul near Tolsta. Whenever his pursuers approached, he threatened to hurl both himself and the boy into oblivion. He said he would only release the boy on one condition, that the chieftain 'should undergo the same torture which had been inflicted on himself':

> The distracted parent submitted to this terrible retaliation; but still the avenger insisted on some evidence which might satisfy him that it had actually been

inflicted. He required to know, ere he quitted his refuge, what particular sensation had been produced. The reply was, an acute and agonizing pain in the lower region of the spine. Having thus ascertained, on testimony which no one but the patient could then produce, that the sentence had been executed, he instantly sprung from the precipice with the child in his arms; they perished together; and thus was the hope of the Macnaughtens blasted for ever.

See also MASSACRE CAVE, THE.

Caterans Highland freebooters and raiders, 'especially such,' says John Jamieson in *An Etymological Dictionary of the Scottish Language* (1808), 'as came down from the Highlands to the low country, and carried off cattle, corn, or whatever pleased them, from those who were not able to make resistance'. The word probably comes from Gaelic *ceatharn*, 'a troop', or *ceathairneach*, 'robber, plunderer'; an alternative (less plausible) suggestion is Welsh *cethern*, 'furies, fiends'.

Ca the coos oot the kailyard, to Literally, 'to call the cows out of the cabbage patch', i.e. to perform some simple task. If something is *no worth ca'in oot o' a kailyard* then it is worthless.

Cathedral of the Seas, the How Keats characterized FINGAL'S CAVE.

Cat in barrel 'A barbarous game,' opines the *Scottish National Dictionary*, 'formerly played at Kelso once a year.' A full account is provided by Ebenezer Lazarus in his *Description of Kelso* (1789):

> This is a sport which was common in the last century at Kelso on the Tweed. A large concourse of men, women, and children assembled in a field about half a mile from the town, and a cat having been put into a barrel stuffed full of soot, was suspended on a crossbeam between two high poles. A certain number of the whipmen, or husbandmen, who took part in this savage and unmanly amusement, then kept striking, as they rode to and fro on horseback, the barrel in which the unfortunate animal was confined, until at last, under the heavy blows of their clubs and mallets, it broke, and allowed the cat to drop. The victim was then seized and tortured to death.

Percy, in his *Reliques of Ancient English Poetry* (1794), asserts:

It is still a diversion in Scotland to hang up a cat in a small cask or firkin, half filled with soot; and then a parcel of clowns on horseback try to beat out the ends of it, in order to show their dexterity in escaping before the contents fall upon them.

A similar 'sport' is referred to by Benedick in Shakespeare's *Much Ado About Nothing* (I.i): 'If I do, hang me in a bottle like a cat, and shoot at me.'

Cat kindness A Northeastern expression for cupboard love.

Cats-an'-kitlins Catkins, the yellow tail-shaped inflorescences of the hazel, pussy willow, etc.

Cat's hair (1) A Northeastern expression for cirrus or cirrostratus cloud. (2) The down of unfledged birds, or on the faces of unbearded boys.

Cats roasted on spit *See* TAGHAIRM.

Cat-witted (1) Hare-brained. (2) Spiteful and irate.

Cauld iron *See* FISHERMEN'S TABOOS.

Cauld parritch is sooner het again than new anes made A saying recorded in Andrew Henderson's *Proverbs* (1832).

Cauld kail Cold cabbage, the epitome of plain fare, as celebrated by Burns:

There's cauld kail in Aberdeen,
And castocks in Strathbogie,
When ilka lad maun hae his lass,
Then fye, gie me my coggie.
   [*castocks*, cabbage stalks; *coggie*, dish]

The association with Aberdeen (the CITY OF BON ACCORD) has persisted:

Cauld kail, and castocks ... never be they scant with those
Wha coup the cog in Bon-Accord.
   – J. Imlah, *Poems and Songs* (1841)

The expression *cauld kail het again* (literally 'warmed-up leftovers') refers to an old story that one has heard many times before.

Celtic Earldoms of Alba, the *See under* MORMAER.

Celtic Homer, the *See* OSSIAN FORGERIES, THE.

Centre of the intelligence of England, the Glasgow, according to Grand Duke Alexis of Russia when he visited the city in 1880 to attend the launch of the *Livadia*, a steam yacht commissioned by Tsar Alexander II and built at the John Elder yard in Govan.

Ceòl Mór *See* PIBROCH.

Ceremonies, rituals, beliefs, customs, celebrations, fairs and festivals The reader is referred to the following entries:

• BACK FEAST
• BANNOCKBURN DAY
• BARTLE FAIR
• BELLS, THE
• BELTANE
• BLACKENING
• BLITHEMEAT
• BLOOD-DRINKING
• BRAW LADS' GATHERING, THE
• BULLION'S DAY
• BURNING THE CLAVIE
• BURNS NIGHT
• BURRYMAN, THE
• CALLANT'S FESTIVAL, THE
• CARROT SUNDAY
• CHRISTENING PIECE
• CHRISTMAS
• CLEIKUM CEREMONIES, the
• *CORP CRIADH* CREAM OF THE WATER, the
• CUMMERS' FEAST
• CURD FAIR
• DAFT FRIDAY
• DOOKING FOR APPLES
• DREAMING BREAD
• DREAMING OF THE DEAD
• DUDS DAY
• FALKIRK TRYST
• FAMINE OF THE FARM
• FIERY CROSS
• FIREBALLS, the

- FIRST FOOT
- FISHERMEN'S TABOOS
- Flitting Day (*see under* FLIT)
- FOUNDING PINT
- GLEN SATURDAY
- GOODMAN'S CROFT
- GRAVEYARD WATCH
- GROZET FAIR
- HALLOWEEN
- HAME-FARE
- HANDFAST
- HANDSEL MONDAY
- HAT AND RIBBON RACE
- HIGHLAND GAMES
- HUMAN SACRIFICE
- HUNTEGOWK
- HUNT OF PENTLAND, the
- ILL EE
- INFAR CAKE
- KATE KENNEDY PROCESSION
- KELTON HILL FAIR
- KIDNEY
- KIRKING SUNDAY
- LAMMAS DAY
- LANIMER DAY
- LEGAVRIK
- LIFTING DAY
- LILIAS DAY
- LIVE BURIAL
- MARYMASS FAIR
- MAY DIP, the
- MEAL AND ALE
- PACE EGG
- PENNY BRIDAL
- PREEN-TAIL DAY
- PULLING THE CORNHEAD FROM THE STACK
- PUT TO THE HORN
- QUARTER DAYS
- RAISING THE WIND
- RAISIN WEEKEND
- RASCAL FAIR
- RED HOSE RACE
- RIDING THE MARCHES
- RIDING THE STANG
- SCOTS CONVOY
- SKIRE THURSDAY
- SMA' SHOT DAY
- STRUAN MICHAEL

- *TAGHAIRM*
- TENANT'S DAY
- THROWING THE STOCKING
- UP-HELLY-AA
- WASHING THE APRON
- WHUPPITY SCOORIE

Cesar The nickname of the footballer Billy McNeill (b.1940), who played for Celtic from 1957 to 1975, and won 29 Scottish caps. He subsequently managed a number of teams, including Celtic, and in 2002 Celtic fans voted him the team's best-ever captain; in 1967 he had led the LISBON LIONS to victory in the European Cup. His nickname derives from the actor Cesar Romero (1907–94), who played the Joker in the *Batman* TV series.

Ceud mile fàilte Gaelic for 'a hundred thousand welcomes', a traditional greeting also found in Irish (*céad míle fáilte*) and Manx (*keead meel failt*), and on innumerable place-name signs. In Scottish Gaelic it is pronounced *kee*-ut *mee*-luh *fah*-il-tya.

Champagne Charlie A nickname of the Liberal Democrat politician Charles Kennedy, born in Inverness in 1959 and raised in Fort William. He became leader of the party in 1999, but was obliged to resign in 2006 after admitting to a drink problem. He was succeeded by fellow-Scot Sir Menzies Campbell (aka MING THE MERCILESS).

Champit or **chappit tatties** Mashed potatoes, which, along with *bashit neeps* (mashed turnip), is an essential accompaniment to HAGGIS, as served, for example, on BURNS NIGHT. If the tatties and the neeps are mixed together, the result is called *clapshot*, which was traditionally served at Halloween and at harvest-home suppers.

Change one's breath, to To take a wee dram. The expression has been recorded in eastern and southern Scotland.

Chapter of Myton, the The name given by the victorious Scots to the Battle of Myton, fought on the River Swale in Yorkshire on 20 September 1319. The Scots, led by the BLACK DOUGLAS, defeated a scratch English army assembled at short notice by

William Melton, Archbishop of York. The nickname refers to the large number of clerics who fought and died for the English – hence its alternative name, the *White Battle*, alluding to the surplices of the hundreds of dead priests.

'Charlie is My Darling' A traditional Jacobite song, with versions by Robert Burns, Lady Nairne, James Hogg and Charles Gray (1782–1851). 'Charlie' is, of course, Prince Charles Edward Stuart, who was known both as the YOUNG CHEVALIER and the YOUNG PRETENDER.

> They've left their bonnie Highland hills,
> Their wives and bairnies dear,
> To draw the sword for Scotland's lord,
> The young Chevalier.
>> Charlie is my darling, my darling, my darling.
>> Charlie is my darling, the young Chevalier.

Charlieoverthewaterism *See* WALLACETHEBRUCE-ISM.

Charms, amulets and spells *See*:
- BARBRECK'S BONE
- CAISEAN-UCHD
- CLACH NA BRATAICH
- CORP CRIADH
- ELF-SHOTS
- FAIRY FLAG, the
- HORSE AND HATTOCK
- LEE PENNY, the
- STITCH STONE
- TOAD STONES

Chaseabout Raid, the The short-lived rebellion of James Stewart, 1st Earl of Moray, in August–September 1565 against Mary Queen of Scots, his half-sister. Moray, a Protestant, objected to Mary, a Catholic, marrying another Catholic, Henry Stewart, Lord Darnley. However, many of the Protestant lords failed to support Moray, and Mary, with a steel cap on her head and a pistol in her saddle holster, personally led her troops around the country in hot pursuit of the rebel earl – a circumstance that gave the episode its name. As the English ambassador Thomas Randolph reported: 'The queen followeth them so near with such forces – and so much the stronger by reason of

her musketeers – that she giveth them no time to rest in any place.' By October Moray was forced to retire into England, but returned to Scotland the following year, after the murder of Rizzio, and was pardoned by the queen. Upon Mary's abdication in 1567 Moray became regent, and defeated her forces at Langside in 1568. Known as 'the GOOD REGENT', he oversaw a period of relative peace in Scotland until his murder in 1570.

Chatty-puss The call by which cats in Fife and the Northeast are summoned by their humans. *Chatty* may be from French *chat*, 'cat'.

Chaud melle or **mella** A former defence in Scottish law against a charge of murder, indicating that the crime was committed in a moment of passion. The term, first recorded in the 14th century, is from French *chaud mellée*, 'heated affray'.

> By our law, says [Sir George Mackenzie, the 17th-century jurist known as BLUIDY MACKENZIE], slaughter and murder did of old differ, as 'homicidium simplex et premeditatum' in the civil law; and murder only committed, as we call it, upon forethought felony, was only properly called murder, and punished as such; for which he quotes the express statute, par. 3, cap. 51. K. James 1, appointing that murder be capitally punished, but *chaud melle*, or slaughter committed upon suddenty, shall only be punishable according to the old laws …
>> – *A Complete Collection of State Trials and proceedings for high treason and other crimes and misdemeanours from the earliest period to the year 1783*, Vol. XVII (1816), ed. T.B. Howell

According to *Bell's Dictionary and Digest of the Law of Scotland* (seventh edition, 1890), 'The person guilty of this offence had the benefit of sanctuary, from which, however, he might have been taken for trial; but if he proved *chaud melle*, he was returned safe in life and limb.' *See also* SANCTUARY.

Chawed moose, to look like a Literally, 'to look like a chewed mouse', i.e. to look careworn, raddled or debauched.

Cheat-the-belly A term applied to any insubstantial food, such as puff pastry.

Cheat-the-wuddy One who has cheated the (wooden) gallows, hence any villain, rogue or ne'er-do-well. In Scott's *Rob Roy* (1818), Bailie Nicol Jarvie addresses the eponymous hero thus:

> Conscience! if I am na clean bumbaized – *you*, ye cheat-the-wuddy rogue – *you* here on your venture in the tolbooth o' Glasgow? – What d'ye think's the value o' your head?
> – chapter xxii

For another literary appearance of the term, *see under* LAND-LOWPER.

Cheeky watter A Glaswegian euphemism for any spirituous liquor. *Silly watter* means the same.

Cheswell one was made in, the One's original social class; the expression is now obsolete. A *cheswell*, literally 'cheese well', is a cheese mould or cheese press.

Cheuchter *See* TEUCHTER.

Cheugh jean A kind of sweet that became a speciality of 'Ball Allan', a 19th-century confectioner known as 'the Candy King of Glasgow', who described them as 'luscious lumps of sweetness that yield themselves into a liquid satisfaction in the warmth of the mouth'. They came in a variety of flavours, including clove, cinnamon, ginger, peppermint and chocolate. *Cheugh* means 'tough' or 'chewy', but the origin of the second element remains obscure.

Chevalier St George, the James Francis Edward Stuart, the OLD PRETENDER (aka DISMAL JIMMY); he was a member of the Confrerie des Chevaliers de Saint-Georges, a French chivalric order created in 1390 by Phillibert de Mollans. His son, the YOUNG CHEVALIER, was also a member.

Cheviot, the Stag and the Black, Black Oil, The One of the best-known plays of the Liverpudlian dramatist John McGrath, long associated with the 7:84 (Scotland) Theatre Company (so-called, like its English namesake, in reference to a statistic published in *The Economist* in 1966 that revealed that 7 per cent of the population of Britain owned 84 per cent of the wealth). The musical show was first performed in village halls in remote areas of the Highlands and Islands, and is a satire on the changes imposed on the area, firstly by the CLEARANCES, in which people were evicted from the land to make way for sheep farming (hence 'the Cheviot', a breed of sheep) and sporting estates (hence 'the stag'), and more recently by tourism and the discovery of oil in the North Sea. *The Scotsman*'s theatre critic, Joyce Macmillan, called the play a 'brilliant ceilidh of rage and laughter against the exploitation of land and people'.

Chevy Chase *See* HUNTING OF THE CHEVIOT, THE.

Chewing one's own shield *See* LEWIS CHESSMEN.

Chicken Balmoral *See* HAGGIS.

Chief of all Scotland, the How the French chronicler Jean Froissart describes Edinburgh in his *Chronicles* (late 14th century).

Chieftain o' the puddin' race *See* GREAT CHIEFTAIN O' THE PUDDIN' RACE.

Children of nature under Robert Burns, and the children of grace under John Knox, the *See* DOURNESS.

Children of the Mist A name given to the MacGregors (from the Gaelic *Clann na Cheo*), presumably after the clan was proscribed (*see* MACGREGOR, PROSCRIPTION OF CLAN).

Children of the Seals In Gaelic, *Sliochd nan Ron*, a name given to the MacCodums of North Uist, who are legendarily descended from the match of a human male and a seal who had transformed herself into human form. Her mate kept her that way for years by hiding her seal skin, preventing her from returning to her own kind. *See also* SILKIE.

Chill looking for a spine to run up, a A phrase deployed by Oliver Brown to describe the shocked Labour reaction to Winnie Ewing (aka MADAME ECOSSE) winning the 1967 Hamilton by-election for the SNP, which thus gained its first MP at West-minster:

> The late Oliver Brown ... put it well. He said that when I won Hamilton, you could feel a chill along the Labour back benches, looking for a spine to run up.
> – Winnie Ewing, quoted in Kenneth Roy, *Conversations in a Small Country* (1989)

Ewing herself famously announced at the time of her election: 'STOP THE WORLD, SCOTLAND WANTS TO GET ON.'

Chitterin bit Literally a 'shivering bite', i.e. a snack or sweetie eaten after a cold swim.

> The same reflected sky, the same blue shout through which a bather plunges, and runs out, his sticky shin rubbed dry with towelled grit, a gravelly biscuit for his chittering bit.
> – Maurice Lindsay, *Collected Poems* (1979)

See also PIECE.

Choccy The nickname of the former Celtic, Motherwell and Scotland footballer Brian McClair (b.1963). Choccy, short for chocolate éclair, is rhyming slang for his surname.

Chooky Embra, ra How Prince Philip is known in parts of Glasgow.

Chowed mouse *See* CHAWED MOOSE, TO LOOK LIKE A.

Christening piece A gift given by a mother to the first person she meets while taking her infant to be christened. Sometimes it has to be a person of the opposite sex to the baby, sometimes it has to be a man, sometimes a child. The PIECE in question usually consists of a snack – for example, a biscuit, a hunk of cheese and some gingerbread, or a couple of buttered biscuits with a silver coin sandwiched in between them – and it was good luck for the recipient to give the mother a silver coin in return. The custom, which dates to at least the early 19th century, appears to have largely died out. *See also* FIRST FOOT.

Christie-Cleek *See* CANNIBALS.

Christis Kirk on the Green A late medieval or early Renaissance poem, variously attributed to James I, James V and Anon., vigorously depicting the rustic revels of a *wappinshaw* or country fair, the wooing, the wild dancing, the quarrels, the boisterous fun:

> The wyvis kest vp ane hiddouss yell,
> Quhen all thir yunkeris yokkit
> Als ferss as ony fyrflaucht fell,
> Freikis to the feild thay flokkit;
> The carilis with clubbis cowd vder quell,
> Quhill blud at breistis out bokkit:
> So rudly rang the commoun bell,
> Quhill all the stepill rokkit,
> For reird,
> At Chrystis kirk of the grene.

The title suggests the congregation of the church let out to play on the village green. Allan Ramsay added two further cantos in 1716 and 1718, and the so-called 'Christis Kirk' genre, and its associated stanza, was added to by both Fergusson and Burns.

Christmas Before it was done away with by the 16th-century Reformers as a papish and/or pagan institution, Christmas was enthusiastically cele-brated in Scotland. In the Outer Hebrides, the fishing boats would donate the catch made that day to the poor and needy, and the fishermen would sing the following Gaelic hymn as they set out:

> I will cast my hook:
> The first fish that I catch,
> In the name of Christ, King of the Elements,
> The poor shall have for his need,
> And the King of Fishers, Saint Peter,
> Will give me his blessing.

Before the Reformation, Scotland had its own rich carol tradition, as the following extract attests:

> Jerusalem, rejois for joy!
> Jesus, the sterne of maist bewté
> In the is risin, as richtous roy,
> Fra derknes to illumine the:
> With glorius sound of angell gle
> The Prince is born in Bethlehem
> Quhilk sall the maik of thraldom fre,
> *Illuminare Jerusalem.*

A law of 1581 banned all the old religious usages as superstition and idolatry, condemning among many other practices 'singing of carolis within and about kirkis at certain seasonis of the yeir'. For a first offence, the culprit could expect a fine; for a second offence, any person convicted was 'to suffer the pain of deid as idolatoris'.

In the absence of Christmas, midwinter celebrations were concentrated at HOGMANAY and NE'ER-DAY, and it was only in the decades after the Second World War that (largely from commercial pressure) Christmas made a comeback in Scotland.

Chronicles of the Canongate The collective title that Sir Walter Scott gave to some of his later novels and stories. The first series (1827) includes *The Surgeon's Daughter*, 'The Highland Widow' and 'The Two Drovers', and the second series (1828) includes *Saint Valentine's Day, or The Fair Maid of Perth*. The fictional narrative framework is that the tales originate in the memory of Mrs Bethune Baliol of the Canongate – the lower part of Edinburgh's ROYAL MILE – as told to and recorded by her friend, Mr Chrystal Croftangry. The name 'Canongate' originates in the 12th century, when David I granted the canons of Holyrood Abbey jurisdiction over the area.

Churchill Barriers, the The four concrete causeways linking the Orkney mainland and the islands of Burray and South Ronaldsay, via the smaller islands of Lamb Holm and Glimps Holm. They were built on the orders of Winston Churchill, then First Lord of the Admiralty, to create a barrier preventing eastern access to the Scapa Flow naval anchorage, after a German U-boat had penetrated the defences and sunk the battleship HMS *Royal Oak* on 14 October 1939. Work began in May 1940 and was completed in September 1944, much of the labour being supplied by Italian prisoners of war (some of whom were responsible for the ITALIAN CHAPEL on Lamb Holm). The barriers now carry a main road.

Cìrein Cròin See SEA SERPENTS.

Cities See FOUR CITIES, THE.

City of Bon Accord A name sometimes applied to Aberdeen. 'Bon accord', the motto of the city, was traditionally the rallying cry of the citizens when, under Robert the Bruce, they fought to take back

their castle. The phrase derives from the French for 'good agreement', and denotes harmony, friendliness and general benignity, thus belying the city's reputation for tight-fistedness (*see* ABERDONIAN JOKES). In the later Middle Ages the town council annually elected an Abbot and Prior of Bonaccord, two officials whose task was to organize sporting events and other entertainments in which all the citizens were expected to take part, or otherwise face a fine. The former was also known as the 'Abbot Out of Reason', and in the early 16th century the pair were elevated to the status of 'Lordis of Bonaccord'.

Today, the passenger train running between Aberdeen and Glasgow is called the Bon Accord, while Aberdeen City Council is located in Bon Accord Street; there is also a Bon Accord Shopping Centre where the good citizens flock to spend their pennies.

> The Guestrow, Gallowgate, and Green,
> Eke Fittie, Broadgate and Broadford,
> A' the four bows o' Aberdeen –
> Our ain 'braif toun' o' Bon-Accord.
> – Quoted in J. Riddell, *Aberdeen and Its Folk* (1868)

City of St Michael, the Dumfries, according to the Revd E. Cobham Brewer in his *Dictionary of Phrase and Fable*, first published in 1870, and revised by him in 1896. The term is preserved in the 18th edition (2009). Although St Michael is the patron saint of Dumfries, the name 'City of St Michael' does not appear to have been widely adopted.

City of St Nicholas, the Aberdeen, whose patron saint is St Nicholas, chosen because of the miracle he performed in rescuing some sailors in a storm – Aberdeen having for long been an important fishing port. In the Middle Ages, the Kirk of St Nicholas was the only burgh kirk in Aberdeen, hence it is also known as 'the Mither Kirk'.

Citz, the The familiar nickname of the Citizens' Theatre in Glasgow. The Citizens' Company, a repertory group founded in 1943, was first based at the Glasgow Athenaeum, but in 1945 moved to its present Gorbals venue, then known as the Royal Princess's Theatre (opened in 1878), and now known as the Citizens' Theatre.

Clach na Brataich The 'banner stone' of Clan Robertson. Prior to joining the forces of Robert the Bruce before Bannockburn, the chief of Clan Robertson, pulling his standard out of the ground, noticed a glittering stone in the hole he had left behind. Taking it as a sign of good omen, he picked up the stone, and after the victory at Bannockburn the chiefs of the clan always carried it with them during times of conflict, and its changes of hue were consulted as indications of the outcome of any forthcoming battle. Just before Sheriffmuir in 1715, a crack was noticed in the stone, taken to betoken the subsequent decline of the clan. The Clach na Brataich was also believed to ward off sickness.

Clachnacuddin (Gaelic, *Clach-na-cudainn*, 'stone of the tubs') A flat slab now built into the Market Cross outside the Town House, Inverness. It was where washerwomen would rest their tubs on the way back from the River Ness, and has become something of a synecdoche of the town itself.

> Then I stopped to have a look at the big flat stone cemented into the pavement outside the Town House, the famous stone, the oldest most important stone in town, the oldest proof of itself as a town that the town I grew up in had. It was reputedly the stone the washer-women used to rest their baskets of clothes on, on their way to and from the river, or the stone they used to scrub their clothes against when they were washing them, I didn't know which was true, or if either of those was true.
> – Ali Smith, *Girl Meets Boy* (2007)

The stone gives its name to a local football team, Clachnacuddin FC, who were founded in 1886, and who play in the Highland Football League.

Claret, the Scottish taste for *See* AULD ALLIANCE, THE.

Clàrsair Dall, An *See* BLIND HARPER, THE.

Clanjamfrie or **clamjamfry** A disorderly rabble; a brouhaha or rumpus; a collection of worthless items. The word famously ends one of Hugh MacDiarmid's best-known early lyrics, in which the Earth is apostrophized as a 'bonnie brookit

bairn' (a bonny, neglected baby) whose cries drown out the 'blethers' of the flashily dressed planets:

> But greet, an' in your tears ye'll droun
> The hail clanjamfrie.
> – 'The Bonnie Broukit Bairn', from *Sangschaw* (1925)

See also GULSOCH.

Clans, Battle of the *See* BATTLE OF THE CLANS.

Clansman, the The passenger train service between Inverness and London.

Clap o' the hass A term for the uvula, recorded in Fife and Angus. The *hass* is the throat, while the *clap* in this context appears to carry the following sense, as defined by John Jamieson in his *Etymological Dictionary of the Scottish Language* (1808):

> A flat instrument of iron, resembling a box, with a tongue and handle, used for making proclamations through a town, instead of a drum or hand-bell.

Hence a *clapman* was a town crier.

Clapshot *See* CHAMPIT TATTIES.

Clarinda *See* AE FOND KISS.

Clartyhole The name of the farm by the River Tweed that Sir Walter Scott purchased in 1811, with a view to gentrification. The word *clarty* being Scots for 'dirty', Scott opted for a more genteel English name for his new property: Abbotsford. *See also* MRS MACCLARTY.

Clash-ma-claver *See* CLISHMACLAVER.

Clatterbags A gossip; *clatter* denotes 'idle chitchat', 'rumour', 'scandal', 'slander', etc. The word has been adopted as the title of the newsletter of 'Highland's Young Carers'.

Claverhouse, John Graham of *See* BONNIE DUN-DEE.

Clavie *See* BURNING THE CLAVIE.

Claw up someone's mittens, to To kill someone, or, figuratively, to best or defeat or scold them. The allusion may be to the curled-up toes of a dead bird.

Clay Davie A term formerly applied in the North-east to an agricultural labourer or other rural manual worker, such as a ditcher.

Claymore A large two-edged, two-handed sword, once favoured by Highland warriors. In his 1772 *Tour*, Thomas Pennant describes it as 'an unwieldy weapon, two inches broad, doubly edged; the length of the blade three feet seven inches; of the handle, fourteen inches'. The name *claymore* – from Gaelic *claidhheamh*, 'sword', and *mór*, 'great' – is also frequently applied to the Highlander's basket-hilted broadsword, which sometimes only had a single edge.

> From Rorie More many of the branches of the [Macleod] family are descended … We also saw his bow, which hardly any man now can bend, and his *glaymore*, which was wielded with both hands, and is of a prodigious size … The broad-sword now used, though called the *glaymore*, is much smaller than that used in Rorie More's time.
> – James Boswell, *A Journal of a Tour to the Hebrides* (1785)

'Clean Pease Strae' *See* PEASE STRAE.

Cleanse-the-Causeway The name given by the citizens of Edinburgh to a bloody affray in the city in April 1520 between two of Scotland's most powerful families, the Douglases and the Hamiltons, who were vying for power during the minority of James V. The cobbles of the streets and wynds were reportedly washed with blood. Such goings-on continued in the city for at least another century, earning Edinburgh the reputation as 'the ordinarie place of butcherlie reuenge and daylie fightis' (as recorded in 1617 in the *State Papers and Miscellaneous Correspondence of Thomas, Earl of Melros*). According to *An Inventory of the Ancient and Historical Monuments of the City of Edinburgh* (1951), the last public assassination committed on a street in Edinburgh occurred in 1608, when Lord Torthorwald was stabbed in the back in conclusion of a family feud dating back to 1581.

Clearances, the The mass eviction of tenants from the land that took place in the Highlands and Islands in the wake of the failure of the 1745 Jacobite Rebellion, and on through the 19th century, often accompanied by considerable brutality. The phenomenon was initially referred to as *clearing*, but by the 1840s the term *clearances* had become established. Some of the worst excesses were carried out in Sutherland, especially in 1814, the YEAR OF THE BURNING. In many instances clan chieftains surrendered their traditional obligations to their clansmen in favour of new ideas of agricultural improvement, replacing people with the more profitable sheep (the FOUR-FOOTED CLANSMEN). Latterly, people were also cleared so that the laird could enjoy better sport in pursuit of deer and other quarry. That being said, population growth in the Highlands had reached the point where the land could no longer sustain the people, so emigration was for many an obvious option – especially during and after the potato famine of the 1840s and 1850s. Those evicted either sought new lives overseas, especially in North America and the Antipodes, joined the army, or moved to the great industrial towns of the Central Belt. In some places, paternalistic lairds established new settlements on the coast, encouraging fishing and other industries, such as kelp. There was little physical resistance, notable exceptions being during the YEAR OF THE SHEEP and at the BATTLE OF THE BRAES, but agitation by the Highland Land League eventually brought about the Crofters' Act of 1886, which gave tenants greater security of tenure. By that time, Scottish Gaeldom had been virtually extinguished.

> A dense cloud of smoke enveloped the whole country by day, and even extended far out to sea. At night an awfully grand but terrific scene presented itself – all the houses in an extensive district in flames at once. I myself ascended a height about eleven o'clock in the evening, and counted two hundred and fifty blazing houses, many of the owners of which I personally knew, but whose present condition – whether in or out of the flames – I could not tell. The conflagration lasted six days, till the whole of the dwellings were reduced to ashes or smoking ruins.
> – Donald McLeod, a Sutherland crofter who reported on the Clearances in letters to the *Edinburgh Weekly Chronicle*. Later, while in exile in Canada, he collected his reports as *Gloomy Memories in the Highlands of Scotland* (1857).

The many ships that left our country
with white wings for Canada.
They are like handkerchiefs in our memories
and the brine like tears ...
  – Iain Crichton Smith, 'The Exiles', from *Selected Poems*
    (1985)

See also GLENDALE MARTYRS, THE; MUTTON IN LIEU OF MAN.

Clear one's crap, to *See* CRAP.

Clear stuff, the A Northeastern euphemism for whisky.

Cleg A horsefly or gadfly. During the RADICAL WAR of 1820 and similar disturbances in the 19th century, the word was also applied to a missile aimed at soldiers or policemen.

Whaur the midges mazy dance,
Clegs dart oot the fiery lance.
  – James Nicholson, *Idylls o' Hame* (1870)

The nervous thistle's shiverin' like
A horse's skin aneth a cleg.
  – Hugh MacDiarmid, *A Drunk Man Looks at the Thistle*
    (1926)

Cleikum Ceremonies, the An annual ceremony held in Innerleithen, on the River Tweed, since 1901, as part of the St Ronan's Border Games, established in 1827. The name goes back to Sir Walter Scott, who in his novel *St Ronan's Well* (1823), set in the town, suggests that the 8th-century St Ronan had visited the area and with his episcopal crook 'cleik't the Deil by the hind leg and banished him'. Accordingly, the hostelry in his novel, prop. Meg DODS, is called the Cleikum Inn.

Clincher, the The byname adopted by Alexander Wylie Petrie (1853–1937), a colourful Glasgow character who from 1897 until his death published his own newspaper, *The Glasgow Clincher*, in which he campaigned tirelessly against the Glasgow Establishment. The byname alludes to his claim that he possessed one particularly brilliant brain cell, which gave him the power to *clinch* any argument. An attempt by the authorities to have him certified as a lunatic came to naught, leading him to claim that he was the only man in Glasgow who was officially sane.

Clishmaclaver or **clash-ma-claver** Nonsense, worthless talk, idle gossip, from *clish*, 'to spread gossip', and *claver*, 'to chatter idly'.

A curse on dull and drawling Whig ...
Wi' heart sae black, and look sae big,
And canting tongue o' clishmaclaver.
  – 'When the King Comes o'er the Water', in James Hogg,
    ed., *Jacobite Relics* (1819)

Clockwork Orange, the A nickname of the Glasgow underground system, playing on Anthony Burgess's 1962 novel and Stanley Kubrick's 1971 film of the same name. The name alludes to the modest dimensions and orange livery of the trains, and the single circular line. Originally built in 1896 (making it the third oldest underground system in the world, after London and Budapest), the Glasgow underground was modernized in the late 1970s, reopening in 1980 with the new orange trains (now being changed to carmine and cream with a thin orange band). The nickname tends only to be used by the media – locals refer to the system as 'the Subway' (hence a *sub crawl* involves visiting a pub adjacent to each of the 15 stations).

Clood o' nicht An obsolete term for the darkness of night (*clood* or *clud* = 'cloud'). Hence *under clood o' nicht* means 'under cover of darkness'.

Cloot A cloth. Hence, for example: *clootie dumpling*, a sweet, dark suet pudding made with dried fruit, and cooked by boiling the mixture in a cloth. Hence also the expression *wi' a face like a cloot* or *fite as a cloot*, 'white as a sheet'. *See also* TONGUE THAT COULD CLIP CLOOTS, A.

Clootie's croft *see* GOODMAN'S CROFT; AULD CLOOTIE.

Close A courtyard or alley (especially in Edinburgh); a farmyard; or a common entrance to a tenement (especially in Glasgow, where a *wallie close* is one with decorative tiles on the walls; *see* WALLIE DUG). If *it's a' up a close* [or *closie*] *wi' someone*, then they are in a pickle or quandary, or in a hopeless situation, as they are if they are *in the wrang close*, which can also mean that they are grievously mistaken about something.

Closeburn, the Swan of *See* SWAN OF CLOSEBURN, THE.

Clout *See* CLOOT.

Clubs and societies *See:*

- ACCIDENTAL CLUB, the
- BANNATYNE CLUB, the
- BEGGAR'S BENISON, the
- COURT OF EQUITY, the
- CROCHALLAN FENCIBLES, the
- HODGE PODGE CLUB, the
- HORSEMAN'S WORD, the
- PIG CLUB, the
- POKER CLUB, the
- SELECT SOCIETY, the
- SIX-FOOT HIGH CLUB, the
- SPEC, the
- TARBOLTON BACHELORS' CLUB

Cludfawer Literally a 'cloud faller', i.e. an illegitimate child. 'A spurious child,' says John Jamieson in his 1825 Supplement to *An Etymological Dictionary of the Scottish Language*, as if 'fallen from the clouds'. He encountered the expression in Teviotdale. *See also* COME-O-WILL.

Cludgie *See* SHANKIE.

Clumsy tea *See* HIGH TEA.

Cluny's Cage A cave on remote Ben Alder, used for some years after Culloden as a hiding place by the Jacobite chief, Ewan Macpherson of Cluny. Some have alternatively located the cave on the crags of Creag Dubh, above the road leading from Newtonmore to Laggan, and thus closer to Cluny's seat at Cluny Castle (the Ordnance Survey marks a Cluny's *Cave* here – Uamh Chluanaidh). The fugitive Bonnie Prince Charlie stayed in the cave for a while, as do David Balfour and Alan BRECK in Stevenson's novel *Kidnapped* (1886). In chapter xxiii Stevenson gives the following imaginative description of the place:

> Quite at the top, and just before the rocky face of the cliff sprang above the foliage, we found that strange house which was known in the country as 'Cluny's

Cage'. The trunks of several trees had been wattled across, the intervals strengthened with stakes, and the ground behind this barricade levelled up with earth to make the floor. A tree, which grew out from the hillside, was the living centre-beam of the roof. The walls were of wattle and covered with moss. The whole house had something of an egg shape; and it half hung, half stood in that steep, hillside thicket, like a wasp's nest in a green hawthorn.

The Prince left Cluny's Cage when news came of a French ship on the west coast, which was to take him to safety. He told Cluny that he was 'the only person in whom he could repose the greatest confidence', and asked him to make preparations for his eventual return. Cluny spent the next eight years in his Cage, waiting fruitlessly for his Prince. *See also* TREASURE OF LOCH ARKAIG, THE.

Clutha The old, perhaps romanticized, Gaelic name for the River Clyde, perpetuated in the names of boats, pubs and locations in New Zealand. In modern Gaelic the name is rendered as *Cluaidh*, and the earliest known reference to the river, as the *Clota*, is found in Tacitus (1st–2nd century AD).

Clyde *See* ANNAN, TWEED AND CLYDE; AS DEEP AND DIRTY AS THE CLYDE; CLYDE-BUILT; D'YE THINK AH CAME UP THE CLYDE ON A BANANA BOAT?; MOOTH LIKE THE CLYDE TUNNEL, A; RED CLYDESIDE; WHAT'S THAT GOT TO DO WI' THE CLYDE NAVIGATION?

Clyde-built Long a guarantee around the world of ship-building quality. Since the 18th century, over 20,000 ships have been produced on the Clyde, including numerous warships and great liners such as the *Queen Mary* (*see* HULL NO. 534) and the *QE2*. Only a residue of this once great industry – which was at its peak before the First World War, when a quarter of the world's ships were built on the Clyde – survives to this day on the river.

Clydebank an' Kilbooie *See* RHYMING SLANG.

Coatbridge Sunnyside Said to be the only oxymoronic station name in the country.

Coats kilted, to have one's To be pregnant.

Cobbler, the A rocky peak (884 m) in the so-called ARROCHAR ALPS. On maps it is also referred to as Ben Arthur, probably from Gaelic *artaich*, 'rocky', or more fancifully *art mòr*, 'big bear'; some even favour a naming in honour of King Arthur. But it is as the Cobbler that it is almost universally known, a term explained by John Stoddart in his *Local Scenery and Manners in Scotland* (1800):

> This terrific rock forms the bare summit of a huge mountain, and its nodding top so far overhangs the base as to assume the appearance of a cobbler sitting at work, from whence the country people call it *an greasaiche cróm*, the crooked shoemaker.

There are in fact three main tops of the Cobbler: the Cobbler himself, Jean the Cobbler's Wife, and His Last, but which is which varies from authority to authority – the Scottish Mountaineering Club, in its guide to the Southern Highlands, asserts that it is the Centre Peak (the highest point) that is the Cobbler, but is agnostic about whether the North Peak is Jean and the South Peak His Last, or vice versa. There is a tradition that in the past each new chief of Clan Campbell (the Earls and later the Dukes of Argyll) had to ascend the Centre Peak; this involves a scramble through 'Argyll's Eyeglass', a natural window through the summit pinnacle that leads to an exposed ledge, from which the top may airily be attained.

> He is a gruesome carle, and inhospitable to strangers. He does not wish to be intruded upon – is a very hermit, in fact; for when, after wild waste of breath and cuticle, a daring mortal climbs up to him, anxious to be introduced, behold he has slipped his cable, and is nowhere to be seen. And it does not improve the temper of the climber that, when down again, and casting up his eyes, he discovers the rocky figure sitting in his accustomed place. The Cobbler's Wife sits a little way off – an ancient dame, to the full as withered in appearance as her husband, and as difficult of access. They dwell in tolerable amity the twain, but when they do quarrel it is something tremendous! The whole county knows when a tiff is in progress. The sky darkens above them. The Cobbler frowns black as midnight. His Wife sits sulking in the mist. His Wife's conduct aggravates the Cobbler –

who is naturally of a peppery temper – and he gives vent to a discontented growl. Nothing loath, and to the full as irascible as her spouse, his Wife spits back fire upon him. The row begins. They flash at one another in the savagest manner, scolding all the while in the grandest Billingsgate. Everything listens to them for twenty miles round. At last the Wife gives in, and falls to downright weeping, the crusty old fellow sending a shot into her at intervals. She cries, and he grumbles, into the night. Peace seems to have been restored somehow when everybody is asleep; for next morning the Cobbler has renewed his youth. He shines in the sun like a very bridegroom, not a frown on the old countenance of him, and his Wife opposite, the tears hardly dried upon her face yet, smiles upon him through her prettiest head-dress of mist; and for the next six weeks they enjoy as bright, unclouded weather as husband and wife can expect in a world where everything is imperfect.
> – Alexander Smith, *A Summer in Skye* (1865)

Cock-a-leekie Chicken and leek soup, one of the staples of the Scottish kitchen. The name is first recorded in the 18th century, but the dish appears to go back to the Middle Ages, when it also contained prunes and/or raisins.

Cockbridge to Tomintoul Often blocked.

Cockie-bendie A small, self-satisfied, pernickety, sometimes effeminate man; also applied affectionately to a small boy, and pejoratively to a woman. It is perhaps related to the term *cockapentie*, which John Jamieson in his 1825 Supplement to his *Etymological Dictionary of the Scottish Language* defines as 'one whose pride makes him live and act above his income'.

> Cockie Bendie had a wife:
> Wow! but she was canty!
> She gaed in below the bed,
> An' knockit ower the chanty.
>
> Cockie Bendie's lyin sick,
> What d'ye think will mend him?
> Twenty kisses in a cloot,
> An' Flora tae attend him.
> – Traditional song [*canty*, 'lively, cheerful'; *chanty*, 'bedpan'; *cloot*, 'cloth']

Cock laird *See* BONNET LAIRD.

Cock of Arran, the The rugged northeast point of the island of Arran, so called from the shape of a geomorphological feature that once graced the place and which was thought to resemble a cockerel. This has since collapsed.

Cock one's wee finger, to To indulge in a dram. To *turn up one's wee finger* is to go further, and become an alcoholic.

Cock o' the North, the George Gordon, 4th Earl of Huntly (1514–62), a turbulent nobleman during the reign of Mary Queen of Scots. Mary sent an expedition against him led by her illegitimate half-brother, James Stewart, Earl of Moray. The two met for battle on 28 October 1562 at Corrichie, on the Hill of Fare, a little to the northwest of Banchory. Huntly had been cheered by the prophecies of the witches of Strathbogie, who had told him that that night he would lie in the Tolbooth of Aberdeen without a wound on him. They proved correct: after the battle, while trying to surrender, the fat and apoplectic Huntly suffered a fatal seizure, and 'without blow or stroke ... suddenly fell from his horse stark dead'. That night his body was duly laid out in the Tolbooth, having been transported thither in a couple of fish baskets. His embalmed corpse was subsequently put on trial for treason, and did not receive burial until 1565. The chiefs of Clan Gordon – the Earls and later Marquesses of Huntly – subsequently adopted the title Cock o' the North. *See also* GORDONS HAE THE GUIDING O'T, THE.

As some kind of tribute, perhaps, Harry Graham (1874–1936) wrote 'The Cockney of the North', a pastiche of Yeats's 'Lake Isle of Innisfree':

I will arise now, and go to Inverness,
And a small villa rent there, of lath and plaster built;
Nine bedrooms will I have there, and I'll don my native dress,
And walk around in a damned loud kilt.

Cock's eye A term used in the Northeast for a small bright circle or halo round the moon, said to foreshadow unsettled weather. The phenomenon is also called a *mune-bow*, and when such a halo appears the moon is said to be *on her back in the midden*.

Cocktail of bubblegum, wet sheep fleece, barley sugar and plastic, a *See* IRN BRU.

Cocktails Lonely Planet's *Best in Travel 2009*, listing Glasgow among the top ten cities in the world, cites 'the cocktails, cuisine and designer chic' as major draws. 'Scotland's biggest city has shaken off its shroud of industrial soot,' the Lonely Planet writers froth, 'and shimmied into a sparkling new designer gown.'

'Twas not always thus. When, in the late 1970s, the city first saw an explosion of cocktail bars, one punter, morosely eyeing a jug full of fruit, miniature umbrellas and something green and orange, was heard to observe, 'D'ye mind when drink wi' food in it wiz called vomit?' *See also* APERITIF; SCOTCH FROG.

Cock the wee finger, to *See* COCK ONE'S WEE FINGER, TO.

Cocky Bung The name awarded by his students to John Young (*c*.1747–1820), professor of Greek at Glasgow University from 1774 until his death. The nickname alluded to the fact that Young's father had been a cooper. Young was an ardent fan of the actor Edmund Kean:

While in the theatre one night, he became so absorbed by witnessing Kean's 'Shylock', that he also commenced to act the part in dumb-show, to the amusement of the audience; and a witty ex-Provost made note of the circumstance in rhyme, as follows.

The very Jew I've surely seen
That Shakespeare painted, played by Kean,
While Plaudits loudy rung;
But what was all his acting fine,
To the diverting pantomime
Displayed by Cocky Bung?
– The 'Rambling Reporter', notes to the 1887 reprint of *Jones's Directory for the Year 1787* – the first Glasgow directory, by Nathaniel Jones

Coinneach Odhar *See* BRAHAN SEER, THE.

Cold ... *See also* CAULD ...

Cold Shoulder of Scotland, the A nickname for Buchan, referring both to its geographical shape, jutting into the North Sea above the main body of Scotland, and to its somewhat chilly climate. *See also* SIBERIA OF SCOTLAND, THE.

Colkitto The anglicized version of the first part of the name of Col Ciotach Mac Domhnaill ('Left-handed Col Macdonald') (1570–1647), also known as Col MacGillespie. Something of an adventurer, Colkitto was involved in the internal struggles between various branches of Clan Donald, and ended up in possession of Colonsay. He is alluded to in Milton's Sonnet XI, 'On the Detraction which Followed upon my Writing Certain Treatises', in which the poet rebukes those who claimed that the title of his book *Tetrachordon* (1645) was too difficult to pronounce:

> Why, is it harder, sirs, than *Gordon, Colkitto*, or
>   *Macdonnel*, or *Galasp*?
> Those rugged names to our like mouths grow sleek,
> That would have made Quintilian stare and gasp.

Col Ciotach's third son, Alasdair MacColla (*c.* 1610–47), in full Alasdair Mac Colla Chiotaich Mac Domhnuill ('Alasdair the son of Colla the Left-handed Macdonald'), is also sometimes (mis-takenly) referred to as *Colkitto*, or (perhaps more permissibly) *Young Colkitto*. He played a notable and complex part in the Wars of the Three Kingdoms, both in Ireland and Scotland, changing allegiance when it suited the interests of his family and clan. At times he joined forces with the Royalist commander in Scotland, the Marquess of Montrose, but at other times concentrated on seizing back Macdonald lands in Argyll from the Campbells. The latter joined with the Covenanters in a campaign against him, and he was obliged to flee to Ireland, where he was killed at the Battle of Knocknanuss in County Cork, possibly after his capture.

Like his father, Young Colkitto was not just left-handed, but ambidextrous. Before one particular fight, it is said, he bragged to his opponent that he had the best sword-hand in all Ireland. The opponent, playing straight man, asked where the next-best could be found. Alasdair tossed the sword into his left hand, declaring, 'Here it is.' Young Colkitto is often credited with refining the tactic of the HIGHLAND CHARGE, which accounted for the majority of Montrose's victories.

Collie, wull ye lick? An invitation to eat (*collie* being the breed of dog):

> 'Burnbrae, yir a gey lad never tae say, "Collie, will ye lick?" for a' hevna tasted meat for saxteen hoors.'
> – Ian Maclaren, *A Doctor of the Old School* (1895)

The phrase is usually used in the negative, as in the following:

> I've sat whole nichts in their hooses an' they never so much as said to me, 'Collie, wull ye lick?'
> – O. Douglas (Anna Masterton Buchan), *Ann and her Mother* (1922)

Collie doug *See* BUTTERY WULLIE COLLIE.

Colliers' Oak, the An oak near Dailly, Ayrshire, where local miners met with the Laird of Dal-quharran to discuss business matters.

Collieshangie A squabble, brawl, animated conversation or dogfight. It has been suggested that the first element refers to the breed of dog, but the earliest usages refer to disputes between people, so it is perhaps more likely that it is from Gaelic *coileid*, 'uproar, loud noise'.

> Kind Sir, I've read your paper through,
> And faith, to me, 'twas really new!
> How guessed ye, Sir, what maist I wanted?
> This mony a day I've grain'd and gaunted,
> To ken what French mischief was brewin;
> Or what the drumlie Dutch were doin;
> That vile doup-skelper, Emperor Joseph,
> If Venus yet had got his nose off;
> Or how the collieshangie works
> Atween the Russians and the Turks ...
> – Robert Burns, 'Lines to a Gentleman who had Sent a Newspaper, and offered to Continue it Free of Expense'

Colonel's Bed, the A rocky ledge hidden in the gorge of the Ey Burn, a tributary of the Dee that cuts into the hills to the southwest of Braemar. The 'Bed' takes its name from Colonel John Farquharson of Inverey, a fiery-tempered Jacobite known as 'the Black Colonel' who in 1689 burnt down Braemar Castle to prevent it from falling into the hands of the Williamite government. In that turbulent year, Farquharson escaped from government troops by riding up the precipitous north side of the Pass of Ballater, and was then obliged to conceal himself in his eponymous bed, while government troops burnt his castle at Inverey to the ground. While in hiding, he was brought sustenance by his beloved mistress Annie Ban ('Fair-Haired Annie'), and before his death, which occurred around 1698, he gave instructions that he was to be buried beside her at Inverey. However, he was interred instead at Braemar. The next morning his coffin was found poking up above the surface; it was then re-buried, but it re-appeared two more times, until, eventually, his wishes were obeyed, and he was buried at Inverey beside Annie Ban.

Colonsay duck A name applied in parts of the Inner Hebrides to the eider duck.

Come all ye *See* 'FREEDOM COME-ALL-YE, THE'.

Come in bye A common invitation to enter the speaker's home.

Come into the body o' the kirk An invitation extended to anyone sitting on their own to join the company.

Comfy? A Glasgow man goes to see a psychiatrist and the psychiatrist ask him to lie down on the couch. The man does as he's told. 'Comfy?' asks the psychiatrist. 'Govan,' the man replies.

A variant of this was related by Brigadier Frank Coutts (1918–2008) of the King's Own Scottish Borderers, who told of the occasion when his men, stationed in Belfast, were visited in their barracks by an English brigadier, who enquired, 'Are you fellows comfy heah?' To which he received the response, 'Naw, wur frae Scotland.' *See also* BOUNTY; MERINGUES.

Come-o-will A plant that grows without having been deliberately planted, or an animal that of its own volition adopts a human; hence also an incomer,

and a euphemism for an illegitimate child (known in Cumbria as a *cum-by-chance*). *See also* CLUDFAWER.

Come paddy owre someone To soften somebody up, get the better of them, or twist them round one's little finger.

Come the peter ower, to To throw one's weight about, exert one's power over others. Similarly, to *pit the peter on* something is to put a stop to it. The origin of *peter* here is obscure.

Comin' thro' the rye The title and refrain of a song attributed to Burns, but which was probably a traditional one dressed up a little by the poet:

> Gin a body meet a body
>> Comin' thro' the rye;
> Gin a body kiss a body,
>> Need a body cry?
>> [*Gin*, if; *body*, person]

It was published in December 1796 in the fifth volume of James Johnson's *Scots Musical Museum*, a collection of folk songs to which Burns was an enthusiastic contributor. There is an earthier version in *The* MERRY MUSES OF CALEDONIA, in which Burns may also have had a hand:

> Gin a body meet a body
>> Comin' throu the rye;
> Gin a body fuck a body,
>> Need a body cry?
>>> *Comin' throu the rye, my jo,*
>>>> *An' comin' throu the rye;*
>>> *She fand a staun o staunin graith*
>>>> *Comin' throu the rye.*
>>> [*fand a staun o staunini graith* found a stand of standing growth]

The Scottish physicist James Clerk Maxwell (1831–79) offered this parody:

> Gin a body meet a body
> Flyin' through the air,
> Gin a body hit a body,
> Will it fly? and where?
> Ilka impact has its measure,
> Ne'er an ane hae I,
> Yet a' the lads they measure me,
> Or, at least, they try.

Common-law marriage See BIDIE-IN; HABIT AND REPUTE; HANDFAST; MARRIAGE *SUBSEQUENTE COPULA*.

Common Riding See RIDING THE MARCHES.

Commotion Lotion A nickname for Buckfast Tonic Wine; *see* BUCKFAST TRIANGLE.

Compagnie Écossaise See GARDE ÉCOSSAISE.

Competitor, the Robert Bruce of Annandale (1210–95), grandfather of ROBERT THE BRUCE. Robert of Annandale was one of 13 claimants to the throne in 1291. His grandson subsequently pursued the claim, with ultimate success.

Connolly, Billy See BIG YIN, THE.

Convoys (Scots, Hielan or Kelso) See SCOTS CONVOY.

Coo clat A cowpat.

Cool the beans A contemporary expression meaning 'calm down'.

Cooncil juice A jocular Glaswegian expression denoting water.

Cooncil telly Free terrestrial television channels, as opposed to satellite or cable television.

Coonter-lowper Literally, 'counter-leaper', a disparaging term for a male shop assistant, particularly a draper's assistant; also known as *lowp-the-coonter*. For an example of a coonter-lowper made good, *see* FIGHTING MAC.

Coo o' Forfar, the There is an old saying: 'Do as the cow o' Forfar did, tak' a stannin' drink.' Sir Walter Scott explains the proverb in *Waverley* (1814):

A cow, in passing a door in Forfar, where a tub of ale had been placed to cool, drank the whole of it. The owner of the ale prosecuted the owner of the cow, but a learned baillie, in giving his decision, said, 'As the ale

was drunk by the cow while standing at the door, it must be considered *deoch an doruis* (stirrup-cup), to make a charge for which would be to outrage Scotch hospitality.'

'Cooper o' Fife, The' A traditional song, the sentiments of which would receive little approbation in our more enlightened times:

There was a wee Cooper wha lived in Fife
Nickety, nackety, noo, noo, noo,
And he had gotten a gentle wife,
   Hey Willy Wallacky, hoo John Dougal,
   Alane, quo' Rushity, roue, roue, roue.

She wadna bake and she wadna brew,
Nickety, nackety, noo, noo, noo,
For spoilin' o' her comely hue …

She wadna wash, nor she wadna wring,
Nickety, Nackety, noo, noo, noo,
For shamin' o' her gentle kin …

The exasperated cooper then places a sheepskin on his wife's back, saying:

'It's I'll no thrash ye for your gentle kin',
Nickety, Nackety, noo, noo, noo,
'But I will skelp my ain sheep's skin …'

This has the desired effect, and the wife vows to perform her duties without complaint.

Coo's meat, ae Literally 'one cow's food', i.e. enough land to feed a single cow.

Coo's quake A spell of cold and stormy weather in May, from the shivering in cattle so caused.

Come it early, come it late,
In May comes the cow quake.
   – James Kelly, *A Complete Collection of Scottish Proverbs* (1721)

Corbett Any mountain in Scotland over 2500 and under 3000 feet (762 and 914.4 m) in height, with a drop of at least 500 feet (152.4 m) between itself and its neighbour. The Corbetts, of which there are 219, are named after John Rooke Corbett, a member of the Scottish Mountaineering Club who compiled a list of them in the 1920s, and who was the first to climb every Scottish mountain over 2000 feet (609.6 m). *See also* DONALD; GRAHAM; MUNRO.

Corbie messenger Literally, 'crow messenger', referring to the raven sent out by Noah (Genesis 8:7), hence any unreliable or unsuccessful messenger.

> His man-servant was accordingly dispatched on horseback to the Well for Dr Quackleben; while ... the wench was dismissed to supplicate the assistance of the gudewife of the Cleikum ... The male emissary proved, in Scottish phrase, a 'corbie messenger;' for either he did not find the doctor, or he found him better engaged than to attend the sick-bed of a pauper, at a request which promised such slight remuneration as that of a parish minister. But the female ambassador was more successful ...
> – Sir Walter Scott, *St Ronan's Well* (1824), chapter xix

In a note in his 1893 edition of Scott's novel, Andrew Lang was perplexed by the expression: 'It seems unlikely that the Scots had a legend like the Greek one concerning the evil "corbie" or raven messenger to Apollo about his false lady-love, but no other explanation suggests itself.'

Corbie steps *See* CRAW STEPS.

Corned-beef legs *See* TINKER'S TARTAN.

Cornkister A species of comic song that succeeded the traditional BOTHY BALLAD. Cornkisters, usually written in Aberdeenshire DORIC, were so-called because supposedly sung by someone sitting on the *cornkist* (corn chest), and beating their heels against it in time to the music. Most cornkisters were in fact written specifically for the music hall, or for recording, and became popular from the late 19th century. Examples include 'A Pair o' Nicky Tams' (*see under* NICKY TAMS) by G.S. Morris, the BUCHAN CHIELD, and 'The Weddin o' McGinnis tae his Cross-eyed Pet' by Willie Kemp (the KING OF THE CORNKISTERS) and G. Bruce Thomson.

Coronach A lament or dirge either sung or played on the pipes at Highland funerals.

> The upper class hire women to moan and lament at the funeral of their nearest relations ... This part of the ceremony is called a *Coronoch*.
> – Edward Burt, *Letters from a Gentleman in the North of Scotland* (1754)

In *Survivals in Belief Among the Celts* (1911), George Henderson tells us that:

> In the Highlands of old the ghosts flitted about if the *coronach* or funeral threnody were unsung; the other side is, when the BANSHEE calls she sings the spirit home. In some houses still a soft low music is heard at death.

Sir Walter Scott inserts a coronach of his own devising into *The Lady of the Lake* (1810). It ends thus:

> Like the dew on the mountain,
> Like the foam on the river,
> Like the bubble on the fountain,
> Thou art gone – and for ever!

The word is from Gaelic *corranach*, 'loud weeping', from *comh-*, 'together', and *rànach*, 'a cry'.

Coronation Scot, the The express passenger train service between London and Glasgow inaugurated in 1937 in honour of the coronation of George VI and running until the outbreak of war in 1939.

Corp criadh Gaelic, 'clay body', a small model of a human employed to inflict harm on one's enemies. Sheila MacDonald, writing in the 1903 issue of *Folk Lore*, gives the following account:

> A rather gruesome relic of a barbarous age which I have heard of as happening within the last few years, is that ugly one known as the *Corp Creagh* [i.e. *criadh*]. As its name indicates, this is a body of clay rudely shaped into the image of the person whose hurt is desired. After a tolerably correct representation is obtained, it is stuck all over with pins and thorns, and placed in a running stream. As the image is worn away by the action of the water, the victim also wastes away with some mortal disease. The more pins are stuck in from time to time, the more excruciating agony the unfortunate victim suffers. Should, however, any wayfarer by accident discover the *Corp* in the stream the spell is broken, and the victim duly recovers. A case of *Corp Creagh* has been known to occur in Uist within the last five years;

and in a parish adjoining ours, it was whispered that the death of a certain young man was due to a spell of this nature.

Corrector, the *See* ALEXANDER THE CORRECTOR.

Corrie-fisted *See* KERRY-MITTED.

Corryvreckan Scotland's very own maelstrom, a whirlpool between the northern tip of Jura and the small island of Scarba (on whose northern side race the GREY DOGS). It is formed by the tide as it squeezes at speeds of up to 10 knots through the narrow strait, the so-called Gulf of Corryvreckan, in which a submarine pinnacle and deep fissure in the seabed contribute to the furious gush of waters, the noise of which can be heard from many miles away. The whirlpool is still sometimes referred to as the Cailleach (Gaelic, 'old woman'), alluding to the hag who allegedly controls the waters, adjudicating as to which ships shall pass by safely (alternatively, she is merely doing her autumn laundry, and when it is white she spreads it across the land as a blanket of snow). The name Corryvreckan itself is from the Gaelic *coire*, 'cauldron', and *bhreacain*, 'speckled' – or alternatively the second element is the personal name Brecan, an ancient Celtic or Norse hero who in legend drowned here when he and his 50 ships were swallowed up. When St Columba later sailed this way, one of Brecan's ribs apparently bobbed to the surface; and Columba's biographer, Adamnan (*fl.* 7th century), referred to the place as *Charybdis Brecani* (Charybdis being the mythical Greek sea monster or whirlpool that almost drowns Odysseus). More recently, in 1949, George Orwell had a lucky escape here while attempting to circumnavigate Jura. Orwell's brother-in-law, one-legged Bill Dunn, was the first person to swim the Gulf. The whirlpool also features in Powell and Pressburger's 1945 film *I Know Where I'm Going!*

Between the north end of Jura, and the isle Scarba, lies the famous and dangerous gulf, called Cory Vrekan, about a mile in breadth; it yields an impetuous current, not to be matched anywhere about the isle of Britain. The sea begins to boil and ferment with the tide of flood, and resembles the boiling of a pot; and then increases gradually, until it appears in many whirlpools, which form themselves in sort of pyramids, and immediately after spout up as high as the mast of a little vessel, and at the same time make a loud report. These white waves run two leagues with the wind before they break; the sea continues to repeat these various motions from the beginning of the tide of flood, until it is more than half-flood, and then it decreases gradually until it hath ebbed about half an hour, and continues to boil till it is within an hour of low water. This boiling of the sea is not above a pistol-shot distant from the coast of Scarba Isle, where the white waves meet and spout up: they call it the Kaillach, *i.e.*, an old hag; and they say that when she puts on her kerchief, *i.e.*, the whitest waves, it is then reckoned fatal to approach her. Notwithstanding this great ferment of the sea, which brings up the least shell from the ground, the smallest fisher-boat may venture to cross this gulf at the last hour of the tide of flood, and at the last hour of the tide of ebb.

– Martin Martin, *A Description of the Western Islands of Scotland* (*c.* 1695)

Corstorphine Sycamore, the A beautiful tree that stood by Corstorphine Dovecot in Edinburgh for some four centuries, before it was blown down in a gale on 26 December 1998. Its appearance was described by the Revd James Oliver in the *Statistical Account* of 1795:

There is growing near the village in a close belonging to Sir William Dick, a sycamore tree of considerable size and the largest in Scotland, which in the end of May and beginning of June exhibits an appearance of the most striking beauty. That side which is exposed to the sun, in the colour of the leaves, is of the richest vivid yellow hue.

The tree was said to have originated in a sapling brought from the East by a monk in the early 15th century, but it is more likely to have been a relic from an avenue of trees leading to Corstorphine Castle, planted in the 16th century. The tree produced no seed, but such was its beauty that many cuttings were taken of it, and it is regarded botanically as a separate sub-species, namely *Acer pseudoplatanus corstorphiense*.

On 26 August 1679 the Corstorphine Sycamore witnessed a notorious crime, as related in James Grant's *Old and New Edinburgh* (issued through the

113

1880s). This was the murder of James, Lord Forrester by a woman with whom he had begun 'a dangerous intrigue', one Christian Nimmo, the wife of an Edinburgh merchant and also the niece of Lord Forrester's first wife. A 'handsome woman', but one of 'violent and impulsive' character, she had learnt that Lord Forrester had in his cups 'spoken of her opprobriously'. In a fury she made for Corstorphine Castle, where she encountered him by the dovecot, and in the ensuing tussle she ran him through with his own sword. When brought before the magistrates, she confessed that she had indeed killed him, but in self-defence, the drunken and furious lord having run at her with his sword, which she took from him, and upon which he impaled himself. This cut no ice with the court, but before her execution she managed to escape from the Tolbooth (the HEART OF MIDLOTHIAN) dressed as a man. Her freedom was short-lived, however, and on 12 November she was beheaded at the Mercat Cross. To mark the occasion she appeared all in black, then drew aside a large black veil to bare her neck and shoulders to the executioner. All were impressed by her courage, and thereafter her wailing ghost, known as the White Lady of Corstorphine, was said to wander around the Corstorphine Sycamore whenever the moon was full, dressed in white and bearing a bloody sword.

Costa Clyde, the Where those sailing DOON THE WATTER go for their holidays.

Couldnae tackle a fish supper Said of an inept footballer, or any person regarded as hopeless.

Could start a fight in an empty house Said of someone who likes a bit of aggro; see, for example, GORGEOUS GEORGE.

Council ... See COONCIL ...

Countess and the gypsy, the See KING OF THE GYPSIES.

Countess instructs gillie to deface phallic statuary See LUSTY MAN.

Counting rhymes and systems A number of counting rhymes are recorded in Walter Gregor's *Folk-Lore of the North-East of Scotland* (1881), including the following:

> Eenrie, twaarie, tickerie, teven,
> Allaby, crockery, ten, or elaiven,
> Peen, pan, fusky dam,
> Wheedlum, whadlum, twenty-one.

There are many variants on the above (from Fraserburgh), such as this from Portsoy:

> Enerie, twaarie, tickerie, ten,
> Allabie, crackabie, ten, or eleevin,
> Pim, pam, musky dam,
> Queevrie, quaavrie, English man.

Here is an example of another strand (also from Portsoy):

> Eetum, peetum, penny pie,
> Cock-a-lorie, jinky jye,
> Staan ye oot by
> For a bonnie penny pie.

Such rhymes are reminiscent of shepherds' counting systems further south, although the latter are more serious in intent. That in use in the Borders, as recorded in *British Archaeology* (issue no. 46, July 1999), is pretty much identical to the better-known version used in Borrowdale in the Lake District.

1. Yan
2. Tyan
3. Tethera
4. Methera
5. Pimp
6. Sethera
7. Lethera
8. Hovera
9. Dovera
10. Dik
11. Yanadik
12. Tyanadik
13. Tetheradik
14. Metheradik
15. Bumfitt
16. Yanabumfitt
17. Tyanabumfitt
18. Tetherabumfitt
19. Metherabumfitt
20. Giggot

Coup the creels or **coup the crans, to** Expressions still heard in Fife and the Northeast, meaning to fall head over heels, or to turn a somersault, or to give birth to an illegitimate child, or to fall into ruin, or to die, while *to coup the creels o'* or *on someone* is to outsmart them or foil their plans. To *coup* means 'to upset, overturn', while a *creel* is a deep basket for carrying fish, peats, etc., and a *cran* a barrel of herrings – or perhaps 'a trivet, on which small pots are placed in cookery, which is sometimes turned with its feet uppermost by an awkward assistant' (John Jamieson, 1825 Supplement to his *Etymological Dictionary of the Scottish Language*). 'Garrin [making] lasses coup the cran' was something that Burns was rather good at:

> But fegs! the Session says I maun
> Gae fa' upo' anither plan
> Than garrin lasses coup the cran,
> Clean heels ower body,
> An sairly thole their mothers' ban
> Afore the howdy.
> – Robert Burns, 'Reply to a Trimming Epistle Received
> from a Tailor' (1786) [*fegs!* 'faith!'; *Session*, 'kirk
> session'; *thole*, 'endure'; *howdy*, 'midwife']

To *coup carls* is synonymous with both expressions, in the sense of 'to fall head over heels'. Jamieson confines it to Galloway, suggests that *carls* is perhaps allied to 'Gaelic *cairl-ean* to tumble, to toss, *cairle*, tumbled', and quotes 'Davidson's Seasons':

> Right winsome was the simmer e'en
> When lads and lasses pingle,
> An' coupis carls on the green,
> An' dancing round the ingle.

Court a Kennedy What one once needed to do if one wanted a bed for the night anywhere in southwest Scotland, where the Kennedys were for long the dominant clan, their head being the Earl of Cassillis. The following rhyme is recorded in *A Description of Carrict by Mr Abercrummie, Minister of Minibole* (1696):

> Twixt Wigtoune and the towne of Aire
> And laigh down be the Cruves of Cree
> You shall not gett a lodging there
> Except ye court a Kennedy.

In *The Monastery* (1820) Sir Walter Scott offers an alternative:

> Twixt Wigton and the town of Ayr,
> Portpatrick and the Cruives of Cree,
> No Man need think for to bide there,
> Unless he court Saint Kennedie.

See also KING OF CARRICK.

Court of Equity A bachelors' club in Mauchline in Burns's time, which held its meetings in the White-foord Arms (prop. John Dove, aka Johnny PIGEON). Its purpose was 'to search out, report, and discuss the merits and demerits of the many scandals that crop up from time to time in the village'. Burns was perpetual president, John Richmond clerk, James Smith fiscal and William Hunter messenger-at-arms.

Covenanters Those many Presbyterian Scots who in the 17th century resisted the attempts of the Stuart kings to impose their own authority on the Kirk via bishops and Anglican styles of worship. The Covenanters took their name from the National Covenant of 1638, which protested against the introduction of the Prayer Book, and the Solemn League and Covenant of 1643, a religious and military alliance between the Scots and the English Parliamentarians, by which the signatories pledged to maintain Presbyterianism in Scotland and to introduce it into the rest of the British Isles. However, the term 'Covenanter' is particularly associated with those who, after the Restoration of 1660, rejected Charles II's attempts to reassert his authority on the Kirk, leading to the debarring of 262 dissenting ministers. They and their followers held secret outdoor conventicles, especially among the remote moors of southwest Scotland (and hence became known as *mountain men* or *mountain folk* or *hill folk*). The government used force to disrupt these gatherings, and in 1678 sent a hugely resented 'Highland Host' into the Covenanting areas. The following year the Covenanters came out in open rebellion, defeating government forces at Drumclog in Ayrshire, but suffering defeat at Bothwell Bridge shortly thereafter. The government adopted a conciliatory policy, but the die-hard CAMERONIANS kept up the fight, and the harshly repressive military action that followed became known as the KILLING TIME. It was not until after the Glorious Revolution of 1689–90 that the government agreed to restore Presbyterianism in Scotland.

Scottish heritage culture is robed in the garb of Highland Jacobitism, the product of a corrupt and venal
monarchy, not the piety of the lowland Covenanter.
How many of us who have visited Culloden, Killiecrankie or Glenfinnan have also visited the monuments at Drumclog or Bothwell Brig?

> – Dr James Coleman, historian at Glasgow University,
> quoted in *The Herald*, 2 November 2007

See also CROP-EAR; WANDERER; WHIG.

Covenanter's Grave A tombstone near the summit
of Black Law, in the southwestern Pentland Hills in
Lanarkshire. The stone, erected in 1841, bears the
following inscription: 'Sacred to the memory of a
Covenanter who fought and was wounded at Rullion Green, Nov 28th 1666, and was buried here by
Adam Sanderson of Blackhill.' The story behind this
brief description is a moving one. During the night
following the rout of the Covenanters at Rullion
Green, Adam Sanderson, a local shepherd, was
woken by a battering on the door of his cottage
below Black Law. On the threshold stood a badly
wounded Covenanter. The man, whose name was
John Carphin, refused to enter, fearing that his
presence would bring disaster on the inhabitants
of the cottage. However, he expressed a wish to die
in sight of his native Ayrshire hills, and to this end
struggled on up the West Water. He did not make it,
dying of his wounds at Oaken Bush. The next
morning Sanderson found his body, and carried
it on up the slopes of Black Law, burying it near the
summit. He left a stone with a simple inscription:
'UNONE COVENANTER 1666'. Sanderson's original stone is now in Dunsyre Kirk.

Covenant made with death and hell, a Cromwell's
description of the proclamation of Charles II as king
by the Scots on 5 February 1649.

Covin tree A particular tree outside a castle or
grand house where the laird met and received
guests, and said farewell to them on their departure.
An example is the old sweet chestnut at Bemersyde
(home of the Haigs), which was painted by Turner.
Covin comes from *covine*, 'a compact, agreement',
ultimately from Latin *convenire*, 'to come together'.
Compare DOOL TREE.

Cow a' green thing, to To outdo everything or
everyone; to excel. *That fair cows a' green thing*
means 'That beats everything'. *Cow* on its own
means 'cut, crop' or 'outdo, surpass', and the expression is used in the Northeast, while the shorter
versions *cow a'* and *cow a'thing* are more general.
Local variants include *cow the cadger* ('itinerant
hawker'), *cow the cuddy* ('donkey') and *cow the
gowan* ('daisy').

Cowgate, the *See* TAM O' THE COUGAIT.

Cows, notable In his *Historie of the Kirk of Scotland*
(1646), David Calderwood records the following
curious event, which took place in March or April
1612: 'A cow brought forth fourteen great dog
whelps instead of calves …'. (It was a spring full
of prodigies, Calderwood tells us, for that same
season 'One of the Earl of Argyle's servants being
sick, vomited two toads and a serpent, and so
convalesced: but vomited after a number of little
toads.')

Several of the BRAHAN SEER's predictions concerned Fairburn Tower, between Muir of Ord and
Strathpeffer: 'The day will come when the Mac-
Kenzies of Fairburn shall lose their entire possessions; their castle will become uninhabited and a
cow shall give birth to a calf in the uppermost
chamber of the tower.' The tower duly fell into ruin,
and in 1851 a farmer was using it to store hay. One
of his cows apparently followed a trail of hay up the
stairs, and then got stuck on the upper floor, where
it gave birth. The farmer waited five days before
bringing cow and calf down, so that people could
come to see the prophecy fulfilled (and no doubt
purchase refreshments from the farmer's wife).

In 1954 a cow escaped a livestock auction in
Inverness, entered a doorway, climbed some stairs,
fell through the floor into the emporium below
where, like a bull in a china shop, it crashed about
and in so doing managed to turn on a tap, resulting
in a flood. The shopkeeper sued the auction firm,
but the judge ruled that 'a gate-crashing, stair-
climbing, floor-bursting, tap-turning cow was something *sui generis* [a unique case] for whose depredations the law affords no remedy unless there was
foreknowledge of some such propensities'.

For other notable cows, *see* COO O' FORFAR, THE;

HALKERTON'S COW, LIKE; WATER COW, THE; TURRA COO, THE; BERNIE THE BULL. For a non-bovine cow, *see* WORRICOW.

Cowp the cadger *See* BOLT THE CADGER.

Crack like a gun, to To talk volubly, to blether on noisily. Variants include *crack like a pen-gun* (a *pen-gun* being a pop-gun or pea-shooter) or *like pea-guns* or *like twa hand guns*.

> 'Od, sic twa sib freens I never saw. They're like lad and lass, cracking awa' like pea-guns a' the hours o' the day an' night.
> – James Ballantine, *The Gaberlunzie's Wallet* (1843)

Crack can also be a noun, meaning much the same as the Irish *craic*, as in expressions such as *Get on the crack*, 'start a conversation', *Gie's yer crack*, 'Tell us your news' and *crack croose* (*see under* CROOSE I' THE CRAW).

Crail capon A species of split and dried smoked haddock, popular in the 19th century and named after the Fife fishing village, which exported it to mainland Europe. The 16th-century Crail Tolbooth sports a copper weathervane in the form of a Crail capon.

Cranachan *See* ATHOLL BROSE.

Crann tàra *See* FIERY CROSS.

Crap Among several meanings should be mentioned (1) crop (as in food crop), (2) crop (as in the craw of a bird), hence (3) throat, and (4) stomach. *Crap an root* means 'root and branch'; to *clear* or *redd one's crap* is to clear one's throat, thus to get something off one's chest; to *get the crap on* is to get the wind up; while to *craw in someone's crap* is to annoy or nag them.

> Ere servant maids had wont to rise
> To seeth the breakfast kettle,
> Ilk dame her brawest ribbons tries,
> To put her on her mettle,
> Wi' wiles some silly chiel to trap,
> (And troth he's fain to get her,)
> But she'll craw kniefly in his crap,

> Whan, wow! he canna flit her
> Frae hame that day.
> – Robert Fergusson, 'Leith Races' (1773)

Crappit heids A dish formerly prepared in coastal areas, and consisting of heads of cod or haddock stuffed with the livers of coley (*crappit heid* means 'stuffed head'). Modern versions use lobster as the stuffing. Walter Scott mentions crappit heids in *Guy Mannering* (1815):

> Ou than, he just said, if there comes such a person to inquire after Mr Brown, you will say I am gone to look at the skaters on Loch Creeran, as you call it, and I will be back here to dinner – But he never came back – though I expected him sae faithfully, that I gae a look to making the friar's chicken mysell, and to the crappit-heads too, and that's what I dinna do for ordinary, Mr Glossin – But little did I think what skating wark he was gaun about – to shoot Mr Charles, the innocent lamb!

Craw bogle *See* BOGLE; TATTIE-BOGLE.

Craw croose *See* CROOSE I' THE CRAW.

Craw in someone's crap, to *See* CRAP.

Craw Road *See* CROW ROAD.

Craws' court A curious ornithological phenomenon ascribed to the hoodie crows of Shetland:

> The crows generally appear in pairs, even during winter, except when attracted to a spot in search of food, or when they assemble for the purpose of holding what is called the *craw's court*. This latter institution exhibits a curious fact in their history. Numbers are seen to assemble on a particular hill or field, from many different points. On some occasions the meeting does not appear to be complete before the expiration of a day or two. As soon as all the deputies have arrived, a very general noise and croaking ensue, and shortly after, the whole fall upon one or two individuals, whom they persecute and beat until they kill them. When this has been accomplished, they quietly disperse.
> – Arthur Edmonston, *A View of the Ancient and Present State of the Zetland Islands* (1809)

The phenomenon has also been recorded by one of Scotland's most distinguished naturalists:

In Shetland an event, known as the 'Craas' court', occurs in spring. A large flock of Hoodies appear from all directions. Apparently the court is held for the purpose of dealing out sentence to certain Crows who have been guilty of some offence, for after an hour or so of deliberation the whole assembly turn fiercely on certain individuals and peck them to death.

– Seton Gordon, *Hill Birds of Scotland* (1915)

Pulling aside the anthropomorphizing, the authors appear to be describing normal flocking behaviour and individual antagonisms displayed by hoodies and their close relatives, carrion crows, observed elsewhere in Britain and Europe.

Craw steps, crow steps or **corbie steps** The small steps in the gables found in many traditional Scottish houses, popularly so-called because suitable for crows to perch upon. The *OED* upbraids John Jamieson for proffering an alternative origin in his *Etymological Dictionary of the Scottish Language* (1808):

Jamieson ... offered the conjecture that *corbie-steps* might be a corruption of 'corbel-steps' (of the existence of which he had no evidence whatever), and this merely fictitious form has been adopted in some Dictionaries, etc.

Cream of the water, the The first water drawn from the well on New Year's morning, also known as the *ream* [i.e. cream], *flooer* or *crap* [crop] *of the water*. Drawing this was called *creaming the well*, and was supposed to bring the young woman who drew it beauty, good fortune and a husband. There was considerable competition after midnight to be the first to the well, and in some places a piece of straw was left in the water to let the other aspirants know that the well had already been creamed. The custom was known from Galloway to Caithness.

Crichton, the Admirable *See* ADMIRABLE CRICHTON, THE.

Crivens *See* JINGS, CRIVENS, HELP MA BOAB.

Creepie chair The STOOL OF REPENTANCE.

Cripple Zaidie *See* CROOKIT ZAIDIE.

Crochallan Fencibles, the An Edinburgh literary club that flourished around the last two decades of the 18th century, and met at the Anchor Tavern, in Anchor Close (situated beneath the present City Chambers). This establishment was, according to James Grant in *Cassell's Old and New Edinburgh* (1880s),

... the famous festive and hospitable tavern of Daniel, or, as he was familiarly named ... Dawney Douglas, an establishment second to none in its time for convivial meetings, and noted for suppers of tripe, mince collops, rizzared haddocks, and fragrant hashes, that never cost more than sixpence a-head; yet on charges so moderate Dawney Douglas and his gudewife contrived to grow extremely rich before they died.

Dawney Douglas was renowned for his renditions of the Gaelic song 'Crodh Chailein' ('Colin's cattle'), which accounts for the 'Crochallan' element in the club's name, while the 'Fencibles' element was a jocular nod to the patriotic fashion for forming militias that had begun at the time of the American Revolution. The club's founder was the printer William Smellie, who wrote much of the first edition of the *Encyclopaedia Britannica*, and it was Smellie who introduced Robert Burns to the club during his 1787 visit to the city to oversee the printing of his poems. When, Grant tells us, 'according to custom, one of the club was pitted against him in a contest of wit and humour, Burns bore the assault with perfect equanimity'. In a note, Burns states that the last verse of the song 'Rattlin', Roarin' Willie' was composed by Burns himself 'out of compliment to one of the worthiest fellows in the world', the club's president or 'colonel', William Dunbar, W.S.:

As I cam by Crochallan,
  I cannily keekit ben:
Rattlin', roarin' Willie
  Was sitting at yon boord-en' –
Sitting at yon boord-en',
  And amang gude companie;
Rattlin', roarin' Willie,
  Ye're welcome hame to me!

It should finally be mentioned that the 1799 edition of the bawdy *MERRY MUSES OF CALEDONIA*, partly at least the work of Burns, claims on its title page to have been 'selected for the use of the Crochallan Fencibles'.

Croesus, the Scots *See* SCOTS CROESUS, THE.

Crofting counties, the The pre-1975 counties of Argyll, Caithness, Inverness-shire, Orkney, Ross and Cromarty, Shetland and Sutherland, which were the beneficiaries of special government grants, etc. The term has continued in use through subsequent local government reorganizations, and following the Crofting Reform Act of 2007, Arran, Bute, the isles of Greater and Little Cumbrae, and Moray were added as crofting areas, and thus able to benefit from the Crofting Counties Agricultural Grants Scheme.

Crooked David *See* BLACK DWARF, THE.

Crookit or **Cripple Zaidie** The name given to the catcher (who imitates a cripple) in a form of tag formerly played by girls. *Zaidie* is a diminutive form of Zed, the last letter of the alphabet.

Crookit stick will throw a crookit shadow, A A proverb cited by Alexander Hislop in *The Proverbs of Scotland* (1868). A *crookit stick* can also be a second-rate suitor; *see* CUT THE CROOKIT STICK, TO.

Crook o' the Forth, a There is a traditional saying that alludes to the rich alluvial soils on either bank of the River Forth between Stirling and the Firth:

A crook o' the Forth
Is worth an earldom o' the North.

Croose i' the craw Literally, 'bold or pleased with oneself in the crowing [as of a cock]', i.e. full of braggadocio and/or garrulous self-satisfaction. To behave in this way is to *craw croose*.

'And this is nae great matter, after a'; just to cut the comb of a young cock that has been crawing a little ower crousely.'
  'Not young Earnscliff?' said the Solitary, with some emotion.
  'No; not young Earnscliff – not young Earnscliff YET; but his time may come …'
    – Sir Walter Scott, *The Black Dwarf* (1816), chapter vi

To *crack croose* is to talk in a vivacious fashion, without necessarily attracting accusations of bump-

tiousness; for example, in 'The Twa Dogs' Burns writes of 'The cantie auld folks crackan crouse' (for *crack, see under* CRACK LIKE A GUN, TO). *Croose* is also spelt *crouse, crowse*, etc.

Crop *See* CRAP.

Crop-ear A disparaging description of a COVEN-ANTER, deriving from the punishment visited on many of them in the pillory during the period of Archbishop Laud's Court of High Commission (abolished in 1641).

I did not think there was a crop-ear of them all could have laid the best cap and feather in the King's Life-Guards on the floor of a rascally change-house.
  – Sir Walter Scott, *Old Mortality* (1816), chapter iv. Sergeant Bothwell speaking.

The Covenanters were also described as 'long-eared' or 'prick-eared', their tight skull-caps and short hair making their ears appear to stick out.

Cross-dressing jockey, a *See* CAMP MEG.

Crouse … *See* CROOSE …

Crow … *See also* CRAW …

Crown of Scotland A hill (1765 ft / 538 m) in the Moffat Hills, a little to the northeast of the DEVIL'S BEEF TUB. The name presumably refers to the fine views to be had from here. *See also* HONOURS OF SCOTLAND, THE.

Crow Road A euphemism for death, as explained by Iain Banks in his 1992 novel *The Crow Road*:

I asked her if she'd ever heard Grandma Margot use the saying: away the Crow Road (or the Craw Rod, if she was being especially broad-accented that day). It meant dying; being dead. 'Aye, he's away the crow road,' meant 'He's dead.'

In this instance, the Crow Road is the one in Glasgow's West End, but there is also a Craw Road in Paisley, and the steep road over the Campsie Fells between Lennoxtown and Fintry is also known as the Craw Road. The latter was originally a drove road, and much used by the MacGregors in their depredations thereabouts. However, it is likely that in many instances no specific road or street is intended:

> Of course, it might be that the fish were for the crow road anyway: nitrates and phosphates from sewage, plus agricultural fertilisers … all drained into the seas.
> – Ian Rankin, *Black and Blue* (1997)

Crow steps *See* CRAW STEPS.

Cruachan! The war cry of Clan Campbell, alluding to Ben Cruachan, the lofty peak in the heart of Campbell country in Argyll. The name comes from Gaelic *cruach*, 'of the stacks', referring to the mountain's several tops. The 14th-century poet John Barbour, in *The Brus*, thought it Britain's highest hill:

> Crechinben hecht yat montane
> I trow nocht yat in all Bretane
> Ane heyar hill may fundyne be.

Cruikit … *See* CROOKIT …

Cry something at the cross, to To announce something to the world at large, *the cross* being the mercat (market) cross where public announcements were traditionally made.

Cuckoo *See* GOWK.

Cuddie-loup-the-dyke *See* LOWP-THE-CUDDIE.

Cullen skink A fish soup named after the fishing port of Cullen on the north coast of Moray. *Skink* (from Middle Dutch *schenke*) is an old Scots word for 'shin' or 'knuckle', and also for a soup made from shin of beef. In Cullen, they made their version of skink with smoked haddock, milk, potatoes, onion and parsley.

Culross girdle The royal burgh of Culross in Fife was once renowned for its iron *girdles* (i.e. griddles). Indeed, so impressed was James VI on a visit to the town in 1599 that he granted the girdlesmiths of Culross the sole right of manufacturing such articles – although it is possible he was just confirming an earlier charter. The method employed in Culross

was apparently as follows: the master smith would hold a lump of iron with his tongs, while two sturdy apprentices went at it with hammers, until the desired flatness had been achieved. The perfect girdle should, it was said, ring like a bell when struck – hence the warning formerly issued to recalcitrant children by distracted mothers: 'Ah'll gar yer lugs ring like a Culross girdle!'

> The hammermen of Edinburgh are to my mind afore the warld for making stancheons, ring-bolts, fetter-bolts, bars, and locks. And they arena that bad at girdles for carcakes neither, though the Cu'ross hammermen have the gree for that.
> – Sir Walter Scott, *The Heart of Midlothian* (1818), chapter xxviii (*Carcakes* were small cakes baked with eggs on FASTERN EVE, i.e. Shrove Tuesday.)

> She took her Culross girdle, which is said to have been extensive enough to toast eighteen bannocks of the Merse's mak at once, and, kneading a large cake full of red Jacobuses, prepared it in the usual manner.
> – Robert Chambers, 'Meg of Tullishill', in *The Picture of Scotland* (1827)

Cumbrays, a prayer for the In September 1827 Sir Walter Scott noted in his journal:

> Prayer of the minister of the two Cumbrays, two miserable islands in the mouth of the Clyde: 'Oh Lord, bless and be gracious to the Greater and the Lesser Cumbrays, and in thy mercy do not forget the adjacent islands of Great Britain and Ireland.'

Cummers' feast Apparently a dinner to which women were also invited, a *cummer* or *kimmer* being a married woman or 'gossip'.

> … the Cummers' Feast. This was a supper, where each gentleman brought a pint of wine to be drunk by him and his wife … There was an eating posset in the middle of the table, with dried fruits and sweetmeats at the sides. When they had finished their supper, the meat was removed, and in a moment everybody flies to the sweetmeats to pocket them. Upon which a scramble ensued, chairs overturned, and everything on the table, wrassalling and pulling at one another with the utmost noise. When all was quieted, they went to the stoups (for there was no bottles) of which the women had a good share. For though it was a disgrace to be

seen drunk, yet it was none to be a little intoxicate in good company.

> – Elizabeth Mure of Caldwell, recording her uncle's memories of the early 18th century, quoted in Agnes Mure Mackenzie, *Scottish Pageant, 1707–1802* (1950)

A *cummer* was also a midwife or a godmother, and a *cummering* or *kimmerin* was a feast to celebrate the birth of a child. In his *Gallovidian Encyclopedia* (1824), John MacTaggart defines *kimmerins* as 'the feasts at births', and continues, 'These, the "*Kimmers*," or gude-wives, have to themselves, no men are allowed to partake along with them.'

Cuntbittin crawdoun Kennedie *See* FLYTING. *See also* AY FUCKAND LYKE ANE FURIOUS FORNICATOR.

Cupar justice A version of JEDDART JUSTICE, named after the former county town of Fife.

> The popular tradition is, that a man, who was confined in prison in Cupar-Fife, obstinately refused to come out to trial; and that water was let into his cell, under the idea of compelling him to forsake it, till he was actually drowned; and that those who had the charge of him, finding this to be the case, brought his dead body into court, and proceeded regularly in the trial, till it was solemnly determined that he had met with nothing more than he deserved.
> – John Jamieson, *An Etymological Dictionary of the Scottish Language* (1825 supplement)

See also HE THAT WILL TO CUPAR MAUN TO CUPAR.

Curd Fair An annual fair that according to the *Ordnance Gazetteer of Scotland* (1882–5) took place in Kilmarnock on the second Tuesday in May. The following Saturday, *Curd Saturday*, was a holiday, on which the inhabitants of the town visited neighbouring farms to eat curds and cream.

Cure for which there is no disease, the Whisky, according to a certain John Ferguson (*fl.* 19th century).

Curly andra A sugared coriander or caraway seed, the name being a corruption of 'coriander'.

Curly Kate The curved top crust of a loaf of bread. The term is also known in the Northeast of England, where the flat crust at the bottom of the loaf is known as *Plain Geordie*.

Curry Alley An obsolescent nickname for Gibson Street in Glasgow's West End, once celebrated for its many curry houses. It was also dubbed the *Khyber Pass*. Many of the street's curry houses have now been replaced by establishments offering alternative cuisines.

Curse of Scotland, the The nine of diamonds. Various theories have been put forward to explain the nickname. Most of these are summarized by Robert Chambers in *The Book of Days* (1862–4), in relation to an article about Sir John Dalrymple, Master of Stair (later 1st Earl of Stair). Dalrymple was instrumental in bringing over William of Orange, was held chiefly culpable for the MASSACRE OF GLENCOE, and was a prime mover in the Union of 1707. His father, James Dalrymple, Viscount Stair, had been president of the Court of Session, while his son, the 2nd Earl, was ambassador to France and active in the anti-Stuart cause:

> The remarkable talents and vigour of three generations of one family on the Whig side, not to speak of sundry offshoots of the tree in eminent official situations, rendered the Dalrymples a vexation of no small magnitude to the Tory party in Scotland. It appears to have been with reference to them, that the Nine of Diamonds got the name of the *Curse of Scotland*; this card bearing a resemblance to the nine lozenges, or, arranged saltire-wise on their armorial coat.

Various other reasons have, indeed, been suggested for this expression – as that, the game of Comète being introduced by Mary of Lorraine [Mary of Guise, mother of Mary Queen of Scots] (alternatively by James, Duke of York) into the court at Holyrood, the Nine of Diamonds, being the winning card, got this name in consequence of the number of courtiers ruined by it; that in the game of Pope Joan, the Nine of Diamonds is the Pope – a personage whom the Scotch Presbyterians considered as a curse; that diamonds imply royalty, and every ninth king of Scotland was a curse to his country: all of them most lame and unsatisfactory suggestions, in comparison with the simple and obvious idea of a witty reference to a set of detested but powerful statesmen, through the medium of their coat of arms. Another supposition, that the Duke of Cumberland [BUTCHER CUMBERLAND] wrote his inhuman orders at Culloden on the back of the Nine of Diamonds, is negatived by the fact that a caricature of the earlier date of October 21, 1715, represents the young chevalier [the CHEVALIER ST GEORGE, i.e. the OLD PRETENDER] attempting to lead a herd of bulls, laden with papal curses, excommunications, &c., across the Tweed, with the Nine of Diamonds lying before them.

Two additional suggestions have been made. Firstly, that the card resembles the coat of arms of the Duke of Argyll, hated by some for his part in bringing about the Union of 1707; this theory was put forward by Francis Grose in his *Dictionary of the Vulgar Tongue* (1811). Secondly, that 'Curse' is a corruption of 'cross', the arrangement of the diamonds representing the SALTIRE cross of St Andrew. As the nines of all suits are arranged thus, this seems implausible.

Curse on Luss, a Robert Andrews (d.1766?) penned a curse on Luss, a village on the west shore of Loch Lomond, where he had lost a book of Milton's poems:

> Luss! be for ever sunk beneath
>   Ben's horrors piled around:
> Sun's livening ray ne'er pierce thy gloom,
>   Thy hideous deep be drained!
>   – 'Mercury. On Losing my Pocket Milton at Luss near
>   Ben Lomond, and other Mountains' (1757)

Curse on Fort William library, a *See* HANGING TREE OF FORT WILLIAM, THE.

Curse on the Laird of Cromarty, a Sir Thomas Urquhart (1611–60), translator of Rabelais and author of *LOGOPANDECTEISION* and other works, had it in for the Laird of Cromarty:

> Scullions, hogge rubbers, kenell brakers and all others of the meanest sort of rascallitie, to spit in your face, kicke you in the breach, to tred on your mushtashes, as also to all those that know yow to curse yow with all the execrations mentioned in the Psalmes of David ...

> from thence furth no honest man will offer to eat drinke or converse with yow nor any above the degree of a hangman's varlet to serve yow.
>   – Sir Thomas Urquart, 'His Letter to the Laird of
>   Cromartie'

Curse on the Reivers, the In 1525 Archbishop Gavin Douglas of Glasgow anathematized the BORDER REIVERS, who had been up to their usual high jinks (burning, pillaging, raping, plundering, stealing, slaughtering and so on). His 'Monition of Cursing' was required to be read by the priests in all the parishes of the Borders. Extracts from a modernized version of the curse were inscribed on a 14-tonne granite boulder designed by Gordon Young and commissioned by the City of Carlisle to mark the millennium. The curse begins thus:

> I curse their head and all the hairs of their head; I curse their face, their brain, their mouth, their nose, their tongue, their teeth, their forehead, their shoulders, their breast, their heart, their stomach, their back, their womb, their arms, their legs, their hands, their feet, and every part of their body, from the top of their head to the soles of their feet, before and behind, within and without.

After another thousand or so words of denunciation and malediction, the archbishop concludes:

> And, finally, I condemn them perpetually to the deep pit of hell, there to remain with Lucifer and all his fellows, and their bodies to the gallows of Burrow moor, first to be hanged, then ripped and torn by dogs, swine, and other wild beasts, abominable to all the world. And their candle [light of their life] goes from your sight, as may their souls go from the face of God, and their good reputation from the world, until they forebear their open sins, aforesaid, and rise from this terrible cursing and make satisfaction and penance.

After the 'Cursing Stone' was placed in Carlisle's Millennium Gallery, locals noted that the city's luck began to decline. First of all there was the 2001 foot-and-mouth epidemic (which was at its worst in the Carlisle area), then, following heavy job losses and derisory performances by the local football team, in January 2005 the city was badly damaged by flooding. Many people blamed the 'Cursing Stone', and in March 2005 Councillor Jim Tootle, reeling from the city's misfortunes, put forward a motion that the Cursing Stone be destroyed. As passions rose, the Bishop of Carlisle intervened, declaring that the stone lacked any ill intent, as the artist had included a blessing on the stone, as well as words from the curse.

Customs and celebrations *See* CEREMONIES, ETC.

Cut the crookit stick, to To settle for a less satisfactory suitor. *Crookit* is 'crooked'. A variant is *tak up wi' the crookit stick*.

Cutty chair The STOOL OF REPENTANCE.

Cutty Sark The nickname of Nannie, the scantily clad young witch in Burns's TAM O' SHANTER (1791). *Cutty sark* means 'short shift' or 'short chemise', and it is to such a garment that comely Nannie has stripped as the witches cavort in the old Alloway Kirk:

> But here my Muse her wing maun cour,
> Sic flights are far beyond her power;

To sing how Nannie lap and flang,
(A souple jade she was and strang),
And how Tam stood, like ane bewitch'd,
And thought his very een enrich'd:
Even Satan glowr'd, and fidg'd fu' fain,
And hotch'd and blew wi' might and main:
Till first ae caper, syne anither,
Tam tint his reason a thegither,
And roars out, 'Weel done, Cutty-sark!'

This alerts the 'hellish legion' to Tam's presence, and they give chase, Cutty Sark herself grabbing hold of the tail of Tam's horse, which comes off in her hand – and so Tam escapes.

The name *Cutty Sark* was given to the famous clipper built at Dumbarton in 1869 (now preserved at Greenwich, although badly damaged in a fire in 2007); a bare-breasted Nannie, with horse's tail in hand, provided the ship's figurehead. The clipper in turn gave its name to a brand of blended whisky, launched in 1923.

Cutty stool The STOOL OF REPENTANCE.

D

Dab, let *See* LET DAB.

Daddies, to be a' their To be the tops, the best. *Daddy* here is the same as in standard English. *Cf.* the modern American expression 'Who's the Daddy?'

Daddy Cloots *See* AULD CLOOTIE.

Daft Ann's Steps A series of rocky pillars extending into the sea on the south side of Hestan Island. This islet in the Solway Firth is linked at low tide on its north side to the mainland at Almorness Point by a natural causeway called the Rack. In the past it was also possible to cross to the island on the south side at low tide from Balcary Point, which saved the long walk around Auchencairn Bay. However, this route was much more dangerous, and when the eponymous Daft Ann, a slow-witted native of Auchencairn village, attempted to make the crossing by laying stepping stones ahead of her, she lost her balance, fell into deep water and was drowned. The island was formerly much used by smugglers, and features as such – under the name Isle Rathan – in S.R. Crockett's novel *The Raiders* (1894).

Daft days Any carefree, fun-filled period, especially one's youth, or the time around Christmas and HOGMANAY. Robert Fergusson's poem entitled 'The Daft Days' evokes the cosy, boozy bonhomie that may be achieved during the festive season, even as 'mirk December's dowie face / Glow'rs owre the rigs wi' sour grimace':

> When merry Yule-day comes, I trow
> You'll scantlins find a hungry mou;
> Sma' are our cares, our stamacks fou
>   O' gusty gear,
> And kickshaws, strangers to our view,
>   Sin Fairn-year.

> Ye browster wives, now busk ye bra,
> And fling your sorrows far awa';
> Then come and gie's the tither blaw
>   Of reaming ale,
> Mair precious than the well of Spa,
>   Our hearts to heal.

In 1907 Neil Munro published a novel entitled *The Daft Days*, set in a small town in Argyll (based on Inveraray).

Daft Friday At the University of Glasgow, the day of boozing and larks celebrating the end of the Martinmas term, culminating in an all-night black-tie ball. It originated in 1909 as a sing-song organized by the honorary secretary of the Glasgow University Union, Osborne Henry Mavor (later better known as the playwright James Bridie).

Daft laddie / lassie, to play the To put on a show of naivety and gullibility, in order to get what one wants. For example, when, many decades ago, the present writer was a wet-eared young assistant editor at Collins in Glasgow, he was adjured by his wise old boss to 'play the daft laddie' when attempting to winkle trade secrets out of the production department.

Daft Pate *See* DEVIL ON WHEELS, THE.

Daith candle *See* DEATH CANDLE.

Dalriada The original kingdom of the Scots, who were in fact Irish, although known as Scoti. Dalriada (known as Dál Riata in Ireland) takes its name from the clan who founded it, and initially spanned the North Channel to take in parts of Antrim in Ulster together with much of Argyll and some of the Inner Hebrides. The rulers of Dalriada moved to Scotland in the 5th century AD, after which their power in Ulster was steadily extinguished. Dunadd in southern Argyll was the main seat of the kings of Dalriada, one of whom, Kenneth MacAlpin, defeated the PICTS in 843 and brought them under his rule, so creating ALBA.

> Though thy land is not large this day among thy brothers, yet it is thou shalt be king. From thee shall ever descend the kings of this land.
> – St Patrick prophesies to Fergus Mòr, a 5th-century king of Dalriada, as quoted in a 10th-century life of the saint

Damnable sect, that Sir John Dalrymple's description of the Macdonalds of Glencoe, in a letter dated 11 January 1692:

> Just now my Lord Argyle tells me that Glencoe hath not taken the oaths; at which I rejoice – it's a great work of charity to be exact in rooting out that damnable sect, the worst in all the Highlands.

The MASSACRE OF GLENCOE – for which Dalrymple, as secretary of state, was held responsible by Parliament – followed on 13 February. *See also* CURSE OF SCOTLAND, THE.

Damned Scotch metaphysics *See* NONE OF YOUR DAMNED SCOTCH METAPHYSICS!

Dan or **Danny Boy** A term applied to a Roman Catholic in the West of Scotland; from the archetypal Irish ballad 'Danny Boy', and the fact that Daniel is a popular name among Irish Catholics.

Dancers, the *See* MERRY DANCERS, THE.

Dances *See* GAMES AND DANCES.

Dance the reel o' Bogie, to To have sexual intercourse. *Bogie* here is perhaps 'hobgoblin'. Variants include *dance the reel o' stumpie* (a word with likely phallic connotations) and *dance the miller's reel* (millers notoriously accepted payment in kind).

> Then she fell o'er, an' sae did I,
> An' danced the miller's reel, O,
> Whene'er that bonny lassie comes again,
> She shall hae her maut ground weel, O.

> The mill, mill, O, and the kill, kill, O,
> An' the coggin' o' Peggy's wheel, O,
> The sack and the sieve, an' a' she did leave,
> An' danced the miller's reel, O.
> – 'The Mill, Mill, O', from
> *The Merry Muses of Caledonia*

Dandie Dinmont *See* DINMONT, DANDIE.

Dandy Doctor In 19th-century Edinburgh and environs, a species of bogeyman who would kidnap children and sell them to the anatomists. The notion was inspired by the story of BURKE AND HARE. The Dunbar-born John Muir (1838–1914) – JOHN O' THE MOUNTAINS – recalled the fear they inspired in *The Story of My Boyhood and Youth*:

> The servant girls told us that 'Dandy Doctors', clad in long black cloaks and supplied with a store of sticking-plaster of wondrous adhesiveness, prowled at night about the country lanes and even the town streets, watching for children to choke and sell. The Dandy Doctor's business method, as the servants explained it, was with lightning quickness to clap a sticking-plaster on the face of a scholar, covering mouth and nose, preventing breathing or crying for help, then pop us under his long black cloak and carry us to Edinburgh to be sold and sliced into small pieces for folk to learn how we were made. We always mentioned the name 'Dandy Doctor' in a fearful whisper, and never dared venture out of doors after dark.

So terrified were he and his fellows, Muir recalls, that in mid-winter his school closed early, otherwise the children would refuse to leave the classroom if night had fallen.

Danes, the *See* FOOTBALL CLUB NICKNAMES.

Dang doon *See* DING DOON.

Danny Boy *See* DAN.

Danube Street A street in Edinburgh's New Town, which, from the 1940s to the 1970s, became synonymous with the city's sex industry, owing to the goings-on at Number 17. This was the address of a classy brothel run by Dora Noyce, who, with her fur coat, twin set and pearls, together with her refined Morningside accent, gave the impression of being a genteel Edinburgh lady. She herself rejected the label 'madam', and referred to her establishment as 'a house of leisure and pleasure' or 'a YMCA with extras'. She claimed that business was particularly brisk during the annual GENERAL ASSEMBLY of the Church of Scotland, but she and the women who worked for her maintained complete discretion regarding the identity of their clients, many of whom were almost certainly illustrious figures in the Edinburgh Establishment. Although the authorities were inclined to be tolerant, as Noyce kept such an orderly house, she was still subjected to regular raids, and would greet the policemen at her door with the inquiry, 'Business or pleasure, gentlemen?' She was frequently fined, and occasionally jailed, for living off immoral earnings, but would go straight back to running her business. She died in 1977, and her establishment closed down soon after. *See also* BLYTHSWOOD SQUARE.

Daphne Disaster, the When the SS *Daphne* was launched from the Linthouse yard in Govan into the Clyde on 3 July 1883 there were some 200 workers aboard, ready to start fitting the ship out. Miscalculations regarding stability caused the *Daphne* to capsize and sink almost immediately, drowning 124 men and boys. Only 70 were saved.

Dara-sealladh *See* SECOND SIGHT.

Darien Scheme, the An attempt to establish a Scottish colony on the east side of the Isthmus of Panama at the end of the 17th century. The English Navigation Act of 1661 had barred Scottish vessels from trading with England's colonies in the New World, so Scottish merchants put pressure on the Scottish government to establish its own colonies, resulting in the formation of the Company of Scotland in 1695. The actual scheme, created under the aegis of the company, was devised by William Paterson, and the intention was to create a colony called New Caledonia at Darien, which would serve as a key entrepôt for a new international Scottish trading network. King William III, anxious to restore his image in Scotland after the MASSACRE OF GLENCOE, encouraged English speculators to invest

in the company, but this was withdrawn under pressure from the East India Company and other powerful English trading interests. In addition, William, then at war with France, did not want to alienate Spain, which claimed the area. Inadequate funding together with an absence of organization and knowledge of local conditions led to disaster. The first expedition set sail from Leith on 14 July 1698, with some 1200 settlers aboard five ships. They landed at Darien on 2 November, built Fort St Andrew and named their main settlement New Edinburgh. Agriculture proved difficult, the indigenous people were friendly but unwilling to trade, and within a few months three-quarters of the settlers had died of tropical diseases. In July 1699 a single ship set sail for Scotland, but arrived after a second expedition had embarked, carrying a further 1000 colonists. This landed in November 1699, and found the settlement deserted. The new settlers came under Spanish attack, and early in 1700 surrendered to the Spanish. They were subsequently allowed to leave, and the only evidence of their presence today is the name of a headland: Punta Escocés. The failure of the Darien Scheme, which left Scotland virtually bankrupt, led to two important consequences at home: an increase in support for the Jacobite cause, in reaction to William's perceived neglect of his Scottish subjects' interests; and a pressure for the Union of Scotland and England, which would allow the Scots to participate on equal terms in international trade. Negotiations regarding the Union resulted in the payment of the EQUIVALENT, to wipe out the Scottish national debt. *See also* END OF AN OLD SONG, THE; PARCEL OF ROGUES, A.

Dark Blues, the *See* FOOTBALL CLUB NICKNAMES.

Dark Lochnagar *See under* LAND OF MEANNESS, SOPHISTRY AND MIST.

Dashing White Sergeant, the A Scottish country dance, devised *c.*1890 by David Anderson of Dundee. The origins of the dance are not Scottish: the music is from an operetta by Sir Henry Bishop (1786–1855), the man who gave us 'Home, Sweet Home', and the title is from a song composed by General John Burgoyne (1722–92), who followed his career as an unsuccessful soldier in the American War of Independence (he surrendered at Saratoga) with that of successful playwright. The chorus goes:

If an army of Amazons e'er came in play,
As a dashing white sergeant I'd march away,
A dashing white sergeant I'd march away,
March away, march away, march away,
March away, march away, march away,
March away, march away, march away!

Daughter of debate, the Elizabeth I's description of Mary Queen of Scots:

The daughter of debate, that eke discord doth sow.
– Quoted in George Puttenham (ed.), *The Art of English Poesie* (1589)

Daughter of Edward Formerly a propitiatory name for the adder in Argyll and Perthshire, according to John G. Campbell in *Superstitions of the Highlands and Islands of Scotland* (1900). Campbell suspects that the name might have been suggested by the rhyme in a popular saying about the creature.

Daughter of the manse *See* SON OF THE MANSE.

Daylicht for someone, he or she canna see A Northeastern expression, meaning that one is blinded to someone's faults.

Day of the Seven Sleepers *See* BATTLE OF THE SEVEN SLEEPERS.

Days of the week *See* HANDSEL MONDAY; MEAL MONDAY; MURK MONDAY; SKIRE THURSDAY; BLACK FRIDAY; Bloody Friday (*under* BATTLE OF GEORGE SQUARE); DAFT FRIDAY; FLATTERIN FRIDAY; Flitting Friday (*under* FLIT); Rascal Friday (*under* RASCAL FAIR); BLACK SATURDAY; BLOWING SATURDAY; Curd Saturday (*see under* CURD FAIR); GLEN SATURDAY; Grozet Saturday (*under* GROZET FAIR); LITTLE SATURDAY; BONNY SUNDAY; KIRKING SUNDAY; STOOKIE SUNDAY.

Deacon Brodie William Brodie (1741–88), a respectable Edinburgh cabinet-maker, member of the town council and deacon of the guild of wrights and masons, who by night led a secret life as a burglar, employing his skills to copy the keys of the doors of his wealthier clients. He used the money he thereby obtained to maintain two mistresses, five illegitimate children and a gambling habit. Brodie was eventually caught, and died on the gallows that he himself, as a town councillor, had earlier approved and funded. His career (perhaps combined with that of MAJOR WEIR) inspired Robert Louis Stevenson's novella, *The Strange Case of Dr Jekyll and Mr Hyde*, and he is commemorated in the name of a pub on the Royal Mile, Deacon Brodie's Tavern.

Dead woman bites not, a The argument said to have been put forward in 1587 by Patrick, Lord Gray (d.1612) in favour of executing Mary Queen of Scots. Sometimes the Latin version is cited: '*Mortua non mordet*' ('Being dead, she will not bite').

Deaf as Ailsa Craig How Robert Burns describes Meg in his poem 'Duncan Gray', the simile referring to the great rock in the Firth of Clyde nicknamed PADDY'S MILESTONE.

Duncan fleech'd and Duncan pray'd
(Ha, ha, the wooing o't!),
Meg was deaf as Ailsa Craig
(Ha, ha, the wooing o't!)

Presumably John Keats had not read his Burns when he began his 1818 sonnet on Ailsa Craig with the line 'Hearken, thou craggy ocean-pyramid ...'

Deafness, a cure for In 1771 an Irvine man was struck by lightning, which instantly cured the deafness he had suffered from for 20 years.

Deal o' fine confused feedin', a *See* HAGGIS.

Deans, Jeanie *See* HEART OF MIDLOTHIAN, THE.

Dear Green Place A sobriquet for Glasgow, sentimentally derived from the Gaelic name *Glaschu*, which itself is from Brythonic *glas cau*, meaning 'green hollow'. Despite the city's industrial heritage, it is also famed for the extent of its parks and other green places.

The Dear Green Place was the much celebrated but only completed novel of Archie Hind (1928–2008). Published in 1966, it tells the story of the struggle of a young working-class man from Glasgow's Southside to become a writer, and is regarded as one of the finest novels to come out of Glasgow. The phrase has also been borrowed for *Dear Green Place*, a BBC Scotland TV sitcom broadcast in 2007–8 and set in a park in central Glasgow.

> Glas Chu! Glasgow! The dear green place! Now a vehicular sclerosis, a congestion of activity.
> – Archie Hind, *The Dear Green Place* (1966)

Deasil *See* DEISEIL.

Death candle or **dede-candle** A will o' the wisp, i.e. a flare of marsh gas, thought to forecast doom. John Jamieson, in his 1825 Supplement to *An Etymological Dictionary of the Scottish Language*, defines it thus:

> A preternatural light, like that of a candle, seen under night by the superstitious, and viewed as the presage of the death of someone. It is said to be seen for a moment only, either within doors, or in the open air; and, at other times, to move slowly, from the habitation of the person doomed to death, to the churchyard where he is to be interred.

See also DEID-LICHTS.

Debatable Lands Those once blood-soaked areas on either side of the Border that were for centuries fought over by Scots and English armies, and, in an unofficial capacity, by generations of lawless BORDER REIVERS. The term is especially applied to the relatively small area between the Dumfriesshire Esk and the Sark Water, which now forms part of the western Border. There is an early occurrence of the term in an official document from 1494: '... a myle of land nixt about it of the debatabill land betuix us and Ingland'. A little later, in 1530, another document mentions typical goings-on hereabouts: 'The Irwynnis of the Staikheuch and Armstrangis duelland upon the debatable landis ...' In 1552 there are official complaints about the inhabitants of the debatable lands, who 'makis quotidiane reiffis [forcible seizures, as in 'reivers'] and oppressionis upon

the pur'. That same year Monsieur D'Oysel, French ambassador to Scotland, determined the division between Scotland and England of the Esk–Sark Debatable Land, and later that century, along the line of the division, a few miles to the north of Gretna, was built the earthwork known as the Scots Dyke, supposedly the first man-made frontier in Europe since the time of the Romans.

> And as we crossed the Debatable land,
> And tae the English side we held,
> The first of men that we met wi',
> Whae should it be but fause Sakelde?
> – 'Kinmont Willie' (traditional ballad; *see* KINMONT WILLIE)

> Ye ken Highlander and Lowlander, and Border-men, are a' ae man's bairns when you are over the Scots Dyke.
> – Sir Walter Scott, 'The Two Drovers' (1827)

> I sit, being helplessly
> lugged backwards
> through the Debatable Lands of history, listening
> to the execrations, the scattered cries, the
> falling of roof-trees
> in the lamentable dark.
> – Norman MacCaig, 'Crossing the Border' (1968)

Today, at the southern end of the Debatable Land, across the Esk from Longtown, there is (perhaps appropriately enough) a massive munitions factory – although this is but a fragment of the explosives manufacturing complex built here in the First World War, which extended nine miles west past Gretna to Eastriggs. It is said to have been the most extensive factory ever built, and employed 30,000 workers – and it was to control the alcoholic intake of these men and women that the government brought all the pubs and the brewery in Carlisle under public ownership for the duration of hostilities.

Declaration of Arbroath, the A document, probably drafted by Bernard de Linton, Abbot of Arbroath, and signed by the Estates of Scotland when they met in the town on 6 April 1320. In the Declaration they vowed loyalty to King Robert the Bruce, and asserted Scotland's independence from England (something they had secured *de facto* at

Bannockburn six years previously). The purpose of the Declaration was to attempt to persuade the pope to accept Scottish independence, and end Bruce's excommunication, imposed after his murder of the RED COMYN in church in 1306. The most famous passage was originally rendered in Latin as:

> Quia quamdiu Centum ex nobis viui remanserint, nuncquam Anglorum dominio aliquatenus volumus subiugari. Non enim propter gloriam, diuicias aut honores pugnamus set propter libertatem solummodo quam Nemo bonus nisi simul cum vita amittit.

The passage is more familiar in English translation:

> For so long as but a hundred of us remain alive, we will in no way yield ourselves to the dominion of the English. For it is not for glory, nor riches, nor honour that we fight, but for Freedom only, which no good man lays down but with his life.

In the United States, the date of the signing of the Declaration, 6 April, is celebrated as TARTAN DAY. See also FREEDOM IS A NOBLE THING; LIBERTAS OPTIMA RERUM; SCYTHIA.

Dede-candle See DEATH CANDLE.

Dede-lights See DEID-LICHTS.

Dee, River See DEE VS DON.

Dee, the See FOOTBALL CLUB NICKNAMES.

Deedle-doddle, deetle-dottle See EEDLE-DODDLE.

Deedle-dawdle See DIDDLE-DODDLE.

Deep-fried Mars bar The epitome of the healthy Scottish diet, according to the popular press. Deep-fried Mars bars appear to have been first served by the Haven Chip Bar in Stonehaven in 1995, at the request of local schoolchildren. This was reported in the *Aberdeen Evening Express*, and was quickly picked up by the nationals and the BBC. Within days deep-fried Mars bars were on offer in chip shops all over the country.

Dee vs Don A number of traditional rhymes compare the two great Aberdeenshire rivers:

> River Dee for fish and tree
> But Don for ham and corn.

> Ae mile o' Don's worth twa o' Dee
> Except for salmon, stone and tree.

For their relative appetite for human victims, *see* BLOODTHIRSTY DEE.

Degenerate Douglas See OLD Q.

Deid as a mauk Literally, 'dead as a maggot', i.e. utterly lifeless.

Deid-lichts 'The name given by the peasantry,' according to John Jamieson in his 1825 Supplement to *An Etymological Dictionary of the Scottish Language*, 'to the luminous appearance which is sometimes observed over putrescent animal bodies, and which arises probably from the disengagement of phosphorated hydrogen gas.' The sight of such strange lights at night was thought to be as ominous as that of a DEATH CANDLE.

> At length, it was suggested to the old man, that there were always *dead lights* hovered over a corpse at night, if the body was left exposed to the air; and it was a fact that two drowned men had been found in a field of whins, where the water had left the bodies, by means of the *dead lights*, a very little while before that.
> – *Blackwood's Magazine*, March 1823

Deid-man's-sneechin See DEIL'S SNUFFBOX, THE.

Deil ... See also DEVIL ...

Deil haet Literally, 'the Devil have it', used to denote 'not even the tiniest jot or smidgen', or used simply as an imprecation, sometimes reduced to a simple *haet*, *het* or *hate* on its own ('Het! she's far ower young'). Various other words, such as *fiend* or *fule* or *plague*, may be substituted for *deil*.

> I wad find some chields should speak Greek and Latin weel, at least they got plenty o' siller for doing de'il hae't else, if they didna do that.
> – Sir Walter Scott, *Rob Roy* (1818), xxiv

Deil's applerennie, the Camomile (*Anthemis* and *Chamaemelum* spp). *Applerennie* or *aippleringie* is southernwood, the aromatic shrubby wormwood *Artemisia abrotanum*, which has an apple-ish odour – as does camomile, a name that derives from Greek *khamaimelon*, literally meaning 'earth-apple', referring to the apple-like smell of the flowers.

'Deil's awa' wi' th'Exciseman, The' A celebrated song by Robert Burns, written in 1792 when he himself was working as an exciseman.

> There's threesome reels, there's foursome reels,
> There's hornpipes and strathspeys, man,
> But the ae best dance ere cam to the land
> Was the deil's awa wi' th' Exciseman!
> > The Deil's awa', the Deil's awa,
> > The Deil's awa' wi' th' Exciseman!
> > He's danc'd awa', he's danc'd awa,
> > He's danc'd awa' wi' th' Exciseman!

In his 1877 annotated edition of Burns's works, William Scott Douglas supplies the following note on the circumstances of the creation of the song, based on the account given by John Gibson Lockhart in his *Life of Burns* (1828):

> In the early part of 1792 a great deal of contraband traffic, chiefly from the Isle of Man, was going on along the coasts of Ayrshire and Galloway, and all the revenue-officers from Gretna to Dumfries were placed under the orders of a superintendent residing in Annan, who exerted himself zealously in intercepting the descent of the smuggling vessels. On 27th Feb. a suspicious looking brig was discovered in the Solway Firth, and Burns was one of the party whom the superintendent conducted to watch her motions. Lewars was dispatched to Dumfries for a guard of dragoons, and Mr Crawford, the superintendent, proceeded himself on a similar errand to Ecclefechan, while Burns was left with some men to watch the brig and prevent landing or escape. The poet manifested considerable impatience while thus kept waiting for several hours in a wet salt-marsh, with a force which he knew to be inadequate to the purpose it was meant to fulfil. One of his comrades hearing Burns abusing Lewars for being so slow on his mission, remarked that he wished the devil had him for his pains, and suggested that Burns should indite a song upon the

> sluggard. Burns said nothing; but after taking a few strides by himself among the reeds and shingle, rejoined his party and chanted to them the following well-known ditty.

This is much better than the common story, which states the song was first produced at an Excisemen's dinner when a toast was asked from him. Lockhart proceeds to tell that Lewars arrived shortly after with the dragoons, and Burns was one of the first to board the brig, sword in hand. The crew lost heart and submitted: the vessel was condemned, and all her arms and stores sold next day in Dumfries; upon which occasion the poet purchased four carronades by way of trophy, for which he paid £3, and sent them as a present to the French Convention, with a letter testifying his admiration and respect, which gift and letter were intercepted at the custom-house at Dover, and the issue produced a good deal of trouble to Burns.

(In February of the following year Britain went to war with Revolutionary France.)

Deil's Barn Door A subsidiary top of Whitelaw Brae in Lanarkshire.

Deil's breath or **wind** The winnowing machine, so condemned by Scottish Luddites:

> The winnowing-machine … was testified against as the 'Deil's Wind', invented to overreach Nature, and take the bread out of the mouths of honest families.
> – Henry Johnston, *The History of Glenbuckie* (1889)

Deil's Caldron ('Devil's cauldron') A dramatic defile and waterfall north of Comrie, Perthshire, on the River Lednock. Legend has it that it was the lair of a water spirit called Uris-chidh, who lured passers-by down into the cauldron to destruction.

Deil's dizzen Thirteen, apparently the required quorum for a witches' Sabbath, in mockery of Jesus and his twelve disciples.

Deil's Heid, the A sandstone sea stack on the Angus coast, near Arbroath, so named because of its grotesque shape.

Deil's Jingle A linear earthwork extending intermittently for some distance along the hillside above

Castle O'er, south of Eskdalemuir, Dumfriesshire. It was probably a medieval estate boundary, and *jingle* here denotes gravel or shingle. Nearby is KING SCHAW'S GRAVE.

Deil's mark 'Pigs have from three to five round marks ranged in the shape of a crescent on the foreleg a little above the ankle', according to Walter Gregor's *The Folklore of the North-East of Scotland* (1881). 'They go by the name of the "Devil's mark".'

Deil's metal Mercury.

Deil's milk The bitter white sap of a number of plants, such as the dandelion. The milky sap of the spurge family is particularly poisonous.

Deil's ower Jock Wabster, the It's all gone to pot, things are in a hell of a mess. A variant is the *Deil gaes* [etc.] *ower Jock Wabster* or *Wobster*.

> Ae wean fa's sick, ane scads itsell wi' broe,
> Ane breaks his shin, anither tines his shoe;
> The Deel gaes o'er John Wobster, hame grows hell,
> When Pate misca's ye war than tongue can tell.
> – Allan Ramsay, *The Gentle Shepherd* (1725), I.ii

In chapter xiv of Scott's *Rob Roy* (1817), the phrase is used by Andrew Fairservice, the Scottish gardener at Osbaldistone Hall, to perplex the young English narrator, Frank Osbaldistone:

> 'Than, if ye maun hae't, the folk in Lunnun are a' clean wud about this bit job in the north here.'
> 'Clean wood! what's that?'
> 'Ou, just real daft – neither to haud nor to bind – a' hirdy-girdy – clean through ither – the deil's ower Jock Wabster.'
> 'But what does all this mean? or what business have I with the devil or Jack Webster?'
> 'Umph!' said Andrew, looking extremely knowing …

Deil's Putting Stone A small rock on Windy Standard, a hill southeast of Dalmellington. There is a hollow in the top of the rock, in which passersby leave coins, presumably as some sort of propitiation of the *genus loci*. The term is also used generically for any boulder.

Deil's snuffbox, the The common puffball, so called from the spores, which were thought to make one blind, and which in some places were called *deid-man's-sneechin* (*sneechin* being a pinch of snuff).

Deil's testament Playing cards; *cf.* the English Puritans' condemnation of cards as 'the Devil's picture-book'.

Deil's wind *See* DEIL'S BREATH.

Deirdre of the Sorrows The legendary Celtic heroine, one of the best-known figures in Irish mythology. Deirdre may have been born in Scotland, and certainly in the story she spends an idyllic interlude with her lover Naoise in Argyll, on the shores of Loch Etive (or in other versions in Benderloch or Glendaruel). She and Naoise, under a promise of safe conduct, then sail for Ulster, where she is to marry her betrothed, King Conchobar. The jealous king has Naoise and his brothers put to death, and Deirdre dies of a broken heart. The earliest version of the story is in *The Fate of the Sons of Usneach*, which dates from the 8th or 9th centuries. The version in the 12th-century *Red Branch Cycle* includes the moving verses of 'Deirdre's Farewell to Alba' [i.e. Scotland]:

> Glen Etive! Glen Etive! where dappled does roam,
> Where I leave the green shieling I first called a
>   home;
> Where with me my true love delighted to dwell,
> The sun made his mansion – Glen Etive, farewell!
> – translated by Samuel Ferguson

See also FINGAL.

Deiseil A Gaelic word literally meaning 'southward' or 'sunward', and used to denote a sunwise turn, an ancient propitiatory rite of the Gaels; the word is often anglicized as *deisil*, *deasil*, etc. An instance of its performance is given by Martin Martin, in his *Description of the Western Isles of Scotland* (1703). Describing the rituals considered necessary after making the difficult and dangerous landing on the remote and rocky Flannan Isles (some 20 miles west of Lewis and sacred to the 7th-century Saint Flannan), Martin writes that:

when they are got up into the island, all of them uncover their heads, and make a turn sun-ways round, thanking God for their safety.

He adds:

The first injunction given after landing, is not to ease nature [i.e. urinate] in that place where the boat lies, for that they reckon a crime of the highest nature, and of dangerous consequence to all their crew; for they have a great regard to that very piece of rock upon which they first set their feet, after escaping the danger of the ocean.

Scott, in *The Fair Maid of Perth* (1828), describes the use of 'the deasil' in Highland funerary rites:

Various ceremonies were gone through, while the kindred of the deceased carried the body ashore, and, placing it on a bank long consecrated to the purpose, made the deasil around the departed.

Thomas Pennant, in his *Tour in Scotland* (1771), quotes the Revd L. Shaw of Moray, to the effect that 'at marriages and baptisms they make a procession around the church, *Deasoil, i.e.* sunways, because the sun was the immediate object of the Druids' worship'. Compare WIDDERSHINS. *See also* CAISEAN-UCHD.

Delting Disaster, the A tragedy that occurred on 21 December 1900 when four boats from the old Delting parish of northern Mainland, Shetland were lost in a northwesterly storm some 20 miles off shore. A memorial near the turn-off to Mossbank lists the names of 22 men drowned, and includes the following words attributed to the widow of Charles Nicolson, who also lost her son in the disaster: 'You see dey wirna mine, Da Loard gae dem tae me fir a time and dan he took dem back ageen.'

Demon's Penis, the *See* DEVIL'S POINT, THE.

Demonstration of Satan's subtlety, a *See* WITCH OF LAUDER, THE.

Dense black substance, inimical to life *See* BLACK BUN.

Deoch-an-dorus A Gaelic phrase literally meaning a 'drink at the door', i.e. a stirrup-cup, a drink to toast

a departure, 'one for the road'. Although the phrase occurs in Sir Walter Scott's *Bride of Lammermoor* (as *doch-an-dorroch*; other variants include *doch-an-doris* and *deoch-an-doruis*), it became more widely known to an Anglophone audience largely through the endless renditions by Sir Harry Lauder of R.F. Morrison's 1911 song 'Just a Wee Deoch an Dorus', in which it is shamelessly claimed that 'wherever Scots forgather' it is the custom just before saying goodnight to raise a glass and sing:

Just a wee deoch an dorus,
Just a wee dram that's a'.
Just a wee deoch an dorus,
Before we gang awa'.

More FAUX JOCKERY follows: not only is 'a wee BUT AND BEN' evoked, but also the famous shibboleth 'IT'S A BRAW BRICHT MUNELICHT NICHT'. Deoch-an-doruses are also to be found in abundance in Will Fyfe's 'I BELONG TO GLASGOW':

I've been wi' a couple o' cronies,
One or two pals o' my ain;
We went in a hotel, and we did very well,
And then we came out once again;
Then we went into anither,
And that is the reason I'm fu';
We had six deoch-an-doruses, then sang a chorus,
Just listen, I'll sing it to you:

I belong to Glasgow,
Dear old Glasgow town ... [etc.]

In medieval Scots, the equivalent of the *deoch-an-dorus* was the *bonaily*, from French *bon aller*, 'go well':

Bonailis drank richt gladlie in a morrow,
Syne leif thay tuik ...
– Blind Harry, *The Wallace* (late 15th century)

Dere Street The Roman road that ran from York to the Firth of Forth. To the south and north of the Border, it follows the modern A68, notable for giving in places a straight-as-a-die, belly-bunching rollercoaster ride, so typical of Roman roads. The *Dere* element is from Anglo-Saxon *deora*, meaning 'of the stags'; alternatively some have suggested a connection with the ancient Northumbrian kingdom of Deira. *See also* VIA REGIA.

Devorgilla's Bridge *See under* SWEETHEART ABBEY.

Deserving bedlam rather than the gallows *See* SWEET SINGERS, THE.

Destitution Road The stretch of the A832 in Wester Ross between Dundonnell and Braemore Junction. It was so-called as it was built under the auspices of the Central Board for the Destitute Highlands during the potato famine of 1846–7 by starving locals, who were paid in oatmeal. Its highest point is at over 1000 feet. Various other roads built at the same time are also referred to as 'destitution roads'.

Deucaledonian Ocean The name given by Ptolemy, the 1st-century Alexandrian geographer, to the sea that bounds the island of Britain to the north.

Devil ... *See also* DEIL ...

Devil, the The Scots have come up with a worryingly large number of names for the Devil, many of them propitiatory and/or euphemistic, including:

- Ancient
- Auld Ane, the
- Auld Bobbie
- Auld Black Lad, the
- Auld Boy, the
- Auld Chiel, the
- AULD CLOOTIE
- AULD ENEMY, the
- Auld Harry
- Auld Hornie
- Auld Man, the
- Auld Mishanter (*mishanter*, 'disaster')
- Auld Nick
- Auld Nicky Blue-Thooms (*thooms*, 'thumbs')
- Auld Roughy
- Auld Sandy
- Auld Simmy
- Auld Sootie
- Auld Thief, the
- Auld Whaap-neb ('old curlew-beak')
- Auld Yin, the
- BAD MAN, the

- BLACK DONALD
- BLACK THIEF, the
- *CAOMHAN* (Gaelic, 'dear one')
- Daddy Clouts
- EARL O' HELL, the
- FOUL THIEF, the
- GUID MAN, the
- HALYMAN
- Ill Thief, the
- LITTLE GUID, the
- LUCKY PIPER, the
- The Man on the Chain (*AM FEAR TH'AIR AN T-SLABHRUIDH*)
- MUCKLE CHIELD, the
- PLOTCOCK
- Ragman (*see under* RAGMAN ROLLS)
- THRUMMY CAP or Thrum or Thrummy
- UNCLE GEORDIE
- The Wee Man (*see* IN THE NAME OF THE WEE MAN)
- WORRICOW, the

There are also many Scottish topographical features that include the word 'Devil's' or 'Deil's' in their names (quite a number of which are included in the present volume).

Devil on wheels, the The nickname applied to the first pedal-driven bicycle, invented in 1839 by the Dumfriesshire blacksmith Kirkpatrick Macmillan (1812–78) – known as 'Daft Pate' by his neighbours, who thought he was soft in the head. In 1842 Macmillan pedalled all the way to Glasgow, where, travelling at 8 mph (13 kph) through the Gorbals, he knocked down a small girl. Although she was only grazed, Macmillan was arrested and fined five shillings – although it is thought the magistrate, impressed by Macmillan's machine, paid the fine himself. The local paper opined that 'This invention will not supersede the railway.'

Devil's Beef Tub, the A steep-sided semicircular corrie, some 600 feet deep, on the south side of Annanhead Hill in Dumfriesshire, a few miles north of Moffat. It forms the source of the River Annan (*see* ANNAN, TWEED AND CLYDE), and gained its name from the fact that the Johnstones, the local BORDER REIVERS, used to hide their stolen cattle here. It is also called the Marquis of Annandale's Beef-stand, for the same reason. On its west side is an ancient road pass (the route of the modern A701), linking Annandale with Tweeddale, and some of Bonnie Prince Charlie's Highlanders retreated this way during the '45. There is a story that one of them, MacLaren of Invenenty, hotly pursued by redcoats, evaded capture by wrapping himself in his plaid and rolling down the steep slopes to the bottom of the Devil's Beef Tub – hence yet another name for the place: MacCleran's Loup ('leap'). This story inspired an incident in Sir Walter Scott's *Redgauntlet* (1824), in which, in chapter xi, he gives the following description of the Devil's Beef Tub:

> It looks as if four hills were laying their heads together, to shut out day-light from the dark hollow space between them. A d—d deep, black, blackguard-looking abyss of a hole it is, and goes straight down from the roadside, as perpendicular as it can do, to be a heathery brae. At the bottom, there is a small bit of a brook, that you would think could hardly find its way out from the hills that are so closely jammed round it.

The Laird of Summertrees goes on to give an account of his escape here:

> And so, just when we came on the edge of this Beef-stand of the Johnstones, I slipped out my hand from the handcuff, cried to Harry Gauntlet, 'Follow me!' – whisked under the belly of the dragoon horse – flung my plaid round me with the speed of lightning – threw myself on my side, for there was no keeping my feet, and down the brae hurled I, over heather and fern, and blackberries, like a barrel down Chalmer's Close, in Auld Reekie. G—, sir, I never could help laughing when I think how the scoundrel redcoats must have been bumbazed; for the mist being, as I said, thick, they had little notion, I take it, that they were on the verge of such a dilemma. I was half way down – for rowing is faster wark than rinning – ere they could get at their arms; and then it was flash, flash, flash – rap, rap, rap – from the edge of the road; but my head was too jumbled to think anything either of that or the hard knocks I got among the stones. I kept my senses thegither, whilk has been thought wonderful by all that ever saw the place; and I helped myself with my hands as gallantly as I could, and to the bottom I came. There I lay for half a moment; but the thoughts of a

gallows is worth all the salts and scent-bottles in the world for bringing a man to himself. Up I sprang, like a four-year-auld colt. All the hills were spinning round with me, like so many great big humming-tops. But there was nae time to think of that neither; more especially as the mist had risen a little with the firing. I could see the villains, like sae mony craws on the edge of the brae; and I reckon that they saw me; for some of the loons were beginning to crawl down the hill, but liker auld wives in their red cloaks, coming frae a field preaching, than such a souple lad as I was. Accordingly, they soon began to stop and load their pieces. Good-e'en to you, gentlemen, thought I, if that is to be the gate of it. If you have any further word with me, you maun come as far as Carriefraw-gauns. And so off I set, and never buck went faster ower the braes than I did; and I never stopped till I had put three waters, reasonably deep, as the season was rainy, half a dozen mountains, and a few thousand acres of the worst moss and ling in Scotland, betwixt me and my friends the redcoats.

Devil's bird, the The magpie. The name is explained by Walter Gregor in *The Folklore of North-East Scotland* (1881):

> It was sometimes called the 'Devil's bird' and was believed to have a drop of the Devil's blood in its tongue. It was a common notion that a magpie could receive a gift of speech by scratching its tongue, and inserting into the wound a drop of blood from the human tongue.

The magpie was also called *maggie, pyardie, pegpie* or *pyot*, and Gregor records the following saying:

> 'Ye're like the pyot, ye're a' guts and gyangals.' It is applied to a person of slender form and much given to talking and boasting.

Another name is *pickie-turds*, as in the children's rhyme:

> Tell-pye, pickie-turds, sittin on a tree
> Tellan doun the peerie burds, one, two, three.

There is an equivalent counting rhyme to the English magpie rhyme 'One for sorrow, two for joy':

> Ane is ane, twa is grief,
> Three's a wedding, four's death.

See also MESSENGER OF THE CAMPBELLS, THE.

Devil's Bridge A natural feature on the rocky Burrow Head, at the tip of the Machars, Wigtownshire. It was in this 'dysart' place, just south of Howe Hill of Haggagmalag, that St Ninian (the 4th–5th-century missionary) went into retreat.

Devil's Burdens A scattering of large rocks on the southwest slopes of West Lomond, Fife.

Devil's Elbow, the A section of the old Blairgowrie–Braemar road on the south side of the 2199 ft (670 m) Cairnwell Pass (location of the Glenshee Ski Centre), so called because of the double-hairpin bend with a 1 in 3 gradient. This difficult passage – which brought many a car to a full stop – has, since the 1960s, been by-passed by the modern A93.

Devil's Fingermarks, the Some parallel grooves incised by a person or persons unknown into the parapet of the ruined Kirk of Lady near Overbister on Sanday, Orkney.

Devil's Hole, the A system of trenches in the floor of the North Sea some 120 miles (200 km) east of Dundee. The seabed around here is about 300 ft (90 m) under the surface, while the trenches extend to a depth of 750 ft (230 m). The trenches were first detected in 1931, and the name derives from the damage the trenches cause to fisherman's trawl nets.

Devils in Skirts See LADIES FROM HELL, THE.

Devil's Point, the The bowdlerized English name for Bod an Deamhain (Gaelic, 'the demon's penis'), a subsidiary peak of Cairn Toul on the southwest side of the Lairig Ghru, in the Cairngorm Mountains. In the early 19th century the Gaelic was sometimes deliberately corrupted to Poten Duon, to obscure the true meaning; the story that the modern English name resulted from a query put by Queen Victoria to her gillie John Brown as to the meaning of the Gaelic is probably apocryphal. However, it is known that it was a pious Victorian gentleman, a Mr Copland, who came up with the phoney name 'the Angel's Peak' for another of Cairn Toul's tops, in Gaelic Sgòr an Lochain Uaine ('peak of the green lochan').

Devil's Ridge The elegant, sharp ridge on the south side of Sgurr a' Mháim, the second highest peak in the Mamores. There are some exposed sections where care is needed.

Devil's Staircase, the The route of the old military road between the Kingshouse in Glen Coe over an 1800 ft (550 m) shoulder to the Blackwater Reservoir and then down to Kinlochleven. The name particularly applies to the steep zigzags on the south side of the pass. It now forms part of the West Highland Way.

Devil's Thrashing Floor An area of mudflats in Kirkcudbright Bay, forming part of the estuary of the River Dee.

Diamonds, the See FOOTBALL CLUB NICKNAMES.

Dichty water Formerly a pejorative term for the sort of affected southern English attempted by some Scots. The term apparently refers to the Dighty or Dichty Water, a small river that rises in the Sidlaw Hills, flows through Dundee and enters the Firth of Tay between Broughty Ferry and Monifieth.

Dico tibi verum ... See *LIBERTAS OPTIMA RERUM*.

Diddle-doddle or **deedle-dawdle** Rhyming slang for model, i.e. model lodging house, as set up for the homeless by various philanthropists in the 19th century.

Diddling See *PORT-A-BEUL*.

Did he die a natural death, or was the doctor sent for? A saying once current in Annandale, according to Charles Rodgers in his *Familiar Illustrations of Scottish Life* (1866).

Die facing the monument, to See YE'LL DIE FACING THE MONUMENT.

Die for the law, to Formerly a euphemism for being hanged for some crime. Edmund Burt, in his *Letters from a Gentleman in the North of Scotland* (1726–37), tells of a Highland woman who was asked how many husbands she had had, to which the answer was three:

And being further questioned, if her husbands had been kind to her, she said the first two were honest men, and very careful of their family, for they both 'died for the law' – that is, were hanged for theft. 'Well, but as to the last?' 'Hout!' says she, 'a fulthy peast! He dy'd at hame, like an auld dug, on a puckle o' strae.'

Ding doon What the Reformers of the 16th and 17th centuries did to any manifestation of idolatry. For example, here is a description of the iconoclasts at work in Aberdeen Cathedral in June 1642:

> They ordained the back of the High Altar in Bishop Gavin Dunbar's Aisle, curiously wrote in wainscot, matchless within all the kirks of Scotland, to be dung down as smelling of idolatry.
> – John Spalding, *History of the Troubles and Memorable Transactions in Scotland* (compiled 1624–45)

Spalding also describes how, two years previously, Aberdeen's Old Town Cross was 'dung down', as was the crucifix on the west end of St Nicholas Kirk in New Aberdeen, 'whilk was never troubled before'. Some of the most energetic dinging doon had occurred in 1559, after John Knox had preached a particularly fiery sermon in St Andrews. The results were described by William Tennant (1784–1848) in 'Papistry Storm'd':

> Great bangs of bodies, thick and rife,
>   Gaed to Sanct Androis town,
> And, wi' John Calvin i' their heads,
> And hammers i' their hands and spades,
> Enrag'd at idols, mass, and beads,
>   Dang the Cathedral down.

Ding doon Tantallon, to A proverbial saying, meaning to achieve the impossible, or to behave in some excessive fashion. The allusion is to the mighty Douglas castle of Tantallon that stands (now in ruins) on a cliff above the sea in East Lothian. One version of the origin of the expression is as follows:

> Tantallon Castle ... was famous, in the Scots history, for being the seat of rebellion, in the reign of King James V. And hence came the old, and odd fancy among the soldiers, that the drums beating the Scots March, say, 'Ding down tan-tallon.' That beat or march

being invented by King James the Vth's soldiers (or, perhaps, drummers).
> – Daniel Defoe: *A Tour Through the Whole Island of Great Britain* (1724–6)

A similar expression is 'to mak a brig to the Bass', i.e. to build a bridge to the Bass Rock.

Dinmont, Dandie A rough farmer from Liddesdale in Sir Walter Scott's novel *Guy Mannering* (1815). Scott apparently modelled him on a certain Willie Elliot. Dinmont's surname derives from the word *dinmont*, a wether between its first and second shearing, while the man himself is noted for his breeding of terriers:

> 'I have six terriers at hame, forbye twa couple of slow-hunds, five grews, and a wheen other dogs. There's auld Pepper and auld Mustard, and young Pepper and young Mustard, and little Pepper and little Mustard. I had them a' regularly entered, first wi' rottens, then wi' stots or weasels, and then wi' the tods and brocks, and now they fear naething that ever cam wi' a hairy skin on't.'
> 'I have no doubt, sir, they are thoroughbred; but, to have so many dogs, you seem to have a very limited variety of names for them?'
> 'O, that's a fancy of my ain to mark the breed, sir. The Deuke himsell has sent as far as Charlie's Hope to get ane o' Dandy Dinmont's Pepper and Mustard terriers ...'

By the middle of the 19th century the name Dandie Dinmont was being applied to a real breed of terriers, characterized by short legs, long body and rough coat. Such dogs – also known as *pepper-and-mustard terriers* – had been bred in the Borders since the 17th century as hunters of otters and badgers. The Dandie Dinmont Terrier Club, founded in the Fleece Hotel in Selkirk on 17 November 1875, is one of the oldest pedigree dog clubs in the world. The Dandie Dinmont is the only breed of dog named after a fictional character.

Dinnae fash yersel Don't trouble yourself; don't get into a state.

> 'Hout, Bauldie,' replied the principal, 'tak ye that dram the landlord's offering ye, and never fash your head

about the changes o' the warld, sae lang as ye're blithe and bien yoursell.

– Sir Walter Scott, *The Black Dwarf* (1816), chapter i

The word *fash* derives from Old French *fascher*, 'to annoy or trouble (someone)'; compare modern French *fâcher*.

Dirdum *See* DREE THE DIRDUM, TO.

Dirk Hatteraick's Cave A cave on the eastern shore of Wigtown Bay, named after the Dutch smuggler in Scott's *Guy Mannering* (1815). Hatteraick was modelled on a certain Captain Yawkins, a larger-than-life Dutchman about whose smuggling escapades around the Solway Firth in the later 18th century many tales were told – including the occasion when he sailed directly between two revenue cutters, so close that he could toss his hat onto the deck of one and his wig onto the deck of the other. Dirk Hatteraick's Cave was reputedly used by Yawkins, and once boasted a sleeping platform and special pigeon holes for storing Dutch flagons – but no traces of these remain. Torrs Cave on the east side of Kirkcudbright Bay – which formerly had a stone doorway and has signs of having been occupied from the Iron Age through to the 18th century – is also known as Dirk Hatteraick's Cave. Yawkins appears as himself in S.R. Crockett's novel *The Raiders* (1894).

Discoverer of the Principle of Natural Selection How the Scottish arboriculturalist and gentleman farmer Patrick Matthew (1790–1874) described himself on his calling cards, following the publication of Darwin's *On the Origin of Species* in 1859. In 1831 Matthew had published *On Naval Timber and Arboriculture*, based on his own experiences of managing the orchards of his family estate at Gourdiehill in the Carse of Gowrie. In this work he decried the practice of harvesting only the trees of highest quality for the Royal Navy's warships, as this would leave only trees of inferior quality to reproduce. From such artificial selection, he extrapolated an outline of natural selection:

As nature, in all her modifications of life, has a power of increase far beyond what is needed to supply the place of what falls by Time's decay, those individuals who possess not the requisite strength, swiftness, hardihood, or cunning, fall prematurely without reproducing – either a prey to their natural devourers, or sinking under disease, generally induced by want of nourishment, their place being occupied by the more perfect of their own kind, who are pressing on the means of subsistence ... [The] progeny of the same parents, under great differences of circumstance, might, in several generations, even become distinct species, incapable of co-reproduction.

It is almost certain that Darwin was unaware of Matthew's publication until in 1860 Matthew himself read a review of *On the Origin of Species* and wrote a letter to the *Gardener's Chronicle*, drawing attention to his own earlier theory. When Darwin saw this letter, he wrote that Matthew 'completely anticipates the theory of Nat. Selection', and in subsequent editions of *Origin* he acknowledged Matthew's claim to priority. However, historians of science have pointed out that Matthew, unlike Darwin, amassed very little evidence to back up his theory, nor did he assemble an array of arguments that convinced most of the scientific world. Furthermore, in *On Naval Timber and Arboriculture* he had spoken of a 'beauty and unity of design in this continual balancing of life to circumstance', which betrays a belief in a purposeful Providence, at odds with the Darwinian universe, from which such teleological musings have been forever banished. Thus Matthew's own claim to have been 'The Discoverer of the Principle of Natural Selection' has not been widely endorsed. *See also* EVOLUTION.

Matthew's other sobriquet, 'the Seer of Gourdiehill', was awarded posthumously, and has more merit. From 1869 Matthew campaigned against the plans for the first Tay Bridge, expressing doubts both about the location (where it would be difficult to build sound foundations) and the quality of the cast-iron to be used. He argued that the money would be better spent improving the appalling quality of workers' housing in Dundee. Despite his objections, the bridge opened in 1878, four years after his death. The following year it broke up in a storm as a train was crossing it, killing 75 people (*see* TAY BRIDGE DISASTER).

Diseases Here are a few Scots terms for various diseases:

Bellythraw Colic.

Blabs Chickenpox or nettlerash (a *blab* is a bubble or a drop of liquid).

Boat cough or **strangers' cold** Terms used on St Kilda for either the common cold or influenza, outbreaks of which would follow the arrival of a vessel from the Outer Hebrides.

Branks Mumps (possibly related to BRANKS, a halter or bridle).

The GOOD WIFE Smallpox.

GRANDGORE or **glengore** Syphilis (from Old French, *grand gorre*, 'great pox'). The disease was also referred to as the *seiknes of Napillis* ('the sickness of Naples'), and as *viroll* (from French *vérole*, pox).

GULSOCH Jaundice.

Haingles Influenza (to *haingle* is to hang around feebly, as if convalescing)

Inbred fever Various chest diseases, including bronchitis and tuberculosis.

JAW-PISH Urethritis.

Kinkhoste Whooping cough (to *kinke* is to suffer a coughing fit).

Knot in the pudding, a A strangulated hernia.

MACDONALDS' DISEASE Some type of chest infection.

Meselrie, meselne or **messall** Leprosy (from Anglo-Norman *mesel*, 'leprous', 'a leper'; ultimately from Latin *miser*, 'wretched').

Mort cauld A severe cold, influenza (literally 'death cold').

Nirls Measles (a *nirl* is a small lump).

Phtisik or **teesick** Any wasting disease, especially consumption, i.e. pulmonary tuberculosis (from Medieval Latin *phthisis*).

Ripple A disease affecting the back and loins; also applied to gonorrhoea.

Rush fever Scarlet fever (a *rush* is a rash), which is sometimes also referred to as *flurisfever* (*fluris* is the blossom of fruit trees or hawthorn) or simply as *fivver* or *fiver*.

Scaw Any scaly skin disease, apparently formerly treated using brimstone and butter.

Stourie lungs The name given in Fife and the Lothians to pneumoconiosis, aka black lung, a disease of miners caused by the inhalation of coal dust. It can also denote silicosis, a similar disease suffered by stone grinders and quarrymen, and caused by the inhalation of tiny fragments of silica. *Stourie* means 'dusty'.

Timmer-tongue Literally, 'timber-tongue', i.e. the cattle disease actinomycosis, also known as lumpy jaw, in which the tongue is rendered hard and swollen, while abscesses develop on the head and neck.

Worm Toothache, colic or any other ailment believed to be caused by a worm.

Ydrope or **ydropesie** Dropsy.

A girl on her arrival was asked whether she had had the smallpox. 'Yes, mem, I've had the sma'pox, the nirls, the blabs, the scaw, the kinkhost and the fever, the branks and the worm.'

> – Dean E.B. Ramsay, *Reminiscences of Scottish Life and Character* (1864)

But Man's a fiky bairn
Wi' bellythraw, ripples, and worm-i'-the-cheek!

> – Hugh MacDiarmid, *A Drunk Man Looks at the Thistle* (1926)

Dish of Spurs A symbolic offering at the table by the womenfolk of certain families among the BORDER REIVERS to tell the menfolk that the larder was empty and it was time to saddle up and set off in quest of fresh plunder.

Dismal Jimmy A nickname applied by the Scots to King James VII and II, whose stiff and formal manner was quite different from that of his flamboyant, humorous and charming brother, Charles II. The Irish were less polite: after James fled the field at the Battle of the Boyne, they referred to him as *Séamus an Chaca* ('James the Shit'). The name *dismal Jimmy* is now more widely applied to anyone taking a jaundiced or otherwise pessimistic view of things.

> We have these dismal Jimmies who are quite convinced that all is lost and that never again will this country be the country it was. I don't believe a word of it.
>
> – J.W. Belcher, Parliamentary Sectretary to the Board of Trade, quoted in the *Glasgow Herald*, 14 October 1948

This use of the term appears to have first appeared during the First World War, and is not specifically Scottish.

Disneyland Any institution or workplace where nothing runs as it should, so-called because *this disnae work an' that disnae work*, and so on.

Disruption of 1843 The split in the Church of Scotland during the GENERAL ASSEMBLY of 1843. The issue was patronage rather than theology, and it led the evangelical wing to break away to form the Free Church of Scotland, asserting that the appointment of new ministers should be in the hands of the presbytery, not the local landowner. Thomas Chalmers, the Free Church's first Moderator, was anxious to avoid suspicions of sectarianism:

> Who cares about the Free Church, compared with the Christian good of Scotland? Who cares about any church but as an instrument of Christian good?

The breakaway Free Church of Scotland was known as the 'Free Kirk' (and later nicknamed the WEE FREES), while the rump became known as the 'AULD KIRK'. *See also* FORTY THIEVES, THE.

Dissy ... *See* DIZZY ...

Diver, The *See* TAY BRIDGE DISASTER.

Divination, methods of *See* ANT-TOSSING; DRAPPING GLASSES; HALLOWEEN; MOON; RIDDLE AND THE SHEARS, THE; SOWANS; *TAGHAIRM*. For the use of the shoulder-blade of a sheep, *see under* SECOND SIGHT. *See also* SEERS.

Dizzy or **dissy, give someone a** To stand up a date; *see* BOOTS CORNER.

Dizzy Corner *See* BOOTS CORNER.

Dobbie Another term for a BROWNIE; the name is a familiar version of Robbie, as in Robin Goodfellow. The word *dobbie* is also applied to a foolish or clumsy person.

Doc, the A nickname of the footballer and manager Tommy Docherty (b.1928), who played for Celtic, Preston North End, Arsenal and Chelsea, and won 25 caps for Scotland. As a manager his teams included Chelsea, Aston Villa, Manchester United, Derby County and Queens Park Rangers, and he also managed Scotland in 1971–2.

Docken A dock, a broad-leaved weed, which features in a number of expressions as something worthless, e.g. 'Ah couldna gie a docken', 'That's nae worth a docken'.

> Combing his locks and preening himself, and brushing out his finery as if God would care a docken what he looked like when He cast him into the furnace.
> – James Robertson, *The Fanatic* (2000)

Doctor Finlay's Casebook A BBC TV series (1962–71) based on *Country Doctor*, a novella by A.J. Cronin (1896–91), together with a number of his short stories, collected in *Adventures of a Black Bag* (1969). The town of Callander took the part of the fictional Tannochbrae (although the first few episodes were shot in Milngavie), while Bill Simpson played the country GP Dr Alan Finlay, Andrew Cruickshank his older partner Dr Angus Cameron, and Barbara Mullen their housekeeper Janet MacPherson. The TV series was followed by a radio series (1970–8). A second TV series, entitled *Doctor Finlay* and produced by Scottish Television, was aired in 1993–6. This time Auchtermuchty stood in for Tannochbrae, while the title role was taken by David Rintoul, Ian Bannen played a semi-retired Dr Cameron, and Annette Crosbie was Janet.

Doctor Subtilis (Latin, 'the subtle doctor') The sobriquet of the Scottish scholastic philosopher and Franciscan friar John Duns Scotus (c.1266–1308), who was born in the Berwickshire town of Duns. The sobriquet reflects the high regard in which he was held in his own time. Duns Scotus argued against Aquinas, asserting that it is the essential rather than accidental properties of a thing that distinguishes it from another thing. He studied and taught at Oxford, Cambridge and Paris, and died in Cologne, hence his epitaph:

> *Scotia me genuit, Anglia me suscepit, Gallia me docuit, Colonia me tenet.*
> ('Scotland bore me, England took me, France taught me, Cologne holds me.')

There is a tradition that when his grave was later opened he was found outside his coffin, his hands torn and bloody as if he had made some desperate effort to escape. He and his followers were later ridiculed as thick-headed nitpickers, hence the word

'DUNCE'. Erasmus himself observed of Scottish scholars in general that 'They plume themselves on their skill and dialectic subtleties.'

Dods, Meg In Sir Walter Scott's *St Ronan's Well* (1824), the shrewish landlady and superb cook of the Cleikum Inn, near Peebles, who discourages both over-indulgence and late hours. The character is said to have been based on Miss Marian Ritchie, landlady of the Cross Keys in Peebles. The name, gentrified to 'Mrs Margaret Dods', was adopted as a pseudonym by Mrs Isobel Johnston, novelist and journalist, author of *The Cook and Housewife's Manual* (published in Edinburgh in 1826), famous for its recipe for HAGGIS (quoted in full in that entry). It has frequently been suggested that Scott himself may have been responsible for the quirky introduction and intriguing footnotes. *See also* CLEIKUM CEREMONIES, THE.

Doe or die The motto of the Douglases; *see* BLACK DOUGLAS, THE.

Dog afore his maister, the In the Northeast, the swell that precedes a storm. The swell that remains after a storm is passed is called 'the dog ahint his maister'.

Doggie in heaven that has dung them all down, a *See under* WILLIE WASTELL.

Dog Pyntle and Buggerback Nicknames (*pintle*, 'penis') for two notorious BORDER REIVERS, Archie and George Elliott, according to George Macdonald Fraser's history of the Borderers, *The Steel Bonnets* (1971).

Dogs *See* DINMONT, DANDIE; GORDON SETTER; GREYFRIARS BOBBY; LUATH; WEST HIGHLAND TERRIER. For dogs rendered hairless by their speleological exploits, *see* MACKINNON'S CAVE; WIZARD OF REAY, THE.

Dog's Pillar, the A large rock on the shore near Dunollie Castle, just north of Oban, associated with the mythic Irish hero Finn McCool (known as FINGAL in Scotland):

... a huge upright pillar, or detached fragment of that sort of rock called plum-pudding stone [conglomerate], upon the shore, about a quarter of a mile from the castle. It is called *Clack-na-can*, or the Dog's Pillar, because Fingal is said to have used it as a stake to which he bound his celebrated dog Bran.
> – Sir Walter Scott, note to Canto I of *The Lord of the Isles* (1815)

Dolly the Sheep The world's first cloned mammal, born in 1996 at the Roslin Institute near Edinburgh. She had three mothers: one supplied the egg, the second the DNA, and the third was implanted with the cloned embryo and carried it to term. Ian Wilmut, a member of the team that produced her, explains the name: 'Dolly is derived from a mammary gland cell and we couldn't think of a more impressive pair of glands than Dolly Parton's.' Dolly died in 2003, and she has been stuffed and put on display in the National Museum of Scotland, Edinburgh.

Domestic Scots *See* WILD SCOTS.

Domhnall Dubh *See* BLACK DONALD.

Domnall Bán The Gaelic nickname of Donald III (reigned 1094–7), younger brother of MALCOLM CANMORE. It means 'Donald the Fair', and is often anglicized as *Donalbain*.

Domnhuill Dubh or ***Domnuill-dhu*** *See* BLACK DONALD.

Don, River *See* BLOODTHIRSTY DEE; DEE VS DON.

Donalbain *See* DOMNALL BÁN.

Donald Any hill in the Scottish Lowlands over 2000 ft (609.6 m), including those in the Southern Uplands and the Ochil Hills. There are 89 listed by the Scottish Mountaineering Club, and they are named after Percy Donald, who first compiled the list. The highest of the Donalds, which are all, by definition, either CORBETTS or GRAHAMS, is Merrick, at 843 m (2766 ft). Among the more memorably named Donalds are Molls Cleuch Dod, Shalloch on Minnoch, Gathersnow Hill, Curleywee and Louise Wood Law.

'Donald, Where's Yer Troosers?' An innuendo-laden song playing on the old chestnut as to what a Highlander wears beneath his kilt. For Andy Stewart, presenter of *The WHITE HEATHER CLUB*, it was a tremendous hit in 1961 on both sides of the Atlantic, and a re-worked version reached number five in the UK charts at Christmas 1989, four years before Stewart's death. Shy, small Donald, arriving in the big city from Skye, finds himself much admired by the ladies:

> Let the wind blow high,
> Let the wind blow low,
> Through the streets in my kilt I'll go
> All the lassies say hello –
> Donald, where's your troosers?

From the 19th century *Donald* or *Donal* had been used to denote a Highlander, the name being common in those parts.

Donn, Rob See ROBERT BURNS OF GAELDOM, THE.

Donnchadh Bàn nan Orainn ('Fair Duncan of the Songs') The Gaelic poet Duncan Ban Macintyre; *see* PRAISE OF BEN DORAIN.

Don Roberto See UNCROWNED KING OF SCOTS, THE.

Dons, the See FOOTBALL CLUB NICKNAMES.

Don't be vague, ask for Haig! A long-running advertising slogan used by John Haig and Company Ltd, the whisky distillers founded in 1824 by John Haig (1802–78), and now part of the Diageo group. The earliest known form, dating from 1933, is 'Don't be vague, order Haig', which by 1935 had become 'Why be vague? Ask for Haig.' The present form appears to have emerged around 1936, although this is not certain as many of the Haig archives were destroyed during the Second World War. The advertising agency behind the slogan was probably C.J. Lytle Ltd.

Dooking for apples A traditional HALLOWEEN game, in which the participants *dook* ('duck') their heads in a tub of water in which apples are floating. The aim is to retrieve an apple in one's teeth without using one's hands. In recent years, many

primary heads have banned the game from their schools on the grounds of hygiene, only permitting the variant in which participants hold a fork between their teeth and drop it into the water in the hope of spearing a fruit.

> Experts, however, insisted dooking was perfectly safe. Bacteriologist Hugh Pennington dismissed the notion of any real danger. 'It is sort of unhygienic, but no more unhygienic than breathing air,' the retired Aberdeen University professor said. 'Dooking for apples on my scale of risk is so low that the fun you get from it far outweighs any possible risks.'
> – *The Scotsman*, 2 November 2008

One head teacher, when asked why dooking had been banned, told *The Herald* (9 October 2000), 'It's too big a temptation for the staff just to hold some of the kids' heads under until they drown.'

The other popular food-related Halloween game is the one in which participants, with their hands held behind their backs, attempt to take a bite out of treacle scones hanging from strings.

Dookit folk Members of the Baptist Church, who are entirely *dooked* (immersed) when they are baptised.

Dool tree A hanging tree (*dool* or *dule* = 'sorrowful, mournful'). Such trees, on which the executed criminals were left hanging in public view, were found on many estates until the mid-18th century. Extant examples include an old sycamore at Blairquhan Castle, near Straiton in Ayrshire, which was planted in the early 16th century, and the Gallows Tree on Gallow Hill near Monikie, Angus. *See also* HANGING TREE OF FORT WILLIAM, THE; and, for the Hanging Ash of Tushielaw, *see under* KING OF THE BORDER, THE. *Compare* COVIN TREE.

Doom-ray A nickname adopted by anti-nuclear campaigners for the experimental nuclear-power installation at Dounreay, Caithness, set up in 1955.

Doon, bonnie See YE BANKS AND BRAES O' BONNIE DOON.

Doon-moued Literally 'down-mouthed', i.e. miserable looking, down in the mouth.

Doonhamers A nickname applied to people from Dumfries, who, when elsewhere in Scotland, refer to their home town as *doon hame* (i.e. 'down home', Dumfries being in the far south of Scotland). The nickname is also applied to the town's football team, QUEEN OF THE SOUTH. *See also* HAME.

Doon the watter A popular holiday destination for Glaswegians from the later 19th century, involving a cruise down the Firth of Clyde to resorts such as Dunoon or Rothesay. It may either be a day trip, or a week or so may be endured in a boarding house at the destination.

> In search of lodgins we did slide,
> To find a place where we could bide,
> There was eighty-twa o' us inside
> In a single room in Rothesay, O.
>
> We a' lay doon tae tak our ease,
> When somebody happened for tae sneeze –
> An' he wakened hauf a million fleas
> In a single room in Rothesay, O.
> – Anon.: 'The Day We Went to Rothesay, O'

Today, the SS *Waverley*, a paddle-steamer launched in 1946, is the only remaining regular cruise ship on the Clyde, and fewer and fewer people take advantage of the pleasures she offers, opting instead for sunnier climes abroad. Yet sailing *doon the watter* still has its devotees, one of whom evokes its particular magic:

> This was the Clyde steamer's great trick: that within an hour or two it could take you from one of the world's densest cities into the heart of one of its most intricate and beautiful landscapes, and give you companionship as well as food and drink, and shelter from the rain.
> – Ian Jack, in the *Guardian*, 30 July 2011

See also BATTLE OF GARELOCHHEAD, THE; FAIR FORTNIGHT; HAMELLDAEME; MADEIRA OF THE NORTH, THE.

Doric or **the Doric** The Scots language. Sometimes the term is restricted to vernacular versions, and/or the dialects of the Northeast, particularly Aberdeenshire. The term derives from ancient Greece, where the Athenians thought the Dorians to be uncivilized

rustics, hence the Doric is the simplest of the three orders of architecture. From the 18th century, the term began to be applied to rustic versions of English, particularly in Northumbria and the Lowlands of Scotland.

> Many people think that Scots possesses a rich vocabulary, but this is a view not wholly borne out by a close examination … It is as if the Doric had been invented by a cabal of scandal-mongering beldams, aided by a council of observant gamekeepers.
> – George Malcolm Thomson, *The Rediscovery of Scotland* (1928)

See also PLASTIC SCOTS.

Dornoch Firth Disaster *See* MEIKLE FERRY DISASTER.

Do school *See* DOUGH SCHOOL.

Dott, Graeme *See* POCKET ROCKET, THE.

Doubting with Dirleton, and resolving those doubts with Stewart According to the Revd E. Cobham Brewer, in the 1896 edition of his *Dictionary of Phrase and Fable*, this saying means 'Doubting and answering those doubts, but doubting still. It applies to law, science, religion, morals, etc.' The allusion is to two works on Scottish law: *Some Doubts and Questions in the Law* by the judge and politician Sir John Nisbet, Lord Dirleton (1610–88), comprising his comments on the decisions of the lords of council and session between 1665 and 1677, published posthumously in 1698; and *Dirleton's Doubts and Questions in the Law of Scotland, Resolved and Answered* (1715) by the politician and judge Sir James Stewart of Goodtrees (1635–1713). Brewer says that both are 'works of established reputation in Scotland, but the *Doubts* hold a higher place than the *Solutions*'.

Dough School How colleges of domestic science were affectionately referred to, *dough* (pronounced 'doh') being short for 'domestic', and punning on the *dough* used in bread-making. The name is still applied to what was the Glasgow & West of Scotland College of Domestic Science, founded in 1908. It became The Queen's College, Glasgow in 1975, and merged with Glasgow Polytechnic in 1993 to become Glasgow Caledonian University.

Douglas The noted Scottish family ultimately derives its name from the name of a river in Lanarkshire, which was originally Gaelic *dubh*, 'black', and *glais*, 'stream'. Their now ruined stronghold, Douglas Castle, was the original of Sir Walter Scott's Castle Dangerous, in the 1831 novel of that name. In chapter iii, Scott refers to the traditional derivation of the name:

> ... the complexion of the day is congenial with the original derivation of the name of the country, and the description of the chiefs to whom it belonged – Sholto Dhu Glass – (see yon dark grey man) ...

Those of a facetious bent will tell you that 'Douglas' means 'a man without a dog'. *See also* ARCHIBALD THE GRIM; BLACK DOUGLAS, THE; HUGH THE DULL; MOTTOES; OLD Q. For John Home's romantic tragedy *Douglas*, *see* WHAUR'S YER WULLIE SHAKESPEARE NOO?

Douglas grot A groat minted in 1525–8 during the later part of the minority of James V when Archibald Douglas, Earl of Angus, was the power in the land.

Douglas Larder, the An episode during the Wars of Independence when Sir James Douglas (the BLACK DOUGLAS) slaughtered the English garrison occupying his own Douglas Castle in Lanarkshire. On Palm Sunday 1307 or 1308, as the English troops were attending a church service, Douglas and his followers fell on them, killing some and taking others prisoner. These latter were led to the castle, where the stores in the cellar were piled together, and then the prisoners were beheaded and their heads and bodies placed on top of the pile, which was then set alight. Aware that he did not have the men to hold the castle, Douglas withdrew, having poisoned the wells with salt and the cadavers of dead horses.

Dourness A disposition often attributed to the Scots, especially by others. The adjective *dour* originates in Scots; the earliest usage is that of Barbour in the 1370s in *The Brus*:

> He wes a stout carle and a sture,
> And of him-self dour and hardy.

Some believe the word derives from Latin *durus*, 'hard', and it is generally taken to mean sullen and stern, or hard and obstinate, or determined, resolute and hardy. There are greater subtleties, however:

> The word is a hard one to define, but it carries with it a distinct suggestion of severity dashed with melancholy. The dour man is ever observant of the rugged side of human life. He notes that all the sounds of inanimate Nature, the voices of the woods and of the streams, are in the minor key. The tragedy of the world afflicts him, and he is willing that others should call him austere rather than stand in his own eyes an optimist on false pretences. This is a dour world, he says, and I will be dour to match it. That was a shrewd critic of national character who divided the Scotch into two families, 'the children of nature under Robert Burns, and the children of grace under John Knox'; but who shall count the number of the souls whom their very dourness drove into these opposite companionships, some that they might find an antidote for their melancholy in sensuous delights, and other some that they might find warrant for it in the eternal decrees of a predestinating God.
> – Revd William Reed Huntingdon, 'The King's Cup-Bearer', a sermon preached in memory of the Revd E. Winchester Donald, 20 November 1904

Others have been more succinct, and less sympathetic to the mood:

> The whole nation hitherto has been void of wit and humour, and even incapable of relishing it.
> – Horace Walpole, letter to Sir Horace Mann, 1778

> It requires a surgical operation to get a joke well into a Scotch understanding.
> – Sydney Smith, quoted in Lady Holland, *A Memoir of Sydney Smith* (1855). When Smith's observation is made to a Scotsman in J.M. Barrie's play *What Every Woman Knows*, the man replies: 'What beats me, Maggie, is how you could insert a joke with an operation.'

> It is never difficult to distinguish between a Scotsman with a grievance and a ray of sunshine.
> – P.G. Wodehouse, *Blandings Castle and Elsewhere*, 'The Custody of the Pumpkin' (1935)

To *tak the dourles* is to take umbrage, to go off in a sulk. *See also* MEANNESS; MISERY FROM THE MANSE, THE; *PRAEFERVIDUM INGENIUM SCOTORUM*.

Dout or **dowt** A cigarette end.

> Q. Why is life like an ashtray?
> A. It's full o' wee douts.

See also NIP.

Dove of Dunbar, the Elizabeth Dunbar (1425–94), who around 1442 married Archibald Douglas, the 6th Earl of Moray. The name derives from the *Buke of the Howlat*, an allegorical poem written in 1450 by the Earl's chaplain or secretary, Richard Holland, who dedicated the work to the Countess:

> Thus for ane Dow of Dunbar drew I this Dyte,
> Dowit with ane Dowglass, and boith war thei dowis.
> [*dow*, 'dove'; *dyte*, 'composition, work'; *dowit*, 'endowed through marriage'; *dowis*, 'doves']

Do you ... *See* D'YE ...

Dracula's Castle The castle of the count in Bram Stoker's *Dracula* (1897) may have been partly inspired by Slains Castle in Aberdeenshire, where Stoker had stayed as a guest of the Earl of Erroll. The castle was begun in 1597, and was subsequently extended and modified. It is now in ruins.

Dragons Not a common sight in Scotland, but in his *Historie of the Kirk of Scotland* (1646), David Calderwood has the following entry for the year 1622:

> Upon Monday the 3rd of June, there was a fiery dragon, both great and long, appeared to come from the south to the north, spouting fire from her, half an hour after the going to of the sun.

See also COWS, NOTABLE; MORAG; LOCH NESS MONSTER; SEA SERPENTS.

Drap i' the ee, a Literally, 'a drop in the eye', i.e. just enough alcohol to make one slightly merry. The expression is now obsolete.

Drapping glasses The procedure of telling the future by dropping an egg white into a glass of water, also known as *casting eggs*.

Draw in one's chair an' sit doon, to To become rich through the hard work of others rather than through one's own efforts.

Draw straes afore someone's een, to Literally, 'to draw straws in front of someone's eyes', i.e. to pull the wool over their eyes, or make fun of them.

Dreaming bread A name formerly given to the piece of wedding cake that young girls traditionally placed under their pillows in the hope of dreaming of their future husbands. Sometimes it was thought necessary to first pass the piece of cake three (or nine) times through a wedding ring. Similar beliefs attached to pieces of christening cake. *See also* INFAR CAKE.

Dreaming of the dead In Highland superstition, dreaming of the dead was to be avoided, as it encouraged the departed to return as revenants. Various rituals might be deployed to prevent such dreams, as described by George Henderson in *Survivals in Belief Among the Celts* (1911):

> In the etiquette of paying one's parting respects to the dead, before the corpse is buried, no custom is more tenacious in the Highlands than that of touching the body with the finger. To neglect doing so is thought to expose a person to dreaming of the deceased, and by consequence to the danger of being visited by the dead, and of being open to the dread haunting of the ghost. This is the relic of the old ordeal upon the corpse of the murdered – a custom not confined to present Gaeldom, but current in a wider area. For instance, the minister of Pitsligo [the Revd Walter Gregor, *Folk Lore of North-East Scotland* (1881)] testifies: 'The opinion prevailed till not very long ago, and even yet lingers, that in case of murder, if the murderer touches the corpse, blood flows from the wounds [*see* ORDEAL BY BLOOD].' To touch the body is therefore a sort of folk-ritual to signify that one is at peace with the deceased.

Other rituals might be employed. In the same book Henderson gives an account of what happened after the execution of Alexander Mackintosh of Borlum for assaulting a cattle-dealer from Beauly, who was suspected of having misidentified his assailant. As the crowd, filled with horror and sorrow, slowly and silently dispersed after witnessing the hanging, many of them placed a small piece of bread under a stone, to 'prevent after-dreams of the unfortunate Alexander Mackintosh'. As for the cattle-dealer, he was ostracized in Beauly, and in the end killed himself.

Dree one's weird To endure one's fate, accept one's lot.

> For it's nae choice, and ony man s'ud wish
> To dree the goat's weird tae as weel's the sheep's!
> – Hugh MacDiarmid, *A Drunk Man Looks at the Thistle* (1926)

Dree the dirdum, to To endure the consequences, bear the punishment; a *dird* is a hard blow.

Dreme, The A poem of 1134 lines written by Sir David Lindsay in 1528 to mark the assumption of power by the 16-year-old James V. In the poem, the poet is brought a vision by Dame Remembrance of Scotland's full potential, given the richness of its resources, which could be realized under a brave and wise ruler – for example:

> The rich riveris, pleasand and profitabill,
> The lustie lochis, with fische of sindrie kindis,
> Hunting, hawking, for nobillis convenabill,
> Forestis full of da, ra, hartis and hindis,
> The fresche fountains, quhais halesum cristal
>   strandis
> Refreschis sa the flourischit grein medis:
> So lak we nothing that to nature neidis.

Dreyfus, the Scottish *See* SCOTTISH DREYFUS, THE.

Dribbly beards Long strips of curly kale boiled in greasy broth.

Drink For a list of drink-related articles, *see* FOOD, DRINK, FEASTING AND COOKING. *See also* DRUNKENNESS.

Drink oot o a toom cappie, to Literally, 'to drink out of an empty cup', i.e. to be in a state of hunger and/or penury. The expression derives from the Northeast, and is found, for example, in the following wedding blessing: 'May you aye be happy and ne'er drink oot o' a toom cappie.'

Drink siller Literally 'drink silver', i.e. a tip intended to be spent on drink. *Cf.* the French word for a tip, *pourboire*, literally 'for to drink'.

Drive pigs or **swine, to** To snore loudly.

Dromedaries *See* CAMEL OF THE CANONGATE, THE.

Drongs, the A group of sea stacks off the west coast of the Ness of Hillswick, Mainland, Shetland. The highest, at 60 m (200 ft) is Main Drong, and the others include Slender Drong, Slim Drong and Stumpy Drong. From a distance they are said to resemble a group of vessels under sail.

Droon the miller Literally, 'drown the miller', i.e. to put too much water in one's whisky, as in the phrase 'Dinnae droon the miller' – the miller being the man who provided the grain to make the whisky.

Drove of Dunbar, the *See* RACE OF DUNBAR, THE.

Drowned owing to lack of skill in verse *See* BLUE MEN OF THE MINCH.

Drum, the The local nickname for Drumchapel, the massive postwar housing scheme on the west side of Glasgow.

> 'Naw,' he says, 'I come fae Outer Space, ye know.'
>   Well ah thought he wis jokin. Ah mean, who wouldny? So ah says, 'Ah come fae the Drum. Same thing, intit?'
>   'Naw,' he says, 'ah'm serious.'
> – David Crooks, 'Spaced Out', a short science fiction story first published in the *Glasgow Herald*, 29 March 1986

See also WHERE DREAMS COME TRUE.

Drum-major A bossy woman (in the army, a drum-major is the NCO in charge of the regimental drummers). The word is also used as a verb, meaning 'to boss people about'.

Drunkenness In Scotland, a lexically rich condition. Synonyms for being intoxicated include:

> **Aff one's face**
> **Awa wi' it**
> **Bevvied**
> **Birlin** (i.e. spinning)
> **Bitchify'd** ('Gude forgie me, I gat myself sae notour-

iously bitchify'd the day after kail-time that I can hardly stotter but and ben.' Robert Burns, Letter to William Nicol, 1 June 1787 ('or I believe the 39th o' May rather')

Blazin, bleezin or **bleezin fou**

Blootered

Bongo'd or **heavy bongo'd**

Disnae ken whether it's New Year or New York (also said of a person in any kind of confused state)

Dunted (mildly tipsy)

FOU

Full o' it

Jaked up or **oot** (*jake* is meths)

Hammered

Lillian Gished (rhyming slang for *pished*)

Lummed up (presumably from *lum*, 'chimney', possibly alluding to the fumes coming off the drinker)

Mad wi' it (sometimes abbreviated to MWI)

Miraculous, miraklous or just plain **maroc**

On the bash (engaged in a drinking session)

On the rammle (ditto)

On the skelp (ditto; a *skelp* is a smack)

On the spin (ditto)

Oot o' one's brain or **face**

Pished

Puggled (perhaps only mildly tipsy)

Rubber

Scotch mist (rhyming slang for 'pissed')

Slaughtered

Steamin, hence also **steamboats** (although there is a story that the latter expression derives from family trips DOON THE WATTER, when fathers would tell their dear ones that they were just going to inspect the steam engines, when in fact they were off to the bar)

Stenked

Stoated, stoatin or **stottin** (literally 'staggering' or 'bouncing')

Stocious

The maut's abune the meal ('he's drunk')

Unable to bite one's thoum ('thumb')

Wankered

Well- or **over-refreshed**

Zebadee'd

The fondness of the Scot for the bottle is both a stereotype and a statistical reality. *See also* BEER; WHISKY; STAIRHEID SHANDY.

Duds Day Literally 'clothes day', originally the hiring fair at Kilmarnock held around Martinmas (11 November), and later denoting a number of other hiring fairs in Ayrshire, held at various dates until the Second World War. Duds Day was so-called because the servants attending would buy new clothes at the fair.

Duff's luck Good fortune. The origin of the expression is explained by Walter Gregor in his *Folk-Lore of the North-East of Scotland* (1881):

> Duff is the family name of the Earl of Fife. The family has gone on for several generations, adding, from a beginning not at all large, land to land, so that the estates now bulk largely in the shires of Banff, Aberdeen, and Moray. Hence, probably, has arisen the proverb 'Duff's luck'.

Dufftown For its boast to rival Rome, *see* SEVEN HILLS OF EDINBURGH, THE.

Dughall Mor The name given to what was formerly thought to be Britain's tallest tree, a Douglas fir planted in 1882 in Reelig Glen, 13 km (8 miles) west of Inverness. In 2009 the tree was reported to be 62.02 m (203.4 ft) high, and the Gaelic name means 'big, dark stranger'. On 19 February 2009 the Stronardon Douglas fir near Dunans Castle in Argyll was subjected to accurate measurement and came out as Britain's tallest tree, with a height of 63.79 m (209 ft). The Douglas fir was introduced to Britain from North America in the 1820s by the Scottish plant collector, David Douglas; *see* EPONYMS.

Duke of Argyle's Bowling Green *See* ARGYLL'S BOWLING GREEN.

Dumbarton youth A 19th-century term for a person, usually female, of a certain age – at least past their mid-30s. Why such a person should be considered characteristic of Dumbarton is obscure.

> She had been allowed to reach the discreet years of a Dumbarton youth in unsolicited maidenhood.
> – John Galt, *The Entail; or, The Lairds of Grippy* (1823)

Dumf The familiar name for the Dunfermline College of Physical Education, founded in Dunfermline in 1905. The institution moved to Edinburgh in 1966, but kept its name until 1987.

Dumfries *See* ALOREBURN; CITY OF ST MICHAEL, THE; QUEEN OF THE SOUTH, THE.

Dunbar, Race of *See* RACE OF DUNBAR.

Dunbar Martyrs *See* RACE OF DUNBAR.

Dunbar wether A salted herring (a wether is a castrated male sheep).

> They have here [in Dunbar] a great herring-fishery, and particularly they hang herrings here, as they do at Yarmouth in Norfolk, for the smoking them; or, to speak the ordinary dialect, they make red herrings here ...
> – Daniel Defoe, *Tour Through the Whole Island of Great Britain* (1724–7)

Dunblane, the Flower of *See* FLOWER OF DUNBLANE, THE.

Dunblane Massacre On 13 March 1996 a former Scout leader called Thomas Hamilton made his way into Dunblane Primary School armed with four handguns and opened fire, killing 16 young children and a teacher, before shooting himself. Among those who survived was Andy Murray, the tennis-player, then aged eight. Privately owned handguns were subsequently banned in Britain.

Dunce The word 'dunce' derives from the Scottish scholastic philosopher, John Duns Scotus (*c.*1266–1308), known as DOCTOR SUBTILIS, who was born in the Berwickshire town of Duns. By the 16th century the humanists had begun to deride what they considered the pedantry and sophistry of the followers of Duns Scotus, known as Dunses or Dunsmen, who were regarded as blockheads for resisting the new learning. During the Reformation the reformers joined in the attack, as Duns Scotus had asserted the superior power of the papacy over secular rulers. Hence 'dunce' came to mean a dull, stupid person.

Dundas, Henry 'Starvation' *See* HENRY THE NINTH.

Dundee cake A rich fruitcake, first made in the city in the 19th century by the Keiller family, who added to the cake-mix excess orange peel not required in their DUNDEE MARMALADE. An 1892 *Encyclopedia of Practical Cookery* mentions among the ingredients a pound of butter and thirteen eggs.

Dundee marmalade A type of marmalade with thick bits of peel, manufactured in the city. The name was registered as a trademark in 1880 by the Dundee firm of James Keiller & Son (founded by Mrs Janet Keiller in the 1790s), although it is mentioned some decades earlier by Dickens in *Household Words* for 28 June 1856: 'Anchovy Paste, Dundee Marmalade, and the whole stock of luxurious helps to appetite.' It may have been Janet Keiller who, thrifty body that she was, watered down marmalade – hitherto a thick citrus-based conserve that was cut into chunks – to create the spread we know today. The old chestnut, that the word 'marmalade' comes from *Marie malade* ('sick Mary'), alluding to the seasickness of Mary Queen of Scots as she returned to Scotland from France, has no basis in truth. In fact 'marmalade' comes from the Portuguese word for quince jelly: *marmelada* (from *marmelo*, 'quince').

Dundee steak Spam. The term seems to have arisen in Edinburgh in the 1990s, presumably as some kind of barbed reference to Dundee's supposed poverty.

Dunedin The anglicized form of *Dùn Éideann*, the old Gaelic name for Edinburgh. *Dùn* is Gaelic for 'fort', while *Éideann* may derive from *eiddyn*, Brythonic (the language of the ancient Britons, ancestral to Welsh) for 'crag', referring to Castle Rock. Before the Gaels moved in, Castle Rock was the stronghold of the people the Romans referred to as the Votadini, a British tribe who moved their capital here from Traprain Law in East Lothian around AD 500. These were presumably the people whom the 6th-century proto-Welsh poet Aneirin referred to as the GODODDIN, who feasted and drank at a place he called *Dineiddyn*. Thus chronology renders nonsensical the assertion that the second element refers to Edwin, Anglo-Saxon king of Northumbria from 617 to 633. The first recorded version of the Anglo-

Saxon (Old English) form of the name, *Edenburge*, dates from 1126; in this form Gaelic *dùn* has simply been replaced by Old English *burh*, meaning the same thing, i.e. 'fortified place'. The name Dunedin survives in the name of the capital of Otago province, New Zealand.

> My dear Sir, do not think I blaspheme when I tell you that your Great London as compared to Dun-Edin 'mine own romantic town' is as prose compared to poetry, or as a great rumbling, rambling, heavy Epic – compared to a lyric, bright, brief, clear and vital as a flash of lightning.
> – Charlotte Brontë, letter, 20 July 1850

Dung down *See* DING DOON.

Dun Kenneth *See* BRAHAN SEER, THE.

Dunlop cheese A mild cheese made from 'sweet' (i.e. unskimmed) milk, resembling a soft cheddar. It was first made in Scotland in the Ayrshire village of Dunlop around the end of the 17th century by a farmer's wife called Barbara Gilmour, who had in fact acquired the recipe in Ulster, where she had lived for a while before returning to Scotland and settling in Dunlop in 1688. Dunlop cheeses were subsequently made in other parts of Scotland.

Dunse dings a' Literally, 'Duns beats all' – referring to the former county town of Berwickshire, known as Dunse until 1882. The phrase originates in the first BISHOPS' WARS, when in 1639, at the hill near the town called Duns Law, an army of Covenanters defied the forces of Charles I, who was obliged to desist from his attempt to impose bishops on the Scots. Some wag at the time came up with the following saying as a consequence:

> The bishops were discharged in Scotland neither by Canon Law nor by Civil Law but by Dunse Law.

Dunsinane *See* BIRNAM WOOD.

Duns Scotus *See* DOCTOR SUBTILIS; DUNCE.

Dutchman's Cap The familiar name for Bac Mor, one of the Treshnish Isles in the Inner Hebrides, so-called because of its shape (although some would say it more closely resembles a sombrero).

Dwam, awa in a *See* AWA IN A DWAM.

Dwarfie Stane, the A large rock-cut chambered tomb on the Orkney island of Hoy, dating from *c*.3000 BC, and of a type rare in northern Europe. Local legends associate it both with giants and with TROWS – i.e. trolls or dwarves, who would fit better than giants into its cramped interior. The Dwarfie Stane features in Scott's *The Pirate* (1821), in which Norna of the Fitful-head says it was the dwelling place of 'Trollid, a dwarf famous in the northern Sagas'. *See also* CARBUNCLE OF WARD HILL, THE.

D'ye think ah came up the Clyde on a banana boat? Do you think I am completely gullible/innocent/naïve? The Aberdonian variant is 'D'ye think ah came doon the Dee on a digestive?'

D'ye think ma heid buttons up the back? Do you consider me a fool? The allusion is to a scarecrow, whose head is stuffed with straw. Sometimes *zips* is substituted for *buttons*.

E

Eagle, abducted by an The following account of the abduction of an infant by an eagle is reported by William Daniell in his *Voyage Round Great Britain* (1815–25):

> In conversing on the strength of these formidable animals, he [Dr Jura, the son of the laird of that isle] stated that an eagle once took up a child which its mother had wrapped up in a piece of flannel and laid down by a stook of oats (it being harvest time) and flew with it from Scarba to Jura [a flight of at least a mile, over the Gulf of CORRYVRECKAN]. Some of the people of Jura observing the eagle descend, with what they supposed to be a lamb in his talons, hastened to the place where he alighted, and, to their surprise, found the infant unhurt, with the wrapping around it scarcely discomposed.

Earl Beardie A legendary character associated with Glamis Castle, Angus. He has variously been identified with Alexander Lyon, 2nd Lord Glamis (d.c.1486), and Alexander Lindsay, 4th Earl of Crawford (d.1453), the so-called TIGER EARL. The story goes that Earl Beardie was one night playing cards, when someone suggested he should stop because either he was losing heavily, or it was the Sabbath. At this unwonted interruption Earl Beardie lost his temper and swore he would go on playing till Judgement Day. This gave the Devil his cue to enter and claim his victim's soul. Earl Beardie is supposedly still playing cards with the Devil and/or his cronies, perhaps in a hidden room – for Glamis Castle supposedly has a secret chamber, which no one can find, although it has a window. The ghost of Earl Beardie can still be heard, it is said, swearing and stamping his foot in a rage.

Another story about the secret chamber says that it was built to house an heir to the Strathmore family who was born a deformed monster. This was supposedly in the early 19th century, and the creature was said to have lived into the 1920s. The secret was passed down the family from father to son – which rather begs the question as to how the story became so widely known in the first place.

A third explanation of the secret-chamber-whose-existence-cannot-be-established-because-no-one-has-ever-found-it is that in it are hidden the bones of a number of Ogilvies who came to Glamis for aid during a feud with the Lindsays, but were locked in the room and starved to death instead. The relevant Lord Strathmore was so ashamed of what he had done that he had the place bricked up.

'Earl of Erroll, The' *See under* WALY.

Earl of Mar's Grey Breeks, the A nickname for the Royal Scots Fusiliers; *see* REGIMENTAL NICKNAMES.

Earl of Moray will not be long in debt to the Earl of Mar, the A traditional Northeast saying when a southern wind carries large heavy clouds northward (Moray being north of Mar).

Earl o' Hell, the The Devil, hence the expression *black as the Earl o' Hell's waistcoat*, meaning 'pitch dark'. The title *Earl o' Hell* was also apparently awarded to a chief of a band of Yetholm gypsies in the later 18th century.

Earth hound *See* ERTH HUN.

Earthquake Capital of Scotland, the Comrie in Perthshire; *see* SHAKY VILLAGE, THE, under which heading an account will be found of the notable earthquake of 1816, experienced over much of Northeast Scotland.

East Fife four, Forfar five An apocryphal but long awaited football result. The two teams came close in the 1963–4 season when playing in the old Second Division: the result was Forfar five, East Fife four. It is said in Aberdeenshire that the result of one local match was 'Echt five, Fyvie echt'.

East Neuk, the The eastern corner (*neuk*) of Fife, which juts into the outer reaches of the Firth of Forth and the North Sea beyond. The area is renowned for its old fishing villages, such as Crail, Anstruther and Pittenweem, with their brightly painted harled walls and crow-stepped gables (*see* CRAW STEPS).

> East Neuk of Fife, the fishers' margin,
> driftnet of villages pursing the shore ...
> – Stephen Scobie, 'Dunino' (1985)

East Neuk Disaster, the A fishing tragedy that took place on 19 November 1875, when two boats from Cellardyke and three from St Monans – each with some six crew aboard – were lost in a great storm on their way home from the East Anglian herring fishery.

Eastward Hoe A satirical play in the 'city comedy' genre by Ben Jonson, George Chapman and John Marston, first performed and printed in London in 1605. Its anti-Scottish barbs made it offensive to James VI and I and his Scottish courtiers, who were not greatly loved in the English capital. As a consequence, Jonson and Chapman served a spell in jail, while Marston managed to make himself scarce until things calmed down. The most notorious passage comes in Act III, scene iii, in which Captain Seagull is outlining the attractions of Virginia:

> And then you shall live freely there, without sergeants, or courtiers, or lawyers, or intelligencers, only a few industrious Scots, perhaps, who indeed are dispers'd over the face of the whole earth. But, as for them, there are no greater friends to Englishmen and England, when they are out on't, in the world, than they are. And, for my part, I would a hundred thousand of 'em were there, for we are all one countrymen now, ye know; and we should find ten times more comfort of them there than we do here.

It is thought that Chapman was responsible for this scene, although he blamed Marston. When he visited William Drummond of Hawthornden at Christmas 1618, Jonson, who prided himself on his Scottish ancestry, talked about the episode, confiding that 'The report was that they should have had their ears cut and noses.' As it was, he and Chapman were released by November 1605. By 1614, when *Eastward Hoe* was performed at court, all appears to have been forgiven, and when Jonson made his visit to Scotland to see Drummond, he was made an honorary citizen of Edinburgh.

Eat the breid o' idleseat, to To be lazy; *breid* is 'bread', and *idleseat* 'idleness'. The expression is more often heard in the negative, e.g. *He disnae eat the breid o' idleseat*, 'He works hard for his living.'

Eat the cow and worry on the tail, to To spoil the ship for a pennyworth o' tar; to spoil a project, etc., by standing on a point of minor principle; to be hung up on details.

Echt five, Fyvie echt *See* EAST FIFE FOUR, FORFAR FIVE.

Eck *See* BIG ECK; WEE ECK.

Eclipses *See* MURK MONDAY.

Écossaise Short for *danse écossaise* (French, 'Scottish dance'), a dance in duple time, or the music for such a dance, popular in the early 19th century. Beethoven and Schubert both wrote examples. It is unclear whether there was ever any connection with Scotland. *Cf.* SCHOTTISCHE.

Edgewell Tree, the A prophetic oak that grew by Dalhousie Castle, the seat of the Ramsays near Bonnyrigg in Midlothian. According to Allan Ramsay in his *Poems* (1721), it was

> ... very much observed by the country people, who give out, that before any of the family died, a branch fell from the Edgewell Tree. The old tree, some few years ago, fell altogether, but another sprung from the same root, which is now tall and flourishing.

Sir James Frazer mentions it in *The Golden Bough*, and records that 'on seeing a great bough drop from the tree on a quiet, still day in July 1874, an old forester exclaimed, "The laird's deid noo!" and soon after news came that Fox Maule, eleventh Earl of Dalhousie, was dead.'

Edina, the A 19th-century brand of water closet, the name being inspired by a line in Burns's 'Address to Edinburgh': 'Edina! Scotia's darling seat!' The design, in white porcelain, has relief mouldings at the base.

Edina's roses *See* AULD REEKIE.

Edinburgh *See* ATHENS OF THE NORTH, THE; AULD REEKIE; DUNEDIN; FLOWERS OF EDINBURGH; GUID TOUN, THE; SUMMER HAS LEAPED SUDDENLY UPON EDINBURGH LIKE A TIGER.

Edinburgh duck, the *See* SALTER'S DUCK.

Edinburgh gingerbread A rich gingerbread that includes dried fruit and nuts. How and when it acquired its name is unclear.

Edinburgh method, the The now generally accepted method of treating tuberculosis with a combination of three different antibiotics, to prevent the development of resistance by the bacteria responsible. The highly successful method was developed in the 1950s by an Edinburgh team headed by Dublin-born John Crofton (1912–2009), professor of respiratory diseases at Edinburgh University. Prior to the development of the method, TB was the leading cause of death in young people in Edinburgh, but in six years Crofton and his team had got TB in the city under control, and the method was subsequently adopted around the world, saving millions of lives.

Edinburgh Review The first periodical of this name was a short-lived affair, surviving for just two issues in 1755, but notable for including an unfavourable notice of Dr Johnson's *Dictionary* by Adam Smith. Its much more famous successor was founded in 1802 by Francis Jeffrey, Sydney Smith and Henry Brougham, and published by Archibald Constable. Jeffrey remained as editor until 1829. Its motto was *Judex damnatur ubi nocens absolvitur* (Latin, 'The

judge is damned when the guilty is acquitted'), and its stated intention was to be 'distinguished rather for the selection than for the number of its articles'. Politically its sympathies were Whiggish and pro-reform, although in literary matters Jeffrey was dismissive of 'the Lake School', and began his review of Wordsworth's *The Excursion* with the words, 'This will never do ...' The magazine's politics prompted the foundation of the Tory-leaning *Quarterly Review* (published by John Murray in London from 1809) and the more acerbic Edinburgh-based *Blackwood's Magazine* (dubbed 'MAGA') in 1817. The *Edinburgh Review* continued in existence until 1929, publishing many of the leading writers of the era, including Scott, Carlisle, Hazlitt, Leigh Hunt, Macaulay and Bertrand Russell. Hazlitt declared that 'to be an Edinburgh Reviewer is, I suspect, the highest rank in modern literary society'.

The magazine was revived in 1969 as the *New Edinburgh Review*, and changed its name to *Edinburgh Review* in 1984. Its motto is 'To gather all the rays of culture into one', and it carries work by both established and new writers, from Scotland and elsewhere (for example, issue 128 was devoted to Czech literature).

Edinburgh rock A stick-shaped confection, coming in a variety of pastel shades. It is crumblier than Blackpool rock, and is made from sugar, cream of tartar and water, with various colourings and flavourings. Edinburgh rock was first made by Alexander Ferguson, who was born in Doune, Perthshire in 1789, and who learnt his trade in Glasgow before going on to set up a confectionery business in Edinburgh. This was so successful that he became known as 'Sweetie Sandy', and he was able to retire to Doune on the fortune he made from Edinburgh rock.

Edinburgh Royal High School riot *See* ROYAL HIGH SCHOOL RIOT.

Edinburgh's Folly The popular name for the National Monument that stands atop Calton Hill in Edinburgh; it is also known as Scotland's Disgrace or Scotland's Pride and Poverty. It takes the form of an incomplete Parthenon, so bolstering the capital's aspiration to be the ATHENS OF THE NORTH.

Originally, in the wake of the victorious conclusion of the Napoleonic Wars, it had been intended to erect such a monument in London, but this never came to fruition. The idea subsequently migrated northward, and in 1819 in Edinburgh a meeting of patriotically minded persons determined

> ... to erect a Temple of Gratitude to God, for the protection he had, in the day of peril, afforded to the Land, and for the Glory he had, in the day of Battle and of Victory, shed around the Warriors of Caledonia; and also to render pious tribute of gratitude and affection to those gallant Scotsmen, Officers and Men, who, by their signal heroism on the great Military Arena of a conflicting world, had maintained the Martial Fame of their Ancestors, and attracted the marked notice and approbation of the greatest Monarchs and first Generals of the Age.

As far as the form that such a Monument should take, some favoured a copy of the Pantheon in Rome, others a 'Modern Church', others again a triumphal arch, while the avant-garde were all for 'a fanciful Gothic Edifice', but in the end it

> ... occurred at length to a few public-spirited individuals, of more refined taste, that a restoration of the Parthenon of Athens would be the most eligible; and that Calton Hill from its resemblance to the Acropolis of Athens, should be chosen as the site.

Supporters included Sir Walter Scott, Francis Jeffrey and Lord Cockburn, and it was proposed to raise the funds by public subscription: target £42,000; minimum contribution 1 guinea. The renowned Hellenophile architect Charles Robert Cockerell was commissioned, assisted by William Henry Playfair, and it had been hoped that the foundation stone would be laid by George IV during his visit to Scotland in 1822 (the first by a reigning monarch since 1641), but George found himself otherwise engaged; it has been suggested that this enabled him to avoid coughing up a contribution to the building costs. That indeed turned out to be the trouble: the citizens of Edinburgh proved unable to dig deep enough in their pockets, and although construction began in 1826 it was abandoned in 1829, leaving the building in its present unfinished state. Many think it turned out for the best: for example, Sir Nikolaus

Pevsner, in *A History of Building Types* (1971), stated that the National Monument had 'acquired a power to move which in its complete state it could not have had'.

Edinburgh School, the A loose but influential grouping of painters all of whom taught in the interwar years at Edinburgh College of Art, and who broadly drew their inspiration from the Fauves and the Expressionists. Their numbers include William Gillies, William Johnstone, John Maxwell, Anne Redpath and William MacTaggart.

Education, Salvation and Damnation The nickname for the Central Library, St Marks Church and His Majesty's Theatre, three neighbouring buildings on Rosemount Viaduct, Aberdeen.

Edward Longshanks *See* HAMMER OF THE SCOTS, THE.

Eechie nor ochie (Neither) one thing nor another; from the exclamations *ech* and *och*. It is also found in the form *ichie nor ochie*. Applied to a person, it means that they are a ditherer.

> Wha gangs hauvers wi' a thief,
> Daes the warst for his ain saul:
> He's weel eneuch awaur o' the wrang,
> But hauds his thoom on the ploy,
> An' ne'er says eechie nor ochie.
> – Proverbs 29:24, as rendered by T. Whyte Paterson

Eedle-doddle or **needle-noddle** Carefree, slapdash, laidback, lacking initiative; or a person demonstrating such characteristics. The expression appears to derive from the English word 'idle', and gives rise to the similar *deetle-dottle*, 'dawdling', 'messing about', where the *dottle* element on its own indicates a state of dotage, as in *dottle-headed*. The similar-sounding *deedle-doddle* means 'spineless', with *deedle* probably coming from *daidle*, 'to idle', and *doddle* meaning 'to lumber slowly along'.

Eeksy-peeksy or **icksie-picksie** Evenly balanced, both the same. The expression *equal-aqual* is synonymous.

Eel-drooner Literally, someone who can drown eels, in other words, someone capable of seemingly impossible feats, a very clever person. The expression, usually used ironically and in the negative (e.g. 'He's nae eel-drooner'), was in use into the early 20th century.

Eels In the Highlands eels were formerly thought to grow from horse hairs, and were not considered suitable for human consumption (John G. Campbell, *Superstitions of the Highlands and Islands of Scotland*, 1900). The *nine-eed eel* was the lamprey (*see* WIZARD SHACKLE).

E'en do and spare nocht A motto of Clan MacGregor. It is said to have originated some time in the 12th century, when Sir Malcolm MacGregor was out hunting with the king. After the latter was attacked by a wild boar, Sir Malcolm requested leave to take on the animal. The king replied, 'E'en do and spair nocht.' Sir Malcolm duly killed the boar. The more familiar motto of the clan is *Rioghal Mo Dhream*, Gaelic for 'Royal is my race', alluding to the MacGregors' claim to be descended from a high king of Ireland and the father of Kenneth MacAlpin, first king of Scotland.

Een like penny bowls, to have To stare with wide-open eyes (*een*), as if with astonishment or fright. A *penny bowl* is a small, inexpensive dish, so the expression is similar to having 'eyes like saucers'.

Eenty-teenty *See* ZEENTY-TEENTY.

Eggs, aff one's *See* AFF ONE'S EGGS.

Eightsome reel A Scottish country dance in 4/4 time involving four couples dancing in a broadly circular formation.

Eildon Tree, the A tree that formerly stood on the slopes of the Eildon Hills above Melrose, its location now marked by a stone. It was at the Eildon Tree that THOMAS THE RHYMER entered the land of the fairies (ELFAME) that lay under the hills, as recounted in the old ballad (itself based on a 15th-century romance):

True Thomas lay on Huntly Bank,
A ferlie he spied with his e'e;
And there he saw a ladye bright,
Came riding down by the Eildon Tree.

According to legend, Thomas the Rhymer still sleeps under the Eildons, along with his host of warriors. (In other legends, it is King Arthur and his knights who sleep here, if not under ARTHUR'S SEAT or elsewhere.)

Aneath the hills the gigants turn
  In their ayebydan dwaum –
Finn under Nevis, the great King
Under Arthur's Seat, True Tammas
  Neth the Eildons steers again ...
    – Sydney Goodsir Smith: '23rd Elegy: Farewell to
      Calypso', *Under the Eildon Tree* (1948) [*ayebydan
      dwaum* 'everlasting sleep', *steers* 'stirs']

The triple-peaked Eildon Hills were the sight of a large Iron Age fort, and also a Roman signal station – the Romans called the hills *Trimontium*. According to another legend, the hills were once one hill, until the wizard Michael SCOT got one of his demons to split it into three. The Eildons figure prominently in SCOTT'S VIEW.

Eilean a' Cheò *See* MISTY ISLE, THE.

El D Eldorado, an inexpensive brand of fortified wine, often consumed from dawn till dusk, and beyond.

During my own teenage days, young people used to get hold of all sorts of things such as Eldorado sherry, which is probably quite pleasant, but is not supposed to be drunk in pints at a time, as some of my young friends used to do.
  – Doug Henderson MP, during a House of Commons
    debate, 28 February 1997

Elder An officer in the Church of Scotland and other Presbyterian churches. *Ruling elders* are lay people (exclusively men until 1966) who take part in the government of the church, while ministers are known as *teaching elders*. To *keep to elders' hours* was to make sure that one was safely and respectably home at a decent hour, usually around ten o'clock; formerly the elders would patrol the streets to enforce this curfew. In various places, cormorants were known as *elders o' Cowend* or *Mochrum elders* (*see under* FAUNA CALEDONIA).

Elderslie Oak and Yew *See* WALLACE'S OAK.

Electric Brae, the A section of the A719 traversing the coastal hills between Ayr and Turnberry. It is the location of a famous optical illusion, as outlined in an inscription on a stone by the roadside:

> The 'Electric Brae', known locally as Croy Brae. This runs the quarter mile from the bend overlooking Croy railway viaduct in the west (286 feet Above Ordnance Datum) to the wooded Craigencroy Glen (303 feet A.O.D.) to the east. Whilst there is this slope of 1 in 86 upwards from the bend at the Glen, the configuration of the land on either side of the road provides an optical illusion making it look as if the slope is going the other way. Therefore, a stationary car on the road with the brakes off will appear to move slowly uphill. The term 'Electric Brae' dates from a time when it was incorrectly thought to be a phenomenon caused by electric or magnetic attraction within the Brae.

Don Paterson, in the section of his poem 'Exeunt' entitled 'The Electric Brae', recalls a trick played by generations of drivers:

> On an easy slope, his father lets the engine
> cough into silence. Everything is still.
> He frees the brake: the car surges uphill.
>   – from *Nil Nil* (1993)

Andrew Greig borrowed the name *Electric Brae* for the title of a 1992 novel, described by the author as 'a modern romance without heather or hardmen'.

Electric soup Any particularly potent, cheap liquor, such as BUCKFAST, CALLY, EL D, LANNY or RED BIDDY. The name was adopted as the title of a Glasgow-based underground comic that ran from 1989 to 1992, featuring such strips as *The Greens*, a parody of *The BROONS*.

Elephant Man The nickname of the footballer David Dodds (b.1958), who played for Dundee United, Aberdeen and Rangers, and won two Scottish caps. The unkind nickname refers to Dodds's fancied resemblance to Joseph Merrick (1862–90), whose facial disfigurement earned him the name 'the Elephant Man'.

Elephant of Broughty Ferry, the An Indian elephant of unknown name which in April 1706, approaching Dundee on the road from Broughty Ferry, collapsed and died. A local physician, Patrick Blair, seeing an opportunity for scientific fame, set about dissecting the beast – the first person to do so. He recorded the results in a paper, 'Osteographia Elephantina, or a Full and Exact Description of all the Bones of an Elephant etc.', published in *Philosophical Transactions of the Royal Society*, Volume 27, London, 1710. After the dissection, the bones were mounted and the skin stuffed, both being exhibited in Dundee. Blair's work had the desired result, and in 1712 he was made a fellow of the Royal Society. Three years later he found himself on the wrong side in the Jacobite Rising, and was within hours of being hanged when interventions by friends and colleagues brought about a reprieve. He died in 1728. *See also* BLUE WHALE OF BRAGAR, THE; CAMEL OF THE CANONGATE, THE; WALRUS OF THE HEBRIDES, THE.

Elfame The land of Faerie, the country of the elves; also spelt *Elfhame, Elfan, Elfin, Elphame* or *Elphyne*. The name is also sometimes used as a euphemism for Hell, and there are cases from the later 16th century of women being convicted of witchcraft for having conversed with the 'Queen of Elfame', or other denizens of the otherworld. For example, in the 1571 trial of Bessie Dunlop of Lyne in Ayrshire, who was charged with curing illness and finding lost objects through supernatural means, the court records tell how Bessie encountered 12 men and women:

> The men wer cled in gentilmennis cleithing, and the wemen had all plaiddis round about thaim ... thay wer the Guid Wichtis that wonnit in the Court of Elfame; quha cum thair to desyr hir to go with thaim ... Sche answerit that sche dwelt with hir awin husband and bairnis, and culd nocht leif thaim.

Even conversing with the 'Guid Wichtis of Elfame' was enough to seal Bessie's fate: she was 'convict and brint'.

In the legend of THOMAS THE RHYMER, Elfame is located under the Eildon Hills (*see* EILDON TREE, THE), and is neither Heaven nor Hell:

I'm not the Queen of Heaven, Thomas,
That name does not belong to me;
I am but the Queen of fair Elphame
Come out to hunt in my follie.

The name Elfhame was formerly applied by the locals to Cleeves Cove, a cave on the Dusk Water in Ayrshire, between Dalry and Kilwinning, in the belief that supernatural beings had once made the limestone cave complex their home. Excavations in the 19th century revealed evidence of habitation by prehistoric people; the cave was also used as a refuge by Covenanters in the 17th century.

In the fantasies of Sylvia Townsend Warner (1893–1978), Elfhame is the fairy castle of Queen Tiphaine, situated near Eskdalemuir. In 'The Five Black Swans' she describes it thus:

Tiphaine's Kingdom lay on the Scottish border, not far from the romantic and lonely Eskdalemuir Observatory (erected in 1908). Her castle of Elfhame – a steep-sided grassy hill, round as a pudding basin – had great purity of style. A small lake on its summit – still known as the Fairy Loch, and local babies with croup are still dipped in its icy, weedless water – had a crystal floor, which served as a skylight. A door in the hillside, operated by legerdemain, opened into a complex of branching corridors ...

Although visitors to Eskdalemuir may find it tricky locating Elfhame, they can visit the equally unlikely Kagyu Samye Ling Buddhhist monastery, founded here in 1967.

Elf-arrows *See* ELF-SHOTS.

'Elfin Knight, The' A ballad dating back to the early 17th century. In the oldest versions the elfin knight seeks out a young human woman to take as his lover, a fate she can only avoid if she performs the series of impossible tasks he sets her. She responds by demanding that he perform her own set of impossible tasks. In later versions, it is she who desires the elfin knight, who will only agree if she carries out the impossible tasks.

The elfin knight sits on yon hill,
Ba, ba, ba, lilli ba.
He blaws his horn both loud and shrill,
The wind hath blown my plaid awa.

Elf-shots or **elf-arrows** Thomas Pennant, in his *Tour of Scotland 1769* (1772), gives the following account:

Elf-shots, i.e. the stone arrow-heads of the old inhabitants of this island, are supposed to be weapons shot by Fairies at cattle, to which are attributed any disorders they have: in order to effect a cure, the cow is to be touched by an elf-shot, or made to drink the water in which one has been dipped. The same virtue is said to be found in the crystal gems, and in the adder-stone, our *Glein Naidr*; and it is also believed that good fortune must attend the owner; so, for that reason, the first is called *Clach bhuaidh*, or the powerful stone (recte, stone of virtues). Captain Archibald Campbell showed me one, a spheroid set in silver, which people came for the use of above a hundred miles, and brought the water it was to be dipt in with them; for without that, in human cases, it was believed to have no effect. These have been supposed to be *magical* stones or gems used by the Druids to be inspected by a chaste boy, who was to see in them an apparition informing him of future events.

Another mention is made in a 1795 entry in the *Statistical Account*:

On examining the cow-doctor, he said he had often seen elveshot cows, some of which he had cured ... That he had frequently picked up those arrows, which were smooth triangular small pointed stones or pebbles, like flints; and it was his belief, that those who do the mischief are our *goodly neighbours*.

(The 'goodly neighbours' being, of course, the GUID FOLK.)

Elizabeth of Bohemia *See* WINTER QUEEN, THE.

Emmerteen's meat The plant heath bedstraw, *Galium saxatile*. An *emmerteen* is a Northeastern term for an ant, the word being a diminutive variant of the English dialect term *emmet*, which shares the same Old English root as 'ant'. There was a traditional rhyme spoken when an ant nest was disturbed, and the ants seen carrying off their eggs:

Emerteen, emerteen, laden yir horse,
Yir father and yir mither is ded in Kinloss.

End of an old song, the The curt elegy uttered by James Ogilvy, Lord Seafield (1664–1730), Lord Chancellor of Scotland, as he signed the 'engrossed exemplification' of the Act of Union in 1706, the year before the act abolished the Scottish Parliament. As recorded in the *Lockhart Papers* (1817), his actual words were:

Now there's ane end of ane old song.

The dying fall of this cadence is echoed by Scott in *OLD MORTALITY* (1816). Mrs Wilson, the housekeeper, is recounting the last words of the hero's uncle, who believes as he lies dying that he is dying heirless:

The name o' Morton of Milnwood's gane out like the last sough of an auld sang.

When the new Scottish Parliament held its first meeting on 12 May 1999, it fell to Winnie Ewing (aka MADAME ECOSSE), as the eldest MSP, to preside over the opening with the following words: 'The Scottish Parliament, adjourned on the 25th day of March in the year 1707, is hereby reconvened.' Thus the old song was found not to have ended, merely to have suffered an interruption. *See also* EQUIVALENT, THE; PARCEL OF ROGUES, A.

End o' a French fiddle *See* FAR AWA END O' A FRENCH FIDDLE.

Enemy, the *See* AULD ENEMY, THE.

Engagers Supporters of the 'Engagement' of 1647, Charles I's proposal to impose Presbyterianism throughout Britain in return for military aid from the Scots. The Engagers were defeated by Cromwell at the Battle of Preston in 1648.

English Comics' Grave, the The Glasgow Empire; *see* HOUSE OF TERROR, THE.

Enjoying the dry of the house What one may be said to be doing when not venturing out on a wet day.

Eoghan of the Little Head (Gaelic *Eoghan a chinn bhig*) A Maclean of Lochbuie on Mull who was killed in battle some time in the 16th or early 17th century, having had his head cut off with a claymore while charging full tilt at his enemies. His horse ran off with his body still mounted upon it, so that all his family could bury of him was his head. As a consequence, his restless (and headless) spirit still rides abroad at night, presumably in search of its missing member. According to some accounts, the reason Eoghan's ghost is unquiet is that he was killed before he had broken his fast. An early version was recounted in the periodical *Teachdaire Gaelach* (August 1830).

Ephor A prefect at the Edinburgh Academy. The original Ephors were the five magistrates of ancient Sparta.

Epilepsy, cures for *See* LIVE BURIAL; SUICIDES.

Epitaphs A selection follows:

WO. bE. TO
HIM. yAT. PU
TIS. yIS, TOO
Any. WDER.
WS. WHA
desecit. in. a
noa. mxclx
xxlv. yN. yAR
['Woe be to him that puts this to any wider use. Who deceased in anno 1660, 24 in years.']
  – For an unknown blacksmith, Maryton, Angus

There lies interred beneath this sod,
A sycophantish man of God,
Who taught an easy way to Heaven,
Which to the rich was always given.
If he gets in he'll look and stare,
To find some out that he put there.
  – For Dr McCulloch, Bothwell, Lanarkshire

Tam Samson's weel worn clay here lies,
Ye canting zealots spare him;
If honest worth in heaven arise,
Ye'll mend or ye win near him.
  – For Thomas Samson (d.1795), Kilmarnock

Stop, passenger, until my life you read:
The living may get knowledge of the dead.
Five times five years I lived a virgin's life:
Ten times five years I was a virtuous wife:
Ten times five years I lived a widow chaste;
Now, weary'd of this mortal life, I rest.
Between my cradle and my grave have been
Eight mighty kings of Scotland and a queen.
Four times five years the Commonwealth I saw;
Ten times the subjects rose against the law.
Twice did I see old Prelacy pull'd down;
And twice the cloak was humbled by the gown.
An end of Stuart's race I saw: nay, more!
My native country sold for English ore.
Such desolations in my life have been,
I have an end of all perfection seen.

    – For Margaret Scott, Dalkeith, Midlothian. She died in
    1738, supposedly at the age of 125 years.

Stop traveller as you go by,
I once had life and breath;
But falling from a steeple high
I swiftly passed through death.

    – For James Hunter, wright, Jedburgh, 1765

He was a peaceable, quiet man, and to all appearances a
sincere Christian. His death was much regretted which
was caused by the stupidity of Laurence Tulloch of
Clothister (Sullom) who sold him nitre instead of
Epsom Salts by which he was killed in the space of
five hours after taking a dose of it.

    – For Donald Robertson, Eshness, Shetland. Robertson
    died on 14 June 1848, at the age of 63.

Alexander Monteith, druggist in Edinburgh, a man
remarkably distinguished in true greatness of soul,
and by far the most eminent in the surgical art –
whose sepulchral mound might be termed a pile of
virtues, the lofty eulogies upon which, pronounced on
the non-professional, and contained in all the foregoing
epitaphs, unless they were confined within their own
lines and limits, having formed themselves into a
ph[a]lanx would pass over and through force of kin,
would emulously rush in and fly troops to him [&c, &c,
&c ...] He departed this life on December 23rd 1713,
two days before the festival of the birth of Christ, lest
the mourning and the sadness on account of the
decease of the former might interrupt the joy and
exultation of the nativity of the latter.

    – Greyfriars Kirkyard, Edinburgh

Gow an' time are even now;
Gow beat time, now time's beat Gow.

    – For Niel Gow (1727–1807), the famed Dunkeld
    fiddler, in the *Scots Magazine*, July 1812

Lament him, Mauchline husbands a',
He often did assist ye;
For had ye staid whole weeks awa',
Your wives they ne'er had miss'd ye!

Ye Mauchline bairns, as on ye pass
To school in band thegither;
O tread ye lightly on his grass,
Perhaps he was your father.

    – Robert Burns, 'Epitaph on a Wag in Mauchline'.
    The 'Wag' is said to have been Burns's crony,
    James Smith.

She was – but words are wanting
    To say what –
Think what a wife should be –
    She was that.

    – For Susan Gibson, Barry, Angus. She died in 1835,
    aged 29.

I do my best to leave aboon
The grave's lang, lanely hame,
A poor man' richest legacy,
And that's an honest name.

    – Epitaph of Alexander Maclagan, Balmoral, 1871

           Eternity is
        A wheel that turns
      A wheel that turned ever,
        A wheel that turns
    And will leave turning never.

    – For an unknown miller, Campsie, Dunbartonshire

Erected to the memory of
John MacFarlane
Drowned in the Water of Leith
By a few affectionate friends.

    – Anon.

Here lies my good and gracious Auntie
Whom Death has packed in his portmanty,
Three score and ten years God did gift her,
And here she lies, wha' de'il daurs lift her?

    – Possibly apocryphal, said to have once stood in Crail,
    Fife

Within this circular Idea
Called vulgarly a Tomb

The Ideas and Impressions lie
That constituted Hume.

> – Not to be found on David Hume's grave on Calton
> Hill, Edinburgh. His monument bears nothing more
> than his name and the years of his birth and death, as
> requested in his will, 'leaving it to Posterity to add the
> Rest'.

This be the verse you grave for me:
Here he lies where he longed to be,
Home is the sailor, home from sea,
And the hunter home from the hill.

> – Robert Louis Stevenson, 'Requiem'

Who're youse lookin at?

> – Apocryphal inscription on the gravestone of a hardman
> from Shettleston

See also WORST OF KINGS AND THE MOST MISER-
ABLE OF MEN, THE; and for the epitaph of Duns
Scotus, *see under DOCTOR SUBTILIS.*

Eponymous places *See:*
- AGASSIZ ROCK
- ARCHIE'S ROCK
- ARGYLL'S BOWLING GREEN
- ARTHUR'S OON
- ARTHUR'S SEAT
- BALFOUR BAY
- CLUNY'S CAGE
- DAFT ANN'S STEPS
- Numerous DEIL'S X and DEVIL'S Y
- DIRK HATTERAICK'S CAVE
- FINGAL'S CAVE
- FRANK LOCKWOOD'S ISLAND
- GRANNY KEMPOCK STONE
- HADDO'S HOLE
- LADY'S ROCK
- MACGREGOR'S LEAP
- MAIDEN HAIR
- MAIDEN STACK
- MERLIN'S GRAVE
- OSSIAN'S CAVE
- PADDY'S MARKET
- PADDY'S MILESTONE
- PHILIP AND MARY
- PUCK'S GLEN
- QUEEN OF SCOTS' PILLAR
- QUEEN VICTORIA'S ROCK
- RANDOLPH'S LEAP
- ROB ROY'S PRISON
- SALISBURY CRAGS
- SLAIN MEN'S LEA
- THE SOLDIER'S LEAP
- WITCH'S HOLE

Eponyms Here is a selection of items named after
Scots:

Argyll Robertson pupils Pupils that do not constrict
when exposed to bright light, a symptom of neuro-
syphilis. The eye surgeon Douglas Argyll Robertson
(1837–1909) taught ophthalmology at the University of Edinburgh.

Beilby layer A disorganized molecular layer that forms
on the surface of finely polished metals. The chemist George Beilby (1850–1924) was born and educated in Edinburgh.

Bell's palsy Paralysis of the muscles on one side of the
face. The condition is named after one of the
founders of neurology, the Scottish anatomist, physi-
ologist and surgeon Sir Charles Bell (1774–1842),
who gained his medical degree from Edinburgh
University in 1799. He first described the condition
in an 1821 paper entitled 'On the Nerves ...'.

Brewster's angle The angle of incidence at which light
with a particular polarization is perfectly transmitted
through a transparent dielectric surface, with no
reflection. The physicist Sir David Brewster (1781–
1868) was born in Jedburgh, and is also remembered for his invention of the kaleidoscope.

Brownian motion The random movement of particles
suspended in a fluid, first described by the botanist
Robert Brown (1773–1858), who was born in
Montrose, and studied at Aberdeen and Edinburgh
universities.

Clerk cycle The cycle performed by the two-stroke
engine invented by the Glasgow-born engineer Sir
Dugald Clerk (1854–1932).

Cnemophilus macgregorii A bird of paradise named
after Sir William MacGregor (1846–1919), governor of Papua, who hailed from Towie in Aberdeenshire.

Cudbear A purplish dye derived from various lichens.
The name is a fanciful alteration of the first name of the
industrial chemist who patented it, Dr Cuthbert
Gordon (baptized in Kirkmichael, Banffshire in
1730; d. 1810).

Dewar flask The vacuum flask, invented in 1892 by
the Scottish scientist Sir James Dewar (1842–1923).

It consists of a double wall of metal or silvered glass, with a vacuum in between the two layers.

Douglas fir A North American conifer, grown as an exotic on many Scottish estates, and named after the Scottish naturalist and explorer David Douglas (1798–1834), who first introduced it to cultivation in 1826. Somewhat contrarily, its species name, *Pseudotsuga menziesii*, honours another Scot, the naval surgeon and naturalist Archibald Menzies (1754–1842) who sailed on board HMS *Discovery* with George Vancouver on his circumnavigation in the 1790s. Douglas himself met an unfortunate end while collecting on the island of Hawaii. He fell into a pit intended to catch wild cattle, and was gored to death by an angry bull that had preceded him into the trap.

Drummond light A light used in the 19th century in surveying, using the principle of limelight, which combines both incandescence and candoluminescence. It was the Scottish civil engineer Thomas Drummond (1797–1840) who, after seeing a demonstration of limelight by Michael Faraday, built a working version in 1826 for use in the trigonometric survey of Great Britain and Ireland.

Forbes The US business magazine was founded in 1917 by the financial journalist Bertie Charles Forbes (1880–1954). Forbes was born in New Deer, Aberdeenshire, and emigrated to the USA in 1904.

Gordon setter A breed of gun dog, with a black and tan coat, named after Alexander Gordon, 4th Duke of Gordon (1743–1827), who kept many such dogs in his kennels. The name Gordon setter was recognized by the Kennel Club in 1924.

Graham's law A physical law that states that the rate of diffusion of a gas is inversely proportional to the square root of its molecular weight. It takes its name from the Scottish chemist Thomas Graham (1805–69), who proposed the law in 1831.

Greenockite The mineral sulphate of cadmium, named after Charles Murray, Lord Greenock (later 2nd Earl of Cathcart; 1783–1859), who found it on his land near Port Glasgow in 1841.

Gregorian telescope A type of reflecting telescope described in 1663 by James Gregory (1638–75), who was born in Drumoak, Aberdeenshire.

Kelvin temperature scale The scale in which 0 degrees is absolute zero. William Thomson (1824–1907), later Lord Kelvin, although born in Belfast, spent most of his life in Glasgow.

Kerr effect A physical effect by which the refractive index of certain materials changes in an electric field. It was discovered in 1875 by the Scottish physicist John Kerr (1824–1907).

Lawson's cypress A conifer, *Chamaecuparis lawsonia*, native to southwestern Oregon and northwestern California, whose seeds were first collected in 1854 by the Scottish botanist Andrew Murray (1812–78). Murray named the tree in honour of Peter (d.1820) and Charles (1794–1873) Lawson, the proprietors of the Edinburgh nursery Lawson and Son, which introduced the species to cultivation.

macadam A type of smooth, hard road surface developed by the Scottish civil engineer John Loudon McAdam (1756–1836) in the early 19th century, which replaced the earlier muddy tracks that passed for roads. By the end of the 19th century bitumen (tar) had been added (hence the surface became known as tarmacadam), and most of the main roads in Europe had been 'macadamized'. Tarmac is a trademark, registered in 1903, for a particular type of tarmacadam that incorporates iron slag and creosote. The poet Thomas Hood (1799–1845) apostrophized McAdam in the following terms:

> McADAM, hail!
> Hail Roadian! hail Colossus, who dost stand
> Striding ten thousand turnpikes in the land!
> Universal Leveller, all hail!

macadamia nut The nut of the macadamia tree, genus *Macadamia*, of Australia and Southeast Asia. The plant was named by his colleague Ferdinand von Müller after the Scottish-born chemist John Macadam (1827–65), who emigrated to Australia in 1855.

macfarlane A type of overcoat with a cape and slits in the sides to give access to one's pockets in the layers underneath. It originated in the mid-19th century. The identity of the eponymous Macfarlane is unknown, although such a coat gets a mention both in Joyce's *Finnegans Wake* and in Beckett's *Embers*.

macgillivraii A species name given to a number of animals, including the North American birds *Ammodramus macgillivraii*, a bunting, *Sylvia macgillivraii*, a warbler, and *Fringilla macgillivraii*, a finch.

They are named after William Macgillivray (1796–1852), professor of botany at Marischal College, Aberdeen, who assisted J.J. Audubon in the publication of *Birds of America*.

mackintosh A waterproof coat, originally incorporating the method of rubberizing fabric invented by the Scottish chemist Charles Macintosh (1766–1843).

Maclagan diesel A type of diesel engine designed by John C.M. Maclagan (1886–1962), and incorporated into many CLYDE-BUILT ships.

Maclaurin's theorem A mathematical formula beyond the comprehension of the present author, named after the brilliant mathematician and physicist Colin Maclaurin (1698–1746). Maclaurin was appointed professor of mathematics at Aberdeen at the age of 19, was elected a fellow of the Royal Society at 21, and became professor of mathematics at Edinburgh at 27, having been recommended for the post by Newton. He helped prepare the defences of Edinburgh against the advancing Jacobites in 1745, and fled to England when they seized the city. He returned the following year, but died shortly thereafter.

maclurin A chemical found in various trees, including mulberry, and used in dyes. It is named after the Ayr-born American geologist William Maclure (1763–1840), who also gave his name to maclurite, a mineral better known as chondrodite.

Macquarie pine A tree of the yew family, native to Tasmania, and named after Lachlan Macquarie (1762–1824), who was born on Ulva, off Mull, and who as governor of New South Wales did much to transform the colony from a mere penal settlement. Various other plants and animals are also named after Macquarie.

Maxwell's demon A hypothetical creature posited in 1871 by the great Scottish physicist James Clerk Maxwell (1831–79) as the only way of breaking the second law of thermodynamics, which states that it is not possible for heat to pass from a cold body to a hot body. In a thought experiment, Maxwell imagined his creature as possessing the remarkable ability to identify slow from fast-moving particles, and opening and shutting a hole between two parts of a vessel containing air at uniform temperature so that all the fast-moving particles would end up in one part, making it warmer than the other part.

monteith an ornamental wineglass cooler, made either of silver or from porcelain (there is a Sèvres example in the Fitzwilliam Museum, Cambridge). The wineglasses are suspended from the notched rim, the bowls dipping into iced water, while the bases stay dry. The term is said to derive from the name of a 17th-century Scot who wore a cloak with a scalloped hem:

> Such a bason was called a 'Monteigh', from a fantastical Scot called 'Monsieur Monteigh', who at that time or a little before wore the bottome of his cloake or coate so notched …
> – Anthony Wood, *Life, from 1632 to 1672, written by himself* … (1683)

Monteith A red handkerchief with white spots, named after the 19th-century Scottish dyer Henry Monteith, who manufactured them.

Munro A Scottish mountain over 3000 feet in height, named after Sir Hugh Munro (1856–1919), who published a list of such mountains in 1891. *See* MUNRO.

Napier's bones A calculating device consisting of graduated rods, named after the Scottish mathematician John Napier (1550–1617), and described by him in *Rabdologiae* (1617). Natural logarithms, discovered by Napier, are sometimes called Napierian logarithms.

Nicol prism The earliest device for polarizing light, invented in 1828 by the Scottish physicist and geologist William Nicol (1770–1851). It consists of a rhombohedral crystal of calcite split diagonally at an angle of 68 degrees and then cemented together again using Canada balsam.

Phlox drumondii A brightly coloured North American flowering plant, popular with gardeners. It is named after the Scottish botanist Thomas Drummond (1780–1836).

Playfair cipher An encryption technique based on pairs of letters. It was devised in 1854 by the English scientist Charles Wheatstone, but named after Sir Lyon (later Lord) Playfair (1818–98), the Indian-born Scottish chemist and Liberal politician who promoted the system. Playfair also advocated the use of poison gas against the Russians during the Crimean War.

Rankine scale A temperature scale in which 0 degrees is absolute zero, as in the Kelvin scale (*see above*);

but whereas in the Kelvin scale a degree Kelvin is equal to a degree Celsius, in the Rankine scale a degree is equal to a degree Fahrenheit. The Rankine scale was proposed in 1859 by the Scottish engineer and physicist William John Macquorn Rankine (1820–72).

Stevenson screen A box with louvred sides used to house meteorological instruments, designed by the Scottish lighthouse engineer Thomas Stevenson (1818–87), father of RLS.

Stirling engine A highly efficient type of external-combustion engine incorporating a heat exchanger. It was invented by the Scottish engineer and minister the Revd Dr Robert Stirling (1790–1878), who patented his design in 1816. Nearly two centuries later it is attracting interest for its potential in domestic combined heat and power units. The thermodynamic cycle employed in the Stirling engine is known as a Stirling cycle.

Stirling formula A mathematical formula for approximating large factorials, devised by the Scottish mathematician James Stirling (1692–1770). He also gave his name to Stirling numbers of the first kind, and, indeed, to Stirling numbers of the second kind.

Tarmac *See* MACADAM *above.*

Thomson's gazelle A gazelle, *Gazella thomsoni*, native to the savannas of eastern Africa, named after the Scottish geologist and explorer Joseph Thomson (1858–95). It is sometimes familiarly known as the 'tommy'.

watsonia Any plant of the genus *Watsonia*, also known in English as the bugle lily. It belongs to the iris family, is native to South Africa, and was named in honour of the Scottish naturalist William Watson (1715–87).

watt The SI unit of power, named in 1882 in honour of the Scottish engineer and improver of the steam engine, James Watt (1736–1819).

Wilson cloud chamber A device filled with super-cooled, supersaturated vapour used to detect alpha and beta particles. These ionize the vapour, and the resulting ions form condensation nuclei around which a mist forms, so allowing the passage of the particles to be traced. The cloud chamber was invented by the Scottish physicist, meteorologist and Nobel laureate C.T.R. Wilson (1869–1959), who was apparently inspired by the sight of a Brocken spectre on the summit of Ben Nevis in 1894.

Wilson's storm petrel A small dark seabird, *Oceanites oceanicus*, which breeds on the coasts and offshore islands of Antarctica and spends the rest of the year wandering the world's oceans. It is named after the Paisley-born poet, ornithologist and illustrator Alexander Wilson (1766–1813), who emigrated to America in 1794. Wilson is also honoured in the names of a number of other birds, including Wilson's plover (*Charadrius wilsonia*), Wilson's phalarope (*Phalaropus tricolor*) and Wilson's warbler (*Wilsonia pusilla*), all New World species.

See also BUCHANITE; CANT; CAMERONIAN; CAMP-BELLITE; CORBETT; DONALD; GRAHAM.

Eppie Callum's Oak An ancient oak in Crieff, reputed to have sheltered both ROB ROY and the YOUNG PRETENDER. It was named after the hostess of the Oakbank Inn, who is said to have planted an acorn in a teapot, and then replanted the sapling in the garden when it became too large. The tree is actually more ancient than this story suggests, being some 600 years old.

Equal-aqual *See* EEKSY-PEEKSY.

Equivalent, the The money paid by the new British government at the time of the Union in 1707 to pay off the Scottish national debt, valued precisely at £398,085 10s. 0d. For their part, the Scots shouldered their own share of the British national debt. It was widely suggested that some of the money was diverted into the coffers of pro-Union members of the Scottish Parliament, which had voted for its own abolition. *See also* END OF AN OLD SONG; PARCEL OF ROGUES, A.

Erchie The central character in a series of humorous stories by Neil Munro, which began to appear in the Glasgow *Evening News* in 1902, and continued to appear until 1926. Erchie MacPherson is a waiter and kirk deacon, and he and his wife Jinnet and friend Duffy the coal merchant have something to say about almost everything, from sport, politics and fashion to Harry Lauder, Andrew Carnegie and Robert Burns. In 1904 a collection of these stories was published as *Erchie, My Droll Friend*, but many of the newspaper stories were not published in book form until Birlinn brought out two further volumes in 1993 and 2005.

> 'I'm nae phenomena; I'm jist Nature; jist the Rale Oreeginal.'
> – Neil Munro, *Erchie, My Droll Friend* (1904)

Erebus (1) The Greek god of darkness, (2) Glaswegian for 'There's the bus'. This observation may be elaborated in various ways, e.g. *Erenurrerbus*, 'There's another bus'; *Snowurbus*, 'It's not our bus', etc.

Errata In his *Unlikely Stories, Mostly* (1983), Alasdair Gray instructed the printers to insert an erratum slip with the following wording: 'This slip has been inserted by mistake.' *See also* BOOKMARKS.

Errol's aik *See* OAK OF ERROL, THE.

Erse many times harder than flint, an *See* HARD AS HINNERSON'S ERSE, AS.

Erth huns Literally 'earth hounds', mysterious creatures said to burrow through the graveyards of the Northeast:

> The kirkyard … was also said to be tenanted by a hideous ghoul, termed the 'erth-hun' who feasted on the dead, and whose teeth could be heard crunching the coffins ere the mould was covered in.
> – G.W. Anderson, *Lays of Strathbogie and the Story of the Strath* (1891)

These creatures were also known as *yird pigs* (*yird* meaning 'earth', hence also a grave). The unimaginative have dismissed them as either rats or moles.

Eternal snows of Braeriach, the In the 20th century, the snow only melted completely in the Garbh Choire Mor of Braeriach (1296 m / 4248 ft), in the summers of 1933, 1959 and 1996. *See also* SNOWS OF BEN WYVIS.

Eton, the Scots *See* SCOTS ETON, THE.

Ettrick Shepherd, the A nickname and pseudonym of the poet and author James Hogg (1770–1835), who was born the son of a peasant farmer at Ettrickhall Farm, near the village of Ettrick in Selkirkshire, and who worked for a while as a shepherd. Today his most admired creation is his innovative and psychologically perceptive novel, *The Private Memoirs and Confessions of a Justified Sinner* (1824). His friend Sir Walter Scott, with whom he collaborated on MINSTRELSY OF THE SCOTTISH BORDER, punningly described Hogg as 'the honest grunter' (*Journal*, December 1825), while Byron, in a letter to Thomas Moore, opined: 'The said Hogg is a strange being, but of great, though uncouth, powers.' The character of 'the Ettrick Shepherd', speaking in a broad dialect, figured large in the *Noctes Ambrosianae* colloquies in *Blackwood's Magazine* (*see* MAGA), mostly penned by Professor John Wilson, though Hogg had a hand in some of them, making it difficult to distinguish the man from the literary character. Wordsworth, who had visited Hogg many years previously, mourned his death in 1835 with an 'Extempore Effusion':

> When first, descending from the moorlands,
> I saw the Stream of Yarrow glide
> Along a bare and open valley,
> The Ettrick Shepherd was my guide.
>
> When last along its banks I wandered,
> Through groves that had begun to shed
> Their golden leaves upon the pathways,
> My steps the Border Minstrel led.
>
> The mighty Minstrel breathes no longer,
> Mid mouldering ruins low he lies;
> And death upon the braes of Yarrow,
> Has closed the Shepherd-poet's eyes.

Et tu quoque mi fili 'And you too, my son?' – the Latin words supposedly spoken by Julius Caesar to Brutus as the latter wielded his knife. Suetonius reports the story, giving the phrase in Greek, but says Caesar said nothing as he died; Shakespeare adapts the phrase as '*Et tu, Brute?*' In the Scottish context, the words were borrowed by Lord Belhaven during a speech in the debate on the Union in the Scottish Parliament in November 1706:

> But above all, my lord, I think I see our Ancient Mother Caledonia, like Caesar sitting in the midst of the Senate, ruefully looking around her, covering herself

with the royal garment, attending the fatal blow, and breathing out her last with *Et tu quoque mi fili*.

Evening effluvia of Edinburgh *See* GARDYLOO.

Evil eye, the *See* ILL EE.

Evil mélange of decrepit Presbyterianism and imperialist thuggery *See* LAST MINISTER STRANGLED WITH LAST COPY OF *SUNDAY POST*.

Evolution Three Scottish contributions to the theory of evolution may be mentioned. The first was that made by the philosopher and judge James Burnett, Lord Monboddo (1714–99), who in his six-volume *Of the Origin and Progress of Language* traced the ancestry of modern humans back to the orang-utan, and in the process asserted that the human inhabitants of the Nicobar Islands still possessed tails. His theory that the ape is the 'brother of man' anticipated Darwin, but on this point he was opposed by the great French naturalist, the Comte de Buffon, who also had evolutionary ideas but who rejected a human–ape link. Monboddo's contemporaries thought him eccentric at the least, if not outright mad. Posterity took a different view, and in 1875 Lord Neaves, a successor of Monboddo on the bench of the High Court, penned the following:

> Though Darwin now proclaims the law
> And spreads it far abroad, O!
> The man that first the secret saw
> Was honest old Monboddo.
> The architect precedence takes
> Of him that bears the hod, O!
> So up and at them, Land of Cakes,
> We'll vindicate Monboddo.

There is no evidence that Darwin ever read Monboddo, and scholars are divided as to the extent to which he should be credited. Monboddo certainly never came up with natural selection, the key that cracked the puzzle of evolution, but he was aware of the power of selective breeding – artificial selection. He also believed that humans and apes, although related, were distinct from the rest of the animals; he posited no ancestor common to all creatures.

The second contribution to evolutionary thought was that made by Patrick Matthew (1790–1874), the self-styled DISCOVERER OF THE PRINCIPLE OF NATURAL SELECTION, who, in *On Naval Timber and Arboriculture* (1831), anticipated Darwin's theory, but provided little evidence.

The third contribution was *Vestiges of the Natural History of Creation* (1844), written by Robert Chambers, but published anonymously. In this, Chambers outlined a form of evolutionary theory, while dismissing Lamarck's theory of evolution by the inheritance of acquired characteristics, stating that 'we only can place it with pity among the follies of the wise'. Darwin, in his introduction to the first edition (1859) of *On the Origin of Species*, gently criticized Chambers's woolly science. Being the astute publisher and journalist that he was, Chambers took the opportunity to issue a new edition of his own work, stating that Darwin's book 'in no essential respect, contradicts the present: on the contrary … it expresses substantially the same general ideas'. Never one to willingly cause offence, in the third edition (1861) of *Origin*, Darwin credited *Vestiges* with preparing the mind of the public for his own theory.

Export *See* BEER.

Extreme case of necrophilia, an The Scottish Tories, according the historian and Scottish Nationalist politician Professor Christopher Harvie in his *Cultural Weapons: Scotland in a New Europe* (1992). The decline of the Scottish Conservatives through the Thatcher and Major years culminated in a complete wipe-out in the 1997 general election, after which they held no seats at all in the Westminster Parliament. Ironically, they subsequently achieved some representation in the new Scottish Parliament, whose creation they had opposed. In the general elections of 2001, 2005 and 2010, the Conservatives have only won a single Scottish seat in Westminster.

Eyemouth disaster of 1881 *See* BLACK FRIDAY (2).

Eyemouth fish pie A fairly standard fish pie, consisting of white fish in a white sauce with hardboiled eggs and tomatoes, with a topping of mashed potatoes and cheese. It is named after the Berwickshire fishing village

Eyes like dug's baws Bloodshot eyes (supposedly resembling the testicles of a dog).

Eynhallow A tiny islet between Orkney Mainland and the island of Rousay; the name is from the Old Norse for 'holy island', referring to the cells of early Irish monks found here. According to local legend it was the summer home of the Fin Folk, an undersea people whose offspring were mermaids. It was said the island itself disappeared from time to time, until the Fin Folk were expelled after stealing the wife of a local farmer.

That might not be the end of the story, however.

In 1990 a cruise organized by the RSPB and the Orkney Heritage Society visited the island. As was the normal practice, the passengers were counted off the boat, and counted again as they boarded for the return trip to the Mainland. After the second count, two passengers were found to be missing, and an extensive search involving police and coastguards failed to find them. Those of a whimsical disposition suggested that the two were the Fin Folk come to reclaim their ancient summer home, while others wondered if the missing pair, like others before them, had been taken as mortal lovers by the people who live under the sea. *See also* SILKIE FOLK.

F

Faa clan See KING OF THE GYPSIES.

Face like a skelpit erse, a A face like a smacked bottom, presumably suggesting a ruddy complexion, or a blush, or an outburst of anger. In *The Complete Patter* (1996), lexicographer Michael Munro lists a whole range of things to which unattractive faces are compared in Glasgow, including *a bulldog chewing a wasp*, *a burst couch* or *a burst tomato*, *a camel eating sherbet*, *a half-chewed caramel*, and, most unpleasantly of all, *a wee hard disease*.

Face like a wet nicht lookin fer a dry mornin, a Said of one bearing a doleful expression.

Faculty of Advocates An independent body comprising those lawyers who have been admitted to practise as advocates (the Scottish equivalent of English barristers) in Scotland's higher courts. Founded in 1532 as part of the College of Justice, the Faculty is based in Edinburgh, where the famous Advocates' Library is situated in Parliament Square. It was originally a general library, and in 1709 was granted the right to a copy of every book published in the British Isles. In 1925 the Advocates' Library donated all its non-legal collection to the newly founded National Library of Scotland (Scotland's present copyright library).

Fag-ma-fuff A gossipy old woman; perhaps from *fag*, 'to exhaust' and *fuff*, 'puff of wind'.

Fair, the See FAIR FORTNIGHT.

Fair City, the Perth. As it happens, one of the earliest references to Perth as the 'Fair City' is in Scott's *FAIR MAID OF PERTH* (1827). Later in the century the city was praised in the following terms:

Beautiful Ancient City of Perth,
One of the fairest on the earth,
With your stately mansions and scenery most
    fine,
Which seems very beautiful in the summer time.
   – William McGonagall, 'The City of Perth'

Fair Duncan of the Songs The Gaelic poet Duncan ban Macintyre; *see* PRAISE OF BEN DORAIN.

Faire chlaidh See GRAVEYARD WATCH.

Fair forfochen See SAIR OR FAIR FORFOCHEN.

Fair Fortnight The two weeks of the annual summer holiday. In Glasgow, where it is often referred to simply as *ra Ferr*, it starts on the second Monday in July; in Edinburgh (where, as elsewhere, it is often referred to as *the Trades*, i.e. the trades holiday) it takes place earlier in the month. During the fair, factories close down and the workers take their annual holiday; popular destinations include Blackpool and various resorts DOON THE WATTER, although these days many are lured by the Spanish Costas and similar drier, hotter localities – for, as Stanley Baxter points out in *Parliamo Glasgow*, the beginning of the Fair is traditionally greeted with the following doleful chant: 'Errarainoanu. Scummindooninbuckits.' Offices and other places of work close down for Fair Holiday Monday. Until after the First World War, the holiday was generally restricted to one week, and the Glasgow Fair was originally just that: a fair held on Glasgow Green where livestock and other goods were offered for sale; later, circuses and other fairground attractions and travelling shows (known as 'the geggies', from the theatrical term *gag*) provided entertainment for the punters.

We stood by Clyde at the Broomielaw
and I spoke o' steamers for Doun the Watter
and happy holidays at the Fair.
– Duncan Glen, 'Stranger in Toun', from *Realities* (1980)

Fairies For detailed descriptions, *see under* SECRET COMMONWEALTH, THE.

Fairies o' Carlops The supernatural agencies who were blamed in 1997 when a mobile telephone mast at the village of Carlops, south of the Pentland Hills, was mysteriously dismantled during the night. The locals had apparently objected to its presence. For the witches of Carlops, *see under* CARLIN.

Fair Isle pattern A traditional style of knitting, especially popular for jumpers, involving complex patterns and bright colours, and using Shetland wool. The style gained a wider popularity in the 1920s after the Prince of Wales (later Edward VIII) began to sport Fair Isle tank-tops. Legend has it that the style was introduced by Spanish sailors after their ship, *El Gran Grifon*, part of the storm-tossed Spanish Armada, was wrecked on Fair Isle in 1588. However, it is more likely the style derives from traditional Nordic designs.

Fair Maiden Lilliard The supposed heroine of the Battle of Ancrum Moor (27 February 1545), where the Scots temporarily held up the progress of Henry VIII's ROUGH WOOING. According to the story, Lilliard, maddened by the death of her lover in the fighting, took up his sword and entered the fray. Her 'grave' on the moor carries the following inscription:

Fair Maiden Lilliard
Lies under this stane:
Little was her stature,
But muckle was her fame.

Upon the English loons
She laid monie thumps,
An' when her legs were cuttit off
She fought upon her stumps.

In 1743 the Revd Adam Milne, minister of Melrose from 1711 to 1747, noted that the memorial was broken, and its inscription illegible. He proceeded

to collect the above wording from various aged inhabitants of the locality, who claimed they had heard the story in their youth. However, it seems that the name of the actual location of the battle, Lilliard's Edge, predates 1545, and thus it is likely that the heroic Maid Lilliard is a back-formation from the place-name. Similar stories of legless fighting furies occur elsewhere in northwestern Europe, and even in the 19th century there were sceptics:

I need hardly point out that it [the inscription] bears a wonderful likeness to the famous deed of one of the heroes of 'Chevy Chase':–

For Witherington I needs must wail
As one in doleful dumps;
For, when his legs were smitten off,
He fought upon his stumps.

And, unless we concede that such an abbreviated method of fighting was not unusual in Border conflicts, we must set down the fair maiden, Lilliard, as being a vile plagiarist.
– Cuthbert Bede, *A Tour in Tartan-land* (1863)

Fair Maid of Galloway, the Margaret Douglas, the sister of William Douglas, 6th Earl of Douglas, who was murdered with his younger brother at the notorious BLACK DINNER of 1440. In 1449 or 1450 she married William Douglas, 8th Earl of Douglas, son of the 7th Earl who was probably involved in the murder of her brothers. After her husband William's death in 1452 or 1453 Margaret married William's brother James, 9th Earl of Douglas. She divorced him after his attainment in 1455, and in 1459 or 1460 married John Stewart, 1st Earl of Atholl.

Fair Maid of Norway, the *See* MAID OF NORWAY, THE.

Fair Maid of Perth, The A novel by Sir Walter Scott, published in 1828, and largely inspired by the BATTLE OF THE CLANS, which took place on the North Inch of Perth in 1396. The 'Fair Maid' is Catherine or Kate Glover, and although there is a 'Fair Maid's House' (rebuilt in the late 19th century) in Blackfriars Wynd in Perth, there is no evidence that such a person ever existed. Scott's novel inspired Bizet's opera, *La jolie fille de Perth* (1867). The passenger train service between Perth and London via Edinburgh was formerly called the Fair Maid.

Fairs and festivals *See* CEREMONIES, ETC.

Fairy Boy of Leith, the The story of this character, a boy of 10 or 11 in possession of 'a cunning much above his years', was related by Captain George Burton to Richard Bovet, who included it in his *Pandemonium, or the Devil's Cloister* (1684). When Burton met the boy in a certain house in Leith where he was used to take refreshment, the latter was drumming his fingers on the table, so Burton asked him whether he could beat a drum. The boy replied:

> Yes, sir, as well as any man in Scotland; for every Thursday night I beat all points to a sort of people that used to meet under yonder hill …

With this he pointed at Calton Hill, which stands between Edinburgh and Leith. Burton continues:

> How, boy? quoth I, what company have you there? There are, sir, said he, a great company both of men and women, and they are entertained with many sorts of music, besides my drum; they have, besides, plenty of variety of meats and wine, and many times we are carried into France or Holland in a night, and return again, and whilst we are there we enjoy all the pleasures the count [this character remains unexplained] doth afford. I demanded of him how they got under that hill? To which he replied that there was a great pair of gates that opened to them, though they were invisible to others; and that within there were brave large rooms, well accommodated as most in Scotland. I then asked him how I should know what he said to be true? Upon which he told me he would read my fortune, saying I should have two wives, and that he saw the forms of them sitting on my shoulders; that both would be very handsome women. As he was thus speaking, a woman of the neighbourhood, coming into the room, demanded of him what her fortune should be? He told her that she had two bastards before she was married, which put her in such a rage that she desired not to hear the rest.
>
> The woman of the house told me that all the people

in Scotland could not keep him from the rendezvous on Thursday night; upon which, by promising him some more money, I got a promise of him to meet me at the same place, in the afternoon, the Thursday following, and so dismissed him at that time. The boy came again, at the place and time appointed, and I had prevailed with some friends to continue with me, if possible, to prevent his moving that night. He was placed between us, and answered many questions, until, about eleven of the clock, he was got away unperceived by the company; but I suddenly missing him, hasted to the door, and took hold of him, and so returned him into the same room; we all watched him, and, of a sudden, he was again got out of doors; I followed him close, and he made a noise in the street, as if he had been set upon; but from that time I could never see him.

Thus concludes Burton's letter, and all we know of this mysterious lad.

Fairy Flag, the (Gaelic *An Bratach Sith*) An ancient fragment of cloth in the possession of the chiefs of Clan MacLeod, and preserved in Dunvegan Castle on Skye. There are a number of legends as to the origin of the flag, suggesting that in the Middle Ages a MacLeod chieftain took a fairy woman for a wife. In one version she is obliged to return to her own folk after a number of years, and leaves her son wrapped in the flag at the bridge linking our world to the Land of Faery (the place, near Dunvegan, is still called Fairy Bridge; grid reference NG 277 513). In another account, she briefly returns to comfort her crying child, wrapping him up in the flag and singing to him what has become known as 'The Dunvegan Lullaby'. This was overheard by the boy's nurse, and the lullaby was thereafter sung to all infant MacLeod heirs by their nurses. Perhaps more plausibly, it has been suggested that the Fairy Flag is in fact Land-Ravager, the famed flag of the traditional ancestor of the MacLeods, the Norwegian king Harald Hardrada, who met his doom at Stamford Bridge in 1066, prior to which the flag had guaranteed him certain victory. Experts say the material is silk from Syria or Rhodes, and dates from the 4th–7th centuries AD, so it may be a saintly relic. Harald Hardrada did have a connection with the Middle East, as he had served with the Varangian Guard of the Byzantine emperor in Constantinople. A further tradition associated with the flag is that if Clan MacLeod is ever faced with disaster it will be saved if the flag is waved; but this can only work three times. The records are not altogether clear how many times this has been tried – perhaps twice or thrice in the 15th and 16th centuries when the MacLeods faced annihilation at the hands of their traditional enemies, the Macdonalds (*see* MASSACRE CAVE, THE). During the Second World War MacLeod servicemen were said to carry a photograph of the flag into action to keep them from harm. For a prophecy concerning the flag, *see under* MACLEOD'S MAIDENS.

Fairy Minister, the *See* SECRET COMMONWEALTH, THE.

Faith, Hope and Charity The nickname of the three wind turbines at the southern end of the island of Gigha, which was subject to a community buyout in 2001. *Compare* EDUCATION, SALVATION AND DAMNATION; JAM, JUTE AND JOURNALISM.

Falkirk, bairns o' *See* BAIRNS O' FALKIRK.

Falkirk Triangle, the An area, extending from Stirling in the west to the outskirts of Edinburgh in the east, noted for its high incidence of UFO sightings (supposedly some 300 a year). The hottest spot is the town of Bonnybridge, where the first reported sighting was made in 1992. Some in Bonnybridge have sought to capitalize on the town's reputation for extraterrestrial activity as a means of attracting visitors, and Bonnybridge is now twinned with Roswell in New Mexico, site of the famous alleged 'flying saucer' crash of 1947.

Falkirk Tryst, the Once Scotland's biggest cattle market, held near Falkirk, probably established shortly after the 1707 Union, when demand from England increased. Initially, the Tryst was held at Reddingmuir, but in the 1770s the location moved southwest of Roughcastle. The construction of the Forth and Clyde Canal provided an obstacle to the drovers, so the Tryst moved again to Carmuirs, then shortly afterwards to Stenhousemuir. Drovers would bring cattle down from all parts of the

Highlands for sale, while many of those purchased would be driven southward over the drove roads of the Southern Uplands to the Border and beyond. The big sale days were the first Tuesday in August, September and October, and as many as 150,000 animals could be traded in a single day. The Tryst declined with the advent of the railways, which could take fattened animals (unfit for long walks) straight from the farmer who bred them to the final purchaser. The Tryst had all but disappeared by the end of the 19th century.

False Men *See* FIR CHREIG.

Famine of the farm An old superstition, described by the Revd J.G. Campbell, minister of Tiree, whose account is quoted in Sir James Frazer's *The Golden Bough* (1890):

> In harvest, there was a struggle to escape being the last done with the shearing, and when tillage in common existed, instances were known of a ridge being left unshorn (no person would claim it) because of it being behind the rest. The fear entertained was that of having the 'famine of the farm' (*gort a bhaile*), in the shape of an imaginary old woman (*cailleach*), to feed till next harvest. Much emulation and amusement arose from the fear of this old woman … The first done made a doll of some blades of corn, which was called the 'old wife,' and sent it to his nearest neighbour. He in turn, when ready, passed it to another still less expeditious, and the person it last remained with had 'the old woman' to keep for that year.

'Famine Song, The' A song sung by supporters of Glasgow Rangers FC, to the tune of the Beach Boys' 'Sloop John B'. The title refers to the Great Famine that devastated Ireland (and also parts of the Highlands and Islands) in 1845–52, which led to a million deaths in Ireland and mass emigration to the colonies and the West of Scotland. The deeply offensive, anti-Irish, anti-Catholic lyrics include the chorus:

> Well the famine is over
> Why don't they go home?

Singing the song has been widely condemned – by Celtic supporters, by the Scottish Premier League, by the Scottish and Irish governments and by Rangers FC itself – and is likely to lead to charges of breaching the peace, aggravated by religious and racial prejudice.

> ... this is a pretty vile song and I don't think that any reasonable person who has read the words of this song can see it as anything other than a pretty vicious, racist song. It combines racism and sectarianism and goes beyond a lot of other things that we have seen in the past.
> – Dr John Reid, chairman of Celtic FC, addressing the club's AGM, November 2008

See also BILLY BOYS; NINETY-MINUTE BIGOTS.

Famous Five, the The celebrated Hibernian FC forward line of the late 1940s and early 1950s, comprising Eddie Turnbull (*see* TURNBULL'S TORNADOES), Gordon Smith, Bobby Johnstone, Lawrie Reilly and Willie Ormond. They helped the club to win the Scottish Football League three times. In 1995 the new north stand at Easter Road was named in their honour.

Fanatics with demented enthusiastical delusions *See* SWEET SINGERS, THE.

Fancy yer barra *See* BARRA.

Fanny Toosh A woman who is regarded as getting above herself, and thus likely to be seen in the company of TEENIE FAE TROON. The expression probably derives from *fantoosh*, an adjective applied to anyone thought of as over-dressed and/or flashy, and in its turn deriving from French *fantoche*, a puppet (*cf.* Italian *fantoccino*).

Faraday in the Campsies? On 4 November 2009 the *Herald* carried the following story, in relation to a bid to make the Campsie Fells a regional park:

> It is claimed that in 1841 electric pioneer Michael Faraday spent 36 hours lost on the upper slopes of the Campsies, during which time he came up with the theory of electromagnetic induction and developed his life-long fondness for sheep.

This story appears to have derived from a letter from 'Andrew McCloy of Yougrave' to the offbeat hillwalking magazine *The Angry Corrie* 43 (October–November 1999), and you can believe it if you like:

> Dear TAC,
> The editor's revelations about Albert Einstein in TAC42 come as no surprise to me, for this is a phenomenon that I have spent some years looking into, and the sadly over-looked results of my studies ('Clever but clueless: famous people lost and found on Scottish Mountains', University of Aviemore, 1996) make for fascinating reading.
> Take the case of Michael Faraday, who in 1841 spent 36 hours lost on the upper slopes of Campsies, during which time he came up with the theory of electromagnetic induction and developed his lifelong fondness for sheep. Or composer Edward Elgar, who toured the Scottish Borders during the mid-1880s and spent a week living in a cave below Dollar Law eating grubs and lichen after he got lost during a hillwalk. He was eventually found and taken in by local shepherds, who made such an impact on the young Englishman with their whimsical tales and riddles, and their baffling south of Scotland philosophizing, that he later translated his experiences into the now famous *Enigma Variations* ...

The editor was moved to comment: 'That's just nonsense.' The clipping from the *Herald* made it on to that week's *News Quiz* on BBC Radio 4.

Far awa end o' a French fiddle What one is said to look like if one is pulling a long face (also known as a *fiddle face*), or if one looks sour and disapproving. The phrase is sometimes abbreviated to *far end o' a fiddle*. Although it may well be that it is a violin that is being referred to here, it should be born in mind that *fiddle* was formerly a euphemism for the female pudendum:

> An armfu' o' love is her bosom sae plump;
> A span o' delight is her middle sae jimp,
> A taper white leg, and a thumpin' thie,
> And a fiddle near by ye can play a wee!
> – 'Muirland Meg', from The MERRY MUSES OF CALEDONIA

Far i' the book Learned, well-educated, scholarly. The phrase may still be heard in Orkney.

Fash *See* DINNAE FASH YERSEL.

Fastern Eve or **Fastern's Een** Shrove Tuesday, the eve of Lent, the period of fasting leading up to Easter. The term is first recorded in the 14th century as *fasteryn evyn*, and other old forms include *fasternevin*, *fasterevin* and *fasterniseven*. Hence also *fasteneven hen*, i.e. a hen paid as rent on Shrove Tuesday. In the *Lay of the Last Minstrel* (1805), canto 4, Scott gives it as 'Fastern's night'. Special cakes called *carcakes*, made of eggs and oatmeal and baked on a CULROSS GIRDLE, were eaten – just as in other places pancakes were cooked to use up any eggs. In various places in the Borders, Fastern Eve was celebrated with games of football or handball, while in rural schools the schoolmaster customarily organized cockfights:

> Every minister in his boyish days had indulged in it [cock fighting], when on Fastern Eve or Shrove Tuesday he had proudly brought his own favourite cock under his arm to pit against those of his schoolmates, while the master looked on and annexed the corpses of the slaughtered fowls to replenish his own scanty table.
> – H. Grey Graham, *The Social Life of Scotland in the Eighteenth Century* (1899)

In Aberdeenshire, Shrove Tuesday was also called *Bannock Nicht* (*see under* BANNOCK).

Fastest knife in the West End, the A characterization of the Scottish surgeon Robert Liston (1794–1847) in *Great Medical Disasters* (1983) by Richard Gordon (better known for *Doctor in the House* and its sequels). The description is apt. Liston began his career as a surgeon at the Edinburgh Royal Infirmary, but managed to antagonize his colleagues to such an extent that he moved south, to London, where he became professor of surgery at University Hospital, built up a profitable practice, and attained a reputation for the speed with which he could carry out amputations – a useful skill in the days before general anaesthesia. On one occasion Liston cut off a man's leg in two and a half minutes, although unfortunately the man's testicles came off as well – as did the fingers of Liston's assistant, and both patient and assistant subsequently died of gangrene. In addition, Liston managed to slash the coat tails of a fellow surgeon who was observing the operation, and the man, believing that he had been stabbed, died of shock on the spot.

Fathers and brethren *See* GENERAL ASSEMBLY.

Fatlips A supernatural spirit that was said to dwell in a dark vault in the ruins of Dryburgh Abbey, as reported in Scott's *Minstrelsy of the Scottish Border* (1802–3), in a note to 'The Nun who never saw the day'. After the '45 Jacobite Rising this vault apparently became the lodging of an unfortunate woman who had vowed she would never look on daylight again until her lover returned from the wars. She emerged only at night time, when she would go begging at the nearby houses, and during her absence she claimed her dwelling was kept in order by a small man called Fatlips, who stamped the ground with his heavy iron shoes to dispel the damp. This latter circumstance might suggest that Fatlips was a REDCAP, although he did not appear to share the malevolence of this latter species.

There is a ruin on the south side of Tinto in Lanarkshire called Fatlips Castle, and another Fatlips Castle, now restored, on Minto Craigs near Denholm on the River Teviot.

> What the origin or meaning of the name may be, seems quite inexplicable, but some ingenious antiquary may perhaps be able to deduce it from, or connect it with, a custom which has from time immemorial obtained among parties of pleasure visiting the top of Minto – that every gentleman, by indefeasible privilege, kisses one of the ladies on entering the ruin.
> – Robert Chambers, *The Picture of Scotland* (1827)

Fattest hog in Epicurus' sty, the How William Mason (1724–97) characterized David Hume in 'An Heroic Epistle to Sir William Chambers'. Hume was a self-confessed devotee of the culinary art:

> Cookery, the Science to which I intend to addict the remaining years of my Life ... for Beef and Cabbage (a charming dish) and old Mutton, old Claret, no body excels me.
> – David Hume, letter to Sir Gilbert Elliot, October 1769

See also TURTLE-EATING ALDERMAN, A.

Fauna Caledonia There follows a selective list of Scots names for various mammals, birds, reptiles, amphibians, fish and sundry invertebrates. Fuller details of the currency and geographical spread of these names will be found in the *Dictionary of the Scottish Language. See also* BEASTS AND BEAST LORE.

AILSA COCK The puffin (once common on Ailsa Craig).

Ainster craw 'Anstruther crow', i.e. the herring gull.

Baggie (minnie) The minnow.

Barbarian haddie The common sea bream (*haddie* is haddock).

Bass cock The puffin (common on the Bass Rock).

Black chacker The ring ousel (from its colour and imitative of its call).

Black coaly hood The reed bunting.

Black jock The blackbird.

Black ox-eye The coal tit.

Blethering Tam The whitethroat. Other names include **Jenny-cut-throat, Meg-cut-throat, moosy-whitebeard, nettle-creeper, wheetie-whitebeard** (also the **willow warbler**).

Blin ee ('blind eye') The dogfish.

Bog-bleater The bittern (also **bull o' the bog**).

Bonnet fleuk The brill.

Bonxie The great skua.

BUBBLY-JOCK The turkey-cock.

Buckhaven pie The edible crab (from the Fife fishing village).

Buckie The whelk.

Caain whaal The pilot whale (in Shetland) or (in the Highlands and Islands) the porpoise, which was thought to grow from a dogfish – hence its Gaelic name *mucun bearraich* ('dogfish pigs'). The pilot whale is also known as the **pot-heid**, alluding to its rounded forehead.

Canny ca The woodworm.

Canny nanny A stingless species of bumblebee.

Cat gull The herring gull, so called by gamekeepers in Galloway because of 'their cat-like depredations amongst the newly-hatched young birds and eggs on the moors'.

Cattyface The short-eared owl (Orkney).

Chackie The stonechat (imitative of its call).

CLEG The horse fly.

Clipshears The earwig. Other names include **forkie-tail, coachbell, scodgebell** or **switchbell**.

Clock leddy The ladybird (a *clock* is a beetle).

Coal-and-candlelight or **col-candlewick** The long-tailed duck (imitative of its plaintive call).

Colonsay duck The eider duck.

Corbie The crow; the raven.

Cushie-doo The woodpigeon.

DAUGHTER OF EDWARD The adder.

Deil's bird, the The magpie; for more details, and more names for the magpie, *see* DEVIL'S BIRD, THE.

Deil's buckie The whelk.

Deil's butterfly The tortoiseshell butterfly.

Deil's darning needle The dragonfly.

Deil tak you The yellowhammer.

DEVIL'S BIRD, THE The magpie.

Dirdy-lochrag The lizard, from the Gaelic *dearc-lua-chrach*.

Dirt bee The common dung beetle.

Dirten Tammie The skua.

Dovekie The black guillemot (diminutive of 'dove').

Elders o' Cowend Cormorants (referring to the ELDERS of the Kirk in their dark clothes, and the coastal parish of Colvend in Kirkcudbrightshire). Another name is **Mochrum elder** (alluding to the parish on Luce Bay in Wigtownshire). There was an old Gaelic saying to the effect that the cormorant spent seven years as a shag, seven years as a black-throated diver and seven years as a cormorant (*Seachd bliadhna 'na sgarbh, seachd bliadhna 'na learg, 's seachd bliadhna 'na bhallaire bodhain*).

Elf-mill The death-watch beetle.

Emmerteen The ant (see under EMMERTEEN'S MEAT).

Foggie bummer or **foggie toddler** The bumblebee.

Goloch or **golach** Applied variously to ground beetles, earwigs and centipedes. The latter is denoted in the following traditional rhyme:

A goloch is an awesome beast,
Souple an' scaly,
Wi' a horny heid an' a hantle o' feet,
An' a forky tailie.

In the Northeast, an earwig is a **horny-golach**. The word derives from Gaelic *gobhlach*, applied to an earwig or anything forked.

Gowdie duck or **goldeine** The goldeneye.

Gowd spink The goldfinch.

GOWK The cuckoo.

Grey back The hooded crow.

Grey cheeper The meadow pipit.

Grey horse The head louse.

Grey willie The herring gull.

Hairy bummer The wild bee *Bombus muscorum*.

Hairy heid The red-breasted merganser.

Hairy minister or **hairy woobit** or **hairy Willie** or **hairy worm** The woolly bear caterpillar. If something *gaes roun yer hert like a hairy worm* then it thoroughly delights you.

Heather blackie The ring ouzel.

Heather bleater The common snipe.

Heather cock The grouse, whether red or black.

Heather peeper The meadow pipit or the sandpiper.

Hielan pyot The mistle thrush. The name *pyot* is applied to a number of piebald birds, e.g. the magpie, the dipper (*water pyot*) and the oystercatcher (*sea pyot*). *See also* DEVIL'S BIRD, THE

Holland hawk The great northern diver.

HORSE OF THE WOODS The capercaillie.

Hose-fish The cuttlefish.

Jennaniver The skate.

Jenny Forster The female long-tailed duck.

Jenny Gray The black guillemot, or the wren.

Jennie-hunner-feet or **Maggie wi the mony feet** The centipede; the latter name is also given to crabs and lobsters.

Jenny lang-legs or **Johnnie Piper** The cranefly, daddy longlegs.

Jerusalem haddie The opah or kingfish (*haddie*, 'haddock').

Jerusalem traveller The louse (possibly an allusion to the pilgrim's grey garb).

Johnnie Scatan The fulmar (*scattan*, 'herring').

Johnny Mainland The angler fish.

Kae The jackdaw. A person of limited intelligence is said to be *kae-witted*.

Kail jockie The hedge sparrow.

Katie-beardie The hedge sparrow; also applied to the wren and the loach.

Killie-leepie The common sandpiper (from its call).

King coll-awa The ladybird.

King fleuk The turbot (*fleuk*, 'flounder').

King of the herrings The rabbitfish (*Chimaera monstrosa*), or the allis shad (*Alosa alosa*). It was once the custom to present such a fish, if caught, to the oldest member of the crew, who would pass it round the 'skudding-pole' while the others petitioned Providence for good catches.

King's fisher The dipper.

Lady of Heaven's hen The wren. In *The Golden Bough* (1890), Sir James Frazer records the following children's rhyme:

Malisons [curses], malisons mair than ten,
That harry the Lady of Heaven's hen!

Land moose The field vole.

LANG LUGS The donkey; also the hare.

Lang neb The curlew (literally 'long nose').

Lang Sandy The heron.

Laverock The skylark.

Lintie The linnet, hence the phrase 'singin' like a lintie', i.e. singing melodiously.

Loch-liver or **loch-lubbertie** The jellyfish.

Lowper dog The porpoise; also the dolphin (literally 'leaping dog').

LOWRIE The fox.

Maggie-lickie-spinnie The spider.

Mallimoke or **mallduck** The fulmar.

Man-keeper Applied to both newts and lizards.

Man's face The sea urchin.

Mason's ghost The robin.

Mauk flee The bluebottle (*mauk*, 'maggot').

Maukin or **malkin** The hare (and formerly also the female pudendum).

Mavis The songthrush.

May-bird The whimbrel (referring to the month of the migrants' arrival).

May-skate The sharp-nosed ray.

Meer-swine The dolphin or porpoise (literally 'sea-pig').

Meg wi' the mony feet A name applied both to various beetles and the lobster.

Ye lie whar the meg-o-mony-feet crawls on green and yellow carrion.
– *Wilson's Tales of the Borders* (1836)

MESSENGER OF THE CAMPBELLS The magpie.

Mire-drum The bittern.

Mire-duck or **moss-duck** or **muir-duck** The mallard.

Moss-bleater The common snipe.

Moss-cheeper or **muir-cheeper** The meadow pipit.

Moss-trout The brown trout.

Mowdiewort The mole (and also jocularly applied to moles or warts on the skin).

Muir-fowl The red grouse.

Mup-mup The rabbit (imitative of nibbling).

Needlach A young eel (from its resemblance to a needle).

Nine-eed eel The lesser lamprey (*see* WIZARD SHACKLE).

Peewit The lapwing.

Pellock The porpoise, and possibly also the dolphin.

Peter's bird or **Petricock** The storm petrel, which flies low over the waves. The name alludes to Matthew 14:29: 'And when Peter was come down out of the ship, he walked on the water, to go to Jesus.'

Pewlie Willie The herring gull.

Pin-heids The fry of the minnow or stickleback.

Plover's page The dunlin (which often accompanies plovers in flight).

Pluffy The porpoise (from the noise emitted through its blowhole). The animal is also known in the Northeast as the **puffy dunter**.

Pollywags Tadpoles.

Poverty fish The lumpsucker – regarded by the fishermen of the Moray Firth as a poor substitute for herring.

Pricker The basking shark (alluding to its prominent dorsal fin).

Puddock The frog.

> A puddock sat by the lochan's brim,
> An' he thocht there was never a puddock like
>   him …
>   – J.M. Caie (1878–1949), 'The Puddock'

In the 17th century, tortoises (presumably then not a common sight in Scotland) were known as **shell paddocks**.

Puddock-spittle Cuckoo-spit (*puddock*, 'frog').

Puggie Any monkey. *See* FOU; GET YER PUGGIE UP.

Pyot The magpie.

Queen of Heaven's hen or **Our Lady of Heaven's hen** The skylark. The first name features in a traditional rhyme, recorded by Walter Gregor in *Folk-Lore of the North-East of Scotland* (1881):

> Mailisons, mailisons mehr nor ten
> That hairries the Queen o' Heaven's hen.
> Blissins, blissins mehr nor thoosans
> That leuks on her eggies an lats them alane.

Quink goose The brent goose or the greylag goose (imitative of the bird's call).

Red-coat The ladybird. In the Borders, children used to pick up ladybirds and throw them into the air, accompanied by the following rhyme:

> Red-coat, red-coat, flee away
> And make the morn a sunny day.

Red hawk The merlin or the kestrel.

Red-legged crow The chough.

Red-legged horseman The redshank.

Red-neb The oystercatcher (alluding to its red bill).

Red-nebbit pussy The puffin.

Red Rab The robin.

Reid-arsie A species of bee with red markings on the rear.

Reid-gibbie The stickleback (from the colour of the male's *gibbie* or belly).

Rock blackbird or **rock starling** The ring ouzel.

Rock cadie The cod.

Rock cock The wrasse.

Rock hawk The merlin.

Rock lintie The rock pipit.

Rock owl The barn owl.

Rose lintie The male linnet (from its breeding plumage).

Rushyroo The shrew.

Sandy dorbie The sandpiper (a *dorbie* is a stonemason, although the connection, if any, to the bird is unclear).

Sandy laverock or **sandy lairick** The ringed plover or the sandpiper (*laverock*, 'skylark').

Sandy swallow The sand martin.

Scotch nightingale Either the woodlark or the sedge warbler.

Sea cat The wolf fish.

Sea dog The dogfish.

Sea doo The black guillemot (*doo*, 'dove').

Sea goos Seagulls.

Sea hen The common guillemot.

Sea lark The dunlin.

Sea lintie The rock pipit.

Sea paps Sea anemones.

Sea pudding The great sea cucumber (so-called in Shetland).

Sea pyot The oystercatcher (the *pyot* is the magpie).

Sea soo or **sea swine** The small-mouthed wrasse.

Seed bird or **seed lady** The pied wagtail.

Shear mouse The shrew.

Sheer dog The tope shark (possibly a corruption of *sea dog*, influenced by *sheer dog*, 'a wag').

Siller willie The pyramid shell.

Skaitbird The Arctic skua, so called because formerly thought to feed on the *scat* (excreta) of other birds, hence also known as **skatie-goo, scoutiallan** or

Dirty Allan. In his *Description of Orkney, Zetland, Pightland-Firth and Caithness* (1701), the Revd John Brand describes:

> … a Fowl there called Scutiallan, of a black colour, and as big as a Wild Duck, which doth live upon the Vomit and Excrements of other Fowls.

The inhabitants of the parish of Hope on South Ronaldsay are referred to disparagingly as *Scooties* (*see* TEU-NEEMS).

Skate bubbles Jellyfish.

Skeppie or **skep bee** The honeybee (*skep*, 'straw basket, beehive').

Skirly wheeter The oystercatcher (from its call, a *skirl* being a high-pitched cry).

Skittery feltie The fieldfare. *Skittery* here appears to mean 'footering about' or possibly 'producing diarrhoea', while *feltie* is an abbreviation of *feltifare* or *feltiflier*, alternative names for the bird.

Snawflake The snow bunting.

Sodger, soldier The ladybird; the red-breasted minnow.

Sookie bleedie The red sea-anemone (*sook*, 'suck'). More generally, sea anemones are known as **souk paps**.

Speeder jenny or **speederlegs** The cranefly or daddy-long-legs.

Speug or **spug(gie)** The sparrow.

Spricklybag The stickleback.

Stane chacker or **chackart** The stonechat.

Stane chipper The wheatear.

Stankie hen The moorhen (*stank*, 'pool, ditch').

Stinker The white-backed dolphin.

Swankie's doo A jocular name for a seagull in Arbroath, where Swankie is a common surname (*doo*, 'dove').

Tammie-cheekie or **Tammie-noddie** or **Tammie-(o'-) Norrie** The puffin. The last name (perhaps alluding to Norrie Law in Fife) gave rise to a saying, 'Tammie Norie o' the Bass 'Canna kiss a bonny lass.' Robert Chambers, in his *Popular Rhymes of Scotland* (1826), explains it thus:

> This is said jocularly, when a young man refuses to salute a rustic coquette. The puffin, which builds in great numbers on the Bass Rock, is a very shy bird, with a long deep bill, giving him an air of stupidity, and from these two things to-

gether the saying probably has arisen. It is also customary to call a stupid-looking man a *Tammie Norie*.

Tammie Herle The heron.

Tammie-nid-nod or **Tammie-noddie-heid** A tadpole, or the chrysalis of a butterfly (alluding to its movements prior to metamorphosing), or the cranefly.

Tee-oo The lapwing (Orkney).

Teuchit The lapwing (Aberdeenshire).

Tibbie Thiefie The sandpiper (imitative of its call, elided with the personal name Tibbie).

Titlin The meadow pipit, as in the expression GOWK AND TITLIN.

Tobacco fleuk The lemon sole (*fleuk*, 'flounder').

Tod The fox; *see* LOWRIE.

Tree-speeler The tree creeper (*speel*, 'climb').

Virgin Mary Applied to the ladybird in northeast Scotland, where it is also the **golden calfie**; in Angus, it is the **doctor**, as it is supposed to cure cuts if placed on them; in southwest Scotland the insect is **Queen Chronicle**. The ladybird traditionally brings good luck, as in this rhyme:

> Reid-spottit jeckit
> An' polished black e'e;
> Land on my luif, an' bring
> Siller tae me.

Waggie or **waggitie** The pied wagtail.

Wallopie or **wallopiewheet** The lapwing (imitative of its call).

Ware goose The brent goose (*ware* is a kind of seaweed used to fertilize the fields).

Water blackbird/bobbie/cockie/craw/meggie/pyot The dipper.

Water clearer The pondskater.

Water dog or **mouse** The water vole.

Watery wagtail The yellow wagtail.

Weet-my-fit The corncrake (literally, 'wet my feet', imitative of the bird's cry).

Whaal-bubble The jellyfish (*whaal*, 'whale')

Whaup The curlew. The name may relate to English 'whelp', suggesting the bird whines like a puppy.

Wheelie-o The willow warbler (imitative of the last notes of the bird's song).

Whin sparrow The hedge sparrow.

White houlet The barn owl.

Whitrat or **whitrick** Literally 'white rat', i.e. the weasel, and also applied to the stoat, ferret and polecat.

> Said the whitrick to the stoat,
> 'I see ye've on your winter coat;
> I dinna see the sense ava!
> Ye're shairly no expectin' snaw?'
>   – J.K. Annand (1908–93), 'Fur Coats'

Whitterick The curlew (imitative of its cry, and perhaps influenced by the preceding).

Willie goo The herring gull.

Willie wagtail The pied wagtail.

Willie-whip-the-wind The kestrel.

Wuid-lark The tree pipit.

Wunda-swalla 'Window swallow', i.e. the house martin.

Yella-neb lintie The twite.

Yella plover The golden plover.

Yella wagtail The grey wagtail (which is indeed almost as yellow as the yellow wagtail).

Yella taid A frog.

Yella yite The yellowhammer.

Fause Menteith See LAKE OF MENTEITH.

Faux Jockery The Scots equivalent of Stage Oirish, as practised by entertainers long before Harry Lauder trod the boards, and still encountered on stage and screen. Two centuries ago, Henry Mackenzie (1745–1831), author of *The Man of Feeling*, was bemoaning the fact that 'The imitated Scots of the stage is seldom a happy imitation', while as recently as 1989, James Campbell, in *Invisible Country*, observed that: 'It's a strange state of affairs when even in Scotland the use of Scots is taken by audiences as a signal to laugh.' Such expressions are also encountered in the sentimentalizing works of the KAILYARD SCHOOL and their successors. There is inevitably an overlap with genuine Scots expressions, some of which have been hijacked by the pedlars of quaintness. Notable examples of the genre include:

- DONALD, WHERE'S YER TROOSERS?
- HASTE YE BACK
- HOOTS MON!
- IT'S A BRAW BRICHT MUNELICHT NICHT
- JINGS, CRIVENS, HELP MA BOAB

- LANG MAY YER LUM REEK
- MICHTY ME!
- THE NIGHTS ARE FAIR DRAWIN IN
- OCH AYE THE NOO
- ROAMIN' IN THE GLOAMIN'
- A WEE BUT AND BEN
- A WEE DEOCH AN DORUS

See also BALMORALITY; *BROONS, THE*; OOR WULLIE; PLASTIC SCOTS; RHYMING SLANG (for 'Jockney'); WALLACETHEBRUCEISM; *WHITE HEATHER CLUB, THE*.

Feathers in Gentle Annie's hat, the See GENTLE ANNIE.

Fecht wi' his ain taes, he'd Literally, 'He'd fight with his own toes,' i.e. he's extremely touchy and quarrelsome. A variant is *He'd fecht wi' the wind*.

Féilead-beg See PHILABEG.

Fell twa dugs wi' ae bane Literally, 'fell two dogs with one bone', i.e. kill two birds with one stone (indeed, in some variants, *stane* and/or *burds* are substituted).

> He can fell twa dogs wi' ae bane,
> While ither fock
> Maun rest themselves content wi' ane.
>   – Robert Fergusson, 'The Rising of the Session' (1773)

Ferntickle or **fernietickle** A freckle, thought to resemble the spore of a fern. It was formerly believed that freckles resulted from being touched or tickled by a fern. The world is found as *farntikylle* in Middle English.

Ferry-looper A term applied to an incomer in Orkney – one who has 'looped' (walked) off the ferry. The Shetland equivalent is SOOTH-MOOTHER.

Fiddle face See FAR AWA END O' A FRENCH FIDDLE.

Fiddler-fou See FOU.

Fiddler's biddin' or **fiddler's invite** A last-minute invitation to a social event. The origin of the expression is obscure; perhaps in the past a wandering fiddler might turn up at one's house unannounced and be invited to join the company at table in return for a tune.

> Then, when it comes tae the bit, the weddin'
> Can aye be pit aff at a fiddler's biddin'.
> – Liz Lochhead, *Tartuffe* (1985)

A *piper's bidding* is the same thing.

Fiddler's or **piper's news** The same as CADGER'S NEWS.

Fiddlers' rally A satirical label for a meeting of a local council, with the imputation that those foregathered are not entirely incorruptible. The phrase is a waggish application of a perfectly respectable term for a number of violin players gathered together to make music.

Fierce, stubborn and warlike nation, a The description of the Scots by the French diplomat Michel de Castelnau, Seigneur de Mauvissière et de Concressault, who in 1560 accompanied Mary Queen of Scots when she returned from France to Scotland after the death of her first husband, Francis II. Castelnau recorded his view in his *Mémoires*:

> The Scots are a fierce, stubborn and warlike nation, who cannot be dominated by force, unless one should completely wipe them out, which would be too difficult, considering the nature of the country: and one cannot tame their wild spirit with the rod, but by treating them gently and with courtesy.

Fier comme un Écossais An old French saying meaning 'proud as a Scotsman', dating back to the Middle Ages, the time of the AULD ALLIANCE. It occurs in Rabelais' *Gargantua and Pantagruel* (1532–52), and Hugh MacDiarmid uses the phrase as a refrain in a section of *A Drunk Man Looks at the Thistle* (1926). The GARDE ÉCOSSAISE, the royal bodyguard in France, were known as *les fiers Écossais*.

Fiery cross (Gaelic *crann tàra, croishtarich, crosstarrie*, etc.) A signal formerly carried from place to

place to summon the warriors of a clan to rally round their chief and go to war. It was passed from one runner to the next, so that great distances could be traversed in a relatively short time.

> A person is sent out full speed with a pole burnt at one end and bloody at the other, and with a cross at the top, which is called Crosh-tairie, the cross of shame, or the fiery cross; the first from the disgrace they would undergo if they declined appearing; the second from the penalty of having fire and sword carried thro' their country, in case of refusal.
> – Thomas Pennant, *A Tour in Scotland in MDCCLXIX* (1771)

There is a dramatic description in Canto III of Sir Walter Scott's *The Lady of the Lake* (1810), including the following passage:

> Angus, the heir of Duncan's line,
> Sprung forth and seized the fatal sign.
> In haste the stripling to his side
> His father's dirk and broadsword tied;
> But when he saw his mother's eye
> Watch him in speechless agony,
> Back to her opened arms he flew
> Pressed on her lips a fond adieu, –
> 'Alas' she sobbed, – 'and yet be gone,
> And speed thee forth, like Duncan's son!'
> One look he cast upon the bier,
> Dashed from his eye the gathering tear,
> Breathed deep to clear his labouring breast,
> And tossed aloft his bonnet crest,
> Then, like the high-bred colt when, freed,
> First he essays his fire and speed,
> He vanished, and o'er moor and moss
> Sped forward with the Fiery Cross.

In a note, Scott gives some explanation of the custom:

> When a chieftain designed to summon his clan, upon any sudden or important emergency, he slew a goat, and making a cross of any light wood, seared its extremities in the fire, and extinguished them in the blood of the animal. This was called the Fiery Cross, also Crean Tarigh, or the Cross of Shame, because disobedience to what the symbol implied, inferred infamy. It was delivered to a swift and trusty messenger, who ran full speed with it to the next hamlet,

where he presented it to the principal person, with a single word, implying the place of rendezvous. He who received the symbol was bound to send it forward, with equal despatch, to the next village; and thus it passed with incredible celerity through all the district which owed allegiance to the chief, and also among his allies and neighbours, if the danger was common to them. At sight of the Fiery Cross, every man, from sixteen years old to sixty, capable of bearing arms, was obliged instantly to repair, in his best arms and accoutrements, to the place of rendezvous. He who failed to appear suffered the extremities of fire and sword, which were emblematically denounced to the disobedient by the bloody and burnt marks upon this warlike signal.

Scott goes on to describe how, during the 1745 Jacobite Rebellion, a fiery cross 'passed through the whole district of Breadalbane, a tract of thirty-two miles, in three hours'. The symbol was later, regrettably, adopted by the Ku Klux Klan.

Fiery Face The nickname of James II (reigned 1437–60), whose face bore a livid crimson birthmark – 'an ominous forecast of what was to happen to the uneasy kingdom he inherited', according to John Prebble (*The Lion in the North*, 1971).

Fiery Mine, the A nickname for the Blantyre Colliery, alluding to two major explosions that took place there; *see* BLANTYRE PIT DISASTER.

Fife, Gentlemen Adventurers of *See* GENTLEMEN ADVENTURERS OF FIFE, THE.

Fifer A person from the KINGDOM OF FIFE. Fifers have somehow acquired a reputation as a bunch of chancers: the *DSL* states that the word Fifer is 'sometimes used opprobriously to denote a greedy, rather unscrupulous person', and cites the following:

> The Fifer is quite aware that unfortunate folk who do not happen to have been born in the ancient kingdom, relieve their feelings by tacking on a long string of opprobrious epithets to his name; they call him 'canny Fifer,' 'pawky Fifer,' 'Fifer with an eye to the main chance.'
> – Jessie Patrick Finlay, in the *Edinburgh Evening Dispatch*, 18 September 1897

To heap insult onto injury, the Edinburgh-born journalist Euan Ferguson has this to say:

> Fifers make the rest of Scotland look like a living sculpture designed to carry across the concepts of optimism, balance, health and good humour. Cold scabby bars, cold sea, cold grey hearts, rampant unemployment, cold grey knife-scars, and that's just from the tourist brochure ...
> – The *Observer*, 13 January 2002

As if this wasn't bad enough, the term *Fifish* is used to mean 'eccentric, daft, slightly deranged':

> Ye shouldna ca' the Laird daft, his bannet has a bee,
> He's just a wee bit Fifish, like some Fife lairds that be.
> – Lady Nairne, 'The Fife Laird' (*c*.1800)

Scott, in *The Pirate* (1822), attributes the expression to 'east-country fisher-folk'.

Why Fifers should be regarded in this way is unclear – for, according to the following nursery rhyme, they appear to be entirely normal:

> In a cottage in Fife
> Lived a man and his wife,
> Who, believe me, were comical folk;
> For, to people's surprise,
> They both saw with their eyes,
> And their tongues moved whenever they spoke!
> [&c.]

See also BEGGAR'S MANTLE FRINGED WI' GOWD, A; KAIL-SUPPER.

Fifers, the *See* FOOTBALL CLUB NICKNAMES.

Fifish *See* FIFERS.

Fifteen, the The failed Jacobite Rebellion of 1715, led by the Earl of Mar (aka BOBBING JOHN) on behalf of the OLD PRETENDER. In the past, it was also known as the SHERRAMOOR.

Fighting Carpenter, the The nickname of the Edinburgh-born boxer Ken Buchanan (b. 1945), formerly world lightweight champion, who was a carpenter before turning professional. During his boxing career, which extended from the later 1960s into the early 1980s, he won 61 out of 69 fights.

Fighting Dominie, the A sobriquet of the school-teacher (Scots *dominie*) and revolutionary socialist John Maclean (1879–1923), one of the leading figures of RED CLYDESIDE. In the early years of the 20th century he drew unsurpassed numbers of workers and socialist activists to his Marxist educa-tion classes. An ardent internationalist, he was imprisoned a number of times for his opposition to the First World War, leading to his dismissal from his school teaching post. After the 1917 October Revolution in Russia, he was appointed an honorary president of the Petrograd Soviet, and also the Bolsheviks' consul in Glasgow. He was arrested again in April 1918, and at his trial for sedition in May he declared: 'I come here not as the accused but as the accuser of capitalism dripping with blood from head to foot.' He was sentenced to five years' penal servitude, but the authorities failed in their intent to have him declared insane, and he was released at the end of the war. He was suspicious of the integrity of those who formed the new Com-munist Party of Great Britain, dismissing them as 'poets, sentimentalists, syndicalists with a sprinkling of Marxists'. His vehement critiques led his enemies on the left to accuse him of mental instability, and he lost the support of Moscow. His political activ-ities led to two more spells in prison, and his last years were marked by failing health and poverty. After his death, however, he was adopted as a hero by British communists and by other revolutionary socialists, and the Soviets named a street in Lenin-grad in his honour: Maklin Prospekt.

As Pilate and the Roman soldiers to Christ
Were Law and Order to the finest Scot of his day,
One of the few true men in our sordid breed,
A flash of sun in a country all prison-grey.
– Hugh MacDiarmid, 'John Maclean (1879–1923)'
(1934), published in the 1956 edition of *Stony Limits and Other Poems*

Hey, mac, did ye see him as he cam doun by Gorgie,
Awa owre the Lammerlaw an north o the Tay?
Yon man is comin an the hail toun is turnin out,
We're aa shair he'll win back tae Glesca the day.
The jiners an hauders-on are merchin fae
    Clydebank,
Come on nou an hear him, he'll be owre thrang tae
    bide.

Turn out Jock an Jimmie, leave yer cranes an yer
    muckle gantries,
Great John Maclean's comin hame tae the Clyde.
– Hamish Henderson, 'The John Maclean March'

Tell me whaur he's been, lad,
An why has he been there?
They've had him in the prison
For preachin in the Square.
For Johnny held a finger up
Tae aa the ills he saw,
He was right side o the people,
But the wrang side o the law.
    Dominie,
    Dominie
    There was nane like John MacLean,
    The fightin' Dominie.
    – Matt McGinn, 'The Ballad of John Maclean'

Fighting Mac The nickname of the soldier and popular hero Sir Hector Archibald MacDonald (1853–1903), on account of his bravado and flair in battle. The son of a crofter from Easter Ross, as a youth MacDonald became a COONTER-LOWPER in a Dingwall draper's shop. Lying about his age, in 1870 he joined the 92nd Gordon Highlanders as a private and went on to achieve the rare distinction of being commissioned from the ranks as a second lieutenant. He won considerable military glory in a number of actions in the Second Afghan War, the First Boer War, and in the campaigns against the Mahdists in Egypt and the Sudan. In 1900 he was put in command of the Highland Brigade in the Second Boer War with the rank of major-general. The war correspondent G.W. Steevens described him as 'one of the soundest soldiers in the Egyptian or British armies' with 'a rare gift for the handling of troops', and 'so sturdily built that you might imagine him to be armour-plated under his clothes'. Sir Arthur Conan Doyle described him as 'a bony, craggy Scotsman, with a square fighting head and a bulldog jaw'. His career came crashing down in 1903 amidst rumours of homosexual affairs, and MacDonald shot himself in a Paris hotel. Some 30,000 people visited his grave in Edinburgh in the first week, while a massive sum was raised by subscription to erect a great tower in Dingwall in his memory. That same year, James Scott Skinner wrote a fiddle tune entitled 'Hector the Hero', which has since gained considerable popularity. Many blamed English snobbery for MacDonald's disgrace and demise, some even insisting he was not dead at all – there were even suggestions during the First World War that the German general August von Mackensen was, in fact, Fighting Mac in disguise.

Fighting upon one's stumps *See* FAIR MAIDEN LILLIARD.

Filibeg *See* PHILABEG.

Fine-gabbit or **nice-gabbit** Fussy or pernickety, particularly about food (*gabbit*, 'mouthed').

Fin Folk *See* EYNHALLOW.

Fingal The name by which the hero of ancient Irish legend Finn McCool (or Finn Mac Cumhal, etc.) was normally known in Scotland. Various topographical features in Scotland, such as the DOG'S PILLAR, KING'S CAVE and (more doubtfully) FINGAL'S CAVE, are associated with him. One of James Macpherson's OSSIANIC FORGERIES was entitled *Fingal, An Ancient Epic Poem in Six Books* (1762). *See also* DEIRDRE OF THE SORROWS.

Fingal's Cave The celebrated cave on the island of Staffa, surrounded by hexagonal and pentagonal basalt pillars and topped with amorphous lava – 'a soufflé stiffening in a crystal dish', according to the contemporary Shetland poet Christine de Luca. The place was unknown to the English-speaking world until Sir Joseph Banks visited in 1772, and it was he who reported that the locals called it 'the Cave of Fingal' (after the hero of ancient Irish legend) – although the only Gaelic name otherwise recorded is An Uamh Binn ('the melodious cave'). It is likely that Banks was swept along by the tide of Ossianic fervour then sweeping Europe (*see* OSSIANIC FORGERIES, THE); he was certainly ravished by this geological masterwork of Nature:

> Compared to this what are the cathedrals or the palaces built by men! Mere models or playthings, imitations as diminutive as his works will always be

when compared with those of nature. Where now is the boast of the architect! Regularity, the only part in which he fancied himself to exceed his mistress, Nature, is here found in her possession, and here it has been for ages undescribed.

> – Joseph Banks, quoted in Thomas Pennant's *A Tour of Scotland and a Voyage to the Hebrides; MDCCLXXII* (1773)

Fingal's Cave became a must-see for the more adventurous tourist, and among those who visited was the poet John Keats, who dubbed it 'the Cathedral of the Seas', and replaced Fingalian with Olympian imagery in his description:

> Suppose now the Giants who rebelled against Jove had taken a whole Mass of black Columns and bound them together like bunches of matches – and then with immense Axes had made a cavern in the body of these columns … For solemnity and grandeur it far surpasses the finest Cathedral.
> – Letter to Tom Keats, 23/26 July 1818

In 1831 J.M.W. Turner painted the island and its cave in stormy weather from the unsteady deck of a steamship; when the man who purchased the painting complained that it was 'indistinct', Turner replied, 'Indistinctness is my forte.' Two years later Wordsworth visited, resulting in an unmemorable effusion. The most celebrated artistic work to be inspired by the place is, of course, Mendelssohn's 1832 concert overture *The Hebrides*, subtitled *Fingal's Cave*, which followed his visit in 1829, when the composer was violently seasick. On that occasion Mendelssohn was accompanied by a Herr Klingemann, a Hanoverian diplomat in London, who felt that the pillars made the cave 'look like the inside of an immense organ, black and resounding, and absolutely without purpose, and quite alone, the wide grey sea within and without'.

Finger, to cock one's wee *See* COCK ONE'S WEE FINGER, TO.

Finnan haddie Split haddock lightly smoked over peat or green wood, giving it a delicate flavour. It is often poached in milk and served with a poached egg. There seems to be a consensus that Finnan haddie comes from the little Aberdeenshire coastal village of Findon, on the coast south of Aberdeen, and not Findhorn on the Moray Firth (which the *Oxford English Dictionary* favours, albeit cautiously).

> *Customer:* Piece of smoked haddock, please.
> *Fishmonger:* Finnan?
> *Customer:* No, a nice thick 'un, please.
> – Old Tommy Trinder joke

Compare ARBROATH SMOKIE.

Fir Chreig Gaelic for 'false men', the local name for the stone circle at Callanish, Lewis. The story is that the stones are the petrified forms of the giants who inhabited the place in ancient times. When St Ciaran came to evangelize them, they would neither build a church nor let themselves be baptized, so the holy man turned them to stone. It was formerly believed that at midsummer the chief stone, known as the 'Shining One', came back to life, and paraded along the main avenue of stones.

Fireballs, the An annual ceremony held in Stonehaven to welcome in the New Year. Watched by thousands of spectators, some 50 or 60 participants parade along the High Street of the Old Town, swinging balls of fire around their heads. The balls, which are finally thrown into the harbour, comprise all sorts of combustible and oily waste, held together in a spherical wire mesh. The participants were originally all local fishermen, but now the only qualification is that they must reside in the burgh. The origins of the Fireballs (like UP-HELLY-AA in Shetland and BURNING THE CLAVIE in Burghead) lie in pagan midwinter fire festivals

Fire burn or **water burn** Phosphorescence seen on the surface of the sea at night.

Fireside tartan *See* TINKER'S TARTAN.

Fir Ghorm, Na *See* BLUE MEN OF THE MINCH.

First and Worst, the A nickname for the Royal Scots; *see* REGIMENTAL NICKNAMES.

First family, Scotland's *See* BROONS, THE.

First foot To make the first visit to friends and neighbours after the BELLS on Hogmanay. The first visitor to cross one's threshold after midnight is called the first foot, and traditionally brings with them a gift such as shortbread, BLACK BUN, whisky, or coal for the fire. In return, they are plied with a bite to eat and a dram. There are various superstitions associated with the tradition, for example, some regard it as unlucky to leave one's house and come back in without a first foot having called. Misfortune can be circumvented, however, if one first sends a child out of the back door and then invites them in by the front door. First footing, though regarded as archetypically Scottish, was previously also practised south of the Border. There are no records of the custom prior to the 19th century. One account, from later in that century, tells how:

> Each girl is expecting the first-foot from her sweetheart, and anxious to be the first to open the door to him, and many a quiet stratagem is sometimes spent in the endeavour to outwit her, and get the old grandmother, or some dooce serving-lass, to be the first to meet the kiss-expecting lover.
> – *All the Year Round*, 31 December 1870

See also CHRISTENING PIECE.

First younger Sister to the Frozen Zone Daniel Defoe's characterization of Scotland in his 'Caledonia, A Poem In Honour of Scotland', published in 1707, the year of the Union.

> First younger Sister to the Frozen Zone
> Battered by Parent Nature's constant frown.
> Adapt to hardships, and cut out for toil;
> The best worst climate, and the worst best soil.
> A rough, unhewn, uncultivated spot,
> Of old so fam'd, and so of late forgot.
> Neglected Scotland shows her awful brow,
> Not always quite so near to Heaven as now.

Fish dishes A culinary genre for which Scotland is celebrated. The reader is referred to the following entries for some of the more interestingly named items:

- ARBROATH SMOKIE
- CABBIECLAW
- CRAIL CAPON
- CRAPPIT HEIDS

- CULLEN SKINK
- DUNBAR WETHER
- EYEMOUTH FISH PIE
- FINNAN HADDIE
- GLASGOW MAGISTRATES
- GLASGOW PALES
- HAIRY MARY
- HUGGA-MUGGIE
- PARTAN BREE
- PIN-THE-WIDDIE
- STAP
- TWA-EE'D STEAK
- TWEED KETTLE
- WELL-HUNG FISH
- WIND-BLOWN FISH

See also FAUNA CALEDONIA; SALMON, ON THE UNACCEPTABILITY OF.

Fishermen's taboos Like many seafarers around the world, Scottish fishermen have a number of taboos, particularly in relation to certain words, in place of which 'lucky words' (as they are called in Shetland) must be substituted. Hence, a minister or priest must be referred to as *the black coat*, rabbits are *little feeties*, pigs *grumphies, guffies, curly tails* or *the four-fitted beasties*, salmon *charlies* or *the big fish*, and the church is *the bell hoose*. If any of the forbidden words should be inadvertently uttered, disaster may be avoided by crying 'Cauld iron', and grabbing onto the nearest bit of metal. Activities to be avoided include counting ships at sea or nets on land, burning fish bones, or having a woman aboard, while good luck may be brought by sprinkling the house with salt water at New Year, spitting in the fire, or hanging seaweed over the door. One anthropologist writes of his experience in the last quarter of the 20th century on board a fishing vessel sailing out of Buchan:

> When [he] mentioned the word pig in front of crew members, their reaction was first to look at one another, then to laugh. They made it clear, however, that he should not say that word on board the boat or the skipper might get angry enough to steam back to port and put him ashore. While they regarded such prohibitions as silly, they were not willing to test the tolerance of the skipper and therefore avoided using taboo words.
> – Edward E. Knipe and David G. Bromley, 'Speak No Evil: Word Taboos Among Scottish Fishermen', in Ray

B. Browne, ed., *Forbidden Fruits: Taboos and Tabooism in Culture* (1984)

See also DEISEIL.

Fish that never swam, the See TREE THAT NEVER GREW, THE.

Fithich dhubha Loch Carrann See BLACK RAVENS OF LOCHCARRON.

Five Articles of Perth James VI's attempt to impose Anglican liturgical practices on the Kirk in Scotland, to the disgust of Presbyterians. The provisions of the articles insisted that participants kneel during communion, that children at confirmation should be examined and blessed by a bishop, and that the festivals of Christmas, Good Friday, Easter and Pentecost should be observed; they also allowed for private baptism and private communion, at odds with the Presbyterian view of the primacy of the congregation. Kneeling in particular – a reminder of the ceremonial of the Catholic Mass – filled many with horror, and the General Assembly meeting at St Andrews in November 1617 rejected the Articles. The angry king summoned another General Assembly at Perth in August 1618, and, having been subjected to considerable duress, the majority accepted the provisions, and Parliament ratified them on 4 August 1621 – a day marked by a violent storm and thereafter referred to as Black Saturday. The Articles were condemned by the General Assembly meeting in Glasgow in 1638, and the act ratifying them was repealed in 1690.

Five Sisters Bing See WEST LOTHIAN ALPS.

Five Sisters of Kintail, the Five pointy, endlessly photographed peaks above Glen Shiel: Sgùrr na Mòraichd, Sgurr nan Saghead, Sgùrr na Càrnach, Sgùrr na Cìste Duibhe and Sgùrr Fhuaran. Only two are MUNROS, but the traverse of the ridge – originally known as Beinn Mhòr ('big mountain') – is a favourite among hillwalkers. The English name 'the Five Sisters' may go no further back than the earlier 20th century, possibly coined on the model of the THREE SISTERS OF GLENCOE, or even that of the Seven Sisters, the celebrated chalk cliffs on the Sussex coast.

Flanders frost A southeasterly gale (i.e. from the direction of Flanders) accompanied by a hard frost.

Flannan broth Bread soaked in hot milk, sweetened with sugar or treacle. *Flannan* here is 'flannel'.

Flannan Isles Mystery, the A notorious and unsolved case, in which three lighthouse keepers disappeared from Eilean Mór, one of the remote Flannan Isles, which lie some 20 miles (30 km) west of Lewis. The lighthouse on Eilean Mór had been built in 1899, and on Boxing Day 1900 the *Hesperus*, a vessel of the Commissioners of Northern Lights, arrived at the island to relieve one of the three keepers. On the night of 15 December, a ship heading for America had noticed that no light was showing, but this news only reached Oban after the *Hesperus* had set sail. The arrival of the relief ship, scheduled for 20 December, was delayed by severe storms, and when three men from the *Hesperus*, including the relief keeper Joseph Moore, did land on Eilean Mór, they noted that there was no answer to their ship's whistle, nor was there any flag flying from the flagpole. The gate leading to the lighthouse was carefully closed, as was the door to the lighthouse itself. On entering the building, the visitors found the table laid with an untouched meal, the lamp ready for lighting, and notes in the log up to the morning of 15 December. There were just two clues that something untoward had happened: an upturned chair, and the absence of two sets of oilskins. But arching over all of this was the fact that – despite a thorough search of the entire island – there was absolutely no sign of any of the three keepers, James Ducat, Thomas Marshall and Donald McArthur. There was evidence, however, of the severe storms that had delayed the *Hesperus*, and signs that giant waves had smashed over the top of the 200 ft (60 m) cliffs.

The official report by the superintendent of the Commissioners of Northern Lights, issued on 8 January 1901, concluded that the men had been swept away by a giant wave while attempting to secure some equipment. However, sceptics have asked why one man would have gone out in such conditions without his oilskins. And if two men had been in trouble, how would the third have heard their cries in the storm? And even if he had heard

them, and if he had rushed out to answer some emergency, would he have closed the door and the gate so carefully? The mystery inspired the famous poem 'Flannan Isle', written in 1912 by Wilfred Wilson Gibson, and narrated as if by Joseph Moore, the relief keeper. The poem ends:

> We seemed to stand for an endless while,
> Though still no word was said,
> Three men alive on Flannan Isle,
> Who thought on three men dead.

The story also provides the basis for the opera *The Lighthouse* (1979) by the Orkney-based composer Peter Maxwell Davies.

Flatterin' Friday According to Walter Gregor's *Folk-Lore of the North-East of Scotland* (1881), 'A Friday with fine weather during a time of wet is called a "flatterin' Friday", and is supposed to indicate a continuance of wet weather.'

Fleein' merchant Literally 'flying merchant', an obsolete term for a commercial traveller or CADGER; *fleein'* here means 'flying'.

Flee-up or **flee-up-i'-the-air** Someone who is thought to be either superficial and trivial, or who is all mouth and no trousers, or who puts on airs and graces; for example, in Nan Shepherd's *The Quarry Wood* (1928), 'the beautiful Mrs K', who is 'mostly frocks and fal-la-la-la', is described as a *flee-up*. *Flee* here means 'fly'. Used adjectivally, the phrase means 'lightweight' and/or 'here-today-gone-tomorrow'.

Fling A throw or kick; thus to *get the fling* or to be *flung* is to be jilted, while to *gie someone the fling* is to jilt them. *See also* HIGHLAND FLING.

Flit To move house, usually taking one's possessions with one. Thus to do a *moonlight flit* is to vacate the premises (especially rented accommodation) surreptitiously at night, leaving unpaid bills, etc., behind one. *Flit* or *Flitting Friday* was the day at Whitsun or Martinmas that farm labourers moved on to new employment. *Flitting Day*, also at Whitsun, seems to have been more generally observed:

Flitting-Day in Scotland. The 25th of May, as the Whit Sunday term (old style), is a great day in Scotland, being that on which, for the most part, people change their residences. For some unexplained reason the Scotch 'remove' oftener than their southern neighbours. They very generally lease their houses by the year, and are thus at every twelve-month's end able to shift their place of abode. Whether the restless disposition has arisen from the short leases, or the short leases have been a result of the restless disposition, is immaterial. That the restlessness is a fact, is what we have mainly to deal with.

It happens accordingly, that at every Candlemas a Scotch family gets an opportunity of considering whether it will, in the language of the country, sit or flit. The landlord or his agent calls to learn the decision on this point; and if 'flit' is the resolution, he takes measures by advertising to obtain a new tenant ...

– Robert Chambers, *The Book of Days* (1862–4)

In Glasgow they have a saying, *A Saturday flit's a short sit*, meaning that if you move on a Saturday, you won't stay long in your new abode. The origin of the superstition is obscure.

Flodden Wall, the A defensive wall round Edinburgh constructed after the Scots defeat at Flodden in 1513. Its ability to resist attackers was never tested. Parts can still be seen.

The walls of the city are built of little and unpolished stones, and seem ancient, but are very narrow, and in some places exceedingly low, in other ruined.

– Fynes Morison, *Itinerary* (1617)

Flog poussy, to *See* WHIP THE CAT.

Flooer, flouer ... *See* FLOWER ...

Flora Caledonia There follows a selection of some of the more colourful flower names from various parts of Scotland. More details regarding currency and geographical spread will be found in the *Dictionary of the Scottish Language*.

Auld wife's mutch or **granny's mutch** Columbine (a *mutch* was a close-fitting cap, as formerly worn by married women).

Bad man's bonny floo'er, the White campion (the BAD MAN is the Devil).

Blackheid, bumblekite or **lady's garter** Blackberry.

BLUEBELL OF SCOTLAND, THE Harebell. Others Scots names for the harebell include **blue-blavers**; **gowk's thummles** ('cuckoo's thimbles'); **ladies' thimbles**; **thunderbell** (the flowers supposedly ward off thunder); **witch-bell**.

Blue-blavers, cuckoo-hood or **witch-bell** Corn flower.

Bluidy fingers Foxglove. There are a host of other Scots names for the foxglove, including: **deid men's bells**; **dog's lugs** (ears); **fairy** or **granny's** or **ladies'** or **witches' thummles** (thimbles); **KING'S ELLWAND, THE**; **lady's** or **witch's fingers**; **mappie's mou** ('rabbit's mouth'; also applied to the snapdragon); **Scotch mercury**; **tod mittens** (from Tod LOWRIE, the fabular name for a fox); **trowie girse**, from TROW, the Orkney and Shetland version of a troll; **witches' paps**.

Bog-aiples, misk nits or **meadow nuts** Marsh cinquefoil (the roots were eaten by children; *misk*, 'marsh'; *nits*, 'nuts').

Bull's bags Purple orchid (presumably alluding to the same fancied resemblance of the root as the English name, which derives from Greek *orkhis*, 'testicle').

Carlin heather Bell heather (a CARLIN being an old hag or witch).

Carlin spurs or **cat-whins** Gorse.

Cat cleuk, catten-clover, cat-in-clover or **craw-taes** Bird's foot trefoil (*cleuk*, 'claw'; *craw-taes*, 'crow's toes').

Cat's een Germander speedwell (*een*, 'eyes').

Cat's lugs, cat's tails or **MOSS TROOPERS** Bog cotton.

Cat's milk Sun spurge (alluding to the poisonous white sap). Other names include **deil's appletrees** and LITTLE GUID.

Chastain, chasten or **chestane** Chestnut (compare French *châtaigne*). A conker is a *cheggie*, while in the game of conkers a conker that has broken another is a *gully o' wan* (*gully* being analogous to 'bully'), one that has broken two is a *gully o' twa*, and so on. Chestnut wood is *she-oak*.

Cockaloorie Common daisy.

Comfort-knit-bane Tuberous comfrey (a salve prepared from the root was formerly used to aid the healing of fractures).

Coo-paps Bladder campion (from the shape of the petals).

Cowsmouth, lady's fingers or **spink** Cowslip.

Craw-bell or **yellow lily** Daffodil.

Craw-nebs Kidney vetch ('crow beaks', from the shape of the flower).

Craw-peep, craw-tae, paddock flower or **SIT-SICCAR** Buttercup (*paddock*, 'frog').

Cuckoo cheese-an'-breid Cuckoo flower, aka lady's smock.

Curl-doddy or **curlie-daddy** Devil's-bit scabious ('round head'). Robert Chambers, in *Popular Rhymes of Scotland* (1826), records the following rhyme from Fife:

> Curly doddy, do my biddin',
> Soop my house, and shool my midden.
> [*soop*, 'sweep'; *shool*, 'shovel'?]

Cushy-cows The seeds of the dock. The name comes from the game by which children draw their hands up the stalks to collect the seeds, as if milking a cow.

Daft-berries or **deil's cherries** The berries of the deadly nightshade.

Dandillie, dent-de-lyon or **dentylion** Dandelion (from French *dent de lion*, 'tooth of the lion'). There are numerous other Scots names for the flower, including: **bum-pipe** (from *bum*, 'to buzz, hum', possibly from the children's use of the stalks to make a noise); **Deil's milk-plant** (referring to the bitter white sap); **doon-head-clock** or **what-o'clock-is-it?** (from the children's game in which the seedhead cluster is used as a 'dandelion clock': the number of puffs taken to blow off all the seed heads tells you the time); **heart-fever-grass**; **Langholm lily** (a jocular coinage); **pee-the-bed** or **pish-the-bed** (the plant is a noted diuretic; compare English *piss-a-bed*, French *pissenlit*); **Stink Davie**; **witch-gowan**.

Deid man's bellows Bugle.

DEIL'S APPLERENNIE, THE Camomile.

Deil's barley Crimson stonecrop.

DEIL'S SNUFFBOX, THE The common puffball.

Dog's carvie or **shepherd's needle** Chervil (*carvie*, 'caraway').

Dog-pintle or **dog's pintle** Yarrow or milfoil (*pintle*, 'penis').

Duke's meat, mouse lug or **shukkinwort** Chickweed.

EMMERTEEN'S MEAT Heath bedstraw.

Feverfoylie or **featherfooly** Feverfew (alluding to its actions in dispelling fevers). Another name is **fle-chie Nellie** (*flechie*, 'flea-ridden').

Fiddles March marigold.

FLOWER WHICH GREW AT THE FOOT OF THE CROSS Redshank.

Fox-fit Creeping buttercup (*fit*, 'foot').

Fuff-daisy Wood anemone.

GOWKINSPINTIL Cuckoo pint.

Gowk's hose Canterbury bell ('cuckoo's stockings').

Gowk's meat Wood sorrel ('cuckoo's food').

Grundiswallow or **watery drums** Groundsel.

Gulsa girse Buckbean or marsh trefoil (*see under* GULSOCH).

Hairy Davie Round-leaved mint.

Hard-heid or **horse's knot** Knapweed.

Hert o' the yearth Self-heal ('heart of the earth'). It is also known as **puir man's clover**.

Hielanman's garters Ribbon grass.

Hillberry Crowberry.

Honey blobs Gooseberries.

Horse-gladdening or **Jacob's sword** Yellow flag.

How-doup Medlar ('hollow buttocks', referring to the fruit's fancied resemblance to the anus; *cf. open-arse*, an English dialect term for the fruit, and Sir Thomas Urquhart's translation of Rabelais' *au cul sallé* as 'at the salt doup').

Hundred-fald Lady's bedstraw.

King's hood or **king's head** Wood cranesbill.

Kirrie dumplins The flower-heads of the drumstick primula (seemingly the plant, from the Himalaya, flourishes in the vicinity of Kirriemuir).

Lad's or **ploughman's love** or **auld maid's comfort** Southernwood.

Lady nit Larger plantain (*nit*, 'nut').

Lamb's lugs Lamb's ear or hoary plantain.

Lammie sourocks Sheep's sorrel.

Lazier Ox-eye daisy (because they do not open until the sun shines on them).

Links o' love or **maid-in-the-mist** Navelwort.

Love links or **queen's cushion** Yellow stonecrop.

Luck lilac White lilac.

Mad dog's berries Woody nightshade.

Mammy-flooers Forget-me-not.

Moorfowl berry or **moss-brummle** Cranberry (*brummle*, 'bramble').

Ox-toung Bugloss.

Paddy's rhubarb Butter-burr.

Puddock's spindle Spotted orchid (*puddock*, 'frog').

Puddock-pipes Horsetails.

Queen of the meadows or **meadow queen** Meadowsweet. Other Scots names include **blacking grass** and **molarie-tea** (a corruption of the species name, *Spirea ulmaria*; the plant is used for making infusions).

Rabbit's thistle Sow thistle.

Rosidandrum Rhododendron (from an imagined resemblance of the flower to a rose). The shrubs are more commonly known simply as **rhodies**.

Seachdamh aran, an Silverweed (Gaelic, 'seventh bread': the root was formerly dried and ground into a type of flour).

Seel-o-downs Celandine (of which *seel-o-downs* is a corruption).

Shepherd's club Mullein.

Siller shakers Quaking grass (*siller*, 'silver').

Sit-siccar A Buchan name for the buttercup. The term literally means 'sit sure, fixed', as the plant is difficult to eradicate once established.

Slattyvarrie Edible seaweed (from Gaelic *slatmhara*).

Sleepin Maggie Night-scented stock.

Sleepy dose or **Stinkin Davie** or **Stinkin Willie** Ragwort.

Smear docken Good King Henry (an ointment made from it was smeared onto the skin as a herbal treatment).

Sodger or **stinkin' puppy** Red poppy (*sodger*, 'soldier'; *puppy*, 'poppy').

Sodger's bluid Common sorrel. It is also known as **rantie-tantie**, and children call the seeds *rabbit's sugar*.

Sodger's buttons Water avens or the burnet-leaved rose; also applied to the burrs of burdock.

Sodger's feather Honesty.

Son-afore-the-faither A name applied to various plants, such as coltsfoot, butterbur and cudweed, where the flowers appear before the leaves.

Souky mammy or **souky soo** Clover (because the flowers are sucked by children for the nectar). The flower of the white clover was sometimes called *sheepie mae*, borrowing a familiar name for a sheep, with the second element being imitative of a bleat.

Sticky Willie or **Robbie-rin-the-hedge** Goose-grass. The first name alludes to its adhesive properties; the name is also applied to sundew, which uses a sticky exudation to trap insects.

Stinkin Billy Sweet William (*see* BUTCHER CUMBERLAND).

Stinkin nettle Dead-nettle.

Stinkin Tam Tansy.

Sweet Willie Red campion.

Wild jessamine Wood anemone.

William and Mary or **Jock and Jennie** Lungwort (the two names reflecting the presence of both pink buds and blue flowers on the same plant). It is also known as **deil's ain** and **thunner-an-lichtenin**, the latter because of the white spots on its leaves.

Witch's thorn A gnarled old hawthorn standing on its own, a suitable location for the performance of the dark arts. Haws (the berries) are *cat-haws* or *haw-haws*, while the young leaves and buds are *lady's meat* or *cheese-an-breid*.

Withershins Honeysuckle (*see under* WIDDERSHINS).

See also HEATHER; THISTLE; WHITE ROSE OF SCOTLAND, THE.

Flounders In *Superstitions of the Highlands and Islands of Scotland* (1900) John G. Campbell provides two explanations as to why the flounder has a wry mouth. The first, from Sutherland, is that it arose when the flounder was making faces at the rock-cod, and its face got stuck. In Tiree and Iona it was believed that the wry mouth was caused by St Columba:

> Colum-Kil met a shoal of flounders and asked: 'Is this a removal, flounder?'
> 'Yes it is, Colum-Kil crooked legs,' said the flounder.
> 'If I have crooked legs,' said St. Columba, 'may you have a crooked mouth,' and so the flounder has a wry mouth to this day.

Flower of Dunblane, the One Jessie, the subject of a fine love song, 'Jessie, the Flower o' Dunblane', by the WEAVER POET Robert Tannahill (1774–1810), with music by his friend, Robert Archibald Smith.

> She's modest as ony, and blythe as she's bonny;
> For guileless simplicity marks her its ain;
> And far be the villain, divested o' feeling,
> Wha'd blight, in its bloom, the sweet flower o' Dunblane.
> Sing on, thou sweet mavis, thy hymn to the evening,
> Thou'rt dear to the echoes of Calderwood glen;
> Sae dear to this bosom, sae artless and winning,
> Is charming young Jessie, the flower o' Dunblane.

Tannahill's song proved very popular, and throughout the 19th century there appeared a host of poems and songs following the formula 'X, the flower o' Y'.

Flower of Galloway, the Jane Maxwell (?1749–1812), a celebrated beauty, painted by George Romney. She was the daughter of Sir William Maxwell, 3rd Baronet of Monreith, and in 1767 married Alexander Gordon, 4th Duke of Gordon. She became the leading society hostess among the Scottish Tories, and seems to have been something of a character, one contemporary writing:

> The Duchess triumphs in a manly mien;
> Loud is her accent, and her phrase obscene.

Her marriage was tempestuous, and neither party was faithful to the other. A story circulated that when she was marrying off one of her daughters to Marquess Cornwallis (three others married dukes), he expressed some reservations on account of the streak of madness that supposedly ran through the Gordon family. However, the Duchess was able to put his mind at rest by assuring him that her daughter possessed not a drop of Gordon blood. Her son, later the 5th Duke, raised the 92nd Highlanders, and she famously sought to encourage recruitment on his behalf by placing the king's shilling between her teeth.

'Flower of Scotland' A song by Roy Williamson of the folk duo The Corries, first performed in 1967, and celebrating the Scottish victory at Bannockburn. It has subsequently become one of Scotland's unofficial national anthems, sung at international football and rugby matches, and largely replacing SCOTLAND THE BRAVE.

> O Flower of Scotland, when will we see your like again
> That fought and died for your wee bit hill and glen
> And stood against him, proud Edward's army
> And sent him homeward tae think again.

The anthem is alluded to in another song much favoured by the TARTAN ARMY, 'The Happy Hooligans o' Wembley':

> Oh, I wear a tartan bunnet and a scarf around my
> throat
> And I can sing the Flower of Scotland every single
> note.

> For we're gan doon tae London toon
> Tae paralyse the undergroond
> And we're just the happy hooligans o' Wembley.

'Flower of Scotland' does not appeal to all Scots:

> God, it was a miserable little dirge. The song reeked of chippy victimhood. It wasn't even a traditional song ... But to me, it has come to represent invented heritage, in a country with a tendency to go much further back than it needs to, in order to assert identity. Flower of Scotland is sentimental and ersatz. But back in the 70s, I was well into it. It filled my heart with something that felt like wounded yet triumphant pride.
> – Deborah Orr, in *Guardian*, 20 May 2011. Orr grew up in Motherwell.

Flower of Strathearn, the A sobriquet awarded to Carolina, Lady Nairne, née Oliphant (1766–1845), the celebrated writer of Scottish songs. The name alludes to her grace and good looks, and her birthplace at Gask House, in the valley of the River Earn in Perthshire. Her father and grandfather were both staunch Jacobites, and had been obliged to go into exile after the '45. At the age of 41 she married William Murray Nairne, her second cousin and also a Jacobite sympathizer, whose barony had thus been forfeited. This was eventually restored by Parliament in 1824, following much lobbying by Sir Walter Scott.

Lady Nairne herself thought 'this queer trade of song-writing' not quite respectable for a lady, and published either anonymously or under the pseudonym Mrs Bogan of Bogan. Her songs include bowdlerized renditions of traditional songs (for example, 'The LAIRD O' COCKPEN'), and versions of old Jacobite songs such as 'CHARLIE IS MY DARLING' and 'Will ye no' come back again?' Many of them were published in *The Scottish Minstrel* (1821–4). *See also* CALLER HERRIN.

Flower of Teviot, the *See* LAY OF THE LAST MINSTREL, THE.

Flower of the water, the *See* CREAM OF THE WATER, THE.

Flower of Yarrow, the Mary Scott of Dryhope in the Yarrow valley, whose family lived in Dryhope

Tower, at the northeastern end of St Mary's Loch. Reputedly the most beautiful woman of her time, she married AULD WAT Scott of Harden (d.1629), the notorious and venerable BORDER REIVER, and was thus an ancestor of Sir Walter Scott, who writes of Auld Wat and Mary in *The Lay of the Last Minstrel*:

Marauding chief! his sole delight
The moonlight raid, the morning fight;
Not even the Flower of Yarrow's charms
In youth, might tame his rage for arms.

John Leyden (who assisted Scott in the compilation of *Minstrelsy of the Scottish Border*) recounts a story in his *Scenes from Infancy* about Mary and the infant she discovers among the booty brought back by Auld Wat in a cross-Border raid:

The waning harvest-moon shone cold and bright,
The warder's horn was heard at dead of night;
And as the massy portals wide were flung,
With stamping hoofs the rocky pavement rung.
What fair, half-veiled, leans from her lattice hall,
Where red the wavering gleams of torchlight fall?
'Tis Yarrow's fairest flower, who through the gloom
Looks wistful for her lover's dancing plume.
Amid the piles of spoil that strew'd the ground,
Her ear, all anxious, caught a wailing sound
With trembling haste the youthful matron flew,
And from the hurried heaps an infant drew.
Scared at the light his little hands he flung

Around her neck, and to her bosom clung;
While beauteous Mary soothed, in accents mild,
His fluttering soul, and clasped her foster-child.
Of milder mood the gentle captive grew,
Nor loved the scenes that scared his infant view;
In vales remote, from camps and castles far,
He shunned the fearful shuddering joy of war;
Content the loves of simple swains to sing,

Or wake to fame the harp's heroic string.
His are the strains, whose wandering echoes thrill
The shepherd, lingering on the twilight hill,
When evening brings the merry folding hours,
And sun-eyed daisies close their winking flowers.
He lived o'er Yarrow's Flower to shed the tear,
To strew the holly leaves o'er Hardens bier;
But none was found above the minstrel's tomb,

Emblem of peace, to bid the daisy bloom;
He, nameless as the race from which he sprung,
Saved other names, and left his own unsung.

A different, and male, Flower of Yarrow appears in the Revd John Logan's version of the ballad 'The Braes of Yarrow', printed in Robert Chambers's *The Scottish Ballads* (1829):

Thy braes were bonnie, Yarrow stream,
When first on them I met my lover;
Thy braes how dreary, Yarrow stream,
When now thy waves his body cover!
For ever, now, Oh, Yarrow stream,
Thou art to me a stream of sorrow!
For ever, on thy banks shall I
Behold my love, the flower of Yarrow.

This melancholy effusion appears to owe something to other ballads set in the Yarrow valley that mourn the deaths of young lovers, such as 'The Dowie Houms o' Yarrow' and 'Rare Willie Drowned in Yarrow'.

Flowers of Edinburgh, the The smells resulting from the habit of the city's maids of emptying bed pans out of upper-storey windows onto the streets below, after crying GARDYLOO. In 1819 the poet Robert Southey wrote of 'the windes, down which an English eye may look, but into which no English nose would willingly venture, for stinks older than the Union are to be found there'.

At the warning call of 'Gardy loo' from servants preparing to outpour the contents of stoups, pots and cans, the passengers beneath would agonizingly call out 'Haud yer hand'; but too often the shout was unheard or too late ... the dreaded hour when the domestic abominations were flung out, when the smells (known as 'the flowers of Edinburgh') filled the air.
– H. Grey Graham, *The Social Life of Scotland in the Eighteenth Century* (1899)

'The Flowers of Edinburgh' is also the name of a popular reel, first published in 1753.

'Flowers of the Forest, The' A traditional Scottish folk tune, known from at least the early 17th century. In 1756 Jean Elliot supplied words to the tune in the form of an elegy on the loss of James IV and some 10,000 of his fellow countrymen at the Battle of Flodden in 1513:

> I've heard the lilting, at the yowe-milking,
> Lassies a-lilting before dawn o' day;
> Now they are moaning on ilka green loaning,
> The flowers of the Forest are a' wede away.

A decade later Alison Cockburn published her own lyrics, of a more personal nature (thought to reflect her parting from a certain John Aikman, who had left for London):

> I've seen the smiling
> Of fortune beguiling,
> I've tasted her pleasures,
> And felt her decay;
> Sweet is her blessing,
> And kind her caressing,
> But now they are fled
> And fled far away.

Today the tune is often played on the solo pipes as a lament at funerals or Remembrance Day ceremonies.

Flower which grew at the foot of the Cross, the A description formerly applied in the Borders to redshank (*Polygonum persicaria*), a member of the dock family. The red flowers were presumably thought to resemble drops of Christ's blood.

Flying Abbot, the *See* BIRDMAN OF STIRLING CASTLE, THE.

Flying Flea, the A nickname of the diminutive (5 ft 4 in / 1.6 m)) footballer James Connolly ('Jimmy') Johnstone (1944–2006), who scored 82 goals for Celtic between 1962 and 1975, and won 23 Scottish caps. In 1967 he was in the Celtic team that won the European Cup in Lisbon, helping to earn them the sobriquet the LISBON LIONS. In 2002 Celtic supporters voted him the club's greatest-ever player. It was the French press who dubbed Johnstone 'the Flying Flea', after he had tormented Nantes with his dribbling skills during a European Cup tie – his colleague Bobby Lennox remembered that 'Jimmy must have kept the ball for an hour that night.' Ironically, given his nickname, Johnstone had a terrible fear of flying. He was also known as 'the Wee Flea', but to most Celtic fans he was simply 'Jinky', because of the way he could 'jink' round opponents.

Flying Scotsman (1) The 'Special Scotch Express' (as it was originally described) linking the capitals of Scotland and England. It has simultaneously left Edinburgh Waverley and London King's Cross at 10 a.m. since 1862, when the journey took 10½ hours, including half an hour for lunch in York. Now it takes around 4½ hours, and on the southbound run the name is applied to the 13.00 from Waverley. (2) The name of an LNER A3-class locomotive, number 4472, built in 1923, which took its name from the above express service. It was retired in 1963, and went on tours of the USA and Australia. It is now in the care of the National Railway Museum in York. (3) The nickname of the athlete and rugby international Eric Liddell (1902–45), who won the men's 400 metres at the 1924 Olympics, and was portrayed in the film *Chariots of Fire*. (4) A nickname of the cyclist Graeme Obree (b.1965), who twice broke the world one-hour distance record, in 1993 and 1994. *The Flying Scotsman* is both the title of his autobiography and of a 2006 film drama based on his life. (5) *See* HAGGIS. *See also* BIRDMAN OF STIRLING CASTLE, THE.

Flyting A bout of mutual name-calling, especially as practised by the poets of the early Renaissance period in Scotland. The most notable example is 'The Flyting of Dunbar and Kennedie', in which rival MAKARS (poets) William Dunbar (*c.*1460–*c.*1520) and Walter Kennedy (*c.*1455–?1518) indulge in a war of words, resulting in a tour de force of vituperation and technical dexterity. It is thought to have been performed at the Court of James IV in the early years of the 16th century. Among many other things, Kennedy calls Dunbar:

> Ignorant elf, aip, owll irregular,
> Skaldit skaitbird, and commoun skamelar;
> Wanfukkit funling, that natour maid ane yrle ...
> [*skaldit*, scabby; *skaitbird*, skua, thought to feed on the excrement (scat) of other birds; *skamelar*, scrounger, sycophant; *wannfukkit funling*, misbegotten foundling; *yrle*, dwarf]

For his part, Dunbar calls his opponent:

> Cuntbittin crawdoun Kennedie, coward of kind …
> [*cuntbitten*, pox-ridden, ?hen-pecked; *crawdoun*, dwarf]

– not to mention a 'vyle beggar', a 'mismaid monstour', and:

> The fathir and moder of morthour and mischeif,
> Dissaitfull tyrand, with serpentis tung, unstable;
> Cukcald cradoun, cowart, and commoun theif …

And so it continues for dozens of stanzas, each poet addressing the other's personal appearance, ancestry, disgusting habits, moral failings and lack of poetic skill. The tone soars from the lofty to the scatological, and the allusions range from the theological and classical to the contemporary and political.

For some more flyting, *see* AY FUCKAND LYKE ANE FURIOUS FORNICATOR.

Folks in Orkney are plucking geese, the A traditional saying in the Northeast when snow was falling in flakes.

Follyrood *See* HOLYROOD.

Food, drink, cooking and feasting *See:*

- ALCOHOLISM VS COMMUNISM
- ARBROATH SMOKIE
- ATHOLL BROSE
- AYRSHIRE SHORTBREAD
- BACK FEAST
- BANNOCK
- BAWD BREE
- BEER
- BERWICK COCKLES
- BLAAND
- BLACK BUN
- BLACK CORK
- BLACK DINNER, the
- BLACK MAN
- BLACK-STRIPPIT BA
- BLITHEMEAT
- BLOODY PUDDINGS
- BLUBBER-TOTUM
- BOUNTY
- BROSE

- BUCKFAST TRIANGLE
- BUTTERY
- CABBIECLAW
- CALLY
- CHAMPIT TATTIES
- CHEEKY WATTER
- CHEUGH JEAN
- CHITTERIN BIT
- CHRISTENING PIECE
- CLEAR STUFF, the
- COCK-A-LEEKIE
- CRAIL CAPON
- Cranachan (*see under* ATHOLL BROSE)
- CRAPPIT HEIDS
- CULLEN SKINK
- CULROSS GIRDLE
- CUMMERS' FEAST
- CURLY ANDRA
- CURLY KATE
- CURRY ALLEY
- DREAMING BREAD
- DRIBBLY BEARDS
- DUNBAR WETHER
- DUNDEE CAKE
- DUNDEE MARMALADE
- DUNDEE STEAK
- DUNLOP CHEESE
- EDINBURGH GINGERBREAD
- EDINBURGH ROCK
- EL D
- ELECTRIC SOUP
- EYEMOUTH FISH PIE
- FINNAN HADDIE
- FLANNAN BROTH
- FORFAR BRIDIE
- FOUSTIE
- FREEDOM AND WHISKY GANG THEGITHER
- FREE KIRK PUDDING
- FUR COAT
- GLASGOW MAGISTRATES OR BAILLIES
- GLASGOW PALES
- GLASGOW TOFFEE
- GREAT CHIEFTAIN O' THE PUDDIN'-RACE
- GROANING MALT
- HAGGIS
- HAIRY MARY
- HAPPY DAY
- HAUF AN A HAUF

- HAWICK BA
- HAWICK GILL
- HEATHER ALE
- HELENSBURGH TOFFEE
- HIGHLAND HONOURS
- HIGH TEA
- HOLYROOD PUDDING
- HOWTOWDIE
- HUGGA-MUGGIE
- INDESCRIBABLES
- INFAR CAKE
- IRISH STEAK
- IRN BRU
- JEDDART SNAILS
- JENNY LIND
- KAIL
- KAIL BROSE
- KIDNEY
- KILL-THE-CARTER
- KINGDOM OF FIFE PIE
- KIRRIEMUIR GINGERBREAD
- LANG ALE
- LANNY
- LORNE SAUSAGE
- LOW-FLYER
- MEAL AND ALE
- MOFFAT TOFFEE
- NIPPY SWEETIE
- OATS, DR JOHNSON ON
- ONION JOHNNIE
- PACE EGG
- PAIL ALE
- PALLY ALLY
- PAN LOAF
- PEASE BROSE
- PETTICOAT TAILS
- PIN-THE-WIDDIE
- POCK-PUDDING
- POKEY-HAT
- PORRIDGE
- QUAICH
- RED BIDDY
- REESTIT MUTTON
- RUMBLEDETHUMP
- SAIR HEIDIE
- SCOTCH BROTH
- SCOTCH CHOCOLATE
- SCOTCH COFFEE

- SCOTCH EGG
- SCOTCH FLUMMERY
- SCOTCH FROG
- SCOTCH MIST
- SCOTCH MUFFLER
- SCOTCH PIE
- SCOTCH WOODCOCK
- SCOTS COLLOPS
- SINGIN GINGER
- SKATE BREE
- SKINNY TATTIES
- SKIRL-I'-THE-PAN
- *SLÀINTE MHATH*
- SLIM JIM
- SMA' DRINK
- SNAP AN' RATTLE
- SOOKIE SWEETIES
- SOOR PLOOM
- SORE HAND
- SOWANS
- SPEEL-THE-WA'
- STAIRHEID SHANDY
- STAP
- STRUAN MICHAEL
- SUMPTUARY LAWS
- SWEETIE-WIFE
- TAPPIT HEN
- TATTIES AND POINT
- TEA, COFFEE AND CHOCOLATE
- TEVIOTDALE PIE
- TWA-EE'D STEAK
- TWEED KETTLE
- WELL-HUNG FISH
- WHISKY
- WIND-BLOWN FISH
- WOMLE AND BREES

Foonin' pint *See* FOUNDING PINT.

Football club nicknames

The Accies Hamilton Academicals.
The Bairns Falkirk; from the town's motto, 'Better meddle wi' the Deil than the bairns o' Falkirk.'
The Bankies Clydebank.
The Bears or **the Teddy Bears** or **the Gers** or **the Light Blues** Glasgow Rangers. *Bears* is rhyming slang for the second syllable 'gers' (and the area

round their ground at Ibrox is referred to as *Teddy Bear Country*). Their strips are not a particularly light shade of blue, but are paler than those of Dundee, the Dark Blues. Their supporters are referred to by rival fans as Huns or Bluenoses.

The Bhoys or **the TIMS** or **the Hoops** Celtic (Irish Catholic origins / strip pattern). Sometimes they are simply **the 'Tic.**

The Binos Stirling Albion.

The Blue Brazil Cowdenbeath, perhaps because, as one supporter has said, 'Cowden play in blue and have debts like a Third World country'. There is also the suggestion that the team aspires to world-class status.

The Blues Stranraer (from the strip).

The Borderers or **the Wee Rangers** Berwick Rangers (although stranded on the wrong side of the Border, they play in the Scottish League; not to be confused with Glasgow Rangers).

The Bully Wee Clyde ('bully' as in 'good' or 'jolly', and 'wee' as in not a major team).

The Cabbage Hibernian (rhyming slang Cabbage and Ribs = Hibs).

Caley Inverness Caledonian Thistle (*see* SUPER CALEY GO BALLISTIC, CELTIC ARE ATROCIOUS).

The Danes Rothesay Brandane AFC (an abbreviation of BRANDANE).

The Dee or **the Dark Blues** or **the Taysiders** Dundee (from the name/strip colour/geographical location).

The Diamonds or **the Waysiders** Airdrie (the red diamond design on their strip; one of its players called it 'the Wayside Club').

The Dons Aberdeen. The name *may* refer to the River Don, but is more likely be short for 'Aberdonians'. It has also been suggested that it refers to the fact that the founders of the club were teachers.

The Doonhamers QUEEN OF THE SOUTH (Dumfries people when away refer to their home town as 'doon hame').

The Fifers (1) East Fife, (2) Methil.

The Gable-endies Montrose (*see* GABLE-ENDIE).

The Hibees or **Hibs** or (via rhyming slang) **the Pen Nibs** Hibernian.

Hi Hi or **the Warriors** Third Lanark (the former possibly from a supporters' chant when a ball was kicked so high that it left the ground entirely; the latter as it was founded, in 1872, as the 3rd Lanarkshire Volunteer Rifles Football Club).

The Honest Men Ayr United (in Burns's 'Tam o' Shanter', Ayr is unsurpassed 'for honest men and bonnie lasses').

The Jags or **the Maryhill Magyars** Partick Thistle (thistles being spiky; the latter name alludes to the location of the club's ground, and the successful Hungarian international side of the early 1950s).

Killie Kilmarnock.

The Lilywhites CLACHNACUDDIN FC of Inverness, who wear white strips.

Livi Lions Livingstone.

The Loons Forfar Athletic (Scots, 'young men').

The Maroons or **Hearts** or **the Jam Tarts** or **the Jambos** Heart of Midlothian (from the colour of the strip/rhyming slang).

The Miners Cowdenbeath (a former mining town).

The Pars Dunfermline Athletic. (There are a number of not altogether convincing theories about the origin of this nickname, first recorded in the early 20th century: (1) It is an abbreviation of 'paralytics', the team playing badly at the time. (2) English sailors from the nearby Rosyth naval base displayed a banner at a Dunfermline game reading 'Plymouth Argyle (Rosyth) Supporters'. (3) After the team had been promoted to the League, it was 'on a par' with other senior teams. (4) The black-and-white-striped strip resembles the markings of the parr, the name given to an immature salmon.)

The Rabs or **the Roy** Kirkintilloch Rob Roy FC.

The Red Lichties Arbroath (from the rose window in Arbroath Abbey, once used as a navigation aid when it was lit up at night; *see* O OF ARBROATH, THE).

The Saints (1) St Johnstone. (2) St Mirren (also known as **the Buddies**; *see* BUDDY).

The Shire East Stirling(shire).

The Sons of the Rock or **the Warriors** Dumbarton (from Dumbarton Rock; *see* SONS OF THE ROCK).

The Spiders Queen's Park (from the black and white hoops on their strip).

The Staggies Ross County, from the stag's head on their badge, taken from the regimental badge of the Seaforth Highlanders, in which many local men had fought in the First World War.

The Terrors or **the Tangerines** Dundee United (strip colour). The club's supporters are known, for reasons unknown, as 'Arabs'.

The Ton Morton (Greenock Morton FC).

The Toons Peterhead (from the town's nickname, 'the BLUE TOON').

The Warriors Stenhousemuir; also Third Lanark (*see* HI HI *above*) and Dumbarton (*see* SONS OF THE ROCK *above*).

The Wasps Alloa (their strip is gold and black).

The Wee Rangers Berwick Rangers (*see* BORDERERS *above*).

The Wee Rovers Albion Rovers.

The Well or **the Steelmen** Motherwell (former local industry).

See also LISBON LIONS, THE.

Foreign parts There follows a selection of Scots versions of foreign place names and peoples, used at various times in the past (most pre-date the 19th century):

Bertane, Bartane	Britain or Brittany
Burdeaulx, Burdeous	Bordeaux
Cashub	Kaszubia, a province of Poland
Cisteus, Systeus	Cîteaux, site of the mother-house of the Cistercian order
Crocko, Crocavia	Kraków
Danskin, Danskene	Danzig (Polish *Gdansk*)
Denes, Dens, Densmen	Danes
Druntin	Trondheim
Easter Seas, the	the Baltic
Eastlan, Estland, Eistland	Estonia, or other regions of the eastern Baltic
Goddis inymyes	the Saracens
Gregiouns	Greeks
Hispaniarts	Spaniards
The Ingies	The Indies
Ingland	England
Janis	Genoa (cf. Old French *Jannes*)
Leonis	Lyon
Lymmistar	Leominster (source of fine black woollen cloth)
Machometists	Mohammedans, i.e. Muslims
Massedone	Macedonia
Mauchlyne	Mechelen (Belgium)
Muscovia	Russia

Napillis	Naples
Norroway, Northway	Norway
Osnaburg	Osnabrück (Germany)
Pairis, Pareis	Paris
Pass of Calies, the	the Straits of Dover
Pikkardie	Picardy
Rooshians	Russians
Sciennes	Sienna (the Sciennes area of Edinburgh is named after the Dominican convent of St Catherine of Sienna that once stood there)
Spaingie, Spangyie, Spengie	Spain
Swadan, Swane, Suethin	Sweden
Tallies	Italians (a modern jocular or disparaging term)
Yacks	Eskimos (a disparaging term formerly used by whalers, perhaps deriving from 'Jack', or imitative of their speech)

Forester, muckle the *See* MUCKLE FORESTER, THE.

Forester of the Fairy Corrie, the The story of this figure (*Forsair Choir' an t-Sidhe* in Gaelic) and his fairy lover, who took the form of a white hind, was told by Alexander Macpherson of Kingussie in the *Glasgow Herald* (20 August 1910):

Somewhere in this Garden of Sleep [Kingussie Cemetery] hallowed by St Columba, although no trace can now be found of the actual grave, there rests the dust of the celebrated forester of the Fairy Corry, a native of Cowal in Argyllshire. This hero was of a branch of the MacLeods of Raasay, and being fair-haired his descendants were called Clann Mhic-ille bhain – that is, children of the fair-haired man, who now call themselves by the surname of Whyte. The forester was universally believed to have had a Leannan-Sith (a fairy sweetheart), who followed him wherever he went.

Mr Duncan Whyte, of Glasgow, one of the eighth generation in direct descent from the forester, communicated to me in Gaelic sundry very interesting traditions which have come down regarding his famous

---

ancestor. In the year 1644 the Earl of Montrose was in the field with an army on behalf of King Charles I; while the Earl of Argyll had the chief command of the Covenanters' forces. Montrose was burning and pillaging in the north when Argyll received instructions to go in pursuit of him. The forester was in Argyll's army, and the fairy sweetheart, in the shape of a white hind, followed the troops wherever they went. While they were resting in the neighbourhood of Ruthven Castle, in Badenoch, some of the officers began to mock Argyll for allowing the hind to be always following the army. Their ridicule roused his wrath, and he commanded his men to fire at the hind. This was done without a particle of lead piercing her hair. Some observed that the forester was not firing, although pointing his gun at the hind like the rest, and he was accused to Argyll. He then received strict orders to fire at the hind. 'I will fire at your command, Argyll,' said the forester, 'but it will be the last shot that I shall ever fire,' and it happened as he said. Scarcely was the charge out of his gun when he fell dead on the field. The fairy gave a terrific scream and rose like a cloud of mist up the shoulder of the neighbouring mountain, and from that time was never seen following the army. It has been believed by every generation since that the fairy left a charm with the descendants of the forester, which shall stick to them to the twentieth generation.

Forfar bridie The full name of the *bridie*, a type of meat pie originating in Forfar, probably in the early decades of the 19th century, and now ubiquitous in Scotland. The bridie consists of a semicircular pie of pastry covering minced or diced steak and onions, usually well seasoned. In Forfar, the pastry is short-crust, while elsewhere it is flaky. According to one tradition, bridies were originally made by a certain Margaret *Bridie* of Glamis, who sold them at Forfar. Another explanation of the word is that it derives from 'bride's pie', the suggestion being that this served as the feast at PENNY WEDDINGS. Apparently only Dundonians can say: 'Twa bridies, a plen ane and an ingin [onion] ane an a'.'

Forfar bridle A famous example of the BRANKS, preserved in Forfar's Town House. It was worn in the 17th century by local witches on their way to execution.

Forfar four, East Fife five *See* EAST FIFE FOUR, FORFAR FIVE.

Forfochen *See* SAIR OR FAIR FORFOCHEN.

For love and favour and affection A common legal formula in the 18th and 19th centuries to denote that the transfer of property alluded to in the document was a gift.

Fornication ... but a pastime Prior to the passage by the Reformation Parliament of laws against adultery in 1563 and fornication in 1567, Sir Antony Weldon, an Englishman, observed of the Scots:

> Fornication they hold but a pastime wherein man's ability is proved and woman's fertility is discovered.

After the law was tightened up, the punishment was to stand in sackcloth with bare feet and bare head, at the door of the kirk and then on the STOOL OF REPENTANCE within the kirk. This went on each Sunday for six months, sometimes longer, and whipping and fines were also administered. An alternative punishment took the form of BUTTOCK-MAIL.

For stark love and kindness *See* ROB GIB'S CONTRACT.

Fort, the A familiar name for Fort William, sometimes also known as *the Bill*. *See also* HANGING TREE OF FORT WILLIAM, THE.

Fortingall Yew, the An ancient tree growing in the kirkyard of the Perthshire village of Fortingall, a few miles west of Aberfeldy. Estimates of its age range from 2000 to 5000 years old. The younger figure appears to be more likely, but this still makes it the oldest known tree in Europe. In 1769 its circumference was measured at 52 ft (15.85 m), but subsequently much of its wood was cut away by the locals to make QUAICHS and other souvenirs to sell to the tourists. Today the tree, surrounded by a stone wall, consists of a number of apparently separate elements, but its former girth is marked out on the ground with white pegs. Local tradition has it that Pontius PILATE was born under its shelter.

Fort Weetabix A nickname for the St Mungo Museum of Religion, in Cathedral Square, Glasgow, a building dating from 1989 but resembling a traditional Scottish tower house with ecclesiastical ambitions. The nickname – possibly coined by some journalist, and apparently rarely used by the Glaswegian public – alludes to the colour and texture of the stonework.

Forty-five, the The failed Jacobite Rebellion of 1745–6; for details see YOUNG PRETENDER, THE.

Forty Thieves, the The name given by their enemies to a group of Glasgow ministers – the self-proclaimed 'Forty' – who, as the DISRUPTION OF 1843 loomed, drew back from the brink of secession and tried to find a compromise. The allusion is to the story of 'Ali Baba and the Forty Thieves' from *The Arabian Nights*.

Forty-twa, the See BLACK WATCH, THE.

Fou Literally 'full', hence 'drunk'. *Fou as a puggie, fou as a wulk* and *fiddler-fou* all mean 'dead drunk', though why this state should be associated with *puggies* (monkeys; see GET YER PUGGIE UP), whelks or players of the violin is unclear; pipers are similarly slandered in the expression *as fou as a piper*. If someone is *as fou as cap or staup'll mak them* (literally, 'as drunk as cup or cask will make them'), then they are as drunk as it is possible to be. Prior to achieving that state, a drinker might for a while be *greetin-fou*, in which state lachrymose sentimentality is tiresomely indulged. Hugh MacDiarmid's *A Drunk Man Looks at the Thistle* (1926) opens with the oft-heard excuse: 'I amna' fou' sae muckle as tired – deid dune.'

Foukies, little See LITTLE FOLK, THE.

Foul-mouthed duchess, a See FLOWER OF GALLOWAY, THE.

Foul Thief, the 'If we can trust the testimony of the author of *Scots Presbyterian Eloquence* [1692],' opines John Jamieson in the 1825 supplement to his *Etymological Dictionary of the Scottish Language*, 'some of the old Scottish ministers gave the devil this name in their discourses'. It seems that Robert Burns was more familiar with the Foul Thief than Jamieson:

> Ye little skelpie-limmer's face!
> I daur you try sic sportin',
> As seek the foul thief ony place,
> For him to spae your fortune.
> Nae doubt but ye may get a sight!
> Great cause ye hae to fear it;
> For mony a ane has gotten a fright,
> And lived and died deleeret
>   On sic a night.
> – Robert Burns, 'Halloween' (1786)

Founding pint The drink presented to the construction team after they have finished the foundations of a building. For example, in the accounts for the building of the new tolbooth in North Berwick in 1728, there is an entry reading 'To the masons a quart of ale, 4s'. The practice was thought to ensure good luck, or at least to avert ill fortune: there is a 19th-century account of the minister of Knockando in Moray refusing – despite the plethora of distilleries in the vicinity – to give the builders of the new church a founding pint, 'upon which they are said to have pronounced a malison against future incumbents'. The custom persisted into the 20th century. The stonemason Ian Cramb, who in 1959 was given the task of rebuilding the 13th-century cloisters of Iona Abbey, recalls:

> Before starting the Cloisters, I had one traditional stonemasons' ceremony to perform, the 'founding pint'. You put the names of all involved in the building, also a newspaper and some other details of our way of life at that date into an empty whisky bottle, after we had consumed the contents. It was all blessed by Lord MacLeod and placed within the foundations. I knew then everything was going to be alright. A little party was given in the evening to celebrate this historic occasion. This was to be the last time I would celebrate this old custom.
> – Ian Cramb, 'Rebuilding the Cloisters of Iona Abbey', in *Stonexus Magazine*, summer 2004

Four Cities, the A collective term for Edinburgh, Glasgow, Aberdeen and Dundee. Scotland now has seven cities, Inverness having been granted city status in 2001, Stirling in 2002 and Perth in 2012.

Four-footed clansmen The mocking name given during the CLEARANCES by the Highlanders to the Cheviot sheep that their chiefs and their new tenants – shepherds and graziers from the Borders – had introduced to replace the two-legged clansmen and their black cattle. The bard of Clan Chisholm bemoaned the new dispensation:

> Our chief has lost his feeling of kinship, he prefers sheep
> in the glen and his young men in the Highland regiments.

When, at the time of the Crimean War, recruiters visited the deserted glens to replenish these Highland regiments, they were told, 'Since you have preferred sheep to men, let sheep defend you.' The sentiment was echoed in the poem 'Skye' by Alexander Nicolson (1827–93):

> Woe be to them who choose for a clan
> Four-footed people.

See also YEAR OF THE SHEEP.

Four Maries or **Marys, the** Four ladies-in-waiting of Mary Queen of Scots: Mary Seton, Mary Beaton, Mary Fleming and Mary Livingston. In Scots, the word *marie* (cognate with Icelandic *maer*, a maid or virgin) formerly denoted a maid-of-honour to the queen. All of Mary's Marys were of noble birth, and had been picked by Mary's mother, Mary of Guise, to be the queen's companions when she was sent to France as a girl. Many years later, when the queen lay ill in Jedburgh following her desperate moorland ride to see Bothwell at Hermitage Castle in 1566 – after he had been wounded by Little Jock Elliot (*see* WHA DAUR MEDDLE WI ME?) – she was looked after exclusively by the Four Marys.

In some versions of the ballad 'Mary Hamilton' (aka 'The Fower Maries' or 'The Queen's Maries') – about a lady-in-waiting to a queen of Scots who bears the king's child, kills it, and is subsequently hanged – the eponymous heroine is one of the 'Four Maries':

> Last nicht there was four Maries,
> The nicht there'll be but three;
> There was Marie Seton, and Marie Beton,
> And Marie Carmichael, and me.

However, neither Mary Hamilton nor Mary Carmichael were among the historical 'Four Maries'. Mary Carmichael may have been introduced in preference to Mary Livingston for the sake of euphony, while the ballad collector Francis J. Child identified Mary Hamilton herself with a woman of that name who was a maid of honour to the Russian empress and who was executed for murdering her own child on 14 March 1719. The balladeers may

subsequently have conflated her fate with the story of Mary Queen of Scots' ladies. Others have pointed out that there are versions of the ballad that date from before the 18th century.

Four pleas of the Crown, the The offences of murder, rape, arson and robbery, which in feudal times could not be tried in baronial courts (*see* PIT AND GALLOWS) but only in a royal court. Since the 17th century, this has meant the High Court of Justiciary, although these days that court has exclusive jurisdiction only over murder and rape; robbery and arson can be tried in sheriff courts.

Four stoups o' misery, the In the 19th century, a bitter appellation for the handloom, which could not compete with the industrial power-looms in the mills. The allusion is to the four posts or *stoups* of the handloom.

Four Towns of Lochmaben, the *See* KING'S KINDLY TENNANTS, THE.

Foustie or **fowstie** A species of breakfast roll, originally known as a *fustian scone*. They are substantial, white and floury, although their original name referred to the fact that they were once coarser in texture, containing oatmeal; *fustian* is a coarse fabric of cotton mixed with flax or wool.

Fox, the Red *See* APPIN MURDER, THE.

Francie and Josie A pair of shiftless but sharp-suited Glasgow lads, the comic creations of Rikki Fulton (1924–2004) and Jack Milroy (1915–2001). They first appeared on stage in 1958, and transferred to TV in 1962 with the series *The Adventures of Francie and Josie*. One of their catchphrases was 'nyuch nyuch', an appreciative comment on viewing an attractive young woman.

Frank Lockwood's Island A tiny island off the south coast of Mull, to the east of the mouth of Loch Buie. It was named after the brother-in-law of the 21st Maclean of Duart, the English lawyer and Liberal politician Sir Frank Lockwood (1846–97), who briefly served as solicitor-general in 1894–5.

Fred the Shred The nickname of Paisley-born Fred Goodwin (b.1958), chief executive of the Royal Bank of Scotland from 2001 until his resignation on 31 January 2009, a month before RBS announced a loss of £24 billion, the largest corporate loss in UK history. Goodwin had by this time secured himself an annual pension of £703,000, despite the government having to bail out the bank. He earned his nickname while chief executive of the Clydesdale Bank in the later 1990s, on account of his ruthless cost cutting. He has also been described as 'a corporate Attila'. Goodwin was awarded a knighthood in 2004 for services to banking, but this was rescinded in 2012 – leading to many headlines along the lines of 'A reputation shredded'.

Free Church of Scotland *See* WEE FREES.

Freedom and whisky gang thegither An assertion made by Burns at the conclusion of 'The Author's Earnest Cry and Prayer, to the Right Honourable and Honourable, the Scotch Representatives in the House of Commons' (1786) regarding the activities of 'damn'd Excise-men' in regard to 'that curst restriction / On AQUAVITAE'. The following year Burns himself became an exciseman. Burns's association of alcohol and freedom has proved a popular one with Scots, although there is no mention of whisky in the DECLARATION OF ARBROATH. A contrary view is supplied by Hugh MacDiarmid in *A Drunk Man Looks at the Thistle* (1926):

> The wee reliefs we ha'e in booze,
> Or wun at times in carnal states,
> May hide frae us but canna cheenge
> The silly horrors o' oor fates.

See also ALCOHOLISM VS COMMUNISM.

'Freedom Come-All-Ye, The' A modern folk song composed in 1960 by Hamish Henderson, the great radical songwriter, for CND demonstrators. It is sung to the tune of 'The Bloody Fields of Flanders' – a tune first heard by Henderson at the beachhead at Anzio, while serving in Italy during the Second World War. Henderson explains that in the Come-All-Ye 'I have tried to express my hopes for Scotland, and for the survival of humanity on this beleaguered planet.'

> So come all ye at hame wi' Freedom,
> Never heed whit the hoodies croak for doom.
> In your hoose a' the bairns o' Adam
> Can find breid, barley-bree and painted room.

Some claim 'The Freedom Come-All-Ye' as Scotland's national anthem, but this ignores the anti-imperialist internationalism of the song – which has, indeed, become known as 'the Scots Internationale'. In one verse it commemorates the communist RED CLYDESIDE hero John Maclean, the FIGHTING DOMINIE ('When Maclean meets wi' his freens in Springburn ...'). A 'Come-all-ye' is a type of folk song beginning 'Come all ye (young gentlemen, brave ladies, etc., etc.) and listen to my song.'

Freedom is a noble thing A famous line from John Barbour's *The Brus* (*c.* 1375), which celebrates Scotland's victory in the Wars of Independence:

> A! fredome is a noble thing!
> Fredome maiss man to haif liking:
> Fredome all solace to man giffis,
> He levis at ease that freely levis!
> A noble heart may haif nane ease,
> Nae ellis nocht that may him please,
> Gif fredome failye.

See also DECLARATION OF ARBROATH; *LIBERTAS OPTIMA RERUM.*

Free Kirk *See* DISRUPTION OF 1843; WEE FREES.

Free Kirk pudding A steamed pudding including mixed spice, raisins and currants, and sometimes also lemon and orange zest. Its association with the Free Kirk is not altogether clear.

Free trade A 19th-century euphemism for smuggling, which was also known jocularly as the *gentle traffic*, as some of those involved were gentlefolk.

> '... I am fully persuaded that they are a' hand in glove with notorious Freetraders ... And for aught that I ken they may be art and part in supplying undutied stuff to various law-breaking, king-contemning grocers and even baillies. I am resolved that I'll lodge informations with the officers of His Majesty's Preventive forces and get the reward.' ... Then I minded that the Maxwells of Craigdarroch, all the seven big sons of them, and even the dour Cameronian father, were said to be deeper in the Gentle Traffic, as it was called, than any others in the locality.
> – S.R. Crockett, *The Raiders* (1894), chapter v

French leach, the *See* BIRDMAN OF STIRLING CASTLE, THE.

Freuchie and fry mice, Gang tae *See* GANG TAE BUCKIE!

Friend Mother in the Lord *See* BUCHANITES.

Frighten the French, she'd An ability attributed in Glasgow to the fiercer sort of woman.

Froissart's toponymy The 14th-century French chronicler Jean Froissart found Scottish place names somewhat challenging. In *Scottish Pageant* (volume 1, 1946), Agnes Mure Mackenzie collected a few choice examples of his versions:

Alquist	Dalkeith
Astroderne	Strathearn
Auercegne	Erskine
Bredane	Aberdeen
Estremelan	Stirling
Fii	Fife
Gedeours	Jeddart (Jedburgh)
Monshie	Menteith
Morette	Moray
Surlancke	Sutherland

As for personal names, Froissart rendered Sir John Sandilands as Sir John de Saynt de Laux, and Sir Archibald Douglas as Sir Ancebance de Duglas.

Two centuries later, Jean de Beaugué, who served with the French forces in Scotland in 1548, recounted his experiences in his *Histoire de la guerre d'Ecosse*. His rendering of certain Scottish place names is also worth recording:

Aberdim	Aberdeen
Dondy	Dundee
Montrosts	Montrose
Saint Ian d'Eston	St Johnstoun (i.e. Perth)

From Maidenkirk to John o'Groats *See* MAIDENKIRK TO JOHN O'GROATS.

FTP An abbreviation for 'fuck the pope', a sentiment expressed by the more bigoted sort of anti-Catholic in Scotland. It is often seen as graffiti or in internet chat forums. In the cyber world, FTP more inoffensively stands for 'file transfer protocol'.

Fuckand lyke ane furious fornicator *See* AY FUCKAND LYKE ANE FURIOUS FORNICATOR.

Fucking Halkirk *See* BLOODY ORKNEY.

Fundin' pint *See* FOUNDING PINT.

Funeral tea *See* HIGH TEA.

Fungle Road, the A hill track over the Mounth in Aberdeenshire, linking Aboyne in Deeside with Tarfside in Glen Esk. Its curious name may derive from Scots *fung*, describing the action of a restive horse in kicking up its legs, or alternatively meaning 'hurl violently'. It was formerly a busy trade route, but these days it is mostly frequented by mountain bikers. It was one of the many Scottish place names celebrated in Edwin Morgan's 'Canedolia: An Off-Concrete Scotch Fantasia':

> *what do you do?*
> we foindle and fungle, we bonkle and meigle and
> maxpoffle ...

Fur coat The 'winter hitch-hikers' friend'. Not an article of clothing but

> ... a particularly virulent cocktail of strong beers: a Fowlers Wee Heavy and a Carlsberg Special Lager. This brew did not keep the hitch-hiker warm, but it numbed his brain, thus serving for him a similar reality-blocking function as do coca leaves for Bolivian tin miners. Its name comes from the texture of the tongue after an over-indulgence in such refreshment.
> – Dave Brown and Ian Mitchell, *Mountain Days and Bothy Nights* (1987)

Fur coat and nae knickers *See* AW FUR COAT AND NAE KNICKERS.

Furry Boots City A nickname for Aberdeen coined in the 1980s by the journalist Tom Shields, then diarist on the *Glasgow Herald*. It refers to the habit of Aberdonians of inquiring as to the origin of outsiders: 'Fur aboots are ye from?' – *fur* being the local way of saying 'where'. *See also* GRANITE CITY, THE.

Fustian scone *See* FOUSTIE.

G

Gaberlunzie A word of obscure origin, originally denoting a licensed beggar, also known as a *King's Bedesman* or *Blue Gown*. Such a man, according to Scott in his introduction to *The Antiquary* (1816), 'belonged ... to the aristocracy of his order, and was esteemed a person of great importance'. Scott continues:

> These Bedesmen are an order of paupers to whom the Kings of Scotland were in the custom of distributing a certain alms, in conformity with the ordinances of the Catholic Church, and who were expected in return to pray for the royal welfare and that of the state. This order is still kept up. Their number is equal to the number of years which his Majesty has lived; and one Blue-Gown additional is put on the roll for every returning royal birthday. On the same auspicious era, each Bedesman receives a new cloak, or gown of coarse cloth, the colour light blue, with a pewter badge, which confers on them the general privilege of asking alms through all Scotland, – all laws against sorning, masterful beggary, and every other species of mendicity, being suspended in favour of this privileged class.

At the start of chapter iv, Scott quotes 'The Gaberlunzie Man', a traditional poem that supposedly recounts an adventure of James V in his disguise as the GOODMAN OF BALLENGEICH:

> The pawkie auld carle cam ower the lea,
> Wi' mony good-e'ens and good-morrows to me,
> Saying, Kind Sir, for your courtesy,
> Will ye lodge a silly puir man?
>   The Gaberlunzie Man.

Later, the word was applied to any beggar, peddler or tinker, and also to a beggar's bag or wallet. In *The Gaberlunzie's Wallet* (1843), James Ballantine includes a song called 'The Gaberlunzie', of which the following lines comprises the first verse:

> Blythe be the auld Gaberlunzie man,
> Wi' his wallet o' wit, he fills a' the lan';
> Wi' his blinks o' fun, and his blauds o' lear,
> O' a'thing that's gude he has walth to spare;
> Has a warm Scotch heart, and a braid Scotch
>   tongue,
> He has a' the auld sangs that ever were sung;
>   His daffin and quaffin, his glory and glee,
>   Lichts up the auld spunk o' the North Countrie.

Gaberlunzie is also the name of a Scottish folk band founded in the early 1970s by Robin Watson and Gordon Menzies.

Gable-endie An inhabitant of Montrose, so called because in the 19th century many houses in the town were built with their gable ends facing the street, owing to the shape and size of the plots of land being leased. Montrose FC are nicknamed the Gable-endies.

Gab o' May A spell of wintry weather in May (usually early in the month). *Gab*, literally 'mouth', is here probably used figuratively for 'opening', 'beginning'.

> The weather doesn't really turn until after the Gab o' May, the last snow storm that sweeps across the hills in the middle of May killing newborn lambs, nesting birds and the first spring flowers; a Calvinistic reminder that we shouldn't relax until the end of May.
> – *The Sunday Herald*, 28 March 1999

Gaelic Mafia, the The supposed network of Gaelic-speaking people from the Highlands and Islands who, it is said, monopolize jobs in the Gaelic media, especially BBC Scotland. It is said that the *eminence grise* behind it all is a shady figure known as the Modfather.

Gaick, the Loss of *See* LOSS OF GAICK, THE.

Gàidhealtachd, A' The Scottish Gaeltacht, i.e. the area where Gaelic is spoken as the native tongue.

Galloglasses *See* GALLOWGLASSES.

Gallous or **gallus** A Scots version of the word 'gallows', hence also denoting one who deserves a hanging; also used adjectivally of such a person. The word has come to acquire an air of approbation, and is now applied, especially in Glasgow, to any high-spirited, bold, cheeky, somewhat wild and un-law-abiding person.

Gallovidian Encyclopaedia, The *See* STAR O' DUN-GYLE, THE.

Gallowgate Gourmet, the A comic character created by Rikki Fulton in his television show *Scotch and Wry* (1978–92). The name parodies *The Galloping Gourmet*, a BBC TV show starring wine-slurping playboy chef Graham Kerr, first broadcast in 1968. In contrast, the Gallowgate Gourmet (taking his name from Gallowgate, a street in Glasgow) is a chain-smoking and utterly filthy and unhygienic chef. He presents his programme from Dirty Dick's Delicat'messen, and the recipes he offers the viewer are of an unsurpassed revolt-ingness.

Gallowglasses or **galloglasses** Heavily armed Gaelic-Norse mercenaries from the Hebrides who between the 13th and 16th centuries fought in various wars in Ireland. The word derives from the Irish *gallóglach*, from *gall*, 'foreigner', and *óglach*, 'young warrior-servant'. Formations of gallowglasses, armed with long spears and wearing knee-length mail shirts and conical iron helmets, were known for their iron discipline in resisting cavalry charges. One contemporary described them as 'grim of counten-ance, tall of stature, big of limb ... chiefly feeding on beef, pork and butter'.

> Turloch O'Neill ruled Tyrone in general with satisfac-tion to the government. But as dowry with his wife Agnes Campbell, daughter of the fourth Earl of Argyll, he got two thousand Hebridean Scots, and the enlist-ment of these professional fighters aroused suspicion. 'One Scot,' it was said, 'was worth two of the Irish.'
> – Edmund Curtis, *A History of Ireland* (1936)

Gallows Slot, the A feature on the shores of Carlingwark Loch, Castle Douglas.

> On the west side of Carlingwark Loch, between it and the public road, near to Lochbank House, there is still pointed out a small piece of rising ground, supposed to have been the pit into which the remains of the victims of Douglas cruelty or revenge were thrown. It is to this day called the 'Gallows Slot', or 'Gallows Pit'; and notwithstanding the time which has elapsed since the downfall of the Douglases in Galloway, it is recorded that human bones were turned up there in abundance, when making the present highway, about the beginning of the present century.
> – Malcolm McLachlan Harper, *Rambles in Galloway* (1876)

Gallus *See* GALLOUS.

Galshachs *See* GULSOCH.

Game's a bogey, the A children's expression in-dicating that something's gone wrong in the game, which should be restarted or abandoned. *Bogey* (or *bogie*) in this context denotes a hobgoblin or similar ghoul.

> That game was a bogey. Pub rules son, if a game doesn't get finished all bets are cancelled.
> – James Kelman, *A Chancer* (1985)

John McGrath's 1974 musical play *The Game's a Bogey* is a satire on the class struggle using a game-show format, in which the participants never get ahead of the game sufficiently to escape the poverty trap.

Games and dances *See*:
- BABBITY BOWSTER
- BAR-THE-DOOR
- BELLY-BLIND
- BLOCK, HAMMER AND NAIL
- BONSPIEL
- CAT IN BARREL
- CROOKIT ZAIDIE
- DASHING WHITE SERGEANT, the

- EIGHTSOME REEL
- GAY GORDONS
- HACKY-DUCK
- HANDBA
- HAP-THE-BEDS
- HAT AND RIBBON RACE
- HAWICK BA
- HEADIM AND CORSIM
- Passing through the mires of HECKLEBIRNIE
- HET BEANS AND BUTTER
- HIGHLAND FLING
- HIGHLAND GAMES
- JOCKIE BLINDIE
- KING'S BA
- LONDONS
- LOWP-THE-DYKE
- PAPA STOUR SWORD DANCE
- RED HOSE RACE
- The ROARING GAME
- SCOTCH AND ENGLISH
- SCOTCH HORSES
- SHUFFLE-THE-BROGUE
- SKIN-THE-CUDDY
- SMUGGLE THE GEG
- SWORD DANCE
- TAM O' REEKIE
- TAPPIE-TEENIE
- TWISTING THE FOUR LEGS FROM A COW
- WILLIE WASTELL

Gane ... *See* GONE ...

Gang agley Go astray.

> The best laid schemes o' mice an' men
> Gang aft a-gley.
> – Robert Burns, 'To a Mouse' (1786)

Gang by oneself To abandon normality for madness; to throw a major wobbly.

Gang doon the brae To go downhill (*brae*, 'hillside', 'slope'), either physically through ageing, or owing to a decline in one's fortunes. Hence the proverb, 'If a man's gaun doun the brae, ilka ane gies him a jundie' (Andrew Henderson, *Scottish Proverbs*, 1832), i.e. if a man's on the way down, everyone gives him a shove.

Gang owre the march *See* MARCH, THE.

Gangrel scrape-gut A vagrant fiddler. The 19-year-old Walter Scott was so called by his father, Walter Scott WS. At this time the younger Scott preferred to wander the countryside roistering than working as an apprentice in his father's law firm in Edinburgh.

Gang tae Buckie! Go away, with the small Moray fishing port standing in for hell. Banff (in Aberdeenshire) and Freuchie (in Fife) are also deployed as infernal euphemisms; a colourful variant is 'Gang tae Freuchie an fry mice!'

Garde Écossaise The 'Scots guard', the personal guard formed by Charles VII of France in 1418, reflecting the AULD ALLIANCE between the two countries. The Compagnie Écossaise remained the senior company of the Gardes du Corps (royal bodyguard) until the Revolution, although from the 16th century recruits were mostly French. Their captain stood at the king's right hand during coronations, and they were known as *les fiers Écossais* ('the proud Scots'; *see* FIER COMME UN ECOSSAIS). The Compagnie Écossaise was revived after the overthrow of Napoleon, and finally disbanded following the abdication of Charles X in 1830. There is a story that after the defeat of Francis I at Pavia in 1525, a remnant of the Garde Écossaise were retreating over the Alps near the Simplon Pass when they found themselves trapped in a storm, and ended up settling in the area. Their descendants became known as 'the Lost Clan'.

Garden of Scotland, the The Carse of Gowrie, a stretch of fertile land on the north side of the Firth of Tay, between Perth and Dundee. It is renowned for its cultivation of soft fruit, especially raspberries. *Carse* denotes water-meadows, from Old Norse *kjarr*, while Gowrie is Gaelic *gaibhre*, 'of the goat'.

> 'Twas on a simmer's afternoon,
> A wee afore the sun gaed doun,
> A lassie wi' a braw new goun
> Cam' owre the hills to Gowrie.
>
> The rosebud washed in simmer's shower
> Bloomed fresh within the sunny bower;
> But Kitty was the fairest flower
> That e'er was seen in Gowrie.

To see her cousin she cam' there;
And oh! the scene was passing fair,
For what in Scotland can compare
Wi' the Carse o' Gowrie?
  – Lady Carolina Nairne (the FLOWER OF STRATHEARN),
  'The Lass o' Gowrie'

Garden of Shetland, the The isle of Fetlar, so called because of its particularly fertile soil.

Garden party Formerly, an ironic Glaswegian term for a gathering of drunks and down-and-outs in a park or on wasteland. The preferred beverage was usually some sort of ELECTRIC SOUP. Such gatherings are now rare, as even civilized al fresco drinking is against the law in Glasgow.

Gardyloo The famous warning cry formerly uttered by servants in the Old Town of Edinburgh as they tipped the contents of the household's chamber pots from high windows into the street below.

> At ten o'clock at night the whole cargo is flung out of a back window that looks into some street or lane, and the maid calls *Gardy loo* to the passengers.
>   – Tobias Smollett, *Humphry Clinker* (1771)

If a passerby, on hearing the shout, should feel that he or she was in imminent danger of inundation, the thing to do was to cry 'Haud yer hand!' The word *gardyloo*, which was also applied to the contents of the pots, is first recorded in 1662 as *gardelue*, and is assumed to derive from French *gardez (vous de) l'eau* or *(prenez) garde à l'eau*, 'beware the water'. In his *Journal of a Tour to the Hebrides* (1785), James Boswell describes his embarrassment when accompanying Dr Johnson to Edinburgh in 1773:

> Mr Johnson and I walked arm-in-arm up the High Street, to my house in James's Court: it was a dusky night: I could not prevent his being assailed by the evening effluvia of Edinburgh. I heard a late baronet, of some distinction in the political world in the beginning of the present reign, observe, that 'walking the streets of Edinburgh at night was pretty perilous, and a good deal odoriferous'. The peril is much abated, by the care which the magistrates have taken to enforce the city laws against throwing foul water from the windows; but, from the structure of the houses in the old town, which consist of many stories, in each of which a

different family lives, and there being no covered sewers, the odour still continues. A zealous Scotsman would have wished Mr Johnson to be without one of his five senses upon this occasion. As we marched slowly along, he grumbled in my ear, 'I smell you in the dark!'

On Ben Nevis, the couloir below the old summit observatory was dubbed Gardyloo Gully, for reasons that do not need explaining. *See also* AULD REEKIE; FLOWERS OF EDINBURGH.

Garelochhead, the Battle of *See* BATTLE OF GARELOCHHEAD, THE.

Garret exposed to the north wind, a Scotland, according to John Arbuthnot; *see under* BULL, PEG. The metaphor presumably alludes to Scotland's geographical position, vis à vis its southern neighbour. For his part, the Revd Sydney Smith called Scotland 'That garret of the earth – that knuckle-end of England'; *see* LAND OF CALVIN, OATCAKES AND SULPHUR.

Garvellachs, the *See* ISLES OF THE SEA, THE.

Gathering of the clans Formerly the assembling of a clan or group of allied clans, often summoned by a FIERY CROSS, as a prelude to war. Such a gathering occurred at Glenfinnan on 19 August 1745 when the Marquess of Tullibardine raised the young pretender's standard to mark the start of the '45 Jacobite Rebellion. In more recent times, the term has denoted a peaceful reunion of the members of a particular clan, or a group of clans, for example the march through Edinburgh of representatives of some 130 clans during the HOMECOMING SCOTLAND celebrations in 2009. Such gatherings are usually accompanied by massed pipers, HIGHLAND GAMES and other manifestations of tartanry.

Gaun fit's aye gettin', a An expression from the Northeast, literally 'a going foot is always getting', i.e. those who put the effort in get the good results.

Gaup-the-lift Literally, 'gawp at the sky', a term applied to someone who walks along with their nose in the air.

Gay Gordons Originally a nickname of the Gordon Highlanders, and subsequently the name of a lively Scottish country dance, supposedly once popular in the regiment. The 'Gay' in the name predates the denotation 'homosexual'. *See also* REGIMENTAL NICKNAMES.

Geddes, Jenny The (possibly legendary) old woman who, according to tradition, on 23 July 1637 hurled her stool at John Hanna, Dean of Edinburgh, in St Giles's Kirk, when he first started to use Charles I's hated new prayer book. A general riot ensued. As she hurled the stool (or, in another account, as she hit her neighbour with her bible as he began one of the prescribed responses), she is said to have shouted:

> Deil colic the wame o' ye, fause thief! Daur ye say Mass in my lug?
> ('The Devil give you stomach ache, false thief! Dare you say Mass in my ear?')

David Masson, appointed Professor of Rhetoric and English Literature at the University of Edinburgh in 1865, and known both for his Free Kirk principles and his promotion of university education for women, opined:

> Jenny Geddes and her stool are precious articles of our national belief not to be given up without danger of sapping the foundations of society in our beloved Scotland.
> – Quoted in G. Donaldson, *Four Centuries: Edinburgh University Life* (1983)

Gee one's beaver, etc., to *See* JEE ONE'S BEAVER, TO.

Geg, geggie *See* FAIR FORTNIGHT; SHUT YER GEGGIE; SMUGGLE THE GEG.

General Assembly The governing court and legislative body of the Church of Scotland, which meets annually in May in Edinburgh. Large numbers of ministers, elders and others (collectively known as 'commissioners', or, informally, as 'fathers and brethren') foregather, representing their presbyteries and presided over by the Moderator, who holds the post for a year. In the past, the General Assembly (which first met in 1560) was held in different cities, such as Perth, St Andrews and Glasgow, but since 1929 it has nearly always been held in the Assembly Hall on the Mound in Edinburgh. Being a highly representative body, the Assembly has long had an important political function, often finding itself at odds with the impositions of the secular power – whether Stuart absolutism in the 17th century or hard-hearted Thatcherism in the 20th.

> The Scots had no reason to set any value on their Parliament. The Scots Parliament was a time-serving institution and echoed the voice of whoever was in power. It was to the General Assembly of the Church that the Scots looked for their liberty.
> – Norman Maclean, *The Years of Fulfilment* (1953)

When the General Assembly is in session, it is not all hard work and no play. In 1784, for example, when Mrs Siddons appeared on the Edinburgh stage, the General Assembly was obliged to arrange its business so as not to coincide with her performances; while a survey in 1842 found that Edinburgh's 200 brothels were at their busiest when the General Assembly was in session (*see also under* DANUBE STREET). Today the commissioners must content themselves with tea and cucumber sandwiches at the garden party laid on for them at Holyrood by the Queen or her representative.

> I saw twa items on
> The TV programme yesterday.
> 'General Assembly of the Church of Scotland'
> Said ane – the ither 'Nuts in May'.
> I lookit at the pictures syne
> But which was which I couldna say.
> – Hugh MacDiarmid, 'Nuts in May' (1953)

See also DISRUPTION OF 1843; PLAYPEN, THE; SERMON ON THE MOUND, THE.

Geneva print, to read *See* READ GENEVA PRINT, TO.

Gentle Annie A propitiatory name in the Northeast for the southwesterly gales that come around the time of the spring equinox, preventing the fishermen from setting out to sea. Hence the proverbial advice to 'Pit a saxpence in thee pooch for Gentle

Annie', i.e. put some money aside for a rainy day. Foam-flecked waves were known as the *feathers in Gentle Annie's hat*.

Gentle Lochiel, the The sobriquet of Donald Cameron of Lochiel (*c*.1700–48), chief of Clan Cameron. In 1745 he tried to persuade the YOUNG PRETENDER to return to France, believing his expedition was doomed, but when the prince determined to go through with the rebellion, Lochiel supported him loyally, declaring 'I shall share the fate of my prince and so shall every man over whom nature or fortune has given me any power.' Clan Cameron suffered many casualties at Culloden, and Lochiel himself was badly wounded, although he eventually escaped to France. His sobriquet refers to his gallantry and magnanimity; for example, he made sure that the Hanoverian prisoners taken at Prestonpans received decent treatment, and ordered that no reprisals be made against the Whigs of Edinburgh or Glasgow.

Gentleman in Black Velvet *See* 'LITTLE GENTLEMAN IN BLACK VELVET, THE'.

Gentleman Jim *See* SLIM JIM.

Gentlemen Adventurers of Fife, the A group of 12 Fife merchants whom James VI authorized to settle Lewis, the inhabitants of which he considered 'ALLUTERLIE BARBARES'. In 1598 an act of Parliament had required all those who claimed land in the Highlands and Islands to produce their deeds before the Privy Council. The Macleods of Lewis could not do so, because their deeds had been stolen by their bitter rivals, the Mackenzies. James gave the Adventurers and their small army permission to pacify the natives by all means necessary, including 'slauchter, mutilation, fyre-raising, or utheris inconvenieties'. In the face of this onslaught, the Macleods and Mackenzies temporarily buried their differences, and succeeded in expelling the Adventurers. The two clans then resumed hostilities, with the Mackenzies coming out as top-dogs on Lewis.

Gentle Persuasion, the The Episcopalian Church in Scotland, so-called in the 18th and 19th centuries because many of its adherents, especially in the Northeast, were members of the gentry or aristocracy.

Gentle Poet of Lochleven, the The sobriquet of the weaver's son Michael Bruce (1746–67), who was born in the village of Kinnesswood, overlooking Loch Leven in Fife. As a boy he spent his summers herding cattle on the Lomond Hills, and later attended Edinburgh University. He went on to work as a schoolteacher at Forest Mill near Clackmannan, but suffered from poverty and isolation, and gradually succumbed to consumption. Shortly before his death, at the age of only 21, he wrote 'Lochleven', contrasting memories of his idyllic youth with his present miserable state:

> Thus sung the youth, amid unfertile wilds
> And nameless deserts, unpoetic ground!
> Far from his friends he stray'd, recording thus
> The dear remembrance of his native fields,
> To cheer the tedious night, while slow disease
> Prey'd on his pining vitals, and the blasts
> Of dark December shook his humble cot.

Gentle traffic, the *See* FREE TRADE.

George Square, Battle of *See* BATTLE OF GEORGE SQUARE.

German lairdie, a wee wee *See* WEE, WEE GERMAN LAIRDIE, A.

Gers, the *See* FOOTBALL CLUB NICKNAMES.

Get aff at Paisley, to To practise coitus interruptus, Paisley being the last stop before Glasgow Central. In Edinburgh they *get off at Haymarket* (the stop before Waverley Station).

Get one's pennyworths oot o' someone, to To get one's own back, to wreak revenge.

Get roun the mou wi' an English dishclout, to To adopt an anglicized manner of speech.

Get stuck in like twa men an a wee fella An adjuration to tuck in heartily.

Get the crap on, to *See* CRAP.

Get the jile, to To receive a prison sentence. In 2007 the following exchange occurred on kintyreforum.com regarding that year's Miss South Carolina:

> *Bobbie En Tejas (from the USA):* The unfortunate thing about this competition is that she is from the south, where there is a stereotype of ignorance, and what she did is probably reinforce that to a lot of people! She did handle herself well in the follow-up interview though. *Pete Reek:* Is ah this hanlin yersell, whether well done or naw, allowed on the telly ower therr Bubba? Yi mite get the jile ower here if yi wur lake that on the box.

Get the road, to A Glaswegian expression meaning to be given the sack.

Get the smit, to To be smitten with love, or, more literally, to become infected with some disease. To *gie someone the smit* is to infect them.

Get yer heid in yer hands an' yer teeth tae play wi', to To be subjected to a severe telling off. In some circumstances, it may be one's *lugs* ('ears') that one is given to play with.

Get yer puggie up or **take a puggie** or **lose yer puggie** To lose one's temper. *Puggie* is a diminutive of *pug*, 'monkey'. *Fou as a puggie* means 'dead drunk' (*see* FOU). Perhaps unrelatedly, a *puggie* is contemporary Glaswegian for a fruit machine or a cash dispenser.

Get Younger Every Day An advertising slogan used in the 1950s by the Scottish brewer William Younger & Co.

Ghillie *See* GILLIE.

Ghost-bird, the The name given by the St Kildans to the last great auk (or 'garefowl') in the British Isles, caught on Stac an Armin in July 1840:

> It was described as being about the size of a year-old lamb, with a head like a razor-bill, and short wings, so that it could not fly. The men caught the bird, tied a rope to its leg, and kept it for two or three days. The extraordinary appearance of the bird impressed the men so much that they thought it was a ghost, and looked upon it as the cause of the bad weather they were experiencing. They, therefore, killed the poor bird, and threw it at the back of the house, covering it with stones. It has ever since gone by the name of the 'ghost-bird'.
> – J. Wiglesworth, M.D., F.R.C.P., *St. Kilda and its Birds* (1903)

In other accounts, the men believed it to be a witch, rather than a ghost.

Ghoulies and ghosties The subject of a traditional prayer:

> From ghoulies and ghosties
> And long-leggedy beasties
> And things that go bump in the night,
> Good Lord, deliver us!

Giant MacAskill The sobriquet of Angus MacAskill (1825–63), who, at 7 ft 9 in (2.36 m) tall, is thought to have been the largest 'natural' giant (i.e. one without medical abnormalities) ever to have lived. Known also as Gille Mòr (Gaelic, 'big lad') or the Cape Breton Giant, he was born on the island of Berneray in the Sound of Harris, and around 1831 emigrated with his family to Cape Breton Island in Canada. He was formidably strong, and it was said could lift a horse over a 4 ft (1.2 m) fence.

Gibbites *See* SWEET SINGERS, THE.

Gibble-gabble Tittle-tattle. As the Revd T. Whyte Paterson so sapiently points out in *The Wyse-Sayin's o' Solomon Rendered into Scots* (1917), 'The gibble-gabble o' a fule is the cause o' mony a COLLIE-SHANGIE.'

Gie it laldie, to To go at it hammer and tongs; said of a range of activities, from fighting to drinking. A *laldie* was originally a beating or thrashing, but the word was also applied to any energetic action; it may ultimately derive from Old English *læl*, 'whip'.

> He focht alane for Israel against the Philistine,
> An' fairly gied them laldie wi' the jaw-bane o' a cuddie.
> – W.D. Cocker, *Further Poems: Scots and English* (1935)
> [*cuddie*, 'ass']

Gie's-a-piece What today's metropolitan glitterati would call a ligger, i.e. a flattering freeloader or parasitic hanger-on. *See also* PIECE.

Gie someone his or her character, to To tell someone exactly what you think of them.

Gie someone his or her coffee, to To give someone a real telling off.

> 'I'll gie him's coffee for yon trick!' ... A shrill scream from the person who was getting his coffee showed what sort of larking was going on.
> – Neil Roy, *Horseman's Word* (1895)

Gie someone rhubarb, to To administer a severe beating. To *gie someone a sackfu' o' sair banes* means the same.

Gift of one Edinburgh lad to another, the *See* MY ELDER BROTHER IN MISFORTUNE.

Gigelorum An elusive creature described by John G. Campbell in his *Superstitions of the Highlands and Islands of Scotland* (1900):

> The giolcam-daoram, or gigelorum, is the smallest of all animals. It makes its nest in the mite's ear and that is all that is known about it.

Gilderoy or **Gillie Roy** (Gaelic *Gille Ruadh*, 'the red-haired lad') The byname of Patrick Roy MacGregor, a notorious CATERAN or outlaw active in Deeside and elsewhere in the 1630s. He and a band of his fellow MacGregors from Perthshire had been hired to deal with an outbreak of looting and plundering, but, once they had dealt with the raiders, they turned cattle rustlers themselves. Their hiding place was supposedly the rocky gorge called the Vat in the Vat Burn on the flanks of Culblean Hill above Loch Kinord, a few miles west of Aboyne. Gilderoy extended his depredations as far as apparently Lennox and Strathspey. His exploits came to the attention of the Privy Council, which in March 1636 issued the following proclamation:

> Patrick MacGregor and others hes associat and combynned themselves togidder, hes thair residence neere to the forests of Culblene [Culblean] ... and from these parts they come in darknes of the night down to the incountrie, falls unaware upon the houses and goods of his Majesties poore subjects and spoyles theme of their goods, and, being full handed with

the spoyle they goe backe agane to the bounds forsaids where they keepe mercat of thair goods peaceablie and uncontrolled, to the disgrace of law and order. For the remeid whairof the Lords of Secreit Counsell charge all landslord and heretours, where thir brokin lymmars has thair resset, abode, and starting holes, to rise, putt thamselffes in armes, and to hunt, follow and persew, shout and raise the fray, and with fire and sword to persew the said theeves, and never leave aff thair persute till they be ather apprehended or putt out of the countrie.

Gilderoy was eventually captured, and he and five of his companions were brought to trial in Edinburgh on 7 June 1636. Sentence having been passed, Gilderoy was given the distinction of being hanged from a higher gibbet than his fellows, a fate that expressed the extremity of his crimes; hence the expression (largely US) *higher than Gilderoy's kite*, meaning 'so high as to be out of sight'.

For reasons that are unclear, Gilderoy was heavily romanticized by the balladeers, who had him mourned by many a young lady. One ballad starts thus:

> My love he was as brave a man
>   As ever Scotland bred;
> Descended from a Highland clan,
>   A kateran to his trade.
> No woman then, or womankind,
>   Had ever greater joy,
> Than we two when we lodged alone,
>   I and my Gilderoy.

Another ballad contains the following:

> O sic twa charming een he had,
>   A breath as sweet as rose,
> He never ware a Highland plaid,
>   But costly silken clothes;
> He gained the love of ladies gay,
>   None e'er to him was coy;
> Ah, wae is me! I mourn this day
>   For my dear Gilderoy.

A number of improbable legends arose around Gilderoy, as related, for example, by Captain Charles Johnson (*fl.*1730) in his *Lives and Exploits of English Highwaymen, Pirates and Robbers*, in which Gilderoy becomes a gentleman-thief and pan-European celebrity. In one episode, he picks the purse of

Cardinal Richelieu in sight of the French king, while in another, disguised as the household steward, he makes off with the valuable plate of the Duke of Medina-Celi in Madrid. Johnson even has Gilderoy playing the highwayman with Oliver Cromwell in Galloway:

> ... the first mischief he did was shooting Oliver's horse, which, falling on his side as soon as wounded, broke the Protector's leg; as for his servants, he shot one of them through the head, and the other begging quarter, it was granted; but Oliver being disabled, he had the civility to put him on an ass, and, tying his legs under his belly, sent both of them to seek their fortune.

In reality, the MacGregors were particularly notorious for lawlessness; *see* MACGREGOR, PROSCRIPTION OF CLAN; ROB ROY.

Gille Mòr *See* GIANT MACASKILL.

Gillie, ghillie or **gilly** A word (derived, like KEELIE, from Gaelic *gille*, 'lad' or 'servant') formerly denoting a manservant or personal attendant of a Highland chieftain. A *gillie-mor* (Gaelic *mór*, 'big') was an attendant who carried the chief's armour, while the lowlier *gillie-casflue* (from Gaelic *cas fhliuch*, 'wet foot') had the job of carrying his master over wet places, such as bogs and fords; the term *gilliwetfit* was subsequently used pejoratively. Since the 19th century the word *gillie* has more commonly denoted a man who attends a fisherman or a sportsman out shooting, proffering advice and local knowledge.

Gillie Callum The name often given to the Highland sword dance, from the first two words of the song that gives the tune.

Gillie Roy *See* GILDEROY.

Gillies Hill A low eminence above the Bannock Burn. According to Barbour in *The Brus* (1370s), during the 1314 battle, Robert the Bruce ordered all the GILLIES (lads and servants) and other camp followers to conceal themselves behind the hill. When the battle was clearly turning to the advantage of the Scots, the gillies emerged from hiding to benefit from plunder, waving their clothes like flags

and banging their pots and pans. The English, taking them for a second Scottish army, took to their heels and fled.

Gilmerton Cove A series of mysterious underground passages and chambers carved out of the sandstone under the village of Gilmerton, now part of Edinburgh. George Patterson, a local blacksmith who died in 1737, claimed that he had carved them out himself between 1719 and 1724. He and his family certainly lived in them, and may have used one of the chambers as a pub (on one occasion Patterson was obliged to appear before Liberton Kirk Session on a charge of supplying liquor on the Sabbath). However, the excavations are thought to be older, and are too extensive for one man to have made in just five years – although the beds and tables carved out of the rock may well have been Patterson's work. Various theories have been put forward as to the origin of Gilmerton Cove. It may have been dug by miners in search of coal seams, and/or been used by smugglers or as a hiding place by Covenanters. More outlandish theories link it to the Hellfire Club, the Freemasons (a square and compasses are carved into the rock), a witches' coven (on the basis of a crude carving of a cat), and even the Knights Templar.

Ginger *See* SINGIN GINGER.

Girdle A griddle. *See* CULROSS GIRDLE; HEN ON A HET GIRDLE, LIKE A.

Girth *See* SANCTUARY.

Give ... *See* GIE ...

Glack someone's mitten To tip or bribe someone. *Glack* is literally a glen, defile or hollow, and as a verb means to make such a hollow in someone's hand, so to *glack someone's mitten* is to drop a coin into it.

Glamis, Monster of For this and other legends associated with the castle, *see under* EARL BEARDIE.

Glamour Although now borrowed by the English, and associated with the superficialities of contemporary celebrity culture, *glamour* was originally a Scots word meaning magic or enchantment, especially if it involves deceiving the eyes.

> Glamour ... this beautiful word had been bludgeoned to death by modern showmanship ... and English importation from Scotland where it had long signified magic with magical effect.
> – Ivor Brown, *A Word in Your Ear* (1942)

The word, often in the form *glamourie*, is found in old ballads such as 'Johnnie Faa':

> She came tripping down the stairs
> And all her maids before her,
> As soon as they saw her weel-far'd face,
> They coost their glamourie owre her.

It is also found in the work of a number of 18th-century poets, such as Allan Ramsay, Robert Fergusson and Burns:

> Ilk ghaist that haunts auld ha' or chaumer,
> Ye gipsy-gang that deal in glamour,
> And you, deep-read in hell's black grammar,
> Warlocks and witches ...
> – Robert Burns, 'On the Late Captain Grose's Peregrinations' (1789)

Glamour is in fact a corruption of 'grammar', which in the Middle Ages was taken as encompassing all learning, including the occult sciences.

> My one October night without a roof was bland as silk, with a late moon rising in the small hours and the mountains fluid as loch water under a silken dawn: a night of the purest witchery, to make one credit all the tales of *glamourie* that Scotland tries so hard to refute and cannot. I don't wonder. Anyone caught out of doors at four or five on such a morning would start spelling wrong. *Faerie* and *glamourie* and *witcherie* are not for men who lie in bed till eight. Find an October night warm enough to sleep out, and a dawn all mixed up with moonshine, and you will see that I am right. You too will be mis-spelled.
> – Nan Shepherd, *The Living Mountain* (1977)

See also CANT; JOCKEY; SLOGAN.

Glasgow *See* DEAR GREEN PLACE, THE; NO MEAN CITY; SECOND CITY OF THE EMPIRE; TINDERBOX CITY; TREE THAT NEVER GREW, THE.

Glasgow atheists According to the journalist Sandy Strang, these are people who go to OLD FIRM games to watch the football.

Glasgow bailies *See* GLASGOW MAGISTRATES.

Glasgow belongs to me *See* 'I BELONG TO GLASGOW'.

Glasgow Boys, the A loose grouping of Glasgow painters, including James Guthrie, Joseph Crawhall, E.A. Hornel, George Henry and John Lavery, active especially in the 1880s and 1890s. Although sometimes referred to as 'Scotland's Impressionists', they were more influenced by earlier French *plein-air* painters such as Corot, Millet and Jules Bastien-Lepage. Rather than depicting modern urban life, as the French Impressionists did, they belied their urban origin and their name and became what Tom Nairn has characterized as 'valedictory realists', painting scenes of women and children involved in agricultural work, scenes that towards the end of the 19th century represented a vanishing way of life. East Lothian and the Berwickshire countryside round Cockburnspath were particularly popular destinations for the Glasgow Boys' *plein-air* expeditions, and their depictions of cabbages are so precise that the actual varieties can be identified: as Ian Jack has written, 'Nobody painted brassica better or so often – these young men were to cabbage plots what RA portraitists were to kings' (*Guardian*, 30 October 2010).

Glasgow Empire Theatre *See* HOUSE OF TERROR, THE.

Glasgow Fair, the *See* FAIR FORTNIGHT.

Glasgow Girls, the A group of female designers and artists active at the turn of the last century, including Margaret and Frances MacDonald (also members of the GLASGOW SCHOOL), Norah Neilson Gray, Ann Macbeth and Jessie Wylie Newbery.

Glasgow Glutton, the Robert Hall (d.1843), more familiarly known as Rab Ha' or Haw, a celebrated vagrant of the city, who lived by taking bets as to how much he could consume at a sitting. In a famous competition held in the Saracen's Head Inn (see SARRY HEID, THE), he defeated a rival tren-cherman billed as 'the Yorkshire Pudding', and on another occasion ate an entire calf, served up in pies. His feats gave rise to the following children's rhyme:

Rab Ha', the Glesga Glutton,
Et ten loaves an' a leg o' mutton.

Subsequently, the term *Rab Ha'* has been applied to any person of prodigious appetite. The name has also been borrowed by a restaurant in Glasgow's Merchant City.

Glasgow grin A blackly humorous term for a razor (or knife) slash across the cheeks, from the lips to the ears. Before inflicting this injury, the perpetrator may first ask the victim 'Kin yer mammy sew?' *Cf.* LOCKERBIE LICK.

Glasgow humour As Chic Murray so wisely ob-served, 'There's many a joke told in Glasgow that they won't laugh at in London. You know why? They can't hear it.' *See also* HOUSE OF TERROR, THE.

Glasgow Keelies A nickname for the Highland Light Infantry. *See* KEELIE; REGIMENTAL NICK-NAMES.

Glasgow kiss A headbutt, also known as a *Glasgow nod* or a Govan or GORBALS KISS.

The sound of bygone battles was steel on steel,
Even cannon's roar had some appeal.
There is one thing I'll never miss,
The sickening sound of a Glasgow kiss.
  - Frank McNie, 'A Glasgow Kiss'

Glasgow magistrates or **bailies** Red herrings, in other words, kippers. They were said to have been invented or introduced by the Glasgow merchant Walter Gibson, who was provost of the city in 1687–8.

Glasgow's Miles Better The SLOGAN of a cam-paign launched in 1983 by Lord Provost Michael Kelly, with the intention of encouraging tourism and inward investment. Landmarks in the city's subsequent regeneration included the opening of

the magnificent new building housing the Burrell Collection, the erection of the Scottish National Exhibition and Conference Centre (aka the BIG RED SHED), the Glasgow Garden Festival of 1988, and the nomination of the city as the 1990 European City of Culture. The slogan and the campaign – one of the first to successfully rebrand a city – were developed by Struthers Advertising.

Glasgow pales Small haddock that have been split, brined and then lightly smoked, until they have acquired the colour of pale straw.

Glasgow Plague, the Glasgow had, like most other parts of Britain, been visited by the plague in the 14th century at the time of the Black Death, and thereafter had suffered renewed outbreaks in the 16th and 17th centuries. But the city also experi-enced a visitation as recently as 1900, involving 48 reported cases, mostly in the slums south of the river. There were 16 deaths. It was presumed that the outbreak was caused by an infected rat disem-barking from a ship from the Far East, where an epidemic of bubonic plague had broken out in 1893–4.

Glasgow School, the A small group of Art Nouveau artists and designers active at the turn of the last century, including Charles Rennie Mackintosh, his wife Margaret MacDonald, her sister Frances and Herbert MacNair. They were sometimes dubbed by philistines the *Spook School*, alluding to their fond-ness for depicting otherworldly figures. The name Glasgow School is also sometimes applied to the GLASGOW BOYS.

Glasgow screwdriver Jocular slang for a hammer, suggesting Glaswegian joiners preferred to hammer in screws, only giving them a couple of turns at the end. Alternative terms are *Paisley screwdriver* or *Irish screwdriver*.

Glasgow toffee A species of toffee made with chocolate, golden syrup and vanilla essence.

Glenara *See* LADY'S ROCK.

Glenbogle *See* MONARCH OF THE GLEN.

Glen Cinema Fire, the The worst cinema disaster in Britain. It occurred on 31 December 1929 during a children's matinée at the Glen Cinema, Paisley. Some nitrocellulose film had caught fire in the spool room, and smoke spread into the auditorium, causing panic and a rush for the exits. The escape door into Dyers Wynd was padlocked, and 71 children died in the crush.

Glencoe, Lost Valley of *See* LOST VALLEY OF GLENCOE, THE.

Glencoe, Three Sisters of *See* THREE SISTERS OF GLENCOE, THE.

Glencoe Massacre *See* MASSACRE OF GLENCOE.

Glendale Martyrs, the Five crofters from Glendale, a settlement to the west of Dunvegan on Skye, who in 1883 refused to pay their rents, and then saw off both sheriff-officers and the police. As a consequence they were imprisoned for two months, leading to an outburst of public sympathy, which, like that attending the BATTLE OF THE BRAES the previous year, helped to bring in the Crofters Act of 1886.

Glenelg The village on the mainland opposite Skye is possibly the only palindromic place name in Scotland (though in the international stakes it comes way behind Madagascar's Anahanahana).

Glengarry A thick woollen cap with flat sides, and pointed fore and aft, similar to a forage cap. Sometimes there are a couple of ribbons at the back, and a chequered band round the bottom (the inspiration of the SILLITOE TARTAN). It is often worn with Highland dress, and forms part of the uniform of various regiments: the first to do so were the Glengarry Fencibles, formed by Alasdair Ranaldson MacDonell of Glengarry in 1794. This style of bonnet became more widely popular after Colonel Alastair MacDonell of Glengarry wore one when George IV (resplendent in kilt and flesh-coloured tights) visited Edinburgh in 1822. The Colonel (the model for Fergus Mac-Ivor in Scott's *Waverley; see* HIGHLAND PRIDE) was famously painted by Henry Raeburn wearing such a cap, in which he has stuck a feather or two. *See also* BALMORAL BONNET; BLUE BONNET; SCOTCH BONNET.

Glen Golly An improbably named, waterfall-filled defile in Sutherland, to the southeast of Foinaven and to the northeast of Gobernuisgach Lodge. The name is from the Gaelic *Gleanna Gallaidh*, meaning 'glen of the stranger', and the place is celebrated in the song '*Gleann-gallaidh, aig ceann Loch-Eireabuill*' by the 18th-century Gaelic bard Rob Donn ('brown-haired Rob'), who was born in nearby Strathmore, and who is sometimes referred to as 'the ROBERT BURNS OF GAELDOM'.

Glengore *See* GRANDGORE.

Glen of Sorrow, the A by-name of Glen Fruin, north of Helensburgh, site of the 1603 Slaughter of Lennox; *see* MACGREGOR, PROSCRIPTION OF CLAN.

Glen Saturday A special day in the Kilmarnock calendar:

> Many of my readers will have sunny memories of *Glen Saturday* (the third Saturday of April) and Craufurd-land Castle. On that day it was and still is customary for the children of the town to go in droves to the castle to gather 'glens' – as they term the yellow daffodils that grow in great abundance on a lawn behind the mansion. The later Mrs Craufurd of Craufurdland delighted to welcome the little people, and to load them with bouquets of the coveted flowers. None were sent away empty handed, the crop being often so abundant that hundreds more could be supplied.
> – Archibald R. Adamson, *Rambles Round Kilmarnock* (1875)

Glen Tilt, Battle of *See* BATTLE OF GLEN TILT.

Glesca or **Glesga** For phrases beginning thus, look under GLASGOW ...

Gloup Disaster, the On 20 July 1881, ten open fishing boats from the Gloup area of northern Yell, Shetland, were caught in a sudden storm, and 58 men lost their lives, leaving behind 34 widows and 85 orphans.

Glower at the mune till one falls i' the midden, to *See under* MOON.

Glunimie or **Glunyie-man** 'A rough unpolished boorish-looking man,' according to John Jamieson in his *Etymological Dictionary of the Scottish Language* (1825 Supplement), 'a term generally applied to a Highlander.' Jamieson cites some lines from the burlesque poet William Meston (?1688–1745):

> Upon a time, no matter where,
> Some Glunimies met at a fair,
> As deft and tight as ever wore
> A dirk, a targe and a claymore.

The word, not heard since the days of Sir Walter Scott, may come from Gaelic *glùineanach*, 'someone wearing garters', from *glùn*, 'knee'. Some 200 years earlier, a Highlander might have been contemptuously addressed as a *gluntoch* or *gluntow*, from Gaelic *glùn dubh*, 'black knee', implying his knees were hairy. *See also* HEEDRUM-HODRUM; HEUCHTER-TEUCHTER; TEUCHTER. *Compare* SASSENACH.

Go ... *See also* GANG ...

Goat's hair A rural term for cirrus cloud.

Goats, supernatural In his *Survivals in Belief Among the Celts* (1911), George Henderson gives the following version of a Hebridean tale, told to him by Hugh McLennan in 1895:

> A story is told of a he-goat having been seen very often in a certain part of the islands and of people who met with violence and sometimes with death when they came to the spot frequented by him. There was a suspicion that the goat was only a form assumed by a weaver (*breabadair*) in the place. A man called at the weaver's one day on his way through the country. The weaver asked where he was going to. The man told him. The weaver asked if he were not afraid of passing the spot where the goat was seen – a spot fatal to many. The man replied that he was not, that he bore his help on his hip ('*tha cobhair chruachainn agam*'). When he came to the spot the goat stood above him and began to attack him. The man was being worsted when the goat said: '*Cà 'eil do chobhair air chruachainn a nisd?*' 'Where is the help on your hip now?' The man replied as he drew forth a dagger he had on his hip: "'*S ann air a chuimhne bha'n diùlanas*,' 'It was thy memory that had the fortitude.' He killed the goat, and when he returned

to the weaver's house the blood of the weaver had frozen ('*bha fuil a' bhreabadair air reothadh*').

Goblin Ha' A magnificent underground Gothic vault – all that remains unruined of Yester Castle, near Gifford, East Lothian. The castle was built by the so-called Wizard of Yester, Sir Hugh or Hugo de Gifford or Giffard (d.1267), who had the reputation as a necromancer, and whose army of hobgoblins supposedly built the castle. The Goblin Ha' features in Sir Walter Scott's *Marmion* (1808):

> Of lofty roof, and ample size,
> Beneath the castle deep it lies:
> To hew the living rock profound,
> The floor to pave, the arch to round,
> There never toiled a mortal arm –
> It all was wrought by word and charm;
> And I have heard my grandsire say,
> That the wild clamour and affray
> Of those dread artisans of hell,
> Who laboured under Hugo's spell,
> Sounded as loud as ocean's war
> Among the caverns of Dunbar.
>   – Canto III, xix

God Bless the Duke of Argyll A rather contrived piece of 19th-century humour. It was then the custom, if one saw one's companion shrugging, to utter these words, the imputation being that one's companion was lousy. Alternatively one might say it while scratching oneself. The allusion was to the iron posts that George Douglas Campbell, 8th Duke of Argyll (1823–1900), had had erected to mark the bounds of his estates, which proved popular as scratching posts with verminous livestock.

God destroying Glasgow, on the necessity of *See* HEROD OF HILLHEAD, THE.

Gododdin An ancient British kingdom in Lothian, named after the Gododdin, the Welsh name of a tribe whom Ptolemy named the *Otadinoi*, and the Romans the *Votadini*. Their first capital was on Traprain Law near Haddington, but then they moved it to Edinburgh, which they called Dineiddyn (*see* DUNEDIN). The ancient Welsh poem *Y God-*

oddin, preserved in a 13th-century manuscript but traditionally ascribed to the 6th-century bard Aneirin, tells how 300 warriors of the Gododdin spent a year feasting and drinking in Dineiddyn before marching south to be annihilated by the Anglo-Saxons at the Battle of Catraeth or Catterick (*c.* AD 580–600). The kingdom of Gododdin collapsed when the Anglo-Saxons took Edinburgh in 638.

God's silly vassal What the radical reformer Andrew Melville called James VI to his face in 1592 during the latter's attempts to reassert a measure of royal authority over the Kirk. At this period 'silly' had a range of meanings, from 'lowly' to 'weak' to 'piteous', as well as 'foolish' (*see also* SILLIE REGENT, THE). The confrontation was recorded by Melville's nephew James in his diary:

> Mr Andro boir doun and utterit the commissioun as from the michtie God, calling the King bot Goddis sillie vassal, and taiking him be the sleive … 'I maun tell yow, thair is twa kingis and twa kingdomis in Scotland. Thair is Christ Jesus the King, and His kingdom the kirk, quhais subject King James the saxt is, and of quhais kingdom nocht a king, nor a lord, nor heid, bot a member.

For his part, James VI, a believer in the divine right of kings, put a rather different interpretation on his position in his *Trew Law of Free Monarchies* (1598), in which he stated that kings 'sit upon God his Throne in the earth, and have the count of their administration to give unto him'. In *Basilikon Doron* he went further, calling the monarch a 'little God'. Such beliefs were to lead his son Charles I to the scaffold. *See also* WISEST FOOL IN CHRISTENDOM, THE.

Golden Act, the The fond name given to the Charter of the Presbytery, a piece of legislation passed by James VI's Parliament in June 1592, by which the liberties and privileges of the Kirk were confirmed, and a Presbyterian form of government for the Kirk established in place of episcopacy.

Golden Horse of Loch Lundie, the A legendary horse, sometimes described as yellow, thought to be the Devil in disguise. Horses of this type feature in a number of tales from Caithness, eastern Sutherland

and Aberdeenshire. Such horses were possibly inspired by the herds of wild horses that survived in these areas into the 16th century. The story of the Golden Horse of Loch Lundie was retold a century or so ago by a Mr D.M. Rose in a letter to the *Scotsman*:

> Two men from Culmailie went one Sunday to fish on Loch Lundie, and they saw, pasturing in a meadow, one of the most lovely golden coloured ponies they had ever seen. One of the men determined to seize the animal and bring it home. His companion, in a state of great alarm tried to dissuade him, assuring him that the animal was none other than the devil in disguise. The man, nothing daunted, began to stalk the pony, declaring that if he could get a chance he would mount on the beast, even if it were the Evil One. At length he managed to get within reach, and making a bound he seized the bristling mane, and leaped on the animal's back. In an instant the pony gave one or two snorts that shook the hills, fire flashed from its eyes and nostrils, and tossing its tail into the air, it galloped away with the man to the hills, and he was never again seen by mortal being.
>
> According to another version, the yellow horse of Loch Lundie was last seen in a meadow near Brora by two boys who broke the Sabbath. They tried to mount the animal, and one of them succeeded in doing so. The other boy, getting alarmed, tried to withdraw, but found to his horror that his finger had stuck in the animal's side. With great presence of mind, he immediately pulled out his knife and cut off his finger. The pony immediately gave an appallingly shrill neigh and galloped madly away with his rider, who was never seen again.
>
> – Quoted in George Henderson, *Survivals in Belief Among the Celts* (1911)

See also BOOBRIE; KELPIE.

Golden Square, the The sobriquet of Edinburgh's St Andrew's Square, on account of the number of banks and insurance companies that have their major offices there.

Gonnae no dae that? or **Goannistoapa'?** Pray desist.

Gone tae potterlow A now rather dated North-eastern expression to describe food that has been spoilt in the cooking, or any other mess or shambles. A situation that has gone pear-shaped is also said to have *gone tae potterlow*, as is a person who has fallen on hard times. The phrase combines the expression *gone to pot* with a possible allusion to Napoleon's defeat at Waterloo. A similar phrase is *gone tae potterneeshin*, derived from the word *crockanition*, 'smithereens' (as in a broken *crock*, perhaps combined with per*dition*), with *pot* being substituted for *crock*.

Good ... *See also* GUID ...

Good God in Govan! A common Glasgow ejaculation. It was adopted as the title of Joe Sharp's 2005 memoir of working-class life.

Goodman of Ballengeich, the The name adopted by James V (remembered as 'the Poor Man's King') when he wandered in disguise among the common people in order to discover their complaints – for he did not trust his courtiers to give him true reports of the state of his kingdom. A *goodman* is a tenant, while Ballengeich (or Ballengiech) is, according to Scott in *Tales of a Grandfather*, 'a steep pass which leads down behind the castle of Stirling'. Apparently James's disguise was none too successful, as an English spy reported that the urchins would cry after him, 'There goes the King of Scotland!' However, the tale survives of how the Goodman was set upon by five gypsies on Cramond Brig, and to his aid came one John Howieson, a worker on the nearby farm of Braehead, a crown property. To express his thanks, James, pretending that he was a servant at the palace, invited Howieson to take a sneak look at the royal apartments. After the tour, Howieson eventually realized whom he had rescued when they entered the Great Hall, where all the courtiers doffed their hats except the Goodman. For his service to the king, James made Howieson the new owner of Braehead Farm.

Vis à vis the king's clandestine peregrinations, it is perhaps because of these that he is credited as the author of 'The Jolly Beggar':

> And we'll gang nae mair a roving
> Sae late into the night
> And we'll gang nae mair a roving, boys,
> Let the moon shine ne'er so bright.

This poem was famously imitated by Byron:

> So, we'll go no more a-roving
> So late into the night,
> Though the heart be still as loving,
> And the moon be still as bright.

It was perhaps the king's moonlit rovings that led Sir David Lindsay to accuse him of 'AY FUCKAND LYKE ANE FURIOUS FORNICATOR'. *See also* KING OF KIPPEN.

Goodman's croft An area of land left untilled to propitiate the Devil, a custom known from at least the time of the Reformation, and found in many parts of Britain, but particularly common in Northeastern Scotland. The Goodman or Guidman was, of course, the Devil himself. Other terms include *halyman's ley* (*see* HALYMAN), *Goodman's fauld*, *Clootie's croft* (*see* AULD CLOOTIE), and *the black faulie*.

> ... the Scotch are a nation of pessimists. They have found their religious vocation in Calvinism, the gloomiest and most terrible of creeds; and the spirit which embraced Calvinism like a bride informs their mythology and their fireside tales. Their tendency to devil-worship – to the propitiation of evil spirits – is illustrated by the hideous usage of the Good-man's Croft – a plot of ground near a village which was left untilled, set apart for, and dedicated to, the Powers of Evil, in the hope that their malignity might be appeased by the sacrifice, and that so they might be induced to spare the crops on the surrounding fields.
> – Sir George Douglas, *Scottish Folk and Fairy Tales* (1901), introduction

The custom had long been abominated by the Kirk, and in the 17th century the presbyters of Garioch in Aberdeenshire resolved to lobby Parliament for an act:

> Anent the horrible superstitioun used in Garioch and diverse parts of the countrey, in not labouring ane parcell of ground dedicate to the Devil, under the name of the Good-ans Craft: The Kirk, for remedie therof, hes found meitt that ane article be formed to the Parliament, that ane act may proceid from the Estates therof, ordaining all persons, possessours of the saids lands, to cause labour the samein betuixt and ane certane day appointit therto; utherwayes, the case of

dissobedience, the saids lands to fall in the Kings hands, to be disponit to such persons as pleases his Majestie, quho will labour the samein.

> – *The Book of the Universal Kirk of Scotland: Acts and Proceedings of the General Assemblies of the Kirk of Scotland from the year MDLX* (1845)

Good Regent, the James Stewart, 1st Earl of Moray (*c*.1531–70), bastard son of James V, who as regent of Scotland following his half-sister Mary Queen of Scots' abdication in 1567 oversaw a period of relative tranquillity. *See also* CHASEABOUT RAID.

Good Sir James, the *See* BLACK DOUGLAS, THE.

Good Wife, the (Gaelic *A' Bhean Mhath*) Formerly a propitiatory name for smallpox in Inverness-shire, according to George Henderson's *Survivals in Belief Among the Celts* (1911).

Gorbals kiss Another term for a GLASGOW KISS, i.e. a headbutt. The Gorbals is an area on the south side of Glasgow once notorious for its slums, poverty and violence.

Gorbals Mick A nickname attached by various parliamentary sketch writers at Westminster to Michael Martin (b.1945), one-time Glasgow sheet-metal worker and Speaker of the House of Commons from 2000 until his resignation in 2009, in the wake of his inept handling of the MPs' expenses scandal. The nickname is particularly favoured by the *Daily Mail* and the *Mail on Sunday*: 'How much longer can Gorbals Mick cling to power?' (19 February 2008), 'Gorbals Mick clings on as Speaker ...' (26 February 2008), but it has also been found in the *Guardian*: '... the knives are out for the man dubbed Gorbals Mick' (Iain Dale, 30 November 2009). The nickname is intended to be jocularly derogatory, but to some betrays both a lack of research (Martin has never lived in the Gorbals; he was brought up in Anderston) and the snobbishness of those who use it, who apparently cannot accept that the post of Speaker should be held by a man with a working-class Glasgow accent.

The question now arises as to what designation the Speaker will adopt when he takes up his seat in the

Lords. Connections with the Gorbals having been revealed as the vile slander that they are, some name suggesting an architectural feature of his native Anderston is surely required. The smart money must be on Lord Martin of Bridge to Nowhere.

> – Geoff Woollen, letter published in the *Guardian*, 20 May 2009, the day after Martin's resignation.

See also BRIDGE TO NOWHERE, THE; LOW-FLYING JIMMIES.

Gorbals Vampire, the An elusive creature that became the focus of a *cause célèbre* in the 1950s. On 23 September 1954 hundreds of local primary schoolchildren flooded into Glasgow's Southern Necropolis, adjacent to the Gorbals, lured by a rumour that there they would find a seven-foot vampire with iron teeth that had killed and eaten two small boys. The broken-down Victorian cemetery was a compelling location for such a rumour, its haunted atmosphere intensified by the smoke and flames from the steelworks at its back. Tam Smith, one of the boys present that day, described the scene to the BBC in 2010: 'The red light and the smoke would flare up and make all the gravestones leap. You could see figures walking about at the back all lined in red light.' The children milled about for hours, some wielding stakes, and only a heavy downpour dispersed them. However, gangs of children returned to the cemetery for the next two nights. The incident fuelled a campaign by an unlikely alliance of Christians, communists and the National Union of Teachers against imported American horror comics, which were blamed for the outbreak of mass hysteria. The campaign reached Parliament, where it was championed by Alice Cullen, Labour MP for the Gorbals, and resulted in the 1955 Children and Young Persons (Harmful Publications) Act – a piece of legislation that is still on the statute book. There was, as it happens, a story in a contemporary American horror comic entitled 'The Vampire with the Iron Teeth', although the campaigners failed to produce this as evidence. Nor did they draw attention to the horrifying creatures that people the Bible:

> After this I saw in the night visions, and behold a fourth beast, dreadful and terrible, and strong exceedingly; and it had great iron teeth: it devoured and brake in

pieces, and stamped the residue with the feet of it: and it was diverse from all the beasts that were before it; and it had ten horns.
– Daniel 7:7

The children may equally have been inspired by tales of an old woman who haunted Glasgow Green in the early 19th century, whom the local urchins dubbed 'Jenny wi' the Iron Teeth'. And naughty children were customarily threatened by their parents with a visitation of a local bogeyman – the Iron Man.

Gordon setter A breed of dog previously known as the black and tan setter, but renamed by the Kennel Club in 1924 [sic] after Alexander Gordon, 4th Duke of Gordon (1743–1827), who helped to popularize an existing breed, and formalized the breed standard in 1820.

Gordons hae the guiding o't, the A traditional Aberdeenshire saying, referring to the dominant role played in the Northeast by the Gordon clan, whose chiefs were Earls and later Marquesses of Huntly. See also COCK O' THE NORTH.

Gored to death by an angry bull in Hawaii The fate of the botanist David Douglas; see under EPONYMS.

Gorgeous George The nickname of the colourful politician George Galloway (b.1954), so called because he and his moustache are always so perfectly groomed. Galloway became a Labour MP in 1987 (firstly for Glasgow Hillhead, then for Kelvin), but was expelled from the party in 2003 following his ardent opposition to the Iraq war. He went on to found the Respect Party and won the seat of Bethnal and Bow from New Labour in 2005, while in a 2012 by-election he secured the seat of Bradford West. One of his former Labour colleagues in his old Hillhead constituency observed: 'George could start a riot in an empty house.'

Go to Banff! See GANG TAE BUCKIE!

Govan kiss A version of a GLASGOW KISS.

Gowk A cuckoo; a fool. An *April gowk* is the victim of an April fool; see HUNTEGOWK. In the Highlands, the cuckoo was once often referred to as *bradog*, 'rascal', owing to its neglect of its young, and in St Kilda it was a bird of ill omen:

It is said the Cuckoo is rarely to be seen in Hirta, and then only upon such extraordinary occasions as the death of MacLeod, his steward, or the arrival of some notable stranger upon the island. This venerable superstition is more than two centuries old, and is still believed in as firmly as ever. In fact, its truth is said to have been verified only a year or two back, when a bird visited the island as a presage of the late proprietor's death.
– Richard Kearton, *With Nature and a Camera* (1898)

The ominous nature of the bird was believed in elsewhere in the Highlands and Islands, and in places it was euphemistically referred to as *ian glas a Chéitein* ('grey bird of May-time'). It was regarded as unlucky to hear the first call of the cuckoo before having broken one's fast, and if one called on one's roof, it signified the imminent death of one of the inhabitants of the house. See also GOWK AND TITLIN; GOWKISPINTIL; GOWK'S CHEESE; GOWK'S NEST; GOWK STORM.

Gowk and titlin An inseparable pair, or a large person next to a small one, like the *gowk* (cuckoo) and the *titlin* (meadow pipit), in the nest of which the former often lays its eggs.

Charles ... was sent to the master's school, where he and Andrew soon became inseparable ... the gouk and the titling ... (as the two boys were called).
– John Galt, *Sir Andrew Wylie of That Ilk* (1822)

Gowkispintil Cuckoopint (aka lords and ladies), *gowk* being the cuckoo, and *pintle* a penis, referring to the plant's poker-shaped inflorescence or spadix.

Gowk's cheese Wood sorrel, supposedly food for the cuckoo (*gowk*).

Gowk's nest A castle in the air; something wonderful but absurd. The *gowk* (cuckoo) famously does not make a nest, but rather lays its eggs in those of other species.

Gowk storm An untimely spring storm of short duration, sometimes involving snow. *Gowk* is the standard Scots word for a cuckoo, so may imply the time of year when the song of the cuckoo is heard, and when such sudden short-lived storms may occur; but *gowk* also means a fool or simpleton, or a trick, so the phrase *gowk storm* may imply that there is something unseasonal and 'mad' about the meteorological phenomenon. The expression dates back to at least the 16th century, and seems to be associated with weather lore as far south as Craven, in the Yorkshire Dales, where there used to be a saying: 'In the month of Averil, the gowk comes over the hill in a shower of rain.' The phrase provided the title for Nancy Brysson Morrison's much admired 1930 novel *The Gowk Storm*. Narrated by the youngest of three daughters of a minister in a remote parish on the edge of the Highlands, the novel tells of the passionate affairs ('gowk storms') of the two elder sisters, and the disapproval they provoke in this parochial society.

Gowrie Conspiracy, the A peculiar incident in the reign of James VI, who in 1600 broke off from a hunting expedition mounted from his palace at Falkland to ride to Perth, where he paid an unexpected visit to Gowrie House, home of John Ruthven, 3rd Earl of Gowrie, and his brother Alexander. James claimed that they then lured him up into a turret with a story about a pot of gold, and then threatened his life. The king's attendants heard him shout 'Treason, treason' out of the turret window, and, strange to say, found the room he was in was bolted from the inside. During the rescue bid, both Ruthven brothers were killed. James's account was not widely credited, and no evidence of a conspiracy on the part of the Ruthvens has come to light. However, the king had long been suspicious of their militantly Protestant family: William Ruthven, the 1st Earl of Gowrie, had been put to death for his leading part in the RUTHVEN RAID of 1582. But against the doubts regarding James's account of events must be placed his own response to a sceptical Edinburgh minister: 'It is known very well that I was never bloodthirsty. If I would have taken their lives, I had causes enough; I needed not to hazard myself so.' In the wake of the Gowrie Conspiracy, the very name of Ruthven was proscribed, and Ruthven Castle became known by its present name, Huntingtower.

Go yer dinger To go at a tremendous rate, to do something in a vigorous fashion. A *dinger* is a powerful blow. *See also* ACME WRINGER *under* RHYMING SLANG.

Graham Any Scottish hill over 2000 ft (609.8 m) and under 2500 ft (762.2 m). They are named after Fiona Graham, who published a list of such hills in 1991, prior to which they were known as 'Lesser CORBETTS', LCs or Elsies. There are a total of 224 Grahams. *See also* DONALD; MUNRO.

Graham's Dyke *See* GRYME'S DYKE.

Grain or **grayne** A branch of a Border clan. For example, at the time of the BORDER REIVERS, the Crichtons and Douglases were grains of the Maxwells. A *grain* was originally the branch of a tree, and the word was also applied to the tine of a fork. In the Highlands, the equivalent was a *sept*.

Grain after grape ... The following anecdote is told of John Wilsone, ironmonger of the Trongate in Glasgow and president of the Beefsteak Club, presumably around the turn of the 19th century:

> At a meeting of the club, on a particular occasion, Mr Wilsone observed a member tossing off a glass of whisky, and following it up immediately by a bumper of brandy. The witty president at once exclaimed, 'Good God, sir! what you about? You have disgraced yourself and the club, by putting a fiddling Frenchman above a sturdy Highlander.' The copper-nosed delinquent instantly started to his feet, swallowed another jorum of Ferintosh, and laying his hand upon his heart, said, 'Brand me not with being a democrat, sir; for now I've got the Frenchman between two fires!'
> – The 'Rambling Reporter', notes to the 1887 reprint of *Jones's Directory for the Year 1787*

Grandgore or **grangoir** or **glengore** Sexually transmitted disease, specifically syphilis. The term, from Old French *grand gorre*, 'great pox', is first recorded in 1497 in the minutes of a meeting of the Edin-

burgh Town Council, which mention 'This conta-
gius seiknes callit the Grandgor'. In response to the
epidemic the Town Council in Aberdeen issued an
edict that 'all licht women decist fra thar vicis and
syne of venerie'. In his *Memoirs of My Own Life*, Sir
James Melville, a member of Mary Queen of Scots'
household and an opponent of her marriage to
Bothwell, noted that the earl was 'a man full of
reproach and grangoir' – and, indeed, Bothwell was
to be rendered insane by the disease, dying chained
to a pillar in a Danish dungeon in 1578. The word
grandgore had died out by the 18th century, but its
altered form, *glengore*, persisted into the 19th.

Granite City, the Aberdeen, so-called for the stone
used in so many of its older buildings. The city is, in
the poet Robert Crawford's words, 'Howked out of
the Rubislaw Quarry's / Undiamandiferous granite.'
Marischal College, built in the 19th century, is the
second largest granite-built building in the world,
after Madrid's Escorial Palace, while Aberdeen Art
Gallery (1885) boasts a score of pillars each made
from a different type of granite. One of the passenger train services between Aberdeen and London is called the Granite City.

Grannies *See* YE CANNAE SHOVE YER GRANNY AFF
A BUS; YER GRANNIE!

Granny Kempock Stone A prehistoric megalith
that stands above Kempock Street in Gourock, its
shape apparently resembling someone's granny. It is
also known as the *Lang Stane*. Sailors about to
embark on a long voyage and couples about to
wed would attempt to ensure good luck by per-
ambulating seven times around the stone. In 1662
Mary Lamont and some other women were convicted of witchcraft and burned to death for dancing
around the stone, with the alleged intention of
casting it into the sea and thus causing passing
ships to founder. Local legend has it that on a full
moon Mary may be seen dancing round the stone,
in the company of the Devil.

Granny Made Me An Anarchist The 2002 memoirs
of Stuart Christie (b.1946), the Glaswegian anarchist who in 1964, at the age of 18, went to Spain to
blow up the dictator Francisco Franco, and as a

consequence spent three years in Spanish jails. He
was subsequently acquitted of involvement with the
Angry Brigade's bombing campaign in Britain. A
full-length portrait of Christie by Blantyre artist
Michael Fullerton was hung in Tate Britain in 2006.

Granny's tartan *See* TINKER'S TARTAN.

Graveyard of English comics, the The Glasgow
Empire Theatre; *see* HOUSE OF TERROR, THE.

Graveyard watch (Gaelic *faire chlaidh*) It was
formerly believed that the most recent person to
be buried in a churchyard had to undertake tasks on
behalf of the others buried there, such as fetching
water or keeping watch over the graveyard. The
person would be relieved of these duties when the
next person was buried. There are records of disputes and even brawls between rival funeral parties,
both attempting to ensure that their corpse was
buried first. Conversely, it was held to be dangerous
to be the first to be buried in a new churchyard, as
the following testimony from Aberdeenshire, dating
from 1866, bears witness:

> There was great difficulty in bringing the new church-
> yard into use. No one would be the first to bury his
> dead there, for it was believed that the first corpse laid
> there was a teind [tenth part, i.e. tithe] to the Evil One.
> At last a poor tramp who was found dead in the road
> was interred, and after this there was no further
> difficulty.

Grazier King, the The sobriquet of William
McCombie (1805–80), tenant farmer of Tillyfour
in Aberdeenshire, renowned breeder of Aberdeen
Angus cattle, and author of the definitive *Cattle and
Cattle Breeders* (1867). A champion of the interests
of small farmers and farm labourers, from 1868 to
1876 he sat as Liberal MP for West Aberdeenshire,
the first Scottish tenant farmer to take a seat at
Westminster.

Great auk mistaken for ghost (or witch) *See*
GHOST-BIRD, THE.

Great Cause, the The process by which Edward I,
the HAMMER OF THE SCOTS, was to decide – at the

request of the Guardians of Scotland – who was to be king of Scotland, following the deaths of Alexander III in 1286 and of his heir, the young MAID OF NORWAY, in 1290. The two main rivals were John de Balliol (aka TOOM TABARD), who was supported by the RED COMYN, and ROBERT THE BRUCE. In 1292 Edward came out in favour of Balliol.

Great chieftain o' the puddin'-race How Burns apostrophizes the haggis in his 'Address to a Haggis':

> Fair fa' your honest, sonsie face,
> Great chieftain o' the puddin-race!
> Aboon them a' ye tak your place,
> Painch, tripe, or thairm:
> Weel are ye wordy o' a grace
> As lang's my arm.
>> [*sonsie*, 'ruddy'; *painch*, 'paunch', 'stomach'; *thairm*, 'intestine']

The poem is almost invariably recited at BURNS NIGHT suppers.

Greatest gentleman in the House of Commons, the How Winston Churchill described James Maxton (1885–1946), ILP (Independent Labour Party) MP for Bridgeton from 1922 until his death. Although Maxton was a revolutionary socialist who adopted an internationalist, pacifist stance during both world wars, his charisma and sincerity drew admiration from all points of the political spectrum. 'With all who knew him,' wrote Churchill to his widow on 17 August 1946, 'I mourn your husband's death. I always said he was "the greatest gentleman in the House of Commons".'

Greatest speech since President Lincoln's Gettysburg Address, the *See* RAT RACE IS FOR RATS, THE.

Great Michael A formidable warship, which was, according to Lindsay of Pitscottie writing some 50 years later, 'the greitest schip and maist of strength that evir sailit in Ingland or France'. Commissioned by James IV around 1505 as part of his new navy, the *Great Michael* was named after the Archangel Michael. It was built at Newhaven (just west of Leith), launched in 1511 and completed the following year, at which point it was indeed the largest warship in Europe, with a length of possibly 150 ft (46 m), four masts and a displacement of 1000 tons. Pitscottie claims that its construction consumed 'all the woods of Fife', and apparently timber was also imported from elsewhere in Scotland, as well as from France and the Baltic. The total cost was £30,000 Scots. The ship had a crew of 300 sailors, plus 120 gunners to man its two or three dozen guns, and could carry up to 1000 soldiers. It was, in today's parlance, a formidable weapons-platform:

> To wit, scho bure mony canonis, xii on every side with thair greit bassellis, two behind in hir deck and ane befoir, with iii c schott of small artaillzie, that is to say moyen and bastard falconis and quarter falconis, slingis, pestelent serpentines and doubill doggis, with hagbut and culverin, croce-bowis and hand-bowis.

In response, Henry VIII commissioned his own monster-ship, the *Great Harry*. After the disaster at Flodden in 1513, the *Great Michael* was sold to the French for a knock-down 40,000 livres, and thereafter seems to have rotted unused in a French harbour, either Brest or Dieppe.

Great music, the *See* PIBROCH.

Great Pedestrian, the The sobriquet awarded to Robert Barclay Allardice of Ury (1779–1854), also known as Captain Barclay, who walked 51 miles (82 km) and back twice a week, exercised his dogs daily for 20 or more miles (32 km), and on one occasion completed a distance of 90 miles (144 km) in just over 20 hours. His greatest achievement came in 1809, when, between 1 June and 12 July, he walked 1000 miles (1600 km) at Newmarket in 1000 hours for a wager of 1000 guineas. During the course of his walk he lost 2 stone 4 lb (14.5 kg). *See also* LUGLESS WILLIE; PEDESTRIAN TRAVELLER, THE.

'Great Silkie of Sule Skerry, The' *See* SILKIE FOLK.

Great Unknown, the *See* AUTHOR OF *WAVERLEY*, THE.

Great White Shark, the The nickname of the rugby union player John Jeffrey (b.1959), alluding to his thatch of blond hair. As flanker, he was capped 40 times for Scotland between 1984 and 1991.

'Greek' Thomson The nickname of the architect Alexander Thomson (1817–75), who was responsible for many of the finest neo-classical buildings in Glasgow.

Green Lady, the Any of various apparitions once thought to haunt certain old castles, mansions, lonely spots, etc. The old Craig House, at Craiglockhart in Edinburgh, was supposedly infested with such a spectre, as was Fernie Castle in Fife, Castle of Park in Banff, and Fyvie Castle in Aberdeenshire. In this last case, the Green Lady has been identified as Lilias Drummond, who as a teenager in 1592 married Alexander Seton, later 1st Earl of Dunfermline, who was some 20 years her senior. She died on 8 May 1601, and on 27 October Seton married his step-niece, Grizel Leslie. Lilias apparently made her posthumous displeasure felt by scratching her name on the windowsill of the bridal chamber, and sightings of her in her green guise have been reported from around the castle ever since. In reference to such imaginings, children in Glasgow formerly played a game in which one would stand at the top of the dark stair in a dark close on a dark night and summon his or her companions one by one with the call, 'Green Lady, Green Lady, come up for your tea.'

In more recent times, the health visitors employed by Glasgow Corporation were known as 'green ladies', in reference to the colour of their uniforms.

Greetin face A face so miserable it is *greetin*, i.e. crying. Also described as a 'torn face'.

Greetin Teenie A Moaning Minnie of either sex; anyone of a lachrymose disposition. *Teenie* is a shortened form of Christina. *See also* TEENIE FAE TROON.

Gretna Green A Dumfriesshire village (now absorbed into the larger village of Gretna) that was long the destination for eloping couples from England, owing to its proximity to the Border. Its fame followed the Hardwicke Marriage Act of 1753,

which aimed to end the clandestine marriage of minors in England. In Scotland, however, couples could be legally married without a licence, banns or a priest. All that was necessary was that the couple make a declaration *de praesenti*, i.e. before witnesses – a role that the landlords and blacksmiths of Gretna were only too pleased to fulfil, for a fee. There are a number of mentions of Gretna Green as a destination for eloping couples in the novels of Jane Austen, and by that time the place had become notorious:

> Their town was large, and seldom pass'd a day
> But some had fail'd, and others gone astray;
> Clerks had absconded, wives eloped, girls flown
> To Gretna-Green, or sons rebellious grown …
> – George Crabbe: *Tales in Verse* (1812)

An Act of 1856 required that at least one of the parties to be married should be resident in Scotland for at least 21 days, but marriage by declaration continued to be legal until abolished by the Marriage (Scotland) Act of 1939. Nevertheless, young English couples continued to journey north of the Border, as minors over the age of 16 could still be married in Scotland without parental assent, until the age of majority was fixed at 18 in 1969.

Gretna Green Rail Disaster Britain's worst-ever rail accident, which occurred on 22 May 1915. A southbound troop train collided with a stationary local train at Quintinshill, near Gretna, and one minute later a northbound express hit the wreckage. A terrible fire ensued, engulfing two other trains as well, and a total of 226 people were killed and 246 injured; 214 of the dead were on the troop train, most of them soldiers from the 7th ('Leith') Battalion of the Royal Scots, en route for embarkation to Gallipoli. They are buried in Rosebank Cemetery in Edinburgh. After the disaster, two signalmen were convicted of culpable homicide due to gross neglect of duties, and sentenced respectively to three years and eighteen months in prison.

Grey Auld Toon, the *See* AULD GREY TOON, THE.

Grey Dogs, the The fierce tidal race, reaching speeds of 8 knots, in the narrows between Scarba and Lunga, two small islands to the north of Jura.

The name comes from the Gaelic name of this channel: Bealach a' Choin Ghlais, meaning 'pass of the grey dog'. To the south of Scarba lies the even fiercer Gulf of CORRYVRECKAN.

Greyfriars Bobby A Skye terrier who, after the death in 1858 of his master, the night watchman John ('Old Jock') Gray, guarded his grave in Greyfriars Kirkyard, Edinburgh, for 14 years. He was fed by the doting citizenry, and in 1867 the Lord Provost, Sir William Chambers, paid for the renewal of his licence. Bobby died on 14 January 1872, and was buried in unconsecrated ground near the entrance to the Kirkyard, not far from his master's grave. Shortly afterwards a statue of Bobby, with separate fountains for humans and dogs on its plinth, was raised at the south end of George IV Bridge, where it can still be seen in front of the local hostelry named Greyfriars Bobby's Bar. Bobby was lauded as the epitome of Fido-like devotion, and became the subject of a 1912 novel by Eleanor Atkinson and of a couple of films (1961 and 2006).

Grey Man of Ben Macdui, the An apparition that is said to frequent Britain's second-loftiest mountain, Ben Macdui (4294 ft/1309 m). The summit of Macdui rises above a remote, high, sub-arctic plateau in the Cairngorm Mountains, surrounded by a number of huge cliffs – the Shelter Stone Crag, Carn Etchachan, Coire Sputan Dearg and Craig na Coire Etchachan. The higher reaches of the mountain are said, when the mist is down, to be haunted by a giant shadowy presence, known in Gaelic as *Am Fear Mòr Liath* ('the Great Grey Man') or *Ferlas Mor*. One of the most celebrated reports of the Grey Man was given in 1925, 34 years after the event, by the veteran mountaineer and distinguished scientist Professor Norman Collie:

> I was returning from the cairn on the summit in a mist when I began to think I heard something else than merely the noise of my own footsteps. For every few steps I took I heard a crunch, and then another crunch as if someone was walking after me but taking steps three or four times the length of my own. I said to myself this is all nonsense. I listened and heard it again but could see nothing in the mist. As I walked on and the eerie crunch, crunch sounded behind me I was

> seized with terror and took to my heels, staggering blindly among the boulders for four or five miles nearly down to Rothiemurchus Forest. Whatever you make of it I do not know, but there is something very queer about the top of Ben Macdui and I will not go back there myself I know.

Other solitary walkers have also reported mysterious footsteps, and sometimes a great grey shadow in the mist, and in every case they have been stricken by panic and fled. The giant shadow may perhaps be explained by the phenomenon known as the Brocken spectre, by which the sun projects the viewer's shadow onto cloud, but the footsteps and the terror induced are more mysterious. The climber and writer Alistair Borthwick recounts in his mountain memoir, *Always a Little Further* (1939), how he once asked the local gamekeepers and stalkers what they thought of the stories. 'They looked at me for a few seconds, and then one said: "We do not talk about that."'

Grim's Dyke *See* GRYME'S DYKE.

Groaning malt Ale specially brewed in former times to celebrate a birth, presumable so named in reference to the strains of labour. Burns mentions the custom in the poem with which he greeted the birth of his illegitimate child by his 'Bonny Bettie':

> O wha will own he did the faut?
> O wha will buy the groanin' maut?
> O wha will tell me how to ca't?
> The rantin dog, the daddie o't.
> – Robert Burns, 'The Rantin Dog' (1790)

Grozet or **Groset Fair** An agricultural fair once held in late July or early August in various localities, including Kilmarnock, Callander, Doune and Rutherglen. A *grozet* is a gooseberry (from Old French *groselle*; cf. Modern French *groseille*), and such fairs were held when gooseberries were in season. In Kilmarnock, *Grozet Saturday* in early August was a holiday, later extended into a week's break.

Gruelly-belkie *See* MEAL-BELLY.

Gruinard Island *See* ANTHRAX ISLAND.

Gryme's Dyke The name applied in medieval histories to the Antonine Wall, the defensive wall built c.AD 142/3 by the Romans between the Forth and the Clyde in the reign of the Emperor Antoninus Pius. The 14th-century chronicler John of Fordun states that Gryme was the grandfather of a legendary king called Eugenius (a Latinization of Old Irish Eochaid), while other early histories mention a Gryme or Grimus who in the early 11th century raised an army against his relative, Malcolm II, and who agreed to a partition of the kingdom with the wall as the boundary. Alternatively, Gryme may be a corruption of the name of a 9th-century Scottish king, Giric mac Dúngail, who in medieval times was credited with many a famous victory. The section of the wall near Bo'ness is still known as Graham's Dyke, probably a corruption of Gryme, although there is a local story of a soldier called Robert Graham who supposedly mounted an assault on the defences between Chapel Hill and Elf Hill. It is most likely that the name Gryme's Dyke is the same as that found in the various earthworks called Grim's Ditch in England, where Grim is thought to be a byname of the pagan god Woden.

Guid folk, the A propitiatory name for fairies, BROWNIES, dwarfs, etc.

> The dwarfs of Shetland, then, who dwell among the hills, are to be considered as the same malevolent beings who are to be found in the Scandinavian Edda; and as it is deemed dangerous to offend them by any terms of obloquy, however well merited, they are also named the 'guid folk'.
> – Samuel Hibbert, *A Description of the Shetland Islands: comprising an account of their geology, scenery, antiquities and superstitions* (1822)

A day in which rain was followed by sun was known in some places as the *guid folk's baking day*, the rain being used to make the leaven, and the sun to bake the bread.

The guid folk were also known as *guid neighbours*:

> There is a statute in the laws of Fairyland which expressly forbids the use of the term Fairy by mortal lips. In the north of Scotland, about twenty years ago, this statute was strictly observed; and I recollect, in my boyish days, that while roaming over the green knowes

and valleys in search of flowers, my youthful companions were perfectly acquainted with its provisions. The popular form of the statute ran thus –

> If ye ca's guid neighbours, guid neighbours we
> will be;
> But if ye ca's fairies, we'll fare you o'er the sea.

And, in order to give weight to this mysterious announcement, it was always sagely added that they did, on one occasion, make good their threat. Having been detected using the misnomer, a person was actually fared o'er the sea; and what was still more terrible to youthful imagination to contemplate, the vessel in which he was conveyed was no other than an egg shell.
> – James Paterson, *The Ballads and Songs of Ayrshire* (1847)

Guid gear gangs in sma' buik Literally, 'Good stuff goes in small book', i.e. all the best things come in small packages (said of people of lowly stature).

Guid grip o' Scotland If one has or takes a *guid grip o' Scotland*, one has large, flat feet; or, figuratively, one has one's feet firmly on the ground, eschewing all flightiness and whimsy.

Guid Man, the A children's name for God. The term also makes the occasional saccharine appearance in sentimental Victorian verse.

> Nae doot it was the Good Man wha made the
> flowerets wee.
> – James Nicholson, *Idylls o' Hame, and Other Poems* (1870)

Conversely, *the Guid Man* could also be a propitiatory name for the Devil (*see* the last quotation under HECKIBIRNIE).

Guid neighbours *See* GUID FOLK, THE.

Guid Nychburris Festival *See* RIDING THE MARCHES.

Guid Schir James, the *See* BLACK DOUGLAS, THE.

Guid Toun, the Edinburgh. The term seems to have been particularly popular among the city's self-satisfied worthies, and was in use well into the 20th century. An early instance comes in the minutes of the Town Council in 1567 when Sir Simon Preston made a gift to the city of 'the Trinity College Kirk, houses, biggins, and yards adjacent thereto, and by and contigue to the samyn, to be ane Hospital to the Puir, and to be biggit and uphaldane by the Guid Toun …' Four centuries later, when the recently crowned Queen Elizabeth II visited the city in June 1953, she was offered 'the keys of Your Majesty's good town of Edinburgh'.

Guide the gullie, to To control things; a *gullie* or *gully* is a large knife. Proverbially, 'He who guides the gullie' is God.

Guisers Originally mummers or masqueraders, but now the word denotes children who go around in fancy dress and masks, especially at HALLOWEEN, singing songs, reciting poems, etc., in return for gifts such as sweets or money. Guising has largely been superseded by trick-or-treating, an American import, in which children need do nothing more than dress scarily and make implicit threats. The *Herald* diary carried the following item on 2 November 2011:

> 'A wee lad,' says Craig Bradshaw in Saltcoats, 'turns up at the doorstep on Hallowe'en and says, "Trick or Treat? And by the way, mister, I'm diabetic, so it's cash only."'

Gulsoch Originally applied to jaundice, which in Middle English was *gulesought*, from *gowyl* or *gule*, 'yellow', and *suht*, 'disease'. Subsequently the word was applied to a surfeit, or nausea due to overeating, or a gargantuan appetite. Hence *gulsa girse*, buckbean or marsh trefoil, and *gulsa-shall*, snail's shell, both formerly used as cures for jaundice. Hence also *galshachs*, any unhealthily sweet foodstuff, such as confectionary, iced cakes, sweet biscuits; also applied to a treat, or anything trashy or worthless, a CLANJAMFRIE.

> An' halesame is the hamely fare in ilka hoose an' ha',
> For galshachs an' clamjamfry trash we canna thole ava'.
> – J. Mitchell, 'Bydand' (1918)

Gust the gab, to To indulge the appetite and treat the palate to culinary delights; *gab* is the mouth, and gust comes from Latin *gustare*, 'to taste'.

Guttie ba A golf ball, made from the type of rubber known in Scots as *gutty-perky*, i.e. gutta-percha (from Malay *getah*, 'gum', and *percha*, the tree from which it comes). Gutta-percha was also used to make the soles of gym shoes, which became known as *gutties*, as did children's catapults, from the rubber band used in the missile-delivery system.

Guttit Haddie, the The 'gutted haddock', a name applied to two Edinburgh features. The first is the aerial or plan view of the Old Town, from the map of the city drawn by James Gordon of Rothiemay in 1647, which depicts the wynds and closes spreading out on either side of the ROYAL MILE like ribs extending from the spine of a fish. The name is also applied to a great rift in the western flank of ARTHUR'S SEAT. The *Old Statistical Account* (1791–9) tells us somewhat improbably that it was formed by a waterspout on 13 September 1744: 'Dividing its force, it discharged one part upon the western side, and tore up a channel or chasm, which still remains a monument of its violence; the other division took its direction towards the village of Duddingston, carried away the gable of the most westerly cottage, and flooded the loch over the adjacent meadows.'

> … as a laddie,
> ye skliddert doun, for scarts no caring,
> the Guttit Haddie.
> – Robert Garioch, 'To Robert Fergusson'

Gypsies, king of the See KING OF THE GYPSIES.

Gypsy Palace See KING OF THE GYPSIES.

H

Ha', Rab *See* GLASGOW GLUTTON, THE.

Haar A term, related to the Dutch dialect word *harig*, 'damp' and Middle Dutch *hare*, 'bitterly cold wind', used in Scotland and parts of eastern England since at least the 17th or 18th centuries to denote the chill sea mist that sometimes comes in off the North Sea. It can squat on cities such as Aberdeen, St Andrews and Edinburgh for days at a time, depressing the spirits and chilling the flesh, although if one were to travel a few miles inland one would be likely to find bright sunshine.

> But it's just your ain vile, vapoury, thick, dull, yellow, brown ... easterly haur o' Embro' that gies me the rheumatics.
> – John Wilson ('Christopher North'), *Noctes Ambrosianae* (1827)

> Gurlie an gray the snell Fife shore,
> Frae the peat-green sea the cauld haar drives ...
> – Sydney Goodsir Smith, 'Armageddon in Albyn', VII, The War in Fife [*gurlie* 'stormy', *snell* 'fiercely cold']

> The haar was in, that cold fog that rises so thick from the Forth that, given a hammer, you could beat the sound of doom on its skin.
> – Ruaridh Nicoll, writing about Edinburgh in the *Observer*, 25 September 2005

Habbie A resident of Kilbarchan in Renfrewshire. The name comes from Habbie Simpson (1550–1620), the famous Kilbarchan piper, whose statue stands in the town and who is commemorated every year on LILIAS DAY. Simpson famously inspired *The Life and Death of the Piper of Kilbarchan, or, The Epitaph of Habbie Simpson* (*c.*1640) by Robert Sempill. In this elegy, first printed around 1700, Sempill pioneered a stanza form with the rhyming scheme *aaabab*:

> Kilbarchan now may say alas!
> For she hath lost her game and grace,
> Both Trixie, and the Maiden Trace:
> But what remead?
> For no man can supply his place,
> Hab Simpson's dead.

This form – dubbed 'the standard Habbie' by Allan Ramsay – was much used by Robert Fergusson and Burns, for example in the latter's 'Poor Mailie's Elegy' (1786):

> Lament in rhyme, lament in prose,
> Wi' saut tears trickling down your nose;
> Our Bardie's fate is at a close,
> Past a' remead!
> The last, sad cape-stane of his woes;
> Poor Mailie's dead!

Habbie's Howe A wooded defile in the valley of the North Esk, a little to the northeast of the village of Carlops (*see* CARLIN; FAIRIES O' CARLOPS), on the south side of the Pentland Hills. It is the scene of Allan Ramsay's pastoral, *The Gentle Shepherd* (1725), in which Peggy says to Jenny:

> Gae far'er up the burn to Habbie's Howe,
> Where a' the sweets o' spring and summer grow:
> There 'tween twa birks, out ower a little lin,
> The water fa's and maks a singin' din;
> A pool breast-deep, beneath as clear as glass,
> Kisses, wi' easy whirls, the bord'ring grass.
> We'll end our washing while the morning's cool;
> And when the day grows het, we'll to the pool,
> There wash oursells.

'Habbie's Howe' appears to have been Ramsay's coinage; topographico-literary sleuths subsequently set to work to identify the actual location of his scene, with some suggesting the Vale of Glencorse, also on the south side of the Pentlands, but a little closer to Edinburgh. However, the consensus plumps for the valley of the North Esk, and here the Ordnance Survey unequivocally marks the spot (grid reference NT 175 565). Also marked in the vicinity are other appropriately pastoral place names: Amazondean, Peggy's Pool, Turtle Bank, Lonelybield.

Ha' binks are sliddery A now defunct saying, literally 'the seats in a great man's house are slippery', glossed by James Kelly in *A Complete Collection of Scottish Proverbs* (1721) as 'Great Men's Favour is uncertain'.

Habit and repute A term used in Scots law, and explained thus by A.D. Gibb in *Legal Terms* (1946):

> Habit and repute, in the law of theft, means the reputation of being a thief, the words being used in aggravation of the particular charge. In civil law it is the reputation of being married which, coupled with cohabitation, constitutes an irregular marriage.

The phrase comes from the medieval Latin *habitus et reputatus*. *See also* BIDIE-IN; HANDFAST; MARRIAGE *SUBSEQUENTE COPULA*.

Hacky-duck A children's game once popular in Dundee:

> ... 'Hucky-duck' a team game, where a line of bent backs formed a pier stretching from the wall. The opposition's aim, to pile up by running leaps to those backs, in the hope it would collapse. The mounted then chanted 'Hucky-duck three times on and off again.' Should the pier's legs hold, the positions had to be reversed, with the riders as cuddies [donkeys].
> – Norman Lynn, *Row Laddie Sixty Years On* (1987)

A similar game was played in Glasgow, where it was known as *hunch-cuddy-hunch* (a *cuddy* being a donkey).

Had Cain been Scot ... In 'The Rebel Scot', the English poet John Cleveland (1613–58) levelled the following barb at England's northern neighbour:

> Had Cain been Scot, God would have changed his doom
> Not forced him wander, but confined him home.

Cleveland, a staunch Royalist, was inspired by the Scottish invasion of England in 1643 in support of the Parliamentarians in the Civil War.

Haddie or **Aiberdeen haddie** A Glaswegian name for an Aberdonian, *yellow haddie* (smoked haddock) being a major product of Aberdeen. *See also* FINNAN HADDIE.

Haddingtonus Scotus (Latin, 'the Scot from Haddington') A byname of John Mair or Major (1496–1550), also known as Joannes Majoris, a noted historian and one of the leading European philosophers of his day. Mair was born at Gleghornie, near North Berwick in East Lothian, and attended the grammar school in Haddington, 'the town which fostered the beginning of my studies, and in whose kindly embrace I was nourished as a novice with the sweetest milk of the art of grammar'. He later studied at Cambridge and at the University of Paris, where he became acquainted with the likes of Erasmus and Rabelais. Mair went on to become professor of logic and theology at Paris, Glasgow and St Andrews, and numbered among his pupils the future Protestant reformers John Knox, Patrick Hamilton and George Buchanan. His works were all written in Latin, the most celebrated being *Historia Majoris Britannae* (1521), which translates as 'history of the greater Britain' or, punningly, 'Major's history of Britain'. In this he anticipates the social-contract ideas outlined in the following century by Thomas Hobbes and John Locke. 'It is the free people who first give power to the king,' writes Mair, 'and his power depends on the whole people.' He continues:

> If the state is in such case that it is invaded by an enemy, and King A cannot guard it and consents to its conquest, but B protects it and breaks the enemy's grip and keeps it safe, then A should be deposed and B put in his place.

See also WILD SCOTS.

Haddo's Hole A now demolished part of St Giles Cathedral in Edinburgh. It took its name from Sir John Gordon of Haddo, a Royalist commander who was here imprisoned – or, in the words of John Spalding's contemporary *History of the Troubles*, 'most shamefully wairdit and straitlie kepit, to his grayt greif and displeasour' – by the Covenanters prior to his execution on the MAIDEN in 1644. Haddo's Hole was subsequently used to house those found guilty of adultery.

Haet *See* DEIL HAET.

Haggis The archetypal Scottish dish, comprising finely chopped offal (heart, liver, lungs) of a sheep, together with oatmeal, suet, seasonings and diced onion, all stuffed into the animal's stomach lining and boiled. Calf's meat is sometimes substituted. The word – which was also formerly applied, figuratively, to a man's paunch – perhaps derives from Old English *haccian*, 'to hack', or Old Norse *hoggva*, 'to hew'; Norman French *hachis*, 'minced meat', has also been suggested.

Until the early 18th century haggis was also eaten in England: the earliest known recipe comes not from Scotland but from a 15th-century manuscript from Lancashire, while the earliest printed recipe is in Gervase Markham's *The English Huswife* (1615). Haggis is customarily the main dish at BURNS NIGHT suppers, when its ceremonial entrance is accompanied by the pipes, followed by a recitation of the poet's 'Address to a Haggis', in which the subject is apostrophized as GREAT CHIEFTAIN O' THE PUDDIN'-RACE – 'for,' as James Hogg (the ETTRICK SHEPHERD) says in *Noctes Ambrosianae*, 'what's better than a haggis?'

One of the most celebrated recipes for haggis is that to be found in *The Cook and Housewife's Manual* (1826) by Mrs Margaret Dods (*see* DODS, MEG):

Clean a sheep's pluck [heart, liver, lungs and windpipe] thoroughly. Make incisions in the heart and liver to allow the blood to flow out, and parboil the whole, letting the wind-pipe lie over the side of the pot to permit the phlegm and blood to disgorge from the lungs; the water may be changed after a few minutes' boiling for fresh water. A half-hour's boiling will be sufficient; but throw back the half of the liver to boil till it will grate easily; take the heart, the half of the liver, and part of the lights [lungs], trimming away all skins and black-looking parts, and mince them together. Mince also a pound of good beef-suet and four onions.

Grate the other half of the liver. Have a dozen of small onions peeled and scalded in two waters to mix with this mince. Toast some oatmeal before the fire for hours, till it is of a light-brown colour and perfectly dry. Less than two-cupfuls of meal will do for this quantity of meat. Spread the mince on a board, and strew the meal lightly over it, with a high seasoning of pepper, salt, and a little cayenne, well mixed. Have a haggis-bag perfectly clean, and see that there be no thin part in it, else your whole labour will be lost by its bursting. Some cooks use two bags. Put in the meat with a half-pint of good beef-gravy, or as much strong broth, as will make it a thick stew. Be careful not to fill the bag too full, but allow the meat room to swell; add the juice of a lemon, or a little good vinegar; press out the air, and sew up the bag; prick it with a large needle when it first swells in the pot, to prevent bursting; let it boil slowly for three hours if large.

Haggis has been subjected to a number of culinary variants: deep-fried haggis in batter is a staple of Scottish chip shops; haggis bhaji are served in some Indian restaurants in Glasgow; some of the more pretentious restaurants serve 'Flying Scotsman' (chicken breast stuffed with haggis) or 'Chicken Balmoral' (the same, but wrapped in bacon); and in 2010 Nadia Ellingham, an Edinburgh chocolatière, came up with haggis-flavoured chocolate truffles. Between 1989 and 2010, haggis was not available in the USA, for fear that it might be infected with scrapie, the ovine version of mad cow disease. In 2001, during the foot-and-mouth epidemic, a haggis was confiscated at Seattle airport from a Scottish journalist by US customs officers. The offending item was taken outside, shot five times, soaked in petrol and incinerated. *See also* SHEEP'S HEID.

There is an old joke played by the pawkier kind of Scot upon gullible tourists, who are solemnly informed that the haggis is a species of animal (*Haggis scoticus*), the males having the left legs shorter than the right, and the females vice versa, so that the males circumambulate steep-sided Highland hills anticlockwise (WIDDERSHINS), and the females clockwise (DEISEIL). In this way their meeting, and the continuation of the species, is ensured. A poll conducted in 2003 purported to reveal that a third of American visitors believed this story, while nearly a quarter said they'd come to Scotland with the intention of catching a haggis. Quite who was pulling whose leg in these responses is unclear. *See also* WOMLE AND BREES.

> 'Dish or no dish,' rejoined the Caledonian, 'there's a deal o' fine confused feedin' about it, let me tell you.'
> – John Brown, *Horae Subsecivae* (1858), on the haggis

Haggisland A jocular term for Scotland, first coined in the 19th century. How we laughed.

Haig shall be Haig of Bemersyde One of the prophecies of the 13th-century seer, THOMAS THE RHYMER:

> Betyde, betyde, whate'er betyde
> Haig shall be Haig of Bemersyde.

Bemersyde, near Newton St Boswells in the Borders, has been the traditional home of the Haig family since the 12th century, although the oldest part of the present house is the rectangular tower built around 1535. The estate passed to a different branch of the family in the 19th century, but in 1921 the British government bought the house for Field Marshal Earl Haig in gratitude for his role as commander-in-chief of British forces on the Western Front in the First World War. Not all have been so appreciative of Haig's contribution: his apparent indifference to mass casualties earned him the sobriquet 'Butcher of the Somme', while Lloyd George later condemned Haig as 'intellectually and temperamentally unequal to the task', describing him as 'brilliant – to the tops of his boots'. In a Swiftian aside, the Glasgow-born historian Norman Stone has praised Haig as the greatest of Scottish generals, on the grounds that he was responsible for the deaths of vastly more Englishmen than any other soldier in Scottish history. Haig was a scion of the well-known whisky family; *see* DON'T BE VAGUE, ASK FOR HAIG.

Hail ... *See also* HALE ...

'Hail to the Chief' A march frequently played to announce the appearance at a formal occasion of the president of the United States. It owes its origins to 'The Boat Song' in Sir Walter Scott's *The LADY OF THE LAKE* (1810), in which the chief in question is Roderick Dhu:

> Hail to the Chief who in triumph advances!
> Honoured and blessed be the evergreen pine!
> Long may the tree in his banner that glances,
> Flourish, the shelter and grace of our line.
> Heav'n send it happy dew,
> Earth lend it sap anew,
> Gaily to bourgeon and broadly to grow;
> While ev'ry Highland glen,
> Sends our shout back again,
> 'Roderigh Vich Alpine dhu, ho! i-e-roe!'
> – Canto 2, stanza 19

Stage versions of Scott's poem soon appeared, and in one of the London productions a musical setting of 'The Boat Song' was supplied by James Sanderson, conductor of the orchestra at the Surrey Theatre. A production featuring this setting opened in Philadelphia in 1812, and the sheet music was published in the USA at about the same time, under the title 'March and Chorus, "Hail to the Chief", in the Dramatic Romance of *The Lady of the Lake*'. It was first associated with an American president when it was played in 1815 at a ceremony to honour the memory of George Washington and the end of the War of 1812, and first played to honour a living chief executive on 9 January 1829, the president in question being Andrew Jackson. It featured among the pieces played during the inauguration of Martin Van Buren on 4 March 1837, and during the presidency (1841–5) of John Tyler, Mrs Tyler requested that it be played to announce the arrival of the president – a tradition that persists to this day. There are some specifically US lyrics, penned by Albert Gamse:

> Hail to the Chief we have chosen for the nation,
> Hail to the Chief! We salute him, one and all.
> Hail to the Chief, as we pledge cooperation
> In proud fulfillment of a great, noble call.
>
> Yours is the aim to make this grand country grander,
> This you will do, that's our strong, firm belief.
> Hail to the one we selected as commander,
> Hail to the President! Hail to the Chief!

Fortunately, these words are rarely heard, the music more typically being played by a military band.

Haims *See* PIT THE HEMS ON.

Hairless dogs *See* MACKINNON'S CAVE; WIZARD OF REAY, THE.

Hair like a burst couch An expression denoting disorder in the tonsorial department. Such hair might also be described as *like straw hingin oot a midden*.

Hairy, wee *See* WEE HAIRY.

Hairy Bible, the A 1773 bible in Birnie Kirk, Moray, so-called because bound in calfskin with the hair still attached.

Hairy coos Contemporary urban slang for Highland cattle.

Hairy Hand *See* MEG MULLACH.

Hairy-Leggit Irishmen, the A nickname for the Highland Light Infantry; *see* REGIMENTAL NICKNAMES.

Hairy Mary A pie of mashed potatoes and flakes of boiled fish, popular in the Northeast. If the fish is salt cod, then the dish is called *Hairy Willie*.

Hairy Willie The woolly-bear caterpillar. *See also under* HAIRY MARY.

Hale closhach, the *See* HALE JING-BANG, THE.

Hale jing-bang, the The entire kit and caboodle; the whole lot. The phrase is often used dismissively.

> This is to compensate for the fact that a number of Westminster MPs are surplus to requirements; the hale jing bang o' them are, in our view, apart from our own noble SNP members!
> – *The Scots Independent*, 2 March 2001

A variant is *the hale rickmatick* (from 'arithmetic'), which can also apply to a group of people; while in the Northeast they say *the hale closhach* (from Gaelic *closach*, 'carcass'; a *closach* can also be a pile of money).

Hale rickmatick, the *See* HALE JING-BANG, THE.

Half and a half *See* HAUF AN A HAUF.

Half-hangit Maggie The nickname of Margaret Dickson, an Edinburgh woman who in 1721 survived a hanging, as described by Robert Chambers in his *Book of Days* (1862–4):

> On the 2nd of September 1721, a poor woman named Margaret Dickson, married, but separated from her husband, was hanged at Edinburgh for the crime of concealing pregnancy in the case of a dead child. After suspension, the body was inclosed in a coffin at the gallows' foot, and carried off in a cart by her relatives, to be interred in her parish churchyard at Musselburgh, six miles off. Some surgeon apprentices rudely stopped the cart before it left town, and broke down part of the cooms, or sloping roof of the coffin, – thus undesignedly letting in air. The subsequent jolting of the vehicle restored animation before it had got above two miles from the city, and Maggy was carried home a living woman, though faint and hardly conscious. Her neighbours flocked around her in wonder; a minister came to pray over her; and her husband, relenting under a renewed affection, took her home again. She lived for many years after, had several more children creditably born, and used to be pointed out in the streets of Edinburgh, where she cried salt, as Half-hanget Maggy Dickson.

Half-shut knife, to look like a *See* LOOK LIFE A HALF-SHUT KNIFE, TO.

Halkerton's Cow, like Said of anything that turns out to be the opposite of what is expected, or to what one has been led to believe. The expression survived into the early 20th century. James Kelly, in *A Complete Collection of Scottish Proverbs* (1721), explains it thus:

> Hackerton was a Lawyer, who gave leave to one of his Tenants to put a weak Ox into his Park to recruit; a Heifer of Hackerton's run upon the Ox and gor'd him; the Man tells him that his Ox had kill'd his Heifer: Why then, says Hackerton, your Ox must go for my Heifer, the Law provides that. No, says the Man, your Cow kill'd my Ox. The Case alters there, says he.

The said Hackerton appears to have taken his name from Halkerton near Laurencekirk, in the Howe of the Mearns.

A prodigal beast called 'Halkerton's Calf' is the subject of a song by Alex Laing, contributed to WHISTLE-BINKIE (3rd series, 1842), and sung to the tune of 'The Corby and the Pyet'. Halkerton's Calf not only has 'the rare gift o' speech', but ...

Has scripture by heart, as the gowk has its lied,
An' fechts wi' his tongue for a kirk an' a creed.
    An' fechts, &c.

At alehouse an' smiddy he rairs an' he cracks,
'Bout doctrines, an' duties, an' statutes, and acts;
At blythemeat, an' dredgy, yulefeast, an' infare,
He's ready aff-hand wi' a grace or a prayer.
    He's ready, &c.

Hallelujahs, the A disparaging Glaswegian nickname for the Salvation Army. *Compare* BUBBLY BABIES.

Halloween All Hallows' Eve, celebrated on 31 October, the day before the Christian festival of All Saints' Day, which honours all the saints, both known and unknown. Halloween has traditionally been more widely celebrated in Scotland than in England, until in the later 20th century the latter took up the heavily commercialized US custom of trick-or-treating. Scottish Halloween pastimes include the making of turnip lanterns (a tougher proposition than the American pumpkin lantern), DOOKING FOR APPLES, attempting to eat treacle-soaked scones hanging from threads with one's hands tied behind one's back, and dressing up as GUISERS. In Scotland (and Ireland) Halloween coincides with the old Celtic festival of SAMHAIN, when the veil between this world and the otherworld is supposedly at its thinnest. As Robert Burns explains in a note to his poem 'Halloween' (1786), 31 October 'is thought to be a night when Witches, Devils and other mischief-making beings are all abroad on their baneful, midnight errands: particularly, those aerial people, the Fairies, are said, on that night, to hold a grand Anniversary'. He goes on to describe how on this night the peasantry of the west of Scotland would use KAIL (cabbages) to divine the future, explaining in another note:

The first ceremony of Halloween, is, pulling each a *Stock*, or plant of kail. They must go out, hand in hand, with eyes shut, and pull the first they meet with: it's being big or little, straight or crooked, is prophetic of the size and shape of the grand object of all their Spells – the husband or wife. If any *yird*, or earth, stick to the root, that is *tocher*, or fortune; and the taste of the *custoc*, that is, the heart of the stem, is indicative of the natural temper and disposition. Lastly, the stems, or to give them their proper appellation, the *runts*, are placed somewhere above the head of the door; and the Christian names of the people whom chance brings into the house, are, according to the priority of placing the *runts*, the names in question.

Burns then describes various other traditional means of divining one's future spouse, via drawing straws of oats, burning nuts, and so on. Overall, the spirit was one of jollity, as Burns's final verse attests:

Wi' merry sangs, an' friendly cracks,
    I wat they did na weary;
And unco tales, an' funnie jokes
    Their sports were cheap an' cheery:
Till butter'd sowens, wi' fragrant lunt,
    Set a' their gabs a-steerin;
Syne, wi' a social glass o' strunt,
    They parted aff careerin
        Fu' blythe that night.

Contra Burns, not all the spirits abroad at Halloween are thought to be malevolent:

Hallowe'en, the night which marks the transition from autumn to winter, seems to have been of old the time of year when the souls of the departed were supposed to revisit their old homes in order to warm themselves by the fire and to comfort themselves with the good cheer provided them in the kitchen or the parlour by their affectionate kinsfolk. It was, perhaps, a natural thought that the approach of winter should drive the poor, shivering, hungry ghosts from the bare fields and the leafless woodlands to the shelter of the cottage with its familiar fireside ... could the goodman and the good-wife deny to the spirits of their dead the welcome which they gave to the cows?
    – Sir James Frazer, *The Golden Bough* (1890)

Hall, Robert *See* GLASGOW GLUTTON, THE.

Hal o' the Wynd *See* BATTLE OF THE CLANS, THE.

Halyman 'Holy man', a propitiatory name for the Devil, especially in the context of such terms as *Halyman's ley*, another name for GOODMAN'S CROFT.

Ham a haddie! A likely story! The expression may arise, according to the *Dictionary of the Scottish Language*, from a music-hall gag from the turn of the 20th century, and apparently refers to the popular Scottish breakfast dish of a slice of ham or bacon served with smoked haddock (especially FINNAN HADDIE), sometimes with a poached egg – hence *ham 'n' haddie* came to refer to a mix-up, and thence a confused story, and thus an incredible tale.

Hame How Campbeltown is known locally (*cf.* DOONHAMERS). Locals also refer to the town as the NEAREST PLACE TO NOWHERE.

Hamebiders Literally 'stay-at homes', a nickname given to the inhabitants of both Anstruther and Bo'ness.

Hame-fare In Orkney and Shetland, the journey of a bride to her new home, and the festivities laid on by her for friends and relatives when she arrives there. *See also* BACK FEAST.

Hamelldaeme 'Home-will-do-me', the holiday destination of choice for those unable to afford a sojourn on the Costas, or even a trip DOON THE WATTER. Many prefer to avoid the crowds at Cap d'Antibes by taking their holidays sunning themselves on the BACK GREEN.

Hammer, the The nickname given by the *Scottish Daily Express* to the policeman David McNee (b.1925) for his tough approach while Chief Constable in Glasgow in the 1970s. McNee went on to become Commissioner of the Metropolitan Police from 1977 to 1982.

The nickname was later applied to the Bellshill-born Labour politician John Reid (b.1947), who held a number of cabinet posts under Tony Blair, and who is currently chairman of Celtic FC. Reid acquired something of a reputation as an aggressive enforcer, and displayed a certain dogged skill in his ability to swipe aside unwelcome questions from journalists. He is apparently fond of the saying, 'Better a broken nose than a bended knee.' Having served as an MP since 1987, he was ennobled in the 2010 dissolution honours as Baron Reid of Cardowan.

Hammer of the Nats, the *See under* TARTAN TORIES.

Hammer of the Scots, the King Edward I of England, who aggressively attempted to impose his will on Scotland, although he died before he could fully achieve his aim. His grave in Westminster Abbey bears the following Latin inscription: '*Hic est Edwardvs Primus Scottorum Malleus*', meaning 'Here is Edward the First, Hammer of the Scots'. When his grave was opened in 1774, his skeleton was found to measure 6 ft 2 ins (1.85 m) – hence his other nickname, Edward Longshanks ('long legs'). It may have been Edward's ultimate failure to 'hammer' the Scots that led the 14th-century Scottish chronicler John of Fordun to label the BLACK DOUGLAS, Bruce's right-hand man, 'a brave hammerer of the English'.

Hampden roar, the The noise generated by the spectators at Hampden Park, Scotland's national football stadium, and also the home ground of Queen's Park FC. Up to the 1980s the ground, located in Glasgow, could hold up to 150,000 people, and the noise generated by them, audible over several miles, was said to intimidate opponents:

> English football players have been quoted as saying that the Hampden Roar is the equivalent of two goals for Scotland. Unfortunately this has not always proved true.
> – Jack House, *The Third Statistical Account of Scotland: Glasgow* (1958)

The phrase has become RHYMING SLANG for 'score', as in 'What's the Hampden roar?'

> It's aw oor poppy! Lenny snapped. – Granty kens the fuckin Hampden roar.
> – Irvine Welsh, *Trainspotting* (1993)

Handba An apparently anarchic game played annually in Jedburgh with a moss-stuffed leather ball, bigger than a tennis ball and smaller than a football, and decorated with ribbons. The men of the town are divided into two teams, the Uppies (from the south end) and the Doonies (from the north end). The Uppies score a *hail* (goal) if they manage to throw the *ba* over the railings surrounding Jedburgh

Castle, while the Downies score if they get the ball across the Skiprunning Burn, a tributary of the Jed that flows invisibly under the streets through a culvert. All forms of brute force and subterfuge seem to be permissible. James Hepburn, Earl of Bothwell and third husband of Mary Queen of Scots, was reputedly a fearsome player, and in those days the game might end with a handful of dead men littering the field.

Handba was also formerly played between Uppies and Doonies in Hawick, the match being held on the first Monday after the new moon in February, and with portions of the game being played in the River Teviot.

There is still a similar mass-participation game played in Kirkwall every Christmas Day and New Year's Day. The Orkney game uses a handmade, cork-filled leather ball weighing some 3 lbs (1.36 kg) and with a circumference of 28 in (70 cm). The two sides in the Kirkwall Ba' are also known as the Uppies and Doonies (or Up the Gates and Down the Gates, from Norn *gata*, 'road'); the former aim to touch the ball against a wall in the south part of the town, while the latter try to get it into the waters of the harbour on the north side. Games have been known to last up to eight hours.

Handfast To contract (by a joining of hands) to undertake a trial period of cohabitation prior to marriage. The idea was to test compatibility, and also the woman's fertility; it was commonly a condition that she should bear a man-child within a year and a day. Thomas Pennant, in his *Tour in Scotland and Voyage to the Hebrides* (1774), recounts:

> In the upper part of *Eskdale* ... was held an annual fair, where multitudes of each sex repaired. The unmarried looked out for mates, made their engagements by joining hands, or by *handfisting* [sic], went off in pairs, cohabited till the next annual return of the fair, appeared there again, and then were at liberty to declare their approbation or dislike of each other. If each party continued constant, the handfisting was renewed for life.

The Kirk disapproved of the practice, but it persisted in rural parts of the Borders into the last decades of the 19th century. *See also* MARRIAGE *SUBSEQUENTE COPULA.*

Handsel Monday The first Monday of the New Year, formerly a holiday, on which it was traditional to give a *handsel*, a good-luck gift (such as also given at housewarmings).

> My prince in God, gif thee guid grace,
> Joy, glaidnes, confort, and solace,
> Play, pleasance, myrth, and mirrie cheir
> In hansill of this guid New Yeir.
> – William Dunbar, 'To the King'

See also HOGMANAY.

Handy, Para The central character in a series of humorous stories by Neil Munro (using the pen name Hugh Foulis), the first of which appeared in the Glasgow *Evening News* in 1905. The name Para Handy is an anglicized form of Para Shandaidh ('Peter son of Sandy'), the Gaelic nickname of one Peter Macfarlane, a 'short, thick-set man, with a red beard, a hard round felt hat, ridiculously out of harmony with a blue pilot jacket and trousers and a seaman's jersey ...' Para Handy is the skipper of the *Vital Spark*, 'the most uncertain puffer that ever kept the Old New Year in Upper Lochfyne', and in this small, unreliable coaster he and his characterful crew carry cargo up and down and around the Firth of Clyde and along the west coast of Argyll, becoming involved in a variety of scrapes and high jinks. BBC TV made three series of dramatizations of the tales, with the part of Para Handy played successively by Duncan MacRae, Roddy McMillan and Gregor Fisher, while other parts were played by such notables as John Grieve and Rikki Fulton.

> 'If you're goin' to speak aboot love, be dacent and speak aboot it in the Gaalic. But we're no talkin' aboot love: we're talkin' aboot my merrage.'
> – Neil Munro, *The Vital Spark* (1906)

Hang ... *See also* HING ...

Hanging Tree of Fort William, the An old oak that used to grow outside the walls of Fort William, and which was used to hang malefactors. It was cut down in the 1970s to make way for the town's new public library, and this act of vandalism, according to some locals, provoked a *buidseachd* or curse.

Accordingly, so the press reported, the morning after the new library was opened staff found books and paintings strewn across the floor, heard toilets flushing and strange dog-like snuffling noises, and witnessed their precious electric typewriter chuntering along on its own – and printing out characters upside down. For another hanging tree, *see* KING OF THE BORDER, THE.

Hangman's Craig or **Knowe** A cliff on ARTHUR'S SEAT above Duddingston Loch in Edinburgh. It gained its name from the following circumstance:

> About the reign of Charles II, the office of public executioner was taken by a reduced gentleman, the last member of an old family that had long possessed an estate near Melrose. His earlier years had been passed in profligacy; his patrimony was gone, and at length for the sake of food, he was compelled to accept this degrading office, 'which in those days,' says Chambers, 'must have been unusually obnoxious to popular odium, on account of the frequent executions of innocent and religious men. Notwithstanding his extreme degradation, this unhappy reprobate could not altogether forget his former tastes and habits. He would occasionally resume the garb of a gentleman, and mingle in the parties of citizens who played at golf in the evenings on Bruntsfield Links. Being at length recognized, he was chased from the ground with shouts of execration and loathing, which affected him so much that he retired to the solitude of King's Park, and was next day found dead at the bottom of a precipice, over which he is supposed to have thrown himself in despair. The rock was afterwards called *Hangman's Craig*.
>
> – James Grant, *Cassell's Old and New Edinburgh* (1880s)

Hang them a'! *See* JEDDART JUSTICE.

Hanover, House of *See* IDIOT RACE, AN.

'Happy Hooligans o' Wembley, The' *See* 'FLOWER OF SCOTLAND'.

Hap-the-beds or **hoppin beds** The game of hopscotch, also known as *peevers* or *beds*. It is, according to John Mactaggart in his *Gallovidian Encyclopaedia* (1824),

> A singular game, gone through by hopping on one foot, and with that foot sliding a little flat stone out of an oblong bed, rudely drawn on a smooth piece of ground; this bed is divided into eight parts, the two of which at the farther end of it are called the *kail pots*; if the player then stands at one end, and pitches the smooth stone into all the divisions one after the other, following the same on a foot, (at every throw) and bringing it out of the figure, this player wins not only the game, but is considered a first-rate daub at it; failing, however, to go through all the parts so, without missing either a throw or a hop, yet keeping before the other gamblers (for many play at one bed), still wins the curious rustic game.

Hap weel, rap weel The (now obsolete) Scots equivalent of the Spanish *Qué será será*, 'Whatever will be, will be.' The derivation of the phrase is uncertain; it may be a corruption of something else.

Happy day A drink consisting of a bottle of wee heavy poured into a pint glass and topped up with ordinary heavy (for heavy and wee heavy, *see under* BEER).

Hard as Hinnerson's erse, as Very hard indeed; intolerably tough. The expression is popular in the Northeast. Hinnerson (i.e. Henderson) is said to be a term for the Devil, but the name may have been chosen for its euphonic quality. It has been averred that the *erse* in question is ten or even fifty times harder than flint, and some add that it whistles when he runs. In politer circles, the expression is simply *as hard as Henderson*.

Hares It was formerly believed that witches could transform themselves into these creatures. Even in the early years of the 20th century, the Gaelic scholar and folklorist George Henderson was writing:

> I have personally heard of and known many women who were regarded as having the power of shifting themselves into hare-shape. It was most uncanny to see a hare pacing a thatched cottage in the gloaming, still more to see several of them capering at cross-roads ... There are numerous stories in the Highlands of hares having been shot at with a gun having a 'silver

sixpence', the creature shot being reputed to be some local witch afterwards found suffering of secret wounds.

> – George Henderson, *Survivals in Belief Among the Celts* (1911)

Harl o' bones An emaciated person, a *harl* being a scraping together of bits and pieces.

Harry the Minstrel *See* BLIND HARRY.

Harry the Ninth *See* HENRY THE NINTH.

Haste ye back A standard form of goodbye, equivalent to '*au revoir*', 'till next time', but now somewhat tinged with FAUX JOCKERY. The song 'Haste Ye Back', sung by the entire company, was the standard closing number in each episode of *The WHITE HEATHER CLUB*:

Haste ye back, we loue you dearly,
Call again you're welcome here.
May your days be free from sorrow,
And your friends be ever near.

In the world of retail and marketing, a *haste-ye-back* is a little something extra (or perhaps a discount) offered by the shopkeeper to encourage repeat visits.

Hat and Ribbon Race A foot race held in early August along Hope Street, Inverkeithing, the winner being awarded a hat and ribbons to present to his beloved. It is one of the oldest of such races held in Scotland, dating back several centuries, and was originally a competition for shepherds. It is part of the Lammas Fair celebrations (*see* LAMMAS DAY).

Hatteraick, Dirk *See* DIRK HATTERAICK'S CAVE.

Hattock *See* HORSE AND HATTOCK.

Haud yer wheesht! Be quiet. *Wheesht* or *whisht* is the Scots equivalent of 'shhh'.

Hauf an a hauf Literally 'a half and a half', i.e. a whisky served with half a pint of beer as a chaser. In whisky terms, a *hauf* was originally half a gill, but the word was later applied to any small measure. A *wee*

hauf is now taken to be a fifth of a gill, the commonest measure of spirits in Scottish pubs.

Haw, Rab *See* GLASGOW GLUTTON, THE.

Hawick ba The version of HANDBA formerly played in the Borders town; now the name is restricted to a locally made boiled sweet, brown in colour and peppermint in flavour. In *Scottish Regional Recipes* (1981), Catherine Brown attributes the invention of Hawick ba's (aka *Hawick bools* or *balls*, and formerly also known as *rock bools*) to two 19th-century Hawick sweet-shop owners, Jessie McVittie and Aggie Lamb:

> Little did they imagine that the bools would become so famous; not only do Hawick Balls allegedly inspire prowess at rugby, a tin of the sweets has also been buried at the South Pole during an Antarctic expedition … Jessie made the Rock Bools in her shop in Drumlanrig Square, Hawick, in the 1850s, as well as Black Sticky Taffy and White Peppermint Taffy. It is said that she stretched her Rock Bool mixture and hung it on a nail stuck in the wall, where she could keep an eye on it from her shop counter. As the mixture slowly slid to the ground, Jessie carried on with her housework and tended to customers, until such time as the mixture fell close to the floor when she would suddenly get hold of it, give it a twist and a stretch and hang it over the nail again. The method of 'pulling' was repeated over and over.

Hawick gill A commendably generous but sadly obsolete measure of spirits, equivalent to half a pint.

Headim and corsim An old game involving pins:

> Pins are hid with fingers in the palms of the hands; the same number is laid alongside them, and either *headim* or *corsim* called out by those who do so; when the fingers are lifted, if the heads of the pins hid, and those beside them, be lying one way, when the crier cried *headim*, then that player wins; but if *corsim*, the one who hid the pins wins. This is the king of all the games at the *preens* [pins], and let it not be thought that it is a *bairn's play*; by no means; it is played by lads and lasses as *big* as ever they will be, and by those whom age has again made young; the game is simple and harmless, and not uninteresting; the Peasant is as anxious about

gaining a preen, as my *Lord Duke* would be ten thousand pounds ... *Cheatery* is sometimes heard of in this game too; then is the saying sounded, 'They wha begin to steal needles and pins, end wi' stealing horned kye [cattle].'

– John Mactaggart, *The Scottish Gallovidian Encyclopaedia* (1824)

A similar game is called *headicks and pinticks*.

Headless Horseman of Mull, the *See* EOGHAN OF THE LITTLE HEAD.

Heart of Midlothian, the The nickname for Edinburgh's Tolbooth prison, demolished in 1817. The location, close to St Giles on the Royal Mile, is today marked by red paving stones in the shape of a heart, and it was formerly a tradition to spit on it, to demonstrate one's opinion of the old Tolbooth. Sir Walter Scott took *The Heart of Midlothian* as the title of one of his most admired novels, published in 1818. The name is explained in the first chapter:

'Then the tolbooth of Edinburgh is called the Heart of Midlothian?' said I. 'So termed and reputed, I assure you.'

In the novel, the Tolbooth features both as the place of incarceration of the historical figure of Captain Porteous (*see* PORTEOUS RIOTS), and of the fictional heroine's sister, Effie Deans. The suggestion is that the heroine herself, the kindly and virtuous Jeanie Deans, is the true 'heart of Midlothian'. Jeanie Deans was based on a historical woman, Helen Walker (*c*.1710–91), a farmer's daughter from Kirkcudbrightshire, who, like Jeanie, walked to London to obtain a pardon for her sister, who had been convicted of infanticide.

The Edinburgh premier-league football club, Heart of Midlothian (Hearts for short), was founded in 1874; *see also* FOOTBALL CLUB NICKNAMES. One of the passenger services between Edinburgh and London is called the Heart of Midlothian.

Heart-roastit Exasperated, anguished, irritated, at the end of one's tether. The expression has been in use in Glasgow since the mid-20th century.

Hearts *See* FOOTBALL CLUB NICKNAMES.

Heather One of Scotland's national flowers, along with the THISTLE, the BLUEBELL OF SCOTLAND (the harebell) and the WHITE ROSE OF SCOTLAND. It was formerly used to flavour ale (*see* HEATHER ALE), and to make bedding, brooms, rope, thatch for roofs, fuel, baskets and an orange dye, and it still provides the basis of much honey. Heather is the plant-badge of Clan Donald, which gives rise to one of the clan's mottoes, *Fraoch Eilean* ('the heathery isle'). There are two common species in Scotland: common heather (*Calluna vulgaris*) and bell heather (*Erica cinerea*). Rare white varieties occur of both, and finding them is considered lucky. A third species, cross-leaved heath (*E. tetralix*), is also found, but in less abundance.

I love a lassie, a bonnie, bonnie lassie,
She's as pure as the lily in the dell,
She's as sweet as the heather,
The bonnie bloomin' heather,
Mary, ma Scotch Bluebell.
    – Harry Lauder, 'I Love a Lassie'

Heather has not appealed to everybody. Edmund Burt, in his *Letters from a Gentleman in the North of Scotland* (1726–37), writes of the heather-clad landscape thus:

There is not much variety in it, but gloomy spaces, different rocks, and heath [heather] high and low. To cast one's eye from an eminence towards a group of them, they appear still one above the other, fainter and fainter according to aerial perspective, and the whole a dismal brown drawing upon a dirty purple, and most of all disagreeable when the heath is in bloom.

See HEATHER ALE; HEATHER LEGS; NO' THE HEATHER; TAKE TO THE HEATHER; SET THE HEATHER ON FIRE.

Heather ale A potion supposedly brewed by the PICTS, who did in fact make a form of crude ale from wild barley, flavoured with other ingredients such as rowan berries and heather. In legend, the recipe was lost when the last Pict leapt from the cliffs of the Mull of Galloway, following his people's final defeat there at the hands of the Scots. There is, however, no historical record of a battle here. In another version of the story, the only survivors of the battle on the Pictish side are a father and son.

When the king of the Scots threatens them with torture, the father says:

> My son ye maun kill,
> Before I will you tell
> How we brew the yill
> Frae the heather bell!

The son is immediately put to death, whereupon the father says to the king that is the secret now safe, as the son who might have given away the secret under torture is dead, but the father will never give it away:

> And though you may me kill,
> I will not tell,
> How we brew the yill
> Frae the heather bell.

Contrary to this legend, heather continued to be used to flavour beer in Scotland up to at least the 17th century.

Heather legs Legs that take high and wide strides, as if walking through dense, high heather.

> He was a thick-made, square-built, sturdy Highlander, with what are commonly called heather-legs.
> – J.G. Lockhart, *The Life of Adam Blair, Minister of Gospel at Cross Meikle* (1824)

The term *heather-lowper* ('leaper') is applied to someone who lives and works among the hills.

Heave Awa' House A block in Edinburgh's High Street constructed in 1862 on the site of a 17th-century tenement that collapsed on 24 November 1861, resulting in the deaths of 35 people. The name alludes to a young boy called Joseph McIvor who was trapped in the ruins, and who encouraged his rescuers with the words, 'Heave awa', lads, I'm no deid yet.' He was the only survivor. The tragedy caused an outrage, leading to an inquiry into the appalling living conditions in the Old Town, and to the appointment of the first medical officer of health in Scotland.

Heaven-taught ploughman *See* PLOUGHMAN POET, THE.

Heavy *See* BEER.

Hech how *See* AULD HECH HOW, THE.

Heckiebirnie or **Hecklebirnie** A euphemism for Hell. John Jamieson, in his *Etymological Dictionary of the Scottish Language* (1825 Supplement), has this to say:

> A strange sort of imprecation is used, into which this term enters: *I dinna care though ye were at Heckiebirnie* ... The only account given of this place is, that it is three miles beyond *Hell*. In Aberdeenshire it is used nearly in a similar manner. If one says, 'Go to the D—l,' the other often replies, 'Go you to *Hecklebirnie*.'

The suggestion is that Hell is to Hecklebirnie as the frying pan is to the fire:

> For a' we see, we may be running out of the latitude of Hell, into that of Hecklebirnie – a place that is hotter still!
> – James Grant, *The White Cockade, or, Faith and Fortitude* (1868)

Jamieson goes on to describe an Aberdeenshire game, in which thirty or forty children form two lines, each joining hands with his or her opposite number. As a child runs between the rows, he or she is struck by each of the paired hands in turn. This running of the gauntlet was called 'passing through the mires of Hecklebirnie'.

Jamieson suggests that the first element of the term may derive from Hekla, the Icelandic volcano that was known by the islanders in the Middle Ages as the 'gateway to Hell'; however, it is more likely that the first element is the same as *heck*, a 19th-century euphemism for Hell, while the second element suggests 'burning'.

There is a real place called Hecklebirnie (grid reference NS 897 381), not 'three miles beyond Hell', but rather three miles south of Lanark, in the valley of the Douglas Water. Nearby is a somewhat mysterious archaeological site, probably an Iron Age settlement, described as follows by the Royal Commission on the Ancient and Historical Monuments of Scotland:

> The severely wasted remains of a circular enclosure, about 50m in internal diameter, occupy the level summit of a slight rise in arable ground, 168m N of

Hecklebirnie. Originally the enclosure, noted as in good preservation in 1858, was formed by what was evidently a substantial stone wall as 'an enormous quantity of stones' is said (D Christison 1890) to have been removed from it.

This account has a strange congruence with the following tale:

> The surmises and suspicions regarding the agency employed in the removal of the stones [of a new church] ... rested on the guid-man of Hecklebirnie, the only dissatisfied parishioner ... The common adage, 'Gae to Hecklebirnie' ... would imply anything but a place of rest ... if we may judge from the speedy migration of the stones intended for the Kirk.
> – Robert Sim, *Legends of Strathisla and Strathbogie* (1849)

He couldnae get a wumman in Paisley Said of a man who has little success with the opposite sex. The saying casts no aspersions on the modesty and virtue of Paisley womanhood, but rather reflects the era when the town's textile mills predominantly employed women workers.

Hedges of Death, the The site near the M90/A823 (M) interchange near Pitreavie, Fife, where two Highland regiments were said to have been massacred by English Commonwealth forces in the aftermath of the Scots defeat at the Battle of Inverkeithing (20 July 1651). In defence of their chief, Colonel Hector Maclean of Duart, his loyal clansmen rallied in front of him, being cut down one by one, crying 'Another for Hector!' In fact, Maclean's regiment probably only suffered 140 casualties out of 800 men.

He'd take the sugar oot yer tea He's about as trustworthy as an old fox.

Heedrum-hodrum An expression, supposedly imitative, applied pejoratively by Lowlanders to the sound of Gaelic singing and other forms of Highland music. *Compare* HEUCHTER-TEUCHTER.

Hee-haw Nothing at all (used disparagingly); sweet FA.

I'd grown up with the assumption that Scotland was a poor, wee deprived place that had never had a fair kick of the ball and could certainly never stand on its own two feet. ... And then I read a lot and thought a lot and decided that assumption was based on hee-haw, apart from an ingrained indoctrination and pessimism.
– Alex Salmond, interviewed by Ian Jack in the *Guardian*, 31 January 2009

Heels owre gowdie or **heelster gowrie** Head over heels, topsy-turvy – both literally and figuratively. *Gowdie* may originally have denoted a head of *gowden* ('golden') hair.

> Soon, heels-o'er-gowdie! in he gangs,
> And like a sheep-had on a tangs,
> Thy girning laugh enjoys his pangs
>   And murdering wrestle,
> As, dangling in the wind, he hangs
>   A gibbet's tassel!
> – Robert Burns, 'To Colonel de Peyster' (1796)

Heid on someone, to stick or **put the** To give someone a GLASGOW KISS, i.e. a headbutt.

Heid in one's hands, to get or **gie one's** To be at the receiving end or to administer a right telling off, or even sharper punishment.

Heidsman The chief of a Border family or clan; *see* BORDER REIVERS. The word was formerly also applied to a foreman, or a person appointed by a trade to inspect the quality of workmanship of its members.

Heid-the-ba Literally 'head the ball', a phrase denoting someone considered a bit simple; it perhaps alludes to the supposed brain damage that might ensue if one was to head an old-fashioned heavy leather football too often. *See also* BA-HEID.

Heid under one's oxter, to have one's Literally, 'to have ones' head under one's armpit', i.e. looking the very picture of misery.

Helensburgh toffee A confection more akin to fudge than toffee, containing butter, sugar, golden syrup, milk, condensed milk and vanilla essence.

Hell, Ladies from *See* LADIES FROM HELL.

Hell a mere fiction of priestcraft *See* ST ORAN'S CHAPEL.

Hell's Glen A steep-sided pass in the ARROCHAR ALPS, linking Loch Goil and Loch Fyne. The name appears to be a misreading of its Gaelic name, *Gleann Aiffrin*, 'glen of offering', as *Iffrin*, 'Hell'.

Hell shall have her ain again this nicht An old oath of the BORDER REIVERS when about to embark on a raid, according to Robert Louis Stevenson in *Weir of Hermiston* (1896), chapter v.

Hell's Latest Invention A nickname for the Highland Light Infantry; *see* REGIMENTAL NICKNAMES.

Hell's Lum A prominent rock 'chimney' (Scots *lum*) or fissure in the great cliff known as Hell's Lum Crag, on the south flank of Cairn Lochan, overlooking Loch Avon in the northern Cairngorms.

Help ma boab *See* JINGS, CRIVENS, HELP MA BOAB.

Hems *See* PIT THE HEMS ON.

Hen Ogledd *See* OLD NORTH, THE.

Hen on a het girdle, like a Literally, 'like a hen on a hot griddle', i.e. hopping from foot to foot. The simile denotes a general state of agitation.

> The Bailie, whom this reference regarded, and who had all this while shifted from one foot to another with great impatience, 'like a hen,' as he afterwards said, 'upon a het girdle'; and chuckling, he might have added, like the said hen in all the glory of laying an egg, now pushed forward.
> – Sir Walter Scott, *Waverley* (1814), chapter lxxi

Henry the Minstrel *See* BLIND HARRY.

Henry the Ninth A mocking nickname given to the reactionary politician Henry Dundas, 1st Viscount Melville (1742–1811), also known as 'the Uncrowned King of Scotland'. From the time he was appointed Lord Advocate in 1775, and through his

time as a cabinet minister until his impeachment in 1805, he was the regarded by many as the absolute dictator of Scotland, controlling as he did virtually all the political patronage in the country – as described by Lord Cockburn, in *Memorials of His Time*:

> Within this Pandemonium sat the town council, omnipotent, corrupt, impenetrable. Nothing was beyond its grasp; no variety of opinion disturbed its unanimity, for the pleasure of Dundas was the sole rule of every one of them.

Dundas earns a mention in Burns's 'The Author's Earnest Cry and Prayer' (1786):

> ... a chap that's damn'd auldfarran,
> *Dundas* his name.
> [*auldfarran*, 'old-fashioned, droll, quaint; wise, witty, clever']

He was also the subject of a famous quip in Parliament by Sheridan:

> The Right Honourable Gentleman is indebted to his memory for his jests, and to his imagination for his facts.

Horace Walpole reports that an alternative nickname was 'Starvation Dundas', owing to his coining (or popularizing) the word 'starvation' in a parliamentary debate in 1775 regarding trade restrictions with the American colonies. His statue has stood atop a pillar in St Andrew's Square, Edinburgh, since 1828.

For Jacobites, the real Henry IX was Henry Stuart, Cardinal of York (1725–1807), younger brother of the YOUNG PRETENDER.

Here's to us The beginning of a popular traditional toast:

> Here's to us, wha's like us?
> Gey few, and they're a' deid.

Sometimes 'Damn' is substituted for 'Gey', and 'Mair's the pity' added at the end.

Hermaphroditism *See* THING NOT ORDINAR IN THIS KINGDOM, A.

Hermit of Hawthornden, the A romantic sobriquet of the poet William Drummond of Hawthornden (1585–1649), who on his father's death in 1610 became laird of Hawthornden, above the River North Esk at Roslin Glen, south of Edinburgh, where his house still stands. Drummond expressed the intention of living within his means (or, as he put it, *Vivere infra fortunam*) and aimed at a Horatian ideal of rural – albeit gentlemanly – simplicity. His penchant for solitude was strengthened (according to romantic legend) after the death in 1616 of Euphemia Kyninghame or Cunningham of Barns, whom he supposedly had intended to marry – although modern scholars are sceptical of any amorous connection. His enjoyment of the 'sweet solitary life', as one of his friends described it, was famously interrupted in the winter of 1618–19 by a three-week visit from Ben Jonson, who drank his cellar dry and opined that his host's poems 'smelled too much of the Schooles, and were not after the fancie of the tyme'. Drummond's hermit-like tendencies did not prevent him from taking a mistress, by whom he had three children, and his solitude came to a complete end in 1632, when he married Elizabeth Logan, possibly the daughter of the minister of Eddleston near Peebles. Elizabeth bore him nine children, and survived him by thirty years.

> Drummond, lang syne o' Hawthornden,
> The wiliest an' best o' men.
> – Robert Fergusson, 'To the Principal and Professors of the University of St Andrews, on their Superb Treat to Dr Samuel Johnson'

Herod of Hillhead, the Just one weapon in the oratorical armoury of Pastor Jack Glass (1936–2004), the extreme Protestant preacher, anti-papist and denouncer of the nation's morals. This particular barb was aimed at Roy Jenkins during the campaign for the 1982 Hillhead (Glasgow) by-election, which Jenkins won on behalf of the new Social Democratic Party. It presumably referred to the fact that abortion had become legal during Jenkins's period as Labour Home Secretary in the 1960s. Glass himself stood in the Hillhead by-election on behalf of the 'Protestant Crusade Against the Papal Visit Party', winning 388 votes. When, despite this popular endorsement of Glass's views, Pope John Paul II still had the temerity to press ahead with his visit, Glass, joined by the Revd

Ian Paisley, greeted the pontiff's arrival in Bellahouston Park with cries of 'The Beast is coming!', 'No surrender', etc. Paisley subsequently came to regard Glass as 'a bit of an extremist'.

Glass was well known for picketing plays and performers that he regarded as mocking the Christian religion; a particular target was the comedian Billy Connolly, whom he described as a 'blasphemous buffoon'. When Glass was diagnosed with the cancer that was eventually to kill him, he stated that it was a personal attack on him by the Devil. 'I don't hate anyone,' he said shortly before his death. 'I'm just trying to bring people to Christ. Glasgow has turned its back on God. Sadly, God will have to punish it.'

Herring Road, the An old trade route by which herring was carried from Dunbar on the Firth of Forth over the Lammermuir Hills to market at Lauder. It fell out of use with the coming of the railways.

Herschip of Buchan, the The harrying of Buchan by Robert the Bruce following his victory over John Comyn, Earl of Buchan, at Barra in 1308. It involved the seizure and looting of castles, and the killing of their garrisons. *Herschip*, a word going back to the 14th century and related to Old Scandinavian *herskapr* 'harrying', can denote either a raid for the sake of plunder or more general pillaging and punitive harrying by an army.

> Now ga we to the king agayne
> That off his victory wes rycht fayn,
> And gert his men bryn [burn] all Bowchane
> Fra end till end and sparyt nane,
> And heryit thaim on sic maner
> That eftre weile fyfty yer
> Men menyt [grieved] the herschip off Bouchane.
> – John Barbour, *The Brus* (c.1375)

Herschips were something of a feature of medieval Scottish history: for example, the *Asloan Manuscript* (a 16th-century collection of earlier texts) recounts events in 1444 during the turbulent minority of James II, when 'thair was ane richt greir herschip maid in Fyff' by the Earl of Crawford, the Ogilvies, and others. *See also* ROUGH WOOING, THE.

Het ... *See also* HOT ...

Het beans and butter A children's game, resembling hunt the slipper:

A game in which one hides something, and another is employed to seek it. When near the place of concealment, the hider cries *Het*, i.e. hot on the scent; when the seeker is far from it, *Cald*, i.e. cold. He who finds it has the right to hide it next.

– John Jamieson, *An Etymological Dictionary of the Scottish Language* (1825 supplement)

He that will to Cupar maun to Cupar Literally, he that will go to Cupar must go to Cupar, i.e. the strong-willed (or pigheaded) will have their way. The expression is first recorded in James Kelly's *Scottish Proverbs* (1721), and turns up in chapter xviii of Scott's *Bride of Lammermoor* (1819):

'And you will go, then?' said Caleb, loosening his hold upon the Master's cloak, and changing his didactics into a pathetic and mournful tone – 'and you WILL go, for a' I have told you about the prophecy, and the dead bride, and the Kelpie's quicksand? Aweel! a wilful man maun hae his way: he that will to Cupar maun to Cupar ...'

The reference in the saying is to the former county town of Fife, or perhaps to Coupar-Angus, but why either should be associated with obduracy is unclear. *See also* CUPAR JUSTICE.

Heuchter-teuchter An adjectival phrase applied pejoratively by Lowlanders to music, dancing and other cultural phenomena from the Highlands and Islands, or, as a noun, to a devotee of such things. The expression derives from the supposed cries of 'Heuch!' uttered by Highland dancers and the word TEUCHTER, a contemptuous term for a Highlander. *Compare* HEEDRUM-HODRUM. *See also* GLUNIMIE; SASSENACH.

He who guides the gullie God. *See* GUIDE THE GULLIE, TO.

Hey, Johnnie Cope, are ye wauken yet? The opening line of the well-known song by Adam Skirving (1719–1803), celebrating – with consider-

able poetic licence – the Jacobite victory at Prestonpans (21 September 1745) over a Hanoverian force led by Sir John Cope, commander-in-chief in Scotland. The chorus goes:

Hey, Johnnie Cope, are ye wauken yet?
Or are your drums a-beating yet?
If ye were wauken I wad wait
To gang to the coals i' the morning.
[*wauken*, 'waking']

The Jacobites began their attack in this, the first engagement of the '45, at four o'clock in the morning, but contrary to the song, Cope was not asleep, and ordered his men into position when the alarm was raised. However, his inexperienced troops fled before the HIGHLAND CHARGE, despite Cope's admonitions as he rode among them, shouting: 'For shame, gentlemen, behave like Britons!' The action was all but over within five minutes, leaving the battlefield 'a spectacle of horror, being covered with heads, legs and arms, and mutilated bodies'. It was said – inaccurately – that Cope was the first to bring the news of his own defeat:

When Johnnie Cope tae Dunbar came,
They speired at him, 'Where's a' your men?'
'The deil confound me gin I ken,
For I left them a' i' the morning.'

Now Johnnie, troth, ye are na blate
To come wi' the news o' your ain defeat,
And leave your men in sic a state,
Sae early in the morning.
[*speired*, 'asked'; *blate*, 'backward, timid']

Cope himself reported to Lord Tweeddale, secretary of state for Scotland:

I cannot reproach myself; the manner in which the enemy came on was quicker than could be described, and ... possibly was the cause of our men taking a most destructive panic.

Hey-you A Glaswegian name for any particularly unrefined person, of the sort likely to address a stranger with the phrase 'Hey you!'

Hibs or **Hibees, the** *See* FOOTBALL CLUB NICKNAMES.

Hide-i'-the-heather A vagabond. *See also* TAKE TO
THE HEATHER, TO.

Hide the geggie *See* SMUGGLE THE GEG.

Hielan ... *See also* HIGHLAND ...

Hielan convoy *See* SCOTS CONVOY.

Hielanman's Umbrella, the A nickname of the
wide railway bridge spanning Argyle Street in Glasgow, next to Central Station. The area underneath
the bridge was once a rendezvous for TEUCHTERS.

High doh *See* UP TAE HIGH DOH.

Higher than Gilderoy's kite *See* GILDEROY.

High heid yin Literally 'high head one', i.e. the top
dog in an organization; she who must be obeyed.
The term was first recorded in the 1920s.

Highland ... *See also* HIELAN ...

Highland charge A battle tactic employed by the
Highland clans, involving a headlong rush wielding
broadsword and targe, while letting out wild yells to
terrify the enemy. Some say the tactic was perfected,
if not invented, by Alasdair MacColla (aka Young
COLKITTO), during the Wars of the Three Kingdoms in the mid-17th century. The charge would
begin with a trotting advance towards the enemy
until within range of firearms, followed by a brief
halt to discharge a volley. Firearms would then be
cast aside and swords drawn before the onrush. The
enemy, presumably having discharged their own
firearms, would be denied the opportunity to
reload. The shock tactic proved effective so long
as the enemy panicked and stopped fighting as a
unit, as happened at Killiecrankie in 1689 and
Prestonpans in 1745 (*see* HEY, JOHNNIE COPE,
ARE YE WAUKEN YET?), but by the time of the
Battle of Culloden in 1746 the anti-Jacobite forces
had learnt how to counter the charge by a combination of musket fire and disciplined use of the
bayonet. Prior to the battle, the Duke of Cumberland addressed his troops thus: 'Depend, my lads,
on your bayonets; let them mingle with you; let

them know the men they have to deal with.' This
advice proved horribly effective. Although the Highlanders charged 'like troops of hungry wolves',
within less than an hour, according to one contemporary account, 'the soldiers' bayonets were
stain'd and clotted with the blood of the rebels
up to the muzzles of their muskets'.

Highland fling A lively solo Scottish country dance,
in which the dancer stays above the same spot while
executing some nifty footwork and raising his or her
hands in the air. It is thought to be one of the oldest
of Scotland's traditional dances, and was said to
have originally been performed by victorious warriors on a targe – the traditional small, round shield
of the Highlander, which sometimes had a spike in
the centre. The dance appears to have embodied
everything that the Lowlander considered wild,
outlandish and unrestrained about the Highlander:

> Miss Bonnyrigg ... had made the company at the Well
> alternately admire, smile and stare, by dancing the
> highest Highland fling, riding the wildest pony, laugh-
> ing the loudest laugh at the broadest joke, and wearing
> the briefest petticoat of any nymph of St Ronan's.
> – Sir Walter Scott, *St Ronan's Well* (1824)

> ... at Acharacle ... in front of a croft a young fellow was
> dancing the Highland fling, with such whole-souled
> consuming zeal that I stood transfixed with wonder
> and awe. He was alone, and I came suddenly upon him
> at a sharp bend of the road. He threw his legs about
> him with such regardless glee that for a moment I was
> afraid that one of them might come spinning through
> the air to hit me. I watched him, fascinated, for fully ten
> minutes. When at length he saw me, the glory flowed
> suddenly off his legs; he subsided into a country
> bumpkin, and beat a hasty retreat indoors.
> – D.T. Holmes, *Literary Tours in the Highlands and
>   Islands* (1909)

By the 19th century the dance had acquired an
international reputation; Mark Twain, for example,
in his *Letter from Hawaii*, describes a woman's
reaction on discovering a scorpion: 'Well, she just
got up and danced the Highland Fling for two hours
and a half.'

Highlanders' Umbrella, the *See* HIELANMAN'S
UMBRELLA, THE.

Highland games or **Highland gathering** An annual event held in a number of locations and featuring a variety of competitions, such as dancing, bagpipe playing, and various heavyweight athletic contests, such as TOSSING THE CABER, stone-putting and throwing hammers. The most famous is the Braemar Gathering, founded in 1832 by the Braemar Wrights' Friendly Society, and given a boost from the time that Queen Victoria first attended in 1848. The Braemar games are said to have their origins in the 11th century, when MALCOLM CANMORE supposedly summoned the clans to Braemar for an athletic competition to establish which men would make the fastest royal messengers. However, the institution, wallowing as it is in tartanry, is largely Victorian in origin, and there are probably more Highland games held in the USA than there are in Scotland itself. *See also* GATHERING OF THE CLANS; NORTHERN MEETING, THE.

Highland honours The mode of drinking a toast formerly favoured by Highland clansmen (or at least so the post-Scott Scots seem to have imagined), in which all the company placed one foot on a stool or chair, and the other on the table.

Highland Host, the *See* COVENANTERS.

'Highland Laddie, The' A traditional song, dating back to the '45. The eponymous laddie is sometimes taken as a generic Highlander, and sometimes as Charles Edward Stuart, the YOUNG PRETENDER:

Where ha' ye been a' the day?
Bonnie laddie, Hielan' laddie,
Saw ye him that' far awa',
Bonnie laddie, Hielan' laddie.

On his head a bonnet blue,
Bonnie laddie, Hielan' laddie,
Tartan plaid and Hielan' trews,
Bonnie laddie, Hielan' laddie.

When he drew his gude braid-sword,
Then he gave his royal word,
Frae the field he ne'er wad flee,
Wi' his friends wad live or dee.

Geordie sits in Charlie's chair
But I think he'll no bide there.
Charlie yet shall mount the throne,
Weel ye ken it is his own.

The tune subsequently became one of the most popular regimental marches among Highland regiments.

James Hogg rewrote the words for George Thomson to celebrate the part played by Highland regiments in the victory of Wellington over Napoleon at Waterloo, and Thomson published this version, with a musical setting by Ludwig van Beethoven, in the fifth volume of his *A Select Collection of Original Scottish Airs* in 1818:

Where got ye that siller moon,
Bonny laddie, Highland laddie,
Glinting braw your belt aboon,
Bonny laddie, Highland laddie?
Belted plaid and bonnet blue,
Bonny laddie, Highland laddie,
Have ye been at Waterloo,
Bonny laddie, Highland laddie?

Highland Land League *See* CLEARANCES, THE.

Highland Lass The 'Solitary Reaper' of Wordsworth's poem, encountered by the poet on his 1803 tour of Scotland:

Behold her, single in the field,
Yon solitary Highland Lass!
Reaping and singing by herself;
Stop here, or gently pass!
 – 'The Solitary Reaper'

For Burns's 'Highland Lassie', *see* HIGHLAND MARY.

Highlandman, the One of the passenger train services running between Inverness and London.

Highland Mary Burns's beloved Mary Campbell (1763–86), who was born in Argyll, on the farm of Auchnamore near Dunoon (which has a statue to her). Burns began an affair with Mary in the summer of 1786 during a hiatus in his relationship with Jean Armour, the BELLE OF MAUCHLINE. It is possible that Mary became pregnant, and even that she and Burns married. They planned to move to Jamaica, where the poet intended to become a bookkeeper on a plantation, but in October Mary died of typhus. Burns himself recalled the event in a note:

At the close of autumn she crossed the sea [the Firth of Clyde] to meet me at Greenock, where she had scarce landed, when she was seized with a malignant fever, which hurried my dear girl to the grave in a few days, before I could even hear of her illness.

Burns addressed a number of poems to Mary, including 'The Highland Lassie', 'Highland Mary' and 'To Mary in Heaven'.

> That sacred hour can I forget,
>   Can I forget the hallow'd grove,
> Where, by the winding Ayr, we met,
>   To live one day of parting love!
> Eternity will not efface
>   Those records dear of transports past,
> Thy image at our last embrace,
>   Ah! little thought we 'twas our last!
>   – 'To Mary in Heaven' (1789)

> O pale, pale now, those rosy lips,
>   I aft hae kissed sae fondly!
> And closed for aye the sparkling glance
>   That dwelt on me sae kindly:
> And mouldering now in silent dust
>   That heart that lo'ed me dearly!
> But still within my bosom's core
>   Shall live my Highland Mary.
>   – 'Highland Mary' (1792)

George Henderson, in his *Survivals in Belief Among the Celts* (1911), provides an intriguing footnote:

> ... when Burns's Highland Mary (Mary Campbell) fell ill, her friends at Greenock supposed, it is said, that she had come under the malign power of the evil-eye. To avert this, seven smooth stones were procured from the junction of two streams. These were placed in milk, which, after being boiled, was administered, but without success.

(For other beliefs concerning the evil eye, *see* ILL EE.)

Highland pride An inflated sense of the importance of one's birth and genealogy, combined with a touchiness in all matters pertaining to honour. One might cite Sir Thomas Urquhart of Cromarty, who in 1652 published *Pantochronachanon; or, A Peculiar Promptuary of Time*, in which he traced his forbears back through 153 generations, via Noah, to the lump of clay from which God formed Adam. Of course Sir Thomas, a man of wild and whimsical humours, might have had his tongue in his cheek (he made a notably inventive translation of Rabelais, created a cod language called LOGOPANDECTEI-SION, and laughed so much on hearing of the Restoration of Charles II that he fell down dead). Less ambivalent examples of Highland pride include the post-prandial pomposity of MacNeil of Barra (*see* MACNEIL OF BARRA HAS EATEN, THE), or the pre-prandial preening of a certain Macdonald chieftain visiting Ireland (*see* WHEREVER MACDONALD SITS ...). On his brief tour of the Western Highlands, Burns ascribed insufferable *hauteur* to the Duke of Argyll:

> Whoe'er he be that sojourns here,
>   I pity much his case,
> Unless he come to wait upon
>   The Lord their God – his Grace.

> There's naething here but Highland pride,
>   And Highland scab and hunger;
> If Providence has sent me here,
>   'Twas surely in an anger.
>   – Robert Burns, 'Epigram at Inveraray' (1787)

Then there is that almost-unsurpassed peacock, Colonel Alastair MacDonell of Glengarry, who in Raeburn's famous full-length portrait of 1812 cuts such a dash in his Highland dress, complete with his own creation, the GLENGARRY BONNET. Glengarry insisted that wherever he went he was followed by a train of kilted servants, including a personal bard, weapon-bearer (*gillie-mor*), and *gillie-casflue* ('wet foot') to carry him over bogs and burns (*see also* GILLIE). It was MacDonell who inspired one of the most striking characters in Scott's *Waverley*, Fergus Mac-Ivor of Glennaquoich, who on his first appearance is described thus:

> The eyebrow and upper lip bespoke something of the habit of peremptory command and decisive super-iority. Even his courtesy, though open, frank, and unconstrained, seemed to indicate a sense of personal importance; and, upon any check or accidental excita-tion, a sudden, though transient lour of the eye showed a hasty, haughty, and vindictive temper, not less to be dreaded because it seemed much under its owner's command. In short, the countenance of the Chieftain resembled a smiling summer's day, in which, notwith-

standing, we are made sensible by certain, though slight signs that it may thunder and lighten before the close of evening.

> – Sir Walter Scott, *Waverley* (1814), chapter xviii

In more recent times, one might mention as an example of Highland pride the genealogist Sir Iain Moncreiffe of that Ilk, known to the press as the WORLD'S GREATEST SNOB.

High Road See TAKE THE HIGH ROAD.

High School riot See ROYAL HIGH SCHOOL RIOT.

High tea A meal that includes a cooked savoury dish as well as bread, cakes, etc., all washed down by tea. Although not a peculiarly Scottish institution, it is (or at least was) something of a speciality. Lewis Grassic Gibbon, in *Scottish Scene* (1934), gives an account of high tea in Aberdeen, which 'is like no other meal on earth':

> Tea is drunk with the meal, and the order of it is this: first, one eats a plateful of sausage and eggs and mashed potatoes; then a second plateful to keep down the first. Eating, one assists the second plateful to its final home by mouthfuls of oatcake spread with butter. Then you eat oatcake with cheese. Then there are scones. Then cookies. Then it is really time to begin on tea – tea and bread and butter and crumpets and toasted rolls and cakes. Then some Dundee cake. Then, about half past seven, someone shakes you out of the coma into which you have fallen and asks you persuasively if you wouldn't like another cup of tea and just *one* more egg and sausage.

In some places, the cooked, savoury element of a high tea was called *kitchen*. A *funeral tea* is a particularly splendid high tea, as served to mourners after a funeral. Other synonyms include *tea and eating*, *tea and till't* – i.e. 'tea accompanied by (something)' – and *meat tea*. John Galt in *The Last of the Lairds* (1826) called it *clumsy tea*, claiming the term was Renfrewshire usage:

> ... by clumsy tea ... is meant a very substantial meal of jellies marmalades short bread puffs cookies the cheese and ham always appear and at the time of the killing of the *mart* cowheel with tripe and onions are sometimes superadded.

Hi Hi See FOOTBALL CLUB NICKNAMES.

Hill folk A term applied to COVENANTERS, especially the CAMERONIANS, who during the KILLING TIME were obliged to seek refuge in the wilds of Galloway.

> That person is never of a great character who laughs at the hill-fowk; there is less patriotic blood in the veins of such than would fill a nut-shell, and the heart is as rotten as a yellow puddock stool.
> – John MacTaggart, *The Scottish Gallovidian Encyclopaedia* (1824)

The term is also applied to the hill fairies.

Hillfoots, the The appropriately named area of Clackmannanshire between the Ochil Hills and the Firth of Forth, including the towns of Alloa, Alva, Dollar and Tillicoutry, sometimes referred to as the Hillfoots Villages.

Hillman Imp The 'Scottish car', so called because assembled at Linwood, outside Glasgow. Manufactured by the Rootes Group as a rival to the Mini, the Imp went into production in 1963, government pressure and grants having persuaded Rootes to build the Imp in an area of high unemployment north of the Border. The engine castings were also made at Linwood, although they then had to be sent 300 miles (480 km) to Rootes' plant at Ryton, near Coventry, to be machined, before being sent back up to Linwood to be inserted into the cars. The huge investment in Linwood, and the failure of the Imp to compete with the Mini, led to large losses, and in 1967 Rootes was taken over by Chrysler, who ended production of the Imp in 1976.

> Scotland the wee ...
> land of the millionaire draper, whisky vomit
> and the Hillman Imp
> – Tom Buchan (1931–95), 'Scotland the Wee'

Hill of Reproach, the See PROPHET PEDEN.

Hills of Home Robert Louis Stevenson's beloved Pentlands, among which he wandered as a boy while staying at Swanston, to the south of Edinburgh. He wrote about them in exile in Samoa in 'To S.R. Crockett':

Be it granted me to behold you again in dying,
Hills of home! and to hear again the call;
Hear about the graves of the martyrs the peewees
    crying,
And hear no more at all.
    [*peewees*, 'lapwings, peewits']

The 'martyrs' were those Covenanters killed in the PENTLAND RISING of 1666. *Hills of Home* was adopted as the title of the fourth of MGM's Lassie films (1948), set in 'the Glen'.

Hingin' by the breers o' the een Hanging by one's eyebrows, i.e. on the verge of catastrophe, especially bankruptcy. The expression was common in the Northeast into the 20th century.

Hingin' mince Some non-existent absurdity; the object of a wild goose chase or fool's errand. Unlike a solid joint of beef, for example, mince cannot be hung from a hook with any degree of success. Thus the *DSL*, at any rate. However, on the Fraserburgh message board of the knowhere.co.uk website, in response to an enquiry as to the meaning of 'hinging mince', one respondent responds:

> are u hivin a laugh or sumthing, abody kens fit the fuck hingin mince is. and if ye dinna then ye really dinna want te ken and its nae for a lady te tell ye ats for sure.

It would appear that in these circles the expression is a term for the labia minora, especially if protuberant. *The Cassell Dictionary of Slang* (1998), compiled by that most urbane of lexicographers, Jonathan Green, remains uncharacteristically silent on the matter.

Hingin' the cat Working to rule, lounging about. The expression comes from Dundee and thereabouts.

Hing the lugs Literally, 'to hang the ears', i.e. to look downcast.

Hing the petted lip To sulk; literally 'to hang the offended lip', i.e. to protrude the lower lip, as a sulking child would. *Pet* is Scots for 'to take umbrage'.

Hinny an' jo If someone is (or a couple are) said to be *a' hinny an' jo*, or *nuthin' but hinny an' jo*, then they are full of kindness, speaking nothing but words of endearment – such as *hinny* ('honey'), a term of affection applied particularly to women and children, and *jo*, a term of affection for a man (as in the famous song 'John Anderson, My Jo'; *see* MERRY MUSES OF CALEDONIA, THE).

> I hae indeed an auld aunt, – but she's no muckle to lippen to, unless it comes frae her ain side o' the house; an' then she's a' hinny and joe.
>   – James Hogg, *The Brownie of Bodsbeck and Other Tales* (1818)

His Polyonymous Omnipotence A disparaging nickname (*polyonymous*, 'known by a variety of names') for Donald Munro, a local solicitor whom Sir James Matheson made his factor when he acquired the island of Lewis in 1844. Munro's high-handedness with the crofters eventually led to the Bernera Riot of 1874, when the crofters of Great Bernera, a small island off the west coast, resisted attempts to evict them after they had refused to obey an order to move their animals to make way for a sporting estate. The crofters pelted the bailiffs with clods of earth, and tore the coat of the sheriff officer – who declared that if he had had a gun, many Bernera mothers would be in mourning for their sons. Three crofters were arrested, but were acquitted after hundreds of Bernera men, led by pipers, marched to Stornoway to demand an audience with the aged Matheson. The laird condemned his factor's actions, and Munro was sacked the following year.

Hobbe, King *See* KING HOBBE.

Hobbema, the Scottish *See* SCOTTISH HOBBEMA, THE.

Hochmagandy *See* HOUGHMAGANDIE.

Hodge Podge Club A prominent gentlemen's club in Glasgow in the 18th century, described a century later by the librarian of the Chamber of Commerce and Manufactures in Glasgow as follows:

> The Hodge Podge Club ... was composed of gentlemen holding a high social position. They met in a tavern in Trongate, kept by one Cruikshank. It was

originally constituted with the object of assisting the members to form correct views upon matters of a literary, political, or philosophical nature, and also of improving them in the practice of public speaking. With these laudable objects the members met once a fortnight; but, as might have been expected, the purposes of the club were found rather heavy and uninteresting, and it is wickedly reported that latterly its principal attractions consisted in a jolly Scotch dinner, where the dish from which the club took its name was an invariable accompaniment [*hodge-podge* is a thick vegetable broth], the whole seasoned with wit and laughter, followed by profuse libations of the celebrated Glasgow Punch, in which the now forgotten beauties of that day were uproariously toasted. Dr Moore, author of 'Zeluco', and father of Sir John Moore, was, in the palmy days of the 'Hodge Podge', the chief spirit of the club, and its poet laureate; and at its anniversary dinners produced graphic sketches of the members after the manner of Goldsmith's 'Retaliation', which kept the table in a roar, and many of which are still preserved.

– George Stewart, *Curiosities of Glasgow Citizenship* (1881)

See also ACCIDENTAL CLUB; PIG CLUB, THE.

Hogboon A variety of BROWNIE or elf found in Orkney; *hog* is from Old Norse *haugr*, 'mound, hillock', while *boon* is from *bui*, 'dweller' or 'farmer'. Nearly every significant ancient burial mound was thought to have its own hogboon dwelling there, and such creatures, sometimes regarded as ancestral spirits, were collectively known as *hogfolk*. Similarly, a dwarf or any unusual-looking person was known as a *hjogfinni*.

There is a tale from the Orkney island of Sanday of a hogboon whose nose had been put out of joint by the failure of a farmer's wife to leave out food for him. As a consequence, he made life so difficult for the farmer that the latter decided to move himself and his family to another part of the island. As they drove their cart to their new home, they were severely put out when the hogboon poked its head out of the top of a milk churn and exclaimed, 'What a grand day for a flittin'!'

Hogmanay New Year's Eve, for long the most important festival in the Scottish calendar – although in recent decades CHRISTMAS, once condemned as papist and thus banned after the Reformation, has loomed larger and larger. Hogmanay, falling in the midst of what used to be called the DAFT DAYS, is marked by parties, the BELLS at midnight, followed by kissing and the singing of AULD LANG SYNE, first footing (*see* FIRST FOOT) and the consumption of BLACK BUN and considerable quantities of alcohol. Some people believe one should clean the house, empty the grate of ashes and clear one's debts before midnight. In certain parts of Scotland fire ceremonies are conducted, for example, in Biggar there is an enormous bonfire in the main street, while in Stonehaven they 'swing the FIREBALLS', and in many places there are fireworks and torchlit processions (*see also* BURNING THE CLAVIE). In his *Book of Days* (1862–4), Robert Chambers observes:

> Whilst … the inhabitants of South Britain are settling down again quietly to work after the festivities of the Christmas season, their fellow-subjects in the northern division of the island are only commencing their annual saturnalia, which, till recently, bore, in the licence and boisterous merriment which used to prevail, a most unmistakable resemblance to its ancient pagan namesake. The epithet of the Daft Days, applied to the season of the New Year in Scotland, indicates very expressively the uproarious joviality which characterized the period in question. This exuberance of joyousness – which, it must be admitted, sometimes led to great excesses – has now much declined.

That was then, this is now, and all the inhibitions observed by Chambers are long forgotten.

The word *hogmanay* itself first appears in Scots at the beginning of the 17th century as *hagmonay*, denoting a New Year's gift, typically of oat cakes or bread and cheese, requested by children touring the streets with a cry of '*Hagmonay*'. (The custom of giving such gifts led to New Year's Eve also being referred to as *Cake Day*, while the musical offerings of the children gave rise to the alternative name, *Singin' E'en*, and their rewards were known as *singin' cakes*.) Chambers records various rhymes that were used by children in his day, for example:

Get up, goodwife, and shake your feathers,
And dinna think that we are beggars;
For we are bairns come out to play,
Get up and gie's our hogmanay!'

and:

Get up, goodwife, and dinna sweir,
And deal your bread to them that's here;
For the time will come when ye'll be dead,
And then ye'll neither need ale nor bread.

and:

My feet's cauld, my shoon's thin;
Gie's my cakes, and let me rin!

Some children dressed up as GUISERS and put on performances, while in certain places in the Highlands and Islands groups of lads would roam about, beating one of their fellows dressed up in a cowhide with sticks.

There have been all kinds of speculations regarding the origin of the word *hogmanay*. For example, Robert Chambers mentions the unlikely suggestion that it is from the French *homme est né*, 'man is born', referring to the birth of Christ. Chambers also mentions the theory that:

… the term under notice is derived from *Hoggu-nott*, *Hogenat*, or *Hogg-night*, the ancient Scandinavian name for the night preceding the feast of Yule, and so called in reference to the animals slaughtered on the occasion …

Another suggestion is Flemish *hoog min dag*, 'great love day', while John MacTaggart, in his *Gallovidian Encyclopaedia* (1824), charmingly offers the following:

On the happy nights of *hog-ma-nay* the kissing trade is extremely brisk, particularly in AULD REEKIE; then the lasses must kiss with all the stranger lads they meet, while phrases not unlike to 'John, come kiss me now' or 'John, come *hug me now*' are frequently heard. From such causes, methinks, *hog-ma-nay* has started. The *hugging day*, the time to *hug-me-now*.

However, it is most likely that the word derives from the northern French dialect term *hoginane*, in turn deriving from Old French *aguillanneuf*, the last day of the year, and also a New Year's gift; the second

element is clearly *l'an neuf*, the New Year, but the first element remains obscure, Chambers proffering *au gui*, 'to the mistletoe', suggesting a Druidical link (highly unlikely). *See also* CAISEAN-UCHD; CREAM OF THE WATER, THE; HANDSEL MONDAY; NE'ER-DAY.

Hold . . . *See* HAUD . . .

Hologram Tam The nickname of Thomas McAnea, who in 2007 was jailed for his part in the sophisticated forgery of large numbers of Bank of Scotland £20 and £50 notes. The centre of operations was the Print Link shop in Maryhill, Glasgow, which normally specialized in printing leaflets and menus for local takeaways. McAnea's particular skill lay in his ability to place holograms and watermarks in the forged notes.

Holy Corner The nickname for a crossroads in Edinburgh marking the boundary between Bruntsfield and Morningside. The sanctity of the locality derives from the four churches at or near each corner of the junction: Christ Church (Scottish Episcopal), Morningside United (Church of Scotland and United Reformed), Morningside Baptist Church, and what is now the Eric Liddell Centre, a Christian community centre set up in memory of the Olympic athlete known as the FLYING SCOTSMAN. Formerly standing near the northwest corner was the garden centre known euphoniously as Mulhearn and Brotchie. As is the way of such things, the site is now occupied by a Tesco Metro.

Holy Island A small, hilly island off the east coast of Arran. It was here, according to legend, that the Irish monk St Molaise (aka Laserian, d.639) set up a hermitage in a cave on the western shore. It was said that Molaise voluntarily accepted 30 diseases at the same time, as a way of expiating his sins and so avoiding Purgatory. The island is now home to a small Buddhist community. For another 'holy island', *see* EYNHALLOW.

Holy Loch, the An arm of the Firth of Clyde by Dunoon, which takes its name from the story that a ship carrying earth from the Holy Land intended for the foundations of Glasgow Cathedral sank here.

The sanctity of the place was hardly enhanced by the presence, from 1960 to 1992, of a base for nuclear-armed US submarines.

Holyrood A name that now primarily denotes the Scottish Parliament, in the same way that 'Westminster' denotes the UK Parliament. The name was originally applied to the Abbey of Holyrood (*see also* ABBEY LAIRDS), built at the foot of Edinburgh's ROYAL MILE in the 12th century by David I. The name means 'holy cross', alluding to the story that when David was out hunting one day, he fell from his horse and was on the verge of being skewered by an affronted stag, when, in answer to his prayer, a cross appeared between the deer's antlers. The king was saved, founding an abbey in gratitude. The name was subsequently transferred to the nearby Palace of Holyroodhouse, the building of which was commenced by James IV in 1498, and from thence to the new Scottish Parliament building, designed by Enric Miralles and opened opposite the palace in 2004. The fact that the Parliament building cost ten times more than budgeted, and opened three years late, led the press to dub it *Follyrood*.

An intriguing footnote regarding Holyroodhouse was provided by the Edinburgh-born eccentric William Money (1809–83), who built a version of the palace near Los Angeles in brick and adobe as the headquarters of his fundamentalist Reformed New Testament Church of the Faith of Jesus Christ, of which he was bishop, spiritual leader and sole member.

Holyrood pudding A pudding involving semolina, milk, eggs, butter, sugar, ratafia biscuits and orange marmalade. How and when the dish acquired its name is unclear.

'Holy Willie's Prayer' A poem by Robert Burns, written in 1785. In addressing God, Holy Willie outlines his belief in the Calvinist doctrine of predestination:

Oh Thou, wha in the heaven dost dwell!
Wha, as it pleases best thysel',
Sends ane to heaven, and ten to hell,
    A' for thy glory,
And no' for ony gude or ill
      They've done afore thee!

He goes on to express his conviction that he is one of the Elect, a 'chosen sample / To show thy grace is great and ample' – for Willie then confesses that he is 'fash'd wi' fleshly lust', and in consequence has lifted a 'lawless leg' against a certain MEG, not to mention trifling with 'Lizzie's lass'; but then in mitigation he pleads that he was drunk at the time. Of course, being one of the Elect, he is convinced of his own salvation, and proceeds to demand that God smite down his enemies for their various sins –

An' a' the glory shall be thine,
    Amen, Amen!

The inspiration for Holy Willie was William Fisher, 'a rather oldish bachelor elder in the parish of Mauchline', who had demanded that the kirk session bring actions against various parishioners – notably Burns's friend Gavin Hamilton – for such crimes as failing to attend church, or digging potatoes on the Sabbath. Burns himself noted that the appearance of his poem 'alarmed the kirk-session so much, that they held several meetings to look over their spiritual artillery, if haply any of it might be pointed against profane rhymers'. In fact, the poem was not printed until 1799, after the poet's death. As for William Fisher, according to Robert Chambers, he 'was afterwards found guilty of secreting money from the church offerings, and he closed his miserable life in a ditch, into which he had fallen in going home after a debauch'. Ever since, the name 'Holy Willie' has been applied to any person whose excess of piety raises suspicions of hypocrisy and hidden sin. *See also* UNCO GUID, THE.

Homecoming Scotland A campaign launched by the Scottish government on 25 January 2009, the 250th anniversary of the birth of Robert Burns, to encourage expatriate Scots and descendants of Scottish emigrants from around the world to revisit their ancestral homeland. The programme of events included celebrations of Scottish contributions to the world such as golf and whisky, as well as intellectual and technological innovations. The day of the launch was marked by an appearance by First Minister Alex Salmond, alongside Prime Minister Gordon Brown, in the *Sunday Post*'s cartoon strip, *The Broons* (for more on this, *see* BROON, THE).

Home vs Hume *See* HUME VS HOME.

Honest Allan The name given by Thomas Carlyle to the poet and man of letters Allan Cunningham (1784–1842). The son of a land-steward in Dumfriesshire, Cunningham became apprenticed to his brother, a mason, and both became friends with James Hogg, the ETTRICK SHEPHERD. In 1809 Cunningham was commissioned by the antiquarian R.H. Cromek to collect contributions for his *Remains of Nithsdale and Galloway Song* (1810). Failing in his quest for old ballads and songs, young Cunningham decided to make up some new ones, and these so delighted Cromek that he included them in his collection as if they were of genuine antiquity. The truth was not generally known until John Wilson ('Christopher North') revealed it in *Blackwood's Magazine* in 1819. Thus began a distinguished literary career, the best-known product of which is the poem 'A Wet Sheet and a Flowing Sea' (1825). *See also* WEE, WEE GERMAN LAIRDIE, A.

Honest Grunter, the *See* ETTRICK SHEPHERD, THE.

Honest Lad and Honest Lass *See* HONEST TOUN, THE.

Honest man's the noblest work of God, An Perhaps the best-known line in Burns's 'The Cottar's Saturday Night' (1786):

From scenes like these old Scotia's grandeur springs,
That makes her loved at home, revered abroad:
Princes and Lords are but the breath of kings,
'An honest man's the noblest work of God.'

The line is in fact a quotation from Pope's *Essay on Man*, epistle 4 (1734), although Burns gives it a more democratic spin than is found in Pope's original:

A wit's a feather, and a chief's a rod;
An honest man's the noblest work of God.

The American agnostic, Robert G. Ingersoll, inverted the line in his book *The Gods* (1876):

An honest God is the noblest work of man.

Honest Men, the *See* FOOTBALL CLUB NICKNAMES.

Honest Toun, the Musselburgh, from its motto *Honestas* (Latin, 'honesty'). This dates back to 1322, when Randolph, Earl of Moray, regent for David II, died here, having been cared for assiduously by the citizens in his final illness. The new regent, the Earl of Mar, offered them a reward, which they declined, declaring that they were simply doing what was right. Mar declared they were a set of honest men, and to this day the Honest Lad and Honest Lass are the leading figures in the town's annual festival, held since 1936.

Honey frae the dunny, a A label applied to any woman who has emerged from an impoverished background (a *dunny* is the basement or cellar of a tenement) into greater affluence and refinement, but who has a tendency to betray her humble origins.

Honours of Scotland, the The Scottish crown jewels, consisting of a crown, sceptre and sword of state. According to tradition, the sceptre was given to James IV by Pope Alexander VI in 1494, and the sword by Pope Julius II in 1507. The crown probably dates from the late 15th century, but was extensively refurbished in 1540 by order of James V. There had been a crown and other royal regalia before the reigns of James IV and James V; the earliest written record, by Andrew of Wyntoun, refers to the 'septure, suerde, crowne and rynge' taken from John Balliol in 1296 as he was forced by Edward I of England to surrender the throne of Scotland (*see* TOOM TABARD). The regalia were taken by Edward back to England, along with the STONE OF SCONE.

The present Honours of Scotland have had their share of adventures. Charles II bore them when he was crowned at Scone on 1 January 1651, an event that prompted Cromwell's invasion of Scotland. The Honours were safeguarded on Charles's behalf by Sir George Ogilvy, governor of Dunottar Castle. When Cromwell laid siege to the castle (from September 1651), Mrs Grainger, the wife of the minister at nearby Kinneff, was given permission by Cromwell's forces to visit Lady Ogilvy inside the besieged castle. She succeeded in smuggling out the crown in her petticoats, while her maid concealed the sceptre and sword in a bundle of flax. The Honours remained buried under the floor of Kinneff Church until after the Restoration.

Following the Union of 1707, the Honours were locked in an iron-bound oak chest and placed in the Crown Room of Edinburgh Castle, which was then sealed up. Over a century later, Sir Walter Scott obtained permission from the Prince Regent (later George IV) to recover the Honours, and so on 4 February 1818, accompanied by various worthies, Scott entered the Crown Room and approached the chest – with some anxiety, for some believed the chest could well be empty. Scott himself described what happened next:

> The chest seemed to return a hollow and empty sound to the strokes of the hammer, and even those whose expectations had been most sanguine felt at the moment the probability of disappointment ... The joy was therefore extreme when, the ponderous lid of the chest being forced open, the Regalia were discovered lying at the bottom covered with linen cloths, exactly as they had been left in the year 1707.

The Honours were presented to George IV at Holyroodhouse when he came to Scotland in 1822, a visit orchestrated and choreographed by Scott himself. They were then returned to the Castle.

The Honours had not quite finished their adventures, however. On 12 May 1941, to prevent them from falling into enemy hands, the Regalia were buried in secret locations deep beneath the Castle's Half-Moon Battery, in the ancient ruins of St David's Tower. Only four people were informed of the exact locations: King George VI, the Secretary of State for Scotland, the King's and Lords' Treasurer's Remembrancer, and the Governor General of Canada. The Honours were unburied after the war, and on 24 June 1953 were presented to Queen Elizabeth II in the High Kirk of St Giles. They are now on view in Edinburgh Castle.

Hoops, the See FOOTBALL CLUB NICKNAMES.

Hoots, mon! An ejaculation, expressive of dismissive incredulity, akin to 'Get away with you!', that has long been a standard in the repertoire of FAUX JOCKERY, providing, for example, the title of a 1950s hit single by Lord Rockingham's XI (which contains the immortal faux jockery line 'There's a moose loose aboot this hoose.') However, the origins of the expression (as *hout, hut, hoot* or *hoots*) are more *echt* than *ersatz*, as attested by the following:

> Hoot, Johnnie Rousseau man, what for hae ye sae mony figmagairies.
>> – James Boswell, diary, 1764 (published as *Boswell and the Grand Tour*)

> Hout! hout! Mrs Flockhart, we're young blude, ye ken.
>> – Sir Walter Scott, *Waverley* (1814), chapter xlii

> 'Hout tout, mither,' cried Cuddie, interfering and dragging her off forcibly, 'dinna deave the gentlewoman wi' your testimony! ye hae preached eneugh for sax days ...'
>> – Sir Walter Scott, *Old Mortality* (1816), chapter viii

Hoppin beds See HAP-THE-BEDS.

Horn, at the See PUT TO THE HORN.

Horse and hattock The cry supposedly uttered by the fairies when they are about to go back to their own land, or to transport some mortal or object by magical means. A *hattock* is a little fairy hat. In a witch trial in 1662 the following testimony was given:

> I haid a little horse, and wold say 'Horse and hattock, in Divellis name'. And than ve vold flie away, quhair we vold.

From the same century comes the story of Lord Duffus, told to the English antiquarian and gossip John Aubrey by a 'learned friend' in Scotland, in a letter dated 25 March 1695. Lord Duffus had been walking one day in the fields near his Morayshire home when

> ... he heard the noise of a whirlwind, and of voices crying Horse and Hattock (this is the word which the Fairies are said to use when they remove from any

place), whereupon he cried Horse and Hattock also, and was immediately caught up, and transported through the air, by the Fairies ...

When Duffus came to his senses he found himself in the cellar of the king of France in Paris, with a silver cup in his hand. When brought before the king and asked to account for himself, he offered the above explanation, which was graciously accepted, and he was allowed to return home, with the cup.

Horseman's Word, the A secret society formed in the Northeast of Scotland in the late 18th century. It was effectively a guild or trade union to maintain the skills and protect the pecuniary interests of men who worked with horses, particularly draught horses on farms. As in the Freemasons, new members had to undergo various quasi-religious initiation rites, such as breaking bread and drinking whisky in imitation of the sacraments, while being put through a mock catechism. Once the candidate was accepted, he was given a secret Word, which supposedly had a magical effect in charming horses. He was then taught various genuinely effective techniques for training and controlling horses and treating their ailments, many involving herbs. The society also functioned as a social club, involving much drinking, bonhomie and anticlerical jesting, and there seems to have been a nod backward to the old beliefs that humans who could control animals had somehow entered into a compact with the Devil:

> In Renfrewshire, Thomas Lindsay, a young lad apprehended on a charge of witchcraft, in 1664, boasted that he would for a halfpenny make a horse stand still in the plough at the word of command by turning himself widdershins or contrary to the course of the sun.
> – Francis Grant, *Narratives of the Sufferings of a Young Girl* (1698)

Membership of the Horseman's Word declined after the Second World War, as farming became increasingly mechanized, but new members were still being initiated in the 1960s. One of these, Billy Rennie of Buchan, who was initiated in September 1961, published a book about the society in 2009. He told the *Buchan Observer*:

> It wasn't the Word that really gave the power, but a knowledge handed down through history. There are

many concoctions to be mastered and many powerful drugs which a horsemen had to learn. Using various herbs and potions, the horsemen could make the wildest of horses follow him without halter or bridle, and make it so that the horses would not leave the stables without him.

When Rennie found there were no more Clydesdales to work with in Buchan, he and his brother Bobby pursued successful careers in show jumping, and then trained and sold horses across Scotland and Ireland.

See also MASON-WORD, THE.

Horse of the woods The literal translation of the Gaelic *capull coille*, the capercaillie, so-called because of its size (they can grow up to weights of 15½ lb / 7 kg). Other names include wood grouse and heather cock (Gaelic *an coileach-fraoich*). The bird became extinct in Scotland in the late 18th century owing to the depletion of its pine-wood habitat, but was successfully reintroduced into Perthshire from Scandinavia in 1837 by the Marquess of Breadalbane. Despite its rarity and its disgusting taste (of turpentine, due to a winter diet of pine needles), it was formerly valued as a game bird.

Hot ... *See also* HET ...

Hot an' reekin' If one *gies it hot an' reekin'* ('smoking') one is handing out a severe dose of verbal or physical chastisement. The recipient thus *gets it hot an' reekin'*. Similarly, to *gar someone's rumple reek* (literally, 'make someone's rump smoke') is to administer a severe thrashing.

Hotspurs of the Kirk How the *Mercurius Politicus*, Oliver Cromwell's official newspaper, characterized the disputing parties within the Church of Scotland in November 1653:

> Here hath been a thin meeting of divers Hotspurs of the Kirk, to little purpose, save thwarting and crossing one another, being of different parties and opinions to show that the quarrel is everlasting between the Assembly man and the Remonstrator, and that no feud is more mortal, and immortal, than that which is upon account of religion.

Houghmagandie or **hochmagandy** A euphemism for sexual intercourse, perhaps jocularly composed from *hochle*, 'to walk or do something awkwardly', hence 'to fornicate', from *hough*, 'hock' (i.e. that part of the horse homologous to the human ankle; alternatively, the hamstring); and *canty*, 'happy, cheerful, full of vim and vigour'. The word is best known from Burns's 'The Holy Fair':

> There's some are fou' o' love divine;
> There's some are fou' o' brandy;
> And many jobs that day begin
> May end in 'houghmagandie'
> Some ither day.

Householding or Domestic Scots See WILD SCOTS.

House of Terror, the The nickname awarded by the Liverpudlian entertainer Ken Dodd to the Glasgow Empire Theatre (1897–1963), a well-known graveyard for comics, especially those from England. On one occasion someone mentioned to Dodd the theory enunciated by Freud that jokes result in elation and relief from tension. 'The trouble with Freud,' Dodd retorted, 'is he never played the Glasgow Empire Saturday night.' Unpopular acts might be pelted with diverse objects by the unpropitiated audience, and legend has it that if men from the shipyards were in the objects might be rivets. One well-worn joke about the taciturnity of Empire audiences recounts the night when a talented and enthusiastic performer starts juggling with four then five then six balls. Silence. Then, while still juggling, he starts to ride a unicycle. Silence. Then he's riding the unicycle along a high wire while singing highlights from *Carmen* and juggling eight footballs, all simultaneously. The silence is deathly – until, from the darkness at the back of the stalls, a lugubrious voice demands, 'Is there nae end to this man's fuckin' talent?'

House with the Green Shutters, The A novel (1901) by George Douglas (George Douglas Brown, 1869–1902). Grim and realistic, it represents a reaction against the rural sentimentality of the KAILYARD SCHOOL. The eponymous house of the title, located in the fictional Ayrshire village of Barbie (based on the author's native Ochiltree), embodies the pride and prosperity of the central character, dour local businessman Jock Gourlay. It all ends very badly indeed:

> No man dared to speak. They gazed with blanched faces at the House with Green Shutters, sitting dark there and terrible, beneath the radiant arch of dawn.

Howe-dumb-deid The dead silent depth (*howe*, 'hollow, hole'), usually of the night, or the winter:

> I' the how-dumb-deid o' the cauld hairst nicht
> The warl' like an eemis stane
> Wags i' the lift …
> > – Hugh MacDiarmid, 'The Eemis Stane' (1925) [*hairst*, 'harvest'; *eemis*, 'unsteady'; *lift*, 'sky']

The *howe o' the nicht* is midnight, or the WEE SMALL HOURS.

Howtowdie A plump young chicken before it has begun to lay, especially one destined for the pot. The word comes from Old French *hétoudeau* or *estaudau*, meaning the same thing. *Howtowdie* is also a dish of boiled chicken with spinach and poached eggs, and in the 19th century the word was applied to an unmarried woman.

Hugga-muggie A Shetland dish, comprising a sort of fish haggis, using the fish's stomach. *Hugga* is from Shetland dialect *uggen*, 'delicacy', 'snack', possibly related to Old Norse *hugga*, 'to soothe, comfort'.

Hugh of the Little Head See BODACH GLAS, EOGHAN OF THE LITTLE HEAD

Hugh the Dull Hugh, Lord of Douglas (1294–c.1345), so called because, as a cleric, he led a less swashbuckling life than many other medieval Douglases, such as his elder brother the BLACK DOUGLAS or the latter's bastard son ARCHIBALD THE GRIM. In his *History of the House of Douglas and Angus*, David Hume of Godscroft (1558–1629) writes:

> Of this man, whether it was by reason of the dullness of his mind, we have no mention at all in history of his actions.

Hull No. 534 The hull of the giant Cunarder which during the worst years of the Great Depression, from December 1931 to 1934, stood unfinished and abandoned in the John Brown yard at Clydebank. Work had begun in 1930 and was resumed in May 1934, once a government loan had been secured. It was launched as the *Queen Mary* on 26 September 1934, and made its maiden voyage in May 1936. Regarding the name, legend has it that Cunard intended to call the ship *Victoria*, but when representatives of the company sought George V's permission to name the ship 'after Britain's greatest queen', the king replied that his wife, Queen Mary, would be delighted.

Human sacrifice Scottish folklore contains a few accounts of human sacrifices being made in order to cure diseases. In *Social and Religious Life in the Highlands* (1902), the Revd K. Macdonald of Applecross relates the following story:

> The most horrible of sacrificial remedies was that in vogue at one time for the cure of cattle-madness. It is reported that a farmer in Kinlochewe had his cattle infected with that disease, and was unable to heal them by ordinary means. He was told that if he could get the heart of a man who did not know his parents, and dip it in a tub of water, that he would have his remedy. By sprinkling the water on the cattle the trouble would be washed away. He could not expect to get that, but the idea got hold of him, and kept him on the alert for the charm. A travelling pack merchant or pedlar happened to come to his house one evening, and he was hospitably entertained. In course of conversation the man gave as much of his history as he remembered at the time. Among other things, he said that he knew nothing of his people, that he did not know even the names of his parents. He got up next morning and set out on his journey towards Torridon. When about half-way through the glen he was overtaken by his host of the previous evening who demanded his life. The poor man said that he might have all his goods without a struggle on his part if that was what he was after. But the murderer told him plainly that he wanted no less than his life, that he followed him for his heart to cure his cattle. He took out his heart there and then and prepared the remedy. It is said that the cattle had been cured, but that the disease was transferred to his family.

Some of his descendants, who inherited the transferred madness, were spotted up to the middle of last century as families who were under a more terrible ban than that of Gehazi [2 Kings 5:27].

In Breadalbane, as recounted in the *Transactions of the Gaelic Society of Inverness*, volume xxv, 1901–03 (1907),

> ... there is a tradition that, once upon a time, when a pestilence raged among the herds on the south side of Lochtay, a ghastly tragedy was enacted. Actuated by a heathenish desire to propitiate some evil spirit or other, the people seized a poor 'gangrel body', bound him hand and foot, and placed him in the ford of Ardtalnaig burn ... a little further up the stream than the present bridge. All the cattle in that district were then driven over his body, and the poor creature's life was crushed out.

In 1588 a witch was accused of advising Hector Munro, 17th Baron of Fowlis, that his illness would only be cured if 'the principal man of his bluid should die for him'. Despite these tales, there does not appear to be any hard evidence of human sacrifice in Scotland in historical times; and even Roman, Greek or later Christian accounts of Celtic sacrificial customs must be taken with a pinch of salt. *See also* ST ORAN'S CHAPEL, LIVE BURIAL IN.

Humble cot shaken by blasts of dark December *See* GENTLE POET OF LOCHLEVEN, THE.

Hume vs Home Regarding the spelling of this surname, Robert Chambers, in his *Book of Days* (1862–4), relates the following anecdote:

> Amongst jocular bequests, that of David Hume to his friend John Home, author of *Douglas* [*see* WHAUR'S YER WULLIE SHAKESPEARE NOO?], may be considered as one of the most curious. John Home liked claret, but detested port wine, thinking it a kind of poison; and the two friends had doubtless had many discussions on this subject. They also used to have disputes as to which of them took the proper way of spelling their common family-name. The philosopher, about a fortnight before his death, wrote with his own hand the following codicil to his will: 'I leave to my friend, Mr John Home, of Kilduff, ten dozen of my old claret at his choice, and one single bottle of that other liquor called

port. I also leave him six dozen of port, provided that he attests under his hand, signed John Hume, that he has himself alone finished that bottle at two sittings. By this concession, he will at once terminate the only two differences that ever arose between us concerning temporal matters.'

Humle or **hummel cow** A cow that is either naturally without horns, or which has been polled. The word is first recorded in the 15th century, and is cognate with Old German *hummel*, 'hornless animal'.

I gat the humle cow, that's the best in the byre, frae black Frank Inglis and Sergeant Bothwell, for ten pund Scots ...
– Sir Walter Scott, *Old Mortality* (1816), chapter iv

Humour, the Scottish sense of *See* DOURNESS; GLASGOW HUMOUR; HOUSE OF TERROR, THE.

Hun A disparaging name for a supporter of Glasgow Rangers FC. *See* FOOTBALL CLUB NICKNAMES.

Hunch-cuddy-hunch *See under* HACKY-DUCK.

Hundred Years' Peace, the The century of harmony that prevailed between Scotland and England from 1189 until the death of Alexander III in 1286, an event that ushered in the Wars of Scottish Independence and which was dubbed the BEGINNING OF ALL SORROW by the 15th-century *Liber Pluscardensis*.

Huntegowk Literally 'hunt the cuckoo', i.e. to go on a fool's errand. A *gowk* is also a fool, or a trick, and *Gowk's Day* (or *Magowk's Day*) is April Fool's Day, on which one lets out the cry 'Huntegowk' when one has successfully *gi'en someone the gowk* or *magowked someone*, i.e. duped one's victim, who may be dubbed an *April gowk*.

It would look unco-like, I thought, just to be sent out on a hunt-the-gowk errand wi' a land-louper like that.
– Sir Walter Scott, *Guy Mannering* (1815), chapter xlv

See also GOWK AND TITLIN; GOWKISPINTIL; GOWK'S CHEESE; GOWK'S NEST; GOWK STORM; PREEN-TAIL DAY.

Hunter's Bog A shallow valley on Arthur's Seat, between the hill itself and the northeast flank of SALISBURY CRAGS, leading down from the GUTTIT HADDIE towards Holyrood. It is mentioned in *WEIR OF HERMISTON* as the place Archie flees in disgust after witnessing his father's brutal performance in court:

He lay and moaned in the Hunter's Bog, and the heavens were dark above him and the grass of the field an offence.
– Robert Louis Stevenson, *Weir of Hermiston* (1896), chapter iii

Hunting of the Cheviot, the Another name for the Battle of Otterburn, fought on 15 August 1388 in Redesdale in Northumberland, to the south side of the Cheviot Hills. The battle, which is also known as Chevy Chase (the name of a local hunting ground) and which is the subject of various ballads, saw the Scots under James, Earl of Douglas, defeat the English under Henry Percy (aka Harry Hotspur). According the 15th-century ballad, 'The Battle of Chevy Chase', Douglas was infuriated when Percy boasted that he intended to hunt for three days on the Scottish side of the Border, which Douglas regarded as a mortal insult. As it turned out, Douglas was fatally wounded in the fight, and ordered that he be hidden in a stand of bracken so that the enemy would not take heart from hearing of his death. Despite the loss of their leader, the Scots were victorious, and it was to this stand of bracken that Hotspur acknowledged defeat – hence the celebrated verse in 'The Battle of Otterbourne':

But I hae dream'd a dreary dream,
Beyond the Isle of Skye;
I saw a dead man win a fight,
And I think that man was I.

These lines provide the epigraph for the film *The Man Who Never Was* (1956), the true story of how in 1943 British intelligence dressed up a corpse as a major in the Royal Marines, and jettisoned the body into the sea off Spain (where they knew German spies would hear of it). Attached to the body was a briefcase containing documents that suggested the Allies were about to launch a double-pronged invasion, of Sardinia and Greece, rather than the actual target, Sicily. The deception was successful.

Hunt of Pentland, the An episode (also known as the Royal Hunt of Roslin) during the reign of Robert the Bruce, when the king challenged his knights to kill 'a white faunch deer' that always evaded him when he went hunting on the Pentland Hills. The deer was eventually killed by Help and Hold, two hounds of Sir William Sinclair of Roslin and Penicuik, who was granted the lands of Glencorse as a reward and built a chapel to mark the place where the stag had been brought down. In another version of the story, the man responsible for slaying the deer was Randolph de Clerc, who was given the lands of Penicuik as a consequence. During the hunt, the royal standard was raised in the Buckstane, an old march stone that used to stand on Braid Road, Comiston, and after granting the lands Bruce declared:

> When I, or any succeeding kings, shall come to hunt on the Pentlands or Burgh Muir, your huntsman shall attend the gathering, and from the top of the Buckstane shall wind three blasts on the bugle horn, and I wish you and yours long life to enjoy it.

This is the origin of 'Free for a Blast', the motto of the Clerks of Penicuik. Since 1936, Penicuik's annual gala – modelled on the traditional Border common ridings (*see* RIDING THE MARCHES) – has seen the installation of the 'Penicuik Hunter and Lass', who become ambassadors for the town.

Hurricane Bawbag The informal name given to the fierce storm that hit Scotland on 8 December 2011, with winds reaching over 100 mph (160 kph). The name rapidly went global on Twitter, prompting one user to comment, 'Hurricane Bawbag is trending? This is the kind of thing that makes me proud to be Scottish.' *Bawbag* (literally 'ball bag') is Scots for 'scrotum'; the word is also applied disparagingly to a person regarded as complete idiot. Within hours of the storm hitting the country, Hurricane Bawbag t-shirts were being offered for sale, with the tag line 'a load of old wind'.

Hydro boys, the *See* TUNNEL TIGERS, THE.

Hyne *See* MERRY HYNE TO YE, A.

I ... *See* AH ...

Iain Lom *See* LOM, IAIN

Iain Ruaidh nan Cath *See* RED JOHN OF THE BATTLES.

'I Belong to Glasgow' One of the better-known songs of the music-hall entertainer Will Fyffe (1885–1947). The chorus goes as follows:

> I belong to Glasgow, dear old Glasgow town;
> But there's something the matter wi' Glasgow,
> For it's goin' roun' and roun'!
> I'm only a common old working chap,
> As anyone here can see,
> But when I get a couple o' drinks on a Saturday,
> Glasgow belongs to me!

Apparently Fyffe had been inspired while helping a man a little the worse for wear, who claimed 'The way I feel tonight is that Glasgow belongs to me.' Fyffe offered the song to Sir Harry Lauder, who declined it on the grounds that he did not wish to endorse alcoholic indulgence. When it was pointed out to Lauder that he showed no such diffidence when singing 'Just a Wee DEOCH AN DORUS', he asserted that the emphasis in that song was on the word 'wee'. As for Fyffe himself, the critic James Agate wrote he 'was not so much a sober man trying to appear drunk as a drunk man trying to appear sober'.

Ibrox Tragedy, the A disaster that occurred at Ibrox Park, home of Glasgow Rangers FC, on 22 January 1971, when 66 fans were killed in a crush on Stairway 13 while attempting to leave at the end of an OLD FIRM game. An earlier disaster occurred at the stadium on 5 April 1902, during a Scotland–England match, when the back of one of the stands collapsed, and hundreds of spectators fell to the ground, resulting in 25 deaths.

Ice-Cream Wars, the A series of violent turf wars in Glasgow in the 1980s between rival operators of ice-cream vans. It was generally believed that the selling of ice cream was a cover for dealing in drugs and stolen goods. The police detailed to deal with the conflict were punningly dubbed 'the Serious Chimes Squad', and the Ice Cream Wars feature (light-heartedly) in Bill Forsyth's 1984 comedy film, *Comfort and Joy*. However, the violence was no laughing matter, culminating as it did on 16 April 1984 in the deaths of several family members of one van driver in a deliberate arson attack.

Iceman A nickname of the snooker player Stephen Henry (b.1969), born in South Queensferry, who became the youngest ever snooker world champion in 1990, at the age of 21.

Ichie nor ochie *See* EECHIE NOR OCHIE.

Idiot race, an How Robert Burns described the ruling House of Hanover in his lines inscribed with a diamond 'On the Window of an Inn in Stirling', on 27 August 1787:

> Here Stuarts once in glory reigned,
> And laws for Scotland's weal ordained;
> But now unroof'd their palace stands,
> Their sceptre's sway'd by other hands;
> The injured Stuart line is gone,
> A race outlandish fills their throne –
> An idiot race, to honour lost;
> Who know them best despise them most!

In his 1877 annotated edition of Burns's works, William Scott Douglas (1815–83) notes that these subversive lines 'eventually caused so much excitement, and not a little trouble to their author', that about two months later Burns returned to the inn 'and dashed out the pane with the butt-end of his riding-switch; but, meanwhile, the epigrams had been copied into travellers' note-books, and widely circulated'.

If Ah don't see ye through the week Ah'll see ye through the windae A jocular Glaswegian way of saying goodbye. Another version is *If Ah don't see ye aboot, Ah'll see ye a sanny* – with a pun on *boot* and *sanny* ('sandshoe').

If at first ye don't succeed, / In wi' the boot an' then the heid The Glaswegian version of 'If at first you don't succeed, / Try, try and try again', with the suggestion that a little light violence might just do the trick.

If he's big enough, he's auld enough A Border saying, now heard when a young lad first plays for a senior rugby team, but probably originating in the days of the BORDER REIVERS. One such lad was Robert Johnstone of Raecleugh, who in 1593 was only 11 years old when he bloodied his lance during the slaughter of the Maxwells by the Johnstones at Dryfe Sands near Lockerbie.

If it's for ye, it'll no go by ye If it's got your number ... *Qué será será.*

If it's no' the skitter, it's the spew If it's not one thing (diarrhoea), it's another (vomiting). *See also* THERE'S AYE A SOMETHING.

If it wisnae for the weavers The opening of the refrain of the well-known song 'The Wark o' the Weavers' by David Shaw (1786–1856):

If it wisnae for the weavers whit wid we do,
We wadna hae claith made o' oor woo',
We widnae hae a coat, neither black nor blue
If it wisnae for the wark o' the weavers.

The song was parodied by Billy Connolly and Tom McGrath in *The Great Northern Welly Boot Show* (1972):

If it wisnae fur yer wellies where wid ye be
You'd be in the hospital or infirmary

Cos you would have a dose o' the flu or even
   pleurisy
If ye didnae have yer feet in yer wellies.

If you wish to be blamed, marry; if you wish to be praised, die A saying still current in the Highlands and parts of Ireland in the early 20th century. In Gaelic it is:

Mas maith leat do cháineadh, pós;
Mas maith leat do mholadh, faigh bás.

Île de Dieu, l' The name (French for 'the island of God') given by Mary of Guise, mother of Mary Queen of Scots, to Inchkeith, a small island in the Firth of Forth taken by the English in 1547 and recaptured by a Franco-Scots force two years later, on 29 June, the French *Fête Dieu* ('festival of God'). It was on Inchkeith (or possibly on the tiny island of Inchmickery, also in the Forth) that James IV assayed an experiment to see whether an infant brought up in isolation by a deaf-mute nurse would speak Hebrew. It didn't.

Ilk, of that *See* OF THAT ILK.

Ilka body's body Literally, 'every person's person', i.e. everybody's friend. The phrase can either denote a genuinely popular, helpful, friendly type, or an insincere flatterer who merely displays the semblance of friendship to all and sundry.

Ill-Beloved, the How the Scottish nobility referred to James V, who, mistrusting the great magnates, had appointed men of lesser rank to positions of power in the land. The ordinary people had a greater affection for 'the Poor Man's King'; *see* GOODMAN OF BALLENGEICH, THE.

Ill comes upon waur's back Literally, 'ill comes upon the back of worse', i.e. it's one damn thing after another; it never rains but it pours. The proverb has been traced back to Robert Henryson's 'The Trial of the Fox', from *The Morall Fabilis* (later 15th century):

Off evill cummis war, off war cummis werst of all.

Ill ee The evil eye. Although largely associated with the cultures of the Mediterranean, belief in the evil eye as a cause of illness or other misfortune was once widely held in Scotland. In *Daemonologie* (1597), for example, James VI speaks of 'such kind of charms as commonly daft wives use, for healing of forspoken goods, for preserving them from evil eyes', while official records from 1617 talk of a child 'quha haid tane ane brash of seiknes thrugh ane ill ee'. The belief appears to have endured longest in the Highlands and Islands, as recounted by George Henderson in his *Survivals in Belief Among the Celts* (1911):

> Young infants are frequently believed to be over-looked; likewise cattle; a man may lay the evil eye even on what is his own property, as when a husband must on no account see the churning operations, as his glance would prevent the butter coming. The great remedy is *bùrn airgid*, 'water into which silver coins have been put', as also gold and copper if you like, but silver by all means. The water has to be raised with a wooden ladle from a stream over which pass the living and the dead, in the name of the Trinity; the sign of the cross is made over the contents of the ladle, and a rhyme is repeated wherein the opening word of the Lord's Prayer, *Pater*, in G[aelic] *Paidir*, is repeated seven times, but alternately in name of the Virgin and of the King (or Lord) ...

Henderson goes on to quote the observations of the Revd Allan MacDonald regarding various rituals practised on South Uist:

> If a person came and saw a cow or other creature belonging to you, and he began to praise it, e.g. if he were to say, *tha ùth mór aig a' bhoin*, 'the cow has a big udder', or anything similar of a complimentary nature, this act of praising was called *aibhseachadh*; and as it might lead accidentally to *gonadh*, or evil eye, or wounding of the cattle, as a preventative it was cus-tomary to say to the person making the complimentary remarks: *Fliuch do shùil* = 'Wet your eye.' This wetting of the eye was generally performed by moistening the tip of the finger with saliva, and moistening the eye with it thereafter.

Fire also played a part in averting the evil eye. Henderson cites Thomas Pennant, traveller to the Hebrides in the mid-18th century:

> It has happened that, after baptism, the father has placed a basket, filled with bread and cheese, on the pothook that impended over the fire in the middle of the room, which the company sit around; and the child is thrice handed across the fire, with the design to frustrate all attempts of evil spirits or evil eyes. This originally seems to have been designed as a purifica-tion.

Henderson also describes ceremonies involving passing a candle three times round a mother and newly born child, and others involving passing a toddler who was failing to thrive through a burning hoop, a ceremony known as *Beannachd Na Cuairte* ('the blessing of the round or of the circle'). Similar ceremonies were recorded in the Lowlands. *See also* HIGHLAND MARY.

Ill Raid, the The name given to the precursor to the disaster at Flodden. In August 1513, in response to an English raid across the Tweed into southeast Scotland, Alexander Home, Lord Warden of the Scottish Marches, led 3000 horseman into North-umberland, where they put seven villages to the torch and drove off large numbers of horses. But an English force under Sir William Bulmer circled ahead of the returning raiders and on 13 August set an ambush at Milfield, close to the present-day A697 between Wooler and Coldstream. The Scots rode straight into it, losing 500 men and perhaps a similar number of prisoners. Thomas Ruthal, Bishop of Durham, gleefully recorded how the English 'sette upon and venquysched the chamberlayn of Scotland' (i.e. Home), who fled, leaving his standard with the enemy. Ten days later James IV marched his royal host across the Tweed, en route to annihilation at Flodden – which was fought within a mile or two of Milfield on 9 September 1513.

Ill skin If one is said to put one's food, meat, etc., in an *ill skin*, one is all skin and bones, giving the appearance of malnourishment.

> Having inquired for the Laird, Jenny replies, 'Deed, sir, he's no right.'
> 'Ay, Jenny, I'm sorry for that – what ails him?'
> 'Ails! I canna say mickle's the matter wi' him, poor bodie, but he's dwining, and he's no ill either – trowth, ony ha'd o' health he has, is aye at meal-time, and yet he puts a' in an ill skin.'
> – John Galt, *The Last of the Lairds* (1826), chapter i

Ill-trickit A Northeastern expression meaning naughty or mischievous.

Ill Week A massive raid by Scottish BORDER REIVERS into Cumbria in April 1603, while James VI was en route to London to ascend the throne of England. During the raid, parties of Grahams, Armstrongs and Elliots plundered some 5,000 cattle from Cumbria, perhaps realizing that this was going to be their last chance for such booty, as James decreed the very name 'the Borders' be abolished, to be replaced by the MIDDLE SHIRES.

Ill Years, the *See* SEVEN ILL YEARS, THE.

Imminent destruction of the City of Edinburgh by fire and tempest *See* SWEET SINGERS, THE. For a similar threat to Glasgow, *see* HEROD OF HILLHEAD, THE.

Immortal Memory, the *See* BURNS NIGHT.

I'm ower auld a cat to draw that strae before me A proverbial saying (this version is from Scott's *Old Mortality*, chapter xl), literally meaning 'I'm too old a cat to play with the straw put in front of me', i.e. I'm too experienced to be taken in by that trick.

In a case In a state of vexation or excitement. The expression is found in the Northeast, and here *case* denotes 'state'.

Inaccessible Pinnacle, the A fearsome rock fang that forms the summit of Sgurr Dearg in the Black Cuillin of Skye. The first ascent was made on 18 August 1880 by the brothers Charles and Lawrence Pilkington, the latter recalling many years later:

> I shall always remember that as the noisiest climb I ever had. There was a foot or more of loose rock which had been shattered by the lightning and frost of ages. This formed the edges of the pinnacle and had to be thrust down as we climbed up. The noise was appalling: the very rock of the pinnacle itself seemed to be vibrating with indignation at our rude onslaught.
> – *Scottish Mountaineering Club Journal*, April 1939

The Inaccessible Pinnacle is the only MUNRO that requires rock-climbing skill (and a rope) in order to

ascend it. It is said to have 'an infinite drop on one side, and an even longer one on the other', and thus has a tendency to strike terror into the timider sort of Munro-bagger. Those on more familiar terms refer to it as *the In Pin*.

In a coupla hurries In two ticks; immediately.

In airts and pairts If one is found guilty *in airts and pairts*, one is convicted of being an accessory to the crime. For an example of such a conviction, *see under* APPIN MURDER, THE.

Inchcape Rock *See* BELL ROCK.

In Defens *See* IN MY DEFENS GOD ME DEFEND.

Independent Companies *See* BLACK WATCH.

Indescribables Glasgow slang for pakora, a speciality of CURRY ALLEY in its heyday.

In 1832 on this spot nothing happened A sign on a house in the historic Fife burgh of Culross.

Infar cake Wedding cake, *infar* or *infare* being the feast put on by the bridegroom to welcome his bride to her new home (*cf.* HAME-FARE). The cake is broken over the head of the bride as she enters.

> A decorated form of shortbread is still the national bride's-cake of rural Scotland, and was formerly used as infar-cake. The breaking of infar-cake over the head of the bride, on the threshold of her new home, is a very ancient custom, having its origin in the Roman rite of *confarratio*, in which the eating of a consecrated cake by the contracting parties constituted marriage. (Scots law, unlike English, is based on the old Roman Law.) Portions were distributed to the young men and maidens 'to dream on'.
> – F. Marian McNeill, *The Scots Kitchen* (1929)

(For this last custom, *see* DREAMING BREAD.)

Ingan Johnnie *See* ONION JOHNNIES.

In manus tuas, Domine The last recorded words of Mary Queen of Scots as she placed her head upon the executioner's block at Fotheringhay on 8 February

1587. The words are from Psalm 31, verse 5, which in the version authorized by her son reads: 'Into thine hand I commit my spirit: thou hast redeemed me, O Lord God of truth.' Mary's words were recorded in the official eyewitness account prepared for Lord Burghley, Elizabeth I's chief minister, by 'Ro. Wy.' (probably Robert Wingfield):

> Then groping for the block, she laid down her head, putting her chin over the block with both her hands, which holding there still, had been cut off had they not been spied. Then lying upon the block most quietly, and stretching out her arms, cried 'In manus tuas, Domine,' three or four times. Then she lying very still upon the block, one of the executioners holding of her slightly with one of his hands, she endured two strokes of the other executioner his axe, she making very little noise or none at all, and not stirring any part of her from the place where she lay; and so the executioner cut off her head, saving one little gristle, which being cut in sunder, he lift up her head to the view of the assembly, saying, 'God save the Queen.'

The writer goes on to describe how 'Her lips stirred up and down for a quarter of an hour after her head was cut off.' He also relates how Mary's little dog had crept under her clothes and 'could not be got forth but by force, yet afterwards would not depart from the dead corpse but came and lay between her head and her shoulders'.

In My Defens God Me Defend The motto above the royal coat of arms of Scotland, and also used on the royal coat of arms of the UK as used in Scotland. It is sometimes abbreviated to 'In Defens' or 'In Defence'. It is known to have been used during the reign of James IV, and may have been adopted by earlier Stewart kings. The phrase also appears in various old Scottish prayers, such as:

> In my defence God me defend
> And bring my soul to ane good end.
> When I am sick and like to die
> Father of Heaven have mercy on me.

The motto *NEMO ME IMPUNE LACESSIT* was added to the foot of the royal arms during the reign of Charles II.

In my end is my beginning (originally in French: *En ma fin git mon commencement*) The motto of Mary Queen of Scots, embroidered on her clothing. The motto is mentioned in a letter dated 1619 from William Drummond (the HERMIT OF HAWTHORNDEN) to Ben Jonson. T.S. Eliot may have been aware of the motto when, in one of his *Four Quartets* ('East Coker', 1940), he wrote 'In my beginning is my end'.

Innocent Railway, the Edinburgh's first railway, linking the city to Dalkeith, with its surrounding coalmines. Other branches were later added. After receiving royal assent in 1826, the line was constructed by the civil engineer Robert Stevenson. It was dubbed 'innocent' because of its good safety record; originally the carriages were horse-drawn, steam locomotives being regarded as too dangerous. Although originally intended just for coal, it was soon carrying 300,000 passengers per year. Part of the original track has been turned into a cycle path.

Inspired butler, an William Hazlitt's description of Sir Walter Scott in his essay on Mrs Siddons, published in the *Examiner*, 15 June 1816:

> Sir Walter Scott (when all is said and done) is an inspired butler.

In the bowels of Christ, think it possible that you may be mistaken Cromwell's plea to the Scots, who persisted in supporting Charles II despite their differences over religion. The plea was contained in a letter to the General Assembly of the Kirk, 3 August 1650. The theocrats who held sway in Scotland had not ever thought that they might be mistaken, and were not about to doubt themselves now. The result was Cromwell's invasion at the head of an army 16,000 strong, who won a great victory at Dunbar (*see* RACE OF DUNBAR). The Scottish army had been weakened by the purge of many experienced soldiers on theological grounds – an intriguing parallel to the weakened state of the Red Army at the time of Operation Barbarossa in June 1941, following Stalin's purges of the later 1930s.

In the name o' the wee man! An exclamation of mild outrage, surprise, annoyance, etc. It was among the catchphrases of the Glasgow comedian Tommy Lorne (*see* LORNE SAUSAGE). The 'wee man' is a euphemism for the Devil.

> It turns out that whatever we're really about it's not playing football. 4–0, in the name of the wee man! (What are we good at? Curling, drinking and asthma.)
> – *The Scotsman*, 20 February 2004

In the sheuch *See* UP THE SHEUCH.

Inverness cape A heavy tweed coat with a removable cape, favoured by Highland sportsmen (and Sherlock Holmes) in the 19th century. *Mackenzie's Guide to Inverness* (1893) credits Messrs A. Macbean & Sons of that town as 'inventors of the far-famed deer-stalking cloak', although it is not absolutely certain that the garment originated in the town.

Inverness Formula The basis of the Anglo-Irish Treaty of 1921, formulated on 7 September 1921 when the first British Cabinet meeting to be held outside London took place in Inverness – Lloyd George then being on holiday in Gairloch.

Inversneckie *See* SNECK, THE.

Inverurie The local train stopped at a station long enough for the passengers to stretch their legs. Sniffing the pure, clean air with appreciation, a passenger said to the guard: 'Invigorating, isn't it?' 'No,' he replied. 'Inverurie.'

Iolaire Disaster An appalling maritime disaster that took place on 1 January 1919 in the Minch, involving the Admiralty yacht *Iolaire* (Gaelic for 'eagle'), which was carrying servicemen home to Lewis after the First World War. The *Iolaire* left Kyle of Lochalsh on the evening of 31 December 1918, and just a mile out from the safety of the harbour of Stornoway hit the rocks known as the Beasts of Holm. Over 200 men were drowned – the exact figure may never be known, as the vessel was severely overcrowded, and records of who was on board were not complete. Only 75 passengers survived. A stone pillar now marks the site of the wreck.

Irish steak Glaswegian slang for cheese, presumably with a pejorative allusion to the supposed poverty of the Irish.

Irn Bru An orange-coloured carbonated soft drink made by the Scottish firm of A.G. Barr, and described by Jack House, in *The Heart of Glasgow* (1965), as 'the wee boy's Drambuie'. It is one of the best-selling soft drinks in Scotland, where it is reputed to be an effective cure for hangovers, perhaps owing to its caffeine and sugar content. It was first produced in 1901 in Falkirk and called Strachan's Brew, but a change in the law in 1946 meant that, as it was not brewed, it had to change its name: the spelling Irn Bru removed the legal difficulty. The recipe, which is kept in a bank vault, is known only to two people: the chairman – who mixes the key ingredients once a month in a sealed room – and one other unnamed employee. The two are never allowed to fly on the same plane together.

In the 1960s the drink was advertised on television by two cartoon youths, one a Scot in a kilt, the other an Indian in a turban, who would sing:

> I'm very thirsty.
> I'm thirsty too.
> Here's the drink that's made for you –
> Barr's Irn Bru!

In more recent decades a number of well-known slogans have been associated with the drink, for example, 'Scotland's Other National Drink' and 'Made in Scotland From Girders' (although the only iron is the 0.002 per cent ammonium ferric citrate listed in the ingredients). Not everybody is a fan: the wine critic Jilly Goolden once likened the taste of Irn Bru to a cocktail of bubblegum, wet sheep fleece, barley sugar and plastic.

Irn Brun *See* MISERY FROM THE MANSE, THE.

Iron Brew *See* IRN BRU.

Iron, touching *See* FISHERMEN'S TABOOS.

I.R. Wray The nickname bestowed by *Private Eye* magazine on Jimmy Wray (b.1938), formerly Labour MP for Glasgow Baillieston. The nickname alludes to his support for the nationalist cause in Northern Ireland.

Isles of the Sea, the An alternative name for the Garvellachs, a group of small islands north of Jura. In AD 542, some 20 years before his nephew Columba established his mission on Iona, the Irish churchman St Brendan of Clonfert founded a monastery on one of the islands, Eilach an Naoimh ('rocky place of the saint'). It is thought that this is the island referred to in the 7th century by Adamnan, abbot of Iona, when he mentioned *Hinba*, the 'isles of the sea'.

Italian Chapel, the An ornately decorated Catholic Chapel built in their spare time during the Second World War by Italian prisoners of war on the small Orkney island of Lamb Holm. The prisoners were housed on the island while working on the construction of the CHURCHILL BARRIERS. The Italian Chapel, which basically comprises two Nissen huts joined end to end and disguised by plasterboard and concrete, is now something of a tourist attraction.

It came with a lass and it will pass with a lass Reportedly the last words of James V, on being brought the news in December 1542 that his wife had been delivered of a baby daughter, who was to become Mary Queen of Scots. James was referring to the Stewart (later Stuart) dynasty, which owed its claim to the throne to the marriage of Walter Stewart (1293–1326), High Steward of Scotland, to Marjorie, daughter of Robert the Bruce. Their son became Robert II, the first Stewart king of Scotland, on the death in 1371 of Robert the Bruce's childless son David II. James V was convinced that a female monarch would be a disaster, and bring the line to an end. His words were reported by Robert Lindsay of Pitscottie (*c.*1500–65) in his *Historie and Cronicles of Scotland*:

> Be this, the post cam out of Linlithgow, showing the king good tidings, that the queen was deliverit. The king inquired whedder it was a man or woman. The messenger said it was ane fair dochter. He answered and said, 'Fairwell, it cam with ane lass and it will pass with ane lass.'

As it turned out, James was correct – not about his daughter being the last Stewart monarch, but about the fact that the last Stewart monarch, Queen Anne (d.1714), was indeed 'ane lass'.

Itchland or **Scratchland** Derogatory names given to Scotland from the later 17th to the early 19th century, perhaps alluding to the voracious denizens infesting the mattresses in Scottish inns, or possibly to the supposed sexual incontinence of the human inhabitants.

It's a braw bricht munelicht nicht A famous example of FAUX JOCKERY; in Sir Harry Lauder's 'Just a Wee DEOCH AN DORUS' the phrase becomes a shibboleth to test one's Scottishness:

> If you can say
> It's a braw bricht munelicht nicht,
> Well, you're all right, you ken.

The phrase is sometimes extended to 'It's a braw bricht munelicht nicht the nicht', or even, 'It's a braw bricht munelicht nicht the nicht, Mrs Wricht, how's yer dochter?'

It's a far cry to Lochawe! A traditional motto of Clan Campbell, vaunting the unlikelihood of their enemies penetrating to their heartland.

It's drappin suit Literally, 'it's dropping soot', used as a warning to one's interlocutor that one might be overheard.

It's Scotland's oil A campaign slogan adopted by the Scottish National Party in 1972, referring to the discovery of oil and natural gas in the North Sea off the coast of Scotland. The slogan was deployed through the 1970s to buttress the SNP's argument that Scotland could be economically as well as politically independent.

It's yer meat that maks ye bonny *See* MEAT, TO LOOK LIKE ONE'S.

I went to Scotland but I could find nothing that looked like Scotland *See* BRIGADOON.

J

Jacobite A supporter of the exiled James VII, or his successors, the OLD PRETENDER (another James) and the YOUNG PRETENDER; hence the *Jacobite* Rebellions of 1715 and 1745, after which the Jacobites were a spent force. The word comes from *Jacobus*, the Latin for 'James'.

Jacob's Stone *See* STONE OF SCONE, THE.

Jags, the *See* FOOTBALL CLUB NICKNAMES.

Jag-the-flea *See* PRICKER.

Jaicket on a shoogly peg, to have one's Literally, 'to have one's jacket hanging on a wobbly peg', i.e. to be in danger of losing one's job.

Jambos, the *See* FOOTBALL CLUB NICKNAMES.

James of the Glens *See* APPIN MURDER, THE.

James Ryall *See* SWORD DOLLAR.

James the Gross *See* BLACK DINNER, THE.

Jam, jute and journalism The three pillars of industry in Dundee. Jute was woven here from the early 19th century (*see* JUTEOPOLIS), while the jam industry grew up from the soft-fruit production in the nearby Carse of Gowrie, and the city is also famous for its DUNDEE MARMALADE. Journalism is largely under the aegis of D.C. Thomson (founded 1905), publishers of the *Sunday Post* (wherein appear The *BROONS* and *OOR WULLIE*), the *Courier*, the *Beano*, the *Dandy*, the *People's Friend*, *Jackie*, the *Scots Magazine* and many other periodicals. For its part, Aberdeen has EDUCATION, SALVATION AND DAMNATION.

Jam Tarts, the *See* FOOTBALL CLUB NICKNAMES.

Jaw-box A sink in a kitchen or common stair, from *jaw*, to pour or splash water (hence a *jaw* in the Northeast is a wave or breaker). Hence also *jaw-hole*, a drain or sewer.

Jaw-pish A now archaic term for inflammation of the urethra, from French *chaude*, 'hot', and *pisse*, 'piss'.

Jaws The nickname of the footballer Joe Jordan (b.1951), who won 52 Scottish caps. Much of his career was spent outside Scotland, with teams such as Leeds United and Manchester United, although he managed Hearts between 1990 and 1993. His nickname refers to his resemblance to Jaws, the giant steel-toothed Bond villain; Jordan is 6 ft 1 in (1.825 m), and is missing his front teeth.

Jean's Hut A mountain shelter erected in 1951 in Coire Cas on the north side of Cairn Gorm. It was built as a memorial to Jean Smith, the daughter of a Hebridean doctor, who had been killed while skiing in Coire Cas in the spring of 1948. The plaque on the door read:

> In memory of Jean MacIntyre Smith, who trod this way joyfully *Cha till i tuilidh* ['she will not return'].

When in the 1960s skiing infrastructure was introduced to Coire Cas, the hut was moved west, to the more remote Coire an Lochain. Ironically, like other such high-mountain shelters, it proved a tragic lure to climbers attempting to reach it in conditions where they would have done better to turn back. It was eventually dismantled.

Jeddart justice A procedure by which the accused was punished first (usually by hanging), and tried afterwards. Alternatively, the phrase was applied to a trial in which a number of persons were accused together, and the jury was asked to determine not the guilt or innocence of each, but to deliver a collective verdict, so all would either hang or be spared. Such procedures were traditionally associated with Jedburgh (aka Jeddart or Jethart), especially during the time of the repression of the BORDER REIVERS by James VI. Robert Chambers, in *Popular Rhymes of Scotland* (1826), provides two different accounts:

> Jethart justice – first hang a man, and syne judge him. According to Crawford, in his *Memoirs*, the phrase Jedburgh justice took its rise in 1574, on the occasion of the Regent Morton there and then trying and condemning, with cruel precipitation, a vast number of people who had offended against the laws, or against the supreme cause of his lordship's faction. A different origin is assigned by the people. Upon the occasion, say they, of nearly twenty criminals being tried for one offence, the jury were equally divided in opinion as to a verdict, when one, who had been asleep during the whole trial, suddenly awoke, and being interrogated for his vote, vociferated: 'Hang them a'!'

John Jamieson, in the 1825 Supplement to his *Etymological Dictionary of the Scottish Language*, also mentions this last explanation. *Compare* CUPAR JUSTICE.

Jeddart snails Dark brown toffees with a mild peppermint flavour, and formed in the shape of a snail. They were supposedly first made for a Jedburgh (aka Jeddart or Jethart) baker by a French prisoner of war during the Napoleonic Wars.

Jeelie-eaters A nickname for the inhabitants of Alexandria in the Vale of Leven. Apparently during the Industrial Revolution the town's only grocery store experienced a great demand for *jeelie*, i.e. jam, perhaps because the locals could afford to eat nothing more than bread and jam.

Jee one's beaver, ginger, jundie, noddle, etc To be bothered to do something; to rouse oneself. To *jee* or *gee* is to bestir oneself, while the *beaver* that Margaret fails to *gee* in the following extract was, of course, her hat (made from beaver pelt):

> Now here, thinks I, is a bonny kettle of fish, for Margaret was sitting with us, but for all the suddenness of it she never geed her beaver, and I kent then that she had word some way.
> – John Sillars, *The McBrides: A Romance of Arran* (1922), chapter xxix

Ginger was what one *jeed* for the sake of alliteration (and subsequently *ginger* became a word for the posterior, so *jeeing one's ginger* was 'getting off one's backside'); one's *jundie* was one's regular stride; while one's *noddle* was the back of one's head, as in the following from a versifying Paisley weaver, later a hotel keeper and publican:

> For me, I never geed my noddle,
> Nor car'd I Snip, or Tib a boddle.
> – George MacIndoe, *The Wandering Muse, A Miscellany of Original Poetry* (1813)

Jekyll and Hyde For two Edinburgh characters who may have inspired R.L. Stevenson's London-set tale of split personality, *see* DEACON BRODIE and MAJOR WEIR.

Jellyfish, land with the consistency of a *See* ULTIMA THULE.

Jenkin's hen 'A hen that never knew the cock,' says John MacTaggart in his *Gallovidian Encyclopaedia* (1824), continuing that the phrase is

> … metaphorically used for an old maid – 'she pined awa like *Jinkin's hen*,' – saith Nicholson; the old maids are great favourites of mine, but not so bachelors …

Who Jenkin was has been lost in the mists of time, but the fate of *dying like Jenkin's hen* continued to be feared by spinsters (some of them, at any rate) into the 20th century. By transference, the name *Jenkin's hen* was also applied to an effeminate man.

Jenny A generic term for a woman, the female equivalent of JOCK. *Catch yer Jenny* was a version of blind man's buff. *Jenny* is also found as part of a variety of names for various animals; *see* FAUNA CALEDONIA. *See also* JENNY-A'THING; JENNIE-REEKIE; JESSIE; TEA JENNY.

Jenny-a'-thing(s) The female owner of a shop selling all kinds of little bits and pieces, or the shop itself. The male version is *Johnnie-a'-thing*.

Jenny Lind A type of fancy loaf, round and flat in shape and glazed with egg. It was popular in the mid-19th century and was named after the opera singer Jenny Lind (1820–87), known as 'the Swedish Nightingale'.

Jenny-reekie The operative item in a Halloween prank once popular in rural parts. It comprised a hollowed-out kail stem which was filled with tow and ignited. The jennie-reekie, thus armed, was applied to the keyhole of the victim's house, which then filled with acrid smoke. A good time was had by all.

Jenny Wullock *See* JESSIE.

Jessie An effeminate man, a sissy, typically heard in the expression 'Ya big Jessie', directed at anyone thought to be acting wimpishly. Variants include *Jessie Ann, Jessie Bell* and *Jessie Fisher*. Why this particular girl's name should have been singled out is unclear, although in some places the name *JENNY* plays a similar role, denoting a man who meddles in matters traditionally regarded as belonging to the feminine domain. The expression *Jenny Wullock* denotes a hermaphrodite, or an effeminate man, or a castrated bull.

Jesus and no quarter! The battle cry of the Covenanters at the Battle of Tippermuir, fought on 1 September 1644, a Sunday. The Covenanters ended up being slaughtered by the Royalists under the Marquess of Montrose.

Jesus wrong to have travelled on a Sunday *See* SABBATH.

Jethart A form of the place name Jedburgh. For *Jethart justice* and *Jethart snails, see under* JEDDART ...

Jethart Callant *See* RIDING THE MARCHES.

Jimmy or **Jim** The name used, especially in the West of Scotland conurbation, to address any male stranger. The appellation may be friendly, neutral or threatening – the latter is usually the case in the expression 'See you, Jimmy?', which may be followed by a summary of Jimmy's moral shortcomings and/or a GLASGOW KISS. The tartan-bonnet-with-ginger-wig-attached sold in joke shops and favoured by members of the TARTAN ARMY and others is known as a 'See You Jimmy' ensemble.

> In my dream I am trapped in one of those peculiarly tacky gift shops ... Garish tartan is flowing down from the walls; blue and white nylon Saltires are wrapping themselves around my shocked shoulders; there is a ginger see-you-Jimmy wig clamped to my head and everywhere I look, I see a sea of tat – whisky miniatures, imitation bagpipes, shortbread tins, postcards of Highland cows with their tongues exploring up their nostrils. Why, there are even plastic models of Mel Gibson – press the button and he shouts '*Freeee*-dom' and his kilt flies up.
> – *Melanie Reid, in* The Times, 3 December 2007

A *jimmie* or *mealie jimmie* is a white or MEALIE PUDDING, of the sort sold battered in fish-and-chip shops. *See also* LOW-FLYING JIMMIES; MAC; MRS WUMMIN.

Jimmy Johnstone The jocular name given by some Glaswegians to the green man at pedestrian lights. The reference is to the footballer Jimmy Johnstone (the FLYING FLEA), who was of short stature and who played for Celtic, and who was thus the archetypal 'wee green man'.

Jing-bang *See* HALE JING-BANG, THE.

Jinglin' Geordie The nickname of the wealthy Edinburgh burgess George Heriot (1563–1624), goldsmith to James VI and his consort Anne of Denmark. In 1603 Heriot moved with the court to London, where he died, and in his will endowed the Edinburgh school that bears his name. Originally founded as Heriot's Hospital, a charitable foundation for 'faitherless bairns', it is now a fee-paying independent school, although looked down upon by some of the snobbier educational establishments of the city – hence the following:

> Knock knock.
> Who's there?
> Humphrey.
> Humphrey who?
> Humphrey Heriots.

Heriot's name is also commemorated in that of Heriot-Watt University, and his nickname was given greater currency by Scott's use of it in *The Fortunes of Nigel* (1822):

> Such was the monarch, who, saluting Heriot by the name of Jingling Geordie (for it was his well-known custom to give nicknames to all those with whom he was on terms of familiarity), inquired what new clatter-traps he had brought with him, to cheat his lawful and native Prince out of his siller.

Jings, crivens, help ma boab Expressions of astonishment, all catchphrases of the D.C. Thomson cartoon character OOR WULLIE (b.1936), and otherwise these days heard only on the lips of stage Scotsmen, along with phrases such as HOOTS, MON (*see* FAUX JOCKERY). *Jings* appears to be related to 'jingo' (as in 'by jingo'), possibly a euphemism for Jesus (it originated in the 17th century), while *crivens*, which has been traced back to the 19th century, may be a euphemistic version of 'Christ [de]fend us'. *Help ma boab* is a Glaswegian speciality; *help* in this context is an old Scots word (traced to the 15th century) for 'repair, mend', but the identity of *boab* is obscure.

> 'Aw, help ma boab!' exclaimed Willie, 'Ah'm no' a traivellin' dictionary.'
> – H.W. Pryde, *McFlannels United* (1949)

> Crivens, jings and help my boab,
> Let's put Thatcher oot o' a job.
> – Quoted in *The Scotsman*, 1 December 1989

Jinky *See* FLYING FLEA, THE.

Jock The Scottish equivalent of Jack, a familiar form of John. Today, where not being used as a personal name, it is most commonly heard as a slang term for a Scotsman, sometimes specifically a Scottish soldier (also formerly JOCKEY). It is used mostly by English people, and sometimes with a certain dismissive or offensive intent (for an example, *see under* BLACK WATCH, THE; *see also* various nicknames for the Scots Guards *under* REGIMENTAL NICKNAMES). In the past in Scotland, *Jock* was used as a generic term for an ordinary man (*cf.* English *Jack*), and such *Jocks* were typically paired with *Jennies* or *Jeanies* (hence the name *Jock and Jennie* for the lungwort,

which bears pink and blue flowers on the same plant). A *Jock* or *country Jock* could more specifically be an agricultural labourer or a miner, while a *Jock Hock* (or *Hack* or *Muck*) was, in the Northeast, a ploughman, and a *Jock Hornbook* was a teacher. *Jock* may also denote a bull or a pig, and forms part of the names of various animals, such as BUBBLY-JOCK; *see* FAUNA CALEDONIA. *See also* the various JOCK-entries below; DEIL'S OWER JOCK WABSTER, THE; FAUX JOCKERY; and PLAY JOCK NEEDLE JOCK PREEN.

Jockey A word of Scottish origin, literally meaning 'little Jock', in the sense of an ordinary fellow; *-y* or *-ie* is a diminutive suffix. The word *Jockie* was originally (in the 16th century) applied to stable lads, before coming to denote a professional rider. In the 17th and 18th centuries it was also used in English broadside ballads as a name for a Scottish soldier, as attested by the following from the reign of William III:

> Valiant Jockey's marched away,
> To fight the foe, with great Mackay,
> Leaving me, poor soul, alas, forlorn,
> To curse the hour I e'er was born ...
> – 'The Maiden Warrior or The Damsel's Resolution to Fight in Field by the side of Jockey her Entire Love'

See also CANT; GLAMOUR; SLOGAN.

Jockney *See* RHYMING SLANG.

Jock Hornbook *See* JOCK.

Jockie Blindie The game of blind man's buff; also, any short-sighted person.

Jock-nip-the-neb The Scottish equivalent of Jack Frost (*neb*, 'nose'). A *Jock-frosty-neb* was a hook-like implement for howking neeps out of frost-hardened ground.

'Jock of Hazeldean' A song by Sir Walter Scott, in which the heroine's attachment to the eponymous Jock is rebuked by her father:

> 'Now let this wilfu' grief be done,
> And dry that cheek so pale;
> Young Frank is chief of Errington
> And lord of Langley-dale;

His step is first in peaceful ha',
His sword in battle keen' –
But aye she loot the tears down fa'
For Jock of Hazeldean.

However, when it comes to the day of her wedding with 'Young Frank', she's nowhere to be found, for –

She's o'er the Border, and awa'
Wi' Jock of Hazeldean.

(Hazeldean is a small settlement in Lanarkshire, just to the east of Strathaven; and there is a Hazeldean House in East Renfrewshire, just south of Newton Mearns.)

Jock o' the Slates or **Jockie o' the Sclates** The name given by James VI to his childhood companion, John Erskine of Mar (1562–1634), on account of his studious application to his lessons. Their childhood friendship did not stop Mar, together with the Earls of Gowrie and Glencairn, abducting James in the RUTHVEN RAID of 1582, in which the conspirators told their terrified, sobbing captive, still only 16, 'Better bairns weep than bearded men.'

Jock Scott A small fisherman's fly, comprising gold and black feathers with a hackle. It is named after its inventor, Jock Scott of Branxholm (1817–93), a keeper on the Tweed; hence also *Jock Scott's gloamin'*, a twilit evening ideal for angling.

Jock's Road The high-level path and former drove road between Glen Clova and Braemar, via Glen Doll, Tolmount and Glen Callater. It takes its name from one John ('Jock') Winter, who in the 19th century challenged the local landowner's attempts to bar people from using it. The cause was taken up by the Scottish Rights of Way Society, and the case went all the way to the House of Lords, who in 1888 declared the route a right of way. Appropriately enough, 'Jock' is also the Scottish Everyman.

Jock Tamson's bairns The Scottish nation collectively, or humanity as a whole, with a suggestion of equality, as in the saying, 'We're a' Jock Tamson's bairns [i.e. children]', i.e. we're all the same under the skin, 'A MAN'S A MAN FOR A' THAT', 'WE'RE A' AE OO'.

Scotland is a less fragmented society [than England] ... The fact that 90-plus per cent of children go to the same schools – in terms of public rather than private education – is a good way to start. That doesn't mean Scotland is a happy utopia where everybody links arms and we're all Jock Tamson's bairns.
– Alex Salmond, interviewed by Ian Jack in the *Guardian*, 31 January 2009

Jock Tamson may be a kind of Everyman, although it has also been suggested that the name is a euphemism for God; it is also used as a jocular name for whisky; *cf.* John Barleycorn in England. Various suggestions have been made as to the origin of the phrase. One theory traces it to the Revd John Thomson (1778–1840), who was Church of Scotland minister in Duddingston, and who used to welcome his congregation with the words, 'Come in, all ma bairns'; alternatively, he was so respected in his parish that even those belonging to other denominations would say 'We're all Jock Tamson's bairns.' Another theory holds that the Jock Tamson in question was the John Thompson (1787–1839) who kept an inn in Montrose that was a centre of smuggling, poaching and other illegal activities; when the law came a'calling, his daughter would deny there was anybody in the inn bar the family: 'We're all Jock Tamson's bairns,' she would supposedly protest. In the song 'We're A' John Tamson's Bairns' by Dr Joseph Roy (born in Glasgow in 1841), Tamson is from Aberdeenshire:

John Tamson was a merry auld carle,
And reigned proud king o the Dee;
A braw laird, weel-to-dae i' the warl'
For mony a farm had he,
And mony a servant-maid and man,
Wham he met aft a year;
And fu' proud and jolly he wav'd his han',
While they sang wi' richt gude cheer –

Chorus:
O! We're a' John Tamson's bairns,
We're a' John Tamson's bairns;
There ne'er will be peace till the warld again
Has learned to sing wi' micht an' main,
We're a' John Tamson's bairns.

See also AH KENT HIS FAITHER; JOHN TAMSON'S MAN; *MEROUR OF WYSSDOME, THE.*

Jockteleg The word applied to the new-fangled table knife in the 16th century, after its inventor Jacques de Liège.

Jock-the-liar A former term for an almanac, of the sort once used by farmers, and so called because of the unreliable predictions regarding the weather contained in such publications.

'John Anderson, My Jo' *See* MERRY MUSES OF CALEDONIA, THE.

John Gunn A Northeastern euphemism for a latrine or privy.

John Knox cap A soft, square cap, as worn by the 16th-century Reformer and sported to this day on ceremonial occasions by the graduates and doctors of certain Scottish and Commonwealth universities.

John Knox's man *See* JOHN TAMSON'S MAN.

Johnnie-a'-thing *See* JENNY-A'-THING.

Johnnie Cope *See* HEY, JOHNNIE COPE, ARE YE WAUKEN YET?

Johnnie-stan'-still A scarecrow.

Johnnie Ged Death, a *ged* being a pike (the fish), and figuratively a glutton. Hence *Johnnie Ged's hole* is the grave.

> 'Waes me for Johnnie Ged's-Hole now,'
> Quoth I, 'If that thae news be true!
> His braw calf-ward whare gowans grew,
> Sae white an' bonie,
> Nae doubt they'll rive it wi' the plew;
> They'll ruin Johnnie!'
> – Robert Burns, 'Death and Dr Hornbook' (1787)

Johnnie Pyot's term day The day after the Day of Judgement, i.e. never, or for eternity. A *pyot* is a magpie, or other pied bird.

John o' Groats A small settlement near the northeastern tip of Caithness, at one end of the longest distance (873 miles/1397 km) between two in-habited localities on the mainland of Great Britain, Land's End in Cornwall being at the other end. As such it is a destination for long-distance walkers, cyclists and tourists, although it has little more to recommend it, being described by the *Lonely Planet* guide as a 'seedy tourist trap'. The most northerly point on the mainland is in fact Dunnet Head, while the most northeasterly point is Duncansby Head, 3 km (2 miles) to the east of John o' Groats. The wholly Scottish proverbial equivalent of 'Land's End to John o' Groats' is MAIDENKIRK TO JOHN O'GROATS.

> It is no further from the north coast of Spitsbergen to the North Pole than it is from Land's End to John of Gaunt.
> – Revd William Spooner, remark to Julian Huxley, quoted in William Hayter, *Spooner* (1977)

The name John o' Groats comes from that of Jan de Groot, a Dutchman who, along with his brothers Malcolm and Gavin, settled here during the reign of James IV and established a ferry service to Orkney, which had been acquired from Norway in 1496. (Local legend confuses the matter by claiming that the fare on the ferry was one groat.) Eventually eight families of de Groots lived here, and on one occasion they could not agree to who should have precedence when they gathered together, so an eight-sided house was built, each side with its own door, and within the house was placed an eight-sided table, so that no individual should be 'head of the table' (broadly the same principle as lay behind King Arthur's Round Table). Although this house no longer exists, the hotel (established in 1875 and now disused) has an octagonal tower. In the 2010 CARBUNCLE AWARDS, John o' Groats was awarded the 'Plook on the Plinth' trophy as Scotland's 'most dismal town' (although it has barely 300 inhabitants). *See also* RHYMING SLANG.

John o' the Mountains The byname of John Muir (1838–1914), the Scottish-born US naturalist, writer, pioneer conservationist and advocate of the preservation of America's wild places, especially its mountains. 'In God's wilderness,' he wrote in his journal, 'lies the hope of the world.' Muir was born in Dunbar, East Lothian, and emigrated to the USA with his family in 1849. The *John Muir Trust*, founded in 1983, is concerned with the conservation of Scottish wild places, together with their flora and fauna. Its properties include Ben Nevis, Sandwood Bay, Schiehallion and Quinag, and it has helped in a number of community buyout schemes, such as that of the Knoydart estate (*see also* SEVEN MEN OF KNOYDART).

Johnson on Scotland and the Scots, Dr In his *Life of Samuel Johnson* (1791), James Boswell, a Scot, gleefully recorded his English friend's animadversions regarding his country and his countrymen. For example:

> Seeing Scotland, Madam, is only seeing a worse England. It is seeing the flower fade away to the naked stalk.

> God made it, but we must remember that He made it for Scotchmen; and comparisons are odious, but God made Hell.

> Much ... may be made of a Scotchman, if he be *caught* young.

> Their learning is like bread in a besieged town: every man gets a little, but no man gets a full meal.

> Sir, let me tell you, the noblest prospect which a Scotchman ever sees is the high road that leads him to England.

> *Boswell:* I do indeed come from Scotland, but I cannot help it ...
> *Johnson:* That, Sir, I find, is what a very great many of your countrymen cannot help.

> Sir, it is not so much to be lamented that Old England is lost, as that the Scotch have found it.

In Johnson's own *Journey to the Western Islands of Scotland* (1775) we find:

> A Scotchman must be a very sturdy moralist who does not love Scotland better than truth.

See also OATS, DR JOHNSON ON.

John Tamson's man A henpecked husband.

> 'The deil's in the wife!' said Cuddie. 'Dye think I am to be John Tamson's man, and maistered by a woman a' the days o' my life?'
> – Sir Walter Scott, *Old Mortality* (1816), chap. xxxviii

J.A. Nicklin, in his notes to his 1906 edition of *Old Mortality*, suggests that 'John Tamson' was originally 'Joan Thompson', and cites a proverb:

> Better be John Tamson's man than Ring and Ding [corruption of St Ringan] or John Knox's.

– which Nicklin explains thus: 'better a wife who wheedles than one who scolds or beats her husband'. (A *John Knox's man* is – punningly – one who is beaten or *knocked* by his wife.) In the 1894 edition of his *Dictionary of Phrase and Fable*, the Revd Brewer suggests 'Tameson – i.e. spiritless, the slave even of a Tame-son'. It is possible that John Tamson is the same Everyman figure as in the phrase JOCK TAMSON'S BAIRNS.

Jolly, the Revd I.M A character created by the Glaswegian comedian and actor Rikki Fulton (1924–2004) in his long-running television show *Scotch and Wry* (1978–92). A quiet talk from the Revd Jolly, an earnest-to-miserable Church of Scotland minister, became a Hogmanay tradition, broadcast just before the BELLS. The format was a parody of BBC Scotland's late-night religious slot, *Late Call*. A rarer guest on *Scotch and Wry* was the Revd W.E. Free, of the Free Church of Scotland (the WEE FREES), who made Jolly seem positively ... jolly. Jolly subsequently appeared in a number of TV specials, such as *'Tis the Season to be Jolly* (1993), and *Jolly: A Man for All Seasons* (1994). Fulton himself was an elder of the Kirk, and in 1993 he and his friend the Revd Alastair Symington published a book containing their discussions on religious matters, entitled *For God's Sake, Ask!* In 2008 First Minister Alex Salmond appeared on the BBC's *Children in Need* programme as the Revd Jolly, but reportedly one of his lines was cut. He had been complaining that his predecessor, the Revd McConnell, had taken all the light bulbs with him, and Salmond would then have said, 'You see, the Revd McConnell has always been at heart a Leninist – gonnie len' us this, and gonnie len' us that.'

Judex damnatur ubi nocens absolvitur The Latin motto of the EDINBURGH REVIEW, meaning 'The judge is damned when the guilty is acquitted'.

Judge, the A nickname awarded to the footballer Ally McCoist (b.1962) in 1991, because that season 'he was always on the bench'. The name stuck. He played for Rangers from 1983 to 1998, becoming their record goal scorer; he also gained 61 international caps.

Julius' Hoff *See* ARTHUR'S OON.

Jungle, the The stand in Celtic FC's Parkhead stadium where the club's most vocal supporters take up residence. The name may derive from the rhyming slang *Jungle Jim* = TIM, the latter being Glasgow slang for a Catholic.

Juteopolis A 19th-century sobriquet for Dundee, famed for JAM, JUTE AND JOURNALISM. Dundee was already a centre for weaving flax and wool when jute was first imported from India in the early 19th century. It also had a large whaling fleet, and it was found that if jute was treated with whale oil it became sufficiently pliant to be woven into sacks and carpet-backing. Such were the fortunes to made by the nabobs of jute that neighbouring Broughty Ferry, where they built their mansions, became known as the RICHEST SQUARE MILE IN EUROPE.

> What tho' their foundation is built on the sand,
> They dash and they dare like lords o' the land,
> What is readily got they mak merrily flee,
> The splendid Jute Lords o' Bonnie Dundee.
> – Anon. parody of Scott's 'BONNIE DUNDEE', in the *Dundee Weekly News*, January 1856

> The streets are waiting for a snow
> that never falls:
> too close to the water,
> too muffled in the afterwarmth of jute ...
> – John Burnside (b.1955), 'Dundee'

'Just a Wee Deoch an Dorus' *See* DEOCH AN DORUS.

Juvlo-mengreskey tem The Romany name for Scotland, according to George Borrow's *Romano Lavo-Lil* ('word book of the Romany', 1874). It apparently translates as 'lousy fellows' country'. *Cf.* ITCHLAND.

K

Kail Cabbage – the epitome of plain fare. The word is also applied to other vegetables of the genus *Brassica*, and to various dishes made with kail, and sometimes denotes food more generally – as in *kail-bell*, a bell rung to signify dinner is served. *See also* CA THE COOS OOT THE KAILYARD; CAULD KAIL; JENNIE-REEKIE; KAIL BROSE; KAIL KIRK; KAIL-YARD SCHOOL; and, for the use of kail in divination, *see under* HALLOWEEN.

Kail brose Brose (oatmeal or peasemeal porridge) made with the stock left over after boiling kail (cabbage). It is a pot of hot kail brose that Jenny Dennison deploys to repel her suitor, Cuddie, in Scott's *Old Mortality* (chapter xxv). To some, it is a hallmark of nationhood:

> Each true-hearted Scotsman, by nature jocose,
> Can cheerfully dine on a dishfu' o' brose,
> And the grace be a wish to get plenty of those;
> And it's O for the kail brose o' Scotland,
> And O for the Scottish kail brose.
> – Alexander Watson, quoted in Charles Mackay, *Poetry and Humour of the Scottish Language* (1882)

See also ATHOLL BROSE; PEASE BROSE.

Kail Kirk The Glasite sect, a breakaway Church founded in 1728 by the Revd John Glas (1695–1773), who desired to return to the earliest form of Church organization, and who emphasized equality and unanimity within the Church. The sect are also known as the Sandemanians, after Glas's son-in-law Robert Sandeman, who spread Glas's beliefs to England and America. The origin of the disparaging appellation 'the Kail Kirk' is explained thus:

> Since the breaking of bread had been one act performed when Christ's disciples came together on the first day of the week, they would observe this ordinance weekly. Thus began the Love-Feast, the sitting-down after the morning service on Sunday to a common table, which resulted in the name 'The Kail Kirk'.
> – *The Scots Magazine*, August 1936

The 'Love-Feast' was not just the normal symbolic sips of wine and nibbles of communion wafers, but rather a substantial meal. This was no doubt most welcome to the Church's mostly impoverished members, who were referred to by outsiders as *kail-sippers* (a term also formerly applied to people from Fife; *see* KAIL-SUPPER).

Kail-supper or **kail-sipper** A former nickname for a FIFER (a person from Fife), with the imputation that they lived off (or were particularly partial to) kail-based broth. Aiken Drum in Scott's *The Anti-quary* is described as 'ane o' the kale-suppers o' Fife'. The term was also applied to members of the KAIL KIRK.

Kailyard School A disparaging term applied to certain Scottish writers of the later 19th century, including J.M. Barrie, 'Ian Maclaren' (John Watson) and S.R. Crockett, in particular those parts of their oeuvres that consist of sentimental, nostalgic, escapist tales set in idealized pre-industrial rural parishes, in which virtue and hard work triumph. These tales – including Barrie's *A Window in Thrums* (1890; Thrums was Barrie's fictionalized version of his native Kirriemuir) and Crockett's *The Stickit Minister* (1893) – were sufficiently smattered with the vernacular to give an 'authentic' feel, but not so impenetrable as to alienate a non-Scottish readership. A *kailyard* is a cabbage patch, and the term was inspired by Maclaren's 1894 collection, *Beside the Bonnie Brier Bush*, which he prefaced with lines from the traditional song 'THERE GROWS A BONNIE BRIER BUSH' (as polished by Carolina, Lady Nairne, the FLOWER OF STRATHEARN):

There grows a bonnie brier bush in our kail-yard,
And white are the blossoms o't in our kail-yard.

The following year, the Edinburgh academic J.H. Millar wrote in W.E. Henley's *New Review* that Barrie was 'fairly entitled to look upon himself as *pars magna* if not *pars maxima* of the kailyard movement'. Some believed that the publication in 1901 of George Douglas Brown's grimly realist rural novel *The HOUSE WITH THE GREEN SHUTTERS* would ring the death knell of the genre – 'Into this cosy chamber of fiction,' wrote J.B. Priestley, 'Brown let in the East wind.' Subsequently, the SCOTTISH RENAISSANCE of the early to mid-20th century looked to wider horizons and more uncomfortable subjects than would have been palatable to the kailyarders:

> Now is the yaird kail boiled and hashed
> While Muses feed in slums;
> The Ball of Kirriemuir has smashed
> The window-pane of Thrums.
>> – A.H. Emslie-Smith, 'Scottish Renaissance', quoted in
>> Douglas Young, *Scottish Verse 1851–1951* (1952)

But the shadow of the kailyard continued to hang over Scottish fiction, from A.J. Cronin's DOCTOR FINLAY stories onward, and it was a shadow that Lewis Grassic Gibbon, author of perhaps the finest novel of rural life in 20th-century Scottish literature, was all too aware of:

> ... he was to say it was the Scots countryside itself, fathered between a kailyard and a bonnie brier bush in the lee of a house with green shutters. And what he meant by that you could guess at yourself if you'd a mind for puzzles and dirt, there wasn't a house with green shutters in the whole of Kinraddie.
>> – Lewis Grassic Gibbon, *Sunset Song* (1932)

Kate Barlass *See* BARLASS, KATE.

Kate Kennedy Procession An annual pageant by students at St Andrew's University, in which the leading role is taken by a male student dressed up in female attire as Kate Kennedy, the beautiful niece of Bishop James Kennedy, who founded St Salvator's College in 1450. There was also a bell in the college tower named 'Katherina' in her honour. Quite when the annual student festivities in her name began is lost in the mists of time, but by the later 19th century they had become increasingly boisterous, with unwelcome caricaturing of various members of the university staff, leading to the authorities imposing a ban in 1881. Inspired by a rectorial address on 'Courage' by J.M. Barrie, a number of students formed the Kate Kennedy Club and revived the annual procession, with the approval of the university and with strict rules and regulations. Its stated aims are to maintain the traditions of university and town, to improve town and gown relations, and to raise money for local charities. The number of members cannot exceed 60, and only male students are eligible. The aim of the procession, which takes place in March, is 'to celebrate the lives and contributions of some of the great men and women of the town and university'.

Katie Bairdie A name given to a woman with facial hair (*baird* being a Scots form of 'beard'). 'Katie Bairdie' is also the title of a song and dance tune that goes back to the early 17th century. Among the verses is the following, suggesting the transgender persona of the eponymous heroine:

> Katie Bairdie hid [had] a wife,
> She could use baith fork an' knife,
> Wasna that a dentie wife?
> Dance, Katie Bairdie!

The name is also applied to various animals (*see* FAUNA CALEDONIA).

Kebbie-lebbie *See* CABBY-LABBY.

Keelie A tough urban male, especially one from Glasgow. The term is considered derogatory by some, especially as the name (dating from the early 19th century) originally carried connotations of violent and/or criminal tendencies. However, others wear it as a badge of pride. The Highland Light Infantry were nicknamed the *Glasgow Keelies* (*see* REGIMENTAL NICKNAMES), while the boys of George Heriot's School in Edinburgh (*see* JINGLIN' GEORDIE) formerly called those who did not attend the school *keelies*. The word, like GILLIE, derives from Gaelic *gille*, 'youth', 'lad', and was presumably first applied to the penniless young men who flocked from the Highlands to the big cities in the wake of the CLEARANCES. *See also* WEEGIE.

Keep elders' hours, to *See* ELDER.

Keep the puddin' het Keep the pot boiling; maintain the pace.

Keep yer ain fish guts for yer ain sea maws Look after your own; charity begins at home (*sea maws*, 'seagulls'). The saying is recorded in Allan Ramsay's *Collection of Scotch Proverbs*, published posthumously in 1776.

> He said it behoved us to gi'e our ain fish guts to our ain sea-maws, and that he designed to fee Thomas Birlpenny's hostler for our coachman, being a lad of the parish.
>
> – John Galt, *The Ayrshire Legatees* (1821), chapter x

Kellas cat *See under* WILDCAT.

Kelpie or **water kelpie** A malevolent water sprite, in the form of a horse, prone to carrying people off in order to devour them in its underwater lair. The kelpie is said to be related to the Irish *phooka*, although it lacks the latter's shape-shifting propensities. Etymologically, it may connect to Gaelic *cailpeach*, 'heifer'. Although often associated with the Highlands, kelpies may also be encountered in Lowland streams, as the following verses attest:

> The side was steep, and the bottom deep;
> From bank to bank the water pouring;
> The bonny grey mare she swat for fear,
> For she heard the water-kelpie roaring.
> – Anon., 'Annan Water'

> Downward we drift through shadow and light,
> Under yon rock the eddies sleep,
> Calm and silent, dark and deep.
> The Kelpy has risen from the fathomless pool,
> He has lighted his candle of death and of dool.
> – Sir Walter Scott, 'On Tweed River'

The kelpie's *modus operandi* is explained by Patrick Graham in his *Sketches Descriptive of Picturesque Scenery of the Southern Confines of Perthshire* (1806):

> Every lake has its Kelpie, or Water-horse, often seen by the shepherd, as he sat in a summer's evening upon the brow of a rock, dashing along the surface of the deep, or browsing on the pasture-ground upon its verge. Often did this malignant genius of

the waters allure women and children to his subaqueous haunts, there to be immediately devoured. Often did he also swell the torrent or lake beyond its usual limits, to overwhelm the hapless traveller in the flood.

The poet William Collins, in his posthumously published fragment, 'An Ode Upon the Popular Superstitions of the Highlands of Scotland, Considered as the Subject of Poetry', written in 1750, gives himself the willies, and an occasion for drear sentiment, in imagining a Highland swain 'Drown'd by the kelpie's wrath':

> What though far off, from some dark dell espied,
> His glimm'ring mazes cheer th' excursive sight,
> Yet turn, ye wand'rers, turn your steps aside,
> Nor trust the guidance of that faithless light;
> For watchful, lurking, mid th' unrustling reed,
> At those mirk hours the wily monster lies,
> And listens oft to hear the passing steed,
> And frequent round him rolls his sullen eyes,
> If chance his savage wrath may some weak wretch
>   surprise.

> Ah, luckless swain, o'er all unblest indeed!
> Whom late bewilder'd in the dank, dark fen,
> Far from his flocks and smoking hamlet then!
> To that sad spot [his wayward fate shall lead]:
> On him, enrag'd, the fiend in angry mood,
> Shall never look with pity's kind concern,
> But instant, furious, raise the whelming flood
> O'er its drown'd bank, forbidding all return.
> Or, if he meditate his wish'd escape,
> To some dim hill that seems uprising near,
> To his faint eye the grim and grisly shape,
> In all its terrors clad, shall wild appear.
> Meantime the wat'ry surge shall round him rise,
> Pour'd sudden forth from ev'ry swelling source.
> What now remains but tears and hopeless sighs?
> His fear-shook limbs have lost their youthly force,
> And down the waves he floats, a pale and breathless
>   corse.

In some stories, the kelpie is not entirely malevolent, but, taking the form of a handsome youth, captures the heart of a maiden. But one day she comes upon him asleep at their wonted trysting place, and notices a bunch of rushes in his hair. Realizing the true nature of her lover, she flees to her father's door, just crossing the threshold in time to bar the door in the kelpie's face. The kelpie then sings:

Ann an là 's bliadhna,
Mo bhean òg, thig mi dh' iarraidh.
In a day and a year,
I'll come seeking my dear.

Sure enough, a year and day later, as the maiden leaves the church where she has just been married to an earthly suitor, a big black horse appears, seizes the maiden, and gallops off with her. No more is seen of either, save for the occasional glimpse in the gloaming of a pale face in the water, crooning a low, sweet love song. In similar tales, all that is found of the unfortunate young woman are some shreds of clothing and a pool of blood, or 'a little bit of one of her lungs on the shore of the lake'. *See also* BOOBRIE, THE; GOLDEN HORSE OF LOCH LUNDIE, THE.

Kelso convoy *See* SCOTS CONVOY.

Kelso Laddie *See* RIDING THE MARCHES.

Kelton Hill Fair The traditional horse fair at Kelton Hill near Castle Douglas in Kirkcudbright-shire, which was held on the first Tuesday after 17 June, Old Style. Well into the 19th century it drew horse dealers from Scotland, England and Ireland, together with chapmen, hawkers, pickpockets, sellers of sweatmeats and spirituous liquors, and vast crowds of punters out for a good time. The fair became a byname for rowdiness, in much the same way as Dublin's Donnybrook Fair:

> At Kelton Hill Fair may be lifted a tolerable idea of the Donnybrook of Erin; at one time in danger of having a skull bared with a cudgel, at other times hemmed in with rowly-powly men flinging sticks, and sweetie-wives.
>
> – Unnamed observer, quoted in Sir Andrew Agnew, *The Hereditary Sheriff of Galloway*, Vol. II (1893)

The expression *Kelton Hill Fair* was subsequently applied to any riotous gathering:

> Nor cou'd ye ken, wi' nicest care,
> The victors frae the vanquish'd there:

> Like Kelton-Hill, that feghting Fair,
>   The hubbleshew,
> Wi' neeves, and staffs, and rugging hair
>   Sae awsome grew!
>
> – John Mayne, *The Siller Gun: a poem in five cantos* (1836)

In a similar way, the riotous fair at Kirkdamdie near Barr in Ayrshire gave rise to the word *kirdandy* for a row, rumpus or tumult. *See also* LEVELLERS' RISING.

Kelvinside accent The Glasgow equivalent of a MORNINGSIDE ACCENT, Kelvinside being a well-to-do area of the city's West End. *See also* SEX.

Ken? Know what I mean? The word is often added as a suffix to a proposition, and for some becomes something of a conversational tic, along the lines of: 'Ah wis walkin' doon the road, ken, when this big guy, ken, he comes up tae me, ken, an' he says …. [etc.]'

Kennedy, court a *See* COURT A KENNEDY.

Kennedy, cuntbittin crawdoun *See* FLYTING.

Kennedy, Kate *See* KATE KENNEDY PROCESSION.

Kenny's from heaven *See* KING KENNY.

Kent face An old acquaintance (*kent* meaning 'known'); the phrase is most commonly found as WEEL-KENT FACE.

Ken the richt side o' a shillin', to To be canny with money. The coin concerned may alternatively be a BAWBEE or a *saxpence*.

Kentigern, St *See* TREE THAT NEVER GREW, THE.

Kerry-mittit or **kerr-handit** or **corrie-fisted** Left-handed. The term is still heard, and is said to refer to the Kerrs, a powerful Border family in whom left-handedness was supposedly so common that they would build the spiral staircases in their castle towers to turn anti-clockwise. This meant that when they were retreating up the stair, they could fight with their sword arms while the inside wall protected their bodies – while their right-handed attackers would have to expose their bodies in order to wield their swords. It is of course possible that the Kerr connection was concocted as a consequence of the fact that the Gaelic word for awkward or left-handed is *cearr*, which in Scots (up to at least the end of the 16th century) was rendered as *ker* or *kar*, or *car* or *caur*.

Kertin Mary or **Cairter Mary** A phrase used in Moray for a glare of light like a rainbow on the surface of the sea, said to anticipate an easterly wind. It derives from the Gaelic *caoir na mara*, 'flame of the sea'.

Kettle-biler A Dundonian term for a man who stays at home while his wife works – once a not uncommon occurrence in Dundee, where at least into the mid-20th century a higher proportion of women worked than in any other Scottish city, most of them employed in the jute mills. There was relatively less work for men. According to Tom Devine in *The Scottish Nation 1700–2000* (1999):

> Dundee had a reputation as a 'women's town', where women not in paid employment were regarded as lazy and the men who remained at home were referred to as 'kettle boilers' who prepared the meals.

Key keep the castle James I's promise to restore order in Scotland when he returned to his homeland for his coronation in 1424:

> If God gives me but a dog's life, I will make the key keep the castle and the bracken bush keep the cow through all Scotland.

James had been held by the English since 1406, the year of his accession, and the country had degenerated into lawlessness in his absence.

Kick one's own arse, to An emphatic Glaswegian way of kicking oneself, as in experiencing violent regret.

Kick up Dublin, to To make a big fuss, a Glaswegian expression alluding to the supposed hot tempers of the Irish.

Khyber Pass, the *See* CURRY ALLEY.

Kick with the left foot, to To be a Roman Catholic, from the belief originating in Ulster that Catholics used their left foot to push the spade while digging. Catholics are thus called *left-footers*. Catholics and Protestants say of each other that they *kick with the wrong foot*.

Kidnapped A novel by Robert Louis Stevenson, published in 1886. He who is kidnapped is the hero, young David Balfour: to cheat him out of his inheritance his wicked Uncle Ebenezer has him abducted and put aboard a ship bound for the Carolinas, where he is to be sold into servitude. The ship is wrecked off the Isle of Mull, and David escapes in the company of the 'bonnie fighter', Alan BRECK. They have many adventures together across the Highlands in the wake of the '45 Jacobite Rebellion. A key event of this novel, and of its sequel *Catriona* (1893), is a real historical event, the notorious APPIN MURDER. The story of Balfour's kidnap was also, it turns out, inspired by a real incident, which Stevenson probably came across in a book published in 1743 and entitled *Memoirs of an Unfortunate Young Nobleman, Returned from Thirteen years' Slavery in America, where he had been sent by a Wicked Contrivance of his Cruel Uncle; A Story founded on Truth, and address'd equally to the Head and Heart*. This volume had largely been dismissed as a sentimental fiction, but in *Birthright: the True Story that Inspired* Kidnapped (2010), the American historian Roger Ekirch shows that it tells the true story of James Annesley, the Anglo-Irish heir to a fortune and the earldom of Anglesey, who as a lad was kidnapped by his Uncle Richard and sent to Delaware as an indentured servant. Annesley eventually returned to Britain, and spent years fighting for his rightful inheritance in the courts, but died in 1760 before he could secure it. Wicked Uncle Dick died the following year, and the earldom was declared extinct in the 1770s. *See also* BALFOUR BAY; CLUNY'S CAGE.

Kidney An organ regarding which there are various traditional beliefs:

> The kidney ... is specially an organ of the soul, and there are certain prescriptions regarding it: children

must not partake of it until they can pronounce the word or name for it (Inverness-shire); if you eat a whole kidney it will come out on the body (Sutherland).

> – George Henderson, *Survivals in Belief Among the Celts* (1911)

Kilbarchan Piper, the *See* HABBIE.

Killie *See* FOOTBALL CLUB NICKNAMES.

Killing Time, the The period of most intense persecution of the COVENANTERS, especially the extreme CAMERONIANS, between 1679 and 1688, most especially 1685: Patrick Walker, in his hagiographic *Some remarkable passages of the life and death of Mr John Semple, Mr John Welwood, Mr Richard Cameron* (1727), mentions that 'The Eighty five was ev'n a killing Time.' The period was also known as the *Persecuting Time*.

Kill-the-carter An informal term for a peculiarly potent species of cheap whisky formerly found in the Northeast. In some manifestations, it was infused with porter.

Kill-the-coo A serious matter. The phrase, from the Borders, is usually used in the negative, e.g. 'It's nae great kill-the-coo.'

Kilmarnock bonnet Another name for a BLUE BONNET (although it might also be black or red), taking its name from the Ayrshire town. A *Kilmarnock hood*, in contrast, was a conical woollen cap worn by indoor workers.

Kilmarnock mittens If one is wearing these, one has one's hands in one's pockets.

Kilmarnock shot Any unsporting play in a variety of games, such as kicking the ball into touch in football in order to waste time. The original *Kilmarnock shot* was in bowling, whereby one placed one's bowl well away from the jack so as not to risk knocking away the bowls already played. Why people from Kilmarnock should be regarded as unsporting is unclear.

Kilmaurs whittle *See* SHARP AS A KILMAURS WHITTLE.

Kiln's on fire, the A hornets' nest has been stirred up; something unpleasant has hit the fan. A variant is *the kiln's in a bleeze*.

> Aweel, when my mother and him forgathered, they set till the sodgers, and I think they gae them their kale through the reek! Bastards o' the hure o' Babylon was the best words in their wame. Sae then the kiln was in a bleeze again, and they brought us a' three on wi' them to mak us an example as they ca't.
>
> – Sir Walter Scott, *Old Mortality* (1819), chapter xiv

Kiltie kiltie cauld bum A chant aimed by urban urchins at any man in a kilt. Sometimes it is continued with the line 'cannae keep a warm wan'. There is also a more extended children's rhyme that goes:

> Kiltie kiltie cauld bum
> Three sterrs up,
> The wummin in the middle door
> Hit me wi' a cup.
>
> Ma heid's a' bleedin,
> Ma face is a' cut,
> Kiltie kiltie cauld bum
> Three sterrs up.

King, the The nickname of the footballer Denis Law (b.1940), whose club career was mostly in England, notably playing for Manchester United, for whom he scored 46 goals in a single season. He played for Scotland 55 times, and his record 30 goals for Scotland has only been equalled by Kenny Dalglish (KING KENNY). Fans also called him *the Lawman*. In 1964 Law became the only Scot ever to be named European Footballer of the Year.

Kingdom of Fife, the Why the county of Fife should be dubbed a 'kingdom' is uncertain. Some say it is because until the mid-9th century it was an independent Pictish kingdom (called *Fib*); others say it alludes to Fife's isolation (at least before the construction of bridges across the Firths of Tay and Forth), and the resultant independent-mindedness of the FIFERS. *See also* BEGGAR'S MANTLE FRINGED WI' GOWD, A.

Kingdom of Fife pie A hearty meat pie, with the pastry enclosing rabbit, bacon, gravy and balls of stuffing that include rabbit liver and bacon fat. How and when the dish acquired its name is unclear.

Kingdom of the Rock, the A name for the Dark-Age Kingdom of Strathclyde, one of the kingdoms of the Brythonic-speaking OLD NORTH. The allusion is to Dumbarton Rock (*Alt Clut* in Brythonic), where the kings of Strathclyde had their capital from the 5th to the 9th centuries. *See also* SON OF THE ROCK.

King Hobbe The mocking nickname given by the English to ROBERT THE BRUCE, as in this song from *c.*1325:

> Now Kyng Hobbe in the mures ȝongeth,
> For te come to toune nout him ne longeth.

Hobbe or *Hob* was a familiar form of Robert or Robin, and the name became a generic term for a rustic clown.

Kingis Quair, The A long poem by James I, written during his captivity in England (1406–24), and influenced by Chaucer's translation of a French allegory.

> The bird, the beste, the fisch eke in the see,
> They lyve in fredome everich in his kind;
> And I a man, and lakkith libertee ...

A *quair* in this context simply means a poem, although with an aspect of self-deprecation, as the word more commonly denoted a bundle of sheets of paper. The poem itself marks the transition from French to Scots as the language of the Scottish court, and earned James the sobriquet 'the Scottish Orpheus'.

King James II Holly, the An ancient tree in the grounds of Floors Castle near Kelso, said to mark the spot where James II met his end, killed by his own cannon misfiring during the siege of Roxburgh Castle in 1460, as described by Robert Lindsay of Pitscottie in his *Historie and Chronicles of Scotland 1436–1565*:

> ... his thigh-bone was dung in two with a piece of misframed gun that brake in shooting, by the which he was stricken to the ground and died hastily.

King Kenny A nickname of the Scottish footballer and manager Kenny Dalglish (b.1951). As a player he had great success with Celtic then Liverpool, and won 102 caps for Scotland, scoring 30 goals for his country (making him joint record holder with Denis Law, aka the KING). As a player-manager at Liverpool in 1985–6, he led Liverpool to its first-ever 'double' (League Championship and FA Cup). In total, under his management Liverpool won the League Championship nine times, the League Cup four times and the FA Cup twice, leading fans to wave banners declaring 'Kenny's from Heaven' (playing on the title of the old song, 'Pennies from Heaven'). Dalglish continued his successful managerial career with Blackburn Rovers, Newcastle United and Celtic. Asked on one occasion what he said to his players in the dressing room, he replied: 'Nothing really. Most of the time I don't even know what they are going to do myself.'

King of Carrick A sobriquet of Gilbert Kennedy, 4th Earl of Cassilis (*c.*1541–76), awarded because of the power he wielded in the Carrick region of southern Ayrshire. Typical of his tyrannous carryings-on was his abduction of Allan Stewart, whom he confined in the Black Vault of Dunure Castle. There he roasted him over a fire until his 'flesch was consumed and brunt to the bones', at which point Stewart agreed to cede his rights over the lands of Crossraguel Abbey. Kennedy was fined by the Privy Council, and obliged to pay a pension to his victim, but he nevertheless kept the lands he had extorted. *See also* COURT A KENNEDY.

King of Kippen The facetious name by which the Laird of Arnprior became known, as described by Sir Walter Scott in *Tales of a Grandfather* (1831):

> When James the Fifth travelled in disguise, he used a name which was known only to some of his principal nobility and attendants. He was called the Goodman (the tenant, that is) of Ballengeich. Ballengeich is a steep pass which leads down behind the castle of Stirling. Once upon a time when the court was feasting in Stirling, the king sent for more venison from the neighbouring hills. The deer was killed and put on horses' backs to be transported to Stirling. Unluckily they had to pass the castle gates of Arnprior, belonging

to a chief of the Buchanans, who chanced to have a considerable number of guests with him. It was late, and the company were rather short of victuals, though they had more than enough liquor. The chief, seeing so much fat venison passing his very door, seized on it, and to the expostulations of the keepers, who told him it belonged to King James, he answered insolently, that if James was king of Scotland, he (Buchanan) was king in Kippen; being the name of the district in which Arnprior lay. On hearing what had happened, the king got on horseback, and rode instantly from Stirling to Buchanan's house, where he found a strong fierce-looking Highlander, with an axe on his shoulder, standing sentinel at the door. This grim warder refused the king admittance, saying that the laird of Arnprior was at dinner, and would not be disturbed. 'Yet go up to the company, my good friend,' said the king, 'and tell him that the Goodman of Ballengeich is come to feast with the King of Kippen.' The porter went grumbling into the house, and told his master that there was a fellow with a red beard at the gate, who called himself the Goodman of Ballengeich, who said he was come to dine with the King of Kippen. As soon as Buchanan heard those words, he knew that the king was come in person, and hastened down to kneel at James's feet, and to ask forgiveness for his insolent behaviour. But the king, who only meant to give him a fright, forgave him freely, and, going into the castle, feasted on his own venison which Buchanan had intercepted. Buchanan of Arnprior was ever afterwards called the King of Kippen.

See also GOODMAN OF BALLENGEICH, THE.

King of the Border, the Adam Scott of Tushielaw, a notable BORDER REIVER and HEIDSMAN of the early 16th century, whose stronghold lay in the Ettrick valley. Scott was also known as 'King of Thieves'. He suffered eventually from James V's determination to bring order to the Borders, and according to local tradition the king had him hanged from a branch of an ash tree that grew within the walls of his own castle – a tree on which he had hanged so many others. The ash is now gone, but it was still around when *Chambers Gazetteer* was published in 1832:

It is curious to observe that along its principal branches there are yet visible a number of nicks, or hollows, over

which the ropes had been drawn wherewith he performed his numerous executions.

Unfortunately for poetic justice, history recounts that Scott was actually beheaded in Edinburgh on 27 July 1529, a month before James's expedition into the lawless Borders. Scott, in his *MINSTRELSY OF THE SCOTTISH BORDER*, notes:

A path through the mountains, which separate the vale of Ettrick from the head of Yarrow, is still called the 'King's Road', and seems to have been the route which he followed. The remains of the tower of Tushielaw are yet visible, overhanging the wild banks of the Ettrick; and are an object of terror to the benighted peasant, from an idea of their being haunted by spectres.

King of the Cocos The title claimed by the Shetland-born sea captain John Clunies-Ross (1786–1854) and his descendants, who owned the remote Indian Ocean archipelago of the Cocos (Keeling) Islands from 1827 until 1978. The Clunies-Ross family had supported the 1715 Jacobite Rebellion, after which they had fled to Shetland. John Clunies-Ross had explored the Cocos Islands (first discovered by Captain William Keeling in 1609) in 1825, returning two years later to settle his family, together with his crew and a Malay workforce, establishing coconut plantations and exporting copra. Britain formally annexed the islands in 1857, but in 1886 Queen Victoria granted the islands to the Clunies-Ross family in perpetuity. In 1955 the islands were transferred to Australia, and in 1978 Australia bought out the Clunies-Ross family, under threat of compulsory acquisition.

King of the Cornkisters The sobriquet of Willie Kemp (1888–1965), whose family owned a hotel in Oldmeldrum and who became one of the most celebrated writers and performers of CORNKISTERS (comic songs in the DORIC). He collaborated on some songs with his brother-in-law, G.S. Morris, the BUCHAN CHIELD.

King of the Forest, the A mighty Scots pine in Muirwood Wood, near New Scone, Perthshire. It has the largest girth of any such Scots pine in the UK: 6.09 m (20 ft). In 1883 it was said to be some 300 years old.

King of the Gypsies A title claimed in Scotland through the ages by the leaders of various gypsy clans, notably the Faa family of Kirk Yetholm, one of the main centres of the Scottish gypsies. In 1540 James V recognized 'oure louit' Johnnie Faa as 'lord and erle of Litill Egipt', and granted him jurisdiction over his people, calling on all sheriffs to support him 'in executione of justice upoun his company and folkis'.

This historical character became associated with the Johnnie Faa of a popular ballad, sung in many versions across Scotland, typically beginning 'The gypsie's cam' to the Castle yett [gate]', and telling the story of a noble knight whose lady-love marries a powerful lord. While the husband is away from his castle, the knight disguises himself as a gypsy, and runs off with the lady. The version of the ballad sung in Ayrshire began 'The gypsie's cam' tae Cassillis yett', referring to Cassillis House on the River Doon near Maybole, and the lady in the ballad become associated with a Countess of Cassillis, the earldom of Cassillis having been created in 1509 for the 3rd Lord Kennedy (*see* COURT A KENNEDY). 'Cassillis' is pronounced 'cassels', so it is easy to see how the change from 'Castle yett' to 'Cassillis yett' came about. Furthermore, there was a tradition that Johnnie Faa and his people sometimes set up camp at nearby Culroy, 'the glen of the king'. A local legend thus grew up, recounted by Robert Chambers in his *Picture of Scotland* (1827), that 'a gallant young knight, a Sir John Faa of Dunbar' was enamoured of a Countess of Cassillis, identified by Chambers (without historical evidence) with Lady Jean Hamilton, the daughter of Thomas, 1st Earl of Haddington, who in 1621 married John Kennedy, 6th Earl of Cassilis (d.1668), 'a stern Covenanter'. In Chambers's version, while the earl was attending the Assembly of Divines in Westminster, Faa took his opportunity, and turned up at Cassillis disguised as a gypsy, and in company with a band of gypsies who (in the words of an old ballad) 'cuist the glaumourye ower her' (*see* GLAMOUR).

The Countess condescended to elope with her lover. Most unfortunately ere they had proceeded very far, the Earl came home, and, learning the fact, immediately set out in pursuit. Accompanied by a band which put resistance out of the question, he overtook them,

and captured the whole party, at a ford over the Doon, still called the Gypsies' Steps, a few miles from the castle. He brought them back to Cassillis, and there hanged all the gypsies, including the hapless Sir John, upon 'the Dule Tree' [*see* DOOL TREE], a splendid and most umbrageous plane, which yet flourishes on a mound in front of the Castle Gate, and which was his gallows-in-ordinary, as the name testifies. As for the Countess, whose indiscretion occasioned all this waste of human life, she was taken by her husband to a window in front of the Castle, and there, by a refinement of cruelty, compelled to survey the dreadful scene – to see, one after another, fifteen gallant men put to death, and at last to witness the dying agonies of him who had first been dear to her, and who had imperilled all that men esteem in her behalf. The particular room in the stately old house where the unhappy lady endured this horrible torture, is still called 'the Countess's Room'. After undergoing a short confinement in that apartment, the house belonging to the family at Maybole was fitted for her reception, by the addition of a fine projecting staircase, upon which were carved heads representing those of her lover and his band; and she was removed thither and confined for the rest of her life – the Earl in the meantime marrying another wife.

Thus the legend, but Lady Jean in fact died in 1642, the year before the 6th Earl attended the Westminster Assembly, and was sorely mourned by her husband, who in a letter shortly after her death referred to her as 'my deir bedfellow'. The earl did remarry, in 1644, but not bigamously as Chambers suggests. As a footnote to the fictional career of Johnnie Faa, a 'king of the gyptians' of this name appears in Philip Pullman's celebrated novel *Northern Lights* (1995).

Other notable members of the Faa clan include Patrick Faa, whose wife Jean Gordon was the main inspiration for Scott's character Meg MERRILIES, and William Faa II (d.1847), who lived in Kirk Yetholm in the 'Gypsy Palace', a cottage built on land given to the gypsies in the 18th century by the local laird, Bennet of Grubbit and Marlefield, whose life had been saved by a Scottish gypsy at the Battle of Namur in 1695. When William Faa died, aged 96, the *Kelso Mail*, under the headline 'Death of a Gypsy King', declared him 'a more respectable character than any of his tribe, and could boast of never having been in gaol during his life'. Among his successors was Queen Esther Faa Blyth (d.1883), and her son, Charles Faa Blyth (d.1902), the last of the gypsy kings in Scotland.

Finally, mention must be made of Billy Marshall (1671/2–1792), known as *King of the Galloway Tinkers*. One of his many wives, Flora Marshall, was another inspiration for Scott's Meg Merrilies. For more on Billy Marshall's fabulous career, *see* CAIRD O' BARULLION, THE.

King of the Wood, the A mighty old oak near Jedburgh. It is 24 m (79 ft) high, and its bole has a girth of 5.42 m (17 ft 9 in). Nearby is the even older CAPON TREE.

King over the Water, the The Jacobite toast to the exiled James VII and his successors, the OLD PRETENDER and the YOUNG PRETENDER. In circumstances when uttering the words would betray one's sympathies, such as dinners when the 'loyal toast' was being proposed to the Hanoverian monarch, discreet Jacobites would pass their glasses over the finger bowl. *See also* LITTLE GENTLEMAN IN BLACK VELVET, THE.

King's ba A children's game recorded in Fife and Angus in which a ball is passed between players, who may only throw or catch the ball between their fists. If a player drops the ball, he or she is out, but may try to get other players out by throwing the ball (using the hands) to hit them below the knees. They may use their fists to try to defend themselves from being hit.

King's Bedesman *See* GABERLUNZIE.

King's Cave A cave on the southwest coast of Arran, said to have been a hiding-place of the legendary Fingal, and where Robert the Bruce supposedly took refuge in 1307, before returning to Carrick. However, the cave in which he watched the spider was probably on Rathlin Island, between Kintyre and the mainland of Ulster (*see* BRUCE AND THE SPIDER). There is another King's Cave on the coast northeast of the North Sutor of Cromarty (*see* SOUTAR).

King Schaw's Grave A prehistoric cist on a hilltop near to the DEIL'S JINGLE, above Castle O'er, south of Eskdalemuir, Dumfriesshire. It was formerly enclosed by a large cairn in the form of a SALTIRE, but 150 cartloads of stones were removed in 1828 to make drystane dykes. A crouched skeleton was apparently found within. King Schaw was supposedly a king of the Picts.

King's Ellwand, the A former name for Orion's Belt, in the constellation Orion, also known as Our Lady's Ellwand. The King's Ellwand also formerly denoted the foxglove (*see under* FLORA CALEDONIA). An ellwand is a rod measuring an ell, the Scots ell being a yard, i.e. four-fifths of the English ell (45 inches). *See also* PETER'S STAFF.

King's errand may come in the cadger's gate, the A proverb noted by Allan Ramsay in *Scots Proverbs* (1737), meaning the great man sometimes has use of the small man. A *cadger* is a hawker or beggar, while here *gate* means 'road'. *See also* BOLT THE CADGER.

King's keys, to make To make a forced entry to a house, chest, etc., in pursuance of a court order or warrant, the *king's keys* being the tools (such as crowbars and sledgehammers) used to gain access.

'And I warn you,' continued Earnscliff, 'that your only way to prove your son's innocence is to give us quiet admittance to search the house.'

'And what will ye do, if I carena to thraw the keys, or draw the bolts, or open the grate to sic a clamjamfrie?' said the old dame, scoffingly.

'Force our way with the king's keys, and break the neck of every living soul we find in the house, if ye dinna gie it ower forthwith!' menaced the incensed Hobbie.

– Sir Walter Scott, *The Black Dwarf* (1816), chapter ix

King's Kindly Tenants, the A former name for the inhabitants of four Dumfriesshire villages – Greenhill, Heck, Hightae and Smallholm, known collectively as 'the Four Towns of Lochmaben' – who claimed descent from the vassals of Robert the Bruce.

Kings of Scotland, descended from *See* ABYSSI-
NIAN, THE; UNCROWNED KING OF SCOTS, THE.

King's road, the *See* KING OF THE BORDER, THE.

King's weather The shimmers seen in the air above
the ground on a hot day.

King William's Dear Years *See* SEVEN ILL YEARS,
THE.

Kinmont Willie William Armstrong of Kinmont
(*c.*1530–*c.*1610?), perhaps the most notorious of a
notorious clan of BORDER REIVERS. His notoriety is
largely due to the ballad 'Kinmont Willie', collected
by Walter Scott in his *MINSTRELSY OF THE SCOT-
TISH BORDER*. From his castle at Kinmont, near
Canonbie in Dumfriesshire, Armstrong often led
several hundred horsemen – known as 'Kinmont's
Bairns' – in his raids across the Border or against his
fellow countrymen (Border allegiances were to clan
not king), and reputedly would drive back up to
3000 head of sheep and cattle at a time. Eventually,
on 17 March 1596 Lord Thomas Scrope, the
English Warden of the West March, violated a
TRUCE DAY to apprehend Armstrong, and subsequently imprisoned him in Carlisle Castle. Outraged
at this treachery, Walter Scott of Buccleuch, Keeper
of Liddesdale (and an ancestor of his namesake, the
writer), demanded Armstrong's release, and when
this was refused, he led a small band of men in a
daring rescue attempt, which on 13 April successfully broke Armstrong out of Carlisle Castle against
considerable odds.

> Buccleuch has turn'd to Eden water,
> Even where it flowed frae bank to brim,
> And he has plunged in wi' a' his band,
> And safely swam then thro' the stream.

> He turn'd him on the other side,
> And at Lord Scrope his glove flung he;
> 'If ye like na my visit in merry England,
> In fair Scotland come visit me!'

> All sair astonished stood Lord Scrope,
> He stood as still as rock of stane;
> He scarcely dared tae trew his eyes,
> When through the water they had gane.

> 'He is either himsel' a devil frae hell,
> Or else his mother a witch maun be;
> I wadna hae ridden that wan water,
> For a' the gowd in Christendie.'

For his audacity Walter Scott earned the sobriquet
BOLD BUCCLEUCH, while Scrope was so incensed
that he marched into Scotland, burnt the towns of
Annan and Dumfries, and marched some 200 prisoners back to England, 'naked, chained together on
leashes'. The whole affair set back the process of
rapprochement between James VI and Elizabeth I,
and the two embarked on a diplomatic damage-
limitation exercise. As for Armstrong, he was never
retaken, and it was said that he lived to a ripe old age
and died peacefully in his bed.

Kintail, Five Sisters of *See* FIVE SISTERS OF KIN-
TAIL, THE.

Kintyre taken by trickery The following account
of an infamous 11th-century land-grab is from
William Daniell's *A Voyage Round Great Britain*
(1815–25):

> When Magnus the Barefooted, king of Norway, ob-
> tained, from Donald-Bane of Scotland, the cession of
> the Western Isles, or all those places that could be
> surrounded in a boat, he added to them the peninsula
> of Cantyre by this fraud: he placed himself in a boat,
> held the rudder, was drawn over this narrow tract [the
> isthmus separating Kintyre and Knapdale, between
> Tarbert and West Tarbert], and by this species of
> navigation wrested the country from his brother mon-
> arch.

Kipper's knickers, the A Glaswegian equivalent of
the cat's pyjamas or the bee's knees. The kipper's
knickers were once more widely invoked, and, like
the cat's pyjamas, the bee's knees and a host of other
nonsense phrases, appear to have originated in
1920s America.

Kirdandy *See* KELTON HILL FAIR.

Kirking A ceremony performed by women following childbirth. In Scotland this was not quite the
same as the churching of a woman in the Church of
England, which involves official Church ceremonial:

The mother never sets about any work till she has been *kirked*. In the Church of Scotland there is no ceremony on the occasion; but the woman, attended by some of her neighbours, goes into the church, sometimes in service time, but oftener when it is empty; goes out again, surrounds it, refreshes herself at some public-house, and then returns home. Before this ceremony she is looked on as unclean, never is permitted to eat with the family; nor will any one eat of the victuals she has dressed.

    – Thomas Pennant, *A Tour in Scotland in 1769* (1771)

Kirking Sunday The Sunday after a wedding when the bride and groom would attend church together for the first time, dressed in their finery. Not until after the bride was *kirked* were the couple regarded as properly married.

Kirk Malignant, the A term applied by the Covenanters in the 17th century to the Roman Catholic Church. *See also* MALIGNANT.

'Kirkcudbright Grace, The' *See* 'SELKIRK GRACE, THE.'

Kirkwall Ba *See* HANDBA.

Kirkyaird deserter Literally, someone who has deserted the graveyard, i.e. someone who looks like they are not long for this life. The semi-jocular expression comes from the Northeast.

Kirn-milk Geordie A Jacobite nickname for George I, from the song 'Kirn-Milk Geordie' (1715); *kirn-milk* is buttermilk. To avoid charges of sedition, the identities of the protagonists are thinly disguised in an allegory – not that any contemporary would have been left in any doubt:

It's James and George, they war twa lords,
    And they've coosten out about the kirn;
But Geordie he proved the strongest loon,
    And he's gart Jamie stand ahin'.
And hey now, Geordie, Geordie, Geordie,
    Ply the cutty as lang as ye can;
For Donald the piper will win the butter,
    And nought but kirn-milk for ye than.
    [*cutty* as a verb means 'to sup greedily']

James is the OLD PRETENDER, and presumably 'Donald the piper' is the Highland host that comes out in his favour. The song ends with Geordie being tied up in a rope (*tow*) and hanged up high, while his enemies celebrate with a wild drinking spree:

Then up wi' Geordie, kirn-milk Geordie,
Up wi' Geordie high in a tow:
At the last kick of a foreign foot,
We'se a' be ranting roaring fou.

Kirrie dumplins *See under* FLORA CALEDONIA.

Kirriemuir gingerbread A rich loaf cake, also known as *starry rock*, containing spices such as cinnamon as well as ginger, muscavado sugar, golden syrup, treacle and buttermilk. It is often eaten spread with butter.

Kishorn Commandos, the The name adopted by the workers on the vast oil-rig construction site located on Loch Kishorn in the 1970s and 1980s, after the song by Gordon Menzies of the folk group Gaberlunzie:

We're the Kishorn Commandos way up in Wester
    Ross,
We've never had a gaffer, we've never had a boss,
But we'll build the biggest oil-rig you've ever come
    across,
Remember we're the Kishorn Commandos.

Cf. TUNNEL TIGERS, THE.

Kiss-ma-luif Literally, 'kiss-my-hand', i.e. a fawner or fop.

As we left the king's ship astern, old Father Yawkins sprang on our taffrail, and waved his hand – 'Out-sailed, out-fought, out-witted – such a set of kiss-my-loofs, you king's men. That's what I think of ye! Hae!'
    – S.R. Crockett, *The Raiders* (1894), chapter x

If one *disnae gie a kiss-ma-luif*, one doesn't give a damn.

Kist o' whistles A term formerly applied by disapproving Presbyterians to the pipe organ, a *kist* being a chest, and the whistles being the organ pipes. Until the later 19th century organs were only found in Episcopalian churches, which were disparagingly referred to as *whistle kirks,* and their clergy as *whistle-kirk ministers.* The term is also applied jocularly to a congested (human) chest. *A Kist of Whistles* is the title of a volume of poetry by Hugh MacDiarmid, published in 1947.

Klondyke To preserve herring in ice for export to mainland Europe. The expression, first used in the 1920s, alludes to the Klondike Gold Rush in Yukon in the late 1890s, and refers to the profitable nature of the Scottish herring-export business. Today, the word *Klondyker* is applied to the big foreign (mostly Eastern European) factory-ships that buy fish at sea from Scottish fishermen and process it on board before returning to their home ports. Crew members are also referred to as *Klondykers.*

Knickerbocker Politician, the The nickname of the anarcho-communist Guy Alfred Aldred (1886–1963), alluding to his distinctive style of dress, as described by his contemporary, John Taylor Caldwell:

He wore a Norfolk jacket, pleated and high-lapelled. He had a starched Eton collar and a starched shirt front. The ends of his black bow tie were tucked under his wide collar. He wore knickerbockers, thick grey stockings and heavy, highly polished black boots.

Though born in London, Aldred settled permanently in Glasgow after the First World War, where he set up the Bakunin Press and became a key figure in the Anti-Parliamentary Communist Federation (nicknamed the Anti-Panties). Aldred stood in many elections, urging people not to vote for him and instead to take back control over their own lives from Parliament. He continued to campaign against injustice until his death.

Knight of Elderslie, the How BLIND HARRY refers to William Wallace. Elderslie in Renfrewshire was traditionally Wallace's birthplace, and the site of WALLACE'S OAK and Yew.

Knot in the puddin, a *See under* DISEASES.

Knot o' the thrapple The Adam's apple (*thrapple,* 'throat'); also known as the *knot o' the craig,* ('neck').

Knox cap *See* JOHN KNOX CAP.

Knox's Liturgy The popular name for *The Forms of Prayers in the Ministration of the Sacraments used in the English Congregation at Geneva,* published in that city in 1556, during John Knox's exile there. As *The Book of Common Order,* it was adopted by the General Assembly of the Church of Scotland in 1562. Among the prayers included therein is the 'Prayer to be said before a man begin his work', which contains the following:

And if it please thee to try and exercise us by greater poverty and need than our flesh would desire, that thou wouldest yet, O Lord God, grant us grace to know that thou wilt nourish us continually through thy bountiful liberality, that we be not so tempted that we fall into distrust: but that we may patiently wait till thou fill us, not only with corporal graces and benefits, but chiefly with thine heavenly spiritual treasures, to the intent that we always have more ample occasion to give thee thanks and wholly to rest upon thy mercies.

In 1567 the prayers were translated into Gaelic, becoming the first book to be printed in that language. The translator, John Carswell, Superintendent of Argyll, seems to have had little stomach for his task, stating in his introduction:

Great the blindness and sinful darkness and ignorance and evil will of those who teach, write, and foster the Gaelic speech; for to win for themselves the empty rewards of the world, they both choose more and use more to make vain and misleading tales, lying and worldly, of the Tuath De Danann, of fighting men and champions, of Fionn MacCumhal and his heroes, and many more whom now I will not number.

Knox's man, John *See* JOHN TAMSON'S MAN.

KOBs or **Kosbees, the** Nicknames for the King's Own Scottish Borderers; *see* REGIMENTAL NICKNAMES.

Krankies, the A comedy duo comprising Janette Tough (b.1947) in the role of schoolboy Wee Jimmy Krankie, and Janette's husband Ian (b.1947) as Wee Jimmy's father. They worked the club circuit in the 1970s and emerged into the limelight in 1979 with a slot at the Royal Variety Performance. The Krankies had a number of TV shows in the 1980s, and still make appearances on stage in variety and panto, and on TV. In 2003 a readers' poll in the *Herald* voted Wee Jimmy Krankie 'The Most Scottish Person in the World'.

Kyle for a man A saying relating to the parts of Ayrshire:

Kyle for a man, Carrick for a coo,
Cunninghame for butter, Galloway for woo.

Kyle has rich ground for arable farming, Carrick is more suitable for cattle, while Cunninghame provides richer grazing for dairy herds. As for Galloway (part of which is in Ayrshire), it is fit only for sheep (*woo*, 'wool'). Burns was a native of Kyle.

I had no conception that the native place of Burns was so beautiful – the idea I had was more desolate, his rigs of barley seemed always to me but a few strips of green on a cold hill – O prejudice! it was rich as Devon.
– John Keats, letter to J.H. Reynolds, 1818

L

Labour pains, transference of The phenomenon by which the father rather than the mother suffers the pains of childbirth was in the past known in various parts of Europe, including Scotland, and was reported by Sir James Frazer in *Totemism and Exogamy* (1910). As far as Scotland is concerned, George Henderson, in his *Survivals in Belief Among the Celts* (1911), claims to have personally encountered one such instance, and attributed it to 'a power ascribed to certain wise mid-wives of transferring the mother's pains to the father'. He continues:

> For resorting to such enchantments Eufame Macalyne was burned alive on the Castle-hill at Edinburgh in 1591. When James VI was born, a lady of rank, Lady Reirres, complained 'that she was never so troubled with no bairn that ever she bare, for the Lady Athole had cast all the pain of her child-birth upon her'. At Langholm, in Dumfriesshire, in 1772, [Thomas] Pennant found a belief that 'the midwives had power of transferring part of the primeval curse bestowed on our great first mother, from the good wife to her husband. I saw the reputed offspring of such a labour; who kindly came into the world without giving her mother the least uneasiness, while the poor husband was roaring with agony in his uncouth and unnatural pains.'

Ladies from Hell, the The description of the kilted soldiers of the Highland regiments awarded them by their German enemies in the First World War, and subsequently adopted as a nickname by the BLACK WATCH. The Germans also called the Highland soldiers 'Devils in Skirts'. Marshal Joffre opined of the kilt: '*Pour l'amour, oui. Mais pour la guerre, non.*' ['For love, yes. But for war, no.']

> Join a Highland regiment, my boy. The kilt is an unrivalled garment for fornication and diarrhoea.
> – John Masters, *Bugles and a Tiger* (1956)

Ladies' Rock A rock in the Old Town Cemetery, Stirling, so-called as from here the ladies would watch the tournaments taking place in the 'Valley' below.

Lad o' pairts A young man, usually from a poor background, who shows particular promise, for example in intellectual capabilities or business acumen. The popularity of the phrase derives from its use as the title of a story in Ian Maclaren's *Beside the Bonnie Brier Bush* (1894; *see* 'THERE GROWS A BONNIE BRIER BUSH'). A *lass o' pairts* is the female equivalent.

Lady of Heaven's hen, the The wren. *See* FAUNA CALEDONIA.

Lady of Lawers, the (Gaelic, *Baintighearn Labhuir*) A seer who lived in the old and now abandoned village of Lawers, on the west shore of Loch Tay, close to the modern village of Lawers. She probably flourished in the mid-17th century, and is thought to have been a Stewart of Appin who married a Campbell laird of Lawers. As regards her prognostications, the Revd William Gillies of Kenmore writes in his book *In Famed Breadalbane* (1938):

> One or two of the prophecies ascribed to the Lady may be echoes of sayings credited to other well known Scottish seers: some relate to the church of Lawers, others to social and economic changes on Lochtayside, and a few to happenings in the history of the Breadalbane Campbells. The sayings were uttered in Gaelic, and have been handed down in that language from one generation to another. A saying of a general nature is to the effect that the feather of the goose would drive the memory from man, which no doubt referred to the destructive influence of writing upon the power of remembrance. In olden days when people in the

Highlands could neither read nor write many persons were to be found who could recite thousands of lines of poetry from memory. With the introduction of printing and of books this gift has to a great extent been lost.

Among other things the lady was also said to have predicted the DISRUPTION OF 1843 in the Church of Scotland, the building of the railway over Drumochter Pass (she talked, in Gaelic, of 'fire-coaches'), and the CLEARANCES:

> The Lady further said that the jaws of the sheep would drive the plough out of the ground, that many holdings would become one holding, that the homesteads on Lochtayside yet would be so far apart that the one cock would not be able to hear his neighbour crow …

She also made a number of predictions regarding events that would occur when an ash tree she planted by the church in Lawers reached certain heights:

> The Lady further predicted with regard to this fateful tree that whoever should cut it down would be sure to come to an evil end. About sixty years ago John Campbell the tenant of the Milton farm along with a neighbour had the temerity to lay an axe to the stem of the tree. As they did so the neighbours shook their heads, feeling assured that they were courting disaster. The neighbours' fears were shortly confirmed. John Campbell was gored to death by his own Highland bull, while his assistant lost his reason, and had to be removed to the district asylum.

According to George Henderson, in his *Survivals in Belief Among the Celts* (1911), 'Children were dipped in the Lady of Lawers' Well at Beltane, and sprinkled when the sun was visible.'

Lady of the Lake, The A long narrative poem set in the 16th century by Sir Walter Scott, published in 1810. The eponymous heroine is Ellen Douglas, daughter of Lord James Douglas, who has fallen out with the king. The lake in question is Loch Katrine, the first view of which in the poem is had by a hunter pursuing a stag:

> And thus an airy point he won,
> Where, gleaming with the setting sun,
> One burnish'd sheet of living gold,
> Loch Katrine lay beneath him roll'd,

> In all her length far winding lay,
> With promontory, creek, and bay,
> And islands that, empurpled bright,
> Floated amid the livelier light,
> And mountains, that like giants stand,
> To sentinel enchanted land.
> – Canto 1, stanza 14

The Lady of the Lake herself first appears rowing a skiff:

> A ne'er did Grecian chisel trace
> A Nymph, a Naiad, or a Grace,
> Of finer form, or lovelier face!
> – Canto 1, stanza 18

The poem was a sensation not just in Britain, but across the Continent, inspiring Rossini's opera *La Donna del Lago* (1819), while in 1825 Schubert provided settings for three of Ellen's songs. In the wake of publication, Loch Katrine and the Trossachs became a major tourist magnet – which did not please everybody, least of all a man who operated a ferry across Loch Lomond:

> That d—d Sir Walter Scott … I wish I had him to ferry over Loch Lomond: I should be after sinking the boat, if I drowned myself into the bargain; for ever since he wrote his Lady of the Lake, as they call it, everybody goes to see that filthy hole Loch Katrine … and I have only had two gentlemen to guide all this blessed season.

See also 'HAIL TO THE CHIEF'.

Lady's Rock A small rock (grid reference NM 775 345) in the narrows traversed by the Oban–Craignure ferry between the southwest point of Lismore and Duart Castle on Mull. The name refers to the wife of the 11th Chief of Maclean, and the story of her abandonment on the rock and subsequent rescue provides the subject for Joanna Baillie's tragedy, *The Family Legend* (1810). She outlines the tale in her preface:

> In the fifteenth century a feud had long subsisted between the lord of Argyle and the chieftain of Maclean; the latter was totally subdued by the Campbells, and Maclean sued for peace, demanding, at the same time, in marriage, the young and beautiful daughter of Argyle. His request was granted, and the lady was carried home to the island of Mull. There

she had a son; but the Macleans were hostile to this alliance with the Campbells. They swore to desert their chief if they were not suffered to put his wife to death, with her infant son, who was then at nurse, that the blood of the Campbells might not succeed to the inheritance of Maclean. Maclean resisted these threats, fearing the power and vengeance of Argyle; but at length fear for his own life, should he refuse the demands of his clan, made him to yield to their fury, and he only drew from them a promise that they would not shed her blood. One dark winter night she was forced into a boat, and, regardless of her cries and lamentations, left upon a barren rock, midway between the coasts of Mull and Argyll, which, at high water, is covered with the sea. As she was about to perish she saw a boat steering its course at some distance; she waved her hand, and uttered a feeble cry. She was now upon the top of the rock, and the water as high as her breast, so that the boatmen mistook her for a large bird. They took her, however, from the rock, and, knowing her to be the daughter of Argyle, carried her to the castle of her father.

The Earl rewarded her deliverers, and desired them to keep the circumstance secret for a time, during which he concealed her till he should hear tidings from Mull. Maclean solemnly announced her death to Argyle, and soon came himself with his friends, all in mourning, to condole with the Earl at the castle. Argyle received him, clad also in black. Maclean was full of lamentations; the Earl appeared very sorrowful; a feast was served with great pomp in the hall; every one took his place, while a seat was left empty on the right hand of Argyle; the door opened, and they beheld the lady of Maclean enter, superbly dressed, to take her place at the table. Maclean stood for a moment aghast, when, the servants and retainers making a lane for him to pass through the hall to the gate of the castle, the Earl's son, the Lord of Lorne, followed him, and slew him as he fled. His friends were detained as hostages for the child, who had been preserved by the affection of his nurse.

The lady of Maclean later marries 'an amiable young nobleman who adored her'.

The story of Lady's Rock also provided the inspiration of the ballad 'Glenara' by Thomas Campbell, in which the youth 'who had loved the fair Ellen of Lorn' declares:

'I dreamt of my lady, I dreamt of her grief,
I dreamt that her lord was a barbarous chief;
On a rock of the ocean fair Ellen did seem;
Glenara! Glenara! now read me my dream!'

In dust low the traitor has knelt to the ground,
And the desert revealed where his lady was found;
From a rock of the ocean that lady is borne;
Now joy to the house of fair Ellen of Lorn.

Lager Lovelies, the The photographs of well-up-holstered and sometimes scantily clad young women that graced the backs of cans of Tennent's Lager (made in Glasgow's Wellpark Brewery) from the 1960s until 1991, comforting many a lad's lonely teenage years. Now that such lads have grown to middle age and beyond, the cans have become collector's items. For those with nothing better to do, a full catalogue may be found at http://www.cannyscot.com/.

Laimh Dearg (Gaelic, 'red hand') A bloody-handed, broadsword-wielding apparition that supposedly haunts the forests of Glen More below Cairn Gorm, challenging anyone he comes across to a fight.

Laird, bonnet or **cock** See BONNET LAIRD.

Laird in the Abbey See ABBEY LAIRDS.

'Laird o' Cockpen, The' A song by Carolina Oliphant, Lady Nairne, the FLOWER OF STRATHEARN, published in *The Scottish Minstrel* (1821–4).

The laird o' Cockpen, he's proud an' he's great,
His mind is ta'en up wi' things o' the State;
He wanted a wife, his braw house to keep,
But favour wi' wooin' was fashious to seek.

The cocksure laird decides on Jean, the daughter of MacCleish of Clavers Ha' Lee, 'a penniless lass wi' a lang pedigree'. So he rides over and summons her to his presence:

An' when she came ben she bobbit fu' low,
And what was his errand he soon let her know;
Amaz'd was the Laird, when the lady said, 'Na!'
An' wi' a laigh curtsie she turned awa'.

Dumbfounded was he, but nae sigh did he gie;
He mounted his mare an' he rode cannilie;
And aften he thocht, as he gae'd thro' the glen,
'She was daft to refuse the Laird o'Cockpen.'

The lady in question subsequently comes to the same conclusion, and

Next time that the laird and the lady was seen,
They were gaun arm-in-arm to the kirk on the
    green;
Now she sits in the ha' like a weel-tappit hen,
But as yet there's nae chickens appear'd at Cockpen.

Cockpen is a parish near Dalkeith in Midlothian, and the character of the laird is perhaps based on a 17th-century gentleman called Mark Carse, although others say it was Ramsay of Dalhousie, whose Edinburgh townhouse was the Outlook Tower (which houses a famous camera obscura). The tune of the song is an old one, having been traced to a manuscript dated 1692, but the original words were thought too vulgar, so Lady Nairne provided her own version. The song was popular enough to be the subject of a parody, dating from the second half of the 19th century, which begins:

The Laird o' Cockpen he's puir and he's duddy
Wi' daidling and drinking his head is aye muddy
But he was determined to hae a bit wife,
Although she should vex him the rest o' his life.

Laird of Auchtermuchty, the The byname of Jimmy Shand (1908–2000), the most famous Scottish country dance-band leader of the 20th century. Although born in East Wemyss, Fife, he settled in Auchtermuchty, where he raised his family. Among the honours bestowed upon him towards the end of his life, he was made a knight and the first ever Freeman of the Kingdom of Fife.

In the toon o Auchtermuchty naethin er'e will be
    the same
Nou the Laird o Auchtermuchty haes gaed back frae
    whaur he came.
Aa the heavenly harps o Paradise hae got a different
    beat
As they play a tune bi Jimmy Shand, an angels tap
    thir feet.
    – Bob Peffers, 'Tune bi Jimmy Shand (On the sad loss of
    The Bandleader)'

Laird of Bladnoch and Lochanbards, the A recent holder of this title was an Austrian aristocrat, whisky expert and promoter of heraldry and humanitarianism, known in full as His Excellency Colonel Professor Chevalier Helmut Bräundle-Falkensee GCJ, FMA, MEASc, Grand Master of the Order of St Joachim and The Much Honoured the Laird of Bladnoch and Lochanbards (1950–2007). Bladnoch is a small village near Wigtown, but Lochanbards is nowhere to be found on the Ordnance Survey's 1:50,000 series.

Laird of Inversnecky, the *See* SNECK, THE.

Lake of Menteith The only loch in Scotland that is called a lake. As a lad, the present author was instructed at school that it was given this English name to dishonour Sir John Menteith, who in 1305 handed William Wallace over to the English, so earning the sobriquet 'Fause Menteith'. In fact, *lake* here is a corruption of *laicht*, Gaelic for 'low-lying land'. *See also* BONSPIEL.

Laldie, gie it *See* GIE IT LALDIE, TO.

Lallans *See* PLASTIC SCOTS.

Lally's Palais A nickname for the Glasgow Royal Concert Hall, in the development of which Lord Provost Pat Lally (*see* PAT LAZARUS) played an important part. It has been suggested that the coinage – like FORT WEETABIX and the CLOCK-WORK ORANGE – is more journalese than *echt* patter; it has now fallen out of use. *See also* RHYMING SLANG.

'Lament for the Makaris' Perhaps the best-known poem by William Dunbar (?1456–?1513). MAKAR is an old Scots word for a creative artist, particularly a poet, and Dunbar's poem is an elegy for a number of dead poets, including Chaucer, Gower, Barbour, Blind Harry and Henryson. After the title, Dunbar wrote a note indicating that he wrote the poem 'when he wes seik' ('when he was unwell'):

Sen he hes all my brether tane,
He will nocht let me live alane;

On forse I man his next prey be:

Timor mortis conturbat me.

> ['Since he has taken all my brothers, he will not let me
> live alone; perforce I must be his next prey: the fear of
> death confounds me.']

Lammas Day 1 August, one of the QUARTER DAYS
in Scotland, and a Christian festival also celebrated
in England up to the early 18th century. The word
Lammas originally comes from Old English *hlâf-
mæsse*, 'loaf mass', and it was traditional on Lammas
Day to bring to church a loaf made from the new
crop. *Lammas Fairs* are held in various parts of
Scotland; that at Inverkeithing features the HAT
AND RIBBON RACE.

Lammermuir lion A jocular name for a sheep,
which in the 18th century began to overrun the
Lammermuir Hills of East Lothian and Berwickshire.

Lamp of Lothian, the Originally the name given to
the Franciscan priory in Haddington, East Lothian,
on account of its stained glass and tracery. This
building was destroyed by the English during the
BURNT CANDLEMAS of 1356, and the name Lamp
of Lothian was transferred to St Mary's Parish
Church, begun in 1375 and completed in 1462.
This too was largely destroyed by the English, in
1548, during the ROUGH WOOING, although a major
restoration was carried out in the 1970s. In the case
of St Mary's, the name may allude to the bright red
of its sandstone masonry, or to the stonework
'lantern' that once topped its tower.

Land-lowper Literally, 'land-leaper', i.e. a vagrant or
vagabond. In a letter from 1787, Robert Burns wrote
of his 'landlowper-like stravaiguin [roaming, gad-
ding about]', and the term was still in use a century
or so later: for example in S.R. Crockett's *The
Raiders* (1894), chapter xiii, the narrator describes
Hector Faa as 'a broken land-loupin' cheat-the-
wuddy' (*see also* CHEAT-THE-WUDDY) – although
Crockett may have been striving for period effect in
employing the term.

Land o' Cakes Scotland, referring to its oatcakes.
The usage has been traced back to the 17th century.

As the Lowlanders call their part of the country the
land of cakes, so the natives of the hills say they inhabit
a land of milk and honey.

> – Edmund Burt, *Letters from a Gentleman in the North of
> Scotland* (1726–37)

Hear, Land o' Cakes, and brither Scots
Frae Maidenkirk to John o' Groats.

> – Robert Burns, 'Grose's Peregrinations' (1789), i

And for my dear lov'd Land o' Cakes,
I pray with holy fire:
Lord, send a rough-shod troop o' Hell
O'er a' wad Scotland buy or sell,
To grind them in the mire!

> – Robert Burns, 'Election Ballad'

See also LAND OF CALVIN, OATCAKES AND SULPHUR.

Land of meanness, sophistry and mist Byron's
characterization of Scotland in *The Curse of Minerva*
(1812):

And well I know within that bastard land
Hath Wisdom's goddess never held command;
A barren soil, where Nature's germs, confined
To stern sterility, can stint the mind;
Whose thistle well betrays the niggard earth,
Emblem of all to whom the Land gives birth;
Each genial influence nurtured to resist;
A land of meanness, sophistry and mist.
Each breeze from foggy mount and marshy plain
Dilutes with drivel every drizzly brain,
Till, burst at length, each wat'ry head o'erflows,
Foul as their soil, and frigid as their snows:
Then thousand schemes of petulance and pride
Despatch her scheming children far and wide;
Some East, some West, some – everywhere but North!
In quest of lawless gain, they issue forth.

The cause of all this vituperation was the seizure
by Lord Elgin, the PICTISH PEER, of his eponymous marbles from the Parthenon in Athens. Of
course, Byron was far from uniformly antipathetic
to his mother's native land, as attested by the
following:

England! thy beauties are tame and domestic
To one who has roved o'er the mountains afar:
O for the crags that are wild and majestic!
The steep frowning glories of dark Loch na Garr.

> – Lord Byron, 'Lachan y Gair' (1807)

Land of Calvin, oatcakes and sulphur A characterization of Scotland by the English clergyman and wit Sydney Smith, who spent five years in Edinburgh (1798–1803), where he edited the first number of the *Edinburgh Review*:

> That garret of the earth – that knuckle-end of England – that land of Calvin, oatcakes and sulphur.
> – Quoted in Lady Holland, *A Memoir of Sydney Smith* (1855)

Land of Mists A romantic name sometimes given to the Highlands and Islands, and more specifically to Skye (also known as the MISTY ISLE).

> 'S iomadh Gàidheal tha fo bhròn,
> A thogadh ann an Tìr a' Cheò,
> 'Ga thacadh anns a' bhaile-mhór,
> Le stùr agus le ceò a' ghuail.

> Bowed with sadness many a Gael
> bred up in the Land of Mists,
> smothers now in urban streets
> from the city dust and reek of coal.
> – Mary Macpherson (1821–98), '*Soraidh leis an Nollaig ùir*' ('Farewell to the New Christmas')

Land of the leal Literally, 'land of the loyal or faithful', i.e. heaven. An earlier form of the phrase appears to have been *lands o' leal*:

> Ye maun mak o'er her, kiss her o'er and o'er,
> Say ye're in love, and but her cannot cowr;
> But, for her sake, maun view the lands o' leal,
> Except she pity, and your ailment heal ...
> – Alexander Ross, *Helenore, or the Fortunate Shepherdess* (1768)

The popularity of the phrase (particularly in the pious and sentimental 19th century) is largely due to the moving 1798 poem 'The Land o' the Leal' by Carolina, Lady Nairne (the FLOWER OF STRATHEARN):

> I'm wearin' awa', John
> Like snaw-wreaths in thaw, John,
> I'm wearin' awa'
>   To the land o' the leal.
> There's nae sorrow there, John,
> There's neither cauld nor care, John,
> The day is aye fair
>   In the land o' the leal.

Land of the mountain and the flood Sir Walter Scott's characterization of Scotland in *The Lay of the Last Minstrel* (1805), Canto 6, stanza 2:

> O Caledonia! stern and wild,
> Meet nurse for a poetic child!
> Land of brown heath and shaggy wood,
> Land of the mountain and the flood,
> Land of my sires! what mortal hand
> Can e'er untie the filial band
> That knits me to thy rugged strand!

Byron quotes the phrase in *Don Juan*:

> I '*scotch'd* not kill'd' the Scotchman in my blood,
> And love the land of 'mountain and of flood'.

The phrase also gave the Scottish composer Hamish MacCunn (1868–1916) a title for his concert overture *The Land of the Mountain and the Flood*, which he wrote in 1887 at the age of 19. It has long been a standard in Scottish concert halls, and provided the theme music for the BBC Scotland 1970s TV drama series, *Sutherland's Law*, with Iain Cuthbertson in the role of the eponymous Sutherland, a procurator fiscal in a small Highland town (the series was filmed in Oban).

Land of the omnipotent No A characterization of Scotland by Alan Bold (1943–98) in his poem 'A Memory of Death'.

Lang ale Up to the middle of the 20th century or so, the name given in the Northeast to ginger beer, lemonade and other soft drinks, because they were sold in taller bottles than alcoholic ale or beer.

Lang Day, the The Day of Judgement. The expression is cited in James Kelly's *Complete Collection of Scottish Proverbs* (1721), so was presumably by then long in use, but by the 20th century it was becoming obsolescent.

> What *you* are, Maister Rashleigh, and what excuse ye hae for being *what* you are, is between your ain heart and the lang day.
> – Sir Walter Scott, *Rob Roy* (1818), chapter viii

Lang-lippit Literally 'long-lipped', i.e. sulky.

Lang Lourie *See* LOWRIE.

Lang-lugs Literally 'long-ears', i.e. an eavesdropper and gossip. The term also denotes a donkey, and was used as a name for a hare, especially in areas such as Caithness where it was taboo to call the animal by its proper name.

Lang may yer lum reek 'Long may your chimney smoke', a blessing traditionally offered to newly-weds. It has been said that in Edinburgh they add '... wi' ither folks' coal'. The expression these days is tainted with FAUX JOCKERY.

Lang Raw, the Literally 'the long row (of houses)', the local nickname for the village of Eaglesham in Renfrewshire. In 1962 the *Third Statistical Account* said that Eaglesham consisted 'chiefly of two rows of houses, with a public green ... between'.

Lang Sandy The nickname of the Edinburgh surgeon Alexander Wood (1725–1807), whose eccentricities were described by John D. Comrie in his *History of Scottish Medicine* (1927):

> At a time when personal peculiarity was widely affected by Edinburgh people, Wood especially distinguished himself by going to see his patients accompanied by a pet sheep and raven.

Nevertheless, such was his reputation that Sir Walter Scott's parents consulted him regarding their son's lameness, and Robert Burns was also a patient. Wood was widely popular with the people of Edinburgh on account of his philanthropy and personal kindness, which on one occasion saved him from an unfortunate end. On a dark night, when the mob were after the blood of the provost, Sir James Stirling, they mistook Wood for their intended victim and were about to hurl him over the parapet of the North Bridge when he cried out 'I'm Lang Sandy Wood; tak' me to a lamp and ye'll see!' Byron remembered him fondly in a fragment of a fifth canto for *Childe Harold*, published in *Blackwood's Magazine* in 1818:

> Oh! for an hour of him who knew no feud,
> The octogenarian chief, the kind old Sandy Wood!

Lang Sandy is also a name for the heron.

Lang Stane, the *See* GRANNY KEMPOCK STONE.

Lang Thrums *See* THRUMS.

Lang Toun, the 'The long town', a name applied to Kirkcaldy, originally alluding to its High Street, and now to its 4-mile (6 km) long esplanade. The name is also applied to various other Scottish towns, such as Auchterarder.

Language in which it appears impossible to tell lies, a Scots, or at least English spoken with a Scottish accent, according to Simon Gray in *The Smoking Diaries* (2004):

> Of course the great thing about Scotty [apparently Gray's coinage] is that it's a language in which it appears impossible to tell lies, which is why so many of our most successful current politicians speak it, whether they're from Scotland or not.

This is also why people with a Scottish accent are often selected to work in call centres, as their way of speaking supposedly represents 'the voice of trust'.

Lang Whang, the The traditional name (meaning 'long whip' or 'whack') for the road between Edinburgh and Lanark (now the A70), particularly the long stretch across the moorland north of the Pentland Hills, between Balerno and Carnwath.

> But the far-flung line o' the Lang Whang Road,
> Wi' the mune on the sky's eebree,
> An' naething but me an' the wind abroad,
> Is the wuss that's hauntin' me.
> – Hugh Haliburton (James Logie Robertson, 1846–1922), 'The Lang Whang Road' [*eebree*, 'eyebrow'; *wuss*, 'wish']

Lanimer Day An annual celebration held on a Thursday in early June in Lanark, in which school-children parade through the town in costume, accompanied by brass bands, pipe bands and floats, culminating in the crowning of the year's Lanimer Queen. Lanimer Day is the culmination of Lanimer Week, in which there is both a perambulation and a RIDING OF THE MARCHES, *lanimers* or *landimures* being an old term for the boundaries of a burgh's land. The inspection of the marches is said to have been carried out every year since David I awarded the town its charter as a royal burgh in the 12th century.

Lanny A nickname for Lanliq, a brand of inexpensive South African fortified wine formerly popular in Glasgow among those who found themselves down on their luck. It was supposedly just one step above Brasso.

> A blizzard of authors was sweeping through Glasgow. To get into the boozers you'd to plod through drifts of Hemingways and Mailers. Kerouacs by the dozen could be found lipping Lanny on Glesca Green.
> – Jeff Torrington, *Swing Hammer Swing* (1992)

> There was a drink in Glasgow called Lanliq ... and it was pure firewater. Young people who could not afford more expensive forms of intoxication often got dragged into the Lannie queues.
> – Doug Henderson MP, during a House of Commons debate, 28 February 1997

The trade name Lanliq is said to be derived from 'Lang's Liqueur', and it inspired the following street ditty:

> Lan liq liq liq
> It's sure to make you sick.

It also features in 'Cod Liver Oil and the Orange Juice', a song by Ronnie Clark and Carl MacDougall, sung by Hamish Imlach:

> He went intae a pub, cam oot paralytic
> Oh oh, Lanliq and the cider
> Ah haw, what a helluva mixture
> Cod liver oil and the orange juice ...

See also BUCKFAST TRIANGLE; RED BIDDY.

Lantern of the North, the A former sobriquet of Elgin Cathedral, founded in 1224, completed by the end of that century, and reduced to ruins by a vengeful WOLF OF BADENOCH in 1390.

Lash A nickname of the footballer Peter Lorimer (b.1946), who played for Scotland 21 times, but whose club career was mostly with Leeds United. His nickname refers to the record speed of his 76 mph (122 kph) strike, which left goalkeepers standing.

Last great auk in the British Isles, the *See* GHOST-BIRD, THE.

Last minister strangled with the last copy of the *Sunday Post* In his 1968 essay 'The Three Dreams of Scottish Nationalism' (*New Left Review*, I/49, May–June 1968), Tom Nairn expressed the radical zeitgeist of the day thus:

> Scotland will be reborn when the last minister is strangled with the last copy of the *Sunday Post*.

He was adapting for local consumption the sentiment expressed in the French Revolutionary periodical *La Bouche de Fer* ('the iron mouth'), on 11 July 1791:

> When the last king is hanged with the bowels of the last priest, the human race can hope for happiness.

In the same essay Nairn fretted against:

> This evil mélange of decrepit Presbyterianism and imperialist thuggery, whose spirit may be savoured by a few mornings with the Edinburgh *Scotsman* and a few evenings watching Scottish television ...

He went on to say that this spirit 'appears to be solidly represented in the SNP'.

Last Stuart claimant to the throne of Scotland, the The current claimant is Franz Bonaventura Adalbert Maria Herzog von Bayern, Duke of Bavaria (b.1933), the great-grandson of the last king of Bavaria, Ludwig III, who was deposed in 1918. He is recognized by Jacobites as the rightful Stuart heir to the throne of Scotland, England and Ireland, though he himself dismisses the claim. He lives alone in the Nymphenburg Palace near Munich.

Last wolf in Scotland, the As elsewhere, wolves were long persecuted in Scotland, as attested in this 1457 act of James II's Parliament:

> Item, it is ordainit for the destruccioun of wolfis that in ilk cuntré quhair ony is, the Scheriff or the Bailzie of that cuntré sal gadder the cuntré folk thre tymis in the year, betuix Sanct Merkis Day and Lammess, for that is the tyme of the quhelpis ... And he that slayis ane wolf, than or any other tyme, he sal haif of ilk hous halder of that parochine that the wolf is slain within, i d.

By 1621 inflation had set in, and James II's reward of one penny had grown to £6 13s 4d. Some wolf hunts were conducted on a massive scale. In 1563 Mary Queen of Scots participated in a hunt organized by the Earl of Atholl that involved 2000 Highlanders, and which accounted for five wolves and 360 deer. Felling and burning of the OLD CALEDONIAN FOREST deprived the wolf of its habitat, and wolf kills became rarer and rarer.

Various claims were made as to the slaying of the 'last wolf'. Sir Ewen Cameron of Lochiel made a kill in 1680 near Loch Arkaig, at a place called Glac-a'-Mhadaidh ('wolf's hollow'). This may have been the last wolf killed in Lochaber, but when this specimen, stuffed, came up for sale in London in 1818 it was claimed as 'the last wolf killed in Scotland'. Further to the north, the last wolf in Sutherland was dispatched in 1700 in the following circumstances:

> A man named Polson, and his two sons, having found a wolf's den in a cairn, the two lads crept in and found a family of cubs which they proceeded to kill, the father of the lads remaining without. To his horror he perceived the furious mother rushing homeward, attracted by the cries of the cubs. As it dashed past him into the entrance of the cave, Polson luckily succeeded in seizing it by the tail and holding it fast, thus darkening the aperture, on which one of the sons asked what was keeping out the light. 'If the tail breaks you will soon know that,' said the father, who succeeded, however, in killing the animal with repeated stabs of his dirk.
> – Charles Henry Alston, *Wild Life in the West Highlands* (1912). Alston attributes this account to William Scrope, *Days of Deer-Stalking in the Scottish Highlands* (1839).

The generally accepted tradition is that the very last wolf in Scotland was killed in 1743 by a certain MacQueen of Poll-a'-Chrocain in the Findhorn country near the Monadhliath mountains. (Poll-a'-Chrocain may be Ballachrochin on the upper River Findhorn in Strathdearn.) Alston picks up the tale:

> The story is that a message was brought to MacQueen, a man of gigantic stature and noted for his courage and prowess as a hunter, that a 'large black beast' had killed two children, and requiring him to join his chief, the MacIntosh of that day, with his dogs for a great hunt on the following day. In the morning all were at the

gathering place, except MacQueen, whose non-appearance greatly irritated the Chief; and when at last MacQueen made his appearance he was received with impatience and remonstrance. 'What is the hurry?' said MacQueen, unfolding his plaid and throwing down the newly severed head of the wolf at the MacIntosh's feet. 'There it is for you'; and the tradition further tells how he was rewarded by his Chief with the grant of the lands of Seann-achan ...

Today, wolves may be seen within the confines of the Highland Wildlife Park near Kingussie. Proposals to reintroduce wolves into the wild in places such as Alladale in the Northwest Highlands have met with mixed responses.

Lauchin rain, a Literally 'a laughing rain', a term traditionally applied in the Northeast to rain coming from the southwest with a clear horizon behind. This appears to suggest that the rain will soon be over, whereas in fact it is believed that in such circumstances the rain will last for some time.

Laud to the Devil *See* LITTLE LAUD TO THE DEVIL.

Laureate of the Chemical Generation, the A label sometimes applied to the novelist Irvine Welsh (b.1958), Leith-born author of *TRAINSPOTTING* and other drug-fuelled fictions.

Laureate of the Nursery, the The sobriquet of William Miller (1810–72), author of WEE WILLIE WINKIE.

Laurie, Annie *See* 'BONNIE ANNIE LAURIE'.

Lavellan A vole- or shrew-like creature (Gaelic *labhallan*) that features in the folklore of Caithness and Sutherland. It has the power of hurting cattle at distances of up to 40 paces.

> *Na leigibh o bhail' e*
> *do mhòinteach no coille*
> *mun tig an labhallan*
> *'s gum buail i e.*
> Let him not go away from the houses,
> to moss or wood,
> lest the Lavellan come and smite him.
> – Robb Donn (the ROBERT BURNS of GAELDOM), 'Mac Rorie's Breeches'

Law's Bubble *See* PAPER KING, THE.

Lawman, the A nickname for the footballer Denis Law; *see* KING, THE.

Lawnmarket The section of Edinburgh's ROYAL MILE between Castlehill and the High Street. The name is a corruption of *land market*, a generic term in the 17th and 18th centuries for a place where agricultural produce was sold.

Law of Clan Macduff *See* LEGEM DE CLANMACDUFF.

Lawrightman or **lawrikman** A former law officer in Orkney and Shetland, acting as a constable. One or more lawrightmen served under each local bailiff (magistrate).

> These *Lawrightmen* have a Privilege inherent to their Office, by the Custom of the Country, which is not usual elsewhere; which is, if there be any Suspicion of Theft, they take some of their Neighbours with them, during the Silence of the Night, and make Search for the Theft, which is called *Ransacking*, from *Ransaka*, which is to make Enquiry, in the ancient *Danish*: They search every House they come to, and if the Theft be found, they seize him upon whom it is found, and bring him to the Seat of *Justice*.
> – Revd James Wallace, *A Description of the Isles of Orkney* (1693)

The name derives from the Old Norse *lawting*, 'general assembly' or 'law court', to which the lawrightmen were originally delegates.

Laymedoonandeeism A species of Scottish sentiment, according to James Bridie (*see* WALLACE-THEBRUCEISM), its name deriving from a line in the song 'BONNIE ANNIE LAURIE':

> … for bonnie Annie Laurie
> I'd lay me doon and dee.

Lay of the Last Minstrel, The A long narrative poem by Sir Walter Scott (1771–1832), published in 1805. The 'last minstrel' of the title is the narrator of the romantic and violent tale set in the Scottish Borders in the 16th century, in which Baron Henry

of Cranstown woos 'the flower of Teviot', Lady Margaret of Bransome Hall. A 'lay' is an old word for a ballad. Byron for one was not impressed:

> Thus Lays of Minstrels – may they be the last! –
> On half-strung harps whine mournful to the blast.
> …
> And think'st thou, Scott! by vain conceit perchance,
> On public taste to foist thy stale romance.
> – Lord Byron, *English Bards and Scotch Reviewers* (1809)

As a child Lord Macaulay could recite the whole of the *Lay of the Last Minstrel* after just one reading. (Macaulay later boasted that if all the copies of *Paradise Lost* and *Pilgrim's Progress* were destroyed, he could reconstruct the texts from memory.) *See also* THIS IS MY OWN, MY NATIVE LAND!

Lazy bed An area of land in which potatoes were placed on the top of a ridge, then covered with kelp or manure mixed with soil from the trench or *sheuch* (*see* UP THE SHEUCH) on either side. Remains of lazy beds can be seen in many parts of the Highlands and Islands, and also in Ireland. The name is inaccurate, as it required considerable effort to dig the trenches.

Leave-o *See* BAR-THE-DOOR.

Leave someone the likeness of a dog, to not To thoroughly disparage someone, so that they are left lower than a dog.

> … he cast a look to his wife that spoke unutterable things; but finding that his joke did not take, after so serious a prayer, he turned again on Brownie, and, as his own wife said, 'didna leave him the likeness of a dog'.
> – James Hogg, *The Brownie of Bodsbeck and Other Tales* (1818)

Lee Penny, the An amulet belonging to the Lockharts of Lee, situated between Carluke and Lanark. The amulet consists of a small, triangular semi-transparent red stone, somewhat in the shape of a heart, which is set in a worn silver groat, thought to date from the reign of Edward I of England (the HAMMER OF THE SCOTS). It is now housed in Lee Castle in a gold and enamel snuffbox given to James Lockhart of Lee and Carnwarth, an exiled Jacobite,

by the Empress Maria Theresa, who in 1782 ennobled him as Count Lockhart-Wisecheart of the
Holy Roman Empire in recognition of his military
service.

The charm was formerly used to treat various
diseases of both man and beast:

> The method employed was one of extreme simplicity.
> The celebrant, holding the 'Penny' with its magic gem
> by the chain attached to it, proceeds to plunge the
> amulet three times into pure spring water and then
> gives it a swirl round once, but no more, a procedure
> popularly known as 'three dips and a sweel'.
>
> – Thomas Reid, 'The Lee Penny', *Proceedings of the*
> *Society of Antiquaries of Scotland*, 12 February 1923

In this same article, Reid recounts how he himself
had tasted a glass of water in which the Lee Penny
had been given 'three dips and a sweel'. He reported
that it had ' a perceptibly peculiar flavour', but, being
in good health at the time, he had no opinion as to
its curative properties.

The stone itself was supposedly brought back
from southern Spain in 1330 by Sir Simon Lockhart
of Lee, who had accompanied the BLACK DOUGLAS
and the heart of Robert the Bruce on Crusade
against the Moors. The Lee Penny inspired the
story of the talisman in Scott's 1829 novel of that
name, set during the Third Crusade (1189–92). In
his introduction to *The Talisman*, Scott gives the
following account of the traditions associated with
the acquisition of the charm:

> He [Sir Simon Lockhart] made prisoner in battle an
> Emir of considerable wealth and consequence. The aged
> mother of the captive came to the Christian camp, to
> redeem her son from his state of captivity. Lockhart is
> said to have fixed the price at which his prisoner should
> ransom himself; and the lady, pulling out a large
> embroidered purse, proceeded to tell down the ransom,
> like a mother who pays little respect to gold in compar-
> ison of her son's liberty. In this operation, a pebble
> inserted in a coin, some say of the Lower Empire, fell out
> of the purse, and the Saracen matron testified so much
> haste to recover it as gave the Scottish knight a high idea
> of its value, when compared with gold or silver. 'I will
> not consent,' he said, 'to grant your son's liberty, unless
> that amulet be added to his ransom.' The lady not only
> consented to this, but explained to Sir Simon Lockhart
> the mode in which the talisman was to be used, and the

uses to which it might be put. The water in which it was
dipped operated as a styptic, as a febrifuge, and possessed other properties as a medical talisman.

Back in Clydesdale the Lockharts continued to use
the amulet to cure diseases, especially those of
cattle, but after the Reformation such practices were
condemned as popish, and the case of the Lee
Penny was brought before a Kirk assembly held
in Glasgow in 1638, with the following outcome:

> ... the Assemblie having inquired of the manner of
> Using thereof and particularlie onderstood be exam-
> inationne of the Laird of Lee, and otherwise that the
> custome is only to cast the stone in sume water and
> give the diseasit cattell thereof to drink and yt the same
> is done without using onie wordes such as charmers
> and sorcerers use in their Unlawful Practicess and
> considering that in nature they are many thinges sain
> to work strange effect qr of no humane wit can give a
> reason, it having pleased God to give unto stones &
> herbes a special Vertue for the healings of mony
> Infirmities in man and beast, advises the Brethern to
> surcease thair process as qrin they perceive no ground
> of offence and admonishes the Laird of Lee in the
> Using the said stone to tak heed that it be Ust heir after
> wt the least scandall that possiblie may be.

So the Lee Penny continued to be used, and its fame
spread as far as Northumberland and Yorkshire,
where it was known as the *Lockerlee Penny*. During
the reign of Charles I (whether before or after the
judgement by the Kirk assembly is unclear), the
corporation of Newcastle-upon-Tyne borrowed the
amulet to deal with the plague then rampant in the
city, and were so impressed by its efficacy that they
offered to surrender the £6000 surety they had
deposited with Sir James Lockhart. The latter refused the offer. In Scott's day the powers of the Lee
Penny were still sometimes called upon:

> Of late [Scott writes], they have been chiefly restricted
> to the cure of persons bitten by mad dogs; and as the
> illness in such cases frequently arises from imagination,
> there can be no reason for doubting that water which
> has been poured on the Lee-penny furnishes a con-
> genial cure.

Leery-light-the-lamps A generic term for the man
who used to light the street lamps, initially fuelled by

whale oil, then by gas. The name, probably coined for its alliterative quality, originates in a children's rhyme recorded by Robert Chambers in 1826:

Leerie, leerie, light the lamps,
Lang legs and short shanks.
Tak' a stick and break his back,
And send him through the Nor-gate!

Leery makes his most famous poetical appearance towards the end of the century:

My tea is nearly ready and the sun has left the sky;
It's time to take the window to see Leerie going by;
For every night at tea-time and before you take
    your seat,
With lantern and with ladder he comes posting up
    the street.

   – Robert Louis Stevenson, 'The Lamplighter' (1885)

By the time Stevenson wrote this poem, the lamplighters were on the way out, as gas lamps began to be replaced by electric lighting. Four years earlier Stevenson had described gas lamps as 'biddable, domesticated stars':

It is true ... that they did not unfold their rays with the appropriate spontaneity of the planets, coming out along the firmament one after another, as the need arises. But the lamplighters took to their heels every evening, and ran with a good heart. It was pretty to see man thus emulating the punctuality of heaven's orbs; and though perfection was not absolutely reached, and now and then an individual may have been knocked on the head by the ladder of the flying functionary, yet people commended his zeal in a proverb, and taught their children to say, 'God bless the lamplighter!' ...

God bless him, indeed! For the term of his twilight diligence is near at hand; and for not much longer shall we watch him speeding up the street and, at measured intervals, knocking another luminous hole into the dusk. The Greeks would have made a noble myth of such an one; how he distributed starlight, and, as soon as the need was over, re-collected it; and the little bull's-eye, which was his instrument, and held enough fire to kindle a whole parish, would have been fitly commemorated in the legend. Now, like all heroic tasks, his labours draw towards apotheosis, and in the light of victory himself shall disappear.

   – Robert Louis Stevenson, 'A Plea for Gas Lamps',
    Virginibus Puerisque (1881)

Left-footer *See* KICK WITH THE LEFT FOOT.

Legavrik A fair held in Inverness on 1 February in the 16th and 17th centuries. The name comes from Gaelic *Leth-gheamhraidh*, literally 'half winter', i.e. the winter half of the year, 1 November to 30 April.

Leg bail *See* TAK LEG BAIL, TO.

Legem de Clanmacduff Latin for 'law of the Clan Macduff', which from the later 14th through to the 16th century specified that kin of the Macduff Earls of Fife, or any Fife man, would be immune from the usual punishment for manslaughter on condition that he paid *kinbut* or *kynbutt*, i.e. monetary compensation, to the victim's kin, at the rate of 24 marks if the deceased was a gentleman, and half that if a woman. *See also* LETTERS OF SLAINS.

Leith police dismisseth us, The *See* TONGUE-TWISTERS.

Lennoxlove *See* BELLE STUART, LA.

Leopard Man of Skye, the The sobriquet of the Suffolk-born Tom Leppard, 99.2 per cent of whose body is covered in tattoos to make him look like a leopard. Even his eyelids are tattooed, and he was for long the most tattooed person in the world. After nearly three decades serving in the armed forces, he decided to adopt this new persona as a way of making appearance money, choosing spots not because of any affinity with big cats, but because they were cheap to do. For 20 years, in between appearances on TV and in the *Guinness Book of Records*, he lived the life of a reclusive ascetic in an earth-floored, windowless, tin-roofed bothy on the shores of Loch na Bèiste, near to Kyleakin in Skye, from where he would kayak across the strait to Kyle of Lochalsh to do his weekly shopping. (Not infrequently, while queuing at the chemist, people would inquire whether he was after something to clear up his spots.) In 2008, at the age of 73, he retired to sheltered housing in Broadford. 'I never bothered people when I lived in the bothy,' he says, 'and they didn't bother me, and I'm not really that interested in what else is going on outside.' He has no time for cats: 'They are the most selfish creatures out, and they only care about themselves.'

Let dab Let something be known, usually used negatively, e.g. 'Ah'll no' let dab.' *Dab* itself has a number of meanings. As a verb it can denote 'peck', 'strike lightly', 'pierce lightly', 'aim (a marble, etc.)'. As a noun, it can mean 'blow, slap', 'light stroke', 'throw (e.g. of a marble)' or 'relish or sauce (in which to dip one's potatoes)'.

Let Glasgow Flourish The motto of the city of Glasgow, whose citizens have largely forgotten the latter part: '... by the preaching of the word'; *see* TREE THAT NEVER GREW, THE.

Letters of cursing Prior to the Reformation, a writ of excommunication issued by a Church court.

Letters of fire and sword A commission formerly issued by the central authority (the monarch, Privy Council or Parliament) to a powerful individual to deal with crime or disorder in his locality, particularly in the Highlands where central government had little direct control. Such letters were often used by clan chiefs and fractious nobles to eliminate their rivals, and the powers granted were draconian, involving at the very least confiscation of property and eviction. Summary execution, the burning down of houses and the slaughter of anyone daring to resist were par for the course (*see*, for example, WELL OF THE HEADS). During the 17th century, central government increased its regulation and control of these commissions, and, according to the *Juridical Review* (vol. LXVII, 1935), 'The last Commission of Fire and Sword was issued on 27th September 1703, at the instance of Lady Emila, Dowager of Lovat, against "Captain Simion Fraser of Beaufort".' The latter was Simon Fraser, 11th Lord Lovat (SIMON THE FOX), who had forcibly married Lady Amelia in 1696 and abandoned her the following year. By the time the commission was issued, Lovat – involved as he was in Jacobite intrigues – had already fled to France.

Letters of slains A formal legal document issued in the name of the relatives of someone killed in a private feud, acknowledging that *assithment* (compensation) had been received from the killer, and that therefore the relatives granted 'a remission of their malice, revenge, and resentment' (Gilbert Stuart, *Observations Concerning the Public Law and Constitution of Scotland*, 1779). The custom survived into the 18th century. *See also* LEGEM DE CLAN-MACDUFF.

Let the tow gang wi' the bucket, to To drop or give up on something impetuously (a *tow* is a winding rope, as used for example in a well or mine).

Let yon flee stick tae the wa' Literally, 'let that fly stick to the wall', i.e. let's drop the subject, it's getting embarrassing. For example, in the penultimate chapter of Scott's *Waverley*, Mr Macwheeble implores the Colonel, 'O whisht, Colonel, for the love o' God! let that flee stick i' the wa'.'

Levellers' Rising A popular protest by tenant farmers in Galloway in 1724 against the recent enclosures. The protest largely involved 'levelling' the stone walls that had been erected to mark the boundaries of newly enclosed land. The leader of the Levellers was Billy Marshall, the CAIRD O' BARULLION and self-styled king of the Galloway gypsies, and it was said that the plan was first hatched at KELTON HILL FAIR, near Castle Douglas. Although the disorders were suppressed by dragoons summoned from Edinburgh by the landowners, the support for the protestors amongst the clergy, lesser gentry and merchant classes mitigated the severity of the punishments meted out when those arrested were brought to trial the following year.

Lewd and profligate life, a The summary by George Lockhart (1673–1731) in *The Lockhart Papers* (published 1817) of the career of Archibald Campbell, 10th Earl and 1st Duke of Argyll (*c*.1658–1703). Although Argyll stood by when his father joined Monmouth's Rebellion against James VII in 1685, he became a prominent supporter of the Glorious Revolution, and it was the regiment he raised in 1689 that perpetrated the MASSACRE OF GLENCOE. Lockhart's verdict on Argyll was that although he was 'in outward appearance a good-natur'd, civil, and modest gentleman':

   ... his actions were quite otherwise, being capable of
   the worst things to promote his interest, and altogether

addicted to a lewd profligate life: he was not cut out for business, only applying himself to it in so far as it tended to secure his Court interest and politicks, from whence he got great sums of money to lavish upon his pleasures.

Argyll married Lady Elizabeth Tollemache in 1678, but they separated in 1696, and Argyll set up home in Chirton, Northumberland, with his mistress Peggie Allison. He was by no means faithful, and his death in 1703 followed a brawl in a brothel in which he received a number of stab wounds. Argyll was also a keen follower of the turf, and has been credited (erroneously) with the invention of the condom.

Lewis Chessmen A collection of 78 assorted chess pieces found in a kist (stone chamber) hidden in a sandbank at Uig Bay, Lewis, in 1831. The pieces are made from walrus ivory (apart from a few that are carved from whale teeth), and come from a number of different sets. They date from the 12th century, when Lewis was part of the kingdom of Norway and within the archbishopric of Trondheim, and the style of the carving links them to other similar pieces made in Trondheim. The kings sit on thrones with swords across their knees; the largest is 3 inches (7.5 cm) high, and would nestle within one's fist. The queens hold their chins in one hand while staring into the distance; they appear glum, but in fact the posture denotes wise counsel. Instead of castles there are berserkers, those bearskin-clad Norse warriors famed for the insane and reckless frenzy of their fighting; here they are shown chewing their own shields. The pawns are simple geometric tokens. Most of the pieces are today in the British Museum, and the remainder in the National Museum of Scotland. There have been calls for the chessmen to be returned to Lewis.

Lewis goes extraterrestrial Alginate extracted from brown seaweed from Lewis was used to fireproof the notebooks of US astronauts, and thus a little bit of the Hebrides visited the Moon.

Libertas optima rerum (Latin, 'freedom is the best of things') A phrase from a couplet said by the 14th-century chronicler John of Fordun to have been taught to the young William Wallace by his uncle, the parish priest of Dunipace:

> *Dico tibi verum, libertas optima rerum:*
> *Nunquam servile sub nexo vivito, fili.*
> ['I tell you truly, freedom is the best of things, so never live under the bond of slavery, my sons.']

See also DECLARATION OF ARBROATH; FREEDOM IS A NOBLE THING.

Lichts, Auld and New *See* AULD LICHTS AND NEW LICHTS.

Lick-birse *See* SOUTAR.

Licking of wounds Scotland's second national sport, according to Tom Nairn, writing in the *Guardian* (May 1986):

> Among the Scots, licking of wounds is second only to football as a national sport, ecstasy occurring when the two activities merge (as they often do) into one.

Hugh McIlvanney has written in a similar vein:

> The game is hopelessly ill-equipped to carry the burden of emotional expression the Scots seek to load upon it. What is hurting so many now is the realization that something they believed to be a metaphor for their pride has all along been a metaphor for their desperation.
> – *McIlvanney on Football* (1994)

Lick-ma-doup or **lick-the-dowp** Literally, 'lick my/the backside'. The phrase can function as an adjective, denoting arse-licking, unctuous; or as a noun, denoting an arse-licker or fawning toady. Dr Johnson's biographer James Boswell was described as a 'lick-ma-doup' in *Fraser's Magazine* in 1832.

Lick the white out of someone's eye, to To cheat someone while pretending to help them.

> O'er lang, in Troth, have we By-standers been,
> And loot Fowk lick the White out of our Een:
> Nor can we wyt them, since they had our Vote;
> But now they'se get the Wistle of their Groat.
> – Allan Ramsay, 'A Poem on the North-Sea Fishery' (1721)

Lick thumbs, to To seal a bargain. The origin of the expression is explained by John Erskine of Carnock in his *Institutes of the Law of Scotland* (published posthumously in 1773):

> Another symbol was anciently used in proof that a sale was perfected, which continues till this day in bargains of lesser importance among the lower rank of people, the parties licking and joining of thumbs.

The practice was still known within living memory; schoolchildren would lick thumbs to 'seal' a bet.

Liddesdale drow A drenching drizzle (although *drow* can also denote a squall), presumably often experienced in the remote Border valley. It has been described as 'a shower that wets an Englishman to the skin'.

Liege poustie A legal term denoting the state of being sound in both body and mind, the test of which, according William Bell's *Dictionary and Digest of the Law of Scotland* (1838), was the ability to go to kirk or market unsupported. The term derives from medieval Latin *ligia potestas*, 'free power'.

Lie wrang, to To lose one's virtue.

> Ye hae lien wrang, lassie,
> Ye hae lien a' wrang,
> Ye've lien in some unco bed,
> And wi' some unco man.
>
> Your rosy cheeks are turn'd sae wan,
> You're greener than the grass, lassie,
> Your coatie's shorter by a span,
> Yet deil an inch the less, lassie. [etc.]
> – 'Ye Hae Lien Wrang, Lassie', sung to the tune of 'Up and waur them a', Willie', from *The* MERRY MUSES OF CALEDONIA

Lifting Day In the Highlands, a day nominated in spring when, in former times, the animals were taken outside to pasture after the long winter. In the days before there was adequate winter feed for livestock, the animals were so emaciated that they needed to be lifted out of the byre and carried to the grass to recover their strength.

Light Blues, the *See* FOOTBALL CLUB NICKNAMES.

Like . . . Similes are listed under what the subject is being compared to, e.g. HEN ON A HET GIRDLE, LIKE A.

Lilias Day An annual festival held in June in Kilbarchan, Renfrewshire, named either after St Liliosa, a 9th-century Spanish saint with a feast day on 27 July (according to the *DSL*), or Lilias Cunninghame, daughter of a local laird in the 18th century (according to the inhabitants of Kilbarchan, who each year select a young woman to take the part of 'Miss Lilias'). There was formerly a cattle market on Lilias Day, accompanied by races and processions of the local trades. The tradition died out at the end of the 19th century, but has been revived in recent years, a notable feature being the grand procession telling the history of the town from the 6th century to the present day. Much is made of the local celebrity, the famous piper Habbie Simpson (1550–1620); *see* HABBIE.

Lilliard's Edge *See* FAIR MAIDEN LILLIARD.

Lilywhites, the *See* FOOTBALL CLUB NICKNAMES.

Lindsay's Well *See* PRISONER OF PAPA STOUR, THE.

Linguae Hiberniae Lumen *See* SECRET COMMONWEALTH, THE.

Link in one's tail, to put or have a To be bent on deceit, to be full of craft and guile. A *link* here is a vertebra, and the allusion is presumably to an increase in one's ability to wriggle and manoeuvre.

> Then my Lord Moray, wha was head judge that day, was just gaun to address the jurymen, an' direct them to hang me, when up gat Geordie Lockie again for the hindmost time; (he had as mony links an' wimples in his tail as an eel, that body,) an' he argyed some point o' law that gart them a' glowr . . .
> – James Hogg, *The Brownie of Bodsbeck and Other Tales* (1818) [*wimple*, 'twist, turn']

Lion of Justice, the *See* WILLIAM THE LION.

Lion of Liddesdale How James Hogg (the ETTRICK SHEPHERD) describes the BORDER REIVER

Jock Elliot (*see* WHA DAUR MEDDLE WI ME?) in his 1811 poem 'Lock the Door, Lariston' (Larriston being Elliot's home in Liddesdale):

> Lock the door, Lariston, lion of Liddesdale,
> Lock the door, Lariston, Lowther comes on,
>> The Armstrongs are flying,
>> Their widows are crying,
> The Castletown's burning, and Oliver's gone.

In an 1832 edition of his *Songs*, Hogg himself was modest about this early effort: 'I look upon it as having no merit whatever, excepting a jingle of names, which Sir Walter's good taste rendered popular, and which in every other person's hand has been ludicrous.'

Lion of the Covenant, the *See* CAMERONIANS.

Lion Rampant The central item in the Royal Standard of Scotland, and often used as a synecdoche thereof (i.e. the flag itself is often referred to as the Lion Rampant); beyond that, the term is sometimes used as a synecdoche of the nation as a whole. It is thought that WILLIAM THE LION (William I, ruled 1165–1214) was the first to display it, but the earliest recorded use dates from 1222, when it appeared in the seal of William's son, Alexander II. The Lion Rampant (i.e. lion rearing up on its hind legs) itself is red, with blue claws and teeth, on a yellow background, and with a double 'tressure' (border) featuring floral motifs resembling fleurs-de-lys, the French royal emblem – all as described by Richard Holland in his *Buke of the Howlat*, an allegorical poem written in 1450 and dedicated to the DOVE OF DUNBAR:

> Thairwith linkit in a lyng, be lerit men approvit,
> He bure a Lyon as lord, of gulis full gay,
> Maid maikles of micht, on mold quhair he movit,
> Rich rampant as a roy, rich of aray.
> Of pure gold wes the grund, quhair that grim hovit,
> With double tressure about, flourit in fay,
> And flour de lices on loft, that mony leid lovit,
> Of gulis signit and set, to schawe in assay
> Our Soveraine of Scotland, his armes to knawe ...

Habbakuk Bisset, in *Rolment of Courtis* (*c*.1620) suggests that the fleurs-de-lys echoed the AULD ALLIANCE, and were:

... to signifie that the said Lyoun wes then armit, keipt, an defendit with the lilleis, richis, and freindschip of that nobill and most puissant kingdom of France.

The great Italian Renaissance poet Ariosto, in his epic *Orlando Furioso* (1532), gives a somewhat fanciful description of 'the banner of the King of Scots':

I saw between the two unicorns the great Lion who bears a sword of silver in his paw.

Because the Lion Rampant is the Royal Standard of Scotland, there are strict rules as to when, where and by whom it may be displayed. These rules are blithely ignored by most Scots, especially on international sporting occasions – no doubt to the consternation of the LYON COURT. The Lion Rampant features in the Royal Standard of the United Kingdom (twice in that flown in Scotland, once in that flown elsewhere). *See also* SALTIRE, THE.

Lisbon Lions, the The nickname given to Celtic's victorious team in the European Cup Final on 25 May 1967, when they beat Inter Milan 2–1 at the National Stadium in Lisbon, Portugal, becoming the first British team to win the trophy.

Liston, Robert *See* FASTEST KNIFE IN THE WEST END, THE.

Little Belsen The nickname of Camp 165, a military camp built in 1943 at Watten, a village between Wick and Thurso in Caithness. After the war the camp held a number of senior Nazis, kept here for denazification. Among the inmates were Gunter d'Alquen, chief editor of the SS weekly *Das Schwarze Korps*; Max Wunsche, Hitler's personal aide; and Paul Werner Hoppe, commandant of Stutthof concentration camp, where 85,000 were killed. Some of the prisoners were repatriated, while others were sent to trial.

Little door to the wide House of England, the How James VI described the Border town of BERWICK-UPON-TWEED, through which he travelled in 1603 en route south to be crowned as James I of England. Concluding that the small wooden bridge via which he was obliged to cross the Tweed was insufficient to his dignity, James had a new stone bridge built, which was completed in 1634 and which still stands.

Little feeties *See* FISHERMEN'S TABOOS.

Little folk, the A euphemistic or propitiatory name for the fairies, also known as 'the good neighbours' or 'the honest folk', in case any offence should be taken.

> And O the gath'ring that was on the green
> Of little foukies, clad in green and blue!
> – Alexander Ross, *Helenore, or the Fortunate Shepherdess*
> (1768)

'Little Gentleman in Black Velvet, The' A Jacobite toast, referring to the mole that had dug the molehill over which the horse of William III had stumbled, so throwing the usurper of the Stuarts to the ground. Shortly afterwards, on 8 March 1702, William died of complications resulting from his fall. *See also* KING OVER THE WATER, THE.

Little Guid, the Literally, 'the little good', a euphemism for the Devil particularly favoured by the novelist John Galt (1779–1839). The term also denotes the sun spurge.

Little Jock Elliot *See* LION OF LIDDESDALE; WHA DAUR MEDDLE WI ME?

Little laud to the Devil There is a possibly apocryphal story regarding the enmity between Archbishop Laud and Archy Armstrong, originally (it was said) a sheep-stealer from the Borders, who became jester to both James VI and Charles I. Being a favourite of both, Armstrong incurred the enmity of many. Accompanying Prince Charles and the Duke of Buckingham to Spain in 1623 on the former's pursuit of the Infanta, he outraged his hosts by crowing about the defeat of the Armada. Buckingham said he would have him hanged, to which Armstrong riposted that 'dukes had often been hanged for insolence but never fools for talking'. According to another story, at a banquet in Whitehall, when asked to say grace, Armstrong uttered the following words: 'Great praise be given

to God and little laud to the Devil.' As a consequence of the feud with Archbishop Laud, in 1637 Armstrong was banished from court. He set up shop as a money-lender and eventually retired to his estate in Cumberland, where he died in 1672.

Little Saturday Wednesday, once commonly a half-day for shopkeepers.

Little Sparta The name given to the Arcadian garden created out of bare moorland at Stonypath, near Dunsyre in Lanarkshire, by the concrete poet and artist Ian Hamilton Finlay and his wife Sue Finlay. Work started in 1966, and the name was chosen in 1983, in rivalry to Edinburgh's claim to be the ATHENS OF THE NORTH. Finlay filled the 5-acre site with artworks, many having classical allusions, including temples, sculptures and inscribed aphorisms, created in collaboration with a range of craftspersons. In 1983 Strathclyde Region informed Finlay that it was increasing the rates on the site, insisting that it was an art gallery. Finlay claimed that, to the contrary, the garden was a temple, and refused to pay up. The authorities were not amused and sent in the bailiffs, whom Finlay and his supporters successfully resisted. The confrontation became known as the First Battle of Little Sparta. In 2004 a panel of Scottish artists, gallery directors and critics voted Little Sparta 'the nation's greatest work of art'. After Finlay's death in 2006, the garden came under the care of the Little Sparta Trust.

Little Willie *See* ORPHAN WILLIE.

Live and Let Live Monument, the The nickname of the Panmure Testimonial, a tower on Cambustane Hill near Monikie, Angus, erected in 1839 by grateful tenants of William Ramsay Maule, 1st Lord Panmure, who had let them off paying rent during several years of bad harvests in the 1820s.

Live burial Live burial of animals appears to have occasionally been practised to treat various diseases. A cure for epilepsy was recorded in Ross-shire and Lewis in the 19th century, involving the live burial of a perfectly black barnyard cock at the spot where a child experienced its first seizure. Sir James Simpson, the discoverer of chloroform, recalled that at the end of the 18th century his own father 'was in early life personally engaged in the offering up and burying of a poor live cow as a sacrifice to the spirit of Murrain [a disease of cattle]'. This was done near Edinburgh, and the man who undertook the sacrifice also maintained a GOODMAN'S CROFT, an area left untilled to propitiate the Devil.

Live burials of humans are rare and usually accidental (for an exception, see ST ORAN'S CHAPEL, LIVE BURIAL IN). One case recorded from Chirnside in Berwickshire in 1674 recounts how one Marjorie Halcrow Erskine was buried in a shallow grave by the sexton, who intended to return later to steal her jewellery. When he attempted to put this plan into effect by cutting off her finger to obtain a ring, the unfortunate woman recovered consciousness. Fully restored, she went on to give birth to two sons. For another possible live burial, see under DOCTOR SUBTILIS.

Live hawks for dead Herons See REDESWIRE FRAY.

Livi Lions See FOOTBALL CLUB NICKNAMES.

Living cats roasted on a spit See TAGHAIRM.

Lizzie See WESTLOTHIANA LIZZIAE.

Lochaber axe A fearsome sort of two-handed axe with a hooked tip, going back to the 12th or 13th centuries, and originating in Lochaber, an area of the Western Highlands. John Taylor, the London 'waterman-poet', who visited the Highlands in 1618, described the typical armaments of the clansmen thus:

> Now, their weapons are long bows and forked arrows,
> swords and targets, harquebuses, muskets, durks, and
> Loquhabor axes.

Lochaber axes were later adopted as semi-ceremonial weapons by Edinburgh's town guard, as recorded by Robert Fergusson in his poem 'Hallow-Fair' (1773):

> Jock Bell gaed furth to play his freaks,
> Great cause he had to rue it,
> For frae a stark Lochaber aix
> He gat a clamihewit [heavy blow] ...

'Lochaber No More' A song by Allan Ramsay, published in his *Tea Table Miscellany* (1724), to a 17th-century Irish tune, possibly composed by a certain Myles O'Reilly, who was born in County Cavan around 1636. The tune on its own is a favourite piper's lament, and in Ireland is known as 'Limerick's Lament' or 'Sarsfield's Lamentation', Patrick Sarsfield having held Limerick for James VII until obliged to surrender it to the besieging Williamites in 1691. Ramsay's words – about a soldier leaving for distant wars – evoke the pain of exile, a fate suffered by so many Highlanders during the CLEARANCES that were to follow:

> Then glory, my Jeanie, maun plead my excuse;
> Since honour commands me, how can I refuse?
> Without it, I ne'er can have merit for thee;
> And losing thy favour, I'd better not be.
>
> I gae then, my lass, to win honour and fame:
> And if I should chance to come glorious hame,
> I'll bring a heart to thee with love running o'er.
> And then I'll leave thee and Lochaber no more.

The artist John Watson Nicol gave the title *Lochaber No More* to his famous 1883 painting of a heartbroken Highland couple on board a ship bound for distant lands.

Loch Arkaig See TREASURE OF LOCH ARKAIG.

Lochgelly See TAWSE.

Lochiel, the Gentle See GENTLE LOCHIEL, THE.

Lochiel's lantern See MACFARLANE'S BOWAT.

Lochinvar See YOUNG LOCHINVAR.

Lochmaben Stone A Neolithic granite megalith south of Gretna, near the mouth of the River Sark and the English border, at the inner end of the Solway Firth. The *maben* element in the name is Mabon, a Celtic god, while its alternative name, Clochmabenstane, probably includes Gaelic *clach*, 'stone' (as in Clackmannan, which means 'stone of Manau', another Celtic god). The Lochmaben Stone was formerly part of a stone circle, but the other stones were removed in the early 19th century to make way for the local farmer's plough. Prior to the Union of the Crowns in 1603, the Lochmaben Stone was a meeting point for the Wardens of the Western Marches (*see* MARCH, THE).

Loch ma Nàire *See* LOCH OF SHAME, THE.

Loch Ness Monster, the A creature, more familiarly known as Nessie (or, in Gaelic, *Niseag*), that supposedly inhabits Loch Ness, and which has become an icon of popular culture not just in Scotland, but around the world. Although St Adamnan, the biographer of St Columba, mentions an *aquatilis bestia* in the loch, the first known 'sighting' was on 22 July 1933, after which (strangely enough) the local tourist industry experienced a sustained boom. Despite numerous subsequent claimed sightings, and a rash of 'scientific' expeditions, no firm evidence of the creature has been produced, although believers suggest that the beast may be a relict plesiosaur that somehow escaped the mass extinction of 65 million years ago. Appropriately enough, it was Edwin Morgan, the first 'Scots Makar', who first gave the creature voice:

> Sssnnnhufffffll?
> Hnshuffl hhnnwfl hnfl hfl?
> Gdroblboblhobngbl gbl gl g g g g glbgl.
> – 'The Loch Ness Monster's Song' (1973)

Loch of Shame, the The supposed meaning of Loch ma Nàire, a lochan in Strath Naver, Sutherland, a few miles south of Bettyhill. The Revd David McKenzie, in the *Statistical Account for the Parish of Farr*, written in 1834, gives the following explanation:

> A woman, either from Ross-shire or Inverness-shire, came to the heights of Strathnaver, pretending to cure diseases by means of water into which she had previously thrown some pebbles, which she carried about with her. In her progress down the strath, towards the coast, a man in whose house she lodged wished to possess himself of the pebbles; but, discovering his design, she escaped, and he pursued. Finding at the loch referred to that she could not escape her pursuer any longer, she threw the pebbles into the loch, exclaiming in Gaelic, *Mo nar*, that is, 'shame', or 'my shame'. From this exclamation the loch received the

name which it still retains, *Loch-mo-nar*, and the pebbles are supposed to have imparted to it its healing efficacy. There are only four days in the year on which its supposed cures can be effected. These are the first Monday (old style) of February, May, August and November. During February and November no one visits it; but in May and August numbers from Sutherland, Caithness, Ross-shire, and even from Inverness-shire and Orkney, come to this far-famed loch. The ceremonies through which the patients have to go are the following: They must all be at the loch side about twelve o'clock at night. As early on Monday as one or two o'clock in the morning the patient is to plunge, or to be plunged, three times into the loch; is to drink of its waters; to throw a piece of coin into it as a kind of tribute; and must be away from its banks so as to be fairly out of sight of its waters before the sun rises, else no cure is supposed to be effected.

Regarding the meaning of the name of the lochan, some poo-poo the above explanation, and suggest that it means 'loch of the serpent', *nathair* ('serpent') being pronounced in the same way as *nàire* ('shame'); others suggest that *nàire* comes from a word for the moon. Other theories hold that Mo-Nair was a Celtic demi-goddess, or that *ma Nàire* is a contraction of Mo-Fhinn-Bharr, i.e. St Findbarr or Barr, a saint once venerated in Sutherland.

Loch of the Clans *See* MUIR OF THE CLANS.

Lockerbie Bombing, the On the night of 21 December 1988, a Pan Am Boeing 727, flight number PA 103, blew up high over the town of Lockerbie, en route from London to New York. All 259 people on board died, and 11 people on the ground were killed by falling debris, which destroyed a number of houses in the town. Examination of the wreckage confirmed that a terrorist bomb was responsible, and after considerable diplomatic manoeuvring, in 1999 two Libyan suspects were sent for trial by a Scottish court sitting in the Netherlands. In 2000 one of the accused was acquitted, while the other, Abdelbaset al-Megrahi, was found guilty and sentenced to life imprisonment in Scotland. In 2009 Megrahi, diagnosed with terminal cancer, was released on compassionate grounds and returned to Libya. The decision, by the Scottish Justice Secretary Kenny MacAskill, was widely criticized in America.

Lockerbie lick or **wipe** Darkly humorous terms for a cut or wound on the face. Lockerbie in lower Annandale was in the 16th and 17th centuries frequently the venue for skirmishes between the local rivals, the Johnstones and the Maxwells, and the former had a reputation for slashing the faces of their enemies. *Cf.* GLASGOW GRIN.

Logopandecteision An artificial language proposed by Sir Thomas Urquhart in his 1653 book of that name. The title page reads:

> *Logopandecteision,*
> OR AN
> INTRODUCTION
> TO THE
> UNIVERSAL LANGUAGE.
> Digested into these Six several Books,
> *Neaudethaumata, Chrestasebeia,*
> *Cleronomaporia, Chryseomystes,*
> *Neleodicastes, & Philoponauxesis.*
> BY
> Sir THOMAS URQUHART of *Cromartie*, Knight.
> Now lately contrived and published
> both for his own utilitie, and that of all
> pregnant and ingenious Spirits.

The 'Epistle Dedicatorie' was addressed 'To Nobody'.

Urquhart's language was to have twelve parts of speech, eleven genders, eleven cases, eleven tenses, seven moods, four numbers and four voices. What is more, the author promises, 'One word thereof, though but of seven syllables at most, shall comprehend that which no language else in the world is able to express in fewer than four score and fifteen several words.' Despite its apparently complex grammar, Urquhart assures us, 'The greatest wonder of all is that of all the languages in the world, it is the easiest to learn, a boy of ten years old being able to attain to the knowledge thereof in three months' space.' It was all, no doubt, one of Urquhart's more elaborate jokes. *See also* HIGHLAND PRIDE.

Lom, Iain 'Bald Iain', the noted Gaelic poet Iain Lom MacDonald, scion of the MacDonalds of Keppoch – hence he is also known as 'the Bard of Keppoch'. The sobriquet Lom may allude to the story that he was born hairless, and remained in that state for the rest of his life; but the word can also mean 'outspoken'. His dates are unknown, but he was present at the Battle of Inverlochy in 1645, and wrote about the 1707 Treaty of Union (*see under* PARCEL OF ROGUES, A). Charles II made him his Gaelic laureate. *See also* WELL OF THE HEADS.

Londons, London ropes or **londies** A skipping game involving two ropes being spun in opposite directions.

Longevity, exceptional *See* CAIRD O' BARULLION, THE; OLDEST MAN IN SCOTLAND, THE?

Longshanks, Edward *See* HAMMER OF THE SCOTS, THE.

Look like a half-shut knife, to To appear depressed and generally pig-miserable.

Look like Wattie to the worm, to An expression explained thus by John Jamieson in the 1825 supplement to his *Etymological Dictionary of the Scottish Language*:

> Ye look like Watty to the worm, a proverbial phrase, expressive of the appearance of disgust, or great reluctance ...

Jamieson goes on to quote he following:

> His father says, Lay by, man, thir humdrums,
> And loukna mair *like Watty to the worm*;
> Gin ye hae promis'd, what but now perform?
> – Alexander Ross, *Helenore, or The Fortunate Shepherdess* (1768)

Wattie is a short form of the name Walter.

Loon A common Northeastern word for a youth or young lad; the female equivalent is a *quean*. More specifically, a *Loon* is an inhabitant of Forfar. *See also* PLAY THE LOON, TO.

Loons, the *See* FOOTBALL CLUB NICKNAMES.

Lord High Constable of Scotland A title created by David I in 1147. Since the reign of Robert the Bruce it has been held by the Earls of Erroll.

Lord Lyon King of Arms *See* LYON COURT.

Lord of Erection A layman who at the Reformation was awarded former Church lands and benefices.

Lord of the Isles An ancient title, going back to the time when the Hebrides and the western seaboard were ruled by chiefs of mixed Norse and Gaelic blood, who owed their allegiance (nominally at least) to the kings of Norway, until sovereignty over the area was transferred to the Scottish kings in 1266, following the defeat of Haakon IV at Largs in 1263. The origins of the title go back to Somerled (*c.*1126–64), whose seat of power was on Islay and who, with the aid of 80 war galleys, consolidated his control over the area. Somerled, whose mother was Norse and who on his father's side traced his ancestry to the ancient kings of DALRIADA, adopted the title *Ri Innse Gall is Cind tire* (Gaelic, 'ruler of the islands of the strangers and of Kintyre') or *Rex Insularum* (Latin, 'king of the isles'). Somerled's grandson Donald gave his name to Clan Donald, and the chiefs of Clan Donald went on to assume the title Lord of the Isles – the first to do so was John of Islay (d.1387), son of ANGUS OG, Lord of Islay. At the inauguration of each Lord of the Isles, the incumbent placed his foot in a 'footstep stone' (now lost), to symbolize that he would tread in the footsteps of his predecessors. During the ceremony he wore a white tunic to represent his purity and integrity, while carrying a white rod to signify his right to rule, and a sword to signify his duty to protect his people.

John's son Donald fought the Crown over the disputed earldom of Ross at the REID HARLAW in 1411. His grandson John (d.1503) also came into conflict with the Crown, after it was discovered he had signed a secret treaty with the English. In addition he fought his own son, another ANGUS OG, at BLOODY BAY, and by 1493 King James IV had had enough and forfeited all the lands of the Lord of the Isles. In 1540 the title was taken over by the Crown and given to the eldest son of the reigning monarch (thus Prince Charles is the current holder of the title).

Donald Dubh, grandson of John, was held captive in Edinburgh Castle from 1506, but after his escape in 1544 he was recognized as Lord of the Isles by all of Clan Donald and by many other chiefs, but he died in Ireland of a fever in 1545 before he could mount his planned invasion of Scotland. Four years later Donald Munro, High Dean of the Isles, looked back to the era of the independent Lords of the Isles as a golden age:

> In thair time thair was great peace and welth in the Iles throw the ministration of Justice.
> – *A Description of the Western Isles of Scotland Called Hybrides* (1549)

Sir Walter Scott's long narrative poem *The Lord of the Isles* (1815) follows the fortunes of Robert the Bruce, whose story is interwoven with that Edith of Lorne and her love for the fictional Lord Ronald, Lord of the Isles, who is betrothed to Bruce's sister. However, disguised as a mute page, she follows Bruce and Ronald, and after saving their lives is rewarded by Ronald's love.

Lord Preserve Us A title once suggested as suitable for an ambitious advocate who intended himself for the bench:

> When Lord Meadowbank was yet Mr Maconochie, he one day approached his facetious professional brother, John Clerk of Eldin, and after telling him he had prospects of being raised to the bench, asked him to suggest what name he should adopt. 'Lord Preserve Us,' said Clerk, and moved on.
> – Robert Ford, *Thistledown* (1901)

Allan Maconochie (*c.*1748–1816), later Lord Meadowbank, was, as a student at Edinburgh University, one of the founders of the Speculative Society (the SPEC) in 1764. He was appointed Regius Professor of Public Law and the Law of Nature and Nations at Edinburgh in 1779, resigning his chair in 1796, the year he took his seat on the bench as an ordinary lord of session. Henry Brougham described him as 'one of the best lawyers … and … the most diligent and attentive judge'.

Lords of the Congregation The pro-Reformation faction in Scotland during the minority of Mary Queen of Scots. In December 1557 five Protestant noblemen, calling themselves the Congregation of Jesus Christ, signed a covenant committing them to 'apply our whole power, substance and very lives to maintain and forward and establish the most blessed Word of God'. The Congregation developed into a powerful faction in Scottish politics, at odds with the staunchly Catholic regent, Mary of Guise, and forming its own Army of the Congregation of Christ. After initial setbacks, the intervention of the English helped the Congregation to victory, leading in 1560 to the establishment of the re-formed Kirk in Scotland. The Congregation had its final triumph with the defeat of Mary Queen of Scots at Langside in 1568, so assuring the security on the throne of her Protestant son, the infant James VI, in whose favour she had been forced to abdicate the previous year.

Lord's Throat, the The picturesque (rather than dramatic) gorge of the River Don on the south side of Bennachie, Aberdeenshire. It is perhaps so named because of its beauty; nearby is Paradise Wood.

Lorn, Brooch of *See* BROOCH OF LORN, THE.

Lorne sausage A beef sausage shaped in a block with a cross-section some 4 ins (10 cm) square (hence its alternative name, *square sausage*). It is served in slices, and may or may not have taken its name from the Glasgow music-hall comedian Tommy Lorne (1890–1935), who used to joke that eating this type of sausage was like chewing a doormat, and among whose catchphrases was 'Sausages is the boys!' (not to mention 'IN THE NAME O' THE WEE MAN!') One Scottish newspaper once offered the following recipe for lending Lorne sausage an aura of haute-cuisine sophistication:

> Take one slab finest Lorne saucisse. Fry till almost burnt on one side. Slice well-fired petit pain. Spread with Lurpak and insert saucisse. Garnish with coulis de ketchup. Serve with chilled can of vintage Irn-Bru.
> – *Sunday Mail*, 30 May 2004

Lose yer puggie *See* GET YER PUGGIE UP.

Loss of Gaick, the (Gaelic *Call Ghàdhaig*) A famous disaster that took place in early January 1800, when an enormous avalanche overwhelmed a bothy at Gaick Lodge, a remote spot in the Cairngorms between Drumochter and Glen Feshie. The remains of five men and their dogs who had been on a deer-hunting expedition were later recovered from the ruined building. One of the victims, Captain John MacPherson of Ballachroan (1724–1800), was not widely liked, being known locally as *an t-Oifigeach Dubh*, 'the Black Officer', for his forcible recruitment techniques, and some said the disaster was the result of MacPherson's compact with the Devil. MacPherson had his friends though, and one of these, Malcolm Macintyre (Calum Dubh nam Protaigean), commemorated him in an elegy. The Loss, according to the Revd Alexander Cameron writing later in the century, gave a 'rude shock' to 'the popular imagination', and the site is now marked by a small monument.

Lost Clan, the *See under* GARDE ÉCOSSAISE.

Lost Valley of Glencoe, the A high hidden valley clenched between the precipitous flanks of Bheinn Fhada and Geàrr Aonach, two of the THREE SISTERS OF GLENCOE. It is approached by a steep climb up through a narrow, wooded defile, choked with giant boulders, then suddenly the valley's bottom broadens and flattens out. The English name may only have been coined in the earlier 20th century; in Gaelic it is known as Coire Gabhail, 'the corrie of capture', traditionally because it was here that the local Macdonalds hid their rustled cattle. Another peculiarity of the place is that the river, the Allt Coire Gabhail, disappears underground for much of the length of the valley (an unusual circumstance in non-limestone areas). Recalling a visit he made in March 1939, the mountaineer and writer W.H. Murray wrote (from the German prison camp where he spent the last three years of the war):

> Spring or autumn – for these have greatest charm – a man might come here for a week and be alone. He might pitch a tent on that meadow and be as much out of sight and sound of civilization as if he dwelt on the North Pole.
> – W.H. Murray, *Mountaineering in Scotland* (1947)

Loup ... *See* LOWP ...

Loup de Mer, le (French, 'the wolf of the sea') Napoleon's name for Admiral Thomas Cochrane

(1775–1860), later 10th Earl of Dundonald. Cochrane's considerable success against the French in the Mediterranean during the Napoleonic Wars was followed by an equally successful career in the 1820s as a freelance admiral, in which role he helped the Chileans, Peruvians and Brazilians to rid themselves of their Spanish and Portuguese colonial masters, and then assisted the Greeks against the Turks. He was the inspiration behind C.S. Forester's dashing naval hero, Horatio Hornblower, and also Patrick O'Brian's Jack Aubrey. He is commemorated by a bust in Culross, Fife, where he spent his boyhood.

Louseland A derogatory term applied by the English in the later 17th century to Scotland, which later became known as ITCHLAND. The lice in question were dubbed *Scots greys*, or simply *Scotchmen*.

Lousy fellows' country See JUVLO-MENGRESKEY TEM.

Love-dotterel A dotard in love, i.e. an old man or woman in the grip of an unseemly passion.

Love is on me for you According to Charles Mackay (1814–89), in 'The Poetry and Humour of the Scottish Language', the introductory chapter to his *Dictionary of Lowland Scotch* (1888), 'The Highlanders do not say, "I love you," but "Love is on me for you."'

Lovely incurable disease, a Tommy Docherty's description of football, speaking on the 1985 BBC TV documentary *It's Only a Game.*

Lowest of the fuckin low, the The Scots, according to Irvine Welsh's novel TRAINSPOTTING (1993):

> We're ruled by effete arseholes. What does that make us? The lowest of the fuckin low, the scum of the earth. The most wretched, servile, miserable pathetic trash that was ever shat intae creation. Ah don't hate the English. They just git oan wi the shite thuv goat. Ah hate the Scots.

Low-flyer Contemporary slang for a measure of The Famous Grouse, a brand of blended whisky, alluding to the flight of the red grouse. Such a measure may also be denoted by the rhyming slang *Mickey Mouse*.

Low-flying Jimmies A disparaging nickname applied to those Scottish Labour MPs who have no hope of attaining high office, but who provide the party with useful parliamentary cannon fodder at Westminster. Once numbered among them was Michael Martin (inaccurately dubbed GORBALS MICK), MP for Glasgow Springburn until appointed Speaker in 2000 – to the surprise of all those who had barely noticed his political career up to that point. *See also* JIMMY.

Lowpin an leevin Literally, 'leaping and living', an expression applied to freshly caught fish, and also to sprightly persons.

Lowp-the-coonter See COONTER-LOWPER.

Lowp-the-cuddie or **cuddie-lowp-the-dyke** The game of leapfrog (*lowp*, 'leap'; *cuddie*, 'donkey', 'stupid person').

Lowrie, Lourie or **Laurie** A fabular name for a fox, often combined with the name *Tod*, which on its own can also denote a fox (as for example in the name of the board game *tod and lambs*, a version of fox and geese).

> And slee Tod Lowrie says: 'Come here, wee Robin, and I'll let ye see a bonny spot on the tap o' my tail.' But wee Robin says: 'Na, na! slee Tod Lowrie; na, na! Ye worry't the wee lammie; but ye'se no worry me.'
> – Robert Chambers, 'The Marriage of Robin Redbreast and the Wren', from *Popular Rhymes of Scotland* (1826)

Lowrie is a familiar form of the name Lawrence, which in the 15th and 16th centuries was also applied to foxes, notably by Robert Henrysson (d.1500), who in his *Morall Fabillis* uses *Lowrence* or *Schir Lowrence* as the equivalent of the English and French *Reynard*. The name *Lowrie* or *Tod Lowrie* can also be applied to a cunning human:

> Archie haed a maist awfu ill-will to Tod-Lowrie, oor coonty member. 'A braw speaker, ye tell me?' he wad say; 'nae dout: speakin's his trade. Gin a laayer haesna the gift o the gab. he's no worth caain oot o a kail-yaird ...'
> – P. Hay Hunter, *James Inwick: Ploughman and Elder* (1894)

The name *Lourie* or *Lang Lourie* was also sometimes given to the great bell of a church (for example, that in St Nicholas in Aberdeen), such bells often being dedicated to St Lawrence.

Luath The hunting dog of the Irish hero Cuchullain in James Macpherson's *Fingal* (1761; *see* OSSIAN FORGERIES, THE). The name is the Gaelic word for 'swift' or 'nimble'. Luath was also the name of Burns's favourite collie, who at a wedding tripped up Jean Armour, the BELLE OF MAUCHLINE, giving the poet an opportunity to pay his respects to the young woman who would later become his wife. Sadly, Luath was 'killed by the wanton cruelty of some person, the night before his father's death' (according to William Scott Douglas in his 1877 annotated edition of Burns). Burns commemorated Luath as one of 'The Twa Dogs' (the other is called Caesar), and describes him thus:

He was a gash an' faithfu' tyke
As ever lap a sheugh or dyke.
His honest, sonsie, baws'nt face,
Ay gat him friends in ilka place.
His breast was white, his touzie back
Weel clad wi' coat o' glossy black;
His gawsie tail, wi' upward curl,
Hung o'er his hurdies wi' a swirl.
  [*gash*, 'wise'; *lap*, 'leapt'; *sheugh*, 'ditch'; *sonsie*, 'good,
  honest, lucky'; *baws'nt*, 'white-streaked'; *touzie*, 'shaggy';
  gawsie, 'jolly'; *hurdies*, 'haunches']

The name has also been adopted by the Scottish publisher, Luath Press.

Luckenbooth Literally, 'locked booth', a lockable market stall of a type once common in Scottish towns. The luckenbooths in Edinburgh comprised a row of shops in the High Street, to the north of St Giles, demolished in 1817 for reasons that may be discerned from the following:

He stood now before the Gothic entrance of the ancient prison [the Tolbooth], which, as is well known to all men, rears its ancient front in the very middle of the High Street, forming, as it were, the termination to a huge pile of buildings called the Luckenbooths, which, for some inconceivable reason, our ancestors had jammed into the midst of the principal street of the town ...
  – Sir Walter Scott, *The Heart of Midlothian* (1818),
  chapter vi

The luckenbooths in Edinburgh gave their name to *luckenbooth brooches*, love-tokens or betrothal brooches, often in the form of a heart, or two hearts intertwined, made by Edinburgh silversmiths in the late 17th and 18th centuries.

Luck penny A sixpence, shilling or larger sum returned by the vendor to the purchaser (especially of agricultural produce, livestock, etc.), as a way of sealing the bargain.

Luckie Buchan, the witch-wife *See* BUCHANITES.

Lucky Piper, the A euphemism for the Devil.

Lugless Willie The nickname of the Lanark-born traveller William Lithgow (1582–?1645). According to tradition, his *lugless* (earless) condition came about in the following circumstances: some time before his 21st birthday he became involved with a woman whose brothers turned upon him violently, like 'foure blood-shedding wolves' devouring 'one silly stragling lambe' (as Lithgow himself put it), and it was during this incident that Lithgow had his ears cropped or cut off entirely, earning him the sobriquet Cutlugged Will or Lugless Willie. In 1609 Lithgow began two decades of wandering, visiting – largely by foot – Germany, Poland, Bohemia, the Low Countries, France, Spain, Italy, the Balkans, Greece and the Greek islands, Palestine, Turkey, Syria, Egypt, Libya, Algiers, Morocco and Malta. His *Totall Discourse of the Rare Adventures and Painfull Peregrinations of Long Nineteen Years Travayles from Scotland to the most famous Kingdomes in Europe, Asia and Africa* was published in London in 1632. In it he recounts his many adventures (some no doubt exaggerated), and claims to have walked a total of 36,000 miles. For other great pedestrians, *see* GREAT PEDESTRIAN, THE; PEDESTRIAN TRAVELLER, THE.

Lumber, to get a To enter into a physical relationship with a person of the opposite sex. The expression is a modern one.

Lusty man An English version of the Gaelic *Séamas-an-bhuid*, the name given to a medieval stone carving of a man holding his erect penis. It is the male equivalent of a Sheela-na-gig (Irish *Síle na gcíoch*, 'Julia of the breasts'), a depiction of a woman displaying her genitals. Such carvings are fairly common in Ireland, but rare in Scotland. A lusty man on the west wall of Iona's nunnery disappeared at some point in the last century, while another, horizontal figure on the wall of St Clement's Church in Rodil, Harris, was, according to W.H. Murray's *The Islands of Western Scotland* (1973), disfigured when the Countess of Dunmore ordered her gillie to fire his gun at it.

Lyer Honor Acquyred, A *See* SAY NO TREUTH.

Lyon Court, the The public body responsible for all matters relating to heraldry in Scotland. It is more formally known as the Court of the Lord Lyon, and is headed by the Lord Lyon King of Arms, who has the status of a judge, and who is also responsible for overseeing all state ceremonies in Scotland. His court has considerable legal powers, with a dedicated procurator fiscal ready to prosecute any infringements. The Lyon King of Arms is assisted on a full-time basis by the Lyon Clerk and Keeper of the Records. On ceremonial occasions, other officers of the court, bearing titles such as Albany Herald of Arms in Ordinary and Carrick Pursuivant of Arms in Ordinary, creep out from under the woodwork and don their finery. It is the Lyon Court that decrees on such matters as when, where and by whom the SALTIRE or the Royal Standard (the LION RAMPANT) are permitted to be flown. The populace quakes in their collective boots. *See also* WORLD'S GREATEST SNOB, THE.

Lyon in Mourning, The A collection of speeches, journals, letters, speeches and eyewitness accounts pertaining to Prince Charles Edward Stuart and the '45 Rising, assembled by the Revd Robert Forbes, the Episcopalian Bishop of Ross and Caithness. The 'Lyon' in question is Scotland (presumably an allusion to the LION RAMPANT). Forbes, a Jacobite sympathizer, was arrested in 1745 on his way to join the Prince, and was released in May of the following year. Shortly afterwards he began what was to become his life's work, stating his intention was

> ... to make up a collection of papers relative to the affairs of a Certain Young Gentleman and of those who followed his fortunes ... establishing the truth both as to facts and men ... for a strict and impartial examination, that so they may be carefully recorded and transmitted to posterity according to truth and justice.

'Now is the time or never,' Forbes declared, realizing that fading memories and mortality made his task – largely undertaken in secret, to protect his sources – that much more urgent. He was working on the tenth volume at his death in 1775. Extracts from the work – which is an important source for the period – were published by Robert Chambers in 1834 as *Jacobite Memoirs of the Rebellion of 1745*, and the full text was published by the Scottish History Society in 1895.

M

Mac- or **Mc-** A Gaelic prefix in many surnames, meaning 'son of'. *Mac* is also commonly used, like JIMMY, as a familiar form of address to any man whose name one does not know. A variant is *MacTavish*.

No McTavish
Was ever lavish.
– Ogden Nash, 'Genealogical Reflection', *Hard Lines* (1931)

See also MRS WUMMIN.

Macadam *See under* EPONYMS.

Macallum Raspberry-flavoured ice cream. The name is said to derive from some horrendously devious wordplay: *mak* ('make') + *cauld* ('cold') + *'em* ('them'). An alternative theory (but lacking any culinary connection or other corroboration) suggests that the reference is to one John McCallum of Bridgeton, who played for Clyde FC and went on to become provost of Rutherglen in the late 19th century.

Mac an t-Srònaich A fugitive from justice, alleged murderer and reputed cannibal who at some vague time in the past (possibly the early 19th century) fled from Garve in Wester Ross, where his father was innkeeper, and haunted the hills and moors of Lewis. For generations his name was invoked to scare children into behaving themselves: 'Mac an t-Srònaich is going to get you!' He was said to have ended his life on a gibbet on the mainland, lamenting:

A mhointich riabhaich Leodhais:
Agus fhad's a ghleidh mi' thus'
Ghleidh thusa mis'.
['O brown moors of Lewis, as long as I kept to you, you preserved me.']

The anglicized version of his surname is Stronach.

Macbeth The anglicized version of Mac Bethad mac Findlaích, King of the Scots (1040–57), whose actual career was not quite as depicted in Shakespeare's tragedy. In 1032 he became ruler of Moray after killing his cousin, who had in turn killed Macbeth's father. Having married his cousin's widow, Gruoch, in 1040 Macbeth became king after killing his cousin Duncan I in battle (rather than in bed, as Shakespeare has it), probably at Pitgaveny near Elgin. His reign seems to have been a strong and stable one, and, according to the chronicler Marianus Scotus, in 1050 he was able to make a pilgrimage to Rome, where he 'scattered money to the poor like seed'. His rule was challenged in 1054 when Duncan's son MALCOLM CANMORE invaded from England, and after a fierce battle at Dunsinane in Perthshire (*see* BATTLE OF THE SEVEN SLEEPERS), Macbeth was obliged to offer Malcolm concessions. Three years later, on 15 August 1057, Malcolm killed Macbeth in battle, not at Dunsinane as in Shakespeare's play, but probably at Lumphanan, near Banchory in Aberdeenshire. For a few months the throne was occupied by Lulach, Gruoch's son and Macbeth's stepson, but he was killed by Malcolm on 17 March 1058.

Shakespeare's source was principally the *Chronicles* (1577) of Ralph Holinshed, who based his work on the *Historia Gentis Scotorum* (1527) of Hector Boece, who in turn borrowed from and enlarged upon the *Orygynale Cronykil of Scotland* (*c*.1410) of Andrew Wyntoun. It was Wyntoun who introduced the 'Thre werd sisteris', who prophesy thus:

The first he herd say gangand by:
'Lo, yonder the thayne of Crumbaghty [Cromarty]!'
The tother sister said agane:
'Off Murray yonder I see the thayne.'
The third said: 'Yonder I see the king.'
All this herd he in his dremyng.

Sone efter that, in his youth heid,
Off thai thayndomes he thayne wes maid;
Than thocht he nixt for to be king,
Fra Duncanis dais had tane ending.

Incidentally *werd* or *weird* originally meant 'fate', so the 'weird sisters' were women thought to have power over a person's fate. It was through the application of the term to the witches in *Macbeth* that the word *weird* took on its modern meaning of 'uncanny' or 'bizarre'. *See also* BIRNAM WOOD; SCOTTISH PLAY, THE.

McChattering classes A term applied in February 2008 by David Cairns, a minister in the Scotland Office, to those who supported increased fiscal powers for the Scottish Parliament. He was obliged to backtrack following a *volte face* by his boss, Gordon Brown, on the issue. The term 'chattering classes' is thought to have been first coined by the political commentator Alan Watkins in the early 1980s, and is disparagingly applied to those members of the liberal-left intelligentsia who have a fondness for pronouncing on issues of the day, both in the media and at the dinner table. The prefix 'Mc' deployed by Cairns, although obviously intended to denote the Scottish sept of Clan Chatter, carries an additional burden of odium by association with such terms as 'McJob' and 'McMansion', where the 'Mc' derives from the fast-food chain McDonald's.

MacClarty *See* MRS MACCLARTY.

MacCleran's Loup *See* DEVIL'S BEEF TUB, THE.

MacCulloch's Tree A 40 ft (12 m) fossilized conifer of the genus *Cupressinoxylon*, located in the Wilderness of Mull, near Burg. It is set amidst basalt columns similar to those on nearby Staffa, and appears to have been overwhelmed by a massive lava flow some 60 million years ago. It was first identified by the geologist John MacCulloch (1773–1835), who began a Scottish tour in 1811 and published *A Description of the Western Isles of Scotland* in 1819. Like many other old things, MacCulloch's Tree is now looked after by the National Trust for Scotland.

Macdonalds' disease Some kind of chest infection, formerly believed to be curable by the touch of certain members of the Macdonald clan. In Gaelic it was called *tinneas nan Domhnullach*, and was also known as *glacach*.

> The common diseases of this country (I may say of the Highlands in general) are fevers and colds ... The *Glacach*, or, as it is sometimes called, the *Macdonalds disorder*, is not uncommon. The afflicted finds a tightness and fullness in his chest, as is frequent in the beginning of consumptions. A family of the name of Macdonald ... pretend to the cure by *glacach*, or handling of the part affected, in the same manner as the Irish Mr Greatrack [the faith healer Valentine Greatrakes, 1629–83], in the last century, cured by stroking. The Macdonalds touch the part, and mutter certain charms; but, to their credit, never accept a fee on any entreaty.
> – Thomas Pennant, *A Tour in Scotland and Voyage to the Hebrides*, 1772 (1776)

Macdonnil fato hic A Latin inscription said once to be common on Macdonald gravestones, implying only fate could lay a Macdonald in his grave. A variant is *Nec tempore, nec fato* ('neither time nor fate').

MacFarlane's bowat The moon; a *bowat* is a hand-held lantern, and the reference is to the usefulness of the moon's light to Highland cattle rustlers.

> The Highlander eyed the blue vault, but far from blessing the useful light with Homer's, or rather Pope's benighted peasant, he muttered a Gaelic curse upon the unseasonable splendour of MacFarlane's buat (i.e. lantern).
> – Sir Walter Scott, *Waverley* (1814), chapter ix

Scott appends the following note: 'The clan of Mac-Farlane, occupying the fastnesses of the western side of Loch Lomond, were great depredators on the Low Country, and as their excursions were made usually by night, the moon was proverbially called their lantern.' Another jocular name for the moon, for the same reasons, was *Lochiel's lantern*, Lochiel being a name for the chief of Clan Cameron. *See also* THERE WILL BE MOONLIGHT AGAIN.

MacFarlane's geese like their play better than their meat An old proverb, explained thus by Sir

Walter Scott in a footnote in chapter xiii of *The Monastery* (1820):

> A brood of wild-geese, which long frequented one of the uppermost islands in Loch-Lomond, called Inch-Tavoe, were supposed to have some mysterious connexion with the ancient family of MacFarlane of that ilk, and it is said were never seen after the ruin and extinction of that house. The MacFarlanes had a house and garden upon that same island of Inch-Tavoe. Here James VI was, on one occasion, regaled by the chieftain. His Majesty had been previously much amused by the geese pursuing each other on the Loch. But, when one which was brought to table, was found to be tough and ill fed, James observed – 'that MacFarlane's geese liked their play better than their meat,' a proverb which has been current ever since.

McGregor, Mr The fearsome, bunny-hunting Scottish gardener in Beatrix Potter's *Tale of Peter Rabbit* (1902), *Tale of Benjamin Bunny* (1904) and *Tale of the Flopsy Bunnies* (1909). The character is thought to have been inspired by Charles McIntosh (1839–1922), postman at Dunkeld, where Potter spent many holidays. McIntosh, a noted amateur naturalist, had a great knowledge of fungi, an enthusiasm shared by Potter.

> Don't go into Mr McGregor's garden: your father had an accident there, he was put into a pie by Mrs McGregor.
> – Beatrix Potter, *The Tale of Peter Rabbit* (1902)

MacGregor, proscription of Clan The Mac-Gregors were first proscribed by James VI in 1603 following the so-called Slaughter of Lennox, in which they set upon the Colquhouns of Luss in Glen Fruin with 'hagbuttis, pistolettis, murrionis, mailzie-coittis, pow-aixes, twa-handit swoirdis, bowie, darloches, and utheris wappones invasive', carried off hundreds of cattle, sheep and horses, and massacred 'seven scoir personis or thereby'. As a consequence of the proscription, the very name of MacGregor was outlawed, and all MacGregors were obliged to take the surname of neighbouring clans, whether Campbells, Murrays, Grahams or Buchanans. Charles II lifted the ban in 1661, but it was reimposed by William and Mary in 1693, following further outbreaks of lawlessness. *See also* ARROW OF GLEN LYON, THE; GILDEROY; ROB ROY.

MacGregor's Leap A rocky narrows just west of Fortingall, Perthshire, on the River Lyon, across which in 1565 Gregor MacGregor of Glenstrae supposedly made a heroic jump from north to south to escape the pursuing bloodhounds of his sworn enemies, the Campbells of Glenorchy. His enemies eventually caught up with him, however, and he was beheaded in April 1570. There is a Gaelic song supposedly sung by his widow, Marion Campbell, after his death:

> Oh that Finlarig were in flames, proud Taymouth lying in ashes, and Red Gregor of the White Hands in my arms again ...
> Other men's wives sleep soft in their houses; I stand by the wayside wringing my hands.

See also ARROW OF GLEN LYON, THE; SOLDIER'S LEAP, THE.

Machair A stretch of low, flower-rich grassland adjacent to a sandy shore, often used for grazing. Such areas are found particularly on the northwestern seaboard, and in the Hebrides. The word is Gaelic in origin, meaning 'low-lying plain', and also gives rise to the name of the Machars, the broad peninsula between Luce Bay and Wigtown Bay on the Solway Firth.

> Until a man has seen good machair, like that of Berneray, or of the Monach Isles, or of Tiree, he may find it hard to realize that although the crofters call it 'gress' it grows not grass but flowers.
> – W.H. Murray, *The Islands of Western Scotland* (1973)

Mac-Ivor of Glennaquoich, Fergus The haughty Highland chief in Sir Walter Scott's novel *Waverley*; *see under* HIGHLAND PRIDE.

Mackay, the real *See* REAL MACKAY, THE.

Mackenzie's Shirt of Mail A byname of Clan Macrae, long the close friends and allies of the chiefs of Clan Mackenzie, who became the Earls of Seaforth. Hence Clan Macrae was also known as *Seaforth's Shirt*. *See also* Seaforth Highlanders *under* REGIMENTAL NICKNAMES.

Mackinnon's Cave A sea cave on the west coast of Mull, near the Gribun Rocks, visited by Johnson and Boswell in 1773. It is only accessible at low tide.

At Gribune there is a natural curiosity, which Dr Johnson considered one of the greatest that he saw during his tour. It is called Mackinnon's Cave, from a tradition that a gentleman of that name, whose curiosity had been excited by various reports of its amazing extent, went in to explore it, and was never again heard of. As the place has been investigated with greater success in later times, the conclusion is, that he must have been killed by persons who had taken shelter there, and who considered him as a dangerous spy or intruder.

– William Daniell, *A Voyage Round Great Britain* (1815–25)

Daniell fails to mention some of the key aspects of the Mackinnon legend, which states that he was a piper who entered the cave with his dog with the intention of demonstrating his superior piping skills to the local fairies. The latter must have been displeased by such hubris, as only the dog – now without its hair – ever emerged from the dark depths. Similar tales of pipers and their dogs meeting such fates are told of other caves in the Hebrides (for the case of the hairless dog of Smoo Cave, *see under* WIZARD OF REAY, THE).

Macleod's Maidens A group of three sea stacks off Idrigill Point, at the mouth of Loch Bracadale on Skye, in the heart of Macleod territory. They comprise a 'mother' (over 60 m/200 ft) high, and two 'daughters', and their shapes are said to represent women wearing crinolines. There is an old Gaelic prophecy, related by the writer Norman Macleod to his daughter shortly before his death in 1862, that if the FAIRY FLAG of Dunvegan should no longer be displayed, and a fox be seen to whelp in a turret of the castle, and Macleod's Maidens come into the possession of a Campbell, 'then the glory of the Macleod family should depart'.

Macleod's Tables The popular name given to Healaval Mhor and Healaval Bheag, a pair of flat-topped hills near Dunvegan on Skye. The story behind the name is that when Macleod of Dunvegan was being feasted by James V in Edinburgh, he boasted to the king that when the latter came to Dunvegan he would find more splendid hospitality. When James took him up on his offer, Macleod led him at dusk to the summit plateau of Healaval

Bheag, which was spread with a splendid banquet, while all around his clansmen stood in a great circle bearing torches, outshining any candles. Above them all twinkled the Milky Way, finer than any painted palace ceiling.

Macmillanites *See under* CAMERONIANS.

MacNab, the A term applied to any self-appointed 'big cheese', possibly in allusion to the notoriously conceited and bossy Archibald MacNab of McNab (d. 1860), 17th chief of Clan MacNab.

MacNeil of Barra has eaten, the It was once apparently the custom, at Kisimul Castle on the isle of Barra, for a herald to announce that the local chief had finished his dinner with the following proclamation: 'The MacNeil of Barra has eaten, and now the princes of the earth may dine.' James Boswell recounts how the Earl of Argyll was sorely irritated with a letter he had received from MacNeil, who had written it in such a high-flown style that it was 'as if he were of another kingdom'.

McNotty, Mr How the Italian-American opera composer Gian Carlo Menotti (1911–2007) referred to himself after his purchase in 1974 of Yester House, an elegant Robert Adam mansion in Gifford, East Lothian, where he lived for over 30 years.

Macphee's Hill A modest eminence on the now-deserted Outer Hebridean island of Mingulay. The story is that long ago MacNeil of Barra wondered why nothing had been heard from his tenants on the island, and sent a boat to investigate. On arriving at Mingulay the crew dispatched a man (or lad) called Macphee ashore, who went from house to house and then shouted the dreadful news that all the inhabitants had died of some disease. The crew refused to allow Macphee back on board, fearing the plague, and sailed off. For six weeks (or a year) Macphee survived on sheep and shellfish, climbing his eponymous hill every day to look out for rescue. Eventually, when rescue came, MacNeil promised Macphee that thereafter he and his family could live on Mingulay rent-free.

Macpherson, James *See* OSSIAN FORGERIES.

Macpherson, origin of the name *See* SON OF THE PARSON.

Macpherson's law An expression introduced and explained by Wilfred Taylor in *The Scotsman* on 27 February 1952:

> We met a citizen of Edinburgh whom we shall call Macpherson. Macpherson propounded to us what he called 'Macpherson's law of economics'. It greatly appealed to us. Briefly put, Macpherson's law holds that in any economic relationship Macpherson will always come worse off. If Macpherson has a modest meal, the bill will invariably be greater than the bill presented to his fellow-diners who have consumed more than he has. If Macpherson shares a taxi, the driver will, without hesitation, ask him for payment, and, if it comes to the point, Macpherson's taxi will almost certainly break down on the way to catch an important train.

Two years later Taylor returned to his theme, to assure us that 'the law only affects those who are basically decent, friendly and well-disposed people', and cited the 1953 annual dinner of Clan Macpherson, during which 'all the lights in the city went out'.

'M'Pherson's Rant' A tune composed by the notorious freebooter and fiddler James M'Pherson, who was hanged in Banff in November 1700. He supposedly played the tune on his fiddle as he was marched to the gallows, and then offered his instrument to the crowd. No one took up his offer, and he broke the fiddle in two before meeting his doom. A ballad to the tune was produced shortly afterwards, but the best-known version, entitled 'M'Pherson's Farewell', is that supplied by Burns in 1787. It begins:

> Farewell, ye dungeons dark and strong,
> The wretch's destinie!
> M'Pherson's time will not be long
> On yonder gallows-tree.
>
> *Sae rantingly, sae wantonly,*
> *Sae dauntingly gaed he;*
> *He play'd a spring, and danc'd it round,*
> *Below the gallows-tree.*

> O, what is death but parting breath?
> On many a bloody plain
> I've dared his face, and in this place
> I scorn him yet again!
>
> *Sae rantingly, &c.*

McRonaldo An imaginary creature conjured up by Scotland manager Craig Brown in anticipation of the 1998 World Cup:

> Unless we can find a McRonaldo or a Hamish Zidane, we'll have to make do with what we've got.

The allusions were, of course, to the Brazilian Ronaldo and the Frenchman Zinedine Zidane, the only two players to have been named FIFA World Player of the Year on three occasions each. Scotland were, as is customary, knocked out in the first round.

MacSycophant, Sir Pertinax The central character in Charles Macklin's comedy *The Man of the World* (1781), which he adapted from his earlier, unpublished play *The True Born Scotchman* (performed 1764). The latter had widely been seen as a satire on John Stuart, Earl of Bute, George III's Scottish tutor whom the king made his prime minister, leading to a wave of antipathy in England towards Scots in general. The first production of *The Man of the World* saw the Irish-born Macklin taking the part of MacSycophant, an ambitious and highly placed politician who has reached his eminent position through a willingness to fawn and do others' bidding. He here describes to his son Charles how he made both himself and his fortune:

> Sir, I booed, and watched, and hearkened, and ran about, backwards and forwards, and dangled upon the then great mon, till I got intill the very bowels of his confidence; and then, sir, I wriggled, and wrought, and wriggled, till I wriggled myself among the very thick of them. Ha! I got my snack of the clothing, the foraging, the contracts, the lottery tickets, and aw the political bonuses, till at length, sir, I became a much wealthier mon than one-half of the golden calves I had been so long a-booing to ... But, Charles, ah! while I was thus booing, and wriggling, and raising this princely fortune, ah! I met with many heart-sores and disappointments fra the want of literature, eloquence, and other popular

abeelities. Sir, guin I could but have spoken in the Hoose, I should have done the deed in half the time, but the instant I opened my mouth there, they aw fell a-laughing at me; aw which deficiencies, sir, I detearmined, at any expense, to have supplied by the polished education of a son, who I hoped would one day raise the house of MacSycophant till the highest pitch of ministerial ambition. This, sir, is my plan ...

Macklin denied in his preface that he was attacking the Scots, claiming his aim was merely 'to explode the reciprocal national prejudices that equally soured and disgraced the minds of both English and Scots men'.

MacTavish *See* MAC-.

Macwhachle, Wee *See* WEE MACWHACHLE.

Madame Ecosse A nickname (French for 'Mrs Scotland') initially applied disparagingly, and now affectionately and respectfully, to the Scottish Nationalist Winnie Ewing after she became an MEP in 1979. Ewing welcomed the nickname, and it has been used by headline-writers ever since. *See also* CHILL LOOKING FOR A SPINE TO RUN UP, A; STOP THE WORLD, SCOTLAND WANTS TO GET ON.

Mad dogs, a cure for the bite of *See* LEE PENNY, THE.

Made in Scotland from Girders *See* IRN BRU.

Madeira of the North, the The Firth of Clyde resort of Rothesay, on the Isle of Bute, much visited by those sailing DOON THE WATTER.

As the capital and only town of the island of Bute, it has a court, a pier, two putting greens, a cinema, a fine weekly newspaper (the *Buteman*), a bookshop, no fewer than two wet fish shops (long may they survive) and enough palm trees to justify its old title as 'the Madeira of the North' in the days when it had electric tramcars.
  – Ian Jack, 'Lay of the Last Duchess', the *Guardian*, 12 March 2005

Rothesay's romantic nicknames – Madeira of the North and Madeira of Scotland – sound too snobby.

The old Red Guide had the right idea – Rothesay: the Margate of Glasgow.
  – Mike Whitley, letter to the *Guardian*, 19 March 2005

Mad Mitch The nickname of Lieutenant-Colonel Colin Mitchell (1925–96), awarded to him in 1967 when he commanded the 1st Battalion of the Argyll and Sutherland Highlanders during the re-taking of the Crater district of Aden from Arab nationalist fighters. His strong-arm methods proved controversial, and he resigned from the army the following year. He went on to campaign against the disbanding of his old regiment, and was Conservative MP for Aberdeenshire West from 1970 to 1974. Although his parents were Scottish, he himself was born and raised in south London.

Mad Piper, the The nickname of Bill Millin (1922–2010), aka Piper Bill, originally from Sandyhills, Glasgow. During the Second World War he was personal piper to Lord Lovat, commander of 1st Special Service Brigade. Against strict orders from British high command, Lovat asked Millin to pipe his men ashore on Sword Beach on D-Day, 6 June 1944, playing 'Hielan' Laddie' and 'The Road to the Isles'. The practice of piping troops into battle had been banned following the First World War, as so many regimental pipers had been picked out by German snipers. But apparently on D-Day the German defenders simply thought that Millin, marching up and down the beach unarmed and wearing a kilt, was mad, and left him alone. Later the same day, Millin played 'Blue Bonnets over the Border' (*see under* BLUE BONNET) as Lovat's commandos crossed Pegasus Bridge. Millin later recalled his experience of the Normandy Landings:

I could see people lying face down in the water going back and forwards with the surf. Others to my left were trying to dig in just off the beach. A low wall, and they were trying to dig in there. It was very difficult for them trying to dig in the sand. Yet when they heard the pipes, some of them stopped what they were doing and waved their arms, cheering. But one came along, he wasn't very pleased, and he called me 'the Mad Bastard'. Well, we usually referred to Lovat as a 'mad bastard'. This was the first time I had heard it referred to me.
  – http://www.pegasusarchive.org/normandy/
     bill_millin.htm

It has often been said that Millin played himself in the 1962 film about D-Day, *The Longest Day*, but in fact the role of the 'Mad Piper' was taken by Pipe-Major Leslie de Laspee, official piper to the Queen Mother. When Lovat was asked why Millin hadn't played himself in the film, he said, 'My old piper works in a bar in Glasgow now, I believe, and is too fat to play the part.' Millin piped a last time for Lord Lovat in 1995, at the latter's funeral. In 2004 the famous photo of Millin stepping ashore on Sword Beach was featured on an Isle of Man postage stamp to mark the 60th anniversary of D-Day.

Maga The nickname of *Blackwood's Magazine*, the sharp-tongued, often satirical, Tory-orientated periodical founded in Edinburgh in 1817 by William Blackwood (1776–1834). The name reputedly referred to Blackwood's proud pronouncement as he presented his wife with a copy of the first issue: 'There's ma maga-zine.' Blackwood's intention was to take on the Whig-supporting EDINBURGH REVIEW with a 'more nimble, more frequent, more familiar' rival than the staid *Quarterly Review*, published by John Murray in London. Early contributors included J.G. Lockhart (Sir Walter Scott's son-in-law and first biographer), William Maginn, James Hogg (the ETTRICK SHEPHERD), John Galt, Thomas de Quincey and John Wilson, principal author of the *Noctes Ambrosianae* colloquies under the pseudonym Christopher North. In the August 1818 issue Lockhart greeted Keats's *Endymion* with the following dismissal (alluding to the poet's profession as a surgeon's apprentice):

> It is a better and a wiser thing to be a starved apothecary than a starved poet; so back to the shop, Mr John, back to 'plasters, pills, and ointment boxes'.

Over the years the magazine attracted numerous notable (and not always Tory) contributors, from Coleridge and Shelley to George Eliot and Joseph Conrad. It remained in the possession of the Blackwood family until its closure in 1980.

Magna Farta How the Earl of Lauderdale, Charles II's chief minister in Scotland in the earlier part of his reign, referred to Magna Carta, thus betraying his – and his master's – contempt for constitutionality and the rule of law. The expression had already been deployed by Cromwell in the 1650s. Lauderdale himself attracted much odium, such as this anonymous verse:

> This is the savage pimp without dispute
> First bought his mother for a prostitute;
> Of all the miscreants ever went to hell,
> This villain rampant bears away the bell.

Magowk *See* HUNTEGOWK.

Maiden, the A precursor of the guillotine, introduced into Scotland in 1564 by Regent Morton, who, according to Sir William Sanderson's *Complete History of Mary and James VI* (1656), had been inspired by an English precedent: 'The fatall Axe (called the maiden) himself had Patterned from that at Halifax in Yorkshire, which he had seen, and liked the fashion.' The Halifax Maiden (also known as the Halifax Gibbet) was used to dispatch perpetrators of even minor misdemeanours – hence the saying 'From Hell, Hull and Halifax, Good Lord, deliver us' – whereas the Edinburgh Maiden was for the exclusive use of those of higher social status. Morton's first intended victim was the Laird of Penicuik, although the first to die on it, in 1566, was Thomas Scott, one of the murderers of Rizzio, Mary Queen of Scots' Italian secretary. Morton himself, having fallen from favour, suffered on the Maiden in 1581 when he was convicted of involvement in the murder of Lord Darnley 14 years previously. Subsequent victims included Archibald Campbell, 8th Earl of Argyll, executed in 1661 after the Restoration, and his son, also Archibald, the 9th Earl, who rebelled against James VII in 1685. Just before the blade fell the 8th Earl declared:

> This is the sweetest maiden I ever kissed, it being the mean to finish my sin and misery, and my inlet to glory, for which I long.

For his part, on the scaffold the 9th Earl complained that the block was uneven, and pulled out a ruler to prove it, demanding that a carpenter be fetched. 'I die not only a Protestant,' he then declared, 'but with a heart-hatred of popery, prelacy, and all superstition whatever.' The Maiden was retired in 1708, having severed some 150 heads, and is now in the National Museum of Scotland.

Maiden Castle Although today this phrase is now more familiar as the name of various Iron Age hill forts in England (especially the fort near Dorchester, Dorset, taken by the Romans in AD 43), the first recorded use of the name– in 1659 – was in reference to Edinburgh Castle. A slightly different form, 'the Castle of the Maids or Virgins', had already appeared in Fynes Morison's *Itinerary* of 1617. This was a direct translation of the Latin *Castrum Puellarum* ('castle of the maidens'), which had been in use in relation to Edinburgh Castle from at least the 13th century, and thought to be the result of a misunderstanding of an earlier Gaelic or even Brythonic name. There is also a tradition that in the early medieval period the castle was used as a safe refuge for princesses of the royal line, and that there was also a convent here. Edinburgh's coat of arms now sports a maiden as one of its supporters.

Maiden Hair A rocky islet off the south tip of the Isle of May in the Firth of Forth. It is said to take its name from the story of a princess called Thenaw or Enoch, the unmarried daughter of the chief of the Votadini, an ancient British tribe whose capital was on Traprain Law, East Lothian, until they moved to Castle Rock in Edinburgh around AD 500. According to legend, the chief was so incensed when he found his daughter was pregnant that he had her thrown down the cliffs of Traprain Law. When she survived, he concluded she was a witch and had her taken out to sea and dumped in the water near the Isle of May. Here she clung onto the rock now called Maiden Hair, until swept up the Firth of Forth to Culross, where she gave birth to St Kentigern or Mungo, who was to become Glasgow's patron saint (*see* TREE THAT NEVER GREW, THE).

Maidenkirk to John o' Groats The whole of Scotland. JOHN O' GROATS is popularly regarded as the most northeasterly point in the country, while Maidenkirk – more commonly known as Kirkmaiden – on the Rhinns of Galloway, is the most southwesterly parish in Scotland.

> Hear, Land o' Cakes, and brither Scots
> Frae Maidenkirk to John o' Groats.
> – Robert Burns, 'Captain Grose's Peregrinations' (1789), i

> From John o' Groats to Maidenkirk
> You'll never find a truer
> For loyal faith and dauntless deeds,
> Than the Lady of Kenmure.
> – Traditional, 'The Lady of Kenmure'

> Sae on the cod I see't in you
> Wi' Maidenkirk to John o' Groats
> The bosom that you draw me to.
> – Hugh MacDiarmid, *A Drunk Man Looks at the Thistle* (1926) [*cod*, 'pillow']

Maiden Stack A sea stack off the east coast of Papa Stour, Shetland. It takes its name from the daughter of Lord Tirval Thoresson, who in the 14th century was confined by her father in a house on top of the stack to prevent her from eloping with her beloved, a poor fisherman. In this intention, Lord Thoresson was unsuccessful. *See also* PRISONER OF PAPA STOUR, THE.

Maid of Norway, the Margaret, granddaughter of Alexander III, and daughter of his daughter Margaret and King Eric of Norway. Four years after Alexander's fatal fall from his horse in 1286, the seven-year-old heir to the Scottish throne set sail for Scotland and an agreed marriage with the oldest son of Edward I of England. The young girl died on the voyage, and so began a decades-long struggle for the Scottish throne and Scottish independence. She is sometimes referred to as 'the Fair Maid of Norway'. *See also* GREAT CAUSE, THE.

Maids of Bute Two painted rocks on the northwest shore of Bute, just south of Buttock Point. They are said to have been first painted in the early 20th century (legend has it that Para HANDY was responsible), and they are given new coats every now again, in a variety of patterns.

Maister and mair *See* MISTRESS AND MAIR.

Maitland Club *See* BANNATYNE CLUB.

Maitland of Lethington, William *See* MICHAEL WYLIE.

Major-mindit Stuck-up, arrogant, domineering. The allusion is to the military rank.

Major Weir Thomas Weir (1599–1670), strict Covenanter, commander of the city guard in Edinburgh, persecutor of Royalists (he mocked and abused Montrose just before his execution), and alleged witch. He lived with his sister Jean in a turreted house in Edinburgh's West Bow, and was renowned for his sanctity and punctilious religious observance, earning him the nickname 'the Bowhead Saint', while various doting women called him 'Angelical Thomas'. He cut an austere figure:

> A tall, thin man, with lean and hungry look, big, prominent nose, severe, dark, gloomy countenance, which grew yet more gloomy when one of the conforming ministers crossed his path. Then, with expressive gesture, be would draw his long black coat tighter about him, pull his steeple-hat over wrathful brows, and turn away with audible words of contempt. And as he went his Staff, with an indignant rat-tat, beat the stones of the street. That Staff was to become in after years a terror to all Edinburgh; it was of one piece, with a crooked head of thorn wood. When curiously examined afterwards it was seen to have carved on it the grinning heads of satyrs.
>
> – Francis Watt, *Edinburgh and the Lothians* (1912)

In 1670 the facade of respectability crumbled when Weir fell ill and suddenly confessed to a series of horrendous crimes, and with cries and roars demanded that he be punished. Weir went on to tell his inquisitors that he had felt the Devil in the dark, that Satan had appeared to him in the guise of a beautiful woman, that he had sinned beyond all possibility of repentance, that he was already damned, that he could find nothing within himself but blackness and darkness, brimstone and burning to the bottom of hell. His sister Jean joined in to create a *folie à deux*, confessing to all sorts of dealings with the powers of darkness. Some judged him out of his mind, but such confessions were taken very seriously in those days, and when a witness testified that Weir's notorious staff had walked down the street ahead of him, the couple's fate was sealed. He was strangled and burnt, she hanged. It was noted that Weir's staff, committed to the flames, gave 'rare turnings, and was long in burning'. After the executions, Weir's house in the West Bow, which many believed haunted, remained empty, gradually falling into ruin until finally pulled down around 1830.

> Sure Major Weir, or some sic warlock wight,
> Has flung beguilin' glances owre your sight.
> – Robert Fergusson, 'The Ghaists: a Kirkyard Eclogue' (*c.*1771)

In Sir Walter Scott's story, 'Wandering Willie's Tale' (contained within *Redgauntlet*, 1824) there is a malicious pet monkey – 'a great, ill-favoured jackanape' – that goes by the name of Major Weir, 'after the warlock that was burnt':

> A cankered beast it was, and mony an ill-natured trick it played; ill to please it was, and easily angered – ran about the haill castle, chattering and rowling, and pinching and biting folk, specially before ill weather, or disturbance in the state.

In Scott's story there is certainly something demonic about the laird's simian companion, that mocks the agonies of its master's death:

> Sir Robert sat, or, I should say, lay in a great arm-chair, wi' his grand velvet gown, and his feet on a cradle, for he had baith gout and gravel, and his face looked as gash and ghastly as Satan's. Major Weir sat opposite to him, in a red-laced coat, and the laird's wig on his head; and aye as Sir Robert girned wi' pain, the jackanape girned too, like a sheep's head between a pair of tangs – an ill-faur'd, fearsome couple they were.

In his editorial note to the 1924 Tusitala Edition of the works of R.L. Stevenson, Sir Sidney Colvin informs us that W.E. Henley, Stevenson's friend, had told him that the name of the cruel judge Adam Weir, Lord Hermiston, in WEIR OF HERMISTON, was inspired by that of Major Weir. The latter, alongside the likes of DEACON BRODIE, may well have inspired Stevenson's *The Strange Case of Dr Jekyll and Mr Hyde*.

Mak a bauchle o' something To make a botch of something, or turn something into an object of derision. A *bauchle* is a broken old shoe or slipper, and hence anything or anyone who has seen better days, or who has become a laughing-stock.

Mak a brig to the Bass, to *See* DING DOON TANTALLON, TO.

Mak a fraik aboot something, to To make a fuss about something, especially something one doesn't want to do. If you *mak a fraik o' someone*, then you make a fuss of them.

Mak a kirk or a mill o' it It's up to you what you make of circumstances; the choice is yours. To *mak a kirk or a mill out o nowt* is to make a mountain out of a molehill.

Makar An old word, literally a 'maker', hence occasionally applied to God ('the first makar') but more usually to a writer, specifically a poet, as in William Dunbar's 'LAMENT FOR THE MA-KARIS'. In literary history, the term *the Makars* refers to the poets of the Scottish Renaissance, such as Dunbar, Robert Henryson and Gavin Douglas. The word was revived in the early 21st century, when various Scottish cities (starting with Edinburgh in 2002) appointed their own makars. In 2004 the Scottish Parliament made Edwin Morgan (1920–2010) the first 'Scots Makar', i.e. national poet. He was succeeded in the post in 2011 by Liz Lochhead.

Mak mice feet o' something, to To smash something to smithereens; to confound. The expression comes from the Northeast and the Northern Isles. A variant is *to mak like mice feet*.

Mak one's feet one's freens, to To run off at speed (*freens*, 'friends'). Sometimes *heels* is substituted for *feet*. The expression comes from the Northeast.

Mak one's mercat, to *See* MERCAT.

Mak siccar, to *See* RED COMYN, THE.

Malagrowther, Malachi The pen name adopted by Sir Walter Scott in three letters to the *Edinburgh Weekly Journal* in 1826, arguing in favour of the right of Scottish banks to continue printing £1 notes. The government had proposed, in the wake of a series of bank failures in England, that private banks should not be allowed to issue notes smaller than £5. Scott argued that this would be disastrous to Scotland's economy, where small-denomination notes were the principle means of exchange. No one was in any doubt of the identity of Malachi, who claimed to be a descendant of Sir Mungo Malagrowther in

Scott's novel *The Fortunes of Nigel*. Scott's campaign was successful, and in recognition his portrait still appears on Bank of Scotland notes.

Malcolm Canmore Malcolm III (*c.*1031–93), king of Scotland from 1058, the year after he defeated and killed MACBETH. His nickname *Canmore* is generally taken to mean 'big head', from Gaelic *ceann*, 'head', and *mor*, 'great', although *ceann* can also mean 'chief'. His reign was prophesied by St Berchan many centuries before:

> No woman bore or will bring forth in the east
> A king whose rule will be greater over Alban;
> And there shall not be born forever
> One who had more fortune or greatness.

In 1069 Malcolm married Margaret, an Anglo-Saxon princess who had taken refuge at his court following the Norman Conquest. They were buried together in Dunfermline Abbey, and she was canonized in 1250 on account of her piety and almsgiving. At the Reformation, both bodies were exhumed and taken to Spain, where they were reburied in a special chapel in the Escorial Palace, Madrid.

Malcolm the Maiden The nickname of Malcolm IV (reigned 1153–65), given to him by later chroniclers. His health was poor and he was still unmarried when he died at the age of 24.

Malignant A term applied by the COVENANTERS in the 17th century to their religious opponents – Episcopalians and Roman Catholics. Thus the Roman Catholic Church was dubbed 'the Kirk Malignant'. In 1649 the Scottish Parliament passed an act ordaining that 'no person that is Malignant or disaffected to the present work of Reformation and Covenants ... nor any person given to drunkenness, swearing, uncleanness or any other scandalous offence' should be 'employed in any place of power or public trust within this kingdom'.

> 'Think ye,' he continued, 'to touch pitch and remain undefiled? to mix in the ranks of malignants, papists, papa-prelatists, latitudinarians and scoffers ...?'
> – Sir Walter Scott, *Old Mortality* (1816), chapter iv

Malkie *See* RHYMING SLANG.

Man i' the mune, the According to popular belief, this character ended up on the moon for failing to observe the SABBATH (he had gathered sticks on a Sunday). It is recorded that a servant girl in Ayrshire, rebuked for sewing on a button on a Sunday, retorted, 'Ah'll be getting ma face i' the mune.'

Man on the chain, the The Devil; *see* AM FEAR TH'AIR AN T-SLABHRUIDH.

Man o' one's meat, to be To be possessed of a hearty appetite and a sound digestion.

Man's a man for a' that, A Perhaps Burns's best-known sentiment, from the song 'For a' that and a' that', written in January 1795. The song embodies the new egalitarian ideals that had emerged from the Enlightenment and the American and French Revolutions, and apparently includes various Masonic symbols (Freemasonry being a child of the Enlightenment; Burns was initiated in 1781).

What though on hamely fare we dine –
    Wear hoddin grey, and a' that?
Gie fools their silks, and knaves their wine –
    A man's a man, for a' that:
For a' that, and a' that,
    Their tinsel show, and a' that;
The honest man, tho' e'er sae poor,
    Is king o' men for a' that.

There are also anticipations of the international socialism that was to emerge in the 19th century:

Then let us pray that come it may,
    As come it will for a' that,
That sense and worth, o'er a' the earth,
    May bear the gree, and a' that:
For a' that, and a' that,
    It's comin' yet for a' that,
That man to man, the warld o'er,
    Shall brothers be for a' that.

In his *Life and Works of Robert Burns* (1851), Robert Chambers opines that 'This song may be said to embody all the false philosophy of Burns' time, and of his own mind.' Time has perhaps taught us that Chambers was the dinosaur here. The song was sung at the opening of the Scottish Parliament on 12 May 1999, reflecting the egalitarian spirit of the Scottish body politic rather than any particularly nationalist sentiment. Burns himself was modest about his production. In a note accompanying the manuscript he wrote:

A great critic [Aikin] on songs says, that love and wine are the exclusive themes for song-writing. The following is on neither subject, and consequently is no song, but will be allowed, I think, to be two or three pretty good prose thoughts inverted into rhyme. I do not give it for your book, but merely by way of *vive la bagatelle*; for the piece is not really poetry.

See also AH KENT HIS FAITHER.

Man who lost his shadow to the Devil, the *See* WIZARD OF REAY, THE.

Man With No Name, the The sobriquet awarded by the press (after the Clint Eastwood character in various Spaghetti Westerns) to the body found in June 1996 sitting near the top of Ben Alder, on the edge of a cliff overlooking a lochan. It had been there for some months. At first it was thought the dead man must have been an unlucky victim of the fierce storms that can lash this remote and lofty peak at any time of the year, but then it was found that his heart was pierced by a single, spherical lead bullet, like an old-fashioned musket ball. He had lying beside him a replica Remington .44 of the kind favoured by the Clint Eastwood character, wore slip-on shoes (hardly suitable for the rough terrain) and carried a sleeping bag, full water bottles, £21 in cash and a map with his route outlined in pencil. But he had no credit cards or other means of identification, and all the labels had been cut from his clothes. The police eventually worked out that the clothes mostly came from French supermarkets, and in November 1997 cranio-facial reconstruction led investigators to the conclusion that the body was that of a young Parisian called Emmanuel Caillet. Caillet was an introverted, melancholic young man, somewhat at odds with the world, who was obsessed with chivalry and spent his weekends dressed in chainmail in historical re-enactments. His parents had last seen him on 14 August 1995. He had crossed the Channel the following day, sold his car, and made his way north, eventually leaving the train at Rannoch station, from where he had trudged the 10 miles (16 km) or so across the wilds to the place of his death. It was his parents who had suggested that he might like to holiday in Scotland, and after he disappeared they hired a private detective to find him, but to no avail. Subsequently his parents came several times to Scotland, but found nothing. They do not accept the official verdict that their son's death was suicide; his father has a variety of alternative theories, one of which has Emmanuel going to his death in fulfilment of some dark role-playing game.

See also BEN ALDER COTTAGE.

Many ... *See* MONY ...

March, the A former name for the areas on either side of the Border; often used in the plural. The word comes from French *marche*, 'frontier, boundary', and there were also Marches along the Anglo–Welsh frontier. The Anglo–Scottish Border was divided into the East, Middle and West Marches, each with its warden on both sides, typically a local nobleman. The wardens of each march, accompanied by their retainers, would meet on a regular basis to iron out any little local difficulties, often occasioned by the doings of the BORDER REIVERS. Sometimes tempers flared on these *march days* or TRUCE DAYS and things got out of hand, resulting in skirmishes such as the REDESWIRE FRAY. The job of the wardens became redundant at the Union of the Crowns in 1603.

Associated terms include: *marchman*, a Borderer, specifically a warrior; *laws of the march*, the regulations governing proceedings along the Border; *march treason*, a breach of the above; and *gang owre the march*, to elope from England into Scotland (typically to GRETNA GREEN), with the intention of contracting an *owre-the-march marriage*. *See also* RIDING THE MARCHES.

Marching through water, an insistence on *See* BLACK BOB.

March sud come in like a boar's head, an gang oot like a peacock's tail A Northeastern version of 'March comes in like a lion and goes out like a lamb.' Sometimes it is an adder's rather than a boar's head that marks the month's commencement.

Mare Scoticum See SCOTCH SEA.

Margaret of Scotland, St *See* MALCOLM CANMORE.

Margate of Glasgow, the *See* MADEIRA OF THE NORTH, THE.

Maroons, the *See* FOOTBALL CLUB NICKNAMES.

Marquis of Annandale's Beef-stand *See* DEVIL'S BEEF TUB, THE.

Marriage *subsequente copula* A form of irregular marriage, in which a couple were legally deemed to be married if the man promised to marry a woman as a means to have sexual intercourse with her. Irregular marriages could also arise if both parties agreed to marry at that moment (marriage *per verba de praesenti*). Both these forms of irregular marriage were abolished by the Marriage (Scotland) Act 1939, although a third form of irregular marriage, in which a couple living together are deemed to be married 'by HABIT AND REPUTE', remains valid in Scottish common law (a man in such a situation is referred to as a 'common-law husband', and a woman a 'common-law wife'). *See also* BIDIE-IN; HANDFAST.

Marrow Controversy, the A doctrinal dispute within the Kirk occasioned by the reissue in 1718 of *The Marrow of Modern Divinity* by 'E.F.' (believed to be the English Calvinist theologian Edward Fisher), first published in two parts in 1645 and 1649. In 1719 the General Assembly instructed its Committee for Purity of Doctrine to examine the book, and in May 1720 the Committee issued its report, condemning *The Marrow* as Antinomian (the view that the Elect regard existing laws as inapplicable to themselves, a view supposedly implicit in the AUCHTERARDER CREED) – to the consternation of its supporters, the *Marrow-folk* or *Marrow-men*. The theology of *The Marrow* was adopted by the Associate Presbytery when it seceded from the Church of Scotland in 1732.

Martin of Bullion, St *See* BULLION'S DAY.

Marvellous Merchiston *See* NAPIER'S BONES.

Marvels of infernal agency *See* WITCH OF STOER, THE.

Maryhill Magyars, the *See* FOOTBALL CLUB NICK-NAMES.

Marymass Fair A fair held in Inverness on the nearest Saturday to 15 August, the Feast of the Assumption of the Virgin Mary. The tradition was revived in 1986. The name is also said to commemorate the time that Mary Queen of Scots spent in the city in 1562, during the rebellion by the Earl of Huntly (the COCK O' THE NORTH). The governor of Inverness Castle was of the Huntly faction, and refused Mary admission, so she took up residence in a house in Bridge Street (demolished in the 1970s) until Clan Munro and Clan Fraser took the castle for her. The governor was hanged.

Irvine in Ayrshire also has a Marymass Fair, held since the 12th century and originally connected to the town's church of St Mary. However, the festival has been linked to Mary Queen of Scots since she visited the town in 1563, with the annual Queen of the Fair dressed up to resemble her.

Mary Queen of Scots' Pillar *See* QUEEN OF SCOTS' PILLAR.

Mary the Jewel The sobriquet of the Gaelic poet Màiri nighean Alasdair Ruaidh (Mary McLeod; *c.*1615–*c.*1707), who was born at Rodel in Harris and became bard to MacLeod of Dunvegan, and also acted as nurse to several generations of the family.

Mason-word, the According to a 1696 pamphlet described as 'a true narrative of the wonderful expressions and actions of a spirit which infested the house of Andrew Mackie of Ringcroft in the County of Galloway', the said Mackie, being a mason, was suspected by his neighbours of having 'devoted his first child to the Devil at taking the mason-word'. The London publisher of the pamphlet explains that the 'mason-word' is

... a secret reserved by some of that trade in Scotland to themselves, which entitles those that have it to some sort of privileges in the Society: but some way or other

the common people have entertained an ill idea of it, as an enchantment, devilism, etc.

See also HORSEMAN'S WORD, THE.

Massacre Cave, the A dank recess in the sea cliffs on the south coast of Eigg, near Galmisdale, where in 1814 Sir Walter Scott found 'numerous specimens of mortality'. These were presumed to have been the remains of some 200 MacDonalds who had taken refuge here in 1577 when a marauding band of MacLeods from Skye had landed on the island. The latter were determined to revenge some of their fellow clansmen who, on a previous visit, had been castrated by the MacDonalds after pressing their unwelcome attentions on the maidens of the island. The cave proved to be no refuge, however: when the MacLeods discovered it they lit a fire at the entrance and suffocated all those inside. The MacDonalds took their revenge the following year, on the first Sunday in May, when they landed on Skye and barred the door of the church at Trumpan before setting it alight and killing all but one of the MacLeods inside. The girl who escaped alerted the MacLeods at Dunvegan, who unfurled the FAIRY FLAG, thus guaranteeing that their enemy was doomed. The bodies of the slaughtered MacDonald invaders were lined up beneath a turf wall, which was then pushed over them; the encounter was thereafter known as the Battle of the Spoiled Dyke.

The 1577 outrage was by no means the first massacre on the island of Eigg, which up till the 16th century was known as *Eilean Nimban More*, meaning 'island of the powerful women'. This was thought to refer to the episode in AD 617, when St Donan, who had established a monastery on the island, was killed along with 67 of his monks by a band of wild warrior women.

Massacre of Glencoe, the An infamous episode following the Glorious Revolution that ousted James VII and brought William and Mary to the throne. After the defeat of the Jacobites in the fighting that followed, the Highland chiefs were obliged to swear allegiance to William and Mary by the last day of 1691. Most of the chiefs complied, but MacIan, chief of the Macdonalds of Glen Coe, was unavoidably delayed, and did not reach Inverary to take the oath until 6 January. It seems that the government decided to make an example of the Glencoe Macdonalds, who had no powerful allies but something of a reputation for lawlessness. The principal author of the Macdonalds' downfall was the Scottish secretary of state, Sir John Dalrymple, Master of Stair, a Lowlander who nursed a hatred of all things Highland. He drew up an order, signed by William, to 'extirpate that sect of thieves', and to this end a regiment raised by the Duke of Argyll (*see* LEWD AND PROFLIGATE LIFE, A) and largely composed of Campbells, the traditional enemies of the Macdonalds, were quartered in Glencoe. On the night of 13 February 1692 the troops – who for a fortnight had been enjoying the hospitality of the Macdonalds, eating, drinking and playing cards with every sign of amity – turned on their hosts with fire and sword, killing 38 men, women and children and forcing the rest to flee into the wintry wilderness, where more of them died of exposure. It was said that some of the troops forewarned their hosts, and that their commander, Campbell of Glenlyon – who was related by marriage to MacIan – tried to save a boy, who was then killed by Captain Drummond. Drummond, who had earlier been instrumental in delaying MacIan's journey to Inverary, coldly explained that 'a nit may grow into a louse'. Two lieutenants broke their swords rather than carry out their orders, and were arrested but later released. When news of the massacre got out, there was an uproar. The massacre was regarded as a shocking incident of 'murder under trust', and a commission of inquiry was established. The government was deeply implicated, and the Master of Stair was obliged to resign – though he was never charged with any crime. No blame was apportioned by the commission to the king, but William's reputation in Scotland plummeted, and the Jacobite cause was strengthened. *See also* CURSE OF SCOTLAND, THE.

Massacre of Tranent, the An incident that took place in the East Lothian mining town in 1797. On 29 August local men protesting against the Militia Act, which allowed for forcible conscription, confronted the recruiting officer, Major Wight, who ordered his troops to open fire. Several protestors were killed, including their leader, Jackie Crookston.

As the protestors fled, they were pursued by dragoons, and several more people were cut down. Women and children were among the dead, and estimates of the number killed range from 12 to 20. A memorial was unveiled in 1995.

Mass of moral putrescence, a How St Andrews was described by the missionary Alexander Duff (1806–78), who had studied arts and theology there. Duff was described by one contemporary as 'humourless and austere', and went on to spend much of his life in India, where he exhibited 'a burning desire to convert the souls of the heathen'.

Master of Mortifications A member of Aberdeen's town council whose role it is to look after the city's *mortified* property, i.e. property that has been bequeathed to it in perpetuity. The position arose in the 16th century, and still survives; today the Master chairs the Guildry and Mortification Funds Sub-Committee.

Maximum Eck *See* WEE ECK.

Maxwell's demon *See under* EPONYMS.

Maybe aye and maybe och aye An expression of uncertainty or ironic disbelief.

Maybe was ne'er a gude honeybee A proverb cited in Andrew Henderson's *Scottish Proverbs* (1832), meaning that a dubious promise or possibility may not necessarily be fulfilled.

May Dip, the A tradition at St Andrews University in which students stay up all night on the eve of May Day, then at dawn throw themselves into the North Sea, to the accompaniment of a choir singing madrigals. The May Dip supposedly nullifies any curse invoked by stepping on the PH COBBLES.

May prick nor purse ne'er fail you *See* BEGGAR'S BENISON, THE.

Meal and ale A dish of ale, oatmeal and sugar, formerly served at harvest suppers in the Northeast. When the creamy mix was served out, a tot or two of whisky was poured into each bowl, together with a ring or a button. The phrase was also applied to the celebration itself.

Meal-belly or **gruelly-belkie** A nickname for a man from Sanday, Orkney. In this context, both *meal* and *gruel* denote porridge.

> The gentlemen of Sanday were specially famous because of the capacity they had for consuming whisky, and they generally wound up their festivities with a mixture of boiling water, oatmeal, and strong spirits. This failing of theirs came to be so well known that they were at length named 'gruelly-belkies' – a cognomen which has stuck to the natives of that island to the present day.
> – W.R. Mackintosh, *Around the Orkney Peat Fires* (*c.*1890)

Another explanation is that Sanday was once regarded as the 'granary of Orkney'. *See also* TEU-NEEMS.

Mealie pudding or **white pudding** A traditional sausage, still widely sold in chip shops, composed of oatmeal, pork meat and fat, stuffed into a tubular skin. They are white in contrast to black or bloody puddings, and are sometimes also known as *jimmies* or *mealie jimmies*. White puddings were among the Scottish dishes that Robert Fergusson suggested that the professors of St Andrews should have served to Dr Johnson, in retaliation for his disparaging remarks in his dictionary regarding OATS (*see also* SHEEP'S HEID):

> What think ye neist, o' gude fat brose
> To clag his ribs? a dainty dose!
> And white and bloody puddins routh,
> To gar the Doctor skirl, O Drouth!
> – 'To the Principal and Professors of the University of St Andrews on their Superb Treat to Dr Samuel Johnson'

In 1946, during the period of postwar rationing, Dr Edith Summerskill, parliamentary secretary at the Ministry of Food, announced to Parliament that mealie puddings 'come within the definition of flour confectionery' and would require coupons, while haggis would remain unrationed. *See also* SKIRL-I'-THE-PAN.

Meal mob A crowd rioting in protest at shortages of oatmeal deliberately engineered by producers or speculators hoarding supplies in order to push up prices. Such riots were not uncommon in the 18th and earlier 19th century.

Meal Monday A day's holiday formerly observed on the second Monday of February at the universities of Edinburgh, St Andrews, Aberdeen and Glasgow, originally so that impoverished students from rural parts could return home to stock up on oatmeal – for, as the Revd James Sharp noted in the later 19th century, 'the liberal arts, sciences and theology were cultivated on oatmeal, with an occasional glass of beer on a Saturday night' (quoted in Laurence Hutton, *Literary Landmarks of the Scottish Universities*, 1904). At Edinburgh until the 1880s, such holidays were given on the first Monday of every month, while at St Andrews Meal Monday is still maintained as a holiday for 'manual staff'.

Meanness A stereotypical component of the Scottish character – at least according to a common English prejudice. The Scots themselves would prefer to refer to this characteristic as probity.

> The Scotsman is mean, as we're all well aware,
> And bony, and blotchy, and covered with hair,
> He eats salted porridge, he works all the day,
> And he hasn't got Bishops to show him the way.
> – Michael Flanders (with Donald Swann), 'A Song of Patriotic Prejudice', from *At the Drop of Another Hat* (1964)

See also ABERDONIAN JOKES; DOURNESS; LAND OF MEANNESS, SOPHISTRY AND MIST.

Measure Miller The nickname of the London-born book collector William Henry Miller (1789–1848), the son of William Miller, a wealthy Quaker, Jacobite and nurseryman who had acquired Craigentinny House, near Edinburgh, in 1764. A diehard reactionary, Miller *fils* sat in Parliament as a Tory from 1830 to 1841, opposing the Reform Bill of 1832, the admission of dissenters to the universities, and the abolition of flogging in the navy. His nickname comes from his passion for collecting rare books, in the pursuit of which he always carried in his hand a foot-rule to measure prospective purchases, the size and thickness of which became something of an obsession with him. Sir Frederic

Madden noted that Miller was 'known to be a very strange sort of person', and some suggested that he might even be a changeling or even a woman (he never married, and had no beard). He died at Craigentinny, leaving instructions that he be buried in a pit 20 feet (6 m) deep, topped by a lavish Roman mausoleum designed by David Rhind and with marble panels by Alfred Gatley.

Meat, to look like one's To appear well-nourished. In contrast, *to fa frae one's meat* is to go off one's food. Meat is a generic term for food generally as well as flesh, hence a *meat house* is a house where there is always plenty to eat; hence also the words of wisdom imparted to children, 'It's yer meat that maks ye bonny.'

Meat and one's mense, to have both one's Said when one's hospitality has been declined, so that one has the advantage of saving on *meat*, i.e. food, while preserving one's *mense*, i.e. honour. Sometimes the word *manners* is substituted for *mense*.

Meat tea A synonym for HIGH TEA.

Mee-maws Contemporary slang for the police, alluding to the sound of a siren. Hence the joke about the proud mother of three young policeman who asks which of them would like second helpings, and is greeted by a chorus of me-maws.

Meet the cat i' th' mornin', to To suffer a stroke of bad luck. The expression comes from the Northeast.

Meet wi' a myresnipe, to To become stuck in a bog; figuratively, to encounter some misfortune. A *myresnipe* is the common snipe.

Meg A familiar abbreviation of Margaret, formerly used as a generic name for any simple country girl.

> O Lord! yestreen, Thou kens, wi' Meg –
> Thy pardon I sincerely beg –
> O! may't ne'er be a livin' plague
>   To my dishonour,
> An' I'll ne'er lift a lawless leg
>   Again upon her.
> – Robert Burns, 'Holy Willie's Prayer' (1785)

Meg Dods *See* DODS, MEG.

Meg Merrilies *See* MERRILIES, MEG.

Meg Mullach Literally 'hairy Meg' (Gaelic *molach*, 'hairy'). According to *Ane Account of the Rise and Offspring of the Name of Grant* (1876), she was 'a little familiar spirit, a little hairy creature in the shape of a female child', who was reputed 'to have followed the family and served for great drudgery to them'. These were the Grants of TULLOCHGORUM on the Spey, and their familiar was mentioned in the late 17th century by the English antiquarian John Aubrey in his *Miscellanies*. Other accounts describe how 'the BROWNIE of Tullochgorum' would light the 'Goodman' home on dark nights, and how she never failed to warn the family of death or danger. Meg Mullach or Mag Molach seems to have had a wider presence in that part of the world. In his *History of the Province of Moray* (1775), Lachlan Shaw translates the name as 'one with the left hand all over hairy', and continues:

> I find in the Synod Records of Moray, frequent orders to the Presbyteries of Aberlaure and Abernethie, to enquire into the truth of Maag Moulach's appearing. But they could make no discovery, only that one or two men declared they once saw in the evening a young girl whose left hand was all hairy, and who instantly disappeared.

In his *Survivals in Belief Among the Celts* (1911), George Henderson (who quotes the above passage from Shaw) refers to her as 'Hairy Hand' and says that 'Hairy Hand was supposed to come down the chimney and take children away.' *See also* BODACH GLAS.

Meg's hole A break in the clouds to the southwest, heralding brighter weather.

Meg wi' the mony feet *See under* FAUNA CALEDONIA.

Meikle Ferry Disaster, the A maritime tragedy that occurred on the calm night of 16 August 1809, when the overcrowded Meikle Ferry crammed with people heading for the market at Tain sank in the middle of the Dornoch Firth, drowning 99 passengers. Among the dead was Sheriff Hugh MacCulloch of Dornoch, who had prevented more people from embarking on the boat. The disaster resulted in the construction of Bonar Bridge in 1812.

Meikle John *See* SWEET SINGERS, THE.

Melville, Viscount *See* HENRY THE NINTH.

Men of Mey *See* MERRY MEN OF MEY, THE.

Mercat Any market, but often in the past specifically the marriage market, hence to *mak one's mercat* meant to become engaged, while to *lose one's mercat* was to blow one's chances of connubial bliss. An eligible young woman might be described as *mercat-ripe*.

Merchant Company schools A number of Edinburgh schools originally set up by the Merchant Company of Edinburgh, a body instituted to protect the trading rights of the city and awarded its charter by Charles II in 1681. The schools were originally termed 'hospitals', and run as charitable trusts: the Merchant Maiden Hospital (founded 1694; now the Mary Erskine School), George Watson's Hospital (founded 1741; now George Watson's College), Daniel Stewart's Hospital (founded in 1855; now part of Stewart's Melville College) and James Gillespie's Hospital and Free School (founded 1803; now James Gillespie's High School). The first three are all now independent day schools and are still managed by the Merchant Company, while the fourth, which in 1908 was handed over to the Edinburgh School Board, is now a state-run comprehensive. (For a reference to 'merchant school old boys', *see under* SCHEME.)

Mercurius Caledonius Scotland's first newspaper, launched on 31 December 1660, and running to 12 issues before folding. Its editor was the playwright Thomas Sydserf, who had served under Montrose, and its aim was to report 'the affairs now in agitation in Scotland with a survey of foreign intelligence'. Sydserf himself quoted Cicero, declaring that he would 'assert no falsehood and hide no truth'. A second *Caledonian Mercury* was launched in 1720, and continued to publish until 1867. A third *Cale-*

donian Mercury, an online newspaper, was launched in 2010.

Meringues An Englishman walks into a Glasgow bakery and points at an item. 'Is that a marshmallow or a meringue?' 'Nah, yer right,' says the salesgirl. 'It's a marshmallow.' *See also* BOUNTY; COMFY?

Merlin's Grave According to tradition, the burial place of the Arthurian wizard is near Drumelzier, on the Tweed in Peeblesshire; today the Ordnance Survey marks 'Merlindale' just across the river from the village, but not the site of the grave. (According to another tradition, he is buried near Carmarthen in Wales.) Merlin had himself predicted that he would die by falling, hanging and drowning, and so it turned out (according to the story of 'Lailoken and Kentigern'): he was chased over the bluffs on the banks of the Tweed, fell onto the salmon nets below, was caught by his ankles, and, hanging upside down, was drowned in the river. His grave played a part in another prophecy, one of those uttered by THOMAS THE RHYMER:

> When Tweed and Powsail meet at Merlin's grave,
> England and Scotland shall one monarch have.

Alexander Penecuik, in his *Geographical, Historical Description of Tweedale* (1715), says:

> The particular place of his grave, at the root of a thorn-tree, was shown me many years ago, by the old and reverend minister of the place, Mr Richard Brown, and here was the old prophecy fulfilled.

For, says Penecuik, on the day when James VI of Scotland became James I of England, the Tweed overflowed here into the nearby Powsail Burn. Robert Chambers – himself a Peebles man – would have none of it, commenting that 'there is nothing in the local circumstances to make the meeting of the two waters at that spot in the least wonderful, as Merlin's Grave is in the haugh or meadow close to the Tweed, which the river must of course cover whenever it is in flood' (*Popular Rhymes of Scotland*, 1826).

Mermaid In addition to the mermaids and mermen described below, *see also* BLUE MEN OF THE MINCH;

EYNHALLOW (for Fin Folk); SILKIE FOLK; TROW (for sea-trows).

Mermaid of Benbecula, the In 1830 it was reported that a boy throwing stones into the sea had fatally injured a small mermaid off the coast of Benbecula. Her body was washed up on the shore two days later, and seventy years later was described as follows by the Gaelic scholar Alexander Carmichael:

> The upper part of the creature was about the size of a well-fed child of three or four years of age, with an abnormally developed breast. The hair was long, dark and glossy, while the skin was white, soft and tender. The lower part of the body was like a salmon, but without scales.

The local sheriff organized for the creature's burial, but no funeral service was held.

Mermaid of Galloway, the According to R.H. Cromek in his *Remains of Nithsdale and Galloway Song* (1810), this mermaid lived in a pool where Dalbeattie Burn flows into Urr Water. At night she would sit on a rock and give the local populace the benefit of her medical knowledge, until one local woman, a religious zealot, pushed the rock into the pool – only to find on her return home that her baby lay dead in its cradle. Thereafter the mermaid was heard to sing:

> Ye may look i' yere toom [empty] cradle,
> And I'll look to my stane;
> And meikle we'll think, and meikle we'll look,
> But words we'll ne'er hae nane!

After that the woman made the pool uninhabitable for the mermaid by throwing in all kinds of weeds and filth – but she herself was left barren.

Mermaid of Knockdolian Castle, the The ruined tower of Knockdolian Castle stands by the River Stinchar in Ayrshire, and the story of the local mermaid is told by Robert Chambers in his *Popular Rhymes of Scotland* (1870 edition). She used to sit at night upon a black stone by the water, singing while she combed her long yellow hair. But this would disturb the slumbers of the infant heir of Knockdolian, so his mother ordered that the stone upon

which the mermaid sat be broken. When the mermaid returned the next night to find her throne in pieces, she sang:

> Ye may think on your cradle – I'll think on my
> stane;
> And there'll never be an heir to Knockdolian again.

And so it transpired: soon afterwards the infant heir was found dead beneath his overturned cradle, and this marked the extinction of the family line.

Mermaid of Port Glasgow, the The subject of a local legend. The mermaid in question apparently appeared out of the waves as the funeral of a girl who had died of consumption passed the shore, and smugly pronounced:

> It they wad drink nettles in March,
> And eat muggins [mugwort] in May,
> Sae mony braw maidens
> Wadna gang to the clay.

Mermaid of Sandwood Bay, the *See under* SANDWOOD BAY.

Mermaids of the River Dee, the These creatures, apparently both pious and patriotic, are described in the *Aberdeen Almanac; or, New Prognostications of the Year 1688*:

> To conclude for this year 1688. Near the place where the famous Dee payeth his tribute to the German Ocean [the North Sea], if *curious observers of wonderful things in nature* will be pleased thither to resort the 1, 13, and 29 of May, and in divers other times in the ensuing summer, as also in the harvest time, to the 7 and 14 October, *they will undoubtedly see a pretty company of* MARMAIDS, creatures of admirable beauty, and likewise hear their charming sweet melodious voices:
>> In well tun'd measures and harmonious lays,
>> Extol their Maker and his bounty praise;
>> That godly honest men, in everything,
>> In quiet peace may live, GOD SAVE THE KING!

Merman of Kintyre, the On 29 October 1811 John McIsaac gave the following deposition before the sheriff-substitute at Campbeltown, regarding a merman he had seen on the shores of Kintyre:

The animal, upon the whole was between four and five feet long, as near as he could judge … it had a head, arms and body down to the middle like a human being, only that the arms were short in proportion to the body which appeared to be about the thickness of that of a young lad, and tapering gradually to the point of the tail … for the first time he saw its face, every feature of which he could see distinctly marked, and which, to him, had all the appearance of the face of a human being, with very hollow eyes.

See also BLUE MEN OF THE MINCH.

Meroure of Wyssdome, The A discourse on the duties of a sovereign, written in 1490 for James IV by Dr John Ireland, his private chaplain, who had earlier studied at the University of Paris and conducted diplomatic missions on behalf of Louis XI of France. It is one of the earliest surviving literary prose works in Scots. At one point, while discussing the Lord's Prayer (beginning Pater Noster, 'Our Father'), Ireland asserts a typically Scottish egalitarianism (echoed in later centuries in the assertion that 'We're a' JOCK TAMSON'S BAIRNS'):

This haly and plesand word Noster teichis us that we all, hie and law, riche and puir, yonge and auld, hail and seik, kingis, emperiouris, men and wemen of quhatsumevir state, are sonnies and dochtiris of a Fader, God Omnipotent, and a Moder, the Haly Kirk, and evirilkane sould luif and help othir as brether, sisteris, membris and partis of ane body.

Merrick hills, the See AWFUL HAND, THE.

Merrilies, Meg The tall, awesome prophetess who plays a heroic role in Scott's Guy Mannering. Although described by another character, Dominie Sampson, as 'harlot, thief, witch and gypsy', Meg is also marked by a loyal heart and a fiery eloquence. On her first appearance Scott describes her thus:

She was full six feet high, wore a man's great-coat over the rest of her dress, had in her hand a goodly sloe-thorn cudgel, and in all points of equipment, except her petticoats, seemed rather masculine than feminine. Her dark elf-locks shot out like the snakes of the gorgon between an old-fashioned bonnet called a

bongrace, heightening the singular effect of her strong and weather-beaten features, which they partly shadowed, while her eye had a wild roll that indicated something like real or affected insanity.

In his introduction to the novel, Scott discusses the original of this character: she was one Jean Gordon of Kirk Yetholm, the market town on the north side of the Cheviots that was for long the centre of Scottish gypsy life. She had, Scott says, 'great sway among her tribe … and possessed the savage virtue of fidelity in the same perfection' as Meg Merrilies. As an example of this, she protected a farmer whose hospitality she had once enjoyed from the depredations of her nine sons, notable plunderers who all went to the gallows in Jedburgh on the same day. Jean herself met her end in 1746 in Carlisle. A staunch but incautious Jacobite, she had expressed her sympathies loudly one market day, and been seized by the mob and ducked to death in the River Eden:

It was an operation of some time, for Jean was a stout woman, and, struggling with her murderers, often got her head above water; and, while she had voice left, continued to exclaim at such intervals, 'Charlie yet! Charlie yet!' When a child, and among the scenes which she frequented, I have often heard these stories, and cried piteously for poor Jean Gordon.

In his 'additional note' to the novel, Scott says 'Meg Merrilies is in Galloway considered as having had her origin in the traditions concerning the celebrated Flora Marshal, one of the royal consorts of Willie Marshal, more commonly called the Caird of Barullion, King of the Gipsies of the Western Lowlands.' (See CAIRD O' BARULLION, THE.)

Scott's character inspired a poem by John Keats, written in 1818, but Keats's Meg is an insipid creature compared to Scott's original:

Old Meg she was a Gipsy,
And liv'd upon the Moors:
Her bed it was the brown heath turf,
And her house was out of doors.

See also DINMONT, DANDIE.

Merry-begotten Illegitimate, or at least conceived out of wedlock.

Merry Dancers, the A term, in use since at least the 17th century, for the livelier sort of northern lights or aurora borealis. They are also known as the *Pretty Dancers*, or just the *Dancers*, while in Gaelic they are called *na fir-chlis*, and there is a Gaelic saying that translates as:

When the Merry Dancers play
They are like to slay.

The belief was that the dance of the aurora often ended in violence. The term Merry Dancers is known from Shetland as far south as the Isle of Man:

The merry dancers are out to-night,
In the northern heavens they skip and go;
Manx Jane says they're fairies tripping it light,
On their own fantastic fairy toe.
　　– The Rev. J.E. Pattison, 'The Merry Dancers', from
　　Manxiana: Rhymes and Legends (1870)

The more diffuse and arc-like form of the aurora is known as the *Northern Dawn*. In some places, the Northern Lights are known as *the Streamers. See also* 'NORTHERN LIGHTS OF OLD ABERDEEN, THE'.

Merry hyne to ye, a According to John Jamieson, in his *Etymological Dictionary of the Scottish Language* (1825 Supplement), this is an Aberdeenshire 'mode of bidding good b'ye to one, when the speaker is in an ill humour; as equivalent to "Pack off with you." ' *Hyne* in Old Scots was an adverb meaning 'hence' or 'away', for example, from this life or this world, but in this expression, which survived at least into the 20th century, it is a noun denoting 'departure'.

Merry Men of Mey, the The most extensive and dangerous tidal race in the Pentland Firth. It forms during the west-going tidal stream off the rocks known as the Men of Mey on St John's Point, near the Castle of Mey on the north coast of Caithness. When it really gets going the tidal race extends across the entire Firth, and is at its most violent to the west of the island of Stroma, where large waves can come with no warning from any direction. Regarding the dangers of navigating these waters, Daniel Defoe, in *A Tour Through the Whole Island of Great Britain* (1724–6), wrote that 'the tides are so fierce, so uncertain, and the gusts and sudden squalls of wind so frequent, that very few merchant-ships care to venture through it'. The same might be said to this day. *See also* SWELKIE, THE.

Merry Muses of Caledonia, The A collection of bawdy verses and songs found in one of Burns's notebooks after his death in 1796. Most of them were probably not original to Burns, although it is likely that he improved and polished some of them. The collection was discreetly published in 1799, and was subtitled 'A Collection of Favourite Scots Songs, Ancient and Modern, selected for the use of the CROCHALLAN FENCIBLES', the Edinburgh literary club into which Burns had been enrolled in 1787; only two copies of this edition survive. It wasn't until 1965, five years after the Lady Chatterley trial, that a modern edition was published, edited by James Barke and Sydney Goodsir Smith. In his introduction, Barke wrote of 'the great leaven that breaks through all Scots bawdry. It is never sneering or sly or sexy or prurient or titillating. It is lusty like a good broad female buttock.' Among the pieces in the collection is a version of COMIN' THRO' THE RYE replete with many a 'fuck' and a single 'cunt', and the beautiful love song, 'John Anderson, My Jo', in which an elderly wife tenderly recalls the lost vigour of her man (*jo* means 'sweetheart'):

John Anderson, my jo, John,
　When first that ye began,
Ye had as good a tail-tree
　As ony ither man;
But now it's waxen wan, John,
　And wrinkles to and fro;
I've twa gae-ups for ae gae-down,
　John Anderson, my jo.

See also MUIRLAND MEG.

Mes or **Mess John** A former nickname for a minister. *Mes* is an abbreviation of master – clergymen often held the degree of master of arts – and was used as a title in a similar fashion to 'Reverend' until supplanted by the latter in the later 19th century.

Nae dominie, or wise Mess John,
Was better lear'd in Solomon;
He cited proverbs one by one
　Ilk vice to tame;
He gar'd ilk sinner sigh an' groan,
　And fear hell's flame.
　　– Robert Fergusson, 'Elegy on John Hogg, late Porter to
　　the University of St Andrews' (1773) [*lear'd*, 'learned']

Messages, to do the To do the shopping. More generally, a *message* is an errand, while *the messages* are more specifically the routine items purchased on a regular basis.

> For the first time in my life I had no messages to go, either for Grannie, or anybody else. No duties of any kind.
>> – Molly Weir, *Best Foot Forward* (1974)

Messenger of the Campbells, the The magpie (*pyot* in Scots).

> The pyet (*piaghaid*) is called 'the messenger of the Campbells' (*gille ruith nan Caimbeulach*), a name also given (for what reason the writer has not been able to ascertain) to a person who is 'garrulous, lying, interfering with everybody' (*gobach, briagach, 'g obair air na h-uile duine*). It is said of a meddling chatterbox, 'What a messenger of the Campbells you have become!'
>> – John G. Campbell, *Superstitions of the Highlands and Islands of Scotland* (1900)

See also DEVIL'S BIRD, THE.

Mester Stoor Worm In Orkney lore, a sea monster, one of the curses of humankind, whose story was first preserved in the late 19th century by the Orcadian folklorist Walter Traill Dennison. The Stoor Worm – a creature possessed of poisonous breath and a habit of smashing ships as if they were eggs – was given the honorific title 'Mester' to denote its complete mastery of malevolence. Its forked tongue was so powerful it could swipe away castles and even whole cities, and any kingdom near which the Stoor Worm took up its habitation found that it could only prevent such eventualities by supplying the monster with a weekly diet of seven virgins. The king of one such kingdom was advised by a wizard that this would only stop if the king offered up his own daughter to the monster. To avoid losing his daughter, the king promised his kingdom to any man who could kill the Stoor Worm. Many tried in vain. In the end, there came to the court a farmer's son called Assipattle – a lazy male version of Cinderella, who 'pattles' his feet in the ashes while dreaming up heroic fantasies. Assipattle succeeds in destroying the monster, having sailed a boat into the Stoor Worm's vast interior and inserted a burning peat into a wound in the crea-

ture's liver. As the fire grew it began to consume the mighty Stoor Worm, whose falling teeth became the islands of Orkney and Shetland. *Stoor* may perhaps come from Old Norse *stour*, 'battle, conflict'.

Meteorological and other natural phenomena
See:
- BANFF BAILLIES
- BUCKIEMAN'S TOOTH
- COCK'S EYE
- COO'S QUAKE
- CORRYVRECKAN
- DEATH CANDLE
- DEID-LICHTS
- DOG AFORE HIS MAISTER, THE
- EARL OF MORAY WILL NOT BE LONG IN DEBT TO THE EARL OF MAR, THE
- FIRE BURN
- FLANDERS FROST
- FLATTERIN' FRIDAY
- FOLKS IN ORKNEY ARE PLUCKING GEESE, the
- GAB O' MAY
- GENTLE ANNIE
- GOAT'S HAIR
- GOWK STORM
- GREY DOGS, the
- The guid folk's baking day (see under GUID FOLK)
- HURRICANE BAWBAG
- JOCK-NIP-THE-NEB
- KERTIN MARY
- KING'S WEATHER
- LAUCHIN RAIN
- LIDDESDALE DROW
- MARCH SUD COME IN LIKE A BOAR'S HEAD, AN GANG OOT LIKE A PEACOCK'S TAIL
- MEG'S HOLE
- MERRY DANCERS, the
- MERRY MEN OF MEY, the
- MOON
- MUCKLE FORESTER, the
- MURK MONDAY
- PARALLEL ROADS OF GLEN ROY, the
- RAINBOWS AND RELATED PHENOMENA
- RAININ' AULD WIVES AN' PIKE STAVES
- RAISING THE WIND
- ST CAUSLAN'S FLOW
- SHAKY VILLAGE, the

- SILK NAPKIN
- SONG OF THE SEA, the
- SUMMER HAS LEAPED SUDDENLY UPON EDINBURGH LIKE A TIGER
- SWELKIE, the
- WITCH'S HOLE
- WOLF'S TEETH
- YOWE TRUMMLE

Methane bubbles from the Witch's Hole *See* WITCH'S HOLE.

Methodome, the The nickname awarded by the citizens of Paisley to St Mirren FC's new ground in Greenhill Road, where they moved for the 2008–9 season. The nickname puns on methadone, as the new St Mirren Park borders Ferguslie Park, an estate apparently notorious for its troubles with drug dependency. *See also* BUDDY; FOOTBALL CLUB NICKNAMES.

Mice and rats, a charm against *See* PEST CONTROL.

Michael or **Mickey** Formerly a jocular euphemism for a chamber pot or privy. The name may be an abbreviation of *micturation*. The name *Michael* also formerly denoted a boor or bumpkin of either sex.

Michael Wylie The nickname, derived from Machiavelli and punning on 'wily', of William Maitland of Lethington, emissary to the English during the negotiations resulting in the Treaty of Berwick (1560).

Michty me! Goodness me! *Michty* is Scots for 'mighty', and the expression is a euphemism for 'God Almighty!' Sometimes the word is used on its own, or in expressions such as *Michty be here!* or *Michty on's!* These days such expressions smack of FAUX JOCKERY.

Mickey *See* MICHAEL.

Midden A dunghill or refuse heap. For *midden-raker* and *midden mavis, see under* MIDGIE-RAKER. For *either i' the mune or the midden* and *glower at the mune till one falls i' the midden, see under* MOON. *See also* ANNACKER'S MIDDEN.

Midden, flight ends ingloriously in a *See* BIRDMAN OF STIRLING CASTLE, THE.

Midden, preferring to be buried at the bottom of a *See* WORST OF KINGS AND THE MOST MISERABLE OF MEN, THE.

Middle Shires The name that James VI and I decreed be given to the Borders following the Union of the Crowns in 1603, having asserted that 'the late marches and borders of the two realms of England and Scotland are now the heart of the country'. This marked James's determination, following ILL WEEK, to end the era of the BORDER REIVERS, as stated in a decree issued once James had arrived in London in the early summer of 1603:

> He ordered all places of strength in those parts to be demolished except the habitation of noblemen and barons; their iron yetts [gates] to be converted into plough irons and their inhabitants to betake themselves to agriculture and other works of peace.

James wasted little time in enforcing his will: hundreds of known reivers were rounded up, taken to Dumfries, Carlisle and Jedburgh, and hanged, with little regard for due process – hence (possibly) the expression JEDDART JUSTICE.

Midgie-raker Someone who goes through other people's rubbish, in the hope of discovering a pearl beyond compare. The term *midgie* for rubbish or refuse came into use in the later 20th century, hence dustmen are *midgie-men*. The earlier name for a *midgie-raker* was a *midden-raker* (a *midden* being a dunghill or refuse heap), and the female equivalent was a *midden mavis* (*mavis*, 'song thrush'). *See also* ANNACKER'S MIDDEN.

Mighty Mouse The nickname of the rugby union player Ian McLauchlan (b.1942), who played for Scotland as loose-head prop between 1969 and 1979. He was capped 43 times, and captained Scotland on 19 occasions, 10 of which were Scottish victories. His nickname refers to the fact that he was relatively small but immensely powerful – like the cartoon character of the same name.

Mile, Scots *See* SCOTS MILE.

Mill yin Literally 'mill one', i.e. a factory worker.

Mim as a May puddock Literally, 'prudish as a frog in May', a simile applied to 'a mincing, ultra-modesty-affecting manner in a woman', according to J. Riddell in *Aberdeen and Its Folk* (1868). Frogs supposedly remained silent from May till the advent of autumn.

Minch, Blue Men of the *See* BLUE MEN OF THE MINCH.

Mincy heid A crazy person, from slang *mince*, 'nonsense', as in 'Yer talkin' mince.'

Miners, the *See* FOOTBALL CLUB NICKNAMES.

Ming the Merciless How the press dubbed Sir Menzies ('Ming') Campbell (b.1941), after he had taken over the leadership of the Liberal Democrats from fellow-Scot Charles Kennedy (aka CHAMPAGNE CHARLIE) in March 2006. Campbell himself was ousted from the leadership in October 2007 by a CLEG(G). The nickname refers to Ming the Merciless, the tyrannical emperor of the Planet Mongo in the pre-war strip cartoon *Flash Gordon* (and the 1980 feature film of the same name). Incidentally, the pronunciation of 'Menzies' as 'Mingis' (hence *Ming*) is explained by the fact that the 'z' in Menzies (and in some other names) is actually an attempt to depict the obsolete character ȝ (called a 'yogh'). This state of affairs has given rise to the following limerick:

There wis a young lassie named Menzies,
That asked her aunt whit this thenzies.
Said her aunt wi a gasp,
'Ma dear, it's a wasp,
An you're haudin the end whaur the stenzies!'

Ministers' Altar, the The satirical nickname given to the scaffold in Edinburgh upon which the Marquess of Montrose and other Royalist officers were executed in 1650.

After Montrose's death, the scaffold which was set up at the Cross for the mangling of his body was, contrary to all former custom, kept unremoved near two months, for the execution of the Scots officers who were taken with him … so that it became all covered with blood and gore, and was called the Ministers' Altar, of whom is was sarcastically observed … that they delighted not in unbloody sacrifices.
– John Skinner, *The Ecclesiastical History of Scotland* (1788). Skinner, Episcopalian dean of Aberdeen, was also the author of 'TULLOCHGORUM'.

Minstrelsy of the Scottish Border A collection of Border ballads published in three volumes in 1802–3, compiled by Sir Walter Scott with the aid of others, including James Hogg (the ETTRICK SHEPHERD), John Leyden, Robert Surtees and many old women, including Hogg's mother, Margaret Laidlaw. Scott himself outlined his purpose in the introduction:

By such efforts, feeble as they are, I may contribute somewhat to the history of my native country; the peculiar features of whose manners and character are daily melting and dissolving into those of her sister and ally.

Not everything was as authentic as more modern folklorists and ethnomusicologists might wish: Scott was not above 'improving' on the originals to varying degrees, and at least one contribution from Surtees ('The Death of Featherstonhaugh') was entirely his own creation. Hogg himself felt that, in committing the old ballads to print, something had died:

These songs had floated down on the stream of oral tradition, from generation to generation, and were regarded as a precious treasure belonging to the country; but when Mr Scott's work appeared their arcanum was laid open, and a deadening blow was inflicted on our rural literature.
– James Hogg, 'On the Changes in the Habits, Amusements and Condition of the Scotch Peasantry', in *The Quarterly Journal of Agriculture*, 1831–2

Hogg's mother was not impressed by Scott's efforts, and told him so – at least according to Hogg's *Familiar Anecdotes of Sir Walter Scott* (1834):

… there war never ane o' my songs prentit till ye prentit them yoursel', an' ye hae spoilt them awthegither. They war made for singing an' no for reading; but ye hae broken the charm now, an' they'll never be sung mair. An' the worst thing of a', they're nouther right spell'd nor right setten down.

Scott himself, later in life, regretted his methodology:

I think I did wrong myself in endeavouring to make the best possible set of an ancient ballad out of several copies obtained from different quarters, and that, in many respects, if I improved the poetry, I spoiled the simplicity of an old song.

– Letter to Motherwell, 3 May 1825

Nearly a century later, Lauchlan Maclean Watt, in his *Scottish Life and Poetry* (1912), opined:

It was unfortunate for the Scottish ballads that so many who collected such things were able to write creditable verse, while the master of romance himself was the head of the enterprise.

Mirror of Wisdom, The *See* MEROURE OF WYSS-DOME, THE.

Misery from the Manse, the A nickname given to Gordon Brown (b.1951), Glasgow-born and Kirk-caldy-raised Labour prime minister from 2007 to 2010. In the role of Chancellor of the Exchequer from 1997 to 2007, he earned, owing to his much-vaunted prudence, the sobriquet 'The Iron Chancellor' – or 'Irn-Brun' (*see* IRN-BRU). Brown's father was a minister of the Church of Scotland, so Brown himself is a SON OF THE MANSE, while his public persona was thought by some to convey a certain joylessness, possibly related to his frustration during the ten years that Tony Blair occupied Downing Street – hence another nickname, 'The Incredible Sulk' (after the American comic-book character, the Incredible Hulk). He was also known as 'The BROON'.

In 2006 Brown won the Miserabilist of the Year award from Spiked Online. 'With his dour personality, dour politics and dour outlook on life, he is a more than deserving winner', the judges opined.

Mississippi Bubble, the *See* PAPER KING, THE.

Mistress and mair Literally 'mistress and more', a term applied to the preeminent and not-to-be-questioned authority who lords it over a household. If it is the man of the house who wears the trousers, he is *maister and mair*.

'She [her sister Jeanie] wad hand me nae better than the dirt below her feet,' said Effie to herself, 'were I to confess I hae danced wi' him four times on the green down by, and ance at Maggie Macqueens's; and she'll maybe hing it ower my head that she'll tell my father, and then she wad be mistress and mair. But I'll no gang back there again ...'

– Sir Walter Scott, *The Heart of Midlothian* (1818), chapter x

Misty Isle, the A rough translation of *Eilean a' Cheò* ('island of mist'), by which the island of Skye is known in Gaelic song and verse. Strangely enough, the English version has been picked up by the tourism promoters, unabashed at the island's reputation for wet weather. In 2007 there was a rumour that Highland Council were replacing the name 'Skye' with *Eilean a' Cheò*, which caused considerable consternation until it transpired that the latter name was simply to be used for a new electoral ward, encompassing the islands of Skye and Raasay. *See also* LAND OF MISTS.

Mither o' the Sea *See* SEA MITHER.

Mither's Carritch *See* CARRITCH.

Mixter-maxter or **mixtie-maxtie** Jumbled, confused, chaotic, or a collection of items in such a condition.

Yon mixtie-maxtie queer hotch-potch.
– Robert Burns, 'The Author's Earnest Cry and Prayer' (1786)

Mod, the An annual festival of Gaelic culture, featuring competitions in areas such as choral singing, instrumental performance and poetry reading. The Mod (from Gaelic *mòd*, 'meeting, assembly') was founded by An Comunn Gàidhealach (the Gaelic Association) and was first held in 1892 in Oban. The equivalent of the Welsh Eisteddfod, it is now officially known as Am Mòd Nàiseanta Rìoghail (the Royal National Mod). Many a Gaelic singer's professional career begins with winning a gold medal at the Mod.

Moderator, the The minister who presides over the GENERAL ASSEMBLY.

Tall, ruffed and gaitered, the Moderator
of the General Assembly of the Church of Scotland
waltzes the minute figure of Ernie Finnie
across the dead water.

    – Tom Buchan, 'Iona', from *Dolphins at Cochin* (1969)

Moffat toffee Not really a toffee, more of a boiled sweet, striped amber and gold and with a tangy centre. It was first made commercially in Moffat in the late 19th century by Janet Cook Johnstone.

Moladh Beinn Dòbhrainn See PRAISE OF BEN DORAIN.

Mole aboot or **mollach aboot** To wander about aimlessly; to loiter without intent. The reference is to the apparently random patterns of molehills in a field. The phrase comes from Aberdeenshire, where *mollach* is a word for 'mole'.

Monarch Country See *MONARCH OF THE GLEN*.

Monarch of the Glen A portrait of a magnificent red deer stag by Sir Edwin Landseer, painted in 1851 from studies he made in Glen Quoich. When the painting was first exhibited at the Royal Academy in London, the catalogue entry included the following lines from an unknown poem entitled 'Legends of Glenorchay':

> Up rose the Monarch of the Glen
> Majestic from his lair,
> Surveyed the scene with piercing ken,
> And snuffed the fragrant air.

The painting was commissioned as one of three panels on hunting themes to hang in the Refreshment Rooms of the House of Lords, but when payment was not forthcoming, Landseer sold it to a private collector. It later came into the possession of the whisky firm John Dewars & Sons, now part of Diageo.

Compton Mackenzie borrowed the title for his 1941 comic novel about a Highland laird fallen on hard times, trying to maintain his castle of Glenbogle. This in turn provided the basic premise for the BBC TV Sunday-night drama *Monarch of the Glen*, which ran to seven series between 2000 and 2005. It starred a number of celebrated character

actors such as Richard Briers, Susan Hampshire, Tom Baker and Julian Fellowes, and was filmed in around Badenoch and Strathspey (which for a while became known as 'Monarch Country'). Glenbogle House was played by Ardverikie House, a magnificent Scottish baronial pile on Loch Laggan, while the village of Glenbogle was played by the village of Laggan, with walk-on parts for Newtonmore, Kingussie and Carrbridge. Fans of the show dubbed themselves 'Boglies'.

Monday's haddie See WELL-HUNG FISH.

Mondegreen See 'BONNIE EARL O' MORAY, THE'.

Monks' Road The old path over the Pentlands from Balerno to Nine Mile Burn. Quite what the monastic connection might have been is unknown, but the path passes near to Spittal Hill and Spittal Farm, names that suggest the lands hereabouts once belonged to a hospital or hospice run by monks.

Mons Graupius The site of a battle fought in AD 84 somewhere in northeast Scotland, in which the Romans under Agricola defeated the Caledonians. Although resounding, the Roman victory achieved little, and after the battle the Romans marched back south to the Tweed. It was the last documented battle the Romans fought in Britain.

Where the battle was fought is uncertain, and its location has long been debated by historians. The name does not help: *Mons* is Latin for 'hill', but the meaning of *Graupius* is obscure, although it is from this that the Grampians take their name (possibly via a mistranscription made by the historian Hector Boece in 1520). One of the more likely contenders for the location of the battle is a site on the northern side of Bennachie, 20 miles (32 km) northwest of Aberdeen.

Tacitus, in his life of Agricola, puts a famous prebattle speech into the mouth of the Caledonian commander, a chief he calls Calgacus (possibly from Celtic *Calgaich*, 'swordsman'), who weighs into the *modus operandi* of the Romans thus:

> To us who dwell on the uttermost confines of the earth
> and of freedom, this remote sanctuary of Britain's glory
> has up to this time been a defence. Now, however, the

furthest limits of Britain are thrown open, and the unknown always passes for the marvellous. But there are no tribes beyond us, nothing indeed but waves and rocks, and the yet more terrible Romans, from whose oppression escape is vainly sought by obedience and submission. Robbers of the world, having by their universal plunder exhausted the land, they rifle the deep. If the enemy be rich, they are rapacious; if he be poor, they lust for dominion; neither the east nor the west has been able to satisfy them. Alone among men they covet with equal eagerness poverty and riches. To robbery, slaughter, plunder, they give the lying name of empire; they make a wilderness and call it peace [*Ubi solitudinem faciunt pacem appellant*].

The criticism of the Roman way is perhaps surprising in a history that lauds the successes of Agricola, Tacitus's own father-in-law. However, throughout the work Tacitus points up the love of freedom of the inhabitants of Britannia as a way of criticizing the corruption and tyranny of the Roman empire.

Mons Meg A massive 15th-century cannon mounted on the ramparts of Edinburgh Castle, pointing out over the New Town. It weighs over 6 tons, and its cannonballs have a diameter of 21 inches (52.5 cm). Mons Meg takes the first part of its name from the town of Mons in Flanders, where it was made. The second part, 'Meg', subsequently became a popular name for artillery pieces: a Roaring Meg cut swathes through the Roundhead lines at the Battle of Hopton Heath in 1643, and another of that name saw action at the Siege of Londonderry in 1689. In Galloway there is an alternative explanation of the name 'Mons Meg'. This holds that it was made in 1435 at the behest of James II by a smith of Castle Douglas called Mouncey (or McKim), with the aim of knocking down the walls of Threave Castle, the stronghold of the rebellious Douglases; it was supposedly nicknamed 'Mouncey's Meg' (or 'McKim's Meg') after the smith's noisy wife.

Mons Meg's useful life came to an end in 1680, when the Duke of Albany and York (later James VII and II) visited Edinburgh. Lord Fountainhall takes up the tale:

A little after his arrival, having visited the Castle of Edinburgh, and for a testimony of joy the gun called

Mons Meg, being charged by the advice of an English cannoneer, in the shooting was riven, which some foolishly called a bad omen. The Scots resented it extremely, thinking the Englishman might of malice have done it purposely, they having no cannon in England so big as she.

Mons Meg was removed to London in 1754, but in 1829 its return to Scotland was secured by Sir Walter Scott, who in March of that year noted in his Journal:

Mons Meg is a monument of our pride and poverty. The size is immense, but six smaller guns would have been made at the same expense, and done six times as much execution as she could have done.

The great cannon was celebrated by Robert Fergusson:

Oh willawins! Mons Meg, for you,
'Twas firing crack'd thy muckle mou;
What black mishanter gart ye spew
        Baith gut and ga'?
I fear they bang'd thy belly fu'
        Against the law.
    – 'The King's Birth-Day in Edinburgh'

Monster Butler, the The Glasgow-born serial killer Archibald Hall (1924–2002). He began his criminal career as a jewel thief, and studied the mores of the aristocracy while serving a prison term, enabling him to launch a parallel career as a butler. Thereafter he divided his time between butling and thieving. His first victim was David Wright, a former lover of Hall's who threatened to reveal his criminal past to his employer. Hall subsequently became butler to an elderly couple, Walter and Dorothy Scott-Elliott, whom he murdered when they interrupted him while he discussed with his associate Michael Kitto how they were going to steal the couple's money. The killers drove the bodies up to Scotland to bury them, aided by a prostitute called Mary Coggle. When Coggle herself started drawing too much attention by wearing Dorothy's clothes and jewellery, Hall and Kitto decided that she too must go. Hall's final victim was his hated half-brother Donald, a paedophile whom he drowned in the bath. Kitto and Hall put the body in the boot of their car, where it was discovered by the police, who had been following up on a number of leads pointing at Kitto and Hall. The police told Kitto that he was lucky to be arrested, as Hall had intended him as his next victim. Both were sentenced to life imprisonment, Hall receiving a whole-life tariff. While in prison, Hall published his autobiography, entitled *A Perfect Gentleman* (1999).

Monster of Glamis, the *See under* EARL BEARDIE.

Monstrous Regiment of Women A phrase coined by John Knox in his work *The First Blast of the Trumpet Against the Monstrous Regiment of Women*, published in 1558 from the safety of his exile in Geneva. In this context 'regiment' means 'rule' or 'government', and Knox is referring to the Catholic queens regnant of Scotland and England, Mary Queen of Scots and Mary Tudor.

> To promote a woman to bear rule, superiority, dominion or empire above any realm, nation or city, is repugnant to Nature, contumely to God, a thing most contrary to his revealed will and approved ordinance, and finally it is a subversion of good order, of all equity and justice.

Shortly afterwards, Mary of England was succeeded by the Protestant Elizabeth, who took exception to Knox's diatribe, and prevented his involvement in the English Reformation.

Month o' munes, a A very long time.

Mony a mickle maks a muckle An old proverb, taken to mean 'Many small things add up to a big thing', 'Every little helps', and thought to encapsulate the virtues of financial prudence, saving for a rainy day, etc. In 1793 George Washington, a cautious commander if ever there was one, referred to 'a Scotch adage, than which nothing in nature is more true "that many mickles make a muckle"'. Somewhat confusingly, *mickle* is in fact a variant of *muckle*, so also, like *muckle*, means (in this context) a large quantity, thus seemingly draining the proverb of sense. In his *Scottish Proverbs* (2nd edn, 2000), Colin Walker states that the proverb was originally 'Mony a pickle maks a mickle', a *pickle* being a grain of cereal or salt, or any small amount. Another variant, in standard English, is 'Many a little makes a

mickle', recorded in this form in William Camden's *Remaines of a Greater Worke, Concerning Britaine* (2nd edn, 1614); *mickle* (from Old English *micel*, 'much') is now archaic in Britain apart from Scotland and northern England.

Moon Regarding the new moon, John Jamieson has this to say in his *Etymological Dictionary of the Scottish Language* (1808):

> It is considered an almost infallible presage of bad weather, if the new moon lies sair on her back, or when her horns are pointed towards the zenith.

There is also the famous stanza from 'Sir Patrick Spens', describing the 'auld mune in the airms o' the new', i.e. when the disc of the full moon can just be descried within the crescent moon, thought to herald a storm:

> I saw the new moon late yestreen
> Wi' the auld moon in her arm;
> And if we gang to sea master,
> I fear we'll come to harm.

For another presage of bad weather relating to the moon, *see* COCK'S EYE.

The appearance of the new moon gave an opportunity for love divination. In *Popular Rhymes of Scotland* (1826), Robert Chambers records that young women in the Lowlands would, on seeing the new moon, utter the following rhyme:

> New mune, true mune, tell unto me,
> If [naming their favourite lover], my true-love, he
>   will marry me.
> If he marry me in haste,
> Let me see his bonnie face;
> If he marry me betide,
> Let me see his bonnie side;
> Gin he marry na me ava,
> Turn his back and gae awa.

Chambers also records that:

> The young women in Galloway, when they first see the new moon, sally out of doors and pull a handful of grass, saying:

> New mune, true mune, tell me if you can,
> Gif I hae here a hair like the hair o my gudeman.

The grass is then brought into the house, where it is carefully searched, and if a hair be found amongst it, which is generally the case, the colour of that hair determines that of the future husband.

To be *mune-brunt* ('moon-burnt'), is to be moon-struck, i.e. half mad, while to be *either i' the mune or the midden* ('dunghill') suggests one is suffering from bipolar disorder. To *glower at the mune till one falls i' the midden* is to be lost in a maze of dreams and fantasies

See also BACK O' THE MUNE, AT THE; MACFAR-LANE'S BOWAT; MAN I' THE MUNE, THE; MONTH O' MUNES, A; THERE WILL BE MOONLIGHT AGAIN; TWA MEENS I' THE LIFT.

Moonlight flit See FLIT.

Moor of the Clans See MUIR OF THE CLANS.

Moorpark See WINE ALLEY.

Moose's meat A disparaging name for cheese (*moose*, 'mouse').

Mooth like the Clyde Tunnel, a A gaping maw.

Morag The familiar name given to the monster that supposedly inhabits Loch Morar, which, with a depth of 309 m (1017 ft) is the deepest body of freshwater in Britain, and thus an inspiration to the credulous. Various sightings of a long serpent-like creature have been claimed, beginning in 1887, but investigations have provided no evidence of the beast's existence. See also LOCH NESS MONSTER.

Morave An old name for an inhabitant of Moray, from the medieval Latin *Moravus*, derived in turn from Gaelic *Moireabh*. Hector Boece, in his *History of Scotland* (1527), distinguishes between 'Scottis, Pichtis, Moravis and Britouns', and suggested that the 'Moravis' were 'pepill of Germany'.

'Moray, The Bonnie Earl of See 'BONNIE EARL O' MORAY, THE'.

More hair on their thievish faces than clothes to cover their nakedness See PICTS.

Mormaer An ancient Celtic office of uncertain rank. The word probably comes from Gaelic *mór*, 'great' + *maer*, 'steward', and is translated in medieval Latin documents as *comes*, 'earl'. There were mormaers of Buchan, Mar, Moray, Angus and Lennox, but their precise role is not known. They may have been the precursors or successors of the 'sub-kings' of the so-called seven Celtic earldoms of ALBA: Angus, Atholl, Fife, Mar (including Buchan), Moray (including Ross) and Strathearn; the identity of the seventh is uncertain, possibly Caithness or Argyll or Menteith or Lennox.

Morningside accent An overly refined version of a Scottish accent, as traditionally affected by the upwardly aspirational residents of Morningside, an affluent southern suburb of Edinburgh (hence cocaine is sometimes referred to as *Morningside speed*). The Glasgow equivalent is the KELVINSIDE ACCENT. See also AW FUR COAT AN NAE KNICKERS; SEX.

Moscow Disappointingly, the village of this name near Kilmarnock has nothing to do with the capital of Russia. The name derives from Brythonic *magos* (*cf.* Welsh *maes*), 'open field, plain', and *collen* (*cf.* Gaelic *coll*), 'hazel'.

Moss laird A facetious term for a tenant farmer who took over poor moorland for a nominal rent in return for improving it. The term was in use in the 18th and 19th centuries, and was particularly applied to those attempting to work the marshy ground of Flanders Moss in the upper Forth valley to the west of Stirling. The Flanders Moss scheme was initiated in the 1770s by Henry Home, Lord Kaimes, who offered tenants (mostly from the Highlands) a spade and as much land as they could drain up to ten acres, with no rent payable for the first 19 years.

Moss troopers Irregular troops, deserters or other BROKEN MEN who during the turbulence of the mid-17th century pursued careers as raiders along the Border, after the suppression of the traditional families of BORDER REIVERS. The name derives from their natural habitat among the moors and bogs of the Border hills. In his *Letters and Speeches of*

Oliver Cromwell (1845), Thomas Carlyle talks of 'Rebellion ... with much mosstroopery and horse-stealing.' In the Borders, clumps of bog cotton were also formerly called moss troopers.

Most Ancient Order of the Thistle, the *See* ORDER OF THE THISTLE.

Most beautiful if not the most romantic village in Scotland, the Sir Walter Scott's description of the Border market town of Kelso, where he spent six months studying at the grammar school while living with his Aunt Jenny.

Most Scottish Person in the World, The Wee Jimmy Krankie (apparently). *See* KRANKIES, THE.

Most signposted nowhere on the planet, the Crianlarich, according to Jim Crumley in his *Gulfs of Blue Air: A Highland Journey* (1977). The village is little more than a railway station and a road junction, but signs to it may be seen as far away as Perth.

Most unpopular visitor to Scotland since Rudolf Hess crash-landed, the The description by 'Clogger' in the *Guardian* newspaper (24 February 2004) of Berti Vogts, the German manager of Scotland's international football team, after it went down 3–0 to Wales. Vogts, who took up the job in 2002, resigned in November 2004 after Scotland's draw with Moldova ended its hopes of qualifying for the 2006 World Cup.

Most wretched, servile, miserable pathetic trash that was ever shat intae creation, the *See* LOWEST OF THE FUCKIN LOW, THE.

Motherwell vs Hamilton The rivalry of the two Lanarkshire towns, which scowl at each other across the great divide of the M74, is summed up in the following saying, once popular in Motherwell:

What's Motherwell famous for? Coal and steel. What's Hamilton famous for? Stealin' coal.

Both coal and steel are now long gone.

Mottoes For some of the more interesting Scottish mottoes (both formal and informal), *see*:

- ALOREBURN
- BIGGAR'S BIGGER
- DOE OR DIE
- E'EN DO AND SPARE NOCHT
- Free for a Blast (*see under* HUNT OF PENTLAND, THE)
- IN MY DEFENS GOD ME DEFEND
- IN MY END IS MY BEGINNING
- IT'S A FAR CRY TO LOCHAWE!
- *JUDEX DAMNATUR UBI NOCENS ABSOLVITUR*
- LET GLASGOW FLOURISH
- *MACDONNIL FATO HIC*
- Mak Siccar (*see under* RED COMYN, THE)
- MAY PRICK NOR PURSE NE'ER FAIL YOU
- *NEC TAMEN CONSUMEBATUR*
- *NEMO ME IMPUNE LACESSIT*
- NEVER BEHIND!
- TOUCH NOT THE CAT BUT A GLOVE
- WHA DAUR MEDDLE WI ME?

Mountain dew A fanciful term for whisky distilled in some remote spot among the mountains, perhaps illicitly.

I tell him, that I never saw, or tasted, a glass of unlawful aqua vitae in the house of my Landlord; nay, that, on the contrary, we needed not such devices, in respect of a pleasing and somewhat seductive liquor, which was vended and consumed at the Wallace Inn, under the name of mountain dew.
  – Sir Walter Scott, *Old Mortality* (1816), introduction

Mountain Dew, *clear* as a Scot's understanding,
Pure as his conscience wherever he goes,
Warm as his heart to the friends he has chosen,
Strong as his arm when he fights with his foes!
  – Charles Mackay, *Poetry and Humour of the Scottish Language* (1882)

See also ARRAN WATER.

Mountain folk *See* COVENANTERS.

'Mouse, To a' *See* BEST-LAID SCHEMES.

Moy, Rout of *See* ROUT OF MOY.

Mr McNotty *See* MCNOTTY, MR.

Mrs Barbour's Army The nickname given to the protestors involved in the Glasgow rent strike of

1915, who were largely organized by Mary Barbour, née Rough (1875–1958), the daughter of a carpet weaver. In 1920 she was elected to Glasgow town council, the first-ever Labour woman councillor, and went on to campaign for improved health and welfare provision for her constituents in Govan.

Mrs MacClarty A name given to any housewife considered below par in the cleanliness stakes. *Clarty* means 'mucky, filthy', and the original Mrs MacClarty was a character in Elizabeth Hamilton's novel, *The Cottagers of Glenburnie* (1808), a popular and improving satire on the manners of the Scottish peasantry. The novel was greeted by the *Edinburgh Review* as 'a specimen of the purest and most characteristic Scotch which we have lately met with in writing'.

> 'And cannot you be fash'd to go to the end of the house to throw out your dirty water? don't you see how small a drain would from that carry it down to the river, instead of remaining here to stagnate, and to suffocate you with intolerable stench?'
> 'O, we're just used to it,' said Mrs MacClarty, 'and never mind it. We cou'dna be fash'd to gang sae far wi' a' the slaistery.'
> – Elizabeth Hamilton, *The Cottagers of Glenburnie* (1808), chapter 7

See also CLARTYHOLE.

Mrs Wummin A form of address, in Glasgow and elsewhere, to a woman whose name one does not know; the female equivalent of MAC or JIMMY.

Muck By convention, the laird of the Inner Hebridean island of Muck (from Gaelic *Eilean nam Muc*, 'isle of pigs') would have been known as 'Muck', just as the laird of Coll was known as 'Coll'. However, in Dr Johnson's time, this convention caused the then laird of Muck some embarrassment, as Johnson explains:

> Among other guests, which the hospitality of Dunvegan brought to the table, a visit was paid by the Laird and Lady of a small island south of Sky, of which the proper name is Muack, which signifies swine. It is commonly called Muck, which the proprietor not liking, has endeavoured, without effect, to change to Monk. It is usual to call gentlemen in Scotland by the name of their possessions, as Raasay, Bernera, Loch Buy, a practice necessary in countries inhabited by clans, where all that live in the same territory have one name, and must be therefore discriminated by some addition. This gentleman, whose name, I think, is Maclean, should be regularly called Muck; but the appellation, which he thinks too coarse for his Island, he would like still less for himself, and he is therefore addressed by the title of, Isle of Muck.
> – Samuel Johnson, *A Journey to the Western Islands of Scotland* (1775)

Muckle *See* (in addition to the following entries) MONY A MICKLE MAKS A MUCKLE.

Muckle chield Literally, a big (i.e.) well-built boy (or girl). The term was also applied to senior boys at Heriot's School in Edinburgh, and to the Devil.

Muckle forester, the Literally, 'the head forester', i.e. the wind, so characterized in Moray and thereabouts. If this character has been in action, then a lot of trees have been blown down.

Muckle Mou'd Meg Literally, 'big-mouthed Margaret', a character who features in a story from the Borders. In the 16th and 17th centuries the Scotts of Harden and the Murrays of Elibank were constantly at each others' throats, and on one occasion William Scott, the heir of Harden, was caught by the Murrays while trying to steal their cattle. Sir Gideon Murray was about to string up his uninvited guest when his wife interceded, saying, 'Hout, na, Sir Gideon, would you hang the winsome young laird of Harden when you have three ill-favoured daughters to marry?' Sir Gideon saw that Lady Murray had a point, and presented his captive with a choice: either he should hang, or marry Muckle Mou'd Meg – the nickname of his daughter Agnes. Young Harden was all for resisting the young lady's charms, until he was brought to the very foot of the scaffold. There he underwent a last-minute conversion, and so agreed to exchange one noose for another. As it turned out, the marriage – which was contracted in 1611 – was a happy one, and among their descendants was Sir Walter Scott.

The story became the subject of 'Muckle-Mouth

Meg', one of Robert Browning's less successful poetic efforts, in which young Wat is confined to 'the Hole' to consider his answer:

Soon week came to end, and, from Hole's door set
    wide,
Out he marched, and there waited the lassie:
'Yon gallows, or Muckle-mouth Meg for a bride!
Consider! Sky's blue and turf's grassy:

'Life's sweet: shall I say ye wed Muckle-mouth Meg?'
'Not I,' quoth the stout heart: 'too eerie
The mouth that can swallow a bubblyjock's
    [turkey's] egg:
Shall I let it munch mine? Never, Dearie!'

Perhaps more successful is 'Muckle Mou'd Meg' by James Ballantine (1808–77), of which the following is the last verse:

Meg's tear touch'd his bosom, the gibbet frown'd
    high,
An' slowly Wat strode to his doom;
He gae a glance round wi' a tear in his eye,
Meg shone like a star through the gloom.
She rush'd to his arms, they were wed on the spot,
An' lo'ed ither muckle and lang;
Nae bauld border laird had a wife like Wat Scott;
'T was better to marry than hang.
So saddle an' munt again, harness an' dunt again,
Elibank hunt again, Wat's snug at hame.

Muckle Spate, the The 'great flood' that occurred in the Northeast in August 1829. Torrential rains began on 2 August; over the next 24 hours, 3.75 inches (9.5 cm) were recorded in Huntly, while on 3 August a great thunderstorm broke over the Cairngorms. To the south of the massif, the River Dee rose in excess of 15 ft (4.5 m), while to the north the Findhorn rose nearly 50 ft (15 m) in places; the Nairn, Lossie and Spey were also affected. There were few fatalities, but whole villages were swept away. The episode was commemorated in a lengthy poem written in the DORIC around 1851 by a local man, David Grant. It begins thus:

Tho' I was only but a bairn
In auchteen twentynine,
The mem'ry o' the Muckle Spate
Has never left my min'.

We had a byous weety time,
A week, or maybe mair,
The eident rain kept pelting on,
Nae single hoor wis fair;

An' then for fouran'twenty hoors
There followed a doonfa'
The like o' which, sin' Noah's flood,
The warl' never saw.

The thunner rum'lt roon the hills,
The howes were in a soom,
We thocht the warl', owergaen wi' age,
Drew near the crack o' doom ...
    [*byous weety*, 'extraordinarily wet'; *eident*, 'persistent';
    howes, 'valleys'; *soom*, 'flood']

Muckle Toon, the 'The big town', the name awarded by its inhabitants to Langholm in Dumfriesshire. For Hugh MacDiarmid's celebration of his native place, *see under* RIDING THE MARCHES.

Muckle White Hope *See* BLACK HOPE.

'Muirland Meg' An old song, a copy of which was found in Burns's handwriting and included in *The MERRY MUSES OF CALEDONIA*. It is sung to the tune of 'Eppy Macnab'. There follows the first two verses:

Amang our young lasses there's Muirland Meg,
She'll beg or she'll work, and she'll play or she'll
    beg;
At thretteen her maidenhead flew to the gate,
An' the door o' her cage stands open yet.

*And for a sheep-cloot she'll do't, she'll do't,
And for a sheep-cloot she'll do't;
And for a toop-horn she'll do't to the morn,
And merrily turn and do't, and do't.*

Her kittle black een they wad thirl ye thro',
Her rosebud lips cry kiss me just now;
The curls and links o' her bonny black hair,
Wad put you in mind that the lassie has mair.

And for a sheep-cloot &c., &c. ...

Muir of the Clans An area of moorland (now drained for agriculture) just north of Cawdor.

The name apparently derives from the march made by 3000 Jacobite troops on the night of 15/16 April 1746, en route to attack the Hanoverian camp at Nairn. However, the attack was abandoned and the men ordered back to Culloden, some miles to the southwest, where they met their fate the following day. On the moor is also to be found the miniature Loch of the Clans.

Mune *See* MOON.

Mungo, St *See* TREE THAT NEVER GREW, THE.

Munro The generic term for any mountain in Scotland of 3000 ft (914.4 m) or more. They are named after Sir Hugh Munro (1856–1919), who published the first list of such mountains (*Munro's Tables*) in 1891. When he died, Munro had still to climb just two of his namesakes: the INACCESSIBLE PINNACLE, and Carn Cloich-mhuillin, the Munro nearest to his own home (but now demoted; see below). The first 'compleater' (the spelling being a nod to that sporting classic, Izaac Walton's *The Compleat Angler*) was the Revd A.E. Robertson, who topped his final Munro, Meall Dearg in Glen Coe, in 1901. It was another 22 years before the next compleation, and it was not until 1970 that the 100th person finished the round. The 1000th compleation came in 1989, while by 2011 the number was approaching 5000 – a graphic demonstration of the accelerating popularity of 'Munro-bagging'.

Quite what constitutes a full Munro as opposed to a 'Top' over 3000 ft is a tricky business, adjudicated upon by the Scottish Mountaineering Club, but the general rule appears to be that there must be a distance of at least 1 mile (1.6 km) between one Munro and another, and/or a re-ascent of at least 500 ft (152.4 m). Re-surveying over the years has seen various Munros demoted, and other hills promoted. As it happens, the total number in late 2011 was 283, the same number as Sir Hugh had listed 120 years before. *See also* CORBETT; DONALD; GRAHAM.

> 'I am patient, young man,' Munro bagger said,
> 'For I have enjoyed a long life through;
> It is not the ones left that are keeping me going
> But the new ones they are making me do.'

> – Anon., 'The Old Munro Bagger', recorded in the bothy book at Shenavall, in the wilds to the south of An Teallach

See also CORBETT; DONALD; GRAHAM.

Munro, Donald *See* HIS POLYONYMOUS OMNIPOTENCE.

Munter hunter A Glaswegian expression for a man who woos unattractive women (*munters*).

Murder Hole, the An inlet on Loch Neldricken, a small loch among the craggy hills above Glen Trool in Galloway. It is marked as such on Ordnance Survey maps, and was so dubbed by S.R. Crockett in his historical novel *The Raiders* (1894), as a hiding place for murdered corpses:

> Now we were on a platform on the north side of Loch Neldricken, but close down by the waterside. There was a strange thing beneath us. It was a part of this western end of the loch, level as a green where they play bowls, and in daylight of the same smooth colour; but in the midst a black round eye of water, oily and murky, as though it were without a bottom, and the water a little arched in the middle – a most unwholesome place to look upon.
> As she knelt over me May Maxwell pointed it out to me, with the knife which was in her hand.
> 'That is their Murder Hole,' she said, 'but if we are to lie there we shall not lie there without company.'
> – chapter xxix

Crockett got the idea from the story of a woman and her son who lived on a lonely stretch of the road between Glen Trool and Straiton, who would rob and murder travellers and dump their bodies in a boggy pool up on the moors.

Murk Monday The name that in Scotland for long commemorated the total solar eclipse that occurred on 29 March 1652 (8 April New Style). The eclipse tracked a diagonal course across west Wales, Cumbria and then from southwest to northeast Scotland, taking in most of the main centres of population. In England, the eclipse of 1652 was known as Black Monday, and, following Cromwell's defeat of the Scots, was used by the Parliamentarian press as an occasion to discredit that nation; for example,

Perfect Passages of Every Daies Intelligence claimed that the Scots, in their simplicity, believed that the sun was going to go out. Remarkably, Scotland was affected by two other total solar eclipses in the second half of the 17th century: that on 12 August (NS) 1654 passed near Aberdeen, while that on 23 September (NS) 1699 affected the far northeastern corner, including Wick.

Mutton in lieu of man How Stewart Mackenzie of Seaforth characterized the CLEARANCES in an 1819 letter requesting financial aid to facilitate the transportation of tenants from Lewis:

> If it becomes necessary for me, as I fear it will, to carry through the measure of dispossessing a population overgrown and daily becoming more burdensome to pave the way for the grand improvement of the introduction of mutton in lieu of man, the numbers almost appal me and will astonish you.

'My Ain Folk' A sentimental, pseudo-traditional song, subtitled 'A Ballad of Home', by William Alfred Braund, writing under the pen name Wilfred Mills. It was published in 1904, with music by Laura Lemon.

> Far frae my hame I wander, but still my thoughts return
> To my ain folk ower yonder, in the shieling by the burn.
> I see the cosy ingle, and the mist abune the brae,
> And joy and sadness mingle, as I list some auld-warld lay.
>
> *And it's oh! but I'm longing for my ain folk,*
> *Tho' they be but lowly, puir and plain folk:*
> *I am far beyond the sea, but my heart will ever be*
> *At home in dear auld Scotland, wi' my ain folk.*

Braund lived in South London, working for a piano maker, and never visited Scotland. He explained his adoption of a pen name thus:

> … there is somewhat of a prejudice on the part of employers against the writing of verses by those following commercial avocations. It is deemed that such verse-writing is apt to conduce to less zeal being shown in their routine employment.

Bill Douglas entitled the second part of his autobiographical film trilogy *My Ain Folk* (1973). For the species of Scottish sentiment known as Myainfolkism, *see* WALLACETHEBRUCEISM.

My elder brother in misfortune How Robert Burns addressed Robert Fergusson in his inscription on the stone he raised in 1789 over the poet's grave in Canongate Churchyard, Edinburgh:

> Curse on ungrateful man that can be pleased
> And yet can starve the author of the pleasure!
> O thou my elder brother in misfortune,
> By far my elder brother in the muses,
> With tears I pity thy unhappy fate!
> Why is the bard unpitied by the world,
> Yet has so keen a relish of its pleasures?

Fergusson had died, broken in mind and body, in an Edinburgh lunatic asylum on 17 October 1774, aged only 24. In the 19th century Robert Louis Stevenson paid for the grave to be repaired, and added his own inscription:

> This stone originally erected by Robert Burns has been repaired at the charge of Robert Louis Stevenson and is by him rededicated to the memory of Robert Fergusson as the gift of one Edinburgh lad to another.

Thus Scotland's THREE ROBBIES, to use Stevenson's own phrase, are poignantly united.

N

Nabobs o' the Ferry *See* RICHEST SQUARE MILE IN EUROPE, THE.

Nae bad A prudent mode of saying 'Quite good, actually.'

Nairrrrrn Where Scottish racing drivers come from. *See also* BRIGHTON OF THE NORTH, THE.

Nane the waur o' a hanging *See* WEIR OF HERMISTON.

Napier's bones Calculating rods made of bone, ivory or wood, described (but not invented) in 1617 by the mathematician John Napier (1550–1617), 8th Laird of Merchiston. Napier, who invented logarithms and was nicknamed 'Marvellous Merchiston', gave his name to Napier Technical College, founded in Edinburgh in 1964 and incorporating the tower in which Napier was born. It is now Napier University.

Narra-nebbit Literally, 'narrow nosed', i.e. bigoted, especially as far as religion is concerned.

Nat Basher in Chief *See* STALIN'S GRANNY.

National Covenant *See* COVENANTERS.

Nation of Gentlemen How George IV characterized the Scots on his visit in 1822, the first visit to Scotland by a reigning monarch since Charles II was crowned king in 1651. The visit was orchestrated by Sir Walter Scott, and the king was greeted enthusiastically (and with considerable tact, no public mention being made of the flesh-coloured tights George wore beneath his kilt).

Natural phenomena For a list of entries, *see* METEOROLOGICAL AND OTHER NATURAL PHENOMENA.

Nazis in Caithness *See* LITTLE BELSEN.

Nearest place to nowhere, the How locals describe Campbeltown, the remote burgh near the foot of the Kintyre peninsula.

Necrophilia, an extreme case of *See* EXTREME CASE OF NECROPHILIA, AN.

Nec tamen consumebatur 'And yet it was not consumed', the motto of the Church of Scotland. The allusion is to the story of Moses and the Burning Bush in Exodus 3:2:

> And the angel of the Lord appeared unto him in a flame of fire out of the midst of a bush: and he looked, and, behold, the bush burned with fire, and the bush was not consumed.

The motto, accompanied by the emblem of the Burning Bush, made its first appearance in 1691 on the title page of that year's *Principal Acts of the General Assembly*, and the innovation was down to the printer, George Mossman, who borrowed the Latin from the 1597 edition of Tremellius and Junius, rather than the earlier Vulgate. Calvin had taken the Burning Bush as a symbol of the people of God.

Ned A disparaging term for a poorly educated, hard-drinking, hard-fighting working-class youth, usually with criminal tendencies; the Scottish equivalent of the English term *chav*. It has been suggested, fallaciously, that the word is an acronym for 'non-educated delinquent'. In fact, it is the familiar form of the name Edward, with an allusion to *teddy-boys*, and possibly also to *neddy*, a donkey. The female version of a ned is a *nedette*. *See also* SENGA.

Needle-noddle *See* EEDLE-DODDLE.

Ne'erday New Year's Day. In Scotland it was not until 1600 that it officially occurred on 1 January; prior to that, the New Year was not thought to begin until 25 March. Most countries in western Europe had already adopted 1 January as the first day of the new year, and the change, made by order of the Privy Council in 1599, was made 'that thair sall be na disconformitie betwix His Majestie his realm and liegis and uthiris nichtbour countreyis in this particular'. In Neil Munro's Para HANDY stories, one particular Loch Fyne village is always described as Cairndow 'where they keep the two New Years'. *See also* HOGMANAY.

Neither biggin' kirks nor placin' ministers Literally, 'neither building churches nor appointing ministers', i.e. up to no good. The expression is recorded by J. Riddell in *Aberdeen and Its Folk* (1868).

Neither here nor there As Chic Murray pertinently asked, 'If something's neither here nor there, where the hell is it?'

Nemo me impune lacessit The Latin motto of the ORDER OF THE THISTLE, and of the kingdom of Scotland; it means 'no one provokes me without impunity', and in Scots is often rendered as WHA DAUR MEDDLE WI ME? The motto was added to the arms of the king of Scotland during the reign of Charles II, and since the Union has appeared in Scottish versions of the arms of the monarch. It is also the motto of the Royal Regiment of Scotland, the Scots Guards and the Royal Scots Dragoon Guards, and was also the motto of various former regiments: the Royal Scots, the Royal Scots Greys, the Royal Highland Fusiliers and the BLACK WATCH. The motto is associated with the Scottish symbol of the THISTLE. *See also* IN MY DEFENS GOD ME DEFEND.

Neologisms, Scots *See* WABSTEID.

Neptune's Staircase The sequence of eight locks constructed by Thomas Telford at the southwest end of the Caledonian Canal, which was opened in 1822. The height difference is nearly 20 m (66 ft).

Nesbitt, Rab C *See* RAB C. NESBITT.

Nessie *See* LOCH NESS MONSTER, THE.

Never behind! The Douglas family motto, in accordance with which the clock in the tower of St Bride's Church in the town of Douglas (presented by Mary Queen of Scots) strikes three minutes before the hour. Another Douglas motto is 'Doe or Die', referring to the last charge of the BLACK DOUGLAS.

New Caledonia (1) The Scottish colony set up in the late 17th century in what is now Panama; *see* DARIEN SCHEME. (2) The name given to the fur-trading district broadly occupying the area now covered by British Columbia in western Canada. The name is generally attributed to Simon Fraser, who, working for the North West Company, explored the area in 1805–8. Although Fraser was born in New England, his parents were from Easter Ross. (3) *Nouvelle-Calédonie*, a French island group in the southwest Pacific. In 1774 Captain James Cook landed on the largest island and named it New Caledonia. On the same voyage he gave the name New Hebrides to the islands to the north (now Vanuatu).

New Firm, the *See* OLD FIRM, THE.

New Hebrides *See* NEW CALEDONIA (3).

New Lichts *See* AULD LICHTS AND NEW LICHTS.

New moon *See* MOON.

New tout in an auld horn, a A now archaic expression denoting stale news or an old idea dressed up as fresh news or a new idea. *To tout on anither horn* is to change the subject, while *to tout on one's ain horn* is to blow one's own trumpet.

Next year in Scotland A toast made by the Carbonari ('charcoal burners'), an Italian secret society of the early 19th century devoted to securing the independence and unification of Italy. The Carbonari had no particular ambition to visit Scotland, but their mythology claimed that their organization had Scottish origins, when, at some rather vague time in the past of 'great disturbances' in Scotland, various illustrious men took refuge in the forests from the prevailing tyranny, adopted the role of charcoal burners as cover, and evolved a mystical discipline. In addition, the Carbonari regarded Scotland as the origin of esoteric knowledge – in perhaps the same way that various European Freemasons adopted the 'Ancient and Accepted Scottish Rite' as their model. The Carbonari reappear in Scotland in Robert Louis Stevenson's story, 'The Pavilion on the Links' (1880):

> 'Tell me one thing,' said I. 'What are they after, these Italians? What do they want with Mr Huddlestone?'
> 'Don't you know?' he cried. 'The black old scamp had Carbonaro funds on a deposit – two hundred and eighty thousand; and of course he gambled it away on stocks. There was to have been a revolution in the Tridentino, or Parma; but the revolution is off, and the whole wasp's nest is after Huddlestone. We shall all be lucky if we can save our skins.'
> 'The Carbonari!' I exclaimed; 'God help him indeed!'

Nice-gabbit *See* FINE-GABBIT.

Nicknames In addition to a variety of miscellaneous nicknames scattered throughout the volume, *see also:*

- FOOTBALL CLUB NICKNAMES
- NICKNAMES, BY-NAMES AND SOBRIQUETS OF PERSONS
- NICKNAMES, BY-NAMES AND SOBRIQUETS OF PLACES
- NICKNAMES FOR INHABITANTS OF TOWNS, CITIES AND REGIONS
- REGIMENTAL NICKNAMES
- SPORTSPERSONS' NICKNAMES

Nicknames, by-names and sobriquets of persons
See also SPORTSPERSONS' NICKNAMES.

- The ABYSSINIAN — James Bruce
- The ADDISON OF THE NORTH — Henry Mackenzie
- The ADMIRABLE CRICHTON — James Crichton
- ADVERSITY HUME — Joseph Hume
- ALEXANDER THE CORRECTOR — Alexander Cruden
- Angelical Thomas — MAJOR WEIR
- The APOSTLE OF THE HIGHLANDERS — St Columba
- The Apothecary — ADVERSITY HUME
- ARCHIBALD THE GRIM — Archibald, Earl of Douglas; also Archibald Campbell, 7th Earl of Argyll
- The ARIOSTO OF THE NORTH — Sir Walter Scott
- The ARROW OF GLEN LYON — Alasdair MacGregor
- AULD BLEARY — Robert II
- AULD RINGAN OLIVER
- AULD WAT — Walter Scott of Harden
- The AUTHOR OF *WAVERLEY*, aka the Wizard of the North aka the Great Unknown — Sir Walter Scott
- BADGER — Alistair Darling
- BAILLIE VASS — Sir Alec Douglas-Home
- Bald Iain, aka the Bard of Keppoch — Ian LOM
- The BARD OF THE SILVERY TAY — William McGonagall
- The BAWLING CAMPBELLS — the daughters of the 2nd Duke of Argyll
- The BELLE OF MAUCHLINE — Jean Armour
- La BELLE STUART — Frances Teresa Stuart
- BELL GEORDIE — George Gibson
- BELL-THE-CAT — Archibald Douglas, Earl of Angus
- BENDY WENDY — Wendy Alexander
- BIBLE JOHN

- BIG SAM — Samuel McDonald
- The BIG YIN — Billy Conolly
- The BIRDMAN OF STIRLING CASTLE — John Damian
- BLACK AGNES — Agnes, Countess of Dunbar
- BLACK BOB — General Robert Craufurd
- The BLACK DOUGLAS — Sir James Douglas
- The BLACK DWARF — David Ritchie
- BLACK JOCK — Johnnie Armstrong of Gilnockie
- The Black Colonel — Colonel John Farquharson of Inverey (see COLONEL'S BED, THE)
- The Black Officer — Captain John MacPherson of Ballachroan (see LOSS OF GAICK, THE)
- The BLIND HARPER — Roderick Morrison
- BLIND HARRY
- Bloody or Bluidy Clavers — John Graham of Claverhouse (see BONNIE DUNDEE)
- BLUIDY MACKENZIE aka the Bluidy Advocate — Sir George Mackenzie of Rosehaugh
- BLUIDY TAM aka the Muscovy Deil — General Tam Dalyell
- BOBBING JOHN — John Erskine, Earl of Mar
- BOLD BUCCLEUCH — Walter Scott of Buccleuch
- The BONELESS WONDER — Ramsay MacDonald
- BONNIE DUNDEE — John Graham of Claverhouse, 1st Viscount Dundee
- The BONNIE EARL — James Stewart, 2nd Earl of Moray
- The Bow-head Saint — MAJOR WEIR
- The BOY DAVID — David Steel
- The BRITISH SOLOMON — James VI and I
- The BROON — Gordon Brown
- BUFF THE BEGGARS — Dr William Porteous
- BUKHARA BURNES — Sir Alexander Burnes
- BUTCHER CUMBERLAND — William Augustus, Duke of Cumberland
- The CAIRD O' BARULLION — Billy Marshall
- CAMP MEG
- The Candy King of Glasgow — 'Ball Allan' (see CHEUGH JEAN)
- CAPTAIN BURLY — John Balfour of Kinloch
- The Celtic Homer — Ossian (see OSSIAN FORGERIES, THE)
- CHAMPAGNE CHARLIE — Charles Kennedy
- The CHEVALIER ST GEORGE — James Francis Edward Stuart
- The CLINCHER — Alexander Wylie Petrie
- Ra CHOOKY EMBRA — Prince Philip
- The COCK O' THE NORTH — George Gordon, 4th Earl of Huntly
- COCKY BUNG — Professor John Young
- The COMPETITOR — Robert Bruce of Annandale
- Daft Pate — Kirkpatrick Macmillan (see DEVIL ON WHEELS, THE)
- DISCOVERER OF THE PRINCIPLE OF NATURAL SELECTION (aka the Seer of Gourdiehill) — Patrick Matthew
- DISMAL JIMMY aka *Séamus an Chaca* ('James the Shit') — James VII and II
- *DOCTOR SUBTILIS* — John Duns Scotus
- DOMNALL BÁN (Donald the Fair) — Donald III
- The DOVE OF DUNBAR — Elizabeth Dunbar, Countess of Moray

- The ETTRICK SHEPHERD   James Hogg
- Fair Duncan of the Songs   Duncan ban Macintyre; *see* PRAISE OF BEN DORAIN
- The FAIR MAID OF GALLOWAY   Margaret Douglas
- The FASTEST KNIFE IN THE WEST END   Robert Liston
- The FATTEST HOG IN EPICURUS' STY   David Hume
- FIERY FACE   James II
- The FIGHTING DOMINIE   John Maclean
- FIGHTING MAC   Sir Hector Archibald MacDonald
- The FLOWER OF GALLOWAY   Jane Maxwell
- The FLOWER OF STRATHEARN   Lady Nairne
- The FLOWER OF YARROW   Mary Scott of Dryhope
- The GENTLE LOCHIEL   Donald Cameron of Lochiel
- The GENTLE POET OF LOCHLEVEN   Michael Bruce
- GIANT MACASKILL aka Gille Mòr aka the Cape Breton Giant   Angus MacAskill
- GILDEROY OR GILLIE ROY   Patrick Roy MacGregor
- The GLASGOW GLUTTON   Robert Hall aka Rab Ha'
- GOD'S SILLY VASSAL   James VI
- The GOODMAN OF BALLENGEICH, aka the Poor Man's King   James V
- The GOOD REGENT   James Stewart, 1st Earl of Moray
- GORBALS MICK   Michael Martin
- GORGEOUS GEORGE   George Galloway
- The GRAZIER KING   William McCombie
- The GREATEST GENTLEMAN IN THE HOUSE OF COMMONS   James Maxton
- The GREAT PEDESTRIAN   Robert Barclay Allardice of Ury
- 'GREEK' THOMSON   Alexander Thomson
- *HADDINGTONUS SCOTUS*   John Major
- HALF-HANGIT MAGGIE   Margaret Dickson
- The HAMMER   (1) David McNee, (2) John Reid
- The Hammer of the Nats   Willie Ross (*see under* TARTAN TORIES)
- The HAMMER OF THE SCOTS   Edward I
- HENRY THE NINTH aka the Uncrowned King of Scotland   Henry Dundas, 1st Viscount Melville
- The HERMIT OF HAWTHORNDEN   William Drummond of Hawthornden
- The HEROD OF HILLHEAD   Roy Jenkins
- The HIGHLAND LADDIE   Charles Edward Stuart, the YOUNG PRETENDER
- The HIGHLAND MARY   Mary Campbell
- HIS POLYONYMOUS OMNIPOTENCE   Donald Munro
- HOLOGRAM TAM   The forger Thomas McAnea
- HONEST ALLEN   Allan Cunningham
- HUGH THE DULL   Hugh, Lord of Douglas
- I.R. WRAY   Jimmy Wray
- JAMES OF THE GLENS   James Stewart (*see* APPIN MURDER, THE)
- James the Gross   James Douglas, 1st Earl of Avondale (*see* BLACK DINNER, THE)
- JINGLIN' GEORDIE   George Heriot
- JOCK O' THE SLATES   John Erskine of Mar
- JOHN O' THE MOUNTAINS   John Muir
- KING HOBBE   Robert the Bruce
- The KING OF CARRICK   Gilbert Kennedy, 4th Earl of Cassilis

• KING OF KIPPEN	the Laird of Arnprior
• KING OF THE BORDER	Adam Scott of Tushielaw
• KING OF THE COCOS	John Clunies-Ross
• KING OF THE GYPSIES	Johnnie Faa and others of his clan
• KINMONT WILLIE	William Armstrong of Kinmont
• KIRN-MILK GEORDIE	George I
• The KNICKERBOCKER POLITICIAN	Guy Alfred Aldred
• The KNIGHT OF ELDERSLIE	William Wallace
• LANG SANDY	Alexander Wood
• The LAUREATE OF THE CHEMICAL GENERATION	Irvine Welsh
• The LAUREATE OF THE NURSERY	William Miller
• The LEOPARD MAN OF SKYE	Tom Leppard
• The Lion of Justice	William the Lion
• The LION OF LIDDESDALE	Jock Elliot
• The Lion of the Covenant	Richard Cameron (see CAMERONIANS)
• LORD PRESERVE US	Lord Meadowbank
• *LE LOUP DE MER*	Admiral Thomas Cochrane
• The Luckie Buchan, the witch-wife	Elspeth Buchan (see BUCHANITES)
• LUGLESS WILLIE	William Lithgow
• MADAME ECOSSE	Winnie Ewing
• MAD MITCH	Lieutenant-Colonel Colin Mitchell
• The MAD PIPER	Bill Millin
• The MAID OF NORWAY	Margaret, granddaughter of Alexander III
• Marvellous Merchiston	John Napier (*see under* NAPIER'S BONES)
• MARY THE JEWEL	Mary McLeod
• MEASURE MILLER	William Henry Miller
• MICHAEL WYLIE	William Maitland of Lethington
• MING THE MERCILESS	Menzies Campbell
• The MISERY FROM THE MANSE	Gordon Brown
• The MONSTER BUTLER	Archibald Hall
• MUCKLE MOU'D MEG	Agnes Murray
• OLD BORLUM	Brigadier William Mackintosh of Borlum
• OLD MISTER MELANCHOLY	James Francis Edward Stuart
• OLD MORTALITY	Robert Paterson
• The OLD PRETENDER	James Francis Edward Stuart
• OLD Q	William Douglas, 4th Duke of Queensberry
• ORPHAN WILLIE	Willie Douglas
• The PAPER KING	John Law
• PARAFFIN YOUNG	James Young
• PAT LAZARUS	Pat Lally
• The PEASANT POET	(1) Robert Burns, (2) James Hogg
• The PEDESTRIAN TRAVELLER	Captain John Dundas Cochrane
• PICKLE THE SPY	Alestair Ruadh MacDonnell
• The PLOUGHMAN POET	Robert Burns
• The POOR MAN'S KING	James V
• The PRISONER OF PAPA STOUR	The Hon. Edwin Lindsay
• PROPHET PEDEN	Alexander Peden
• QUEER HARDY	Keir Hardy
• The RED COMYN	Sir John Comyn
• The RED DUCHESS	Katherine Stewart-Murray, Duchess of Atholl

- The Red Fox — Roy Campbell of Glenure (*see* APPIN MURDER, THE)
- RED JOHN OF THE BATTLES — John Campbell, 2nd Duke of Argyll
- The SAGE OF CHELSEA — Thomas Carlyle
- The SCOTS CROESUS — Sir William Dick of Braid
- The SILLIE REGENT — The Earl of Lennox
- SIMON THE FOX — Simon Fraser, Lord Lovat
- The SKATING MINISTER — The Revd Robert Walker
- SLUDGE THE MEDIUM — Daniel Dunglas Home
- STALIN'S GRANNY aka Attila the Hen aka Nat Basher in Chief — Helen Liddell
- The STAR O' DUNGYLE — Miss Heron
- The STAR-SPANGLED SCOTCHMAN — Andrew Carnegie
- STEENIE — George Villiers, Duke of Buckingham
- STIRLING THE VENETIAN — James Stirling
- Sweetie Sandy — Alexander Ferguson (the inventor of EDINBURGH ROCK)
- TAM O' THE COUGAIT — Thomas Hamilton
- The TARTAN PIMPERNEL — The Revd Donald Caskie
- The TINCLARIAN DOCTOR — William Mitchel
- The TINEMAN — Archibald, 4th Earl of Douglas
- TOOM TABARD — John Balliol
- TUSITALA — Robert Louis Stevenson
- The UNCROWNED KING OF SCOTS — Robert Bontine Cunninghame Graham
- WATER WILLIE — Sir William Collins

- The WEAVER POET — (1) Robert Tannahill (2) William Thom
- WEE ECK — Alex Salmond
- A WEE, WEE GERMAN LAIRDIE — George I
- Willie Winkie — William III (*see under* WEE WILLIE WINKIE)
- WILLIAM THE LION — William I
- The WINTER QUEEN — Elizabeth of Bohemia
- The WISEST FOOL IN CHRISTENDOM — James I
- The WIZARD EARL — Francis Stewart, Earl of Bothwell
- The WIZARD OF REAY — Sir Donald Mackay, 1st Baron Reay of Reay
- The Wizard of Yester — Sir Hugh de Gifford (*see under* GOBLIN HA')
- The WOLF OF BADENOCH — Alexander Stewart, Earl of Buchan
- The WORLD'S GREATEST SNOB — Sir Iain Moncreiffe of that Ilk
- The WORST OF KINGS AND THE MOST MISERABLE OF MEN — Robert III
- The WREN OF NORTH BRITAIN — Sir William Bruce
- The YOUNG CHEVALIER — Prince Charles Edward Stuart
- The YOUNG PRETENDER — Prince Charles Edward Stuart

Nicknames, by-names and sobriquets of places

- Da AALD ROCK — Shetland
- ANTHRAX ISLAND — Gruinard Island
- The ATHENS OF THE NORTH — Edinburgh
- AULD REEKIE — Edinburgh
- The AWFUL HAND — The Merrick hills
- The BAR-L — Barlinnie Prison
- The Bill — Fort William

- The BLUE TOON — Peterhead
- The BRAIF TOUN — Aberdeen
- The BROCH — (1) Fraserburgh, (2) Burghead
- The BOAR OF BADENOCH — An Torc
- The BONNET TOUN — Stewarton
- The BUCKFAST TRIANGLE — The triumvirate of Cumbernauld, Coatbridge and Airdrie
- The CITY OF BON ACCORD — Aberdeen
- The CITY OF ST MICHAEL — Dumfries
- The CITY OF ST NICHOLAS — Aberdeen
- The COBBLER — Ben Arthur
- The COCK OF ARRAN
- The COLD SHOULDER OF SCOTLAND — Buchan
- The COLONEL'S BED
- The DEAR GREEN PLACE — Glasgow
- DOOM-RAY — Dounreay
- The DRUM — Drumchapel
- The EARTHQUAKE CAPITAL OF SCOTLAND — Comrie
- The FAIR CITY — Perth
- The FIERY MINE — Blantyre Colliery
- The FORT — Fort William
- FURRY BOOTS CITY — Aberdeen
- The GOLDEN SQUARE — St Andrew's Square, Edinburgh
- The GRANITE CITY — Aberdeen
- The GUID TOUN — Edinburgh
- HAME — Campbeltown
- HOLY CORNER
- The HONEST TOUN — Musselburgh
- ÎLE DE DIEU, L' — Inchkeith

- The ISLES OF THE SEA — The Garvellachs
- ITCHLAND OR SCRATCHLAND — Scotland
- JUTEOPOLIS — Dundee
- JUVLO-MENGRESKEY TEM — Scotland
- LAND O' CAKES — Scotland
- LAND OF MISTS — The Highlands and Islands; Skye in particular
- The LANG RAW — Eaglesham
- The LANG TOUN — Kirkcaldy (and various other towns)
- The MADEIRA OF THE NORTH — Rothesay
- The MISTY ISLE — Skye
- The MOST SIGNPOSTED NOWHERE ON THE PLANET — Crianlarich
- The MUCKLE TOON — Langholm
- The NEAREST PLACE TO NOWHERE — Campbeltown
- NODDY TOWN — Cumbernauld
- NO MEAN CITY — Glasgow
- POLOMINT CITY — East Kilbride
- The PUBIC TRIANGLE
- The QUEEN OF THE BORDERS — Hawick
- The QUEEN OF THE HEBRIDES — Islay
- The QUEEN OF THE NORTH ISLES — Westray
- The QUEEN OF THE RINNS — Port Charlotte
- The QUEEN OF THE SCOTTISH PEAKS — Ben Loyal
- The QUEEN OF THE SOUTH — Dumfries
- The REAL BIG BEN — Ben Nevis
- The RICHEST SQUARE MILE IN EUROPE — Broughty Ferry

• The SECOND ALEXANDRIA	Berwick-upon-Tweed
• The SECOND CITY OF THE EMPIRE	Glasgow
• The SHAKY VILLAGE	Comrie
• The SIBERIA OF SCOTLAND	The Cabrach
• SILICON GLEN	
• The SLOCH	Portessie
• The SMALLEST CITY IN SCOTLAND	Perth
• The SNECK	Inverness
• The Sow of Atholl	Meall an Dòbhraichean (*see under* BOAR OF BADENOCH)
• TINDERBOX CITY	Glasgow
• *TÌR A'MHURAIN*	South Uist
• TONGLAND	Calton
• VILLAGE OF MOURNING	Balfron
• WINE ALLEY	Moorpark, Govan
• WINE CITY	Greenock–Port Glasgow

Nicknames for inhabitants of towns, cities and regions A selection is given below. For the nicknames given to the inhabitants of various parts of Orkney, *see* TEU-NEEMS.

Aberdeen	HADDIES (or Aberdeen haddies); SNECKS (disparaging)
Alexandria	JEELIE-EATERS
Anstruther	HAMEBIDERS
Arbroath	RED LICHTIES
Bo'ness	HAMEBIDERS
Carnwath	WHITE CRAWS
Ceres (Fife)	Sodgers (they claimed for centuries that their ancestors fought at Bannockburn)

Clydebank	Bankies
Dumbarton	SONS OF THE ROCK
Dumfries	DOONHAMERS
Forfar	LOONS
Freswick (Caithness)	Tammie-fuds
Galashiels	Braw Lads and Lasses (*see* BRAW LADS' GATHERING)
Glasgow	KEELIES, WEEGIES
The Highlands	GLUNIMIES, TEUCHTERS
Kilbarchan	HABBIES
Linlithgow	BLACK BITCHES
Lochcarron	BLACK RAVENS OF LOCHCARRON
The Lowlands	SASSENACHS
Montrose	GABLE-ENDIES
North Uist	CHILDREN OF THE SEALS
Paisley	Buddies (*see* BUDDY) or Bodies
Peterhead	Blue Mogganers (*see* BLUE TOON, THE)
Scalloway	Scallowa' SMA' DRINK.
Stirling	SONS OF THE ROCK
Stromness	BLOODY PUDDINGS
Turriff	Turra Neeps or Turra Tatties (*see* TURRA)

Nicky tams A pair of leather straps or pieces of string tied by farm labourers around the trousers just below the knee, to help keep the cloth out of the mud. *Nicky* comes from *knickerbockers*, which the trousers so gartered resembled, while *tam* is from *taum*, a cord. To some, nicky tams represented the height of sartorial sophistication:

> I'm coortin' Annie noo, Rab Tamson's kitchie deem;
> She is five and forty, and I am seventeen,
> She clorts a muckle piece tae me, wi' different kinds o' jams,
> And tells me ilka nicht that she admires my Nicky Tams.
> – G.S. Morris (1876–1958), 'A Pair o' Nicky Tams'

Nicolay Rutter The name given to the first accurate chart of the Scottish coastline. *Rutter* is a corruption of the French word *routier*, 'route finder', and Nicholas de Nicolay was the French cartographer responsible for the final chart. However, the Rutter's origins are Scottish, and lie with the 1540 voyage round Scotland made by James V, intended partly as a show of strength to the fractious clans of the Hebrides, and partly as a survey of the seas and coasts of his realm. James was accompanied by the pilot Alexander Lyndsay, who charted details of headlands, islands and inlets. His original was somehow obtained by the English, who passed it on to Nicolay in 1546. The French put the chart to use almost immediately, when they sent a fleet to besiege St Andrews after the murder of Cardinal Beaton. In 2007 a copy of the Nicolay Rutter sold for £22,610.

Nights are fair drawin in, the An opening conversational gambit, to be heard at any time between midsummer and the winter solstice. The hackneyed observation has joined the ranks of FAUX JOCKERY.

Nine-eed eel *See* WIZARD SHACKLE.

Nine Maidens Well A site near Dundee, marked on old maps but now covered over. The story behind it is told by Robert Chambers in his *Book of Days* (1862–4):

> Near Dundee, in Forfarshire, there is a well called The Nine Maidens' Well, and adjoining are places named respectively Pittempton, Baldragon, Strathmartin, and Martinstane. From these simple circumstances we have a dragon story, which may be thus abridged. A dragon devoured nine maidens at the well near Pittempton. Martin, the lover of one of the maidens, finding life a burden, determined to kill the reptile, or perish in the attempt. Accordingly, he attacked it with a club, striking the first blow at Strath – pronounced by the country people Strike – martin. The venomous beast was scotched, not killed, by this blow; but as it dragged – Scottice, *draiglet* – 'its slow length along' through a morass, the hero of the adventure followed up the attack, and finally killed the monster at Martinstane. The dragon, like other great criminals of the olden time, made a 'last speech, confession, and dying declaration,' in the following words:

> I was tempit [tempted] at Pittempton,
>   Draiglit [draggled] at Baldragon,
> Stricken at Strikemartin,
>   And killed at Martinstane.

There is an old stone at Balkello, on the way to the Sidlaw Hills, called Martin's Stone, on which there is a representation of a dragon and a horseman. Baldragon Academy possesses a series of paintings illustrating the story, which were originally commissioned by the Nine Maidens public house.

Nineteen canteen Some unspecified (usually distant) year in the past. A variant is *nineteen oatcake*.

Ninety-minute bigots A phrase suggesting that many of those supporters of Rangers, Celtic and other religiously aligned football clubs in Scotland who sing offensive sectarian songs such as 'The BILLY BOYS' during matches are models of toleration and ecumenical understanding the rest of the time. Speaking at a 2005 conference on dealing with sectarianism, head of safety at Rangers, Lawrence Macintyre, stated:

> There's a thing in a football ground called a 90-minute bigot, someone who has got a friend of an opposite religion next door to them. But for that 90 minutes they shout foul religious abuse at each other, and we've got to handle in the first instance the 90-minute bigot. If we can get the person that doesn't mean it then we'll isolate the real racists and real bigots in numbers that are manageable to deal with.

Ninety-minute patriots Those Scots who only get worked up about being Scottish during an international football match. The phrase was coined by the politician Jim Sillars, who started his career as a Labour MP, then formed the breakaway Scottish Labour Party in 1976, and joined the SNP in the early 1980s. He made the comment when he lost his Govan seat in the 1992 general election.

99 An ice-cream cone with a chocolate flake bar stuck in the top. It has been claimed that it took its name from 99 Portobello High Street, Edinburgh, where an ice-cream shop was located from the 1920s until 2005. Various other ice-cream shops around the UK with '99' in their address have made the same claim, and the origin of the name remains uncertain.

Ninety-third! Damn all that eagerness *See* THIN RED LINE, THE.

Nip A fag-end (*see* DOUT) or a cigarette that has been put out for later by pinching it. In *The Complete Patter* (1996), Michael Munro records the following Glasgow rhyme:

> Samson was a strong man,
> He lived on fish and chips,
> He went along the Gallowgate
> Pickin up the nips.

Nip someone's heid, to To irritate, scold or constantly nag someone. The part of the body nipped may sometimes be the *lug* (ear).

Nippy sweetie A sharp-flavoured sweet, such as a lemon drop or a Fisherman's Friend, and hence a sour, bad-tempered or disapproving person. The expression is also jocularly applied to a shot (*nip*) of spirits.

Nitsie, the A nickname for Nitshill, an area of southwest Glasgow. The name has nothing to do with the eggs of headlice; rather *nit* is a Scots version of 'nut'. Nitshill was formerly a mining village, and the scene of a major mining disaster on 15 March 1851, in which 61 men were killed.

No ... *See also* NAE ...

No bishop, no king James VI's remark to a delegation of Scottish Presbyterians demanding religious toleration in England, quoted in *Sum and Substance of the Conference* (1604). At this same conference at Hampton Court, James declared: 'A Scottish presbytery agreeth as well with monarchy as God and the Devil.'

Noddy Town Cumbernauld, so-called by Glaswegians partly from a play on the last syllable of its name and partly because, as a New Town, it is not a 'real' town.

No feud more mortal than that which is upon account of religion *See* HOTSPURS OF THE KIRK.

No Language, No Nation! A slogan coined by the left-wing Scottish nationalist Ruaraidh Arascain is Mhàirr – as the Hon. Ruaraidh Stuart Joseph

Erskine of Mar (1869–1960), second son of the 5th Lord Erskine, preferred to be known. Erskine learnt Gaelic as a child from his Hebridean nanny, and in 1892 became a vice-president of the Scottish Home Rule Association. He called for a Gaelic national movement in Scotland similar to that in Ireland, and was lauded by Hugh MacDiarmid as 'one of the most remarkable personalities of modern Scottish history, the very core and crux of the *Gaeltacht*'. Nevertheless, language has not played such a central part in Scottish nationalism as it has in either Irish or Welsh nationalism, and Erskine ended up a somewhat marginalized figure.

Nollie, the A Glaswegian nickname for the Forth and Clyde Canal – or *ca-noll*, as it is pronounced locally.

No mean city The phrase, from Acts of the Apostles (in which St Paul of Tarsus describes himself as 'a citizen of no mean city'), was applied to Glasgow in the title of the 1935 novel *No Mean City: A Story of the Glasgow Slums*, which tells the story of Johnnie Stark, 'Razor King' of the Gorbals. It was written by an unemployed Glasgow man, Alexander McArthur, in collaboration with a London journalist, H. Kingsley Long. Such was its shock value that libraries in Glasgow refused to stock it when it first appeared, but the *Times Literary Supplement* was impressed: 'Sometimes a "human document" finds its way into print, forcing itself on public attention by the sheer weight of its sincerity, in spite of literary failings. When such a document has artistic value, too, its importance is doubled.'

None of your damned Scotch metaphysics! A reproof issued by George III to Henry Dundas (HENRY THE NINTH), a Scottish minister in the government of the Younger Pitt. Pitt had raised the prospect of Catholic Emancipation as a *quid pro quo* for the Union of Great Britain and Ireland in 1801, but the king declared that to grant Catholic Emancipation would be to breach his coronation oath to uphold the Protestant religion. When Dundas suggested that His Majesty was only bound by the oath in his executive and not in his legislative role, the king angrily retorted: 'None of your damned Scotch metaphysics, Mr Dundas!'

No pudding, and no fun! Queen Victoria's verdict, inscribed in her journal on 8 October 1861, after a night spent at an inn in Dalwhinnie, the loftily situated village on the north side of the Drumochter Pass:

> Unfortunately there was hardly anything to eat, and there was only tea, and two miserable starved Highland chickens, without any potatoes! No pudding, and no fun!

North Berwick Witches A number of people who were accused in 1590 of conspiring to kill James VI by attempting to sink the ship in which he was returning from Norway with his new queen, Anne of Denmark. Interrogated by the king himself, and suffering extreme torture, the supposed conspirators admitted that they had held their covens in the Auld Kirk of North Berwick, where Francis Stewart, Earl of Bothwell (the so-called WIZARD EARL), played the part of the Devil. Their method for raising a storm to sink the king's ship was said to have involved tying gobbets of flesh ripped from the corpse of a hanged man to the paws of a cat, which was then thrown alive into the Firth of Forth. Something must have gone wrong, because the king's ship was unharmed (though another vessel sailing with it foundered). Three people were executed: the schoolteacher Dr John Fian, the midwife Agnes Simpson (or Sampson or Tompson), and Euphemia Maclean, daughter of Lord Cliftonhall. They suffered appalling tortures before being strangled and their bodies then burnt: Fian had his head crushed by a rope twisted round his skull, his legs shattered in the SCOTTISH BOOT, and his fingernails torn out, pins then being inserted into his raw fingertips. Although apprehended, Bothwell escaped from Edinburgh Castle, and continued in more or less open rebellion against the king. *See also* 'BONNIE EARL O' MORAY, THE'.

North Briton How some pro-Union Scots described themselves after 1707, although to many it smacked of the 18th-century equivalent of newspeak:

> I am by birth a *North Briton*, as a *Scotchman* must now be called.
> – James Boswell, letter to the *Public Advertiser*, April 1779

The appointment in 1762 by George III of his former tutor, John Stuart, 3rd Earl of Bute, as prime minister, led to considerable resentment among some English Whigs, who suspected the country was being overrun by a coterie of 'North Britons' – hence the title of John Wilkes's scurrilous political periodical *The North Briton*, one issue of which landed him in the Tower of London. The term long survived in the name of Edinburgh's North British Hotel, built by the North British Railway Company next to Waverley Station, but this historical name was dropped in 1991 in favour of 'The Balmoral', a name the marketing people no doubt considered more in tune with the spirit of tartanry.

Northern Dawn, Northern Lights *See* MERRY DANCERS.

'Northern Lights of Old Aberdeen, The' A song much favoured by Aberdonians. The chorus is as follows:

> The Northern Lights of old Aberdeen mean home sweet home to me,
> The Northern Lights of old Aberdeen are what I long to see.
> I've been a wanderer all of my life and many a sight I've seen –
> God speed the day when I'm on my way to my home in Aberdeen.

The song was composed in 1952 by Mel and Mary Webb, an English couple who had never visited the city. *See also* MERRY DANCERS, THE.

Northern Meeting, the A society formed in Inverness in 1788 by 13 Highland gentlemen, who agreed to hold an annual week-long meeting 'for the purpose of promoting a social intercourse', together with 'pleasure and innocent amusement'. Dining and dancing were initially the principal activities, but in the 19th century all the appurtenances of a full-blown HIGHLAND GAMES were added, which continued until the Second World War. The Northern Meeting continues in slimmed-down form to this day, with grand formal balls in autumn and at Christmas, and a highly prestigious piping competition.

North Ronaldsay Known for its SEAWEED-EATING SHEEP.

No' the full tattie A potato short of plateful, i.e. suffering from learning difficulties.

No' the heather Not the genuine article.

Not proven A third choice available to Scottish juries, implying they know you did it, but there's not enough evidence to convict you. At the start of proceedings, persons in the dock are not, however, asked, 'How do you plead: guilty, not guilty, or not proven?'

> ... that bastard verdict, *Not proven*. I hate that Caledonian *medium quid*. One who is not proven guilty is innocent in the eye of the law.
> – Sir Walter Scott, Journal, 1827

One of the most famous 'not proven' verdicts was that in the case of Madeleine Smith, a young woman from the Glasgow haute bourgeoisie charged in 1857 with poisoning her lover, Pierre Emile l'Angelier, a clerk from Jersey, in order to clear the way for a more advantageous match. Although it was shown that she had purchased arsenic, and that l'Angelier had threatened to show her letters to her father, it could not be proved that she had met him to administer the dose. In 1861 Miss Smith married George Wardle, an artist and colleague of William Morris, and after his death she emigrated to America and remarried. She continued to profess her innocence up to her death in 1928.

Not worth the king's unlaw A phrase used in court proceedings in the 18th century to suggest that a witness was so poor that their testimony could not be relied upon (*unlaw*, 'fine').

Nova Scotia Latin for 'New Scotland', and the name of the colony in eastern Canada chartered by James VI and I on 29 September 1621. The French had already established a settlement in the area (which they called Acadia) in 1604, and struggles for control continued until the Treaty of Paris ending the Seven Years War in 1763 confirmed the colony as British. Nova Scotia became a province of Canada in 1867. In French it is *Nouvelle-Écosse*, and in Gaelic *Alba Nuadh*.

Nuckelavee The 'Devil of the Sea' in Orkney mythology, who takes the form of a malevolent centaur, man above and horse below. The terror inspired by the Nuckelavee was enhanced by its grotesque appearance: it had no skin, so its raw, red flesh and the black blood in its veins was exposed; it had a single burning eye; and its vast mouth jutted forward from its head, which was ten times the size of that of a man. The Nuckelavee was regarded as the source of all distress, from disease to drought, and it was said that, had it not been restrained by the SEA MITHER, its depredations would have caused the end of human habitation in the Northern Isles.

The Nuckelavee had only one vulnerability – its horror of fresh water. This gives rise to an account published in the 19th century in *The Scottish Antiquary* by the Orkney folklorist W. Traill Denison of an encounter between a man called Tammas and the Nuckelavee, in which Tammas only manages to save himself (like TAM O' SHANTER fleeing the witches) by crossing a stream:

> As he reached the near bank another clutch was made at him by the long arms. Tammie made a desperate spring and reached the other side, leaving his bonnet in the monster's clutches. Nuckelavee gave a wild unearthly yell of disappointed rage as Tammie fell senseless on the safe side of the water.

Nulli Secundus Club, the A nickname of the Coldstream Guards. The regiment's motto is *Nulli Secundus* (Latin, 'second to none'): although ranked second in order of precedence behind the Grenadier Guards, the Coldstream Guards, raised in 1650, is the older regiment.

Nyaff An expressively dismissive term for a contemptible and irritating person. Nyaffs are conventionally *wee*, and often *shilpit* ('puny'). The word is thought originally to be imitative of the bark of a small dog. The lexicographer Michael Munro, in *The Complete Patter* (1996), comments:

> Partridge's *Dictionary of Slang* refers to a Parisian slang word *gniaffe* (a term of a abuse for a man) which would have a similar pronunciation. Perhaps the Académie Française would cite this as an example of the Auld Alliance corrupting the French language.

O

Oak of Errol, the This 'immemorial oak' was, according to THOMAS THE RHYMER, bound up with the fortunes of the Hays of Errol:

> While the mistletoe bats on Errol's aik,
>   And the aik stands fast,
> The Hays shall flourish, and their good grey hawk
>   Shall nocht flinch before the blast.
>
> But when the root of the aik decays,
>   And the mistletoe dwines on its withered breast,
> The grass shall grow on Errol's hearth-stane
>   And the corbie roup in the falcon's nest.

Oary boat A Glaswegian term for a rowing boat (i.e. one with oars).

Oath of allegiance MSPs may opt to declare their loyalty in Scots, as follows:

> I depone aat I wull be leal and bear aefauld alleadgance tae her majesty, her airs an ony fa come aifter her anent the laa.

Oats, Dr Johnson on Samuel Johnson famously used his definition of oats as the occasion for a dig at the Scots:

> *Oats.* A grain which in England is generally given to horses, but in Scotland supports the people.
> – Samuel Johnson, *A Dictionary of the English Language* (1755)

Some Scots were inclined to take offence. In response to the definition, Robert Fergusson penned a satire entitled 'To the Principal and Professors of the University of St Andrews, on their Superb Treat to Dr Samuel Johnson', referring to Johnson's visit to the university in 1773. Outraged that the good doctor had been offered such Frenchified delicacies as 'snails and paddocks [frogs]', Fergusson rouses his compatriots to indignation:

> But hear me lads! gin I'd been there,
> How I wad trimm'd the bill o' fare!
> For ne'er sic surly wight as he
> Had met wi' sic respect frae me.
> Mind ye what Sam, the lying loun!
> Has in his Dictionar laid down?
> That aits in England are a feast
> To cow an' horse, an' sican beast,
> While in Scots ground this growth was common
> To gust the gab [please the mouth] o' man and
>   woman.

The poet goes on to suggest a more suitable menu for the English visitor, including HAGGIS, SHEEP'S HEID, trotters, white puddings (i.e. MEALIE PUDDINGS) and BLOODY PUDDINGS.

The rivalry of frogs and porridge seems to have been an enduring one:

> The Frenchman offended the old Scottish peeress by some highly disparaging remarks on Scottish dishes ... All she would answer was, 'Weel, weel, some fowk like parritch, and some fowk like paddocks.'
> – Dean E.B. Ramsay, *Reminiscences of Scottish Life and Character* (1861)

Oban Sesame The name of a whole-food shop in Oban.

Och aye the noo Apparently an ejaculation of affirmation, but in fact a concocted modern expression ironically playing on FAUX JOCKERY and intended to signify that a Scots person is speaking. It should be pointed out, however, that *och* on its own is *echt* Scots, originally, like OCHONE, an interjection expressing sorrow, regret, etc., but now usually expressing lack of patience, exasperation, disdain, etc. Sometimes it comes out as *ach*, which somehow manages to sound a bit more testy.

> To say *ach!* correctly you need generations of Scots blood behind you, and you must have been born with

the peat-reek in your nostrils, and the sight of the hills as the first thing you ever clapped eyes on.
– Ronald MacDonald Douglas, *The Scots Book* (1935)

Ochone or **ochane** An interjection, originally Gaelic, expressing grief and anguish.

Quhen scho ouircome, with siching sair & sad,
With mony cairfull cry and cald ochane ...
– Robert Henryson, *The Testament of Cresseid* [*scho ouircome*, 'she recovered'; *siching sair*, 'sighing sore']

But what's this I see, ochone for me,
It's a vision to make your blood freeze.
It's the police afloat in a dirty big boat
And they're shouting: 'Time, gentlemen, please!'
– 'Campbeltown Loch', as sung by Andy Stewart in the 1960s

See also WALY.

Octavians, the The group of eight men of lesser rank whom James VI appointed in 1596 to look after the royal finances, having vowed that he would 'no longer use chancellor or other great men in those his causes, but such as he might convict and were hangable'. The Octavians (from Latin *octo*, 'eight') were David Carnegie of Culluthie, James Elphinstone, Thomas Hamilton (TAM O' THE COUGAIT), John Lindsay, Alexander Seton, Sir John Skene, Walter Stewart and Peter Young.

O'er-the-march marriage *See* MARCH, THE.

Of mice and men *See* BEST LAID SCHEMES.

Of that ilk A phrase, meaning 'of the same', used in various Scottish titles, especially those of clan chiefs, e.g. David Wemyss of that Ilk means 'David Wemyss of Wemyss', i.e. he is the laird of Wemyss.

Og, Angus *See* ANGUS OG.

Oily Peter *See* REEKIE PETER.

Old ... *See also* AULD ...

Old Borlum The nickname of Brigadier William Mackintosh of Borlum, one of the Jacobite commanders at the Battle of Preston (1715). He was

described by one contemporary as 'a brute beast ... as obstinate as a mule and as savage as a tiger'.

Old Caledonian Forest, the The vast forest that once covered much of the Highlands, consisting principally of Scots pine, intermingled with birch, rowan, juniper and, particularly in the west, oak. In the 17th century Sir Robert Gordon described the forest as being 'full of reid deer and roes, woulffs, foxes, wyld catts, brocks [badgers], skyurells, whittrets [stoats], weasels, otters, martrixes [pine martens], hares and fumarts [polecats]'. A few patches of forest remain, most extensively around the Cairngorms, but the ability of these areas of forest to regenerate is under constant threat from overgrazing by red deer.

Scotland rises as the border of the world,
And there, amid the dense Caledonian Wood,
In the close ancient shadows of the oaks
Is heard the echoing of warlike steel.
– Ariosto, in *Orlando Furioso* (1532)

The golden edging of a bough at sunset, its pantile way
Forming a double curve, tegula and imbrex in one,
Seems at times a movement on which I might be borne
Happily to infinity ...
– Hugh MacDiarmid: 'In the Caledonian Forest', from *Stony Limits and Other Poems* (1934, 1956)

Oldest man in Scotland, the? William Daniell reports in his *Voyage Round Great Britain* (1815–25) on a remarkable phenomenon found in Jura:

The climate, owing to the prevalence of westerly winds from the Atlantic, is humid, but the air in general is so temperate as to be favourable to longevity. Several instances are mentioned of natives who have passed their hundredth year, but the most remarkable is that of Gillour Macrain, who is said to have kept 180 Christmases in his own house, and died in the reign of Charles I.

The 1799 *Statistical Account* found a similar tendency to great age prevailed in Maybole, Ayrshire, noting 'the schoolmaster ... died at the age of 104, three years ago a woman died here aged 105 and there are at present 10 persons whose ages put together amount to upwards of 900 years'. For another example of unusual longevity, *see* CAIRD O' BARULLION, THE.

Old Firm, the A collective term, originating in the late 19th or early 20th century, for Rangers and Celtic, the leading football clubs in Glasgow, regarded as a kind of footballing establishment – and a successful money-making venture.

> We've no chance, I thought, you never do at Hampden against one of the Old Firm, with the crowd and the referees firmly behind the establishment clubs.
> – Irvine Welsh, *Trainspotting* (1993)

The fans of Glasgow's other club, Partick Thistle, have an even-handed approach to the Old Firm teams, as attested in their chant:

> Hello, hello, how do you do?
> We hate the boys in royal blue,
> We hate the boys in emerald green,
> So fuck the Pope and fuck the Queen!

In the 1980s, the success of Aberdeen and Dundee United led to them being sometimes referred to as the *New Firm*.

Old Man The name given to a number of sea stacks and other rock pillars round Scotland. The grand-daddy of them all is the Old Man of Hoy, in Orkney, which is 450 ft (137 m) high, and which was first climbed by Tom Patey, Rusty Baillie and Chris Bonington in 1966. The Old Man of Stoer (200 ft/60 m) in Sutherland, off the Point of Stoer, was also first ascended by Patey, while the Old Man of Storr (160 ft/50 m) is on the flanks of the mountain called the Storr in Skye, and was first climbed in 1955 by Don Whillans.

Old Mister Melancholy A nickname for James Francis Edward Stuart, the OLD PRETENDER, who lacked the charisma of his son, the YOUNG PRE-TENDER. Old Mister Melancholy was the son of DISMAL JIMMY, i.e. James VII.

Old Mortality A novel by Sir Walter Scott, published in 1816. The story is largely set in 1679, at the time when the more extreme COVENANTERS came out in armed rebellion against the efforts of Charles II to suppress Presbyterianism in Scotland. There is a clear dialectic in the novel, with cruel Stuart absolutism set against the zealotry of theocratic Calvinists, while the hero Morton represents the spirit of what Scott depicts as sensible compromise, as later embodied, the author implies, in the Glorious Revolution, the Union of 1707 and the Hanoverian succession.

'Old Mortality' himself only appears briefly in the framing narrative of the novel. He was an actual historical character, who travelled round Scotland repairing the graves of Covenanting 'martyrs'. Scott tells us that he himself had met him, some three decades previously, in Dunnottar churchyard in Kincardineshire:

> This remarkable person, called by the title of Old Mortality, was well known in Scotland about the end of the last century. His real name was Robert Paterson. He was a native, it is said, of the parish of Closeburn, in Dumfries-shire, and probably a mason by profession – at least educated to the use of the chisel.

Paterson was born in 1715, the son of a farmer near Hawick, and served his stonemasonry apprentice-ship in a quarry near Lochmaben, Dumfriesshire. The circumstances of his death in 1801 were described by John MacTaggart in his *Gallovidian Encyclopedia* (1824):

> One night, as he wandered through Annandale, with his old shelty, he took too much of the 'Cratur' [whisky] that 'doiter'd' him, and made him lose his way; and having wandered on until he and his companion became quite exhausted, he alighted off the back of his faithful comrade, for the last time, and betook himself to a quarry-hole for shelter and there, with the fatigue and the 'nappie' he fell asleep – no more to awake in this world – for a stormy night of sleet came on, and the cold froze the warm blood in the heart of Auld Mortality; but his memory shall not perish ...

The Italian composer Vincenzo Bellini drew on the story of Scott's novel (rather loosely, and via a French play called *Têtes Rondes et Cavaliers*) for his 1835 opera *I Puritani di Scozia*. The action is shifted to Plymouth, and the period to that of the English Civil War, cuing appearances by Queen Henrietta Maria and Oliver Cromwell. The *Spectator* was not impressed, concluding that the piece amounted to 'a mass of drivelling imbecility'.

Old North, the (Welsh, *Yr Hen Ogledd*) The name by which the Welsh in the Middle Ages knew southern Scotland and northern England, where in the Dark Ages Old Welsh (Brythonic) was spoken. The inhabitants of this area were *Gwyr y Gogledd*, 'Men of the North'. The most notable of the Brythonic kingdoms in Scotland included that of the GODODDIN in Lothian and, in the west, Strathclyde, known as *Alt Clut* or the KINGDOM OF THE ROCK.

Old Pretender, the James Francis Edward Stuart (1688–1766), the Jacobite claimant ('pretender') to the throne, who was regarded by his supporters as King James VIII of Scotland and III of England following the death of his father James VII in 1701. He was 'old' in comparison to his son, the YOUNG PRETENDER, and lacked the latter's charisma – indeed, he was dubbed OLD MISTER MELANCHOLY on account of his lugubrious piety and lack of vim and vigour. One of his main English supporters, Viscount Bolingbroke, who joined him in exile in France, declared that James 'dwelt in a maze of unrealities', and that he was fatally indecisive: 'He was a man who expected to set sail for England or Scotland, but who did not very well know for which.' In 1708 James got as far as the Firth of Forth, before scuttling back to France on the appearance of the Royal Navy. When the Earl of Mar (BOBBING JOHN) came out for him in the '15, James arrived just in time to be crowned James VIII in Perth, but by this time the rebellion had petered out. Once again, and for the last time, he turned tail for France. He spent his later years in Rome, playing no part in the '45 Rebellion, though informing his son he would abdicate in his favour should he be successful. The circumstance did not arise.

The byname 'Old Pretender' gave Philip Guedalla the following bon mot about one of our more distinguished novelists:

The work of Henry James has always seemed divisible by a simple dynastic arrangement into three reigns: James I, James II, and the Old Pretender.
– *Supers and Supermen* (1920), 'Some Critics'

Old Q The nickname of William Douglas, 4th Duke of Queensberry (1725–1810), who, on inheriting the Queensberry estates in 1778, became one of the wealthiest men in Britain. He was notorious for his sybaritic lifestyle, his pursuit of young women (he never married) and for his disregard of public opinion – notably when he began to clear-fell the woodlands on his Scottish estates. This prompted Burns to pen 'Verses on the Destruction of the Woods Near Drumlanrig' (1791), in which the 'genius of the stream' (the River Nith) informs the poet of the reasons for his bare banks:

'Nae eastlin blast,' the sprite replied;
'It blaws na here sae fierce and fell,
And on my dry and halesome banks
Nae canker-worms get leave to dwell:
Man! cruel man!' the genius sighed –
As through the cliffs he sank him down –
'The worm that gnaw'd my bonie trees,
That reptile wears a ducal crown.'

William Wordsworth was similarly outraged when Old Q cleared the woods around Neidpath Castle, on the Tweed near Peebles:

Degenerate Douglas! O the unworthy lord!
Whom mere despite of heart could so far please
And love of havoc (for with such disease
Fame taxes him) that he could send forth word
To level with the dust a noble horde,
A brotherhood of venerable trees,
Leaving an ancient dome, and towers like these,
Beggar'd and outraged!
– 'Composed at Neidpath Castle, the Property of Lord Queensberry, 1803'

Old Rock, the *See* AALD ROCK, DA.

Old Tom and Young Tom The nicknames given to distinguish the celebrated St Andrews father-and-son golfers, both called Tom Morris. Old Tom (1821–1908) won the Open four times (the last time, in 1867, at the age of 46), and gave his name to the final hole at the ROYAL AND ANCIENT. Young Tom (1851–75) also won the Open four times, the first time at the age of just 17. He died tragically young, apparently heartbroken by the death of his wife in childbirth.

Oliver, Ringan *See* AULD RINGAN OLIVER.

One foot in the grave How John Knox described himself to Sir William Cecil in January 1570, in an addendum to a request by the Regent Moray to Elizabeth I to send back Mary Queen of Scots. 'If ye strike not at the root,' Knox wrote, 'the branches that appear to be broken will bud again ... More days than one would not suffice to express what I think.' Then he signed himself off thus: 'John Knox, with his one foot in the grave.' Within two years he was dead. The *OED*'s earliest citation for the phrase dates from 1632 ('When one foot's in the grave', from Massinger and Field's *Fatal Dowry*), so it is possible that Knox coined the phrase.

One o'Clock Gun Every day (except Sunday) at 1 p.m. a gun fires a blank round from Edinburgh Castle. This custom originated in 1861, when a Captain Wauchope arranged for a large ball on the flagpole on top of Nelson's Monument on Calton Hill to drop at 1 p.m., giving a visual signal of the time to ships anchored in the Firth of Forth, enabling them to check the accuracy of their marine chronometers. However, it was realized that when the HAAR was in, such a visual signal was of no use, and so the practice of firing a gun was introduced that same year. Originally an 18-pound cannon, fired from the Half-Moon Battery, provided the signal; this was replaced with a 25-pounder field gun in 1953, fired from Mill's Mount Battery. In charge of operations between 1979 until his death in 2005 was 'Tam the Gun' – Staff Sergeant Thomas McKay MBE. The gun is also fired to mark the New Year.

One singer, one song See WAN SINGER, WAN SONG.

Onion Johnnies Itinerant sellers of onions (*ingans* in Scots, hence they were also referred to as *Ingan Johnnies*; history also records a single *Onion Jenny*). Onion Johnnies first came over from Brittany in 1828, touting their wares from house to house. In due course – with their onion-laden bicycles and their berets, striped pullovers and neat moustaches – they created a stereotype of the typical Frenchman, bringing a twinkle into the eye of many a romance-starved housewife. The last of the Scottish Onion Johnnies, André Quemener – who first

landed in Leith in 1951 at the age of 14 – hung up his beret for good in 2005. The tradition is commemorated in La Maison des Johnnies et de l'Oignon in Roscoff.

Only breed of dog named after a fictional character, the See DINMONT, DANDIE.

Only football team to be mentioned in the Bible, the See QUEEN OF THE SOUTH.

On the box In receipt of weekly monetary assistance from a poor fund, such as a friendly society or church collection; the more modern equivalent is *on the broo* (see BROO).

On the broo See BROO.

On the ran-dan On the razzle; out on the town. 'Ran-dan' first appears in the 18th century, denoting rowdy behaviour or a spree; it may derive from the more chaotic side of the word 'random'.

> You've been on the ran dan you couple of wee tinkers and your mother's up to high doe.
> – Alan Warner, *Morvern Callar* (1995)

On the skite Painting the town red; on a spree, often a drunken one. To *skite* is to skid, slip or slide, or to rebound or ricochet, or to spray, splash or squirt.

Oo The Scots term for wool. The word gave rise to the following (probably apocryphal) conversation, recorded by E.B. Ramsay in his *Reminiscences of Scottish Life and Character* (1862):

> Customer (inquiring the material): Oo?
> Shopman: Ay, oo.
> Customer: A' oo?
> Shopman: Ay, a' oo.
> Customer: A' ae oo?
> Shopman: Ay, a' ae oo.

See also WE'RE A' AE OO.

O of Arbroath, the The nickname of the great rose window in Arbroath's 12th-century abbey. The window is positioned above a round-arched triforium, and in the Middle Ages was used as a navigational beacon by boats far out at sea. It also gave the inhabitants of Arbroath (and Arbroath FC) their nickname, the Red Lichties.

Oor Wullie A comic strip that has appeared in D.C. Thomson's *Sunday Post* every week since 8 March 1936 – the same day the paper launched *The BROONS*. Dudley D. Watkins, who created *The Broons*, also drew *Oor Wullie* until his death in 1969, after which the paper re-ran old strips for some years before commissioning new artists and writers. *Oor Wullie* also features in an annual every other year, alternating with *The Broons*. The eponymous Wullie, a young citizen of AUCHENSHOOGLE (or Auchentogle), is a nine-year-old urchin with spiky hair, dungarees and a cheeky grin, often to be seen sitting on an upturned bucket, and who often ends up getting into some kind of trouble. His most frequent catchphrase is JINGS, CRIVENS, HELP MA BOAB. Wullie now has his own Myspace entry (www.myspace.com/Oorwullie), where he describes himself as 'Male, 73 years old, Auchenshoogle, Scotland', and lists among his 168 friends Jimmy Shand (the LAIRD OF AUCHTERMUCHTY), Andy Stewart, Robert Burns, GREYFRIARS BOBBY, Sir Walter Scott, Mary Queen of Scots and Paw Broon – who sometimes appears in Wullie's strip.

Oot like a pot fit *See* POT FIT.

Orcadian An inhabitant of Orkney, from *Orcades*, the Latin name for the islands first recorded in the 1st century AD (although much earlier, in 330 BC, there is a Greek reference to *Orkas*). There is a well-known saying that 'An Orcadian is a farmer with a boat, while a Shetlander is a fisherman with a croft.'

Ordeal by blood A method (also known as *bier-richt*) of finding the guilty party in a murder mystery, advocated by James VI in *Daemonologie* (1597):

> In a secret murther if the dead carcase be at any time thereafter handled by the murtherer, it will gush out of blood, as if the blood were crying out to heaven for revenge of the murtherer.

In *Old Church Lore* (1891), William Andrews recounts a case from 1688:

The body of Sir James Stanfield, of New Mills, was found in a stream near Haddington. It appeared that he had met his death by strangling. James Muirhead, a surgeon, and another person swore that when Philip Stanfield [Sir James's disinherited son] was helping to place the body of his father in a coffin, blood started from the left side of his neck upon his touch, and that he exclaimed, 'Lord have mercy upon me!' On this slight evidence he was, 7th February, 1688, pronounced guilty of parricide, and was publicly executed on the 24th of the same month, and his body hung in chains. He protested his innocence to the last.

See also DREAMING OF THE DEAD.

Order of the Thistle, the Most Ancient The exclusively Scottish order of knighthood, founded in 1687 by James VII and II, and second in precedence only to the English Order of the Garter. James claimed he was reviving an ancient order founded by Achaius, a legendary king of Scots in the 8th or 9th century, but there are no grounds to support such a claim. Suggestions that the order originated in the reigns of James III or James V again have little supporting evidence. Membership, awarded on the sole discretion of the monarch, is restricted to 16 knights or ladies (including the Lord Lyon King of Arms; *see* LYON COURT, THE), plus the sovereign and sundry other royals, both foreign and home-grown. The only knight ever to have been expelled from the order was the Jacobite Earl of Mar, aka BOBBING JOHN. The motto of the order is *NEMO ME IMPUNE LACESSIT*, and its master of ceremonies is called the Usher of the Green Rod.

Ordinarie place of butcherlie reuenge and daylie fightis, the Edinburgh; *see* CLEANSE-THE-CAUSE-WAY.

Orphan Willie The affectionate name given by Mary Queen of Scots to 'Little Willie' Douglas, the 16-year-old pageboy who in May 1568 helped her to escape from Lochleven Castle. Mary had been imprisoned by the Confederate Lords in the castle, built on a small island in the loch, since June 1567, and was forced to abdicate shortly thereafter. Little Willie was an orphaned cousin (or possibly an illegitimate child) of Sir William Douglas, the laird of the castle and thus the queen's jailer, and had succumbed to the queen's undoubted charms. Among the other young men who had succumbed was Sir William Douglas's younger brother George, and he and Little Willie hatched a plan to get the queen out of her prison on 2 May 1568. While on the shore George assembled Sir William Douglas's best horses (which had been 'borrowed' for the occasion), Little Willie managed matters on the island. Taking on the role of ABBOT OF UNREASON to celebrate the Mayday weekend, he carried out a series of drunken escapades as cover for certain actions – such as holing all the boats bar one – that would otherwise invite suspicion. That evening, while serving Sir William at table, he somehow managed to get hold of the laird's keys, and thus escorted Mary out of the main gate, depositing the keys in the mouth of a cannon before taking the only serviceable boat and rowing the queen to the shore. Mary's liberty was short-lived, however. After her defeat at Langside on 13 May, she was forced to seek refuge in England, where her cousin Elizabeth was to keep her in confinement for another two decades. Right up to the end she was attended by faithful Orphan Willie, who was rewarded with a mention in her will.

Ossian forgeries, the Scotland's greatest literary scandal. In 1759 the poet James Macpherson (1736–96), the son of a farmer from Ruthven near Kingussie, showed the dramatist John Home (*see* WHAUR'S YER WULLIE SHAKESPEARE NOO?) a fragment entitled 'The Death of Oscar'. He told Home that the fragment was the work of Ossian, the legendary Gaelic bard whose father was FINGAL (or Finn), hero of ancient Irish myth. Encouraged by Home and Hugh Blair, who raised money to help fund his researches, Macpherson toured the Western Highlands and the Hebrides collecting and translating more manuscripts, and in 1760 published *Fragments of Ancient Poetry, Collected in the Highlands of Scotland, and Translated from the Galic or Erse Language*. Here is a fragment of one of these fragments:

My love is a son of the hill.
He pursues the flying deer.
His grey dogs are panting

around him; his bow-string sounds in
the wind. Whether by the fount of
the rock, or by the stream of the
mountain thou liest; when the rushes are
nodding with the wind, and the mist
is flying over thee, let me approach
my love unperceived, and see him
from the rock …

Such simple, unadorned lines – which do have a flavour of genuine Gaelic poetry – provoked great excitement, many Scots feeling that their nation should possess an ancient epic poet to rival Homer or Virgil (indeed, Ossian was hailed as 'the Celtic Homer'). Macpherson duly obliged, and in 1762 published *Fingal, An Ancient Epic Poem in Six Books*, followed the next year by another epic, entitled *Temora*. These works caused a sensation, not only in Britain but right across Europe – especially in those parts of northern Europe where intellectuals were increasingly seeking to establish a national identity independent of the classical, Mediterranean traditions of Greece or Rome. Among the throng of admirers was no less a figure than Goethe, who in *The Sorrows of Young Werther* (1774) sings Ossian's praises:

Ossian has superseded Homer in my head. To what a world does the illustrious bard transport me! To wander over pathless wilds, surrounded by impetuous whirlwinds, where by the feeble light of the moon, we see the spirits of our ancestors: to hear from the mountain tops, mid the roar of torrents, their plaintive sounds issuing from deep caverns …

But back in Britain there was growing scepticism. In *A Journey to the Western Islands of Scotland* (1775), Dr Johnson opined that Macpherson had collected numerous fragments of genuine Gaelic poems and tales, then worked them into epics of his own composition. Boswell records Johnson as saying 'I look upon M'Pherson's Fingal to be as gross an imposition as ever the world was troubled with.' Johnson's comments prompted Macpherson to issue a written challenge, which Johnson dismissed thus:

I received your foolish and impudent letter. Any violence offered me I shall do my best to repel; and what I cannot do for myself, the law shall do for me …

I thought your book an imposture; I think it an imposture still ... what I hear of your morals, inclines me to pay regard not to what you shall say, but to what you shall prove.

David Hume, in a letter to Edward Gibbon dated March 1776, declared:

It is indeed strange that any man of sense could have imagined it possible, that above twenty thousand verses, along with numberless historical facts, could have been preserved by an oral tradition during fifty generations, by the rudest, perhaps, of all the European nations, the most necessitous, the most turbulent, and the most unsettled.

Several Irish historians also doubted the authenticity of the works, Charles O'Connor for one pointing out problems with Macpherson's chronology, and in his formation of Gaelic names. To none of these objections did Macpherson have an answer, and when asked to produce the original manuscripts, he had to resort to forging them. After his death a committee of inquiry chaired by Henry Mackenzie, author of *The Man of Feeling*, concluded in 1805 that Johnson had been correct in his judgement as to the provenance of the 'Ossianic' works, and later generations of scholars have concurred with this verdict. The revelation of the fraud did not dent the popularity of the poems, which were among the favourite books of Napoleon (in an Italian translation), and in 1866 Matthew Arnold praised the 'apparition of newness and power' in the better passages. *See also* FINGAL'S CAVE.

Ossian's Cave A cave high on the north face of Aonach Dubh, one of the THREE SISTERS OF GLENCOE. It was supposedly the birthplace of the Gaelic bard Ossian, son of the hero FINGAL. It is something of a rock climb (albeit a damp and vegetated one) to reach the cave, and the first recorded visitor was a local shepherd, Neil Marquis, who made the ascent in 1868. Some 30 years later, a subsequent ascentionist recorded his impressions of the route thus:

No good cragsman will make much of Ossian's Cave, but at the same time no honest one will despise it. When [William] Tough and I climbed into it in July,

the rocks were running with moisture, and the vegetation which grows profusely upon them was like a well-watered market-garden. It was simply impossible at places to get a firm hold of the solid rock. Hands, knees, toes, and eyelids had to be awkwardly spread over a mixture of mud and vegetable, which affords a support as treacherous as it is dirty, and which no respectable mountaineer, having regard to his Norfolk [jacket], will care to depend on.
  – William Brown, 'Climbing in Glencoe', *Scottish Mountaineering Club Journal*, Volume 4, Number 1 (January 1896)

Otterburn, Battle of *See* HUNTING OF THE CHEVIOT, THE.

Our Lady's Ellwand *See* KING'S ELLWAND, THE.

Over the sea to Skye The refrain of the famous 'Skye Boat Song', written in 1908 by Sir Harold Edwin Boulton, a Hertfordshire baronet, to an older tune collected by Miss Annie MacLeod, who heard it from the men rowing her boat across Loch Coruisk on Skye in the 1870s.

Speed, bonnie boat, like a bird on the wing,
'Onward!' the sailors cry;
Carry the lad that's born to be king,
Over the sea to Skye.

The refrain was not original to Boulton, however, having been used earlier by Robert Louis Stevenson in 'Sing me a song of a lad that is gone', from *Songs of Travel* (1896):

Sing me a song of a lad that is gone,
Say, could that lad be I?
Merry of soul he sailed on a day
Over the sea to Skye.

The subject, of course, is the voyage made by Bonnie Prince Charlie, the YOUNG PRETENDER, in 1746 from the Outer Hebrides to Skye, disguised as his companion Flora MACDONALD's maid, Betty BURKE, and the song has since become one of the most famous of a dribble of sentimental, nostalgic Jacobite songs that flowed out of Scotland from the later 18th century.

Owre-the-march marriage *See* MARCH, THE.

P

Pace egg A hard-boiled egg painted or dyed in bright colours, and rolled down a slope at Easter (*Pace*) – possibly in commemoration of the rolling aside of the rock in front of Christ's tomb, although originally probably associated with Eostre, the pre-Christian Germanic goddess of spring whose name is the origin of the word 'Easter'. The custom of *pace-egging* was particularly popular among the Episcopalians of the Northeast, where it was carried out on Easter Sunday. Elsewhere in Scotland, Pace Egg Day might be Easter Monday, or the Saturday before Easter. The custom is also known in parts of northern England. Variants of *Pace* include *Pasche*, *Pask* and *Pax*, ultimately from Latin *Pascha*, the Jewish festival of Passover, which occurs around the same time.

Pacification of Perth, the A peace agreement drawn up by the powerful Earl of Argyll and agreed by the Privy Council meeting in Perth on 23 February 1572, by which the Huntly and Hamilton factions, supporters of the exiled Mary Queen of Scots, were obliged to 'submit themselves to the King's obedience and to the government of James, Earl of Morton, Regent, and other Regents during the King's minority'. The Pacification thus ended some years of civil war in Scotland.

Pack of tatterdemalions, a A description of the Jacobite army in the '45 by James Gilchrist, postmaster of Dumfries, who had joined the army as a Hanoverian double agent. He wrote to his masters in London:

> Now that we have seen the army it gives us no small concern to think that a whole kingdom should have been so shamefully intimidated with such a pack of tatterdemalions, for two thirds of them are not better and great numbers of them marching without breeches, stockings or shoes.

A contrasting view of the Jacobite army is provided by John Ramsay of Ochtertyre (1736–1814):

> It was perhaps one of the most innocent and orderly hosts ever seen, considering they had no discipline and not much pay.
> – Letter to Elizabeth Dundas, 1810

Paddy's Market A second-hand clothes and furniture market in Glasgow. It was established in the 1820s at the foot of the Saltmarket, mostly by Irish traders (hence the name), and in the 1850s moved to a covered market south of Bridgegate, until this was demolished in 1866, since when it has been an outdoor market again – noted for its cheapness and chaotic layout. Following an increase in drug dealing and illegal street trading in the vicinity, one councillor has described it as a 'crime-ridden midden', and in 2008 the council announced its intention of transforming it into Glasgow's answer to London's Camden Market. No change then.

Paddy's Milestone A nickname for Ailsa Craig, a large lump of granite in the lower Firth of Clyde, south of Arran. It is approximately halfway between Glasgow and Belfast, and was thus a marker for Irish immigrants heading for the Broomielaw – hence the nickname. It is also known as a source of fine curling stones, and as home to the AILSA COCK – the puffin. *See also* DEAF AS AILSA CRAIG.

Pad the road or **streets, to** To travel about in search of work.

> Says I, 'My dearest Molly,
> Come let us fix the time
> When ye and I will married be
> And wedlock us combine,
> When ye and I get married, love,
> Richt happy we will be

For ye are the bonnie lassie
That's tae pad the road wi' me.'

'To pad the road wi' you, kind sir;
Cauld winter's coming on,
Besides my aged parents
Have ne'er a girl but one;
Besides, my aged parents
Have ne'er a girl but me,
So I'm no the bonnie lassie
That's to pad the road wi' thee.'
    – 'Pad the Road wi' Me' (traditional song)

Pail ale The name formerly given by Glasgow barmen to the slops they poured into a bucket for recycling into the bottom of 'fresh' pints of Guinness. The name punned on 'pale ale' (*see under* BEER).

Painting the Forth Bridge An expression that has spread far beyond Scotland, denoting any endless task. The allusion is to the (apparently erroneous) belief that as soon as the painters have finished giving the 1.5-mile rail bridge over the Firth of Forth (completed in 1890) one coat of paint, they have to start again at the other end. Thanks to new materials, the coat applied in the early years of the 21st century should last 25 years. *See also* BRIGGERS, THE.

Paisley, to get aff at *See* GET AFF AT PAISLEY, TO.

Paisley, unable to obtain a woman in *See* HE COULDNAE GET A WUMMAN IN PAISLEY.

Paisley bodie *See* BUDDY.

Paisley pattern A distinct curvilinear pattern, Mughal in origin, based round a comma-shaped motif. The pattern is characteristic of Kashmiri shawls, and when such shawls were brought back by Scottish soldiers around the turn of the 19th century the pattern was copied by the weavers of Paisley. It was particularly characteristic of *Paisley shawls*, fine shawls of wool, cashmere or silk manufactured in the town in the 19th century.

Yet Paisley's name is widely spread,
And history doth show it's
Been famed alike for shawls and thread,
For poverty and poets.
    – John Kent, himself a Paisley poet, alongside the likes of Robert Tannahill, the celebrated WEAVER POET

Paisley Rocketeers An amateur society founded in 1936 by John D. Stewart, inspired by the writings of H.G. Wells and others. Their achievements include what is thought to have been the first three-stage rocket, which took to the skies in 1937.

Paisley screwdriver *See* GLASGOW SCREWDRIVER.

Paisley shawl *See under* PAISLEY PATTERN.

Palace of Scottish blackguardism, the Dundee, according to Lord Cockburn (1779–1854) in his *Circuit Journeys*:

Dundee, the palace of Scottish blackguardism, unless perhaps Paisley be entitled to contest this honour with it.

Palindromic place names *See* GLENELG.

Pally ally A colloquial version of pale ale (*see under* BEER). Not to be confused with London's Ally Pally (Alexandra Palace), glimpsed from the train by those heading from Edinburgh to King's Cross.

Pan Am Flight 103 *See* LOCKERBIE BOMBING, THE.

Pandemonium, two minutes of What Norman MacCaig suggested the nation should observe following the death in 1978 of the poet Hugh MacDiarmid, a great stirrer of hornet's nests.

I'll ha'e nae hauf-way hoose, but aye be whaur
Extremes meet – it's the only way I ken
To dodge the curst conceit o' bein richt
That damns the vast majority o' men.
    – Hugh MacDiarmid, *A Drunk Man Looks at the Thistle* (1926)

My job, as I see it, has never been to lay a tit's egg; but to erupt like a volcano, emitting not only flame, but a load of rubbish.
    – Hugh MacDiarmid, letter to George Bruce, June 1964

Pan loaf A loaf of bread with a smooth crust, more expensive than a *plain loaf*, which has a hard black crust on top. Hence, to *speak pan loaf* is to affect a 'posh' accent and/or manner of speech; Michael Munro, in *The Patter* (1985), suggests that this may arise from rhyming slang with 'toff', which rhymes with loaf in Glasgow and environs. *Pan loaf* may also imply 'posh' people generally, as in the put-down 'There's pan loaf folk sure, bit yer jist plain breid.'

Papa Stour, the Prisoner of *See* MAIDEN STACK; PRISONER OF PAPA STOUR, THE

Papa Stour sword dance A traditional Shetland dance named after the small island off the west coast of Mainland, and involving a number of performers accompanied on the fiddle. The dancers, joined to each other by swords (or pieces of wood), perform a variety of complex circular and knot-like figures. In the version described by Sir Walter Scott in *The Pirate* (1822), the dancers represent the Seven Champions: St George of England, St James of Spain, St Denis of France, St David of Wales, St Patrick of Ireland, St Anthony of Italy and St Andrew of Scotland. At the end they intermesh their swords to form a shield. *See also* SWORD DANCE.

Paper King, the A nickname of the Edinburgh-born financier and economist John Law (1671–1729), whose father, a banker and goldsmith, had acquired the estate of Lauriston near the city. Law's abilities as a mental calculator of probabilities drew him to gambling, which he pursued as a career in England. In 1694 he killed a man in a duel and was sentenced to death, but escaped to the Continent, where he led a peripatetic life for many years, eventually, in 1716, becoming a naturalized French subject. He earned his nickname from his advocacy of paper banknotes, backed by gold, silver or land, and he was also a staunch proponent of the establishment of the Banque Générale, the French national bank. His ideas appealed to the French regent, and Law was made controller general of finances. He went on to devise a notorious financial scheme that ballooned and then went bust – the infamous Mississippi Bubble (also known as Law's Bubble). As a consequence of this scandal, Law was

obliged to resume his wanderings, and some years later he died of pneumonia and in relative poverty in Venice, his vast paper assets having proved worthless.

Paper minister A disparaging term in the 18th and 19th centuries for a minister who read his sermon, generally regarded as 'a proof of disgraceful incapacity'.

Paradise How Celtic supporters refer to their club's ground at Parkhead.

Paraffin Young The nickname of the Glasgow-born chemist James Young (1811–83), the first oil entrepreneur. Young conducted his first experiments in distilling lamp oil from natural petroleum seepage in a Derbyshire coalmine, and subsequently found that he could distil a variety of fractions from various coals and shales, including one product he called 'paraffine oil'. In 1851, in partnership with others, he began extracting and refining oil from a deep brown shale called torbanite, or Boghead coal, named after Torbane Hill on the Boghead estate near Bathgate, where it was mined. Eventually other companies became involved in exploiting the oil shales of West Lothian, resulting in the great red spoil heaps known as the WEST LOTHIAN ALPS. By 1870 Young had retired from business, and devoted himself to philanthropy, leisure, and scientific pursuits.

Para Handy *See* HANDY, PARA.

Parallel Roads of Glen Roy, the A remarkable geomorphological feature in Glen Roy in Lochaber. There are three parallel terraces on the hillsides on both sides of the glen, which from a distance resemble man-made roads, but which actually mark the varying levels of an ice-dammed lake that filled the valley towards the end of the last Ice Age. When Charles Darwin visited in June 1838 he concluded that the 'roads' were marine in origin – a conclusion he later conceded had been a 'gigantic blunder'.

Parcel of rogues, a How Burns characterized the members of the Scottish Parliament who voted for the Union in 1707; the phrase 'Such a parcel of rogues in a nation' forms the last line of each verse in the poem of the same name. According to William Scott Douglas in his 1877 annotated edition of the poet's works, Burns found the line 'in old "Musical Repositories", and he, believing it to apply to the national indignation in regard to the question of *The Union,* conceived and executed the present lyric accordingly'.

> Fareweel to a' our Scottish fame,
>   Fareweel our ancient glory;
> Fareweel ev'n to the Scottish name,
>   Sae fam'd in martial story!
> Now Sark rins o'er the Solway sands,
>   And Tweed rins to the ocean,
> To mark where England's province stands –
>   Such a parcel of rogues in a nation!

(For the significance of the Sark, *see* DEBATABLE LANDS.) Burns picks up on the common perception in Scotland that some of the EQUIVALENT (money supplied by the new British government to cancel the Scottish national debt) found its way into the pockets of 'a coward few' – the pro-Union members of the Scottish Parliament:

> We're bought and sold for English gold
> Such a parcel of rogues in a nation!

Burns is quite restrained in his condemnation in comparison to an earlier poet, Iain LOM, who, in his 'Song Against the Union' (originally in Gaelic) wrote:

> If I had my way
> I would melt your gold payment,
> Pour it into your skull
> Till it reached your boots.

It was the Jacobite sympathizer and anti-Union politician George Lockhart of Carnwath (1673–1731) who had done much to expose the bribery. In his *Memoirs of the Affairs of Scotland* (1714) he recalled the words of Robert Harley, Queen Anne's first minister, during a parliamentary debate on the taxation of linen exports in 1710 or 1711:

> After a long debate, Mr Harley said he admired the debate should last so long. 'For have we not bought the Scots and a right to tax them? And pray, for what did we give the Equivalent?'

I took him up, and said I was glad to hear the truth, which I never doubted, now publicly brought to light and owned: for the honourable gentleman acknowledged that Scotland was bought and sold ... I would be extremely glad to know what this price amounted to, and who received it.

Another strongly anti-Union politician, Andrew Fletcher of Saltoun, described Scotland after the Union as 'only fit for the slaves who sold it'. *See also* END OF AN OLD SONG, THE.

Parliamo Glasgow A series of sketches, broadcast by STV from the later 1960s, in which Stanley Baxter played the part of a language teacher imparting to viewers the Glasgow patois (or PATTER). He would start by introducing a Glaswegian phrase, such as the following that might be heard at a local market: 'Izzatamarraonyerbarra, Clara?' This was then given a standard English translation: 'Is that a marrow on your barrow, Clara?'. Other examples include 'Errarainoanu, scummindooninbuckits', which phrase heralds FAIR FORTNIGHT, while at Glasgow weddings it is traditional for the bride's mother to utter the following cry: 'O molasses! O molasses! O molassesmerritaheidcase!' The title and format parodied the BBC's *Parliamo Italiano* ('Let's speak Italian'). In his 1971 production of *Mother Goose,* Baxter sang a song that triumphantly ended thus:

> Anif yuzkin say ramorra
> Orrabest an itznae borra
> Yezkin parliamo Glasgow orratime!

Parritch *See* PORRIDGE.

Pars, the *See* FOOTBALL CLUB NICKNAMES.

Partan bree A crab soup from the Northeast, *partan* being a crab and *bree* a stock. Other ingredients include milk, cream, chives and rice.

Particularly disagreeable What the Scots are, according to the English essayist William Hazlitt (1778–1830):

> Among ourselves, the Scotch, as a nation, are particularly disagreeable. They hate every appearance of comfort themselves, and refuse it to others. Their

climate, their religion and their habits are equally averse to pleasure. Their manners are either distinguished by a fawning sycophance (to gain their own ends, and conceal their natural defects), that makes one sick; or by a morose, unblending callousness, that makes one shudder.

– 'On Disagreeable People', published in the *Monthly Magazine*, August 1827

For other ill-judged tirades, *see* SOUR, STINGY, DEPRESSING BEGGARS; TULLIETUDLESCLEUGH.

Parts, pendicles and pertinents An old legal term, denoting all the items associated with a piece of land that formed part of the conveyance when it was sold.

Pat Lazarus A nickname of Pat Lally (b.1926), Lord Provost of Glasgow from 1995 to 1999, referring to his various political comebacks. *See also* LALLY'S PALAIS; RHYMING SLANG.

Patter, the The colourful, inventive and constantly evolving dialect of Glasgow and environs. It has been masterfully and entertainingly recorded by the lexicographer Michael Munro in his books *The Patter* (1985), *The Patter – Another Blast* (1988) and *The Complete Patter* (1996). The word *patter* itself denotes 'talk', but especially flamboyant, persuasive talk, and anyone who specializes in the latter is known as a *patter merchant*. If any aspirant patter merchant is deemed insufficiently skilled in this respect, they may, as Munro points out, be put down with such lines as 'Yer patter's like watter', or 'Yer patter's like toothpaste – it comes oot a TUBE.' *See also* PARLIAMO GLASGOW.

Peasant Poet, the An epithet sometimes applied either to Robert Burns (the PLOUGHMAN POET) or to James Hogg (the ETTRICK SHEPHERD).

Pease-bogle *See* TATTIE-BOGLE.

Pease brose A kind of porridge made from dried peas. It was very basic fare, hence the phrase was often used to denote poverty. *Pease brose and pianos* indicates genteel poverty (*cf.* AW FUR COAT AN NAE KNICKERS). *See also* ATHOLL BROSE; KAIL BROSE.

Pease strae The dried remnants (*strae*, 'straw') of the pea plant after harvest, used as fodder or bedding for animals – or impoverished humans:

When John and I were married,
Our hau'ding was but sma',
For my minnie, canker't carline,
Wou'd gi'e us nocht ava';
I wair't my fee wi' canny care,
As far as it would gae,
But weel I wat our bridal bed
Was clean pease-strae.
– Robert Tannahill (the WEAVER POET), 'When John and I Were Married' [*hau'ding*, 'holding' (i.e. small farm); *minnie*, 'mother'; *carline*, 'old woman'; *wat*, 'know']

'Pease Straw' or 'Clean Pease Strae' is a traditional hornpipe or reel; the associated tune is first found in print in 1757.

Peculiar disguisements of print An allusion to the complexities and perplexities (at least to the outsider) of Gaelic orthography:

The regrettable thing about Gaelic is its hopelessly bewildering spelling. The sounds are pleasing and melodious in a high degree but they hide themselves behind the most peculiar disguisements of print.
– D.T. Holmes, *Literary Tours in the Highlands and Islands* (1909)

Peden the Prophet *See* PROPHET PEDEN.

Pedestrian, the Great *See* GREAT PEDESTRIAN, THE.

Pedestrian Traveller, the The byname of Captain John Dundas Cochrane (1780–1825), grandson of the 8th Earl of Dundonald and illegitimate son of the MP, gun-runner, fraudster and general bad egg, Andrew James Cochrane-Johnstone. After a career in the Royal Navy, Cochrane Junior applied to the Admiralty to mount an expedition to the Niger, but was rebuffed. In 1820 he set off from London with the intention of walking round the world, his mode of transport being largely dictated by financial constraints. Reaching St Petersburg by way of Paris and Berlin, he was offered assistance by the Russian government and so parts of his onward journey across Siberia were made by horse, sledge and canoe. Hardship was ever at his heels, however, and he recalled how he had spent 20 nights sleeping in the snow 'without even the comfort of a blanket – a great oversight'. Reaching the Pacific, he fell in love with a 14-year-old native of Kamchatka, whom he married. Rather than completing his circumambulation via North America, he returned with his bride by way of St Petersburg to Britain. In 1824 Cochrane travelled to South America, intending to walk across the continent and to visit the copper-mining venture of his cousin, Captain Charles Stuart Cochrane, but died of a fever in Valencia, Colombia. Shortly afterwards, his cousin returned to Britain, styling himself 'Señor Juan de Vega, a Spanish Minstrel'. *See also* GREAT PEDESTRIAN, THE; LUGLESS WILLIE.

Peebles for Pleasure The slogan of the Border town of Peebles, which set itself up as a holiday destination in the 19th century, offering such attractions as golf, fishing in the River Tweed, and the Peebles Hydro spa.

Peeled egg, a A stroke of luck, something handed to one on a plate. The expression was recorded by James Kelly in his *Complete Collection of Scottish Proverbs* (1721):

> *You have come to a peel'd egg.* Spoken to those who have got an estate, place or preferment ready prepar'd for their hand; or as the English say, *Cut and dry.*

A number of farms in the Northeast apparently once bore the name Peeled Egg, and the expression continued in use into the 20th century.

Peel tower *See* PELE TOWER.

Peely-wally Pale, emaciated and generally unhealthy-looking.

> And damn it, if before a twelvemonth was up she didn't have a bairn, a peely-wally girl.
> – Lewis Grassic Gibbon, *Sunset Song* (1932)

The *DSL* suggests that *peely* is 'probably imitative of a whining, feeble sound', but remains silent regarding *wally*; there may possibly be a connection with WALLIE, 'porcelain', a material known for its pallor.

Peerie heels High heels, especially women's stiletto heels. A *peerie* is a child's spinning top, which has a sharply pointed base. There is a children's rhyme that goes:

> Oh there she goes,
> Oh there she goes,
> Peerie heels and pointed toes.
> Look at her feet,She thinks she's neat,
> Black stockings and dirty feet.

Peg Bull *See* BULL, PEG.

Pele tower A defensive stone tower, many of which litter the Borders, and which, at the time of the BORDER REIVERS, provided a refuge for people and cattle. Some were supposedly haunted by REDCAPS. The word *pele*, which has been applied to such towers since at least the 14th century, comes from *pale*, a wooden stockade – originally the towers were surrounded by such stockades, before being replaced by stone-built barnekin walls. The word *pale* in turn comes from Latin *palus*, a sharpened stake (as carried by Roman legionaries to make their temporary camps). Hence also the Pale, the area of English settlement in Ireland in the Middle Ages.

Pen-gun *See* CRACK LIKE A GUN, TO.

Pen Nibs, the *See* FOOTBALL CLUB NICKNAMES.

Penny bridal or **penny wedding** or **siller bridal** The rowdy celebrations formerly conducted on the eve of a wedding, involving drinking, feasting and dancing. Contributions were also made by the guests towards the cost of the wedding feast. At one point the bride-to-be was taken by her female friends to the best room in the house, where they washed her feet in a tub of water into which a woman who had been long happily married dropped her wedding ring. The women then grabbed the bridegroom and forced him to sit at the tub while they rubbed his legs with cinders and soot (*see also* BLACKENING).

The ritual of washing the bride's feet may be behind a story recounted by Thomas Love Peacock in his *Memoirs of Shelley* (1858–62). In 1811 Shelley had eloped with Harriet Westbrook to Edinburgh, where they were married.

> Their journey had absorbed their stock of money. They took a lodging, and Shelley immediately told the landlord who they were, what they had come for, and the exhaustion of their resources, and asked him if he would take them in, and advance them money to get married and to carry them on till they could get a remittance. This

the man agreed to do, on condition that Shelley would treat him and his friends to a supper in honour of the occasion. It was arranged accordingly; but the man was more obtrusive and officious than Shelley was disposed to tolerate. The marriage was concluded, and in the evening Shelley and his bride were alone together, when the man tapped at their door. Shelley opened it, and the landlord said to him – 'It is customary here at weddings for the guests to come in, in the middle of the night, and wash the bride with whisky.' 'I immediately,' said Shelley, 'caught up my brace of pistols, and pointing them both at him, said to him, – "I have had enough of your impertinence; if you give me any more of it I will blow your brains out;" on which he ran or rather tumbled down stairs, and I bolted the doors.'

The custom of washing the bride with whisky is more likely to have been so made known to him than to have been imagined by him.

Penny dog A dog that is always at its owner's heels; hence also a sycophant or other fawning creature. The term may be a corruption of *pirrie-dog*, which has the same meaning – *to pirrie* is to follow someone around or dog their footsteps.

Penny-rattler The equivalent of a pound shop in the Northeast, before inflation set in.

Penny wedding *See* PENNY BRIDAL.

Pentland, the Hunt of *See* HUNT OF PENTLAND, THE.

Pentland Rising The Covenanter insurrection of 1666, rapidly suppressed by BLUIDY TAM Dalyell at the Battle of Rullion Green, below Turnhouse Hill on the south side of the Pentland Hills.

> Blows the wind to-day, and the sun and the rain are flying,
> Blows the wind on the moors to-day and now,
> Where about the graves of the martyrs the whaups [curlews] are crying,
> My heart remembers how!
> – Robert Louis Stevenson, 'To S.R. Crockett' ('Hills of Home')

Penure-pig An archaic term for a piggy bank, *penure* (or sometimes *pinner*) being a version of 'penury'.

People's Palace, the A museum of Glasgow life from 1750 to the present, situated on Glasgow Green. Attached are the Winter Gardens, glasshouses containing a variety of palms and other exotic plants. The People's Palace was opened in 1898, and was initially used as a cultural centre for the poor of the city's East End, with reading and recreation rooms, as well as a picture gallery and museum. From the 1940s it has been a museum of Glasgow social history.

Pepper-and-mustard terrier *See* DINMONT, DANDIE.

Perfervid Scots, the *See* PRAEFERVIDUM INGENIUM SCOTORUM.

Perish the pack, to A 19th-century expression meaning to blow one's fortune, *perish* being to kill or dissipate.

Persecuting time, the *See* KILLING TIME, THE.

Perth *See* FAIR CITY, THE; *FAIR MAID OF PERTH, THE*; FIVE ARTICLES OF PERTH, THE; PACIFICATION OF PERTH, THE; SMALLEST CITY IN SCOTLAND, THE.

Pest control In the 4th edition of his *Popular Rhymes of Scotland* (1870), Robert Chambers describes the following charm against rats and mice:

> When these creatures become superabundant in a house of the humbler class, a writ of ejectment, in the following form, is served upon them, by being stuck up legibly written on the wall:

> > Ratton and mouse,
> > Lea' the puir woman's house;
> > Gang awa' owre by to 'e mill,
> > And there ane and a' ye'll get your fill.

> A correspondent says: 'I have seen the writ served on them, but cannot tell the result.'

Similar devices – known as rat or mouse satires – were employed in the Gaelic-speaking parts of Scotland:

> When the islet of Calv (*an Calbh*, the Inner Door), which lies across the mouth of Tobermory harbour,

was let in small holdings, the rats at one time became so numerous that the tenants subscribed sixpence a-piece, and sent for *Iain Pholchrain* to Morven, to come and satirize the rats away. He came and made a long ode, in which he told the rats to go away peaceably, and take care not to lose themselves in the wood. He told them what houses to call at, and what houses (those of the bard's own friends) to avoid, and the plenty and welcome stores – butter and cheese, and meal – to be got at their destination. It is said that after this there was an observable decrease in the number of rats in the island!

– John G. Campbell, *Superstitions of the Highlands and Islands of Scotland* (1900)

It seems that in some parts of the country, such remedies may have proved effective:

Not only are we told by the credulous Hector Boece, that there are no rats in Buchan (Aberdeenshire), but a later and more intelligent author, Sir Robert Gordon, makes the same statement regarding Sutherlandshire: 'If,' says he, 'they come thither in ships from other parts, they die presently, how soon they do smell the air of that country.' Sir Robert at the same time asserts, that the species abounds in the neighbouring province of Caithness. But this is not all. The reverend gentlemen who contributed to Sir John Sinclair's *Statistical Account of Scotland*, about 1794, the articles on Morven and Roseneath, the one in the north, the other in the south of Argyle-shire, avouch that rats have been introduced into those parishes in vain.

– Robert Chambers, *The Book of Days* (1862–4)

Peter *See* COME THE PETER OWER, TO.

Peterhead *See* BLUE TOON, THE.

Peter's bird *See* FLORA CALEDONIA.

Peter's Plough The Plough constellation, Ursa Major.

Peter's Staff The 'sword' in the constellation Orion. *See also* KING'S ELLWAND, THE.

Peter's thumb or **mark** A term used by East Coast fishermen for the dark mark below the gills of a haddock, supposed to be the thumbprint of St Peter

when he caught the fish with a coin in its mouth (Matthew 17:27).

Petted lip *See* HING THE PETTED LIP.

Petticoat tails A round shortbread with a scalloped edge, cut into triangular pieces. A recipe is provided in Mrs Frazer's *The Practice of Cookery, Pastry and Confectionery* (5th edition, Edinburgh, 1806), and they are mentioned by Scott in *The Bride of Lammermuir*. In *The Cook and Housewife's Manual* (1826), Margaret DODS (Mrs Isobel Johnston) remarks that 'the name *Petticoat tails* has its origin in the shape of the cake, which is exactly that of the bell-hoop petticoat of our ancient Court ladies'. Petticoat tails became popular in courtly circles in the 16th century when Mary of Guise was queen consort and then regent of Scotland. The word actually derives from the French *petites gatelles*, 'little cakes'.

Pet-willed Stubborn, wilful. The expression comes from the Northeast.

PH Cobbles The monogram 'PH' written in cobblestones outside St Salvator's College, St Andrews, marking the site where the Protestant martyr Patrick Hamilton was burnt at the stake in 1528. There is a student tradition in the town that it is bad luck to step on these cobblestones, and that anyone doing so will fail their degree. The only known ways of shaking off the curse, apparently, are either to walk three times round the post at the end of the pier, or to participate in the MAY DIP.

Philabeg or **filibeg** The kilt. The term is an anglicized form of Gaelic *féilead-beg*, 'little kilt', from *féileadh*, the full plaid from which the modern kilt evolved (the first recorded example of the latter dates from 1692).

Philip and Mary The name of some rocks on the east coast of Luce Bay, on the Solway Firth. Local legend has it that the name was that of a Spanish galleon wrecked here after the Armada of 1588. Another suggestion is that a ship of the same name was wrecked here in 1558 during the course of a punitive expedition to the Clyde sent by Mary I of England, who was married to Philip II of Spain.

Pibroch The 'art' music of the Highland bagpipes, and also sometimes played on the fiddle or clarsach (Gaelic harp). This music is known in Gaelic as the *Ceòl Mór* ('great music'), and consists of laments (*cumha*), salutes (*fàilte*), marches and gatherings (*port tionail*) – in contrast to the *Ceòl Beag* ('little music'), which comprises reels, strathspeys and other dance tunes. An individual piece of the *Ceòl Mór* is also known as a *pibroch*, and consists of an *urlar* (literally 'floor', i.e. theme) and variations. The word *pibroch* derives from Gaelic *piobaireachd*, 'piping', and the origins of the *Ceòl Mór* are sometimes traced to the 17th century and the hereditary pipers to the MacLeods of Dunvegan, the MacCrimmons.

> Thy chanter's shout gives pleasure,
> Sighing thy bold variations.
> Through every lively measure;
> The war note intent on rending,
> White fingers deft are pounding,
> To hack both marrow and muscles,
> With thy shrill cry resounding.
> – Alasdair mac Mhaighstir Alasdair (c. 1695–1770),
> 'Moladh air Piob-Mhor Mhic Cruimein' ('In Praise of MacCrimmon's Pipes')

> My duty done, I will try to follow you on the last day of the world,
> And pray I may see you all standing shoulder to shoulder
> With Patrick Mor MacCrimmon and Duncan Ban MacCrimmon in the centre
> In the hollow at Boreraig or in front of Dunvegan Castle ...
> – Hugh MacDiarmid, 'Lament for the Great Music, from *Stony Limits and Other Poems* (1934)

> Let me play to you tunes without measure or end,
> Tunes that are born to die without a herald,
> As a flight of storks rises from a marsh, circles,
> And alights on the spot from which it arose.
> – Hugh MacDiarmid, 'Bagpipe Music', from *Lucky Poet* (1943)

Pibroch of the Confederacy, the A name given to the 'Rebel yell' uttered by Confederate soldiers during the American Civil War. One theory holds that the yell derived from that of charging Highlanders (*see* HIGHLAND CHARGE); certainly many Highland Scots had settled in the South, especially in the Carolinas. The yell was also called 'the Pibroch of Southern fealty'.

Pickie-turds See DEVIL'S BIRD, THE.

Pickle the Spy The *nom de guerre* of a Hanoverian double agent who was close to the Jacobite leaders, and in the wake of the failed '45 Rebellion informed the government of George II of the plots and plans of Bonnie Prince Charlie and his supporters. In his 1897 book *Pickle the Spy* Andrew Lang identified Pickle – the name the man used to communicate with his Hanoverian masters – with Alestair Ruadh MacDonnell (*c.*1725–61), chief of the MacDonnells of Glengarry. As a boy MacDonnell had gone to France to serve with the Royal Scots, a regiment in the service of the French king, and in 1744 was sent to Scotland as a Jacobite agent. He was captured the following year, and spent nearly two years in the Tower of London before being released and going abroad again. He returned to London in 1749, and it may have been then that he offered his services as a double agent. He is thought to have been responsible for the capture of the brother of Cameron of Lochiel, Dr Archibald Cameron, who was executed for treason in 1753.

Pick one's wulk, to To pick one's whelk, i.e. nose (presumably so dubbed because the nose, like the shellfish, is not only pointed, but hard on the outside and squidgy on the interior).

Pictish peer, the Byron's characterization of Thomas Bruce, Lord Elgin, who, starting in 1801, removed his eponymous marbles bit by bit from the Parthenon. In *The Curse of Minerva* (1812), Byron compares Elgin with Alaric the Goth, who sacked Rome in AD 410:

> The Gothic monarch and the Pictish peer:
> Arms gave the first his right, the last had none,
> But basely stole what less barbarians won.
> So, when the lion quits his fell repast,
> Next prowls the wolf, the filthy jackal last.
> Flesh, limbs, and blood the former make their own,
> The last poor brute securely gnaws the bone.

The Parthenon was, of course, sacred to Athena, whom the Romans called Minerva.

Picts A group of Celtic tribes who inhabited much of Scotland north of the Forth and Clyde before the coming of the Scots from Ireland. Their language was probably related to the Brythonic language of the ancient Britons who lived to the south. In the 6th century AD, one of these southern Britons, the chronicler and cleric Gildas, described the Picts as 'a set of bloody freebooters, with more hair on their thievish faces than clothes to cover their nakedness'. In 685 the overlordship claimed by the Northumbrians over the Picts was ended when the former were defeated at the Battle of Nechtansmere in Angus, leading the Northumbrian chronicler Eddi to write, in his *Vita Wilfridi Episcopi* (*c.*710) that 'The bestial people of the Picts with savage mind despised subjection to the Saxons.' Once the Scots established the kingdom of DALRIADA in the west, the Picts were confined to the northeast of the country, and they ceased to exist as a separate power after Kenneth MacAlpin, king of Dalriada, unified most of Scotland in the 9th century, to form the kingdom of ALBA. The DECLARATION OF ARBROATH says that the Scots 'utterly destroyed' the Picts, but it is more likely to have been a process of assimilation.

'Discussion of the meaning of the word "Pict",' says Agnes Mure Mackenzie in the first volume of *Scottish Pageant* (1946), 'can rouse mild elderly gentlemen, even today, to a bubbling pitch of fury.' In the 14th century John of Fordun, in his *Scotichronicon*, states:

> Some maintain that the people of the Picts were called Picti either from their beauty, the graceful stature of their body, or their embroidered garments … or that perhaps other people called them Picti in derision, by antiphrasis, because they were so shabby.

In his *Historia Gentis Scotorum* (1527), Hector Boece says that the 'name Pictis … may be interpret payntit owder becaus of the plesand forme of thare persouns or fra the variant coloure of thare clething'. Both these authorities assume that the word *Picti* is Latin, meaning 'painted ones', given to the Picts because of their tattoos (*picti* is the past participle of the verb *pingere*, 'to paint'), although there is no strong evidence that tattooing *was* a widespread practice. More recently some scholars have questioned the 'painted ones' theory, suggesting that the name is the same as the 'Pit-' element in many place names in eastern Scotland north of the Forth, such as Pitlochry, Pitcur, Pitscottie, Pitmedden and Pittenweem, in which the element represents the Old Celtic word *pett*, 'portion' or 'area'.

Picts' houses A name once given to various prehistoric underground dwellings:

> There are in most of the parishes Picts houses as they call them; they are some of them of a pyramidal form.
> – Robert Sibbald, *Description of the Isles of Orkney and Shetland* (1711)

This attribution prompted the following definition of 'Pict' in an old edition of *Chambers Dictionary*: 'one of a dwarfish race of underground dwellers, to whom (with the Britons, the Druids and Cromwell) ancient monuments are generally attributed'.

Piece A sandwich or other portable snack; *black piece*, for example, is gingerbread. A *playpiece* is any snack taken by a child to school for consumption during break, while a *bairn's piece* is bread and cheese offered to those who meet or visit a baby after it has been christened, a custom still observed in the late 19th century. The following song by Adam McNaughtan was inspired by the plight of the many slum-dwellers who were moved into high-rise blocks in the 1960s (the number of weans may vary considerably from version to version):

> O ye cannae throw a piece frae a twenty-storey flat,
> Fifty thousand hungry weans'll testify tae that.
> If it's butter, cheese or jelly,
> If the bread is plain or pan,
> The odds agin it reaching earth
> Ur ninety-nine to wan.

There is also a children's counting-out game that goes:

> Eetle ottle black bottle,
> Eetle ottle out,
> If you want a piece and jam,
> Just march right out.

Some prefer crisps as a filling:

> A piece on crisps. Aye beautiful. Crunchy and munchy.
> – James Kelman, *A Disaffection* (1989)

Elgin has a sandwich shop called Blessed R., as in 'blessed are the peacemakers' (with a pun on 'piece'). *See also* CHITTERIN BIT; GIE'S-A-PIECE.

Pig and Whistle Light Infantry, the A nickname for the Highland Light Infantry; *see* REGIMENTAL NICKNAMES.

Pig Club, the A gentlemen's club in Glasgow, that flourished between 1798 and 1807. Membership, drawn largely from the city's sugar barons, was limited to twenty. 'From the proud position attained in society by its several members,' opines John Strang in *Glasgow and its Clubs* (1856), this club 'may well be designated a truly aristocratic fraternity.' Strang goes on to discuss the name of the club:

> It has ... been suspected, and perhaps with some truth, that the origin of the fraternal symbol might be attributed to the necessary appearance of a roasted suckling, of six weeks old, being placed before the president at every Club dinner; but if this be found to be apocryphal, it is at least known for certainty, that the president was bound to wear round his neck, at every meeting, a silver chain, to which was attached the figure of a pig; and so strictly was this enforced, that on every occasion when the member occupying the chair appeared in the Club-room, either from hurry or neglect, without exhibiting the Club jewel, he was instantly fined in a bottle of rum for the benefit of the Club.

See also ACCIDENTAL CLUB; HODGE PODGE CLUB.

Pigeon, Johnny Burns's nickname for John Dove, landlord of the Whitefoord Arms in Mauchline, where the poet, then known as 'Rob Mossgiel', met with the other members of the bachelors' club called the COURT OF EQUITY. On 4 June 1786 Burns penned the following 'Epitaph' for 'my landlord':

> Here lies Johnny Pigeon:
> What was his religion,
>   Whae'er desires to ken,
> To some other warl
> Maun follow the carl,
>   For here Johnny Pigeon had nane.
>
> Strong ale was ablution,
> Small beer persecution,
>   A dram was *memento mori*;
> But a full flowing bowl,
> Was the saving his soul,
>   And port was celestial glory.

More commonly, John Dove was known by his customers as 'Johnnie Doo' (*doo* being the Scots word for 'dove').

Pigs and whistles Bits and pieces, fragments, odds and sods, hence figuratively, matters of no consequence. A *pig* is an earthenware pot or other container, and *pigs* are shards.

Pike Plot, the At a time of radical agitation, the discovery of a store of pikeheads in Edinburgh in 1794 led to the arrest of one Robert Watt, formerly a government spy. He had acquired the weaponry supposedly on the orders of the British Convention of Delegates to Obtain Universal Suffrage and Annual Parliaments. His hanging before the Tolbooth helped to inspire the formation of the UNITED SCOTSMEN.

Pilate, Pontius An unlikely Scot, but nevertheless legend has it that the Roman procurator of Judaea who washed his hands of Jesus' fate was born in the village of Fortingall, in Glen Lyon, Perthshire. The story is that Pilate's father was on an embassy to Metallaus or Metellanus, a local Caledonian chief, and that his mother, who had accompanied her husband, gave birth to Pontius in the shelter of the venerable FORTINGALL YEW, which even then may have been several thousand years old. Further elaborations of the legend suggest that Pilate's mother was not a Roman at all, but rather a Menzies, or perhaps a MacLaren. *See also* PONTIUS PILATE'S BODYGUARD.

Pillory coat bespattered all over with dirt and rotten eggs, a A description of the map of Scotland by 'An English Gentleman', in *A Modern Account of Scotland* (1679):

> The country is full of lakes and loughs, and well stocked with islands, so that a map thereof looks like a pillory coat bespattered all over with dirt and rotten eggs ... The people are proud, arrogant and vainglorious boasters, bloody, barbarous and inhuman butchers. They show their pride in exalting themselves and depressing their neighbours. The women dislike Englishmen because they have no legs.

Presumably this particular English gentleman had suffered a rebuff ...

Pineapple, the A curious building, 14 m (45 ft) high, with a roof in the shape of a giant pineapple, built in 1761 in the grounds of the Dunmore estate, near Falkirk. It was commissioned by John Murray, 4th Earl of Dunmore, from an unknown architect, and pineapples (among other tender exotics) were actually grown on the south-facing ground floor, with the aid of a furnace-driven heating system. The upper floor contained living accommodation for the gardeners. The building is now a holiday let run by the Landmark Trust.

Pin-the-widdie A small haddock hung up whole to smoke in the chimney; hence the expression *as reekit as a pin-the-widdie*. A *widdie* is a willow wand.

Pintle The penis, as in Burns's paean to the 'guid weel-willy pintle' (*see* WEEL-WILLY). On its own the word was also once found south of the Border, but its appearance in a number of older Scots phrases may be mentioned here, e.g. *pintle-conneckit*, related by marriage, and *pintle-keek*, a lascivious leer. The *pintle-hide* is the foreskin, while, in the flora, *dog's pintle* is yarrow, and GOWKISPINTIL is cuckoo pint. Among fish, the *pintle-fish* is the sand eel, and the plain *pintle* is the ling.

Piper, as fou as a The same as *fiddler-fou; see under* FOU.

Piper Alpha Disaster On 6 July 1988 the Piper Alpha oil rig, located in the North Sea 110 miles (176 km) off Aberdeen, suffered a major explosion followed by a fire. There were 226 men on board, and a total of 167 men perished. It was by far the worst disaster to hit the North Sea oil industry.

Piper Bill See MAD PIPER, THE.

'Piper of Kilbarchan, The' See HABBIE.

Piper's biddin' See FIDDLER'S BIDDIN'.

Piper's or **fiddler's news** The same as CADGER'S NEWS.

Pirrie-dog See PENNY DOG.

Piscinata Scotia 'Fish-rich Scotland', apparently an established Latin saying by 1498, when Don Pedro de Ayala, Spanish ambassador to James IV, reported:

> It is impossible to describe the immense quantity of fish. The old proverb says already 'piscinata Scotia'. Great quantities of salmon, herring, and a kind of dried fish, which they call stock fish [*stoque fix*], are exported. The quantity is so great that it suffices for Italy, France, Flanders and England.

Pish pundit A Glaswegian term denoting a bookmaker.

Pisky A derogatory appellation for a member of the Scottish Episcopal Church (previously the Episcopal Church in Scotland); *see* PRESBY VS PISKY.

Pit and gallows The former right of capital jurisdiction held by barons within their own lands. The phrase is a translation of the Latin *furca et fossa*, a term used in medieval Scottish law. The *pits* referred to were water-filled holes in which women convicted of capital offences were drowned. The power of barons over life and death was diminished through the 17th century, and finally abolished by the Heritable Jurisdictions Act of 1746. Not all punishments meted out by the barons were as severe. In 1629 a man was brought before the baron court of the Campbells of Glenorchy and found guilty of vomiting on someone's floor. He was merely fined. *See also* FOUR PLEAS OF THE CROWN, THE.

Pitcaithly bannock See BANNOCK.

Pit (someone's) gas at a peep To deflate someone, put them in their place. To *pit oot someone's pipe* means the same thing. To *pit the gas at a peep* literally means to turn the gas in a light or cooker down to the minimum, so only a tiny flame burns.

Pit the hems on (someone or something) To restrain someone from doing something, to put a stop to something, to make something impossible; to impose a restraining order. *Haims* or *hems* are the parts of the collar of a draught horse to which the traces are attached.

Pit the peter on, to See COME THE PETER OWER, TO.

Plain loaf See PAN LOAF.

Plastic Scots How its detractors styled the 'Synthetic Scots' developed by Hugh MacDiarmid and other poets of the SCOTTISH RENAISSANCE, who gathered words and phrases from varieties of Scots scattered across both space and time, thus including terms from different dialects and words that had been long extinct. MacDiarmid's main quarry was John Jamieson's *Etymological Dictionary of the Scottish Language* (1808, with 1825 Supplement), and the Synthetic Scots created by him and others has become known as Lallans (i.e. Lowland Scots). James Fergusson, in the introduction to his 1946 anthology *The Green Garden: A New Collection of Scottish Poetry*, describes experiments in Synthetic Scots as legitimate but unsuccessful. Synthetic Scots is, he says:

> ... a debased form of modern Scots, of somewhat Balkan appearance on the printed page, styled by some of its practitioners 'Lallans' ... I cannot but suspect that the motive in each case has been political rather than literary: a desire to find a medium of expression, which should not be English.

It was Fergusson, according to his brother Bernard in his book *Hubble Bubble* (1978), who 'happily dubbed' Lallans 'Plastic Scots'.

> ... the present century has seen the conscious creation of a 'mainstream' variety of Scots – a standard literary variety ... referred to as 'synthetic Scots' ... In its grammar and spelling, it shows the marked influence of Standard English, more so than other Scots dialects.
> – David Crystal, *The Cambridge Encyclopedia of the English Language* (1995)

See also DORIC; SOME MAIR.

Playing cards with the Devil, on the perils of See BLUIDY TAM; EARL BEARDIE.

Play Jock needle Jock preen or **pin** To play fast and loose; to act in an underhand manner.

Playpen, the A fenced-off area in the Assembly Hall on the Mound in Edinburgh. When the GENERAL ASSEMBLY of the Church of Scotland is in session, this area, in front of the Moderator, is where the clerks and other officials sit.

Play the daft laddie, to See DAFT LADDIE, TO PLAY THE.

Play the loon, to To behave lewdly, to commit fornication. The expression survived into the 20th century. Although today the word *loon* is most familiar as a Northeastern word for a young lad, in the past it could mean a sexually promiscuous person of either sex.

Pleas of the Crown, the See FOUR PLEAS OF THE CROWN, THE.

Plook on the Plinth See CARBUNCLE AWARDS.

Plotcock An obsolete name for the Devil. The name is a variant of Plutock, itself a version of Pluto, Roman god of the underworld. There is a small ruined 16th-century tower called Plotcock Castle in the gloomy defile known as Plotcock Glen, a mile or so west of Larkhall in Lanarkshire.

Ploughman Poet, the Robert Burns, who spent much of his life as a humble tenant farmer. In a letter, Alison Cockburn (1712–94) described his reception in Edinburgh in 1786 thus:

> The town is at present agog with the ploughman-poet, who receives adulation with native dignity, and is the very figure of his profession – strong and coarse – but has a most enthusiastic heart of LOVE.

Ploughmen, it seems, had something of a reputation as lusty lovers, perhaps deriving from the imagery of their occupation – as suggested in this anonymous 18th-century farm song:

> But the plooman laddie's my delight,
> The plooman laddie loe's me;
> When a' the lave gang tae their bed,
> The plooman comes an' sees me.

The novelist Henry Mackenzie (1745–1831), an acquaintance of Burns, patronizingly and sentimentally described him as the 'heaven-taught ploughman', while T.W.H. Crosland, in his 1902 broadside *The*

Unspeakable Scot, debunked him as 'a superincontinent yokel with a gift for metricism'. A.E. Housman was no kinder, and no more accurate, when he wrote: 'If you imagine a Scotch commercial traveller in a Scotch commercial hotel leaning on the bar and calling the barmaid *Dearie*, then you will know the keynote of Burns' verse.' *See also* WEAVER POET, THE.

Pocket Rocket or **Pocket Dynamo, the** Nicknames for the Larkhall snooker player Graeme Dott (b. 1977), who won the world championship in 2006. Other nicknames include 'Pot the Lot Dott'.

Pock-pudding A pudding or dumpling steamed in a cloth bag (*pock* or *poke*), hence formerly a jocular name for an Englishman, on account of the supposed fondness of that race for such stolid fare.

> My countrymen, not only here, but all over Scotland, are dignified with the title of *poke pudding*, which, according to the sense of the word among the natives, signifies a glutton.
> – Edmund Burt, *Letters from a Gentleman in the North of Scotland* (*c*.1730; published 1815)

Poison Dwarves, the A nickname for the Cameronians; *see* REGIMENTAL NICKNAMES.

Poker Club, the A political and social club founded in Edinburgh in 1762, as a sort of successor to the SELECT SOCIETY. Its political aims were firstly the establishment of a Scottish national militia, and secondly parliamentary reform, which would 'let the industrious farmer and manufacturer share at last in a privilege now engrossed in by the great lord, the drunken laird and the drunkener bailie'. The name seems to have derived from the fact that the first chairman, on his election, grasped hold of a poker and adopted it as his insignia of office. Members of the club included many prominent figures in the Scottish Enlightenment, including Adam Smith, David Hume, John Home, Lord Elibank, William Robertson, Hugh Blair and Joseph Black.

Pokey-hat An ice-cream cone. The first element comes from *hokey-pokey*, a colloquial English term for ice cream, with the *hat* element alluding to the shape of the cone, which resembles a dunce's cap.

Polomint City A nickname for East Kilbride, so-called because of the number of roundabouts.

Polwarth Thorns, the Two old hawthorns that formerly stood on the green in the now barely extant Borders village of Polwarth, southwest of Duns. For some 300 years it was the custom to dance round these trees to celebrate every local marriage.

> At Polwarth on the Green,
> If you'll meet me in the morn,
> Where lads and lasses do convene
> To dance around the thorn.
> – 'Polwarth on the Green', a traditional song elaborated by Allan Ramsay

Pontius Pilate *See* PILATE, PONTIUS.

Pontius Pilate's Bodyguard A nickname for the Royal Scots, raised in 1633 and thus the oldest infantry regiment of the line in the British Army. When in the 17th century the French Regiment of Picardy boasted that it had stood watch over Christ's tomb prior to the Resurrection, the Royal Scots responded with the boast that they had provided a guard for that unlikely Scot, Pontius PILATE (allegedly born in Fortingall). In 2006 the regiment merged with the King's Own Scottish Borderers to form the Royal Regiment of Scotland.

Poor Man's King, the A name by which James V was remembered, for his concerns for the common people. *See* GOODMAN OF BALLENGEICH, THE.

Porridge Although now strongly associated with Scotland (where it is vernacularly known as *parritch* or *porritch*, and to children as *posh* or *poshie*), historically porridge can be viewed as a form of frumenty, a medieval dish made from boiled wheat (or other grains) mixed with cow's milk (or almond milk on fast days). The use of oats in such a dish was not exclusive to Scotland, but in the Middle Ages was common across the north of England. When mentioning the use of oats, an Italian cookbook from this period refers to it being in 'the English tradition'. The first mention of oatmeal porridge in Scotland is in an account by the English traveller

Richard James (1592–1638), who writes that the common people, children and ladies eat a *pottage* made from oatmeal flour and water, accompanied by butter or milk or ale. By the Victorian era the English who persisted in eating porridge – but also persisted in finding the Scots to be coarse peasants – called their breakfast dish 'cream of oatmeal'.

Although described by Burns as 'The healsome porritch, chief of Scotia's food' (in 'The Cotter's Saturday Night', 1786), and by the *Guardian* (30 March 2011) as 'a well-known Scottish substitute for central heating', not all Scots have shown complete loyalty to the dish:

> Though we're fearful fond o' oor parritch in Scotland, and some men mak' a brag o' takin' them every mornin' just as if they were a cauld bath, we're gey gled to skip them at a holiday and just be daein' wi' ham and eggs.
> – Neil Munro, *Erchie* (1904). It was once common to refer to porridge as 'them' (as in the above), presumably from 'oats' being plural.

The traditional Scottish insistence that porridge should be eaten with salt alone, and that all sweeteners such as sugar or golden syrup must be eschewed, appears to be dying out. Regarding the (presumably Presbyterian) preference for salt, Dean E.B. Ramsay, in *Reminiscences of Scottish Life and Character* (1862), has the following anecdote:

> The Rev. Mr Monro of Westray, preaching on the flight of Lot from Sodom, said: 'The honest man and his family were ordered out of the town, and charged not to look back; but the old carlin, Lot's wife, looked owre her shouther, for which she was smote into a lump of sawt.' And he added with great unction, 'Oh, ye people of Westray, if ye had had her, mony a day since ye wad hae putten her in the parritch-pot!'

See also AULD CLAITHS AND CAULD PORRICCH; CAULD PARRITCH IS SOONER HET AGAIN THAN NEW ANES MADE; OATS, DR JOHNSON ON; SAE PLAIN AS PARRITCH; SAVE YOUR BREATH TO COOL YOUR PORRIDGE.

Port-a-beul Gaelic, literally 'music from mouth', i.e. the singing of simple or nonsense words to a fast-paced tune (typically a jig or reel), sometimes used to accompany dancing in the absence of an instrumentalist. According to tradition, the practice arose

after the bagpipes were banned by the 1746 Act of PROSCRIPTION, passed in the wake of the '45 Jacobite Rebellion. In non-Gaelic-speaking areas, singing in this style is known onomatopoeically as *diddling*, and competitions are held to establish who is the champion *diddler*. Scat singing in jazz and beatboxing in contemporary youth culture are analogous.

Port Charlotte *See* QUEEN OF THE RINNS, THE.

Porteous Riots A series of civil disturbances that took place in Edinburgh in 1736. After the hanging in the Grassmarket of a popular smuggler, there was a degree of violent unrest among the crowd, prompting Captain John Porteous of the city guard to order his men to open fire. Several in the crowd were killed, and Porteous was later arrested, tried, and sentenced to death. Suspecting he might be reprieved, an outraged mob broke into the Tolbooth where Porteous was being held, dragged him out into the street, and hanged him from a dyer's pole with a rope taken from a draper's shop. The riots are vividly recreated in the early part of Scott's *HEART OF MIDLOTHIAN*.

Portessie *See* SLOCH, THE.

Port Glasgow *See* WINE CITY.

Portobello This Edinburgh seaside suburb owes its improbable name (Spanish for 'beautiful port') to Puerto Bello in Panama, captured by Admiral Vernon in 1739. A sailor who participated in this famous victory subsequently built a cottage called Portobello Hut on what was then called Figgate Muir, on the shores of the Firth of Forth. It was this house (which survived until 1851) that gave the later suburb – once a fashionable bathing resort – its name.

Pot and gallows A variant of PIT AND GALLOWS.

Pot fit A Northeastern term for the leg of a cauldron. Hence to *stick oot like a pot fit* means to stick out like a sore thumb, while if two people are *oot like a pot fit*, they have fallen out with each other.

Potterlow, potterneeshin *See* GONE TAE POTTER-
LOW.

Pot the Lot Dott *See* POCKET ROCKET.

Pound Scots The principal unit of currency in
Scotland until after the Union of 1707 and the
closure of the Scottish mint two years later. Even by
the Union of the Crowns in 1603, the pound Scots,
once possessed of the same value as its English
equivalent, had become so debased that one pound
sterling was worth twelve pounds Scots. This was
still the exchange rate in 1707.

Powsowdie *See* SHEEP'S HEID.

Praefervidum ingenium Scotorum 'The perfervid
[i.e. fervently serious] disposition of the Scots', a
Latin phrase coined by the French Huguenot theologian André Rivet (1572–1651). In those former
times when it was fashionable to discover the
history and nature of a nation through what was
thought of as its native genius, the phrase had a
particular currency:

> The history of Scotland is not to be found in the
> chronicles of her kings, or in the narrative of her
> contendings with a powerful neighbour; not even in
> the records of her commerce. While by the blending of
> Celt and Teuton a distinctive nationality was formed,
> its development was effected by those who in conflict
> with a rugged soil and a rigorous climate, struggled
> diligently for subsistence. What were the earlier and
> latter surroundings of those who so struggled; how
> from inconsiderable beginnings the nation acquired
> that moral and intellectual superiority which induced
> Professor Rivet, a learned foreigner, early in the
> seventeenth century, to speak of the *praefervidum
> ingenium Scotorum*, it has been my object to discover.
> – Revd Charles Rogers, *Social Life in Scotland* (1884)

The quality most central to Scottish character is
intensity. The people of that stock know how to
love, and they know how to hate, – for hatred, the
obverse of love, is sometimes a virtue:– 'Ye that love
the Lord, see that ye hate the thing which is evil.' The
Scotch can be good haters as well as ardent lovers.
'Perfervid' was the epithet a controversial divine of the
seventeenth century fastened upon the race, and it has

stuck. When they care for anything or any person,
they care a very great deal, – 'Praefervidum ingenium
Scotorum'.

> – Revd William Reed Huntingdon, 'The King's Cup-
> Bearer', a sermon preached in memory of the Revd E.
> Winchester Donald, 20 November 1904

Huntingdon goes on to contrast this Scottish quality
of enthusiasm with that other national characteristic, DOURNESS.

Praise of Ben Dorain (Gaelic *Moladh Beinn Dòbhrainn*) One of the most celebrated of descriptive
Gaelic nature poems, written by Duncan Ban Macintyre (Donnchadh Bàn Mac an t-Saoir; 1724–
1812), known in his lifetime as Donnchadh Bàn
nan Orainn ('Fair Duncan of the Songs'). The
eponymous Ben is a noted conical mountain in
Argyll, standing a little north of Tyndrum; for a time
Macintyre, who was born in nearby Glen Orchy,
worked in the vicinity as a gamekeeper for the Duke
of Argyll. He later moved to Edinburgh, and is
buried in Greyfriars Kirkyard.

> An t-urram thar gach beinn
> Aig Beinn Dòbhrain;
> De na chunnaic mi fon ghrèin,
> 'S i bu bhòidhche leam …
> (Praise over every other mountain
> To Ben Dorain,
> Of all I have seen under the sun
> The most beautiful …)

Preen-tail Day or **Tailie Day** 'Pin-tail Day', the day
after April Fool's Day (*see* HUNTEGOWK), on which
those who had been successfully duped (or other
unsuspecting victims) had paper tails pinned onto
their backs.

Prent-buik *See* SPEAK LIKE A PRENT-BUIK, TO.

Prentice Pillar, the An ornately carved Gothic pillar
in the 15th-century Roslin Chapel, Midlothian. The
tale attaching to it, although often repeated, is almost
certainly apocryphal, and similar legends are told of
ornate windows at Melrose Abbey and at the cath-
edrals of Lincoln and Rouen. The September 1817
issue of the *Gentleman's Magazine* reproduced the
spiel delivered by Mrs Annie Wilson, the ancient

landlady of the Roslin Inn, who over the decades had entertained such notable visitors as Dr Johnson and James Boswell, Sir Walter Scott, William and Dorothy Wordsworth, Robert Burns and the painter Alexander Nasmyth, and shown them and countless others around the chapel:

> There ye see it with the lace bands winding sae beautifully roond aboot it. The maister had gane away to Rome to get a plan for it, and while he was away his prentice made a plan himself and finished it. And when the maister came back and fand the pillar finished, he was sae enraged that he took a hammer and killed the prentice. There you see the prentice's face up there in the corner, wi a red gash in the brow, and his mother greetin for him in the corner opposite. And there, in another corner is the maister, as he lookit just before he was hanged; it's him wi a kind o ruff roond his neck.

The *Gentleman's Magazine* described the story as 'twaddle, which Annie had told for fifty years without every hearing a word of it doubted, and never once doubting it herself'.

Presbyterian Cat, the *See* PUSSY-BAUDRONS.

Presby vs Pisky In the 19th century, Episcopalian (PISKY) urchins would cry:

> Presby, Presby, never bend.
> Sit on your seat on Man's chief end!

Meanwhile the Presbyterian children would taunt:

> Pisky, Pisky, Amen.
> Down on your knees and up again!

For an earlier encounter between the sects, *see* RABBLING OF DEER, THE.

Pretenders, Old and Young *See* OLD PRETENDER; YOUNG PRETENDER.

Pretty Dancers, the *See* MERRY DANCERS, THE.

Pricker or **Prick-the-clout** or **Prick-the-louse** Disparaging terms for a tailor in the 18th and 19th centuries.

> Cou'd *Prick-the-louse* but be sae handy
> To make the breeks and claise to stand ay,

> Thro' thick and thin wi' you I'd dash on,
> Nor mind the folly of the fashion …
> – Robert Fergusson, 'To My Auld Breeks'

Burns, in his 'Reply To A Trimming Epistle Received From A Tailor' (1786), adds an additional term of contempt:

> Gae mind your seam, ye prick-the-louse,
> An' jag-the-flea!

The tailor in question was one Thomas Walker of Poole, near Ochiltree, who had had the temerity to write to Burns in verse, beginning his epistle thus:

> Folks tell me ye're gaun aff this year, out owre the
>   sea,
> And lasses, whom ye lo'e sae dear, will greet for
>   thee!

Burns would have none of this impertinence, beginning his 'Reply' as he meant to go on:

> What ails ye now, ye lousie bitch
> To thresh my back at sic a pitch?

Prin … *See* PREEN …

Prince Charlie's rose *See* WHITE ROSE.

Principality of Scotland Those lands in Scotland held by the monarch's eldest son, who bears the title of Prince and Great Steward of Scotland, as well as Duke of Rothesay, Earl of Carrick, Baron of Renfrew and LORD OF THE ISLES.

Prisoner of Papa Stour, the The Hon. Edwin Lindsay, the son of Alexander Lindsay, 6th Earl of Balcarres and *de jure* 23rd Earl of Crawford. In 1809, after Lindsay, an officer in the Indian Army, had refused a challenge to fight a duel, his father declared him insane and confined him on the small Shetland island of Papa Stour. There he remained for 26 years, bathing in a spring now known as Lindsay's Well, until rescued by a Quaker preacher called Catherine Watson. Balcarres himself was a colourful character, who had fought in the American War of Independence until obliged to surrender at Saratoga. As lieutenant-governor of Jamaica from 1795 to 1801, he attracted controversy by employing hunting dogs in the suppression of a rebellion of freed slaves (and for keeping a pet pig at Government House). Back in Britain, he was introduced by George III to the American general and turncoat Benedict Arnold, and reputedly exclaimed, 'What, the traitor Arnold?' A duel followed, but after Arnold had fired and missed, Balcarres turned on his heels and left the field. When Arnold demanded why he had not fired, Balcarres retorted, 'Sir, I leave you to the executioner.' *See also* MAIDEN STACK.

Prisoner of St Kilda, the Lady Grange (née Rachel Chiesley; 1679–1745), the beautiful, hot-tempered wife of James Erskine, Lord Grange. After the breakdown of their marriage, Lady Grange, who had Hanoverian sympathies, threatened to disclose her husband's role in the 1715 Jacobite Rebellion. To prevent this eventuality, in April 1732 Lord Grange, along with his fellow Jacobites Lord Lovat (SIMON THE FOX) and Macleod of Dunvegan, kidnapped his estranged wife from her lodgings in Edinburgh. After a long and uncomfortable journey, she eventually found herself incarcerated on the remote Monach Islands, off the west coast of North Uist. After two years there, she was moved to the even more remote islands of St Kilda (part of the Macleod fiefdom), where she remained until 1742, her husband having in the meantime announced her death and arranged a corpseless funeral for her in Edinburgh. From St Kilda Lady Grange managed to smuggle a note to her cousin, the Lord Advocate, who sent out a rescue party. But before it arrived, she was moved first to Assynt, and then to Skye (also both part of the Macleod lands), where it was said she ended her days living in a cave. She died in May 1745, and was buried at Trumpan on Skye. Her case was noted by Boswell and Johnson, the latter ungallantly commenting '... if M'Leod would let it be known that he had such a place for naughty ladies, he might make it a very profitable island'. She also supplied a subject to many later writers.

'They say I'm mad, but who would not be mad
on Hirta, when the winter raves along
the bay and howls through my stone hut ...'
– Edwin Morgan, 'Lady Grange on St Kilda', from
Sonnets from Scotland (1984)

Proclaimers, the *See* 'SUNSHINE ON LEITH'.

Prood as bull-beef Very proud indeed; the phrase was once common in the Northeast.

Prophet Peden A byname of the COVENANTER and charismatic preacher Alexander Peden (*c.*1626–86). He became minister of New Luce in Galloway in 1660, but was ejected from his parish three years later. He became a peripatetic preacher, wearing a cloth mask, false beard and wig as a disguise, but was eventually arrested in 1673, imprisoned on the Bass Rock and then in the Edinburgh Tolbooth. In 1678 he was sentenced to be transported to the Americas, but the captain of the ship on which he and his fellows were to cross the Atlantic sympathized with his principles and released him. He spent his last days living in a cave, still a fugitive, near his birthplace of Auchinleck, Ayrshire. After his death in 1686 his body was exhumed from its secret burial place by government dragoons, and hanged from the gallows at Cumnock, before being reburied at the foot of the gallows, like a common criminal. The gallows hill became known as 'the Hill of Reproach', and in Peden's honour many villagers subsequently opted to be buried at his side.

During Peden's lifetime there were many reports of his prophecies coming true. For example, in 1682 he presided over the wedding of John Brown and Isabel Weir, and afterwards told the bride:

You have a good man to be your husband, but you will not enjoy him long; prize his company, and keep linen by you to be his winding sheet, for you will need it when ye are not looking for it, and it will be a bloody one.

On 30 April 1685 Brown was shot through the head by John Graham of Claverhouse ('Bluidy Clavers', aka BONNIE DUNDEE) for failing to acknowledge the king as head of the Kirk. Another story of Peden's powers of foreknowledge is recounted in John Howie's *Scots Worthies* (1775):

In the year 1684, being in the house of John Sloan ... about ten o'clock at night, seated by the fireside, discoursing with some honest people, he started to his feet and said, 'Flee off, Sandy, and hide yourself, for Colonel —— is coming to apprehend you, and I advise you all to do the like, for they will be here within an hour.' This came to pass, and when they had made a most inquisitive search, without and within the house, and gone round the thornbush where he was lying concealed, they came off without their prey. Mr Peden then came in, and said, 'And has this gentleman given poor Sandy such a fright, and other poor things? For this night's work, God shall give him such a blow within few days, as all the physicians in the world cannot cure.' In this likewise his words came to pass, for the person alluded to soon after died in great misery, vermin issuing from all the pores of his body.

Peden and his like have proved less sympathetic to more recent generations:

Hoodicrow Peden in the blighted corn
Hacked with his rusty beak the starving haulms.
Out of that desolation we were born.
– Edwin Muir, 'Scotland' (1941)

Proscription, Act of A law passed in 1746 in the wake of the Jacobite rising. Its aim was to destroy the clan system and Highland Gaelic culture in general, and in particular it decreed that:

No man or boy within that part of Great Britain called Scotland ... shall on any pretence whatsoever wear or put on the clothes commonly called the Highland clothes, the plaid, philebeg or little kilt, trowse, shoulder belts.

The act was not repealed until 1782. On the Inner Hebridean island of Seil, next to the famous BRIDGE OVER THE ATLANTIC, is the inn called Tigh na Truish (Gaelic, 'house of the trousers'), where, in the wake of the act, islanders would change into acceptable dress before crossing over to the mainland.

Proscription of Clan MacGregor *See* MAC-GREGOR, PROSCRIPTION OF CLAN.

Protestant Crusade Against the Papal Visit Party *See* HEROD OF HILLHEAD, THE.

Protestants of the yellow stick *See* RELIGION OF THE YELLOW STICK.

Provost The Scottish equivalent of a mayor. The cities of Edinburgh, Glasgow, Aberdeen and Dundee have a lord provost, just as the City of London has a lord mayor. The word ultimately derives from Latin *praeponere*, 'to place first'.

Sir, there is something incompatible between greatness and the provostship of a Scottish burgh.
– John Davidson, *Perfervid: The Career of Ninian Jamieson* (1890)

Pubic Triangle, the A jocular name for an area of Edinburgh around the Grassmarket, Lothian Road and Tollcross, in which are concentrated what local authorities now define as 'sex-encounter venues', such as lap-dancing clubs.

Puck's Glen An enchanting and popular walk located between Dunoon and Loch Eck in the Cowal Peninsula, Argyll. The path meanders up a steep, narrow gorge through mixed woodland, following a tumbling burn crossed by arched wooden bridges. The area was landscaped in 1870 by the Younger family (of brewing fame), and the path once led to a folly on the hill, now in the nearby Benmore Botanic Gardens. The name is a Victorian importation from English folklore, the character of Puck being familiar from Shakespeare's *A Midsummer Night's Dream*.

Puggie A monkey. *See* FOU; GET YER PUGGIE UP.

Puirrabbieburnsism *See* WALLACETHEBRUCEISM.

Pulling the cornhead from the stack The extraction of an entire stem of oats, the head included, from a stack. This custom was apparently once practised in the west of Scotland as a proof of virginity.

To pu' the corn-head frae the stack;
For it would seem, on Hallowe'en,
That Virtue's test could thus be seen.
– 'Young Glasgow', *Deil's Hallowe'en* (1856)

Pultes Scottorum *See* SCOTIA.

Punny eccy A curiously fond diminutive deployed by schoolchildren to denote 'punishment exercise', i.e. a piece of written work set for the purposes of chastisement.

Pure dead brilliant Exceedingly good. The phrase became popular in Glasgow from the later 1970s, and forms the title of one of Debi Gliori's darkly comic *Pure Dead* trilogy for older children, concerning the eccentric Strega Borgia family who live in StregaSchloss in Argyll. *Pure Dead Brilliant* was first published in 2003.

Pussy-baudrons A pet or fabular name for a cat; often simply *baudrons*, a pet name also given to a hare (Scots *bawd*).

> Then that curst carmagnole, auld Satan,
> Watches like baudrons by a ratton,
> Our sinfu' saul to get a claut on
>   Wi' felon ire ...
> – Robert Burns, 'To Colonel de Peyster' (1796)

> And Poussie Baudrons says: 'Come here, wee Robin, and I'll let you see a bonny white ring round my neck.' But wee Robin says: 'Na, na! grey Poussie Baudrons; na, na! Ye worry't the wee mousie; but ye'se no worry me.'
> – Robert Chambers, 'The Marriage of Robin Redbreast and the Wren', from *Popular Rhymes of Scotland* (1826)

'As quiet as pussy-baudrons' was formerly a familiar simile, with 'quiet' sometimes replaced with a variety of similar adjectives:

> She listened, innocent as pussy-bawdrons thinking on the cream jug.
> – S.R. Crockett, *The Raiders* (1893)

An early appearance is in this anonymous satire, originating in the 17th century:

> There was a Presbyterian cat
> Went seeking for her prey;
> She caught a moose, within the hoose,
> Upon the Sabbath Day ...

> Then unto execution
> Poor Baudrons she was drawn;
> And on a tree, there hanged she:
> The minister sang a psalm.

Put ... *See also* PIT ...

Put doon a broo, to To express dissatisfaction; *broo* denotes 'eyebrow' or 'forehead'.

Put in thee hand 'The traditional Orkney invitation to a visitor,' according to the Orcadian poet Edwin Muir in his autobiography, *The Story and the Fable* (1940).

Put legs and arms to, to To embellish (a story) or adorn (a tale).

Put to the horn, to To declare someone to be an outlaw, rebel or bankrupt, a process formerly accompanied by three blasts on a trumpet. A person who had been put to the horn would be described as *at the horn*. If someone was put to the horn, they would be cast out from their clan, lose their name and become a broken man (*see* BROKEN MEN). After the entire Clan MacGregor was put to the horn by James VI in 1603, the very name was banned, and anyone who bore it forfeited their life (*see* MACGREGOR, PROSCRIPTION OF CLAN).

> You suppose, now, a man's committed to prison because he cannot pay his debt? Quite otherwise: the truth is, the king is so good as to interfere at the request of the creditor, and to send the debtor his royal command to do him justice within a certain time – fifteen days, or six, as the case may be. Well, the man resists and disobeys: what follows? Why, that he be lawfully and rightfully declared a rebel to our gracious sovereign, whose command he has disobeyed, and that by three blasts of a horn at the market-place of Edinburgh, the metropolis of Scotland. And he is then legally imprisoned, not on account of any civil debt, but because of his ungrateful contempt of the royal mandate.
> – Sir Walter Scott, *The Antiquary* (1816), chapter xxxix

Pyot The magpie; *see* DEVIL'S BIRD, THE.

Quaich A shallow two-handled drinking cup. The word derives from Gaelic *cuach*, 'cup, bowl'. In the past most quaichs were made from wooden staves hooped with metal, and were used for drinking whisky, although in Tobias Smollett's *The Expedition of Humphry Clinker* (1771), J. Melford writes to Sir Watkin Phillips, recounting how the Lowlanders would drink beer from a 'quaff', which he describes as:

> . . . a curious cup made of different pieces of wood, such as box and ebony, cut into little staves, joined alternately, and secured with delicate hoops, having two ears or handles – It holds about a gill, is sometimes tipt round the mouth with silver, and has a plate of the same metal at bottom, with the landlord's cypher engraved.
> – J. Melford to Sir Watkin Phillips, Sept. 3.

In a letter dated 1824, Sir Walter Scott told how he had been making quaichs out of various 'scraps of remarkable wood as I have chanced to collect' – including a fragment of WALLACE'S OAK. Today quaichs are largely produced as prizes or ornamental or commemorative items, made in pewter or silver.

Quallie or **Quali, the** Formerly, the 'qualifying examination' that pupils took at the end of their primary education. Those who were successful proceeded on to secondary school. In celebration, pupils would attend a *quallie dance* or *quallie party*.

Quarter days Those Christian festivals on which rents were due and servants were hired. In Scotland they were: Candlemas (2 February), Whitsunday (fixed by statute on 15 May for this purpose; sometimes BELTANE was substituted, often on 1 or 3 May), LAMMAS (1 August) and Martinmas (11 November).

Quean *See* LOON.

Queen Mary, RMS *See* HULL NO. 534.

Queen of Hearts *See* WINTER QUEEN, THE.

Queen of Heaven's hen The skylark; *see* FAUNA CALEDONIA.

Queen of Scots One of the passenger train services running between London and Glasgow via Edinburgh.

Queen of Scots' Pillar or **Mary Queen of Scots' Pillar** A massive flowstone feature in Poole's Cavern near Buxton, Derbyshire. The story is that in 1580 Mary Queen of Scots, suffering from rheumatism, was taken by her kindly jailer, the Earl of Shrewsbury, to the spa town of Buxton to take the waters. While there she reputedly visited the cavern, although the only evidence for this is the following verse:

> The fairest, brightest Queen, that ever
> On English ground unhappy footing set,
> Having to th' rest of th' Isles eternal shame;
> Honoured this stone with her own splendid name.
> – Charles Cotton, *The Wonders of the Peak* (1681)

Queen of the Borders, the *See* AULD GREY TOON, THE.

Queen of the Hebrides, the A title claimed by Islay.

Queen of the North Isles, the A name by which Westray, the most northwesterly island in Orkney, is sometimes known. An alternative title (apparently a registered trade mark) is simply 'Queen of the Isles':

> Westray has often been described as 'The Queen of the Isles' , the second largest of the North Isles and is in many ways a miniature Orkney.
> – visitorkney.com

Queen of the Rinns, the A title sometimes bestowed on the village of Port Charlotte, on the Rinns of Islay (one of the island's peninsulas, from Gaelic *rinn*, 'sharp point'). Port Charlotte was built for distillery workers by Walter Frederick Campbell, laird of Islay, in 1828, and named after his mother.

Queen of the Scottish Peaks, the Ben Loyal in Sutherland, so styled not because of its height (a modest 2506 ft / 764 m), but because of its elegant appearance, and perhaps from a misunderstanding of the second part of its name, which actually comes from Old Norse *laga*, 'law', and *fjall*, 'mountain', alluding to the fact that in ancient Scandinavia laws were often proclaimed from the summits of mountains.

Queen of the South, the A sobriquet of Dumfries, coined by the poet David Dunbar, who, while campaigning to be elected to Parliament in 1857, referred to Dumfries as 'the Queen of the South'. This name was adopted by Dumfries's new football club on its formation in 1919. It is often observed that Queen of the South is the only football team to be mentioned in the Bible, alluding to the following passage:

> The queen of the south shall rise up in the judgement with this generation, and shall condemn it ...
> – Matthew 12:42

The club is nicknamed the DOONHAMERS.

Queensbury Plot Another name for the SCOTCH PLOT.

Queen's Maries, the *See* FOUR MARIES, THE.

Queen Victoria's Rock A rock formation by Bàgh a Tuath on the northeast coast of the island of Barra, said to resemble the older Queen Victoria in profile.

Queer Hardy A disparaging nickname for Keir Hardy (1856–1915) the Lanarkshire-born founder of the Independent Labour Party. In 1892 he was elected to Parliament, becoming one of Britain's first socialist MPs. The name alludes to what his detractors regarded as his unconventional behaviour, such as attending Parliament in a tweed suit, red tie and deerstalker, rather than the standard frock coat and top hat.

Quintinshill Rail Disaster *See* GRETNA GREEN RAIL DISASTER.

R

R&A *See* ROYAL AND ANCIENT.

Rabbling of Deer, the A riot in the Aberdeenshire village of Old Deer on 23 March 1711, when Episcopalians (who were strongly represented in the Northeast) and Presbyterians went head to head over the installation of the new Presbyterian minister, John Gordon, the first to be appointed here by the local laird rather than by the bishop. According to one account, 'the presbytery and their satellites were soundly beat off by the people, not without blood on both sides'. More usually in the later 17th and early 18th centuries, *rabbling* involved the expulsion of Episcopalian clergy by a Presbyterian mob.

Rab C. Nesbitt A blackly humorous TV sitcom launched by BBC Scotland in a one-off special in 1988 (although the title character had appeared in sketches in BBC2's *Naked Video*, starting in 1986). Several series followed, beginning in 1990. Nesbitt, an impoverished, hard-drinking and utterly unreconstructed Glaswegian (albeit 'sensitive by Govan standards'), was created by the writer Ian Pattison, and is played by Gregor Fisher. Perennially unshaven, and sporting a dirty string vest, torn jacket and bloody head bandage, Nesbitt will do anything to avoid employment and to obtain a drink. Fisher recalls that he was helped in shaping his role when he was sitting in his van one day, and 'a real Glasgow gentleman who'd had one or two sherbets too many started hitting the side of the van and saying, "You're giving this place a bad name, by the way."' At one stage the programme was investigated by the Broadcasting Standards Council, which commissioned a report on the views of 600 Scottish teenagers:

> There was national solidarity behind the argument that while it may be all right for Scottish people to enjoy the comedy, English people should not be given the opportunity to laugh at us.

Rabs, the *See* FOOTBALL CLUB NICKNAMES.

Race of Dunbar, the The second Battle of Dunbar, fought on 3 September 1650 between Cromwell's Parliamentary army and the Scots, who were commanded by David Leslie. The battle is also known as the *Drove of Dunbar*. Despite differences over religion, the Scots had given their allegiance to Charles II, and Cromwell's plea to the General Assembly to change their minds had fallen on deaf ears (*see* IN THE BOWELS OF CHRIST, THINK IT POSSIBLE THAT YOU MAY BE MISTAKEN). Cromwell then led his army into Scotland and proceeded to inflict an overwhelming defeat on the Scots at Dunbar, which ended in a rout in which 3000 Scots were killed and 10,000 taken prisoner. Those of the latter who were not wounded (about half the total) were marched south into England under appalling conditions, and when they eventually arrived in Durham, only 3000 were still alive. These were imprisoned in the cathedral, but lack of food and fuel resulted in another 1600 deaths by the end of October. The bodies were dumped in an unmarked mass grave beside the cathedral, while the survivors were packed off in chains to work on the plantations of the New World. In 2007 a campaign was launched to construct a memorial at Durham to the 'Dunbar Martyrs'.

Rach-ma-reeshil In a muddle; all over the place. The origin of the expression is obscure, although it has been suggested that the last element may be *reesle*, 'rustle, crackle'.

Radge, to go To go 'mental', to lose it completely, sometimes with manifestations of violence. *Radge* is

383

a variant of standard English *rage*, and possibly also influenced by Romany *raj*, meaning the same thing. As an adjective, *radge* can mean 'crazy' or 'sexually excited' or 'feeble-witted', while as a noun, a *radge* is a wild, untameable person or animal, or a promiscuous woman.

Radical Road, the The pathway constructed along the foot of SALISBURY CRAGS in Edinburgh in 1820, so named from 'the destitute and discontented west-country weavers being employed on its construction under a committee of gentlemen' (James Grant, *Cassell's Old and New Edinburgh*, 1880s). The scheme was initiated by Sir Walter Scott. It is to the construction of the Radical Road that the tongue-twister

> Round the rugged rocks the ragged rascals ran

is said to allude, with the suggestion that 'ragged' may have originally been 'radical'. It was originally planned to plant the crags themselves with 'the rarest heaths from the Cape of Good Hope and other foreign parts', but this idea was never implemented.

Radical War, the The name given to an abortive and small-scale rising in April 1820, a time of economic depression, unemployment and increasing calls from the disenfranchised for political reform. At the same time as tens of thousands of workers went on strike in the West of Scotland, a few score Radicals marched from Stirling and Glasgow to seize arms from the Carron Iron Works. They were intercepted on 5 April by government troops and local volunteers, resulting in the skirmish known as the 'Battle of Bonnymuir'. Three of the Radical leaders – Andrew Hardie, John Baird and James Wilson – were executed for treason, and 19 others (the so-called 'Scottish Insurrectionists') transported to Australia. *See also* PIKE PLOT, THE; SCOTTISH MARTYRS, THE; UNITED SCOTSMEN, THE.

Ragman Rolls The various documents by which the nobility and gentry of Scotland expressed their fealty to Edward I of England in 1291 and again in 1296. The documents were returned by Edward III in 1328. The word *ragman*, of obscure origin, denotes a document with seals attached. Coinciden-

tally, but apparently unrelatedly, *Ragman* was once used as a name for the Devil.

Raid of Ruthven, the *See* RUTHVEN RAID, THE.

Rain blue snaw Said of something impossible or highly unlikely, e.g. 'It'll rain blue snaw afore he'll lift a finger tae help.'

Rainbows and related phenomena A rainbow is also called a *rainy bow* or a *rainbro* (Ayrshire), and was once known as an *arch of heaven*:

> A cyrkyll ... That tyll ane arche off hewyn wes
> Apperand lyk on lyklynes.
>   – Andrew of Wyntoun, *Orygynale Cronykil of Scotland*
>   (early 15th century)

A watery, indistinct rainbow is called a *watergaw*, as in Hugh MacDiarmid's early lyric of that name:

> A weet forenicht i' the yow-trummle
> I saw yon antrin thing,
> A watergaw wi' its chitterin' licht
> Ayont the on-ding ...
>   – 'The Watergaw', from *Sangschaw* (1925) [*forenicht*,
>   'early evening'; *yow-trummle*, 'ewe-tremble', i.e. a cold
>   snap after the sheep are sheared; *antrin*, 'rare'; *chitterin'*,
>   'shivering'; *on-ding*, 'onset' (of rain)]

Gaw is the Scots word for a parhelion or mock sun, also called a *dog*; a *weather gaw*, according to the *New Statistical Account* (1834–45), 'resembles the rainbow in colour, but ... is much shorter and hangs in a vertical line'. In the Northeast, a *rawn* or *silk napkin* or *boar's head* is a fragmented or imperfect rainbow, and is said to herald a rising wind; in the same region, the fragment of the lower end of a rainbow, usually seen out at sea and also heralding bad weather, is called a *tuith* or *teeth* or a *Buckieman's tooth* or a *wolf's teeth* or *stuthe*; further down the East Coast, in Angus and Fife, this is called a *stob*, while in Shetland the phenomenon is called a *brennik* or *brynics*. The Shetlanders also note another phenomenon, called a *skafer*, which is like a rainbow appearing through mist, and indicates that the mist will soon clear.

> Rainbow, rainbow, haud awa' hame,
> A' yer bairns are dead but ane,
> And it lies sick at yon grey stane,
> And will be dead ere you win hame.

Gang owre Drumaw and yont the lea,
And down the side o' yonder sea;
Your bairn lies greeting like to die,
And the big teardrop's in his e'e.
– Traditional Berwickshire rhyme, from John Holloway
(ed.), *The Oxford Book of Local Verses* (1987)

The Northeast also has a number of rhymes regarding rainbows, several of which are quoted in Walter Gregor's *Folk-Lore of the North-East of Scotland* (1881), for example:

Rainbow, rainbow,
Brack an gang hame,
The cow's wi' a calf,
The yow's wi' a lam,
An the coo 'ill be calvt
Or ye win hame.

and:

Rainbow, rainbow,
Brack an gang hame,
Yir father an mither's aneth the grave stehn.

Rainin' auld wives an' pike staves Raining cats and dogs. Sometimes *puir men* are substituted for *auld wives*.

Raise a reek, to To cause a commotion, to raise a stink (*reek*, 'smoke').

Raising the wind In *The Golden Bough* (1890), Sir James Frazer recounts how Scottish witches used to raise the wind 'by dipping a rag in water and beating it thrice on a stone', while chanting the following rhyme:

I knock this rag upon this stane
To raise the wind in the divellis name,
It sall not lye till I please againe.

For a more gruesome method of raising a wind, *see under* NORTH BERWICK WITCHES, THE.

Raisin Weekend An 'ancient' tradition at St Andrews University, said to date from the early 20th century. It takes place on the Sunday and Monday of the second week of November. On the Sunday, BEJANS (as freshers are known) attend tea parties given by their student 'mothers' (3rd or 4th year students who take a pastoral interest in their charges), and then accompany their 'fathers' for further partying, liquid refreshment, and associated high jinks. For their part, the freshers present their 'parents' with a gift – originally a pound of raisins (hence 'Raisin Weekend'), but now usually a bottle of wine. In return they are given 'raisin receipts', usually in the form of some bulky and awkward object such as a piece of old furniture or a stuffed animal, which they are obliged to carry to the Monday morning fancy-dress foam fight in the Quad.

Ramsay Mac *See* BONELESS WONDER, THE.

Rampage To riot, behave boisterously, paint the town red. Like GLAMOUR and SLOGAN, it was originally a native Scots word, before being absorbed into standard English. The word is thought to derive from *ramp*, 'to rear' (as in LION RAMPANT), with an admixture of 'rage'.

His Wife did Reel,
And Rampadge in her Choler.
– Allan Ramsay, additional canto to *CHRISTIS KIRK ON
THE GREEN* (1718)

Ran-dan, on the *See* ON THE RAN-DAN.

Randolph's Leap A narrow rocky defile on the course of the River Findhorn. It is named after Thomas Randolph, Earl of Moray (d.1332), to whom Robert the Bruce gave land hereabouts that he had confiscated from the Comyns (*see* RED COMYN, THE). However, it was not Randolph who made the leap, but rather the man he was pursuing: Alastair Comyn of Dunphail. Randolph was the father of BLACK AGNES.

Rascal Fair Formerly, a hiring fair in Aberdeenshire for agricultural labourers who had been unable to get a job at the Muckle Fair – the bi-annual hiring fair – or who had been fired from their previous job or were dissatisfied with their current employment. It was held on *Rascal Friday*, in early December.

Rash bush keeps the cow, the A proverbial saying traditionally ascribed to James I (reigned 1406–37),

385

suggesting a period of peace when the peasantry is free from depredation. A *rash bush* is a clump of rushes.

Rashiecoat 'Rush-coat', the Scottish Cinderella, who wears a coat made of rushes. In the version of the story in Robert Chambers's *Popular Rhymes of Scotland* (1826), just as the prince is riding away with the hen-wife's daughter, who has 'nippit and clippit' her feet to fit the slipper, a bird sings to him:

> 'Nippit fit and clippit fit
> Ahint the king's son rides
> But bonny fit and pretty fit
> Ahint the caudron hides.'

And when the king's son heard this, he flang aff the hen-wife's dochter, and cam hame again, and lookit ahint the caudron, and there he faund Rashie-coat greetin' for her slipper. And he tried her fit wi' the slipper, and it gaed on fine. Sae he married her.

> And they lived happy and happy,
> And never drank oot o' a dry cappy.

As Rushiecoat, the character is also found in Appalachian folk tales.

Rat race is for rats, the A celebrated expression of defiance by Jimmy Reid (1932–2010), a shop steward and charismatic public speaker, who rose to national prominence in 1971–2 as the public face of the work-in at Upper Clyde Shipbuilders, threatened with closure following the withdrawal of subsidies by the Conservative government. As Reid announced that the workers had taken control, he addressed the men as follows:

> We are not going to strike. We are not even having a sit-in strike. Nobody and nothing will come in and nothing will go out without our permission. And there will be no hooliganism, there will be no vandalism, there will be no bevvying because the world is watching us, and it is our responsibility to conduct ourselves with responsibility, and with dignity, and with maturity.

The success of the work-in and the public sympathy generated by Reid forced the government into a U-turn. Reid was subsequently elected rector of Glasgow University. 'From the very depth of my being,' he declared in his inaugural address, 'I

challenge the right of any man or group of men, in business or in government, to tell a fellow human being that he is expendable ... The rat race is for rats. We're not rats, we are human beings.' The address was reprinted in full in the *New York Times*, which called it 'the greatest speech since President Lincoln's Gettysburg Address'. In 1974 Reid stood as the Communist Party candidate in Central Dunbartonshire; he lost, although he polled nearly 6000 votes. He later joined the Labour Party, standing as their candidate in Dundee East in 1979. He lost again (this time to the SNP), and became known as 'the best MP Scotland never had'. He subsequently pursued a career as a journalist and broadcaster. From 1983 he became associated with the reforming leadership of Neil Kinnock, and was dismissed during the 1984–5 Miners' Strike by Mick McGahey, the Communist miners' leader, as 'Broken Reid'. After Tony Blair became Labour leader in 1994 Reid became increasingly disillusioned with New Labour, urging people to vote for the Scottish Socialist Party or the SNP. He joined the latter party in 2005.

Rats, eating live *See* BOSJESMAN.

Rats and mice, charms and satires against *See* PEST CONTROL.

Rattle-skulled half-lawyer, a Sir Walter Scott's description of himself:

> A rattle-skulled half-lawyer, half-sportsman, through whose head a regiment of horse has been exercising since he was five years old.
> – Quoted in L. Maclean Watt, *Scottish Life and Poetry* (1912)

Rattlin', roarin' Willie *See* CROCHALLAN FENCIBLES, THE.

Ray of sunshine, distinguishing Scotsmen with a grievance from a An easy task, according to P.G. Wodehouse:

> It is never difficult to distinguish between a Scotsman with a grievance and a ray of sunshine.
> – 'The Custody of the Pumpkin', *Blandings Castle and Elsewhere* (1935)

In Milne's Bar in Edinburgh there used to be a notice stating

No dancing
No singing

to which someone had appended 'Nae enjoyin yersel.'

Read Geneva print, to To get drunk, punning on the Geneva Bible (the famous English translation of 1557–60) and Dutch *genever*, 'juniper', the berry used to flavour gin.

'Why, John,' said the veteran, 'what devil of a discipline is this you have been keeping? You have been reading Geneva print this morning already.'

'I have been reading the Litany,' said John, shaking his head with a look of drunken gravity, and having only caught one word of the Major's address to him; 'life is short, sir; we are flowers of the field, sir – hiccup – and lilies of the valley.'

– Sir Walter Scott, *Old Mortality* (1816), chapter xi

Readie-ma-deezy, reediemadeasy, reed-a-ma-daisy, etc. A child's term for a first school reading book (literally, 'reading made easy').

But the bairns were reasonably weel cared for in the way of air and exercise, and a very responsible youth heard them their Carritch [catechism], and gied them lessons in Reediemadeasy.*

*'Reading made Easy', usually so pronounced in Scotland. [Scott's note]

– Sir Walter Scott, *Chronicles of the Canongate* (1827), Introductory, chapter iv

Real Big Ben, the How the Scottish Tourist Board once tried to promote Ben Nevis.

Real Mackay, the The genuine article. The phrase was adopted as a slogan in 1870 by the Edinburgh whisky distillers G. Mackay and Co., but is known to predate this (the *Dictionary of the Scottish Language* has an 1856 citation, 'a drappie o' the real McKay'). One suggestion is that *real* is a corruption of Reay, the area of Sutherland giving its name to Lord Reay, chief of the Clan Mackay (*see* WIZARD OF REAY, THE). Hence the Reay Mackays were the senior branch of the clan, in contrast to upstarts such as the Aberach Mackays.

When the Mackay whisky was exported to North America, the phrase became transformed into 'the real McCoy', and appears as such in James S. Bond's *The Rise and Fall of the 'Union Club'; or, Boy Life in Canada* (1881), in which a character says 'By jingo! yes; so it will be. It's the "real McCoy", as Jim Hicks says. Nobody but a devil can find us there.' Subsequently, in the 1890s, the US middleweight boxer Charles 'Kid' McCoy (1872–1940) was nicknamed 'the Real McCoy'. There is a story, probably apocryphal, that when the slight and dapperly dressed McCoy was drinking at a bar one day, he was harassed by a local tough, who expressed doubts that he was the famous boxer, and challenged him to a fight. When he recovered consciousness, the tough supposedly exclaimed, 'Oh my God, that *was* the real McCoy.'

Ream of the water, the *See* CREAM OF THE WATER, THE.

Reay, Lord *See* WIZARD OF REAY, THE.

Rebellious bugger the Duke of Montrose, that *See under* ROB ROY.

Rebellious Scots The nation was thus characterized in a verse added to 'God Save the King' in the wake of the '15 Rebellion:

Lord, grant that Marshal Wade,
May by thy mighty aid,
Victory bring.
May he sedition hush
And like a torrent rush,
Rebellious Scots to crush,
God save the King.

This, of course, ignores the fact that the great majority of Lowland Scots were anti-Jacobite in sentiment and deed. In 2007 Lord Goldsmith, the former attorney general, reviewing the 'future of Britishness and citizenship', questioned whether the verse should still be included in the national anthem of the United Kingdom. Few realized that it still was.

Rebus, Inspector The hero of a series of best-selling detective novels by Ian Rankin, largely set in Edinburgh, beginning with *Knots and Crosses* (1987). They are regarded as exemplars of the

TARTAN NOIR genre. Rebus, whose first name is John, not only has to battle with the city's criminals, but also with his superiors and his own inner demons. He has been played in TV dramatizations by John Hannah and Ken Stott. A *rebus* is a sort of puzzle, in which a word or phrase is represented by a series of pictures, symbols, letters and so on.

Red . . . *See also* REID . . .

Red biddy A tipple comprising methylated spirits mixed with cheap red wine such as LANNY or buckie (*see* BUCKFAST TRIANGLE), or sometimes just the cheap red wine on its own. The earliest references date from the 1930s. *Biddy* here is the familiar form of the Irish female first name Bridget; it has been suggested that the drink gets its name from its supposed popularity among the Glasgow Irish.

> Hidderie-hetterie stouteran in a dozie dwaum
> O' ramsh reid-biddie – Christ!
> The stink
> O' jake ahint him . . .
> > – Sydney Goodsir Smith, 'The Grace of God and the Meth-Drinker', from *Collected Poems 1941–1975* (1975) [*jake*, 'meths']

Redcap A species of malevolent sprite that formerly haunted castles and PELE TOWERS in the Borders. William Henderson, in his *Notes on the Folk-lore of the Northern Counties of England and the Borders* (1879), describes the Redcap as:

> A short thickset old man, with long prominent teeth, skinny fingers, armed with talons like eagles, large eyes of a fiery red colour, grisly hair streaming down his shoulders, iron boots, a pikestaff in his left hand and a red cap on his head.

This latter he would use to catch the blood of his victims, mostly travellers caught out on the open road after nightfall. However, if they pronounced the 'Holy Name', he would flee in a flash of fire, leaving behind a tooth. The most notorious Redcap was the familiar of Lord Soulis of Hermitage Castle, whose story was told by John Leyden in his ballad 'Lord Soulis', published in Scott's *MINSTRELSY OF THE SCOTTISH BORDER* (1802). The original Lord Soulis was William, Lord Soulis, who in the early 14th century conspired against the king and died a prisoner in Dumbarton Castle. In legend Soulis is a warlock who harries his neighbours mercilessly, and is told by Redcap that he cannot be killed by either 'forged steel, nor hempen band'. The last straw comes when Soulis seizes the Laird of Branxholm and his betrothed, whom Soulis desires for himself. But the young couple are rescued and Soulis is taken prisoner. Given his immunity to sword, axe or hangman's rope, he is bound in a sheet of lead and boiled to death in a cauldron. Many centuries later, after Hermitage Castle had been abandoned, the local lads would hurl stones into the ruins, crying, 'Redcappie-dossie, come oot if ye daur!' A related species is the THRUMMY CAP.

Red Clydeside A term referring to the strongly socialist working class who once laboured in the shipyards along the River Clyde. 'Red Clydeside' first came to prominence during the First World War, when radical firebrands such as Willie Gallacher, John Maclean (the FIGHTING DOMINIE) and James Maxton (later dubbed the GREATEST GENTLEMAN IN THE HOUSE OF COMMONS) were all arrested for anti-war activity. Another feature of the period was the rent strike organized by women such as Mary Barbour (*see* MRS BARBOUR'S ARMY). After the war, a massive rally held in George Square, Glasgow, in January 1919 prompted the government to send in English troops, fearing a Bolshevik revolution was about to break out (*see* BATTLE OF GEORGE SQUARE). In the 1922 general election, several Red Clydesiders, including Maxton and Manny Shinwell, and mostly members of the Independent Labour Party, were elected to Parliament. The spirit of Red Clydeside has continued to the present, a notable landmark being the work-in at Upper Clyde Shipbuilders in 1971, organized by the communist shop steward Jimmy Reid (*see* RAT RACE IS FOR RATS, THE).

Red cock crow on the rooftree, to make the To burn someone's house down; an expression associated (at least in literature) with the lawless wilds of Galloway, smugglers, BORDER REIVERS, etc.

> We'll see if the red cock crow not in his bonnie barn yard ae morning before day-dawing.
> > – Sir Walter Scott, *Guy Mannering* (1815), chapter iii

> Be the day dark or clear, the nicht starshine or pit-mirk,

an' the Red Cock craw not on the rooftree of Richard Maxwell by the heuchs of Craigdarroch, may I turn for ever and ever frae side to side between the red coal and the brimstone flaming blue ayont the bars o' muckle hell.

– S.R. Crockett, *The Raiders* (1894), chapter x

The phrase is not unique to Scotland, however:

Fire is described as a *red cock*: H. Sachs has the phrase 'to make the red cock ride on one's rooftree', and the Danes '*den röde hane galer over taget*', the red cock crows on the thack (the fire crackles).

– Jacob Grimm, *Teutonic Mythology* (1835)

Red Comyn, the The nickname of Sir John Comyn, Lord of Badenoch (d.1306), so called because of his red hair and complexion. His father, also John Comyn (d.1302), was known as the Black Comyn for similar reasons (although, confusingly, some sources say he was also known as the Red Comyn). He took part in the rebellion against English overlordship, but, owing to his support for his uncle, John de Balliol, he came into conflict with Robert the Bruce, who also claimed the throne. The invasion of Scotland by Edward I, the HAMMER OF THE SCOTS, forced most of the Scottish magnates to submit, and Comyn negotiated the terms. The rivalry between Comyn and Bruce culminated on 10 February 1306, when the two met in Greyfriars Church in Dumfries. It seems that both suspected the other of treachery; hot words turned to violence, and Comyn was killed; in one account, he was first stabbed by Bruce, then finished off by his supporters. (According to legend, one of these, Sir John Kirkpatrick, gave the fatal blow, saying 'To mak siccar [to make sure].' The phrase 'Mak siccar' was adopted as the motto of the Kirkpatricks in the 15th century.) On 25 March Bruce had himself crowned king, and proceeded to wage war against the Comyn power base in the Northeast (*see* HERSCHIP OF BUCHAN), as well as against the English. The murder – in a church, before the high altar – led to Bruce being excommunicated, and the DECLARATION OF ARBROATH issued in 1320 was partly an attempt to have this excommunication lifted. It was to atone for his killing of the Red Comyn that on his deathbed Bruce asked the BLACK DOUGLAS to take his heart with him on crusade.

Redd one's crap Literally, 'to clear one's crop (i.e. throat)', i.e. to get something off one's chest.

Red Douglases *See* BLACK DOUGLAS, THE.

Red Duchess, the A somewhat misleading nickname of Katherine Stewart-Murray, Duchess of Atholl (1874–1960), wife of the 8th Duke. She was Scottish Unionist (i.e. Conservative) MP for Kinross and West Perthshire from 1923, but her support for the Republicans during the Spanish Civil War and her opposition to Chamberlain's appeasement of Hitler led her to resign her seat in 1938. In the subsequent by-election she stood as an independent, but lost.

Redeswire Fray, the A bloody altercation (also known as the Redeswire Raid) that broke out during the TRUCE DAY held on 7 July 1575 at Carter Bar, the hill pass on the Border now taken by the A68. The Redeswire is the local name for the source of the River Rede, just over the English side (the Old English word *swire* means a hollow on top of a ridge). On this particular truce day, the Scottish Warden of the Middle March (*see* MARCHES), Sir William Kerr of Cessford, was unable to attend, so his deputy, Sir John Carmichael, Keeper of Liddesdale, stood in for him. Heading up the English side was 'Old' Sir John Forster (then aged 74), Warden of the English Middle March, supported by his deputy, Sir George Heron of Ford. All went well until the case of a certain 'Farnstein' (probably Harry Robson of Falstone) came up. The man had been accused of some crime by the Scots, and the English had promised to hand him over at a previous meeting, but now failed to produce him, although Old Sir John promised that he would deliver the man at the next truce day. Carmichael seems not to have accepted this, and tempers flared as Old Sir John goaded his younger counterpart, accusing him of knowing nothing of this part of the Border, and being generally wet behind the ears in Border affairs. Mutual insults led to violence, and a contingent of Fenwicks loosed their bows at the Scots, who were driven down the slope back into Scotland. Here the English encountered the men of Jedburgh, who were arriving late for the meeting, and who vigorously turned the tables.

Heron was killed, several leading Englishmen taken prisoner, and (to make the day a bit more profitable) a few hundred cattle reived from Redesdale.

Both Regent Morton of Scotland and Queen Elizabeth of England were furious with their respective wardens, whose actions had endangered diplomatic relations at a delicate moment. Morton sent back the English prisoners with gifts of hawks – leading to the tart observation that the Scots were giving 'live hawks for dead Herons' – and Carmichael was surrendered to the English (who returned him honourably to Scotland). On the English side, Lord Killigrew, Elizabeth's ambassador, declared that 'the English warden was not so clean in this matter as he could wish'. However, Old Sir John – whose allegiances were more local than national, and who had informal alliances with a number of Border families on the Scottish side, and thus turned a blind eye to their raids – continued as warden until 1595, despite suffering what his English critics called 'imbecility and weakness'. He died in 1602, the year before the Union of the Crowns brought an end to the era of the BORDER REIVERS.

The events of the Redeswire Fray are remembered annually by the Redeswire Ride, during which a large number of riders from Jedburgh head for the Border to celebrate the role of the men of the borough in the affair.

> Then raise the slogan with ane shout –
> 'Fy, Tindaill [Tynedale], to it! Jedburgh's here!'
> But anis his stomach was asteir.
> With gun and genzie, bow and speir,
> Men might see mony a cracked crown!
> But up amang the merchant geir,
> They were as busy as we were down.
> – 'The Raid of the Reidswire', from Scott's *MINSTRELSY OF THE SCOTTISH BORDER*

Red Etin, the A three-headed giant, the villain in an old Scottish fairytale, known at least as early as the 16th century. He imprisons women (including 'King Malcolm's daughter') and turns men to stone, or devours them, and as he searches for his prey he growls:

> Snouk butt, and snouk ben,
> I find the smell of an earthly man;

> Be he living or be he dead,
> His heart shall be kitchen to my bread.
> [*Snouk butt, and snouk ben*, 'Sniff or smell in the outer part of the house and the inner part of the house']

It is a somewhat long and tediously repetitive tale, but in the end the hero, the son of a poor widow, slays the Red Etin and frees the princess, whom he marries. The similarity of the names has led the Red Etin to be associated (baselessly) with Edin's Hall Broch near Abbey St Bathans in Berwickshire.

Red Fox, the *See* APPIN MURDER, THE.

Red Hector of the Battles *See* REID HARLAW, THE.

Red Hose Race A foot race held annually in Carnwath, Lanarkshire, for some 500 years, and supposedly the oldest such race in Britain. The prize, supplied by the local laird, is a pair of red stockings ('hose'), and the winner used to be announced at the Mercat Cross in Edinburgh. On 13 March 1508 James IV gave a charter for the barony of Carnwath to John, 3rd Lord Somerville, with the following condition:

> Paying thence yearly … one pair of hose containing half an ell of English cloth at the feast of St John the Baptist, called Midsummer, upon the ground of the said barony, to the man running most quickly from the east end of the town of Carnwath to the Cross called Cawlo Cross.

Permission to cancel the race (such as happened during the 2001 foot-and-mouth outbreak) has to be secured from the Crown. *See also* WHITE CRAW.

Red John of the Battles A translation of Iain Ruaidh nan Cath, the Gaelic byname of John Campbell, 2nd Duke of Argyll (1680–1743). He played a prominent role in the War of the Spanish Succession, in which he entered into a bitter rivalry with Marlborough, who wrote 'I cannot have a worse opinion of any body than I have of the duke of Argyle.' Nevertheless, he was promoted to field marshal, and commanded the Hanoverian forces against the Jacobites under BOBBING JOHN at Sheriffmuir in 1715. His shrill-voiced daughters were known as the Screaming Sisterhood or the BAWLING CAMPBELLS.

Red Lichties The nickname for inhabitants of Arbroath, and thus of the town's football team, Arbroath FC. The allusion is to the O OF AR-BROATH.

Red-shank A Highlander, or more specifically a Highland soldier, alluding to the colour of his *shanks* ('legs') below the kilt. The term was also applied to the Irish. It was already an archaism when Stevenson put it in the mouth of David Balfour in the following passage:

> We can leave these Hielandmen behind us on the rock, and one of your boats from the Castleton can bring them off to-morrow. Yon Neil has a queer eye when he regards you; maybe, if I was once out of the gate there might be knives again; these red-shanks are unco grudgeful.
> – Robert Louis Stevenson, *Catriona* (1893), chapter xvi

Red thread *See* ROWAN.

Reduplicate words Scots has a large number of words and expressions in which the second element somehow echoes the first, either through internal rhyme or other euphonious device, such as assonance or consonance. Some examples follow:

CABBY-LABBY
Catter-batter An altercation.
Clish-clash The same as CLISHMACLAVER.
Clitter-clatter A clattering noise; chatter.
COCK-A-LEEKIE
Currie-wurrie A dispute in which blows are exchanged. The expression may refer to the *wurr* (growl) of a *cur* (female dog).
Cushle-mushle Speaking sotto voce.
Deedle-doddle *See under* EEDLE-DODDLE.
Deetle-dottle *See under* EEDLE-DODDLE.
Dibber-dabber To argue, dispute.
Diddle-daddle A lot of faffing about with little to show for it.
Ding-dang Rapidly or confusedly.
EECHIE NOR OCHIE
EEDLE-DODDLE
EEKSY-PEEKSY
Eenty-teenty *See* ZEENTY-TEENTY.
Equal-aqual *See* EEKSY-PEEKSY.
Feery-farry A kerfuffle.

Fick-facks Bothersome details; a fuss about nothing (from *fyke*, 'fidget, fret').
Fiddle-diddle The noise a violin makes.
Flumgummery Flim-flam, frippery or flightiness; flashy and meretricious adornment.
GIBBLE-GABBLE
Giff-gaff Give and take; reciprocation (*gif* being 'give').
Gilly-gawkie A foolish young thing (especially female).
Glim-glam Blind man's buff (from *glaum*, 'snatch').
Hackum-plackum Equal (e.g. of portions); equally, evenly (e.g. of the way something is doled out).
Haggerty-taggerty Ragged.
Haggle-baggle or **hargle-bargle** Haggle; indulge in some argy-bargy.
HAIRY MARY
Heckum-peckum A species of fisherman's fly.
HEEDRUM-HODRUM
Heeliegoleerie Topsy-turvy.
HEUCHTER-TEUCHTER
Hickertie-pickertie Higgledy-piggledy.
Hickery-pickery The *OED* calls this a 'vulgar perversion' of the medieval Latin pharmacological term *hiera picra*, a purgative composed of aloes and canella bark.
Hiddie-giddie Topsy-turvy.
Hiddie-kiddie Common sense; the state of having a *hiddie* (i.e. head) on one's shoulders.
Hi Hi *See* FOOTBALL CLUB NICKNAMES.
Hingum-tringum Shoddy or dodgy.
Hinkie-pinkie or **inkie-pinkie** Weak beer.
Hippertie-skippertie Frivolous and flighty.
Hipsie-dipsie A right thrashing.
Hirdum-dirdum Riotous revelry. Used adjectivally, the expression is synonymous with *hiddie-giddie* or *heeligoleerie* (see above).
Hirdy-girdy Much the same as *hirdum-dirdum* (see above).
Hirrie-harrie The cry put up when a thief has been detected; 'Stop thief!'
Hish-hash Much the same as a 'hash', i.e. a mess or muddle.
Hixy-pixy Synonymous with *hiddie-giddie* or *heeligoleerie* (see above).
Hockerty-cockerty Sitting on someone's shoulders.
Hodge-podge A thick vegetable soup; *see* HODGE-PODGE CLUB.

HOWTOWDIE

Hudderie-dudderie Mucky; scruffy.

Hudge-mudge Secrecy; cushle-mushle (see above).

Huggery-muggery Secretive; messy.

Hurry-burry A rumpus, a busy confusion.

Icksie-picksie *See* EEKSY-PEEKSY.

Inkie-pinkie Hinkie-pinkie (see above).

Jennie Meggie The cranefly.

Kebbie-lebbie *See* CABBY-LABBY.

Kiggle-caggle To make a curling stone zigzag between others.

Mixter-maxter or **mixtie-maxtie** In a chaotic, jumbled state.

Molly-Dolly A fairground Aunt Sally.

Needle-noddle *See* EEDLE-DODDLE.

Nick-nacket A knick-knack.

Niffnaff Something or someone of no consequence (probably related to the word nyaff).

Pavey-waveys A children's skipping game, in which a rope is made to form *waves* above the *pavement*.

Peerie-weerie Dwindled to a thread of sound:

An' the roarin' o' oceans noo'
Is peerieweerie to me ...
 – Hugh MacDiarmid, 'Moonstruck' (1925)
 [Any small creature could also be called a peerie-weerie.]

Peesie-weesie Sharp-faced; wheedling.

Pilliewinkies A form of thumbscrew in use in the 16th and 17th centuries.

Pitter-patter To recite prayers, etc., rapidly and without conscious thought.

Ramstam Hurriedly or carelessly.

Rickietickie A button on a thread, used by children to irritate their elders by rattling it against a window.

Rim-ram Higgledy-piggledy.

Rump and stump or **stump and rump** Entirely.

SKITTERY WINTER

Snochter-dichter A handkerchief (*snochter*, 'snot, phlegm', *dichter*, 'wiper').

Tail-toddle Sexual intercourse.

Tappietourie Anything that forms an ornament on top of something, from a turret to a topknot of hair.

Tapsie-teerie Topsy turvy.

Teerie-orrie A game in which a ball is bounced against a wall.

Tippeny-nippeny A variety of leapfrog.

Tirlie-whirlie A knick-knack or trinket; a trill, turn or grace note in music; a gadget or ingenious device; the female pudendum. (From *tirl*, 'spin, twirl'.)

Tirr-wirr An uproar; to speak angrily.

Titbore-tatbore Peekaboo.

Too-hoo A to-do or fuss; a pathetic, useless person.

Toot-moot or **teet-meet** To carry on a conversation *sotto voce*; or such a conversation itself.

Towdy-mowdy An archaic term of affection, apparently equivalent to something like 'Bum-cheeks', *towdy* being an obsolete word for the buttocks.

Trittle-trattle Trash.

Whittie-whattie Temporizing obfuscation.

Wiffer-waffer A nobody, a useless waste of space.

Wiggletie-waggletie Wobbly; shaky on one's legs.

Yiff-yaff Chatter; an insignificant blether-mouth.

ZEENTY-TEENTY

See also COUNTING RHYMES AND SYSTEMS.

Reediemadeasy, reed-a-ma-daisy, etc. *See* READ-IE-MA-DEEZY.

Reekie, Auld *See* AULD REEKIE.

Reekie Peter A Northeastern term for a holder for a fir candle or an open oil lamp with a rush wick, otherwise known as an *Oily Peter* or a *cruisie*. *Reekie* means smoky (as in AULD REEKIE). *See also* TAM O' REEKIE.

Reekin', hot an' *See* HOT AN' REEKIN'.

Reek in the house, a Something Rotten in the State of Domesticity, especially an atmosphere of discord attributed to a shrewish wife.

'It is a sour reek, where the good wife dings the good man.' A man ... coming out of his house with tears on his cheeks, was ask'd the occasion; he said that there was a sour reek in the house; but upon farther inquiry, it was found that his wife had beaten him.
 – James Kelly, *A Complete Collection of Scottish Proverbs* (1721)

Reestit mutton Cured mutton, a Shetland delicacy. Traditionally in Shetland the older sheep were slaughtered in the autumn and then the meat was *reestit* by soaking it in brine for a fortnight; it was then hung up to dry for a week or so, usually above a peat fire. Reestit mutton is still popular, although in some shops the meat is actually lamb. The word *reest*, meaning 'to cure by smoking or drying', is of Norse origin, but is not confined to the Northern Isles. In its literary appearances it has a strong association with the Devil: Burns, in 'To the Deil' (1795), refers to Satan's *reestit gizz* ('smoked wig'); in Sir Walter Scott's *The Black Dwarf* (1816) Hobbie declares, 'Let us cut up bushes and briers, pile them before the door and set fire to them, and let us smoke that auld devil's dam as if she were to be reested for bacon'; while in James Hogg's *Private Memoirs and Confessions of a Justified Sinner* (1824) the weaver greets the narrator thus: 'What now, Mr Satan? What for art ye roaring that gate? Are you fawn inna little hell, instead o' the big muckil ane? Deil be in your reistit trams [machinations].'

Regalia, Royal *See* HONOURS OF SCOTLAND, THE.

Regimental nicknames A selection of nicknames of Scottish regiments past and present is given below.

Argyll and Sutherland Highlanders: the SWINGING SIXES; the Agile and Suffering Highlanders; the Thin Red Line (it was the Sutherland Highlanders who provided the 'THIN RED LINE' of resistance against a Russian cavalry attack at the Battle of Balaclava in 1854).

Black Watch: the LADIES FROM HELL; *see also* BLACK WATCH.

Cameronians: the Poison Dwarves (apparently so-named by Kaiser Wilhelm II during the First World War).

Coldstream Guards: the NULLI SECUNDUS CLUB.

Gordon Highlanders: the GAY GORDONS (it was the regiment that gave its name to the dance); the Ninety Twa (from their designation as the 92nd Regiment of Foot).

Highland Light Infantry (the HLI): the Assaye Regiment (from the name of a victory in India in 1803); the Pig and Whistle Light Infantry; the Glasgow KEELIES; Hell's Latest Invention; the Hairy-Leggit Irishmen.

King's Own Scottish Borderers: the KOBs; the Kosbees; the Botherers.

Queen's Own Cameron Highlanders: the Cia mar thas (Kamarhas); the Cams.

Royal Midlothian Yeomanry Cavalry (mid-19th century): SOOR-DOOK SODGERS.

Royal Scots: the First and Worst (it was the oldest infantry regiment of the line in the British Army, raised in 1633); PONTIUS PILATE'S BODYGUARD.

Royal Scots Fusiliers: the Earl of Mar's Grey Breeks (the regiment was raised by the Earl of Mar in 1678, and their trousers were grey).

Royal Scots Greys: the Bird-Catchers or Bubbly Jocks (i.e. turkeys; *see* BUBBLY-JOCK), referring to the eagle on their badge, which recalls their capture of a French eagle standard at Waterloo. 'Greys' in the regiment's name may have referred to their uniforms, or their grey horses.

Scots Guards: the Jocks; the Jock Guards; the Surrey Highlanders; the Bairns; the Kiddies. These last two names derive from an episode in 1678 when James VII and II stationed three Guards regiments on Hounslow Heath to deter unrest in London; the Scots Guards were the most junior of the three.

Seaforth Highlanders: the Wild MacRaes, possibly alluding to a mutiny in the regiment in Edinburgh in 1778; the regiment drew many of its recruits from the Macraes of Kintail (*see* SEAFORTH'S SHIRT). Incidentally, in one of various 'unofficial alphabets', the regiment makes an appearance in third place: "Ay for 'orses, Beef or mutton, Seaforth Highlanders ...'

Reid ... *See also* RED ...

Reid Harlaw, the The bloody (*reid*, i.e. red) Battle of Harlaw, fought near Inverurie, Aberdeenshire, on 24 July 1411, between the Earl of Mar (serving under the Regent Albany) and Donald, Lord of the Isles, over the disputed earldom of Ross. The battle, also known as *Bluidy Harlaw*, stopped Donald's advance on Aberdeen, but at the cost of high casualties (estimated at 1500), including the Mac-Lean chief, Red Hector of the Battles. In fact, both sides thought the other victorious, and withdrew.

In doubtsome victory they dealt;
The bluidy battle lasted long;
Ilk man his neighbour's force there felt
The weakest oft-times go the wrong.
    – Anon., 'The Battle of Harlaw'

Another version of the ballad suggests (inaccurately) that the battle went on for several days:

On Monaday, at mornin',
The battle it began;
On Saturday, at gloamin',
Ye'd scarce ken wha had wan.

The balladeers go on to tell of the cost of the battle: 'And sic a weary burying/The like ye never saw …' See also BRAIF TOUN, THE.

Reivers See BORDER REIVERS.

Religion of the yellow stick, the (Gaelic *creideamh a' bhata bhuidhe*) Presbyterianism, as enforced by the laird on Rum. Dr Johnson explains the term thus, in his description of the island:

The inhabitants are fifty-eight families, who continued Papists for some time after the Laird became a Protestant. Their adherence to their old religion was strengthened by the countenance of the Laird's sister, a zealous Romanist, till one Sunday, as they were going to mass under the conduct of their patroness, Maclean met them on the way, gave one of them a blow on the head with a *yellow stick*, I suppose a cane, for which the Earse had no name, and drove them to the kirk, from which they have never since departed. Since the use of this method of conversion, the inhabitants of Eigg and Canna, who continue Papists, call the Protestantism of Rum, the religion of the Yellow Stick.

 – Samuel Johnson, *A Journey to the Western Islands of Scotland* (1775)

Repentance stool See STOOL OF REPENTANCE.

Repentance Tower A watchtower on an eminence above the River Annan near Hoddam Castle, a few miles to the northwest of the town of Annan. It was built in the mid-16th century by John Maxwell, 4th Lord Herries of Terregles, and on its lintel is inscribed the single word 'REPENTANCE'. There are two explanations as to why Herries should feel the need to atone. The first suggests that in the course of building Hoddam Castle he demolished an old chapel. The second recounts how Maxwell accepted an English pension in return for supporting English efforts against the powerful Douglases.

However, when in 1548 an English expedition up Nithsdale was brutally repulsed, the English suspected Maxwell of treachery and hanged a number of Scottish hostages, including, it is said, Maxwell's 12-year-old nephew.

Rest and be Thankful The pass (804 ft/245 m) between Glen Croe and Glen Kinglass in the ARROCHAR ALPS. The original road, which takes a very steep route up the head of Glen Croe, was built by government soldiers in 1753, in the wake of the 1745 Rebellion, and it was some of these men who erected a stone seat at the summit, on which they inscribed the words 'Rest and be Thankful'. Wordsworth, coming this way in 1803, concurred:

Doubling and doubling with laborious walk,
Who that has gained at length the wished-for height,
This brief, this simple wayside call can slight,
And rest not thankful?

The summit proved a disappointment to Keats on his 1818 walking tour:

We were up at 4 this morning and have walked to breakfast 15 miles through two tremendous Glens – at the end of the first there is a place called rest and be thankful which we took for an Inn – it was nothing but a Stone and so we were cheated into 5 more miles to breakfast.
 – John Keats, letter to Tom Keats, 17 July 1818

The present A83 takes a less steep route up the flank of Glen Croe.

Resurrectionists See BURKE AND HARE.

Rhapsody of ill-invented nonsense, a Theology, according to Thomas Aikenhead (1676–97), a young student at Edinburgh University. As a consequence he was charged with blasphemy, the indictment asserting:

That … the prisoner had repeatedly maintained, in conversation, that theology was a rhapsody of ill-invented nonsense, patched up partly of the moral doctrines of philosophers, and partly of poetical fictions and extravagant chimeras: That he ridiculed the holy scriptures, calling the Old Testament Ezra's fables, in profane allusion to Esop's Fables; That he railed on Christ, saying, he had learned magick in Egypt, which enabled him to perform those pranks which were called miracles: That he called the New Testament the history of the imposter Christ; That he said Moses was the better artist and the better politician; and he preferred Mahomet to Christ: That the Holy Scriptures were stuffed with such madness, nonsense, and contradictions, that he admired the stupidity of the world in being so long deluded by them: That he rejected the mystery of the Trinity as unworthy of refutation; and scoffed at the incarnation of Christ.

– *A complete collection of state trials and proceedings for high treason and other crimes and misdemeanors* … (1809–28, vol. 13, ed. T.B. Howell)

The case was prosecuted by the Lord Advocate, Sir James Stewart, who demanded the death penalty. Aikenhead had made a full recantation before his trial, but he was found guilty and hanged on 8 January 1697. On the morning of his execution he declared:

It is a principle innate and co-natural to every man to have an insatiable inclination to the truth, and to seek for it as for hid treasure … So I proceeded until the more I thought thereon, the further I was from finding the verity I desired.

Aikenhead was the last person in Britain to be executed for blasphemy.

Rhyming slang Scottish rhyming slang has been dubbed 'Jockney', suggesting an imitation of Cockney rhyming slang (in which, incidentally, Sweaty Sock = Jock, i.e. a Scotsman, and SCOTCH MIST = pissed, i.e. drunk). However, Scottish rhyming slang may have arisen independently, and certainly has its own unique lexicon, often dependent on Scottish pronunciation. There has been a considerable increase in new coinages over recent years, especially in Glasgow. For a more exhaustive list of Glaswegian rhyming slang, readers are referred to the relevant appendix in Michael Munro's *The Complete Patter* (1996).

Acme wringer = FINGER. *Go yer Acme wringer* = GO YER DINGER. Acme was a brand of clothes wringer.

Barry White = shite (alluding to the American soul singer)

Berryhuckle = Huckleberry (Hound) = round, as in 'It's no ma berryhuckle.' (The allusion is to the US cartoon character.)

Bertie Auld = cold. The reference is to the footballer Robert ('Bertie') Auld (b.1938), who joined Celtic FC in 1955 and was a member of the LISBON LIONS team in 1967. Sometimes the reference was even more obscure, as in 'It's fair Burlington the day' (Burlington Bertie = Bertie Auld).

Bob Hope = dope

Cabbage (and ribs) = Hibs, i.e. Hibernian FC

Carolina = China (plate) = mate

Chic Murray = curry (referring to the comedian, 1919–85)

Choccy = chocolate éclair = Brian McClair, the footballer (*see* CHOCCY)

Chorus (and verse) = erse, i.e. arse.

Clydebank an' Kilbooie = Shooey, a Glaswegian version of the name Hugh

Collie (dug) = mug.

Corned beef = deif, i.e. deaf.

Cowdenbeath (the former mining town in Fife) = teeth

Cream bun = Hun (i.e. a Rangers supporter)

Crossmyloof (an area of Glasgow once known for its ice rink) = poof

Currant bun = nun

Dan Dares or **Tony Blairs** = flares (i.e. flared trousers; Dan Dare was a spaceman in the *Eagle* comic)

Diddle-doddle = model, i.e. a 'model lodging house', a hostel for the homeless, along the lines first established in the 19th century by various philanthropists.

Donald (Duck) = luck

Duke of Argylls = piles, i.e. haemorrhoids.

Elkie Clark = mark, as in 'Get aff yer Elkie'. Elkie (Alec) Clark (1898–1956) was a noted Glasgow boxer.

Easter egg = beg

Frankie Vaughan = hawn (i.e. hand). Frankie Vaughan (1928–99) was the Liverpool-born crooner known as 'Mr Moonlight' who in the 1960s did much work on behalf of disadvantaged youths in Glasgow's Easterhouse estate.

Friar Tucked = in deep trouble

Gas-cookered = snookered, i.e. thwarted

Gone an dunnit = bunnit, i.e. flat cap

Good looks = books, i.e. one's form P45, presented to one on leaving one's employment, whether voluntarily or otherwise. **Pansy Potters** = jotters, means the same.

Govan ferry = Mary (pronounced 'Merry' in Glasgow)

Green or **wine (grape)** = pape, a derogatory term for a Catholic

Gregory Pecks = specs

HAMPDEN ROAR = score (from the venue for Scottish football internationals).

Ham shank = wank, i.e. an act of masturbation

Harry Wraggs = Jags (i.e. Partick Thistle FC), alluding to the successful jockey and trainer Harry Wragg (1902–85)

Hielan or **disco dancer** = chancer (**Bengal lancer** means the same)

Hillbilly = chilly

Hoosie Fraser = razor (after the department store House of Fraser)

Jack and Jill = the Pill

Jambos = **Jam Tarts** = Hearts, i.e. Heart of Midlothian FC

John Greigs = legs (referring to John Greig (b. 1945), the Rangers player and manager)

John o' Groat = coat

John o' Groats = oats, as in 'Are ye gettin' yer John o' Groats?' i.e. 'Are you having regular sexual intercourse?'

Jungle Jim = TIM (i.e. a Catholic), particularly applied to Celtic supporters (*see* JUNGLE, THE)

Kenneth McKellar = cellar (referring to the popular tenor, 1927–2010)

Legal Aid = lemonade

Lemon curd = burd, i.e. a young woman, especially one's girlfriend

Lillian Gish = pish

Malkie = (in Glasgow gangster slang) a razor used as a weapon, from an unknown person by the name of Malkie (Malcolm) Fraser.

Manfred Mann = tan (alluding to the 1960s pop group)

Mars Bar = scar

Some Mars Bar you've got yourself there, man, Donny says. – You should see the other guy, I say, all cocky.
– Irvine Welsh, *Acid House* (1994)

Mick (Jagger) = lager

Mickey Rooney = loony

Mr Happy = nappy (alluding to the logo of the GLASGOW'S MILES BETTER campaign)

Moby (Dick) = sick

Nat King Cole = hole, i.e. sex (as in 'Are ye getting yer Nat King Cole?')

Oscar (Slater) = later. Oscar Slater, wrongfully convicted of murder in 1909, became known as the SCOTTISH DREYFUS.

Pan breid = deid, i.e. dead (*see also* PAN LOAF)

Paraffin (ile, i.e. oil) = style

Parkheid smiddies = diddies, i.e. titties (the allusion is to the *smiddies* or engineering works – such as that of Beardmore – that formerly stood in the Parkhead area of Glasgow)

Pat 'n' Mick = (on the) sick, i.e. off work with a sick note

Pat Lally = swally, i.e. a drink. Pat Lally (b.1926) was Lord Provost of Glasgow from 1995 to 1999. *See also* PAT LAZARUS; LALLY'S PALAIS.

Pea pod = tod (Sloane) = own, as in 'on one's pea pod'

Pearl diver = fiver, i.e. £5

Pen Nibs = Hibs (Hibernian FC)

Pineapple = chapel (i.e. a Catholic church)

Pottit heid = deid, i.e. dead

Radio Rental = mental (alluding to the TV hire company)

Rothesay docks = socks

Salisbury Crag = scag, i.e. heroin (after Edinburgh's SALISBURY CRAGS).

Salvador (Dali) = swallie, i.e. swallow, drink

Scooby (Doo) = clue (from the American cartoon dog)

Scotch mist = pissed, i.e. drunk

Shammy (leather) = blether, i.e. chat, gossip.

Single (fish) = pish (what one takes out of the gullible)

South of the Border = out of order

Tackety bits or **tacketies** = tits (*tackety bits* are hobnail boots)

Tarry rope = the pope

Teds = **Teddy Berrs** = **Gers** = Rangers FC (*see* FOOTBALL CLUB NICKNAMES)

Tin flute = suit

Tony (Blair) = hair

Varicose veins = weans (i.e. children)

Whodunnit = bunnet, i.e. hat

Richest Square Mile in Europe, the In the 19th century Broughty Ferry had this (no doubt exaggerated) reputation, owing to the concentration of wealthy industrialists who built their mansions here, having made their fortunes in nearby Dundee, aka JUTEOPOLIS (*see also* JAM, JUTE AND JOURNALISM). Their abandonment of the city in which they accumulated their riches attracted some opprobrium, as in this anonymous rhyme printed in the *City Echo* in 1907:

When the city merchants, cool an' cute,
Have fortunes made frae jam or jute
They flee tae scape the smeel an' soot
Awa tae Broughty Ferry.

Tae 'scape the smeel an' but the tax
(Oor laws are shuir a trifle lax)
They tak' the honey, lave the wax
These Nabobs o' the Ferry.

An' thus we see braw villas stand
Wi' whigmaleeries on ilk hand
As raised by some enchanter's wand
Round bonnie Broughty Ferry.

Riddle and the shears, the A method of divination, involving a *riddle* (a coarse-meshed sieve) and a pair of scissors:

The riddle is set on its side, the points of a pair of large scissors being so fixed in it (separate from each other), that the riddle may be suspended by the hold taken of it by the scissors. One handle of the scissors is placed on the finger of one person, and the other on that of another. Some words, to the same purpose with the following are repeated; By St Paul and St Peter, did A.B. steal my yarn? or whatever is lost. If the person mentioned be innocent, the riddle remains motionless; if guilty, it immediately turns round ...

This, among the other superstitious customs common on *Halloween*, is also used as a mode of divination in regard to marriage. When two persons are *evened*, or named in relation to the connubial tie, if the riddle turns round, it is concluded that they are to be united in this bond. Sometimes a good deal of art is practised in this ceremony.

– John Jamieson, *An Etymological Dictionary of the Scottish Language* (1825 supplement)

Jamieson says that this method of divination was well known in France, and cites Sir Thomas Urquhart's translation of Rabelais: 'Let us have a sive, and

a paire of shiers, and thou shalt see devils.' In the early 18th century the practice was still thought to have a dangerous whiff of the occult, the records of the court sessions of Minnigaff referring in 1702 to 'that pice of devilrie commonly called turning the riddle'.

Riddrie Hilton, the Another nickname for HM Prison Barlinnie; *see* BAR-L, THE.

Riding the Marches An annual civic ceremony in a number of Scottish burghs, particularly in the Borders. It is also known as the Common Riding in places such as Selkirk and Hawick, while in Dumfries it forms the highlight of the Guid Nychburris Festival (a 20th-century creation, borrowing some Old Scots spelling). The ceremony involves a band of people on horseback, led by an annually elected Cornet (or variously known as the Jethart [Jedburgh] Callant, Kelso Laddie, etc.), who rides around the marches or boundaries of the burgh (*see* MARCH, THE) to check that no neighbouring landowners are encroaching on the territory, privileges or liberties of the burghers. Each town has a variety of traditions associated with the Riding. For example, in Langholm, where the ceremony is held on the last Friday in July, the riders traverse the burgh boundaries asserting the right of the townspeople to cut peat and bracken on the surrounding common land. In some towns, the riders carry banners, while in Langholm they carry three standards: a wooden fish nailed to a bannock, a giant crown woven out of roses, and a giant thistle woven out of many actual thistles. Hugh MacDiarmid, a native of Langholm, recalled the Riding in the 'Muckle Toon' in *A Drunk Man Looks at the Thistle* (1926):

A' as it used to be, when I was a loon
On Common-Ridin' Day in the Muckle Toon.
The bearer twirls the Bannock-and-Saut Herrin',
The Croon o' Roses through the lift is farin',
The aucht-fit thistle wallops on hie ...

See also BRAW LADS' GATHERING; HUNT OF PENTLAND, THE; LANIMER DAY.

Riding the stang An informal punishment formerly administered by the mob to men who violently mistreated their wives, or to others who offended against local convention, such as scolds or adulterers. The perpetrator was forced to sit astride a *stang* – a pole or rough tree branch – and was then carried in a jolting fashion around the town or village for a prescribed distance. In 1734 the women of Huntly petitioned the authorities that the custom might be tolerated, after a Mr John Fraser, a notorious wife-beater, had complained that his neighbours had threatened him with the stang in an effort to prevent his wife being 'butchered'. The petition concluded:

> May it please your Lordships to take this our more than most lamentable case into your most serious consideration by granting a toleration to the Stang which has not only ever been practicable in this place but in most parts of this Kingdom being we know of no act of Parliament to the contrary. Or else if your Lordships can fall on a more prudent method we most humbly beg your opinion for preventing more fatal consequences. Otherwise upon the least disobligement given we must expect to fall victims to our husbands' displeasure, from which *libera nos, Domine.*

Sometimes riding the stang might be crowned with a ducking in the local loch, although in Leith and Restalrig this latter practice was abandoned in the 18th century when a gentle gardener called Joseph Scott, who turned into a brute when drunk, was drowned in Lochend Loch. The custom was also known in northern England, as this verse from Northallerton, Yorkshire, indicates:

> So all you good people that live in this row,
> I'd have you take warning, for this is our law;
> And if any of your husbands you wives do bang,
> Come to me and my congregation, and we'll Ride
> the Stang.

Riding the stang had died out by the early 19th century.

Right into yer barra *See* BARRA.

Rin ... *See also* RUN ...

Rin the cutter, to Originally, to evade the Excise cutter and land smuggled goods successfully. Subsequently, the phrase was jocularly applied to bring-ing alcohol home without being detected. The word *cutter* was also applied to a hip flask.

Ring of Steall, the A popular hill-walking circuit in the Mamores. Passing under the spectacular Steall Falls (Gaelic An Steall Bàn, 'the white spout') in Upper Glen Nevis, the route ascends An Gearanach, Stob Coire a' Chàirn, Am Bodach, Sgùrr an Iubhair and then traverses the DEVIL'S RIDGE over Stob Choire a' Mhail to the last summit, Sgurr a' Mhàim. The name puns on the name of the waterfall and the quality of the calf muscles required.

Rioghal Mo Dhream *See* MOTTOES.

Rituals and beliefs *See* CEREMONIES, ETC.

Rive one's faither's bonnet, to To surpass one's father's achievements. *Rive* means 'tear up', with the suggestion that the father's bonnet has become too small for the son. The expression was in use into the early 20th century.

Rizzer *See* WELL-HUNG FISH.

Rizzio's blood Since at least 1722, a stain on the floorboards at the entry to the apartments of Mary Queen of Scots in the Palace of Holyrood has been pointed out to visitors as the blood of David Rizzio, Mary's Italian secretary. In 1566 Mary's jealous husband, Lord Darnley, and a group of his followers butchered the little Italian here, stabbing him 56 times. When Mary tried to call for help, one of the conspirators, Lindsay of the Byres, threatened to 'cut her in collops'. John Knox for one had no sympathy for the dead man, writing 'That poltroon and vile knave Davie was justlie punished ...'

Rizzio's Chestnut A tree by the River North Esk, near Melville Castle, said to have been planted by Rizzio (see previous entry) as a token of his love for Mary Queen of Scots.

Roads and Streets *See:*
- BLYTHSWOOD SQUARE
- DANUBE STREET
- DERE STREET
- DESTITUTION ROAD

- DEVIL'S ELBOW, the
- ELECTRIC BRAE, the
- FUNGLE ROAD, the
- HERRING ROAD, the
- JOCK'S ROAD
- King's Road (see under KING OF THE BORDER), the
- LANG WHANG, the
- MONKS' ROAD
- PARALLEL ROADS OF GLEN ROY, the
- RADICAL ROAD, the
- REST AND BE THANKFUL
- ROAD TO THE ISLES, the
- ROSE STREET
- SAUCHIEHALL STREET
- SLUG ROAD, the
- STRING, the
- THIEF'S ROAD
- *VIA REGIA*
- WADE'S ROADS

Road to the Isles, the A traditional route leaving General Wade's road (see WADE'S ROADS) from Stirling to Inverness at Tummel Bridge, and thence proceeding along the north bank of the River Tummel and the north shore of Loch Rannoch, broadly following the present B846 until it ends at Rannoch Station. From here the old road extended across Rannoch Moor, then over the DEVIL'S STAIRCASE past Kinlochleven to Fort William, where it joins the present A830, passing by Glenfinnan, Arisaig and Morar to Mallaig, the ferry port for Skye. Today it is often only the stretch from Fort William to Mallaig – a stretch particularly associated with Bonnie Prince Charlie, who started and ended his rebellion here – that is referred to as the Road to the Isles. However, in Kenneth Macleod's famous song entitled 'The Road to the Isles, Written for the Boys in France, 1914', the chorus goes as follows:

> Sure by Tummel and Loch Rannoch and Lochaber
> I will go
> By heather tracks wi' heaven in their wiles.
> If it's thinkin' in your inner heart, the braggart's in
> my step,
> You've never smelled the tangle o' the Isles.
> Oh the far Cuillins are puttin' love on me,
> As step I wi' my crummack to the Isles.

Roamin' in the gloamin' An activity long conducted by courting couples, and enshrined as a keystone of FAUX JOCKERY in the title of Sir Harry Lauder's 1911 song:

> Roamin' in the gloamin' on the bonnie banks o'
> Clyde,
> Roamin' in the gloamin' wae my lassie by my side.
> When the sun has gone to rest,
> That's the time we love the best,
> O, it's lovely roamin' in the gloamin'!

The *gloamin'* is the twilit end of the evening. The phrase has more recently received a new breath of life in Ali Smith's *Girl Meets Boy* (2007):

> ... we were the tail of a fish were the reek of a cat were the beak of a bird were the feather that mastered gravity were high above every landscape then down deep in the purple haze of the heather were roamin in a gloamin in a brash unending Scottish piece of perfect jigging reeling reel ...

Roaring buckie A whelk (*buckie*) shell, which, when one holds it to one's ear, supposedly gives out the sound of the sea.

Roaring game, the Curling, also referred to as *roaring play*.

> The sun had clos'd the winter-day,
> The Curlers quat their roaring-play ...
> – Robert Burns, 'The Vision' (1786)

> Glorious times they had at the roaring game, with their home-made stones and their heather-cowes or brooms.
> – H.J. Steven, *New Cumnock* (1899)

The name refers both to the cries of participants and spectators, and to the noise of the stones (the *roaring stones*) as they slide across the ice. A *roaring rink* is a curling rink. See also BONSPIEL.

Robbie Burns An old-fashioned sort of plough, assumed to be of the type used by the PLOUGHMAN POET.

Robbie Dye A supporter of Hawick Rugby Football Club, or any partisan for the burgh itself, named after an individual who held such enthusiasms.

Robbie the Pict The *nom de guerre* of the campaigner Brian Robertson (b.1948), who in 1977 founded the Pictish Free State, an internationally unrecognized micronation initially comprising an acre of land that Robertson owned on Skye. In the early 1990s Robertson unsuccessfully sought political asylum in Estonia, and in 1999 stood as MEP for Skye, with a similar lack of success. His greatest triumph came in 2004, when the tolls on the Skye Bridge were abolished, something he had long campaigned for. In 2009 his attempt to have speed cameras declared illegal was rejected by the Scottish Court of Appeal.

Rob Donn *See* ROBERT BURNS OF GAELDOM, THE.

Robert Burns of Gaeldom, the A title sometimes awarded to the Gaelic poet Robert Calder or Mackay (1714–78), universally known as Rob Donn ('brown-haired Rob'), whose poetry, like that of Burns, is celebrated for its sometimes bawdy humour, its wordplay, its social satire and its perceptiveness regarding the foibles of humanity.

Rob Donn was born in Strathmore in Sutherland, later recalling:

> I was born in the winter
> Among the lowering mountains,
> And my first sight of the world
> Snow and wind about my ears.

A humble cowherd, he became a sub-tenant of Iain MacEachainn, himself a third cousin of Lord Reay, the Mackay chief, and MacEachainn became his chief patron. In his earlier years Rob Donn appears to have got into trouble both for poaching deer and for his Jacobite sympathies. He later served for a while with the Sutherland Highlanders, before returning to work for Lord Reay. Towards the end of his life, realizing his strength was failing, he climbed once more to the summit of Beinn Spionnaidh, his favourite hunting ground above Loch Eriboll, and there buried his gun. Rob Donn himself is buried at Balnakeil, and there is a story that shortly after his interment his grave was desecrated by a lesser poet who believed he would inherit the dead bard's genius if he possessed one of his teeth. To this end he dug down into Rob Donn's grave, opened the coffin and extracted a molar. Poetic justice took

its course, of course, and the lesser poet suffered from unbearable toothache until the relic was returned to its proper place.

Rob Donn dictated two manuscript collections of his works during his lifetime, but in 1792 the Revd William Findlater, in the *First Statistical Account*, expressed concern as to their preservation:

> The celebrated bard, Robert Donn, was of this parish. His songs are well known, and discover uncommon force of genius. It is a pity they have not been printed, to secure them from mutilation, corruption and oblivion.

A collected edition of Rob Donn's poems was not published until 1829, and even then in a bowdlerized form. *See also* GLEN GOLLY; LAVELLAN.

Robert the Bruce Robert I, King of Scotland (1306–29), victor of Bannockburn and hero of the Wars of Independence. Of mixed Scottish and Norman descent, he was known in Norman French as *Robert de Brus*, and after his death his deeds were celebrated by John Barbour in the epic poem *The Brus* (*c.*1375), in which he is styled:

> The lord off Anandyrdale
> Robert the Bruys erle off Carryk.

In Old Scots, when 'the' was used before a surname it indicated the chief of a clan or head of an important family. It was a translation of French *le* or a variant on *de*. As for the name Bruce itself, in addition to the Brus version noted above, it was variously rendered, in Scottish and English sources, as Brix, Braose, Breaux, Bruys, Bruyse and Brutz – the name originating in the Norman village of Brix. *See also* BLACK DOUGLAS, THE; BRUCE AND THE SPIDER; DECLARATION OF ARBROATH, THE; GREAT CAUSE, THE; KING HOBBE; RED COMYN, THE; WALLACETHEBRUCEISM.

Rob Gib's contract A toast to faithfulness and selfless love. The expression comes from the name of James V's Master of Horse, who when asked by the king why he served him, answered 'for stark love and kindness' – a phrase that became proverbial.

Robin According to James Napier's *Folk-Lore: Superstitious Beliefs in the West of Scotland within*

This Century (1879), there was a saying that the robin

... had a drop of God's blood in its veins, and that therefore to kill or hurt it was a sin, and that some evil would befall anyone who did so; and, conversely, any kindness done to poor robin would be repaid in some fashion. Boys did not dare to harry a robin's nest.

Conversely, the yellowhammer and the swallow were each said

... to have a drop of the Devil's blood in its veins; so the yellowhammer was remorselessly harried, and the swallow was feared and therefore let alone.

Rob Roy The name, meaning 'Red Rob', adopted by the red-haired outlaw and folk hero Robert MacGregor (1671–1734), who often signed his name thus. Rob Roy, the third son of Lieutenant-Colonel Donald Glas MacGregor of Glengyle, was obliged to take the surname Campbell (his mother's maiden name) after the entire Clan MacGregor was proscribed in 1693, partly owing to their predilection for cattle raiding and BLACKMAIL (*see* MAC-GREGOR, PROSCRIPTION OF CLAN). Rob Roy, although indulging in such pastimes himself, was by and large a legitimate cattle trader, and emerged as something of a leader among the MacGregors. Although initially successful in his business, he ended up unable to collect debts owed to him, and with some powerful creditors, notably the Marquess (later Duke) of Montrose, pursuing him, he was obliged to go underground. With the outbreak of the 1715 Jacobite Rebellion, Montrose having declared his Hanoverian sympathies, Rob Roy came out in favour of the OLD PRETENDER. At the same time he was also supplying intelligence to the government, and his main interest appears to have been in recovering the lands he had lost to Montrose. Rob Roy and his MacGregor followers remained on the sidelines at the Battle of Sheriff-muir, and during the tail-end of the Rebellion they largely indulged in raiding rather than military action in furtherance of the Stuart cause. In May 1716 Rob Roy surrendered his arms, having been assured that he would not be prosecuted, but in June he was attainted for high treason. He now became an outlaw, raiding the estates of the man he

described as 'that rebellious bugger the Duke of Montrose ... who is very far degenerate from his predecessors'. In 1719 Rob Roy and his men came out again in support of the Old Pretender, but were defeated, along with a small Spanish invasion force, at Glenshiel. He resumed his life as an outlaw and raider, until in 1725 the government offered all rebels a pardon in return for submission – an offer that Rob Roy accepted, demonstrating his loyalty by supplying information on continuing Jacobite intrigues in the Highlands. He settled on a farm at Balquhidder, where he died in 1734 and was buried in the churchyard.

Rob Roy's legend as a new Robin Hood began in his lifetime. Though he did not give to the poor, many admired his daring and sympathized with his plight as a persecuted man trying to recover his rights, stolen by rich and unscrupulous magnates. No one ever betrayed him. In 1803 Wordsworth visited what he thought was Rob Roy's grave, and penned a fairly execrable ballad beginning:

A famous man is Robin Hood,
The English ballad-singer's joy!
And Scotland has a thief as good,
An outlaw of as daring mood;
She has her brave ROB ROY!

His fame was further secured by Sir Walter Scott's *Rob Roy* (1817), although he is not the main hero of the novel, and his deeds in it are highly fictionalized – as they have been in various stage and film versions. Rob Roy's son Robin Oig makes an appearance in Robert Louis Stevenson's novel KID-NAPPED, fighting a duel on the bagpipes with his old enemy, Alan BRECK. *See also* GILDEROY.

Rob Roy's Prison A crag on the east shore of Loch Lomond, more or less due west of the summit of Ben Lomond. It was said that Rob Roy used to lower his captives on a rope into the loch here, until they vouchsafed the information he was after. Further north along the east shore, beyond Inver-snaid, may be found Rob Roy's Cave, where, it has been suggested, Robert the Bruce hid in 1306.

Rona Raiders, the The name given to a group of ex-servicemen who in 1919 were evicted from their holdings on the small island of Rona, and landed with their families on the neighbouring island of Raasay. Here they tried to reoccupy the land at North Fearns from which their ancestors had been removed during the CLEARANCES. The men were arrested, tried and sent to prison, but such was the public outcry that they were eventually released and allowed to settle on Raasay. Another consequence was that in 1922 the British government acquired both Rona and Raasay from their private landlord. *See also* SEVEN MEN OF KNOYDART, THE.

Rooney, to have an Annie *See* ANNIE ROONEY, TO HAVE AN.

Rose Street A narrow street in Edinburgh's New Town, between Princess Street and George Street, noted for its plethora of drinking establishments – currently there are 18 or so, but in the 1970s there were nearly 30. These can be linked by the thirsty in the famous Rose Street Challenge, a pub crawl that runs the whole gamut, from Scott's at the western end to The Abbotsford in the east, and taking in many others, including The Kenilworth. Quite what Sir Walter would have made of it all is a matter upon which one can only speculate. The street's literary associations are reinforced by the presence of Milne's Bar, in the past a noted gathering spot for the more leftish of the Scottish literati, such as Hugh Mac-Diarmid, leading to the room they favoured being dubbed 'the Little Kremlin'. For some, the street has proved a place of damnation:

> He taks a funny-turn, begs the Diable
> to gie him leave to quit this aafie place,
> the warstest neuk of Hell, he's like to think;
> as Hell to Rose Street, sae is smell to stink ...
> – Robert Garioch, 'Doktor Faust in Rose Street' (1973)

At one time, Rose Street was promoted as the 'Amber Mile', to complement Edinburgh's more famous ROYAL MILE.

Roslin *See* HERMIT OF HAWTHORNDEN, THE; HUNT OF PENTLAND, THE; PRENTICE PILLAR, THE.

Rottenrow The name by which the Glasgow Royal Maternity Hospital was commonly known, after the street in which it was situated. The institution began its life as the Glasgow Lying-In Hospital and Dis-

pensary in 1834, and moved to the corner of Rottenrow and Portland Street in 1860. In the late 19th century the hospital pioneered the procedure of Caesarian section. The institution relocated to new premises at the Glasgow Royal Infirmary in 2001, and the old buildings were demolished the following year and replaced by a landscaped park, featuring a sculpture of a giant nappy pin by George Wylie entitled *Monument to Maternity*. A number of other streets in the UK are called Rottenrow, and the *rotten* element is thought to be a corruption of the older Scots and English word *ratoun*, 'rat', suggesting the street was rat-infested, while *row* or *raw* denotes a row of cottages. Another suggestion is that the name derives from Gaelic *rat-an-righ*, 'road of the kings', but this is less likely.

Rough Bounds, the A wild, mountainous and sparsely inhabited area of the Western Highlands, extending in the south from Loch Sunart north through Moidart, Arisaig, Morar and Knoydart to Loch Hourn. It is sometimes extended southward through Morvern to the Sound of Mull and north-ward to Glen Shiel and Loch Duich. The name is a translation of the Gaelic *Na Garbhchrìochan*.

Rough Wooing, the A term coined by Sir Walter Scott for the military campaigns conducted by the English in Scotland between 1544 and 1548. The English were attempting to persuade the Scots to honour the 1543 Treaty of Greenwich, by which Henry VIII's young son Edward was betrothed to the infant Mary Queen of Scots. Henry hoped this would lure the Scots away from the AULD ALLI-ANCE with France, with whom he was again at war. Henry vented his fury in 1544 and 1545, when the Earl of Hertford devastated much of southeast Scotland, doing his best to implement Henry's orders:

> Put all to fire and sword, burn Edinburgh town, so razed and defaced when you have sacked and gotten what ye can of it, as there may remain forever a perpetual memory of the vengeance of God lightened upon them for their falsehood and disloyalty. Do what ye can out of hand ... to beat down and overthrow the castle, sack Holyrood house, and as many towns and villages about Edinburgh as ye may conveniently, sack

Leith and burn and subvert it and all the rest, putting man, woman and child to fire and sword without exception, where any resistance shall be made against you ...

Hertford returned after Henry's death in 1547, this time as Protector Somerset, and defeated the Scots at Pinkie on BLACK SATURDAY, but the whole policy predictably only served to put the Scots off any alliance with the invaders, and in 1548 Mary was sent off to France to marry the Dauphin. *See also* ASSURED SCOTS; FAIR MAIDEN LILLIARD.

Roup, brought to the Bankrupt. A *roup* is an auction, and the scenario envisaged is one where all one's goods are put up for sale. Similar expressions for being forced into bankruptcy include *roupit aff* and *roupit to the door*.

Rout of Moy An incident on 16 February 1746, towards the end of the Jacobite Rebellion. Having heard that Bonnie Prince Charlie was staying at Moy Hall, a few miles southeast of Inverness, several hundred Hanoverian troops were dispatched to apprehend him. Suspecting such a move, Lady Anne Farquharson-MacKintosh, the prince's hostess, positioned her son and a few retainers to watch the road from Inverness. When the redcoats appeared after dark, the lookouts made such a noise, beating their swords on rocks, letting off their guns and jumping from place to place shouting out the war cries of various clans, that the redcoats fled, believing they were being ambushed by the entire Jacobite army. The only Jacobite casualty was the Macleod's hereditary Macrimmon piper, who had prophesied his own death before leaving Skye.

Rowan A tree once widely held to protect against witchcraft, and thus often planted around houses. If a red thread was wound round a piece of rowan, it was doubly effective, and there are many traditional rhymes along the following lines:

Rowan tree and red thread
Mak the witches tine their speed.

Rowan was also held to prevent the dead from rising. These beliefs are found in other parts of the British Isles apart from Scotland, but some mani-

festations were peculiarly Scottish. For example, in fishing boats, the halyard was attached to a piece of rowan, while in the Highlands, rowan was built into coffins. On 2 May in the Highlands and Islands, byres, sheepfolds, stables and so on were decorated with rowan twigs, while in Aberdeenshire crosses made from rowan were placed over doors and windows – all as protection against witchcraft.

In some parts, the bitter berries are called *roddens*, hence the Northeastern expression *Ah dinnae gie a rodden*, 'I don't give a damn', while if one has had *roddens tae one's supper*, one is in a foul mood.

Rowie *See* BUTTERY.

Roy, Rob *See* ROB ROY.

Roy, the *See* FOOTBALL CLUB NICKNAMES.

Royal and Ancient The title conferred on the Society of St Andrews Golfers by William IV in 1834. The club, which thereafter became known as the Royal and Ancient Golf Club of St Andrews, traces its origins to 14 May 1754 when 22 'nobles and gentlemen' clubbed together to purchase a silver cup to be played for every year on the links at St Andrews. They drew up rules based on those of Scotland's (and the world's) first golf club, the Honourable Company of Edinburgh Golfers, formed ten years earlier. However, it was the St Andrews club – often referred to simply as the 'R&A' – that came to be regarded as the world's premier club, and also the guardian of the rules of the game.

Royal High School riot of 1595, the A severe breakdown in discipline that occurred at Edinburgh's oldest school, which traces its origins to the 12th century. The rector (headmaster), Hercules Rollock, had been tasked by the town council 'to instruct the youth in pietie, guid maneris, doctrine and letteris', but in September 1595 his charges had been badly neglecting their studies, in favour of roistering and general high jinks. When their request that they be granted the customary autumn week's holiday was rejected, a group of pupils 'tuik the scooll, and provydit thauaeselfis with meit, drink, and hagbutis, pistolit and sword'. The next morning, Rollock was barred from entering by barricades erected by the revolting 'gentilmenis bairnis'. The authorities were consulted, and Baillie John Macmorran led a party of men to force an entrance. As Macmorran approached, one of the most vocal of the youths, William Sinclair, 'wowit to God, he sould schute ane pair of bullettis throw his heid'. He was as good as his word, and 'with ane pistollet schot out at ane window, and schott the said Baillie throw the heid, sua that he diet presentlie'. Eight of the rebels, including Sinclair, were imprisoned, but claimed that as they were sons of barons or landowners from outside the city, the local magistrates had no jurisdiction over them. King James VI granted their request that they be tried in front of peers of the realm; the record of the subsequent trial is lost, but all of the youths were released from prison, and Sinclair was later knighted by James VI. The unfortunate Rollock was dismissed from his post, bitterly observing that after his departure the school descended once again 'into the barbarism from which he recovered it'.

Royal Hunt of Roslin, the *See* HUNT OF PENT-LAND, THE.

Royal is my race *See under* E'EN DO AND SPARE NOCHT.

Royal Mile, the The road that runs down the crest of the hill from Edinburgh Castle to Holyroodhouse, both formerly royal residences, so forming the spine of the GUTTIT HADDIE, as the Old Town was once known. 'Royal Mile' is not a formal designation (the name of the road changes as one descends, from Castle Hill to Lawnmarket to High Street to Canongate), and was first recorded in W.M. Gilbert's *Edinburgh in the Nineteenth Century* (1901), and further popularized in the 1920s as the title of a guide book. However, much earlier it had been referred to as the *Via Regia* (Latin for 'royal way' or 'royal road') by Alexander Hailes in his description of Edinburgh for Sebastian Munster's *Cosmographia* (1544). In 1726 Daniel Defoe considered it 'Perhaps the largest, longest and finest street for buildings and number of inhabitants, not in Britain only, but in the world', while 40 years later, at the peak of the Scottish Enlightenment, Tobias Smollett described it as 'the hot-bed of genius'.

Royal Scot One of the passenger train services running between London and Glasgow. It was inaugurated in 1862, and the name was used up until 2003.

Royal Standard *See* LION RAMPANT.

Rumbledethump(s) or **rummledethump(s)** A dish consisting of mashed (*rumbled*) potatoes pounded (*thumped*) together with cabbage, then baked in the oven. The plainness of the fare may be mitigated by finely sliced and sautéed onion, melted butter, grated cheese and seasoning.

Runrig A former system of common landholding, by which tenants drew lots as to which *rigs* (narrow strips of land) they would cultivate that year, with the intention that tenants would take it in turns to cultivate the most fertile land. In some places the system involved broader pieces of land, in which case it was known as *run-dale*. Runrig persisted into the early 20th century in the Hebrides.

Runrig is also the name of a 'Celtic rock' band, formed in Skye in 1973.

Run the cutter, to *See* RIN THE CUTTER, TO.

Rushiecoat *See* RASHIECOAT.

Ruthven Raid, the The seizure in August 1582 of the 16-year-old James VI by William Ruthven, 1st Earl of Gowrie, the head of Scotland's more militant Protestants. Gowrie and his allies sought to destroy the influence on the boy-king of his favourite, Esmé Stuart, Duke of Lennox, who was suspected of Catholic sympathies, and who fled to France, dying shortly thereafter. James was distraught, provoking the callous Master of Glamis to observe: 'BETTER THAT BAIRNS SHOULD WEEP THAN BEARDED MEN'. Gowrie held James at his castle at Ruthven, near Perth, until June 1583 when supporters of a more conservative faction helped James to escape. Gowrie lost his head, and after the GOWRIE CONSPIRACY of 1600, the very name of Ruthven was proscribed: by royal proclamation, Ruthven Castle became known as Huntingtower.

Sabbath The keeping of the Sabbath has long been a bone of contention in Scotland between the devouter sort of Presbyterian and the more secularly inclined. Strict sabbatarians insist that not only should no one work or travel on a Sunday, but any sort of enjoyment on the Lord's Day should be absolutely ruled out. Lord Neaves (1800–76) offered the following lines on the topic:

> We can't for a certainty tell
> What mirth may molest us on Monday,
> But at least to begin the week well,
> We can all be unhappy on Sunday.

Today, strict sabbatarianism is largely confined to the WEE FREES of the Outer Isles, but they have been fighting a losing battle. When the first Sunday sailing of the ferry service between Stornoway on Lewis to mainland Scotland took place in 2009, only a small group of protestors gathered on the dockside to pray and sing a psalm, while several hundred supporters of the new service applauded. Feelings nevertheless run deep:

> Lord Mackay of Clashfern, Margaret Thatcher's lord chancellor, and himself a Wee Free ..., once found himself stranded there [in Stornoway] on a Sunday, and beseeched a ferry man to take him to the mainland. He was reminded sternly that it was the Sabbath. 'But the Lord Himself travelled on the Sabbath,' protested the peer. 'The Lord was wrong!' came the reply.
> – the *Guardian*, 16 July 2009

See also MAN I' THE MUNE, THE.

Sae plain as parritch 'So plain as porridge', i.e. as clear as crystal.

Saft side Good favour. To be *on* or *up someone's saft side* is to be in their good books, while to *hae a saft side tae someone* or *something* is to be partial to them or it.

Sage of Chelsea, the A sobriquet of the Ecclefechan-born essayist and historian Thomas Carlyle (1795–1881), who in 1834, feeling that his voice was insufficiently heard from his remote Dumfriesshire farm at Craigenputtock, moved to Cheyne Row in Chelsea, London, with his wife Jane. He remained there for the rest of his life, becoming the centre of an intellectual circle including Leigh Hunt, John Stuart Mill, Harriet Martineau, Thackeray, Browning, Tennyson, Dickens, Edward Fitzgerald and Ruskin.

St Andrew The patron saint of Scotland, first adopted as such around the mid-10th century. His feast day, 30 November, is still marked in Scotland. According to legend, in the mid-8th century the Irish monk St Rule or Regulus was shipwrecked on the East Neuk of Fife while carrying some relics of St Andrew from Constantinople. The local Pictish king founded a church at the spot, which came to be known as St Andrews. Alternatively, the relics may have been brought to what became St Andrews when Acca, Bishop of Hexham, was driven north around AD 732. For the legend of how the St Andrews Cross came to adorn the Scottish flag, *see under* SALTIRE. St Andrew, one of the Apostles of Christ, is also the patron saint of Russia, Greece, Ukraine and Romania.

St Andrew's House The home of the Scottish Office from 1939, and thus a metonym for that institution itself. It takes its name from Scotland's patron saint (*see above*). Since 1999, it has been the headquarters of the Scottish government, and includes the office of the first minister. The art deco building, designed by Thomas S. Tait, is situated on the southern flank of Calton Hill, Edinburgh, overlooking Waverley Station.

St Andrew's Square *See* GOLDEN SQUARE, THE.

St Causlan's flaw An old Angus expression for a snow shower in March. A *flaw* is a squall, and *St Causlan* (or *Causnan*) is Constantine, a semi-legendary Scottish king who became a monk. He was martyred in Kintyre in 576, and his feast day was 11 March.

St John's Seat A stone roughly hewn into the shape of a seat, situated at the top of Main Street in Dalry in Kirkcudbrightshire. By tradition, St John the Baptist (an unlikely Galwegian) is supposed to have sat here as he passed by, although the village takes its full name, St John's Town of Dalry, from the fact that the land hereabouts was once owned by the Knights Templar, whose patron saint was St John the Baptist.

St Johnstoun's ribbon The noose of a hanging rope. St Johnstoun or Johnston is an alternative name for Perth, whose patron saint is John the Baptist. The origin of the expression is given in the *Second Statistical Account* (1834–45):

> In 1559, the Earl of Argyle and James Stewart, Prior of St Andrews ... resolved to prosecute the cause of the Reformation or perish in the attempt. They accordingly set out from Perth for Stirling, attended by three hundred citizens; and, that their determination might appear and influence others, they, instead of ribbons, put ropes about their necks, intimating thereby that whoever of their number should desert their colours should be hanged by the ropes. Hence arose the proverb of 'St Johnstoun's Ribbons'.

St Michael's bannock *See* STRUAN MICHAEL.

St Mungo One of the passenger train services running between Aberdeen and Glasgow, named after Glasgow's patron saint, aka St Kentigern (*see* TREE THAT NEVER GREW, THE). In the late 18th and 19th centuries, Glasgow itself was sometimes referred to as 'St Mungo'.

St Oran's Chapel, live burial in The oldest building still standing on Iona is St Oran's Chapel, thought to have been built in the later 12th century

by Somerled, LORD OF THE ISLES. However, legend traces its construction to the 7th century and the beginning of monastic settlement on the island:

> One of the first edifices begun on the island was the chapel of Oran, so called in honour of his [Columba's] friend and associate. The progress of the building was frustrated by the machinations of an evil spirit, by means of which the walls were overthrown as fast as they were erected. Columba in this emergency betook himself to prayer in a remote part of the island, and it was revealed to him, that until a human victim was interred alive, the building would not be completed. Oran magnanimously devoted himself for this sacrifice, and the sepulture was consequently performed. When he had been entombed three days, Columba, desirous of taking a last look at his friend, ordered the earth and stones which covered his sepulchre to be removed, when, to the astonishment of all present, Oran started up and began to reveal 'the secrets of the prison-house', declaring, among other strange things, that hell was a mere fiction of priestcraft, having no real existence. This profane asseveration was interrupted by Columba, who ordered the earth to be thrown in again, and Oran was finally enclosed in his tomb.
> – William Daniell, *A Voyage Round Great Britain* (1815–25)

St Peter's staff The stars that make up the sword in the constellation Orion.

St Rollox Stalk, the *See* TENNANT'S STALK.

Saints, the (1) A somewhat ironic name sometimes given to the more self-righteous and zealous of the Reformers in the 16th century, and the extremer sorts of COVENANTERS in the 17th. (2) A nickname for either St Johnstone FC or St Mirren FC; *see* FOOTBALL CLUB NICKNAMES.

St Trinian's School An educational establishment for extremely scary young ladies, first imagined by the cartoonist Ronald Searle (1920–2011) and then the subject of a number of comedy films. It was inspired by St Trinnean's School in Edinburgh, founded by Miss C. Fraser Lee in 1922. The school, in Palmerston Road, emphasized self-discipline rather than imposed rules, and hence became known as the school 'where they do what they like'. Searle heard of St Trinnean's when he was posted to Scotland during the Phoney War, and drew his first St Trinian's cartoon while a prisoner-of-war of the Japanese.

Sair fecht, a Literally, 'a sore fight', i.e. a great struggle, a terrible tribulation; often heard in the expression *It's a sair fecht*. A variant is *a sair pech*, a *pech* being a gasp or puff, as from exertion.

Sair or **fair forfochen** Sorely or fairly worn out after a great struggle; knackered. *Forfochen* is a past participle of *forfecht*.

> She was sair forfochen for lang wi' an ill cauld she teuk.
> – The Revd William Blair, *The Chronicles of Aberbrothock* (1853)

Sair heidie A small sponge cake with a paper band wrapped around its perimeter. A *sair heid* is a headache, so perhaps the paper band is analogous to a cold compress, or the traditional cure of brown paper soaked in vinegar (as in 'Jack and Jill').

Salisbury Crags The long line of cliffs on the northwest side of ARTHUR'S SEAT in Edinburgh. They are said to be named after William de Montacute, Earl of Salisbury (1301–44), who accompanied Edward III on his invasion of Scotland in 1327, but it seems unlikely that the Scots should commemorate such a person, and the first record of the name dates from the 15th century. At the foot of the crags runs the RADICAL ROAD. *See also* RHYMING SLANG.

Salmon, on the unacceptability of Salmon has not always been a luxury food:

> A large boiled salmon would now-a-days have indicated a more liberal housekeeping; but at that period [the later 17th century] salmon was caught in such plenty in the considerable rivers of Scotland, that instead of being accounted a delicacy, it was generally applied to feed the servants, who are said sometimes to have stipulated that they should not be required to eat a food so luscious and surfeiting in its quality above five times a week.
> – Sir Walter Scott, *Old Mortality* (1816), chapter viii

Salt ... *See also* SAUT ...

Salter's duck A wave-power device invented at Edinburgh University in the 1970s by Stephen Salter (b.1938 in South Africa), now emeritus professor of engineering design. The device, which sits on the surface and bobs up and down on the waves like a duck, is also referred to as the *nodding duck* or the *Edinburgh duck*.

Saltire, the The flag of Scotland, comprising a white X-shaped cross on a blue ground – hence it is also known as *the Blue Saltire*. The X-shaped cross, or *crux decussate*, represents that on which the Apostle Andrew, the patron saint of Scotland, was martyred. The word 'saltire' – originally a heraldic term for a diagonal cross on a shield – first appeared in the 14th century as *sawturoure*, derived from Old French *sauteour*, 'cross-shaped barricade', from Old French *saulter* and ultimately Latin *saltare*, 'to jump'. Legend has it that the Saltire became the Scottish flag after the Battle of Athelstaneford (AD 832) at which the Scots and Picts, having been assured of victory by the appearance of a white St Andrew's cross in the blue sky, defeated an invading English force under Athelstan. The earliest record of the use of the Saltire as a national symbol, however, appears to date from 1385, when the Scottish Parliament decreed that it should be worn by Scottish soldiers. The oldest surviving example of the saltire on a flag is probably the BLUE BLANKET, the banner of the craftsmen of Edinburgh, dating from 1482.

In 1604, the year after the Union of the Crowns, James VI and I ordered that all his subjects' ships, whether from 'South Britain' or 'North Britain', should fly a flag on their maintop that incorporated both the St Andrew's Cross and the St George's Cross – the beginning of what was to become the Union flag.

Today, there are a number of conventions as to where and when the Saltire should be flown on governmental institutions in Scotland, leading to the generation of much heat under a multitude of collars.

> And O! to think that there are members o'
> St Andrew's Societies sleepin' soon,

Wha' to the papers wrote afore they bedded
On regimental buttons or buckled shoon,
Or use o' England whaur the U.K.'s meent,
Or this or that anent the Blue Saltire ...
　　– Hugh MacDiarmid, *A Drunk Man Looks at the Thistle*
　　(1926)

See also LION RAMPANT.

Salvation made easy *See* AULD LICHTS AND NEW
LICHTS.

Saltmarket, all the comforts of the *See* ALL THE
COMFORTS OF THE SALTMARKET.

Samhain An old Celtic festival in both Scotland and
Ireland marking the beginning of winter and the old
new year, starting at sunset on 31 October and
continuing through 1 November. In Scottish Gaelic
it is *Samhuinn*, and it is pronounced 'sown' as in
'frown', or 'sow-in' as in 'cow', or 'sa-win' as in 'pat'.
J.A. MacCulloch, in *Celtic and Scandinavian Religions*
(1949), states that *Samhain* means 'summer end',
but this may just reflect the nature of the festival,
rather than the etymology of the word. Samhain was
celebrated with bonfires and the lighting of great
torches of bog-fir called *sownacks* (from Gaelic
samhnag, 'bonfire', a diminutive form of *Samhuinn*).
Samhain combined elements of harvest festival with
commemoration of the dead, and at this time the
veil separating the world of the living and the
otherworld was supposed to be particularly per-
meable, allowing a certain amount of two-way
traffic. There is a clear overlap with HALLOWEEN
and All Saint's Day, and various Halloween customs,
such as turnip lanterns, GUISING and DOOKING FOR
APPLES, are probably remnants or echoes of the
pagan festival. According to Martin Martin's *Description of the Western Isles of Scotland* (1703), the people
of Lewis observed a particular ritual at Samhain:

　The inhabitants of this island had an ancient custom to
　sacrifice to a sea god, called *Shony*, at Hallowtide, in the
　manner following. The inhabitants round the island
　came to the church of *St Mulvay*, having each man his
　provision along with him; every family furnish'd a peck
　of malt, and this was brew'd into ale; one of their
　number was pickt out to wade into the sea up to the
　middle, and carrying a cup of ale in his hand, standing

still in that posture, cry'd out with a loud voice, saying,
*Shony, I give you this cup of ale, hoping that you'll be so
kind as to send us plenty of sea-ware* [seaweed] *for
inriching our ground the ensuing year*; and threw the
cup of ale into the sea. This was perform'd in the night-
time; at his return to land, they all went to the church,
where there was a candle burning upon the altar; and
then standing silent for a little time, one of them gave a
signal, at which the candle was put out, and immediately all of them went to the fields, where they fell a
drinking their ale, and spent the remainder of the night
in dancing and singing, etc.

See also BELTANE.

Sammy Dreep A term used in various parts of
Scotland for someone who is irrecoverably wet and
lacking in *cojones* – in other words, a 'drip'.

Sanctuary In medieval times, sanctuary from the
law was obtainable in or at certain religious institutions and sites, such as the church in Stow in
Wedale (near Galashiels), Lesmahagow Priory in
Lanarkshire, Torphichen Preceptory in West
Lothian, Holyrood Abbey and environs, the graves
on Iona, and the so-called Immunitie of Tayne (the
sanctuary of St Duthuc of Tain, in Easter Ross).
One might also mention the Sanctuary Cross half-
way across the strip of sand linking Colonsay and
Oronsay at low tide; any law-breaker from Colonsay
who succeeding in reaching the cross was given
sanctuary on Oronsay (the 'island of St Oran', who
founded a priory here in 563), provided he or she
stayed on the island for a year and a day. But
sanctuary was not a sure refuge for all felons:

　The privileges of sanctuary ... did not, by ancient Scottish
　law, indiscriminately shelter every offender; all atrocious
　criminals were excluded, and only the unfortunate delin-
　quent, or the penitent sinner, could here deprecate the
　rigours of justice. They were required to make restoration
　of any property they had stolen, and to make oath that
　they would steal no more. The manslayer was enjoined,
　on pain of banishment, to surrender himself to the law, in
　order that it might be decided whether the slaughter
　amounted to felony or murder. Penalties were exacted to
　defend those refugees intitled to sanctuary from all
　molestation during their retreat.
　　– William Daniell, *A Voyage Round Great Britain* (1815–25)

A place of sanctuary was known as a *girth* up to the early 18th century, and may form part of place names such as Girthhead south of Moffat, and Girthill in Ayrshire. Although most of the sanctuaries ceased to provide a refuge after the Reformation, that at Holyrood Abbey continued to be used by debtors well into the 19th century (*see* ABBEY LAIRDS), its boundary being marked by the old Girth Cross.

Sandwood Bay A beautiful sandy bay on the north coast of Sutherland. The abandoned cottage in the bay is famously said to be haunted by the ghost of a sailor who was shipwrecked here long ago. Many vessels came to grief in the bay before the erection of the lighthouse on Cape Wrath in 1828, and in some versions of the story, the sailor in question died when his galleon came to grief here after the Armada in 1588.

Sandwood Bay is also referred to as 'the Land of the Mermaids', alluding to the sighting of a mermaid here by a local farmer, Alexander Gunn, on 5 January 1900. He later told another man, MacDonald Robertson, of what occurred that day:

> Gunn's collie suddenly let out a howl and cringed in terror at his feet. On a ledge, above the tide, a figure was reclining on the rock face. At first he thought it was a seal, then he saw the hair was reddish-yellow, the eyes greenish-blue and the body yellowish and about 7 ft long. To the day Alexander Gunn died in 1944, his story never changed and he maintained that he had seen a mermaid of ravishing beauty.

Sandy *See* SAWNEY.

Sandy Campbell A jocular name for a pig, or for pork or bacon, alluding to the boar's head in the crest of Clan Campbell. A variant is *Peter Cammel*.

Sandy Munro's Verses Parts of the Scriptures translated into Gaelic verse by the Revd Alexander Munro (1605–53), minister of Durness in Sutherland.

Sanquhar Declaration *See under* CAMERONIANS.

Sarah Bernhardt of Opera, the A sobriquet of the operatic soprano Mary Garden (1874–1967), celebrated as much for her acting as her singing. Although she spent much of her career in the USA, taking American citizenship, when she retired she returned to Aberdeen, her birthplace.

Sarry Heid, the The familiar name of the Saracen's Head, supposedly Glasgow's oldest pub, situated in the Gallowgate but no longer in its original premises, which stood across the road and dated from 1755. It is a popular venue for Celtic supporters when their team are playing at home at nearby Parkhead. The pub exhibits a glass case containing what it claims is the skull of the last witch to be burned in Scotland, one Maggie Wall, who was executed in Dunning on the north side of the Ochils in 1657 (however, the generally accepted claimant to the title, Janet Horne, perished in Dornoch in 1727; *see* WITCH-BURNING IN SCOTLAND, THE LAST). The pub is said to be haunted by the ghost of a former owner, Angus Ross. *See also* GLASGOW GLUTTON, THE.

Sassenach A derogatory term originally applied by Gaelic-speaking Highlanders to English- or Scots-speaking Lowlanders,

> The Highlanders have no other name for the people of the low country, but Sassenaugh, or Saxons.
> – Tobias Smollett, *The Expedition of Humphry Clinker* (1771)

The term is now more commonly applied by the generality of the Scots in a gently disparaging way to the English.

> All loved their McClan, save a Sassenach brute,
> Who came to the Highlands to fish and to shoot.
> – W.S. Gilbert, *Bab Ballads* (1869)

The word comes from Gaelic *Sassunach*, from medieval Latin *Saxones*, 'Saxons'. The Irish also used the word *Sasanach* for the English, while the Welsh use the related word *Seisnig*.

Sauchiehall Street Glasgow's most famous street, familiarly known as *Suckie*. Hence the expression *up Suckie, doon Buckie and alang Argyle*, denoting the route an avid shopper might follow, taking in Sauchiehall Street, Buchanan Street and Argyle Street.

There is a story of a policeman who collars a pickpocket in Sauchiehall Street, but instead of booking him then and there he drags him by the ear a hundred yards and round the corner into Rose Street. 'Whit for did ye dae that?' bleats the aggrieved thief. 'Cos ah kin spell Rose Street, ya wee nyaff,' responds the policeman.

Sausages is the boys! *See* LORNE SAUSAGE.

Saut! quo the sutor, when he ate the coo and worried on the tail 'I suppose this to mean,' says J. Riddell in *Aberdeen and Its Folk* (1868), 'that if it is attempted, by inadequate means, to overcome a difficulty, already almost vanquished, the feat will not be accomplished.' (*Saut*, 'salt'; *sutor*, 'cobbler'.)

Saut someone's brose or **kail** Literally, 'to salt someone's porridge or cabbage', i.e. to get your own back on someone.

Save your breath to cool your porridge A saying now in use across the British Isles, deployed as a retort to those who offer superfluous advice, or whose arguments are refuted or ignored.

> 'Hold your peace, sir,' said the Duke, 'and keep your ain breath to cool your ain porridge – ye'll find them scalding hot, I promise you ...'
> – Sir Walter Scott, *Old Mortality* (1816), chapter xxxvi

Saville Stone, the A massive erratic boulder situated near Scar, on Sanday, Orkney. It was originally located near another settlement, Saville, about a mile away, but in 1879 or 1880 it was taken by cart to Scar, where it was intended that it should provide a landscape feature. However, the cart broke under the weight, and the stone (also known as the *Stone o' Scar*) never quite made it to its destination. According to local legend, the stone originated on the neighbouring island of Eday, but a witch who lived there was so incensed when her daughter ran off with a Sanday man that she lobbed the rock at the eloping couple, who apparently ducked just in time.

Sawney or **Sawnie** A version (used particularly in Ayrshire) of the name Sandy, a short form of Alexander. It was also used as a generic term for a young rustic or country bumpkin, and from the 18th century in both England and Scotland as a disparaging term for a Scotsman:

> No decent Scotchman, at the present day, can enter a Coffee House in London but with the certainty of being put to the blush, by hearing some senseless *Sawnies* slavering about their country, over their cups, imagining, in the vanity of their hearts, that they are actually lustrous with the rays of their country's glory.
> – *The Scots Magazine*, October 1824

See also SANDY CAMPBELL.

Sawney Bean *See* BEAN, SAWNEY.

Say bo to your blanket, to To cast aspersions on your probity, to blacken your character. The phrase was still current in the early 20th century. *Bo* here is the equivalent of 'boo!', while *blanket* denotes 'banner' (*see* e.g. BLUE BLANKET), so the expression is similar to the English phrase 'to blot one's escutcheon'.

Say no Treuth An anagram of 'John Steuarte', i.e. John Stewart, 1st Earl of Traquair (d.1659), devised by his enemies in 1640. Traquair was Charles I's Lord High Treasurer of Scotland from 1636 to 1641, and helped Charles introduce the Anglican liturgy into Scotland. He thus invited the enmity of the COVENANTERS, but neither side fully trusted him. In 1641 the Scottish Parliament issued a warrant for his arrest, and he was sentenced to death in absentia, and dismissed from office. It has been suggested that on the eve of the Battle of Philiphaugh (*see* SLAIN MEN'S LEA) he betrayed Montrose's plans to David Leslie. He was the subject of another condemnatory anagram: Johne, Lord Traquair = A Lyer Honor Acquyred.

Scabby Aggie *See under* BAGGIE AGGIE.

Scald one's lips in other folks' kail, to To interfere in other people's business (*kail*, 'cabbage'), with the suggestion of regrettable consequences.

> 'That's a dawty!' was the delighted old gentleman's exclamation. – 'It's a' settled – it's a' settled!'

'What's settled??' cried Miss Mizy.

'Settle thysel', Mizy, and dinna scaud thy lips in other folks' kail,' retorted the laird.

– John Galt, *Sir Andrew Wylie, Of That Ilk* (1822), chapter cii

Scallowa' sma' drink *See* SMA' DRINK.

Scarecrow *See* TATTIE-BOGLE.

Scart someone's buttons, to To challenge someone to a fight by *scarting* ('scraping', 'clawing') one's fingernails down the buttons of the jacket of one's intended opponent – perhaps in allusion to the mode in which soldiers are disgraced, by having their regimental buttons ceremonially ripped off.

CHALLENGE SECOND

'Sir,

'I scart your buttons. You mocked and disgraced me in your own house; and I dare you to single combat, with muskets, at regular battle distance, such as our seconds shall appoint.

'Yours, &c.

'To Richard M'Ion, Esquire.'

CHALLENGE THIRD

'Sir,

'I scart your buttons; and dare you to fair battle, with any weapons you chuse, from a doubled fist to a munce-meg.

'If one of these challenges are refused, I will brand the whole fraternity of you for dogs, mongrels, ragamuffins and cowards!

'Yours, &c.

'To Lieutenant Callum Gun.'

– James Hogg, *The Three Perils of Women: or, Love, leasing and jealousy* (1823)

Scheme A council housing estate, particularly the vast estates built on the outskirts of Scotland's cities in the 1950s and 1960s, such as Drumchapel (the DRUM) and Easterhouse in Glasgow, and Wester Hailes and Craigmillar in Edinburgh, to house the people from the demolished inner-city slums. It was not all necessarily for the best:

They wanted houses and they got them. Nothing else. Even the name they were to give them was as basic as the featureless areas where they were to be built. They

were called the schemes. And one of these schemes, a place the size of Perth, was so bereft of facilities it had neither a range of shops nor a pub and the number of police would have been stretched to maintain law and order in the smallest of villages.

– John Burrowes, *Mother Glasgow* (1991)

The inhabitants of such places are sometimes derogatively referred to as *schemebos* or *schemies*, terms also applied to anybody supposed to exhibit quasi-criminal tendencies and the symptoms of multiple deprivation.

They'd rather gie a merchant school old boy with severe brain damage a job in nuclear engineering than gie a schemie wi a Ph.D. a post as a cleaner in an abattoir.

– Irvine Welsh, *Trainspotting* (1993)

(*See also* MERCHANT COMPANY SCHOOLS.)

Schottische Short for *der schottische Tanz* (German, 'the Scottish dance'), and denoting a dance like a polka (or the music for such a dance). The dance appears to have no connection with Scotland, and was first introduced to Britain in 1848.

Scone, the Stone of *See* STONE OF SCONE, THE.

Scone o' the day's bakin', a A typical or average thing or person; nothing special. *See also* WHA STOLE YER SCONE?

Schoolmaster of fools, the Experience, according to the poet Alexander Montgomerie (*c*.1545–*c*.1598):

Too late I knaw, wha hewis too hie,
The spail sall fall into his e'e;
Too late I went to schoolis,
Too late I heard the swallow preach,
Too late Experience does teach –
The school-maister of foolis.

– *The Cherry and the Slae* (1597)

Scoring abune the breath Scratching or cutting the forehead of a suspected witch, sometimes in the shape of a cross, as a counter to her supposed evil powers. The practice continued into the 19th century:

In the upper end of Peeblesshire a shepherd, being dissatisfied with the quantity of milk which some of his cows yielded, shrewdly suspected they were bewitched by an old woman who lived about fifteen miles from the spot. *Scoring aboon the breath* being the only remedy prescribed by the superstition which yet remains in that part of the country, for an evil of such a desperate nature, the owner of the cattle, determined to try the cure, set out, and finding the poor old woman at home, cut her severely in the brow.
– *The Scots Magazine* October 1814

Scot A term originally applied to the Irish, which is why some time after the Dark Ages, when the Irish arrived in what was then known as ALBA, the country became known as Scotland. For further details, *see under* SCOTIA.

Scot, a rat, and a Newcastle grindstone, a There is an old saying quoted by John Gibson Lockhart in his *Memoirs of the Life of Sir Walter Scott* (1837–8):

In every corner of the world you will find a Scot, a rat, and a Newcastle grindstone.

Scot, Michael The medieval philosopher, translator of Aristotle, alchemist and astrologer – who died around 1235 – may have been a member of the Scott family of Balwearie in Fife. His reputation extended across Europe: he was admired by successive popes, and spent some time at the court of the Emperor Frederick II. However, in legend his reputation is primarily as a wizard and magician. In the *Inferno* (canto 20), Dante places Scot in the eighth circle of hell reserved for sorcerers, astrologers and false prophets:

That other, round the flanks so slight of form, Is Michael Scot, who verily knew well The lightsome play of every magic fraud.

Scot also appears in Boccaccio's *Decameron* (mid-14th century) as a master of necromancy, while later in the century Benvenuto da Imola relates that Scot had foreknowledge that his death would be caused by a stone falling on his head, and therefore wore an iron cap at all times. This he only doffed on entering a church, whereupon a stone duly fell on his head and killed him. In the second canto of *The Lay of the*

Last Minstrel (1805), Sir Walter Scott mentions some of the stories relating to his namesake:

In these far climes it was my lot To meet the wondrous Michael Scott, A wizard, of such dreaded fame, Than when, in Salamanca's cave, Him listed his magic wand to wave, The bells would ring in Notre Dame! Some of his skill he taught to me; And Warrior, I could say to thee The words that cleft Eildon hills in three, And bridled the Tweed with a curb of stone ...

Regarding these latter feats, Sir Walter adds a note:

Michael Scott was, once upon a time, much embarrassed by a spirit, for whom he was under the necessity of finding constant employment. He commanded him to build a *cauld*, or dam-head, across the Tweed at Kelso; it was accomplished in one night, and Michael next ordered that Eildon hill, which was then a uniform cone, should be divided into three. Another night was sufficient to part its summit into the three picturesque peaks which it now bears. At length the enchanter conquered this indefatigable demon, by employing him in the hopeless and endless task of making ropes out of sea-sand.

According to one tradition, Michael Scot is buried somewhere in Melrose Abbey, along with his books of magic.

Scotch A variant, first recorded in the mid-17th century, of Old Scots *Scottis*, 'Scottish'. Today, the word *Scotch* on its own denotes whisky, although this usage is rare in Scotland itself; elsewhere, the word is used to distinguish Scottish whisky from Irish, American, etc., *whiskey*, which is anyway spelt differently. These days the Scots do not like the word to be used to denote 'Scots' or 'Scottish', except in the context of various foodstuffs and dishes (examples are to be found among the following entries). However, in the past many Scots were quite content to use *Scotch* in other contexts: for example, in 1779 James Boswell stated 'I am by birth a *North Briton*, as a *Scotchman* must now be called'; in 1786 Robert Burns wrote of 'Scotch Representatives in the House of Commons' (*see* FREEDOM AND WHISKY GANG THEGITHER); James Hogg refers to the 'Scotch peasantry' (*see* MINSTRELSY OF THE SCOTTISH BORDER); in his *Book of Days* (1862–4), Robert Chambers speaks of 'Scotch Presbyterians' (*see* CURSE OF SCOTLAND, THE), while in *Virginibus Puerisque* (1881) Robert Louis Stevenson refers to the hanging judge Lord Braxfield as 'the last judge on the Scotch bench to employ the pure Scotch idiom' (*see* WEIR OF HERMISTON). It was the Glasgow solicitor and nationalist William Burns who first insisted that the term 'Scottish' should be preferred to 'Scotch', in an 1854 pamphlet entitled 'Scottish Rights and Honour Vindicated'. The preference in Scotland for 'Scots' or 'Scottish' as opposed to 'Scotch' had become established by the early 20th century:

> The deadly dullness of the recent debates in the British Parliament was enlivened while the Educational bill for Scotland was under consideration by a motion of Mr Gulland of Dumfries that the name of the Scotch Education Department should hereafter be called Scottish. 'Scotch,' he contended, was wrong, and there was laughter in the House of Commons.
> – *New York Times*, 13 December 1908

> My father came from Inverness-shire and certainly never restricted the use of Scotch to the whiskey. It is only in recent years that certain Anglo-American friends have made me feel guilty of committing a particularly bourgeois *faux pas* by using the word. We always looked on Scottish as rather affected, overly poetic.
> – *Baltimore Sun*, 25 June 1943

> Professor Trevor-Roper … tries to irritate and provoke by using the word 'Scotch' knowing well that many decent Scots … have come to regard this as a demeaning adjective.
> – *The Times*, 11 May 1976

The verb *scotch*, meaning 'put a stop to' (and originally denoting 'cut, score, injure'), is etymologically unrelated, although its origin is obscure.

Scotch ale *See* BEER.

Scotch Anacreon, the A sobriquet of the poet Alexander Scott (*c*.1520–82/3), of whom little is known, but to whom are attributed some 35 poems. The allusion is to the Greek poet Anacreon (*fl.* 6th century BC), whose love poems, like Scott's, explore different aspects of human sexuality. The following stanza is from Scott's 'Lament of the Master of Erskine':

> Adew, my ain sweit thing,
> My joy and conforting,
> My mirth and sollasing
>   Of erdlie gloir.
> Fairweill, my ladie bricht
> And my remembrance richt;
> Fairweill, and haif guid nicht.
>   I say na moir.

See also ARIOSTO OF THE NORTH, THE.

Scotch and English The name applied to various games, surviving into the 20th century, in which boys from two different teams competed in various violent pursuits, such as making each other captive, or seizing some prize.

Scotch bonnet or **cap** A brimless cap, such as a BLUE BONNET or BALMORAL BONNET. The distinctive shape of the headwear has led to the name *Scotch bonnet* also being applied to a species of hot pepper, *Capsicum tetragonum*, and to the fairy-ring mushroom, *Marasmius oreades*.

Scotch broth A wholesome soup of beef or mutton stock, winter vegetables and pearl barley.

> At dinner, Dr Johnson ate several platefuls of Scotch broth with barley and peas in it, and seemed fond of the dish. I said, 'You never ate it before?' Johnson: 'No, sir, but I don't care how soon I eat it again.'
> – James Boswell, *Journal of a Tour to the Hebrides* (1785)

Scotch bum 'A kind of bustle', according to the *OED*, which otherwise remains silent on the matter, apart from the following citation, indicating that it had become fashionable in London after James VI transferred his court thither:

> That French gowne, Scotch fals, Scotch bum, and Italian head-tire you sent her.
> – Thomas Dekker and John Webster, *Westward Hoe* (1607), II.ii

Scotch bun *See* BLACK BUN.

Scotch cap *See* SCOTCH BONNET.

Scotch chocolate 'Brimstone and milk', according to Captain Grose's *Dictionary of the Vulgar Tongue* (1785).

Scotch coffee Victorian slang, particularly among seamen, for hot water flavoured with burnt biscuit.

Scotch collops *See* SCOTS COLLOPS.

Scotch cousin or **sister** An archaic term for a distant relative, alluding to the custom apparently observed in former times in Scotland of tracing one's kinship to the *n*th degree.

Scotch cuddy Literally 'Scottish donkey', i.e. a pedlar.

Scotch egg A hardboiled egg coated in sausage meat and dipped in breadcrumbs, then deep-fried. They are usually eaten cold. The London food store Fortnum & Mason claims to have invented Scotch eggs in 1738, possibly in imitation of Indian *kofta*, meatballs that sometimes involve eggs. It is unclear what Fortnum called them, as the first recorded mention of 'Scotch eggs' as such comes in Mrs M.E. Rundell's *New System of Domestic Cookery* (1808):

> *Scotch Eggs.* Boil hard five pullets eggs, and without removing the white, cover completely with a fine relishing forcemeat.

The Scottish connection was perhaps reinforced by the recipe for Scotch eggs given in *The Cook and Housewife's Manual* (1826) by the pseudonymous Meg DODS:

> Five eggs make a dish. Boil them as for salad. Peel and dip them in beat egg, and cover them with a forcemeat made of grated ham, chopped anchovy, crumbs, mixed spices, &c. Fry them nicely in good clarified dripping, and serve with a gravy-sauce in a tureen.

Scotch fiddle A slang expression from the 18th and 19th centuries denoting perhaps either scabies or a sexually transmitted disease, suggesting that the sufferer would be constantly fiddling (i.e. scratching) at the infected parts. *To play the Scotch fiddle*

was to poke the index finger of one hand through a ring made by the thumb and index finger of the other, a gesture suggesting one's companion suffered from such a disease. *Cf.* ITCHLAND.

Scotch flummery A rich egg custard. Elizabeth Cleland gives a recipe in *A New and Easy Method of Cookery*, published in Edinburgh in 1759:

> Take a mutchkin of milk, and one of cream; beat the yolks of nine eggs, with a little rose-water, sugar and nutmeg; put it in a dish, and the dish over a pan of boiling water covered close; when it begins to grow thick, have ready some currants plumped in sack, and strew over it. It must not be stirred while it is over the fire, and, when it is pretty stiff, send it up hot.

Scotch frog A very un-Caledonian cocktail comprising vodka, Galliano, Cointreau, lime juice, maraschino cherry juice and Angostura bitters. *See also* COCKTAILS.

Scotch gravat An embrace or cuddle, a *gravat* being a woolly scarf (or, more sinisterly, the hangman's noose). *See also* SCOTCH MUFFLER.

Scotch hands The wooden bats used for making butter pats.

Scotch horses A group of children running together, grasping each other's hands behind their backs. Sometimes they would chant the following rhyme, recorded in the early 20th century:

> Three Scotch horses gaun awa tae Fife,
> Comin' back on Monday wi' an auld drunk wife.

Scotch mahogany The wood of the alder, from its red colour when exposed to sunlight and the elements.

Scotch metaphysics *See* NONE OF YOUR DAMNED SCOTCH METAPHYSICS!

Scotch mist A soaking, thick mist and/or drizzle, as is often to be found clinging to the hills of Scotland. The American novelist Nathaniel Hawthorne evokes its unpleasantness thus:

This, I suppose, was a genuine scotch mist; and as such it is well enough to have experienced it, though I would willingly never see it again.

Figuratively, the phrase suggests vagueness and obfuscation, and is also rhyming slang for 'pissed', i.e. drunk. Finally, Scotch mist is a cocktail comprising whisky poured on a bed of crushed ice and served with a twist of lemon.

Scotch muffler A dram, so-called from the sensations of warmth it brings.

Scotch ordinary A slang term for a lavatory, in use in England in the 18th and 19th centuries. An *ordinary* was an eating house.

Scotch pie A species of double-crust pie filled with minced mutton, formerly known in Glasgow as a *tuppeny struggle*, and also known as a *mince pie* or, indeed, simply as a *pie* – for if one does not specify otherwise, if one orders a 'pie' in a chip shop or pub, it is a Scotch pie that one will be served with.

> MUTTON PIES. – Vulgarly known in Glasgow as 'Tuppenny Struggles.' They are small pies made with hot-water paste, filled with minced mutton, and served hot with gravy, which is poured into them at the last moment through holes left in the paste lids.
> – Victor McClure *Scotland's Inner Man* (1935)

Scotch Plot The name of a supposed Jacobite conspiracy in 1703, in which Simon Fraser, Lord Lovat (SIMON THE FOX), returned from France with a letter from James VII's widow, Mary of Modena, to an unnamed Scottish nobleman. Lovat addressed it to his enemy, the Duke of Atholl (whose sister he had kidnapped and forcibly married), and then showed it to Atholl's rival, the Duke of Queensberry (the so-called UNION DUKE), in the hope of currying favour with the pro-Hanoverian party. Atholl subsequently lost his position as Keeper of the Privy Seal of Scotland.

Scotch Sea, Scottish Sea, Scottis Se, etc A former name for the Firth of Forth, originally so-called because it separated the Kingdom of the Scots from Lothian, which was settled by Anglo-Saxons and dominated by Northumbria until the 9th century,

when it was conquered by Kenneth MacAlpin, king of Scots:

> *Mare Scoticum* the firth of Forth the Scotsh sea, so called because it was once the march betuix Scotland and England.
> – Manuscript index, *c.*1650, to George Buchanan's *Rerum Scoticarum Historia* (1582)

Scotch snap In music, a rhythmic figure consisting of a stressed semiquaver followed by an unstressed dotted quaver, typical of Scottish dances such as strathspeys.

Scotch Tape The US equivalent to Sellotape, first marketed in 1931 and so named because a little supposedly went a long way – the allusion being to the proverbial thriftiness of the Scots.

Scotch woodcock A jocular name for scrambled eggs on toast, served with anchovies or anchovy paste. The name was coined in the tradition of other culinary misnomers such as Welsh rabbit (cheese on toast) and Bombay duck (a dried fish). The first known mention is in Mrs Beeton's *Book of Household Management* (1861), in which the recipe involves a quarter pint of cream, the yolks of three eggs, and 'hot buttered toast, spread with anchovies pounded to a paste ... serve very hot, and very quickly'.

Scotia A Latin name for Scotland, in use since Kenneth MacAlpin united the Scots and Picts in the 9th century. Originally, Scotia denoted Ireland, whose Gaelic-speaking inhabitants were *Scoti* or *Scotti* – hence the name of the Irish philosopher John Scotus Erigena (*c.*800–*c.*877), and the dismissal of his work *De predestinatione* by his critics as '*pultes Scottorum*' – meaning, in this context, 'Irish porridge'. The use of the term 'Scot' for an Irishman is further attested in the famous exchange between Erigena and Charles the Bald, the Carolingian king, while they sat opposite each other at a feast. When the former asked '*Quid distat inter sottum et Scottum?*' ('What separates a sot from an Irishman?'), Erigena replied, '*Mensa tantum*' ('Only a table'). The word *Scoti* is said by some to have originally meant 'bandits', but in the Irish foundation myths, it was the Milesian settlers of the island who called Ireland

Scotia, after their mother Scota, daughter of the Pharaoh Nectonibus. Historically, when Irish Gaels began to settle in Argyll (*see* DALRIADA), the name came more broadly to designate an ethnic area, the 'land of the Gaels' on both sides of the Irish Sea, and in the Middle Ages there are references to Ireland as *Scotia Maior* and Scotland as *Scotia Minor*. The name gradually became restricted to Scotland, and it provides the root for the word for Scotland in several Romance languages, e.g. Italian *Scozia* and French *Écosse*. The name Scotia for Scotland is now largely only heard in poetic contexts, such as Burns's line, 'From scenes like these old Scotia's grandeur springs', or Scott's 'Oh Scotia, my dear, my native land', or the following from Andrew Greig's 'Last Pibroch in South Queensferry':

Auld Scotia is a bag of wind
in History's oxter.

(Scott's line quoted above was once inscribed in a stone in the middle of the bridge across the Tweed at Coldstream, marking the Border, but was re-moved at the beginning of the Second World War in case it should give too much information to any passing German parachutist.)

Geographically, the name Scotia occurs in NOVA SCOTIA, and in the Scotia Sea, an area of the South Atlantic partially enclosed by the Scotia Arc, which consists of the submarine Scotia Ridge and the South Georgia, South Sandwich and South Orkney Islands, and which extends from Tierra del Fuego to the Antarctic Peninsula. The Scotia Sea was named after the *Scotia*, the vessel of the Scottish National Antarctic Expedition of 1902–4. *See also* ALBA; CALEDONIA; SCOTIA NOSTRA.

Scotia me genuit ... *See* DOCTOR SUBTILIS.

Scotia Nostra A satirical term, mimicking Cosa Nostra (Italian 'our thing' or 'our business', a name for the US Mafia), for the Scots politicians who have, at various stages in history, been perceived of as dominating Westminster. The Scotia Nostra at the turn of the new millennium included at various times the likes of Tony Blair (*see* RHYMING SLANG), Gordon Brown (the MISERY FROM THE MANSE), Alistair Darling (BADGER), John (the HAMMER) Reid, George Robertson, Charles Falconer, Douglas

Alexander, Des Brown, Michael Martin (GORBALS MICK), etc. Parties apart from Labour also had their prominent Scottish figures: Charles Kennedy and Menzies Campbell, successive leaders of the Liberal Democrats; and, amongst the Tories, Liam Fox, Michael Gove, Michael Ancram and Malcolm Rif-kind.

Scotland, names for *See* ALBA; ALBANIA; ALBANY; CALEDONIA; ITCHLAND OR SCRATCHLAND; JUVLO-MENGRESKEY TEM; LAND O' CAKES; SCOTIA.

Scotland, to have a good grip on *See* GUID GRIP O' SCOTLAND.

Scotland for Ever! A well-known painting (1881) by Lady Elizabeth Butler (1846–1933) of the charge of the Royal Scots Greys at Waterloo. The painting is now in Leeds City Art Gallery.

Scotland in Miniature A nickname for the island of Arran, on account of the variety of its landscapes. As the anonymous 12th-century author of the poem 'Arran' declared, 'O, Arran! is delightful at all times.' Other places have also laid claim to being 'Scotland in miniature':

I have nowhere seen loveliness so intense and so diverse crowded into so small a place. Langholm presents the manifold and multiform grandeur and delight of Scotland in miniature.
– Hugh MacDiarmid, 'The Thistle Rises'. The poet was, of course, a native of Langholm.

Scotland's Disgrace *See* EDINBURGH'S FOLLY.

Scotland's first family *See* BROONS, THE.

Scotland's Other National Drink *See* IRN BRU.

Scotland's Pride and Poverty *See* EDINBURGH'S FOLLY.

'Scotland the Brave' For a time Scotland's unoffi-cial national anthem, sung at international sporting events and the like. The stirring tune dates back to the early 20th century, but the words were penned *c.*1950 by the journalist Cliff Hanley for the singer

Robert Wilson. It has been largely supplanted by 'FLOWER OF SCOTLAND', but is still used at the Commonwealth Games.

> Land of my high endeavour,
> Land of the shining river,
> Land of my heart forever,
> Scotland the brave.

The song has been parodied by Billy Connolly:

> Land of the polluted river,
> Bloodshot eyes and sodden liver,
> Land of my heart forever,
> Scotland the Brave.
> – Quoted in Jonathan Margolis, *The Big Yin* (1994)

Scotland the wee A characterization of Scotland in the poem 'Scotland the Wee' by Tom Buchan (1931–95):

> Scotland the wee, crèche of the soul,
> of thee I sing ...

The poem concludes that Scotland is a

> one way street to the coup of the mind.

'Scotland the Wee' is perhaps the only poem in the Scottish canon that contains a reference to the HILLMAN IMP.

Scotland Yard The common metonym for London's Metropolitan Police, especially its Criminal Investigation Department. Great Scotland Yard in Whitehall was the headquarters of the Metropolitan Police in the 19th century, and took its name from the fact that in the Middle Ages the kings of Scotland had their London residence here.

Scots or **Scotch collops** Thin slices of beef stewed with onions and seasoning. Incidentally, when Mary Queen of Scots attempted to call for help following the murder of her secretary David Rizzio (*see* RIZZIO'S BLOOD), one of the conspirators, Lindsay of the Byres, threatened 'to cut her in collops'.

Scots convoy Also known as a *Hielan convoy*, this involves accompanying a party either part of the way to their home, or all the way to their home, whereupon they accompany the accompaniers part of the

way back. There is also the *Kelso convoy*, explained thus by Robert Chambers in his *Picture of Scotland* (1827):

> A *Kelso Convoy* is a common phrase used from time immemorial in the Lowlands of Scotland, to signify the circumstance of being accompanied by one's host no further than the threshold, or rather, as it is commonly phrased, a step and a half owre the doorstane. The origin of this stigma upon the hospitality of Kelso is unknown ...

The *Statistical Account* for Roxburghshire (1845) asserts that Chambers is under a misapprehension:

> A 'Kelso convoy' is not a shabby dismissal of a guest after attending him only to your door. The old Kelsonians did indeed finish the 'convoy' by parting with their guests on the threshold; but then this parting did not take place until they had first hospitably convoyed him [the guest] to *his* door, and been, in return for the compliment, reconvoyed by the latter to *their own*.

Scots Croesus, the Sir William Dick of Braid (1580–1655), an immensely wealthy Edinburgh merchant and financier who twice served as provost of the city. His business interests were wide and varied, including property, coal, salt, herring and soap, and extended as far as London, Paris and Bordeaux. He supported the COVENANTERS to the extent of lending them large sums of money, which they failed to repay, and he died in much reduced circumstances. (The original Croesus was a proverbially wealthy King of Lydia in the 6th century BC.)

Scots Dyke *See* DEBATABLE LANDS.

Scots Eton, the Fettes College, an independent boys' (now co-educational) boarding school in Edinburgh named after the merchant Sir William Fettes (1750–1836), who left £166,000 for the education of orphaned or needy children. The school, housed in an extraordinarily spired gothic extravaganza designed by David Bryce, opened in 1870. Notable alumni include James BOND and Tony Blair.

Scots Internationale, the *See* 'FREEDOM COME-ALL-YE, THE'.

Scots lovage A flowering plant, *Ligusticum scoticum*, that grows among seaside rocks and which was formerly eaten in Scotland (where it is called sea parsley) as a prophylactic against scurvy.

Scotsman, The One of Scotland's national newspapers, founded in Edinburgh in 1817 by William Ritchie and Charles MacLaren. Its chief rival is the Glasgow-based *Herald* (formerly *The Glasgow Herald*). In the first edition of *The Scotsman*, an editorial explained the choice of title:

> We have not chose the name of SCOTSMAN to preserve an invidious distinction, but with the view of rescuing it from the odium of servility. With that stain removed, a Scotsman may well claim brotherhood with an Englishman ...

Scotsman's Cinema, the A nickname for Piccadilly Circus in London, so-called in the 1920s and 1930s because of the advertising light displays which cost nothing to watch.

Scotsmen Behaving Badly See under SHUGGIE.

Scots mile A former unit of measurement, whose length varied in different parts of the country: miles of 1876, 1980 and 1984 yards were all in use. The English mile of 1760 yards was imposed by act of Parliament in 1824, by which time the Scots mile had largely fallen out of use.

> We think na on the lang Scots miles,
> The mosses, waters, slaps, and styles,
> That lie between us and our hame.
> – Robert Burns, 'Tam o' Shanter' (1791)

'Scots wha hae' The version usually given of the title of Burns's 1794 poem, although when translated as 'Scots who have' it is clearly only part of the correct title, 'Scots wha hae wi' Wallace bled'. In 1912 the originator of the *OED*, the Scotsman James Murray, wrote:

> Even Burns thought that Scotch was defiled by 'bad grammar' and tried to conform his Scotch to *English* grammar! Transforming e.g. the Scotch 'Scots 'at hae' to *Scots wha hae* which no sober Scotch man in his senses ever naturally said.

In the poem Robert the Bruce inspires his men before Bannockburn by alluding to the deeds of William Wallace. Hugh MacDiarmid coined the phrase 'Scots Wha Ha'evers' (*haiver*, 'to talk nonsense') to denote the sort of phoney patriots, addicted to BALMORALITY, that he so despised:

> ... the whole gang of high mucky-mucks, famous fatheads, old wives of both sexes, stuffed shirts, hollow men with headpieces stuffed with straw, bird-wits, lookers-under-beds, trained seals, creeping Jesuses, Scots Wha Ha'evers, village idiots, policemen, leaders of white-mouse factions and noted connoisseurs of bread and butter ... and all the touts and toadies and lickspittles of the English Ascendancy, and their infernal womenfolk.
> – Hugh MacDiarmid, *Lucky Poet* (1943)

Scott, Michael See SCOT, MICHAEL.

Scott, Sir Walter Variously known as the ARIOSTO OF THE NORTH, the AUTHOR OF WAVERLEY, an INSPIRED BUTLER and THE WIZARD OF THE NORTH. See also SCOTT MONUMENT; SCOTT'S VIEW; and *passim*.

Scotterati, the A species defined by Pat Kane as 'like the glitterati, only grumpier' (the *Guardian*, 20 May 2011). Among the Scotterati, Kane numbers Sean Connery, Brian Cox, Midge Ure and Jack Vettriano.

Scottish Addison, our See ADDISON OF THE NORTH, THE.

Scottish baronial A style of architecture that formed the Scottish branch of the 19th-century Gothic revival. It can be seen in a host of country mansions and faux castles, from Abbotsford to Balmoral, and features many towers and turrets, CRAW STEPS, battlements, etc., while interiors tend to be decorated with much tartan, armour, weaponry, wooden panelling and stags' heads.

Scottish bluebell See BLUEBELL OF SCOTLAND.

Scottish boot A form of torture. There is a vivid description of its use against Covenanter prisoners by Lauderdale, Tam Dalzell (BLUIDY TAM) and

Claverhouse (BONNIE DUNDEE, aka Bluidy Clavers) in Scott's *Old Mortality* (1816), chapter xxxvi:

> The executioner, with the help of his assistants, enclosed the leg and knee within the tight iron boot, or case, and then placing a wedge of the same metal between the knee and the edge of the machine, took a mallet in his hand, and stood waiting for farther orders. A well-dressed man, by profession a surgeon, placed himself by the other side of the prisoner's chair, bared the prisoner's arm, and applied his thumb to the pulse in order to regulate the torture according to the strength of the patient. When these preparations were made, the President of the Council repeated with the same stern voice the question, 'When and where did you last see John Balfour of Burley?'
>
> The prisoner, instead of replying to him, turned his eyes to heaven as if imploring Divine strength, and muttered a few words, of which the last were distinctly audible, 'Thou hast said thy people shall be willing in the day of thy power!'
>
> The Duke of Lauderdale glanced his eye around the council as if to collect their suffrages, and, judging from their mute signs, gave on his own part a nod to the executioner, whose mallet instantly descended on the wedge, and, forcing it between the knee and the iron boot, occasioned the most exquisite pain, as was evident from the flush which instantly took place on the brow and on the cheeks of the sufferer. The fellow then again raised his weapon, and stood prepared to give a second blow.
>
> 'Will you yet say,' repeated the Duke of Lauderdale, 'where and when you last parted from Balfour of Burley?'
>
> 'You have my answer,' said the sufferer resolutely, and the second blow fell. The third and fourth succeeded; but at the fifth, when a larger wedge had been introduced, the prisoner set up a scream of agony.

Scottish car, the *See* HILLMAN IMP.

Scottish Chaucerians, the A collective term for the MAKARS of the Renaissance period in Scotland, including King James I (1394–1437), Robert Henryson (?1424–?1506), William Dunbar (?1456–?1513) and Gavin Douglas (c.1475–1522). The term is something of a misnomer, as the English poet was only one of many influences, which included the native tradition of Barbour and the courtly poetry of France.

Scottish Colourists, the A loose group of Scottish painters, comprising S.J. Peploe (1871–1935), J.D. Fergusson (1874–1961), G.L. Hunter (1877–1931) and F.C.B. Cadell (1883–1937), whose brightly coloured, painterly works were influenced by the Impressionists and particularly by Post-Impressionists such as Matisse, Cézanne and the Fauves. The term was first coined in 1948.

Scottish Dreyfus, the How Oscar Slater (1872–1948), a German-born Jew, described himself after he was wrongfully convicted of murdering a reclusive Glasgow spinster in 1909. (Captain Alfred Dreyfus was the French army officer of Jewish descent who was wrongly convicted in 1894 of betraying military secrets to the Germans, and sentenced to life imprisonment.) Slater was born Oscar Leschziner in Upper Silesia, and later migrated to Britain, where he moved in underworld circles and came to the attention of the police. At his trial in the High Court in Edinburgh, his past life was paraded before the court, much of the evidence produced was tainted, prejudiced or otherwise unreliable, and there were a number of other irregularities, leading to suggestions of anti-Semitism on the part of the police and legal establishment. His death sentence was commuted to penal servitude for life. Although there were various public campaigns (including a book by Arthur Conan Doyle), it was not until 1928, the year after a court of criminal appeal was first established in Scotland, that Slater's original conviction was quashed, and as a consequence he received £6000 compensation. Such was the notoriety of the case that in Scotland his name became RHYMING SLANG for 'later'.

Scottish Enlightenment, the The great intellectual flowering that took place in Edinburgh and Glasgow in the 18th century, making Scotland one of the key centres of the European Enlightenment. As Voltaire observed, 'We look to Scotland for all our ideas of civilization.' Leading Scottish figures included the economist Adam Smith, philosophers such as Adam Ferguson, David Hume, Frances Hutcheson, Thomas Reid and Dugald Stewart, scientists such as the chemist Joseph Black and the geologist James

Hutton, and inventors such as James Watt. Some historians consider that one of the key factors in the creation of the Scottish Enlightenment was the plethora of clubs in Edinburgh and Glasgow – such as the POKER CLUB and the SELECT SOCIETY – where members could eat, drink and engage in convivial conversation, a perfect milieu for intellectual cross-fertilization.

Scottish Gallovidian Encyclopaedia, The See STAR O' DUNGYLE, THE.

Scottish Hobbema, the A sobriquet of the painter Patrick Nasmyth (1787–1831), whose delicate landscapes were influenced by those of the Dutch painter Meindert Hobbema (1638–1709). Nasmyth, the son of the more celebrated painter Alexander Nasmyth, was born in Edinburgh but spent most of his life in London. Demand for his product boomed as landscapes from the Dutch Golden Age came into vogue among British collectors.

Scottish Hogarth, the A sobriquet of the painter David Allan (1744–96). Although aspiring towards the grandeur of history painting, he had little success in that field, and turned instead to recording everyday life, as in *The Penny Wedding* (1795).

Scottish Insurrectionists, the See RADICAL WAR, THE.

Scottish Martyrs, the A group of Scottish Radicals whose advocacy in 1793–4 of universal male suffrage and annual parliaments, together with their support for the French Revolution, saw them convicted of sedition and transported to Australia. The four men, members of the organization called the Scottish Friends of the People, were Thomas Muir (1765–99), William Skirving (d.1796), Thomas Palmer (1747–1802) and Maurice Margarot (1745–1815). *See also* PIKE PLOT, THE; RADICAL WAR, THE; UNITED SCOTSMEN, THE.

Scottish Orpheus, the See KINGIS QUAIR, THE.

Scottish Ovid, the A sobriquet given to the Latin poet Arthur Johnstone (1587–1641), who was born at his family's seat, Caskieben Castle, near Inverurie, Aberdeenshire.

Scottish Play, the A propitiatory euphemism employed in theatrical circles to denote Shakespeare's tragedy *Macbeth*, the name of which is, according to the superstitious, not to be spoken, nor its lines quoted. Productions of the play are said to be dogged by misfortune, which some attribute to the spells cast by the three witches. In 2009 the press were delighted to report that members of a theatre group attempting to put on the play in Cardiff had suffered a broken toe, a knee operation, two black eyes and a year's delay in putting on the production. For the historical character, *see* MACBETH.

Scottish Renaissance, the A literary movement that arose in Scotland after the First World War, aligning itself with contemporary trends in European Modernism while forging a new kind of Scottish national identity. The movement partly arose as a reaction to the cosiness, sentimentality and parochialism of the earlier KAILYARD SCHOOL. The towering figure was the poet Hugh MacDiarmid (pseudonym of Christopher Murray Grieve), who in the 1920s sought to create a new 'Synthetic Scots' (known by its detractors as PLASTIC SCOTS) as a vehicle for creating something new in literature, akin to the linguistic experimentation of James Joyce in *Ulysses* or that of T.S. Eliot in *The Waste Land*. MacDiarmid's towering achievement in this respect was the long poem *A Drunk Man Looks at the Thistle* (1926). MacDiarmid himself had, in 1922, predicted a 'Scottish Renascence', and the term became more widely used after the French scholar Denis Saurat published an article entitled 'Le Groupe de la Renaissance Écossaise' in the April 1924 issue of the *Revue Anglo-Américaine*. Other key figures in the movement included the poets William Soutar, Sydney Goodsir Smith and Robert Garioch, and the novelists Neil Gunn and Lewis Grassic Gibbon. Not all embraced Scots as a medium: Edwin Muir, for example, argued that Scots could not serve as a vehicle for modern thought (leading to a row with MacDiarmid), while Sorley MacLean turned to his native Gaelic, reinvigorating Gaelic poetry for the 20th century.

Scottish Sea *See* SCOTCH SEA.

Scott Monument, the A tall Gothic spire in Edinburgh's Princes Street Gardens commemorating Sir Walter Scott. After the writer's death a competition was launched to find the best design. The winner was not a professional architect but a joiner from the Borders called George Meikle Kemp, who submitted his entry under the name John Morvo, the medieval master-mason responsible for Melrose Abbey. The monument, which includes a statue of Scott by Sir John Steell, was completed in 1846, two years after Kemp, on his way home from the building site, had fallen into the Union Canal and drowned.

Scott's View A viewpoint from the B6356 east of Melrose, across the River Tweed towards the Eildon Hills. When driving this way on his way home to Abbotsford, Sir Walter Scott would stop his horses to admire the scene. After his death, as his funeral cortège came this way, Scott's horses, now drawing his hearse, stopped of their own accord at this very spot. That is the popular story at least, although apparently in truth the halt was due to 'some accident'.

Scrape, Monarch of the Maunders *See under* SHELLYCOAT.

Scratchland *See* ITCHLAND.

Screaming Sisterhood, the *See* BAWLING CAMPBELLS, THE.

Scutter-hole The exit point for effluence when mucking out a byre or stable. J. Riddell, in *Aberdeen and Its Folk* (1868), records the following reproof delivered to someone displaying 'uncleanly habits in eating, &c.': 'Yer mou' is like the scutter-hole o' a byre.'

Scythia The ancient name for the area of steppes north of the Black Sea, and the supposed original homeland of the Scots, according to medieval chroniclers. The wandering of the ancestral Scots is recorded in the DECLARATION OF ARBROATH thus:

From the chronicles and books of the ancients we find that among other famous nations our own, the Scots,

have been graced with widespread renown. They journeyed from Greater Scythia by way of the Tyrrhenian Sea and the Pillars of Hercules, and dwelt for a long course of time in Spain among the most savage tribes, but nowhere could they be subdued by any race, however barbarous. Thence they came, twelve hundred years after the people of Israel crossed the Red Sea, to their home in the west where they still live today.

Later commentators observed that there were still parallels between the Scythians and at least some of the Scots:

Nowhere will you find people of robuster physique, higher spirited or longer lived, more active in old age and later in reaching it, than among the Highlanders; and that in spite of their entire dependence on cheese, flesh and milk, like the Scythians.

– Sir Thomas Craig, *De Unione Regnorum Britanniae* (1603–5)

Seaforth's Shirt *See under* MACKENZIE'S SHIRT OF MAIL.

Séamas-an-bhuid *See* LUSTY MAN.

Sea Mither or **Mither o' the Sea** In Orkney legend, the benign spirit of the summer seas. Every spring she would do battle with Teran, the spirit of winter, resulting in fearsome storms until the Sea Mither came out victorious, ushering in an era of warmth and calm. Battle recommenced in the autumn, when Teran's rule was restored for the winter. The name Teran may come from Norse *tyrren*, 'angry'. *See also* NUCKELAVEE.

Sea of Darkness, the An ocean to the west of Scotland, according to medieval Arab geographers; *see* SQUTLANDIYAH.

Sea's dearest child, the Benbecula, according to Hector MacIver's piece on 'The Outer Isles' in G. Scott Moncrieff, *Scottish Country* (1936):

In all the Hebrides, Benbecula is the sea's dearest child. That is why the returning tide races so quickly over the sand, hurrying with pouted lips to kiss its shore. And when the night's embraces are over, the sea leaves Benbecula again, like a mother bird going to forage for its young.

Sea serpents One of these, known as *Cìrein Cròin*, features in a Caithness rhyme quoted by John G. Campbell in his *Superstitions of the Highlands and Islands of Scotland* (1900):

> *Seachd sgadain sàth bradain,*
> *Seachd bradain sàth ròin,*
> *Seachd ròin sàth muice-mara,*
> *Seachd mucan-mara sàth Cìrein Cròin.*
> Seven herring are a salmon's fill,
> Seven salmon are a seal's fill,
> Seven seals are a whale's fill,
> And seven whales the fill of a Cìrein Cròin.

'To this,' Campbell continues, 'is sometimes added, "Seven Cìrein Cròin are the fill of the big devil himself."'

Another supposed sea serpent was the so-called Stronsay Beast, a carcass that washed up on the Orkney island of Stronsay in a storm in September 1808. It was reported to have a head like a sheep, a long neck and three pairs of legs. The Natural History Society of Edinburgh deemed it to be a hitherto unknown species, assumed to be some kind of sea serpent, which they dubbed *Halsydrus pontoppidani* ('sea water snake of Pontoppidan', alluding to the 18th-century Norwegian bishop who collected accounts of marine monsters). Later authorities declared that the carcass had the appearance of a basking shark at a certain stage of decomposition, although at 55 ft (16.75 m) long the Stronsay Beast was considerably larger than the largest known basking sharks, which grow to 40 ft (12 m) – so some questions still remain. *See also* DRAGONS.

Seaweed-eating sheep The most famous inhabitants of North Ronaldsay, the northernmost island in Orkney. The members of this unique island breed live on the shore and survive on seaweed. They are kept off the fields by the Sheep Dyke that surrounds the entire island, and their ownership is regulated by the Sheep Court.

Second Alexandria, the A sobriquet of BERWICK-UPON-TWEED in the Middle Ages, when it was a thriving port – in spite of the depredations of both English and Scots attackers.

Second City of the Empire The title given to Glasgow during its industrial heyday in the later 19th and earlier 20th centuries. William McGonagall was more parsimonious when he apostrophized Glasgow:

> ... without contradiction, I will venture to say
> You are the second grandest city in Scotland at the present day.
> – 'Glasgow' (1890)

Second sight (Gaelic *dara-sealladh*) The belief that certain people had inherited the gift of looking into the future was formerly widely held in the Highlands and Islands, and is still not entirely extinct. In the 17th century, at a time when Presbyterian Lowlanders looked askance at all the doings of their wild northern neighbours, there was little doubt of the origin of such gifts, as here outlined by a noted demonologist (who was also the first professor of mathematics at Glasgow University):

> I am undoubtedly informed, that men and women in the Highlands can discern fatality approaching others, by seeing them in waters, or with winding sheets about them ... It is not improbable, but that such preternatural knowledge comes first by a compact with the Devil, and is derived downward by succession to their posterity, many of such I suppose are innocent, and have this sight against their will and inclination.
> – George Sinclair, *Satan's Invisible World Discovered* (1685)

Just a decade later, Martin Martin, himself a Gael, made his famous voyage to the Western Isles, and left the following account of the phenomenon:

> The second sight is a singular faculty of seeing an otherwise invisible object, without any previous means used by the person that sees it for that end; the vision makes such a lively impression upon the seers, that they neither see nor think of anything else, except the vision, as long as it continues; and then they appear pensive or jovial, according to the object which was represented to them.
> – Martin Martin, *A Description of the Western Isles of Scotland* (1703)

In his *Tour in Scotland* (1774), the Welshman Thomas Pennant dismissed the idea of second sight as 'founded on impudence and nurtured by folly', but Dr Johnson, in his *Journey to the Western Islands of Scotland* (1775) was inclined to be more open-minded:

> It is the common talk of the Lowland Scots, that the notion of the Second Sight is wearing away with other superstitions; and that its reality is no longer supposed, but by the grossest people. How far its prevalence ever extended, or what ground it has lost, I know not. The Islanders of all degrees, whether of rank or under-standing, universally admit it, except the Ministers, who universally deny it ...

'Strong reasons for incredulity will readily occur,' Johnson continues, yet 'the Second Sight is only wonderful because it is rare, for, considered in itself, it involves no more difficulty than dreams'. He was impressed by the amount of anecdotal evidence, and 'where we are unable to decide by antecedent reason, we must be content to yield to the force of testimony'.

Where Johnson was inclined to be seduced by the romance of the mysterious Gael, William Daniell, in his *Voyage Round Great Britain* (1815–25), took a more sceptical stance:

> In no very remote times this notion [second sight] retained a strong hold on the minds of the vulgar [in the Highlands]; and, if current testimony may be credited, the race of seers is not wholly extinct. Some of the instances that have been collected by tourists to exemplify the effects of this fearful privilege are suffi-ciently whimsical. An old chieftain in Canna com-plained that his repose was disturbed by the hammering of coffin-nails; and he died within a fort-night. Another possessed the very convenient faculty of foreseeing the approach of all visitors to the little island where he dwelt, and had therefore the option either of providing for their entertainment, or of absenting himself, so that on their arrival they might be con-scientiously told that he was 'not at home'. A sybil of the age of forty could take a view into futurity through the lens of a well-scraped bladebone of mutton, which, on some occasions, figured to her the graves of her friends and relatives.

Instances of divining the future from examining the shoulder-blade of a sheep were still being recorded on Lewis at the end of the 19th century:

> The shoulder-blade of a black sheep was procured by the inquirer into future events, and with this he went to some reputed seer, who held the bone lengthwise before him and in the direction of the greatest length of the island. In this position the seer began to read the bone from some marks that he saw in it, and then oracularly declared what events to individuals or families were to happen. It is not very far distant that there were a host of believers in this method of prophecy.
>
> – John Abercromby, *Traditions, Customs and Superstitions of the* [sic] *Lewis* (1895)

See also BRAHAN SEER, THE; DIVINATION, METH-ODS OF; LADY OF LAWERS, THE; PROPHET PEDAN; *TAGHAIRM*; THOMAS THE RHYMER.

Secret Commonwealth, The A book by Robert Kirk, published in 1691, and subtitled *An essay on the nature and actions of the subterranean (and for the most part) invisible people heretofore going under the name of faunes and fairies, or the lyke, among the low country Scots, as they are described by those who have the second sight.* Kirk (1644–92), later known as 'the Fairy Minister', held that the bodies of fairies (*sith* in Gaelic) are 'so spungious, thin and delecat that they are fed by only sucking into some fine spirituous liquors that pierce like pure air and oil'. They are, he says,

> ... of a middle nature betwixt man and angel, of intelligent studious spirits and light changeable bodies (like those called astral) somewhat of the nature of a condensed cloud, and best seen in the twilight. These bodies be so pliable through the subtlety of the spirits that agitate them, that they can make them appear or disappear at pleasure.

Kirk states that these Celtic fairies could be both male and female, had no kings or queens, and dressed in 'plaids and variegated garments in the Highlands'.

Kirk was minister at Balquhidder and then at Aberfoyle, and was one of the first to record High-land folk beliefs. He also translated the Psalms into Gaelic, as *Psalma Dhaibhidh an meadrachd* (1684), earning him the epitaph *Linguae Hiberniae Lumen* ('Light of the Irish Language'). According to *Sketches of Perthshire* (1812) by Patrick Graham, a later minister at Aberfoyle, Kirk did not die but was taken by the fairies, angered that he had betrayed their secrets, and imprisoned in Doon Hill (also known as Fairy Knowe). According to the story, Kirk had then reappeared in spectral form at the christening of his posthumous child, and begged his brother-in-law, Thomas Graham of Duchray, to release him by throwing a dagger at him, but Duchray, 'in his astonishment', could not, and Kirk remained a captive in fairyland.

Seeing off the Queen of Sheba's husband at pistol point *See* SWEET SINGERS, THE.

Seein' her ain (Of a woman) commencing menstruation. The expression was first recorded in Fife at the start of the 20th century.

See men? Aw the same An oft-heard complaint.

See oursels as ithers see us, To Burns's wish, in 'To a Louse':

O wad some Power the giftie gie us
To see oursels as ithers see us!
It wad frae monie a blunder free us,
And foolish notion.

Seer of Gourdiehill, the *See* DISCOVERER OF THE PRINCIPAL OF NATURAL SELECTION.

Seers *See* BRAHAN SEER, THE; LADY OF LAWERS, THE; PROPHET PEDAN; SPAEWIFE; *TAGHAIRM*; THOMAS THE RHYMER. *See also* DIVINATION, METHODS OF; SECOND SIGHT.

See you? A Glaswegian construction intended to engage the attention of the addressee preliminary to delivering some kind of, usually adverse, character assessment.

Select Society, the A social club founded in the Advocates' Library, Edinburgh, on 22 May 1754. Among its original 15 members were many of the key figures of the SCOTTISH ENLIGHTENMENT, including James and John Adam, Lord Monboddo, Adam Ferguson, Lord Kames, David Hume, Allan Ramsay, William Robertson and Adam Smith. Although its membership rapidly expanded, by

the early 1760s the Select Society had gone into a decline, and many of its members went on to join the POKER CLUB.

Selkirk bannock *See* BANNOCK.

'Selkirk Grace, The' A grace attributed to Robert Burns, said to have been spoken at the table of the Earl of Selkirk during his tour through Galloway in 1793 (hence its other name, 'The Kirkcudbright Grace'):

Some hae meat and canna eat,
And some wad eat that want it;
But we hae meat, and we can eat,
And sae the Lord be thanket.

Sell the jerseys, to To commit an act of betrayal. The metaphor comes from football.

Sell yer pig and buy a can The jocular response to someone who says 'I canna', as an excuse for not performing some task. The expression is recorded by J. Riddell in *Aberdeen and Its Folk* (1868).

Senga A backwards version of the female first name Agnes, found particularly in working-class areas of Glasgow. It is apparently regarded as more exotic than the original. As a generic term, *senga* has also been adopted as a female equivalent of NED, a disparaging term for a working-class youth. *See also* BLACK AGNES.

Sense, good Something that the Scots are supposed to possess in bucketfuls:

In all my travels I never met with any one Scotchman but what was a man of sense: I believe everybody of that country that has any, leaves it as fast as they can.
– Francis Lockier (1668–1740), English churchman and writer, quoted in Joseph Spence, *Anecdotes* (1820)

Sent off at gunpoint *See* WEE BUD.

Serious Chimes Squad, the *See* ICE CREAM WARS.

Sermon on the Mound, the The punning nickname given to Margaret Thatcher's address to the GENERAL ASSEMBLY of the Church of Scotland in

May 1988, at its Assembly Hall at the head of the Mound in Edinburgh. The prime minister had in fact invited herself, and the Kirk thought it only courteous to ask her to say a few words. Mrs Thatcher used the occasion to attempt to restore some support in Scotland for her party, which at the previous year's general election had been reduced to a rump of 9 Scottish MPs, out of 72 Scottish seats. The actual address, which Ludovic Kennedy described as 'a weird amalgam of fundamental Conservatism and simplistic Sunday school homilies', asserted that Christianity was about choice (always a popular concept with free-market ideologues), and that the social teaching of the Bible could be summed up in the phrase 'Create wealth.' Thatcher also quoted St Paul to the effect that 'If a man shall not work he shall not eat.' The whole affair was an embarrassment to the generally leftish-leaning Assembly members. The Moderator that year, the Very Reverend Dr James Whyte, Professor Emeritus of Practical Theology and Christian Ethics at St Andrews University, later commented that the address had been 'quite bizarre'.

Set doon the barra *See* BARRA.

Set the heather on fire To create a great commotion; to cause excitement; to make one's mark.

> What would I not give or do to see Scotland really 'het up'? The heather on fire at last!
> – Hugh MacDiarmid, *Lucky Poet* (1943), chapter ix

> Blow for Royals as Balmoral wedding business fails to set the heather on fire.
> – *The Scotsman*, 11 December 2005, headlining a story that only one couple had made a booking to celebrate their wedding at Balmoral

Seven Celtic Earldoms of Alba, the *See under* MORMAER.

7:84 *See* CHEVIOT, THE STAG AND THE BLACK, BLACK OIL, THE.

Seven Hills of Edinburgh, the Like Rome, and, less glamorously, Sheffield, Edinburgh has seven hills: the Castle Rock, Calton Hill, ARTHUR'S SEAT, Corstorphine Hill, Blackford Hill, the Braid Hills

and Craiglockhart Hill. The whisky-distilling centre of Dufftown, not to be outdone, makes the following boast:

> Rome was built on seven hills;
> Dufftown stands on seven stills.

Compare BIGGAR'S BIGGER.

Seven Ill Years, the A period of poor harvests and famine beginning in 1696 in the reign of William III and extending into that of Queen Anne. The phrase was coined at the time, as attested in a letter dated 1699: 'The laying out much money on work folks and the ill yeers, has made them spend more then ordenarie.' The period – also known as *King William's Dear Years* – cast a shadow right down the 18th century.

Seven Men of Glen Moriston, the A group of BROKEN MEN who had served in the Jacobite army during the '45, but who after Culloden (April 1746) had taken to the hills as outlaws, living off their wits and the land. They owe their fame to the part they played in aiding the fugitive Prince Charles Edward Stuart, the YOUNG PRETENDER. The Prince met them in July 1746 at Corriegoe, north of Loch Cluanie, and they, having sworn eternal enmity to BUTCHER CUMBERLAND, devoted themselves to helping him. For three days they hid him in a cave where he was 'as comfortably lodged as if he had been in a royal palace', before moving him, for another four days, to an equally luxurious cave, all the while sustaining him with stores of mutton, venison, beef, butter, cheese and whisky from their larder. The Seven Men were John MacDonald, Alexander MacDonald, three Chisholm brothers (Alexander, Donald and Hugh), Gregor MacGregor and Patrick Grant; they were later joined by an eighth man, Hugh Macmillan.

Seven Men of Knoydart, the Seven landless crofters, some of them returning servicemen, who after the Second World War tried to seize land from the laird of the remote Knoydart estate, the 2nd Baron Brocket. In the 1930s Brocket had entertained prominent Nazis at Inverie House, his seat on the estate, and had been Hitler's guest at the latter's fiftieth-birthday celebrations in April 1939. On 9 November

1948 Sandy Macphee, Duncan McPhail, Henry Mac-Askill, Jack MacHardy, Archie MacDonald, William Quinn and Archie MacDougall each staked out 65 acres of arable land and 10,000 acres of rough hill land and started farming. Brocket took them to court, but the men argued that the Land Settlement Act passed after the First World War allowed demobilized servicemen to take over land that was being under-used. The Court of Session ruled against them and they were evicted, but eventually the case led to greater crofting rights. Hamish Henderson celebrated the affair in his ballad, 'The Seven Men of Knoydart', who defy Lord Brocket thus:

O we are all ex-servicemen,
We fought against the Hun,
We can tell our enemies by now,
And Brocket you are one!

In 1999 the Knoydart estate, including Inverie, came under community ownership. *See also* BATTLE OF THE BRAES; RONA RAIDERS, THE.

Seven Men of Moidart, the The seven Jacobite adventurers who accompanied the YOUNG PRETENDER when he landed in Arisaig in 1745, and then waited with him at Kinlochmoidart while the clans gathered. They then made their way through Moidart to Glenfinnan, where the prince raised his standard. The seven men included one Englishman, Colonel Francis Strickland, and two Scotsmen: William Murray, Marquess of Tullibardine, formerly Duke of Atholl until his estates were forfeited after his involvement in the 1715 and 1719 risings; and Aeneas Macdonald, a banker. The other four were Irish: Sir Thomas Sheridan, the prince's old tutor; Sir John Macdonald of the Irish Brigade in France; the Revd George Kelly, recently released from the Tower of London; and Captain John William O'Sullivan, who had also fought for the French.

Rather confusingly, the Scottish country dance called 'The Seven Men of Moidart' represents seven men throwing down their work tools and jumping for joy at the approach of the prince. There is also a fiddle tune called 'The Eight Men of Moidart', said to represent seven fishermen who welcomed the prince's arrival with a dance on the shore; being one man short to dance an eightsome reel, they stuck a spade in the sand to make up the numbers.

In the early 19th century, on the north side of Loch Moidart, a row of seven beech trees known as the Seven Men of Moidart was planted in memory of the prince's companions. Today there are only five left.

Seven Sisters, the A set of cannon used by the Scots at Flodden in 1513. Lindsay of Pitscottie, in his account of the battle in his *Historie and Chronicles of Scotland, 1436–1565*, describes 'seven canons that he [James IV] had forth of the Castle of Edinburgh, which were called the Seven Sisters, casten by Robert Borthwick, the master-gunner'. They failed to avert disaster.

The name *Seven Sisters* is still applied in many parts of Scotland to the Pleiades constellation (known in Caithness as the *Knip*, meaning 'bundle' or 'string of things', and in various other places as *the Seven Starn*).

Seven Sleepers, Battle of the *See* BATTLE OF THE SEVEN SLEEPERS.

Seventh son of a seventh son In Gaelic culture, it was believed that such a child would be possessed of SECOND SIGHT. (In contrast, in Argentina it was believed that such a person would turn out to be a werewolf.)

Severed head tells time *See* ARCHIE'S ROCK.

Sex As the Scottish edition of the *Daily Mail* commented in March 1987:

The most frightening fact about AIDS is that it can be spread by normal sex between men and women. This is still rare in Scotland.

In both Morningside and Kelvinside, 'sex' are what the coal is delivered in.

Sex therapists up Arthur's Seat *See* ARTHUR'S SEAT.

Sgian dubh The short, black-hilted dagger (Gaelic *sgian*, 'dagger' + *dubh*, 'black'; sometimes anglicized as *skean dhu*) formerly used for stabbing, cutting meat, gralloching deer, etc., but now often tucked harmlessly into the top of one of the stockings by those sporting full Highland fig. More sinister was the *skean occle*, a weapon concealed in the armpit (from Gaelic *sgian achlais*, 'armpit knife'). Such a knife is sported by the page Callum Beg in Scott's *Waverley*. The sgian dubh has spawned the old visual joke of a pigeon on skis: a 'skiin' doo'.

Shakins o' the poke, the The last remnants (like the last crumbs shaken out of a *poke* or paper bag). The expression is applied figuratively to the last-born of a family.

Shaky Village, the The large Perthshire village of Comrie, which, being positioned on the boundary fault of the Highland Line, has a suffered more earth tremors than is the norm in Scotland. The first earthquake recorded here took place in 1788, and an early seismometer was installed in the village in 1840. However, neither injury nor damage is at all common. One of the best reported earthquakes in Scotland took place on the evening of 13 August 1816, and was felt over much of the Northeast. It lasted six seconds, and cups rattled in saucers, chairs wandered across floors and caged birds fell off their perches. An old sailor in Inverness claimed 'he was tossed in his bed, as he had never been tossed out at sea, for full five minutes', while in Montrose two customs officers, lying in wait to ambush a band of smugglers, jumped up from the ground, fearing the shaking indicated the imminent arrival of armed horsemen.

Shameful Peace, the The name given by the English to the Treaty of Northampton (May 1328), by which – in return for an end to the harrying of the north of England by the Scots – the young Edward III gave up his claim to the Scottish throne, recognized Robert the Bruce as King of Scots, and arranged for the marriage of his own sister Joan to Bruce's young son David. Among the clauses agreed to by the English king were the following (originally in Latin):

That the kingdom of Scotland, divided in all things from the kingdom of England by its right marches, as in the time of Alexander [III] of good memory, King of Scots, shall remain forever entire free, and at peace, without any sort of subjection, servitude, claim or demand whatsoever;

And if we, or our predecessors in past times have sought in any way any rights to the kingdom of Scotland, we renounce and abandon them, by these presents, to the King of Scots, his heirs and successors.

Shankie or **shunky** A toilet bowl, so-called from Shanks of Barrhead, manufacturers of porcelain sanitary ware. John Shanks, a plumber from Paisley, made many innovations in the field, both for domestic and shipboard use. In 1878 he established his first factory in Barrhead, a foundry for making brass fittings for baths and lavatories; it was not until 1900 that the company started making its own china ware. In 1969 the firm merged with Armitage Ware Ltd of Staffordshire, and the Barrhead factory closed in the early 1990s.

The *shunky* famously features in Irvine Welsh's *TRAINSPOTTING* (1993):

Ah whip oaf ma keks and sit oan the cold wet porcelain shunky. Ah empty ma guts, feeling as if everything: bowel, stomach, intestines, spleen, liver, kidneys, heart, lungs and fucking brains are aw falling through ma arsehole intae the bowl.

Our hero then realizes that he has lost his stash of drugs, hitherto secreted in his rectum, down what is also known as the *cludgie* or *cludge* (possibly a conflation of 'closet' and 'lodge'). A retrieval operation is then initiated, and brought to a successful conclusion.

Sharp as a Kilmaurs whittle Sharp-witted, the small Ayrshire town of Kilmaurs being famous in the 18th century for its cutlery, especially its *whittles*, i.e. knives.

Shawfield Riots A violent protest mounted in Glasgow in 1725 against the new malt tax, which increased the price of beer. There was also widespread resentment of the fact that, after the Union, English MPs could vote in favour of taxes imposed in Scotland. The particular target of the Glasgow mob was Shawfield, the mansion of Daniel Campbell, MP for Glasgow Burghs, who had voted for the tax. Troops were called out and opened fire on the mob; the extent of deaths and injuries is unclear, but the Glasgow magistrates arrested Captain Bushel, the commanding officer of the troops. However, the

Lord Advocate, Duncan Forbes, gave Bushel his protection, and arrested the magistrates for failing to control the mob. Although the magistrates were released, some of the leading rioters were sentenced to transportation.

Sheep, Year of the See YEAR OF THE SHEEP.

Sheep's heid A Scottish delicacy, fit, according to its devotees, for any feast. It was celebrated by, among others, Francis Sempell of Beltrees (*c.*1616–82), to whom is attributed 'The Wedding of Maggie and Jock':

> An' there will be partans and buckies,
> And whitins and speldins enew,
> And singit sheep's heid, and a haggis,
> And scadlips to sup till ye spue.
> [*speldins* are sun-dried haddocks; *scadlips* is mutton broth with barley]

The following century Robert Fergusson, irritated that St Andrews University had fed Dr Johnson Frenchified fripperies on his visit there, suggested that next time they should serve him with homelier fare, '*Imprimis*, then, a haggis fat':

> *Secundo*, then a gude sheep's head
> Whase hide was singit, never flead.
> – 'To the Principal and Professors of the University of St Andrews on their Superb Treat to Dr Samuel Johnson' (*see also* MEALIE PUDDING)

Sir Walter Scott shared Fergusson's predilection:

> I wish for sheep's head and whisky toddy against all the French cookery and champagne in the world.
> – Journal, November 1826

The Sheep Heid Inn in Duddingston, Edinburgh, claims to be the oldest in the city, tracing its origins to 'at least 1360'. *Sheep's heid broth* is called *powsowdie* (possibly from *pow*, 'head' + *sowdie*, 'mish-mash'), and was celebrated in 'The Wedding of Maggie and Jock':

> There'll be tartan, dragen and brachen,
> And fouth of good gappocks of skate,
> Pow-sodie and drammock and crowdie,
> And callour nout-feet in a plate ...
> [*tartan* is red cabbage cooked with meal; *dragen, brachen* and *drammock* all appear to be various kinds of preparation of oatmeal; *gappocks*, 'pieces'; *callour*, 'fresh'; *nout*, 'cattle']

In England, sheep's heid became known as *jemmy*, a familiar form of the name James. According to the Revd Dr E. Cobham Brewer in the 1896 edition of his *Dictionary of Phrase and Fable*, this appellation derives from the fact that it was James VI who introduced the dish to England when he went south to become James I. However, the earliest citation in the *OED* for *jemmy* meaning sheep's heid is from Dickens's *Sketches by Boz* (1836). Brewer further asserts that 'a sheep's head not singed' was known as a *sanguinary James*.

Sheep's shoulder-blade, divination by means of a *See under* SECOND SIGHT.

Shellycoat A species of water sprite, with a shell-covered coat that rattles as it moves. They are mischievous rather than malevolent, specializing in misdirecting travellers down the wrong path, as attested by the following tale from the Borders:

> Two men, on a very dark night, approaching the banks of the Ettrick, heard a doleful voice from its waves repeatedly exclaim, 'Lost! Lost!' They followed the sound, which seemed to be the voice of a drowning person, and, to their infinite astonishment, they found that it ascended the river. Still they continued, during a long and tempestuous night, to follow the cry of the malicious sprite; and arriving, before morning's dawn, at the very sources of the river, the voice was now heard descending the opposite side of the mountain in which they arise. The fatigued and deluded travellers now relinquished the pursuit, and had no sooner done so than they heard Shellycoat applauding, in loud bursts of laughter, his successful roguery. The spirit was supposed particularly to haunt the old house of Gorinberry, situated on the River Hermitage, in Liddesdale.
> – Sir Walter Scott, *Minstrelsy of the Scottish Border* (1802)

Alexander Pennecuik mentions Shellycoat in *A Marriage Betwixt Scrape, Monarch of the Maunders, and Blobberlips, Queen of the Gypsies* (1720), which is set 'below fair Peebles' in the Borders:

> No shelly-coat goblin, or elf on the green,
> E'er tripped more nimbly than the beggars' Queen;
> Blobberlips the bride did dance and play,
> (For this, it seems, was her wedding-day).

See also FATLIPS.

Shepherd's tartan or **shepherd's check** A traditional black-and-white check pattern, formerly favoured by shepherds in the Borders and Northumberland.

Sherramoor or **Shirramuir, the** A former name for the 1715 Jacobite uprising (*see* OLD PRETENDER, THE), which petered out at the inconclusive Battle of Sheriffmuir.

> Ae hairst afore the Sherramoor, –
> I mind't as weel's yestreen,
> I was a gilpey then, I'm sure
> I wasna past fifteen …
> – Robert Burns, 'Halloween' (1786)

The term also came to be applied to any rumpus or kerfuffle.

Shetland Bus, the The nickname for the Second World War operation in which small fishing boats ran between Shetland and Norway, carrying supplies and agents for the Norwegian resistance. The operation, set up in 1941, was run jointly be the SIS (Secret Intelligence Service, i.e. MI6) and the SOE (Special Operations Executive), and its deputy commander, the historian David Howarth, later wrote a book about the operation, entitled *The Shetland Bus* (1951). After the small fishing boats proved too vulnerable, in 1943 they were replaced by faster and better-armed submarine-chasers, and the unit became an official part of the Royal Norwegian Navy.

Sheuch *See* UP THE SHEUCH.

Shilling, 60-, 70-, 80-, 90- *See* BEER.

Ship No. 534 *See* HULL NO. 534.

Shire, the Wigtownshire, so-called to distinguish it from the other old division of Galloway, Kirkcudbrightshire, which is known as the STEWARTRY.

> Now it is not often that a Galloway boy takes to lying; but when he does, a mere Nithsdale man has no chance with him, still less a man from the simple-minded levels of the 'Shire'. [Footnote: Wigtonshire is invariably

spoken of in Galloway as the Shire, Kirkcudbrightshire as the Stewartry.]
> – S.R. Crockett, *The Lilac Sunbonnet* (1894), chapter xi

See also FOOTBALL CLUB NICKNAMES.

Shirramuir, the *See* SHERRAMOOR.

Shirts, Battle of the *See* BATTLE OF THE SHIRTS.

Shivery bite The same as a CHITTERIN BIT.

Shoes made at John Brown's, to have one's To be possessed of unusually large feet, with the suggestion that suitable shoes would have to be built by the former Clydebank shipyard of John Brown & Company.

Shony Apparently an ancient sea god, formerly propitiated in Lewis; *see under* SAMHAIN.

Shooey *See* SHUGGIE.

Shoog bog A quaking quagmire, perilous to those attempting to traverse it. To *shoog* is to shake or wobble; hence *shooglie jock*, a dish of brawn in jelly.

Shoot the craw, to To leave hastily, run away, for example if one wishes to escape one's creditors. The expression, which is current in the Central Belt, can also mean to order drinks without paying for them.

Short-Hoggers of Whittingehame A legend attaching to the old village of Whittingehame in East Lothian, to the south of Traprain Law, told by Robert Chambers in his *Popular Rhymes of Scotland* (1826). The village, after many years of decay, was eventually demolished in 1817. The story is that by a tree near the village a mother had long ago murdered her young child, whose ghost was thereafter seen on dark nights running between the tree and the churchyard, crying because, being unbaptized and nameless, it could not obtain entry into heaven. 'Nobody durst speak to the unhappy little spirit,' writes Chambers, 'out of a superstitious dread of dying immediately after; and, to all appearance, the village of Whittingehame was destined to be haunted till the end of time, for want of an exorcist.' Then one night a drunkard reeled by, and, seeing the ghost, hailed it thus: 'How's a' wi' ye this mornin', Short-Hoggers?' The little ghost ran off, joyfully exclaiming:

O weel's me noo, I've gotten a name;
They ca' me Short-Hoggers o' Whittingehame!

The infant spectre was never seen again. Chambers said that its disappearance had only occurred 'little more than half a century' before he wrote, and that he had had the story 'from the lips of an old woman of Whittingehame, who had seen the ghost'. *Hoggers* are footless stockings, worn as gaiters.

Short i' the trot or **pile** Curt, short-tempered, ungracious.

Shot amang the craws, to be To get into trouble through keeping bad company.

Shoulder-blade of a sheep, divining the future by examining *See* SECOND SIGHT.

Shower i' the heids, a 'A flood of tears,' according to John Jamieson in *An Etymological Dictionary of the Scottish Language* (1825 supplement), condemning it as 'a ludicrous phrase used by those in a pastoral district, and borrowed from the proof that rain is falling in the high grounds, or at the *heads* of rivulets, by their swelling below'. A variant is *a shower i' the dam-heids*.

Shuffle-the-brogue A game like hunt-the-slipper, described by A.B. Gomme in *Traditional Games of England, Scotland and Ireland* (Vol. 2, 1898):

One of the players takes a small object, and hands it from one to another under the legs from behind. The players as they pass the brogue repeat the words – 'Shuffle the brogue once, Shuffle the brogue twice, Shuffle the brogue thrice.' ... One player who is blindfolded has to catch it as it is passing along.

Shuggie A familiar version of the name 'Hugh', used in Glasgow and the west of Scotland. Another version is *Shooey*. Shuggie is the eponymous hero of the *Daily Record*'s cartoon strip, 'Shuggie and Duggie: Scotsmen Behaving Badly'.

Shunky *See* SHANKIE.

Shut yer geggie Shut up, *geggie* being Glaswegian for 'mouth'. The word *geggie* also formerly denoted an unsophisticated travelling show or fairground attraction, typically put on in a tent – such as those that prior to the First World War attracted punters to the Glasgow Fair (*see* FAIR FORTNIGHT). *Geggie* in this sense derives from standard English *gag*, a made-up story – which is presumably why someone might be told to shut his or her *geggie* if they were spinning a yarn. *Geggie* also denotes one of those homemade go-karts that children used to construct from pram wheels, wooden fruit boxes, etc.

Siberian mammoth, not unlike the *See* WATER COW.

Siberia of Scotland, the A nickname for the Cabrach, a moorland plateau in Moray, to the north of the Ladder Hills. Eminences around here include Thiefsbush Hill and Dead Wife's Hillock. *Cabrach* in Gaelic means 'antler place'.

Signet Library *See* WRITER TO THE SIGNET.

Signwriter A jocular Glaswegian way of denoting the occupation of an unemployed person – signing on.

Silicon Glen A nickname for an area of the Central Belt, roughly forming a triangle between Dundee, Edinburgh and Inverclyde, where a large number of electronics and computer hardware and software companies began to establish themselves from the 1960s. The name, which also denotes Scotland's high-tech industry generally and which first came into use in the 1980s, echoes that of California's Silicon Valley.

Silkie Folk or **Selkie Folk** In Orkney and Shetland folklore, the seal people (in Scots *silkie* or *selkie* is the name for the common or grey seal). The Silkie Folk lived on remote rocks in the sea and appeared to be seals for most of the time, but were capable of transforming themselves into human shape and sometimes took human lovers. The species is best known from the ballad 'The Great Silkie of Sule

Skerry' (a remote islet some 40 milies / 60 km west of Orkney Mainland):

I am a man upon the land,
I am a Silkie in the sea,
And when I'm far from every strand
My home it is in Sule Skerry.

The Great Silkie takes a mortal woman for his lover, and by her has a child. But things will not work out happily:

It shall come to pass on a summer's day
When the sun shines hot on every stone
That I shall take my little young son
And teach him for to swim the foam.

And thou shalt marry a proud gunner
And a proud gunner I'm sure he'll be
And the very first shot that ever he'll shoot
He'll kill both my young son and me.

Alas, Alas, the maiden cried
This weary fate's been laid for me
And then she said and then she said
I'll bury me in Sule Skerry.

The people of North Ronaldsay, Orkney, are nicknamed *selkies* (*see* TEU-NEEMS). The Silkie Folk are not to be confused with the Fin Folk (*see* EYNHALLOW). *See also* CHILDREN OF THE SEALS.

Silk napkin A Northeastern phrase for a fragmented or imperfect RAINBOW.

Siller bridal *See* PENNY BRIDAL.

Sillie Regent, the A popular sobriquet of Matthew Stewart, 4th Earl of Lennox (1516–71), for, according to the *Oxford Dictionary of National Biography*, 'Opinions concerning Lennox's sagacity and political shrewdness vary.' It should be noted that the sobriquet did not necessarily impute foolishness to the regent, as at this period 'silly' had a range of marginally less opprobrious meanings, from 'deserving pity' to 'feeble' to 'unlearned'.

Lennox was the father of Lord Darnley and thus grandfather of James VI. He became regent for his grandson in 1570, but was killed the following year in a skirmish with the supporters of the deposed Mary Queen of Scots (his daughter-in-law). Richard

Bannatyne, secretary to John Knox, recorded the regent's death in his *Memoriales of Transactions in Scotland, 1570–1573*:

Upon Tuysday the 4 of September, Godis hand struik, as said is, the sillie regent slane, beand schot be ane called Cader, captan of ensignie to the Hamiltonis band, be command gewin befoir so to doe, be the lord Huntlie and Claud Hamiltoun, whilk he confessed befoir he was put to death ...

See also GOD'S SILLY VASSAL.

Sillitoe's Cossacks The Glasgow police under Sir Percy Sillitoe, who was chief constable from 1931 until 1943, when he became head of MI5. Under Sillitoe the Glasgow police forcefully took on the violent gangs, such as the BILLY BOYS and the Norman Conks. Sillitoe himself compared notes with FBI director J. Edgar Hoover on a visit to Chicago in 1933.

Sillitoe tartan The black-and-white chequered band worn round police caps, introduced by Sir Percy Sillitoe, chief constable of Glasgow in the 1930s (*see* SILLITOE'S COSSACKS). It was inspired by the similar band sometimes found on the GLENGARRY bonnet.

Silly Regent, the *See* SILLIE REGENT, THE.

Silly watter *See* CHEEKY WATTER.

Silver City, the A sobriquet of Aberdeen, in full 'the Silver City by the Golden Sands', somewhat flatteringly alluding to the grey stone of the GRANITE CITY. It appears to be a relatively recent coinage.

Silver for the River Dee which ran through it. Silver for the colour of the buildings in sunlight – grey granite transformed into shimmering light. Silver for the money the oil boom had brought. Lumsden explained as Rebus drove them back down on to Union Street.
– Ian Rankin, *Black and Blue* (1997)

Not everybody has embraced the sobriquet:

The ... self-conferred nickname 'Silver City' was another over-reaching feat of turd-polishing euphemism. It was grey. Everything was grey. There was just no

getting away from it. The buildings were all – *all* – made of granite and the sky was covered in a thick layer of permacloud. It. Was. Grey. If Aberdeen was silver, then shite wasn't brown ...
– Christopher Brookmyre, *A Big Boy Did It and Ran Away* (2001)

To add insult to injury, in 2002 the curmudgeonly English novelist Martin Amis described Aberdeen as 'one of the darkest places imaginable – like Iceland'.

Silver darlings An East Coast name for herring, so called from their colour, seen as a flash as the shoal turns over, and also alluding to the money the herring brought in to the fishermen. The term was celebrated by Neil Gunn in his novel *The Silver Darlings* (1941), set in Caithness in the period after the Napoleonic Wars:

They forgot all about the ship; they forgot everything, except the herrings, the lithe silver fish, the swift flashing ones, hundreds and thousands of them, the silver darlings.

In the later 19th and early 20th centuries the Scottish herring fishery became one of the biggest fisheries in the world.

The food of the Herring is said to consist of Crustacea and small fishes, but there is ordinarily so little appearance of food in their stomach that an easier explanation has been found in saying, they live on the foam they make with their own tails!
– John G. Campbell, *Superstitions of the Highlands and Islands of Scotland* (1900)

'There's not much that iss wholesomer than a good herrin',' said Para Handy. 'It's a fush that's chust sublime.'
– Neil Munro, *The Vital Spark* (1906)

Simmer dim The Orkney and (particularly) Shetland version of the 'white nights' of northern Russia, i.e. those nights of midsummer when it never gets completely dark. The joys of the simmer dim can also be enjoyed further south in Scotland, as in this description of bivouacking in midsummer in Coire Leis, high on the northeast side of Ben Nevis:

The colours of a clear simmer-dim sky are almost impossible to describe – faint pinks shading into

delicate blues and greys before the clear pale blue of the pre-dawn.
– Bob Richardson, 'A Night in the Big Bedroom', *Scottish Mountaineering Club Journal*, 2011

Millennia ago, the balance of day and night in the far north proved puzzling to the Romans:

The length of their days is beyond the measure of our world: the night is clear, and in the farthest part of Britain so short one can scarcely tell the twilight from the dawn.
– Tacitus, *Life of Agricola*, describing the visit of the Roman fleet to the Orkneys in AD 84

The downside was described by Julius Caesar:

Very many lesser islands are thought to lie off the coast, of which isles some have written that for thirty days on end, during the winter, it is night there.
– Julius Caesar, *De Bello Gallico*, in which he describes his campaigns in Britain in 55 and 54 BC

Simon the Fox A nickname of Simon Fraser, 11th Lord Lovat (c.1667–1747), who at various stages of his career came out in favour either of the Jacobites or the Hanoverians, depending on which seemed to serve his interests best. After the death of his cousin, the 9th Lord Lovat, he kidnapped and forcibly married the late lord's widow, the sister of the Duke of Atholl, who became his sworn enemy. In 1703, giving the impression that he was a follower of the OLD PRETENDER, Lovat sought to discredit Atholl by implicating him in the supposed Jacobite conspiracy known as the SCOTCH PLOT. During the 1715 Rebellion he supported the Hanoverians, and in 1730 his title as 11th Lord Lovat was confirmed. But with the outbreak of the 1745 Rebellion he guardedly lent his support to the YOUNG PRETENDER, sending his son to fight while he himself stayed at home. After Culloden, the fugitive Prince Charles called on Lovat at Gortleck House in the hope of obtaining shelter; Lovat, it is said, welcomed the prince with a glass of wine, and sent him on his way after another two. Lovat himself went into hiding, but was captured by Loch Morar. Taken to London, he was found guilty of treason and beheaded on Tower Hill, the last man in Britain to suffer this fate.

Simpson, Habbie *See* HABBIE.

Since God left Govan *See* BEFORE THE LORD LEFT PARTICK.

Singin' E'en *See* HOGMANAY.

Singing Butler, The A painting by Methil-born autodidact Jack Vettriano (né Hoggan), rejected in 1992 when submitted to the Royal Academy summer show, but now the most reproduced painting in Britain. The original – which features a young couple in 1930s evening dress dancing on a beach while a butler and maid hold umbrellas up against the inclement weather – sold for nearly £750,000 in 2004. Not to be confused with *The* SKATING MINISTER.

Singin ginger A term applied in Glasgow to any alcoholic beverage, distinguished from plain *ginger* (any non-alcoholic fizzy drink, such as lemonade or cola) by its ability to inspire the consumer to burst into song.

Sing quiet Maggie, to To maintain a discreet silence – also known as *singing dumb*. A similar expression, *to sing sma'*, means to adopt a servile, quiet manner.

Sith The Gaelic name for the fairies. *See also* BROWNIE; *SECRET COMMONWEALTH, THE*; SLUAGH.

Sit on someone's coat-tails, to To make use of someone for furthering one's own aims, or to over-rely or sponge on others.

Sit or flit *See* FLIT.

Sittie-doon or **sittie-in** *See under* CARRY-OOT.

Sittin in the britchin Refusing to move, or, figuratively, refusing to pull one's weight. A *britchin* is the strap fastened round the hindquarters of a draught horse allowing it to push backwards.

Sixes and saxes Six of one and half a dozen of the other. The expression plays on the standard English and the Scots pronunciations.

Six-Foot-High Club, the An Edinburgh club that flourished in the early 19th century, and that included many literary men as members. The conditions for membership were that the candidate should be male and over six feet in height, although exceptions were made for honorary members of lesser stature. The club met at Hunter's Tryst Inn, south of Fairmilehead (not the same as the present Hunter's Tryst, near Dreghorn, which used to be known as Sourhole).

> What a tail of the alphabet I should draw after me were I to sign with the indications of the different societies I belong to, beginning with President of the Royal Society of Edinburgh, and ended with umpire of the Six-foot-high Club!
> – Sir Walter Scott, Journal, 5 March 1829

In a note to this entry in Scott's journal, Scott's son-in-law and biographer J.G. Lockhart described the club as 'a sportive association of young athletes', and recalled (in the same note to Scott's Journal), that James Hogg 'was their Poet Laureate'. Other literary members included 'Christopher North' (John Wilson).

Sixteen Men of Tain, the How the marketing department describes the staff of the Glenmorangie Distillery at Tain in Easter Ross, no doubt alluding to more traditional groupings such as the SEVEN MEN OF MOIDART, etc.

Skairsburn warning *See* SKYRESBURN WARNING.

Skate bree The water in which skate has been boiled, said to have a number of medicinal properties. According to Walter Gregor's *Folk-Lore of the North-East of Scotland* (1881), it 'was accounted an efficacious lotion for sprains and rheumatism in man, gout in pigs, and "crochles" [lameness] in cattle'. Others said it had aphrodisiac qualities.

Skating Minister, The Henry Raeburn's famous full-length portrait, more properly known as *The Reverend Robert Walker Skating on Duddingston Loch* (*c*.1784, National Gallery of Scotland). Walker, a member of Britain's oldest skating club, the Edinburgh Skating Society, had spent time as a child in the Netherlands, where his father had been minister of the Scots kirk in Rotterdam, so he had probably learnt to skate on the Dutch canals. Having an aversion to dishonesty, Walker had a room in his Duddingston manse called 'Edinburgh', so that if an unwelcome visitor called, the servants could say in all truthfulness that the minister was 'in Edinburgh'. In 2005 a curator at the Scottish National Portrait Gallery suggested that the portrait wasn't by Raeburn at all, but rather by a visiting French painter called Henri-Pierre Danloux.

> Carelessly
> as a whore
> raises her shift
> his blades brush
> the frozen loch.
>
> He's left on a whim
> the yoke
> of the sermon
> for Sunday –
> stern words between
> psalm and hymn.
>
> What words, though,
> to send his flock
> to paradise
> if not this sun –
> this air and ice?
>> – Hamish McEwan Hamilton, 'The Rev. Robert Walker Skating from Heaven on Duddingston Loch' (1969)

The Skating Minister, one of the most famous of Scottish (unless it's French) paintings, is not to be confused with another iconic Scottish painting, *The SINGING BUTLER*.

> Was Raeburn's skating parson
> a man of God, poised
> impeccably on the brink;
> or his bland stare
> no more than decorous front?
>> – Stewart Conn, 'Under the Ice' (1978)

Skean dhu, skeen occle, etc. See SGIAN DUBH.

Skinnymalinkie Longlegs The hero of a children's street song:

> Skinnymalinkie Longlegs
> Big banana feet

> Went tae the pictures
> An couldnae find a seat
> So he got on a bus
> But he couldnae pay his fare
> So the rotten old conductor
> Went an threw him doon the stair.

There are several variations; in one version he has 'Umberella feet'. *Skinny malinkie, skinamalink*, etc., are terms applied to any thin creature, human or otherwise.

Skinny tatties Potatoes boiled in their skins.

Skin-the-cuddy or **skin-the-goatie** A variety of leapfrog, in which three of four children would bend over, the front one standing upright, while another child leapt onto the back of the *cuddy* ('donkey'), the aim being to seize the cap of the child standing at the front. Perhaps relatedly, *skin-the-cat* is a movement in gymnastics whereby a somersault is performed over the horizontal bar.

Skire Thursday Maundy Thursday, the day before Good Friday, often the occasion of a fair or market (for example, the one formerly held in Melrose). *Skire*, sometimes given as *Scarce*, means 'bright' or 'gaudy'.

Skirl-i'-the-pan or **skirlie** A dish of onions and oatmeal fried in dripping, similar to MEALIE PUDDING; or sometimes a kind of rissole. In this context *skirl* means 'sizzle'.

Skittery winter The last person to turn up for work on HOGMANAY, or sometimes the last person to leave. *Skittery* here means 'footering about', from *skite*, 'diarrhoea', but the sense of *winter* here is obscure, and may be deployed just for reduplicative effect.

Skulduggery The modern word arose in the later 19th century in the USA, and initially denoted political or financial trickery. The word appears to have derived from the Scots word *skulduddery* or *sculduddery*, first recorded as *sculdudry* in the 17th century, which means fornication, HOUGHMAGANDIE, etc., or obscene talk. The word seems to have been largely confined to tongue-in-cheek literary uses.

They are feared for this, and they are scrupulous about that, and they arena free to tell a lie, though it may be for the benefit of the city; and they dinna like to be out at irregular hours, and in a dark cauld night, and they like a clout ower the crown far waur; and sae between the fear o' God, and the fear o' man, and the fear o' getting a sair throat, or sair banes, there's a dozen o' our city-folk, baith waiters, and officers, and constables, that can find out naething but a wee bit skulduddery for the benefit of the Kirk treasurer.

– Sir Walter Scott, *The Heart of Midlothian* (1818), chapter xv

'Skye Boat Song, The' *See* OVER THE SEA TO SKYE.

Skyresburn or **Skairsburn warning** Any unpredicted catastrophe. The allusion is to the flash floods of the Skyre Burn, which rises on the slopes of Pibble Hill, Meikle Bennan and Stey Fell in Galloway, and flows southward into Fleet Bay.

The little village, or rather mill-town of Skyreburn affords one of the most exquisite little morsels of *burn-side scenery* to be found in Scotland … The burn itself is one of the most unequal and poetical temper. Deriving its waters from the bounteous bosom of a range of lofty hills, it is apt in case of showers to assume suddenly all the consequential airs of a large river, without regard to the good linen webs which may be bleaching, or the bairns that may be plucking gowans or pursuing butterflies on its verdant and copsy banks. This remarkable characteristic has occasioned the proverbial expression – 'Skairsburn Warning;' used throughout Galloway in case of any unexpected calamity.

– Robert Chambers, *The Picture of Scotland* (1827)

The phrase is apparently a Galwegian adaptation of an English expression, *Scarborough warning*. Although the origin of the latter is unknown, it may relate to the unstable coast at the Yorkshire port and resort, where the clifftops not infrequently topple into the sea without warning, carrying buildings with them.

Slain Men's Lea The site of a mass grave on Yarrow Water, near Newark Castle. The burials here followed the defeat on 13 September 1645 of the Royalist commander in Scotland, the Marquess of Montrose, by General David Leslie at Philiphaugh, a few miles downriver from Newark, towards Selkirk. Montrose's army of Highlanders and Irishmen were routed. Around 100 Irish soldiers surrendered, but were summarily executed, while some 300 Irish camp followers – 'boyes, cookes, and a rabble of rascals and women with their children in their arms' (according to a contemporary account by Gordon of Ruthven) – were rounded up, herded into the courtyard of Newark Castle, and shot – seemingly at the urging of zealous chaplains. After the massacre, walking ankle-deep in blood, Leslie seems to have been shocked at how far things had gone, and addressed the following words to the Revd John Nevay, minister of Newmilns: 'Mr John, have you not once gotten your fill of blood?' (Other sources suggest Leslie issued this rebuff after the massacre of 300 MacDonalds who had surrendered at Dunaverty Castle in 1647.) A century and half later, in 1810, while the foundations were being dug for a new school just to the south of Newark Castle, the skeletons of Leslie's victims were uncovered, and the field they lay in, in the 'dowie houms o' Yarrow', has been known ever since as Slain Men's Lea.

Slains Castle *See* DRACULA'S CASTLE.

Slàinte mhath A Gaelic toast, approximately pronounced *slange-vaa*, and broadly meaning 'good health'. It is often abbreviated to *Slàinte*, and is also used in Ireland.

He raised his glass, souked an inch or more out of it. '*Slainte.*' It was only recently that he'd learnt that this was Gaelic for 'health'. For years he'd said 'slange' thinking it was an obscure Scots term signifying 'Slam your drink down your throat and let's get another in.'

– James Robertson, *The Fanatic* (2000)

Slate diamonds Cubic crystals of iron pyrites (aka fool's gold), which are sometimes found in slate, especially that from the island of Easdale.

Slauchter, mutilation, fyre-raising, or utheris inconvenieties *See* GENTLEMEN ADVENTURERS OF FIFE, THE.

Slaughter of Lennox, the *See* MACGREGOR, PROSCRIPTION OF CLAN.

Sleep in, to To lie in, oversleep. Many Scots are surprised to learn that this is a Scotticism.

Sleep in one's shoes, to To die a violent death.

> The dreary eighteenth day of June
> Made mony a ane sleep in their shoon;
> The British blood was spilt like dew
> Upon the field of Waterloo.
> – George Muir, *The Clydesdale Minstrelsy* (1816)

Sleeping Warrior, the A nickname for the island of Arran, from the shape of its mountainous skyline as seen from the Ayrshire shore. Sometimes the name is restricted to the most northerly of the big peaks, Caisteal Abhail, with its infamous Witch's Step.

Sleepy mannies The bits of crystalline matter one sometimes finds in the corners of one's eyes when one wakes up.

Slender Drong, Slim Drong and Stumpy Drong See DRONGS, THE.

Slide on slummir, to An archaic poetical expression meaning to fall asleep (*slummir*, 'slumber'); an alternative is to *slide upon a sleip*.

Slim jim A confection consisting of a long strip of liquorice or coconut.

Slim Jim The nickname of the slender footballer Jim Baxter (1939–2001), regarded by many as Scotland's greatest-ever player. He won 34 Scottish caps between 1960 and 1967, and in the latter year was a key member of the team that beat England – then the world champions – during which game he famously played keepie-uppie with the ball. A left-footed midfielder, he began his senior career with Raith Rovers before joining Rangers, for whom he played from 1960 to 1965; this was followed by stints at Sunderland and Nottingham Forest, before he ended his career at Rangers in 1969–70. Baxter was also known as 'Gentleman Jim' (a nickname previously given to the US heavyweight boxer James J. Corbett, 1866–1933), perhaps alluding to the fact that while playing for Rangers he made a habit of befriending players from the club's arch-rivals,

Celtic. Baxter had the reputation as a heavy drinker, as well as something of a womanizer, and advised players to treat the ball like a woman: 'Give it a cuddle, caress it a wee bit, take your time, and you'll get the required response.' At his funeral in Glasgow Cathedral, Gordon Brown (a Raith Rovers fan) gave one of the readings, and there is a statue of Baxter in his birthplace, the village of Hill of Beath in Fife.

Slip-ma-laaber A Shetland expression for a work-shy, dishonest and unreliable person (*laaber, lauber,* etc., 'labour').

Slip the timmers, to A Northeastern expression, meaning to die (*timmers*, 'timbers').

Sloch, the The nickname of the village of Portessie in Moray, which is situated on a *sloch*, i.e. a rocky inlet.

Slogan A word of Scottish origin, deriving from the Gaelic *sluagh-ghairm*, 'war cry', from *sluagh*, 'army', and *gairm*, 'cry'. The word entered the English language in the 16th century. In the later 18th century the young literary forger Thomas Chatterton, in attempting to pass off his verses as medieval relics, misread the Gaelic as 'slughorn' – hence this line from *The Battle of Hastings* (1770): 'Some caught a slughorne and an onset wounde.' The following century Robert Browning deployed this fabulous instrument in 'Childe Roland to the Dark Tower Came' (1855):

> Dauntless the slug-horn to my lips I set,
> And blew.

See also CANT; GLAMOUR; JOCKEY.

Slorp and greet, to An onomatopoeic expression meaning to weep uncontrollably, with great gulps and sobs.

Sluagh, the In Gaelic culture, the Host of the Dead, the restless spirits of the unforgiven. These airborne wraiths, rejected by the Otherworld (or Heaven and Hell in the post-pagan dispensation) were likely to cause trouble; some said they would fly on the west wind into the houses of the dying in order to claim their souls as their own; hence the custom in some parts of keeping west-facing windows closed (though this was more likely done to shut out the prevailing wind). The whole notion has inspired considerable quantities of froth and whimsy amongst devotees of the Celtic Twilight:

> ... the mouth of the night is the choice hour of the *Sluagh*, the Host of the Dead, whose feet never touch on earth as they go drifting on the wind till the Day of Burning ...
> – Amy Murray, *Father Allan's Island* (1936)

It is none other than the Grey West Wind that brings in his train the Sluagh or Spirit-Multitude, by which the Western Highlands and Hebrides are visited from time to time. In a nebular state, the armies of the Spirit-Host, as it is sometimes called, hover above the places where, when in human form, the individuals composing it transgressed. These armies of the Sluagh manoeuvre in mid-air, where in seeming bewilderment and pother they fly hither and thither, until at length they come into conflict ...
> – Alasdair Alpin MacGregor (1899–1970), *The Peat-Fire Flame: Folk-tales and Traditions of the Highlands and Islands* (1947)

Sludge the Medium How Robert Browning characterized the Scottish spiritualist Daniel Dunglas Home (1833–86). Home, born in Currie, just west of Edinburgh, claimed that as an infant his cradle rocked by itself. He also claimed to be descended on his mother's side from a line of Highland seers, while his father, who worked in a paper mill, claimed to be the illegitimate son of the 10th Earl of Home. As a boy Home moved to America with his aunt and uncle, where the house they lived in was subjected to poltergeist-ish goings-on, leading to complaints from the neighbours and the expulsion of the young Home. Shortly afterwards, aged only 18, Home held his first séance, and proceeded to impress many in New England, though William Makepeace Thackeray, when he saw him in New York, dismissed his performance as 'dire humbug' and 'dreary and foolish superstition'. In 1855 Home set sail for Europe, where he took in a number of eminent persons, including the scientist David Brewster, the novelist Edward Bulwer-Lytton, the Emperor Napoleon III, Queen Sophia of the Netherlands and the poet Elizabeth Barret Browning. The latter's

husband Robert, however, thought the man an utter fraud, and in 1864 penned the dramatic monologue entitled 'Mr Sludge, "The Medium"', which begins:

> Now, don't, sir! Don't expose me!
> Just this once! This was the first and only time, I'll swear, –
> Look at me, – see, I kneel, – the only time,
> I swear, I ever cheated, – yes, by the soul
> Of Her who hears – (your sainted mother, sir!)
> All, except this last accident, was truth ...

Slug Road, the The pass via the A957 between Banchory and Stonehaven, also known simply as *the Slug*. The name has nothing to do with molluscs, but is from Gaelic *slochd*, 'deep hollow' (as in the name of the pass traversed by the A9 between the valleys of the Spey and the Findhorn).

Sma' drink Any weak alcoholic beverage; small beer. Hence to *think oneself nae sma' drink* is to have an inflated opinion of oneself, to consider oneself to be a big cheese.

> Our Johny's nae sma' drink you'll guess,
> He's trig as ony muir-cock,
> An' forth to mak a Deacon, lass;
> He downa speak to poor fock
> Like us the day.
> – Robert Fergusson, 'The Election' (1773)

In contrast, in Shetland an inhabitant of Scalloway is known as a *Scallowa' sma' drink*, presumably because Scalloway is significantly smaller than nearby Lerwick.

Smallest City in Scotland, the Perth, according to the awful old joke, 'because it lies between two inches'. The reference is to the parks known as the North Inch and the South Inch (from Gaelic *innis*, 'island', both parks being adjacent to the River Tay).

Sma' Shot Day A holiday in Paisley, held on the first Saturday in July. Its origins and name are explained as follows:

> Although the weavers dealt separately with the manufacturers for each piece of work, there were some general lists of rates to be maintained against the more selfish of the employers, and hence the Weavers' Trade

Union arose. Many a fierce struggle they had with the manufacturers, more or less successful. In one of these contests over what was called the 'sma' shot', they gained a notable victory, which they commemorated by instituting a holiday under the name of 'Sma' Shot Saturday'. The 'sma' shot', as already explained, was a binding thread not included in the design but necessary for making a perfect fabric. The masters did not wish to pay for this, but the weavers stoutly held to their demand and were successful. This holiday was instituted in 1856 and is still celebrated on the first Saturday of July, although 'sma' shots' are no longer used, or even understood in Paisley.

– Matthew Blair, *The Paisley Shawl and the Men who Produced It* (1904)

In fact, the first Saturday in July was already a holiday in Paisley, but the weavers renamed it to celebrate their victory. Sma' Shot Day was abandoned in 1975, but revived in 1986, since when the citizens have been summoned each year on the relevant day by the Charleston Drum, and then take part in marches, culminating in the burning of 'the Cork', an effigy of one of the despised manufacturers.

Smit, to get the *See* GET THE SMIT, TO.

Smith, Madeleine *See* NOT PROVEN.

Smoo Cave, devilish goings on in *See* WIZARD OF REAY, THE.

Smorin wi' the cauld, to be To be suffering (literally 'stifled, choked') with a nasty cold.

Smuggle the geg or **hide the geggie** A children's game in which the *geg* or *geggie* (an object such as a penknife or a ring, or even a lump of wood) is surreptitiously passed from member to member of one team, while the other team attempts to lay hold of it before the first team succeeds in taking the *geg* to the far end of the playing area.

Ye'll min' how, like birdies, we flew wi' our girdies,
Or play'd at 'kee-how', or at 'smuggle-the-gig'.
– W. Anderson, *Rhymes* (1851)

Snap an' rattle or **snappin' rattle** Oatcakes heated at the fire and crumbled into a bowl of milk.

Snaw aff a dyke, to go like To disappear very quickly, like snow from the top of a wall. Sometimes *ditch* is used instead of *dyke*.

Sneck A disparaging nickname for an Aberdonian, a *sneck* being an acquisitive, greedy person, from the verb *sneck*, 'snatch' or 'steal'.

Sneck, the A nickname of Inverness, being an abbreviation of the alternative nickname 'Inversneckie' or 'Inversnecky'. The latter was originally the name of a fictional Scottish town – based on Banchory – that appeared in the routines of the Aberdonian entertainer Harry Gordon (1893–1957), who became known as 'the Laird of Inversnecky'.

Snite someone's neb, to Literally, 'to pinch or pull someone's nose', i.e. to deflate someone's pretensions, or to snub or jeer at them. If one *snites* one's own nose, one blows it with one's finger and thumb – in relation to which, in his *Collection of Scots Proverbs* (compiled 1736), Allan Ramsay cites the following: 'He snites his nose in his neighbour's dish to get the brose tae himsell.' *Snite* appears to be cognate with 'snot', and as a noun, *snite* or *snot* can denote a small, contemptible person. While on the subject, a *snotter-dichter* or *snochter-dichter* is a handkerchief (*dicht*, 'to wipe'), and in some quarters the nose was formerly vulgarly referred to as the *snotter-box*, which was also applied to a useless, unkempt, disorderly person (also known as a *snotter-cap*).

Snood *See* SON OF THE BONES.

Snot collected at a dirty child's nose, resemblance to *See* BUBBLY-JOCK. For more on snot and snotter, *see under* SNITE SOMEONE'S NEB, TO.

Snows of Ben Wyvis, the The great plateau-topped mountain of Ben Wyvis, rising to 3431 ft (1046 m) to the northwest of Inverness, has long been known for its ability to hold snow, even into the summer. In 1767 James Robertson, a surveyor working for the Commissioners of the Forfeit Estates, made an ascent in June and reported: 'On the summit I was whitened by a fall of snow, and in many lower parts of the mountain it lay underfoot to a considerable depth.' In *The Picture of Scotland* (1828), Robert Chambers records that 'The top of Ben Wyvis was never known to be uncovered by snow till the memorably warm summer of 1826.' He continues:

> Sir Hector Munro of Foulis, the proprietor of Ben Wyvis, holds his estate in Ross-shire by a tenure from one of the early Scottish kings, binding him to bring three wain-loads of snow from the top of that hill whensoever his majesty shall desire.

More recently, various proposals to develop the mountain for skiing have come to nought. *See also* ETERNAL SNOWS OF BRAERIACH, THE.

Social-contract theory, Scottish origins of *See HADDINGTONUS SCOTUS.*

Society Men Members of various dissenting Presbyterian groups calling themselves 'Fellowship Societies' who rejected the Indulgence of 1679 and the Revolution Settlement of 1688. They overlapped with the CAMERONIANS.

Sodger-clad but major-minded An approving description of someone who is in a menial position (*sodger*, 'private soldier') but who has a great sense of responsibility and self-respect.

Soldier's Leap, the A rocky narrowing of the River Garry in the Pass of Killiecrankie, across which, during the Battle of Killiecrankie on 27 July 1689, a Williamite soldier called Donald MacBean is said to have jumped to escape his enemies. The distance is over 18 ft (5.5 m). *See also* MACGREGOR'S LEAP.

Solemn League and Covenant *See* COVENANTERS.

Solitudinem faciunt pacem appellant *See* MONS GRAUPIUS.

Some fowk like parritch, and some fowk like paddocks *See under* OATS, DR JOHNSON ON.

Some mair A phrase whose ambiguity when spoken may lead to unintended consequences, as in this story concerning a renowned proponent of poetry in Scots:

> Douglas Young, anxious to demonstrate the living quality of Scots, held up his empty beer glass and called to the barman, 'Some mair.' To everyone's astonishment, the barman presently came across carrying a long pole and pulled open an upper window.
> – Maurice Lindsay, *Thank You for Having Me* (1983)

See also PLASTIC SCOTS.

Son-afore-the-faither *See* FLORA CALEDONIA.

Song of the sea, the According to Walter Gregor's *Folk-Lore of the North-East of Scotland* (1881), 'Along the Moray Firth the fishermen call the noise of the waves "the song of the sea". If the song is towards the east the wind will shortly blow from east or south-east. If a "long song" is heard from the bar at Banff, the wind will blow from the west.'

Son of the Bones A child fathered on a living woman by the dead. Brian the Hermit, the pagan prophet in Scott's *The LADY OF THE LAKE*, is one such, and Scott derived the idea from an old manuscript written by the Laird of Macfarlane (subsequently edited by Sir Arthur Mitchell and published in 1906 for the Scottish Texts Society as *Macfarlane's Geographical Collection*). In this manuscript, Macfarlane recounts the paternity of *Gille Dubh mac 'Ille Chnàmhlaich*, the Black Child, Son of the Bones:

> The people report of a battell focht in old tymes, hard by thar Church [at Kilmallie, near Fort William], and how long after, hirds feeding ther cattell in that place, in a cold season, made a fyre of dead men's bones ther scattered, who being all removed except one mayd who took up her cloaths and uncovered hirself sum part here, a sudden whirlwind threw sum of the ashes in her privie member. Whereupon she conceaved and bore a sone called Gillie dowmak Chravolick, that is to say the black chyld sone to the bones, who after becam learned and relligious and built this Churche which now standeth in Kilmaillie.

Needless to say, Scott's account beats about the bush, merely recounting:

> His mother watched a midnight fold,
> Built deep within a dreary glen,
> Where scattered lay the bones of men

In some forgotten battle slain,
And bleached by drifting wind and rain.
    – Canto III, v

After this, she:

... ne'er again to braid her hair
The virgin snood did alive wear ...

(A *snood* was a hair-band with which young un-married women in Scotland and the north of England tied up their hair, denoting their virgin status.) Despite the fact that she is with child, she protests no man has touched her:

She said no shepherd sought her side,
No hunter's hand her snood untied.

But the involvement of the bones in the conception of Brian is left hazy.

Son of the manse or **daughter of the manse** The child of a minister of the Kirk, a *manse* being the house lived in by the minister of a parish (from medieval Latin *mansus*, 'ecclesiastical residence'). The phrase has apparently stumped many in Eng-land, at least according to the spoof news website, newsbiscuit.com, which posted the following story on 29 July 2007, a month after Gordon Brown, aka the MISERY FROM THE MANSE, had assumed the premiership:

Scotland's famous 'son of the manse' was apparently deeply disappointed yesterday as a Mori poll revealed that 89% of 18–55-year-olds had absolutely no idea what a 'son of a manse' was. Most respondents believed the phrase to mean 'a man whose father came from the Isle of Man', and 72% in the 18–30 bracket were sure it signified 'someone who has two dads'. Other respondents thought his Dad must have been someone famous called 'Themance' while one person had always presumed some sort of insect connection, based on a mis-hearing of 'son of them ants'.

Brown's father, the Revd John Ebenezer Brown, was a minister in Kirkcaldy, and the younger Brown later explained the influence of being brought up in a manse:

For me, my parents were – and their inspiration still is – my moral compass. The compass which has guided

me through each stage of my life. They taught me the importance of integrity and decency, treating people fairly – and duty to others.

Other notable sons or daughters of the manse include:

- **Douglas Alexander** (b.1967), Labour politician. His father Douglas N. Alexander was a minister in Bishop-ton, Renfrewshire, where Douglas Jnr played bugle in the Boys' Brigade band.
- **Wendy Alexander** (b.1963), aka BENDY WENDY, sister of the above, formerly Labour leader in the Scottish Parliament. In 2006 she told the *Herald* newspaper: 'The children of the manse grew up in an environment where building community is what's going on around your family life all the time.'
- **John Logie Baird** (1888–1946), inventor of the first working television system. His father, John Baird, was minister of the West Parish Church, Helensburgh.
- **Andrew Bonar Law** (1858–1923), Conservative poli-tician and the shortest-serving prime minister of the 20th century (23 October 1922–22 May 1923). His father, the Revd James Law, was an Ulsterman of Scottish descent who was a minister in the Free Church of Scotland in Canada.
- **John Buchan** (1875–1940), novelist, Unionist MP and governor-general of Canada. His father, also John Buchan, was a minister in the Free Church of Scotland in Perth, then Kirkcaldy. Contrary to expectations, the Revd Buchan eschewed WEE FREE Puritanism (although his wife did not), and would regale his family with Border ballads, both sung and played upon the penny whistle.
- **Captain William Kidd** (*c.*1645–1701), pirate. Accord-ing to tradition, he was born in Greenock, the son of a minister; however, the names of his parents are un-known.
- **Cosmo Gordon Lang** (1864–1945), Archbishop of Canterbury. His father, the Revd John Marshall Lang, was Church of Scotland minister in Fyvie, Aberdeen-shire. Cosmo himself was ordained as an Anglican priest in 1891.
- **Eric Liddell** (1902–45), aka the FLYING SCOTSMAN, rugby international and winner of the 400 metres at the 1924 Paris Olympics. He was born in China, where his father the Revd Dunlop Liddell was a missionary. He refused to compete in Paris in the 100 metres, his best event, because he would not run

on a Sunday. In later life Liddell himself became a missionary in China.

- **Sheena McDonald** (b.1954), broadcaster, who, writing in the *Herald* (18 August 2007), recalled: 'I'm told that as a toddler I would stand on the pew at the Sunday morning service and mimic the man in the pulpit – my father (William) – when he rose his arms to deliver the blessing to the congregation ... Today, colleagues can testify that I am no goody-goody or bible-basher or tub-thumper. I am rooted in my Presbyterian upbringing, which I think is always a lively Petri dish for societal contributions and responsibility. "Could do better" is a fact of life that I was brought up to interpret as an encouragement, since mortal perfection is unattainable.'
- **Lord Reith** (John Reith; 1889–1971), first director-general of the BBC. His father, Dr George Reith, was a minister of the United Free Church of Scotland (later reunited with the Church of Scotland) in Stonehaven. Reith Jnr took his strict Presbyterian convictions into his broadcasting career.
- **David Steel** (b.1938), Liberal Democrat peer, and formerly leader of the Liberal Party and presiding officer of the Scottish Parliament. His father, the Revd David Steel, was a minister in Kirkcaldy then Kenya, then Linlithgow, and served as Moderator of the General Assembly of the Church of Scotland in 1974–5.
- **Ena Lamont Stewart** (1912–2006), dramatist, author of plays such as *Men Should Weep* (1947), set in a Glasgow slum of the 1930s, and regarded as a landmark in the depiction of working-class life and gender issues.
- **David Tennant** (David John McDonald, b.1971), actor, whose roles have varied from Dr Who to Hamlet. He was brought up in Ralston, Renfrewshire, where his father, Sandy McDonald, was the Church of Scotland minister. The Revd McDonald also served as Moderator of the General Assembly of the Church of Scotland in 1997–8.
- **John Witherspoon** (1723–94), signatory of the American Declaration of Independence. His father, the Revd James Alexander Witherspoon, was minister at Gifford, East Lothian, and he followed his father into the Kirk, and emigrated to America in 1768 to become president of what later became Princeton University.

Son of the Parson The literal meaning of the name Macpherson (Gaelic *Mac a' Phearsain*). The parson in question was one Muriach, who held this position in Kingussie in Badenoch in the 12th century; in those days the parson was a lay figure, who looked after the Church's property.

Son of the Rock A native of Dumbarton or of Stirling, both noted for their castle-topped crags. The name is recorded from the 19th century. Dumbarton FC are nicknamed Sons of the Rock; *see* FOOTBALL CLUB NICKNAMES. *See also* KINGDOM OF THE ROCK.

Son of William A supporter of Glasgow Rangers FC. The allusion, of course, is to William of Orange, the Protestant hero. Female supporters are sometimes referred to as *Wilmas*. *See also* BILLY BOYS.

Sookie sweeties Boiled sweets, which require much *sooking*.

Soor-dook sodgers A nickname for the Royal Midlothian Yeomanry Cavalry in the mid-19th century. *Soor dook* ('sour dip') is buttermilk, alluding to the fact that many members of the militia were farmers.

Soor ploom A sour-tasting green boiled sweet, long associated with Galashiels. Soor plooms were supposedly first made in 1337 after a group of Galashiels men fell on a band of English raiders eating unripe plums, and killed them. The town's arms show a fox and a plum tree, together with the motto 'Sour Plums'. The incident was also apparently commemorated in an old song.

Soosider One who lives on the *Sooside* or South Side of the River Clyde in Glasgow, regarded as terra incognita by inhabitants of the city's West End.

Sooth-moother The Shetland term for an incomer, and thus the equivalent of the FERRY-LOOPER in Orkney. The term suggests someone who speaks with a southern accent, but the *Independent* (2 February 1991) suggests that incomers are so called because 'the P & O ferry from Aberdeen goes in through the south mouth of Lerwick harbour'. Apparently locals generally consider the term neutral, rather than derogatory.

Sordid race, a The people of Saltcoats, according to John Galt in *The Ayrshire Legatees* (1821).

Sore hand A jocular Glaswegian term for a jam sandwich, the white bread and red jam suggesting bandages and blood.

Sorra, the The Devil, aka *the Big Sorra* or *the Muckle Sorra* (*sorra*, 'sorrow').

Sorras tae seek, Ah've no got ma *See* AH'VE NO GOT MA SORRAS TAE SEEK.

Sosh or **Soshie, the** The Co-op (shop), the term (used in Dundee and Fife) being a back formation from Co-operative *Society*.

Souness, a drink called a The footballer Graeme Souness (b.1953), formerly of Liverpool and Rangers, was the subject of a joke by Tommy Docherty (aka the DOC):

> They serve a drink in Glasgow called a Souness – one half and you're off.

Sour Plums The motto of Galashiels; *see* SOOR PLOOM.

Sour, stingy, depressing beggars In his resumé of 'Foreigners Around the World' (published in *National Lampoon* in 1976), the American right-wing satirist P.J. O'Rourke has this to say of the Scots:

> *Racial characteristics*: sour, stingy, depressing beggars who parade around in schoolgirls' skirts with nothing on underneath. Their fumbled attempt at speaking the English language has been a source of amusement for five centuries, and their idiot music has been dreaded by those not blessed with deafness for at least as long.

Those who like this sort of PARTICULARLY DISAGREEABLE anti-Caledonian slop might also enjoy wallowing in TULLIETUDLESCLEUGH.

Sousider *See* SOOSIDER.

Soutar or **sutor** or **souter** The Scots word for a cobbler. In addition to the mountain known as the

COBBLER, there are a number of geomorphological soutars: the Soutar is a sea stack at Fast Castle, Berwickshire, while the steep headlands that guard the north and south side of the entrance to the Cromarty Firth are the Sutors of Cromarty. In *The Cruise of the Betsey* (1857) the geologist Hugh Miller tells how the Northern Sutor of Cromarty supposedly once bore a 'jewel in its forehead', a 'great diamond' like the CARBUNCLE OF WARD HILL on the island of Hoy:

> But the diamond has long since disappeared; and we now see only the rock. Unlike the carbuncle of Hoy, it was never seen by day; though often, says the legend, the benighted boatman has gazed, from amid the darkness, as he came rowing along the shore, on its clear beacon-like flame, which, streaming from the precipice, threw a fiery strip across the water; and often have the mariners of other countries inquired whether the light which they saw so high among the cliffs, right over their mast, did not proceed from the shrine of some saint or the cell of some hermit. At length an ingenious ship-captain, determined on marking its place, brought with him from England a few balls of chalk, and took aim at it in the night-time with one of his great guns. Ere he had fired, however, it vanished, as if suddenly withdrawn by some guardian hand; and its place in the rock front has ever since remained as undistinguishable, whether by night or by day, as the scaurs and clefts around it.

The residents of Selkirk in the Borders are collectively known as Souters, as the town was once known for its manufacture of light shoes (the inhabitants of Forfar are known as Souters for the same reason). The Souters of Selkirk are celebrated in a song heard at the annual common riding:

> It's up wi' the Souters o' Selkirk,
> An doun wi' the Earl o' Hume,
> An here's tae a' the braw laddies
> That weirs the single-soled shuin.
> It's up wi' the Souters o' Selkirk,
> For they are baith trusty an' leal,
> An up wi' the lads o' the Forest,
> An doun wi' the Merse [Berwickshire] tae the deil.

A somewhat different version of the above is quoted in James Hogg's story, 'The Souters of Selkirk':

Up wi' the Souters o' Selkirk,
An' down wi' the Earl o' Hume,
An' up wi' a' the brave billies
That sew the single-soled shoon!
An' up wi' the yellow, the yellow,
The yellow and green hae doon weel;
Then up wi' the lads of the forest,
But down wi' the Merse to the deil!

The civic pride of the souters is further elaborated in the local saying: 'A day oot o' Selkirk is a day wastit.' Part of the ritual on being made a freeman of the burgh of Selkirk involves *licking the birse*, i.e. licking cobbler's bristles, which on such ceremonial occasions are dipped in wine; a *lick-birse* is another name for a cobbler. *See also* SOUTER JOHNNIE.

Souter Johnnie A drinking buddy of Burns's TAM O' SHANTER:

And at his elbow, Souter Johnnie,
His ancient, trusty, drouthy crony:
Tam lo'ed him like a very brither;
They had been fou for weeks thegither.

The character was based on Burns's friend, the shoemaker (SOUTAR) John Davidson, whose cottage in Kirkoswald is preserved by the National Trust for Scotland as 'Souter Johnnie's Cottage'.

Sowans Formerly a staple dish, along with PORRIDGE and BROSE. It was made by soaking oat husks and *oatsiftins* (fine meal) in water for a week, straining it, then allowing it to ferment. The glutinous mush at the bottom was *sowans*, while the liquor was known as *swats*. The dish, in the form of 'butter'd So'ns', appears in the last verse of Burns's poem 'Halloween' (1785), the poet adding in a note that 'Sowens, with butter instead of milk to them, is always the Halloween Supper.' In the Northeast, sowans with cream played a special role on Christmas Eve (Old Style), which was known as *Sowans Nicht*. *Yule sowans*, like traditional Christmas pudding, would often contain charms such as rings and buttons, from which, if one found one in one's portion, one could supposedly divine the future, especially the identity of the person one was to wed. In *The Scots Kitchen* (1929), Marian McNeill notes

that during the Siege of Mafeking in the Second Boer War, a Scottish soldier was able to keep his companions alive by making sowans from the contents of the horses' feed box.

Sow of Atholl *See* BOAR OF BADENOCH.

Spaewife A female soothsayer or fortune-teller; a male fortune teller is a *spaeman*, and collectively they are *spaefolk*.

Heh, Sirs! what cairds and tinklers come,
An' ne'er-do-weel horse-coupers,
An' spae-wives fenzying to be dumb,
Wi' a' siclike landloupers ...
– Robert Fergusson, *Hallow-Fair* (1772)

These compounds come from the verb *spae*, 'to prophesy, tell fortunes', ultimately deriving from Old Norse *spá*.

The Harpy Celeno Spais onto ws a feirfull takin of wo.
– Gavin Douglas, *Aeneid* (1513), III.vi.28

Spam Valley A term applied to any area – such as Bearsden or Bishopbriggs – where the houses are so expensive that the inhabitants are supposed to have no money left for any food more expensive than spam.

Speak like a prent-buik, to Literally, 'to speak like a printed book', i.e. to talk with an air of authority, or in a pretentious or lah-di-dah fashion.

It's fearsome baith to see and hear her when she wampishes about her arms, and gets to her English, and speaks as if she were a prent book, let a-be an auld fisher's wife. But, indeed, she had a grand education, and was muckle taen out afore she married an unco bit beneath hersell.
– Sir Walter Scott, *The Antiquary* (1816), chapter 39

Spec, the The University of Edinburgh Speculative Society, a debating society established in 1764. Amongst its founders was Allan Maconochie, later Lord Meadowbank (known as LORD PRESERVE US); others who played a part included William Creech, John Bruce, and Henry Mackenzie. In Stevenson's unfinished novel *WEIR OF HERMIS-*

TON, young Weir opposes capital punishment in a debate at the Spec, to the fury of his father, a hanging judge. Stevenson himself had been a member, as was Sir Walter Scott, and, in more recent times, Sir Nicholas Fairburn. Hugh MacDiarmid penned a 'Celebratory Ode for the 200th Anniversary of the Speculative Society of Edinburgh', in which he said of the founders:

> They took three L's and founded us well
> On Law and Literature and Liquor.

Speel-the-wa' Literally, 'climb the wall', a name jocularly given in former times to cheap, low-quality whisky, so called, according to one Victorian commentator, 'from its tragic effect on the temperament'.

Spewin' or **spittin' feathers** Parched; in need of a pint.

Spider, Bruce and the *See* BRUCE AND THE SPIDER.

Spiders, the *See* FOOTBALL CLUB NICKNAMES.

Spit an' gie it ower or **spit an' gie up** Admit defeat; spitting on the ground was formerly a sign that one acknowledged that one had been outwitted. The expression is still current in the Northeast.

Spittin' feathers *See* SPEWIN' FEATHERS.

Spoiled Dyke, Battle of the *See* MASSACRE CAVE, THE.

Spook School *See* GLASGOW SCHOOL.

Sportspersons' nicknames *See:*

- BARRY BACKPASS aka Barry Ferguson Squarebaw
- The BIG MAN — Jock Stein
- BIG ECK — Alex McLeish
- The BROON FRAE TROON aka the Ayrshire Bull — Gordon Brown
- CESAR — Billy McNeill
- CHOCCY — Brian McClair
- The DOC — Tommy Docherty
- ELEPHANT MAN — David Dodds
- The FAMOUS FIVE — Eddie Turnbull, Gordon Smith, Bobby Johnstone, Lawrie Reilly and Willie Ormond
- The FIGHTING CARPENTER — Ken Buchanan
- The FLYING FLEA aka Jinky — Jimmy Johnstone
- The FLYING SCOTSMAN — (1) Eric Liddell, (2) Graeme Obree
- The GREAT WHITE SHARK — John Jeffrey
- ICEMAN — Stephen Hendry
- JAWS — Joe Jordan
- The JUDGE — Ally McCoist
- The KING aka the Lawman — Denis Law
- KING KENNY — Kenny Dalglish
- LASH — Peter Lorimer
- MIGHTY MOUSE — Ian McLauchlan
- The POCKET ROCKET aka Pot the Lot Dott — Graeme Dott
- SLIM JIM aka Gentleman Jim — Jim Baxter
- The TERRIBLE TRIO — Alfie Conn, Willie Bauld and Jimmy Wardhaugh
- TURNBULL'S TORNADOES — The Hibs team of the earlier 1970s
- WEE BUD — Willie Johnston
- The WIZARD OF WISHAW — John Higgins
- YOGI — John Hughes

Spring o' one's ane fiddle, a One's own way, as in 'He'll aye tak a spring o' his ane fiddle'. One can also *play oneself a spring*, with the same meaning. The expression is still current in Shetland. A *spring* is a lively dance, or dance tune; James Boswell recalls in his *Journal of a Tour to the Hebrides* that while on

Coll with Dr Johnson 'We had a spring from the piper at breakfast, at dinner, and at supper.'

Spune in ither folks' brose, to put one's To meddle in other people's business. *See also* THERE'S MAIR IN HIS HEID THAN THE SPUNE PITS IN.

Squadrone Volante An Italian naval expression meaning 'flying squadron', originally applied to a group of cardinals who in the 1650s sought to assert the independence of the papacy from the rival influences of France and Spain. The name was subsequently applied (perhaps originally by the anti-Union politician Andrew Fletcher of Saltoun) in the early years of the 18th century to the 'New Party', an aristocratic Whig faction in the Scottish Parliament, led by the Marquis of Tweeddale. The Scottish Squadrone dithered between the Jacobites and the government party, but in the end their votes proved crucial in securing the 1707 Union. The faction persisted as a power in Westminster politics until 1725, when they were dismissed from office after opposing Walpole's attempt to extend the malt tax to Scotland. As Alexander Murdoch has written in the *Dictionary of National Biography*, 'It could be said that the squadrone originated in an intention to do good during a period of crisis in Scottish public affairs, but instead most of its leadership did well.'

Squarebaw *See* BARRY BACKPASS.

Square go A fair, unarmed, one-to-one fight. The expression is current in the Glasgow area, and beyond.

Square sausage *See* LORNE SAUSAGE.

Squinty Bridge The nickname given to the road bridge across the Clyde in Glasgow between Finnieston and Govan. It was opened in 2006, and formally named the Clyde Arc. The nickname (perhaps more popular with journalists than the general public) refers to the way it crosses the river at an angle, and the eye shape formed by its single arch.

Squtlandiyah The name given by various medieval Arab geographers and historians, such as Ibn Said al-

Maghribi (1213–86), to the king of Scotland. In the *Kitab nuzhat al-mushtaq* (often translated as *A Diversion for the Man Longing to Travel to Far-Off Places*), the Arab geographer Muhammad al-Idrisi (1099–1165), who lived in Sicily at the court of King Roger II, asserts that Scotland 'is uninhabited and has neither town nor village'; there had, apparently, once been three towns, but the inhabitants had fought each other until nearly all were dead. The country is 'bathed on the west by the Sea of Darkness', and

> ... there come continually from that direction mists and rain, and the sky is always overcast, particularly on the coast. The waters of this sea are covered with cloud and dark in colour. The waves are enormous, and the sea is deep. Darkness reigns continually, and navigation is difficult. The winds are violent and towards the west its limits are unknown.

Stage Scotch *See* FAUX JOCKERY.

Staggies, the *See* FOOTBALL CLUB NICKNAMES.

Stairheid shandy Milk through which coal gas has been passed, giving the drink a sickeningly narcotic effect. A *stairheid* is the landing on each floor within a tenement close, and the gas was (long ago) obtained from the stairhead gas-lamps.

Stalag Luft Butlins A nickname for a former Butlins holiday camp on the Ayrshire coast, now the Haven Holiday Park known as Craig Tara, but which until the end of the Second World War was HMS *Scotia*, a Royal Navy base for training telegraph operators. The site was bought in 1946 by Sir Billy Butlin, and the following year it opened to holidaymakers, who apparently did not mind the barrack-like accommodation. It was taken over and completely rebuilt in 1998 by Haven Holidays.

> The karaoke bar is jumping. Packed to the gunnels with glamorous grannies, sozzled dads and quietly-sipping lads, the air is thick with smoke, hilarity and the scent of a hundred cheap perfumes. Children thread through the crowd – dominated by a mixed-sex coach-load of late 40-somethings clad in ill-fitting school uniforms – on a mission to beg more change for the slot machines while a moustachioed heavyweight in

stockings belts out Elvis's American Trilogy to raucous applause.

– Iain S. Bruce describes the camp as it is in the 21st century, in *The Sunday Herald*, 21 July 2002

Stalin's Granny The nickname of the Labour politician Helen Liddell (b.1950), so called on account of her hard-headed, tough-talking style. Other nicknames include 'Attila the Hen' and, because of her antipathy to the SNP, 'Nat Basher in Chief'. At the age of 26 she became General Secretary of the hornet's nest that is the Scottish Labour Party, and entered Parliament in 1994. She was Secretary of State for Scotland 2001–3. In 2005 she left Westminster to become High Commissioner in Australia (until 2009).

Standard, Battle of the *See* BATTLE OF THE STANDARD.

Standard Habbie, the *See* HABBIE.

Stang, riding the *See* RIDING THE STANG.

Stang o' the trump, the Literally, 'the tongue of a jew's harp', formerly applied figuratively in the Northeast to the liveliest and most outspoken person in a group.

Stank-dodger Literally 'drain avoider', a Glaswegian epithet for a person so slender that they might slip between the gratings of a drain cover, were it not for some nifty footwork.

Stap A dish from the Northern Isles involving the flesh of fish-heads boiled with chopped cod's liver, served seasoned. The word comes from Norse *stappa*, 'to mash or pound'.

Stark love and kindness *See* ROB GIB'S CONTRACT.

Starn or **stern o' the ee, the** The pupil of the eye (*starn*, 'star').

Star o' Dungyle, the 'The most beautiful woman in Galloway', according to John MacTaggart in his highly eccentric magnum opus, *The Scottish Gallo-vidian Encyclopaedia* (1824), a work that he alternatively entitles:

> The original, antiquated, and natural curiosities of the South of Scotland; containing sketches of eccentric characters and curious places, with explanations of singular words, terms and phrases; interspersed with poems, tales, anecdotes, &c. and various other strange matters; the whole illustrative of the ways of the peasantry, and manners of Caledonia; drawn out and alphabetically arranged.

Regarding the Star o' Dungyle, the author breathlessly continues:

> … her features ran exactly in the curve of exquisite beauty, and were always kept in the most enchanting animation; her eyes, her hair, her lips, were the most charming objects man could behold – they set the most callous a burning with love!

However, what MacTaggart proceeded to say about this woman, whom he identifies merely as a 'Miss H——', the daughter of a laird, was to cause the withdrawal of MacTaggart's great work within a year of its publication. For, says MacTaggart,

> … the good boxer or bruiser were the only persons who could get to speak to her, and she was always fonder of that class, than of well-bred rich-dressed gentlemen. In short, for all her beauty and elegance, the low and mean were her associates, and she cared not what length she went with them almost; would lay in barns with them at night, put on beggar weeds, and bade farewell to virtue altogether, and bore to some of them bastard children …

One of her heartbroken admirers, a blacksmith, was so bereft that he emigrated to Canada, only to receive a letter from Miss H—— 'inviting him to return to Galloway, and she would surely marry him'. However, when he did return, she 'disdained to look or speak to him', and went on to marry an old cattle dealer. Now, according to MacTaggart, 'her beauty hath entirely fled her', It was apparent to all in Galloway that Miss H—— was a certain Miss Heron, the daughter of the Laird of Inglestone, who threatened to sue, causing MacTaggart to withdraw his work. In a letter dated 24 August 1824, MacTaggart describes how his book 'kicked up a mighty fuss in Galloway, and some of the fiery natives there are determined on blowing out my brains'. He also had to put up with hostile reviewers, the *Scots Magazine* denouncing him as 'an obscene, drivelling blockhead', and expressing sympathy with the dominies who had thrashed MacTaggart so mercilessly at school: 'No one would submit to the laborious task of extinguishing vitality in such a mass of brute matter,' the reviewer opined, 'but from some high and benevolent motive.' Two years later MacTaggart went to Canada to work as a canal engineer, but returned after three years, dying in 1830 at the age of 32.

Starry rock *See* KIRRIEMUIR GINGERBREAD.

Star-Spangled Scotchman, the The sobriquet of Andrew Carnegie (1835–1919), the son of a Dunfermline weaver who emigrated to the USA in 1848. Carnegie himself went on (somewhat ruthlessly) to make a massive fortune out of steel. In 1884 William Black described him in *Harper's New Monthly Magazine* as:

> ... a shrewd and able Scotchman, who went to America a good many years ago, and achieved a fair enough competence there, which he modestly attributes, not to his own brains and business capacity, but to the excellence of republican institutions, toward which he is proportionately and warmly grateful ... The Star-Spangled Scotchman, as we have got to calling him, is abundant and even eager with all his information, and hath a pretty gift of eloquence ...

(The phrase 'Star-spangled' is of course borrowed from the US national anthem, 'The Star-Spangled Banner', the lyrics of which were written in 1814 by Francis Scott Key.) Carnegie became a prominent philanthropist, bestowing his benevolence both in the USA and in Scotland, especially his native Dunfermline, 'the most sacred place to me on earth'. He spent much of his later life at Skibo Castle in Sutherland.

Start, the The name given to Charles II's attempt in October 1650 to escape the COVENANTERS after the RACE OF DUNBAR, and to meet up with the Royalist Episcopalians in the Northeast. In two days the Covenanters had caught up with him in Glen Clova, and subsequently Charles was obliged to agree to various of their demands.

Starvation Dundas *See* HENRY THE NINTH.

Steamboats *See under* DRUNKENNESS.

Steamie A public washhouse, the place where one did one's laundry before the advent of the laundrette. Glasgow's first steamie opened on the banks of the Camlachie Burn on Glasgow Green in 1732. If something is *the talk of the steamie* it is much gossiped about. Tony Roper's celebrated play *The Steamie* (1987) is set in a Glasgow washhouse in the 1950s. *See also* WHERE DREAMS COME TRUE.

Steel, David *See* BOY DAVID, THE.

Steel bonnets A nickname for the BORDER REIVERS, alluding to their helmets. George MacDonald Fraser called his 1971 history of the reivers *The Steel Bonnets*.

Steelmen, the *See* FOOTBALL CLUB NICKNAMES.

Steenie An affectionate Scottish version of the first name Stephen, as in the character Steenie Steenson in Scott's 'Wandering Willie's Tale'. The name Steenie was famously bestowed by James VI and I on his favourite, George Villiers, Duke of Buckingham, the king alluding to St Stephen the Martyr in Acts 6:15:

> And all that sat in the council, looking stedfastly on him, saw his face as it had been the face of an angel.

Stevenson's Yew A tree in the garden of Colinton Manse, Edinburgh. Robert Louis Stevenson's grandfather was the minister at Colinton, and Stevenson spent much time here as a young boy. The marks on the bark where a swing was hung from the branches can still be seen.

> Under the circuit of its wide, black branches, it was always dark and cool, and there was a green scurf over all the trunk among which glistened the round, bright drops of resin.
> – Robert Louis Stevenson, *Memories and Portraits* (1885), 'The Manse'

Stewartry, the A former name for Kirkcudbrightshire, also known as the Stewartry of Kirkcudbright, and now part of Dumfries and Galloway. As a generic term, a 'stewartry' was the equivalent of a county, and denoted an area administered by a steward – as happened in the early 14th century when the Balliol lands of eastern Galloway were brought under the control of a royal steward. Orkney and Shetland were also constituted as 'stewartries' from the late 18th to the early 20th centuries. *See also* SHIRE, THE.

Stickit minister A minister who has been unable to gain a living, either through failure to achieve the necessary qualifications, or by delivering an unsatisfactory probationary sermon. *Stickit* denotes 'stuck', i.e. unable to complete a job, speech or other project.

> He became totally incapable of proceeding in his intended discourse, and was ever after designated as a 'stickit minister'.
> – Sir Walter Scott, *Guy Mannering* (1815), chapter ii

The expression gave S.R. Crockett the title of his 1893 novel *The Stickit Minister*. Other occupations – such as those of shopkeeper or teacher or doctor – also have those who are said to be *stickit*.

Stick oot like a pot fit, to *See* POT FIT.

Sticks and staves, all to In a complete state of ruination and destruction; utterly, absolutely.

Sticky Willie *See* FLORA CALEDONIA.

Stinking Billy *See* BUTCHER CUMBERLAND.

Stinky Bay The local nickname for Poll-na-Crann beach on the west coast of Benbecula, near Griminis, so-called because of the large mounds of rotting seaweed along the shore.

Stirling the Venetian The byname of the mathematician James Stirling (1692–1770), son of Archibald Stirling of Garden in Stirlingshire. After being expelled in 1715 from Oxford University on account of his Jacobite sympathies, he made his way to Venice, where he set himself up as a professor of mathematics. Around ten years later he was obliged to flee the city (with the help of Isaac Newton),

having been threatened with assassination after discovering a trade secret of the Venice glassmakers. After a decade in London, he became manager of the Scots Mining Company in Leadhills, Lanarkshire, and later undertook a survey of the Clyde, prior to the dredging of that river, which made Glasgow into one of the world's greatest ports.

Stitch stone A curative charm, described here by the Revd Kenneth Macdonald of Applecross, Wester Ross:

> The stitch-stone was a charm supposed to give relief in cases of severe pain from sciatica up to acute pleurisy. It was common property, and always kept by the person who used it last till required by another. The last specimen of which I heard about 30 years ago was in Erradale, parish of Gairloch. Mr Matheson, FC [Free Church] minister, got hold of it and took it to the pulpit one day. At the close of the service he held it up before the congregation, remarking that the god of Erradale was the smallest god of which he had ever heard or read. It was a small piece of flint stone, 3 or 4 in. long, found on the shore and highly polished by the action of the waves … Mr Matheson broke it in their presence, and yet no dire results followed.
> – Kenneth Macdonald, *Social and Religious Life in the Highlands* (1902)

Stoat-the-baw Literally, 'bounce the ball', a Glaswegian term for a paedophile, seen as patting children's heads in the same way as one might bounce a ball.

Stonehaven Fireballs Festival, the *See* FIREBALLS, THE.

Stone o' Scar *See* SAVILLE STONE, THE.

Stone of Scone, the The traditional coronation stone of Scottish monarchs, formerly kept at Scone, near Perth. It is also known as *the Stone of Destiny*, and in Gaelic as *An Lia Fàil*. It comprises a rectangular block of red sandstone, inscribed with a simple cross. Geological analysis has shown that the stone was quarried near Scone, which rules out the various legends outlined below as to its overseas origins.

According to one legend, the stone provided

Jacob with a pillow when he dreamt of the angels on their ladder (Genesis 28:11), hence it is sometimes referred to as *Jacob's Stone*. According to this tradition, the stone was given to a Celtic king when he married the daughter of an Egyptian pharaoh, and so ended up at Tara in Ireland around 700 BC, where it was used for the coronations of the High Kings. When Scots from Ireland established the kingdom of DALRIADA in Argyll, they brought the stone with them, keeping it first at their capital Dunadd, then at Dunstaffnage Castle. It was said that if anyone other than the rightful king sat on the stone, it would 'groan aloud as with thunder'. When Kenneth MacAlpin defeated the Picts to unify Scotland in the mid-9th century, he took the stone to Scone, which had been the Pictish capital. Thereafter every Scottish king was crowned while sitting on the stone at Scone until Edward I of England invaded in 1296 and took the stone back to London, placing it under the Coronation Chair in Westminster Abbey as a symbol of his overlordship. By the terms of the SHAMEFUL PEACE of 1328, the stone was to be returned to Scotland, but incensed Londoners prevented its removal from Westminster Abbey, where it duly remained.

When James VI of Scotland became James I of England, he fulfilled an old Latin prophecy regarding the stone:

Ni fallat fatum, Scoti quocunque locatum
Inveniunt Lapidem, regnare tenentur ibidem.

Sir Walter Scot rendered these lines as:

Unless the fates be faulty grown
And prophet's voice be vain
Where'er is found this sacred stone
The Scottish race shall reign.

The stone's continuing residence in England proved a provocation to Scottish national sentiment. To rectify matters, early on Christmas morning in 1950 a group of four Scottish students removed the stone from Westminster Abbey and smuggled it back to Scotland, where, on 11 April 1951, it was found on the altar of Arbroath Abbey – thus symbolically reaffirming the DECLARATION OF ARBROATH. The stone was returned to London, but in 1996 the Westminster government agreed that between coronations it should be kept in Edinburgh Castle.

Stookie Sunday Formerly, the Sunday at the culmination of harvest when all the corn had been gathered into *stooks* – collections of sheaves set up to dry in the fields. On Stookie Sunday in southern Lanarkshire, the locals would climb that fine viewpoint Tinto to survey the progress of harvest across the neighbourhood. Stooks, and Stookie Sunday with them, disappeared with the advent of the combine harvester.

Stool of repentance The stool in the kirk on which those found guilty of fornication (*see* FORNICATION ... BUT A PASTIME) were obliged to sit during Sunday service, sometimes every week for six months. In his *Itinerary* (1617), the English traveller Fynes Morison describes the sinners' seat in St Giles Kirk in Edinburgh:

In this church the king's seat is built some few stairs high of wood, and leaning on the pillar next to the pulpit, and opposite to the same, is another seat very like it, in which the incontinent use to stand to do penance; and some few weeks past a gentleman, being a stranger, and taking it for a place where men of better quality use to sit, boldly entered the same in sermon-time, till he was driven away by the profuse laughter of the common sort, to the disturbance of the whole congregation.

The stool of repentance was also known as the *creepie* (a general term for a low, three-legged stool), *cutty chair* (i.e. short chair) or *cutty stool*, or *black stool*. Burns and his paramour Jean Armour (the BELLE OF MAUCHLINE) were obliged to mount the stool after her pregnancy became known.

When I mount the creepie-chair,
Wha will sit beside me there?
Gie me Rob, I'll seek nae mair –
The rantin dog, the daddie o't!
– Robert Burns, 'The Rantin Dog' (1790)

The bonniest lass that ye meet neist
Gie her a kiss an a' that,
In spite o ilka pairish priest,
Repentin stool, an a' that.
– 'The Bonniest Lass', from The MERRY MUSES OF CALEDONIA

Dean E.B. Ramsay, in his *Reminiscences of Scottish Life and Character* (1862), recalls the case of a young woman obliged to sit upon the cutty stool in St Andrews. When asked who the father of her child was, she responded: 'How can I tell, amang a wheen o' Divinity students?'

Stoor Worm, the *See* MESTER STOOR WORM.

Stop the world, Scotland wants to get on The words with which Winnie Ewing (aka MADAME ECOSSE) greeted her election as an SNP MP in the 1967 Hamilton by-election. Ewing later gave the title *Stop the World* to her autobiography. Ewing's slogan played on *Stop the World – I Want to Get Off*, the title of a musical by Leslie Bricusse and Anthony Newley (1961; film version 1966). *See also* CHILL LOOKING FOR A SPINE TO RUN UP, A.

Storm-damaged Having a few slates missing, i.e. somewhat simple or slightly mad.

Stourie lungs *See under* DISEASES.

Stout hert against a stey brae, to set a To face adversity with determination and equanimity (*stey brae*, 'steep hill').

> In cart or car thou never reestet;
> The steyest brae thou wad hae fac't it;
> Thou never lap, an' sten't, an' breastet,
>   Then stood to blaw ...
> – Robert Burns, 'The Auld Farmer's New-Year-Morning
>   Salutation to his Auld Mare, Maggie' (1786)

Straight-oot-the-gate An Orkney description of someone who tells it like it is.

Strathaven A Lanarkshire town whose pronunciation is best demonstrated by the following limerick:

> There once was a woman from Strathaven
> Who had as a pet a small rathaven.
>   Although small it was strong
>   And when she did wrong
> It knocked her down flat on the pathaven.

The town is celebrated for *Strathaven toffee*, a confection that appears to be a cross between tablet and toffee, like tablet that has been heated too long and becomes almost as chewy as toffee, but not as hard.

Strathclyde, Kingdom of *See* KINGDOM OF THE ROCK, THE

Strathearn, the Flower of *See* FLOWER OF STRATHEARN, THE.

Strathspey A stately Scottish country dance, with steps similar to the HIGHLAND FLING and the reel, but at a slower pace. The earliest records are from the mid-18th century. It takes its name from the broad valley of the River Spey. Numerous tunes have been composed to accompany the dance, traditionally played on the fiddle. They are in four-four time, and usually deploy the rhythmic figure known as the SCOTCH SNAP.

String, the The nickname of the B880, the road that cuts across the hills of Arran along Glen Shurig and Gleannan t-Suidhe between Brodick on the east coast and Blackwaterfoot on the west coast. The road was built by Thomas Telford in 1817, and viewed from out at sea is said to resemble a length of string.

Strip the Willow A popular and straightforward Scottish country dance in jig time, involving much lively spinning of one's partner on one's arm – presumably thought to be akin to stripping the twigs off the side of a willow wand.

> But then Chae cried Strip the Willow, and they all lined up, and the melodeon played bonnily in Chae's hands, and Long Rob's fiddle bow was darting and glimmering, and in two minutes, in the whirl and go of Strip the Willow, there wasn't a cold soul in Blawearie barn.
> – Lewis Grassic Gibbon, *Sunset Song* (1932)

Stroma Pirates, the The nickname for those enterprising inhabitants of the Pentland Firth island of Stroma who boosted their income by specializing in informal salvage operations from the many wrecks that ended up in their waters. Given the wildness of the seas hereabouts, such operations required great feats of seamanship. One of the richest hauls was from the *Pennsylvania*, which came to grief on the west side of the small neighbouring island of Swona in July 1931, en route from America to Copenhagen. The loot is said to have included toys, prams, slot-machines, furniture, sewing machines, watches, ladies' underwear, food, tobacco, typewriters, condoms, a piano and two Cadillacs. The Stroma men proved adept at hiding their booty around the island from customs officials, policemen, coastguards and the Receiver of Wrecks, squirrelling away their trophies in caves and peat stacks and lochs – even under the font in the island's Baptist church. Meanwhile, should the authorities pay a visit, the women of Stroma would attempt to bamboozle them by rushing hither and thither with suspicious looking bundles, often containing innocuous items such as a bag of potatoes, a sack of oatmeal or a baby, but occasionally concealing some genuine loot. One former islander recalls:

> The Stroma pirates, they call them, but they were no pirates in any way. My father never locked the door, nobody ever locked their doors, there was nothing ever under lock and key. But if a ship went ashore, and they thought there was a boat at the bottom of the sea, by jings they would work hard to salvage what they could from the wreck – and quite rightly so. I suppose it was a great provocation for an island to see all these things. These wrecks lasted a couple of days, and then it all went to the bottom of the sea, and nobody got any benefit.
> – James Simpson, quoted in Bella Bathurst, *The Wreckers* (2005)

Stroma's last permanent inhabitants left the island in the early 1960s.

Stronsay Beast, the *See* SEA SERPENTS.

Struan Michael A special cake (Gaelic *srúan*) formerly baked in the Hebrides for Michaelmas (29 September). Martin Martin, in his *Description of the Western Isles of Scotland* (1703), gives the following account:

> They were prepared somewhat after this fashion. The first sheaves of the harvest were taken, dried and ground into meal with the quern. Then the housewife took some eggs, butter and treacle, mixed them up, and into the mixture put the new meal, making a dough. On the stone slab forming her hearth-stone she put some red-hot peats, and when sufficiently heated, swept it clean. On this the dough was placed to cook with an inverted pot over it. During the process of cooking, it was often basted with beaten eggs, forming

a custard-like covering. Finally, after the cake was cooked, a small piece was broken off and cast into the fire. Why? you will ask. Well, as an offering to the *Donas*, or old Hornie, or whatever may be the correct designation of that presiding genius whom we are led to believe inhabits the fiery regions. The housewife did this in order to safeguard herself and her household against the Evil One. After reserving some of the *Struan* for the use of the household, she went round the neighbours in triumph and gave them a bit each, there being usually a great rivalry as to who should be the first to grind the new meal and get the *Struan* ready. The first to do so was generally understood to have the best crops through the coming year.

Struan Michaels were also called *St Michael's bannocks*.

Sub crawl *See* CLOCKWORK ORANGE, THE.

Subtle Doctor, the *See* DOCTOR SUBTILIS.

Suckie *See* SAUCHIEHALL STREET.

Sufferin General, the A jocular nickname for Glasgow's Southern General Hospital.

Suicides The Revd Kenneth Macdonald, for many years Free Church minister at Applecross in the later 19th century, recounted that in Wester Ross it was believed that drinking from the skull of a suicide cured epilepsy. He went on to elaborate on other beliefs concerning those who have taken their own lives:

> Two years ago a man from Shieldaig declared that he used the skull himself for that purpose, and that he knew where it was kept. They [i.e. the suicides] had to be buried in some hole in a hill out of the sight of the sea. If his grave could be seen from the sea it was supposed to be enough to drive all fish from the coast. So strong was this belief that cases are on record in which the remains of suicides which had been buried by their friends in their own burying-ground were exhumed by the neighbours and removed to a spot hidden out of the sight of the sea. And yet by some perversity of human nature the withered skull of a suicide is supposed to be a blessing to mankind.
> – Kenneth Macdonald, *Social and Religious Life in the Highlands* (1902)

Macdonald also describes another cure for epilepsy:

> A live snake was caught and placed in a bottle, which was then filled with pure water and corked. After standing for a short time, the infusion was given to the patient, who was kept ignorant of the nature of the drug.

For yet another supposed cure, *see* LIVE BURIAL.

Summer has leaped suddenly upon Edinburgh like a tiger The opening sentence of *A Summer in Skye* (1865) by Alexander Smith (1830–67). Despite the total implausibility of such a meteorological occurrence, the line was praised by Sir Harold Hobson as 'the perfect opening sentence'.

> Summer has leaped suddenly upon Edinburgh like a tiger. The air is still and hot above the houses; but every now and then a breath of east wind startles you through the warm sunshine – like a sudden sarcasm felt through a strain of flattery – and passes on detested of every organism. But, with this exception, the atmosphere is so close, so laden with a body of heat, that a thunderstorm would be almost welcomed as a relief. Edinburgh, on her crags, held high towards the sun – too distant the sea to send cool breezes to street and square – is at this moment an uncomfortable dwelling-place. Beautiful as ever, of course – for nothing can be finer than the ridge of the Old Town etched on hot summer azure – but close, breathless, suffocating. Great volumes of white smoke surge out of the railway station; great choking puffs of dust issue from the houses and shops that are being gutted in Princes Street. The Castle Rock is grey; the trees are of a dingy olive; languid 'swells', arm-in-arm, promenade uneasily the heated pavement; water-carts everywhere dispense their treasures; and the only human being really to be envied in the city is the small boy who, with trousers tucked up, and unheeding of maternal vengeance, marches coolly in the fringe of the ambulating shower-bath. Oh for one hour of heavy rain! Thereafter would the heavens wear a clear and tender, instead of a dim and sultry hue. Then would the Castle Rock brighten in colour, and the trees and grassy slopes doff their dingy olives for the emeralds of April. Then would the streets be cooled, and the dust be allayed. Then would the belts of city verdure, refreshed, pour forth gratitude in balmy smells; and Fife – low-lying

across the Forth – break from its hot neutral tint into the greens, purples, and yellows that of right belong to it. But rain won't come; and for weeks, perhaps, there will be nothing but hot sun above, and hot street beneath; and for the respiration of poor human lungs an atmosphere of heated dust, tempered with east wind.

A likely story. A more sober account of the capital's climate was offered by Robert Louis Stevenson in his 1878 essay 'Edinburgh':

> Edinburgh pays cruelly for her high seat in one of the vilest climates under heaven. She is liable to be beaten upon by all the winds that blow, to be drenched with rain, to be buried in cold sea fogs out of the east, and powdered with the snow as it comes flying southward from the Highland hills.

Summerisle The fictional, pagan-infested Hebridean island that forms the setting of the cult 1973 horror film, *The Wicker Man*, starring Edward Woodward, Christopher Lee and Britt Ekland. It was in fact filmed in the village of Dundrennan near Kirkcudbright, which now hosts an annual Wickerman Festival.

Sumptuary laws Like many other nations in the later medieval and early modern periods, Scotland had laws restricting conspicuous consumption, whether relating to dress or food, and what one was allowed depended on one's rank. An act of the Scottish Parliament of 1551, for example, limited archbishops, bishops and earls to no more than eight 'dischis of meit' at any one meal; abbots, lord priors and deans could have no more than six; barons and freeholders were limited to four; while burgesses and other 'substantious' men were allowed just three, 'and bot ane kind of meit in everie dische'. Sometimes the motive behind such laws was as much economic as puritanical. For example, in 1672, as money drained out of the country to pay for imported luxuries, Parliament passed an act to prevent people (below a certain rank) wearing gold or silver in their dress, or lace or 'any flowered stuffs, striped stuffs, or brocadoes of silk', and so on and so on. As elsewhere, such laws were no doubt more honoured in the breach than the observance.

Sundials Only of occasional use.

'Sunshine on Leith' The title track of the 1988 album of the same name by the Proclaimers, the music duo comprising the identical twin brothers, Charlie and Craig Reid, who were born in Leith in 1962. The brothers are staunch supporters of Hibernian FC, and 'Sunshine on Leith' has become the club's theme song, played at every home match. Another song on the album, 'I'm Gonna Be (500 Miles)', has become a popular Scottish anthem, heard when Scotland's national football side play a game.

Super Cally Go Ballistic, Celtic Are Atrocious The headline with which *The Sun* gleefully greeted Inverness Caledonian Thistle FC's victory over Celtic in 2000 in the Scottish Cup, masterfully playing on 'supercalafragilisticexpialidocious', the magic word from *Mary Poppins*.

Superincontinent yokel with a gift for metricism, a *See* PLOUGHMAN POET, THE.

Supernatural beings, places and associated phenomena The reader is referred to the following entries:

- BANSHEE
- BIG BOO MAN, the
- BLUE MEN OF THE MINCH, the
- BODHISATTVA OF THE CAIRNGORMS, the
- BOGLE
- BOOBRIE, the
- BROWNIE
- DANDY DOCTOR, THE
- DOBBIE
- DRACULA'S CASTLE
- EARL BEARDIE
- EILDON TREE, the
- ELFAME
- 'The elfin knight'
- EOGHAN OF THE LITTLE HEAD
- ERTH HUNS
- EYNHALLOW (home of the Fin Folk)
- FAIRIES O' CARLOPS
- FAIRY BOY OF LEITH, the
- FATLIPS
- FORESTER OF THE FAIRY CORRIE, the
- GOATS, SUPERNATURAL
- GOLDEN HORSE OF LOCH LUNDIE, the
- GORBALS VAMPIRE, the
- GREEN LADY, the
- GREY MAN OF BEN MACDUI, the
- GUID FOLK, the
- HOGBOON
- HORSE AND HATTOCK
- KELPIE
- LAIMH DEARG
- LAVELLAN
- LITTLE FOLK, the
- MERMAID OF BENBECULA, the
- MERMAID OF GALLOWAY, the
- MERMAID OF KNOCKDOLIAN CASTLE, the
- MERMAID OF PORT GLASGOW, the
- MERMAID OF SANDWOOD BAY, the
- MERMAIDS OF THE RIVER DEE, the
- MERMAN OF KINTYRE, the
- MESTER STOOR WORM
- NUCKELAVEE
- REDCAP
- RED ETIN, the
- SEA MITHER
- SEA SERPENTS
- SHELLYCOAT
- SHORT-HOGGERS OF WHITTINGEHAME
- SILKIE FOLK
- *SLUAGH*, the
- SON OF THE BONES
- THRUMMY CAP
- TROW
- WAG-AT-THE-WA'
- URISK
- WATER COW
- The White Lady of Corstorphine (*see under* CORSTORPHINE SYCAMORE, THE)
- WHUPPITY STOURIE
- WORRICOW

Swabians In Bavaria they say that their westerly neighbours, the Swabians, were thrown out of Scotland as they were too mean even for the Scots.

Swallow A bird once associated with the Devil; *see under* ROBIN.

Swan of Closeburn, the A story associated with the Kilpatricks of Closeburn, in Dumfriesshire, whose crest was a swan's head and neck. Closeburn Castle, built by a small loch, dates to the early 13th century, and by tradition when a pair of swans arrived at the loch, it would herald the miraculous recovery of a sick Kilpatrick. Some time around the 15th century, a certain Robert Kirkpatrick, sceptical of this belief, shot one of the swans with a crossbow. He died soon after, and from that time the appearance of a single white swan with a bloodstain on its breast heralds the death of a head of the Kilpatrick family. The loch was drained in the 19th century.

Swearing Something the Scots have always excelled at, to judge by a law of 1551:

> Item becaus nochtwithstanding the oft and frequent prechingis in detestatioun of the grievous and abominabill execratiounis and blasphematiounis of the name of God, sweirand in vain be His precius bluid, bodie, passioun, and woundis, Devill stick, Cummer gar roist or ryse thaim, and sic utheris ugsome aithis and execratiounis againis the command of God, yit the samyn is cum in sic ane ungodly use amangis the pepil of this realm, baith of greit and small estaitis, that dailie and hourlie may be herd amang thaim opin blasphematiounis of Goddis name and majestie ...

See also JINGS, CRIVENS, HELP MA BOAB.

Sweet Afton Robert Burns thus apostrophized Afton Water, a tributary of the Nith in South Ayrshire:

> How lofty, sweet Afton, thy neighbouring hills,
> Far mark'd with the courses of clear, winding rills;
> There daily I wander as noon rises high,
> My flocks and my Mary's sweet cot in my eye.

The Mary in question was Burns's beloved Mary Campbell, who died in 1786 before they could fulfil their plan to emigrate to Jamaica (*see* HIGHLAND MARY). The fame of the song resulted in various townships in the USA taking the name Afton, while 'Sweet Afton' was subsequently adopted as the name of a brand of cigarettes.

Sweetheart Abbey A ruined Cistercian abbey in Kirkcudbrightshire, founded in 1273 by Devorgilla, widow of John Baliol, the last Celtic lord of Galloway, and mother of the John Balliol who was to be Edward I's nominee for the throne of Scotland (*see* TOOM TABARD). The name of the abbey relates to the story that when her husband died in 1268, Devorgilla kept his casket-enclosed heart with her at all times, and when she dined would give it a place beside her at table, and spread dishes before it, which, left uneaten, would be donated to the poor. The story was related in the early 15th century by Andrew of Wyntoun in his *Orygynale Cronykil of Scotland*:

> Quhen the Baliol, that wes her lord
> Spousit, as ye heard record,
> His saul sent til his Creatour,
> Or he wes laid in sepelture,
> Scho gart open his bodie tyte
> And gart his hert be tane out quyte.
>   With spicerie weil savorand,
> And of kind weil flavorand,
> That ilk hert then, as men said,
> Scho balmit, and gart it be laid
> Intil a coffin of ivoir
> That scho gart be maid thairfoir,
> Enamelit and fitly dicht,
> Lockit and bunden with silver bricht.
>   And alway quhen scho yeid til meit
> That coffin scho gart by her set
> And til her lord, as in presens,
> Ay to that scho did reverens.
>   And thair scho gart set, ilka day,
> As wont befoir hir lord wes ay,
> Al the coursis, coverit weil,
> Into silver bricht veschel,
> Brocht fra the kitchen, and thair set.
> Quhen scho maid hir to rise fra meit,
> All thir courses scho gart then
> Be tane up and delit til puir men ...
>   This scho cessit nevir to do
> Quhile livand in this warld was scho.
>   [*scho*, 'she'; *gart*, 'made'; *yeid*, 'went'; *meit*, 'food, meal']

When Devorgilla died in 1289 she was buried before the altar of the abbey church with the casket placed upon her breast, and thereafter 'New Abbey' became known as 'Sweetheart Abbey'.

Devorgilla's name is commemorated in Devorgilla's Bridge across the River Nith in Dumfries, one of the oldest standing bridges in the country. The present stone structure largely dates from the early 17th century (although it may incorporate the remains of a 15th-century structure), but the first bridge, built of wood, is thought to have been constructed on Devorgilla's instructions in the 1260s.

Sweetie Sandie *See* EDINBURGH ROCK.

Sweetie-wife An itinerant seller of gingerbread, confectionery, etc. Such women must have made a reputation as carriers of news from place to place, as the term came to be applied to a gossip of either sex.

Sweet Singers, the A small but fanatical sect of COVENANTERS, whose leader was a ship's master from Bo'ness called John Gibb (d.1720?) – hence their other name, the Gibbites. Gibb, whose powerful build earned his the nickname 'Meikle John', may have acquired his extreme views from Anabaptists in the Netherlands, where he made a number of voyages, carrying correspondence between ejected ministers in Scotland and their exiled brethren. In 1680, learning that the authorities were about to arrest him, he went underground. Rejecting even such radicals as Donald Cargill as traitors to the cause, Gibb gathered a small group of followers around him, comprising twenty-six women and three men, who acquired the name Sweet Singers on account of their doleful renderings of the psalms, in which they found a parallel between the tribulations of ancient Israel and the woeful fate of the Church in Scotland. Rejecting worldly authority and private property, the Sweet Singers went up into the Pentland Hills to await God's justice in the form of the imminent destruction of the City of Edinburgh by fire and tempest. Even the conventiclers of Galloway condemned Gibb as the Devil in disguise, while Cargill described Gibb's sect as 'fanatics with demented enthusiastical delusions'. The Sweet Singers withdrew to the wild moors between the Pentlands and Tweeddale, praying and fasting and refusing to do any manual labour, which they saw as the work of the Anti-Christ. Gibb, who seems to have possessed considerable sexual magnetism, took the name King Solomon, and gave his followers Old Testament names such as Deborah, Lidiah, and the Queen of Sheba. On one occasion he saw off at pistol point several of his followers' husbands, who had come to reclaim their wives. In May 1681 the government sent troops to round up Gibb and his followers. The Duke of York, Charles II's viceroy in Scotland, opined that they deserved bedlam rather than the gallows, and Gibb himself, who seems to have suffered a complete mental breakdown, denounced his own former 'disloyal principles'. He was sentenced to transportation, and in 1684 sailed for America, where he spent the rest of his days.

Swelkie, the A tidal race and associated whirlpool to the north of the island of Stroma in the Pentland Firth. The name comes from Old Norse *svalga*, 'the swallower', and those sailing too close to it might wish to heed the advice of LUGLESS WILLIE Lithgow:

These distracted tides whirleth ever about, cutting in the middle circle a sloping hole which, if either ship or boat happen to encroach, they must either throw something into it, as a barrel, a piece of timber and such like, or that fatal euripus shall then suddenly become their swalling sepulchre.
– William Lithgow, *Totall Discourse of the Rare Adventures and Painefull Peregrinations of Long Nineteen Years* (1632)

According to Norse legend, the Swelkie was formed in the following circumstances. Frode, King of Denmark, possessed a pair of quernstones that had the enviable property of making anything one wished for. The vast quernstones were operated by two giantesses, and the greedy Frode gave them no rest in grinding out more and more riches. One night while Frode slept, the resentful giantesses ground out an army led by a warrior called Mysinger, who killed the king and sailed off with both the quernstones and the giantesses. He ordered the giantesses to grind out more and more salt, and eventually there was so much salt on board the ship that as it sailed to the north of Stroma it sank. To this day, as the sea races past the massive quernstones it washes out more salt, and in the process forms the Swelkie. *See also* MERRY MEN OF MEY, THE; STROMA PIRATES, THE.

455

Swine has gane through it, the Literally, 'the pig has gone through it', i.e. one's plans have come to nought. The expression, still current in places, may allude to the superstition that it is bad luck if a pig on the loose disrupts some social gathering.

> 'The swine's gone through it'; spoken when an intended Marriage is gone back, out of a superstitious Conceit, that if a Swine come between a Man and his Mistress, they will never be married.
> – James Kelly, *A Complete Collection of Scottish Proverbs* (1721)

Swinging Sixes A nickname for the Argyll and Sutherland Highlanders, referring to the six swinging tassels on their oversize sporrans.

Swings, to get a go at the To achieve coition. The expression is contemporary.

Sword dance A traditional dance in which a solo performer executes some nifty footwork between two swords placed on the ground to form a cross. Sometimes the dancer performs around a targe, a small shield with a metal spike sticking up in the centre. Today, sword dances are a feature of competitions at Highland Games. In the past, various other kinds of sword dance were performed, some involving a number of dancers who held the swords in their hands. A particularly acrobatic version was performed in 1633 before Charles I by the Incorporation of Skinners and Glovers of Perth, as described in an anonymous contemporary account:

> His Majesty's chair being set upon the wall next to the Water of Tay whereupon was a floating stage of timber clad about with birks, upon the which for his Majesty's welcome and entry thirteen of our brethren of this calling of Glovers with green caps, silver strings, red ribbons, white shoes and bells upon their legs, shearing rapiers in their hands and all other abulzements, danced our sword dance with many difficult knots and allapallajesse, five being under and five above upon their shoulders, three of them dancing through their feet and about them, drinking wine and breaking glasses. Which (God be praised) was acted and done without hurt or skaith to any.
> – Quoted in Ebenezer Bain, *Merchant and Craft Guilds: A History* (1887)

See also PAPA STOUR SWORD DANCE.

Sword dollar A silver coin issued at the beginning of the reign of James VI. It had a sword on the reverse, was worth 30 Scots shillings (equivalent to an English half crown), and was also known as a *James Ryall*. It was first minted in 1567 on the orders of the Privy Council:

> That thair be cunyeit ane penny of silver callit the James ryall ... of wecht ane vnce troyis wecht ... havand on the ane syde ane sword wyth ane croun vpoun the same ...

Sylvander *See* AE FOND KISS.

Synthetic Scots *See* PLASTIC SCOTS.

T

Taboos, fishermen's *See* FISHERMEN'S TABOOS.

Taghairm A Gaelic word denoting various rites to obtain knowledge of the future, once supposedly practised in the Highlands and Islands. According to the London *Literary Gazette* in 1824:

> The last time the Taughairm [sic] was performed in the Highlands was in the island of Mull, in the beginning of the seventeenth century, and the place is still well known to the inhabitants. Allan Maclean, commonly styled Allan mac Echain (son of Hector) was the projector of these horrid rites; and he was joined by Lachlan Maclean, otherwise denominated Lachunn Odhar (Lachlann the Dun). They were of resolute and determined character, and both young and unmarried.
>
> The institution was no doubt of pagan origin, and was a sacrifice offered to the Evil Spirit, in return for which the votaries were entitled to demand two boons. The idea entertained of it at the time must have been dreadful, and it is still often quoted for the purpose of terrifying the young and credulous. The sacrifice consisted of living cats roasted on a spit while life remained, and when the animal expired another was put on in its place. This operation was continued for four days and nights without tasting food. The Taughairm commenced at midnight between Friday and Saturday, and had not long proceeded when infernal spirits began to enter the house or barn in which it was performing, in the form of black cats. The first cat that entered, after darting a furious look at the operator, said: 'Lachunn Odhar, thou son of Neil, that is bad usage of a cat.' Allan, who superintended as master of the rites, cautioned Lachunn that whatever he should hear or see, he must continue to turn the spit; and this was done accordingly. The cats continued to enter, and the yells of the cat on the spit, joined by the rest, were tremendous. A cat of enormous size at last appeared

and told Lachunn Odhar that if he did not desist before his great-eared brother arrived, he never would behold the face of God. Lachunn answered that if all the devils in hell came he would not flinch until his task was concluded. By the end of the fourth day there was a black cat at the root of every rafter on the roof of the barn, and their yells were distinctly heard beyond the Sound of Mull in Morvern.

In another account, also featuring *Cluasa Leabhra*, the cat with big ears, a Lochiel in the 15th century performed a *taghairm*, ordering the spit turner:

> Hear you this or see you that,
> Round the spit and turn the cat.

The question he wished to ask was 'What must I do to be saved?' The answer was to build seven churches, one for each of his marauding forays; only this would expiate his sins.

Sir Walter Scott describes a very different sort of *taghairm* ritual – although still involving animal sacrifice – in The *LADY OF THE LAKE*, and explains in a footnote:

> The Highlanders, like all rude people, had various superstitious modes of inquiring into futurity. One of the most noted was the Taghairm, mentioned in the text. A person was wrapped up in the skin of a newly slain bullock, and deposited beside a waterfall, or at the bottom of a precipice, or in some other strange, wild, and unusual situation, where the scenery around him suggested nothing but objects of horror. In this situation, he revolved in his mind the question proposed; and whatever was impressed upon him by his exalted imagination, passed for the inspiration of the disembodied spirits, who haunt these desolate recesses.

Such rituals may owe more to Scott's imagination than anything else.

Tailie Day *See* PREEN-TAIL DAY.

Tak an ug at, to To take a dislike to, or be disgusted or nauseated or horrified by (something).

Tak a puggie *See* GET YER PUGGIE UP.

Take away Aberdeen and twelve miles round and where are you? Apparently a proverbial saying current in the 19th century.

Take one's hand off someone's jaw, to To give someone a good slap or punch, the suggestion being that this will be done with such force that one's hand will rebound with some violence.

Take the High Road A soap opera set in the fictional village of Glendarroch, produced by Scottish Television from 1980 to 2003. It changed its name to just *High Road* in 1994. Outside scenes were filmed in Luss, on the west side of Loch Lomond, and the title comes from the old Jacobite song 'The Bonnie Banks of Loch Lomond'. This exists in a number of versions, including one attributed to Lady John Scott (1810–1900):

> Oh, ye'll tak the high road and I'll tak the low road,
> And I'll be in Scotland afore ye,
> But wae is my heart until we meet again
> On the bonnie, bonnie banks of Loch Lomond.

The words are supposedly sung by a Jacobite soldier sentenced to death following the failure of the '45, whose spirit will return to Scotland before his companion. In one version, the penultimate line is 'But me and my sweetheart will never meet again'. Another, less familiar version ends as follows:

> He'll tak' the high road and I'll tak' the low
> And I'll be in Heaven afore him
> For my bed is prepared in yon mossy graveyard
> 'Mang the hazels o' green Inverarnan.
>
> The thistle shall bloom, and the King hae his ain
> And fond lovers meet in the gloamin'
> But I and my true love shall never [or 'will yet']
>   meet again
> By the bonnie bonnie banks of Loch Lomond.

Take to the heather, to To become an outlaw. In Stevenson's *Kidnapped* (1886), this is what Alan

BRECK advises David Balfour to do, after the latter is suspected of involvement in the APPIN MURDER:

> 'But mind you,' said Alan, 'it's no small thing. Ye maun lie bare and hard, and brook many an empty belly. Your bed shall be the moorcock's, and your life shall be like the hunted deer's, and ye shall sleep with your hand upon your weapons. Ay, man, ye shall taigle many a weary foot, or we get clear! I tell ye this at the start, for it's a life that I ken well. But if ye ask what other chance ye have, I answer: Nane. Either take to the heather with me, or else hang.'
>   – chapter xviii

See also HIDE-I'-THE-HEATHER.

Tak leg bail, to To do a runner in order to avoid unpleasant consequences.

> Sae weel's he'd fley the students a',
> Whan they war skelpin at the ba',
> They took leg bail and ran awa',
>   Wi' pith and speid;
> We winna get a sport sae braw
>   Sin Gregory's dead.
>   – Robert Fergusson, 'Elegy, On the Death of Mr David Gregory, late Professor of Mathematics in the University of St Andrews'

Tak tent Pay attention; be careful; keep a watch out.

> … canny now, lad – canny now – tak tent and tak time – Lord bless ye, tak time – Vera weel!
>   – Sir Walter Scott, *The Antiquary* (1816), chapter vii

Tak the door wi' ye Away with you, and close the door behind you. The expression is from the Northeast.

Tak the sturdies, to To sulk. *Sturdy* is a disease affecting the brains of sheep, caused by the larva of a tapeworm. The disease (known variously in England as turnside, goggles or gid) results in the animal becoming giddy, staggering and eventually collapsing. The word can also denote a sheep so affected.

Tak yer hurry in yer hand Slow down, no need to rush.

Talisman, the One of the passenger train services running between Edinburgh and London, named after Scott's 1825 novel *The Talisman* (*see* LEE PENNY, THE).

Tall Droll and the Small Doll, the How the comedian Chic Murray (1919–85) and his wife Maidie Dickson (1922–2010) were billed when they performed as a double act, she being his much smaller 'straight man'.

Tally van An ice-cream van. The first element refers to the fact that many families of Italian origin are involved in the ice-cream business. *Tally's blood* is the raspberry sauce often poured over a cone, and the phrase was used as the title of a 1990 play by the Scottish dramatist of Italian descent Ann Marie Di Mambro.

Tam o' reekie or **Tammie reekie** A device formerly deployed by boys to annoy the neighbours. It consisted of a hollowed-out cabbage stem filled with material such as tallow, straw, THRUMS or other combustible material. This would then be ignited and the smoke blown through keyholes, to the consternation of those within. Particularly malevolent urchins might add a little sulphur to the mix. *Reekie* means smoky, while *Tam* and *Tammie* are Scots versions of Thomas. *See also* REEKIE PETER.

'Tam o' Shanter' A narrative poem by Robert Burns, published in 1791. Burns had been anxious that the antiquary Captain Francis Grose should include in his forthcoming *Antiquities of Scotland* an account and engraving of the ruined 'Auld Kirk' in the village of Alloway, Burns's birthplace, and to this end composed this poem, in which the old church features largely.

The eponymous hero is a farmer, his character inspired by one Douglas Graham, tenant of the farm of Shanter near Kirkoswald, Ayrshire. In Burns's poem, following a chilly market day in Ayr, Tam indulges in an evening's tippling with his crony SOUTER JOHNNIE, but eventually it is time for Tam to ride home through the cold night. Passing Alloway Auld Kirk, 'Whare ghaists and houlets nightly cry', Tam sees a coven of 'Warlocks and witches in a dance', accompanied by Auld Nick on

the pipes. Tipsy Tam is particularly taken with one scantily clad young witch, whom he dubs CUTTY SARK, and to whom he cries out in encouragement as she frolics around. This alerts the 'hellish legion', who pursue the terrified Tam as he rides off on his old mare Meg. Tam only reaches safety when he crosses the Brig o' Doon, for, as Burns explains in a note:

> It is a well known fact that witches, or any evil spirits, have no power to follow a poor wight any farther than the middle of the next running stream.

The poem was very well received. The critic Alexander Fraser Tytler, later Lord Woodhouselee, who read it in proof, wrote to Burns on 12 March 1791:

> I have seldom in my life tasted of higher enjoyment from any work of genius than I have received from this composition; and I am much mistaken if this poem alone – had you never written another syllable – would not have been sufficient to have transmitted your name down to posterity with high reputation.

Burns himself thought 'Tam o' Shanter' the best thing he'd ever done, writing to Mrs Dunlop in April 1791 that, in his opinion, it showed 'a force of genius, and a finishing polish, that I despair of ever excelling'. Sir Walter Scott compared it favourably to Shakespeare.

'Tam o' Shanter' has inspired a number of pieces of music that share the same title: an overture (1890) by fellow-Scot Learmont Drysdale (1866–1909); the third *Scottish Rhapsody* (1911) by another Scot, Alexander Mackenzie; a 'symphonic ballad' (1911) by the American George Chadwick; and a concert overture (1955) by the English composer Malcolm Arnold.

Sartorially speaking, a *tam-o'-shanter* or *tammie* is a floppy bonnet or beret with a pompom on top, sometimes worn with the kilt, and also referred to as a *Kilmarnock bonnet* or BLUE BONNET. Burns depicts Tam wearing such a 'gude blue bonnet/ Whiles crooning o'er some auld Scots sonnet'. A khaki version is worn by certain Scottish regiments.

Tam o' the Cougait Traditionally the nickname bestowed by James VI on the lawyer and politician Thomas Hamilton, Earl of Melrose and 1st Earl of Haddington (1563–1637), after the king had stayed at Hamilton's mansion in the Cowgate during his visit to Scotland in 1617. However, there is no contemporary evidence that James bestowed this nickname on Hamilton, while there is much to support the other nicknames coined by the king. The Cowgate in Edinburgh was so named as it was originally the route via which cattle were driven from the back greens of the High Street to graze on the Burgh Muir, but by 1529 the theologian Alexander Ales was describing it as the street 'where the nobility and chief men of the city reside, and in which are the palaces of the officers of state, and where nothing is mean or tasteless, but all is magnificent'. By the 20th century the Cowgate had become one of the worst of the city's slums. *See also* OCTAVIANS, THE.

Tam the Gun *See* ONE O'CLOCK GUN.

Tangerines, the *See* FOOTBALL CLUB NICKNAMES.

Tantallon, to ding doon *See* DING DOON TANTALLON, TO.

Tappie-teenie or **tappie-tousie** A children's game, explained thus by John Jamieson in his 1825 supplement to *An Etymological Dictionary of the Scottish Language*:

> In this sport, one taking hold of another by the forelock of his hair, says to him – 'Tappie Tappie tousie, will ye be my man?' If the other answers in the affirmative, the first says – 'Come to me then'; giving him a smart pull towards him by the lock which he holds in his hand. If the one, who is asked, answers in the negative, the other gives him a push backward, saying – 'Gae frae me then.' It represents the mode in which one received another as his bondsman.

In this context, a *tap* or *tappie* is a forelock (more generally it may denote any tuft of hair or wool or feathers); *tousie* means dishevelled, and may also be a pet name for a child with unkempt hair.

Tappit hen A hen with a crest; hence a container for ale or wine, usually made of pewter, with a spherical body, a narrow neck and a wider pouring head, capped by a lid with a protuberance supposedly resembling a hen's crest; the word was also applied to a large claret bottle. The Tappit Hen is now a popular name for restaurants and pubs.

> When they were seated under the sooty rafters of Luckie Macleary's only apartment, thickly tapestried with cobwebs, their hostess ... appeared with a huge pewter measuring-pot, containing at least three English quarts, familiarly denominated a Tappit Hen, and which, in the language of the hostess, reamed (i.e. mantled) with excellent claret just drawn from the cask.
> – Sir Walter Scott, *Waverley* (1814), chapter xi

> 'Oh, drink never disturbs him, Colonel; he can write for hours after he cannot speak. I remember being called suddenly to draw an appeal case. I had been dining, and it was Saturday night, and I had ill will to begin to it; however, they got me down to Clerihugh's, and there we sat birling till I had a fair tappit hen under my belt, and then they persuaded me to draw the paper ...'
> – Sir Walter Scott, *Guy Mannering* (1815), chapter xxxix

Scott helpfully adds a note:

> The Tappit Hen contained three quarts of claret –
>> Weel she lo'ed a Hawick gill,
>> And leugh to see a Tappit Hen.
>
> I have seen one of these formidable stoups at Provost Haswell's, at Jedburgh, in the days of yore. It was a pewter measure, the claret being in ancient days served from the tap, and had the figure of a hen upon the lid. In later times, the name was given to a glass bottle of the same dimensions. These are rare apparitions among the degenerate topers of modern days.

Tarbolton Bachelors' Club A club formed by Robert Burns and his brother Gilbert in 1780, after they had moved to the farm of Lochlea. The rules for membership were outlined as follows:

> Every man proper for a member of this Society, must have a frank, honest, open heart; above anything dirty or mean; and must be a professed lover of one or more of the female sex.

Tartan, tinker's *See* TINKER'S TARTAN.

Tartan Army, the The supporters of the Scottish national football team, now often seen in See You Jimmy ensembles (*see under* JIMMY), their faces painted with the Blue SALTIRE and their bodies cloaked in the Royal Standard of Scotland (*see* LION RAMPANT) – thus inducing an attack of the vapours in the LYON COURT. They were originally, at the time of the World Cup in Argentina in 1978, 'Ally's Tartan Army', referring to Ally MacLeod, the Scottish manager at the time. True to form, Scotland were knocked out in the first round. The World Cup song that year, penned by the Scottish comedian Andy Cameron, was entitled 'On the March with Ally's Tartan Army'. The record reached Number 6 in the charts. One team member, Graham Souness, recalled:

> All that 'On the March with Ally's Army' stuff makes me cringe. And no, I definitely haven't got a copy of the record.
> – *Daily Mail*, 17 October 2007

In July 2006 Cameron expressed indignation when his original words –

> We're representing Britain and we're going to do or die,
> England cannae do it cos they didnae qualify –

... were changed on the website of the Scottish Executive to the more anodyne:

> We're off tae Argentina, we've got to do or die,
> Others cannae do it, cause they didnae qualify.

'It was a joke, for God's sake,' Cameron complained, irritated at this attempt to avoid offending the English.

The Tartan Army also have a number of anonymously authored songs, including the following:

> Everywhere we go-o
> People want to know-ow
> Who the hell we a-are
> And where we come from.
> We're the Tartan Army,
> We're mental and we're barmy.

See also 'FLOWER OF SCOTLAND' (for 'The Happy Hooligans o' Wembley').

Tartan Day 6 April, celebrated in North America every year since the 1980s on the anniversary of the DECLARATION OF ARBROATH. It is part of Scotland Week, during which descendants of Scottish settlers commemorate their links with Scotland.

Tartan Fraud, the Great *See* VESTIARIUM SCOTICUM.

Tartan noir A term applied to the modern crop of Scottish crime fiction, characterized by hardboiled, cynical, flawed heroes, an obsession with sin, corruption and alcohol, and frequent struggles with inner demons. Antecedents include James Hogg's *The Private Memoirs and Confessions of a Justified Sinner* and Stevenson's *Dr Jekyll and Mr Hyde*, with real-life influences coming from the stories of MAJOR WEIR, DEACON BRODIE and BURKE AND HARE, to name but a few. As Val McDermid, a leading exponent, has said:

> We have this sort of dark Calvinist past and it's still in place in the present. We also have this wonderful black sense of humour and we love to party. We've produced some of the greatest thinkers of the Enlightenment, and also some of the worst slag-faced bigots in the history of human thought. So there's always the dark pool of these opposites within us that produces a sort of dramatic tension.

Other writers associated with tartan noir include Ian Rankin (*see* REBUS, INSPECTOR), William McIlvanney, Christopher Brookmyre, Denise Mina and Louise Welsh. The term may have originated with the American crime writer James Ellroy, a major influence on some of the writers, who endorsed Rankin as 'the king of tartan noir' on a book cover, presumably at the behest of the publisher's marketing department. Not all exponents and critics are happy with the term:

> There's an inescapably condescending tinge to the phrase 'tartan noir', devised to describe the contemporary school of Scottish crime writing. It's a touristy phrase, suggesting that there's something quaint about hard-boiled crime fiction that comes from the land of kilts and haggis. The cosy appellation calls up visions of some new niche market of genre fiction ...
> – Charles Taylor, in the *New York Times*, 22 February 2004

See also CALEDONIAN ANTISYZYGY, THE.

Tartan Pimpernel, the The nickname of the Revd Donald Caskie (1902–83), who during the Second World War aided thousands of Allied servicemen to escape from occupied France. In 1938 he became minister of the Church of Scotland's Scots Kirk in Paris, and after the fall of France in 1940 moved south to Marseilles, where he set up a safe house for stranded Britons and escaping servicemen at the British Seamen's Mission. After he was betrayed, he became chaplain to British PoWs and civilian internees in Grenoble, and managed to persuade the Italian commandant of the camp to release the civilians before they were transported to Germany. He was arrested once more and sentenced to death, but saved by the intervention of a German army padre. After the war he resumed his ministry in Paris, and in 1957 published his wartime memoirs as *The Tartan Pimpernel* – the title being inspired by Baroness Orczy's fictional hero the Scarlet Pimpernel, who assists aristocrats to escape the Reign of Terror during the French Revolution.

Tartan Taliban, the The nickname given by the Scottish press to James Alexander McLintock from Dundee, who converted to Islam in the 1980s, married a Pakistani wife and took the name Yaqub Mohammed. In 1988 he joined the US-backed mujahideen fighting against the Soviets in Afghanistan, and in 1994 went to Bosnia to fight the Serbs. In 2001 he was picked up crossing between Afghanistan and Pakistan and interrogated by British intelligence, but released after they were satisfied that he was involved in a charity setting up religious schools. He was arrested and released again in Britain in 2003, and in 2009 was held in Pakistan for some weeks before being released without charge. Regarding his nickname, in 2004 he told the *Scotsman*: 'I'm not that bothered. Under the circumstances, a white middle-class gentleman accused of being an Islamist terrorist – it must have been a shock to the system.'

Tartan, to tear the See TEAR THE TARTAN, TO.

Tartan Tories An entirely inaccurate description of the centre-left Scottish National Party coined by the Labour politician Willie (later Lord) Ross, Secretary of State for Scotland (1964–70, 1974–6). He in turn was nicknamed the 'Hammer of the Nats' for his staunchly pro-Union and anti-devolution views.

Tascal money In former, more lawless times, the reward paid in the Highlands for information regarding cattle rustlers and their booty. The term comes from Gaelic *taisgeal*, meaning the discovery of something that has been lost.

Tattie-bogle A scarecrow standing guard in a field of potatoes (*tatties*), typically with a *neep* (swede) serving for its head. A BOGLE is a ghost or anything similar that might cause a fright, and in the scarecrow sense may be crop-specific, e.g. *pease-bogle*.

> The tattie-bogle wags its airms
> It hasna onie banes or thairms [guts].
> – William Soutar, *Seeds in the Wind* (1933)

The Northeast equivalent is the *tattie-boodie*, a *boodie* being a ghost or hobgoblin, although the word can also denote a small person of limited beauty. *Boodie* derives from Gaelic *bodach*, 'old man' (perhaps also influenced by *bo*, 'hobgoblin'), and in Gaelic a scarecrow is a *bodach-rocais* ('old man of the rooks'). *See also* BODACH GLAS.

Tattie howkers Seasonal workers whose job it is to *howk* (dig out) *tatties* (potatoes). From the 19th century to the early 1980s, many came from Donegal and other parts of the west of Ireland on a yearly basis, sailing to Stranraer or up the Clyde and disembarking at the Broomielaw in Glasgow, hence the following traditional song, sung to tune of the Jacobite air 'Wha wadna fecht for Cherlie?' (notably rendered by Gordon Jackson and Angus Lennie's characters in the film *The Great Escape*,

> Wha saw the tattie-howkers,
> Wha saw them gang awa,
> Wha saw the tattie-howkers,
> Marchin' doon the Broomielaw?
>
> Some of them had bits an' stockin's,
> Some of them had nane at a',
> Some of them had umberellas,
> Marchin' doon the Broomielaw.

Mothers would say to their children if they saw them picking their noses, 'You howkin fer tatties up there then?' A *tattie howker's tan* is one in which only the neck and forearms are browned.

Tatties and point A Spartan meal consisting just of potatoes, in which one points to the space on one's plate where one wishes the meat were. In Lerwick the establishment calling itself Tatties and Point claims to be 'the only dedicated baked potato shop in Shetland'.

Tattie Strike, the The nickname of the 1881 miners' strike, in which the strikers were obliged to rely on donations of potatoes by sympathetic supporters.

> The Ayrshire Miners' Union and the National Union of Scottish Mineworkers had kept up a precarious existence during 1881 and 1882. In August 1881 all the Ayrshire miners struck for a ten per cent increase in wages ... it was in large measure a spontaneous out-burst of indignation. Late summer was a propitious time for a strike. The miners could live off potatoes given or sold on credit by friendly farmers, and the strike, like all autumn strikes, became known as the 'tattie strike'. But winter was less happy, and the miners had to go back to work after ten weeks on strike. Shortly after a wage rise was conceded. But it was a pyrrhic victory. The miners' organization, such as it was, collapsed bankrupt as a result of the strike. Shortly afterwards the Scottish Mineworkers' National Union followed the Ayrshire organization into extinction.
> – Iain McLean, *Keir Hardie* (1975)

Tawse or **taws** A peculiarly Scottish instrument of correction, used in schools until the late 20th century. It comprised a leather strap with one or two long slits at one end, creating a number of tails or tongues (the word is probably the plural form of obsolete *taw*, a strip of leather), the better to deliver pain to the outheld hand (in earlier times bottoms and legs were also targets). A refined version was the *burnt-nebbit tawse*, in which the tails were hardened in the fire. The use of the tawse goes back centuries: in 1619 the Perth Kirk Sessions record of some miscreants that they 'war taikin ... to the grammer scole and scourgeit on the hippis with Sanct Barthilmewis tawis'.

Many such straps were made by the firm of John J. Dick ('Ironmonger, Saddler, Leather Cutter, Sports Outfitter, Oil and Seed Merchant') of Loch-gelly, Fife; hence 'Lochgelly' became a synonym for tawse, although the instrument was most commonly referred to as 'the belt' – as in 'Ah got the belt', 'Ah got six o' the belt', etc. John J. Dick manufactured

straps in two lengths (21 and 24 inches) and four weights (light, medium, heavy, extra heavy); these were 'sold only to the teaching profession for use in the classroom'.

> ... monie a skelp
> of triple-tonguit tawse
> has gien a hyst-up and a help
> towards Doctorates of Laws.
> – Robert Garioch, 'Embro to the Ploy'

The popularity of the tawse among the teaching profession resulted in the term *wag-tawse* being used for a schoolmaster, while a day on which the tawse was deployed frequently was known as a *wheeky-whacky day*. A *tawse* was also formerly a tailed lash used for whipping a spinning top, and in the late 20th century it also became playground slang for 'penis'.

Tay Bridge Disaster The calamity of 27 December 1879, when the first railway bridge across the Firth of Tay was destroyed in a storm while a train was crossing, resulting in the deaths of 90 people. The following year the event was famously commemo-rated by William McGonagall (the BARD OF THE SILVERY TAY):

> Beautiful Railway Bridge of the Silv'ry Tay!
> Alas, I am very sorry to say
> That ninety lives have been taken away
> On the last Sabbath day of 1879,
> Which will be remember'd for a very long time.

The disaster had been anticipated by Patrick Matthew, the so-called Seer of Gourdiehill and self-proclaimed DISCOVERER OF THE PRINCIPLE OF NATURAL SELECTION. The locomotive involved in the disaster, No. 224, was later recovered from the water, refurbished, and informally christened *The Diver*, under which name it remained in service for many years.

Taysiders, the *See* FOOTBALL CLUB NICKNAMES.

Tea and eating or **tea and till't** Synonyms for HIGH TEA.

Tea, coffee and chocolate The subjects of some appalling punning by those who should have known better:

Lord Kelly, a determined punster, and his brother Andrew were drinking tea with James Boswell. Boswell put his cup to his head, 'Here's *t'ye*, my Lord.' – At that moment, Lord Kelly coughed. – 'You have a *coughie*,' said his brother. – 'Yes,' said Lord Kelly, 'I have been like to *choak o' late*.'

> – Henry Mackenzie (1745–1831), in Harold W. Thomson (ed.), *The Anecdotes and Egotisms of Henry Mackenzie* (1927)

Tea jenny A person of either sex addicted to drinking tea.

Team A gang; the term is sometimes used as part of the name of particular gangs, e.g. Anderston Young Team, Govan Team, Pollok Young Team. Other generic terms for gangs include *tongs* (see TONG-LAND), *toi*, *fleet* and *squad*. The term *team-handit* means to face trouble (typically of a violent sort) having assembled a posse of one's mates.

Tear the tartan, to To speak Gaelic (sometimes disparagingly referred to as *the tartan*); to talk in a loud and effusive manner.

Teddy Bears, the *See* FOOTBALL CLUB NICKNAMES.

Tee-names *See* TEU-NEEMS.

Teenie fae Troon A name applied in Glasgow to any flashily dressed woman carrying on with her airs and graces. The name suggests someone wanting to make an impact on a day trip to the big city: Troon is a golfing resort on the Ayrshire coast, and *Teenie* – a familiar form of the name Christina – was formerly applied pejoratively to a lowly female servant or an effeminate man. The equivalent in the Northeast is *Teenie frae the neeps* (*neeps*, 'turnips, swedes'). *See also* GREETIN TEENIE.

Tenant's Day A fair formerly held in Beith, Ayrshire.

> A festival, also, called vulgarly Tenant's day, attended by a great concourse of people, and celebrated for its show of horses, is held yearly on the 18th of August (O.S.), in honour of St Inan, from which name, with the last letter of the word saint, the present appellation has been formed, by corrupt usage. Inan flourished about the year 839, and, though resident chiefly at Irvine, occasionally remained for a time at this place,

where he has left memorials in the name applied to the cleft in a rock, still called St Inan's chair, and in the name of a well, called St Inan's well.
> – *A Topographical Dictionary of Scotland* (1846)

Beith still holds an annual celebration called St Inan's Fete.

Ten-en-a A notable misreading, recorded in *The Bookseller* (17 January 2003):

> *American customer:* Do you have a map of Ten-en-a?
> *Bookseller:* Ten-en-a, sir? Where is that?
> *American customer:* Well, it's a little island off the west coast of Scotland.

Ten Merk Court In 18th-century Edinburgh, the equivalent of the small-claims court, dealing with debts of no more than ten merks (then worth 11s 1⅔d sterling), and also servants' wages (of any amount) that had not been paid.

Tennant's Stalk The nickname of the tall chimney which once stood above the St Rollox Chemical Works in Springburn, Glasgow. The works were established by Charles Tennant in 1800, and the chimney, also known as the St Rollox Stalk, was built in 1842. At 435.5 ft (132.7 m) it was for a while the tallest in Europe. It was dynamited in 1922 after being struck by lightning, and the rest of the works were demolished in the early 1960s.

Terrible Trio, the The collective nickname of three key players of HEART OF MIDLOTHIAN FC in the 1950s, namely Alfie Conn (1926–2009), Willie Bauld (1928–77) and Jimmy Wardhaugh (1929–78). Their most celebrated achievement was to score all the goals in Hearts' record 5–0 victory over their Edinburgh rivals Hibernian in 1955, in the fifth round of the Scottish Cup. The minute book of the Hearts directors describes the trio as 'three men in harmony with no equals'.

Terrors, the *See* FOOTBALL CLUB NICKNAMES.

Testicles, accidental amputation of *See* FASTEST KNIFE IN THE WEST END, THE.

Testicles, deliberate amputation of *See* CASTRATION.

Teuchter or **Cheuchter** A word of obscure origin applied contemptuously by Lowlanders since the early years of the 20th century to anybody from the Highlands and Islands, especially if they are Gaelic-speaking. Teuchters feature in a genre of jokes told by Lowlanders, in which they are depicted as naive, if not slightly (though charmingly) dim. The following is but one example:

> A police constable, based on one of the Outer Isles, phoned the forensic department of Strathclyde Police looking for help. 'If I sent you some of yon skelp, can ye test it for me?' The forensic scientist has never heard of 'skelp' so asks for more details. 'It's that broon powder the kids use,' explained the constable. 'Don't you mean smack?' said the expert. 'Och aye, that'll be right. I kent it had something to dae wi' hittin' folk.'

See also HEUCHTER-TEUCHTER.

Teu-neems or **tou-names** or **tee-names** The nicknames used in Orkney for the inhabitants of different parishes and islands; the word *teu* or *tou* or *tee* may be from 'township'. Tradition has it that some at least of these names refer to the preferred foodstuffs that labourers from different parts brought with them while working on the construction of St Magnus Cathedral in Kirkwall. Other names may refer to totemic animals. During the Second World War, teu-neems were used in ferry timetables instead of the island names, to perplex the enemy.

Birsay (Mainland)	Dogs or Hoes (dogfish)
Burray	Oily Bogies (bags made from sheepskin or whale-stomach, used for holding fish oil)
Deerness (Mainland)	Skate Rumples (skates' rumps, i.e. tails)
Eday	Scarfs (cormorants)
Egilsay	Burstin-lumps (clods of rough meal)
Evie (Mainland)	Cauld Kail (cold cabbage)
Firth (Mainland)	Oysters
Gairsay	Buckies (whelks)
Grimness (South Ronaldsay)	Gruties (apparently referring to the stony ground)
Harray (Mainland)	Crabs
Herston (South Ronaldsay)	Hogs
Holm (Mainland)	Hobblers (people with a limp)
Hoy	Hawks
Kirkwall (Mainland)	Starlings
North Ronaldsay	Selkies or Hides (seals)
Orphir (Mainland)	Yearnings (rennet) or Sheep Grippers (a calumny)
Papa Westray	Dundies (thin or diseased codfish, or codfish after spawning)
Rendall (Mainland)	Sheep Thieves
Rousay	Mares (from the story of the Rousay man who intended to breed horses but purchased only mares)
St Andrew's (Mainland)	Skerry Scrapers
St Margaret's Hope (South Ronaldsay)	Scooties (Arctic skuas, said to feed on the *scat*, i.e. excreta, of other birds)
Sanday	Gruellie-Belkies (porridge bellies; *see* MEAL-BELLY)
Sandwick (Mainland)	Ash Patties (a variant of *assiepattle*, a scruffy urchin)
Sandwick (South Ronaldsay)	Birkies (lively folk)
Shapinsay	Sheep
South Parish (South Ronaldsay)	Teeocks (Lapwings)
Stromness (Mainland)	Bloody Puddings (i.e. black puddings)
Stronsay	Limpets

Walls	Lyres (Manx shearwaters)
Westray	Auks (common guillemots)
Widewall (South Ronaldsay)	Witches
Wyre	Whelks

Teviotdale pie A recipe, possibly originating during the Second World War, that makes a little meat go a long way. The crust is of suet and flour, and the filling includes beef mince, vegetables and Worcestershire sauce. It is not known if there is a specific connection with Teviotdale, the valley of the River Teviot in the Borders.

That's the ticket for tattie soup That's the bee's knees, the cat's pyjamas, etc.

> That's the ticket for tattie soup!' cries a burly ploughman, as he stands by the clean well-set drill that he has chosen. This exclamation expresses the highest form of approbation.
> – Alexander Gordon, *Northward Ho!* (1894)

That's the worst There is an old story in which a young Scottish couple are showing Grandfather the photographs from their wedding. Grandfather, in silence, leafs through them once, and then again, and finally picks out a particular photograph, jabs at it with his finger, and declares, 'That's the wurst.'

Theology *See* RHAPSODY OF ILL-INVENTED NONSENSE, A.

'There Grows a Bonnie Brier Bush' A traditional song, with versions by Robert Burns and Lady Nairne (the FLOWER OF STRATHEARN):

> There grows a bonnie brier bush in our kail-yard,
> There grows a bonnie brier bush in our kail-yard;
> And below the bonnie brier bush there's a lassie
>   and a lad,
> And they're busy busy courting in our kail-yard.

One of the most popular productions of the late 19th-century KAILYARD SCHOOL was Ian Maclaren's *Beside the Bonnie Brier Bush* (1894), a collection of nostalgic tales of Scottish life in a bygone age, based on the experiences of the author during his time as a Free Church minister in rural Perthshire.

There's a Jock for every Jean A consolatory remark addressed to someone who has been unlucky in love, roughly equivalent to 'There's plenty more fish in the sea.'

There's aye a somethin' There's always something to moan about; life's a bitch. The phrase is heard in the Northeast of Scotland, where the speaker's interlocutor is likely to respond, in stoic fashion, 'Aye, there's aye a somethin'.' *See also* IF IT'S NO THE SKITTER, IT'S THE SPEW.

There's aye some water where the stirkie droons A proverb, the equivalent of 'There's no smoke without fire.' A *stirk* is a bullock or heifer, as in the following:

> A set o' dull, conceited Hashes
> Confuse their brains in Colledge-classes!
> They gang in Stirks, and come out Asses,
>   Plain truth to speak …
> – Robert Burns, 'Epistle to J. Laphraik' (1785)

There's mair in his heid than the spune pits in He's got his wits about him; he's a smart one. If he were to have *naethin' but whit the spune pits in*, the reverse would be the case.

There's mair meat on a butcher's pencil An unreconstructed Glaswegian male put-down of a woman regarded as insufficiently curvaceous. Other items that might have more meat on them include *a jockey's whip* and *a well-chowed chicken bone*. Such unreconstructed males might also say of such a woman that she would be *better biled than fried*.

'There's nae Luck about the House' A well-known song that first appeared in print in William Julius Mickle's *Ancient and Modern Scots Songs* (1776), although Mickle may have just produced his own version of an older song. It has also been attributed to Jean Adams (1710–65). The chorus goes (in Mickle's version):

For there's nae luck about the house,
  There's nae luck at a',
There's little pleasure in the house
  When our gudeman's awa.

There will be moonlight again The motto of the Armstrongs and other notorious families of BORDER REIVERS. Raids were largely undertaken at night, and often in the early winter months when the cattle were still fat from the summer's feeding.

There are more than birds on the hill tonight,
And more than winds on the plain!
The threat of the Scotts has filled the moss,
'There will be moonlight again!'
  – Will H. Ogilvie (1869–1963), 'The Blades of Harden'

See also MACFARLANE'S BOWAT.

'These Are My Mountains' A song that became a big hit for the Alexander Brothers in the early 1960s, sentimentally celebrating the pleasures of Scotland:

For these are my mountains and this is my glen,
The braes of my childhood will know me again.
No land's ever claimed me tho' far I did roam,
For these are my mountains and I'm going home.

The work gangs bonnily on A comment said to have been made by the Revd David Dickson on the slaughter by Covenanters of Royalist prisoners of war after the Battle of Dunaverty in 1647. *See also* SLAIN MEN'S LEA.

They haif said: Quhat say they? Let thame say The motto of the Earls Marischal, inscribed on Marischal College, Aberdeen, in 1593.

They'll be dancing in the streets of Hawick/ Melrose/Galashiels tonight *See* VOICE OF RUGBY, THE.

They'll be dancing in the streets of Raith A famous blunder by the sports commentator Sam Leitch in the 1960s, assuming that Raith Rovers must come from a place called Raith, whereas actually they come from Kirkcaldy. Raith is the name of a rural district to the west of the town,

and gives its name to a modern housing estate, built long after the team was founded.

They make a wilderness and call it peace *See* MONS GRAUPIUS.

They wha begin to steal needles and pins, end wi' stealing horned kye *See* HEADIM AND CORSIM.

Thief's Road An old drove road in the Borders, linking Dawyck with Megget over Dollar Law. It was part of a route by which cattle were driven from the FALKIRK TRYST south to England – and was presumably also used by BORDER REIVERS to drive stolen cattle in the opposite direction. There is also a Thief's Road on Horseley Hill east of Abbey St Bathans, while the similarly named Thieves Road, another old drove road, crosses the southwestern Pentland Hills from Harperrig over Cauldstane Slap and Cairn Muir to West Linton.

Thing not ordinar in this kingdom, a According to Robert Chambers in his *Domestic Annals of Scotland From the Reformation to the Revolution* (1874), on 11 February 1653:

A person who was 'both man and woman, a *thing not ordinar in this kingdom,*' was hanged at Edinburgh on account of some irregularities of conduct. 'His custom was always to go in a woman's habit.' This person passed by the name of Margaret Rannie. 'When opened by certain doctors and apothecaries, [he] was found to be two every way, having two hearts, two livers, two every inward thing.'

Thinks he's big, but a wee coat fits him Said of anyone regarded as too big for their boots.

He remembered an expression his mother had used to cut him down to size when he was in his arrogant teens and impressed by the status he felt himself acquiring. 'Aye, ye're a big man but a wee coat fits ye.'
  – William McIlvanney, *The Big Man* (1985)

See also AH KENT HIS FAITHER; JOCK TAMSON'S BAIRNS.

Thin Red Line, the The description by the *Times* journalist William Howard Russell of the formation of the red-coated 93rd Highlanders at the Battle of Balaclava, 25 October 1854, one of the most famous episodes of the Crimean War. In defence of the British camp, the commander of the Highland Brigade, Sir Colin Campbell, ordered the 93rd to form up two deep, rather than the conventional four rows, as he reportedly considered this would be sufficient to hold the Russian cavalry, of which he had a low regard. He then told the troops: 'Men, remember there is no retreat from here. You must die where you stand.' Observing the Russian cavalry charge, Russell wrote 'They dashed on towards that thin red streak topped with a line of steel', and this is how his report appeared in *The Times* on 14 November; however, in his 1877 book *The British Expedition to the Crimea*, he changed the wording to 'They dashed on towards that thin red line tipped with steel.' The Russian commander called off the attack, fearing that the flimsy British formation was a ruse to lure his men into a trap. Seeing the Russians retreat, some of the Highlanders looked like they were about to set off in pursuit, until Sir Colin yelled, 'Ninety-third! Ninety-third! Damn all that eagerness.'

Third Lanark A Glasgow-based football club founded in 1872, and so named because it was originally the 3rd Lanarkshire Volunteer Rifles FC. After considerable early success, the club was relegated from the First Division in 1965, and went bankrupt two years later. *See also* FOOTBALL CLUB NICKNAMES.

This dear paradise How Queen Victoria described Balmoral; *see* BALMORAL BONNET; BALMORALITY; BEAST OF BALMORAL, THE.

This is my own, my native land! A famous affirmation of patriotism in *The LAY OF THE LAST MINSTREL*:

Breathes there the man with soul so dead
Who never to himself has said,
This is my own, my native land!
Whose heart hath ne'er within him burned,
As home his footsteps he hath turned
From wandering on a foreign strand!
— Sir Walter Scott, *The Lay of the Last Minstrel* (1805),
Canto 6, stanza 1

Thistle, the The national badge of Scotland, and one of its national flowers alongside HEATHER, the BLUEBELL OF SCOTLAND and the WHITE ROSE OF SCOTLAND. Which of the many species of thistle is the specifically Scottish one is unclear, although the flowers are purple and the leaves spiky. The origin of the association of the thistle with Scotland seems to go back to a the legend that Scots sentries were alerted to a nocturnal Viking attack when one of the invaders trod on a thistle and let out a yelp. The thistle certainly seems to match the Scottish motto *NEMO ME IMPUNE LACESSIT*. It may have first been adopted as a national emblem during the reign of Alexander III (1249–86), and in 1470 appeared on coins issued by James III. By the time William Dunbar wrote *The THRISSEL AND THE ROIS*, during the reign of James IV, it was firmly established as the national symbol – a role it has continued to play in Scottish literature, as attested by Hugh MacDiarmid's Scots epic, *A Drunk Man Looks at the Thistle* (1926). *See also* ORDER OF THE THISTLE, THE. Of course, in Glasgow 'the Thistle' means Partick Thistle FC.

Thomas the Rhymer Alongside the BRAHAN SEER, Scotland's most famous visionary (*c.*1220–*c.*1297). Thomas, whose historical existence is attested in a number of legal documents and whose surname may have been Rhymour or Learmont, is also known as *True Thomas* or *Thomas of Ercildoune*, Ercildoune being the old name for his native Earlston in Lauderdale, Berwickshire. In the wall of Earlston Kirk there is a stone inscribed with the line 'Auld Rhymer's race lies in this place', while to the south of the town can still be seen the ruins of Rhymer's Tower, where Thomas is said to have lived – apart from the seven years he supposedly spent with the Queen of the Fairies in ELFAME, under the Eildon Hills (*see* EILDON TREE, THE). It was this Fairy Queen who gave him the gift of prophecy, and among his predictions were the Scottish victory at Bannockburn (1314) and defeat at Flodden (1513), the accession of James VI to the throne of England (1603), and, in his own lifetime, the death of Alexander III in 1286. Thomas had been challenged by Earl Patrick of Dunbar to predict the events of the following day, and replied:

Alas for the morrow, day of misery and calamity! Before the hour of noon there will assuredly be felt such a mighty storm in Scotland that its like has not been known for long ages past. The blast of it will cause nations to tremble, will make those who hear it dumb, and will humble the high, and lay the strong level with the ground.

It being a pleasant morning, the earl scoffed at this gloomy prognostication. And then at midday a messenger brought the news that the king had taken a fatal fall from his horse at Kinghorn in Fife. Decades of turmoil were to follow, as the Scots attempted to resist English attempts to fill the power vacuum left by Alexander's death (*see* BEGINNING OF ALL SORROW, THE).

A number of medieval romances were traditionally attributed to Thomas; Sir Walter Scott believed that one of these, *Sir Tristrem*, was indeed Thomas's work. Thomas's own story – that of his dalliance with the Queen of the Fairies under the Eildon Hills – became the subject of a 14th-century romance entitled *Thomas of Erceldoune*, and of a later Border ballad, collected by Scott in MINSTRELSY OF THE SCOTTISH BORDER (1802). Thomas's predictions were first collected in the 15th century, in *Romance and Prophecies of Thomas of Erceldoune*. Robert Chambers observed that in the 14th, 15th and 16th centuries, 'to fabricate a prophecy in the name of Thomas the Rhymer appears to have been found a good stroke of policy on many occasions. Thus was his authority employed to countenance the views of Edward III against Scottish independence, to favour the ambitious views of the Duke of Albany in the minority of James V, and to sustain the spirits of the nation under the harassing invasions of Henry VIII.' The Russian poet Mikhail Lermontov (1814–41) took his surname as evidence that he was descended from Thomas the Rhymer, aka Learmont. *See also* HAIG SHALL BE HAIG OF BEMERSYDE; SECOND SIGHT.

Thomson, 'Greek' *See* 'GREEK' THOMSON.

'Three Craws, The' A traditional children's song, with both ontological and epistemological ramifications:

Three craws sat upon a wa'
Sat upon a wa'
Sat upon a wa'
Three craws sat upon a wa'
On a cauld and frosty morning.

The subsequent verses follow the same pattern, with the following first lines:

The first craw, he couldnae flee at a' ...

The second craw, he fell and broke his jaw ...

The third craw wis greetin fur his maw ...

The fourth craw wisnae there at a' ...

That's a' ah ken aboot the craws
Ken aboot the craws
Ken aboot the craws
That's a' ah ken aboot the craws
On a cauld and frosty mornin.

Three Robbies, Scotland's A phrase coined by Robert Louis Stevenson:

'I am the last of Scotland's three Robbies,' he said once. 'Robbie Burns, Robbie Fergusson, and Robbie Stevenson – and how hardly life treated them all, poor devils!'
– Lloyd Osbourne (Stevenson's stepson), 'The Death of Stevenson', an essay written for the Tusitala edition of Stevenson's works (1924)

See also MY ELDER BROTHER IN MISFORTUNE ...

Three Sisters of Glencoe, the Three precipitous spurs of Bidean nam Bian – Aonach Dubh, Geàrr Aonach and Beinn Fhada – that stand proudly above the south side of Glencoe. The name comes from the title of a celebrated 1864 painting of the scene by Horatio McCulloch. *See also* FIVE SISTERS OF KINTAIL, THE; OSSIAN'S CAVE.

Thrissil and the Rois, The ('The Thistle and the Rose') The first great poem of William Dunbar, an allegory celebrating the marriage of his master James IV to Margaret Tudor, daughter of Henry VII of England. Dunbar was probably a member of the mission sent south in 1503 to fetch Margaret to Scotland. The promise of the union of the national symbols was to be fulfilled by their great-grandson, James VI, who ascended the throne of England exactly a century later, in 1603. The rose in question is undoubtedly the Tudor rose, which combined the white Yorkist rose with the red rose of the Lancastrians, so symbolizing the end of the Wars of the Roses:

> The lark scho [she] sang, 'Haill Rois both reid and quhyt,
> Most plesand flour of michty cullouris twane.'

For its part, the THISTLE is described thus:

> Upon the awful Thrissil scho beheld
> And saw him kepit with a busche of speiris;
> Concedring him so able for the weiris [wars],
> A radius croun of rubies scho him gaif ...

Throwing the stocking A former wedding custom, which probably died out with the advent of Victorian priggishness:

> About the 'noon of night' the bride is put to bed by her maids, in the presence of as many spectators as the bedroom will contain, pressing, squeezing, standing upon tiptoe, and peeping over each other's head for a glance of the blushing fair, who throws the stocking from her left leg over the right shoulder, and the person on whom it falls is to be first married.
> – *Edinburgh Magazine*, November 1818

Thrummy Cap A species of hobgoblin similar to the REDCAP, found on both sides of the Border, and said to be a 'queer-looking little auld man' and to haunt the lower depths of castles. The name refers to his preferred headgear, a cap made from THRUMS. Sometimes the name – often abbreviated to *Thrum* or *Thrummy* – denotes the Devil himself. However, in 'Thrummy Cap', the best known poem of John Burness (1771–1826), a second cousin of Burns, the title character is a harmless enough fellow, who finds himself sharing the only available room in an inn on a cold winter's night with 'a frightful ghaist'.

Thrums (also singular *thrum*) The tattered fringe of warp threads left on a loom when the woven material has been removed; hence any leftover bits and pieces. There was a traditional saying 'He's nae a guid weaver wha leaves lang thrums', and *Lang Thrums* became a nickname for a weaver. More disparagingly, to be of *thrum descent* meant to be of

humble origin, while to *knit on the old thrum* meant to carry on in one's customary way, and to *redd thrums* with someone meant to quarrel with them. James Barrie, the son of a weaver, fictionalized his native Kirriemuir as the town of Thrums in novels such as *Auld Licht Idylls* (1888), *A Window in Thrums* (1889) and *The Little Minister* (1891). The parochial KAILYARD cosiness of these works is firmly rebutted in Hugh MacDiarmid's 1930 poem 'Frae Anither Window in Thrums', in which the likes of Proust and Dostoevsky are invoked in an effort to transcend Barrie's narrow, Thrums-bound vision of Scotland.

> To those who dwell in great cities Thrums is only a small place, but what a clatter of life it has for me when I come to it from my school-house in the glen.
> – J.M. Barrie, *A Window in Thrums* (1889), chapter i

See also THRUMMY CAP.

Thule *See* ULTIMA THULE.

Tibbie Shiel's Inn An old inn between St Mary's Loch and Loch of the Lowes in the Borders, on the road through the hills leading from Selkirk to Moffat. It was established by a young widow called Tibbie (Isabella) Shiel, following the death of her husband, Robert Richardson, a mole-catcher, in 1823. In order to support herself and her six children, she began to take in gentlemen lodgers, who included such literary men as Sir Walter Scott and James Hogg (the ETTRICK SHEPHERD). Regarding the latter, Tibbie had this to say: 'He wrote a deal o' trash, but was a gey sensible man for a' that.' Later visitors included Thomas Carlyle, R.L. Stevenson and W.E. Gladstone.

'Tic, the *See* FOOTBALL CLUB NICKNAMES.

Tiger, like a *See* SUMMER HAS LEAPT SUDDENLY UPON EDINBURGH LIKE A TIGER.

Tiger Earl, the A sobriquet of Alexander Lindsay, 4th Earl of Crawford (d.1453), known for his violence and ferocity. A powerful noble in the reign of James II, Crawford took part in the Douglas rebellion, but was defeated by the king at Brechin in 1452 and submitted. *See also* EARL BEARDIE.

Till a' the seas gang dry A phrase denoting eternity, coined by Burns in 'My Luve is Like a Red, Red Rose':

> But fair thou art, my bonnie lass,
> So deep in luve am I,
> And I will luve thee still, my dear,
> Till a' the seas gang dry.
>
> Till a' the seas gang dry, my dear,
> And the rocks melt wi' the sun,
> O I will luve thee still, my dear,
> While the sands o' life shall run.

Tim Glasgow slang for a Roman Catholic, perhaps from the generic Irish name Tim Malloy. Catholic churches are thus sometimes disrespectfully referred to as *Tim-shops. See also* JUNGLE, THE.

Timor mortis conturbat me *See* LAMENT FOR THE MAKARIS.

Tinclarian Doctor or **Tinklarian Doctor, the** The title awarded himself by the eccentric and prolific pamphleteer William Mitchel (1672–?1740), who from around 1696 lived in the Bowhead, Edinburgh, earning his living as a tinsmith or tinker, and for some years also as superintendent of lamplighters in the city – justifying his claim that his object was 'to give light'. A particular target of his sarcasm were the ministers of the Established Church, whom he suggested should be paid less, and kept from the golf course by means of a tax on clubs. Edinburgh's lord provost, baillies and council also came in for Mitchel's scathing treatment. In *Traditions of Edinburgh* (1824), Robert Chambers describes Mitchel as 'an odd half-crazy varlet of a tinsmith', and his roughly produced pamphlets as a 'strange mixture of fanaticism, humour and low cunning'. A flavour of his style may be gleaned from the titles of some of his works (which in total number over fifty):

> *Dr Mitchel's Strange and Wonderful Discourse concerning the Witches and Warlocks in West Calder* (n.d.)

> *The Great Tincklarian Doctor Mitchel his fearful book, to the condemnation of all swearers. Dedicated to the Devil's captains* (1712)

> *Great News! Strange Alteration concerning the Tinckler,*

> *who wrote his Testament long before his Death, and no Man knows his Heir* (n.d.)

> *The Tinclarian Doctor Mitchel's Letter to the King of France* (?1713)

> *Prophecy of an Old Prophet concerning Kings, and Judges, and Rulers, and of the Magistrates of Edinburgh, and also of the Downfall of Babylon, which is Locusts, who is King of the Bottomless Pit. Dedicated to all Members of Parliament* (1737)

Some of these pamphlets were collected under the title *The whole Works of that Eminent Divine and Historian Doctor William Mitchel, Professor of Tincklarianism in the University of the Bow-head; being Essays of Divinity, Humanity, History, and Philosophy; composed at various occasions for his own satisfaction, Reader's Edification, and the World's Illumination.*

Tinderbox City A nickname applied to Glasgow in the decades following the Second World War, alluding to a number of disastrous fires – such as the blaze in 1951 that destroyed the Arnott Simpson's department store, and the 1960 fire and explosion in a bonded whisky warehouse in Cheapside Street, Anderston, which cost the lives of 14 members of the fire service and five of the salvage corps. The worst loss of life came in 1968, with a fire in an upholstery warehouse in James Watt Street, Anderston. The windows had been barred to prevent break-ins, so that only three of those working inside managed to escape. The remaining 22 all perished.

Tineman or **Tyneman, the** Literally, 'the Loser'; the nickname given to Archibald, 4th Earl of Douglas (1372–1424), commander of the losing side at Homildon Hill in 1402. There he was wounded and captured, and subsequently made a pact with Percy Hotspur and Owain Glendower against Henry IV. This led to another loss, the defeat at Shrewsbury, after which he was ransomed. The verb *tine*, 'to lose', gave rise in the later 18th century to the proverbial phrase, *between the tining and the winning*, denoting a crucial moment in some battle or competition or project.

Tinker's tartan The red marks on one's shins resulting from sitting too close to a fire. The condition is also known as *fireside tartan*, *granny's tartan*, or *corned-beef legs*, and if one suffers from it, one can be described as being *mizzle-shinned* (as in 'measles').

Tinklarian Doctor, the *See* TINCLARIAN DOCTOR, THE.

Tìr a' Cheò *See* LAND OF MISTS.

Tìr a'Mhurain 'Land of bent grass', the Gaelic name traditionally given to South Uist, referring to the swathes of marram grass that flourish along the island's sandy, windswept western shore.

> Tìr a'mhurain tìr an eòrna,
> Tìr 's am pailt a h'uile seòrsa
> Far am bi na gillean òga
> Gabhail òran 's 'g òl an leanna.
>
> Land of bent grass, land of barley,
> Land where everything is plentiful,
> Where young men sing songs,
> And drink ale ...
> – Traditional

The American photographer Paul Strand gave the title *Tìr a'Mhurain* to his celebrated collection of photographs of the island, taken over a period of three months in 1954.

Tirve the kirk to theek the quire, to Literally, 'to rob or strip the church to roof the choir', a proverbial expression equivalent to 'Rob Peter to pay Paul', current from the late 16th to the 19th centuries. Sometimes *pulpit* is substituted for *quire*.

Toad stones It was formerly believed in many parts of Europe that certain toads carried a jewel in their heads, which worked as an antidote to poison and provided protection against sundry malevolent forces. Sir Walter Scott claimed to possess such a stone, writing in *MINSTRELSY OF THE SCOTTISH BORDER*:

> The editor is possessed of a small relique, termed by tradition a toad-stone, the influence of which was supposed to preserve pregnant women from the power of demons, and other dangers incidental to their situation. It has been carefully preserved for several

generations, was often pledged for considerable sums of money, and uniformly redeemed from a belief in its efficacy.

In his poem 'Suilven' (from *Speak to the Earth*, 1939), Andrew Young likens the striking Sutherland mountain to a 'great ruby':

> The mountain in my mind burns on,
> As though I were the foul toad, said
> To bear a precious jewel in his head.

Surviving 'toad stones' have been identified as the fossilized teeth of various extinct fish, such as the ray-finned *Lepidotes*, which lived in the Jurassic and Cretaceous periods.

'To a Mouse' *See* BEST-LAID SCHEMES.

Tobacco Lords Those Glasgow merchants – also known as 'Virginia Dons' – who in the 18th century took advantage of the city's proximity to the Atlantic crossing to make a fortune out of the importation of tobacco from the New World. At this time, more than half of the tobacco brought into Britain came via Glasgow. In his *Enumeration of the Inhabitants of the City of Glasgow* (1832), James Cleland says that the Tobacco Lords, or 'Virginians', were 'looked up to as the Glasgow aristocracy', and that they 'had a privileged walk at the Cross'. Cleland goes on to elaborate on their lofty status:

> When any of the most respectable master tradesmen of the city had occasion to speak to a Tobacco Lord, he required to walk on the other side of the street till he was fortunate enough to meet his eye.

The Tobacco Lords were not averse to showing off their wealth:

> On the 'plainstones' – the only pavement then in Glasgow – in the middle of the street fronting the Trongate piazza, those Virginia traders – known as Tobacco Lords – strutted in business hours, clad in scarlet cloaks, cocked hats and powdered wigs, bearing with portly grace gold-headed canes in their hands.
> – H. Grey Graham, *The Social Life of Scotland in the Eighteenth Century* (1899)

The Virginia trade collapsed during the American War of Independence, but many merchants switched to trading in other commodities, such as cotton grown in the West Indies. Their legacy is found in a number of streets that bear their names, most notably Buchanan Street, named after Andrew Buchanan (1690–1759), tobacco merchant and Lord Provost of Glasgow.

Tobar nan Ceann *See* WELL OF THE HEADS.

Tobermory Treasure, the *See* TREASURE OF TOBERMORY, THE.

Tod Lowrie *See* LOWRIE.

Tomb of the Eagles, the The popular name for the Isbister Chambered Cairn on South Ronaldsay, Orkney. It dates from 3000 BC, and was discovered by a local farmer, Ronnie Simison, in 1958. The tomb contained the bones of some 300 individuals, and also the remains of at least 14 sea eagles, which may have been the totem of the people who built the tomb.

Ton, the *See* FOOTBALL CLUB NICKNAMES.

Tongland A former nickname for the Calton area of Glasgow, dominated in the 1960s by the violent youth gang called the Tongs, known from their ubiquitously daubed slogan, 'Tongs YA BASS'. The Tongs now refer to themselves as the Real Calton Tongs, to distinguish them from other Glasgow gangs that have borrowed the name, e.g. Y. Milton Tongs P. and Ibrox Tongs. It is said that the original Tongs took their name after viewing the 1961 film *Terror of the Tongs*, a blood-spattered melodrama featuring a Chinese secret society known as the Tongs, described in the publicity material as 'Drug-crazed assassins carrying out their hate-filled ritual murders'. The original tongs (from Cantonese *t'ong*, 'meeting place') were formed by Chinese immigrants to America in the 19th century, and were initially intended for mutual support and protection, but soon became involved in criminal activities.

Tongs ya bass *See* TONGLAND; YA BASS.

Tongue-twisters J. Riddell, in *Aberdeen and Its Folk* (1868), offers the following two:

A peacock pykit a peck o' paper oot o' a paper pyock.
[*pykit*, 'picked'; *pyock*, 'magpie']

I snuff shop snuff. Dae ye snuff shop snuff?

From the same part of the world comes:

Patrick Peetrie fae Peterheed plukkit a puckle paitriks an packit a puckle paitriks intae a puckle piles.
[*puckle*, 'small quantity'; *paitriks*, 'partridges']

Robert Chambers suggests 'Clim' Criffel' (the hill in Dumfriesshire), repeated. A celebrated test of sobriety (especially before the advent of the breathalyser) was to be able to enunciate clearly:

The Leith police dismisseth us.

Among Gaelic tongue-twisters should be mentioned:

Balach beag biodach a' bocadaich air bàrr baraille.
['A tiny wee boy jumping about on top of a barrel.']

For 'Round the ragged rocks the ragged rascals ran', *see* RADICAL ROAD. For 'Twa bridies, a plen ane and an ingin ane an a', *see* FORFAR BRIDIE. *See also* IT'S A BRAW BRICHT MUNELICHT NICHT.

Tongue that could clip cloots, a Literally, 'a tongue that could cut cloth'; a phrase applied to anyone thought of as sharp-tongued, abrasive or argumentative.

Haud yer tongue, ye wicked woman, ye, for it wad clip clouts.
– John Mackay Wilson, *Wilson's Tales of the Borders* (1835–40)

She had a fell tongue, they said, that would clip clouts and yammer a tink from the door.
– Lewis Grassic Gibbon, *Sunset Song* (1932)

See also CLOOT.

Tontine face A Glaswegian expression applied to any face that is comically distorted by emotions such as joy or sorrow or anger; thus a parent will admonish a child not to display a tontine face. The phrase refers to the grotesque carved faces on the arches of the piazza frontage of Glasgow's old town hall, opened in 1740 at Glasgow Cross. The first five faces were carved by David Cation, and five more by Mungo Naismith when further arches were added in

1758. In 1781 the building was acquired by the Tontine Society, and became the Tontine Hotel and Coffee Room. (A tontine is a type of life insurance scheme in which the subscribers invest in a common fund, from which they each draw an annuity that increases as each subscriber dies, until the last survivor takes the lot. It was named after the 17th-century Neapolitan banker Lorenzo Tonti.) The fate of the original 'Tontine Faces' is complex. The arcade where they were originally installed was demolished in 1869 when the Tontine Hotel became a draper's shop, and the ten faces – plus some new ones – were incorporated into the frontage of a warehouse at the foot of Buchanan Street. This building burnt down in 1888, and the faces then disappeared until the Glasgow journalist 'Peter Prowler' (James Cowan) began a campaign to locate them in the 1930s. Gradually the faces came to light, and all but one of the original ten were brought together in 1995 in St Nicholas Garden, a recreation of a 15th-century physic garden behind Glasgow's oldest house, Provand's Lordship in Castle Street.

Toom Tabard 'Empty surcoat', the nickname of John Balliol (1249–1313), one of the competitors in the GREAT CAUSE, who was enthroned as king of Scotland in 1292 on condition that he gave his allegiance to Edward I of England, the HAMMER OF THE SCOTS. John eventually rebelled against Edward, but in 1296 was forced to surrender, and the royal arms of Scotland were torn from his surcoat – hence his nickname. He died in exile in Picardy, although his claim to the Scottish throne was continued by his son Edward.

Toon, the Auld Grey *See* AULD GREY TOON, THE

Toon, the Lang *See* LANG TOUN, THE.

Toon, the Muckle *See* MUCKLE TOON, THE.

Toons, the *See* FOOTBALL CLUB NICKNAMES.

Tooth, theft of a dead poet's *See under* ROBERT BURNS OF GAELDOM, THE.

Top-knot, taken up to heaven by one's *See* BUCHANITES.

Torn face *See* GREETIN FACE.

Torquil and Fiona The Scottish version of Henry and Camilla, the archetypal Sloane Ranger couple.

Tossing the caber A sport restricted exclusively to Scottish Highland Games, in which the participants attempt to throw the *caber* – a substantial wooden spar, broadly the size of a telegraph pole – so that it describes an arc through the air of 180 degrees and lands with the end originally held by the tosser furthest away from said tosser. The sport was also formerly known as *kaber-feigh*, and the word *caber*, which also denotes a rafter, comes from Gaelic *cabar*, a long, slender tree trunk.

Totty-peelin Literally 'potato-peeling', a term applied in Glasgow to any accent regarded as refined, or that affects to be so. Quite how such a voice would be able to peel potatoes is unclear, although the expression might allude to the same quality as 'cut-glass accent'.

Touching iron *See* FISHERMEN'S TABOOS.

Touching the corpse *See* DREAMING OF THE DEAD.

Touch not the cat bot a glove The motto of Clan Chattan, whose badge features a cat salient, proper; *bot* means 'without'. In *The Fair Maid of Perth* (1828), Scott describes the warriors of Clan Chattan as they gather for the BATTLE OF THE CLANS on the North Inch of Perth:

> Their pipers marched at the head of their column. Next followed the well known banner, displaying a mountain cat rampant, with the appropriate caution, 'Touch not the cat, but (i.e. without) the glove.' The chief followed with his two handed sword advanced, as if to protect the emblem of the tribe.
> – chapter xxxiv

See also WILDCAT.

Tou-names *See* TEU-NEEMS.

Tourist eagle A jocular name for the buzzard, often mistaken by the non-ornithologist for the much rarer golden eagle.

Trades, the *See* FAIR FORTNIGHT.

Trainspotting The first and most impactful novel of Irvine Welsh, the so-called LAUREATE OF THE CHEMICAL GENERATION. Published in 1993, the book comprises a loosely connected series of episodes in the lives of a group of working-class Edinburgh heroin-users, hardmen and petty crooks, related in uncompromising vernacular with considerable rawness, verve and dark humour (for a typical example, *see under* SHANKIE). A possible key to the title may be found in the passage set in Leith's long abandoned Central Station, where

> ... an auld drunkard ... lurched up tae us, wine boatil in his hand ... 'What yis up tae, lads? Trainspottin, eh?' he sais, laughing uncontrollably at his ain fucking wit.

The title may also allude to the junkie's attempt to find 'tracks' (veins) in which to inject the next fix. The novel was made into a film in 1996, directed by Danny Boyle and starring Ewan McGregor as Mark Renton ('Rentboy'), the principal narrator in the novel, and featuring Robert Carlyle as the psychopathic Begbie.

Tranent Massacre, the *See* MASSACRE OF TRANENT, THE.

Treasure of Loch Arkaig, the A lost hoard of gold coins, together with a cache of arms and brandy, supposedly buried in the area around Loch Arkaig (or deposited at the bottom of the loch). The loot, sent by Spain and France to support the Jacobite rebels, arrived in Scotland in April 1746, just as news came through of the defeat at Culloden. With this change of fortune, the money was to be used to aid fugitive Jacobite leaders, and was entrusted first to Murray of Broughton, then, after his arrest, to Cameron of Lochiel (the GENTLE LOCHIEL), and finally to Macpherson of Cluny, then holed up in CLUNY'S CAGE. The treasure still remained hidden in Arkaig, and quite what happened to it remains murky, although Bonnie Prince Charlie accused Cluny of having appropriated it. The story features in Nigel Tranter's novel, *Gold for Prince Charlie* (1962).

Treasure of Tobermory, the A hoard of 30 million gold ducats that supposedly lies at the bottom of Tobermory Bay, off the coast of Mull. In 1588 in the aftermath of the failed Spanish Armada, a galleon (variously named as the *Florida*, the *Florencia*, the *San Francisco* or the *San Juan de Sicilia*) anchored in the bay in order to purchase provisions. Worried that the Spaniards might be about to make off without paying, Maclean of Duart sent one of his men aboard, who managed to set the powder store alight and send the ship – and its treasure – to the bottom. No one has so far recovered the loot, if it exists at all.

Treaty of Perpetual Peace The treaty between Scotland and England signed in 1502 and consummated by the marriage in 1503 of James IV to Margaret Tudor, daughter of Henry VII (a union celebrated by Dunbar in *The THRISSEL AND THE ROIS*). The treaty was intended to end 200 years of warfare, but after Henry VIII succeeded to the English throne in 1509 he revived the wars with France, obliging James to honour the AULD ALLIANCE and invade England. The result was the catastrophe at Flodden Field, where on 9 September 1513 James and 10,000 of his countrymen were slaughtered.

Trees Among notable Scottish trees should be mentioned:

- ACT OF UNION BEECHES, the
- CAPON TREE, the
- COLLIERS' OAK, the
- CORSTORPHINE SYCAMORE, the
- DUGHALL MOR
- EDGEWELL TREE, the
- EILDON TREE, the
- EPPIE CALLUM'S OAK
- FORTINGALL YEW, the
- Hanging Ash of Tushielaw, the (*see under* KING OF THE BORDER, THE)
- HANGING TREE OF FORT WILLIAM, the
- KING JAMES II HOLLY, the
- KING OF THE FOREST, the
- KING OF THE WOOD, the
- MACCULLOCH'S TREE
- OAK OF ERROL, the

- POLWARTH THORNS, the
- RIZZIO'S CHESTNUT
- The beech trees named after the SEVEN MEN OF MOIDART
- STEVENSON'S YEW
- TREE THAT NEVER GREW, the
- WALLACE'S OAK AND YEW

For more arboreal information, the reader is referred to Donald Rodger, Jon Stokes, James Ogilvie, *Heritage Trees of Scotland* (Forestry Commission, Tree Council, 2006). *See also* COVIN TREE; DOOL TREE; WISHING TREES.

Tree that never grew, the Part of a traditional rhyme about Glasgow's coat of arms:

> There's the tree that never grew,
> There's the bird that never flew,
> There's the fish that never swam,
> There's the bell that never rang.

The coat of arms itself was only approved for use by the Lord Lyon King of Arms in 1866, but the various symbols and motifs – mostly associated with St Mungo (aka St Kentigern) – had long been used on the city's seals. It was St Mungo who in the late 6th century brought Christianity to Strathclyde and founded the city of Glasgow, becoming its patron saint. In a sermon he declared 'Let Glasgow flourish by the preaching of the word' – hence the city's motto, which appears at the foot of the coat of arms: 'Let Glasgow Flourish'. The tree in the coat of arms, depicted as a mighty oak, refers to the legend that as a boy Mungo was entrusted with tending the sacred fire at St Serf's monastery, but other boys, jealous of the favour that St Serf showed to Mungo, put out the fire while he slept. On awakening, Mungo broke some sticks from a hazel tree, placed them in the cold fireplace, and prayed until they burst into flame. The bird in the tree in the coat of arms represents the robin tamed by St Serf; when it died Mungo was again blamed, but prayed over it until it came back to life. The fish – always depicted with a ring in its jaws – refers to the legend of a king of Strathclyde who gave a ring to his queen, who in turn gave it to a knight. The suspicious king demanded that his queen show him the ring, on pain of death. In one version, the knight lost it, while in another the king himself took

the ring from the sleeping knight and threw it into the Clyde. The knight came clean to St Mungo, who dispatched one of his monks to try his luck with his rod in the river. Landing a salmon, the monk took the fish back to St Mungo, who cut it open to reveal the ring; thus king and queen were reconciled. The bell in the tree has a less ancient origin, representing as it does the 'St Mungo's Bell' paid for from an endowment left in 1450 by Glasgow's first Lord Provost, John Stewart, who specified that it be rung through the city to encourage the citizens to pray for his soul. A replacement bell, dating from 1641, can be seen in Glasgow's PEOPLE'S PALACE.

> *Socialism? These days? There's the tree that never grew.*
> *Och, a shower of shites. There's the bird that never flew.*
> – Carol Ann Duffy, 'Politico'

Tron Originally, a *tron* was a public weighing machine employed near a burgh marketplace for weighing the produce. It was also the name of a standard of weight, formally abolished in 1618, but in practice various versions remained in use until imperial avoirdupois weights were adopted in 1824. The location of a burgh's tron sometimes came to denote the area where such weighing took place.

> In 1491 the Bishop of Glasgow negotiated a royal charter which gave him the right to have a free tron, or weighing machine, in the city. At this tron goods coming into Glasgow were weighed and customs were exacted … The place for a tron was, naturally, at the mercat cross of Glasgow.
> – Jack House, *Heart of Glasgow* (1965)

Glasgow's tron gave its name to the street called Trongate (where the TOBACCO LORDS once paraded, and which is now the location of the Tron Theatre, opened in a former church in 1981). The disused Tron Kirk in Edinburgh's High Street, formerly the rendezvous for those wishing to see in the New Year in the company of large numbers of fellow revellers, is named after the salt tron that once stood nearby. In an earlier age, it was the site of one of the pageants put on in June 1633 to welcome Charles I to his Scottish capital:

> At the Tron, Parnassus Hill was curiously erected, all green with birks [birch trees], where nine pretty boys,

representing the nine nymphs or Muses, was nymph-like clad ...

– John Spalding, *History of the Troubles and Memorable Transactions in Scotland and England* (1624–45)

Trot of Turriff, the (14 May 1639) The opening engagement of the BISHOPS' WARS, in which a force of Royalists under Colonel William Johnstone defeated a much larger number of COVENANTERS under Sir William Hay of Delgaty, who were holding the town of Turriff in Buchan. The Royalists appeared at dawn, surprising the Covenanters: 'sum war sleeping in their bedis, uther sum drinking and smoking tabacca' (according to a contemporary account by John Spalding). The defenders retreated in the face of a couple of artillery rounds, and retreat turned into a rout when the Royalist cavalry appeared – hence 'the Trot of Turriff'. However, only three men died. Among the Royalists present was Sir Thomas Urquhart, remembered for his translation of Rabelais and his LOGOPANDECTEISION.

Trouble-the-hoose A name given to a baby or young child whose carryings-on diminish domestic peace and tranquillity.

Trout in the well, a A bun in the oven, especially a bun baked out of wedlock. The expression survives in the Northeast.

Trow The Orkney and Shetland version of a Norse troll. Trows were short, ugly, supernatural and malevolent, and under many circumstances appear to have been invisible. There were hill-trows, land-trows and sea-trows, all of which were capable of inflicting mischief.

They tell us that several such creatures do appear to fishers at sea, particularly such as they call sea-trowes, great rolling creatures tumbling in the waters, which, if they come among their nets, they break them, and sometimes take them away with them; if the fishers see them before they come near, they endeavour to keep them off with their oars or long staves, and if they can get them beaten therewith, they will endeavour to do it: the fishers both in Orkney and Zetland are afraid when they see them, which panic fear of theirs makes

them think and sometimes say, that it is the devil in the shape of such creatures; whether it be so or not as they apprehend, I cannot determine. However it seems to be more than probable, that evil spirits frequent both sea and land.

– John Brand, *A New Description of Orkney, Zetland, Pightland-Firth and Caithness* (1701)

For the Trow of Yell, *see under* WINDHOUSE.

Truce days Days on which, prior to the Union of the Crowns in 1603, the Wardens of the Marches (*see* MARCH, THE) on both sides of the Border agreed to meet peacefully (albeit at the head of troops of armed men) to discuss matters of mutual interest, such as settling local disputes. A description of the custom, dating from some time after 1603, can be found in the manuscript collection known as the Warrender Papers:

There was mutual truce taken, and intimate by sound of trumpets and proclamation of Their Majesties' names to the troops on both sides before their meeting, as the custom was. Wherefore the meetings were called Days of Trews, seeing therethrough parties on both sides, that otherwise were under deadly feud and in quarrel, did usually in peace and assurance meet and do their business one beside another, and converse mutually and in assurance with such as they had occasion withal.

Tensions could often run high, however, not helped by the custom of *bauchling and reproaching*, by which men on one side would accuse someone on the other side of some crime, accompanied by name-calling and pointing of lances (to *bauchle* is to confront an adversary, or to treat someone with contempt). Such undiplomatic behaviour was liable to result in a fracas, and often did, so after 1553 bauchling and reproaching were banned unless one had the permission of both wardens. Of course, the wardens themselves were not immune to hot-headedness, which could lead to a contretemps, such as happened in the famous REDESWIRE FRAY of 1575. *See also* BORDER REIVERS.

True Blue A term originally denoting a COVENANTER, who adopted the blue of the SALTIRE flag, although the blue ribbons they sported allude to a biblical passage (*see* BLUE RIBBON). In the 17th and 18th centuries the True Blues were the WHIGS, and the term also denoted any zealous Presbyterian. The sectarian allegiance that the colour symbolizes survives in the strip of Glasgow Rangers FC. *See also* BLUENOSE.

True Thomas *See* THOMAS THE RHYMER.

Tube A term of abuse, especially in Glasgow, often heard in the phrase 'Ya tube!' (sometimes rendered orthographically as 'Ya choob'). As far as is known, the etymology of the expression remains unknown.

> This week, Gordon Brown appeared on YouTube …
> and that's what everyone said when they saw it.
> – Frankie Boyle, in the *Daily Record*, 9 May 2009

For an effective put-down deploying the term, *see under* PATTER, THE.

Tulchan bishops A disparaging description of the bishops appointed in the 1570s by Regent Morton, who kept all the revenues due to the bishops for himself and his followers. A *tulchan* (from Gaelic *tulachan*) was a calfskin stuffed with straw and placed under a cow to induce her to produce milk.

> The tulchen to wit ane fein3eit counterfeitt bischope … the kingis lordis that obtenit thair beneficeis culd find na way to have proffeit thairof without thay had ane tulchen lyk as the kow had or scho wald gif milk ane calfis skin stoppit with stra.
> – Robert Lindsay of Pitscottie, *The Historie and Chronicles of Scotland* (16th century)

Tullietudlescleugh An archetypically obscure Scottish hamlet, as imagined by that unrepentant hater of all things Caledonian, T.W.H. Crossland, in *The Unspeakable Scot* (1902):

> He is the fine gentleman whose father toils with a muck-fork … He is the bandy-legged lout from Tullietudlescleugh, who, after a childhood of intimacy with the cesspool and the crab louse, and twelve months at 'the college' on moneys wrung from the diet of his family, drops his threadbare kilt and comes south in a slop suit to instruct the English in the arts of civilization and in the English language.

Further regrettable anti-Caledonian rantings may be found under PARTICULARLY DISAGREEABLE and SOUR, STINGY, DEPRESSING BEGGARS.

'Tullochgorum' A song by John Skinner (1721–1807), an Aberdeenshire Presbyterian who converted to Episcopalianism, although, unlike many Episcopalians, he was not a Jacobite. He was ordained in 1742, thereafter looking after the parish of Longside, near Peterhead, until his death. He wrote *The Ecclesiastical History of Scotland* (1788) as well as a number of songs admired by Burns, with whom Skinner corresponded. 'Tullochgorum' became so celebrated that Skinner himself was known as 'Tullochgorum'. His geniality – which made him many friends – is reflected in the lines of the song:

> Come, gie's a sang, Montgomery cried,
> And lay your disputes all aside,
> What signifies't for folks to chide
> For what was done before them:
> Let Whig and Tory all agree,
> Whig and Tory, Whig and Tory,
> Whig and Tory all agree,
> To drop their whig-mig-morum:
> Let Whig and Tory all agree,
> To spend the night wi' mirth and glee,
> And cheerfu' sing alang wi' me
> The Reel o' Tullochgorum.

The cheering power of the reel is attested by Robert Fergusson in his poem about the festive season, 'The DAFT DAYS':

> Fiddlers, your pins in temper fix,
> And roset weel your fiddle-sticks,
> But banish vile Italian tricks
> From out your quorum,
> Nor fortes wi' pianos mix,
> Gie's Tulloch Gorum.

The original Tullochgorum is a tiny settlement on the Spey, just south of Grantown (for the familiar spirit of the Grants of Tullochgorum, *see* MEG MULLACH). Today there is a small housing estate near Skinner's grave at Longside called Tullochgorum.

Tune one's pipes, to To set to wailing and moaning, supposedly like the sound of the bagpipes warming up.

Tunnel Tigers, the The 'hydro boys', the navvies who worked in the postwar years on the many hydroelectric schemes in the Highlands; the term was particularly associated with those involved in blasting the huge tunnels needed. The workers on the schemes included Scots and Irish, and also significant numbers of displaced persons from central and eastern Europe. Pay was relatively high, and the living wild and dangerous. Drinking, fighting and gambling provided a common distraction from the harshness of the conditions and the perils of the job. It was an era when health and safety were put to one side in the race to finish the job – which involved the use of large quantities of gelignite. Alex Ross, then a 16-year-old 'chain man' carrying the surveyor's instruments, remembers one evening when he was working late on the scheme at Loch Mullardoch:

> There was a sudden crump, and the general foreman come round a rock with blood coming out of his ears and says to me: 'For God's sake go and see what you can do for Paddy, though I don't think there's anything we can do for him.' The chief ganger and I went round and Paddy was lying there with his face flapped over on the rock, like a false face, and his stomach blown out between his legs. I was standing there shocked and [the foreman] says to me: 'What are you doing standing there? Get a shovel and bury that' – meaning the entrails.
>
> – Quoted in Emma Wood, *The Hydro Boys: Pioneers of Renewable Energy* (2002)

By way of consolation, in the camps there were huts known as 'hen houses' set aside for visiting prostitutes, while once the working week was over the 'weekend millionaires' (wages could be as high as £200 a week in the early 1960s) would hit the nearest town or village, dressed up in their flashy bespoke suits – and their wellington boots. *Cf.* KISHORN COMMANDOS, THE.

Tup-heidit (Of a man) stupid and obstinate. In the north of England and the Borders, a *tup* is a ram.

Tuppenny *See* BEER.

Tuppeny Faith, the A derisive nickname given to 'Ane Godlie Exhortatioun', a short tract explaining Holy Communion, issued in 1559 under the authority of John Hamilton, Archbishop of St Andrews. It was so-called because of its price when sold by pedlars.

Tuppeny struggle *See* SCOTCH PIE.

Turnbull's Tornadoes The successful Hibernian FC team of the earlier 1970s, under the managership of former player Eddie Turnbull (1923–2011), one of the noted FAMOUS FIVE two decades before. Turnbull took on the job in 1971, and Hibs won the League Cup the following year, and finished second in the league in 1974 and 1975. The team also won the Dryburgh Cup in 1972 and 1973.

Turn up one's wee finger, to *See* COCK ONE'S WEE FINGER, TO.

Turra The local name of the small Buchan town of Turriff. The natives (known as *Turra Neeps* or *Turra Tatties*) have a saying:

> Turra, Turra, faur the sorra idder?

– meaning 'Turriff, Turriff, where the devil else [is there]?' *See also* TURRA COO, THE; TROT OF TURRIFF, THE.

Turra Coo, the A 'fite coo' (white cow) that became something of a celebrity around the Buchan town of Turriff (TURRA) in 1913. That year, Robert Paterson, who farmed at nearby Lendrum, refused to pay the new National Insurance contributions for his workers – the farmers of the area all arguing that their men were rarely sick or out of work. A court ordered the Turriff sheriff George Keith to seize Paterson's property to the value of £22, and lighted upon a chattel that could move itself – Paterson's white milk cow, an Ayrshire-Shorthorn cross. When the cow was led into Turriff, the sheriff's officers were met by a jeering mob and a barrage of cabbages, kale stumps, eggs and other missiles. When the cow was sold to one Alexander Craig for £7, local supporters clubbed together to raise the money to buy the beast back for Paterson. In 2010 a statue was unveiled in Turriff to commemorate the town's most famous daughter, the Turra Coo.

Turtle-eating alderman, a A description of David Hume by Lord Charlemont, who had met the philosopher in 1748 in Turin, where Charlemont was attached to the British embassy:

> Nature, I believe, never formed any man more unlike his real character than David Hume ... His face was broad and fat, his mouth wide, and without any other expression than that of imbecility. His eyes vacant and spiritless, and the corpulence of his whole person was far better fitted to communicate the idea of a turtle-eating alderman than of a refined philosopher.
> – Quoted in E.C. Mossner, *The Life of David Hume* (1954, 1980)

Adam Smith saw behind the outward appearance:

> Upon the whole, I have always considered him, both in his lifetime and since his death, as approaching as nearly to the idea of a perfectly wise and virtuous man, as perhaps the nature of human frailty will permit.
> – Letter to William Strachan, 1776

See also FATTEST HOG IN EPRICURUS' STY, THE.

Tusitala The name given to Robert Louis Stevenson by the Samoan people among whom he lived for the last years of his life. It means 'teller of tales'.

Twa bridies, a plen ane and an ingin ane an a' *See under* FORFAR BRIDIE.

'Twa Corbies, The' An old ballad, known from both sides of the Border, and notable for its bleak, black humour. It recounts how two *corbies* (crows or ravens) are discussing their dining arrangements for the day:

> As I was walking all alane,
> I heard twa corbies making a mane;
> The tane unto the t'other say,
> 'Where sall we gang and dine to-day?'

> 'In behint yon auld fail dyke,
> I wot there lies a new slain knight;
> And naebody kens that he lies there,
> But his hawk, his hound, and lady fair.

> 'His hound is to the hunting gane,
> His hawk to fetch the wild-fowl hame,
> His lady's ta'en another mate,
> So we may mak our dinner sweet.

> 'Ye'll sit on his white hause-bane,
> And I'll pike out his bonny blue een;
> Wi ae lock o his gowden hair
> We'll theek our nest when it grows bare.

> 'Mony a one for him makes mane,
> But nane sall ken where he is gane;
> Oer his white banes, when they are bare,
> The wind sall blaw for evermair.'

'Twa Dogs, The' *See under* LUATH.

Twa-ee'ed steak A jocular term for a herring or kipper, the poor man's sirloin.

Twa meens i' the lift 'Two moons in the sky', a metaphor for impossibility, as in the following expression recorded by J. Riddell in *Aberdeen and Its Folk* (1868): 'When that fa's oot, we'll see twa meens i' the lift, an' anither i' the aiss midden [dunghill].' According to Riddell, this is 'Said to express most forcibly the improbability of better conduct in the future.' A variant is 'twa suns i' the lift'.

Tweed kettle A salmon hash, taking its name from the great salmon river of the Scottish Borders. The dish was apparently popular in Edinburgh in the 19th century. The salmon is simmered in white wine with onions, mushrooms and parsley.

Tweed vs Till *See* BLOODTHIRSTY DEE.

Twinklers, the The Pleiades.

Twisting the four legs from a cow According to the *Reminiscences of My Life in the Highlands* by Joseph Mitchell (1803–83), this was once a competitive sport in parts of the Highlands:

> One feat which I never saw since was twisting the four legs from a cow, for which a fat sheep was offered as a prize. The cow was brought up and felled before the multitude, and the barbarous competition began, several men making the attempt. At last one man succeeded. After struggling for about an hour, he managed to twist off the four legs, and as a reward received his sheep, with a eulogistic speech from the chief in Gaelic.

Tyneman, the *See* TINEMAN, THE.

U

Ubi solitudinem faciunt pacem appellant *See under*
MONS GRAUPIUS.

Ugsome aithis *See* SWEARING.

Ultima Thule The far northern land of the ancients, sometimes referred to as Thule (a name of
obscure origin), sometimes as Ultima ('furthest')
Thule. It has been variously identified with Fair Isle
and Foula, and, beyond the British Isles, with the
coast of Norway, the Faroe Islands, Iceland and
Greenland. Foula, situated 15 miles (24 km) west of
Mainland, Shetland, is said to be Britain's remotest
inhabited island (Michael Powell filmed *The Edge of
the World* here in 1936), although Fair Isle also
makes this claim. The basis of the identification of
Ultima Thule with Foula or Fair Isle is the account
in Tacitus of the Roman general Agricola's visit in
AD 84 to the Orkney Islands, from where he looked
out upon 'Thule':

> Round these coasts of remotest ocean the Roman fleet
> then for the first time sailed, ascertained that Britain is
> an island, and simultaneously discovered and con-
> quered what are called the Orcades, islands hitherto
> unknown. Thule too was descried in the distance,
> which as yet had been hidden by the snows of winter.
> But they say that the sea was sluggish and heavy to the
> rowers, therefore not ever to be raised by the winds.

Formerly, local folk etymology identified the name
'Foula' with 'Thule', although the former in fact
derives from Old Norse *fugle* 'bird' and *ey*, 'island'.
Nevertheless, the identification of Foula with Thule
is preserved in the scientific name of the Foula field
mouse: *Apodemus sylvaticus thuloe*.
    The first mention of Thule was by the Greek
traveller Pytheas, who sailed round Britain in the
later 4th century BC. His account is now lost, but the
Greek historian Polybius in his histories (2nd century BC) was sceptical of Pytheas's description of
Thule, where Pytheas apparently asserted that 'there
was no longer any proper land nor sea nor air, but a
sort of mixture of all three of the consistency of a
jellyfish in which one can neither walk nor sail'. The
Greek geographer Strabo, writing in the 1st century
AD, reports Pytheas's assertion that Thule is 'six
days' sail north of Britain, and is near the frozen sea',
but, like Polybius, he is sceptical of Pytheas's claims.

Uncle Geordie A euphemism for the Devil, as
explained in the following account from Wigtownshire:

> To find out who was to be her husband, the young
> woman took an apple in one hand and a lighted candle
> in the other on Halloween, and placed herself in front
> of a mirror, and then ate the apple in the name of
> 'Uncle Geordie', *i.e.* the devil.
>
> – *Report of the 66th Meeting of the British Association for
>   the Advancement of Science* (1897)

Unco guid, the Those who are smugly pious, and
who look down uncharitably on those they regard as
less righteous than themselves. *Unco* here means
'exceptionally', with a suggestion of oddness or
unnaturalness (strangers or outsiders can be referred to as *unco folk*). The phrase originates with
Burns's 1787 poem, 'Address to the Unco Guid',
which begins:

> O ye, wha are sae guid yoursel,
>   Sae pious and sae holy,
> Ye've nought to do but mark and tell
>   Your neebours' fauts and folly …

So apt was it that the term soon caught on:

> The 'unco guid', with sturdy wrath,
> Hae sworn to banish drinkin'.
>   – J. Barr, *Poems* (1861)

These days the phrase is used in a variety of contexts – political, sporting and social – but always pejoratively. The *unco guid* are not to be confused with their heavy-drinking neighbours, the *unco-nscious*. *See also* HOLY WILLIE'S PRAYER.

Uncrowned king of Scotland, the *See* HENRY THE NINTH.

Uncrowned king of Scots, the How Andrew Lang described his friend Robert Bontine Cunninghame Graham (1852–1936), the South American travel writer, socialist and first president of the Scottish National Party. On his mother's side, Cunninghame Grahame was descended from Spanish nobility – hence his friends referred to him as Don Roberto – while on his father's side he claimed descent from Robert II. 'I ought, madam, if I had my rights,' he once informed an acquaintance, 'to be king of this country – and what a two weeks that would be!' Lang himself declared that his friend should really be Robert IV of Scotland, and Robert I of Great Britain and Ireland.

Understood by none but his own Congregation, and not by all of them *See* CANT.

Unicorn Two unicorns support the Scottish royal coat of arms. In Heraldese, they are described thus:

> Unicorns Argent Royally crowned Proper, armed, crined and unguled Or, gorged with a coronet of the second composed of crosses patée and fleurs de lis a chain affixed thereto passing between the forelegs and reflexed over the back also of the second. Sinister holding the standard of Saint Andrew [the SALTIRE], dexter holding the banner of the Royal arms [the LION RAMPANT].

Since the 1707 Union, the royal coat of arms of the United Kingdom has as supporters a unicorn (representing Scotland) and a lion (representing England).

Unicorn Baa A shoal at the north end of Bressay Sound, guarding the approach to Lerwick harbour, Shetland. *Baa* is the Shetland word for a submerged rock, and the *Unicorn* was the name of a ship wrecked here on 25 August 1567; others have since shared its unhappy fate.

Union, the *See* END OF AN OLD SONG, THE; EQUIVALENT, THE; PARCEL OF ROGUES, A.

Union Beeches *See* ACT OF UNION BEECHES, THE.

Union Duke, the A sobriquet of James Douglas, 2nd Duke of Queensberry (1662–1711), who did much to push through the Union of 1707. As a reward he acquired a number of English titles, being made Duke of Dover, Marquess of Beverley and Earl of Ripon. His eldest son, James Douglas, Earl of Drumlanrig, was a psychopathic maniac, whom the duke kept locked up in Queensberry House in the Canongate of Edinburgh. However, while the family and servants were out celebrating the achievement of the Union, the boy escaped, and when the household returned, they found that the mad earl, though then aged only ten, had killed, spitted and roasted an unfortunate kitchen lad, whose flesh he was slowly devouring. Queensberry's role in the Union had made him many enemies, who saw in the actions of the 'Cannibalistic Idiot' a meet judgement upon the duke's treachery. *See also* SCOTCH PLOT, THE.

United Scotsmen, the A radical secret society formed in 1796–7, in the wake of the PIKE PLOT and the transportation of the SCOTTISH MARTYRS. The United Scotsmen modelled themselves on the United Irishmen, with whom they maintained contact – as they did with the Revolutionaries in France. The United Scotsmen called for universal suffrage and annual parliaments, and appear to have had widespread support among the industrial working classes of the Central Belt. Their main leader, George Mealmaker, was arrested in 1798 (the year the rebellion of the United Irishmen was brutally suppressed) and transported to Australia. The organization was banned in 1799, after which it faded away.

Unitit Kinrick o Great Breetain an Northren Ireland, the The UK rendered in Scots. In Gaelic it is *Rioghachd Aonaichte na Breatainn Mòire agus Èireann a Tuath*.

Unquiet spirit crowing like a cock, an *See under* WIZARD OF REAY, THE.

Unspeakable Scot, The *See* TULLIETUDLESCLEUGH.

Up-Helly-Aa A winter fire festival held in Lerwick and various other parts of Shetland on the last Tuesday of January. The name is derived from Old Norse *Uphalyday*, from *up*, 'over', and *haliday*, 'holy day', indicating that it marked the end of the midwinter festivities (*Uphalieday* formerly denoted Twelfth Night); the *Aa* element is thought to be *A'*, 'all'.

The present form of the ceremonies is of relatively recent origin. Until the 1870s, young men would range around the town dragging sledges loaded with barrels of burning tar – a form of midwinter fire festival found elsewhere in Scotland, for example BURNING THE CLAVIE in Burghead and the FIREBALLS in Stonehaven. The tar barrelling was replaced in 1876 by an organized torchlight procession, and in 1889 the present climax of the ceremonies was instituted, whereby all the torches are thrown into a replica Viking longship. Much partying ensues. The participants, many in fancy dress, are known as GUISERS, and their leader is the Jarl, who heads a Jarl Squad dressed as Vikings.

Uppies and Doonies *See* HANDBA.

Up Suckie, doon Buckie and alang Argyle *See* SAUCHIEHALL STREET.

Up tae high doh Highly wrought; in a state of extreme agitation. The 'doh' may be the musical note, suggesting a high-pitched manner of talking, or, indeed, screaming. The phrase appears to be a 20th-century coinage.

> 'It's my turn to cook tonight,' he said. 'Nell'll be up to high doh if I'm late.'
> – Ian Rankin, *Strip Jack* (1993)

Up the sheuch Having got hold of the wrong end of the stick; entirely mistaken. A *sheuch* is a drainage ditch (such as are dug to make LAZY BEDS), or a furrow made by a plough, or a gutter (hence being

in the sheuch is to be in a condition of misery or utter impoverishment). Figuratively, your *sheuch* is your gullet or your bottom, or more specifically the cleft between your buttocks. In Ulster, the North Channel between Scotland and Ireland is jocularly referred to as *the Sheugh*.

Urisk A species of solitary supernatural being that haunts lonely spots in the Highlands, such as mountains and waterfalls. In John G. Campbell's *Superstitions of the Highlands and Islands of Scotland* (1900), we find that Urisks of both sexes are large and 'lubberly', and are the consequence of unions between mortals and fairies. Campbell continues:

> The Urisk was usually seen in the evening, big and grey (*mòr glas*), sitting on the top of a rock and peering at the intruders on its solitude. The wayfarer whose path led along the mountain side, whose shattered rocks are loosely sprinkled, or along some desert moor, and who hurried for the fast approaching nightfall, saw the Urisk sitting motionless on the top of a rock and gazing at him, or slowly moving out of his way. It spoke to some people, and is even said to have thrashed them, but usually it did not meddle with the passer-by. On the contrary, it at times gave a safe convoy to those who were belated.
>
> In the Highlands of Beadalbane the Urisk was said, in summer time, to stay in remote corries and on the highest part of certain hills. In winter time it came down to the strath, and entered certain houses at night to warm itself. It was then it did work for the farmer, grinding, thrashing, etc. Its presence was a sign of prosperity; it was said to leave comfort behind it. Like Brownie, it liked milk and good food, and a present of clothes drove it away.

See also BROWNIE.

Usher of the Green Rod *See* ORDER OF THE THISTLE, THE MOST ANCIENT.

Usquebaugh *See* WHISKY.

V

Vampires *See* DRACULA'S CASTLE; GORBALS VAMPIRE, THE.

Vermin issuing from all the pores of his body *See* PROPHET PEDEN.

Vestiarium Scoticum (Latin, 'the clothing of the Scots') A book published in 1842 by the brothers John Carter Allen and Charles Manning Allen, under the adopted names John Sobieski Stuart and Charles Edward Stuart. They claimed it was based on a 16th-century manuscript 'formerly in the Library of the Scots College at Douay', and further claimed that they themselves were grandsons of the YOUNG PRETENDER, and that the tartans they illustrated had ancient lineages linked to the great landed families of Scotland. The tartans were in fact modern creations – although subsequently adopted by many clans as their official tartans. The 'Stuart' brothers had circulated a version of *Vestiarum Scoticum* in the 1820s; this had been warmly welcomed by some, but greeted with scepticism by others, including Sir Walter Scott, who in a letter of 19 November 1829 declared that the 'idea of distinguishing the clans by their tartans is but a fashion of modern date'.

Via Regia (Latin, 'royal road') The name given in the Middle Ages to the road between Edinburgh and Jedburgh, connecting the Scottish kings to the great Border abbeys. It was a regular pilgrimage route, and Malcolm IV endowed the Church and Hospital of the Holy Trinity at Soutra Aisle as a resting place at the halfway mark. For much of its route the Via Regia follows what was the Roman DERE STREET and is now the A68. The name was also given to other 'royal roads', including the ROYAL MILE.

Vice more attractive than whisky, a Argument, according to Walter Elliott, who, in a speech to the House of Commons in 1942, declared 'Argument to the Scot is a vice more attractive than whisky.'

Village of Mourning The meaning of the Gaelic place name Balfron, a village in Stirlingshire. The name supposedly alludes to an incident when a pack of wolves attacked the village and took away many children. This may refer to a Viking raid, such as the Norse invasion in 1263 prior to the Battle of Largs.

Villee Vinkee, Der kleine *See* WEE WILLIE WINKIE.

Virginia Dons *See* TOBACCO LORDS.

Visiting one's patients accompanied by one's pet sheep *See* LANG SANDY.

Vital Spark *See* HANDY, PARA.

Voice of Rugby, the The Hawick-born rugby union commentator Bill McLaren (1923–2010), whose broadcasting career stretched from 1953 to 2002. His own promising career as a player (he played in a Scotland trial in 1947) was cut short when he contracted tuberculosis. As a radio and then TV commentator, McLaren was known for his even-handedness, even when Scotland was playing, and for his colourful phrases such as 'It's high enough, it's long enough, it's straight enough', and 'They'll be dancing in the streets of Hawick/Melrose/Galashiels tonight.' His last commentary was at the 2002 Wales vs Scotland match, at which a Welsh supporter held up a banner declaring 'Bill McLaren is Welsh"

Vomit To be sick in Scotland is to *boke, boak,*

bowk or *bock*. Alternatively, it is to *byochy-byochy* or to BOLT THE CADGER. In 1629 the baron court of the Campbells of Glenorchy fined a man for doing just this on the plaintiff's floor. *See also*

COCKTAILS; IF IT'S NO' THE SKITTER, IT'S THE SPEW.

Voodoo of the Hebridean kind *See* CORP CRIADH.

W

Wabsteid A recent Scots neologism, meaning 'web-site'. A *wab* is a piece of woven fabric, while *steid* means 'place'. Other neologisms coined to deal with the modern world include *cauldpress*, 'refrigerator', and *stoor-sooker*, 'vacuum cleaner'.

Wabster, Jock *See* DEIL'S OWER JOCK WABSTER, THE.

Wade's Roads A network of roads built across the Highlands in the 1720s and 1730s by General George Wade (1673–1748), in the wake of the 1715 Jacobite Rebellion. The intention was to enable government troops to deal rapidly with any repeat performance. Ironically, when the 1745 Rebellion broke out, the Jacobites found Wade's roads enabled them to march south more rapidly than would otherwise have been the case.

> Had you seen but these roads before they were
>   made,
> You would hold up your hands and bless General
>   Wade.
> – Old rhyme

Wag-at-the-wa' A species of BROWNIE, described as follows by William Henderson in his *Notes on the Folk-Lore of the Northern Counties of England and the Borders* (1879):

> We are told ... that he is a sort of Brownie, who presided over the Border kitchen, where he acted family monitor, but was a torment to the servants, especially to the kitchen-maid. His seat was by the hearth, or on the crook or bar of iron, terminating in a large hook, which may be seen in old houses hanging by a swivel from a beam in the chimney to hold pots and kettles. Whenever the crook was empty, Wag-at-the-wa' would take possession of it, and swing there with great complacency, only absenting himself when

there was a death in the family. He was fond of children and of household mirth, and hence his attachment to the ingle. When droll stories were told his laugh might be heard distinctly; but if he heard of any liquor being drunk, except home-brewed ale, he would cough and be displeased.

> His general appearance was that of a grisly old man, with short crooked legs, while a long tail assisted him in keeping his seat on the crook. Sometimes he appeared in a grey mantle, with the remains of an old 'pirnicap' on his head, drawn down over that side of the face which was troubled with toothache, a constant grievance of his; but he commonly wore a red coat and blue breeches, both garments being made of 'familie woo [wool]'.

> Altogether there is something uncanny about this ancient sprite, and the mode of his disappearance (for he has passed away from the Scottish ingle) does not speak well for him. A deep cut is now invariably made in the iron of the crook in the form of a cross, and is called the witches' mark, because it warns witches from the fire. This sign also scares away auld Wag-at-the-wa', and keeps him from touching the crook. Still it is deemed wrong and foolish ever to wag the crook, since it is a sort of invitation to the sprite to return. Mr Wilkie says that he has seen a visitor rise up and leave the house, because one of the boys of the family idly swung the crook: she was so horrified, at this 'invokerie' that she declared 'she wad na abide in the house where it was practised'.

The name *wag-at-the-wa'* was also applied to a type of clock from the Black Forest with a pendulum swinging free beneath it, as in the following anonymous song with a music-hall flavour about a man out with his drinking companions who realizes how late it has become:

> She's watchin the wag-at-the-wa',
> Cronies, I'll hae tae be leavin',

My conscience, a quarter tae twa,
And I said I'd be hame at eleeven;
So cronies guid-nicht tae ye aa,
Losh, but I'm sweir tae gae 'wa,
But Mistress McCann's waitin up for her man
And she's watchin the wag-at-the-wa'.

Wages of sin, the Something much pondered upon by ministers and elders of the Kirk down the centuries, as can be seen in the following dialogue recollected by John Buchan in *Memory-Hold-the-Door* (1940):

'Is it true that under the Act there's a maternity benefit, and that a woman gets the benefit whether she's married or no?'
  'That is right.'
  'D'ye approve of that?'
  'With all my heart.'
  'Well, sir, how d'ye explain this? The Bible says the wages of sin is death and the Act says thirty shillins.'

Wag-tawse *See* TAWSE.

Wallace Monument, the A neo-Gothic tower, some 220 ft (67 m) high, designed by John Thomas Rochead, and standing on Abbey Craig near Stirling. It commemorates the national hero William Wallace (d. 1305), and was completed in 1869. It took some time to raise the necessary cash, which was the source of some embarrassment in Scotland, although foreign contributors (including Giuseppe Garibaldi) came to the rescue:

Standing on the ramparts of Stirling Castle, the spectator cannot help noticing an unsightly excrescence of stone and lime rising on the brow of the Abbey Craig. This is the Wallace Tower. Designed to commemorate the war for independence, the building is making but slow progress. It is maintained by charitable contributions, like a lying-in hospital. It is a big beggar man, like O'Connell. It is tormented by an eternal lack of pence, like Mr Dick Swiveller. It sends round the hat as frequently as ever did Mr Leigh Hunt.
  – Alexander Smith, *A Summer in Skye* (1865)

See also BRAVEHEART.

Wallace's Cradle A platform, accessed by a 'scrambling stair', half-way up a fissure in the rock above the 14th-century Well-House Tower, the lowest part of Edinburgh Castle, situated beneath the cliff above West Princes Street Gardens. There does not appear to be any historical link with William Wallace; the alternative name, the Crane Bastion, refers to the fact that on the platform there once stood a crane used to raise water from the Well-House. Hereabouts some gruesome remains have been uncovered:

A human skull, much shattered as though by a fall, was found on the steps near some other bones. A trench on the E. side of the Tower disclosed a deal coffin containing the skeletons of a male and two females, thought to be the remains of a man named Sinclair and his two sisters who, in 1628, had been drowned in the North Loch for incest.
  – The Royal Commission on the Ancient Monuments of Scotland, *An Inventory of the Ancient and Historical Monuments of the City of Edinburgh* (1951)

The name Wallace's Cradle, or Wallace's Bed, is also applied to the Bronze Age fort on Cockleroy Hill, near Beecraigs Country Park south of Linlithgow. Here Wallace is said to have reconnoitred the English encampment prior to the Battle of Falkirk in 1298.

Wallace's Oak A mighty oak that once stood in Elderslie, Renfrewshire, the reputed birthplace of William Wallace (the KNIGHT OF ELDERSLIE). According to legend, it provided a hiding place for Wallace and 300 of his men from the English, and as a consequence 'Wallace's Oak' was supposedly used as a password by Jacobite soldiers during the '45. Sir Walter Scott had a QUAICH made out of a fragment of its wood. In 1825 the tree was 67 ft (20.4 m) high, and its trunk had a diameter of 21 ft (6.4 m) at ground level. It fell in a storm in the middle of the 19th century (one source gives 1845, another 1856). Elderslie is also home to 'Wallace's Yew', which parish records in the 18th century describe as 'this ancient tree', although tree experts judge that it was probably planted around 1729, the year that the Wallace estate was sold to the Speirs family. The current tree – which suffered considerable damage during a storm on 12 January 2005 – may thus be an offspring of an older tree.

A number of other (non-extant) trees have been associated with Wallace, including the Torwood Oak (between Falkirk and Stirling), under which he is reputed to have made camp, and the Bishopton Sycamore (Renfrewshire), where 'Wallace was delivered up to his enemies by the treachery of a pretended friend' (Jacob Stuart Strutt, *Sylva Britannica*, 1830).

Wallacethebruceism A species of Scottish sentiment, according to James Bridie in *A Small Stir* (1949):

> A great deal of what is called Scottish sentiment *is* funny. To anybody who knows the people who indulge in it, Wallacethebruceism, Charlieoverthewaterism, Puirrabbieburnsism, Bonniebonniebanksism, Myainfolkism and Laymedoonandeeism, those not very various forms of Scottish sentiment, are very comical indeed.

Wallie dug or **wally dug** Either of a pair of decorative china dogs that from the 19th century on adorned the mantelpiece of many a Scots living room. *Wallie* means 'fancy, ornamental', and is specifically applied to objects made of porcelain: hence *wallies* are false teeth (*see* APERITIF), and in Glasgow a *wallie close* is a tiled entry to a tenement, regarded as a sign of upward mobility. Thus if you are described as *wallie-close-gless-door* you are regarded as socially pretentious. Mention should also be made of a *wally wall*, which is a porcelain urinal of the uncompartmentalized variety. Finally, *the Wally Dishes* is a nickname for St Aloysius' College, a fee-paying Jesuit school in Glasgow.

Walrus of the Hebrides, the In his *Voyage Round Great Britain* (1815–25), William Daniell describes an unusual visitor to the Western Isles:

> It may not appear extraordinary that along the western side of Harris some fragments of ice have occasionally drifted from the northern latitudes. A short time before the present visit to Rowadill, a walrus found its way on shore, to great consternation of the inhabitants, and was supposed to have been brought hither from his home in the Arctic Circle on one of these natural rafts. The islanders, gradually recovering from their panic, collected their dissipated courage, and at length per-

suading themselves that this formidable visitant had manifested no decided intention of devouring them all, they very manfully destroyed him. The head, which was the only part spared, came into the possession of Macleod, by whom it is preserved as a memorable curiosity. Had he been on the island at the time when the walrus came ashore, it would not have been so wantonly destroyed.

A similar fate befell the last of the British great auks, which in July 1840 was beaten to death on Stac an Armin by St Kildans, who took it for a witch or a ghost; *see* GHOST-BIRD, THE. See also BLUE WHALE OF BRAGAR, THE; CAMEL OF THE CANONGATE, THE; ELEPHANT OF BROUGHTY FERRY, THE.

Waly An exclamation of sorrow, as in the traditional ballad, 'O Waly, Waly':

> O waly, waly up the bank
> And waly, waly doon the brae,
> And waly, waly by yon burn side
> Where I and my first love did gae.

The ballad is said to be based on the sad case of Lady Barbara Erskine, daughter of John Erskine, 20th Earl of Mar, who in 1670 married James Douglas, 2nd Marquess of Douglas. She was unjustly accused of adultery by Douglas's factor, Lowrie of Blackwood, whose suit, it is said, she had previously rejected. Douglas left her, and she returned to her father's house and never remarried.

Waly also appears in the ballad, 'The Earl of Erroll'. This ballad refers to another unfortunate 17th-century marriage, in this case that between Gilbert Hay, 11th Earl of Erroll, and Catherine Carnegie, daughter of James, 2nd Earl of Southesk. They married in 1658, but no issue was forthcoming, and this seems to have resulted in a court case revolving around the question as to whether, if the marriage was unconsummated, the dowry was due.

> O Erroll it's a bonny place,
> It stands in yonder glen;
> The lady lost the rights of it
> The first night she gaed hame.
> A waly and a waly!
> According as ye ken,
> The thing we ca the ranting o't,
> Our lady lies her lane, O.

In another version of 'The Earl of Erroll', *waly* becomes a substantive: 'The waly o't, the waly o't.' *See also* OCHANE.

Wanderer A term for a COVENANTER during the persecutions of Charles II and James II, especially one of those who left their homes to be with the peripatetic preachers who held outdoor conventicles in the wilder parts of Ayrshire and Galloway.

> When he had finished his prayer he arose, and taking Morton by the arm, they descended together to the stable, where the Wanderer (to give Burley a title which was often conferred on his sect) began to make his horse ready to pursue his journey.
> – Sir Walter Scott, *Old Mortality* (1816), chapter vi

Wanfukkit funling A misbegotten foundling; *see* FLYTING.

Wan singer, wan song 'One singer, one song', an adjuration heard in Glasgow not to interrupt the speaker. The expression presumably originated in clubs, where someone might seek to prevent a drunken audience from tunelessly joining in with the performer.

Want a feather in the wing, to To be a few chips short of a fish supper, i.e. a bit dim.

Want a slate, to To be a couple of tiles short of a weatherproof roof.

Want tuppence o' the shillin', to To be a few pieces short of a packed lunch.

'Wark o' the Weavers, The' *See* IF IT WISNAE FOR THE WEAVERS.

Warriors, the *See* FOOTBALL CLUB NICKNAMES.

Washing the apron The ceremony by which apprentices were (at least until the later 19th century) initiated into a trade, or by which apprentices became journeymen. The ceremony, accompanied by much carousing, involved washing the apron of the initiate.

Washing the bride *See* PENNY BRIDAL.

Wasps, the *See* FOOTBALL CLUB NICKNAMES.

Water burn *See* FIRE BURN.

Water cow An amphibious beast of both Highland and Lowland legend, said to live in various lochs. In his unfinished *Scenes of Infancy* (*c.*1803), John Leyden, one of Sir Walter Scott's collaborators in the compilation of *MINSTRELSY OF THE SCOTTISH BORDER*, describes one such loch, that of Alemoor, on the remote road between Hawick and the Ettrick Valley:

> Sad is the wail that floats o'er Alemoor's lake,
> And nightly bids her gulfs unbottom'd quake,
> While moonbeams, sailing o'er her waters blue,
> Reveal the frequent tinge of blood-red hue.

Then in a note he adds:

> The lake, or loch, of Alemoor, whence the river Ale, which falls into the Teviot beneath Ancram, originates, is regarded with a degree of superstitious horror by the common people. It is reckoned the residence of the water-cow, an imaginary amphibious monster, not unlike the Siberian mammoth.

Scott himself recorded another story of the water cow that he had heard at an Edinburgh dinner party:

> Clanronald told us, as an instance of Highland credulity, that a set of his kinsmen, Borradale and others, believing that the fabulous Water Cow inhabited a small lake near his house, resolved to drag the monster into day. With this view they bivouacked by the side of the lake, in which they placed, by way of night-bait, two small anchors, such as belong to boats, each baited with the carcase of a dog slain for the purpose. They expected the Water Cow would gorge on this bait, and were prepared to drag her ashore the next morning, when, to their confusion of face, the baits were found untouched. It is something too late in the day for setting baits for Water Cows.
> – Journal, 23 November 1827

Watergaw *See* RAINBOWS AND RELATED PHENOMENA.

Water Hole, the A detention cell that was once located under the old Guard House in Edinburgh's High Street. It was notorious for its dankness and pools of standing water, present both in summer and in winter.

> Gin we twa cou'd be as auld-farrant
> As gar the council gie a warrant,
> Ilk lown rebellious to tak,
> Wha walks not in the proper track,
> And o' three shilling Scottish suck him;
> Or in the *water-hole* sair douk him;
> This might assist the poor's collection,
> And gie baith parties satisfaction.
> – Robert Fergusson, 'Mutual Complaint of Plainstanes and Causey, in their Mother-tongue' (1773)

Water horse *See* KELPIE.

Water kelpie *See* KELPIE.

Waterspout of Arthur's Seat *See* GUTTIT HADDIE.

Water Willie The nickname of the publisher Sir William Collins (1817–95), who was Lord Provost of Glasgow (1877–80) and, like his father (the founder of the family firm), a zealous temperance campaigner.

Waur to water than to corn Literally, 'worse to water than to corn', i.e. more averse to water than to drink made from grain; in other words, over fond of a dram.

Waverley *See* AUTHOR OF *WAVERLEY*, THE.

Wean *See under* BAIRNS O' FALKIRK.

Weather gaw *See* RAINBOW.

We arra peepul A chant heard on the terraces of Scottish football stadiums, apparently asserting that the people in question are invincible, and that their voices will be heard.

> 'We arra peepul' is the strange, defiant cry heard from some of Scotland's football terraces in the late twentieth century. But which people? A foreign visitor might well be confused.
> – Michael Lynch, *Scotland, A New History* (1991)

The chant is particularly associated with the supporters of Glasgow Rangers FC.

> Every Rangers fan was drinking and singing and drinking some more, and the chant was a celebration of their absolute, unshakeable Rangersness: 'We arra peepul!'
> – Aidan Smith, in *The Scotsman*, 24 December 2001, recalling his first attendance at a Rangers match, 30 years before

> Naively convinced that they are the salt of the earth – 'we arra peepul!' – the Weegies, so devoid of airs and graces, do relish a bit of banter.
> – *Edinburgh Evening News*, 26 July 2002

> When you are dealing with a 'We arra peepul' mentality you are dealing with folk who think they are above the law.
> – 'Greenyodais', ETims Online Celtic Fanzine, 20 February 2009

Some say the phrase originated with a pre-Celtic tribe in Scotland, noted for their exquisitely crafted miniature arrowheads; these were the Wee Arra People. *See also* BILLY BOYS; FAMINE SONG, THE; JOCK TAMSON'S BAIRNS; NINETY-MINUTE BIGOTS; WEEGIES; HERE'S TO US.

Weaver Poet, the Robert Tannahill (1774–1810), who was born in Paisley and was apprenticed to his father as a handloom weaver aged 12. He began to write poetry around this time, composing as he sat at the loom, and subsequently published many poems and songs (some to music by a fellow weaver, Robert Archibald Smith) in periodicals such as the *Scots Magazine* and the *Glasgow Courier*. In 1805 he founded the Paisley Burns Club, and in the same year published a volume of his own poems and songs by subscription, but this was poorly received, and he immediately set about revising it. After the publisher Constable declined to take on a revised edition, Tannahill – who was prone to bouts of depression – burnt his manuscripts and drowned himself in a culvert under a canal outside Paisley at a place now known as Tannahill's Pool. His songs include 'Jessie, the FLOWER OF DUNBLANE', 'Oh, are ye sleeping, Maggie' and 'The Braes o' Glennifer', in which one can find his distinctive feel for genteel bleakness and decorous melancholy:

Keen blaws the wind o'er the braes o' Gleniffer,
The auld castle's turrets are cover'd wi' snaw;
How chang'd frae the time that I met wi' my lover,
Amang the broom bushes by Stanley green shaw:
The wild flow'rs o' simmer were spread a' sae
  bonnie,
The mavis sang sweet frae the green birken tree;
But far tae the camp they ha'e marched my dear
  Johnnie,
And noo it is winter wi' Nature and me.
    [*shaw*, 'thicket, small wood'; *mavis*, 'thrush'; *birken*, 'birch']

A later weaver-poet, who identified himself with Tannahill, was the Aberdeen-born William Thom (?1798–1848), who coped with a hard life by hard drinking – which seems, in the end, to have stemmed his poetic flow. He produced just one volume, *Rhymes and Recollections of a Hand-Loom Weaver* (1844), which includes the radical-minded 'Whisperings for the Unwashed':

Rubadub, rubadub, row dow-dow!
Hark, how he waukens the Weavers now!
Wha lie belair'd in a dreamy steep –
A mental swither 'tween death an' sleep –
Wi' hungry wame and hopeless breast,
Their food no feeding, their sleep no rest.
Arouse ye, ye sunken, unravel your rags,
No coin in your coffers, no meal in your bags;
Yet cart, barge, and wagon, with load after load,
Creak mockfully, passing your breadless abode.

See also PLOUGHMAN POET, THE.

Webster, Jock *See* DEIL'S OWER JOCK WABSTER, THE.

Wee Bud The nickname of the footballer Willie Johnston (b.1946), who played for Rangers, West Bromwich Albion, Birmingham City, Hearts and Scotland. He scored the winning goal for Rangers in the final of the European Cup Winners' Cup in 1972 against Dynamo Moscow, but his international career came to an end after he failed a drugs test at the 1978 World Cup. Johnston was known for his maverick behaviour (during one match, for example, he negotiated the purchase of a greenhouse from a spectator), and his fiery temper sometimes got him into trouble. But in 1976 an FA Disciplinary Report,

investigating one incident, concluded: 'If Johnston had deliberately intended an attack on the referee, his right foot would not have missed its target.' His memoirs are entitled *Sent Off At Gunpoint* – something that happened to him not just once, but twice.

Weedgie *See* WEEGIE.

Wee Eck A nickname of Alex Salmond (b.1954), leader of the Scottish National Party, and Scotland's first minister since 2007. 'Eck' is a standard familiar version of Alec or Alex.

He strides across Scotland like a Caesar, a movie Caesar. More Ustinov than Olivier. A small man with a comfortable paunch, a brilliant mind and a liking for potato chips.
  Meet Wee Eck. Or as he is known to his wife and on Sundays, Scottish nationalist leader Alex Salmond.
    – Nathan Goldberg, on www.wowdewow.co.uk, 9 May 2011

Wee Eck is not to be confused with BIG ECK, aka the footballer and manager Alex McLeish, although, confusingly, Wee Eck *is* sometimes known as Big Eck, alluding to his girth. It is Salmond's portly figure that has prompted the writer Pat Kane to dub him *Maximum Eck*.

Wee finger, to cock or **turn up one's** *See* COCK ONE'S WEE FINGER.

Wee Flea, the *See* FLYING FLEA, THE.

Wee Frees The nickname of the Free Church of Scotland, that part of the original Free Church of Scotland (formed at the DISRUPTION OF 1843) that refused to join with the United Presbyterian Church of Scotland in 1900 to form the United Free Church of Scotland, which in turn reunited with the Church of Scotland in 1929. The current Free Church of Scotland, strongly represented in parts of the Highlands and Islands, is known for its puritanism and strict observance of the SABBATH. An earlier schism in the original Free Church of Scotland in 1893 had led to the formation of the Free Presbyterian Church of Scotland, sometimes nicknamed the Wee Wee Frees. The nickname 'Wee

Frees' may derive from the fact that at the time of the Disruption of 1843 the original Free Church was referred to as the 'wee kirk', as attested in the following anonymous rhyme:

The Free Kirk, the wee kirk,
The kirk without the steeple;
The Auld Kirk, the cauld kirk,
The kirk without the people.

Weegie or **Weedgie** A sometimes derogatory term for an inhabitant of Glasgow, which is in turn sometimes referred to as *Weegie-land*. The word is an abbreviation of *Glasgwegian*. See also KEELIE.

Wee hairy A pejorative term for any young woman whose morals are regarded as sub-standard.

Wee hauf See HAUF AN A HAUF.

Wee heavy See BEER.

Weel-gaithered Affluent; *gaither* in this context means to store up riches.

Weel-kent Well-known, most often in the phrase 'a weel-kent face', i.e. a familiar figure.

Weel-willy Willing, ready, well-disposed.

O what a peacemaker is a guid weel-willy pintle [penis]! It is the mediator, the guarantee, the umpire, the bond of union, the solemn league and covenant, the plenipotentiary, the Aaron's rod, the Jacob's staff, the prophet Elisha's pot of oil, the Ahasuerus' sceptre, the sword of mercy, the philosopher's stone, the Horn of Plenty, and Tree of Life between Man and Woman.
 – Robert Burns, letter to Robert Ainslie, 1788

Wee Macwhachle A jocular name given to a toddler; to *wauchle* is to stumble or stagger.

Wee man, the See IN THE NAME OF THE WEE MAN. *Compare* BIG MAN, THE; BIG YIN, THE.

Wee Rangers, the See FOOTBALL CLUB NICKNAMES.

Wee Rovers, the See FOOTBALL CLUB NICKNAMES.

Wee, sleekit, cow'rin', tim'rous beastie How Burns describes the addressee in 'To a Mouse'. The poet, whose plough has destroyed the mouse's nest, expresses remarkable sympathy with his fellow creature:

I'm truly sorry Man's dominion
Has broken Nature's social union,
An' justifies that ill opinion
     Which makes thee startle,
At me, thy poor, earth-born companion,
     An' fellow-mortal!

William Scott Douglas, in his 1877 annotated edition of Burns's works, says of the poem:

This is, by readers *gentle* and readers *simple*, acknowledged to be one of the most perfect little gems that ever human genius produced.

The poem includes a couplet that has become proverbial; *see* BEST LAID SCHEMES.

Wee small hours An unnecessarily tautological expansion of the phrase 'small hours', denoting the hours soon after midnight (one, two, three o'clock or so), and only finding inclusion here because of the Scots word 'wee'. The first citation in the *Oxford English Dictionary* for 'small hours' is from Dickens's *Sketches from Boz* (1836–7), and for 'wee small hours' from Frederic W. Farrar's *Julian Home* (1859): 'Often beguiled by his studies into the "wee small" hours of night.' Farrar was an Indian-born English theologian, pedagogue and divine, and by his deployment of inverted commas we may assume that the phrase was already current when he used it. The most famous use of the phrase, however, is in the title song of Frank Sinatra's moody 1955 album *In the Wee Small Hours*.

Wee, wee German lairdie, a George I, so dubbed by HONEST ALLAN Cunningham (1784–1842):

Wha the deil hae we got for a King,
But a wee, wee German lairdie?
 – 'The Wee, Wee German Lairdie'

By the time Cunningham was writing this squib on the Hanoverians, the expression of such Jacobite sentiments was regarded as harmless nostalgia.

Wee Willie Winkie A personification of sleep (sometimes just Willie Winkie), as featured in the eponymous nursery rhyme by the Glasgow cabinet maker and poet William Miller (1810–72), 'the Laureate of the Nursery', and published by him in the 1841 volume of the *WHISTLE-BINKIE* anthologies. The first verse, which may be traditional, goes as follows:

Wee Willie Winkie rins through the toun,
Up stairs and doon stairs in his nicht-goun,
Tirling at the window, crying at the lock,
'Are the weans in their bed, for it's now ten
    o'clock?'

'Willie Winkie', as well as being an equivalent of 'the Sandman' who brings sleep to children, was a Jacobite nickname for William III, and the rhyme may refer to curfew regulations under his reign; however, no vestige of political satire remains in Miller's version. The rhyme is also popular in Germany, where it is titled '*Der kleine Villee Vinkee*'. Miller himself died sick and destitute, but subsequently a public subscription was raised to erect a memorial to him in the Glasgow Necropolis.

Miller's younger contemporary, Robert Tennant (1830–79), created a diurnal equivalent of the nocturnal Winkie:

Wee Davie Daylicht keeks owre the sea,
Early in the mornin', wi' a clear e'e;
Waukens all the birdies that are sleepin' soun':
Wee Davie Daylicht is nae lazy loon.

Weird Sisters, the *See under MACBETH.*

Weir of Hermiston An unfinished novel by Robert Louis Stevenson (1850–94), published posthumously in 1896. Hermiston, although physically based on Glencorse in the Pentland Hills, took its name from a farm on the Water of Ale, between Ettrick and Teviotdale. 'Weir' here is not a hydrological feature, but rather the name of the hero, Archie Weir, whose tyrannical father is Adam Weir, Lord Hermiston, a hanging judge. 'I have been the

means, under God,' Hermiston says at one point, 'of hanging a great number, but never such a disjaskit [dejected, shabby, wearied] rascal as yourself.' The name Weir was inspired by that of the 17th-century warlock, MAJOR WEIR, while the character of Lord Hermiston is based on the historical Lord Braxfield (1722–99), a notorious hounder of Scottish radicals, whose pithy remarks from the bench were gleefully recorded by his contemporaries:

[To an eloquent prisoner in the dock] Ye're a vera clever chiel, man, but ye wad be nane the waur o' a hanging.
    – Quoted John Gibson Lockhart, *Life of Scott* (1837–8)

[To a political prisoner who claimed that Christ too had been a reformer] Muckle he made o' that; he was hanget.
    – Quoted Lord Cockburn, *Memorials of His Times* (1856)

Braxfield was equally gracious to the gentler sex, and is said to have addressed his partner at whist thus:

Ye stupid auld bitch ... I beg your pardon, mem, I mistook ye for my wife.

In the 1877 edition of *Kay's Originals*, it is recorded that Braxfield couched his proposal to his second wife in the following terms:

Lissy, I am looking for a wife, and I thought you just the person that would suit me. Let me have your answer, aff or on, the morn, and nae mair about it.

Stevenson himself, in his essay 'Some Portraits by Raeburn' (*Virginibus Puerisque*, 1881), wrote of Braxfield:

He was the last judge on the Scotch bench to employ the pure Scotch idiom. His opinions, thus given in Doric, and conceived in a lively, rugged, conversational style, were full of point and authority. Out of the bar, or off the bench, he was a convivial man, a lover of wine, and one who 'shone peculiarly' at tavern meetings. He has left behind him an unrivalled reputation for rough and cruel speech; and to this day his name smacks of the gallows.

As to the novel itself, critics (including Henry James, a great admirer) have generally agreed that *Weir of Hermiston* shows that at the time of his final illness Stevenson was heading away from juvenile adventures towards something truly great in fiction.

Well, the *See* FOOTBALL CLUB NICKNAMES.

Well-hung fish At one time the Scots seem to have had a taste for fish that was a touch gamey. On Lewis, uncured skate was left hanging for a number of days before being cooked and eaten, and in her *Cook and Housewife's Manual* (1826), Meg DODS (Mrs Isobel Johnston) suggests fish be 'ripened' for two or three days. Haddock that was no longer of the freshest was known in some parts as *Monday's haddie*, while sun-dried haddock was known elsewhere as *rizzer* (from an archaic French word *resorré*, 'dried up, shrivelled').

Well-intentioned but hysterical poodle, a Lewis Grassic Gibbon's characterization of Mary Queen of Scots in *Scottish Scene* (1934):

> The 'heroic young queen' in question had the face, mind, manners and morals of a well-intentioned but hysterical poodle.

Well of the Dead A spring on Culloden Moor where, after the battle on 16 April 1746, many bodies were found, including that of Alexander MacGillivray of Dunmaglass, commander of the Clan Chattan regiment. A memorial stone was erected on the spot in the 19th century.

Well of the Heads (Gaelic, *Tobar nan Ceann*) A well on the west shore of Loch Oich, just south of Invergarry, where in 1812 Colonel Alaistair Mac-Donnell of Glengarry (*see* GLENGARRY; HIGHLAND PRIDE) erected an obelisk with a carving on its top of seven heads, together with a hand holding a large dagger. The monument commemorates a gruesome incident in 1663, when on 25 September seven men murdered Alexander MacDonald, 13th chief of the MacDonalds of Keppoch, along with his brother Ranald. The murdered men had been engaged in a land dispute with Alexander MacDougall Mac-Donald of Inverlair. Justice came two years later, when the Privy Council in Edinburgh issued LETTERS OF FIRE AND SWORD against the perpetrators. Iain LOM, a Keppoch MacDonald and noted poet, with the help of the MacDonalds of Sleat, sought out the murderers and cut off their heads, placing them in a basket to take them back to show the chief of the Glengarry MacDonnells at Invergarry Castle.

On the way, Lom stopped at the well to wash the heads clean of blood – although in later versions of the story it was said that he lowered the basket into the water to put an end to the horrendous grindings of teeth and gnashing of jaws that were emanating from the severed heads. The heads were later sent to Edinburgh, to be displayed upon the gallows.

We'll pay for it The stock response of the stereotypically miserable Scot to fine weather. The line is celebrated in Alastair Reid's poem 'Scotland', in which the poet glories in a day of radiance and sunlight, and seeks to share his enthusiasm with 'the woman from the fish-shop':

> And what did she have to say for it?
> Her brow grew bleak, her ancestors raged in their
>   graves
> as she spoke with their ancient misery:
> 'We'll pay for it, we'll pay for it, we'll pay for it.'

Wells of Wearie, the A collection of springs that once flowed from the side of Arthur's Seat in Edinburgh, near the crag called Samson's Ribs. They were the subject of a number of songs, for example:

> Oh, the sun winna blink in your bonnie blue een,
>   Nor tinge your white brow, my dearie;
> For I will shade a bower wi' rashes lang and green,
>   By the lanesome Wells o' Wearie.

Another, with words by a poet-plumber called Alexander Maclagan (b.1811), commences:

> Come let us climb Auld Arthur Seat,
> When summer flowers are blooming;
> When golden blooms and heather bells
> Are a' the air perfuming.
> When sweet May gowans deck the braes,
> The hours flee fast fu' cheerie,
> Where bonnie lasses bleach their claes
> Beside the Wells o' Wearie.

The Wells were destroyed in 1820 during the construction of a railway tunnel.

Wemyss Madonna, the The byname of Botticelli's *The Virgin Adoring the Sleeping Christ Child*, painted at some time between 1480 and 1485. It was in the possession of the Earl of Wemyss and March until

1999, when it was saved for the nation at a cost of over £10 million and presented to the National Gallery of Scotland. It was acquired by the Wemyss family in the 19th century, and in 1856 the then earl wrote: 'I can truly say that there is not in the whole of the Florentine collections any one picture for which I would exchange this picture of mine.'

Wemyss ware An exuberant and colourful style of pottery, first produced in Fife in 1882 under the patronage of the Wemyss family. In the 1930s manufacture was transferred to Devon, but returned to Fife in the 1980s. Cats, pigs, tableware and tiles are popular products.

We're a' ae oo 'We are all one wool', i.e. we're all made from the same cloth – a sentiment akin to asserting that we are all JOCK TAMSON'S BAIRNS. A 19th-century rhyme goes as follows:

> We're either in or oot wi' folk,
> We're a' ae oo, we're a' ae oo.

See also OO.

We're a' Jock Tamson's bairns *See* JOCK TAM-SON'S BAIRNS.

West Highland terrier A breed of dog first bred by Colonel Edward Donald Malcolm (1837–1930), and originally called the Poltalloch terrier after his estate to the north of Lochgilphead in Argyll. The breed's distinctive white coat originates from the fact that a red terrier owned by the Colonel was mistaken for a fox and shot. The dogs are popularly known as *Westies*.

Westlothiana lizziae One of the oldest known reptiles (or possibly a reptile-like amphibian), dating from 350 million years ago. Its fossil (nicknamed 'Lizzie') was found at East Kirkton Quarry, Bathgate, West Lothian, in 1984, and is now on display at the Museum of Scotland in Edinburgh.

West Lothian Alps The jocular name for the red shale bings that dot the post-industrial countryside west of Edinburgh. The spoil heaps, some of which are now largely covered with grass and trees as nature reclaims them, are a result of the mining of

shale for oil initiated here by PARAFFIN YOUNG in the 19th century – the world's first oil industry. Young built his first paraffin works at Boghead, Bathgate, in 1851, and the last West Lothian shale mine closed in 1963. The spoil heaps have themselves been exploited for hard core for road-making. For a short time the shale waste was also used in the foundations of houses, but it reacted unexpectedly with mortar and cement, and a number of new houses collapsed as a result. One of the most striking of the bings is the many-summitted Five Sisters Bing at Westwood, which is depicted in a sculpture at the Newpark Roundabout in Livingstone, and which features in West Lothian's official logo.

West Lothian question, the A constitutional quandary first raised by Tam Dalyell, Labour MP for West Lothian from 1962 to 1983 (after which he was MP for Linlithgow until 2005). Dalyell posed the question in a Westminster debate on Scottish and Welsh devolution on 14 November 1977:

> For how long will English constituencies and English Honourable members tolerate ... at least 119 Honourable Members from Scotland, Wales and Northern Ireland exercising an important, and probably often decisive, effect on English politics while they themselves have no say in the same matters in Scotland, Wales and Northern Ireland?

Dalyell pointed out the absurdity of the Westminster MP for West Lothian having a say regarding matters affecting Blackburn, Lancashire, but not being able to vote on the same matters that affected Blackburn in West Lothian – his own constituency. Enoch Powell, then an Ulster Unionist MP, responded thus:

> We have finally grasped what the Honourable Member for West Lothian is getting at. Let us call it the West Lothian question.

Wha daur meddle wi me? The usual rendering in Scots of the national motto, *NEMO ME IMPUNE LACESSIT*. The phrase has its origins in a Border ballad, 'Little Jock Elliot', which recounts a 1566 encounter between the eponymous Little Jock Elliot of the Park, a notorious BORDER REIVER in Liddesdale, and James Hepburn, Earl of Bothwell, future husband of Mary Queen of Scots. Bothwell, as Keeper of Liddesdale, was determined to clear the reivers from his home patch, and had already rounded up many Elliots and imprisoned them in Hermitage Castle when he came across Little Jock Elliot and challenged him to single combat. Having shot Little Jock out of the saddle, Bothwell dismounted to finish his victim off, but didn't realize that his opponent had a hidden dagger, with which he wounded Bothwell in the face, chest and hands. Bothwell, bleeding badly, was taken by cart back to Hermitage Castle, only to find the captured Elliots had overpowered their guards and seized the castle. After some negotiation, the Elliots recovered their liberty and the earl his castle. As the ballad gleefully recounts:

> I ne'er was afraid of a foe,
> Or yield I liefer wad die;
> My name is Little Jock Elliot,
> And wha daur meddle wi' me?
>
> I've vanquished the queen's lieutenant,
> And garr'd her troopers flee;
> My name is Little Jock Elliot,
> And wha daur meddle wi' me?
>
> Wha daur meddle wi' me?
> Wha daur meddle wi' me?
> My name is Little Jock Elliot,
> And wha daur meddle wi' me?

See also FOUR MARIES, THE; LION OF LIDDESDALE.

Whale of Bragar, the See BLUE WHALE OF BRAGAR, THE.

Wha stole yer scone? or **Wha shat in yer handbag?** Why are you looking so miserable? See also SCONE O' THE DAY'S BAKIN', A.

What's that got to do wi' the Clyde navigation? What's that got to do with the subject in hand? The reference may either to be to the Forth and Clyde Navigation Company, established in 1768 and involved in canal building; or the Clyde Navigation Trust, formed in 1858 and involved in dredging the river. A variant of the expression is *What's that got to do wi' the price o' spam in Govan?*

Whaur's yer Wullie Shakespeare noo? The famous cry emanating from the stalls at the first performance of John Home's romantic tragedy *Douglas* in Edinburgh in 1756. The play tells the tale of young Douglas, whom his mother thinks to be dead, but who is brought up by Old Norval, a shepherd; in the end Douglas is killed and his mother throws herself off a cliff. Some were scandalized that Home, a minister of the Kirk, should have put his hand to the disreputable business of play-writing, but *Douglas* proved to be a considerable success, and did much to stir Scottish national pride, especially after it had a run at Covent Garden the following year. Adam Smith and David Hume were both keen supporters, the latter writing to the author:

> But the unfeigned tears which flowed from every eye, in the numerous representations which were made of it on [sic] this theatre; the unparalleled command, which you appeared to have over every affection of the human breast: These are uncontestable proofs, that you possess the true theatric genius of Shakespeare and Otway, refined from the unhappy barbarism of the one, and the licentiousness of the other.

Subsequent critics have not been so kind, and the play has faded into obscurity. Hugh MacDiarmid offered the following parody in *A Drunk Man Looks at the Thistle* (1926):

> My name is Norval. On the Grampian Hills
> It is forgotten, and deserves to be.
> So are the Grampian Hills and all the people
> Who ever heard of either them or me.

See also HUME VS HOME.

Wheeky-whacky day See TAWSE.

Where dreams come true Drumchapel, aka 'the DRUM', the massive postwar housing SCHEME on the west side of Glasgow. It was given this ironic accolade by Tony Roper in his play *THE STEAMIE* (1987):

> Dreams come true
> Surely mine is nearly due
> Four apartments and a view
> and an inside toilet too ...
> Me and John will get a new
> House in Drumchapel where dreams come true.

The scheme was built in the 1950s to rehouse 34,000 people moved from Glasgow's inner-city slums, but early hopes of a better life sank beneath a sea of social problems and crumbling housing.

Wherever Macdonald sits ... William Daniell, in his *Voyage Round Great Britain* (1815–25), tells the anecdote of the Macdonald chieftain ...

> ... who, when in Ireland, was invited to an entertainment given by the lord lieutenant. He happened to be one of the last of the guests who arrived, and took the first vacant seat which he found, and which was near the bottom of the table, by the door. The lord lieutenant invited him to come and sit by his side. Macdonald, who spoke no English, asked, 'What says the *carle*?' The answer was, 'His lordship bids you move to the head of the table.' The chieftain replied, 'Tell the carle, that wherever Macdonald sits, *that* is the head of the table.'

See also HIGHLAND PRIDE; MACNEIL OF BARRA HAS EATEN, THE.

Whig In the 17th century, a term applied disparagingly by their enemies to the COVENANTERS, especially those of southwest Scotland, such as the CAMERONIANS, who came out in arms against Charles II and James VII. Towards the end of Charles's reign, the term was applied in both Scotland and England to those who called for the exclusion of the Catholic James from the succession. This Whig faction was instrumental in engineering the Glorious Revolution of 1688–90, by which James was replaced on the throne by William of Orange; their Jacobite enemies were dubbed *Tories*. In Scotland, the term Whig was still being applied in the early 19th century by Episcopalians to Presbyterians, and by mainstream Presbyterians to their more extreme brethren, who had seceded from the established Church.

The origin of the word is not altogether clear. It appears in the 1640s in the north of England as a word for a rustic yokel, and in Scotland for a Presbyterian. Bishop Gilbert Burnet, in his *History of My Own Time* (1724), says that drovers from southwest Scotland encouraged their horses along using the word *whiggam*, and thus became known as *whiggamores*, abbreviated to *whigs*. In 1648 a party of extreme Covenanters from southwest Scotland marched to Edinburgh and overthrew the moderates under the Duke of Hamilton, in an episode mockingly dubbed the *Whiggamore Raid*. The *OED* states there is no evidence to support the supposed existence of the word *whiggam*, and suggests that *whiggamore* comes from the verb to *whig*, 'to urge forward, drive briskly', and *mare*, which originally applied to a horse of either sex. It discounts suggestions of any association of the word *whig* in the political-religious sense with the obsolete word *whig* or *wig*, which denoted whey, buttermilk or sour cream.

Whip the cat A phrase explained thus by Hugh Haliburton (John Logie Robertson, 1846–1922):

> 'Whipping the cat', or, more enigmatically, 'flogging poussy' – it is of tailors that we must be understood to speak – was simply a practice of going from farm-toun to farm-toun, even from cottar-house to cottar-house, and there working for, and meantime messing and lodging with, the inhabitants.
> – Hugh Haliburton, *In Scottish Fields* (1890)

Whisky The national spirit, consumed with HAGGIS on BURNS NIGHT, and without on other occasions. The word is an anglicized form of Gaelic *usquebaugh*, itself from *uisge beatha*, meaning 'water of life' – not to be confused with either *aqua vitae* (Latin for 'water of life'), an archaic term for brandy, nor with the Scandinavian spirit *aquavit* of *akvavit*, based on grain or potatoes and flavoured with aromatic seeds and spices such as caraway. Nor is it to be confused with *whiskey* with an 'e', which is what is drunk in Ireland and America. Outside Scotland, Scottish whisky is frequently referred to as SCOTCH. Much lore and many customs are associated with whisky, although 'washing the bride in whisky' appears to be a spurious one (*see* PENNY BRIDAL). One of the earlier accounts of whisky comes from Martin Martin's *Description of the Western Isles of Scotland* (1703):

> Their plenty of corn was such, as disposed the natives to brew several sorts of liquors, as common usquebaugh, another called trestarig, *id est*, aquavitæ, three times distilled, which is strong and hot; a third sort is four times distilled, and this by the natives is called

497

usquebaugh-baul, *id est*, usquebaugh, which at first taste affects all the members of the body: two spoonfuls of this last liquor is a sufficient dose; and if any man exceed this, it would presently stop his breath, and endanger his life. The trestarig and usquebaugh-baul, are both made of oats.

See also ARRAN WATER; ATHOLL BROSE; FREEDOM AND WHISKY GANG THEGITHER; MOUNTAIN DEW.

Whisky Galore A humorous 1947 novel by Compton Mackenzie, filmed as a celebrated Ealing Comedy in 1949. Mackenzie, who lived on Barra during the Second World War, was inspired by the real-life wreck of the SS *Politician* between Barra and Eriskay on 5 February 1941, en route to America with a cargo of whisky. The islanders of Eriskay salvaged thousands of bottles, but in so doing attracted the unwanted attentions of HM Customs and Excise, and 19 islanders ended up serving prison sentences in Inverness. Fourteen surviving bottles were auctioned for a total of £12,000 in Glasgow in 1993.

Whistle-binkie According to John Jamieson's *Etymological Dictionary of the Scottish Language* (1808), a whistle-binkie is

> ... one who attends a PENNY-WEDDING but without paying anything, and therefore has no right to take any share of the entertainment; a mere spectator, who is as it were left to sit on a *bench* by himself, and who, if he pleases, may whistle for his own amusement.

Whistle-Binkie was adopted as the title of a series of anthologies of humorous and sentimental verse published in Glasgow between 1832 and 1843. The 1842 omnibus edition gives its full title as *Whistle-Binkie, or the Piper of the Party, being a Collection of Songs for the Social Circle, chiefly original*. Contributions were solicited from the general public, who adopted a variety of approaches in pursuit of having their voices heard. Some, according to the publisher's introduction to the 1842 edition, 'speak and act as if your ordinary aliment were alcohol and percussion caps', while others 'have taken an opposite course, and by flattery, direct and indirect, tried to obtain a niche in our temple of the Scottish Muse'. Whatever the approach,

With those beings of vinegar aspect, whose breath would curdle 'the milk of human kindness', the Editor has no sympathy. He believes that there are a thousand blessings under the sun worth living and being thankful for ...

The mood, elevation and intention of the collection are summarized in some introductory lines by John D. Douglas, of which the following is a sample:

> Here's balm in store for every sore,
> Or sorrow e'er sae inky;
> A speedy cure for such, I'm sure,
> You'll find in Whistle-Binkie.

A flavour of the contents may be given by mentioning a few titles, such as 'A British Sailor's Song', 'A Mother's Advice', 'Hurrah for the Thistle', 'My Heather Land', 'Oh! and No!', 'The Evening Drappie', 'The Kail Brose of Auld Scotland', 'The Royal Union' and 'When the Butterfly'. Perhaps the only contribution to have acquired any kind of immortality is William Miller's 'WEE WILLIE WINKIE', first published in the 1841 volume.

The Whistlebinkies are a popular folk band who first emerged in the early 1970s.

Whistle kirk *See* KIST O' WHISTLES.

Whistle on yer thoum Go and play in the corner; *thoumb* is 'thumb'.

Whistle o'er the lave o't A traditional tune, attributed by Robert Burns to the Dumfries dancing master John Bruce (*c*.1720–85), who had been born in Braemar. However, the tune may date back to the 17th century, if the following story is to be believed:

> There was a legend long current in Glasgow that about [1700] as a citizen was passing at midnight through the churchyard which surrounds the Cathedral, he saw a neighbour of his own, lately buried, rise out of his grave and dance a jig with the Devil, who played the air called *Whistle o'er the lave o't* upon the bagpipes: which struck the whole city with so much horror that the town drummer was sent through the streets next morning, to forbid anyone to sing or whistle the tune in question.
> – Charles Kirkpatrick Sharpe, introduction to his 1818 edition of Robert Law's *Memorialls* (17th century)

Burns supplied some words for the tune (apparently replacing a less delicate original):

First when Maggie was my care,
Heav'n, I thought, was in her air;
Now we're married, spier [ask] nae mair,
But – whistle o'er the lave [rest] o't!

Meg was meek, and Meg was mild,
Sweet and harmless as a child:
Wiser men than me's beguiled –
Whistle o'er the lave o't!

How we live, my Meg and me,
How we love, and how we gree,
I care na by how few may see –
Whistle o'er the lave o't!

Wha I wish were maggots' meat,
Dish'd up in her winding-sheet,
I could write (but Meg wad see't) –
Whistle o'er the lave o't!

The tune has been used as a regimental march by the Highland Light Infantry and the Royal Highland Fusiliers.

Whistling bottoms See HARD AS HINNERSON'S ERSE, AS.

White Battle, the See CHAPTER OF MYTON, THE.

White breek An 18th-century nickname for a soldier of the British army, who with their red coats wore white breeches.

White cockade The emblem of the House of Stuart, first adopted by Charles II. It was worn by the Jacobite supporters of the exiled James VII and II and his successors; their enemies, the Hanoverians, wore a black cockade. The white cockade consisted of a piece of white ribbon, about an inch wide, folded and sewn into an equilateral cross, which was then fastened onto one's headgear (or into one's hair if one were a lady). White cockades are clearly visible on the bonnets of the Highlanders in David Morier's famous depiction of Culloden, painted shortly after the battle. Robert Burns, when he was not being a Jacobin, indulged in some Jacobite sentiment, for example in his 1790 song 'The White Cockade':

My love was born in Aberdeen,
The bonniest lad that e'er was seen;
But now he makes our hearts fu' sad,
He's taen the field wi' his white cockade.
    O he's a rantin, rovin blade,
    He's a brisk and a bonny lad,
    Betide what may, my heart is glad,
    To see my lad wi' his white cockade.

The following century James Hogg picked up the strain in 'Cam' Ye By Atholl?':

Cam' ye by Atholl, lad wi' the philabeg,
Down by the Tummel or banks o' the Garry?
Saw ye the lads, wi' their bonnets and white
    cockades
Leaving their mountains to follow Prince Charlie?

See also WHITE ROSE OF SCOTLAND, THE.

White Craw The nickname of an inhabitant of Carnwath, Lanarkshire, home of the RED HOSE RACE. The origin of the name is obscure.

White Heather Club, The An early-evening BBC television variety show with an exclusively Scottish content, produced in Glasgow and broadcast from 1958 to 1968. Andy Stewart was the presenter, and also sang songs and told jokes. Among the musicians were Moira Anderson and the folk groups the Corries and Robin Hall and Jimmy MacGregor, while Jimmy Shand (the LAIRD OF AUCHTERMUCHTY) and his band provided the accompaniment for the tartan-clad Scottish country dancers. Every week the programme ended with a mass rendition of the song 'Haste Ye Back', and special episodes, with guests such as Kenneth McKellar, Jimmy Logan and Stanley Baxter, were broadcast at HOGMANAY. The title alludes to the supposed good luck brought by white HEATHER.

White hind See FORESTER OF THE FAIRY CORRIE, THE.

White Lady of Corstorphine, the See CORSTORPHINE SYCAMORE, THE.

White nights See SIMMER DIM.

White pet A hand-reared lamb. 'The Story of the White Pet' was collected from Mrs MacTavish, widow of the minister of Kildalton, Islay, by J.F. Campbell in his *Popular Tales of the West Highlands* (Vol. 1, 1890). This folk tale, which closely resembles the German story 'The Musicians of Bremen', tells how the White Pet, hearing he is to be killed at Christmas, runs away and is joined by a number of other animals who wish to avoid a similar fate. They succeed in scaring a gang of thieves from a lonely house, and take possession of their ill-gotten gains.

White pudding *See* MEALIE PUDDING.

White Queen, the A nickname for Mary Queen of Scots, on account of the white mourning clothes she wore after the death of her first husband, Francis II of France.

> Just as we see, half rosy and half white,
> Dawn and the morning star dispel the night,
> In beauty thus beyond compare impearled,
> The queen of Scotland rises on the world.
> – Pierre de Ronsard (1524–85), translated by Maurice Baring

White rose of Scotland, the This has been variously identified with the field rose, the burnet rose and the white dog rose, and is described thus by Neil Gunn in *Highland Pack* (1949):

> It grows near the seashore, on banks, in clefts, but above all on the little green braes bordered with hazel-woods. It rarely reaches more than two feet in height, is neither white nor cream so much as old ivory; unassuming, modest, and known as the white rose of Scotland.

It was famously celebrated by Hugh MacDiarmid as

> ... the white rose of Scotland
> That smells sharp and sweet – and breaks the heart.
> – 'The Little White Rose', in *Stony Limits and Other Poems* (1934, 1956)

Bonnie Prince Charlie is said to have plucked a white rose for his bonnet after he landed in Scotland in 1745, and it has been suggested that this gave rise to the Jacobite emblem of the WHITE COCKADE. (In some places, the white rose is still known as Prince Charlie's rose.) However, the white rose had already

been adopted by Jacobites as the emblem of the OLD PRETENDER, whom they served *sub rosa*, 'under the rose', i.e. covertly. The rose as a symbol of secrecy goes back to classical times, when Cupid bribed Harpocrates with a rose to prevent him from telling tales about the amorous exploits of Venus.

For other national flowers, *see* BLUEBELL OF SCOTLAND; HEATHER; THISTLE, THE.

White settlers A disparaging name applied since the 1980s either to English people who have moved to Scotland, or to urbanites who have re-settled in the countryside. The term expresses a similar resentment to that felt by colonial peoples in the British Empire, whose land was taken and farmed by white European settlers.

> The only accommodation I could find that night was in the house of what must have been the earliest white settlers in this part of Lewis. Let us call them Basil and Thelma. They had retired early and were fleeing what they saw as 'Britain going to the dogs': inflation, strikes, comprehensive education. Blinkered and bitter they thought they had found a refuge. Basil fulminated against striking railwaymen who were holding up his DIY materials. Thelma denounced the lazy and untrustworthy locals, for whom she had a racist disdain matching his hatred of the lower classes.
> – Dave Brown and Ian R. Mitchell, *A View from the Ridge* (1991)

Who ... *See* WHA ...

Whole jing bang, the *See* HALE JING BANG, THE.

Whuppity Scoorie A spring festival held in Lanark every 1 March, its name deriving from *whippitie*, diminutive of 'whip', and *scoor*, 'rush about'. In the early evening, children run WIDDERSHINS around St Nicholas Kirk three times, swinging paper balls on strings. Although the tradition may well be older, it is first recorded in print in the mid-19th century. Not to be confused with WHUPPITY STOORIE.

Whuppity Stoorie A folk tale similar to the German Rumplestiltskin, recounted by 'Nurse Jenny' in Robert Chambers's *Popular Rhymes of Scotland* (1826), which is located in the fictional village of

Kittlerumpit, apparently somewhere in the DEBA-TABLE LANDS. When a pig falls ill, the farmer's wife begs the help of a fairy, who cures the pig, but claims the woman's baby unless she can guess the fairy's name. Let Nurse Jenny pick up the tale:

Aweel, the goodwife o' Kittlerumpit could sleep nane that nicht for greetin', and a' the next day the same, cuddlin' her bairn till she near squeezed its breath out; but the second day she thinks o' taking a walk in the wood I tell't ye o'; and sae, wi' the bairn in her arms, she sets out, and gaes far in amang the trees, where was an old quarry-hole, grown owre wi' gerse, and a bonny spring well in the middle o't. Before she came very nigh, she hears the birring o' a lint-wheel, and a voice lilting a sang; sae the wife creeps quietly amang the bushes, and keeks owre the broo o' the quarry, and what does she' see but the green fairy kemping at her wheel, and singing like ony precentor:

'Little kens our guid dame at hame
That Whuppity Stoorie is my name!'

And so when the fairy comes to claim the child, the woman is able to call out her name, and the fairy is obliged to flee, 'scraichin' for rage, like a houlet [owl] chased wi' the witches'. *Whuppity* is a diminutive of 'whip', while *stour* is a commotion or hubbub or storm or a whirl of dust. By transference, the name Whuppity Stourie was subsequently applied to any nimble person, light on their feet.

Wicker Man, The *See* SUMMERISLE.

Widdershins or **withershins** Anti-clockwise, in the opposite direction to the sun (hence the opposite of *DEISEIL*). To move this way is superstitiously regarded as bringing ill fortune, and is supposedly the way that witches move while chanting spells.

A very ancient custom which consists in going three times round the body of a dead or living person, imploring blessing upon him. The Deasil must be performed sunways, that is, by moving from right to left. If misfortune is imprecated, the party moves withershins that is, from left to right.
– Sir Walter Scott, *The Fair Maid of Perth* (1828), chapter xxvii, note

The dance was slow and curiously arranged, for each woman was held close from behind by her partner. And

they danced widdershins, against the sun. To one accustomed to the open movement of country jigs and reels the thing seemed the uttermost evil – the grinning masks, the white tranced female faces, the obscene postures, above all that witch-music as horrid as a moan of terror.
– John Buchan, *Witch Wood* (1927)

Contrarily, the word *withershins* is also applied to plants such as ivy and honeysuckle that are supposed to ward off evil spirits.

Wide boy A gangster, hooligan or rogue, often abbreviated to *wido* or *wide-oh* in Glasgow.

Wigtown Martyrs, the Margaret McLauchlan (aged 62) and Margaret Wilson (aged 18), two Covenanters who died for their beliefs during the KILLING TIME, having refused to swear an oath declaring the king as head of the Church. On 11 May 1685, having been sentenced to be 'tied to palisades fixed in the sand, within the floodmark of the sea, and there to stand till the flood o'erflowed them', they were tied to stakes below high-water mark in Wigtown Bay, and drowned by the incoming tide. Wilson's tombstone tells how

Within the sea tyd to a stake
She suffered for Christ Jesus' sake.

The two women subsequently became major figures in Presbyterian martyrology.

Wildcat A small feline, *Felis silvestris*, resembling a large domestic tabby cat but with a bushier tail, found in scattered populations across Europe, Asia and Africa. In Britain it only survives in northern Scotland, where the subspecies is denominated *F. silvestris grampia*. Wildcats are some 50 per cent larger than the average domestic cat, and fossil specimens have been found measuring 4 ft (120 cm) from head to tail. But none are so large, or fierce, as the following lines suggest:

Thare wyld cattis ar grete as wolffis ar
With ougly ene and tuskis fer scherpare ...
– Gilbert Hay, *The Buik of Alexander the Conquerour* (later 15th century)

Nevertheless, the wildcat was believed to be a man-killer as recently as the 1950s, dropping from branches onto the necks of unsuspecting passersby. It is said to be the only wild animal that can never be tamed, even if raised in captivity. It is unclear whether the creature that features in the crest of Clan Chattan, whose motto is TOUCH NOT THE CAT BOT A GLOVE, is a wildcat or a domestic tabby, although the fact that the former is known to be able to bite clean through a gauntlet suggests it may be the latter.

In some places wildcats have interbred with feral domestic cats, resulting in reports of wild 'black panthers'. These pure black hybrids are called *Kellas cats*, after the village in Moray where such a beast was shot by a local gamekeeper in 1984, and thus shown to be more than a cryptozoological fantasy. Black hybrids may lie behind the large fairy cat, the *Cait Sith*, of Highland legend, which was believed to be the reincarnation of a witch and whose appearance presaged disaster. *See also* BANSHEE; *TAGHAIRM.*

Wilderness, the The popular name for the remote and rugged Ardmeanach peninsula in Mull, the location of MACCULLOCH'S TREE.

Wild MacRaes, the A nickname for the Seaforth Highlanders; *see* REGIMENTAL NICKNAMES.

Wild Scots The generic term applied to the Highlanders by the Scottish historian John Major (aka *HADDINGTONUS SCOTUS*) in his *Historia Majoris Britanniae* (1521). He contrasted these with the Householding or Domestic Scots of the Lowlands:

> The common folk among the Wild Scots go out to battle with the whole body clad in a linen garment sewed together in patchwork, well daubed with wax or with pitch, and with an overcoat of deerskin. But the common people among our Domestic Scots and the English fight in a woollen garment.

The term was taken up by other writers, such as Sebastian Munster, professor of Hebrew and theology at the University of Heidelberg, who in his *Cosmographia* of 1544 (enlarged in a French edition of 1575 edited by François de Belleforêt) wrote:

> In the other part [of Scotland], which is mountainous, dwell a kind of people much tougher and fiercer, who are called the Wild Scots. These are dressed in such a manner and in such shirts dyed with saffron as the

Irish, and go with legs bare to the knee. Their arms are a bow and arrow with a very large sword, and the dagger with a single cutting edge.

Wild warrior women of Eigg *See under* MASSACRE CAVE, THE.

William the Lion A sobriquet given to William I of Scotland (reigned 1165–1214), although not during his lifetime. He was so called not because of his military prowess, but because he is said to have been the first to display the LION RAMPANT on his standard. The Scottish chronicler John of Fordun (d. *c.*1384) called William 'the Lion of Justice', as William used the law to great effect in ruling his kingdom. An Irish annalist nearer to his own time called him 'William the Rough' (Gaelic *garbh*), because of his harsh treatment of those who rebelled against him. The contemporary verse chronicle of Jordan Fantosme (died *c.*1185), dealing with the war between William and Henry II of England, has this to say of the Scottish king:

> The king of Scots was skilled in warfare and in inflicting damage on the enemies he fought; but he was too much in the habit of seeking new advice … He never had much affection for those of his own country whose right it was to counsel him.

Willie Wastell or **Willie Wastle** A children's game, described thus by John Jamieson in the 1825 supplement to his *Etymological Dictionary of the Scottish Language*:

> A piece of ground is chosen for a den, circumscribed by certain bounds. He, who occupies this ground, bears the name of Willie Wastell; the rest, who are engaged in the play, approach the limits of his domain; and his object is to get hold of one of them, who sets his foot within it, and to drag him in. If successful, the person who is seized occupies his place, till he can relieve himself by laying hold of another. He who holds the castle, or den, dare not go beyond the limits, else the capture goes for nothing. The assailants repeat the following rhyme:
>
> > Willie, Willie Wastell,
> > I am on your Castle.
> > A' the dogs in the toun
> > Winna pu' Willie doon.

It is given thus in Scotch Presb. Eloquence, 139.

Like Willie, Willie Wastel,
I am in my castel.
A' the dogs in the town
Dare not ding me down.

This form evidently shows, that the rhythm was formerly repeated by the person supposed to hold the castle.

The rhyme is associated with an actual historical incident. In his *Book of Days* (1862–4), Robert Chambers notes:

Under the date February 3, 1651, we have, in Whitlocke's *Memorials*, intelligence of the siege of Hume Castle in Berwickshire, by Colonel Fenwick, an officer of Cromwell's army.

This seat of a once powerful family occupied a commanding position at the western extremity of the great plain of the Merse. On its being summoned by Colonel Fenwick to surrender to Cromwell (who had recently beaten the Scots at Dunbar and overrun nearly the whole of Scotland south of the Forth), the governor answered, 'That he knew not Cromwell, and for his castle it was built upon a rock.' Four days later, there was intelligence in London, that Colonel Fenwick was playing with his guns upon Hume Castle, and that the governor sent this letter to him:

I William of the Wastle
Am now in my castle,
And awe the dogs in the town
Shand garre me gang down.

So Whitlocke prints or misprints the governor's brave answer, which in reality was only a somewhat confused version of a rhyme used by boys in one of their games.

Chambers goes on to add that the name of the governor was in fact Thomas Cockburn, who, faced with a fierce artillery bombardment, surrendered to Cromwell's forces a few days later. Chambers has more to say regarding Willie Wastle:

The rhyme of Willie Wastle was used later in the century with reference to another public event. Mr William Veitch, a zealous Presbyterian clergyman who had been persecuted under the Stuarts, but after the Revolution became a prominent minister under the new establishment, is stated to have preached one day

at Linton in Roxburghshire, when it pleased him to make allusion to the late episcopal frame of Church government. 'Our bishops,' he said, 'had for a long time thought themselves very secure, like

Willie, Willie Wastle,
I am in my castle;
A' the dogs in the town
Dare not ding me down.

Yea, but there is a doggie in heaven that has dung them all down.'

Another Willie Wastle appears in a poem by Burns, beginning

Willie Wastle dwalt on Tweed,
The spot they ca'd it Linkumdoddie ...

However, the poem is largely about Willie's 'dour and din' wife – 'I wouldna gie a button for her!' Burns wrote the poem at the Crook Inn, Tweedsmuir. Yet another William Wastle appears in *Noctes Ambrosianae* (*see under* MAGA), in which he represents John Gibson Lockhart, Scott's son-in-law and biographer.

Willie Winkie *See* WEE WILLIE WINKIE.

Wilma *See under* SON OF WILLIAM.

Wilson cloud chamber *See under* EPONYMS.

Windae licker A Glaswegian expression for a person with mental-health issues.

Wind-blown fish A traditional method of preparing fish by which, after cleaning and the removal of the eyes, it was threaded and hung up in a draught over night before being cooked slowly over the fire.

Windhouse A striking-looking ruin on a hillside near Mid Yell, Shetland, with the reputation as one of the most haunted houses in Scotland. It was built in 1707 – though said to be a reconstruction of a house built further up the hill in the previous century – and has not been lived in since the 1920s. Its site, according to legend, was that of an ancient burial ground. Among the spectres is the Lady in Silk, said to be the ghost of the woman whose skeleton was supposedly found under the floorboards. There is also an apparition in the form of a tall man in a long black coat (and sometimes a top hat), which has been linked to another, better documented skeleton, discovered by workmen repairing the house in 1887. The skeleton was fully 6 ft (1.83 m) long, and was buried in a shallow grave, with no sign of a coffin, suggesting that he might have been a murder victim.

One of the most famous folk tales associated with Windhouse is that of the Trow of Yell. The story tells how the family then living in the house refused to spend the night before Christmas there. One year, a shipwrecked sailor arrives at their door on Christmas Eve, just as the family are departing. They beg their visitor to come away with them, but he opts to stay in the house. During the night, a monstrous great creature appears at the door, but undaunted the sailor pursues and fells it with his axe. All that is left on the ground is a shapeless mass, and in the morning the ground roundabout has turned a sickly green.

Wine Alley The local nickname for Govan's 1930s Moorpark housing estate, an area stigmatized even within Govan itself. A local, Brian McQuade, recalls:

> I was born in 1950 and brought up in Govan in the Moorpark housing estate or the Wine Alley, as it was commonly known. It was regarded at the time as perhaps the worst slum in Britain, and the people who lived there were treated like vermin by the authorities whom we treated likewise. It was a 'them and us' attitude that persisted right up until the Wine Alley was demolished in the late 1990s.
> – www.citystrolls.com/people/index.htm

Wine City A disparaging nickname given by Glaswegians to the Greenock–Port Glasgow area, with the aspersion that the inhabitants are particularly devoted to such fortified wines as buckie (see BUCKFAST TRIANGLE), LANNY and RED BIDDY.

Win or lose it all, To A line from a poem by James Graham, 5th Earl and 1st Marquess of Montrose (1612–50), the celebrated Scottish soldier. Montrose had, in 1637, signed the National Covenant, by which he swore to defend the Presbyterian religion against Charles I's attempted imposition of episcopacy. However, when in 1644 the COVENANTERS invaded England during the Civil War on the side of Parliament, Montrose's loyalty to the king led him to raise an army of Highlanders on his behalf. Montrose went on to win a succession of brilliant victories in that year against the anti-royalist armies led by Archibald Campbell, 1st Marquess of Argyll. Later the tide of war turned, and Montrose was forced to flee abroad. He returned to Scotland on behalf of the exiled Charles II in 1650 with only 1200 men. He was defeated at Carbisdale in Sutherland, betrayed, and hanged in Edinburgh (see MINISTERS' ALTAR, THE).

> He either fears his fate too much,
> Or his deserts are small,
> That dare not put it to the touch,
> To win or lose it all.
> – James Graham, Marquess of Montrose, 'My Dear and Only Love'

Winter Queen, the Elizabeth Stuart, aka Elizabeth of Scotland (1596–1662), the eldest daughter of James VI and Anne of Denmark. She was born in Falkland Palace, and raised in Linlithgow Palace, until her father succeeded to the throne of England in 1603, after which she spent much of the rest of her childhood at Combe Abbey in Warwickshire. The sobriquet relates to her marriage to the Protestant Frederick V, Elector Palatine, who was briefly (November 1619–November 1620) king of Bohemia, until forced into exile after his defeat by Catholic forces at the Battle of the White Mountain – more or less fulfilling the predictions of his enemies that his rule in Bohemia would not last longer than a single winter. It was through her line that the Hanoverian George I succeeded to the throne of Great Britain in 1714.

Elizabeth's other sobriquet, 'Queen of Hearts', alludes to her ability to inspire devotion in many men, including Sir Henry Wotton (1568–1639), the diplomat and poet, who wrote some of his most famous lines in her praise:

> You meaner beauties of the night,
> That poorly satisfy our eyes
> More by your number than your light;
> You common people of the skies,
> What are you when the sun shall rise?

Wirrikow *See* WORRICOW.

Wise Men In Edinburgh they have a saying *vis à vis* Glasgow: 'All the Wise Men come from the East, and all the Cowboys come from the West.' *See also* CASTLE, A SMILE AND A SONG, A.

Wisest fool in Christendom, the James VI was so called by Henry IV of France, who had heard the phrase from his minister, the duc de Sully. Apparently the phrase was originally applied to a Frenchman, but the identity of this person is unknown. James certainly flattered himself on his learning (which bordered on pedantry), leading sycophants to hail him as 'the British Solomon'. He was the author of a number of books that would probably not be remembered were it not for the identity of the author, for example: *Daemonologie* (1597), *The Trew Lawe of Free Monarchies* (1598), *Basilikon Doron* (1599) and *A Counterblaste to Tobacco* (1604). The question as to whether James was a fool in the political sphere has been much debated by historians. He succeeded in restoring a modicum of stability to Scotland once he began his personal rule, and managed his accession to the English throne with diplomatic finesse – although, when told that his new subjects wished to see his face, he responded: 'God's wounds! I will pull down my breeches and they shall also see my arse!' He kept his new realm out of European wars until his final senility, and the fact that he died peacefully in his bed was in marked contrast to most of his Stuart predecessors. However, his high-handed ways with Parliament ('I will govern according to the common weal, but not according to the common will,' he declared in 1621) taught his foolish son, Charles I, some bad habits that were to lose the latter his head. *See also* GOD'S SILLY VASSAL.

Wishing trees Scotland boasts a number of such trees, into the bark of which people pressed coins in the hope that their wishes would be realized. One of the most notable was the Wishing Tree of Argyll, an old, wind-blasted hawthorn whose remains can still be seen near Ardmaddy Castle a few miles south of Oban. Another was the old oak on Isle Maree in Loch Maree, into which Queen Victoria pushed a coin in 1877.

Witch, great auk mistaken for a *See* GHOST-BIRD, THE.

Witch-burning in Scotland, the last The dubious honour for having hosted the last witch-burning in Scotland is claimed by Dornoch in eastern Sutherland. Here in 1727 one Janet Horne suffered this grisly fate, having been found guilty of turning her daughter into a pony, which was then shod by the Devil. *See also* SARRY HEID, THE.

Witches of North Berwick *See* NORTH BERWICK WITCHES.

Witches' paps A name for the foxglove in the west of Scotland. In the Northeast, the flowers of the foxglove are known as witches' thimbles. *See also* FLORA CALEDONIA.

Witches' spittle Cuckoo spit, the protective froth exuded by the froghopper larva on summer vegetation.

Witch of Eday, the *See* SAVILLE STONE, THE.

Witch of Lauder, the An unfortunate woman, whose name does not survive, who was arrested alongside others in 1649 and charged with witchcraft. She confessed, and was sentenced to burn at the stake. Just before she was to die, she made a shock announcement to the crowd, as recorded in George Sinclair's *Satan's Invisible World Discovered* (1685):

> Now all you that did see me this day know that I am now to die as a witch by my own confession, and I free all men, especially the ministers and magistrates, of the guilt of my blood. I take it wholly upon myself: my blood be upon my own head. And as I must make answer to the God of Heaven presently, I declare that I am as free of witchcraft as any child: but being delated by a malicious woman, and put in prison under that name of a witch, disowned by my husband and friends, and seeing no ground of hope of my coming out of prison nor ever coming in credit again, through the temptation of the Devil I made up that confession on purpose to destroy my own life, being weary of it, and choosing rather to die than to live.

This did not prevent her sentence being carried out, and Sinclair cannot but make a sermon out of this poor woman's fate:

> Which lamentable story, as it did then astonish all the spectators, none of which could restrain themselves from tears, so it may be to all a demonstration of Satan's subtlety, whose design is to destroy all, partly by tempting many to presumption, and some others to despair.

Witch of Stoer, the The story of this unfortunate old woman and her murderers is related by William Daniell in his *Voyage Round Great Britain* (1815–25):

> The promontory of Ru Storr, secluded as it is from the intercourse with the rest of the world, seems to have been one of the last strong-holds in which the gloomy and savage superstitions of the country lingered. There is a tradition, that about sixty years ago an aged woman, named Mhoir Bhein, unhappily incurred the suspicion of being a witch, and became a constant occasion of dread and apprehension to her neighbours. They imputed to her the power of conjuring away the substantial and nutritive part from the milk of their cows, and of enriching with it her own dairy; and they even believed her capable of sinking ships at sea, by a spell peculiar to the weird sisters of the Highlands ... The credulity of the good people of Ru Storr, it seems, was capacious enough to admit, as possible, all these marvels of infernal agency; and it, moreover, invested the unoffending object of their abhorrence with the privilege of assuming at will any shape which might be convenient for her purposes. That of a gray old cat was her favourite guise; and any mischance which occurred in the presence of such an animal was unanimously placed to the discredit of Mhoir Bhein. At length the delusion became so prevalent among this secluded community, that some wicked boys, stimulated, no doubt, by their seniors, determined to kill the poor creature, and accordingly proceeded to her abode, where, after fastening a halter about her neck, they passed the end of it under the door, which they immediately closed, and effected their inhuman purpose by strangling her.

The boys were tried in Inverness, but acquitted. Daniell reports that one still lived, but the others were all dead, none having died a natural death, being 'either killed in battle, or drowned'.

Witch's Hole A 'pockmark' in the seabed, about 330 ft (100 m) across, some 90 miles (150 km) northeast of Aberdeen, just one of several such features scattered across the area known as the Witch's Ground. These depressions in the seafloor sediments are caused by the escape of methane gas. In 2000 an unmanned submarine observed a boat sitting upright in the middle of the Witch's Hole. It was a steel-built steam trawler dating from the early 20th century, and showed no signs of damage. Scientists speculated that the boat might have been engulfed by the sudden release of a large amount of methane from the seabed, in the form of a giant bubble. Methane is even lighter than air, so a boat could not float on it. Marine geologist Alan Judd told the BBC that 'If it was caught in the gas it would have been swamped and gone down as though it were in a lift shaft.' However, he added that there was no firm evidence for this hypothesis.

Witch's Step, the *See under* CARLIN.

Wizard Earl, the Francis Stewart, Earl of Bothwell (1562–1612), the nephew of Mary Queen of Scots' third husband, James Hepburn, the 4th Earl. Francis Stewart often played a double game in the complex power politics of the day, attempting to curry favour both with the young James VI and with the king's enemies. He also earned the king's enmity by espousing a strongly anti-English policy. In April 1591 he was imprisoned in Edinburgh Castle for allegedly playing the part of Satan during the covens of the NORTH BERWICK WITCHES, supposedly aimed at bringing about the king's demise. Bothwell escaped on 22 June, and on 27 December, accompanied by 60 armed followers, he burst into Holyroodhouse, and pursued the king to a remote tower, where he tried to burn down the door behind which James was hiding. The latter was only saved by the intervention of the citizenry of Edinburgh. In July 1593 Bothwell, having been forfeited by Parliament, at last submitted to the king, offering James his own sword with which to strike his head off if the king so desired. Subsequently the turbulent earl was acquitted of treason by witchcraft, but this did not end his rebellions. By 1595 Bothwell's support had trickled away, and in March he went into exile on the Continent, where he pursued a career as a soldier of fortune. But his health failed him, and he died in Naples in 1612, where, as in Scotland, he was suspected of involvement in the dark arts. See also 'BONNIE EARL O' MORAY, THE'.

Wizard Michael Scot, the See SCOT, MICHAEL.

Wizard of Reay, the Sir Donald Mackay (d.1649), chief of Clan Mackay, created 1st Baron Reay of Reay in 1628. Mackay had earlier acquired the village of Reay in Caithness, but it is perhaps surprising that he should have adopted it as his title, the traditional Mackay lands being further to the west, in Sutherland (although this was subsequently referred to as Reay Country). In 1629 Reay raised a regiment to fight in the Thirty Years' War for the Protestant champion, Gustavus Adolphus of Sweden. Back in Scotland, Reay was a (reluctant) signatory of the Covenant, and ended up, like Montrose, fighting for Charles I against the Scots Covenanting army during the English Civil Wars.

It was no doubt his allegiance to king over Covenant that led to Reay's reputation as a man who had dealings with the Powers of Darkness. It was said that he had studied with the Devil in Rome, and that it was the latter's practice to claim as his own whichever of his students was the last to leave his class. Finding himself thus claimed, the cunning Reay, pleading the principle of 'Devil take the hindmost', pointed to his shadow, with which the Devil had perforce to be content. Thereafter it was said that Reay never cast a shadow.

The Devil had not quite done with his former pupil, however. Back in Sutherland, early one morning Lord Reay was approaching the entrance to Smoo Cave, said by some to be a gateway to Hell. When Reay's dog returned howling and hairless from the mouth of the cavern, Reay realized that the Devil awaited him inside. As he hesitated, the sun rose above the horizon, and the Devil and two of his evil spirits were forced to flee through the roof of the cave, leaving the three holes that can be seen today.

In his *Voyage Round Great Britain* (1815–25) William Daniell gives the following account of Reay's experiences here:

> According to a current tradition ... the first attempt to explore this cavern was made in the sixteenth century, by Donald Lord Reay, who entered it in a boat with six attendants and a piper ... After remaining a considerable time, his lordship returned, accompanied only by the piper; and strange to say, the fate of the other unfortunate men was never known, for neither of the two adventurers would reveal what awful scenes they had witnessed; and they were never afterwards seen to smile. One of the dogs which they had taken with them, some time afterwards found egress from this subterranean labyrinth into a small cave, about two miles distant, but the poor animal came forth with scarcely a particle of hair on his skin.

This latter circumstance Daniell ascribes to the dog's 'struggles in the narrow and rocky passages through which he had worked his way', but students of canine speleology know full well that such hairlessness is a consequence of dark forces at work – as evidenced by the fate of the dog in the story of MACKINNON'S CAVE. Daniell himself recounts that the locals hold that the cave is 'the abode of an unquiet spirit, who announces his presence by crowing like a cock every morning till daybreak; thus asserting a privilege over the common herd of ghosts, who are commonly said to vanish at the first summons given by the bird of dawning'.

Wizard of the North, the The nickname given to Sir Walter Scott while he was still publishing his novels anonymously as the 'AUTHOR OF *WAVERLEY*'.

Wizard of Wishaw, the The nickname of the snooker player John Higgins (b.1975), who was world champion in 1998, 2007 and 2009.

Wizard of Yester, the See under GOBLIN HA'.

Wizard shackle A translation of the Gaelic *buarach bhaoi*, applied to a creature that is almost certainly the lamprey, a primitive jawless fish that parasitizes other fish by fastening onto them and sucking their blood.

> The *buarach bhaoi* (lit. wild or wizard shackle), called also *buarach na baoi* (the shackle of the furious one), was believed to be a leech or eel-like animal to be

found at certain fords and in dark waters, that twisted itself like a shackle round the feet of passing horses, so that they fell and were drowned. It then sucked their blood. It had nine eyes or holes in its head and back, at which the blood it sucked came out. Hence it was called *buarach-bhaoi nan sùilean claon* (the furious shackle of the squinting eyes).

> – John G. Campbell, *Superstitions of the Highlands and Islands of Scotland* (1900)

Regarding the 'nine eyes or holes' referred to by Campbell, the lamprey was known as the *nine-eed eel* in Scots, the external gill slits being taken for eyes.

Wobster, Jock *See* DEIL'S OWER JOCK WABSTER, THE.

Wolf, last *See* LAST WOLF IN SCOTLAND, THE.

Wolf of Badenoch, the Alexander Stewart (1343–1405), Earl of Buchan and Lord of Badenoch, the fourth son of Robert II (he was also called Alasdair Mór mac an Righ – 'Big Alexander, son of the king'). His nickname reflects both his ferocity and his remote powerbase, in Badenoch, an area centred on the valley of the Spey; his castle on an island in Lochindorb is known as 'the Wolf's Lair'. In 1382 he vastly extended his territories by his marriage to Euphemia, Countess of Ross, but deserted her to co-habit with Mairead inghean Eachann, who provided him with a number of children. By this time he had also made many enemies, including the Bishop of Moray and one of his older brothers, the Earl of Fife, largely owing to the general lawlessness with which he ruled his territories. The Bishop made Buchan swear to return to his wife, but Buchan failed to stick to his word, and the Church granted Euphemia a divorce, as a consequence of which Buchan lost all the Ross lands he had gained by his marriage. Apparently in retaliation, Buchan and his men burnt Forres in May 1390, and in June destroyed Elgin with its cathedral, the seat of the Bishop of Moray. The Bishop thereupon excommunicated Buchan, who was obliged to appear in Perth to plead for forgiveness, which was granted by the Bishop of St Andrews. Buchan seems to have lived the rest of his life relatively peacefully, although his sons continued to indulge in lawless-

ness (one of them acquired the earldom of Mar by abducting the earl's widow). Buchan died on 20 June 1405. According to legend, he was visited at Ruthven Castle just before his death by a tall stranger, dressed in black, who asked to play a game of chess with his host. Buchan agreed to the match. Eventually the stranger was heard to say 'Checkmate', upon which a terrible thunderstorm commenced, and continued through the night. In the morning Buchan's body was found dead, without a mark, although the nails in his boots had all been torn out. He was buried in Dunkeld Cathedral, where his sarcophagus, with his armoured effigy recumbent upon it, can still be seen.

Wolf's teeth A Northeastern phrase for the fragment of the lower end of a RAINBOW.

Woman clothed with the sun, a *See* BUCHANITES.

Womle and brees A sort of sloppy HAGGIS broth, formerly eaten in the Northeast. A *womle* or *wammle* or *wamble* is a churning of the stomach, while *bree* is soup.

World's Greatest Snob, the A common journalistic description of Sir Iain Moncreiffe of that Ilk (1919–85), an obsessive genealogist who claimed to be descended from Countess Elizabeth Báthory (1560–1614), the Hungarian noblewoman who was said to have bathed in the blood of virgins in order to achieve eternal youth. Moncreiffe's mother was the daughter of the Comte de Miremont, and he himself was Albany Herald at the LYON COURT, the body concerned with heraldry in Scotland. He was awarded a doctorate for his work on Scots law as relating to the succession to peerages (published as *Origins and Background of the Law of Succession to Arms and Dignities in Scotland*), and wrote a popular book on the Highland clans. His first wife was Diana Hay, 23rd Countess of Erroll (daughter of the 22nd Earl, whose unsolved murder in Kenya in 1941 inspired the book and film *White Mischief*), and his second was Hermione Patricia Faulkner, daughter of the present Dowager Duchess of Dundee. Regarding the label of 'World's Greatest Snob', the veteran journalist Roddy Martine wrote in *The Scotsman* (31 July 2010):

In my opinion this couldn't be further from the truth. It was such a misunderstanding because the thing about Iain was that he was obsessed with genealogy and fascinated by people, so when you met him he would start asking you questions about your family, and where they came from. Everyone thought he was a snob, but he wasn't, he was just hugely curious to know where people came from.

Martine proceeds to relate the 'possibly apocryphal' story about Moncreiffe 'dancing with the Queen and suddenly saying "I love you, Ma'am, I love you," and her saying, "Yes I know, but don't tell Philip."'

Worricow or **wirrikow** A malevolent sprite or demon; or even the Devil himself; or merely a scary, horrid-looking person. *Worri-* is the same as standard English 'worry', in the sense of 'pester', 'harass', while *cow* is another word for a hobgoblin or other frightening thing, itself perhaps deriving from the verb *cow* meaning 'to scold'.

> Frae *gudame*'s mouth auld warld tale they hear,
> O' *Warlocks* louping round the *Wirrikow*,
> O' gaists that win in glen and kirk-yard drear,
> Whilk touzles a' their tap, and gars them shak wi'
> fear.
> – Robert Fergusson, 'The Farmer's Ingle' (1773)

> Heh! wha will tell the students now
> To meet the *Pauly* cheek for chow,
> Whan he, like *frightsome wirrikow*,
> Had wont to rail,
> And set our stamacks in a low,
> Or we turn'd tail.
> – Robert Fergusson, 'Elegy on John Hogg, late Porter to the University of St Andrews'

In *Guy Mannering* (1815), Scott puts the word into the mouth of the formidable Meg MERRILIES:

> 'Fule body that thou art,' said Meg, stepping up to him, with a frown of indignation that made her dark eyes flash like lamps from under her bent brows– 'Fule body! if I meant ye wrang, couldna I clod ye ower that craig, and wad man ken how ye cam by your end mair than Frank Kennedy? Hear ye that, ye worricow?'
> – chapter xvii

Worst of kings and the most miserable of men, the The epitaph composed for himself by Robert III

(reigned 1390–1406), the son of AULD BLEARY. Historians have tended to agree with Robert's assessment of his abilities as a ruler, as did his Parliament, which in 1399 passed an act including the following condemnation:

> It is deliverit that the misgovernaunce of the realm and the defaut of the keping of the comoun law sould be impute to the King and his officeris.

Robert's self-assessment comes down to us in the *Scotichronicon* (1440–7) of Walter Bower (1385–1449), Abbot of Inchcolm Abbey, who reports the king's reply when Queen Annabella asked him about his funeral arrangements:

> I have no desire to erect a proud tomb. Therefore let these men who strive in the world for the pleasures of honour have shining monuments. I on the other hand should prefer to be buried at the bottom of a midden, so that my soul may be saved on the Day of the Lord. Bury me therefore, I beg you, in a midden, and write for my epitaph: 'Here lies the worst of kings and the most miserable of men in the whole kingdom.'

His misery was increased when his son, the future James I, was captured by the English (*see* KINGIS QUAIR, THE). When he heard this news, 'his spirit forthwith left him, the strength waned from his body, his countenance grew pale, and for grief thereafter he took no food'. Within three weeks he was dead.

Wrapped up in the skin of a newly slain bullock *See* TAGHAIRM.

Wreck-the-Hoose Juice A nickname for Buckfast Tonic Wine; *see* BUCKFAST TRIANGLE.

Wren of North Britain, the Daniel Defoe's characterization of the architect Sir William Bruce (*c.*1630–1710), who introduced the classical style to Scotland, as attested by a number of magnificent country mansions. Charles II appointed him Surveyor General and Overseer of the King's Works in Scotland, in which role he helped to remodel Holyroodhouse. Defoe described Bruce's own house at Kinross thus:

> At the west end of the lake, and the gardens reaching down to the very water's edge, stands the most

beautiful and regular piece of architecture (for a private gentleman's seat) in all Scotland, perhaps, in all Britain, I mean the house of Kinross. ... The house is a picture, 'tis all beauty; the stone is white and fine, the order regular, the contrivance elegant, the workmanship exquisite. Dryden's lines, intended for a compliment on his friend's poetry, and quoted before, are literally of the house of Kinross.

> Strong dorick columns form the base,
> Corinthian fills the upper space;
> So all below is strength, and all above is grace.

Sir William Bruce, the skilful builder, was the Surveyor-General of the works, as we call it in England, or the Royal Architect, as in Scotland. In a word, he was the Kit Wren of North Britain; and his skill in the perfect decoration of building, has many testimonials left upon record for it ...

– Daniel Defoe, *A Tour Thro' the Whole Island of Great Britain* (1724–6)

Writer to the Signet A member of the Society of Writers to Her Majesty's Signet, a private association of solicitors in Scotland, founded in 1594. The Society formerly had a monopoly on the drawing up of documents requiring the royal signet (private seal), but such privileges exist no more. Members place 'W.S.' after their names. The Society established the Signet Library in 1722; it moved to its current premises in Parliament Square in 1815. Its collection was at first exclusively of law books and statutes, but a general collection was begun in 1778. Formerly, the term *writer* on its own was used to denote a lawyer, leading to the occasional confusion. Tellingly, the *Statistical Account* of 1795 states: 'There are very few law-pleas or disputes in this parish, because we have only one *writer*.' A lucky parish indeed.

WS *See* WRITER TO THE SIGNET.

Wylie, Michael *See* MICHAEL WYLIE.

X *See* SALTIRE, THE.

Ya bass You bastard. This piece of street slang dates from the urban gang culture of the 1960s, hence such slogans daubed onto walls as 'Tongs ya bass' (*see* TONGLAND). The suggestion, mooted in the Glasgow *Evening Times* in 2003, that in this context 'ya bass' is from the Gaelic war cry *aigh bas*, meaning 'battle and die', though appealing, smells distinctly fishy.

Ya beauty! An ejaculation denoting both admiration and exultation, for example if one were to achieve a hole in one.

> Fate's dealt me a trump card. Oh ya beauty!
> And I'll damn well play it. It is my duty.
> – Liz Lochhead, *Tartuffe* (1985)

Ya big Jessie! *See* JESSIE.

Yarrow *See* FLOWER OF YARROW, THE.

Ya tube *See* TUBE.

Yawkins, Captain *See* DIRK HATTERAICK'S CAVE.

Year of the Burning (Gaelic *Bliadhna an Losgaidh*) The name given to the year 1814, when the tenantry of Strathnaver in Sutherland were forcibly evicted, many of the roof-trees of their cottages being burnt, and two or perhaps three people dying in the process. The order for the eviction came from the landowner, George Granville Leveson-Gower, Marquess of Stafford, who had acquired his vast northern estates by marriage to Elizabeth, Countess of Sutherland. He himself was later made Duke of Sutherland. The evictions were carried out by his factor, Patrick Sellar, who was subsequently charged with murder, but acquitted.

> The year that Patrick Sellar came to Strathnaver
> black smoke hung along its length
> from the homes so lately vacated by his tenants;
> too late for one young woman who would not
>   leave,
> so perished in the flames, her unborn child within
>   her.
> Old men, led out in time, were laid
> to die from frost instead of fire.
> – Gerald England, 'The Clearing of the Highlands'
>   (1980)

Year of the Sheep (Gaelic *Bliadhna nan Caorach*) The name given to the year 1792, when, in July, men from across Easter and Wester Ross rounded up the flocks of Cheviot sheep that the landowners had introduced to supplant both their tenants and their black cattle. The intention was to drive the sheep back south again, but the Highlanders were thwarted by soldiers of the Black Watch. It was the only active resistance to the CLEARANCES until the BATTLE OF THE BRAES in 1882.

> My blessing with the foxes dwell,
> For that they hunt the sheep so well!
> Ill fa' the sheep, a grey-faced nation
> That swept our hills with desolation.
> – Duncan Bàn MacIntyre (1724–1812), '*Oran nam
>   Balgairean*' ('Song of the Foxes')

See also FOUR-FOOTED CLANSMEN; YEAR OF THE BURNING.

'Ye banks and braes o' bonnie Doon' A well-known song written by Burns in 1787. The tune, 'Caledonian Hunt's Delight', was composed by an amateur Edinburgh musician called James Miller, 'with a few helping touches from Stephen Clarke the organist', according to William Scott Douglas in his 1877 annotated edition of Burns's works. The song, which refers to the River Doon that flows through Burns's native Alloway, famously begins:

Ye banks and braes o' bonnie Doon,
How can ye bloom sae fresh and fair!
How can ye chant, ye little birds,
And I sae weary fu' o' care!

Apparently Burns had in mind the sad tale of the 17-year-old niece of Mrs Gavin Hamilton of Mauchline, who fatally fell for the charms of one Captain M——, the son of a wealthy landowner and MP from Wigtownshire. Hence the last verse:

Wi' lightsome heart I pu'd a rose,
Fu' sweet upon its thorny tree;
And my fause luver staw my rose,
But, ah! he left the thorn wi' me.

Scott Douglas, who, with typical Victorian double standards calls the young lady 'one of the many frail daughters of Eve', and is inclined to excuse Captain M—— of blame, informs us that:

About ten years after this lyric was composed, and when the minstrel's hand was motionless for ever, the lady was advised, in behalf of her child, to raise against the father an action of *declarator of marriage and legitimacy*, with an alternative claim of *damages* in case of failure. She died shortly after the process was instituted, probably the victim of anguished feelings; but the case continued in her daughter's behalf. In 1798 the judges pronounced in favour of the marriage; but the Court of Session, on review, reversed the judgement, and ordered a payment of £3,000 to the daughter, who was, in 1851, a married lady resident in Edinburgh.

'Ye cannae shove yer granny aff a bus' A playground song, sung to the tune of 'She'll Be Coming Round the Mountain':

O, ye cannae shove yer granny aff a bus
Ye cannae shove yer granny aff a bus
Ye cannae shove yer granny
Fur she's yer mammy's mammy
Ye cannae shove yer granny aff a bus.

An alternative reason for not shoving your granny off a bus is because 'she makes your mince an tatties'. *See also* YER GRANNY!

Ye'd make a better door than a window You're standing in the way of something I'm trying to look at (usually the telly).

Ye'll die facing the monument An old Glasgow insult, meaning you'll be hanged. The allusion is to the view of the Nelson Monument in Glasgow Green seen by those about to die on the gallows that once stood in Jail Square, close to the Justiciary Courts. The last hanging here – and the last public execution in Glasgow – was in 1865, the condemned man being Dr Edward William Pritchard, who had been convicted of poisoning his wife and mother-in-law.

Ye'll have had yer tea What Glasgow people say Edinburgh people say when you turn up on their doorstep.

Yellowhammer A bird (also known as the *yella yite*) once associated with the Devil; *see under* ROBIN.

Yellow Horse of Loch Lundie, the See GOLDEN HORSE OF LOCH LUNDIE, THE.

Yellow stick *See* RELIGION OF THE YELLOW STICK.

Yer a lang time deid *Carpe diem*; enjoy life while you've got it. *Notes and Queries*, 7 December 1901, notes the following version as 'a cheery motto for a house':

Be happy while y'er leevin,
For y'er a lang time deid.

Yer arse! *See* YER GRANNY!

Yer at yer auntie's An expression of indulgence to a young guest, indicating that treats are in store, seconds may be asked for, and minor diversions from the straight and narrow overlooked. Sometimes 'Yer at yer grannie's.'

Yer face is tripping ye You've got a long face.

Yer granny! 'Stuff and nonsense', a contemptuous response, similar in effect to 'My arse!' (or, in Glasgow, *Yer arse in parsley!*). For example, if you were to say 'Please, sir, ma homework wiz eaten by the dug', I might respond, 'Eaten by the dug, yer granny!' *See also* YE CANNAE SHOVE YER GRANNY AFF A BUS.

Yerlston fever A bout of idleness, a fit of sloth. *Yerlston* is the village of Earlston, Berwickshire, whose inhabitants, according to their neighbours, are incorrigibly lazy.

Yer nose is too near yer arse A Glaswegian riposte to someone who claims to have smelt something unpleasant.

Yes I know, but don't tell Philip *See* WORLD'S GREATEST SNOB, THE.

Ye wad be nane the waur o' a hanging *See under* WEIR OF HERMISTON.

Yird pigs *See* ERTH HUNS.

Yogi The nickname of the footballer John Hughes (b.1943), who joined Celtic in 1960 and played with them for 11 seasons. He also won eight Scottish caps. The nickname refers to his build, thought to be similar to that of the cartoon character Yogi Bear.

Yokin' time The time when work starts (originally the time the horses were yoked for work).

You ... *See also* YE ...; YER ...

You must die where you stand *See* THIN RED LINE, THE.

Young, James *See* PARAFFIN YOUNG.

Young Chevalier, the A byname for Prince Charles Edward Stuart, the YOUNG PRETENDER, who was a member of the Confrerie des Chevaliers de Saint-Georges, a French chivalric order created in 1390 by Phillibert de Mollans. His father, the OLD PRETEN-DER (aka DISMAL JIMMY) was also a member, and was often referred to as the Chevalier St George. In 1746 a Whig gave the following report of a christening feast in the Jacobite stronghold of Manchester, in which various royals were represented by figurines at the table:

There was his present Majesty [George II] in the centre of a dish of chickens with their rumps turned

towards him, his late Majesty [George I, aka 'the Turnip-Hoer'] in a dish of unbuttered turnips, the Prince of Wales in a hasty pudding, and the Duke [BUTCHER CUMBERLAND] in a blood pudding ... the elegant treat closed with the young chevalier in the centre of a pyramid of sweetmeats.
– Philip Doddridge, letter, 1746, quoted in *Palatine Note-Book* (1883)

Today, the name is best remembered in the old Jacobite song 'CHARLIE IS MY DARLING':

'Twas on a Monday morning,
Right early in the year,
When Charlie came to our town
The Young Chevalier.
Charlie is my darling, my darling, my darling.
Charlie is my darling, the young Chevalier.

Young Colkitto *See under* COLKITTO.

Young Lochinvar A character who makes a memorable appearance in Canto V of Sir Walter Scott's *Marmion* (1808), carrying off his amour before she can marry another:

O young Lochinvar is come out of the West,
Through all the wide border his steed was the best;
And save his good broadsword, he weapons had none,
He rode all unarm'd, and he rode all alone.
So faithful in love, and so dauntless in war,
There never was knight like the young Lochinvar.

The verses dealing with his adventures became a standard anthology piece. Lochinvar is a small loch in the Galloway hills, and the Gordons of Lochinvar were a local landed family.

Young Pretender, the Prince Charles Edward Stuart (1720–88), known to his admirers as the YOUNG CHEVALIER or Bonnie Prince Charlie. Born in Rome and brought up speaking French, the dashing, impulsive, handsome prince was a complete contrast to his father, the lacklustre OLD PRETENDER, James Francis Edward Stuart, the Jacobite claimant to the throne who had been crowned James VIII of Scotland in Perth shortly before the '15 Rebellion faded out. Charles determined to recover the throne for his father, and, despite the promised French aid failing to materialize, he set sail for Scotland in 1745, landing in Arisaig on 25 July accompanied only by the SEVEN MEN OF MOIDART. Charles had put his faith in the loyalty of the Highland clans to the House of Stuart, but at first the chiefs were reluctant to come out. Several changed their minds once Cameron of Lochiel (the GENTLE LOCHIEL) overcame his misgivings and brought out his 700 clansmen, declaring, 'I'll share the fate of my prince, and so shall every man over whom nature or fortune hath given me any power.' On 19 August the Marquess of Tullibardine raised the prince's standard at Glenfinnan, and the rebellion was underway. Lord George Murray, who had been one of those who had joined the prince only reluctantly, became Charles's field commander. But Charles was a typical Stuart, regarding Murray's robust advice as a disloyal attack upon his person, and, according to one contemporary, he engaged two Irish officers to spy on Murray, 'with orders to murder him should he show any signs of wishing to betray him, a fact he was persuaded was the case'. Lord Elcho summed up the prince's paranoid disposition: 'He could not bear the slightest contradiction which he would put down to a lack of attachment to his person.' Another observer noted: 'Had Prince Charles slept during the whole of the expedition and allowed Lord George to act for him according to his own judgement, there is every reason for supposing that he would have found the crown of Great Britain on his head when he awoke.'

The campaign got off to a good start. The rag-tag Jacobite army, described by one observer as a PACK OF TATTERDEMALIONS, found Edinburgh an open city, and its womenfolk quite entranced with their prince. Morale was boosted by a quick victory at Prestonpans on 21 September (see HEY, JOHNNIE COPE, ARE YE WAUKEN YET?), and the decision was made to press on south into England. But the hoped-for turn-out by thousands of English Jacobites proved to be a chimera, as did the expected French invasion, and on 6 December, BLACK FRIDAY, Murray and others persuaded the prince that there was only one option: turn round and head back north. Murray conducted an effective fighting retreat, winning tactical victories at Clifton (18 December) and Falkirk (17 January 1746). On 16 April the Jacobite army found itself on Culloden

Muir, to the east of Inverness, faced by a reinforced Hanoverian army commanded by the Duke of Cumberland (BUTCHER CUMBERLAND). Colonel John O'Sullivan, one of the prince's Irish officers, insisted that they make a stand. Murray violently disagreed, but was overruled. The Jacobites were routed, and indiscriminate slaughter followed.

The prince then began his five long months in the heather, pursued all over the Highlands and Islands by redcoats, and with a price of £30,000 on his head. No one took up the government offer, and there were many who helped him, at the risk of their own lives (see BURKE, BETTY; CLUNY'S CAGE; OVER THE SEA TO SKYE; SEVEN MEN OF GLENMORISTON). Eventually, on 20 September 1746, Charles boarded a French frigate close to where he had landed with such high hopes just 14 months before, and slipped away to France. Charles spent much of the rest of his life as a wandering exile, declining into alcoholism and bitter disappointment, while one by one the Catholic courts of Europe withdrew their recognition of the Stuart claim. Charles having no legitimate issue, on his death this claim passed to his brother, Cardinal Henry Benedict Stuart. By this time Jacobitism had faded from a force to be reckoned with into a subject for romance, and such was its harmlessness that Cardinal Henry was granted a pension by George III, and his tomb on his death in 1807 was paid for by the Prince Regent.

Young Tom Morris *See* OLD TOM AND YOUNG TOM.

You Pees A nickname for the United Presbyterians, a Protestant denomination founded in Scotland in 1847 from the merger of the United Secession Church with the Relief Church. In 1900 it united with the Free Church of Scotland to form the United Free Church of Scotland, which merged with the Church of Scotland in 1929.

> Not that she [the narrator's mother] was religious or Holy in fact to my knowledge the last time she'd went to Mass she was full and fell off the chair laughing and then was sick in her purse, but Blueskins or 'You Pees' I was acquainted with one or two of their number and they would have made a saint spit.
> – Jane Harris, *The Observations* (2006)

(The term 'Blueskins' for Presbyterians appears to be a North American rather than a Scottish usage, although Rangers supporters and other Protestants are sometimes referred to as BLUENOSES.)

You're ... *See* YER ...

You tube *See* TUBE.

Yowe trummle Literally, 'ewe tremble', a cold snap in early summer. The expression is famously deployed by Hugh MacDiarmid in the opening line of his poem 'The Watergaw' (*see under* RAINBOWS AND RELATED PHENOMENA).

Zaidie, Crookit *See* CROOKIT ZAIDIE.

Zeenty-teenty An obsolete children's counting game or rhyme; possibly from the shepherd's words for 'one' and 'two'. Sometimes *zeenty* is replaced by *eenty*, as in the following:

> Eenty teenty tirry mirry,
> Ram, tam, toosh,
> Crawl under the bed
> And catch a wee fat moose.
> Cut it up in slices,
> Fry it in the pan,
> Be sure and keep the gravy
> For the wee fat man.